French Warships
in the Age of Sail
1626–1786

French Warships
in the Age of Sail
1626–1786
Design, Construction, Careers and Fates

Rif Winfield &
Stephen S Roberts

Seaforth
PUBLISHING

FRONTISPIECE: French naval power under Louis XIV reached its high-water mark at the Battle of Beachy Head (known as Béveziers in France) on 10 July 1690, which resulted in the comprehensive defeat of the main Anglo-Dutch fleet and the allied loss of command of the Channel for two years. In terms of the damage inflicted and its potential strategic value, it was France's greatest victory in the age of sail. This is a Dutch lithograph of the event published about 1830. (Beverley R Robinson Collection, Annapolis 51.7.72)

Copyright © Rif Winfield & Stephen S Roberts 2017

This edition first published in Great Britain in 2017 by
Seaforth Publishing,
An imprint of Pen & Sword Books Ltd,
47 Church Street,
Barnsley
South Yorkshire S70 2AS

www.seaforthpublishing.com
Email: info@seaforthpublishing.com

British Library Cataloguing in Publication Data
A catalogue record for this book is available from the British Library

ISBN 978 1 4738 9351 1 (Hardback)
ISBN 978 1 4738 9352 8 (Kindle)
ISBN 978 1 4738 9353 5 (ePub)

All rights reserved. No part of this publication may be reproduced or transmitted in any form or by any means, electronic or mechanical, including photocopying, recording, or any information storage and retrieval system, without prior permission in writing of both the copyright owner and the above publisher.

Typeset and designed by Neil Sayer
Printed and bound in China

Contents

Preface	vii
Acknowledgments	viii
Structure and Organisation of the Book	1
French Naval Technology and Organisation from Colbert to Castries	4
The Small Three-decked Ship of the Line	4
Mixed Calibres on Gun Decks	4
Changes in Ship Rankings, 1669–1716	4
Appearance and Design	4
Flags	5
Ordnance	5
Manning Levels	7
Administration of the Navy	7
Dockyards and Infrastructure	8
Use of Navy ships for Privateering (*Armements Mixtes*)	11
Historical Overview	13
Chronology	23
French Naval Operations from 1626 to 1786	25
Sources and Bibliography	38
Glossary and Abbreviations	44
Preamble: The Legacy of Richelieu and Mazarin – Ships of the French Navy from 1626 to 1661	49
(A) The French fleet in September 1661.	54

Chapter 1 The First Rank (*Vaisseaux du premier rang*) with 80 or more guns after 1715 — 55
    (A) Vessels in service as at 9 March 1661 — 56
    (B) Vessels acquired from 9 March 1661 — 56
    (C) Vessels acquired from 15 April 1689 — 63
    (D) Three-decked vessels acquired from 1 September 1715 — 69
    (E) 80-gun two-decked vessels (*Vaisseaux de 80*) acquired from 1740 — 74

Chapter 2 The Second Rank (*Vaisseaux du second rang*) with 68 to 78 guns after 1715 — 79
    (A) Vessels in service as at 9 March 1661 — 79
    (B) Vessels acquired from 9 March 1661 — 79
    (C) Vessels acquired from 15 April 1689 — 89
    (D) 74-gun two-decked vessels (*Vaisseaux de 74*) acquired from 1 September 1715 — 97

Chapter 3 The Third Rank (*Vaisseaux du troisième rang*) with 56 to 66 guns after 1715 — 113
    (A) Vessels in service as at 9 March 1661 — 113
    (B) Vessels acquired from 9 March 1661 — 115
    (C) Vessels acquired from 15 April 1689 — 127
    (D) 24pdr- and 36pdr-armed vessels acquired from 1 September 1715 — 139
    (E) 18pdr-armed vessels acquired from 1 September 1715 — 151

Chapter 4 The Fourth Rank (*Vaisseaux du quatrième rang*) with 40 to 54 guns after 1715, sometimes described as Frigates of the 1st Order (*Frégates du 1er ordre*), and 12pdr-armed and larger frigates after 1747 — 155
    (A) Vessels in service as at 9 March 1661 — 155
    (B) Vessels acquired from 9 March 1661 — 157
    (C) Vessels acquired from 15 April 1689 — 163
    (D) Vessels acquired from 1 September 1715 — 170
    (E) 12pdr-armed frigates (*Frégates de 12*) acquired from 1747 — 174
    (F) 12pdr-armed vessels (two-deckers) acquired in 1770 — 184
    (G) 18pdr-armed frigates (*Frégates de 18*) acquired from 1772 — 185

Chapter 5 The Fifth Rank (*Vaisseaux du cinquième rang*) sometimes described as Frigates of the 2nd Order (*Frégates du 2e ordre*), and 8pdr-armed frigates after 1740 — 190
    (A) Vessels in service as at 9 March 1661 — 190
    (B) Vessels acquired from 9 March 1661 — 191
    (C) Vessels acquired from 15 April 1689 — 199
    (D) Vessels acquired from 1 September 1715 — 203
    (E) 8pdr-armed frigates (*Frégates de 8*) acquired from 1740 — 203

Chapter 6 Light Frigates (*Frégates légères*) — 216
    (A) Frigates in service as at 9 March 1661 — 216
    (B) Frigates acquired from 9 March 1661 — 216
    (C) Frigates acquired from 15 April 1689 — 223
    (D) 6pdr-armed *frégates légères* acquired from 1 September 1715 — 234
    (E) 8pdr- and 12pdr-armed *frégates légères* acquired from 1 September 1715 — 236

Chapter 7 Bomb Vessels and other Coastal Warfare Craft (*Galiotes à mortiers, Galiotes à bombes, Prames, Chaloupes-canonnières*, etc) — 239
Bomb Vessels — 239
    (B) Vessels acquired from 9 March 1661 — 239
    (C) Vessels acquired from 15 April 1689 — 242
    (D) Vessels acquired from 1 September 1715 — 243
Prams (*Prames*) — 246
    (D) Vessels acquired from 1 September 1715 — 247
Floating Batteries — 247
    (D) Vessels acquired from 1 September 1715 — 247
Gunboats (*Chaloupes-canonnières*) and mortar boats (*Chaloupes-carcassières*) — 247
    (B) Vessels acquired from 9 March 1661 — 247
    (C) Vessels acquired from 15 April 1689 — 248
    (D) Vessels acquired from 1 September 1715 — 248

Chapter 8 Fireships (*Brûlots*) — 252
    (A) Vessels in service as at 9 March 1661 — 252
    (B) Vessels acquired from 9 March 1661 — 252
    (C) Vessels acquired from 15 April 1689 — 258
    (D) Vessels acquired from 1 September 1715 — 263

Chapter 9 Storeships and Cargo Ships (*Flûtes* and *Gabarres*) — 266
Storeships (*Flûtes*) — 266
    (A) Vessels in service as at 9 March 1661 — 267
    (B) Vessels acquired from 9 March 1661 — 267
    (C) Vessels acquired from 15 April 1689 — 276
    (D) Vessels acquired from 1 September 1715 — 283

Cargo Ships (*Gabarres*)	294	Supply and Patrol Vessels	366
(A) Vessels acquired from 1714	294	(C) Vessels acquired from 15 April 1689	366
		(D) Vessels acquired from 1 September 1715	366
Chapter 10 Corvettes and *Barques Longues*	302	Yachts, *Traversiers*, and *Paquebots*	369
(A) Vessels in service as at 9 March 1661	302	(B) Vessels acquired from 9 March 1661	370
(B) Vessels acquired from 9 March 1661	303	(C) Vessels acquired from 15 April 1689	370
(C) Vessels acquired from 15 April 1689	307	(D) Vessels acquired from 1 September 1715	370
(D) Corvettes with 4pdr guns acquired from December 1715	316	**Addendum** The Galley Corps (*corps des galères*)	372
(E) Corvettes with 6pdr (or heavier) guns acquired from 1763	325	(A) Vessels acquired before 9 March 1661	373
		(B) Vessels acquired from 9 March 1661	374
		(C) Vessels acquired from 15 April 1689	379
Chapter 11 Minor Warships – *Ponant* types (Barques, Brigantines, Snows, Cutters, Luggers, Schooners, Brigs, etc)	332	(D) Vessels acquired from 1 September 1715	381
(A) Vessels in service as at 9 March 1661	332	Appendix A. Strength of the French Navy, 1660–1786	384
(B) Vessels acquired from 9 March 1661	332	Appendix B. Financial Expenditures on the French Navy, 1662–1786	387
(C) Vessels acquired from 15 April 1689	333	Appendix C: French Warship Ranks and Changes in Ranks, 1669–1789	389
(D) Vessels acquired from 1 September 1715	335	Appendix D. Standard Armaments of French Ships, 1674 and 1689	394
Chapter 12 Minor Warships – *Levant* types (Barques, Brigantines, Tartanes, Feluccas, Xebecs, etc)	351	Appendix E. French Monarchs, Political and Naval Leaders, 1626–1786	395
(A) Vessels in service as at 9 March 1661	351	Appendix F. Selected French Master Shipwrights and Master Sculptors, 1661–1786	398
(B) Vessels acquired from 9 March 1661	352	Appendix G. Action stations of the 80-gun ship of the line *Foudroyant* of 1750	403
(C) Vessels acquired from 15 April 1689	353	Appendix H. Colbert's mass ship renamings of 24 June 1671.	404
(D) Vessels acquired from 1 September 1715	357	Appendix J. Lists of the French Fleet as at 1672 – 1682 – 1692 – 1702 – 1712 – 1723 – 1734 – 1743 – 1752 – 1765 – 1772 and 1786	406
Chapter 13 Minor Support Vessels	362		
Cargo Vessels	362		
(A) Vessels in service as at 9 March 1661	362		
(B) Vessels acquired from 9 March 1661	362		
(C) Vessels acquired from 15 April 1689	364	Index to Named Vessels	417
(D) Vessels acquired from 1 September 1715	365		

Preface

This is chronologically the first of two volumes describing ships and other vessels operated by the French Navy (*Marine Royale*) during the Age of Sail, although it is the second to be published. It commences with the development of French naval forces during the reign of Louis XIII under the guidance of Armand Jean du Plessis, Cardinal Richelieu, who became the King's First Minister in 1624, and took over specific responsibility for naval and maritime matters in 1626; this volume concludes with the re-organisation of the Navy at the start of 1786 under the auspices of the then *Secrétaire d'État à la Marine* (Minister of the Navy), Comte de Castries, and thus covers a period of 160 years. A companion volume already published covers the development of the French Navy from 1786 until the conclusion of the Age of Sail (around 1861) – this previously published work is hereafter referred to as Volume II; note that where differences between the two volumes' data are found, this is due to further research subsequent to Volume II's publication, and the current volume should be regarded as correct.

Our aim in this book has been to rescue from their underserved obscurity – for English-speaking readers, whose only acquaintance with these ships is as little-known opponents in naval actions – the identities of the thousands of individual vessels that served under the French flag during these 160 years, and to remind these readers that each of these vessels was the product of skilled design and craftmanship, and each formed a community of hundreds of men, living afloat for periods of years and ranging around the known world.

Inevitably a significant focus is on the ships of Louis XIV – the *Roi Soleil* (Sun King) – as this period served as a Golden Age in French naval history. The Navy created in the 1620s under Cardinal Richelieu's drive for overseas trade, and maintained by his successor Mazarin during the 1640s, declined dramatically during the 1650s to fewer than thirty effective vessels; it was virtually recreated during the following decade (in particular from 1666 to 1671) to reach the intended total of 120 combatant ships (*vaisseaux* and *frégates*, excluding lesser vessels) by 1672, and was maintained at this level (indeed, peaking at over 150 combatant ships in 1692), but went into a fresh decline in the last eight years of Louis XIV's reign to fewer than half the strength.

Following Louis XIV's death in 1715, the much-reduced naval service entered on an era of retrenchment and restructure, and by 1720 was back to its 1660 levels. A slow re-growth began in the 1720s and 1730s, but it was only from 1740 onwards that it again flourished and returned towards anything approaching its former levels. There followed periods of growth in and immediately preceding wartime and decline thereafter (the totals in 1757 briefly reached over 100 effective ships, but fell sharply during and after the Seven Years' War). Another recovery began immediately after the signing of the Treaty of Paris in 1763 and was accelerated under the new king, Louis XVI, in 1774, producing a fleet that performed well against its long-term opponent, Britain, and played a pivotal role in the outcome of the War of American Independence. The fleet was further strengthened during the 1780s, only to be undermined by the collapse of the King's finances in 1788 and the ensuing French Revolution.

The present volume gives a summary of the main technical details of each class of vessel built for or otherwise acquired by the French Navy from 1661 onwards, including its dimensions and tonnage, its complement of men, and its armament. The designers and builders of each vessel are listed, along with its construction dates. A few key highlights of individual ship histories have also been mentioned, notably participation in major battles and naval actions, and – for the latter part of Louis XIV's reign – details of Navy vessels 'lent' for privateering to commercial consortia, usually headed by a senior officer, and numbering Louis himself as one of the partners in the operation, in return for a share (typically a fifth of the net profit).

For vessels built prior to 1661 which were still in existence at that date, we give equal coverage of their details where they are known. Other vessels acquired from 1626 onwards, which had been lost or disposed of prior to 1661, are covered more briefly in the section headed 'Preamble'.

We emphasise below (see 'Dimensions' and 'Tons' below, under 'Structure and Organisation') that all dimensions and other measurements in this book, and in its companion volume covering 1786 to 1861 – unless explicitly described as being in English units – are given in contemporary French units of feet and inches (*pieds* and *pouces*), which were slightly more than 6.5 per cent greater than those used in Britain (or the USA). Conversely tonnages (in terms of tons weight) in French pre-metric units were approximately 3.8% smaller than those units in Britain. To aid the reader, we have given metric equivalents for the French dimensions, although of course the Metric System was not introduced until the 1790s.

Acknowledgments

As with our previous volume covering French Warships of 1786 to 1861, the present book would not have been possible without the many contributions made by colleagues and friends throughout the world. Many of these have been equally helpful with the other volume, but we must again thank them for their continued support and their erudite and well-informed suggestions. Others whose interests have been more related to this earlier period have been vital in ensuring accuracy.

There are several individuals whose expertise has been essential in keeping our work on track, and in encouraging our efforts. We have been delighted to welcome the addition to our research major contributions by *Contre-Amiral* Jean-Yves Nerzic, whose own writings on Louis XIV's navy should be commended to all readers. His helpful discourse on the program initiated by Louis XIV in the 1660s, his exhaustive research on *armements mixtes*, and his knowledgeable and enthusiastic contribution on all sections of our volume (down to a thorough reading through and proof-reading of our text) have made a vast contribution to the quality of this volume. We are also grateful to Larrie Ferreiro who likewise read the entire text and gave us important insights on naval architecture and on the history of the period of the War of American Independence.

We have equally been helped by the consistent support of Frank Fox, the acknowledged guru of seventeenth-century naval construction, who has clarified many contentious or ambiguous matters. In particular, his familiarity with the drawings of the two Van de Veldes (Dutch artists who drew hundreds of ships including some French) and other contemporary documentation has been invaluable in identifying ships (French, English and Dutch) which took part in many of the battles of the seventeenth century.

While both authors of this book have spent time in past years among the archives of the French Navy, neither of us was able to update our knowledge from sources in France during the writing of this book. So we were extremely fortunate that Jane Winfield (Rif's sister), a long-time French resident and professional researcher in Paris, diligently and enthusiastically carried out all the necessary extra research and ferreted out answers to clarify queries and resolve ambiguities in the archives. We also wish to thank the staff at the *Archives Nationales*, the *Bibliothèque Nationale*, the *Service Historique de la Défense*, and the *Musée de la Marine* in Paris (as well as the *Association des Amis de la Musée de la Marine*), as well as those at the *Château de Chantilly*, *Musée Jacquemart-André* and the *Bibliothèque Mazarine*, for the help that they provided to her, and to ourselves in past years.

We are indebted to Grant Walker and his staff at the US Naval Academy Museum at Annapolis for providing a number of illustrations from the Beverley R Robinson collection, as well as for his courtesy and kindness to Steve Roberts on visits to that institution. Staff at the Caird Library in the National Maritime Museum at Greenwich have been an unfailing source of co-operation during many years of research, and our appreciation is also due to the personnel at the Brass Foundry, the NMM's outstation at Woolwich where their vast collection of ship's draughts are stored. The Royal Naval Museum at Portsmouth also contributed to our search for illustrations.

Over a considerable period of time, our information and much helpful advice and support has come from a number of individuals, both in France and around the world, including Jim Bender, Leuewe Bouma, Deb Carlen, J David Davies, James W Davies, Fred Dittmar, David Hepper, John Houghton, Andrew Lambert, Frank Lecalvé, Ian McLaughlan, Byrne McLeod, Charles Moseley, Andy Peters, Stuart Rankin, Christian de Saint Hubert, Eduard ('Ted') Sozaev, John ('Mike') Tredrea and Emir Yener. We offer our apologies to anyone we have inadvertently omitted from this page.

Rif particularly wants to thank his wife Ann for her tolerance of the time he has given to this project, and for putting up with the piles of research documents around the house, while Steve wishes to remember his wife Sue Goetz Ross, who accompanied him on some of his research trips to France but who died long before he got the opportunity to publish his work in this book and its earlier companion.

As we mentioned in connection with our previous book, information in a variety of published works in French has been invaluable in corroborating our information from French archives and in filling in gaps where we lacked details. The comprehensive listings compiled and published over a series of volumes by Cdt Alain Demerliac have been an essential source of data, adding to our information on major ships and helping us to avoid overlooking some of the multitude of smaller craft. The published *répertoire* of Jean-Michel Roche has been a source of copious information, as have the earlier *répertoires* of Frank Lecalvé, Jacques Vichot and Pierre Le Conte. The massive studies of a variety of warship types by Jean Boudriot, the doyen of French sailing warship history are essential references for anyone working in this field. The massive doctoral dissertation of Contre-Amiral Jean-Yves Nerzic on *armements mixtes* has opened up a new dimension of French Navy operational history. Among English-language publications, we recognise Larrie Ferreiro's study of the origins of naval architecture in our period as the authoritative introduction to the evolution of the science. The work of Jean-Claude Lemineur had broken new ground in this field. We have also benefited from the published studies by Henri le Masson, Philippe Masson, Martine Acerra, Jean Peter, Patrick Villiers, Gérard Piouffre and Henri Simoni as well as other volumes referenced in our Bibliography. We gratefully acknowledge our debt to all these authors and their publications.

This publication would again not have been possible without the enthusiastic co-operation and support of our publisher, Robert Gardiner. Robert has not only scoured every possible source for the 220-or-so illustrations which have graced this volume, and contributed many of their captions, but has also been a constant reference point for resolving queries and has settled issues from his own wide-ranging knowledge of the topic. To Rob, to his colleague Julian Mannering, and to the rest of the team at Seaforth, we wish to express our profound thanks.

The whole study of the history of French sailing vessels – both naval and commercial – exists primarily because of the life-long efforts of the late Jean Boudriot, whose work as an architect and as a publisher equally known for his elegant productions on naval architecture and ancient weaponry made him one of the principal movers in the rebirth of the subject matter. Graciously, he gave Steve much support and encouragement during his doctoral research in France in 1973–74.

Structure and Organisation of the Book

This book, like our 1786–1861 volume in the same series, is organised primarily by ship type. Like their rivals across the English Channel, the French Navy classed its vessels since the 1630s according to their functions – primarily as *vaisseaux* (ships of the line of battle), *frégates* (cruising warships), *flûtes* (transports) and *brûlots* (fireships). The sweeping administrative reforms initiated by Colbert in 1669 included the categorising of its principal warships into Rates or *Rangs* (for clarity, this book will use the French term – anglicised to *Rank* – to distinguish it from the English system of Rates). For the French, from mid-1671 there were five Ranks (one fewer than for their cross-Channel rivals) and the criteria for determining the Rank into which ships were placed varied over the years.

Prior to 1669, there was a provisional division of combatants into just three Ranks – those carrying between 60 and 70 guns (1st *Rank*), those carrying between 40 and 50 guns (2nd *Rank*), and those carrying between 30 and 40 guns (3rd *Rank*). A new division into four Ranks was made in 1669 based on both tonnage and number of guns, and this was followed in 1670 with the redistribution of the fleet into five Ranks, (the five ranks first appearing in a *Règlement sur l'Artillerie des Vaisseaux* of 1 December 1669 that governed the distribution of bronze and iron guns to the different ranks). Ranks were initially based primarily on the tonnage of the ships but were subsequently determined in a more complex way than in the British Navy, with consideration also being given to the numbers of guns and decks and the size of the crew (see Appendix C). Vessels were moved from one Rank to another far more frequently than across the Channel, but as far as practical the *vaisseaux* and *frégates* have been divided initially according to the revised five Ranks that were introduced in July 1670 (the 1669 Ranking has been ignored in organising this book, although the 1669 Ranks are shown for individual ships' entries). Vessels which had been deleted by mid-1671 are treated according to how they would have been ranked if still extent at that date.

In this book, the first five chapters are devoted to the corresponding five Ranks (although there are exceptions for various reasons). The Rank system had become less meaningful before 1786, so our Volume II had to be organised somewhat differently. Basically, the 1st Rank comprised the largest two-decked or three-decked warships (including the majority of fleet flagships), which after 1689 comprised 36pdr-armed ships of the line, *i.e.* those carrying batteries of 36 *livres* (French pounds) calibre on the lowest of their three continuous gun decks, although prior to 1689 the lower deck batteries contained guns of lesser calibre.

The 2nd and 3rd Ranks comprised three-decked ships with partial third decks and fewer or lighter guns on their lower deck (these were only built before 1689 and were comparable with contemporary large British two-deckers), plus a range of two-decked ships, *i.e.* those carrying batteries of guns on two continuous gun decks capable of standing in the line of battle. In each case, smaller guns were carried on partial decks above the continuous upper deck. These partial decks consisted on the forecastle (forward) and the quarterdeck (aft) – and sometimes on the largest vessels a poop deck above the quarterdeck; the French used the useful term *gaillards* to group together these partial decks, and the term is adopted in this volume. All the vessels covered by these Ranks were described as *vaisseaux*.

It should be noted that all three Ranks of these *vaisseaux* contained both two-decker and three-decked ships until 1689 according to French definitions, although the definition of 'three-decked' differed from that employed in the English and Dutch Navies. Ships built after 1689 were either three-decked (for 1st Rank ships) or two-decked (for the 2nd and 3rd Ranks); however, from 1740 some two-decked warships of 80 guns were again included in the 1st Rank.

The 4th and 5th Ranks included two-decked ships not generally classed as fit for the battlefleet, normally described as frigates (or *frégates-vaisseaux*) and intended for cruising or for trade warfare (convoy protection or preying on the merchant fleet of France's adversaries in wartime). Smaller frigates which carried fewer guns than the minima set for the 5th Rank or had only a single gun deck were not included in the Rank system, but were classified as light frigates (or *frégates légères*), and these are included in Chapter 6.

During the 1740s the construction of *frégates légères* effectively ceased (it had been in decline for several decades), and they were superseded by what are in modern parlance generally described as 'true' frigates, *i.e.* vessels carrying a single battery of guns on their upper decks (often with a few smaller guns on the *gaillards*), with no openings in the hull on the lower deck level. From 1740 these were built with a battery of 8pdr guns, and these are included in the latter part of Chapter 5, as their role was effectively to replace that of the Fifth Rank ships. Beginning in 1747, frigates were built that carried a battery of 12pdr guns, and later on frigates would adopt a battery of 18pdr guns; these are included in the latter part of Chapter 4, as their role replaced that of the Fourth Rank ships.

The smaller unranked warships and auxiliaries were categorised by a variety of terms, and these are covered by the subsequent chapters.

The French system of grading warships by Rank (or *Rang* in French) according to size and firepower was similar to the Rating system employed for English/British ships, but differed in detail. While there was some separation prior to 1669, when Colbert introduced the first comprehensive structure of Ranks (which was significantly altered a year later), it would be inappropriate to try and apportion pre-1661 ships to a Rank in the way we have done from 1661 onwards. In addition, the amount of reliable data available for ships in service before 1661 is more limited compared to after that year. Our coverage of pre-1661 vessels is thus set out in a Preamble which covers the years from 1626 to 1661, although we have tried to give an account of the development of all significant combatant vessels of those 35 years. In most of the following chapters, the vessels are listed chronologically, subdivided into four periods:

Vessels already in service as at 9 March 1661.
Vessels acquired from 9 March 1661 (up to 1689).
Vessels acquired from 15 April 1689 (up to 1815).
Vessels acquired from 1 September 1715 (up to 1786).

Dates

We must stress that throughout this book we have quoted the dates recorded in the Gregorian calendar (or 'New Style') now used everywhere and which was introduced into France in 1582. In England and its dependent territories the former Julian calendar (or 'Old Style') was retained until September 1752, and this meant that dates in England appearing throughout the seventeenth century were ten days behind those in France and most other countries; in the eighteenth century (until 1753) this disparity increased to eleven days. Also, whereas the Julian year began on 25 March, the Gregorian year – as now – began on 1 January. Finally, in France the day changed over at midnight, whereas for the British Navy, as recorded in the Ships' Logs, the change took place at noon. Thus, there will be these differences between days given in British records and those in this book. The only exception to our policy of using Gregorian calendar dates has been for the construction dates of vessels built in Britain in the period before September 1752, where we have not altered the Julian dates with which English-speaking readers will be familiar.

Dimensions

All the dimensions quoted in this volume (and continued in the subsequent volume, until the introduction of the metric system) are given in French feet (*pieds*) and inches (*pouces*). **Note carefully** that these differ considerably from the English/British (Imperial) and US units of measurement. The French foot measured 32.48394 centimetres compared with the English/British foot of exactly 30.48 centimetres. The French foot was thus 6.5746 per cent longer than the English, and to compare dimensions the French measurement should be multiplied by a factor of 1.065746. The metric equivalents of these dimensions are quoted in parentheses.

- *Length*: This dimension was normally measured in the seventeenth century from the forward face of the stempost to the after face of the sternpost (*de l'étrave à l'étambot*) at the tops of those two verticals, sometimes specified as from head to head (*de tête en tête*). The length of the keel (given here when known after the primary length) consisted of the length of the portion of the keel 'on the ground' (*portant sur terre*). Measurement practices later changed, and by the end of the eighteenth century a ship's length was commonly measured at the level of the gun deck (LD) port sills, or if the designer preferred at the height of the wing transom, instead of at the top of the stem and sternposts. This length is commonly called the length on deck (the gun deck) although it was also called the length between perpendiculars. Length however was also taken in some dockyards at the waterline between the rabbet of the stem and the rabbet of the stern (*de rablure en rablure*), and other measurements could also be taken at the rabbits. (The rabbet, or rabbit or rabbeting, was a wedge-shaped channel or groove cut into the face of the stempost, sternpost, keel, and wing transom to receive the planking.) The various forms of measurement by the end of the eighteenth century make it difficult to interpret lengths recorded then without further detailed explanation, although the measurement of length during the seventeenth century appears to have been relatively consistent.

- *Breadth*: The breadth of the vessel was taken in the seventeenth century at the widest point of the vessel to the outside of the frame and including the hull planking (*hors bordage*). In the eighteenth century it became the common practice to measure it at the same point but to the outside of the frame excluding the planking (*hors membrure*).

- *Depth in hold* (*creux*): For warships the 'construction depth inside the vessel' was usually measured at the point of the maximum breadth of the ship from the top of the keel to a horizontal line drawn between the tops of the ends of the midship beam (*maître-bau*), although another measure was used for merchant vessels. Most of the depth measurements given here are probably of this type. In some cases the French instead measured depth (the load measurement) from the top of the keelson to the under side of the midship beam. The British in contrast measured it from the upper side of the limber strakes to the upper side of the gun deck on the centreline amidships, producing figures that in some cases were significantly different from the French measurements (especially for frigates in the later 1700s). The French measured the *creux* of ships without decks as the vertical distance from the top of the keel to the gunwale at the midship beam.

Tons

The tonnages quoted are in tonnes of 2,000 French pounds (*livres*). The French pound equated to 489.5 grams compared with the English/British pound of 453.6 grams, so that the French weight was 7.916 per cent greater than the English equivalent. Thus, the 2,000-*livre* pre-metric tonne amounted to 979 kilogrammes, whereas the English/British ton of 2,240lbs equalled 1,016.064 kilogrammes; accordingly, the (pre-metrication) tonne should by multiplied by a factor of 0.963522 to give English/British tonnage.

Where known, two tonnages are quoted, separated by an oblique stroke (/). The first figure is the 'port' measurement, approximately equivalent to the British burthen tonnage and essentially an empirical measurement of the volume of the hold of the ship converted to tons by an arbitrary factor. They changed fairly often for individual ships for reasons that remain unclear, and, as the rank of a ship was loosely based on its tonnage until around 1692, re-rankings sometimes accompanied tonnage changes.

The methods of calculating the tonnage (port) of a ship varied from shipwright to shipwright. In 1689 Blaise Pangalo measured the tonnage of the three-decker *Conquérant* by multiplying her length between the stempost and sternpost at their tops (146ft 6in), the width at the midships frame (41ft), and the *creux* (18ft) and then dividing the product by 85, resulting in a measurement of 1,271 tons. At about the same time Laurent Coulomb used essentially the same calculation but divided the product of the dimensions by 60. The calculation was quite different for merchant ships (and presumably naval ships intended to carry cargo). The classic 1745 *Traité du navire* of Pierre Bouguer defined the *tonneau d'arrimage* or the ton in which the 'port' [burthen] of a ship was measured as the space occupied by four barrels of Bordeaux wine, this space being standardised in the *Ordonnance de la Marine* of 1681 at 42 cubic (French) feet = 1 ton. The quick way to calculate this was to measure the depth of hold in three places (amidships and at the ends) and take the average, measure the widths at the same places but three times: high, middle, and low and reducing the nine widths to another average, and then taking the product of the two averages and the length of the hold. He gives an example of a ship measured at 10,000 cubic feet, which at 42 cubic feet per ton measured at 288 tons. He then discourses at some length on the weaknesses of this system, beginning by stating that a ton should really be 48 or 49 cubic feet.

The second tonnage figure, where it appears after the oblique stroke, is a displacement (or weight of water displaced by the ship) at full load, *i.e.* when fully equipped and laden with men, stores and ordnance.

Men

The number of men is from multiple French sources, some of which recorded the established total of officers and ratings and some of which recorded men actually on board. For the period from 1669 to 1692 our primary source for manning data, the *États abrégés de la Marine*, subdivided the number of ratings into three categories – petty officers (*officiers mariniers*), seamen (*matelots*), and marines (*soldats*). These are shown here in the format '(a/b/c)', preceded by the total number of ratings and followed by the number of commissioned officers. For example, the manning of the first ship in Chapter 1, the *Vendôme*, is shown here as '550 (90/340/120) +9 officers', indicating that she had a crew of 550 ratings (90 petty officers, 340 seamen, and 120 marines) plus 9 commissioned officers. Many ships did not carry a contingent of marines and the number for that category is therefore absent.

Guns

Armaments shown in this book are those allocated to a vessel or class of vessel at the time of its entry into service (although sometimes the planned ordnance was altered even before the vessel or vessels entered service). Major subsequent alterations in armament are quoted where possible, but in wartime in particular more guns were probably added for which no records survive.

There is a near-total lack of contemporary data on armaments actually carried by individual ships prior to 1696. To compensate for this, we have in Sections (A) and (B) provided estimated armaments based on the governing directives and the known characteristics of the ships. The two principal directives governing armaments, dating from 1674 and 1689, are provided in Appendix D. Only a handful of armaments given here for ships before 1696 are from actual documentary sources (one example of a documented armament is that of 1666 for *Saint Philippe* in Chapter 1). We feel that the armaments shown here are those most likely to have been carried, but the lack of standardisation during the period, shortages of some types of guns at certain times, and the whims of individual commanding officers and dockyard officials could have led to considerable variation in armaments actually carried.

From 1696 to 1743 detailed information was provided in the annual *États abrégés* concerning the armaments of the navy's ships, and similar information is available for 1746. These armaments changed frequently. We have listed most of these armament changes here, the others being questionable for various reasons. The years given here for armament changes are those of the first *État* in which the changed armament was recorded, the actual change probably occurring early in the year of the *État* or one or two years before.

During the second half of the eighteenth century the armaments of the larger ships tended to become standardised, all 74-gun ships, for example, carrying the same outfit of guns with little variation between ships or during operational careers. We have recorded here the relatively few cases of which we are aware in which the armaments of a ship diverged from the standard or changed during the ship's career.

Construction and Construction Dates

Where known, the dockyard or port of construction of each individual vessel is given, along with its designer and the actual senior shipwright who oversaw the building (in many cases, this was the same person, but where this differed we have tried to give both names). As with shipwrights in Britain and elsewhere, skills were passed down the family generations, and thus surnames are inadequate to identify individuals; as a consequence, we have wherever possible included the first and middle names (*prénoms*) of the individuals. Most of the shipwrights involved are also listed in Appendix F.

The dates of construction given are usually three. 'K' signifies the keel laying date or the start of construction date; 'L' signifies the date of launch (or of entry into the water in the case of vessels built in dry dock); and 'C' signifies the completion date or date of entry into service. Where possible we have also given the date on which the instruction to build was given by the *Secrétaire d'État à la Marine* (Minister of the Navy) and the date upon which the vessel was formally allocated its name ('Named').

French Naval Technology and Organisation from Colbert to Castries

The French Navy in the seventeenth and eighteenth centuries differed in some significant ways from its contemporaries across the Channel or in the Netherlands, whose vessels and naval structures have been described in other volumes in this series. Perhaps the most crucial differences between French and other navies' ships – certainly in the period before 1689 – were in the structural levels of the various ships of the line of battle (*vaisseaux* in French), and in the mixed calibres of cannon which armed these decks.

The Small Three-decked Ship of the Line

While there were certainly small ships with three continuous gun decks in the other major navies (in this book we use the term 'gun deck' to identify *all* the continuous cannon-bearing decks running from stem to stern, rather than simply the British practice of reserving the term for the lowest of these decks), mid-seventeenth century French practice was more widespread in building three-decked warships with as few as fifty guns. We exclude from our definition the fore and aft superstructures above the upper continuous deck – the forecastle (where such existed), quarterdeck and poop as usually described. Note the French did not employ the translations of the terms 'lower deck', 'middle deck' and 'upper deck'; instead they referred to these deck levels as the 'first deck,' 'second deck,' and 'third deck' for three-deckers; as English-speaking readers would not be familiar with this practice, we have retained the more easily understood terms in this book. But we must caution the reader that the French definition of a three-decked ship differed markedly from that employed by the English.

On most three-deckers (prior to 1689), the upper gun deck was not armed with a continuous battery of cannon, but was divided in the waist of the ship. In some ships there was physically a continuous deck at this level (to cover and protect the men on the middle deck below), with continuous bulwarks along the sides (but no gunports), and supported below by transverse deck beams across the full width of the ship to provide structural strength; these ships carried no guns at this level when built, but in 1690 surviving ships of this grade received extra guns to give them a full UD battery.

In other ships, there was a physical gap at the waist, so that the central portion of the middle deck was open to the elements; on a number of ships, this gap was filled by a residual structure (a centreline gangway termed a 'flying bridge') linking the fore and aft sections of this deck. This structure could be (and frequently was) removed in operational practice, turning the type into what would by comprehended by the English as a two-decker. Nevertheless, the French Navy categorised all these ships officially as 'three-deckers', and described their non-continuous upper decks as the 'third deck'. This led to some confusion between the navies, as in 1672 when, during a period of Anglo-French alliance and co-operation, a small French squadron visited Portsmouth, consisting of the 70-gun ships *Superbe*, *Royal Thérèse* (ex-*Paris*) and *Magnanime*.

The main exceptions (prior to 1689) among 1st Rank ships were the massive *vaisseaux du premier rang extraordinaire* – those few vessels of 100 guns of more, which carried three full tiers of guns, plus smaller guns on their forecastles, quarterdecks, and in some cases poops.

These small three-deckers were eliminated in stages. On 22 March 1671, a Regulation was laid down decreeing that ships with fewer than 70 guns should in future by built as two-deckers. In 1689 a fresh decree extended the Regulation to cover all new ships with fewer than 80 guns. Obviously, these regulations applied to new construction rather than to existing ships. In some cases, it was possible to convert an existing three-decker into a two-decker by the simple process of dismantling a 'flying bridge'. On other vessels, a more comprehensive restructuring was required, and clearly on many vessels no changes were carried out and vessels remained three-deckers until the end of their lives. After 1689 all new three-deckers carried three full decks of guns, and none carried fewer than 80 guns.

Mixed Calibres on Gun Decks

The other significant difference, not always clear from certain writings, is that the lower – and on three-deckers the middle – decks on almost all pre-1689 French warships carried a mixture of calibres. The practice was clearly defined in the appropriate regulations, and there seem to have been few exceptions. Thus, a typical three-decker might have had a combination of 24pdr and 18pdr guns on its lower deck, and a combination of 12pdr and 8pdr guns on its middle deck, with 6pdrs on the upper deck (and sometimes 4pdrs on the poop, as a 4th tier). At some date before 1689, single calibres on each deck were adopted, and these became general after 1689 for new construction (and for refitting some older ships), although some older vessels were never re-armed.

Changes in Ship Rankings, 1669–1716

A major complication in determining which chapter should record details of individual ships is that the French Ranks were subject to frequent alteration, with ships being moved from one Rank to another and often back again. This was primarily true with the seventeenth century Ranks, but re-classing also took place during the eighteenth century. This was also a factor with the British Navy, but its more extensive employment by the French may make it difficult for the reader to locate a particular ship. In general, we have tried to describe a ship under the Rank it held when it first entered French naval service, but sometimes we have chosen to position a ship elsewhere when we judged it more helpful to record the development of a particular ship type.

There can be no absolute rule adopted in this matter, and doubtless some readers would have determined matters differently, so we must ask for their indulgence. The individual entries for ships do record what changes took place for that particular ship. A more detailed explanation of the changes in Rank is given in Appendix C of this book, but if the reader cannot find a particular vessel we would recommend referring to the Index to Named Vessels at the back.

Appearance and Design

Further constructional factors contributed to differences between most French-built ships (we shall ignore here French-operated ships built abroad or captured from other countries) and those of other navies. French ships were generally larger, but more lightly built; among smaller ships, this is because they were not expected to remain at sea for such protracted periods as the ships of the maritime powers. It meant also that they tended on average to be faster.

The decoration of French ships, particularly the stern of major ships, was both more prolific and more formalised than in other navies. Under Louis XIV in particular, the carving and painting adorning their structures was designed to be more magnificent and more impressive than that of their likely opponents. The figureheads and sterns were distinct in their iconography and in the skills of their artwork. Many of the artists and sculptors who created the seventeenth century opulence of Versailles and Fontainebleau were equally employed in creating masterpieces afloat. Louis XIV and Colbert established sculpture academies in the three main dockyards, whose graduate craftsmen brought to life the designs of Pierre Puget and others. The navy's senior sculptors are listed at the end of Appendix F.

The ostentatious decoration, particularly the most ornate sculpture which graced the bow and stern of each ship during much of the sevententh century, was subject to radical pruning as the century neared its end. The decorators and sculptors, all gifted and often celebrated artists, outdid each other and indeed themselves to satisfy the vanity of their monarch; but the actual ship commanders, viewing the encumbrance and the fire danger of the ornamental work when at sea – particularly in action – strongly opposed the scale of the decoration, and often took steps to reduce it. The celebrated Pierre Puget, for example, would have been horrified to know that much of his careful artistic work was apt to be quietly jettisoned by a captain as soon as it was out of sight of the dockyard. Obviously this could not happen to the fleet flagships, which were likely to be visited by Louis and his senior ministers; but such carvings clearly suffered in action – witness the description of the ruined state of the magnificent stern sculptures of the *Soleil Royal* when she was grounded in Cherbourg after the Battle of Barfleur (where she would be burnt in a fireship attack a few days later).

Flags

The Royal Standard was white, adorned with fleurs-de-lys and bearing the full royal arms. The flags of ordinary men of war were plain white. Merchant ships flew a blue flag with a white cross that might also bear the royal arms; they also might fly at the main top the flag of their province or of their city. The vessels of the King's commercial companies (*Compagnie des Indes Orientales*, *Compagnie du Sénégal*, etc.) flew a white flag bearing the royal arms. The flags of the galley corps were predominantly red.

Ordnance

The principal weapon carried by all naval ships during this period was the smooth-bore cannon of varying sizes and weights mounted on a truck (wheeled) carriage. All French guns were classified according to the weight of the spherical solid shot that they could fire, but they could also be separated into those manufactured from bronze (*fonte verte*) and those cast from iron. During the seventeenth century, the limitations of foundry technology means that the heavier pieces could only be manufactured in bronze, although this situation changed significantly, when iron 24pdrs and 36pdrs (the abbreviation 'pdr' signifying '-pounder' is used throughout this book) began to be introduced in 1688 and 1691 respectively. Nevertheless, bronze guns remained the preference, and by 1689 it was decreed that the guns in ships of the 1st Rank should all be of bronze.

Colbert's Navy inherited in 1661 a variety of cannon of at least seventeen different calibres, a confusing situation and one which greatly hampered maintenance and supply of ammunition. A start was made in 1661 by restricting the number of calibres to seven, although the changeover took time, and the last 'non-standard' calibre weapons did not disappear until about 1676.

The available supply of guns of the seven 'regular' calibres in 1661 recorded the following totals:

Calibre	English units	Bronze	Iron	Total
36pdr	38lbs 13.6oz	13	–	13
24pdr	25lbs 14.4oz	106	–	106
18pdr	19lbs 6.8oz	85	66	151
12pdr	12lbs 15.2oz	87	146	233
8pdr	8lbs 10.1oz	88	99	187
6pdr	6lbs 7.6oz	12	19	31
4pdr	4lbs 5.1oz	3	19	22

It can be seen that the supply of cannon at this time was barely enough to arm more than a few ships. Colbert's ambition to create within a few years a Navy of some 120 vessels (an aim which he achieved by 1671) required an equal effort in gun manufacture. Including the non-standard calibres the Navy's inventory rose to a total of 5,090 guns in 1671. During the next quarter-century the inventory almost doubled, reaching its peak of 9,514 guns (including 631 *interrompus*, probably unfit for service) in 1696. The other main development during this period was the development of the ability to manufacture large calibre guns of iron (24pdrs in 1688 and 36pdrs in 1691), with the subsequent decline in the production of bronze guns and the near-disappearance in the inventory by 1696 of bronze guns smaller than 18pdrs. The following quantities of guns of the standard calibres were available in 1671 and 1696:

Calibre	1671 Bronze	1671 Iron	1671 Total	1696 Bronze	1696 Iron	1696 Total
36pdr	64	–	64	405	214	619
24pdr	252	30	282	432	554	986
18pdr	391	446	837	315	1,256	1,571
12pdr	372	1,049	1,421	12	1,743	1,755
8pdr	315	828	1,143	3	1,571	1,574
6pdr	105	487	592	3	1,508	1,511
4pdr	39	195	234	8	795	803

By the early 1690s the 36pdr had become the standard heavy weapon of the battlefleet. The Ordinance of 15 April 1689 (see Appendix D) specified a uniform armament of bronze 36pdrs on the LD of first rank ships of 1690, and increased production of these weapons was soon followed by the introduction of iron 36pdrs which gradually supplanted them.

Bronze 36pdrs. These guns had a length of some 10ft (3.04m) and a calibre of 6.88in (17.48cm). They weighed (without carriage) about 3,300 kg (kilos), lighter than their 3,700 kg iron equivalents. They were cast primarily in the dockyard foundries at Toulon and Rochefort. The number of bronze 36pdrs available increased dramatically between 1690 (when 115 were available) and 1692 (when 407 were available). However, bronze guns cost eight to nine times as much to produce as their iron equivalents, and the financial difficulties of the late portion of Louis XIV's reign helped bring about the end of the production of bronze guns of all calibres during the first quarter of the eighteenth century.

Iron 36pdrs. Until the Nine Years War (1688–1697) gunfounding technology was not capable of producing reliable iron weapons of this calibre. Iron guns were produced mostly by contract, especially in the Angumois and Périgord regions in southwest France and at Saint-

Gervais in southeast France. The first iron 36pdrs were successfully cast in late 1691 at Saint-Gervais and by by François de Dans de Hautefort at Ans in the Périgord, and 35 iron 36pdrs were on hand in early 1692. In 1701 the number of iron 36pdrs exceeded the number of bronze 36pdrs for the first time, and in 1712 the Navy had 548 iron 36pdrs compared with 430 of the bronze variety. The importance of 36pdrs (now all being built of iron) increased again after 1715 when they became the standard weapon of 2nd Rank ships of the line as well as 1st Rank. Over the years, the weight of metal increased, so that by 1767 it was 3,643 kg.

The dimensions of French iron naval guns varied over time. The first French Establishment for iron guns was fixed in 1674. It fixed the length of the lesser five of the seven 'standard' calibres from muzzle ring to base ring as follows: 18pdr – 8ft 4½in (2.72m); 12pdr – 7ft 10½in (2.56m); 8pdr – 7ft 4½in (2.40m); 6pdr – 6ft 10¾in (2.24m); 4pdr – 5ft 5in (1.76m). The 36pdrs and 24pdrs were not included as French gunfounding could not reliably produce many guns of those calibres.

However, by the 1690s this had changed, and a fresh Establishment introduced in 1690 included all seven calibres: 36pdr – 9ft 10¼in to 9ft 4¼in (3.20 to 3.04m); 24pdr – 9ft 4¼in (3.04m); 18pdr – 8ft 10½in (2.88m); 12pdr – 8ft 4½in (2.72m); 8pdr – 7ft 11¼in (2.56m); 6pdr – 6ft 10¾in (2.24m); 4pdr – 5ft 11in (1.92m). While their proportions were altered in 1721, 1733 and 1758, and gun weights increased, these lengths remained constant until a new Establishment in 1766 shortened them.

The 1766 revision significantly reduced gun lengths: 36pdr – 8ft 10½in (2.88m); 24pdr – 8ft 4½in (2.72m); 18pdr – 7ft 10½in (2.56m); 12pdr – 7ft 4½in (2.40m); 8pdr – 6ft 9in (2.19m); 6pdr – 6ft 1in (1.975m); 4pdr – 5ft 5in (1.76m).

These lengths were again revised in 1778, when long and short versions of the four smallest guns were introduced: 36pdr – 8ft 10in (2.87m); 24pdr – 8ft 4¾in (2.729m); 18pdr – 7ft 8in (2.492m); 12pdr – 7ft 5.125in (2.413m) and 6ft 8.375in (2.176m); 8pdr – 6ft 9in (2.19m) and 5ft 11in (1.92m); 6pdr – 6ft 2½in (2.015m) and 5ft 4¼in (1.74m); 4pdr – 5ft 4.675in (1.75m) and 4ft 8½in (1.53m).

Finally, right at the close of our period, new lengths were defined in the 1786 reforms brought in by Castries: 36pdr – 8ft 9¾in (2.865m); 24pdr – 9ft 4¼in (2.735m); 18pdr – 8ft 10½in (2.572m); 12pdr – 8ft 4½in (2.43m); 8pdr – 7ft 11¼ft (2.598 and 2.219m); 6pdr – 6ft 10¾in (2.273 and 2.003m); 4pdr – 5ft 11in (1.792 and 1.538m).

The French experimented with cannons larger than the 36pdr without much success. Oversized guns were not entirely new to them – in 1669 they had one 60pdr dating from before 1661 and two 48pdrs at Toulon made in the 1660s. (The former was gone by 1671 and the latter lasted until 1690; two more 48pdrs were briefly listed at Rochefort in 1687–89.) Beginning in 1690 the French developed 48pdr and 64pdr guns in both bronze and iron and a bronze 100pdr.

Bronze 48pdrs. On 10 March 1690 Seignelay recommended building some larger guns to strengthen the ships then being fitted out at Brest – he probably wanted to match the 42pdr 'cannon-of-seven' on the lower decks of the largest British three-deckers. In September 1689 Seignelay ordered the manufacture of 12 bronze 48pdrs at Toulon and Rochefort to fill the Navy's needs for 1690. They weighed about 8,000 pounds and were around ten feet long. Four of them were embarked for trials in *Monarque* in July 1690 and found satisfactory. All twelve guns were at Brest by the end of 1690, eight of them were probably embarked in *Soleil Royal* in 1690–92 and six in *Admirable* in 1692. In 1692 more 48pdrs were ordered from Toulon and Rochefort for the new *Royal Louis* and by early 1693 around twelve of these were already at Brest. However, the flag officer in *Royal Louis*, Victor Marie, Comte d'Estrées, found the huge guns too cumbersome to operate and arranged for them to be replaced with 36pdrs. (The British evidently came to the same conclusion, as they eliminated the 42pdr in their 1703 establishment in favour of the more versatile 32pdr.) The thirty 48pdrs ended up in the battery called *Royale* in the defences of Brest, although on paper they remained assigned to *Royal Louis* through 1723. These guns were then assigned to *Foudroyant* in 1725–42 but not embarked and were later carried in a new *Royal Louis* in 1780–82 and in *Majestueux* in 1782–83.

Iron 48pdrs. On 8 May 1692 the *commissaire général de l'artillerie* at Rochefort, CV Jean-Bernard de Saint-Jean, Baron de Pointis, persuaded Dans to cast an iron 48pdr at Ans in the Périgord and send it to Brest, where it was proved in June 1693. It weighed no more than a bronze 48pdr. He then cast a second one, and these were probably the two listed at Brest in 1696. Although several dozen were made up to 1697 for coast defences, only five more appeared in the naval inventory, at Rochefort in 1698. The two at Brest were embarked on an unidentified ship in 1704 and all seven were still in the inventory in 1723.

Bronze 64pdrs. In December 1689 Seignelay ordered twelve bronze 64pdrs from Toulon and Rochefort. These were *canons-bombes*, designed to fire 64-pound hollow explosive projectiles like those fired from mortars. The bronze 64pdr *canons-bombes* weighed no more than the bronze 48pdr *canons* because their projectiles were lighter. The six cast at Toulon were at Brest by 1692 (four may have been tried there in *Monarque* in mid-1691) and the six cast at Rochefort arrived at Port Louis (Lorient) in late 1692. Some were probably among the 64pdrs embarked in *Pompeux* in 1693. In 1695 Brest proposed mounting two of these guns in the captured British bomb vessel *Tonnerre*. The inventory declined to eight in 1696, six in 1702, four in 1706, and none in 1710.

Iron 64pdrs (60pdrs). The first iron 64pdrs (sometimes called 60pdrs) were cast in 1693 at Saint Gervais and in the Périgord. The weight and recoil of these weapons were similar to those of 36pdrs, they were 7½ feet long instead of 9ft 4in for the bronze guns. On 18 March 1693 two 7-foot and two 9-foot *canons-bombes* were ordered placed on *Phénix*, a 3rd Rank ship then building at Toulon, but they may instead have been among the eight 60pdrs reported on the LD of the older *Pompeux* in the same year. The navy had 15 of these guns in 1696 (all at Toulon) with one added in 1699 plus 8 added at Brest in 1701. The eight at Brest were listed as embarked in 1704; they may have included the four reported in *Victorieux* around this time. In 1709 eight 64pdrs were embarked on ships at Toulon. The navy still had 24 of these guns in 1723: 14 at Toulon, 8 at Brest, and 2 at Rochefort.

Bronze 100pdrs. On 16 October 1689 Rochefort was authorized to cast two 100pdr bronze guns. No details are available on this weapon, although it was most likely a *canon-bombe*. It was listed only intermittently in the inventory, with four in 1696 and 1702, two in 1707, and none after 1709. *Ambitieux* briefly carried four of these guns in around 1704.

Besides conventional cannon, two other items of ordnance deserve mention (other than small arms). The *pierrier* (anglicised to 'perrier' in British usage, although this was also called a 'swivel' by them; but the Ordnance Office generally called them 'bases' or 'murderers'; the Spanish called them 'pedreroes', while the Dutch called them 'kamerstukken', or chamber guns) was – as its name implies – originally evolved to fire stone projectiles rather than metal ones. The term in English originally referred to weapons (of up to 24pdr calibre) firing stone shot. By the mid-seventeenth century the larger calibres had become obsolete, but the *pierrier* survived as a lightweight short-barrelled anti-personnel weapon, usually fitted into a metal stock (between the arms of which it could be elevated or depressed), in turn mounted on a swivelling base on an upright wooden post which was integral with a ship's structure. By the 1660s they used shrapnel ammunition in removable chambers (usually 8 per gun), which were loaded in advance and could be removed and replaced in a few seconds, making quick-firing guns. The name *pierrier* was latterly employed by the French as a term by which to describe all their light swivel-mounted guns.

The other item of heavy ordnance was the sea mortar. This was adopted in the early 1680s as a shore bombardment weapon in vessels specially designed for the purpose. Clearly not applicable for ship-to-ship combat, the mortar-bearing vessel (usually constructed as a galiote) was the seventeenth/eighteenth century version of the twentieth century monitor. Whereas mortar vessels in the English Navy were built with mortars fitted along the centreline of the vessel, usually one ahead of and one aft of the mainmast, in French service the mortars were carried in pairs, mounted side by side before the vessel's mainmast to fire forward over the bows. The weapons were fixed in place, and could not be trained to either side. Furthermore, there were initially cast with an integral base-plate from which they could not be moved, and fixed into the mortar vessel's structure with a fixed elevation of 45 degrees. Consequently, they could not alter their elevation, and the sole means of changing their range was by varying the size of the powder charge used. Later in the eighteenth century mortars were fitted on mountings that could be trained and elevated. For more details on the origins and operational service of French bomb vessels, please see Chapter 7.

Manning Levels

The number of personnel carried by each type of vessel inevitably grew over the decades, as ships increased in size, armament and complexity. Individual vessels' manpower increased or decreased from time to time, but were broadly in line with criteria set down by the Navy, which are summarised in this section.

The number of men assigned to each vessel varied according to the Rank it was graded at, as well as its individual characteristics, notably the number and calibres of the guns carried. The number of men ('ratings' in modern parlance) excluded the numbers of commissioned officers, and in the listing within this volume the officers are shown separately where known.

Excluding commissioned officers, in September 1669, 1st Rank ships each had between 550 and 800 men (the smaller *Henri* had just 450); each 2nd Rank ship had 450 (for ships of 66 guns and above) or 400 (for smaller 2nd Rank ships); each 3rd Rank had from 250 to 350 men; 4th Ranks had between 150 and 230 men; light frigates had between 30 and 80 men (the tiny 2-gun *Laurier* had just 25); and other vessels also varied between 25 and 80 men. From January 1671, 1st Rank ships each had between 450 and 900 men; each 2nd Rank ship had 425 (for ships of 66 guns and above) or 400 (for smaller 2nd Rank ships or large 3rd Rank ships with 60 to 64 guns); ships of 52 to 56 guns had 350 men; those 3rd and 4th Rank ships of 50 guns and below varied from 220 to 300 men; 5th Rank ships had between 120 and 200 men, while light frigates and lesser vessels carried between 25 and 60 men. As with all these figures, there were exceptions which are covered in the individual chapters.

At the start of 1690, ships of 76 guns and above had between 500 and 850 men; ships of 66 to 74 guns had 400 men and those of 60 to 64 guns had 350 (with some exceptions); most 4th Rank ships (with between 40 and 58 guns) had between 200 and 300 men, and 5th Rank ships each had 150 men. Light frigates ranged between 50 and 130 men.

By 1765, the larger 1st Ranks (*Royal Louis* and the new *Bretagne*) each had 1,150 men in wartime, the 90-gun *Ville de Paris* had 950, the 80-gun ships had 850 (except the *Duc de Bourgogne*, which had just 780 because she only mounted 18pdrs on the UD), and the 74-gun 2nd Rank ships had 650 each, while the 56-gun and 64-gun ships each had 480; 50-gun ships had 350 or 400 men, most frigates had 190 or 220. By the start of 1786, the 110-gun ships had 1,037 men (1,098 in the newbuilding 118-gun ships), the 80-gun ships had 839, the 74s had 690 and the 64s had 523; the new 18pdr-armed frigates had 314 men and the lesser frigates 261 each.

As regards commissioned officers, in September 1669, nine were assigned to each 1st Rank ship, six to 2nd Rank ships of 60 to 66 guns, and five to each smaller Ranked ship; light frigates each carried three officers, while lesser vessels carried from one to three officers. From January 1671, the three largest 1st Rank ships (of over 100 guns) each had eight officers, while all other Ranked vessels had five officers, light frigates had two, and lesser vessels (generally *flûtes* and fireships) had either one or two officers.

At the start of 1690, each ship of 66 guns and above had nine officers; ships with 54 to 64 guns had seven officers; ships with 28 to 52 guns (including the larger light frigates) had six; other light frigates (with under 28 guns), *flûtes* and galiotes/*flûtes* had five; and all other vessels (including fireships, corvettes and *barques longues*) had just two.

By the late 1770s, each three-decker had 16 officers (the 90-gun *Ville de Paris* had just 15), the 80-gun ships each had 13, 2nd Rank ships (mainly 74-gun) had 12, 3rd Rank (64s) had 11, 4th Rank (50s) had 9, and frigates had 7 each. By the start of 1786, the three-deckers each had 21 officers, 80-gun ships and other two-deckers had 17, the new 18pdr-armed frigates had 11, and lesser frigates had 10 each.

The foregoing is inevitably simplified; for individual vessels, the reader is referred to the entries in the separate chapters.

Administration of the Navy

The Cardinal de Richelieu began the unification of the administration of the French Navy in 1626. Probably motivated by the imminent threat of English naval intervention in support of the Huguenots, he arranged for the creation of the office of *Grand maître de la navigation et commerce* by an edict of October 1626. The office gave him exclusive authority over maritime affairs throughout France. At the same time, he persuaded the Paris *parlement* to suppress the office of *Amiral de France* (in effect the *Amiral du Ponant* (western and northern France), as the incumbent had obtained the offices of Admiral of Guyenne in 1613 and of Brittany in 1615) held by one of his political rivals, Henri II de Montmorency. Richelieu extended his maritime authority to the Mediterranean when the *parlement* at Aix registered his letters as *grand maître* in August 1632, allowing him to suppress the office of the *Amiral du Levant* (Mediterranean France) held until his exile in 1631 by Charles de Lorraine, duc de Guise. Only the galley fleet (which remained separate until 1748) was excluded from his direct control. The office of *grand maître* passed through several hands after Richelieu died in 1642 and was last held by François de Bourbon-Vendôme, Duc de Beaufort, between 1665 and 1669.

At the time that Richelieu took over in 1626, the Navy consisted of two separate Admiralties, operated by the *Bureau de Levant* (which controlled the Flotte du Levant on the Mediterranean coast of France) and the *Bureau du Ponant*, which controlled the *Flotte du Ponant* on the Atlantic and Channel coasts). In the latter case, control was complicated due to the existence of historic posts of Admiral which were retained by virtually autonomous governors in Brittany, Normandy and Guyenne. It took a considerable period before these could be brought under the control of the central administration.

On 10 March 1661 Louis XIV assumed personal rule of his kingdom and named four Secretaries of State including Michel Le Tellier, for the Army and the *Marine du Levant* (i.e. the Mediterranean fleet) and Louis-Henri de Loménie, Comte de Brienne (succeeded in 1663 by Hugues de Lionne, Marquis de Fresne) for Foreign Affairs and the *Marine du Ponant* (*i.e.* the Atlantic and Channel fleet). At that time the *Secrétaire d'État aux Affaires étrangères* was responsible for the administration of both the Navy (the *Marine Royale*) and civilian (merchant marine) fleets, and for all of France's ports, arsenals, consulates, and colonies, as well as the guardianship of all her commercial companies. The King also appointed Jean-Baptiste Colbert as an *Intendant des Finances* with a mission of working behind the scenes to create a unified naval administration. On 7 March 1669 Louis XIV created the post of *Secrétaire d'État à la Marine* for Colbert, who merged the *Bureau de Levant* and the *Bureau du Ponant* with the Archives Department to form a single *Bureau de la Marine*, while maintaining the administrative division of the Navy into the two geographical Fleets. Following the death in action of the Duc de Beaufort on 25 June 1669 the office of *grand maître* was replaced by the revived office of Admiral of France, which, however, was given to royal infants to limit its power.

Louis XIV died on 1 September 1715, leaving his 5½-year-old younger great-grandson Louis, Duc d'Anjou as the legal heir. To become the Regent for the future Louis XV, Philippe, Duc d'Orléans accepted the replacement of the *Secrétaires d'État* with a *Polysynodie* of seven councils, one of which, the *Conseil de Marine*, was established by a royal ordinance of 3 November 1715. Its chief was Louis-Alexandre de Bourbon, Comte de Toulouse and Admiral of France, and its President was Victor, Comte d'Estrées, the Vice Admiral of the *Ponant*. The *Polysynodie* soon fell into disfavour, with four of the seven councils being abolished in September 1718, and at that time Joseph Fleurieu d'Armenonville received the title of *Secrétaire d'État à la Marine*, which he in turn handed in 1722 to his son, Charles-Jean-Baptiste Fleurieu de Morville. However, the influential Tourville was able to delay the end of the *Conseil de Marine* (the last of the seven to be abolished) until March 1723, leaving the two Fleurieus little to do. In August 1723 Jean-Frédéric de Phélypeaux, Comte de Maurepas (the son of Jérôme) became *Secrétaire d'État à la Marine* and resumed active control of the navy. The navy continued to be run by successive *Secrétaires* (Ministers) until the end of the *ancien régime* with occasional internal reorganisations, including a reconfiguration of the various offices and departments into four major divisions by Marshal de Castries in 1786.

Dockyards and Infrastructure

A shipyard (*chantier*) sufficed to build ships, but a dockyard (*arsenal*) was needed to arm and maintain a fleet. According to the *Encyclopédie méthodique Marine* of 1783 a 'complete arsenal' was an enclosed area that included a seaport belonging to the government where it kept its ships and everything (facilities and supplies) that was necessary to build them, conserve them, fit them out, lay them up, and refit them. The *règlement* of 29 March 1631 in which Richelieu established the regular administration of the navy designated Brouage, Le Havre-de-Grâce

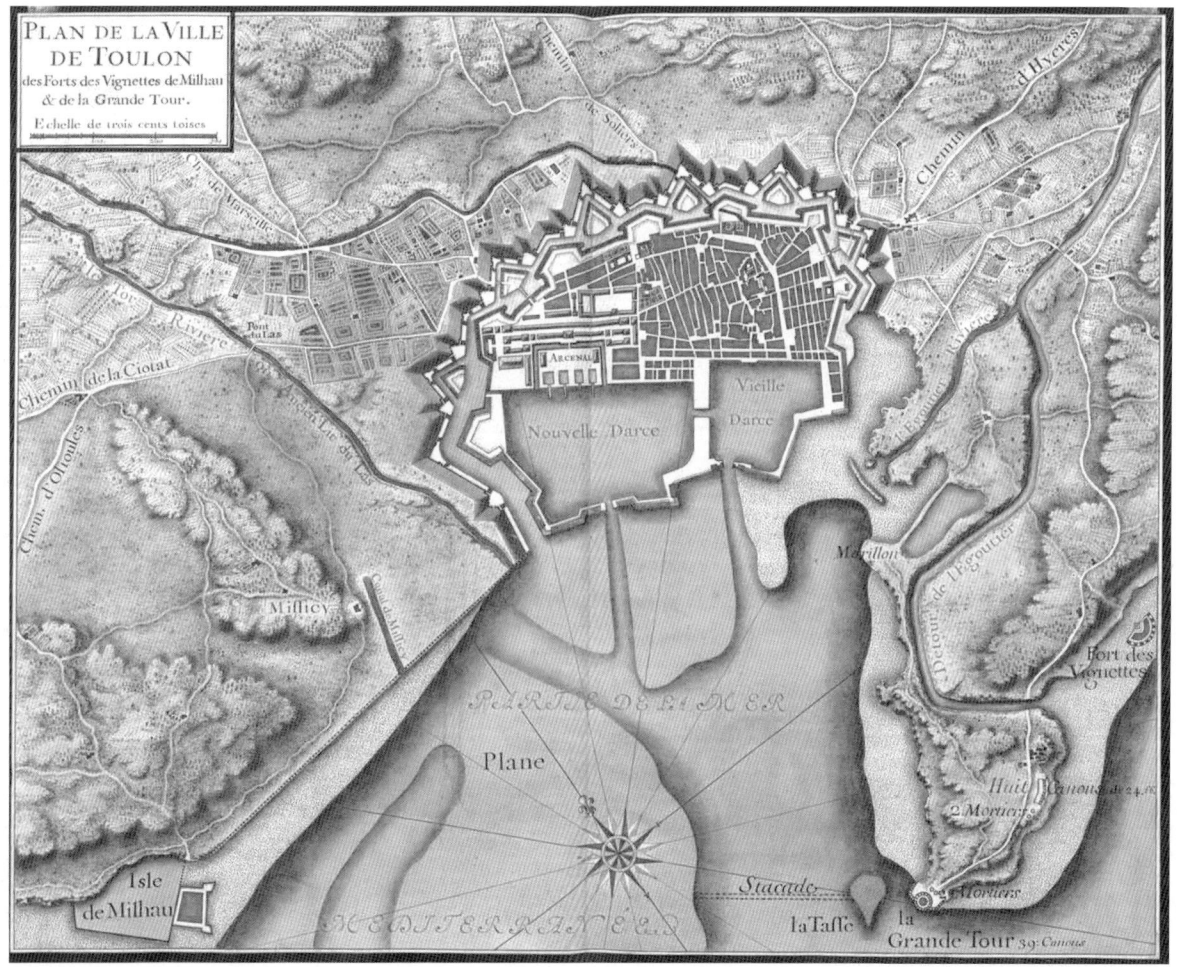

Plan of the city and arsenal of Toulon, the principal French naval base on the Mediterranean, in 1700. The original basin (*darse*) is to the right with the larger new basin and arsenal to the left, all surrounded by elaborate bastioned defences.

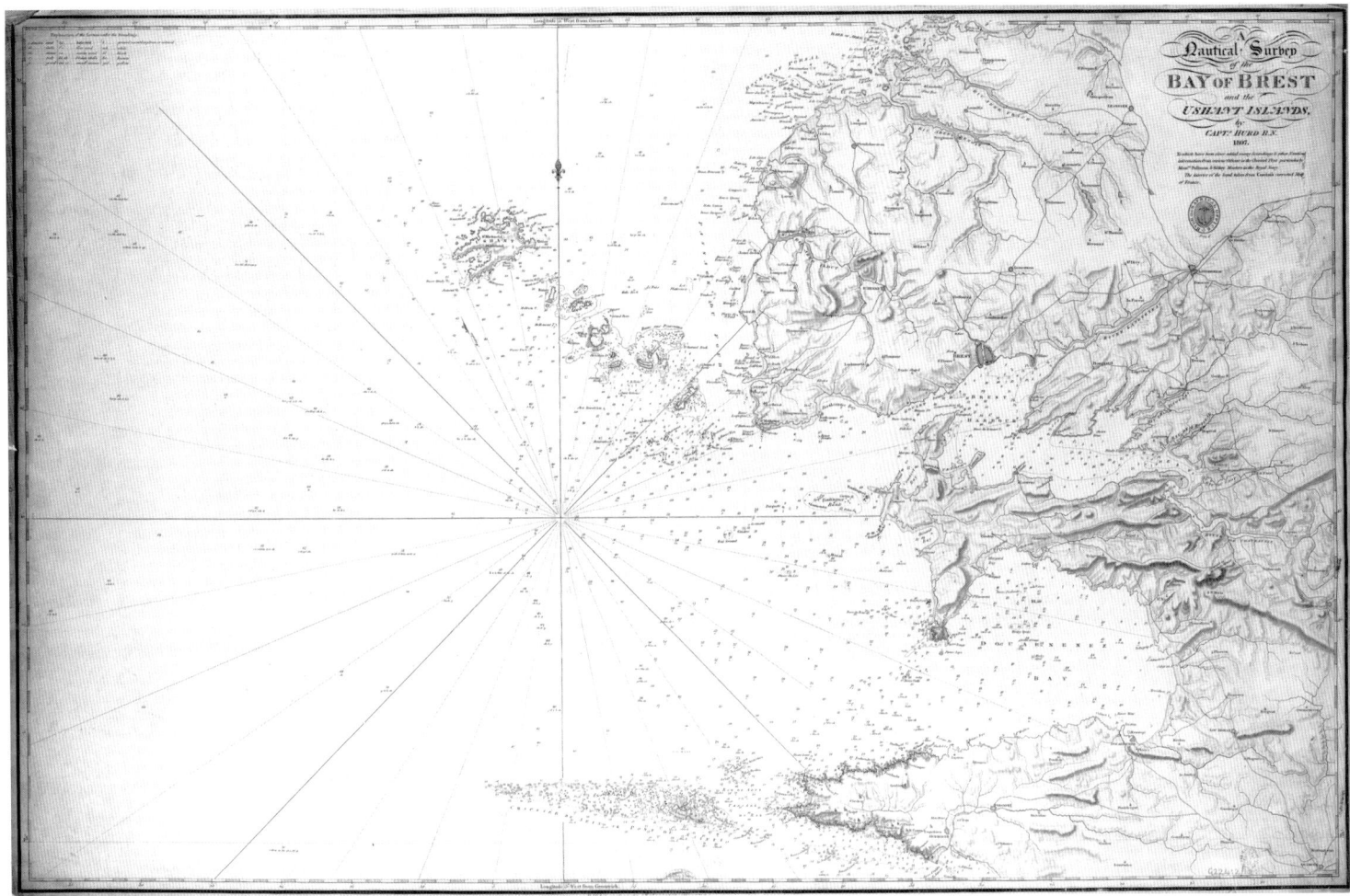

A chart of Brest and its approaches. The most important arsenal for the French *Ponant* fleet, Brest offered a magnificent protected anchorage outside the port itself, and because of its narrow entrance, called the *Goulet*, it was impossible to attack from seaward. However, this geography was a mixed blessing – it made any fleet sortie difficult and protracted (and against the prevailing westerlies, almost impossible), while providing a narrow target for a blockading fleet. However, stopping up the port completely was beyond the technology of the time, and the Royal Navy never mastered the task until late in the eighteenth century – indeed, this British chart of 1807 represents the first comprehensive and reliable information available to blockading forces. (National Maritime Museum, London B8780)

and Brest (all of which he personally controlled) as the three principal military ports for the King's ships in the *Ponant* (western and northern France). Toulon had been France's primary naval position in the *Levant* (Mediterranean France) since the days of King François I (reigned 1515–1547).

Toulon, with one of the best natural roadsteads in Europe, was home during Richelieu's years to the French galley fleet as well as most other French naval vessels in the Mediterranean. Activity there was disrupted by the civil wars of the *Fronde* (1648–1653), and in May 1661 the fleet there consisted of two ships that had sunk at their moorings, three that were only suitable for being broken up to salvage their metal, and six that were still capable of service. Four new ones, however, were under construction, and things rapidly improved under Colbert. The galleys were transferred back to Marseille and the dockyard took a major role in the construction of the first navy of Louis XIV between 1661 and 1671. Expansion of the dockyard began in 1671, and in 1679 excavation began of a new naval basin alongside the existing commercial basin in response to Colbert's desire to be able to moor a fleet of 50 or 60 vessels at Toulon if needed. Concurrently the great military engineer Sébastien Le Prestre, Marquis de Vauban, began in 1678 to transform the urban wall to enhance the protection of the port and arsenal; further improvements to the wall were made between 1760 and 1780.

The development of Brest as a naval dockyard and port effectively started when Richelieu acquired the governorship of Brittany in 1631, but it was then practically abandoned by Mazarin and his successors. Brest had a magnificent natural protected roadstead and an excellent strategic position but suffered from the poverty of the town and surrounding territory, poor land communications with the rest of France, and the prevailing westerly winds that blocked access to the roadstead, sometimes for many days. It was only in 1670 that Pierre Chertemps de Seüil arrived in Brest as *commissaire général de la marine* with a royal *mémoire* designating Brest as the primary port and arsenal of the *Ponant*. The Chevalier Nicolas de Clerville from 1667 and Vauban from 1683 fortified the town and arsenal. Large scale construction of dry docks, warehouses, workshops, building slips and barracks began in 1679 after the signature of treaties of peace with the Netherlands and the Empire and was completed in 1689. Between 1689 and 1696 a fortified tower was erected under Vauban's direction at Camaret-sur-Mer to prevent enemy forces from entering the *goulet* (the channel into the roadstead) at Brest, and the incomplete tower helped to repel an Anglo-Dutch attack in 1694.

Richelieu's other two choices of dockyard locations proved flawed. Richelieu began to turn Le Havre into the King's first naval base and shipbuilding centre in 1627. Although the port was strategically located at the mouth of the Seine River, making it the seaport for Rouen and Paris, it soon became apparent that there was not enough room there for a large dockyard and that the harbour could not be deepened enough for the navy's largest ships. Colbert continued the development of Le Havre but the shallow harbour prevented ships with more than 60 guns from entering and it eventually became a port primarily for frigates. In 1776 Cherbourg was selected for development into a major naval port in the Channel but major construction work began there only in 1784.

Richelieu also began in 1627 to develop Brouage to counter the Protestant port of La Rochelle, but it silted up during the *Fronde* to the extent that it became unusable. Colbert began looking for a replacement in 1661, and after the owners of Tonnay-Charente and Soubise, which already had shipyards, refused to give up their territory, he bought the unoccupied district of Rochefort in 1665 and began building a dockyard and town there in 1666. The new arsenal town was designed by Clerville, although Vauban in 1680–1686 modified the urban wall to encompass the entire arsenal. Rochefort was located fifteen miles up the Charente River, where it was safe from enemy seaborne attack but where it suffered from the fact that the Charente was treacherous to navigate and was too shallow for ships with a full outfit of guns and stores to negotiate. Ships built or commissioned at Rochefort had to descend the Charente (often under tow) to the protected roadstead of the Île d'Aix, where they loaded their guns and stores from service craft that brought them from the dockyard. These limitations restricted the use of Rochefort as an operational base, although it remained one of the navy's leading shipyards.

In 1662 Colbert and Louis XIV bought the former Flemish and Spanish port of Dunkirk from the English, who had captured it in 1658. They then transformed this traditional haven of privateers and pirates into a fortified town with a basin able to hold 30 ships, an arsenal, and a system of locks. Vauban built the citadel in 1662–66 and followed with new ramparts between 1668 and 1683. The naval ships built there were generally limited in size, the largest being of 70 guns, partly because of the extensive sand banks outside the entrance to the port. Naval activities there continued intermingled with commercial and privateering activity, the latter encouraged by the King. Dunkirk thus posed an intolerable threat to the English, who required in the treaties of Utrecht (1713), Aix-la-Chapelle (1748), and Paris (1763) that the fortifications be destroyed and the port blocked. Reconstruction efforts to varying degrees followed each of these treaties, and British restrictions on Dunkirk were finally lifted in the Treaty of Paris of 1783.

On 31 August 1666 the *Compagnie des Indes Orientales* (the French East India Company, founded in 1664) took possession of land across the large estuary of the Blavet River from the small naval port of Port Louis, and established a shipyard which was called L'Orient (later Lorient) from the name of a ship building there for the company. Colbert assigned to Brest the responsibility of overseeing activities at both locations. Activity at Lorient picked up after the company was reorganized in 1684 and during the wars from 1688 to 1713 it worked for both the company and the Navy as an annex to the Brest dockyard. On 28 June 1719 the *Conseil de Marine* in Paris ordered all of the installations at Lorient to be turned over to the new *Compagnie d'Occident*, which merged with the *Compagnie des Indes Orientales* in 1719, becoming the *Compagnie des Indes*. The company, now called the *Compagnie des Indes*, then used Lorient as its exclusive base and shipbuilding centre, but the government suspended

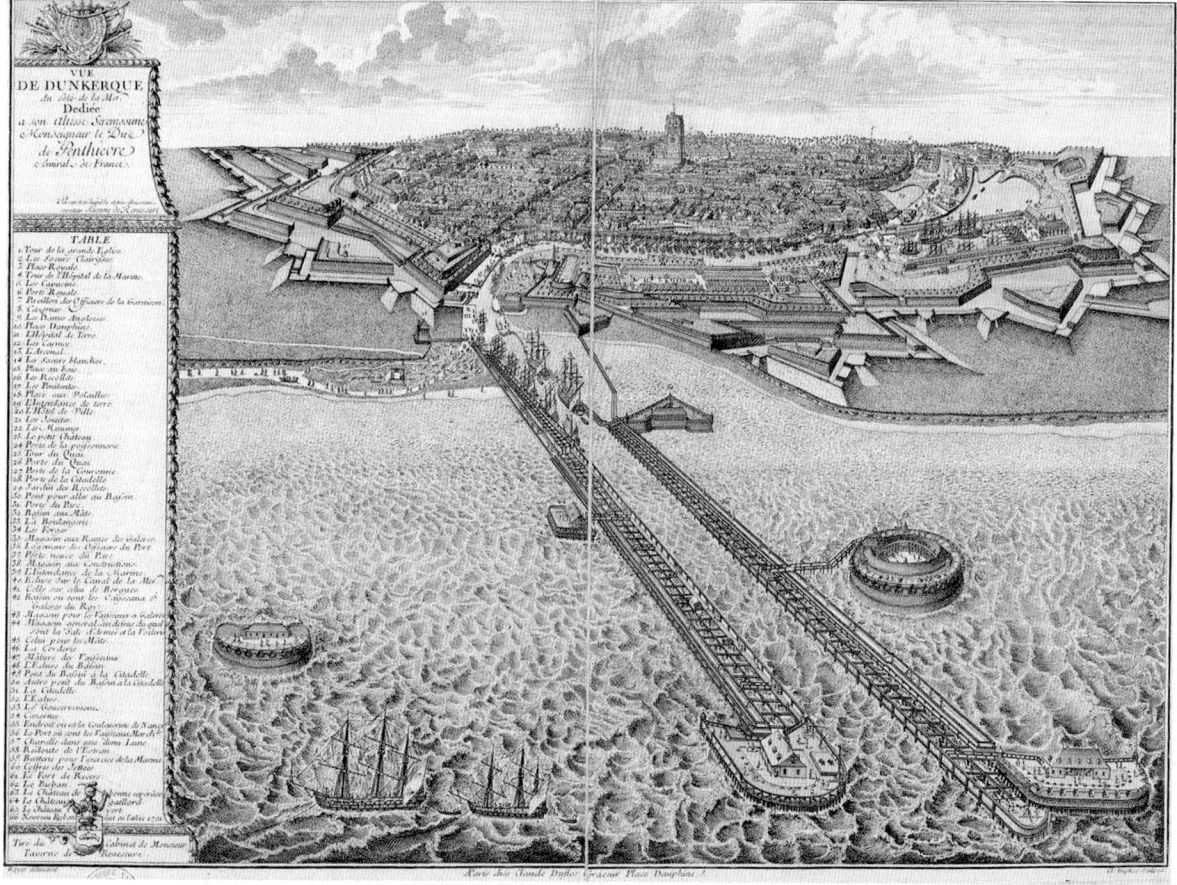

A view of Dunkirk from seaward in the first decade of the eighteenth century. As the main base for the *guerre de course* that did so much damage to British trade in every Anglo-French war, it was important enough to figure in every major peace treaty between the two states. The British regularly demanded the razing of its fortifications, as it was almost impossible to either blockade or attack from the sea, as they soon discovered in the 1690s when a number of assaults by bomb ketches and explosion vessels proved ineffective. At low tide the whole area up to the shoreline was uncovered, so high water was needed to get near enough to bombard the town successfully – and then attackers were kept at bay by the forts either side of the extended mole. Blockade was equally problematic, as extensive shoals and sandbars made lying off the port extremely dangerous, and numerous channels allowed privateers to choose when and in which direction they put to sea.

During the War of the Spanish Succession the concentration of French naval effort on the war against trade – the *guerre de course* – made heroes of the *corsairs*. What made this strategy potent was state involvement, in the form of naval ships and resources lent to privateering consortia, the so-called *armements mixtes*. This produced squadrons that possessed the firepower and confidence to attack even ships of the line, immensely complicating the task of providing adequate defence for convoys. This French etching – one of a series glorifying the exploits of French privateers – depicts the very successful attack on a large convoy bound for Portugal by the joint squadrons of Duguay-Trouin and Forbin in October 1707. The convoy's five escorts included two 80-guns ships, of which *Cumberland* was captured and *Devonshire* (shown second from left, marked 'a') caught fire and blew up. Of the escorts, only the 76-gun *Royal Oak* escaped. (National Maritime Museum, London, detail from PU5206)

its trade monopoly on 13 August 1769 and on 28 February 1770 the Company decided to hand over to the King the dockyard and everything in it, effective 1 April 1770. Although the Navy initially made little use of Lorient, it later became its fourth major port.

In 1668 the *Compagnie des Pyrénées* was founded at Bayonne with close ties to the vast timber forests of the Pyrenees. The French briefly hoped to make Bayonne into another naval port, but these hopes were frustrated in the early 1670s by slow construction there of the 3rd Rank ships *Maure* and *Fendant*, the difficulty of navigating the Adour River, and the stagnation of the new company. As a result Bayonne became primarily a centre for the stocking and onward shipping of timber from the Pyrenees to Rochefort and Brest, although ship construction resumed there in 1688 after the outbreak of the Nine Years' War. Vauban remodelled the citadel and walls here between 1681 and 1685.

Use of Navy ships for Privateering *(Armements mixtes)*

Thanks to *Contre-amiral* Jean-Yves Nerzic, who has written a massive doctoral dissertation on the subject and who has generously helped us enter the data, we are able to present details here on most of the *armements mixtes* in which French Navy ships participated during the reign of Louis XIV. *Armements mixtes* were arrangements whereby warships of the French Navy were contracted out for use in commerce raiding to private individuals or companies who undertook to pay the costs of operating the ships. We describe in the following chapters as 'lent as a privateer' for each of the Navy ships involved; note we exclude fully all other privateers which at no time formed a part of the French Navy.

This procedure of sharing the outfitting and operating costs for naval ships (and sometimes the actual costs of construction) between the State and private shareholders was initiated during the Dutch war of 1672–1678 and was highly developed during the last two wars of the reign, from 1688 to 1713, especially after, for political reasons, the King considered that he no longer needed the whole of the battlefleet to achieve his grand strategy, while for economic reasons he lacked the financial means to maintain it. Louis was an actual partner in each such enterprise, and usually received a fixed share (typically a fifth, although this varied) of the net profits.

Strictly speaking, *armements mixtes* met the following criteria:
- One or more of the king's ships were loaned to private individuals to be fitted out for commerce raiding. These ships, for which the King furnished the necessary military equipment (guns, powder, sometimes soldiers, etc), were fitted out in a royal dockyard and commissions for privateering or for privateering and trading were delivered to the private individuals by the Admiralty with authority at the dockyard.
- A shareholder or a group of shareholders forming a company advanced the funds necessary for the operation of the ship (supplies, salaries, provisions, etc).
- The judgment of prizes taken during the ship's cruise was handled by the Admiralty authority that delivered the commissions.
- Except in special cases the Admiral of France took a tenth of the proceeds.
- The financing of the costs of restoring the ships for naval service and the division of the proceeds from the prizes depended on whether the sovereign wanted to stimulate private interests to mount a greater threat against the maritime lines of communications of the enemy or whether he wanted more actively to enrich the coffers of the State.

This procedure was also used for two kinds of activities whose primary purpose was not commerce raiding. One was assistance to trading companies, in which the King loaned ships to the company to escort the company's fleets or carry additional cargo, the extra ships enhancing the ability of the company's fleets to prevail in any conflict that might arise in the Indies. The *Compagnie des Indes Orientales* was the primary participant in this procedure, but smaller companies also benefited. The other activity was the transport of supplies, generally along the French coast during periods of emergency or for special missions. Examples were the transportation of grain during periods of famine, the transport of provisions for the movement of an army, or the transport of alcohol for tax authorities during times of war (specifically in Brittany in 1711). Finally (although not recorded here), Louis XIV used a similar procedure to loan some of his ships to his grandson, Philip V, King of Spain, during the War of the Spanish Succession.

The campaign against Huguenot La Rochelle convinced Cardinal de Richelieu of the need for a powerful French navy. In the early stages of the conflict the French monarchy did not possess the means to combat the naval forces of the Protestants and had to negotiate foreign naval assistance, and later proved unable to prevent the intervention of English fleets. It was only because the latter failed to break the siege that the city was eventually forced to surrender in October 1628, as depicted in this engraving by Jacques Callot. (National Maritime Museum, London, PU5053)

Historical Overview

Henry IV, the founder of the House of Bourbon, was assassinated in Paris on 14 May 1610 by a Catholic fanatic, François Ravaillac, and was succeeded by his nine-year-old son Louis; a Regency was proclaimed under his mother, Marie de Médicis. While Louis XIII was declared of age in 1614, real power remained with the Queen-mother who remained Regent until 1617.

The Huguenot Uprisings of the 1620s

Religious conflicts across virtually the whole of Europe led to the outbreak of the massively destructive Thirty Years' War in 1618. France contrived to avoid direct involvement in the conflict, but tensions between the Catholic majority and the Huguenot (Protestant) minority, particularly in the southwest of France and around the major Huguenot city of La Rochelle (at that time the third-largest city in France), grew rapidly. Many Huguenot leaders, terrified of the increasing religious intolerance of the French monarchy, began openly to talk of emulating the success of the Protestant population in the Northern Netherlands in breaking away from the control of Catholic Spain to establish the Dutch Republic.

An open rebellion in 1621–22 took place. Conflict ended in stalemate, and a ceasefire was negotiated following the indecisive naval battle of St-Martin-de Ré on 27 October 1622 between the Royalist fleet under Charles, Duc de Guise and the naval forces of La Rochelle. This was ratified in the Treaty of Montpelier, with concessions agreed on both sides which included the dismantling of the fortifications of Fort Louis on the western outskirts of La Rochelle. However, Huguenot fears grew as, rather than dismantling the fort, its commander the Marquis de Toirras commenced strengthening the walls, while Richelieu began negotiation with the Duc de Nevers for the purchase of five warships awaiting crews and munitions in the Breton port of Blavet (modern Port Louis, near Lorient) – this purchase was perceived by the Huguenots as intended to blockade the city of La Rochelle and force its submission.

Led by Benjamin de Rohan, Duc de Soubise, various emissaries were dispatched to Paris to plead for the implementation of the terms of the Treaty of Montpellier, but without any success. Soubise determined on pre-emptive action. Leading a squadron of small ships, he attacked Blavet harbour on 17 January 1625, finding six major French ships at anchor, armed with cannon but without crews or ammunition. This included the *Vierge*, largest warship of the day, with 60 bronze cannon; it was of 800 tons, and had cost the French 200,000 crowns to build. Soubise seized the French warships and returned to La Rochelle, and quickly built up the city's naval forces to some 70 vessels, far exceeding the strength available to Louis's navy. He established garrisons in February on the major offshore islands of Ré and Oléron, and reinforced the fortifications both there and ashore, achieving effective control of the French coast from Bordeaux to the Loire estuary. The city of La Rochelle formally voted to join Soubise's rebellion on 8 August.

The Duc de Vendôme, as Governor of Guyenne, attempted to blockade La Rochelle with a heavy chain across the estuary, and increased fortifications. However, Soubise's fleet broke through the blockade, and anchored off the Ile de Ré. Now thoroughly alarmed at the imminent loss of part of his dominions, Louis XIII ordered a counter-attack by his land forces in September 1625. Lacking ships of his own, Louis was forced to turn to the Dutch and English regimes. Under the terms of the 1624 Franco-Dutch Treaty of Compiegne, the Dutch had supplied a fleet of 20 warships under Adm Willem Haultain de Zoete, and Charles I agreed to the hire of seven English warships under Capt. Pennington, although they were manned by French sailors as it was feared that Protestant sailors would refuse to serve against their Protestant co-religionists. The combined Royalist fleet, under Henri, Duc de Montmorency (the Admiral of France), sailed from Les Sables d'Olonne in September, and defeated the naval forces of the Huguenots off St-Martin-de-Ré on 18 September. By weight of numbers, Ré and Oléron were re-occupied by Royalist forces under the Marquis de Toiras, and Soubise fled to England.

Following protracted negotiations, a Treaty of Paris was signed between representatives of La Rochelle and Louis XIII on 5 February 1626. The terms of the Treaty prevented the city from maintaining a war fleet, and in return Louis guaranteed the religious freedoms of the Huguenots and agreed to dismantle the contentious Fort Louis near the city's western gate. However, Toiras – named as Governor of Ré – began to reinforce the fortresses of La Prée and St-Martin-de-Ré. In October Richelieu was appointed to administer all naval and maritime activities; recognising that Royal authority has only been reimposed through the use of foreign warships, he determined that France needed to establish its own national fleet, and to assume protection of its entire coastline, which until then had been the responsibility of the feudal overlords, noticeably in Normandy, Brittany and Guyenne (southwest France).

On 12 July 1627 an English force of 100 vessels under the command of George Villiers, Duke of Buckingham, arrived and landed 6,000 troops, which laid siege to the citadel of St-Martin-de-Ré. England had now decided that it should secure the approaches to La Rochelle with a view to encouraging rebellion in the city. Toiras stubbornly held out within the citadel, and both sides suffered enormously in the absence of adequate supplies and problems of reinforcement. By September, the citizens of La Rochelle were actively in support, declaring themselves in alliance with Buckingham, but on 10 September Royal troops from Fort Louis, under Louis personally and aided by Richelieu, opened an artillery bombardment of the city, and began work of an encircling entrenchment, reinforced by fortifications which were completed by April 1628.

Meanwhile, Buckingham's forces had been compelled to abandon their campaign at the close of September and return to England. A second expedition in April 1628 under William Feilding, Earl of Denbigh, ended in failure. Buckingham was assassinated at Portsmouth on 23 August, but a third English expedition was organised under the Earl of Lindsey. This likewise failed to relieve the city, which was forced to surrender unconditionally to Louis on 28 October. The resistance's other strongholds succumbed within a few weeks, and – under the terms of the resulting Peace of Alais – the Huguenots were deprived of their territorial, political and military rights, while retaining their rights of religious freedom provided under the Edict of Nantes.

The Franco-Spanish War (1635–1659)

France had fought one war against Spain from 1628 to 1631 ("the War of the Mantuan Succession") over control of northern Italy, as a result of which the Duc de Nevers had succeeded as ruler of Mantua. It had concluded with the Treaty of Cherasco on 19 June 1631.

However, the defeat of France's ally Sweden in 1634 led France to declare war again on Spain in 1635. This war was fought out at sea in both the Western Mediterranean and in the Bay of Biscay. In 1638 France launched an invasion of the Basque Country. A fleet of Spanish warships was sent to break the French blockade, but was forced to anchor off the port of Guetaria. Henri de Sourdis, Bishop of Bordeaux, commanded the French *Flotte du Ponant* in an attack on the Spanish, but as the harbour at Guetaria lacked adequate water to float his larger ships, sent in a number of fireships instead. Virtually every Spanish ship fell victim to the resulting conflagration. By 1639 the *Flotte du Ponant* included 19 fireships, now seen as a key component of success.

By 1640 both France and Spain were concentrating their naval efforts in the Mediterranean. Both Portugal and Catalonia were engaged in revolts against Castillian Spanish control, and both were actively supported by the French. Portugal secured its independence at the start of December almost bloodlessly, under João, Duke of Braganca; both France and the Dutch sent naval forces to protect trade and prevent Spain from defeating the Portuguese. The Catalan Revolt proclaimed a Catalan Republic, under the protection of the French monarchy, on 17 January 1641. The French sent both military and naval forces to assist the Catalan uprising, and its army occupied Catalonia; Louis XIII was proclaimed sovereign Count of Barcelona, as Luís I of Catalonia. The French *Flotte du Levant* attempted to cut off supplies to the Spanish-held ports of Tarragona and Rosas, and a series of naval actions ensued.

At the end of June 1642 the Spanish and French fleets met off Barcelona in a decisive encounter, including both sailing warships and armed galleys. But the fireships again proved the decisive factor. France entered the battle with more than 14 fireships, and on the first day two Spanish galleons were burnt by French attacks, while a third was forced to surrender. The battle was renewed on the following day, with further Spanish losses. Another French victory off Cartagena in 1643 gave French more control of the Western Mediterranean, but French priority moved to assist in freeing the Italian states that were generally under Spanish control.

From mid-1648 the revolts known as the *Fronde* (see below) paralysed the French navy for several years. Spain regained control of the Western Mediterranean, and started counter-offensives both in Catalonia and in Italy. By 1652 the Catalan Revolt was over, and France renounced sovereignty over most of Catalonia, while keeping control of Roussillon; although the war dragged on until the close of the decade, both France and Spain retained little naval strength to propagate the war. The Peace of the Pyrenees between France and Spain, signed on the Island of Pheasants on 7 November 1659, strengthened by the wedding of the young French king Louis XIV to the elder daughter of the Spanish king, Philip IV, on 9 June 1660, opened a new area.

The *Fronde* (1648–1653)

The era of troubles for the young Louis XIV comprised two successive periods of disturbances amounting to virtual civil war and known collectively as the *Fronde* (literally 'sling', after a weapon used in the initial revolts). The first period, known as the *Fronde Parlementaire*, pitted the monarch against his parliament, with its allies the Prince of Conti and the Cardinal de Retz. This lasted from 1648 until 1649, and was followed swiftly by the *Fronde des Princes*, lasting until 1653, during which Condé, Beaufort and Mlle de Longueville, backed by Spain, countered the royal power. While across the Channel English naval forces were massively expanded by the Commonwealth regime, generating the total loyalty of the English Navy (as opposed to Prince Rupert's exiled royal naval force, which often found refuge in French harbours), in France during this period there was no corresponding overhaul of French naval administration, which was to languish until 1661. French naval strength, which in the 1640s had quantitatively rivalled that of England and the Netherlands, declined rapidly. Condé signed a treaty with Spain in 1651, and his Spanish allies stationed a fleet of thirty warships in the Gironde.

César de Bourbon-Vendôme was appointed in 1650 by the Regent, Anne of Austria, to take over her office of Grande-Maitre, but his period of office began badly. In July 1652 a Royal squadron sailing from La Rochelle was defeated at Brouage by the CdE Louis Foucault, Comte du Daugnon, who had switched sides to ally with the *frondeurs* and the Spanish. Vendôme gathered a fleet and managed to overcome du Daugnon's forces, but he was then ordered by Mazarin to take his fleet to the Channel to defend Dunkirk against Spanish forces. On 14 September 1652 the squadron despatched by Vendôme encountered the English fleet (under Blake) off Calais, and lost seven of its eight warships.

The Sun King and Colbert rebuild a Navy (1661–1671)

Following the death of Mazarin on 9 March 1661, Louis XIV decided not to appoint a new Chief Minister for, as he wrote in his *Memoirs* '… *j'étais résolu à ne prendre point de premier ministre, et à ne pas laisser faire par un autre les fonctions de roi* [elsewhere he even used the words '*mon métier de roi*'] *pendant que je n'en aurais que le titre*'. Instead, he chose to act as his own Chief Minister. Notwithstanding that decision, he carefully chose a number of key councillors as his Ministers.

Recognising that the French kingdom needed to establish itself as a maritime power (and to protect its overseas colonies and its trading abilities), Jean-Baptiste Colbert – the King's most capable administrator – persuaded Louis to take an early decision to rebuild his naval forces. They had atrophied during the Mazarin era, partly due to the troubles of the *Fronde* era, and consisted of barely eighteen ships (some with rotting hulls), amongst which was only one 1st Rank of 70 guns, and ten or so galleys. There had been an equivalent deterioration in harbours, shipyards and shore facilities. From 1661 a start was made on creating a great battlefleet to match those of the English and Dutch navies. England had a navy – massively expanded during the Commonwealth era – of some 150 vessels, and the Dutch nearly as many, so a target of building some 120 vessels was set.

Louis adopted a four-fold strategy to achieve this aim of reviving his Navy. First, he appointed a sort of 'shadow' secretary of State for the Navy. At 7 o'clock on 10 March 1661, the day after Mazarin's death, he summoned his councillors and proclaimed he was taking in hand the direction of his Kingdom. He named four Secretaries of State, amongst them, Brienne for Foreign Affairs and the *Marine du Ponant* (i.e. the Atlantic and Channel fleet) and Le Tellier, for the Army and the *Marine du Levant* (i.e. the Mediterranean fleet). Appointed by the *Surintendant des Finances*, Nicolas Fouquet, Jean-Baptiste Colbert was nominally a mere *Intendant des Finances* but he was given the unacknowledged charge of acting behind the scenes to create a *Département de la Marine*, as there was as yet nothing approaching a single Navy.

The second item of Louis's strategy was establishing a genuine Secretary of State for the Navy. This awkward situation of divided control lasted until 18 February 1669, when Colbert, appointed Secretary of State for the *Maison du Roi*, was formally 'given authority' over the new united Navy, allowing him to bring to completion his major expansion program designed to bring France up to the foremost rank amongst the naval powers. During this nine-year 'gestation' from 1661 to 1669, eleven vessels of the 1st Rank were built, twelve of the 2nd Rank, twenty of the 3rd Rank and nineteen of the 4th Rank.

The third item was creating a new strong image of the French Navy. When at sea, warships were the king's ambassadors, so Louis XIV decided to change the names of most of them using generally warlike adjectives

Jean-Baptiste Colbert (1619–1683) is widely regarded as the father of the modern French Navy and was certainly its most influential administrator.

related to the king's triumph and sovereignty. On 24 June 1671, he renamed six out of the twelve vessels of the 1st Rank, seventeen out of twenty-two of the 2nd Rank, eighteen out of twenty-four of the 3rd Rank, fifteen out of twenty-one of the 4th Rank, and nineteen out of twenty-nine of the 5th Rank (see Appendix H). From now on, sculptures and decorations of the actual vessels were made to reflect these symbolic attributes.

Fourthly, Louis XIV ensured the continuity of his legacy. In March 1672, he awarded to Seignelay, Colbert's son, the *survivance* of his father: *i.e.* he was allowed to share the 'signature et aux autres fonctions' of his father; at the latter's death, on 6 September 1683, Seignelay took over the role of Secretary of State for the Navy. Colbert and Seignelay were the co-authors of the two major documents ruling the French Navy – the *Ordonnance de 1681 touchant la Marine* (for the Merchant Navy) and the *Ordonnance du 15 avril 1689 pour les armées navales et arcenaux de marine* (for the Military Navy); they were therefore the founders of the revived French Navy.

The massive increase in the fleet provided by these strategies was achieved primarily during the 1660s, with the expansion in numbers focused on the period from 1664 to 1671 (after 1671 new construction was mainly conceived as replacing worn-out ships). The lead-in time for shipbuilding, and for investments in dockyards and naval arsenals, creating a large permanent officer corps as well as a registration system for seafarers to provide a structure for manning ships, and generally promoting mercantile trade, meant that planning for the navy's infrastructure and personnel also began as early as 1661. By 1671, France had reached its target of 120 ships.

In the same period, France had greatly improved and restocked its primary dockyards – Toulon for the *Levant* Fleet and Brest for the *Ponant* Fleet. While new carpenters and other artisans had to be recruited and trained, Colbert was at least fortunate in having skilled *maître charpentiers* (master carpenters or master shipwrights) in long-term charge at both dockyards – Laurent Hubac at Brest (where most of Richelieu's and Mazarin's new warships had been built) and Rodolphe Gédéon at Toulon (he had been recruited by Mazarin from the Dutch Netherlands in 1645). The third of the Royal Dockyards – Brouage in the estuary of the Oléron – was rapidly silting up, and in 1666 a decision was taken to abandon that port and build a new dockyard at Rochefort on the Charente.

To ensure the future security of the dockyards, other infrastructure such as roads and waterways were renewed, and domestic sources of essential raw materials and allied industries were brought under control – including supplies of shipbuilding timber, hemp for rope, coal and metals for guns, together with the workshops for manufacturing them – so that France would never again be dependent upon foreign supplies. To protect the dockyards from hostile attackers, the renowned military engineer Sébastien Le Prestre, Marquis de Vauban was employed to design and oversee the construction of massive fortifications – a process which continued to the close of the century. Little escaped Colbert's eye, and enormous industries were energetically created.

When *le Grand* Colbert died, on 6 September 1683, Seignelay became Secretary of State for the *Maison du Roi* and for the Navy but, without the *Finances*, he had not his father's stature, particularly in front of Le Tellier's clan who 'owned' the Secretary of State for War. But he was well prepared – he had had the *survivance* for more than a decade – and the Navy did not suffer from this relative lack of power.

The Conflict against North African pirates (*corsairs*)

Predations on French and other European nations' shipping was a constant threat to commerce throughout the sixteenth to nineteenth centuries, and most maritime powers were compelled to take action, not only against the corsairs at sea, but against the ports and harbours along the North African coast where they were based. Algiers, Tunis and Tripoli were nominally under Ottoman rule (Morocco was an independent kingdom), but in practice were ruled by autonomous regents, often titled *Deys*, who ran their territories as military republics, and licensed local privateers to plunder European vessels in return for a fixed share of all prizes, goods and ransom money; besides the three regents' capitals, there were numerous other strongholds along the coast, notably at Derna in Libya, at Bône (Annaba), Bougie (Bejaia), Djidjelli (Jijel) and Cherchell in Algeria; and at Salé and Larache on Morocco's Atlantic coast.

These corsairs ranged far and wide in their voyages, attacking not only shipping, but coastal settlements as far away as Iceland, England and Ireland, sacking towns and enslaving inhabitants. However, the growth of the North European navies, particularly the English and Dutch, who organised to police the northern waters, diminished this traffic and by the mid-seventeenth century it was mainly confined to the Mediterranean and the southern Iberian peninsula. European navies were organised to raid and punish the corsair bases, as with Robert Blake's Parliamentary Navy attack on Porto Farina (in northern Tunisia) in April 1655.

The development of Louis XIV's naval forces, in terms both of sailing warships and of powerful galleys, provided him with the means of attacking at source the corsairs (generally described as '*turcs*'). An attack on one of the Algerian strongholds was decided upon, with the intention of creating a permanent French naval and military base; of several options, the port of Djijelli was chosen. A successful landing was made on 22 July 1664 by 14 vessels under Chevalier Paul, but counterattacks by local and subsequently Ottoman forces strained the unity of the occupiers, and the French were forced to evacuate their forces by late October. Later attacks were organised as raids rather than as permanent occupations. In 1665 the Duc de Beaufort commanded punitive expeditions against the strongholds of La Goulette (Tunisia) in March and Cherchell (Algeria) in August. Agreements to restrict piracy were reached after strong opposition, but were increasingly honoured more in the breach than in the observance.

The War of Devolution (1667–1668)

In late 1665, following the death of Philip IV of Spain, Louis XIV laid claim to large parts of the Spanish Netherlands. The French allied with the Dutch United Provinces in their ongoing war with England (leading to two small naval actions in the Caribbean) and negotiated treaties with German states along the Rhine to block intervention by the Empire. In May 1667 Louis XIV repeated his demands and then sent his armies into the Spanish Netherlands. The Dutch, alarmed by the aggressive strength of France, ended their war with England and negotiated a triple alliance with England and Sweden. Louis XIV felt unable to match the three allies and Spain so gave back some of his gains at the Peace of Aix-la-Chapelle in May 1668. He also felt betrayed by the Dutch, who were also serious commercial rivals, and began diplomatic preparations that led to the Franco-Dutch war of 1672–78.

On 14 November 1669, Colbert proposed a system of classifying by size the component ships of the French Navy, equivalent to the systems used by the English and Dutch. Under his initial proposals, the 1st Rank would include only the largest three-decked vessels which would serve as flagships for French fleets; the 2nd Rank would comprise ships of between 1,400 and 1,500 tons; the 3rd, ships of 1,000 to 1,200 tons; the 4th, ships of 600 to 800 tons, with a '5th Rank' covering lesser vessels. These tonnage ranges differed somewhat as actually applied to the existing fleet in 1669 and 1671.

The Dutch War (1672–1678)

After 1668 French foreign policy focused on breaking up the triple alliance of the War of Devolution and isolating the Dutch United Provinces. Louis XIV negotiated alliances with England and Sweden that included large subsidies. His new English ally declared war on the Dutch in March 1672 followed by Louis himself in April. The French armies penetreated deep into Dutch territory, but in June the Dutch fleet under Admiral Michiel Adriaenszoon de Ruyter held off the combined Franco-English fleet at the Battle of Solebay, saving his country. In 1673 de Ruyter continued his strategic victories in the two Battles of Schooneveldt (Walcheren) and the Battle of the Texel, and in August the Dutch formed a Grand Alliance with Austria, Spain, and the Duke of Lorraine against France. In 1674 most of the German states turned against France, and more importantly in February the English Parliament forced King Charles II to make peace with the Dutch, forcing a French evacuation of Dutch territory.

In February 1675 the French sent a squadron under CV Pierre-Bruno de Valbelle to support Messina in Sicily, which had rebelled against the Spanish. Battles were fought at Messina (Pharo) and the Lipari Islands. In 1676 a French fleet under LG Abraham Duquesne attacked a Dutch fleet that had been sent to help the Spanish off Stromboli (Alicudi) in January and fought a combined Dutch-Spanish fleet at Augusta (Agosta) in April, resulting in the death of de Ruyter. A third battle in June 1676 at Palermo, with the French now under *Amiral* Louis-Victor de Rochechouart, Duc de Vivonne, with Duquesne as *Vice-Amiral,* gave the French control of the western Mediterranean. In October 1676 the Comte d'Estrées, *vice-amiral du Ponant*, sailed from Brest with a small squadron, partially funded by himself, to reinforce a five-ship French force in the Caribbean and counter a Dutch force under Commodore Jacob Binckes which had taken Cayenne and Tobago and pillaged St Domingue. D'Estrées retook Cayenne and then fought a bitter battle at Tobago in March 1677 in which the French lost four ships and the Dutch seven. D'Estrées returned to France, formed a new squadron, and recaptured Tobago (killing Binckes) in December 1677.

In October 1677 Mary of York, niece of Charles II of England, married William of Orange, leading to a rapprochement between the English and Dutch. Louis XIV responded in March 1678 with a new land offensive against the Dutch, and in the same month François-Louis Rousselet, Marquis de Châteaurenault with six ships attacked and beat off a larger Dutch force under Cornelis Evertsen the Younger west of Ushant. These successes and his previous victories enabled Louis to conclude peace with the Dutch on favourable terms at the Treaty of Nijmegen in August 1678 and then with other opponents. Sweden was the last participant in the war to make peace, in November 1679. However, while Louis XIV had achieved many victories, he had not succeeded in conquering the Dutch and he had united all of Europe against him.

On 1 August 1677 Colbert quantified the components by Rank of the intended Navy of 120 ships: there would be 12 of 1st Rank, 30 of 2nd Rank, 30 of 3rd Rank, 24 of 4th Rank and 24 of 5th Rank. This was varied *ad hoc* by Louis XIV, and it was not until 1680 or early 1681 that an improved division was fixed by the King. The figure of 12 ships of the 1st Rank was maintained, but there would now be 26 of 2nd Rank, 40 of 3rd Rank, 26 of 4th Rank and 16 of 5th Rank. A distinction was also made between the true *vaisseaux* which would form the line of battle, comprising the 78 ships of the 1st, 2nd and 3rd Ranks, and the *frégates-vaisseaux* which would (normally) not form part of the battlefleet, comprising the 42 lesser ships of the 4th and 5th Ranks. Clearly this division, while maintained in theory until the Sun King's death, varied in actual practice – and the apportionment of the Navy by Ranks at the start of each year is shown in Appendix A.

The Nine Years' War, or War of the League of Augsburg (1688–1697)

Until the Glorious Revolution of 1688 in England installed William of Orange as King of England, the French Navy had few issues to plan for as the Dutch were only aggressive when France chose to start a war (mainly on land), while the English were allied with France for much of the time. The events of 1688 changed this, uniting the two maritime powers, and for the first time in decades threatening a challenge to the dominant French superpower. Forthwith the role of the French Navy altered from supporting the army in campaigns against the Dutch to safeguarding French commerce against the likely aggression of the combined Anglo-Dutch forces. A building race ensued, while at sea the Navy began its campaign by a successful operation to land and supply the army of King James in Ireland. This culminated in the inconclusive Battle of Bantry Bay in May 1689, an action which led to a formal declaration of war.

France rapidly consolidated its battlefleets, bring the Toulon-based *Flotte du Levant* around to the Atlantic coast and joining the existing *Flotte du Ponant* at Brest. By 1690 France was clearly on its way to equalling, if not overtaking, the combined strengths of the allied English and Dutch Navies in the Channel. William of Orange's priority had been to land his ground forces at Carrickfergus in June 1690, leading to his success in defeating James at the Battle of the Boyne on 11 July. Meanwhile Louis ordered his *Vice-Amiral du Ponant*, Comte de Tourville, to enter the Channel with his 84 ships (and the 15 galleys under the Chevalier de Noailles).

His initial remit had been to attack the English at Plymouth, Torbay and Portland, and then to attack the enemy's main base at Portsmouth before proceeding to the Straits of Dover. However, these instructions were later amended by Louis, instructing Tourville to seek out the enemy fleet and do battle wherever the opponents met. A major battle in the Channel (off Beachy Head – known to the French as Béveziers) on 10 July pitted 70 French *vaisseaux* (plus 5 *frégates légères* and 18 fireships) against 34 English and 22 Dutch ships. The English lost only one ship (the 70-gun *Anne*) while the Dutch lost a total of 7 ships and 3 fireships. While most English ships were undamaged, the majority of the remaining 15 Dutch ships were severely damaged and required dockyard repairs before they could face the French again. The battle demonstrated the capabilities of the French fleet; its victory in that battle gave the French control of the waterway for almost two years.

Seignelay, Colbert's son and successor, died in November 1690. His replacement, the Comte de Pontchartrain (Louis Phélypeaux), who was also the *Contrôleur général des finances*, began by continuing Colbert's strategy, but lacked Seignelay's prime interest in the Navy and long awareness of naval affairs. The French naval campaign of 1691 was dominated by the 'Campagne du Large'; Pontchartrain's instructions to Tourville, issued on 26 May 1691, instructed the latter to cruise for three months in the Western Approaches (the entrance to the Channel) and to try to capture the homebound merchant fleet en route from Smyrna (Izmir). The French fleet, comprising 73 ships (plus 21 fireships) sailed from Brest in June and returned in August from this 'distant cruise' without fighting a fleet action, but since 1690 the Allied strength had improved both in quantity (92 ships) and in quality. The French advantage was lost by 1691. In 1692, without waiting for the completion of the major battlefleet units under construction, Louis ordered the fleet's commander, Comte de Tourville, to put to sea and challenge the Allies, even though the French at that time were numerically inferior to their opponents.

A realisation by Louis soon after of the tactical error came too late, as Tourville had followed his orders, and the countermanding message from Louis failed to arrive in time. The resulting contest off Barfleur resulted in a bruising defeat for the French, even if no ships were lost in the actual battle. The retreating French fleet was split up, with twenty ships making for the safety of Brest, while three heavily damaged ships, including Tourville's flagship *Soleil Royal*, were stranded at Cherbourg, while another twelve sailed east and took refuge in the port of La Hougue. All fifteen were boarded and set on fire a few days later by the Allies.

The losses sustained to the battlefleet at Cherbourg and at La Hougue, while not in themselves catastrophic (French construction was able to fill the gaps with even more powerful 1st and 2nd Rank ships) had significant tactical and strategic consequences. The fact that the destruction at La Hougue had been carried out by ships' boats rather than by fireships convinced the French that building new fireships was a waste of resources; those on order or projected were cancelled, and on the limited occasions France employed fireships thereafter, they were always converted purchases or prizes.

Notwithstanding the major efforts to achieve battlefleet superiority until 1692 (which ironically would have achieved success by 1694 if continued), Louis XIV was always more concerned with continental strategy than maritime dominance, and Pontchartrain's views were closer to the King's than Colbert's and Seignelay's commercial and naval strategy. During the financial crisis of 1693–94, Pontchartrain ceased ordering large battlefleet units, and in October 1693 wrote to the *intendants* at each major dockyard to tell them that no new battlefleet vessels were to be begun, although those already building could continue. The procurement strategy turned instead to vessels which – together with French privateers – could disrupt English and Dutch commerce. Indeed, as part of this strategy, a considerable number of battlefleet units were loaned out to partnerships put together for privateering on a strictly commercial basis. While causing concern in the allies' mercantile interests, this was never enough to affect the outcome of the war.

Moreover, it was now realised that France's strength in naval construction could be undone if their *Ponant* and *Levant* Fleets were kept separate. Initially, the allies maintained a posture of concentrating warships in the Channel, to ward off invasion attempts and control commerce, a strategy held since Elizabethan times; this left France, even with its (temporarily) reduced naval strength, in control of the Mediterranean. William III adopted a policy, against the urging of his Council and naval commanders, that would challenge France in Mediterranean waters and – more importantly – would deter any attempt to deploy the *Levant* Fleet northwards. He dispatched an Anglo-Dutch fleet (under Adm John Berkeley and Lt-Adm Philips van Almonde) into the Mediterranean in 1694, and ensured that it wintered there – in Cadiz Bay, where an English base was established to shelter and repair the fleet. As a consequence, the *Levant* Fleet was confined to port at Toulon, or at best able to operate in the Western Mediterranean only. And as a result, maintaining control of the Straits of Gibraltar became a permanent aim of the English.

Pontchartrain's son, Jérôme Phélypeaux, the new Comte de Pontchartrain, was awarded the *survivance* of his father's office three years later. When Louis de Ponchartrain received the top-ranking position of *chancelier de France* (Minister of Justice), Jérôme in September 1699 became Secretary of State for the Navy, but with only the mere addition of the portfolios of the Colonies, the Sea Fishing, the Maritime Trade and the Consulates: therefore, he was to become the politically weakest Secretary of State for the Navy of the reign.

The War of the Spanish Succession (1702–1714)

Charles II, the last Hapsburg King of Spain, died in October 1700. The rival claimant for the vacant throne were Philip, Duc d'Anjou (supported by his grandfather, Louis XIV) and the Hapsburg prince Charles, son of the Emperor Leopold (who was backed by England and the Netherlands). William III initially recognised the Duc d'Anjou, but French recognition of the Stuart Pretender as James III led to the renewal of hostilities. William's death at Kensington was to delay a formal outbreak, which was declared in April 1702 after Queen Anne's accession to the English throne.

On 8 June 1702 an Anglo-Dutch fleet was despatched to the Mediterranean, a continuation of the policy of William III to force France to split its military and naval strength between southern and northern fronts. The aim was to ensure the opening of the Straits of Gibraltar to allied fleets (and commerce), to secure Allied naval power in the Mediterranean, and to cut off Spain's transatlantic trade. They also wished to support the Austrians, who were pushing for Allied naval power to inspire the anti-Bourbon nobility in Naples, to diminish the Papacy's support for France, and to persuade the Duke of

Savoy to switch sides. The allied fleet consisted of 30 English and 20 Dutch ships of the line, under the overall command of Adm Sir George Rooke.

Following an abortive attempt to attack Cadiz, Rooke learnt that a French fleet, under the LG Louis François de Rousselet, Marquis de Châteaurenault, was in Vigo Bay in support of the Spanish galleons recently arrived from the West Indies. The Allied fleet staged an attack on the port, capturing or destroying every vessel in Redondela Harbour, while land forces under the Duke of Ormonde secured the town and harbour defences. Rooke then sailed for home with the bulk of his fleet, leaving Sir Cloudisley Shovell with a detachment to refit the prizes, with the inclusion of the Spanish treasure, and to destroy those vessels that could not be brought away.

In the summer of 1704, Rooke decided to attack and occupy the peninsula of Gibraltar at Spain's southern tip, which strategically commanded the entrance to the Mediterranean. The attach was launched by an amphibious assault force on 1 August, and on 4 August the Spanish governor surrendered. English control of Gibraltar was challenged on 24 August when a French fleet entered the Straits. An inconclusive battle took place off Vélez-Málaga (the largest naval battle of the War), which both sides claimed as a victory. The French returned to Toulon, where they remained and did not subsequently challenge English control of these waters, and indeed of the Mediterranean.

In 1707 a decision was made to attack Toulon itself. An Allied army crossed the Var from Italy, and laid siege to Toulon. An English fleet under Sir Clowdisley Shovell co-operated by providing the maritime component of the besieging forces during July and August, and carried out a bombardment of the port. In an attempt to prevent their Mediterranean fleet from being burnt, the French Navy – on direction from Louis – arranged to submerge some forty-four of their battlefleet units, including thirteen 1st Rank, nine 2nd Rank and twenty-two 3rd Rank ships. Another two 3rd Rank ships were left afloat; one was destroyed in the bombardment (the *Sage*) and another was so badly damaged (the *Fortuné*) that she was condemned immediately after the

The only major fleet battle of the War of the Spanish Succession was fought off Vélez-Málaga in southern Spain on 24 August 1704 (NS). Tactically inconclusive, it was probably the last fleet engagement in which galleys attempted to play a significant part. In this oil painting by Isaac Sailmaker, one can be seen in the foreground towing a damaged French three-decker stern-first – indeed, towing the badly damaged French flagship *Foudroyant* out of danger was probably the most important contribution galleys made to the outcome of the battle. (National Maritime Museum, London, BHC0340)

siege. Nevertheless, the ground component of the besieging forces was unable to make progress, and after two month Shovell's fleet departed for home. The scuttled ships were all refloated by October, but few of them were ever restored to active service.

The Death of Louis XIV (1 September 1715)

Louis XIV's death in 1715, four days short of his 77th birthday, after 54½ years of absolutist rule, marked the major discontinuity of the Bourbon monarchy prior to the French Revolution. The death of his son (the Grand Dauphin Louis) on 14 April 1711, his grandson Louis, Duke of Burgundy, on 18 February 1712, and his eldest great-grandson Louis, Duke of Brittany, on 8 March 1712, successively removed the three next in legitimate succession to the throne, leaving his 5½-year-old younger great-grandson Louis, Duc d'Anjou as the legal heir. Before his death Louis XIV had in his will legitimised his surviving sons by Madame de Montespan – Louis-Auguste, Duc du Maine and Louis-Alexandre, Comte de Toulouse – but his nephew Philippe, Duc d'Orléans, assuming the Regency, persuaded Parliament to void this part of the will.

The Thirty Years' Peace (1713–1743)

From the signing of the treaties of Utrecht in 1713, France generally remained at peace for thirty years, a period during which a general reconstruction took place. This was briefly interrupted by the War of the Quadruple Alliance (1718–20) which pitted Spain (under Philip V and his wife Elizabeth Farnese) against an alliance of Britain, France, Austria and the Netherlands (later joined by Savoy). By the end of the War of the Spanish Succession in 1713, British and French interests were in common, and from 1716 onwards the two acted in concert to oppose first Spanish and later Russian expansionist intentions. However, this conflict had little naval action in which the French Navy was involved.

Following the death of the Regent Philippe d'Orleans in 1723, Louis XV nominally became of age. He wished his former tutor, André-Hercule de Fleury, to become his First Minister, but the 70-year-old Fleury declined the role in favour of Louis Henri, Duc de Bourbon. However, Fleury remained present as the young King's advisor at all meetings between the King and the Duc de Bourbon. Finally, in June 1726 the Duc was dismissed and exiled from court, and Fleury reluctantly took on the reins of power, albeit disdaining the formal title of First Minister; he was to maintain this role, and to pursue a general policy of excluding France from major wars, until his death in 1743 in his ninetieth year.

With the crushing debts inherited from Louis XIV the *Conseil de Marine*, followed after 1723 by Mazarin as *Secrétaire d'État à la Marine*, could do little more than pay the navy's personnel, and the fleet of Louis XIV rapidly atrophied. During the 1720s the navy did succeed in a small construction effort, launching seventeen ships of the line and two frigates in 1722–24 and eight more ships of the line and three frigates in 1725–28. In contrast, during the 1730s only nine ships of the line and two frigates were launched.

The War of the Polish Succession (1733–1738)

An exception to the strategy of peace took place in 1734, when France was drawn into the politics of Central Europe. On 1 February 1733 Augustus II, King of Poland and Grand Duke of Lithuania, died, leaving two claimants to the vacant throne. France gave support to its preferred claimant, Stanislas Leczinski (Louis XV's father-in-law), who was transported to Danzig by the 44-gun *Argonaute*, as part of a squadron of ten *vaisseaux* and five frigates which included also the *Fleuron* 60 (flagship of LG Francois de Bricqueville, Comte de La Luzerne), *Conquérant* 70, *Saint Louis* 62, *Toulouse* 60, *Heureux* 60, *Triton* 60, *Mercure* 56, *Tigre* 56, *Griffon* 46, *Gloire* 45, *Astrée* 30 and *Méduse* 16), which sailed from Brest on 31 August. The fleet arrived at Copenhagen on 20 September, but advanced no further, receiving orders on 8 October to return to Brest.

Russian and Austrian forces invaded Poland in support of their preferred claimant, Augustus's son. Stanislas Leczinski was forced to retreat to Danzig, where he was besieged by the Russians in early 1734. To relieve him in Danzig, Fleury deployed to Copenhagen a small task force under CV Jean André, Marquis de Barailh, comprising two 64-gun ships, *Achille* and *Fleuron*, plus the 56-gun *Brillant*, 46-gun *Gloire* and 30-gun frigate *Astrée*, carrying a detachment of troops. In May 1734 the *Achille* and *Gloire* landed 1,800 men at Weichselmunde, but these were withdrawn to Copenhagen after four days.

Later that month, the five French warships landed their troops at Danzig, but the arrival of a Russian fleet of fourteen ships of the line (plus smaller vessels) under Adm Thomas Gordon on 1 June caused the French ships to retire, and the French troops surrendered two days later. The 2,400 captured troops were later exchanged in September for the Russian frigate *Mittau*, which the *Fleuron* and *Gloire* of Barailh's squadron had captured on 5 June during their return to Copenhagen. Danzig capitulated to the Russian army on 30 June, and the French squadron returned to Brest on 24 August.

The War of the Austrian Succession (1740–1748)

By 1740 the French Navy, although somewhat recovered from its disastrous condition at the death of Louis XIV in 1715, was still only a fraction of that of Britain, its likeliest naval opponent. This was not the fault of Cardinal Fleury, who gave unstinting support to the Navy and – at the close of his administration – was providing far greater sums to the Navy than his immediate predecessors. Under his office, the naval budget grew from nine million *livres* in 1728 to twenty-seven million in 1742; only after his death was that year's budget reduced to some nineteen million. But even the highest level of expenditure was never likely to allow France to rival Britain in material terms – to do so would have required a doubling of the budget. At the height of the War of the Austrian Succession, the best that Maurepas, the energetic naval minister, could obtain for the Navy was thirty million *livres*.

Maurepas stressed that France needed to maintain a battlefleet of at least sixty ships of the line, but this modest target was not obtained; even in the best year (1745) she had no more than forty-five ships (plus some fifteen frigates).

On the death of Cardinal Fleury in 29 January 1743, Louis XV decided against appointing a new First Minister (Fleury had effectively performed this role since 1726, albeit disdaining use of the title), and he took the role on himself, as Louis XIV had done in 1661. 1661. However, lacking the determination of his great-grandfather, the King vacillated in his policies, and began to change his ministers without allowing them to carry out an effective programme. Maurepas was dismissed in April 1749 and exiled to Bourges, following acrimonious disputes in the Council between the Secretary of War and himself over budgetary priorities.

Late in 1743 France joined with Prussia and other North German states under the Treaty of Frankfurt to take up the cause of Spain, which was already involved in war against Britain. War against Britain was declared on 20 March 1744, and a counter-declaration of war by Britain was issued eleven days later. Admiral Thomas Matthews commanded a fleet of some twenty-eight ships off Toulon when a joint Franco-Spanish fleet exited the port on 20 February 1744. An inconclusive battle took place two days later off Cape Sicié. No major fleet action was to take place during the following five years, but two important actions took place during 1747 which demonstrated British control of the Atlantic.

In August 1746 Vice-Admiral George Anson had assumed personal control of a new Western Squadron comprising seventeen ships of the line and a dozen lesser warships. Maurepas had planned to send reinforcements to sustain the beleaguered French colonies across in North America, in the Caribbean and in India; his problem was to arrange for those reinforcements to get past the blockading British ships. On 14 May Anson's squadron of fourteen ships intercepted a convoy escorted by eight French naval and six *Compagnie des Indes* vessels off Cape Ortégal. The French warships were commanded by CdE Marquis de La Jonquière, who sought battle in a gallant and successful attempt to allow the convoy to escape, but paid the price with a dozen of the escorts being captured by the British.

On 25 October there was virtually a repeat of this, when a squadron under Rear Admiral Edward Hawke intercepted a huge convoy off Cape Finisterre, having sailed from Brest and being escorted by nine French Naval ships and one *Compagnie des Indes* vessel, under the command of CdE Marquis de l'Éstenduère. Six of the French warships were taken, although l'Éstenduère's flagship – the 80-gun *Tonnant* – escaped back into Brest with considerable damage. By the close of the year the French Navy had been virtually crushed, and its maritime trade ruined.

The Seven Years' War (1756–1763)

The 1749 Treaty was perceived by no-one as more than a pause in the contest with Britain, and from then on Antoine-Louis Rouillé, Maurepas's successor as Secretary of the Navy, sought to replace losses and rebuild the Navy, as well as institute administrative controls. Between 1748 and 1758 the French built 52 new ships of the line, while retiring ships built before 1740, and by the outbreak of war the battlefleet was practically all new. Unlike Britain, which tended to over-gun its ships of the line, France increased the size of its warships while maintaining the weight of armament (heavier individual guns, but fewer of them). Her ships' lines became finer, with improvements in speed and ability to operate in distant waters. The smaller units of the battlefleet were phased out, with emphasis given to building 74-gun and 64-gun ships, and no three-deckers added – with a view to developing Maurepas's strategy of trade protection rather than battlefleet combat. By November 1754, 45 of the 55 battlefleet units were 74s or 64s.

Increasing conflicts with the British, notably in North America, signalled an imminent return to war, and the Navy, under new Secretary of the Navy Jean–Bapiste de Machault, was increasingly on a war footing. The capture of the 64-gun *Alcide* and *Lys* in 1755 while both were *en flûte* escorting a convoy across the Atlantic gave a spur to further construction, with six further 74s and the same number of 64s being ordered during that year, as well as more of the new 80-gun two–deckers which were being constructed as the elite flagships of the new Navy – these were longer than earlier three-deckers and, when armed with 24pdrs on the upper deck as well as 36pdrs in the main battery, carrying a weight of broadside identical to the 104-gun *Foudroyant* of 1693, the largest of the post-Barfleur three-deckers. As far as three-deckers were concerned, one was proposed to be built in 1752 at Rochefort, but this was not begun and the first such vessel was only ordered in May 1757, while wartime priorities resulted in the programme being deferred until the war's end.

The much-anticipated war was formally begun in 1756, with a British declaration of war on 17 May. A successful attack on Minorca by the *Levant* Fleet resulted in the capture of the island on 28 June, while in North America the French fortress of Louisbourg on Cape Breton Island was successfully defended, protecting the seaward approaches to the St Lawrence. But by 1758 the tide began to turn. Louisbourg was taken by the British after French reinforcements were blocked by the British naval victory in the Battle of Cartagena (Osborn's Action) on 28 February, and in the same year they captured the French colonies in Senegal.

In 1759 Maurepas had intended to mount an invasion of Britain; the French had consolidated troops around the mouth of the Loire, and endeavoured to bring together their Atlantic and Mediterranean fleets. However, three major setbacks for the French during this *Annus Mirabilis* (as the British termed it) brought havoc to their intentions. On 18 August the Mediterranean fleet under CdE Jean-Francois de Bertet de Sabran, Comte de La Clue, was brought to action by a larger British fleet under Adm Edward Boscawen off Lagos; La Clue's flagship, the 80-gun *Océan*, was burnt along with the 74-gun *Redoutable*, while two other 74s – *Centaure* and *Téméraire* – were captured as well as the 64-gun *Modeste*. In September, the successful British assault on Quebec signalled the beginning of the end to French occupation of the St Lawrence valley (although it would be another year before French forces, now cut off by British naval superiority in the North Atlantic, surrendered at Montreal). On 20 November, the Atlantic Fleet under *Vice-Amiral* Hubert de Brienne, Comte de Conflans, was met by Adm Sir Edward Hawke in Quiberon Bay; in the subsequent action, France lost two 80s (the flagship Soleil Royal burnt and the *Formidable* captured) and four 2nd Ranks (*Thésée*, *Héros*, *Juste* and *Superbe*).

Such early defeats in the Seven Years' War did not deter the French Navy from further construction. A program of reconstruction was begun in 1760–61, although the crushing financial effects of the war meant that the state coffers were empty. To fund the replacements that were required, Étienne François de Choiseul, Duke of Choiseul, Chief Minister of France from 1758 (he also assumed the roles of *Secrétaire d'État* for War in February 1761 and for the Navy in October 1761), had to make an appeal to the various French provincial and civic authorities, and to other institutions, to provide direct funding for the fifteen new ships of the line that were ordered in 1761–62, although some were not completed until after that war.

A second scheme for invading England was put in hand, this time to be arranged in concert with Spain which, in accordance with the Family Compact between the two Bourbon monarchs (signed in August 1761, this was in fact the third such agreement between the Bourbon cousins – the earlier versions had been agreed in 1733 and 1743), entered into the war at the close of 1761, although for various reasons this scheme failed to materialise, as the French and Spanish navies proved unable to coordinate their plans. Also during 1761, the French re-adopted the practice of *armaments mixte*, loaning out nine ships of the line (eight 64s and a single 50) to private contractors for privateering missions or to sail on trading operations *en flute*. This met with varied success: the *Protée* and *Sage* had rewarding captures of prizes, and the *Vaillant* made a safe round trip to India for the *Compagnie des Indes*; but the *Achille*, *Sainte Anne*, *Warwick* and 50-gun *Oriflamme* all fell into British hands, while the *Notre Dame de Rosaire* and *Vierge de Santé* barely avoided the same fate. The Treaty of Paris, bringing a conclusion to the war, was signed in February 1763, chiefly because the combatants on both sides were too exhausted to continue; once again, no lasting peace was envisaged.

Choiseul rebuilds the Navy (1763–1774)

Even before the ink on the Treaty had time to dry, Choiseul put in hand a calculated policy of *revanche* (revenge). The Treaty of Paris had left Britain in a seemingly unassailable position as the global superpower, and inevitably had left both France and Spain horrified that British hegemony – from North America to India – would permanently destroy the balance of power which was the basis of international relations.

Choiseul and his opposite number in Madrid, Jeronimo Grimaldi, were already close allies. They devised a new plan for invading Britain, this time based on a systematic reconstruction of both navies designed to operate as a single Bourbon strike force. They envisaged reconstructing the French Navy to a strength of 80 ships of the line, and simultaneously reorganising and reconstructing the Spanish Navy to include 60 ships of the line built or rebuilt on French lines and capable of acting in concert with the French. The plan provided for an armada of smaller vessels to be escorted by the combined fleets to attack and occupy Portsmouth and the Sussex coast. Simultaneously, other French forces would make a diversionary attack on Scotland, while Spain would seek to capture Gibraltar.

In 1762 the French navy had only 47 ships of the line and 20 frigates, compared to 145 ships of the line and 103 frigates in the British Royal Navy. In 1763 Choiseul set an objective of rebuilding the fleet to a level of 80 ships of the line and 45 frigates. In 1765 he reformed the corps of naval constructors, improving the training of new shipbuilders and giving them the title of *ingénieurs constructeurs*. He put the construction activity in each dockyard under an *ingénieur en chef*, who had a rank equivalent to a *capitaine de vaisseau*. After the monopoly of the *Compagnie des Indes* was suspended in 1769 Choiseul acquired for the Navy some of the company's ships and, more importantly, its arsenal at Lorient. He also took advantage of the period of peace to accumulate large stocks of raw materials in the dockyards.

Choiseul's cousin, César Gabriel de Choiseul–Chevigny, Duc de Praslin, took over the Navy ministry in 1766 (the Duc de Choiseul remained Chief Minister). The naval budget was drastically reduced, and the program of naval construction was cut back; between 1766 and 1774 only eleven ships of the line were launched (the 80-gun *Couronne*, four 74s and six 64s), while three 64s were bought from the bankrupted *Compagnie des Indes*. By 1768 the Navy had reached the strength that it had had at the outbreak of the Seven Years' War and in 1769 it was considered capable of conducting major operations. But by 1771 the number of ships of the line peaked at 68 ships, and then declined slightly. Louis XV wanted to avoid a major war and in 1770 dismissed both Choiseul and Praslin.

Louis XV died in May 1774, and was succeeded by his grandson as Louis XVI (the Dauphin, also named Louis, had died in 1765). Antoine Raymond Jean Gualbert Gabriel de Sartine, Comte d'Alby, *Secrétaire d'État à la Marine* from August 1774, prepared during 1774–75 a long-term program to provide a navy comprising 64 ships of the line and 40 frigates. Sartine had previously been *lieutenant-général de police de Paris* and knew nothing of the Navy, but he was an excellent administrator and on 27 July 1776 issued seven *ordonnances* that constituted a major reform of the Navy, including giving seagoing officers precedence over civilian administrators in the management of the ports and the fleet. In the meantime, increased funding allowed the dockyards to use their

An anonymous wash drawing showing the fleet of Rear Adm Thomas Graves bearing down to attack that of the Comte de Grasse as it emerged from the Chesapeake on 5 September 1781. Graves's failure to break through a stubborn French defence to relieve the besieged British forces at Yorktown left General Cornwallis no option but to surrender. As this capitulation marked the beginning of the end of political will in London to carry on the war, the Battle of the Virginia Capes is often seen as the moment the independence of the United States of America was assured. From this perspective, it is the most significant victory ever won by the French Navy. (National Maritime Museum, London, PY4074)

stocks of raw materials to begin rapid construction of ships towards a target of 80 ships of the line and 60 frigates set by Sartine and Louis XVI. Notwithstanding the fall in numbers, Sartine had inherited a better-resourced fleet than had existed prior to 1756, including eight of the 1st Rank and thirty-two 74s.

The War of American Independence (1778–1783)

On 6 February 1778 France signed an offensive and defensive treaty in Paris with Benjamin Franklin, who had come to France in October 1776 to negotiate such an alliance. This led to open war with England, and on 13 April a French squadron of eighteen vessels (twelve *vaisseaux* and five frigates) under Vice-Amiral Charles Henri d'Estaing left Toulon for Delaware Bay, carrying 4,000 men. Facing difficulties in manning the fleet, and unsure of the French fleet's destination, the British reinforcements (under Vice-Adm John Byron) intended to reinforce Howe's fleet did not sail until 26 May.

The Brest fleet, under LG Comte d'Orvilliers, sailed on 8 July, while the equivalent British fleet, under Adm Augustus Keppel, sailed the following day from Spithead, aiming to bring the French fleet to action. The two forces sighted each other on 23 July, a hundred miles west of Ushant. A four-day chase ensued, but the action which followed on 27 July was fairly indecisive, with both sides claiming that the other left the field of battle first.

Much of the remainder of the naval action over the following four years took place across the Atlantic, both in the Caribbean and off the coasts of the American colonies. Unlike its dismal performance during the Seven Years' War, the French Navy performed well over the next four years, more than holding its own both in fighting qualities and in seamanship; the French Navy was to play a pivotal role in the outcome of the war; Rochambeau brought over 6,000 French trained soldiers in July 1780 which reinforced the rebel forces; and the success of LG Comte de Grasse's fleet in denying control of Chesapeake Bay to the British Navy was the determining factor in General Cornwallis's decision to surrender at Yorktown in October 1781.

In April 1782 the British, under Rodney, succeeded at last in a decisive naval action off the Caribbean islands of Les Saintes (near Guadeloupe) against de Grasse's fleet, but this was too late to influence the outcome ashore. On 20 January 1783 Britain and France signed preliminaries of Peace. News of the agreement reached America on 16 March by the French naval lugger *Triomphe*. French forces in America were repatriated to France in May. The subsequent Treaty of Versailles in September not only secured the independence of the United States, but returned to France control of the Caribbean islands of St Lucia and Tobago (albeit only until the French Revolutionary War) and African territories such as Senegal.

The end of the *Ancien Régime*

Charles Eugène Gabriel de La Croix de Castries, *Secrétaire d'État à la marine* (Minister of the Navy) since 1780, followed the victories of the War of American Independence with a series of reforms. In 1783 and 1784 he ordered a restructuring of the dockyards, and in 1784 he began the construction of a new dockyard at Cherbourg, which was completed only in 1858. At the same time, he adopted the plan of the Inspector of Naval Shipbuilding, Jean-Charles, Chevalier de Borda and the *ingénieur-constructeur* Jacques-Noël Sané to create a homogeneous fleet by adopting standard designs for ships of the line, the ones adopted being the 118-gun three-decker and the 80- and 74-gun two-deckers. These became the core of the French Navy through the Revolutionary and Napoleonic wars and into the post-1815 Restoration. In 1786 Castries divided the fleet into nine squadrons, of which five were at Brest, two at Rochefort, and two at Toulon, and he also reformed the officer corps. The main operation at sea during this period was the departure in 1785 of Jean François de Galaup, Comte de La Pérouse in two *gabarres* promoted to frigates for the occasion, *Boussole* and *Astrolabe*, for a scientific circumnavigation of the world. The expedition disappeared after departing Australia in March 1788; evidence was found in 1826 and confirmed in 1964 and 2005 that the two ships were wrecked in a typhoon at Vanikoro in the Solomon Islands.

The French Navy thus reached new heights of strength and efficiency during the 1780s. However, at the same time the King's finances, drained by massive expenditures including those for the army and navy, were becoming desperate. The year of 1788 saw both a major political crisis and massive crop failures. In August 1788 the King declared bankruptcy and summoned the Estates General to meet in May 1789. The French Revolution broke out two months later, ending the world of the *Ancien Régime*.

Chronology

Note that all dates in this volume are in accord with the Gregorian ('New Style') calendar, and not with the Julian ('Old Style') calendar that was in use in Britain and its territories until September 1752. Julian dates were ten days behind Gregorian dates in the seventeenth century and eleven days behind in the eighteenth century.

Year	Date	Event
1625	(16 July)	Battle of the Pertuis Breton (*Bataille de L'Ile de Ré* in French).
1626	(20 Oct)	Appointment of Cardinal de Richelieu (Armand-Jean du Plessis) as *Grand-Maître, Chef et Surintendant general de la navigation et commerce de France*.
1627	(Nov)	Siege of La Rochelle (to 28 Oct 1628)
1635	(26 May)	Declaration of war against Spain (to 24 Oct 1648)
1637	(24 Mar)	French reconquest of the Îles de Lérins (off Cannes), completed 15 May
1638	(22 Aug)	Battle of Guétaria (off North Spain)
	(1 Sept)	Battle of Genoa – or Battle of Vado (galley combat)
1640	(21 July)	Battle of Cádiz
1641	(4 July)	1st Battle of Tarragona (to 6 July)
	(20 Aug)	2nd Battle of Tarragona (to 25 Aug)
1642	(29 June)	1st Battle of Barcelona (to 3 July)
	(4 Dec)	Death of Cardinal de Richelieu; appointment of Cardinal Jules Mazarin as Chief Minister.
1643	(9 Aug)	2nd Battle of Barcelona
	(3 Sept)	Battle of Cartagena (or Battle of Cap de Gata)
1646	(14 June)	Battle of Orbetello (off Tuscany)
1647	(21 Dec)	Battle of Castellammare
1648	(26 Aug)	Start of the *Fronde* uprisings (to 21 Oct 1652)
	(24 Oct)	Peace of Westphalia brings end to the wider Thirty Years' War
1650	(23 Nov)	Action off Cambrils
1652	(9 Aug)	Battle of Pertuis d'Antioche
1653	(20 Oct)	Battle of Bordeaux
1659	(7 Nov)	Treaty of the Pyrenees brings end to war between France and Spain
1661	(9 Mar)	Death of Cardinal Mazarin; Louis XIV assumes regnal powers as his own Chief Minister.
1664	(23 July)	Landings at Djidjelli (Algeria)
1665	(3 March)	Battle of La Goulette (Tunisia)
	(24 Aug)	Battle of Cherchell (Algeria)
1666	(23 Feb)	France declared war (as Dutch allies) against England
1667	(24 May)	French invasion of the Spanish Netherlands opens War of Devolution.
	(30 May)	Battle of Nevis
	(5 July)	Battle of Martinique
	(31 July)	Treaty of Breda ends Anglo-Dutch War.
1668	(23 Jan)	Peace of Aix-la-Chapelle ends War of Devolution
1669	(24 July)	French attempt to relieve siege of Candia (Crete)
1671	(24 June)	Mass renaming of French warship (see Appendix X)
	(31 July)	Introduction of ships' names carved on their stern.
1672	(6 Apr)	Start of Franco-Dutch War
	(7 June)	Battle of Solebay
1673	(7 June)	1st Battle of Schooneveldt
	(14 June)	2nd Battle of Schooneveldt (or Battle of Walcheren)
	(21 Aug)	Battle of Texel
1675	(2 Jan)	Battle of Messina (or Pharo)
	(11 Feb)	Battle of the Lipari Islands
1676	(8 Jan)	Battle of Stromboli (or Alicudi Island)
	(22 Apr)	Battle of Augusta (*Agosta* in French)
	(3 June)	Battle of Palermo
1677	(3 Mar)	Battle of Tobago
1678	(17 Mar)	Battle of Ushant
	(10 Aug)	Treaty of Nijmegen ends Franco-Dutch War
1682	(28 July)	1st Bombardment of Algiers (until 5 Sept)
1683	(26 June)	2nd Bombardment of Algiers (until 18 Aug)
	(26 Oct)	Spain declares war on France, beginning War of the Reunions
1684	(18 May)	Bombardments of Genoa (until 28 May)
	(15 Aug)	Truce of Ratisbon ends War of the Reunions
1685	(22 June)	1st Bombardment of Tripoli
1688	(June)	3rd Bombardment of Algiers
	(26 Nov)	Dutch declare war on France, beginning the Nine Years' War
1689	(11 May)	Battle of Bantry Bay
	(27 July)	2nd Battle of Texel
1690	(10 July)	Battle of Beachy Head (*Béveziers* in French)
1692	(29 May)	Battle of Barfleur
	(2 June)	Destruction of French warships at Cherbourg
	(2/3 June)	Destruction of French warships at La Hougue
1693	(27 June)	Battle off Lagos – destruction of the Smyrna convoy
1694	(29 June)	3rd Battle of Texel
1696	(17 June)	Battle of Dogger Bank
1697	(6 May)	Raid on Cartagena de Indias.
	(30 Sept)	End of the Nine Years' War.
1702	(14 May)	Start of the War of the Spanish Succession.
	(29 Aug)	Benbow's Action – Battle of Santa Martha (until 4 Sept)
	(22 Oct)	Battle of Vigo Bay
1703	(22 May)	Battle off Cape de La Roque
1704	(24 Aug)	Battle of Vélez-Málaga
1705	(20 Mar)	Battle of Marbella (or *Bataille de Gibraltar* in French)
1707	(28 July)	Siege of Toulon by Sir Cloudisley Shovell's fleet (until 22 Aug)
	(21 Oct)	2nd Battle of Ushant
1710	(8 Jan)	Action off Toulon
1711	(14 Sept)	Capture of Rio de Janeiro
1713	(12 Apr)	Treaties of Utrecht ends the War of the Spanish Succession
1715	(1 Sept)	Death of Louis XIV, and accession of Louis XV.
1728	(20 July)	2nd Bombardment of Tripoli (to 26 July)
1734	(9 July)	French action to relieve Danzig
1741	(18 Jan)	Battle of Cape Tiburon
1744	(22 Feb)	Battle of Toulon (or Battle of Cap Sicié)
	(11 Apr)	War with Britain (as part of War of Austrian Succession)
1747	(14 May)	1st Battle off Cape Finisterre (*Cap Ortegal* in French)
	(25 Oct)	2nd Battle off Cape Finisterre
1749	(1 Jan)	Final absorbtion of Galley Corps into the French Navy
	(28 Oct)	Peace with Britain
1756	(17 May)	War with Britain (Seven Years' War)

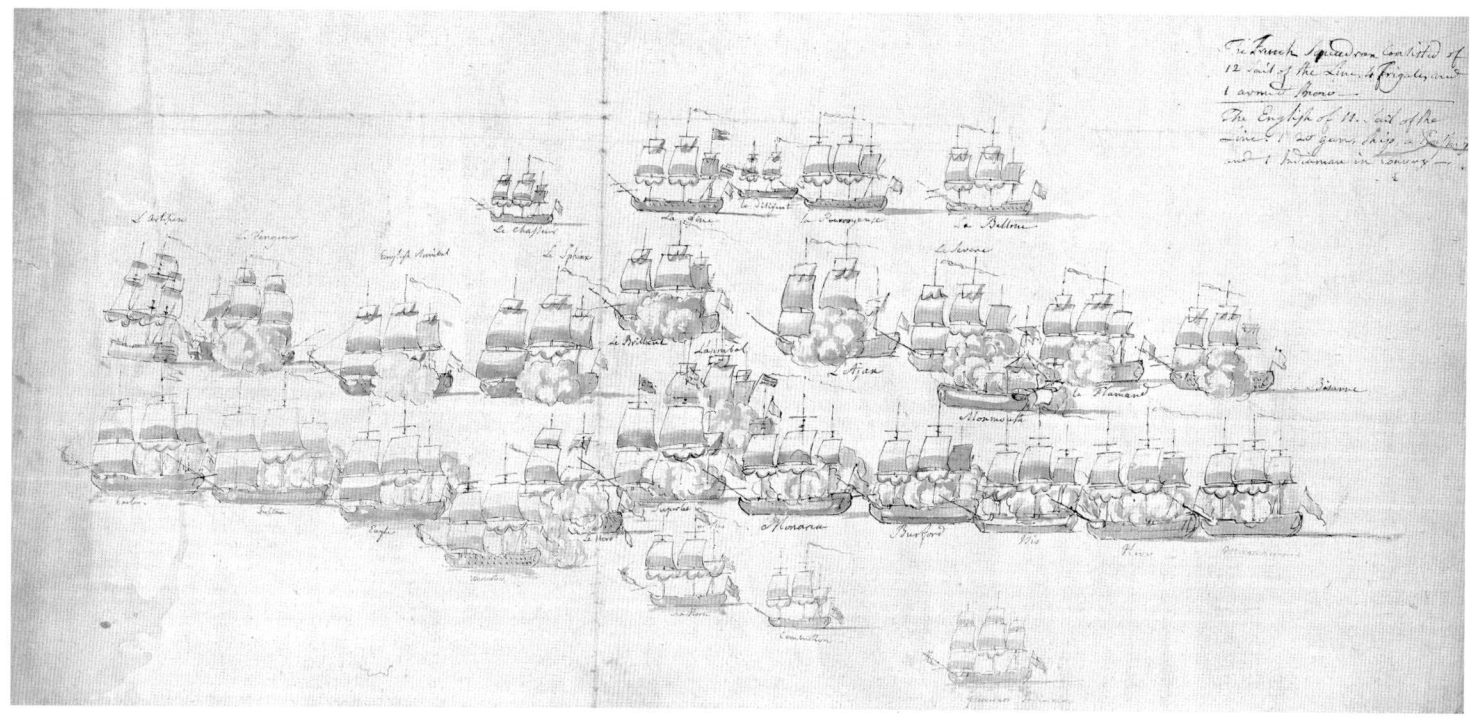

	(20 May)	Battle of Minorca
1758	(28 Feb)	Osborn's Action off Cartagena (capture of *Foudroyant* and *Orphée*)
	(29 Apr)	Battle off Cuddalore (Sadras)
	(17 July)	Fall of Louisbourg to the British
	(3 Aug)	Battle off Negapatam
1759	(18 Aug)	2nd Battle of Lagos
	(10 Sept)	Battle of Pondicherry
	(20 Nov)	Battle of Quiberon Bay (*Les Cardinaux* in French)
1761	(15 Aug)	Third Bourbon 'family' compact between France and Spain.
1762	(3 Nov)	Peace preliminaries signed at Fontainebleu.
1763	(10 Feb)	Peace with Britain (Treaty of Paris)
1774	(10 May)	Death of Louis XV and Accession of Louis XVI
1778	(6 Feb)	France enters the War of American Independence by signing a treaty with Franklin in Paris
	(27 July)	3rd Battle of Ushant
	(8 Sept)	Capture of Dominica
1779	(6 July)	Battle of Grenada
1780	(16 Jan)	Battle of Cape St Vincent ('Moonlight Battle/*Bataille du Clair-de-Lune*')
	(17 Apr)	Rodney's Action with De Guichen off Dominica
1781	(16 Mar)	Battle of Cape Henry
	(16 Apr)	Battle of Porto Praya
	(5 Sept)	Battle of the Chesapeake
1782	(25 Jan)	Battle of St Kitts (or St Christopher)
	(13 Feb)	Capture of St Christopher
	(17 Feb)	Battle off Sadras
	(12 Apr)	Battle of Providien (Trincomalee)
	(12 Apr)	Battle of the Saintes
	(19 Apr)	Battle of the Mona Passage
	(3 July)	Battle of Negapatam
	(3 Sept)	Battle of Trincomalee
1783	(20 Jan)	Britain and France sign preliminaries of peace in Paris
	(20 June)	Battle off Cuddalore (*Gondelour* in French)
	(3 Sep)	Peace of Paris concludes the War of American Independence.

A series of hard-fought battles in Indian waters occurred in both the Seven Years' War and the War of American Independence. In the latter conflict, the British squadron was commanded by Vice-Adm Sir Edward Hughes, who commissioned a series of paintings to celebrate his achievements from the prominent marine painter Dominic Serres. This is a preliminary drawing for one of those paintings, depicting the Battle of Providien on 12 April 1782. As would be expected for such a critical patron, the artist has gone to great lengths to get the details correct. In the centre foreground, he has depicted the fire-fight between the two 74-gun flagships, Hughes's *Superb* and the *Héros* of CdE Pierre André de Suffren, but the main interest is in the upper right where the 64-gun *Monmouth* is in danger of being captured. (National Maritime Museum, London, PY5244)

Subsequent dates (for careers of ships lasting beyond 1792):

1793	(29 Aug)	Occupation of Toulon by Anglo-Spanish-Sardinian forces.
	(18 Dec)	Evacuation of Toulon by the Allied forces.
1794	(1 June)	Battle of 13 Prairial ('Glorious First of June')
1795	(14 Mar)	Battle of Cape Noli ('Hotham's Action off Genoa')
	(23 June)	Île Groix ('Bridport's Action')
	(13 July)	Îles des Hyères ('Hotham's Action off the Hyères')
1798	(1 Aug)	Battle of Aboukir ('the Nile')

French Naval Operations from 1626 to 1786

This section lists the forces of France and her allies involved in naval operations, together (where known) with vessels of its opponents in each major action. Note again that all dates given are in New Style; until 1752, Britain still used the Julian calendar whose dates were 10 days earlier during the seventeenth century (11 days in the eighteenth century); see notes on dates in the Introduction earlier. Also, whereas the Julian year began on 25 March, the Gregorian year – as now – began on 1 January. Finally, in France the day changed at midnight, whereas for the British Navy the change took place at noon. The authors are especially grateful to Frank Fox for sharing his recent research on participants in the Battles of the Texel, Beachy Head and Barfleur, and to David Davies for his assistance on the Texel.

1. BATTLE OF GUÉTARIA – 22 August 1638
The first significant victory of Richelieu's new French Navy, which gained temporary control of the Bay of Biscay as a result. The use of fireships by LG Henri d'Escoubleau de Sourdis in the shallow waters of Guétaria harbour (just west of San Sébastián), which prevented his larger ships from entering, resulted in the destruction of all but one of the 18 Spanish warships, with the loss of 4,000 men (the French lost fewer than a hundred).

De Sourdis's squadron – 21 ships, + smaller vessels
Couronne 72 (flag of acting *Vice-Amiral* Claude de Launay-Razilly), *Navire du Roi* 52 (flag of LG Henri d'Escoubleau de Sourdis), *Vaisseau de la Reine* 38, *Europe* 34, *Vierge* 34, *Cardinal* 30, *Cocq* 30, *Corail* 30, *Cygne* 30, *Faucon* 30, *Licorne* 30, *Triomphe* 30, *Triton* 30, *Trois Rois* 30, *Victoire* 30, *Dauphin du Havre* 28, *Saint Charles* 28, *Espérance en Dieu* 24, *Intendant* 24, *Madeleine de Brest* 24, *Perle* 24, *Renommée* 24.
Also present: *Émerillon, Saint François, Neptune, Petit Saint Jean, Marguerite, Hermine, Grande Frégate de Brest, Cardinale, Royale, Frégate du Havre* and about 4 smaller; plus 7 fireships – *Chasseur, Fortune, Ours, Saint Claude de Honfleur, Saint Jean Baptiste, Saint Louis d'Olonne* (or *de Hollande*), *Soleil*.

2. BATTLE OF ORBITELLO – 14 June 1646
Battle of the Franco-Spanish war (part of the Thirty Years' War). This part of the Tuscan coast – known as the Praesidia – featured the Spanish stronghold of Orbitello under siege by French land forces. A Spanish relief force was sighted off the coast; Maillé-Brézé had his ships towed into position by galleys to avoid being caught at their moorings; the French prevailed, and the Spanish retreated, unaware that Maillé-Brézé had been killed in the closing stage of the fight.

Maillé-Brézé's squadron – 16 ships
Centre division – led by *Grand Saint Louis* (flag of Adm Jean-Armand Maillé, Marquis de Brézé).
Port division – led by *Lune* (flag of Vice-Adm Louis Foucault de Saint-Germain-Beaupré, Comte du Daugnon).
Starboard division – led by *Soleil* (flag of CdE de Montigny).
The other ships present (not available by division) were *Saint Thomas d'Aquin, Admirante, Saint Jacques de Dunkerque, Cardinal, Grand Anglais, Vierge, Sourdis, Triomphe, Triton, Lion Couronné, Saint Charles, Madeleine, Duchesse*.
Reserve division – 6 ships (flag of CdE M. de Montade).
Also 8 fireships (*Deux Aigles, Espérance, Levrette, Lionne, Marguerite de Ponant, Marie, Mecque, Saint Fernand*); 4 *flûtes* (*Cancre Doré, Espérance de Lubeck, Porteur de bois*, and hospital ship *Saint Jacques de Portugal*); 20 galleys.

3. BATTLE OF CASTELLAMMARE – 21/22 December 1647
In 1647, the inhabitants of Naples revolted against Spanish rule and called upon France for support. A fleet of 29 vessels and 5 fireships, under the young Armand-Jean de Vignerot de Plessis, Duc de Richelieu (the Cardinal's nephew) was despatched, which took on a strong Spanish contingent of warships and galleys off Castellammare in the Bay of Naples.

Richelieu's squadron – 29 ships (including 3 Portuguese)
Amiral (flag of Duc de Richelieu), *Lune* (flag of CdE Nicolas Leroy du Mé), *Mazarin* (flag of CdE de Montade), *Grand Saint Louis* (flag of CdE Jean Garnier), *Jupiter* (flag of CE Abraham Duquesne), *Cardinal, Triomphe, Grand Anglais, Dunkerquois, Soleil, Vierge, Dragon, Lion Couronné, Tigre, Cygne, Admirante, Triton, Saint Thomas, Faucon, Léopard, Sourdis, Saint Paul, Postillon, Éminent, Chasseur, Régine*.
Also 5 fireships (*Baleine, Comtesse, Coquette, Elbeuf* and *Saint Fernand*).

4. BATTLE OF LA GOULETTE – 2/3 March 1665
In the attack on La Goulette, near Tunis, the French squadron under the Duc de Beaufort destroyed numerous ships under the overall command of Barbier-Rassam, the Portuguese-born Algerine Admiral (who was killed in the attack).

Beaufort's squadron – 5 ships
Royale 56 (flag of *Amiral* François de Vendôme, Duc de Beaufort), *Écureuil* 38, *Étoile* 38, *Perle* 38, *Mercure* 36.
Also fireships *Saint Cyprien* and *Sainte Anne*.

5. BATTLE OF CHERCHELL – 24 August 1665
In the attack on Cherchell, on the Algerian coast, the French squadron destroyed two ships ('Flowerpot' and 'White Horse') and captured three others – *Chems* 33, *Hillell* 33 and *Nekhla* 22 (added to the French Navy as *Soleil d'Afrique, Croissant d'Afrique* and *Palmier* respectively – see Chapter 5).

Beaufort's squadron – 8 ships
Saint Philippe 82 (flag of *Amiral* François de Vendôme, Duc de Beaufort), *Reine* 60, *Royale* 56, *Dauphin* 52, *Saint Antoine* 38, *Hercule* 36, *Perle* 34, *Notre Dame* 28.
Also fireships *Saint Cyprien* and *Sainte Anne*.

6. EXPEDITION TO CANDIA (CRETE) – June 1669
Beaufort's fleet – 16 ships
Monarque 94 (flag of *Amiral* François de Vendôme, Duc de Beaufort), *Bourbon* 66, *Courtisan* 66 (flag of *Vice-Amiral* Damien, Marquis de Martel), *Lys* 60, *Princesse* 60, *Thérèse* 60 (lost in explosion 24.7.1669), *Comte* 50, *Fleuron* 48, *Sirène* 44, *Toulon* 42, *Dunkerquois* 40, *Provençal* 40, *Étoile* 36, *Écureuil* 34, *Croissant* 30, *Soleil d'Afrique* 30.
Also smaller *Concorde* (fireship), *Saint Antoine de Padoue* and *Brigantin*, plus 13 galleys (under Général des Galères Louis-Victor de Rochechouart, Duc de Mortemart et de Vivonne) and 3 *galiotes à rames*.

7. BATTLE OF SOLEBAY (Southwold Bay) – 7 June 1672

Anglo-French fleet – 82 ships (of which the *Royal James* was sunk)

(A) White squadron (French) under d'Estrées
Van division – *Terrible* 70 (flag of LG Abraham Duquesne), *Illustre* 70, *Conquérant* 70, *Admirable* 68, *Téméraire* 50, *Prince* 50, *Bourbon* 50, *Vaillant* 50, *Alcion* 46, *Hasardeux* 38.
Centre division – *Saint Philippe* 78 (flag of Vice-Amiral Jean, Comte d'Estrées), *Foudroyant* 70, *Grand* 70, *Tonnant* 58, *Brave* 54, *Aquilon* 50, *Duc* 50, *Oriflamme* 50, *Excellent* 50, *Éole* 38, *Arrogant* 38.
Rear division – *Superbe* 70 (flag of CdE des Rabesnières-Treillebois), *Invincible* 70, *Sans Pareil* 66, *Fort* 60, *Sage* 50, *Heureux* 50, *Rubis* 46, *Galant* 46, *Hardi* 38.

(B) Red squadron (English) under Duke of York
Van division – *London* 96 (flag of Vice-Adm Sir Edward Spragge), *Old James* 70, *Resolution* 70, *Dunkirk* 60, *Monck* 60, *Bristol* 48, *Diamond* 48, *Sweepstakes* 36, *Dartmouth* 32.
Centre division – *Prince* 100 (flag of HRH James Stuart, Duke of York & Albany), *Saint Michael* 90, *Royal Katherine* 82, *Victory* 82, *Cambridge* 70, *Monmouth* 66, *Dreadnought* 62, *Fairfax* 60, *Yarmouth* 54, *Adventure* 44, *Phoenix* 42.
Rear division – *Charles*, also called *Charles the Second* 96 (flag of Rear-Adm Sir John Harman), *Rainbow* 64, *York* 60, *Anne* 58, *Greenwich* 54, *Advice* 48 (not certain if in this division), *Dover* 48, *Forester* 38.

(C) Blue squadron (English) under Earl of Sandwich
Van division – *Saint Andrew* 96 (flag of Rear-Adm Sir John Kempthorne), *French Ruby* 80, *Saint George* 70, *Warspite* 70, *Gloucester* 62, *Bonaventure* 48, *Antelope* 48.
Centre division – *Royal James* 100 (flag of Adm Edward Montagu, the Earl of Sandwich), *Henry* 82, *Edgar* 72, *Rupert* 66, *Montagu* 62, *Leopard* 54, *Princess* 54, *Mary Rose* 48, *Crown* 48, *Success* 32.
Rear division – *Royal Sovereign* 100 (flag of Vice-Adm Sir Joseph Jordan), *Triumph* 70, *Unicorn* 64, *Mary* 62, *Plymouth* 60, *Ruby* 48, *Tiger* 44.

Dutch fleet – 62 ships (of which the *Jozua* 54 was destroyed and the *Stavoren* 48 captured by the English) and 13 frigates

(A) Van squadron under Banckert
Zevenwolden 76, *Prins Hendrik Casimir* 72 (flag of Hendrik Bruynsvelt, Schout-bij-Nacht of Vriesland), *Groningen* 70 (flag of Enno Doedes Star, Vice-Adm of Vriesland), *Callantsoog* 70, *Oranje* 70 (flag of Jan Matthijszoon, Schout-bij-Nacht of Zeeland), *Oudshoorn* 70 (the former HMS *Swiftsure*), *Walcheren* 70 (flag of Adriaen Banckert, Lieut-Adm of Zeeland), *Steenbergen* 64, *Oostergo* 62, *Wapen van Nassau* 62, *Schieland* 60, *Zieriksee* (flag of Cornelis Evertsen de Jonge, Vice-Adm of Zeeland), *Gelderland* 56, *Kruiningen* 56, *Elf Steden* 54, *Drie Helden Davids* 50, *Kampveere* 50, *Middleburg* 50, *Vlissingen* 50, *Wapen van Medemblik* 46, *Zwanenburg* 44; also frigates *Delft* 34, *Ter Goes* 34, *Popkensburg* 24 and *Schiedam* 20.

(B) Centre squadron under de Ruyter
Zeven Provinciën 80 (flag of Michiel de Ruyter, Lieut-Adm of the Maas), *Westvriesland* 78, *Eendracht* 76 (flag of Aert Janszoon van Nes, Lieut-Adm of Amsterdam), *Reiger[sbergen]* 72, *Maagd van Dordrecht* 68 (flag of Jan vertszoon de Liefde, Vice-Adm of the Maas), *Waesdorp* 68, *Ridderschap van Holland* 66 (flag of Jan Janszoon van Nes, Schout-bij-Nacht of the Maas), *Stad Utrecht* 66, *Gelderland* 64, *Alkmaar* 62, *Delft* 62, *Wapen van Hoorn* 62, *Deventer* 60, *Groot Hollandia* 60, *Provincie van Utrecht* 60, *Westergo* 56, *Wassenaer* 50, *Jozua* 54, *Agatha* 50, *Beschermer* 50, *Jaersveld* 48, *Zeelandia* 44; also frigates *Utrecht* 36, *Windhond* 34, *Brak* 24 and *Postiljon* 24.

(C) Rear squadron under van Ghent
Dolfijn 82 (flag of Baron Willem Joseph van Ghent, Lieut-Adm of Amsterdam), *Oliphant* 82 (flag of Frederik Sweers, Vice-Adm of Amsterdam), *Pacificatie* 76 (flag of Volkhart Schram, Vice-Adm of Noorderkwartier), *Gouda* 72 (flag of Jan de Haan, Schout-bij-Nacht of Amsterdam), *Wapen van Enkhuisen* 72 (flag of David Vlugh, Schout-bij-Nacht of Noorderkwartier), *Komeetster* 70, *Woerden* 70, *Justina van Nassau* 64, *Akerboom* 60, *Amsterdam* 60, *Oosterwijk* 60, *Noorderkwartier* 60, *Gideon* 58, *Essen* 50, *Leeuwen* 50, *Dordrecht* 50, *Caleb* 48, *Stavoren* 48, *Jupiter* 40; also frigates *Asperen* 30, *Overijssel* 30, *Bommel* 24, *Haas* 24 and *Harderwijk* 24.

8. FIRST BATTLE OF SCHOONEVELDT – 7 June 1673

Anglo-French fleet – 76 ships of the line

(A) Van (Red) Squadron under Prince Rupert – 26 (English) ships of the line
Van division – *London* 96 (flag of Vice-Adm Sir John Harman), *French Ruby* 80, *Resolution* 70, *Triumph* 70, *Warspite* 70, *Anne* 58, *Happy Return* 54, *Stavoreen* 48, *Constant Warwick* 42.
Centre division – *Royal Charles* 100 (flag of HRH Prince Rupert), *Henry* 82, *Royal Katherine* 82, *Edgar* 72, *Old James* 70, *Rupert* 66, *Gloucester* 62, *Lion* 62, *Princess* 54, *Crown* 48.
Rear division – *Charles* 96 (flag of Rear-Adm Sir John Chicheley), *Victory* 82, *Revenge* 62, *Newcastle* 54, *Yarmouth* 54, *Mary Rose* 48, *Assurance* 42.

(B) Centre (White) Squadron under d'Estrées – 27 (French) ships of the line
Van division – *Terrible* 70 (flag of CdE Hector des Ardents), *Sans Pareil* 64, *Conquérant* 56, *Téméraire* 52, *Aquilon* 50, *Oriflamme* 50, *Précieux* 50, *Prince* 50, *Sage* 50.
Centre division – *Reine* 104 (flag of Vice-Amiral Jean, Comte d'Estrées), *Foudroyant* 70, *Invincible* 70, *Glorieux* 64, *Tonnant* 64, *Excellent* 60, *Fier* 58, *Aimable* 56, *Vaillant* 50, *Apollon* 50.
Rear division – *Orgueilleux* 70 (flag of CdE François-Bénédict de Rouxel, Marquis de Grancey), *Grand* 70, *Illustre* 70, *Fortuné* 60, *Bon* 52, *Bourbon* 52, *Duc* 50, *Maure* 50.

(C) Rear (Blue) Squadron under Spragge – 23 (English) ships of the line
Van division – *Saint Michael* 90 (flag of Rear-Adm Thomas Butler, the Earl of Ossory), *Rainbow* 64, *York* 60, *Greenwich* 54, *Foresight* 48, *Hampshire* 46, *Sweepstakes* 42.
Centre division – *Prince* 100 (flag of Adm Sir Edward Spragge), *Royal Sovereign* 100, *Cambridge* 70, *Saint George* 70, *Dreadnought* 62, *Henrietta* 62, *Dunkirk* 60, *Advice* 48.
Rear division – *Saint Andrew* 96 (flag of Vice-Adm Sir John Kempthorne), *Unicorn* 64, *Mary* 62, *Monck* 60, *Diamond* 48, *Ruby* 48, *Bonaventure* 48, *Falcon* 42.

De Ruyter's fleet – 52 ships of the line
[Note that the ships and flag officers of the Friesland Admiralty were all absent, as Friesland and Groningen were under land attack by Bernhard von Galen, the Bishop of Munster.]

(A) Van Squadron under Tromp
Gouden Leeuw 82 (flag of Lieut-Adm Cornelis Tromp), *Pacificatie* 80 (flag of Vice-Adm Volkhart Schram), *Hollandia* 80 (flag of Schout-bij-Nacht Jan de Haen), *Kalandsoog* 70, *Delft* 62, *Amsterdam* 60, *Provincie van Utrecht* 60, *Schieland* 60, *Wassenaer* 60, *Geloof* 56, *Prins te Paard* 54, *Agatha* 50, *Zuiderhuis* 48, *Wapen van Holland* 46, *Wakende Kraam* 44, *Zeelandia* 44, *Jupiter* 42.

(B) Centre squadron under Aert van Nes
Vrijheid 80 (flag of Vice-Adm Jan Evertszoon de Liefde), *Zeven Provinciën* 80 (flag of Adm Michiel de Ruyter), *Eendracht* 72 (flag of Lieut-Adm Aert Jansse van Nes), *Spiegel* 70, *Steenbergen* 70, *Maagd van Dordrecht* 68

(flag of Schout-bij-Nacht Jan Janszoon van Nes), *Waesdorp* 68, *Deventer* 66, *Stad Utrecht* 66, *Alkmaar* 64, *Prins van Oranje* 64, *Gelderland* 63, *Beschermer* 50, *Essen* 50, *Caleb* 46, *Dordrecht* 44, *Wapen van Medemblik* 44, *Zeeland* 42.
(C) Rear Squadron under Banckert
Westfriesland 78, *Wapen van Enkhuizen* 72 (flag of Schout-bij-Nacht David Vlugh), *Eenhoorn* 70, *Komeetster* 70, *Walcheren* 70 (flag of Lieut-Adm Adriaan van Trappen Banckert), *Justina van Nassau* 65, *Ridderschap* 65, *Akerboom* 62, *Gideon* 63, *Domburg* 60, *Gelderland* 60, *Noorderkwartier* 60, *Zierikzee* 60 (flag of Vice-Adm Cornelis Evertsen de Jonge), *Wapen van Nassau* 58, *Tijdverdrijf* 56, *Leeuwen* 50, *Ter Veere* 48.

9. SECOND BATTLE OF SCHOONEVELDT (or BATTLE OF WALCHEREN) – 14 June 1673

Prince Rupert's fleet
The only changes from the previous action were that Prince Rupert shifted his flag from the *Royal Charles* to the *Sovereign*, while the *Cambridge*, *Resolution* and French *Conquérant* departed for home, and the *Swiftsure* 70 arrived and was added to the Van (Red) Squadron, reducing the total to 74 ships. The rest of the French contingent was otherwise unchanged.

De Ruyter's fleet
The only changes from the previous action were that the *Prins te Paard*, *Zuiderhuis* and *Deventer* departed for home (the *Deventer* was wrecked en route), while the *Voorsichtigheid* 84 and *Olifant* 82 (flag of Vice-Adm Isaak Sweers) arrived and were added to the Centre and Van Squadrons respectively, reducing the total to 51 ships. However, the *Akerboom* was moved from the Rear to the Van Squadron, and the *Prins van Oranje* from the Centre to the Rear Squadron. As Schram and Vlugh had been killed on 7 June, the former's role in the Van was taken by Sweers, while the latter's role in the Rear was temporarily taken by Capt. Jan Janszoon Dick in the *Eenhoorn*.

10. BATTLE OF THE TEXEL (*Kijkduin* in Dutch history) – 21 August 1673

Anglo-French fleet – 86 ships of the line
(A) White Squadron under d'Estrées – 30 (French) ships of the line
Reine 104 (flag of *Vice-Amiral* Jean, Comte d'Estrées), *Royale Thérèse* 80 (flag of CdE Damien, Marquis de Martel), *Conquérant* 70, *Foudroyant* 70, *Grand* 70, *Illustre* 70, *Invincible* 70 *Orgueilleux* 70, *Pompeux* 70, *Terrible* 70 (flag of CdE Hector des Ardens), *Glorieux* 64, *Sans Pareil* 64, *Tonnant* 64, *Excellent* 60, *Fortuné* 60, *Fier* 58, *Aimable* 56, *Conquérant* 56, *Diamant* 54, *Bon* 52, *Bourbon* 52, *Téméraire* 52, *Vaillant* 52, *Apollon* 50, *Aquilon* 50, *Duc* 50, *Maure* 50, *Oriflamme* 50, *Précieux* 50, *Prince* 50, *Sage* 50.
(B) Red Squadron under Prince Rupert – 28 ships of the line
Van Division – *Constant Warwick* (?) 42, *Anne* 60, *French Ruby* 80, *Lion* 60, *London* 100 (flag of Vice-Admiral Sir John Harman), *Warspite* 68, *Happy Return* 48, *Triumph* 70, and *Stavoreen* 50, plus fireships *Leopard* 6, *Robert* 4, *George* 6, and *Amity* 6.
Centre Division – *Royal Katherine* 100, *Mary* 60, *Henry* 80, *Crown* 50, *Rupert* 64, *Royal Sovereign* 100 (flag of Adm Prince Rupert), *Resolution* 70, *Princess* 54, *Edgar* 74, and *Old James* 70, plus fireships *Ann & Christopher* 8, *Friendship* 6, *Katherine* 6, *Supply* 6, *Hopewell* 6, *Saint Lawrence* 6, *Hawke* 2, and *Thomas & Edward* 6.
Rear Division – *Mary Rose* 48, *Victory* 80, *Assurance* 42, *Fairfax* 72, *Charles* 100 (flag of Rear-Admiral Sir John Chicheley), *Monmouth* 70, *Newcastle* 52, *Nonsuch* 40, and *Yarmouth* 52, plus fireships *True Love* 2, *Dartmouth* 4, *Wivenhoe* 6, and *Olive Branch* 6.
(C) Blue Squadron under Spragge – 28 ships of the line
Van Division – *Hampshire* 46, *York* 62, *Sweepstakes* 40, *Swiftsure* 66, *Saint Michael* 98 (flag of R-Adm the Earl of Ossory), *Greenwich* 60, *Foresight* 52, *Rainbow* 56, *Portsmouth* 48, plus fireships *Firebush* 4, and *Hope Prize* 2.
Centre Division – *Dreadnought* 66, *Saint George* 68, *Bristol* 48, *Henrietta* 60, *Royal Charles* 102, *Prince* 100 (flag of Adm Sir Edward Spragge), *Swallow* 46, *Cambridge* 70, *Advice* 46, and *Dunkirk* 60, plus fireships *Society* 6, *Prudent Mary* 6, *Benjamin* 6, *Blessing* 4, and *Pearl* 6.
Rear-Division – *Diamond* 48, *Unicorn* 64, *Ruby* 48, *Monck* 58, *Saint Andrew* 100 (flag of V-Adm Sir John Kempthorne), *Plymouth* 58, *Falcon* 42, *Gloucester* 60, and *Bonadventure* 52, plus fireships *Hester* 6, and *Jason* 4.
Supporting the English squadrons were the following light frigates and small warships, not in the line - *Nightingale* 34, *Guernsey* 30, *Pearl* 28, *Roebuck* 18, *Henrietta* (yacht) 8, *Roe* (dogger) 6, *Rose* (dogger) 6, *Fox* (shallop), and *John's Advice* (hospital). Also supporting the English were the following sloops - *Bonetta* 4, *Cutter* 4, *Chatham* 4, *Chatham Double* 4, *Dolphin* 4, *Emsworth* 6, *Hound* 8, *Invention* 4, *Lizard* 4, *Prevention* 4, *Spy* 4, *Vulture* 4, and *Woolwich* 4.

De Ruyter's fleet – 60 ships of the line

(A) Van Squadron under Tromp – 21 ships of the line
Amsterdam Admiralty's *Gouden Leeuw* 82 (flag of Lieut-Adm Cornelis Tromp), *Olifant* 82 (flag of Vice-Adm Isaak Sweers), *Hollandia* 80 (flag of Schout-bij-Nacht Jan de Haen), *Kalantsoog* 70, *Komeetster* 70, *Akerboom* 62, *Amsterdam* 60, *Provincie van Utrecht* 60, *Geloof* 56, *Prins te Paard* 54, *Agatha* 50, *Zuiderhuis* 48, *Wapen van Holland* 46, *Wakende Kraan* 44 and *Zeelandia* 44;
Noorderkwartier Admiralty's *Pacificatie* 80, *Noorderkwartier* 60 and *Jupiter* 42;
Maas Admiralty's *Delft* 62, *Schieland* 60 and *Wassenaer* 60.
(B) Centre Squadron under Aert van Nes – 18 ships of the line
Maas Admiralty's *Voorsichtigheid* 84, *Vriheid* 80 (flag of Vice-Adm Jan Evertszoon de Liefde), *Zeven Provinciën* 80 (flag of Adm Michiel de Ruyter), *Eendracht* 72 (flag of Lieut-Adm Aert van Nes), *Maagd van Dordrecht* 68 (flag of Schout-bij-Nacht Jan Janszoon van Nes), *Ridderschap* 65, *Gelderland* 63 (flag of temp. Schout-bij-Nacht Cornelis de Liefde), *Dordrecht* 44 and *Zeelandia* 42;
Amsterdam Admiralty's *Spiegel* 70, *Steenbergen* 70, *Waesdorp* 68, *Stad Utrecht* 66, *Beschermer* 50 and *Essen* 50;
Noorderkwartier Admiralty's *Wapen van Alkmaar* 64, *Caleb* 46 and *Wapen van Medemblik* 44.
(C) Rear Squadron under Banckert – 21 ships of the line
Noorderkwartier Admiralty's *Westfriesland* 78, *Wapen van Enkhuizen* 72, *Eenhoorn* 70 (flag of Schout-bij-Nacht Jan Janszoon Dick), *Justina van Nassau* 66, *Prins van Oranje* 64, *Gelderland* 60 and *Wapen van Nassau* 58;
Friesland Admiralty's *Prins Hendrik Casimir* 72 (flag of Schout-bij-Nacht Hendrik Bruynsvelt), *Groningen* 70 (flag of Vice-Adm Enno Doedes Star), *Oostergo* 68 and *Elf Steden* 54;
Zeeland Admiralty's *Walcheren* 70 (flag of Lieut-Adm Adriaan van Trappen Banckert), *Domburg* 60, *Zierikzee* 60 (flag of Vice-Adm Cornelis Evertsen de Jonge), *Vlissingen* 50, *Dordrecht* 50, *Ter Veere* 48, *Utrecht* 42;
Amsterdam Admiralty's *Gideon* 62, *Tijdverdrijf* 56 and *Leeuwen* 50.
Supporting the ships of the line, there were also 15 frigates – Amsterdam Admiralty's *Edam* 36, *Middelburg* 36, *Oudkarspel* 34, *Damieten* 32, *Bommel* 24, *Haas* 24, *Popkensburg* 24 and *Brak* 22; Maas Admiralty's *Utrecht* 34, *Rotterdam* 30, *Harderwijk* 24 and *Schiedam* 20; Zeeland Admiralty's *Delft* 34 and *Ter Goes* 34; and Friesland Admiralty's *Windhond* 30. There were 18 advice-yachts – Amsterdam's

Egmond, *Kater*, *Kits* and *Triton*; Maas's *Hoop* and *Rotterdam*; Zeeland's *Bruinvis*, *Goes*, *Hazewind*, *Jonge Maria*, *Lapmande*, *Parel*, *Tonijn*, *Waterhond*, *Zwaluw* and one other (name unknown); Friesland's *Hoop* and *Liefde*. And 25 fireships – Amsterdam's *Draak*, *Jacob en Anna*, *Kasteel van Loon*, *Leidster*, *Melkschuit*, *Salvador*, *Vrede*, *Wapen van Velsen*, *Zaaier* and *Zalm*; Maas's *Blackmoor*, *Eenhoorn*, *Jisper Kerk*, *Louise*, *Maria* and *Sint Pieter*; Noorderkwartier's *Catharina*, *Vis* and *Witte Mol*; Zeeland's *Burg*, *Catharina*, *Dadelboom*, *Samuel en Jacob* and *Sevellie*; and Friesland's *Welkomst*.

11. BATTLE OF MESSINA (or BATTLE OF PHARO) – 2 January 1675

A squadron of six ships was despatched from Toulon in 1674 under Valbelle to relieve the city of Messina, which had revolted against Spanish domination and was now under siege by a Spanish fleet of 22 ships and 24 galleys, under Don Melchior de la Cueva. The squadron forced the blockade and relieved Messina.

Valbelle's squadron – 6 ships
Pompeux 70 (commanded by CV Pierre-Bruno de Valbelle), *Fortuné* 58, *Agréable* 56, *Prudent* 54, *Téméraire* 54, *Sage* 50.
Also one frigate (*Gracieuse*, 24) and 3 fireships.

12. BATTLE OF THE LIPARI ISLANDS (or FIRST BATTLE OF STROMBOLI) – 11 February 1675

A prologue to the three battles of 1676, fought between France and Spain. A French victory here, secured when CV Pierre-Bruno de Valbelle sortied from Messina with his 6 ships and attacked the Spanish fleet in the rear, resulted in Spain seeking help from the Dutch, and in December a squadron of 15 Dutch ships under Adm Michiel de Ruyter entered the Mediterranean.

Vivonne's squadron (9 ships)
Sceptre 80 (flag of Am. Louis-Victor de Rochechouart, Duc de Vivonne), *Saint Esprit* 70 (flag of LG Abraham Duquesne, Marquis de Quesne), *Heureux* 60, *Saint Michel* 60, *Triomphant* 60 (flag of CdE Raymond Louis de Crevant, Marquis de Preuilly d'Humières), *Apollon* 56, *Fidèle* 56, *Parfait* 56, *Vaillant* 54.
Also a frigate and 3 fireships.

Valbelle's squadron (6 ships)
Sage 54, *Téméraire* 54. The other 4 are unidentified, but presumably those mentioned under the previous entry.

Viso's fleet (20 ships)
The fleet was commanded by the Marquis of Viso and by Melchior de La Cueva.
The individual ships are not listed. There were also 17 galleys.

13. SECOND BATTLE OF STROMBOLI (or BATTLE OFF ALICUDI ISLAND) – 8 January 1676

The first off three Franco-Dutch battles during 1676 off Spanish-controlled Sicily.

Duquesne's fleet – 20 ships of the line
(A) Preuilly d'Humières's squadron (escadre bleue – avant-garde)
Saint Michel 60 (flag of CdE Raymond Louis de Crevant, Marquis de Preuilly d'Humières), *Fier* 60, *Parfait* 60, *Prudent* 54, *Assuré* 50, *Mignon* 46.
(B) Duquesne's squadron (escadre blanche – centre, or *corps de bataille*)
Sceptre 84 (flag of CdE Anne Hilarion de Costentin, Comte de Tourville), *Pompeux* 72 (flag of CdE Pierre-Bruno de Valbelle), *Saint Esprit* 72 (flag of LG Abraham Duquesne), *Éclatant* 60, *Aimable* 56, *Sage* 54, *Téméraire* 54, *Sirène* 46.
(C) Gabaret's squadron (escadre bleue – arrière-garde)
Grand 72, *Magnifique* 72, *Sans Pareil* 66 (flag of CdE Louis Gabaret), *Vaillant* 54, *Apollon* 52, *Aquilon* 52.
Also 6 fireships (names unknown).

De Ruyter's fleet – 18 Dutch ships
(A) Den Haan's squadron
Gouda 76 (flag of Vice-Adm Jan den Haan), *Provincie van Utrecht* 60, *Vrijheid* 50, *Kraanvogel* 46, *Wakende Boei* 46, *Edam* 34.
There were also 2 snows (snauw) of 8 guns each – *Rouaan* and *Roos* – and 2 fireships – *Sint Salvador*, *Zwarte Tas*.
(B) De Ruyter's squadron
Eendracht 76 (flag of Lt-Adm Michiel de Ruyter), *Steenbergen* 68, *Stad en Lande* 54, *Leeuwen* 50, *Zuiderhuis* 46, *Leiden* 36.
There were also 2 snows (snauw) of 8 guns each – *Kreeft* and *Tonijn* – and 2 fireships – *Melkmeisje* and *Salm*.
(C) Verschoor's squadron
Spiegel 70 (flag of Schout-bij-Nacht Nikolaas Verschout), *Oosterwijk* 60, *Essen* 50, *Harderwijk* 46, *Groenwijf* 36, *Damiaten* 34.
There were also 2 snows (snauw) of 8 guns each – *Prinsen Wapen* and *Ter Goes* – and 1 fireship – *Jakob en Anna*.

14. BATTLE OF AUGUSTA (or AGOSTA) – 22 April 1676

The second battle between Duquesne's and de Ruyter's forces took place in the Bay of Catania; no ships were lost on either side, but the Dutch had numerous casualties, including de Ruyter who died of his wounds a week later.

Duquesne's fleet (29 ships of the line)
(A) Alméras's squadron
Lys 74 (flag of LG Guillaume, Marquis d'Alméras – killed in action), *Magnifique* 72, *Pompeux* 72 (flag of CdE Pierre-Bruno de Valbelle), *Parfait* 60, *Fidèle* 56, *Apollon* 54, *Heureux* 54, *Vermandois* 50, *Trident* 38.
Also fireships *Ardent* and *Orage*.
(B) Duquesne's squadron
Sceptre 80 (flag of CdE Anne Hilarion de Costentin, Comte de Tourville), *Saint Esprit* 72 (flag of *Vice-amiral* Abraham Duquesne), *Éclatant* 60, *Saint Michel* 60 (flag of CdE Raymond Louis de Crevant, Marquis de Preuilly d'Humières), *Aimable* 56, *Fortuné* 56, *Vaillant* 54, *Aquilon* 50, *Joli* 46, *Mignon* 46.
Also fireships Imprudent, *Inquiet* and *Salvador*.
(C) Gabaret's squadron
Grand 72, *Sans Pareil* 70 (flag of CdE Louis Gabaret), *Fier* 60, *Agréable* 56, *Assuré* 56, *Prudent* 54, *Sage* 54, *Téméraire* 50, *Brusque* 46, *Sirène* 46 (the last-named actually took its place in Duquesne's squadron).
Also fireships *Dame de la Mère*, *Dangereux* and *Hameçon*.

De Ruyter's fleet – 17 Dutch and 10 Spanish ships
(A) De Ruyter's squadron
Eendracht 76 (flag of Lt-Adm Michiel de Ruyter), *Spiegel* 70, *Oosterwijk* 60, *Stad en Lande* 54, *Leeuwen* 50, *Zuiderhuis* 46, *Groenwijf* 36, *Leiden* 36, *Damiaten* 34.
Also 3 snows (snauw) of 8 guns each – *Kreeft*, *Prinsen Wapen*, *Tonijn* – and 3 fireships – *Melkmeisje*, *Salm*, *Zwarte Tas*.
(B) Den Haan's squadron
Gouda 76 (flag of Vice-Adm Jan den Haan), *Steenbergen* 68, *Provincie van Utrecht* 60, *Vrijheid* 50, *Harderwijk* 46, *Kraanvogel* 46, *Wakende Boei* 46, *Edam* 34.
Also 2 snows (snauw) of 8 guns each – *Roos*, *Rouaan* – and 2 fireships – *Jakob en Anna*, *Sint Salvador*.

(C) Spanish squadron under La Cerda
Nuestra Senora del Pilar 74 (flagship of Almirante Francisco Pereire Freire de la Cerda), *Santiago* 80, *San Joaquin* 80, *Santa Ana* 60, *Nuestra Senora del Rosario*, *Nuestra Senora de Guadelupe*, *Nuestra Senora del Rosario y Las Animas*, *San Antonio de Napoles*, *San Felipe*, *San Gabriel*, *San Carlo*. (There is some uncertainty as regards the Spanish contingent, which might be one more or one less than the 11 named.)

15. BATTLE OF PALERMO – 3 June 1676
Six weeks later, the French force of 29 warships (now under the Duc de Vivonne, with Duquesne as *Vice-Amiral*) attacked the combined Dutch-Spanish force of 27 warships, 19 galleys and 4 fireships in the Bay of Palermo. The Dutch and Spanish warships were heavily defeated and the French won tactical command of the Mediterranean. The Spanish admiral (Ibarra) was killed in the explosion which destroyed his flagship.

Vivonne's fleet – 29 ships of the line

(A) Van squadron under Duquesne – 10 ships of the line
Saint Esprit 72 (flag of LG Abraham Duquesne), *Grand* 72, *Éclatant* 60, *Parfait* 60, *Aimable* 56, *Fortuné* 56, *Vaillant* 54, *Aquilon* 50, *Joli* 46, *Mignon* 46.
Plus 3 fireships – *Dangereux*, *Hameçon*, *Notre Dame de Hunières*.

(B) Centre squadron under Vivonne – 10 ships of the line
Sceptre 80 (flag of *Amiral* Louis-Victor de Rochechouart, Duc de Vivonne), *Pompeux* 72 (flag of CdE Pierre-Bruno de Valbelle), *Fier* 60, *Saint Michel* 60 (flag of CdE Marquis de Preuilly d'Humières), *Agréable* 56, *Assuré* 56, *Sage* 54, *Téméraire* 50, *Brusque* 46.
Plus 3 fireships – *Ardent*, *Ligournais*, *Orage*.

(C) Rear squadron under Gabaret – 9 ships of the line
Lys 74 (flag of CdE Jean Gabaret), *Magnifique* 72, *Sans Pareil* 70, *Fidèle* 56, *Apollon* 54, *Heureux* 54, *Prudent* 54, *Vermandois* 50, *Trident* 38.
Plus 3 fireships – *Impudent*, *Inquiet*, *Notre Dame de Bon Voyage*.
Also 25 galleys.

Den Haan's fleet – 17 Dutch ships of which 3(*) were burnt
Eendracht 76, *Gouda* 76 (flag of Lt-Adm Jan den Haan), *Spiegel* 70, *Steenbergen** 68 (flag of Schout-bij-Nacht Pieter van Middelandt), *Oosterwijk* 60, *Provincie van Utrecht* 60, *Stad en Lande* 54, *Leeuwen* 50, *Vrijheid** 50, *Harderwijk* 46, *Kraanvogel* 46, *Wakende Boei* 46, *Zuiderhuis* 46, *Groenwijf* 36, *Leiden** 36, *Damiaten* 34, *Edam* 34. Capt Gerard Callenburgh of the *Eendracht* took command of the remaining squadron after both Jan den Haan and Pieter van Middelandt were killed.

Ibarra's fleet – 10 Spanish ships of which 7 (*) were burnt or destroyed by explosion:
(The names are confused, due to Spanish practice of duplicating names)
Nuestra Señora del Pilar* 64/74 (flag of Almirante Don Diego de Ibarra), *Santiago* 80, *San Antonio de Napoles** 44/46, *San Felipe** 40/44, *San Carlo* 40, *Salvator delle Fiandre* 42, *San Salvador** 48, *San Joaquin/San Juan* 80, *San Gabriel* 40, *Santa Ana** 54/60, *Nuestra Señora del Rosario* 50, *San Jose** (flag of Almirante Juan de Villaroel), *San Salvador**. Also possibly the *Nuestra Señora de Guadalupe* and *Nuestra Señora del Rosario y Las Animas*. There were also 4 fireships and 19 galleys – names unknown.

16. ATTACK ON CAYENNE – 17 December 1676

d'Estrées's squadron
Glorieux 60 (flag of *Vice-Amiral* Jean, Comte d'Estrées), *Intrépide* 56, *Fendant* 54, *Précieux* 54, *Marquis* 46, *Soleil d'Afrique* 30, *Laurier* 28.
Also 2 frigates (*Fée* 28 and *Friponne* 16).

17. BATTLE OF TOBAGO – 3 March 1677

d'Estrées's squadron
Glorieux 60 (flag of *Vice-Amiral* Jean, Comte d'Estrées), *Intrépide* 56, *Fendant* 54, *Précieux* 54, *Galant* 46, *Marquis* 46, *Les Jeux* 40, *Émerillon* 36, *Soleil d'Afrique* 30, *Laurier* 28.
Also 1 fireship.

Binckes's squadron – 10 ships
Huis te Kruiningen 56 (flag of Schout-bij-Nacht Roemer Vlacq), *De Berscherming* 50 (flag of Adm Jacon Binckes), *Zeelandia* 44, *Middelburg* 36, *Leyden* 34, *De Gouden Monnik* 31, *De Gouden Star* 28, *Duc d'York* 26, *Alcyon* 24, *Pophesburg* 24.
Also the 12-gun *Sphoera Mundi*, fireship *De Zaayer*, a yacht and various transports.

18. FIRST BOMBARDMENT OF ALGIERS – 23 July–5 Sept 1682

Duquesne's squadron – 11 ships
Saint Esprit 76 (flag of LG Abraham Duquesne), *Vigilant* 52 (flag of LG Chevalier de Tourville), *Vaillant* 52, *Prudent* 52, *Aimable* 50, *Laurier* 46, *Indien* 46, *Éole* 46, *Cheval Marin* 44, *Assuré* 44, *Étoile* 34.
Also bomb vessels *Foudroyante*, *Bombarde*, *Brûlante*, *Cruelle* and *Menaçante*.

19. SECOND BOMBARDMENT OF ALGIERS – 26 June–18 August 1683

Duquesne's squadron – 11 ships
Saint Esprit 76 (flag of LG Abraham Duquesne), *Ferme* 60 (flag of LG Chevalier de Tourville), *Excellent* 54, *Vigilant* 52 (flag of CdE Charles-François Davy, Marquis d'Amfreville), *Prudent* 52 (flag of CdE Henri Cauchon de Lhéry), *Aimable* 50, *Fleuron* 50, *Laurier* 46, *Cheval Marin* 44, *Hasardeux* 44, *Sirène* 44, *Bizarre* 34, *Étoile* 34.
Also bomb vessels *Foudroyante*, *Bombarde*, *Brûlante*, *Cruelle*, *Menaçante*, *Fulminante* and *Ardente*.

20. BOMBARDMENT OF GENOA – 18–28 May 1684

Duquesne's squadron – 13 ships
Ardent 74 (flag of LG Abraham Duquesne), *Assuré* 60, *Ferme* 60 (flag of LG Comte de Tourville), *Parfait* 60, *Fortuné* 56, *Saint Jacques* 56, *Aquilon* 54, *Fleuron* 54, *Vaillant* 54, *Vigilant* 54 (flag of CdE Charles-François Davy, Marquis d'Amfreville), *Aimable* 50, *Bizarre* 44, *Capable* 44, *Indien* 34.
Also bomb vessels *Foudroyante*, *Bombarde*, *Brûlante*, *Cruelle*, *Menaçante*, *Fulminante*, *Ardente*, *Éclatante*, *Terrible* and *Belliqueux*.
Plus 20 galleys (under *Général des Galères* Louis-Victor de Rochechouart, Duc de Mortemart et de Vivonne), 2 fireships, 3 *flûtes* and 26 tartanes.

21. FIRST BOMBARDMENT OF TRIPOLI – 22–26 June 1685

D'Estrées's squadron – 9 ships
Agréable 60 (flag of LG Comte de Tourville), *Prudent* 56 (flag of CdE Charles-François Davy, Marquis d'Amfreville), *Ardent* 50 (flag of *Vice-Amiral* Jean, Comte d'Estrées), *Capable* 48, *Fidèle* 48, *Cheval Marin* 46, *Bizarre* 42, *Aventurier* 40, *Mercure* 20.
Also bomb vessels *Bombarde*, *Menaçante*, *Fulminante*, *Éclatante* and *Terrible*.
Plus 4 *flûtes* (including a hospital ship), 2 fireships, several *galiotes à rames*, tartanes and other small vessels.

22. BATTLE OF BANTRY BAY – 11 May 1689

Châteaurenault's fleet – 24 ships of the line
Ardent 66 (flag of LG Louis François de Rousselet, Comte de Châteaurenault), *Excellent* 60, *Furieux* 60, *Vermandois* 60, *Apollon* 56, *Arrogant* 56, *Courageux* 56 (flag of CdE Job Forant), *Entreprenant* 56, *Fort* 56, *Saint Michel* 56 (flag of CdE Louis Gabaret), *Diamant* 54, *Fendant* 52, *Précieux* 52, *Sage* 52, *Duc* 50, *Modéré* 50, *Capable* 48, *François* 48, *Neptune* 46, *Arc en Ciel* 44, *Emporté* 42, *Faucon* 40, *Léger* 40, *Oiseau* 40. Also five frigates and ten fireships.

Herbert's fleet – 19 ships of the line
Cambridge 70, *Elizabeth* 70 (flag of Adm Arthur Herbert), *Pendennis* 70, *Defiance* 64, *Edgar* 64, *Mary* 62, *Plymouth* 60, *York* 60, *Deptford* 54, *Greenwich* 54, *Woolwich* 54, *Portland* 50, *Saint Albans* 50, *Advice* 48, *Antelope* 48, *Diamond* 48, *Ruby* 48, *Portsmouth* 46, *Dartmouth* 36. Also 16-gun *Saudadoes* and bomb vessels *Firedrake* and *Salamander*.

23. BATTLE OF BEACHY HEAD (*Bataille de Béveziers* in French history) – 10 July 1690

French fleet – 70 ships of the line

(A) Van Squadron under Châteaurenault – 22 ships of the line
Fier 68 (flag of CdE Ferdinand, Comte de Relingue), *Fort* 52, *Maure* 52, *Éclatant* 64, *Conquérant* (flag of LG Philippe Le Valois, Marquis de Villette-Mursay), *Courtisan* 62, *Indien* 50, *Trident* 52, *Hardi* 58, *Saint Louis* 56, *Excellent* 56, *Pompeux* 74, *Dauphin Royal* 110 (flag of LG Louis François de Rousselet, Comte de Châteaurenault), *Ardent* 62, *Bon* 52, *Précieux* 60, *Aquilon* 60, *Courageux* 60, *Couronne* 70 (flag of CdE Joseph Andrault, Marquis de Langeron), *Ferme* 54, *Fendant* 52, *Téméraire* 52; also (not in the line) *Éole* 50, *Solide* 48, *Alcyon* 44 and six fireships (*Hameçon, Fanfaron, Branche d'Olivier, Impudent, Déguisé* and *Dur*).

(B) Centre Squadron under de Tourville – 25 ships of the line
Brusque 50, *Arrogant* 54, *Arc en Ciel* 44, *Henri* 62, *Souverain* 80 (flag of CdE André, Marquis de Nesmond), *Brillant* 66, *Neptune* 46, *Sans Pareil* 58, *Fidèle* 46, *Diamant* 56, *Sérieux* 56, *Tonnant* 70, *Soleil Royal* 98 (flag of *Vice-Amiral* Anne Hilarion de Costentin, Comte de Tourville), *Saint Philippe* 80 (flag of CdE Alain Emmanuel, Comte de Coëtlogon), *Marquis* 80, *Furieux* 60, *Fortuné* 58, *Apollon* 56, *Saint Michel* 54, *Entreprenant* 56, *Magnifique* 76 (flag of LG Charles-François Davy, Marquis d'Amfreville), *Content* 56, *Vermandois* 58, *Cheval Marin* 40, *Fougueux* 58; also (not in the line) *Faucon* 44 and six fireships (*Périlleux, Espion, Insensé, Jolie, Bouffonne* and *Fâcheux*).

(C) Rear Squadron under d'Estrées – 23 ships of the line
Comte 40, *Vigilant* 52, *Parfait* 62, *Triomphant* 70 (flag of CdE Pierre Le Bret de Flacourt), *Bourbon* 62, *Duc* 48, *Vaillant* 48, *Capable* 54, *Brave* 54, *François* 46, *Agréable* 58, *Florissant* 80, *Grand* 80 (flag of LG Victor Marie, Comte d'Estrées), *Belliqueux* 74, *Prince* 56, *Prudent* 52, *Modéré* 50, *Fleuron* 54, *Aimable* 70, *Intrépide* 80 (flag of LG Jean Gabaret), *Glorieux* 60, *Illustre* 66, *Terrible* 74 (flag of CdE François Panetié); also (not in the line) *Léger* 44 and six fireships (*Impertinent, Diligente, Boutefeu, Royal Jacques, Maligne* and *Extravagant*).

Anglo-Dutch fleet – 56 ships of the line

(A) Van (White) Squadron under Evertson – 22 (Dutch) ships of the line
Wapen van Utrecht 64, *Wapen van Alkmaar* 50, *Tholen* 60, *Westfriesland* 82 (flag of Vice-Adm Gerard Callenburgh), *Prinses Maria* 92 (flag of Schout-bij-Nacht Gilles Scheij), *Castricum* 50, *Agatha* 50; *Stad en Lande* 52, *Maagd van Enkhuizen* 72, *Noord Holland* (of Amsterdam Admiralty) 48, *Maagd van Dordrecht* 68, *Hollandia* 74 (flag of Lieut-Adm Cornelis Evertsen the Youngest), *Veluwe* 68 (flag of Schout-bij-Nacht Jan van Brakel), *Provincie van Utrecht* 50, *Maas* 64; *Friesland* 64, *Elswout* 50, *Reigersbergen* 74, *Noord Holland* (of Noorderkwartier Admiralty) 72 (flag of Schout-bij-Nacht Jan Dick), *Elswout* 50, *Gekroonde Burcht* 62 (flag of Vice-Adm Karel van de Putte), *Veere* 60, *Kortgene* 50; also four fireships (*Burg Etna, Kroonvogel, Maagd van Enkhuizen* and *Suikermolen*).

(B) Centre (Red) Squadron under Torrington – 21 ships of the line
Royal Sovereign 100 (flag of Adm Lord Torrington), *Albemarle* 90, *Duchess* 90 (flag of Rear-Adm Sir George Rooke), *Sandwich* 90 (flag of Vice-Adm Sir John Ashby), *Windsor Castle* 90, *Elizabeth* 70, *Expedition* 70, *Grafton* 70, *Hampton Court* 70, *Hope* 70, *Lenox* 70, *Restoration* 70, *Stirling Castle* 70, *Suffolk* 70, *Warspite* 70, *Rupert* 66, *Lion* 60, *Plymouth* 60, *York* 60, *Woolwich* 54, *Deptford* 50; also *Constant Warwick* 36 and eight fireships – *Dolphin, Hound, Owner's Love, Roebuck, Speedwell, Spy, Vulture* and *Wolf*.

(C) Rear (Blue) Squadron under Delavall – 13 ships of the line
Saint Andrew 96, *Coronation* 90 (flag of Vice-Adm Sir Ralph Delavall), *Royal Katherine* 82, *Anne* 70, *Berwick* 70, *Bredah* 70, *Cambridge* 70, *Captain* 70, *Exeter* 70, *Defiance* 64, *Edgar* 64, *Bonaventure* 48, *Swallow* 48; also eight fireships – *Cadiz Merchant, Charles, Cygnet, Fox, Griffin, Hawk, Hunter* and *Thomas and Elizabeth*.

24. 'CAMPAGNE DU LARGE' – June 1691
While not involved in any major set-piece action, the composition of the French fleet which sailed from Brest in June 1691 with the aim of taking on the English/Dutch squadron in included to demonstrate what the French battlefleet would then have been. No listing of the Allied force is attempted as no fleet action ensued.

Tourville's fleet – 73 ships of the line (as departing Brest)

(A) Van (Blue-and-white) squadron under Châteaurenault – 24 ships
Foudroyant 84 (flag of CdE Ferdinand, Comte de Relingue), *Ardent* 70 (flag of flag of LG Charles-François Davy, Marquis d'Amfreville), *Fidèle* 54, *Constant* 70, *Grand* 86 (flag of CdE François Panetié), *Triomphant* 78, *Excellent* 64, *Neptune* 50, *Brave* 62, *Assuré* 64, *Dauphin Royal* 100 (flag of LG Louis François de Rousselet, Comte de Châteaurenault), *Belliqueux* 78, *Fier* 80, *Courtisan* 64, *Vigilant* 54, *Précieux* 60, *Brillant* 64, *François* 52, *Illustre* 76, *Saint Philippe* 84, *Saint Esprit* 70, *Saint Louis* 60, *Téméraire* 62, *Bon* 56.

(B) Centre (White) Squadron under Tourville – 25 ships
Furieux 60, *Perle* 56, *Hardi* 74, *Superbe* 76, *Victorieux* 96, *Terrible* 80, *Arc en Ciel* 54, *Fort* 60, *Arrogant* 60, *Apollon* 62, *Sérieux* 62, *Magnifique* 86 (flag of CdE Alain Emmanuel, Comte de Coëtlogon), *Soleil Royal* (flag of *Vice-Amiral* Anne Hilarion de Costentin, Comte de Tourville), *Conquérant* 84, *Henri* 66, *Gaillard* 66, *Saint Michel* 60, *Aquilon* 56, *Modéré* 56, *Sage* 54, *Aimable* 70, *Magnanime* 84, *Couronne* 60, *Ferme* 64, *Sans Pareil* 60.

(C) Rear (Blue) Squadron under d'Amfreville – 24 ships
Fleuron 60, *Indien* 54, *Entreprenant* 60, *Sirène* 60, *Souverain* 84 (flag of CdE Joseph Andrault, Marquis de Langeron), *Invincible* 70, *Trident* 54, *Diamant* 60, *Entendu* 66, *Florissant* 76, *Orgueilleux* 98 (flag of LG Charles-François Davy, Marquis d'Amfreville), *Tonnant* 82, *Vermandois* 60, *Agréable* 64, *Courageux* 60, *Fendant* 56, *Laurier* 64, *Heureux* 70, *Pompeux* 76, *Monarque* 92 (flag of CdE André, Marquis de Nesmond), *Maure* 60, *Parfait* 66, *Intrépide* 80, *Glorieux* 64.

(D) Fireships, spread among the three squadrons – 18 in all (although 21 names are quoted below).
Boutefeu, Dangereux, Déguisé, Drôle, Dur, Espion, Extravagant, Fâcheux, Fanfaron, Friponne, Hameçon, Impertinent, Inquiet, Insensé, Jolie, Maligne, Pétillant, Renard, Rusé, Serpent, Éveillé.

25. BATTLE OF BARFLEUR – 29 May 1692

Tourville's fleet – 45 ships of the line

(A) Van (Blue-and-white) Squadron under d'Amfreville – 14 ships
Bourbon 64, *Monarque* 90 (flag of CdE André, Marquis de Nesmond), *Aimable* 68, *Saint Louis* 60, *Diamant* 60, *Gaillard* 68, *Terrible* 76, *Merveilleux* 94 (flag of LG Charles-François Davy, Marquis d'Amfreville), *Tonnant* 76, *Saint Michel* 60, *Sans Pareil* 62, *Sérieux* 68, *Foudroyant* 82 (flag of CdE Ferdinand, Comte de Relingue), *Brillant* 68.

(B) Centre (White) Squadron under Tourville – 16 ships
Fort 60, *Henri* 64, *Ambitieux* 96 (flag of LG Philippe Le Valois, Marquis de Villette-Mursay), *Couronne* 76, *Maure* 52, *Courageux* 58, *Perle* 56, *Glorieux* 64, *Conquérant* 84, *Soleil Royal* 104 (flag of *Vice-Amiral* Anne Hilarion de Costentin, Comte de Tourville), *Saint Philippe* 84, *Admirable* 90, *Content* 64, *Souverain* 84 (flag of CdE Joseph Andrault, Marquis de Langeron), *Illustre* 70, *Modéré* 52.

(C) Rear (Blue) Squadron under Gabaret – 15 ships
Excellent 60, *Prince* 60, *Magnifique* 76 (flag of CdE Alain Emmanuel, Comte de Coëtlogon), *Laurier* 64, *Brave* 58, *Entendu* 60, *Triomphant* 76, *Orgueilleux* 94 (flag of LG Louis Gabaret), *Fier* 76, *Fleuron* 58, *Courtisan* 64, *Vermandois* 54, *Grand* 84 (flag of CdE François Panetié), *Saint Esprit* 74, *Sirène* 64.
Also 13 frigates and fireships.
[Note that while there were no ships lost during the battle on 29 May itself, fifteen were subsequently destroyed by fire during the first three days of June at Cherbourg and La Hougue – see Chapter 1 for details.]

Allied fleet – 90 ships of the line

(A) Van (White) Squadron under van Almonde – 27 (Dutch) ships
Van Division – *Zeven Provinciën* 76, *Kapitein Generaal* 84 (flag of Schout-bij-Nacht Philips van der Goes) and *Veluwe* 64, all of the Maas Admiralty; *Wapen van Medemblik* 50, *Noord Holland* 68 and *Kasteel van Medemblik* 86 (flag of Vice-Adm Gerard Callenburgh, all of the Noorderkwartier Admiralty; *Ridderschap* 72 of the Maas Admiralty; and *Harderwijk* 44 and *Keurvorst van Brandenburg* 92, both of the Amsterdam Admiralty.
Also three frigates (*Anna* 36, *Wakende Boij* 26 and *Herder* 10) and two fireships (*Fenix* and *Wijnbergen*).
Centre Division – *Amsterdam* 64, *Prinses Maria* 92 (flag of Vice-Adm Gilles Scheij), *Schattershoef* 50, *Elswout* 72, *Prins* 92 (flag of Lt-Adm Philips van Almonde), *Slot Muijden* 72 and *Edam* 40, all of the Amsterdam Admiralty; *Westfriesland* 88 (flag of Schout-bij-Nacht Jan Gerritszoon Muijs) of the Noorderkwartier Admiralty; and *Leijden* 64 of the Amsterdam Admiralty.
Also three frigates (*Raadhuijs van Haarlem* 38, *Batavier* 26 and *Bruijnwis* 18) and three fireships (*Vesuvius*, *Stromboli* and *Etna*).
Rear Division – *Vlaardingen* 42 of the Amsterdam Admiralty; *Gelderland* 64 of the Maas Admiralty; *Provincie van Utrecht* 62 of the Amsterdam Admiralty; *Eerste Edel* 74 and *Koning Willem* 93 (flag of Vice-Adm Karel van de Putte), both of the Zeeland Admiralty; *Zeelandia* 64 of the Amsterdam Admiralty; and *Ter Goes* 54, *Zeelandia* 92 (flag of Schout-bij-Nacht Geleijn Evertsen) and *Veere* 62, all of the Zeeland Admiralty.
Also two frigates (*Zeijst* 30 and *Neptunis* 18) and two fireships (*Etna* and *Zes Gebroeders*).
(Note the fireship *Etna* in the Centre Division was from Amsterdam, while the fireship of the same name in the Rear Division was from Zeeland)

(B) Centre (Red) Squadron under Russell – 28 (English) ships of the line
Van Division – *Saint Michael* 90, *Lenox* 70, *Bonaventure* 48, *Royal Katherine* 82, *Royal Sovereign* 100 (flag of Vice-Adm Sir Ralph Delavall), *Captain* 70, *Centurion* 48 and *Burford* 70.
Also four fireships (*Extravagant*, *Wolf*, *Vulcan* and *Hound*).
Centre Division – *Elizabeth* 70, *Rupert* 66, *Eagle* 70, *Chester* 48, *Saint Andrew* 96, *Britannia* 100 (flag of Adm Edward Russell), *London* 96, *Greenwich* 54, *Restoration* 70, *Grafton* 70 and *Dragon* 46.
Also four fireships (*Flame*, *Roebuck*, *Vulture* and *Spy*).
Rear Division – *Hampton Court* 70, *Swiftsure* 70, *Saint Albans* 50, *Kent* 70, *Royal William* 100 (flag of Rear-Adm Sir Clowdisley Shovell), *Sandwich* 90, *Oxford* 54, *Cambridge* 70 and *Ruby* 48.
Also four fireships (*Phaeton*, *Fox*, *Strombolo* and *Hopewell*).

(C) Rear (Blue) Squadron under Ashby – 30 (English) ships of the line
Van Division – *Hope* 70, *Deptford* 50, *Essex* 70, *Duke* 90 (flag of Rear-Adm Richard Carter, who was killed in the battle), *Ossory* 90, *Woolwich* 54, *Suffolk* 70, *Crown* 48, *Dreadnought* 64, *Stirling Castle* 70 and *Tiger Prize* 48.
Also four fireships (*Thomas & Elizabeth*, *Vesuvius*, *Hunter* and *Hawk*).
Centre Division – *Edgar* 72, *Monmouth* 66, *Duchess* 90, *Victory* 100 (flag of Adm Sir John Ashby), *Vanguard* 90, *Adventure* 44, *Warspite* 70, *Montagu* 62, *Defiance* 64 and *Berwick* 70.
Also four fireships (*Speedwell*, *Griffin*, *Etna* and *Blaze*).
Rear Division – *Lion* 60, *Northumberland* 70, *Advice* 48, *Neptune* 90 (flag of Vice-Adm George Rooke), *Windsor Castle* 90, *Expedition* 70, *Monck* 60, *Resolution* 70 and *Albemarle* 90.
Also four fireships (*Half Moon*, *Owner's Love*, *Cadiz Merchant* and *Lightning*).
There were eleven frigates and smaller vessels not in the line of battle – *Falcon* 42, *Mary Galley* 34, *Charles Galley* 32, *Portsmouth* 32, *Concord* (hospital ship) 30, *Sally Rose* 22, *Greyhound* 16, *Saudadoes* 16, *Fubbs* (yacht) 12, *Salamander* (bomb) and *Shark* (brigantine) 4.

26. BATTLE OFF LAGOS (destruction of the Smyrna convoy) – 28 June 1693

Tourville's fleet – around 71 ships
The fleet, which had sortied from Brest on 26 May, was composed of 71 ships, plus 29 assorted smaller vessels and fireships, divided into three squadrons; the van (*avant-garde*) was commanded by LG Louis François de Rousselet, Marquis de Châteaurenault, assisted by CdE André, Marquis de Nesmond and CdE Ferdinand, Comte de Relingue; the centre was commanded by *Vice-Amiral* Anne Hilarion de Costentin, Comte de Tourville, assisted by CdE Philippe Le Valois, Marquis de Villette-Mursay and CdE Joseph Andrault, Comte de Langeron; the rear (*arrière-garde*) was commanded by LG Jean Gabaret, assisted by CdE Charles-François Davy, Marquis d'Amfreville and CdE François Panetié.

There are doubts about several of the ships mentioned in available archives – some names listed in contemporary reports (such as *Courrier* and *Maistre*) are plainly in error, and the list is incomplete. The following is a partial list of the vessels known to have taken part (in order of their allocated number of guns):
16 x 1st Rank: *Soleil Royal* 108 (flag of *Vice-Amiral* Anne Hilarion de Costentin, Comte de Tourville), *Dauphin Royal* 104 (flag of LG Louis François de Rousselet, Marquis de Châteaurenault), *Admirable* 106, *Terrible* 100, *Victorieux* 100 (flag of CdE Philippe Le Valois, Marquis de Villette-Mursay), *Merveilleux* 98, *Grand* 90, *Orgueilleux* 90, *Formidable* 90, *Intrépide* 90, *Magnanime* 90, *Magnifique* 96, *Vainqueur* 84,

Conquérant 84, *Souverain* 84, *Ambitieux* 80.
14 x 2nd Rank: *Couronne* 76, *Florissant* 76, *Saint Esprit* 76, *Illustre* 74, *Pompeux* 74, *Aimable* 70, *Bizarre* 70, *Écueil* 70, *Henri* 70, *Ardent* 66, *Glorieux* 64, *Brillant* 64, *Sirène* 64, *Juste* 64.
11 x 3rd Rank: *Agréable* 60, *Capable* 60, *Content* 60, *Courtisan* 60, *Excellent* 60, *Fort* 60, *Marquis* 60, *Parfait* 60, *Prompt* 60, *Sans Pareil* 60, *Vermandois* 60.
[Note that another 20 ships were intended to join up with Tourville's fleet before the action but failed to do so. These included Royal Louis 104 (flag of Vice-Amiral Victor Marie, Comte d'Estrées).]

Rooke's fleet – 21 ships
(2 Dutch 64-gun warships (marked *) were captured and some 92 merchantmen were taken, burnt or sunk)
English ships – *Royal Oak* 64 (flag of Vice-Adm Sir George Rooke), *Breda* 62 (flag of Rear-Adm Thomas Hopsonn), *Monmouth* 58, *Monck* 52, *Lion* 52, *Tiger Prize* 48, *Woolwich* 46, *Newcastle* 46 and *Chatham* 44; also *Sheerness* 28 and *Lark* 16, bombs *Salamander* and *Susanna*, brigantine *Dispatch*, fireships *Speedwell* and *Vulture*; plus hired ships *Lumley Castle* 56, *Loyal Merchant* 50, *Princess Anne* 48 and *Smyrna Factor* 40; and storeship *Muscovia Merchant*.
Dutch ships – *Admiraal Generaal* 84 (flag of Rear-Adm Philips van der Goes), *Gelderland* 72, *Wapen van Medemblik** 64, *Zeeland** 64, *Oost-Stellingwerf* 52, *Nijmegen* 50, *Schiedam* 50 and *Wapen van de Schermer* 44; also 2 fireships.

27. RAID ON CARTAGENA – 6 May 1697
With the agreement of Louis XIV, the following squadron under the command of CV Jean Bernard de Saint-Jean, Baron de Pointis sailed from Brest on 7 January 1697 to attack and loot the rich Spanish city of Cartagena on the Spanish Main (in present-day Colombia); the naval vessels in this expedition were all lent by the Crown as privateers.

De Pointis's squadron – 10 ships
Sceptre 84 (flag of acting CdE Jean Bernard de Saint-Jean, Baron de Pointis), *Fort* 68 (flag of *Contre-Amiral*, under CV Jacques Florimond, Vicomte de Coëtlogon, who was mortally wounded and died on 25 May), *Saint Louis* 64 (flag of *Vice-Amiral*, under CV Louis de Lévy), *Apollon* 60, *Furieux* 60, *Saint Michel* 60, *Vermandois* 60, *Mutine* 40, *Avenant* 42, *Marin* 30.
Also bomb-vessel *Éclatante*, two *flûtes* (*Dieppoise* as hospital ship and *Maison de Ville d'Amsterdam*, also eventually as hospital ship), the brigantine *Providence* and four *traversiers* (*Ester*, *Marie-Anne*, *Saint Pierre*, and *Saint Louis*) for inshore operations. Reinforcement found locally were Des Augiers' prize Christ, eight *frégates flibustières*, two of them being former King's *frégates légères*, and two privateers from St Malo, *Pontchartrain* and *Françoise*. Also 1,700 soldiers from *compagnies franches de la Marine*.

28. BATTLE OF SAINTE MARTHE or SANTA MARTA ('Benbow's Action' in British accounts) – 29 August to 4 September 1702
The action took place off the Caribbean coast of Colombia, just east of the mouth of the Rio Magdalena. Benbow had his leg amputated as a result of the battle, and died of his injuries on 14 November. The captains of the *Defiance*, *Greenwich* and *Windsor* were court-martialled and the first two shot as a result of their failure to support the flagship during the action.

Ducasse's squadron – 4 ships of the line
Heureux 68 (flag of CdE Jean-Baptiste Ducasse), *Phénix* 60, *Agréable* 50, *Apollon* 50.

plus frigate *Prince de Frise* 30, a fireship, a transport and three small craft.

Benbow's squadron – 7 ships of the line
Breda 70 (flag of Vice-Adm John Benbow), *Defiance* 64, *Windsor* 60, *Greenwich* 54, *Ruby* 48, *Pendennis* 48, *Falmouth* 48.

29. BATTLE OF VIGO BAY – 23 October 1702.
Rooke's foray into the Bay of Vigo to attack 20 Spanish merchantmen then in the process of unloading their cargo brought from the Caribbean, under the protection of 17 ships of the French Navy and 3 Spanish warships. The attacking force comprised 49 English and Dutch naval vessels, who between them destroyed 23 of the French/Spanish ships (*) and captured the remaining 17 (#).

Châteaurenault's fleet – 17 French and 3 Spanish ships
Prompt 76#, *Ferme* 72# (flag of CdE André, Marquis de Nesmond), *Espérance* 70*, *Fort* 70* (flag of LG Louis François de Rousselet, Marquis de Châteaurenault), *Superbe* 70*, *Bourbon* 68# (flag of CdE Marquis de Rosmadec), *Assuré* 66#, *Oriflamme* 64*, *Prudent* 62*, *Sirène* 60*, *Modéré* 56#, *Solide* 56*, *Dauphin* 46*, *Volontaire* 46*, *Triton* 42#.
Also 22-gun *Entreprenant*, 18-gun *Choquante* and 3 Spanish vessels – *Jesus-Maria* 70, *Buffona* 54 and *Capitan-de-Assogas* 54.

Rooke's fleet – 15 English and 10 Dutch ships
Two 90-gun ships – *Association* and *Barfleur* – are excluded from the totals as these were not in the line of battle, but were assigned to attack the forts at the mouth of the harbour.
English ships – *Cambridge* 80, *Ranelagh* 80, *Somerset* 80 (flag of Adm Sir George Rooke), *Torbay* 80 (flag of Vice-Adm Thomas Hopsonn), *Bedford* 70, *Berwick* 70, *Essex* 70 (flag of Rear Adm Sir Stafford Fairborne), *Grafton* 70, *Kent* 70, *Monmouth* 70, *Orford* 70, *Northumberland* 70 (flag of Rear Adm John Graydon), *Swiftsure* 70, *Mary* 60, *Pembroke* 60.
Dutch ships – *Unie* 94 (flag of Vice-Adm Jan Gerard Wassenaer), *Zeven Provincien* 92 (flag of Vice-Adm Philips van der Goes), *Reigersberg* 74, *Dordrecht* 72, *Holland* 72 (flag of Lieut-Adm Gerrit van Callenburgh), *Katwijk* 72, *Slot Muiden* 72, *Wapen van Alkmaar* 72 (flag of Vice-Adm Anthonij Pieterson), *Gouda* 64, *Veluwe* 64.
Also fireships *Griffon*, *Hawk*, *Hunter*, *Lightning*, *Phoenix*, *Terrible*, *Vulture* and two Dutch fireships.

30. BATTLE OF VÉLEZ-MÁLAGA – 24 August 1704
A major battle in the Western Mediterranean which saw no ships lost on either side, but while a tactical victory for the French, resulted strategically in the Allies securing control of that Sea for the rest of the war.

Comte de Toulouse's fleet – 51 ships of the line

(A) Van (White-and-blue) Squadron under Villette-Mursay – 10 ships of the line
Saint Philippe 92 (flag of CdE Louis Le Roux, Marquis d'Infreville de Saint-Aubin), *Fier* 90 (flag of LG Philippe Le Valois, Marquis de Villette-Mursay), *Heureux* 72, *Constant* 68, *Éclatant* 66, *Éole* 62, *Oriflamme* 62, *Arrogant* 56, *Marquis* 56, *Rubis* 56.
(B) Centre (White) Squadron under Toulouse – 24 ships of the line
Foudroyant 104 (flag of *Amiral* de France Louis Alexandre de Bourbon, Comte de Toulouse), *Terrible* 102 (flag of LG Ferdinand, Comte de Relingue), *Magnifique* 90 (flag of CdE Jean de Belle-Isle-Érard), *Tonnant* 90 (flag of LG Alain Emmanuel, Comte de Coëtlogon), *Lys* 88, *Vainqueur* 86 (flag of CdE Louis Alphonse Ignace de Lorraine, Chevalier

d'Armagnac), *Intrépide* 84 (flag of CdE Jean-Baptiste Ducasse), *Monarque* 84, *Sceptre* 84, *Magnanime* 74 (flag of CdE Jean Bernard de Saint-Jean, Baron de Pointis), *Parfait* 74, *Orgueilleux* 72, *Écueil* 68, *Henri* 66, *Excellent* 60, *Vermandois* 60, *Entreprenant* 58, *Fendant* 58, *Furieux* 58, *Sage* 58, *Fleuron* 54, *Fortuné* 54, *Mercure* 50.

(C) Rear (Blue) Squadron under de Langeron – 16 ships of the line
Soleil Royal 102 (flag of LG Joseph Andrault, Marquis de Langeron), *Admirable* 92 (flag of CdE Jacques Cadot, Comte de Sébeville), *Triomphant* 92 (flag of CdE François-René de Betz, Comte de La Harteloire), *Couronne* 76, *Saint Esprit* 74, *Invincible* 68, *Ardent* 64, *Toulouse* 62, *Content* 60, *Saint Louis* 60, *Sérieux* 60, *Zélande* 60, *Diamant* 58, *Trident* 56, *Gaillard* 54, *Maure* 54, *Cheval Marin* 44.

Also present were the frigates *Oiseau* (36), *Étoile* (30), *Méduse* (28), *Hercule* (20), 4 small ships of 6–12 guns (*Andromède*, *Diligente*, *Galatée* and *Sibylle*); 12 French galleys under the Marquis de Roye; 12 Spanish galleys under the Duke of Tursis (7 of them formed the Genoa squadron, directly under Tursis; the other 5 of them – the Cartagena squadron – under the Count of Foncalada); 9 fireships (*Aigle Volant*, *Bienvenu*, *Croissant*, *Dangereux*, *Enflammé*, *Etna*, *Lion*, *Turquoise* and *Violent*); and 2 *flûtes*/storeships (*Portefaix* and *Rotterdam*).

Rooke's fleet – 39 ships of the line (including 3 of the 50s)

(A & B) Forming the Van and Centre squadrons
Barfleur 96 (flag of Adm Sir Cloudisley Shovell), *Namur* 96, *Saint George* 96, *Prince George* 90 (flag of Vice-Adm Sir John Leake), *Royal Katherine* 90 (flag of Adm of the Fleet Sir George Rooke), *Saint George*, *Boyne* 80, *Cambridge* 80, *Dorsetshire* 80, *Newark* 80, *Norfolk* 80, *Ranelagh* 80 (flag of Rear Adm George Byng), *Shrewsbury* 80, *Somerset* 80, *Torbay* 80, *Royal Oak* 76, *Bedford* 70, *Berwick* 70, *Burford* 70, *Eagle* 70, *Essex* 70, *Ferme* 70, *Grafton* 70, *Kent* 70 (flag of Rear Adm Thomas Dilkes), *Lenox* 70, *Monmouth* 70, *Nassau* 70, *Orford* 70, *Suffolk* 70, *Swiftsure* 70, *Warspite* 70, *Yarmouth* 70, *Assurance* 66, *Kingston* 60, *Monk* 60, *Montagu* 60, *Nottingham* 60, *Centurion* 50, *Garland* 50, *Panther* 50, *Swallow* 50, *Tilbury* 50, *Triton Prize* 50.
[note that of the 50s, only *Centurion*, *Tilbury* and *Triton Prize* formed part of the line of battle.]
Also present were 2 x 40s (*Lark* and *Roebuck*), 2 x 32s (*Charles Galley* and *Tartar* and 1 x 24 (*Newport*).
There were also 7 fireships (*Firebrand*, *Griffin*, *Hunter*, *Lightning*, *Phoenix*, *Vulcan* and *Vulture*); 2 bombs (*Hare* and *Terror*); 1 yacht (*William & Mary*); and 2 hospital ships (*Jefferies* and *Princess Anne*).

Van Callenburgh's squadron – 12 Dutch ships of the line

(C) Forming the Rear squadron
Wapen van Vriesland 64, *Wapen van Utrecht* 64, *Graaf van Albemarle* 64 (flag of Lt-Adm Gerard Callenburgh), *Vlissingen* 64, *Damiaten* 52, *Leeuw* 64, *Banier* 64, *Nijmegen* 54, *Katwijk* 72, *Unie* 90 (flag of Vice-Adm Baron Jan Gerrit van Wassenaer), *Gelderland* 72, *Dordrecht* 72.
There were also a number of small Dutch vessels (details unknown)

31. RAID ON RIO DE JANEIRO – October 1711

With the agreement of Louis XIV, CV René Duguay-Trouin was given command of a considerable squadron, the naval vessels of which were lent by the Crown as privateers. They sailed from France on 9 June 1711 to attack and loot the rich Portuguese city of Rio de Janeiro, on the east coast of South America (in present-day Brazil).
Lys 72 (CV René Duguay-Trouin, as 'Amiral'), *Magnanime* 72 (CFL Pierre Aubert, Chevalier de Courserac, as 'Vice-amiral') – lost during the return journey 2.1712, *Glorieux* 66 (LV Jean de La Jaille, Seigneur de Thou, as 'Contre-amiral'), *Brillant* 66, *Achille* 64, *Fidèle* 58 (lost during the return journey 2.1712), *Mars* 54, *Amazone* 42, *Argonaute* 42, *Aigle* 38 (lost at Cayenne 2.1712).
Also bomb vessel *Bellone*; three *flûtes*; two *traversiers* for inshore operations; two privateers from St Malo, Also 2,500 soldiers from *compagnies franches de la Marine*.

32. SECOND BOMBARDMENT OF TRIPOLI – 19 July 1728

Grandpré's squadron – 9 ships
Saint Esprit 74 (flag of CdE Étienne Nicolas de Grandpré), *Léopard* 62, *Tigre* 50, *Alcyon* 50, *Astrée* 30.
Also bomb vessels *Foudroyante*, *Ardente* and *Tempête*, the *flûte Seine* and two galleys.

33. BATTLE OF TOULON – 19 February 1744.

Also called the Battle off Cape Sicié, this happened before France joined Spain during the War of the Austrian Succession. A Franco-Spanish joint fleet was blockaded in Toulon by Adm Matthews, but broke out on 16 February and after a three-days chase brought the Allies to action, but the result was inconclusive.

Court de La Bruyère's fleet – 16 ships of the line
Duc d'Orléans 74, *Espérance* 74 (flag of CdE Pierre Gabaret), *Ferme* 74, *Saint Esprit* 74, *Terrible* 74 (flag of LG Charles-Élisée de Court de La Bruyère), *Borée* 64, *Éole* 64, *Sérieux* 64, *Solide* 64, *Trident* 64, *Furieux* 60, *Toulouse* 60, *Alcion* 54, *Diamant* 50, *Tigre* 50, *Aquilon* 48.
Also *Flore*, *Volage* and *Zéphyr* (all 20s) and three unidentified fireships.

Navarro's fleet – 12 ships of the line
Real Felipe 114 (flag of Admiral Don José Navarro), *Isabella* 80, *Constante* 70, *Hercules* 64, *San Fernando* 64, *America* 64, *Brillante* 64, *Poder* 64, *Oriente* 64, *Sobiero* 60, *Neptuno* 54, *Alción* 46.
Also *Volage* 20, and an unidentified fireship.

Mathews's fleet – 33 ships of the line (counting 5 x 50s)
Barfleur 90 (flag of Rear Adm William Rowley), *Marlborough* 90, *Namur* 90 (flag of Adm Thomas Mathews), *Neptune* 90 (flag of Vice-Adm Richard Lestock), *Boyne* 80, *Cambridge* 80, *Chichester* 80, *Dorsetshire* 80, *Norfolk* 80, *Princess Caroline* 80, *Russell* 80, *Somerset* 80, *Torbay* 80, *Princesa* 74, *Bedford* 70, *Berwick* 70, *Buckingham* 70, *Elizabeth* 70, *Essex* 70, *Nassau* 70, *Revenge* 70, *Royal Oak* 70, *Stirling Castle* 70, *Dragon* 60, *Dunkirk* 60, *Kingston* 60, *Rupert* 60, *Warwick* 60, *Guernsey* 50, *Nonsuch* 50, *Oxford* 50, *Romney* 50, *Salisbury* 50.
Also *Feversham* 40, *Diamond* 40, *Winchelsea* 20, *Dursley Galley* 20, fireships *Anne Galley* and *Mercury*, and hospital ship *Sutherland*.

34. FIRST BATTLE OFF CAPE FINISTERRE (*Bataille du Cap Ortégal* in French history) – 14 May 1747

de La Jonquière's fleet – 4 ships of the line (counting 2 x 50s)
Invincible 74, *Sérieux* 64 (flag of CdE Jacques-Pierre de Taffanel, Marquis de La Jonquière), *Rubis* 52 (rated 52, but actually *en flûte*, with 26 guns), *Jason* 50.
Also *Émeraude* and *Gloire* (both 40s); *Chimène* 36; *Apollon*, *Diamant* and *Philibert* (all 30s); *Thétis* 22; *Vigilant* 20; and *Dartmouth* and *Modeste* (both 18s).
[Note all the above ships were taken except *Chimène* and *Émeraude*; the *Chimène*, *Apollon*, *Philibert*, *Thétis*, *Vigilant* and *Modeste* belonged to the *Compagnie des Indes*; *Dartmouth* was a former British privateer.]

Anson's fleet – 14 ships of the line (counting 3 x 50s)
Prince George 90 (flag of Vice-Adm George Anson), *Namur* 74, *Devonshire* 66 (flag of Rear Adm Peter Warren), *Monmouth* 64, *Prince Frederick* 64, *Yarmouth* 64, *Defiance* 60, *Nottingham* 60, *Pembroke* 60, *Princess Louisa* 60, *Windsor* 60, *Bristol* 50, *Centurion* 50, *Falkland* 50.
Also *Ambuscade* 40, sloop *Falcon* 10 and fireship *Vulcan*.
[Note only 8 ships were actually in action – *Namur, Devonshire, Yarmouth, Defiance, Pembroke, Windsor, Bristol* and *Centurion*.]

35. SECOND BATTLE OFF CAPE FINISTERRE – 25 October 1747

de l'Estenduère's squadron – 9 ships of the line (counting 1 x 56)
Tonnant 80 (flag of CdE Henri-François Des Herbiers, Marquis de l'Estenduère), *Intrépide* 74, *Monarque* 74, *Neptune* 74, *Terrible* 74, *Fougueux* 64, *Trident* 64, *Content* 64 (*Compagnie des Indes* ship), *Severn* 56.
Also *Castor* 26.
[Note all were taken except *Tonnant, Intrépide, Content* and *Castor*.]

Hawke's fleet – 14 ships of the line (counting 2 x 50s)
Kent 74, *Edinburgh* 70, *Devonshire* 66 (flag of Rear Adm Edward Hawke), *Monmouth* 64, *Yarmouth* 64, *Defiance* 60, *Eagle* 60, *Lion* 60, *Nottingham* 60, *Princess Louisa* 60, *Tilbury* 60, *Windsor* 60, *Gloucester* 50, *Portland* 50.

36. BATTLE OF MINORCA – 20 May 1756

La Galissonnière's squadron – 12 ships of the line (including 2 x 50s)
Orphée 64, *Hippopotame* 50, *Redoutable* 74 (flag of CdE Pierre-André, Marquis de Glandevèz), *Sage* 64, *Guerrier* 74, *Fier* 50, *Foudroyant* 84 (flag of CdE Rolland-Michel Barrin, Marquis de la Galissonnière), *Téméraire* 74, *Content* 64, *Lion* 64, *Couronne* 74 (flag of CdE Jean-François de Bertet de Sabran, Marquis de la Clue), *Triton* 64.
Also *Junon* 46 and 4 frigates – *Gracieuse* 26, *Nymphe* 26, *Rose* 26 and *Topaze* 24.

Byng's squadron – 13 ships of the line (including 1 x 50)
Defiance 60, *Portland* 50, *Lancaster* 66, *Buckingham* 68 (flag of Rear Adm Temple West), *Captain* 64, *Intrepid* 64, *Revenge* 64, *Princess Louisa* 60, *Trident* 64, *Ramillies* 90 (flag of Vice-Adm John Byng), *Culloden* 74, *Kingston* 60.
Also later *Deptford* 50 (replacing the damaged *Intrepid*).
Also *Chesterfield* 40, *Dolphin* 20, *Experiment* 20, *Phoenix* 20 and *Fortune* 14.

37. BATTLES OFF INDIA – 1758–59
In the East Indies, British and French squadrons under George Pocock and Comte d'Aché respectively fought a series of three battles:

CUDDALORE (usually called SADRAS) – 29 April 1758

D'Aché's squadron
[Note that these vessels were actually French *Compagnie des Indes* vessels, forming its Indian Ocean Squadron, not French Naval vessels.]
Zodiaque 74 (flag of CdE Ann-Antoine, Comte d'Aché de Marboeuf), *Comte de Provence* 74 (not present at action), 64 (actually carrying 54 guns), *Saint Louis* 64 (actually carrying 50 guns), *Bien Aimé* 62 (actually carrying 58 guns; wrecked the same day), *Duc d'Orléans* 60 (actually carrying 56 guns), *Duc de Bourgogne* 60, *Moras* 50 (actually carrying 44 guns), *Condé* 50 (actually carrying 44 guns).
Also *Sylphide* 36, *Diligente* 24 (the latter not present at action).

Pocock's squadron
Yarmouth 64 (flag of Vice-Adm George Pocock), *Elizabeth* 64 (flag of Commodore Charles Stevens), *Tiger* 60, *Weymouth* 60, *Cumberland* 56 (reduced from 66), *Salisbury* 50, *Newcastle* 50.
Also *Queenborough*, 24, and *Protector*, storeship.

NEGAPATAM – 3 August 1758

D'Aché's squadron unchanged except for recent loss of *Bien Aimé* and absence of *Sylphide*.

Pocock's squadron unchanged.

PONDICHERRY – 10 September 1759

D'Aché's squadron
Zodiaque 74 (flag of CdE Ann-Antoine, Comte d'Aché de Marboeuf), *Comte de Provence* 74, *Minotaure* 74, *Centaure* 70, *Vengeur* 64, *Actif* 64, *Illustre* 64, *Fortune* 64, *Saint Louis* 60, *Duc d'Orléans* 60, *Duc de Bourgogne* 60.

Pocock's squadron
Grafton 68 (flag of Rear Adm Charles Stevens), *Elizabeth* 64, *Yarmouth* 64 (flag of Vice-Adm George Pocock), *Tiger* 60, *Weymouth* 60, *Sunderland* 60, *Cumberland* 56 (reduced from 66), *Salisbury* 50, *Newcastle* 50.
Also *Queenborough*, 24.

[Note while no ships were taken or destroyed in these hard-fought battles, they resulted in d'Aché sailing from Indian waters, marking the effective end of French sea power in the subcontinent.]

38. BATTLE OF LAGOS – 18 August 1759

De La Clue's squadron – 7 ships of the line, of which 3 (#) were captured and 2 (*) were destroyed
Océan 80* (flag of CdE Jean-François de Bertet de Sabran, Comte de La Clue), *Centaure* 74#, *Guerrier* 74, *Redoutable* 74*, *Souverain* 74, *Téméraire* 74#, *Modeste* 64#.

[Note that De la Clue's squadron also included 5 other ships of the line and 3 frigates which were absent from the battle – these were the *Fantasque* 64, *Fier* 50, *Lion* 64, *Oriflamme* 50, *Triton* 64; *Chimère* 26, *Gracieuse* 24 and *Minerve* 24]

Boscawen's squadron – 15 ships of the line (including 2 x 50s)
Namur 90 (flag of Adm Edward Boscawen), *Prince* 90 (flag of Vice-Adm Thomas Broderick), *Newark* 80, *Culloden* 74, *Warspite* 74, *Conqueror* 70, *Swiftsure* 70, *Edgar* 64, *Saint Albans* 64, *America* 60, *Intrepid* 60, *Jersey* 60, *Princess Louisa* 60, *Guernsey* 50, *Portland* 50.
Also *Ambuscade* 40, *Rainbow* 40, *Active* 36, *Shannon* 36, *Thetis* 32, *Gibraltar* 24, *Glasgow* 24, *Lyme* 24, *Sheerness* 24, *Tartar's Prize* 24, *Favourite* 16, *Gramont* 16, and two fireships – *Aetna* 8 and *Salamander* 8.

39. BATTLE OF QUIBERON BAY (*Bataille des Cardinaux* in French history) – 20 November 1759

Conflans's fleet – 20 ships of the line of which 1 (#) was taken and 5(*) were sunk or wrecked.
Soleil Royal 80* (flag of *Vice-amiral* Hubert de Brienne, Maréchal and Comte de Conflans), *Tonnant* 80 (flag of CdE Joseph de Bauffremont, Prince de Listenois), *Formidable* 80# (flag of CdE Louis de Saint-André du Verger), *Orient* 80 (flag of CdE Joseph-Marie Budes, Marquis de Guébriant), *Intrépide* 74, *Glorieux* 74, *Thésée* 74*, *Héros* 74*, *Robuste* 74, *Magnifique* 74, *Juste* 70 (former 74)*, *Superbe* 70 (former 74)*,

Northumberland 68, *Dragon* 64, *Sphinx* 64, *Solitaire* 64, *Brillant* 64, *Éveillé* 64, *Bizarre* 64, *Inflexible* 64.
Also two frigates – *Vestale*, 34. *Aigrette*, 36. plus *Calypso*, 16 and *Prince Noir* (chartered storeship).

Hawke's fleet – 23 ships of the line, of which 2 (*) were wrecked:
Royal George 100 (flag of Adm Sir Edward Hawke), *Union* 90 (flag of Vice-Adm. Sir Charles Hardy), *Duke* 90, *Namur* 90, *Mars* 74, *Warspite* 74, *Hercules* 74, *Torbay* 74, *Magnanime* 74, *Resolution* 74*, *Hero* 74, *Swiftsure* 70, *Dorsetshire* 70, *Burford* 70, *Chichester* 70, *Temple* 70, *Revenge* 64, *Essex* 64*, *Kingston* 60, *Intrepid* 60, *Montagu* 60, *Dunkirk* 60, *Defiance* 60.

Commodore Robert Duff's squadron
Rochester 50 (pennant of Robert Duff), *Portland* 50, *Falkland* 50, *Chatham* 50.
Also 6 frigates – *Venus* 36, *Minerva* 32, *Sapphire* 32, *Vengeance* 28, *Coventry* 28, *Maidstone* 28.

40. THIRD BATTLE OF USHANT (Sometimes referred to in Britain as 'Keppel's Action') – 27 July 1778

D'Orvilliers's fleet

(A) Du Chaffault's van division –11 ships of the line
Couronne 80 (flag of LG Louis-Charles de Besné, Comte du Chaffault), *Duc de Bourgogne* 80 (flag of CdE Vicomte de Rochechouart), *Glorieux* 74, *Palmier* 74, *Bien Aimé* 74, *Dauphin Royal* 70, *Vengeur* 64, *Alexandre* 64, *Indien* 64, *Saint Michel* 60, *Amphion* 50.
(B) d'Orvilliers's centre division – 10 ships of the line
Bretagne 110 (flag of LG Louis Gouillouet, Comte d'Orvilliers), *Ville de Paris* 100 (flag of CdE Luc Urbain de Bouexic, Comte de Guichen), *Orient* 74 (an ex-80, flag of CdE Charles Jean Hector), *Fendant* 74, *Magnifique* 74, *Actif* 74, *Réfléchi* 64, *Éveillé* 64, *Artésien* 64, *Actionnaire* 64.
(C) de Chartres's rear division – 11 ships of the line
Saint Esprit 80 (flag of LG Louis-Philippe d'Orléans, Duc de Chartres), *Robuste* 74 (flag of CdE François Joseph Paul, Comte de Grasse-Tilli), *Conquérant* 74 (flag of CdE Francois-Aymar, Comte de Monteil), *Intrépide* 74, *Zodiaque* 74, *Diadème* 74, *Solitaire* 64, *Roland* 64, *Sphinx* 64, *Triton* 64, *Fier* 50.
Also 6 x 32-gun frigates (*Sensible, Andromaque, Sincère, Junon, Iphigénie, Nymphe*), 3 x 16-gun (*Surveillante, Perle, Hirondelle*), 2 x 14-gun (*Écureuil, Sérin*), 2 x 10-gun (*Curieuse, Favorite*) and 1 x 4-gun (*Lunette*).

Keppel's fleet

(A) Harland's van division – 10 ships of the line
Duke 90, *Queen* 90 (flag of Vice-Adm Sir Robert Harland), *Monarch* 74, *Hector* 74, *Centaur* 74, *Shrewsbury* 74, *Cumberland* 74, *Berwick* 74, *Exeter* 64, *Stirling Castle* 64.
(B) Keppel's centre division – 11 ships of the line
Victory 100 (flag of Adm Augustus Keppel and Rear-Adm John Campbell), 90, *Prince George* 90, *Foudroyant* 80, *Courageux* 74, *Thunderer* 74, *Valiant* 74, *Terrible* 74, *Vengeance* 74, *Bienfaisant* 64, *Vigilant* 64.

A dramatic rendition by Dominic Serres of the winter twilight chase into Quiberon Bay on 20 November 1759, which resulted in the loss of six French ships of the line, including the flagship, the 80-gun *Soleil Royal*. It was not a one-sided victory as two British ships of the line were wrecked, but it marked the end of the French attempt to invade England. In the centre of the composition, the *Royal George* 100, flagship of Adm Sir Edward Hawke, is in close pursuit of *Soleil Royal*, flying the flag of *Vice-amiral* Comte de Conflans. (National Maritime Museum, London, BHC0400)

(C) Palliser's rear division – 9 ships of the line
Formidable 90 (flag of Vice-Adm Sir Hugh Palliser), *Ocean* 90, *Elizabeth* 74, *Robust* 74, *Egmont* 74, *Ramillies* 74, *Worcester* 64, *America* 64, *Defiance* 64.
Also 1 x 32-gun (*Arethusa*) and 4 x 28-gun frigates (*Proserpine*, *Milford*, *Fox*, *Andromeda*), 1 x 20-gun (*Lively*), 1 x 12-gun cutter (*Alert*) and 2 x 8-gun fireships (*Pluto*, *Vulcan*).

41. BATTLE OF CAPE HENRY – 16 March 1781

Des Touches's Squadron
Duc de Bourgogne 84, *Neptune* 74 (flag of CdE Charles Sochet, Seigneur des Touches), *Conquérant* 74, *Ardent* 64, *Éveillé* 64, *Fantasque* 64 (*en flûte*), *Jason* 64, *Provence* 64, *Romulus* 44.
Also frigates *Hermione* (36) and *Gentille* (32).

Arbuthnot's Squadron
London 98 (flag of Rear Adm Thomas Graves), *Bedford* 74, *Robust* 74, *Royal Oak* 74 (flag of Vice-Adm Marriot Arbuthnot), *America* 64, *Europe* 64, *Prudent* 64, *Adamant* 50.
Also frigates *Iris* (32), *Pearl* (32), *Guadeloupe* (28) and *Medea* (28).

42. BATTLE OF PORTO PRAYA – 16 April 1781

Suffren's squadron – 5 ships of the line
Annibal 74, *Héros* 74 (flag of CdE Pierre André de Suffren), *Artésien* 64, *Sphinx* 64, *Vengeur* 64.

Johnstone's squadron – 5 ships of the line
Hero 74, *Monmouth* 64, *Isis* 50, *Jupiter* 50, *Romney* 50 (pennant of Commodore George Johnstone).
Also frigates *Active* 32, *Diana* 32 and *Jason* 32, plus *Porto* 16, *Rattlesnake* 14, cutter *Tapageur* 14, fireship *Infernal* 8, bomb *Terror* 8, armed ships *Royal Charlotte* (hired) and *San Carlos*, and armed transport *Pondicherry*.

43. BATTLE OF THE CHESAPEAKE – 5 September 1781.
Sometimes called the Battle of the Virginia Capes, this battle was tactically indecisive but strategically a victory for the French and their American allies, as it prevented the British Navy from reinforcing or evacuating the forces of Lieut-Gen Lord Cornwallis at Yorktown, Virginia.

De Grasse's fleet – 24 ships of the line

(A) Van squadron
Auguste 80 (flag of CdE Louis-Antoine de Bougainville), *Saint Esprit* 80, *Bourgogne* 74, *Diadème* 74, *Marseillais* 74, *Pluton* 74, *Caton* 64, *Réfléchi* 64.
(B) Centre squadron
Ville de Paris 104 (flag of LG François Joseph Paul, Comte de Grasse, and of Chevalier de Vaugiraud), *César* 74, *Citoyen* 74, *Destin* 74, *Northumberland* 74, *Palmier* 74, *Sceptre* 74, *Victoire* 74, *Solitaire* 64.
(C) Rear squadron
Languedoc 80 (flag of CdE François-Aymar, Comte de Monteil), *Hector* 74, *Hercule* 74, *Magnanime* 74, *Scipion* 74, *Souverain* 74, *Zélé* 74.

Graves's fleet – 19 ships of the line

(A) Van squadron
Barfleur 98 (flag of Rear Adm Samuel Hood), *Alfred* 74, *Centaur* 74, *Invincible* 74, *Monarch* 74, *Belliqueux* 64.
(B) Centre squadron
London 98 (flag of Rear-Adm. Thomas Graves), *Bedford* 74, *Montagu* 74, *Resolution* 74, *Royal Oak* 74, *America* 64, *Europe* 64.
(C) Rear squadron
Ajax 74, *Alcide* 74, *Shrewsbury* 74, *Terrible* 74, *Princessa* 70 (flag of Rear Adm Francis Samuel Drake), *Intrepid* 64.
[Note that in the battle, the Van actually served as the Rear, and vice versa.]

44. BATTLE OF ST KITTS – 25/26 January 1782

De Grasse's fleet – 29 ships of the line
Ville de Paris 104 (flag of LG François Joseph Paul, Comte de Grasse), *Auguste* 80 (flag of CdE Louis-Antoine de Bougainville), *Couronne* 80, *Duc de Bourgogne* 80, *Languedoc* 80, *Bourgogne* 74, *César* 74, *Citoyen* 74, *Conquérant* 74, *Destin* 74, *Diadème* 74, *Glorieux* 74, *Hector* 74, *Hercule* 74, *Magnanime* 74, *Marseillais* 74, *Neptune* 74, *Northumberland* 74, *Palmier* 74, *Pluton* 74, *Sceptre* 74, *Souverain* 74, *Zélé* 74, *Dauphin Royal* 70, *Ardent* 64, *Caton* 64, *Éveillé* 64, *Jason* 64, *Réfléchi* 64.

Hood's fleet – 22 ships of the line

(A) Van squadron
Prince George 98, *Ajax* 74, *Alcide* 74, *Torbay* 74, *Princessa* 70 (flag of Rear Adm Francis Samuel Drake), *Intrepid* 64, *Saint Albans* 64.
(B) Centre squadron
Barfleur 98 (flag of Rear Adm Sir Samuel Hood), *Alfred* 74, *Centaur* 74, *Invincible* 74, *Monarch* 74, *Shrewsbury* 74, *Belliqueux* 64, *Prince William* 64.
Also 32-gun *Convert*; 28-gun *Fortunee*, *Lizard*, *Pegasus* and *Triton*; 20-gun *Champion*.
(C) Rear squadron
Bedford 74 (flag of Rear Adm Edmund Affleck), *Canada* 74, *Montagu* 74, *Resolution* 74, *Russell* 74, *America* 64, *Prudent* 64.
Also 28-gun *Sibyl* and *Solebay*.

45. BATTLES OFF INDIA – 1782–1783

In the East Indies, British and French squadrons under Vice-Adm Sir Edward Hughes and CdE Pierre André de Suffren respectively fought a series of five battles:

SADRAS – 17 February 1782

Suffren's squadron – 12 ships of the line
Héros 74 (flag of CdE Pierre André de Suffren), *Annibal* 74, *Orient* 74, *Sévère* 64, *Vengeur* 64, *Brillant* 64, *Artésien* 64, *Sphinx* 64, *Ajax* 64, *Bizarre* 64, *Flamand* 50, *Petit Annibal* 50.
Also 3 frigates – *Pourvoyeuse* 38, *Fine* 32, *Bellone* 32, together with *Subtile* 22, *Sylphide* 16 and *Diligente* 10.

Hughes's squadron – 9 ships of the line
Superb 74 (flag of Vice-Adm Sir Edward Hughes), *Hero* 74, *Monarca* 68 (originally a 70), *Eagle* 64, *Monmouth* 64, *Worcester* 64, *Burford* 64 (originally a 70), *Exeter* 64 (flag of Commodore Richard King), *Isis* 50.
Also *Seahorse* 24, and armed transport *Manilla* 14.

PROVIDIEN – 12 April 1782

Suffren's squadron – 12 ships of the line
Unchanged from 17 February.

Hughes's squadron – 11 ships of the line.
Unchanged from 17 February, with the addition of *Sultan* 74 and

Magnanime 64, both joining 30 March.
also *Seahorse* 24, and fireship *Combustion* 14.

NEGAPATAM – 6 July 1782

Suffren's squadron – 11 ships of the line
Unchanged from 12 April, except for the absence of the *Ajax* because of damage.

Hughes's squadron – 11 ships of the line, unchanged from 12 April (except King's flag now moved to *Hero*).

TRINCOMALEE – 3 September 1782

Suffren's squadron – 14 ships of the line
Unchanged from 12 April (*Ajax* had rejoined), with the addition of *Illustre* 74 and *Saint Michel* 64.

Hughes's squadron – 12 ships of the line
Unchanged from 12 April, with the addition of the *Sceptre* 64.

CUDDALORE (or GONDELOUR) – 20 June 1783

Suffren's squadron – 15 ships of the line.
Héros 74 (flag of CdE Pierre André de Suffren), *Annibal* 74, *Illustre* 74 (flag of Comte de Brugeres), *Fendant* 74, *Argonaute* 74, *Sévère* 64, *Vengeur* 64, *Brillant* 64, *Artésien* 64, *Sphinx* 64, *Ajax* 64, *Saint Michel* 64, *Hardi* 64, *Flamand* 50, *Petit Annibal* 50.
Also 3 frigates – *Apollon* 40, *Cléopâtre* 36, *Coventry* 28.

Hughes's squadron – 18 ships of the line
Gibraltar 80 (flag of Commodore Sir Richard Bickerton), *Superb* 74 (flag of Vice-Adm Sir Edward Hughes), *Hero* 74 (flag of Commodore Richard King), *Sultan* 74, *Cumberland* 74, *Defence* 74, *Monarca* 68 (originally a 70), *Eagle* 64, *Monmouth* 64, *Worcester* 64, *Burford* 64 (originally a 70), *Exeter* 64, *Magnanime* 64, *Sceptre* 64, *Africa* 64, *Inflexible* 64, *Isis* 50, *Bristol* 50.

Also 2 frigates: *Juno* 32 and *Medea* 28, together with *Seahorse* 24.

46. BATTLE OF THE SAINTES – 9/12 April 1782

De Grasse's fleet – 34 ships of the line, of which 7 (#) were taken.
Ville de Paris 110# (flag of LG François Joseph Paul, Comte de Grasse), *Auguste* 80, *Duc de Bourgogne* 80, *Languedoc* 80, *Couronne* 80, *Saint Esprit* 80, *Triomphant* 80, *Souverain* 74, *Hercule* 74, *Northumberland* 74, *Zélé* 74, *Conquérant* 74, *Marseillais* 74, *Hector* 74#, *César* 74#, *Magnanime* 74, *Diadème* 74, *Glorieux* 74#, *Sceptre* 74, *Scipion* 74, *Palmier* 74, *Destin* 74, *Citoyen* 74, *Dauphin Royal* 74, *Neptune* 74, *Bien Aimée* 74, *Brave* 74, *Bourgogne* 74, *Pluton* 74, *Éveillé* 64, *Réfléchi* 64, *Jason* 64#, *Ardent* 64#, *Caton* 64#.

[Note that the battle-damaged *Jason* and *Caton* were captured on 19 April in the Mona Passage by Hood's squadron, along with the frigate *Aimable* and corvette *Cérès*. *César* blew up almost immediately after capture while *Ville de Paris*, *Glorieux*, and *Hector* were lost off Newfoundland on the way to Britain.]

Rodney's fleet – 37 ships of the line
Formidable 98 (flag of Adm Sir George Rodney), *Barfleur* 98 (flag of Rear Adm Sir Samuel Hood), *Duke* 98, *Prince George* 98, *Namur* 90, *Royal Oak* 74, *Alfred* 74, *Montagu* 74, *Valiant* 74, *Monarch* 74, *Warrior* 74, *Centaur* 74, *Magnificent* 74, *Bedford* 74, *Ajax* 74, *Canada* 74, *Resolution* 74, *Hercules* 74, *Russell* 74, *Fame* 74, *Torbay* 74, *Conqueror* 74, *Alcide* 74, *Arrogant* 74, *Marlborough* 74, *Princesa* 70 (flag of Rear Adm Francis Drake), *Yarmouth* 64, *Belliqueux* 64, *Prince William* 64, *Repulse* 64, *St Albans* 64, *Agamemnon* 64, *Protée* 64, *America* 64, *Prudent* 64 (not in action), *Anson* 64, *Nonsuch* 64.
12 frigates (those marked + were not in action) - *Endymion* 44, *Fortunée*+ 40, *Flora* 36, *Nymphe*+ 36, *Santa Monica*+ 36, *Convert*+ 32, *Alarm* 32, *Andromache* 32, *Lizard*+ 28, *Sibyl* 28, *Pegasus*+ 28, *Triton* 28.
Also *Champion*, 24. *Eurydice*, 24. *Zebra*+, 16. *Germaine*+, 16. *Alert*, 14. *Salanander*+, 8. *Blast*+, 8.

Sources and Bibliography

ARCHIVAL SOURCES

États abrégés de la Marine.

These indispensable little books (literally "summary statements of the Navy," referred to hereafter as États, also called *Agendas de Marine*) were prepared annually beginning in 1669 in exquisite calligraphy, initially with coloured ornamentation, in two copies, one for the king and one for the Minister. The 1688 edition is known to have been made by Sieur Belluchau, *conseiller et secrétaire du Roi*, who was paid for his work in May 1688, while between 1735 and 1768 Louis XV assigned the task to Pierre-Benjamin Gallemant, who was to accomplish it between 1 October and 1 January although some were finished a bit later. The États include lists of the officers and ships of the navy and the galley corps, and other information of interest to the top leadership such as the quantities of guns and stores in the dockyards and fleets to be formed during the year. From 1696 to 1743 they also included detailed hull measurements of the ships and enumerations of their armaments, most of which appear in this book. These details disappear after 1743, and later États offer little more than ship names, number of guns, and home port. They generally refer to the situation pertaining as at 1st January, except for 1669 (when it was in September), 1716-17 (1st June), and 1718 (1st September). The dates for the later États are generally not specified except for the year, but they were probably also as at 1st January (although the 1753 one was as at April). These États, which were a vitally important source for this book, are located as follows (those lacking ship lists are excluded):

Archives Nationales, Series G numbers 1–38, 224, and 247–251: 1669, 1671, 1672, 1673, 1675, 1676, 1677, 1679, 1682, 1686, 1688, 1689, 1690, 1692, 1696, 1698, 1700, 1701, 1702, 1704, 1706, 1707, 1708, 1709, 1710, 1712, 1716, 1717, 1718, 1719, 1723, 1729, 1734, 1736, 1738, 1739, 1741, 1742, 1743 1751, 1772, 1773, 1778, 1781, 1782, 1784, 1785, and 1787. Series G also contains two items that, although filed with the États, are not États. One (1763, G-33) is a roster of ships maintained from about 1757 to 1763 that was found at Toulon in 1869, and the other (1767, G-34) is a list of ships attached to Brest, Rochefort, and Toulon in 1767 that, exceptionally, has hull measurements and armaments. The 1772 edition is also at the Musée Jacquemart-André in Paris.

Bibliothèque Nationale de France: 1680 (Rothschild 2364), 1681 (n.a.f. 16588), 1683 (fond français 14284), 1759 (fond français 14286), 1766 (n.a.f. 4373)

Bibliothèque municipale du Havre: 1687 (Ms 274), 1765 (Ms 275)

Bibliothèque municipale de Rouen: 1691 (manuscrit 3278 (5786))

Service Historique de la Défense, département Marine: 1699 (Ms 164), 1777 (Ms 268), 1779 (Ms 23), 1780 (Ms 24), 1783 (Ms 27), 1786 (Ms 30)

Bibliothèque municipale de Versailles: 1753 (Ms P 96, 1412), 1763 (Ms P 145, 1680)

Bibliothèque du Château de Chantilly: 1674 (Ms 1435)

Bibliothèque Mazarine, Paris: 1757 (Ms 2884)

All of the above - except for the 1674, 1680, 1681, 1757, and 1763 editions - were microfilmed in the early 1970s under the Foreign Copying Program of the U.S. Library of Congress, making them available to researchers both in Washington, D.C. and in the Archives Nationales in Paris, where the films are consulted instead of the originals to help conserve the latter. Since the 1970s a few more editions of the États abrégés have come to light including the 1674, 1680, 1681, 1757 and 1763 editions listed above plus the 1684 (Bibliothèque municipale d'Agen, No. 14) and 1756 (Musée de la Marine, Paris, V2311) editions. Others are still missing, including a 1693 edition that was noted in a private collection in 1819 and at Dunkirk in 1861 but has not been reported since.

Archives Nationales

The National Archives (*Archives Nationales,* AN) preserve France's official records and were created in 1790. Other archives elsewhere include those of the Ministry of Defence and the Ministry of Foreign Affairs and Departmental archives. Since 1808 the Archives have been housed in a group of buildings in the Marais quarter of Paris. This centre stores all the documents and records from the Middles Ages up to the Revolution. Naval archives are grouped in the *Fonds de la Marine*. They predominantly cover the period 1670 to 1789. They were intially classified under the direction of Colbert and then definitively classified in their present form in 1887. They comprise seven groupings (*séries*): A Actes du Pouvoir Souverain; B Service général; C Personnel; D Matériel; E Comptabilité: F Invalides et Prises; and G Documents Divers. Most the naval archives are available on microfilm and can be readily accessed without prior arrangement. Original manuscripts must be pre-ordered (using the Internet search engine and booking site http://www.archives-nationales.culture.gouv.fr/fr/web/guest/faire-une-recherche).

FONDS DIVERS: Série AD ARCHIVES IMPRIMÉES
AD-VII-11 *Ordonnance du 15 avril 1689*.

ARCHIVES DE LA MARINE

Série A ACTES DU POUVOIR SOUVERAIN
A1-14-9: *Règlement du 10 février 1674*.

Série B SERVICE GENERALE

B1 DÉCISIONS.
  Documents from 1734, 1748, 1751, 1759, 1760, 1764, 1770, 1771, and 1778.

B2 ORDRES ET DÉPÊCHES
  B2-3: *État des vaisseaux de guerre de l'Armée du Roi composée à Toulon le 29 avril 1666*.
  Correspondence from 1662–69, 1690, and 1746-48.

B3 LETTRES REÇUES
  B3-8: *Mémoire par Jean Baube sur l'artillerie du* Royal Louis (1669) and correspondence from 1747–48.

B4 CAMPAGNES
  Detailed list of ships commissioned at Toulon in 1741 (B4-50) and items from 1747–51 and 1756–57.

B5 ARMEMENTS
  B5-1 to B5-6: Documents from 1644, 1646, and 1661–1769. Tables of total numbers of ships in the fleet, 1660– 1743. Fleet lists for 1715 and 1746 resembling those in the *États abrégés*.
  B5-7 to B5-29: documents from 1770 to 1786. Fleet lists for 1770–1777. Ship registers for vaisseaux and frigates in 1779; vaisseaux, frigates and corvettes in 1780, 1781 and 1782; and frigates in 1783. *Forces Navales* (ship registers) in 1780 (B5-14), 1781 (B5-13), and 1783. Registers of ship movements in 1774–1775 and 1779–1781. Monthly reports of ships and other material in dockyards for Brest in 1772, 1775–1783; Le Havre in 1772–

1781; Lorient in 1774 and 1779–1785; Rochefort in 1774 and 1778–1784; and Toulon in 1776–1783.

Série D MATÉRIEL

D1-13: *Liste des bâtiments de guerre construits de 1659 à 1705 par Coulomb et fils*; Collection of *devis de constructions* notably from Le Havre 1665–1787.

D1-57: Register of *devis* of ships built at Le Havre 1690–1697.

Bibliothèque Nationale de France

The French National Library (*Bibliothèque Nationale de France, BNF*) collects, preserves and publicizes the national documentary heritage. Of the library's 14 million items over 3 million are available on line through the digital library *Gallica*. Most of the BNF's documents are described in the catalogue at *http://catalogue.bnf.fr/index.do*. Manuscripts and archives are partly described in the catalogue. There is a reference service on line, SINDBAD, available through the website (*Service d'Information des Bibliothécaires À Distance*). The collections of the BNF are housed in two different places: the François-Mitterrand Library, Quai François-Mauriac and the Richelieu Library, 58, rue de Richelieu, in the heart of Paris. The Richelieu Library houses several collections including the Manuscript collection of the library.

Manuscrits Français

Fr. 2304: Coulomb, François, *Livre de construction, contenant les proportions de chaque rang de navire, comme aussy les proportions de la masture, manneuvres, canon, les noms de tous les vaisseaux du roi, tant de ponant que de levant*, 1686

Fr. 25377: *Règlements pour l'armement et les équipages des vaisseaux de Louis XIV*, c.1674

Nouvelles Acquisitions Françaises (NAF)

N.A.F. 4223 à 4226: Navy expenditures from 1662 to 1675 in four volumes

N.A.F. 4670: Coulomb, François, *Livre de construction des vaisseaux contenant le nom des pièces, leur liaisons, et les proportions generalles de masture comme aussy pour les fluttes et chaloupes, à Toulon* (1683)

N.A.F. 5399: Table of expenditures on the Navy and the Galley Corps, 1678–1782, Folios 306–313

N.A.F 14284: *Agenda de Marine, ou, Liste générale des vaisseaux du Roi au 1er janvier 1683* (État de 1683)

N.A.F 24447: *Etat général des vaisseaux de guerre de S. M., May 1669* (Folios 296–298)

Ordonnances and Règlements (available on gallica.bnf.fr)

Ordonnance du Roy portant réunion du corps des Galères à celui de la Marine, 27 September 1748

Code des Armées Navales ou Recueil des Édits, Déclarations, Ordonnances et Règlemens sur le fait de la Marine du Roi, from 1669 to 1757 (also published by Torchet de Blois Boismêlé in 1758, see books below)

Ordonnance du Roi concernant les Ingénieurs-constructeurs de la Marine, 25 March 1765.

Ordonnance du Roi concernant la régie et administration générale et particulière des Ports et Arsenaux de Marine, 27 September 1776

Service Historique de la Défense

The Defence Historical Service (*Service Historique de la Défense*, SHD) preserves the archives of the ministries in charge of military affairs from the seventeenth century to the present day. It is also the foremost military library in Europe. It is composed of three centres: the Historical Archives (located in Vincennes, Cherbourg, Brest, Lorient, Rochefort, Toulon, Caen, Le Blanc), the Armaments and Civilian Personnel archives (located in Châtellerault), and the Military Personnel archives (located in Pau). The Historical Archives in the Chateau de Vincennes in the south-east of Paris houses the naval archives. These consist of several collections:

The manuscripts of the library of the Naval Ministry, formerly the Ministry of the Navy and Colonies, whose existence, although official only in 1820, dates to Colbert.

The historical collection of the Royal Naval Academy, founded in 1752, contains the minutes of meetings and reports by French and foreign correspondents and other documents.

The 71 collections (*recueils*) of the Navy Hydrographic Service include international maps and plans, both marine and terrestrial, created between 1550 and 1850.

The Nivard collection includes 850 maps, plans and engravings concerning the navy from the seventeenth century to 1942.

Archives de la Défense, Marine, Fonds anciens (old records)

SH-15: *Mémoires des navires que Maître François Poumet a fait à Rochefort*.

Musée National de la Marine

The Paris branch of the Musée national de la Marine is located in the Palais de Chaillot across the Seine from the Eiffel Tower. It also has branches elsewhere in France. The museum is in the process of moving its reference library to a new facility at Dugny, next to the le Bourget airport.

J-355: Constructions 1690 *Provenant de la collection de Monsieur Henry Ollivier Capitaine de frégate descendant des ingénieurs de ce nom et de leur cousin Coulomb*

B1125: Barras de la Penne, Jean-Antoine, *La science des galères qui renferme tout ce qui regarde la construction, l'armement, la manoeuvre, le combat et la navigation des galères*. Marseille, 1697

PUBLISHED SOURCES

Acerra, Martine, 'Les Constructeurs de la marine (XVIIe-XVIIIe siècle)', *Revue historique* (1985), No 343.

Acerra, Martine, *Rochefort et la construction navale française, 1661–1815*, 4 vols, Librairie de l'Inde Éditeur, Paris, 1992–93

Acerra, Martine (ed), *L'invention du vaisseau de ligne, 1450–1700*, Éditions SPM, Paris, 1997

Acerra, Martine and Meyer, Jean, *La grande époque de la marine à voile*, Éditions Ouest-France, Rennes, 1987

Acerra, Martine and Meyer, Jean, *Marines et Révolution*, Éditions Ouest-France, Rennes, 1988

Acerra, Martine and Zysberg André, *L'essor des marines de guerre européennes 1680–1790*, Paris, Éditions SEDES, Paris, 1997

Aman, Jacques, *Les Officiers bleus dans la marine française au XVIIIe siècle*, Librairie Droz, Paris, 1976.

Anderson, Roger Charles, *Naval Wars in the Levant, 1559–1853*, Princeton University Press, 1952.

Anderson, Roger Charles, *Naval Wars in the Baltic during the Sailing-Ship Epoch, 1522–1850*, C Gilbert-Wood, 1912.

Andrews, Robert J, 'Two Ships – Two Flags: the *Outaouaise/Williamson* and the *Iroquoise/Anson* on Lake Ontario, 1759–1761', *The Northern Mariner/Le marin du nord*, vol XIV no 3 (July 2004), pages 41–55

Anon, *Album de Colbert*, 1670, Éditions Omega, Nice, 1988 (reproduction of an album at the Service Historique des Armées, Marine cote 140-1 513)

Anon, 'Antoine Blaise Pangalo, Maistre constructeur des navires du Roy de 1681–1714', *Bulletin de la Société académique de Brest*, vol 13 (1887–1888), pages 251–276

Anon, *Bi-centenaire du Génie Maritime, 1765–1965*, S.P.E.I., Paris, c.1965

Anon, *Historique de l'Artillerie de la Marine*, D Dumoulin, Paris, 1889

Association des Descendants de Capitaines Corsaires, *Capitaines Corsaires: Audaces, fortunes et infortunes*, Saint-Malo, Éditions Cristel, 2014 (Jean-Yves Nerzic participated in the entry for Duguay-Trouin)

Atauz, Ayşe Devrim, *Eight Thousand Years of Maltese Maritime History: Trade, Piracy and Naval Warfare in the Central Mediterranean*, University Press of Florida, Gainesville, Fla, 2008.

Aubin, Nicholas, *Dictionnaire de Marine contenant les termes de la navigation et de l'architecture navale*, Brunel, Amsterdam, 1702 (later editions in 1742 and 1747)

Aubrey, Philip, *The Defeat of James Stuart's Armada 1692*, Leicester University Press, 1979

Babron, M, 'Les établissements impériaux de la Marine française: Indret', *Revue maritime et coloniale*, vol 23, no 89 (mai 1868), pp 123–148 and vol 24, septembre 1868, pp 495–526, also published separately by Arthus Bertrand, Paris

Bamford, Paul Waldon, *Fighting Ships and Prisons: the Mediterranean galleys of France in the Age of Louis XIV*, University of Minnesota Press, Minneapolis, 1973

Bamford, Paul Waldon, *Forests and French Sea Power, 1660–1789*. University of Toronto Press, Toronto, 1956

Barrachin, Jean, *Tableau des grandes batailles navales qui se sont livrées depuis le règne de Louis XIV jusqu'à la fin du règne de Charles X*, Paris, 1900

Barrey, Philippe, 'Notice sur les constructeurs de navires Havrais', *Recueil des publications de la Société Havraise d'études diverses*, 1907, pp 39–131

Beauchesne, Geneviève, *Historique de la construction navale à Lorient de 1666 à 1770*, Service historique de la Marine, Vincennes, 1980

Bender, James, *Dutch Warships in the Age of Sail 1600–1714: Design, Construction, Careers and Fates*, Seaforth Publishing, Barnsley, 2014

Blackmore, David S T, *Warfare on the Mediterranean in the Age of Sail: A History, 1571–1866*, McFarland & Company, Jefferson, NC, 2011

Blomfield, Sir Reginald, *Sébastien le Prestre de Vauban, 1633–1707*. Paris, 1938.

Blondel, Saint-Aubin, Guillaume (possible author or owner), *Construction des vaisseaux du Roy et le nom de toutes les pièces qui y entrent*, Jacques Hubault, Le Havre de Grace, 1691 (a similar *Nouveau traité des constructions des vaisseaux du Roy* was printed in 1693 at Rochefort by François Lafon)

Bonjean, Antoine Nicolas François, *Nouvelles échelles de déplacement: et de Centre de Gravité de carène, pour les vaisseaux de guerre*, Baudoin, Lorient, 1810.

Bonnefoux, Piere-Marie-Joseph Baron de and Paris, François-Edmond, *Dictionnaire de Marine à voiles et à vapeur, Marine à voiles*, 2nd edition, Arthus Bertrand, Paris, c.1853 (1st edition 1847)

Bonjean, Antoine Nicolas François, Nouvelles échelles de déplacement: et de Centre de Gravité de carène, pour les vaisseaux de guerre, Baudoin, Lorient, 1810.

Bonnel, Ulane (ed), *Fleurieu et la Marine de son temps*, Economica, Paris, 1992

Bouchet, Émile, *Les ports militaires de la France: Rochefort*, Challamel & Arthus Bertrand, Paris, 1865

Boudriot, Jean, and Berti, Hubert, *Brick de 24 Le Cygne de l'ingénieur Pestel (1806–1808), monographie*, Éditions ANCRE, Paris, 1987

Boudriot, Jean, and Berti, Hubert, *Cotre Le Cerf (1779–1780) du constructeur Denÿs, monographie*, Éditions ANCRE, Paris, n.d.

Boudriot, Jean, and Berti, Hubert, *Frégate de 18 La Vénus de l'ingénieur Sané 1782, Monographie*, Éditions ANCRE, Paris, n.d.

Boudriot, Jean, and Berti, Hubert, *Galiote à bombes La Salamandre 1752 du constructeur J M B Coulomb, Monograpie*, Éditions ANCRE, Paris, n.d.

Boudriot, Jean, and Berti, Hubert, *La frégate: Étude historique 1650–1850*, Éditions ANCRE, Paris, 1992 (also available in English)

Boudriot, Jean, and Berti, Hubert, *L'artillerie de mer: Marine française 1650–1850*, Éditions ANCRE, Paris, 1992

Boudriot, Jean, and Berti, Hubert, *Le Bateau de Lanvéoc, Petite marine XVIIe–XVIIIe, Survivances médiévales, Monographie*, Éditions ANCRE, Paris, 1988

Boudriot, Jean, and Berti, Hubert, *Le Requin, 1750: Chébecs et bâtiments Méditerranéens*, Éditions ANCRE, Paris, 1987

Boudriot, Jean, and Berti, Hubert, *Les vaisseaux de 50 et 64 canons, Étude historique, 1650–1780*, Éditions ANCRE, Paris, 1985 & 1994

Boudriot, Jean, and Berti, Hubert, *Les vaisseaux de 74 à 120 canons, Étude historique, 1650–1850*, Éditions ANCRE, Paris, 1995

Boudriot, Jean, and Berti, Hubert, *Lougre Le Coureur (1776) du constructeur D. Denÿs, monographie*, Éditions ANCRE, Paris, n.d.

Boudriot, Jean, and Delacroix, Gérard, *Vaisseau de 64 canons Le Fleuron du constructeur Blaise Ollivier, 1729, monographie*, ANCRE, Nice, 2014.

Boudriot, Jean, *Goélette La Jacinthe, 1825, de l'ingénieur-constructeur Delamorinière*, published by the author, Paris, 1989 (also available in English)

Boudriot, Jean, *John Paul Jones and the Bonhomme Richard, A Reconstruction of the Ship and an Account of the Battle with HMS Serapis*. English translation by David H Roberts, Naval Institute Press, Annapolis, 1987

Boudriot, Jean, *Le vaisseau de 74 canons*, 4 volumes, Éditions des Quatre Seigneurs, Grenoble, 1973–77 (also available in English)

Boudriot, Jean, *Monographie La Créole 1827: Historique de la corvette 1650–1850*, published by the author, Paris, 1990

Boudriot, Jean, 'Constructeurs et constructions navales à Rochefort aux XVIIe et XVIIIe siècles', *Neptunia* No.157, 1985, pp 14–25

Bouguer, Pierre, *Traité du navire, de sa construction et de ses mouvements*, Charles-Antoine Jombert, Paris, 1746

Boulaire, Alain, Boureille, Patrick and Émon-Naudin, Geneviève, *L'arsenal de Brest: 4 siècles d'industrie navale*, Éditions Palantines, Quimper, 2013.

Bourdé de Villehuet, Jacques, *Le manouevrier, ou Essai sur la théorie et la pratique des mouvements du navire et des évolutions navales*, Guerin & Delatour, Paris, 1765 (2nd edition 1769)

Bourdé de Villehuet, Jacques, *Manuel des marins, ou Explication des termes de marine*, 2 vols, Le Jeune, Paris, 1773

Bromley, John Selwyn, *Corsairs and Navies, 1660–1760*, Hambledon Press, London, 1987

Brun, Vincent-Félix, *Guerres maritimes de la France: Port de toulon, ses armements, son administration, dupuis son origine jusqu'au nos jours*, 2 vols, Henri Plon, Paris, 1861

Buti, Gilbert and Hrodej, Philippe (eds), *Dictionnaire des corsaires et pirates*. Paris, CNRS Éditions, 2013 (Jean-Yves Nerzic participated in the entries for Bordenave, Brest, Colbert, Courserac, Dandenne, d'Estrées, Gennes, Nagle, Nesmond, Nesmond de Brie, Pointis, Pontchartrain, and Saupin)

Calvé (Commissire général de la Marine), *Les ports militaires de la France, Toulon*, Challamel & Arthus Bertrand, Paris, c.1865

Chapman, Fredrik Henrik af, *Architectura Navalis Mercatoria*, originally published 1775; reprinted Praeger, New York, 1971.

Chasseriau, F, *Précis historique de la Marine française, son organisation et ses lois*, 2 vols, Imprimerie royale, Paris, 1845

Chernyshev, A A, *Rossiyskiy parusnyy flot, Spravochnik*, 2 vols, Voyennoye Izdatel'stvo, Moscow, 1997–2002

Chevalier, Édouard, *Histoire de la Marine Française pendant la guerre de l'independence américaine*, Hachette, Paris, 1877

Cleirac, Estienne, *Us et Coustumes de la mer*, Millanges, Bordeaux, 1661 (later edition 1671)

Clément, Pierre, *Histoire de la vie et de l'administration de Colbert*, Guillaumin, Paris, 1846

Clément, Pierre, *Lettres, Instructions, et Mémoires de Colbert. Tome III, 1re Partie, Marine et Galères,* Imprimérie Impériale, Paris, 1864

Clowes, Sir William Laird, *The Royal Navy: A History from the Earliest Times to 1900,* Vols 2 & 3, Sampson Low, Marston and Company, London, 1898; republished by Chatham Publishing, London, 1996

Colledge, J J and Warlow, Ben, *Ships of the Royal Navy, The Complete Record of all Fighting Ships of the Royal Navy from the 15th Century to the Present,* Casemate, Philadelphia and Newbury (UK), 2010

D'Houry, Laurent-Charles, *Almanach Royal,* D'Houry, Paris, 1780 and 1781 (first published 1699)

D'Houry, Laurent-Charles, *État de la Marine,* D'Houry, Paris, 1785

Dassié, Charles, *L'Architecture navale,* ANCRE, Paris, 2002 (reprint of the 1695 Paris edition which was identical to the 1677 edition)

Delacroix, Gérard and Berti, Hubert, *Tartane du roi La Diligente, 1738–1761, du constructeur Laurent Marchand,* ANCRE, Paris, 1997

Delacroix, Gérard, *Gabare du roi Le Gros Ventre conçu par Jean-Joseph Ginoux, exécuté à Bayonne par Léon Michel Guignace, 1766–1779,* ANCRE, Nice, 2003

Delacroix, Gérard, *L'Amarante, corvette de 12 canons du constructeur Joseph-Louis Ollivier, 1747,* Éditions Gérard Delacroix, L'Union, France, 2012

Delacroix, Gérard, *La petite marine du roi: Le Rochefort, 1787, Yacht de port.* Éditions Gérard Delacroix, L'Union, France, 2015

Delacroix, Gérard, *Les bâtiments de servitude: Machine à curer les ports, 1750, d'après la description de Bernard Forest de Bélidor, construite à Toulon vers 1745,* Éditions Gérard Delacroix, L'Union, France, 2013

Delacroix, Gérard, *Vaisseau de 118 canons Le Commerce de Marseille,* published by the author, L'Union, France, 2006

Demerliac, Cdt Alain, *La Marine de Louis XIII et de la régence d'Anne d'Autriche: Nomenclature des navires français de 1610 à 1661,* Éditions OMEGA, Nice, 2004

Demerliac, Cdt Alain, *La Marine de Louis XIV: Nomenclature des navires français de 1661 à 1715,* enlarged edition, Éditions OMEGA, Nice, 1995

Demerliac, Cdt Alain, *La Marine de Louis XV: Nomenclature des navires français de 1715 à 1774,* Éditions OMEGA, Nice, 1995

Demerliac, Cdt Alain, *La Marine de Louis XVI: Nomenclature des navires français de 1774 à 1792,* Éditions OMEGA, Nice, 1996

Depeyre, Michel, *Tactiques et stratégies navales de la France et du Royaume-Uni de 1690 à 1805,* Economica, Paris, 1998

Desroches (Officier des Vaisseaux du Roy), *Dictionnaire des termes propres de marine,* Auroy, Paris, 1687

Dessert, Daniel, *La Royale: Vaisseaux et marins du Roi-Soleil.* Librairie Arthème Fayard, 1996.

Dmowska, Aleksandra, *La Marine de guerre en France au XVIIe siècle: Colbert et le Dominium Maris Français,* Warsaw University, Aspra Publishing House, 2011

Duhamel du Monceau, Henri-Louis, *Eléments de l'architecture navale, ou Traité pratique de la construction des vaisseaux,* 2nd ed, Jombert, Paris, 1758

Dull, Jonathan R, *The French Navy and American Independence, A Study of Arms and Diplomacy, 1774–1787,* Princeton University Press, Princeton, 1975

Dull, Jonathan R, *The French Navy and the Seven Years' War,* University of Nebraska Press, Lincoln, 2005

Euler, Leonhard, *Scientia Navalis, seu Tractatus de Construendis ac Dirigendis Navibus Pars Prior Complectens Theoriam Universam de Situ ac Monti Corporam Aquae Innatantium,* St Petersburg, 1749.

Eymin, Eugène and Doneaud (professor), *Les ports militaires de la France, Brest,* Challamel & Arthus Bertrand, Paris, c.1866.

Falconer, William, *An Universal Dictionary of the Marine,* Cadell, London, 1780

Ferreiro, Larrie D, *Ships and Science: The Birth of Naval Architecture in the Scientific Revolution, 1600–1800.* The MIT Press, Cambridge, Mass & London, 2007.

Ferreiro, Larrie D, *Brothers at Arms: American Independence and the Men of France and Spain who saved it.* Alfred A Knopf, New York, 2016.

Fincham, John, *A History of Naval Architecture,* Whittaker, London, 1851.

Fournier, Georges, *Hydrographie, contenant la théorie et la practique de toutes les parties de la navigation,* Soly, Paris, 1643 (reprinted by Éditions des 4 Seigneurs, Grenoble, 1973).

Fox, Frank, *Great Ships, The Battlefleet of King Charles II,* Conway Maritime Press, Greenwich, 1980.

Gardiner, Robert (ed), *The Age of the Galley: Mediterranean Oared Vessels since Pre-classical Times,* Conway Maritime Press, London, 1995.

Gardiner, Robert (ed), *The Line of Battle: The Sailing Warship 1650–1840,* Conway Maritime Press, London, 1992

Gascoin, 'L'Île d'Indret et l'établissement de la Marine nationale', *Cahiers des salorges,* nos 7, 8 and 9 (1964), unpaged

Giorgetti, Franco, *The Great Sailing Ships: the history of sail from its origins to the present.* Edizioni White Star, Vercelli, Italy, 2001.

Glete, Jan, *Navies and Nations: Warships, Navies and State Building in Europe and America, 1500–1860,* 2 volumes, Almqvist & Wiksell, Stockholm, 1993

Glete, Jan, *Warfare at Sea, 1500–1650: Maritime conflicts and the transformation of Europe,* Routledge, London, 2000.

Gréhan, Amédée, *La France Maritime,* 4 vols, published by Dutertre (under the patronage of the Ministry of the Navy, Paris, 1852–53.

Gruss, Robert, *Dictionnaire Gruss de marine,* EMOM, Paris, 1978

Guérin, Léon, *Histoire maritime de France,* 6 vols, Dufour & Mulat, Paris, 1851 (expansion of original 2-vol edition)

Guéroult du Pas, Pierre-Jacob, *Recuëil des veües de tous les différens Bastimens de la mer Méditerrannée et de l'Océan, avec leurs noms et usages,* ANCRE, Nice, 2004 (reproduction of the 1710 edition published by Pierre Giffart in Paris.)

Guillet de Saint George, Georges, *Les Arts de l'homme d'epée, ou le Dictionnaire du Gentil-Homme, Seconde partie contenant L'Art militaire,* Clouzier, Paris, 1680 (other editions 1678 and 1681)

Guilmartin, John Francis, *Galleons and Galleys,* Cassell, London, 2002.

Harding, Richard, *Seapower and Naval Warfare, 1650–1830.* UCL Press, London, 1999.

Harland, John and Myers, Mark, *Seamanship in the Age of Sail,* London and Annapolis, 1984.

Harland, John, *Ships and Seamanship: The Maritime Prints of J J Baugean,* Chatham Publishing, London, 2000

Hayet (Commissaire), *Descrpition du vaisseau le Royal Louis,* Charles Brebion, Marseille, 1677

Hebert, J, *Les ports militaires de la France: Lorient.* Challamel & Arthus Bertrand, Paris, c.1865

Hepper, David J, *British Warship Losses in the Age of Sail, 1650–1859,* Jean Boudriot Publications, Rotherfield, England, 1994.

Hoste, Paul, *L'Art des armées navales, ou Traité des evolutions navales,* Anisson & Posuel, Lyon, 1697 (2nd edition 1727)

Hoste, Paul, *Théorie de la construction des vaisseaux,* Anisson & Posuel, Lyon, 1697

Howard, Frank, *Sailing Ships of War 1400–1860,* Conway Maritime Press, London, 1979

Jal, Augustin, *Glossaire nautique, Répertoire polyglotte de terms de marine anciens et modernes,* 2 vols, Firmin Didot, Paris, 1848

Jal, Augustin, *Abraham Du Quesne et la Marine de son temps,* 2 vols, Henri Plon, Paris, 1873

James, Alan, *Navy and Government in Early Modern France, 1572–1661,* The Boydell Press (for the Royal Historical Society), Woodbridge, Suffolk, 2004

Jenkins, Ernest H, *A History of the French Navy: From its Beginnings to the Present Day*, Macdonald and Jane's, London, 1973

Jouan, René, *Histoire de la Marine française*, Payot, Paris, 1950. (A 1932 edition was in two volumes, before and after 1789)

Jouve, Jean, *Deux albums des bâtiments de l'Atlantique et de la Méditerranée*, edited by Jacques Vichot, Association des Amis des Musées de la Marine, n.d. (reproduction of editions of 1679)

La Roncière, Charles de and Clerc-Rampal, G, *Histoire de la Marine française*, Paris, Librairie Larousse, 1934.

La Roncière, Charles de, *Histoire de la Marine française*, 6 vols, Paris, 1899–1932.

La Roque, Jean-Paul de, *De la théorie de la manouevre des vaisseaux*. Paris, 1689.

La Varende, Jean de, *Les Augustin-Normand: Sept générations de constructeurs de navires*, Imprimerie Floch, Mayenne, 1960

Lacour-Gayet, Georges, *La Marine militaire de la France sous le règne de Louis XVI*, Honoré Champion, Paris, 1905

Lacour-Gayet, Georges, *La Marine militaire de la France sous le règne de Louis XV*, Honoré Champion, Paris, 1902

Lacour-Gayet, Georges, *La Marine militaire de la France sous les règnes de Louis XIII et de Louis XIV, Tome I, Richelieu, Mazarin, 1624–1661*, Honoré Champion, Paris, 1911

Le Conte, Pierre, *Lists of Men-of-War, 1650–1700 Part II, French Ships, 1648–1700*, London, Cambridge University Press, 1935

Le Conte, Pierre, *Repertoire des navires de guerre français*, published by the author, Cherbourg, 1932

Le Moing, Guy, *Les 600 plus grandes batailles navales de l'histoire*, Marines Éditions, Rennes, 2011.

Lecalvé, Frank, *Liste de la flotte de guerre française*, published by the author, Toulon, 1993

Legohérel, Henri, *Les Trésoriers généraux de la Marine (1517–1788)*, Éditions Cujas, Paris, 1965

Lemineur, Jean-Claude and Villiers, Patrick, *L'Aurore, frégate légère de 18 canons, 1697–1720, suivant un plan original de Philippe Cochois*, ANCRE, Nice, 2012

Lemineur, Jean-Claude, *Les vaisseaux du Roi Soleil*, ANCRE, 2015 (first edition 1996, also available in English)

Lemineur, Jean-Claude, *Vaisseau de 5° Rang Le François, Manuscrit de François Coulomb, Toulon 1683*, ANCRE, Nice, n.d.

Lempereur, Charles (Commissaire d'Artillerie de la Marine), *Traité de l'Artillerie de la Marine*, L Baudoin, Paris, 1890 (reprint of original manuscript, Toulon, 1671)

Lescallier, Daniel, *Vocabulaire des termes de marine anglois et françois*, Imprimérie Royale, Paris, 1777 (later editions 1783, 1791, 1797, and 1800)

Levot, Prosper-Jean, *Histoire de la ville et du port de Brest*, 2 vols, Brest (by the author) and Paris, 1864–65

Lewis, James A, *Neptune's Militia: The Frigate South Carolina during the American Revolution*, Kent State University Press, Kent, Ohio, 1999

Little, Benerson, *The Sea Rover's Practice, Pirate Tactics and Techniques, 1630–1730*, Potomac Books, n.d., 2007

Lyon, David, *The Sailing Navy List: All the Ships of the Royal Navy Built, Purchased, and Captured, 1688–1860*, Conway Maritime Press, London, 1993

Mahan, Alfred Thayer, *The Major Operations of the Navies in the War of American Independence*, Cambridge, Mass, 1913

Mahan, Alfred Thayer, *The Influence of Sea Power upon History 1660-1805*, Sampson, Low, London, 1890

Malouet, Pierre Victor, baron, *Collection des opinions de M. Malouet, député à l'Assemblée Nationale*, 3 vols, Paris, 1791–92

Mancel, Émile, 'L'arsenal de la Marine et les chefs maritimes à Dunkerque, 1662–1899', *Société Historique de Dunkerque, Bulletin*, vol 3 (1900), pp 5–174 and 313–550

Marquardt, Karl Heinz, *Eighteenth-Century Rigs and Rigging*, Phoenix Publications, Cedarburg, Wisconsin, 1992.

Mansfield, John Brandt (ed), *History of the Great Lakes*, 2 vols, J H Beers, Chicago, 1899

Martin, Alphonse, *La Marine militaire au Havre (XVIe & XVIIe siècles)*, Durand, Fécamp, 1899

Marzagalli, Silvia (ed), *Bordeaux et la Marine de guerre (XVIIe – XXe siècles)*, Presses Universitaries de Bordeaux, 2002

Mascart, Jean, *La vie et les travaux du chevalier Jean-Charles de Borda (1733–1799)*, Presses de l'Université de Paris-Sorbonne, Paris, 2000

Masson, Paul, *Les galères de France (1481–1781), Marseille, port de guerre*, Hachette, Paris, 1938

Masson, Philippe, *Histoire de la Marine, Tome I, L'ère de la Voile*, Charles Lavauzelle, Paris, 1981

MacLeod, Malcolm, 'French and British Strategy in the Lake Ontario Theatre of Operations, 1754–1760', PhD Thesis, University of Ottawa, 1974

McLaughlan, Ian, *The Sloop of War, 1650–1763*, Seaforth Publishing, Barnsley, 2014

Meirat, Jean, 'Le Siège de Toulon en 1707', in *Neptunia* no 71; Summer 1963.

Mémain, René, *La Marine de guerre sous Louis XIV, Le Matériel. Rochefort Arsenal Modèle de Colbert*, Librarie Hachette, Paris, 1937

Meyer, Jean, and Acerra, Martine, *Histoire de la marine française des origines à nos jours*, Éditions Ouest-France, Rennes, 1994

Mordal, Jacques, *Twenty-five Centuries of Sea Warfare*, Editions Robert Laffont, 1959. Translated into English by Len Ortzen, 1970.

Morineau, Pierre, *Repertoir de construction*, ANCRE, Nice, n.d. (reproduction of a manuscript at the Archives Nationales cote Marine G-246)

Nerzic, Jean-Yves and Buchet, Christian, *Marins et flibustiers du Roi-Soleil, Carthagène 1697*, Éditions PyréGraph, Aspet, 2002

Nerzic, Jean-Yves, *Duguay-Trouin. Armateur malouin, corsaire brestois*, Milon-la-Chapelle, Éditions H & D, 2012

Nerzic, Jean-Yves, *La place des armements mixtes dans la mobilisation de l'arsenal de Brest sous les deux Pontchartrain (1688–1697 et 1702–1713)*, 2 vols, Éditions H & D, Milon-la-Chapelle, 2010. (*Thèse de doctorat*, 1,289 pages)

Neuville, Didier, *État sommaire des archives de la Marine antérior à la Révolution*, Paris, 1898 (Kraus Reprint, 1977).

Neuville, J L, *Les ports militaires de la France: Cherbourg, Brest, Lorient, Rochefort, Toulon*, Hachette, Paris, 1854

Norman, Capt Charles Boswell, *The Corsairs of France*, Sampson Low, Marston, Searle & Rivington, London, 1887

Ollivier, Blaise, *Remarks on the Navies of the English and the Dutch from Observations made at their Dockyards in 1737*. Translated and edited by David H. Roberts, Jean Boudriot Publications, Rotherfield, England, 1992

Ollivier, Blaise, *Traité de construction*, Éditions du Petit Vincent, Brezolles, France, 2013 (transcription by Gérard Delacroix of a manuscript dating from 1736 held by the Service Historique des Armées, Marine cote SH 134)

Ortzen, Len, *Guns at Sea: The World's Great Naval Battles*, BCA, London, 1976.

Ozanam, Jacques, *Dictionnaire mathématique*, Estienne Michallet, Paris, 1691 (with a *Liste de plusieurs termes de Marine* on pages 220–250)

Ozanne, Nicholas-Marie, *Marine militaire, ou recueil des differens vaisseaux qui servent à la guerre*, Paris (by the author), 1762

Padfield, Peter, *Guns at Sea*, Hugh Evelyn, London, 1974.

Pâris, *Vice-amiral* François Edmond, *Souvenirs de marine: Collection de plans ou dessins de navires et de bateaux anciens ou modernes, existants ou disparus avec les élémens numériques nécessaire à leur construction*, 6 vols, Gauthier-Villars, Paris, 1882–1908.

Paullin, Charles Oscar, *The Navy of the American Revolution*, University of Chicago, Chicago, 1906

Peter, Jean, *Le port et l'arsenal de Brest sous Louis XIV*, Economica and the Institut de Stratégie Comparée, 1998

Peter, Jean, *Le port et l'arsenal de Rochefort sous Louis XIV*, Economica and the Institut de Stratégie Comparée, 2001

Peter, Jean, *Le port et l'arsenal de Toulon sous Louis XIV*, Economica and the Institut de Stratégie Comparée, 1995

Peter, Jean, *Le port et l'arsenal du Havre sous Louis XIV*, Economica and the Institut de Stratégie Comparée, 1995

Peter, Jean, *Vauban et Toulon: Histoire de la construction d'un port-arsenal sous Louis XIV*, Economica, 1994

Peter, Jean, *L'artillerie et les fonderies de la Marine sous Louis XIV*, Economica and the Institut de Stratégie Comparée, 1995

Peters, Andrew, *Ship Decorations, 1630–1780*, Seaforth Publishing, Barnsley, 2013

Petiet, Claude, *Le bailli de Forbin, lieutenant-général des galères*, Lanore, Paris, 2003.

Pfister-Langanay, Christian, *Constructeurs, charpentiers et navires à Dunkerque du XVIIe au XXe siècle*, Société Dunkerquoise d'Histoire et d'Archéologie, n.d. (c.2002)

Piouffre, Gérard and Simoni, Henri, *3 siècles de croiseurs français*, Marines éditions, Nantes, 2001

Polak, Jean, *Bibliographie maritime française depuis les temps les plus reculés jusqu'à 1914*, Éditions des 4 Seigneurs, Grenoble, 1976

Poncet de la Grave, Guillaume, *Précis historique de la Marine Royale de France depuis l'origine de la monarchie jusqu'au Roi régnant*, Eugéne Onfroy, Paris, 1780.

Preston, Richard A and Lamontagne, Leopold, *Royal Fort Frontenac*, The Champlain Society, Toronto, 1958

Pritchard, James, *Louis XV's Navy 1748–1762: A Study of Organization and Administration*, McGill-Queen's University Press, Kingston and Montreal, 1987

Randier, Jean, *La Royale, La Vergue et le Sabord, l'histoire illustrée de la Marine nationale française des origines à la fin de la voile*, Éditions de la Cité, Paris, 1978

Renau d'Elissararay, Bernard. *De la Théorie de la manoeuvre des vaisseaux*, Estienne Michallet, Paris, 1689.

Roberts, David H, *Vocabulaire de marine/A Marine Vocabulary* (bilingual dictionary), ANCRE, Nice, 1994

Roche, Lieutenant de vaisseau Jean-Michel, *Dictionnaire des bâtiments de la flotte de guerre française de Colbert à nos jours*, Tome I (1671–1870), Groupe Rezotel - Maury Millau, 2005

Rolt, Richerd *An Impartial Representation of the Conduct of the Several Powers of Europe ... Including a Particular Account of All the Military and Naval Operations from ... 1739 to ... 1748*, 4 vols, 2nd ed, S Birt, London, 1753.

Savérien, Alexandre, *Dictionnaire historique, théorique et pratique de marine*, , Charles-Antoine Jombert, Paris, 1758 (updated edition in 1781)

Severance, Frank H, *An Old Frontier of France: The Niagara Region and Adjacent Lakes under French Control*, 2 vols, Dodd, Mead, New York, 1917

Sottas, Jules, *Histoire de la Compagnie Royale des Indes Orientales, 1664–1719*, Plon, Paris, 1905

Surirey de Saint Remy, Sieur (Commissaire Provincial de l'Artillerie), *Mémoires d'artillerie*, 2 vols, Imprimérie Royale, Paris, 1697 (later editions in 1707 and 1741)

Symcox, Geoffrey, *The crisis of French sea power 1688–1697: from the guerre d'escadre to the guerre de course*, Martinus Nijhoff, The Hague, 1974.

Taillemite, Étienne, *Dictionnaire des marins français*, EMOM, 1992

Taillemite, Étienne, *L'Histoire ignorée de la Marine française*, Perrin, Paris, 1988

Torchet de Boismêlé, Jean Baptiste, with Ch-A. Bourdot de Richebourg and Le P Théodore de Blois, *Histoire générale de la Marine*, 3 vols, 1744–1758 (vol 3 contains the *Code des Armées navales*, a compilation of ordonnances and règlements on the Navy from 1669 to 1757)

Toudouze, Georges, *La bataille de la Hougue 29 mai 1692*, Librairie militaire R Chapelot, Paris, 1899

Tramond, Joannès, *Manuel d'histoire maritime de la France des origines à 1815*, Société d'éditions géographiques, maritimes et coloniales, Paris, 1927.

Tredrea, John, and Sozaev, Eduard, *Russian Warships in the Age of Sail, 1696–1860*, Seaforth Publishing, Barnsley, 2010

Troude, Onésime-Joachim, *Batailles navales de la France*, 4 vols, Challamel Ainé, Paris, 1867

Veres, László and Woodman, Richard, *The Story of Sail*, Naval Institute Press, Annapolis, 1999.

Vergé-Franceschi, Michel, *La Marine française au XVIIIe siècle: guerres, administration, exploration*, Éditions SEDES, Paris, 1996 (1991?)

Vergé-Franceschi, Michel, *Les Officiers généraux de la marine royale (1715–1774)*, Paris 1990

Vérin, Hélène, 'Spectacle ou experimentation : La Préfabrication des vaisseaux en 1679', *Revue de Synthèse* (1987), vol 108

Vial du Clairbois, Honoré-Sébastien, *Encyclopédie méthodique: marine*, 3 vols, Panckoucke, Paris, 1783, 1786 and 1787. (Contributors included Blondeau, La Courdraie, Saverien, Bourdé de la Villehuet, Bellin, Lescalier, and Aubin. The 1793 edition was entitled *Dictionnaire encyclopédique de Marine*)

Viaud, Jean-Théodore and Fleury, Élie-Jérôme, *Histoire de la ville et du port de Rochefort*, 2 vols, Fleury, Rochefort, 1845

Vichot, Jacques (ed.), *L'album de l'Amiral Willaumez*, Association des Amis des Musées de la Marine, Paris, n.d.

Vichot, Jacques, *Répertoire des navires de guerre français*, Association des Amis des Musées de la Marine, Paris, 1967

Villette-Mursay, Philippe Marquis de, *Mes campagnes de mer sous Louis XIV — avec un dictionnaire des personnages et des batailles*, edited by Michel Vergé-Franceschi, Tallandier, Paris, 1991Villiers, Patrick, *La France sur mer: De Louis XIII à Napoléon Ier*, Pluriel (A Fayard), Paris, 2015

Villiers, Patrick, *La Marine de Louis XVI, de Choiseul à Sartine*, Jean-Pierre Debbane (éditeur), Grenoble, 1985

Villiers, Patrick, *Les corsaires du littoral, Dunkerque, Calais, Boulogne, de Philippe II à Louis XIV (1568–1713)*, Presses universitaires du Septentrion, Villeneuve-d'Ascq, 2000

Villiers, Patrick, *Marine royale, corsaires et trafic de l'Atlantique: de Louis XIV à Louis XVI*, (thèse, Lille), ANRT, 1991 (new edition 2007)

Willis, Sam, *The Struggle for Sea Power: A Naval History of American Independence*. Atlantic Books, London, 2015.

Winfield, Rif, and Roberts, Stephen S, *French Warships in the Age of Sail 1786–1861: Design, Construction, Careers and Fates*, Seaforth Publishing, Barnsley, 2015

Winfield, Rif, *British Warships in the Age of Sail 1603–1714: Design, Construction, Careers and Fates*, Seaforth Publishing, Barnsley, 2009

Winfield, Rif, *British Warships in the Age of Sail 1714–1792: Design, Construction, Careers and Fates*, Seaforth Publishing, Barnsley, 2007

Winfield, Rif, *First Rate : The Greatest Warships of the Age of Sail*, Seaforth Publishing, Barnsley, 2010.

Zysberg, André, *Marseille au temps des galères, 1660–1748*, Marseille, Rivages, 1983

Glossary and Abbreviations

This section provides descriptions of many of the terms likely to be encountered in material pertaining to the French Navy with translations when there is an equivalent English term and associated abbreviations used in this book. The French terms are given in italics. In the available space here, only a fraction of the terms found can be given; the reader is encouraged to consult a bilingual maritime/naval directory like the recent one by David H Roberts (see bibliography).

PERSONNEL AND NAVAL RANKS
The whole crew – officers, petty officers, seamen and boys – were termed the *équipage*; the commissioned officers comprised the *état-major*, including the officers of the Garrison (see below), the *chirurgien-major* (chief medical officer), the *aumônier* (chaplain) and (under Louis XIV) the *écrivain* (purser), who later became a supernumerary called the *secrétaire*. The abbreviations that we use in the text for the different grades of officers are shown in parentheses.

In November 1669 Louis XIV suppressed Richelieu's *grande maîtrise*, re-established the *amirauté de France* (although *amiraux* were selected as infants to limit their power), and created the *vice-amirautés* of the *Levant* and *Ponant* as offices of the French Crown. Naval officers could hold the office of *Vice-amiral* (Vice Admiral), making it effectively the most senior naval grade, although Vice Admirals rarely commanded at sea because of age.

Officers of the Crown (see Appendix E for the names of the holders of these offices)
Amiral de France
Vice-amiral ès mer du Ponant
Vice-amiral ès mer du Levant

Commissioned Officers
Lieutenant-général (LG). The highest grade of flag officer normally encountered at sea. The full title was *Lieutenant général des armées navales* to distinguish it from the *Lieutenant général* in the army. It was redesignated in 1791 as *Vice-Amiral* (Vice Admiral).
Chef d'escadre (CdE). Captains of considerable seniority were given this flag-level grade when commanding three-decked ships of the line, or when serving as the senior captain of a small squadron. This grade was redesignated in 1791 as *Contre-Amiral* (Rear Admiral).
Capitaine de vaisseau (CV). Commanded ships of the line and other large ships.
Capitaine de frégate légère (CFL). Officers of this 'intermediate grade' were given precedence over *lieutenants de vaisseau* in 1672 and *capitaines de brûlot* in 1674. They could serve as the second-in-command of a ship of the line as the *Major de vaisseau*. The grade could also be awarded on a temporary basis for a specific mission. It was suppressed in 1786 but reappeared in 1795 as the *capitaine de frégate*.
Lieutenant de vaisseau (LV). The most numerous grade of officer along with the *enseigne de vaisseau*.
Capitaine de brûlot (CB). An 'intermediate grade' created for merchant seamen and naval petty officers who did not qualify for the main officer corps but who demonstrated exceptional courage and skill. When not embarked on a fireship these officers ranked between lieutenants and ensigns. The grade was suppressed at the beginning of the French Revolution.
Enseigne de vaisseau (EV). The lowest rank of commissioned officer, roughly speaking equivalent to the senior midshipman in the British Navy or ensign in the US Navy. Redesignated *sous-lieutenant de vaisseau* in 1786.
Lieutenant de frégate légère (LFL). An 'intermediate grade' created for merchant seamen and naval petty officers who did not qualify for the main officer corps.
Capitaine de flûte. An 'intermediate grade' created for *maîtres pilotes* (master pilots) who were given command of the navy's *flûtes*. They were subordinate to all of the military officer grades.
Garde de la Marine (GM). Young nobles in training to become naval officers. Renamed *élèves de la Marine* in 1786.

Ratings
Officiers-mariniers (petty officers, non-commissioned officers). The senior *officiers-mariniers* were those who were the masters (*maîtres*) in various specialities, including under Louis XIV the *maître entretenu*, *second-maître*, *contremaître*, *capitaine des matelots*, *bosseman*, *quartier-maître*, *maître de chaloupe*, *maître de canot*, *aide*, *pilote côtier*, and *plongeur* (diver). In later periods the *maîtres* included the master of manoeuvre (i.e. sailing master, or *premier maître*), of pilotage (*premier pilot*), of gunnery (*maître-canonnier*), of carpentry (*maître-charpentier*), of caulking (*maître-calfat*) and of sailmaking (*maître-voilier*), together with the boatswain (*maître d'équipage*). The *premier pilot* was the sailing master, and there were several grades of this rate of petty officer.
Matelots (seaman). There were distinctions among the more skilled, including the *timonier* (quartermaster or helmsman) and *gabier* (topman, experienced in reefing or setting topsails); note that a *gabier de port* was a dockyard rigger.
Mousses (boys). The underage members of the crew, such as the powder monkeys. At age 16 the *mousse* would become a *novice* until the time he was able to qualify as a *matelot*.
Officiers non mariniers (supernumeraries). Commonly known as in Britain as the idlers (*fainéants*) as they did not have to stand as part of a watch, comprised the artisans working with weapons and metallic trades, the commissary personnel (stewards, cooks, etc) and the medical personnel.
Soldats de marine (the garrison). As in British ships, there was on each ship a cadre of full-time professional soldiers of marines, separately organised in military regiments, and distinct from the maritime officers and crew, with their own officers who were directly responsible to the *capitaine de vaisseau* and *capitaine de frégate*. They provided the artillery specialists, the infantry (when a landing party was required) and the ship's police force.

The naval artillery had a separate rank structure headed (under Louis XIV) by one *commissaire général de l'artillerie* for the *Levant* and one for the *Ponant* and including *capitaines de galiotes et d'artillerie* (CGA) and *lieutenants de galiotes et d'artillerie* (LGA).

Equivalencies between the grades in the Army and these naval ranks were as follows:

Lieutenant général des armées (army): *Lieutenant général des armées navales*.
Maréchal de camp (army): *Chef d'escadre*
Colonel d'infanterie (army): *Capitaine de vaisseau, Commissaire-général de l'artillerie*
Lieutenant-colonel (army): *Capitaine de frégate légère, Capitaine de galiote et d'artillerie*
Capitaine (army): *Lieutenant de vaisseau, Lieutenant de galiote et d'artillerie, Capitaine de brûlot.*
Lieutenant (army): *Enseigne de vaisseau, Lieutenant de frégate légère, Capitaine de flûte.*

DECK LEVELS IN A WARSHIP (described in ascending order).
Cale. The hold, directly above the ship's keel (*quille*)
Marchepied. Platform; these were (in some vessels) non-continuous deck levels within the upper part of the hold.
Faux pont. Orlop deck; a (mainly) continuous deck level within the ship, usually at or below the waterline.
Premier pont. The lower deck of a two- or three-decked ship of the line (habitually called the gun deck in a British ship), carrying the largest-calibre – and heaviest – carriage-mounted guns.
Second pont. The middle deck in a three-decked ship of the line, or the upper deck in a two-decker.
Troisième pont. The upper deck in a three-decked ship of the line; this was the highest continuous deck of a ship, carrying the smaller carriage guns (although if guns were mounted on the *gaillards*, they were smaller still).
Gaillards. This term describes the superstructure of a warship, above the continuous upper deck, encompassing both the quarterdeck (*gaillard d'arrière* in French) and the forecastle (*gaillard d'avant*) in English equivalent terminology and sometimes including gangways linking quarterdeck and forecastle along the side of the ship
Dunette. On some ships of the line, there was a further level above the quarterdeck equivalent to the poop deck or roundhouse deck in British ships, although this level rarely carried cannon by 1786.

PLEASE NOTE that in this volume we have retained the abbreviations 'LD' (for lower deck), 'MD' (for middle deck), 'UD' (for upper deck), 'Fc' (for forecastle), and 'QD' (for quarterdeck) as more familiar to English-speaking readers.

TOP HAMPER The masts, spars, rigging and sails of a ship.
Mât de misaine. The foremast (also *phare de l'avant* for a square-rigged ship)
Petit mât de hune. The fore topmast
Grand mât. The mainmast (also *phare du milieu* for a square-rigged ship)
Grand mât de hune. The main topmast
Mât d'artimon. The mizzen mast
Mât de perroquet de fougue. The mizzen topmast
Mâtereau or *Mâtreau.* A small mast or vertical spar.
Vergue. A yard, a horizontal spar hoisted and fixed on a mast.
Vergue de misaine. Fore yard
Vergue de petit hunier. Fore topsail yard
Vergue de petit perroquet. Fore topgallant yard
Grand-vergue. Main yard
Vergue de grand hunier. Main topsail yard
Vergue de grand perroquet. Main topgallant yard
Vergue de vigie. Royal yard
Note the masts and spars as a whole were termed the *mâture*.
Basse voile. A lower sail (or course)

Voile à corne. A gaff sail
Voile à livarde, A sprit sail
Voile au tiers, voile à bourcet. A lug sail
Voile aurique. Fore-and-aft sail, including the three above
Voile carrée. Square sail
Voile de cacatois. Royal sail (*i.e.* a sail on a royal yard)
Voile de senault. A try-sail
Voile d'étai. Staysail

OTHER PARTS AND FITTINGS OF A SHIP
Apôtre. Knighthead
Étambot. Sternpost
Étrave. Stempost
Figure de proue. Figurehead
Galèrie de combat. Carpenter's walk
Poulaines. The 'heads'
Roue de gouvernail. Ship's (steering) wheel
Sabord. Gunport
Sainte-Barbe. Gunroom

ARMAMENT / ORDNANCE
Affût. Gun carriage
Boulet. Shot (as in projectile); round shot was *boulet rond*
Canon. A carriage gun, in sizes from 36pdr (occasionally larger) down to 2pdr
Gargousse. Cartridge for use with large-calibre guns
Obusier. Short (33in) bronze 36pdr howitzer firing explosive shells (hence its name) introduced on large French ships in 1787 in response to British carronades but replaced by French iron carronades between 1795 and 1806. Term also used for captured British carronades.
Pierrier. Swivel-mounted gun (a light anti-personnel weapon), originally a primitive weapon loaded from the top near the rear, became in the 1700s a miniature standard cannon, 2pdr or less. From 1786 only a bronze 1pdr model was produced.
Espingole. Swivel-mounted anti-personnel firearm like the English blunderbuss firing multiple small lead projectiles or shrapnel.

TYPES OF VESSEL. The descriptions of certain vessels, notably those with traditional Mediterranean rigs, differed from British usage, and we have attempted here to identify the main types, including translations of the French names where possible. The reader should understand that ship-type definitions are notoriously imprecise, and varied with time and place, so this list necessarily concentrates on vessels of the types and dates found in this book.

1. The following major types carried a ship rig (*i.e.* were three-masted, carrying square sails on the fore and main masts, and with a fore-and-aft sail set on the mizzen but surmounted by a square topsail), although many *barques longues,* corvettes and *gabarres* before the mid-1700s had a two-masted rig.
Vaisseaux. Literally 'vessels', initially a generic word for any seagoing ship with three masts and a bowsprit, the sails being square except for a lateen sail on the mizzen. By the 1770s they were divided into three categories, *vaisseaux de ligne* having 50 or 60 guns or more (meaning that they had two or three full batteries of carriage guns), *vaisseaux de guerre* being a generic term for smaller armed naval ships, and *vaisseaux marchands* or *de commerce* that engaged in trade worldwide.
Frégates-vaisseaux. Ships of the 4th or 5th Rank with two batteries of carriage guns but too small to lie in the line of battle.

Functionally replaced by single-battery 'true' frigates after the 1740s.

Frégates. A new type of frigate introduced in around 1740 with a single continuous battery of carriage guns on its upper deck, the lower or gun deck now being at or below the waterline with no gunports or other openings.

Frégates légères. Vessels with a single battery of carriage guns on their only deck. This type went out of use after around 1740 and was functionally replaced by the corvette. In the 1660s they were called *frégates d'avis*.

Barques longues and *corvettes*. *Barques longues* were initially small vessels that were longer and lower than ordinary *barques*, with sharp lines forward, and propelled by sails and oars. They could have one deck or be open (undecked) with only a narrow platform (*courcive*) along the sides. They typically had a tall mainmast, a short foremast and a bowsprit. By the 1730s, now called corvettes, they had grown into miniature frigates of 50 to 80ft in length with a ship rig and carrying from 4 to 18 guns, usually 4pdrs. By 1780 the largest were of 120ft in length and carried 8pdrs.

Flûtes (*flustes*). Initially large specialized Dutch merchant cargo vessels of 300 tons or more with a very flat floor, tall sterns that were as round as their bows, and rounded sides with a narrow deck. They had a ship rig with masts that were shorter than usual, allowing them to be sailed economically by small crews. By 1680 the French Navy was using the term *flûte* to refer to all of its large cargo ships, including both the Dutch type and conventional ships with square sterns. After about 1715 the French Navy shifted from round to square sterns in its purpose-built *flûtes*. French naval *flûtes* were analogous to British naval storeships.

Gabarres (*gabares*). Initially open (undecked) flat-bottomed lighters or barges, service craft that were used to load and unload seagoing ships, especially in the Loire River. After 1715 the French developed seagoing *gabarres* to carry timber along the coast to naval dockyards. Below the waterline their hulls resembled flûtes with square sterns while above the waterline they resembled corvettes. They had a large hatch amidships for loading timbers. By the 1730s they had a standard ship rig.

2. The following, designated by their rig, hull configuration, or function, illustrate the wide variety of smaller types in French service. When the names of types are similar those designated *Levant* originated in the Mediterranean while those designated *Ponant* originated in the Atlantic or Channel regions.

Barques de l'Océan (*Ponant*). Initially Northern European merchant vessels that rarely exceeded 100 or 200 tons and had a single deck plus a quarterdeck and three masts. Smaller ones had a single mast and a large sail, although they could step a short foremast right forward for long voyages. By the late eighteenth century *barque* was a generic word in Northern Europe for a ship in the 100- to 150-ton range with a single deck that could be rigged in many different ways.

Barques à voiles latines (*Levant*). Relatively short and broad vessels with a single deck and triangular lateen sails on three masts used for trade in Provence and Languedoc and for privateering. *Polacres* were barques with short bowsprits, while *pinques* were barques with narrow poops.

Bateaux-canonniers (artillery boats). Small armed invasion vessels that also transported artillery

Bateaux-plats (flatboats). Flat-bottomed cargo lighters for harbour service and for carrying invasion troops (generally not listed here).

Batteries flottantes (floating batteries). Harbour defence craft, often old ships cut down.

Bélandres (bilanders). Cargo vessels of not over 80 tons generally used on the coasts of Picardy and Flanders. They had flat bottoms like *flûtes* but had only one deck with no upperworks above it. Early bilanders were rigged as hoys with fore-and-aft sails on one or two masts and had leeboards to allow them to sail close-hauled despite their shallow draught. Later ones were rigged as brigantines, snows, or sloops.

Biscayennes (*chaloupes biscayennes*). Basque fishing or whaling craft of from 6 to 20 metres in length, without a deck, rigged with two lugsails, and capable of being rowed.

Bricks (brigs, the term *brigs* was also used quite often in French). Two-masted vessels with a square-rigged foremast and a mainmast with square topsails and a fore-and-aft course. Naval brigs were designed for speed and developed complex rigs.

Brigantins (*Levant*). Essentially feluccas modified for military use as privateers. Levantine brigantines resembled feluccas in typically having no deck, two masts with lateen sails (one amidships and one well forward), around 12 banks of oars, and an armament of two chase guns and some *pierriers*.

Brigantins (*Ponant*). Initially small vessels similar to Levantine brigantines without decks and with low freeboard propelled by oars and sails. They had 12 to 15 banks of oars, one man per oar, and were used for privateering. They were similar to but smaller and lighter than *galiotes à rames*; half-galleys were probably similar. By 1710 in northern Europe the term 'brigantine' was becoming associated with a rig – a two-masted vessel with a mainmast with a fore-and-aft main course and a square topsail, a square-rigged foremast, and a bowsprit. It was used primarily by the British as a merchantman and evolved into the brig (*brick*).

Brûlots (fireships). Generally converted from another type of vessel and fitted with a sallyport to allow the crew to escape after setting fire to the ship alongside an enemy vessel.

Bugalets. Small sailing vessels used in Brittany, particularly at Brest, to carry provisions or other supplies to warships in the roadstead and for coastal navigation and short voyages. Their hulls resembled *double chaloupes* below the waterline and barques above it. They had a single deck, a mainmast with two square sails, a foremast with one, and a small bowsprit.

Caichse (*quaiches*). Small cargo vessels or barques used mostly in the English Channel fitted with single decks and had rigs including fore-and-aft main courses similar to those of hoys and yachts. By the 1730s they ranged from 60 to 150 tons, and a few carried two or four 4pdr guns and had heads like warships. By the 1770s the British word 'ketch' was normally used for this primarily British type, which by then was a two-masted vessel with a mainmast stepped amidships, a mizzen mast well aft, and a long bowsprit.

Caïques. Small oared launches carried by Mediterranean galleys, similar in function to the *chaloupes* carried by *vaisseaux*.

Canonnières or *chaloupes-canonnières*. Gunboats and gun launches.

Chaloupes. Launches or ship's long-boats capable of carrying artillery. The British word 'sloop' shares its derivation with *chaloupe*, reflecting the ancestry of both the British sloop and the French corvette.

Chasse-marées. Vessels of lower (western) Brittany that had fine hull lines, a deck, and two masts each with a lug sail. They were handy and fast under sail, particulary close-hauled. They transported fish and other cargo along the coast.

Chattes (Dutch *kat sonder ooren*). Vessels of 60 to 80 tons that were low and flat and whose ends were low, blunt, and had rounded sides. They probably lacked decks. These roughly built craft had two masts and were used to transport the guns and the provisions of ships, especially at Rochefort.

Chébecs (xebecs or zebecs). Fast heavily-armed three-masted lateen-rigged vessel developed in the mid-eighteenth century to combat Barbary privateers. Xebecs carried from 14 to 22 medium sized carriage guns on a single battery deck with oar ports between the gunports and were military equivalent to contemporary corvettes.

Cotres (cutters). Fast single-masted British vessels extensively used by smugglers whose single-masted rig with a large fore-and-aft main course and several large jibs resembled that of a sloop, except that its mast was usually raked aft and had more spars and sails to maximize its speed. Like luggers, the rig of these vessels became difficult to handle as they increased in size for naval use.

Demi-Galères (half-galleys). Small galleys; in contrast with a typical galley with 26 banks of oars and 5 oarsmen per oar, a half-galley might have 20 banks of oars with 3 rowers per oar. They typically had the usual two-masted galley rig (although a third small mast was later added right aft), one chase gun and two smaller guns forward, and some *pierriers*.

Dogres (doggers). Dutch vessels used for fishing cod and herring on the Dogger Bank and in more distant fishing grounds like Iceland. They had a single mast with two square sails, a bowsprit, and a small mizzen mast with a lugsail. There was a fish tank in the hold.

Double chaloupes. Initially 40 to 50ft long with a complete or partial deck, *pierriers* on the side rails, and rigged with lateen sails in the same manner as a ship' launch or longboat. Larger ones had a two-masted rig and, in Britain, up to 12 guns.

Félouques (feluccas). Coastal Mediterranean merchant vessels initially not much larger than a launch that originated in Italy. They typically had no deck, one or two masts with lateen sails, and twelve banks of oars. Their hull form and rig resembled those of galleys but they were a lot smaller.

Flibots (flyboats, from the Dutch *vlie-boot*). Dutch-style *flûtes* of not over 100 tons and with only two masts, though some had a mizzen mast with a fore-and-aft balancing sail. Sometimes called pinks in England.

Frégates-bombardiers (bomb frigates). A type, of which three (listed in Chapter 7) were built in the mid-1690s, that combined the small 5th Rank two-decked *frégate-vaisseau* and the *galiote à bombes*. They had batteries of 8pdrs like the *frégate-vaisseaux* but also carried two mortars.

Galères (galleys). Low-freeboard warships propelled primarily by oars but also usually having two lateen-rigged masts (the *trinquet* forward and the *arbre de mestre* amidships) and a few forward-firing guns in the bow.

Galiotes (Levant). The Mediterranean *galiote à rames* was a small galley that was used for privateering because of its light weight. It had one or two masts, a few *pierriers*, and 16 to 20 banks of oars with one man per oar. It had minimal upperworks and no deck, thus being little more than a large *chaloupe* or launch.

Galiotes (Ponant). Dutch galiotes (*galiottes*, *galjoots*) or *galiottes hollandoises* were medium sized ships with a hoy rig, *i.e.* a single mast with a fore-and-aft course, a square topsail, and a bowsprit. They also had a small mizzen mast with a fore-and-aft balancing sail. The largest ones reached 300 tons. Galiotes had the underwater lines of *flûtes* and low upperworks. With crews of only five or six men they could make long voyages including to the East Indies. In France they were common at Rouen and other ports of Normandy. Galiotes destined to serve as *yachts d'avis* and not as cargo carriers had lighter, lower hulls and thicker masts with more sails. Those built for fishing were smaller and had large holds for fish.

Galiotes à bombes. Bomb or mortar vessels strongly built, with a flat bottom and without lower decks that carried mortars on a platform in the hold. Their rig consists of a tall mast amidships aft of the mortars and a mizzen mast, similar to the ketch rig of early English bomb vessels. Also called *galiotes à mortiers* and *bombardes*.

Garde-côtes. Coast defence vessels, in the sailing navy generally small converted craft.

Goélettes (schooners). Two-masted vessels of 50 to 100 tons with fore-and-aft courses on both masts, in some cases with square topsails on one or both masts, used mainly by the British, especially in America, and in the French American colonies. Schooners were especially good at sailing close-hauled.

Gribanes. Small vessels of 30 to 60 tons used for commerce along the coasts of Normandy and Brittany and on the Somme River between Saint Valéry and Amiens. They had a mainmast with a topsail, a foremast without a topsail, and a bowsprit, and were built without a keel.

Houcres (*oucres*, hookers). Dutch vessels of 50 to 200 tons with flat bottoms and round hulls like *flûtes* that had a hoy or *quesche* (ketch) rig. Even the smaller ones could sail to the East Indies with only 5 or 6 men.

Heux (hoys, hulks). Vessels of up to 300 tons with flat bottoms, round sterns, a shallow draught, and leeboards to allow sailing close-hauled. In the mid-1600s they were common at Le Havre and in Flanders, Holland, and England. They had a single mast with a large fore-and-aft main course (gaff-headed or *à livarde* on a sprit) and sometimes a square topsail. They also had a bowsprit and a small mizzen mast with a lateen balancing sail.

Lougres (lugger). Vessel the size of schooners or small brigs with two or three masts rigged with *voiles au tiers* or *voiles à bourcet*, sails on yards suspended from the mast at a point on the yard about one third of the distance from one end. The result was a fast vessel in a cross-wind but one that required a large and well trained crew to come about. These military vessels were related to the cargo-carrying *chasse-marées* but had square instead of round sterns.

Mouches. Advice boats or *mouches* used for scouting or carrying messages. The Napoleonic *mouches* were copied from a small Bermuda schooner.

Paquebots (packet boats). Fast galiotes or corvettes that carried passengers and mail between Calais and Dover and other routes including one between Harwich and Brille in Holland and one between Britain and Spain. They were also used in prisoner exchanges.

Pataches. Tenders or advice boats, generally comprising small vessels of varying rigs and types or larger vessels at the ends of their careers. A *patache de santé* was a quarantine ship.

Pinasses (pinnaces). Long, narrow and light vessels with square sterns and three masts that were propelled by sails and oars. They originated around Bayonne (where they were originally called *conques*) and were used for voyages of discovery, to land troops, and for privateeing. The word pinnace was also used for larger three-masted ships similar to Dutch *flûtes* but with high square sterns that were used by the French and British for trade with

America. In Dutch naval usage, the term meant a small warship, in effect the ancestor of the frigate.

Pinques (pinks) (*Levant*). Vessels of the same construction and size as Mediterranean *barques à voiles latines* except that their poop was much narrower. They carried the same rig and armament as barques. They normally carried merchandise but were sometimes armed for war. Their rig resembled that of xebecs but their construction was different in that it was much less low, that it had fuller lines in the bow, and the underwater lines were fuller to carry cargo. They were not fitted with oars and rarely carried guns. The Spanish and Neapolitans had many pinques, some of which reached 200 and even 300 tons.

Pinques (pinks) (*Ponant*). Dutch *flûtes* with a very flat bottom and a long and high stern. English flyboats (*flibots*) were also called pinks.

Polacres. Initially small decked Levantine vessels that used sails and oars like a small tartane. They had a square-rigged mainmast with a topmast, a foremast and a mizzen mast with lateen sails, and a bowsprit. They sometimes carried 4 to 6 guns plus some *pierriers* and were manned by 25 or 30 men. By the 1730s they had shed their oars and grown into merchant vessels of the same size and construction as *barques à voiles latines* or Mediterranean pinks. By the 1770s all three masts were square rigged, and the fore- and mainmasts were single-piece poles (*mâts à pible*), hence 'polacca-rigged' came to denote a vessel with pole masts.

Prames (prams). Flat-bottomed, shallow-draught warships, usually heavily armed, designed for defensive use in harbours and coastal waters.

Senaux (snows) (singular: *senau, senault,* or *snault*; Dutch *snauw*). Initially a *barque longue* with no more than 25 men used by the Flemish for commerce raiding. By the mid-1700s it was an entirely different type of craft, a two-masted merchant vessel developed from the three-masted ship used by the French, British, and especially the Swedish. It resembled the brig but had a 'snow mast', a vertical spar attached behind the mainmast, that allowed it to spread on that mast a square course (mainsail) in addition to the fore-and-aft course.

Sloops. Sloops (also called *bateaux bermudiens* and *bateaux d'Amérique*) were much used in the American colonies, particularly among the English. They carried from 20 to 100 tons and sometimes more. They had a single mast with a fore-and-aft sail and a long bowsprit. This rig was particularly good at sailing close to the wind and it was easy to tack. It was less successful with the wind aft. In contrast with naval cutters and *bateaux*, sloops were primarily merchant vessels, and to avoid their crews becoming too large their size and rigs were limited. In British naval usage a sloop was a cruising warship smaller than a frigate, but the term did not imply a particular rig or hull form.

Smacks (*semaque*, Dutch *smak-schip*). Small Dutch vessels that carried merchandise along the coast and in rivers and canals as far as Antwerp and Flanders. They also transported merchandise to and from large ships. They had single masts with a hoy rig, a relatively narrow beam, shallow draught, and rounded ends.

Tartanes. Small Mediterranean cargo and fishing vessels of 75 to 130 tons with either one lateen-rigged mast with a jib supported by a bow spar or with two lateen-rigged masts. Their hull shape was similar to that of Mediterranean barques except that they had sharp lines aft as well as forward. They had a complete single deck with a cargo hatch amidships and a cabin in the stern. As merchant vessels, they were manned by 3 to 10 men, but as privateers they had up to 80 men and were armed with numerous *pierriers* on the topsides. Tartanes normally did not use oars.

Traversiers. Small cargo vessels for short trips and for fishing. Some had only one mast and three sails: one on the mast, one on a stay, and one on a short pole at the extreme stern. Others had one mast with two square sails and a bowsprit. They were common as fishing vessels around La Rochelle and were also used as harbour and river ferries. Their hulls were built in the same manner as Northern European barques.

Trincadours. Small vessels without decks and with two lugsails on horizontal rather than oblique yards, common in Spanish coastal waters.

Yachts (*Yacs, Yacks*). Decked vessels that usually had a mainmast, a foremast, and a bowsprit. They had a fore-and-aft sail like the hoy and a staysail. Originally intended as pleasure craft, they had a shallow draught and were excellent for short trips and for promenades. They were used as dockyard cargo craft at Rochefort, where they seem to have been counterparts to the *bugalets* at Brest.

Preamble

The Legacy of Richelieu and Mazarin – Ships of the French Navy from 1626 to 1661

This summary describes the ships the French Navy acquired while under the direction of Richelieu and Mazarin. It covers primarily the ships capable of fighting in battle (termed *vaisseaux* by the French), but excludes such ships as were leased/hired rather than owned by Louis XIII and Louis XIV and the French state. Details on many of these are sparse, so that they are summarised below with less data than in the following chapters, although ships which were still in service in 1661 (like the *Reine* of 1647 and *Vendôme* of 1651) will appear in more detail in the Sections (A) of later chapters dealing with 'Vessels in service as at 1 March 1661'. This summary also includes many of the larger escort vessels (*frégates* as they were later termed, although in the late 1620s the French Navy referred to them as '*dragons*'). Space limitations do not permit coverage of lesser naval craft of this period, notably the fireships *brûlots* and storeships (*flûtes*), but the separate galley fleet in the Mediterranean is described in the Addendum.

While the French Navy had been a substantial force during the first half of the sixteenth century, it declined during the second half as France's social and political structures were torn apart by religious and regional divisions. During the sixty years that elapsed between the death of François I on 31 March 1547 and the accession of Louis XIII on 14 May 1610 (following the assassination of his father, Henri IV), the French Navy virtually ceased to exist, and little was done in the next decade to retrieve the situation.

On 29 March 1618 Charles, Duc de Nevers, ordered four ships of 800 tons each to be built in Holland for the Christian Militia (*Ordre de la milice chrétienne*) which he had organised for a campaign in the Balkans; a fifth ship was ordered subsequently. These were all launched in 1620, and completed in November of the same year. The largest of these was the 600-ton *Vierge*, carrying 60 bronze cannon and 20 *pierriers*. The others were the 500-ton *Saint Michel*, and the 300-ton *Saint Jean*, *Saint Charles* and *Saint François*. In 1623 two more ships were purchased for the Order – the 350-ton *Lion d'Or* (renamed *Saint Basile* in July 1624) and the patache *Louise*.

In January 1625 Cardinal Richelieu, Louis XIII's Chief Minister, put pressure on the Duc de Nevers to transfer the seven vessels, then under refit at the Breton port of Blavet (modern Port Louis, near Lorient) to Louis's ownership, and thus his own control, with the intention of using them to blockade the Huguenot city of La Rochelle, a plan of which the Rochellois were fully aware. The ships were intended to become the core of the first permanent royal navy. On 30 January the sale was concluded, for a sum of 150,000 *livres*. However, eleven days earlier the ships had already been seized at anchor in Blavet harbour as a pre-emptive move by a Huguenot squadron under Benjamin de Rohan, Duc de Soubise. The captured ships were taken back to La Rochelle, ironically becoming the core of a secessionist Huguenot naval force.

Louis XIII's Chief Minister tried to close the port of La Rochelle to English support of the rebels there, and found that the only means of so doing was to hire twenty warships from the Dutch in June 1625. Two of these were lost in combat – one (name unknown, but commanded by the Dutch Vice-Adm Philipps van Dorp) was destroyed by the Huguenot's admiral Benjamin de Rohan, Duc de Soubise at the Battle of the Pertuis Breton on 16 July 1625 with the loss of 300 dead, while another (the *Haarlem*) was destroyed in combat by the Huguenot *Vierge* (which was also consumed in the explosion) on 17 September. The remaining eighteen ships were restored to the Dutch on 10 March 1626.

The French also had to hire other foreign ships during 1625. Notable among these was the large English 32-gun warship *Vanguard*, which had been rebuilt (from its Elizabethan origins) by Phineas Pett at Chatham in 1615. She was delivered to the French Navy at La Rochelle in July 1625, but returned to the English off the Isle of Wight on 26 May 1626. Richelieu also chartered six assorted merchant ships on 5/6 August 1625 at Dieppe from the (English) Hon. East India Company – the *Peter-and-John*, *Gift of God*, *Loyalty*, *Industry*, *Marygold* and *Pearl*; these were likewise returned off hire on 26 May 1626. Dubious about how reliable the English Protestant seaman might be in action against their co-religionists, the French provided new crews for these ships during their stay in French service.

Determined that France should never again have to bear the ignominy of relying on hired foreign vessels, Richelieu determined to construct a navy commensurate with French prestige. Facing the problem that French shipbuilding skills and capacity were initially unable to provide the requisite ships, many of the initial acquisitions had to be ordered from Holland. This study commences with the new Navy created by Richelieu from 1626 onwards. However, it is worthwhile mentioning that three warships were begun in French shipyards in 1625 – the *Trois Rois* at Le Havre, the *Espérance en Dieu* at Brouage and the *Saint Louis* at the Basque port of St Jean de Luz. All three served until at least 1640.

The most potent of the new Dutch-built warships were the 1,000-ton *Navire du Roi* (also known as *Vaisseau du Roi*), which served as the *Ponant* Fleet's flagship (termed the *amiral*), the 800-ton *Saint Esprit*, and the 700-ton *Navire de la Reine* (or *Vaisseau de la Reine*), which served as the *vice-amiral*. All three were built in Holland from 1626 until October 1627, but the *Saint Esprit* was promptly captured off Enkhuisen, North Holland, by the English on 7 October, and the other two were not delivered to France (at le Havre) until at least 1629.

The larger *Navire du Roi* measured 148ft 3in, 105ft 0in x 39ft 9in x 15 ft 4in (48.16, 34.11 x 12.91 x 4.98m) and had a complement of 295 men (+5 officers); she initially mounted 52 guns, comprising 6 x 36pdrs, 18 x 24pdrs, 18 x 18pdrs and 10 x 12pdrs – although by 1642 the heavy guns had been reduced to 14 x 36pdrs and just 2 x 24pdrs, with the 18pdrs now numbering 26. She took part in the Battle of Guétaria on 22 August 1638 (as flagship of LG Henri d'Escoubleau de Sourdis). In 1640 she became the flagship of Amiral Jean-Armand Maillé, Marquis de Brézé who, as the designated heir of Richelieu as the *Grand maître de la navigation et commerce*, commanded the *Ponant* Fleet, and took part in the Battle of Cadiz on 22 July 1640 and in the Battle of Orbitello on 16 June 1646, in the course of which Maillé-Brézé was mortally wounded. Renamed *Grand Saint Louis* in 1646, she was sold in December 1649 and BU in 1650. Of the other two ships, the *Saint Esprit* carried 42 guns, and the *Navire de la Reine* carried just 40 guns and had a complement of 245 men; she also took part in the Battle of Guétaria in 1638, but was wrecked off Morbihan in a storm in July 1639.

A number of other warships were also built in Amsterdam (or perhaps elsewhere in Holland) in 1625–27 for the account of the French Navy. They included the 32-gun *Corail*, 30-gun *Fortune* and 34-gun *Europe* – each of 500 tons, laid down in 1625 and delivered in 1626. The *Fortune*

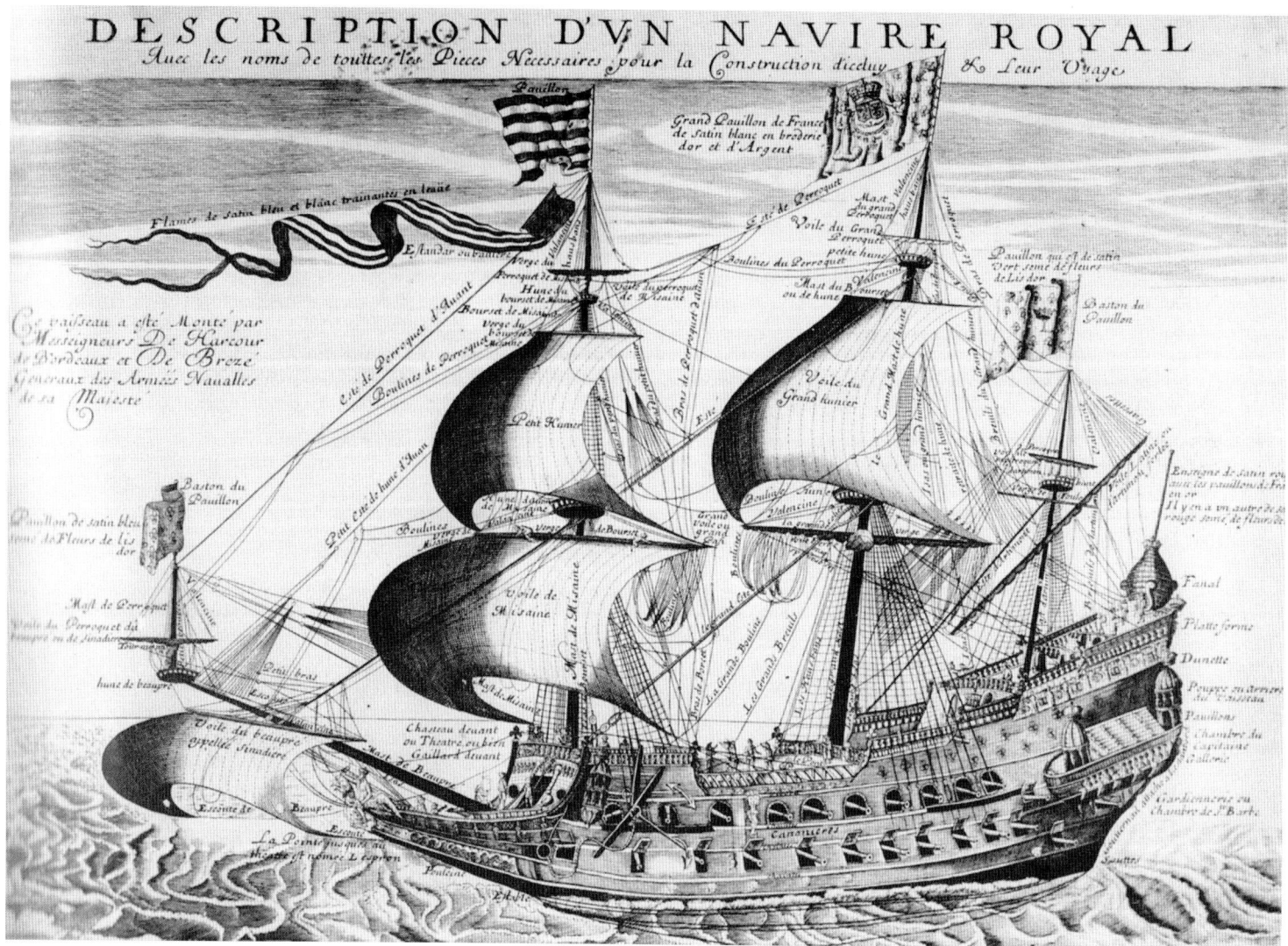

and *Europe* were both lost on 11 September 1629 through collision; the *Corail* was removed from the List by 1641. Begun in 1626 and delivered by November of the same year were the 30-gun *Hercule*, 30-gun *Licorne*, 24-gun *Saint Jean de Hollande* (or *Grand Saint Jean*), and 24-gun *Saint Louis de Hollande* (or *Petit Saint Louis*). The *Grand Saint Jean de Hollande* was renamed *Saint Jean de Bordeaux* in 1638.

A trickle of vessels from French shipbuilders also began in 1626. The *Trois Rois* of 300/500 tons and 26 guns was built at Le Havre. She was renamed *Église* briefly in 1636 but reverted to her former name in the same year; she was finally condemned in January 1641 at La Rochelle and sold.

In November 1626, one month after his appointment as *Grand-Maître*, Richelieu commissioned an investigation of the ports of Normandy, conducted by Nicolas Langlois, his naval lieutenant for that province. Among Langlois's recommendations for improvements at individual ports, he encouraged the construction of new ships. Richelieu took steps to oversee the development of Le Havre (the harbour was dredged, and the inner basin deepened and widened), as well as Brouage in Guyenne; both ports would become bases for the new French Navy, and new fortifications were undertaken at both, with a view to protecting ships there. His uncle, Amador de La Porte (*Intendant Général de la Navigation et Commerce de France*, and acting

In France there was an early interest in the theoretical basis of ship design and hydrodynamics, the scientific investigation of such matters being pursued with intensity by mathematicians, men of letters and even churchmen. One of this last group was the Jesuit Georges Fournier, whose treatise *Hydrographie* of 1643 is widely regarded as the first French maritime encyclopaedia. Fournier had served as a naval chaplain and acquired more than a theoretical knowledge of the sea and ships, so his work is a unique compendium of information about all aspects of early seventeenth century seafaring. This plate, which forms the frontispiece to the work, is a representation of the *Couronne* and, although somewhat caricatured, is generally convincing in its detail.

Governor at Le Havre) was instructed to order the construction of five new ships there, along the lines of the five Dutch-built vessels which had recently arrived at the port. These began from February 1627 at a total contract price of 62,576 *livres*.

These five new ships, called the *dragons du Havre* (the title *dragon* being adopted as a type name) copied many of the attributes used by Flemish shipbuilders in constructing powerful frigates. The design was credited to CdE Isaac de Razilly. The first four, officially listed as *Dragons Nos. 1* to *4*, were generally called *Dragon de Rumare*, *Dragon de La Rochelle*, *Dragon de Puygareau*, and *Dragon de Letier*, mostly bearing the names of their initial commanders. The fifth of the Le Havre units was

Dragon No.6, as a similar vessel built on the south side of the Loire estuary at Honfleur became *Dragon No.5*. Two further units (*Dragons No.7* and *8*) were begun at Le Havre in February 1628, and completed the same year, while other dragons (the names *Griffon* and *Neptune* were recorded) were completed in 1629.

These 200-ton vessels were clearly the direct contemporaries of the 'Lion's Whelps' built in the Thames (plus one in Shoreham) for the English Navy, but were far more sea-kindly. Each of these dragons measured 108ft (85ft keel) x 18ft (or 35 x 6m) and had a draught of 9ft (2.9m). They each carried 12/16 guns and 95 men (plus officers), were heavily armed, and combined good sailing abilities with eleven pairs of oars to give them the speed and flexibility for operations in the Channel. Nor were they alone. On the instruction of Sieur du Mé – appointed as *provéditeur* to oversee the Normandy contracts – four similar ships were arranged to be built by contract at Dieppe and two more from Fécamp, all six constructed by Nicolas Le Roy to the same design. The Dieppe ships appear to have been the *Cerf Volant*, *Aigle*, *Dauphin* and *Madeleine*, while one of the Fécamp pair was seemingly named *Marguerite*.

Further west, Augustin de Beaulieu, appointed Richelieu's *provéditeur* in Brittany, contracted for ten new ships by April 1627, and by 1629 this had risen to thirty vessels, although many were for commercial service. On the orders of de Beaulieu, the shipbuilder Arnaud began four vessels at Auray in March 1627 – the *Catholique*, *Coq*, *Fleur de Lys* and *Triton* – and Charles Mondi began another three at Concarneau at the same time – the *Perle* (500 tons), *Saint Edme* and *Sainte Geneviève* (300 tons each) – while an eighth – the *Madeleine* (also 300 tons) – was built at Couéron on the lower Loire (downriver from Nantes).

Five of these (the Auray and Couéron ships) were launched during 1628, and the Concarneau trio during 1629; all entered service in 1629. The *Catholique* and *Triton* were probably handed over to the *Compagnie de la Nouvelle France* in May 1632, while the *Saint Edme*, *Madeleine* and *Fleur de Lys* were struck in 1633, 1634 and 1636 respectively; the *Coq* lasted until 1643, while the *Perle* and *Saint Geneviève* were struck about 1645.

In addition, Richelieu arranged on 24 January 1629 for the contract with shipbuilder Pierre Gassié for six new warships to be built at Bordeaux – three of 500 tons and three of 450 tons (for a total price of 180,000 *livres*), which were all laid down in February. Three of these – the 500-ton *Henri* and *Concorde*, and the 400-ton *Saint André*, were launched in 1630–31 and completed in 1631–32. Sadly, the other three (the names *Marguerite* and *Saint Vincent* were recorded) were still incomplete when they were destroyed by an accidental fire at Bordeaux in 1633, which may also have claimed the *Concorde*, as her subsequent fate is unknown. The *Henri* and *Saint André* were disarmed at Brouage in 1635–36, and the former was struck a year later, while the latter was restored to service but was taken by the Portuguese in 1640 and became their *Santo André*, later passing into Spanish hands.

The *Couronne* was the first major warship to be built in France, and even she was constructed in a private shipyard – at La Roche-Bernard in Brittany – as there was no state-owned dockyard. She was designed and built by Charles Morieu of Dieppe, who had trained in Holland, and was begun in 1629 – well before Charles I's 1635 order in England to build the *Sovereign of the Seas*. Some 20ft longer than the English ship, she was launched at her Breton yard of La Roche-Bernard in 1632 or 1633, whence she was towed to Brouage where she was completed by shipwright Matthieu Casteau. The French behemoth was however only a two-decker, mounting 72 guns; her portrait shows her pierced for twelve pairs of LD guns, and eleven pairs on the upper deck, while she also had 8 guns firing forwards and 8 firing aft, as protection against the more manoeuvrable galleys encountered in the Mediterranean. She carried a complement of 500 men (+9 officers). She took part in the Battle of Guétaria on 22 August 1636 as the flagship of CV Claude de Launay de Razilly (acting as *Vice-amiral* in Henry de Sourdis's fleet), and served as Henri de Sourdis's own flagship in the campaign of 1639. She measured 165ft (120ft keel) by 44ft x 16ft (or 53.6, 39.0 x 14.3 x 5.2m) and had a tonnage of 1500. The ship was disarmed at Brest in 1641 and BU in 1643–45.

VESSELS ACQUIRED 1635–1642

While the Huguenot revolt might have fizzled out, antagonism between France and Spain (who had actively aided the Huguenots) did not. While France had not taken a major role in the Thirty Years' War, she had generally supported those countries sharing the Bourbon hostility to the Hapsburg monarchies. These notably included Sweden, and Sweden's losses during the early 1630s left Louis fearful of encirclement by Hapsburg enemies. Accordingly, on 26 May 1635 France formally declared war against Hapsburg Spain.

One new French-built ship was begun in 1637 by Rollin le Chevalier at Le Havre; this was the 400-ton *Dauphin*, carrying 24 guns and with a complement of 185 men (plus 5 officers). She measured 80ft by 21ft 6in (26 x 7m) and was launched on 17 March 1638 and completed in the July. She served until condemned at Toulon in May 1661 and was BU in 1662.

Six new ships were ordered from Dutch shipbuilders in 1637, all being built in Amsterdam. They were all launched around February 1638 and completed in June; all six took part in the Battle of Guétaria on 22 August 1638. The largest were the 600-ton *Cardinal* (30 guns), *Triomphe* (30 guns) and *Vierge* (34 guns), each with a crew of 245 men (215 in *Triomphe*), plus 5 officers; the *Vierge* was wrecked at Messina in November 1660, and the *Cardinal* and *Triomphe* – which latterly carried 42 and 40 guns respectively – were condemned at Toulon in May 1661 and BU in 1662. The 500-ton *Triton* (30 guns) and *Victoire* (30 guns) had 190 and 200 men respectively, against plus 5 officers; the *Triton* was captured by the English in the North Sea in September 1652, while the *Victoire* foundered off Naples in October 1652 (with a regiment of French troops lost). Finally, the 400-ton *Faucon*, with 30 guns and 185 men (again, plus 5 officers) was condemned at Toulon in May 1661.

Three further ships were hired from the Dutch in July 1638, each of 30 guns – the 400-ton *Lion* (ex-Dutch *Leeuw*) and the 300-ton *Licorne* (ex-Dutch *Eenhoorn*) and *Nassau*; these were however returned to the Dutch in October 1638 following the capture of another four Spanish warships by Condé in July 1638. These were the 800-ton *Almirante* and *Maquendo*, and the 600-ton *d'Oquendo* and *Olivarez*; while all four were initially stationed at Brest, the *d'Oquendo* and *Olivarez* were moved to the Mediterranean in 1640. Of the four, the *Maquendo* (a name rendered in French as *La Maquaide*), of 40 guns, was burnt at Toulon in April 1644; the *Olivarez*, of 28 guns, was condemned there in 1648. The *D'Oquendo*, of 38 guns, was burnt by the English in 1650, and the 36-gun *Almirante* was struck in the same year and sold.

It was following the completion of the *Couronne* that Richelieu finally recognised the need for France to have a state-owned shipyard, and this was established in 1639 on the Île d'Indret, a few miles downriver from Nantes on the lower Loire. The first ships to be ordered there were the frigates *Baronne* and *Marquise*, launched in 1640. They were followed by the sister-ships *Lune* and *Soleil*, both two-deckers and each carrying between 36 and 46 guns; launched in 1641 and 1642 respectively, and completed in 1643, these measured 117.5ft in length and 700 tons. Both survived into the 1660s, but *Lune* broke in two and foundered off Toulon in November 1664, while *Soleil* remained in service until 1672. A pair of smaller ships – the 28-gun *Léopard* and *Tigre* – were also launched at Indret during 1642; *Léopard* was lost in April 1651, while the *Tigre* survived until September 1664. This first period of construction at Indret then came to an end, and naval construction then moved back to the traditional dockyards or private builders.

VESSELS ACQUIRED 1643–1652

Following Richelieu's death in December 1642, his successor, Cardinal Mazarin, strove to continue his naval policies and for some years the expansion begun by Richelieu was continued. Notwithstanding the state's financial affairs, already parlous by 1642, which continued to worsen during the middle 1640s, the modest growth of the French Navy was carried on. It was not until the outbreak of the *Fronde* – the series of near civil wars that consumed French politics from 1648 to 1652 – that decline set in, and new construction virtually ceased.

An English merchantman (of unknown origin) was captured in August 1643 by four French warships. Re-armed at La Seyne (near Toulon) with 34 guns (28 bronze and 6 iron) and a complement of 245 men (+5 commissioned officers), the 600-ton ship was renamed *Grand Anglais*. Two Spanish ships were also seized in 1643. One was the 600-ton *San Diego*, which was renamed *Saint Jacques* in the French service and given 32 guns (22 bronze, 10 iron) and the same complement as the *Grand Anglais*; she became the *Saint Jacques de Dunkerque* in 1646 (to distinguish her from the other capture from Spain of 1643). Both *Grand Anglais* and *Saint Jacques de Dunkerque* were condemned in December 1649, and were sold a month later. The second Spanish prize, a 400-ton ship renamed *Saint Jacques du Portugal* (her name reflecting her origins)

A reconstructed plan of the *Couronne*, laid down in 1629 and the first major warship built in France, as reproduced in *Souvenirs de Marine*. This monumental, historically invaluable album of material was published in 1882, but its compiler, *Vice-amiral* François-Edmond Pâris, was an avid collector of material on historic ships and craft and headed the French naval archives from 1864 until 1871 when he retired and became curator of the Musée de la Marine, then in the Louvre. The origins of his material were many and various, but the ultimate source for this drawing is a plate and description in Georges Fournier's *Hydrographie* of 1643, the first of many French books attempting to bring science to the craft of shipbuilding. (*Souvenirs de Marine*, Plate 122)

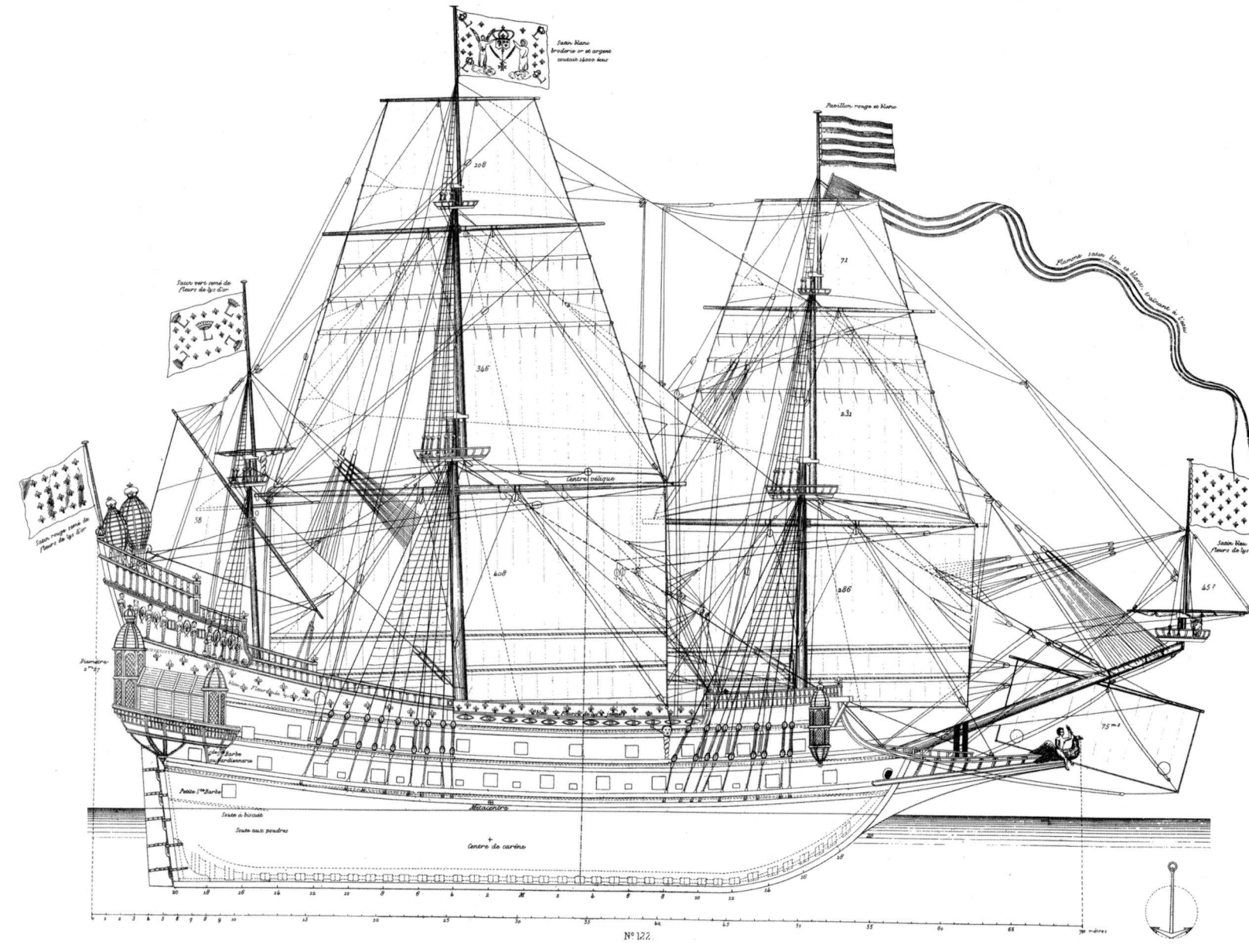

had just 185 men (+5 officers); reduced to a *flûte* in 1646, she became a hospital ship in April 1648 and was out of service in May 1648.

While no new vessels (other than prizes captured from the Spanish and English) were added until late 1645, three ships were purchased in Holland at the close of that year. Two of these seem to have been personal acquisitions by Mazarin and by Vice-Adm François de Nuchèze (*Intendant Général de la Navigation et Commerce de France*, and the first *Lieutenant Général des Mers du Ponant*) respectively – the former being the 500-ton *Fort*, installed with 26 guns and 190 men, and the latter being the 700-ton *Pucelle*, fitted with 48 guns. The third ship, also of 700 tons, was named *Grand Maltais*. All three were brought to Toulon, where they joined de Nuchèze's squadron in August 1646. The *Fort* was captured by the English (Blake's fleet?) on 15 September 1652, and the other two were also taken by the Commonwealth's navy in 1654, although the *Pucelle* was apparently restored to the French, as she was finally sold by them in 1657. A fourth vessel was purchased at the start of 1646 by de Nuchèze, becoming the 36-gun *Vierge*, which was similarly sold in 1657 at La Rochelle.

From late 1645 a number of new ships were ordered. Two were begun at Toulon by Rodolphe Gédéon: the 60-gun *Reine* before the year's end, and the 46-gun *Brézé* in April 1646. Three were begun at Brest by Laurent Hubac during 1646 – the 52-gun *César*, 48-gun *Mazarin* and 42-gun *Dragon*. Three smaller vessels of 26 guns each were ordered in 1646 from the commercial builder Michel Richot at the riverine port of Elbeuf on the Seine, but only one – the eponymous *Elbeuf* – was launched in September, the remaining pair never being built. Finally, in 1647 the 66-gun *Vendôme* was laid down by Hubac at Brest, although she was not to be completed until 1654. She was the largest and most powerful French warship to date, and the first three-decker to be built in France (albeit her upper deck was split at the waist – see Chapter 1). All seven of these ships lasted beyond 1661, and their details will be found in Section (A) of the various following Chapters.

In March 1647 Abraham Duquesne, newly appointed as *chef d'escadre*, arrived in Sweden to negotiate the purchase of four ships – the *Jupiter*, *Smaalands Lejon* (renamed *Lion de Smaaland* by the French, then renamed again as *Éminent* in August 1647), the *Regina* (renamed *Régine*) and the *Jagaren* (renamed *Chasseur*). The *Jupiter* was condemned in June 1658 and BU at Brouage; the *Éminent* was condemned in May 1661 and BU at Toulon. The *Régine* and *Chasseur* were both captured by the Dutch in the Mediterranean on 28 February 1657, being renamed *Koningin* and *Jager* respectively, but were returned to the French on 20 June at Toulon. The *Chasseur* was condemned at Toulon in 1660 and BU in 1661, while the *Régine* was struck in 1667.

A fifth Swedish vessel, the *Julius* (renamed *Jules*) was donated by Queen Christina to Mazarin in 1648, and a sixth, the *Sankt Anna* (name shortened to *Anna*), was similarly gifted by the Swedish monarch to the French Regent, Anne of Austria, in 1650; the *Jules* was captured off Portugal by the English Commonwealth's Fourth Rate *Phoenix* (of Blake's squadron) on 30 October 1650, becoming the *Success* in the English Navy (until sold in September 1662), while the *Anna* was given by the Regent to Mazarin personally, reverting to the Crown on his death (see Chapter 4). Another loss to the English, in September 1652, was the 36-gun *Don de Dieu* – a ship purchased in 1648, which was added to the Commonwealth Navy under the name *Gift*.

Two smallish ships of unknown origins acquired in 1650 were the *Neptune* (armed at Bordeaux with 20 guns, and not retained beyond 1652), and the *Saint Augustin*, armed with 30 guns in Catalonia, but captured by the Spanish on 24 November of the same year off Tarragona. Two larger vessels were captured in November 1651 and placed in service for a short time. The first was the *Marabout*, a sizeable Genoese ship captured off the Bealerics by the *Brézé*; armed with 52 guns, she was converted to a troop transport in October 1654, and was not mentioned after that year. The other was the Spanish *Sanson*, built at Dunkirk, which was captured by the *Soleil*; renamed *Samson*, and armed with 40 guns, she was not mentioned after 1652.

On 26 March 1652 Nicolas Fouchet sold two 'frigates' to the King for 150,000 *livres*. The two were probably the 300-ton *Croissant* (of 26 guns) and the 250-ton *Saint Louis* (of 20 guns). They were armed at Nantes in July 1652, and formed part of the squadron encountered by Blake's Commonwealth Navy on 14 September 1652. Both these ships were captured by Blake's squadron and not recovered.

VESSELS ACQUIRED 1653–1660

Although the long-running conflicts of the *Fronde* came to an end in 1653, the administrative and financial chaos they had caused meant that there was little attempt during the remainder of the 1650s to replace lost or worn-out vessels, although Mazarin's government made considerable efforts to try and keep naval vessels in a good state of repair. In the decade from 1650 to 1659 only sixteen *vaisseaux* and a similar number of frigates joined the French Navy, while many of Richelieu's warships were discarded. The completion in 1654 of the *Vendôme* at Brest provided a new flagship for the *Ponant* (Atlantic) fleet, but no new ships were laid down until 1654.

In March 1654 a Spanish 38-gun ship, the *San Antonio*, was captured by the French in the North Sea; she was added to the French Navy under the name *Saint Antoine*, and retained until wrecked by accident in September 1670 (see Chapter 4). The first new ship to be built for France in 1654 was the 30-gun *Persée*, of which further details are missing. On 9 October 1654 an English fleet sailed for the Mediterranean, under General-at-Sea Robert Blake, with instructions to harry the French vessels there. Sailing via Cadiz, Livorno and Tunis, Blake's fleet arrived off the naval base of Porto Farina, Tunisia (modern Ghat al-Milh, west of the Gulf of Tunis) in February, where they would destroy the nine Tunisian warships there on 14 April. Meanwhile, a squadron of four English frigates (the *Langport*, *Maidstone*, *Hampshire* and *Diamond*) had been detached to cruise off Majorca, and on 23 February these encountered the *Persée*, under CV Jean-Baptiste, Chevalier de Valbelle. After a vigorous defence the *Persée* was driven ashore by her commander and eventually lost.

Five further vessels were newbuilt for the French Navy during the second half of the decade, while France benefited from a treaty signed with Cromwell in October 1655 which ended Anglo-French hostilities. The *Françoise* of 32/36 guns was launched at St Malo in late 1656, and the 48-gun (later 36/40-gun) *Hercule* was built in Brest Dyd. A new 56-gun ship, the *Saint Louis*, was built at Brouage from 1656 onwards, and the 26-gun *Victoire* at Soubise. Another 30-gun vessel, the *Fleur de Lys*, was launched in 1659. All five were still in service in 1661, and thus their details and histories will be found in the appropriate Chapters of this volume.

THE FRENCH NAVY AS AT 1661

By the time that Colbert took office in January 1661, the French Navy consisted of only three ships-of-the-line carrying between 60 and 70 guns (*Reine*, *Vendôme* and *Saint Louis*), eight carrying between 40 and 50 guns, and seven carrying between 30 and 40 guns (these three groups corresponded to the pre-Colbert division of the Navy into three Ranks (First, Second and Third), together with four sloops and eight fireships – a total of thirty vessels.

(A) The French fleet in September 1661

The following list was included in every annual Fleet List (*État abrégé*) between 1675 and 1717 to allow comparison between the fleet of 1661 and the fleet of the current year. The spellings of these names have been altered to correspond with how they appear in the following chapters. Note that they were arranged by tonnage and number of guns. The only one of these ships remaining in the fleet in 1675 was the *Saint Louis* (which had been renamed *Aimable* in 1671).

	Port (tons)	Guns	Built in	see Chapter
18 *Vaisseaux*				
Vendôme	1,500	70	1650	1
Reine	1,000	60	1645	3
Saint Louis	1,000	60	1656	3
César	900	54	1646	3
Brézé	900	54	1646	3
Mazarin	800	48	1646	4
Hercule	800	48	1655	4
Soleil	700	46	1640	4
Lune	700	46	1640	4
Anna	700	46	1645	4
Dragon	600	42	1646	5
Françoise	500	34	1656	4
Notre Dame	450	30	1656	5
Elbeuf	400	30	1646	5
Victoire	400	30	1656	5
Tigre	400	30	1660	5
Fleur de Lys	400	30	1660	5
Sainte Anne	300	30	1646	5
8 *Brûlots*				8
4 *Flûtes*				9

1 The First Rank

(Vaisseaux du premier rang)
with 80 or more guns after 1715

The first classification of the vessels of the French Navy into four Ranks (or *Rangs*) took effect in 1669, but was swiftly altered (with a fifth Rank added) in July 1670. The 1st Rank classification covered the most prestigious ships in the French Navy, embellished with ornate carvings and decoration. They were intended to be employed as as fleet flagships, as strong points in the fleet's formation, and as symbols of Louis XIV's magnificence displaying France's maritime strength. Because of their large crews and requirements for stores they were also very expensive to operate and except during wartime were used sparingly.

The only 'three-decker' of over 60 guns built for the French before 1661 had been the *Vendôme* of 1651. The somewhat smaller *Saint Philippe* which entered service in 1664, and subsequent ships built to the same concept, were officially classed by the French as three-deckers without a forecastle and with a rudimentary quarterdeck (really a poop); they carried no guns or gunports amidships on the third deck, and usually there was a physical break in the deck level (forming a 'waist'), so that the portions of the third deck forward and aft of this interruption served in effect as forecastle and quarterdeck. In a few cases this unarmed portion of the third deck was physically present, complete with deck beams below it, so that the absence of guns and gunports (and sometimes the absence of any bulwarks along each side) left a complete structural level, thus improving the structural integrity of the ship; but in most cases there was a physical gap with the middle portion of this deck not constructed, so that the type was what the English defined as a two-decker.

Accordingly, in this and the following chapter the ordnance on the third deck (UD) of such vessels is described in two batteries – 'aft' and 'fwd'. Most of such 'semi-three-deckers' were eventually re-classed as 2nd Rank, but this applies solely to vessels built before 1689 – after 1689 only three-deckers built with a complete third tier of guns were classed as 1st Rank, until the appearance of 80-gun two-deckers of the 1st Rank in the 1740s.

The last 1st Rank three-decker of this broken-deck type was the *Paris* of 1669, while the last such 2nd Rank vessel was the *Fier* of 1682. It should be noted that the three-deckers with interrupted third tiers of guns retained the two levels of accommodations in the stern typical of three-deckers (the captain's cabin and stateroom on top of the wardroom) while two-deckers had only a single level combining the captain's cabin and the wardroom. Thus while the small three-deckers looked like two-deckers and are perhaps best understood as such, they had some structural features found only in three-deckers.

The first *extra-large* French three-decker with 100 guns or more (rated as a *vaisseau du premier rang extraordinaire*) was the *Royal Louis*, completed in 1669. Prior to 1689, these flagships, generally pierced with fifteen pairs of gunports on the lower deck (excluding the foremost pair or chase ports) were the only vessels fitted with the rare 36pdr bronze guns. Until 1690, these guns were in limited supply – iron 36pdrs did not appear until 1691 – and up to this date, *vaisseaux du premier rang extraordinaire* generally carried a mixture of sixteen 36pdrs and fourteen 24pdrs on the lower deck (all guns in these ships were of bronze). The *vaisseaux du premier rang extraordinaires* were also the only French three-deckers allowed by regulation to have a forecastle as well as a quarterdeck following the unhappy experience of the *Monarque* in 1669.

From 1690, these ships generally carried a uniform battery of 36pdrs (usually fourteen pairs) on the lower deck; initially there were two exceptions – the *Soleil Royal* (after her rebuilding in 1689) carried a mixture of 48pdrs and 36pdrs, while the new *Royal Louis* in 1692 received a complete battery of thirty 48pdrs. The huge 10ft bronze 48pdrs proved too cumbersome to handle, and the ships' commanders (Tourville on the *Soleil Royal* and d'Estrées on the *Royal Louis*) soon arranged for these to be replaced by 36pdrs. The 48pdrs were also briefly carried in *Monarque* (1690) and *Admirable* (1692).

The flagships (*navires amiraux*) of the two fleets were always drawn from the *premier rang extraordinaire*. For the Mediterranean Fleet (*Flotte du Levant*), the flagship was always the most powerful ship based in Toulon: the *Royal Louis* of 1667, its namesake (and replacement) of 1692, until that ship was disarmed in 1716 and taken to pieces in 1727; from 1780 the new *Majestueux* became the *navire amiral* of this fleet, to be superseded by the *Commerce de Marseille* in 1788. For the Atlantic Fleet (*Flotte du Ponant*), the *Soleil Royal* served the same role from 1669, as did its namesake in 1692; the *Foudroyant* of 1724 then held the same responsibility, as did the new *Soleil Royal* in 1749, followed by the *Royal Louis* of 1759; the *Bretagne* of 1766 then fulfilled the role until the 1790s.

The smaller of the 1st Rank ships (those with fewer than 100 guns – in general 84 guns was the maximum) were pierced with thirteen pairs of gunports on the lower deck (again not counting the foremost pair or chase ports). Until 1689, those of 80 guns generally carried a mixture of twelve 24pdrs (bronze) and fourteen 18pdrs (iron) on this deck, and fourteen 18pdrs (bronze) and twelve 12pdrs (iron) on the deck above, with twenty-two 8pdrs (all bronze) on the upper deck, separated into those forward and aft of the unarmed waist, and with six 4pdrs (bronze) on the quarterdeck, the latter effectively being a poop deck; these ships as indicated above had no forecastle. The 84-gun variant had no gap on the upper deck, thus mounting twenty-six 8pdrs there (of which one pair were iron guns). After 1689, a standard armament of 36pdrs was adopted for these ships also, with new 1st Rank ships carrying a similar battery to the largest ships. By 1692, the foremost pair of ports (or chase ports) were no longer cut through on 1st Rank ships, in order to strengthen the head.

Altogether twelve three-decker 1st Ranks were begun during the 1660s. Colbert produced the first French system of rating with his *Règlement* of 4 July 1670, dividing the fleet into '*Rangs*' (i.e. *Ranks*, analogous to the English system of *Rates*), the first of which comprised the three-deckers with more than 70 guns, while the second included the smaller three-deckers (as well as a few large two-deckers). By 1672, several of the smaller 1st Ranks (those with fewer than 80 guns) had been re-classified to the 2nd Rank. More important than actual numbers of guns, all 1st Ranks built after 1689 – see Section (C) – carried a principal (LD) battery of 36pdrs, while the main battery on the 2nd Ranks were generally 24pdrs (although some of this type carried a mix of 36pdrs and 24pdrs on their LD).

In 1680 or early 1681 an 'establishment level' of twelve 1st Rank ships was set, and retained well past the end of Louis XIV's reign. This was the actual number of such ships on the List in January 1681 -- five in the Brest Department, one at Rochefort (the never-completed *Victorieux*), and six at Toulon. This number was roughly adhered to until 1690, when the massive building program of twenty-five 1st Ranks made it irrelevant, but after 1712 the number shrank back and by 1717 most of the remainder had been taken to pieces without replacement.

By the close of the seventeenth century, all 1st Rank ships were three-deckers with three complete gun decks, and this continued well into the eighteenth century. At the same time forecastles were reintroduced in all 1st Rank ships. The relatively few three-deckers built after 1715 are contained in Section (D) of this Chapter. From 1740 onwards a new series of two-deckers armed with 80 guns was introduced; these fulfilled the role of capital ships (and usually the flagships) for the battlefleet, and appear separately, contained in Section (E) of this Chapter.

To compensate for the near total lack of contemporary data on ship armaments prior to 1696, we have in Sections (A) and (B) provided estimated armaments based on the governing directives and the known characteristics of all of the individual ships. This issue is discussed in greater detail in the Introduction.

(A) Vessels in service as at 9 March 1661

While the *Vendôme* (see below) was the largest warship of this size still extent in 1661 that had been built before 1661, from 1626 on there had been other vessels constructed as the '*grands vaisseaux*' of their day, but none of these had carried more than two complete batteries of guns. The first had been the 1,000-ton *Grand Vaisseau du Roi*, built in Amsterdam in 1626–27, which carried 52 guns (6 x 36pdrs and 18 x 24pdrs on the LD, and 18 x 18pdrs and 10 x 12pdrs on the UD and above); she had been sold in December 1649. The first major ship built for Louis XIII in France had been the *Couronne* of 1,400 tons, built in a private yard in Brittany in 1629–34 (see details in the Preamble), which had carried 72 guns; she was BU in 1643–45. No other warship of over 1,000 tons was built until the *Vendôme* in 1647–54 (see Preamble), and after her no more were built until 1661.

VENDÔME. 72, later 66 guns. Designed and built by Laurent Hubac. This elderly vessel (more than a decade older than any other *vaisseau* except the 3rd Rank *Reine*, *Brézé* and *César*) was the smallest to be classed as a 1st Rank when Colbert's rating system was finalised in 1670. Named after César de Bourbon, Duc de Vendôme (a legitimised son of Henri IV), from 1650 the *Grand-Maître, Chef et Surintendant de la Navigation et Commerce de France*. She was significant as the first French vessel to be described as a three-decker, even though the third deck carried no guns in the waist (consequently, the 'third deck' guns are listed below as aft and forward of the waist). The *Vendôme* began to go into commission in March 1665, began reconstruction at Brest in August 1665, became flagship of the *Ponant* Fleet under CdE Abraham Duquesne on 29 April 1666, and completed commissioning in June 1666. Her ordnance listed below is that believed to be carried from that date. Pierced for thirteen pairs of LD gunports (excluding the unarmed chase ports). Under the new rating system, she remained a 1st Rank ship even though by 1669 she carried fewer than the official limit of 70 guns. Well before this date she had ceased to be an effective naval unit, as her timbers were mostly rotten.

Dimensions & tons: 150ft 0in x 40ft 0in x 17ft 6in (48.73 x 12.99 x 5.68m). 1,450 tons. Draught 17½ft (5.54m). Men: 600 in 1665; 550 (90/340/120) in 1669, +9 officers; from 1670, reduced to 450 (66/234/150), +5 officers.

Guns: 72 in 1666: LD 12 x 24pdrs + 14 x 18pdrs; MD 14 x 18pdrs + 12 x 12pdrs; UD (aft) 8 x 8pdrs and (fwd) 6 x 8pdrs; poop 6 x 4pdrs. Reduced to 64 guns from 1669 and then 66 from 1671 (comprising LD 10 x 36pdrs + 16 x 24pdrs; MD 28 x 18pdrs; UD 12 x 6pdrs).

Vendôme Brest Dyd.
K: 1647. L: 1651. C: 1654. Renamed *Victorieux* 24.6.1671 in theory, but this was not put into practice as the ship was condemned 17.7.1671 and became a careening hulk at Brest. Condemned 5.8.1679 as a hulk and BU.

(B) Vessels acquired from 9 March 1661

SAINT PHILIPPE. 74, later 84 guns. Designed and built by Rodolphe Gédéon. Pierced for thirteen pairs of gunports on the LD (excluding the unarmed chase ports), and had no forecastle. Originally ordered under the name *Saint Esprit*, but renamed early in 1662 or 1663 while still on the stocks. Initially (1669) rated as a 70-gun 1st Rank ship, with just 18 guns on her partially-armed UD, but during 1671 was re-classed as 2nd Rank; she remained in the 2nd Rank until returning to the 1st Rank in 1690, shortly before her loss.

Dimensions & tons: 146ft 0in, 121ft 0in x 36ft 6in x 18ft 6in (47.43, 39.31 x 11.86 x 5.01m). 1,450 tons. Men: 500 in 1665, +9 officers; 550 in 1669 (90/340/120), +9 officers. In 1670 reduced to 450 (66/234/150), +9 officers; (1690) increased to 600 (99/304/197), + 9 officers; then (1691) decreased to 500 (84/276/140), +9 officers.

Guns: 74 in 1666 (actual as fleet flagship): LD 8 x 36pdrs + 18 x 24pdrs; MD 26 x 18pdrs; UD (aft) 12 x 8pdrs + (fwd) 6 x 8pdrs; poop 4 x 4pdrs. 70 from 1669, 76 from 1673, 78 from 1674. Increased to 84 guns from 1690.

Saint Philippe Toulon Dyd.
K: early 1661. L: 3.2.1663. C: 15.4.1664. Took part in the Battle of Cherchell 24.8.1665 (as flagship of *Grand-Maître* François de Bourbon-Vendôme, Duc de Beaufort and son of César de Bourbon – see above). The ship attended the (English) Spithead Review on 13.5.1672 and welcomed King Charles II aboard. Flagship of Vice-Am. Jean, Comte d'Estrées at Battle of Solebay 7.6.1672 (with 69 casualties). Refit at Toulon 3.1689–5.1690. Took part in the Battles of Beachy Head (as flagship of CdE Alain Emmanuel, Marquis de Coëtlogon) and of Barfleur 29.5.1692, then was burnt at La Hougue 2.6.1692.

ROYAL LOUIS. 104 guns. A *vaisseau du premier rang extraordinaire*, designed and constructed by Rodolphe Gédéon, with carvings by François Girardon. A full three-decker, with three complete gun decks and an armed forecastle, quarterdeck and poop, and the largest warship built in France to date. Designed for sixteen pairs of gunports on the LD, but the aftermost pair were not pierced and the foremost pair were so near the hawse ports that they were never armed; the MD was pierced for only fourteen pairs, and the UD for just thirteen pairs, to allow space for accommodation at the stern. With five pairs of ports on the QD, four pairs on the Fc and two pairs on the poop, she was pierced for an actual total of 104 guns, well under her notional rating between 1669 and 1677 of 120 guns. When first built, she was intended to serve as the flagship of François de Bourbon-Vendôme, Duc de Beaufort, for the Cretan campaign, but she saw no service until involved in a single campaign (1677), following reconstruction at Toulon from December 1676 to April 1677, during which she was re-rated at her actual 104 guns.

Dimensions & tons: 163ft 0in, 135ft 0in x 44ft 4in x 21ft 0in (52.95, 43.85 x 14.40 x 6.82m). 2,400 tons. Draught 22ft (7.15m). Men:

The great disaster to Louis XIV's fleet at La Hougue made a spectacular subject for marine artists, particularly those hailing from the victorious Netherlands. This oil painting by Adriaen van Diest is stronger on drama than literal accuracy – the ships were beached broadside-on with no canvas set – but appears to represent the 2 June 1692 attack on the northern of the two sheltering groups, which included five 1st Rank ships – *Ambitieux*, *Merveilleux*, *Foudroyant*, *Magnifique*, and *Saint Philippe* – plus the 76-gun 2nd Rank *Terrible*. (National Maritime Museum, London BHC0337)

originally 800 (160/440/200), + 9 officers; later 850 (117/466/267).

Guns: 104 from 1669 (planned): LD 12 x 36pdrs + 16 x 24pdrs; MD 26 x 18pdrs; UD 26 x 12pdrs; QD 12 x 6pdrs; Fc 8 x 6pdrs; poop 4 x 4pdrs. 104 guns from 1677: LD 16 x 36pdrs + 12 x 24pdrs; MD 28 x 18pdrs; UD 26 x 12pdrs; QD 10 x 6pdrs; Fc 8 x 6pdrs; poop 4 x 4pdrs.

Royal Louis Toulon Dyd.

K: 12.1666. L: 1.2.1668. C: 8.1669. Following 1677 reconstruction, sailed from Toulon 11.5.1677 (under LG Abraham Duquesne) to Messina in Sicily, leading squadron (also including *Monarque*, *Magnanime*, *Henri* and *Florissant*) and arrived 14.6.1677 to support rebels opposing Spanish rule there. Out of service 1.1691, and renamed *Royal Louis Vieux* 1692; BU at Toulon 1697.

DAUPHIN ROYAL. 100, later 104 guns. A second *vaisseau du premier rang extraordinaire*, designed and built by François Pomet. A full three-decker, with three complete gun decks and an armed forecastle, quarterdeck and poop. Pierced for thirteen pairs of LD gunports (excluding the unarmed chase ports). Reconstructed at Toulon from January 1680 to August 1681.

Dimensions & tons: 156ft 5in, 130ft 0in x 43ft 6in x 20ft 0in (50.81, 42.23 x 14.13 x 6.50m). 1,800 tons. Draught 21ft/24ft (6.82/7.80m). Men: originally 640 (130/360/150), +9 officers; later 750 (114/391/245); by 1689, 780 war, 600 peace.

Guns: 100 from 1669: LD 12 x 24pdrs + 14 x 18pdrs; MD 14 x 18pdrs + 12 x 12pdrs; UD 24 x 8pdrs; QD 10 x 6pdrs; Fc 8 x 6pdrs; poop 6 x 4pdrs. 104 from 1679: LD 14 x 36pdrs + 12 x 24pdrs; MD 28 x 18pdrs; UD 28 x 8pdrs; QD 12 x 6pdrs; Fc 6 x 6pdrs; poop 4 x 4pdrs. 100 from 1696 (90 peace): LD 26 x 36pdrs; MD 28 x 18pdrs; UD 28 x 8pdrs; QD/Fc 18 x 6pdrs (14 x 6pdrs + 4 x 4pdrs from 1699).

Dauphin Royal Toulon Dyd.

K: 3.1667. L: 29.3.1668. C: 4.1670. Renamed *Royal Dauphin* on 24.6.1671, but resumed *Dauphin Royal* again in 1691. Took part in Battles of Beachy Head 10.7.1690 and of Lagos 28.6.1693 (both as flagship of LG Louis-François de Rousselet, Comte de Châteaurenault). Out of service 11.1699, and sold 6.1700 at Toulon to break up.

HENRI. 70, later 76 guns. Designed and built by Jean-Pierre Brun. This ship was described by the French as a three-decker, but was effectively a two-decker with a partially-armed third deck divided by an unarmed waist, and functioning as a QD and forecastle. The LD was pierced for thirteen pairs of guns (excluding the unarmed chase ports), and the 2nd tier for a similar number. Rebuilt at Rochefort 1678–80; converted to a 76-gun two-decker (with the former broken UD officially becoming a QD and forecastle), and she was re-classed as 2nd Rank in 1678. It was intended that the 3rd deck in the waist be restored around 1689 to turn this back into a complete upper deck (extra 8pdr guns would be added), but instead she was struck in the same year.

Dimensions & tons: 150ft 0in, 125ft 0in x 38ft 0in x 18ft 0in (48.73, 40.60 x 12.34 x 5.85m). 1,500 tons. Draught 18ft/20ft (5.85/6.50m). Men: originally 450 (70/260/120), +6 officers; from 1671, 500 (72/262/166), +5 officers.

Guns: 70 from 1669, then 74 from 1671. 76 from 1672: LD 12 x

The majority of the images in *Souvenirs de Marine* are plans redrawn by *Vice-amiral* Pâris from a variety of sources, but the volumes also contain photographs of models and decoration drawings, such as this one of the stern of *Souverain*, launched in 1669 as the *Henri* and renamed in 1671. The jutting balcony of the stern gallery was a feature much admired by Charles II, and later emulated in English warships. (*Souvenirs de Marine*, Plate 146).

K: 3.1667. L: 4.1669. C: 8.1670. Renamed *Souverain* 24.6.1671, and then *Admirable* 28.6.1678. Struck 1689, and BU at Rochefort.

MONARQUE. 84 guns, later reduced to 80 guns. Designed and built by Laurent Coulomb; decoration sculpted by Pierre Paul Puget (the first of several ships at Toulon for which he carved the figureheads over the next decade). The LD was pierced for thirteen pairs of guns (excluding the unarmed chase ports). Unlike the previous vessels, this ship had a full-length third gun deck, and was completed with a forecastle, although the latter was removed in 1670 after it was judged to have impaired her seaworthiness during the failed relief of Candia (Crete) in 1669. Initially planned to carry 94 guns in three batteries of 26 guns each, plus 10 guns on the QD and 6 on the Fc, and 600 (100/360/140) men + 9 officers, by 1671 she had the complement described below.

Dimensions & tons: 153ft 3in, 127ft 0in x 43ft 6in x 19ft 6in (49.78, 41.25 x 14.13 x 6.33m). Draught 20ft (6.50m). 1,700 tons.

Men: 600 (85/315/200), +5 officers in 1671; 600 (100/303/197), +9 officers by 1676.

Guns: 94 in 1669 (see above). 84 from 1671: LD 12 x 24pdrs + 14 x 18pdrs; MD 14 x 18pdrs + 12 x 12pdrs; UD 26 x 8pdrs; QD 6 x 4pdrs (4 removed in 1678, reducing her to 80 guns).

Monarque Toulon Dyd.

K: 4.1667. L: 28.4.1668. C: 6.1669. Took part in expedition to Candia 6.1669 (as flagship of *Grand-Maître* François de Bourbon-Vendôme, Duc de Beaufort, who was killed in action ashore on 15 June). In 1671 flagship of CdE Guillaume d'Alméras. In 1678 took part in Catalonia campaign (as flagship of LG Abraham Duquesne). Condemned and hulked at Toulon 10.9.1685, but still afloat in 1697.

24pdrs + 14 x 18pdrs; MD 14 x 18pdrs + 12 x 12pdrs; UD (aft) 12 x 8pdrs + (fwd) 6 x 8pdrs; poop 6 x 4pdrs. Increased to 80 guns from 1674 but reverted to 76 from 1676 (the poop guns were removed 1688).

Henri Tonnay-Charente, near Rochefort.

A Van de Velde drawing of the *Royale Thérèse*, probably made during the summer of 1673 when the French fleet was in English waters. When completed, as the *Paris*, the ship sported the elaborate carved works by Pierre Puget found on many Toulon-built ships of this era, but when renamed was fitted with a new sternpiece. Nevertheless, many of the ship's unusual features – such as the gunport arch beneath the quarter-gallery, the four round windows above the quarter-gallery, and the huge winged quarter figure – survived, and confirm the identity of this ship. (National Maritime Museum, London PZ7271)

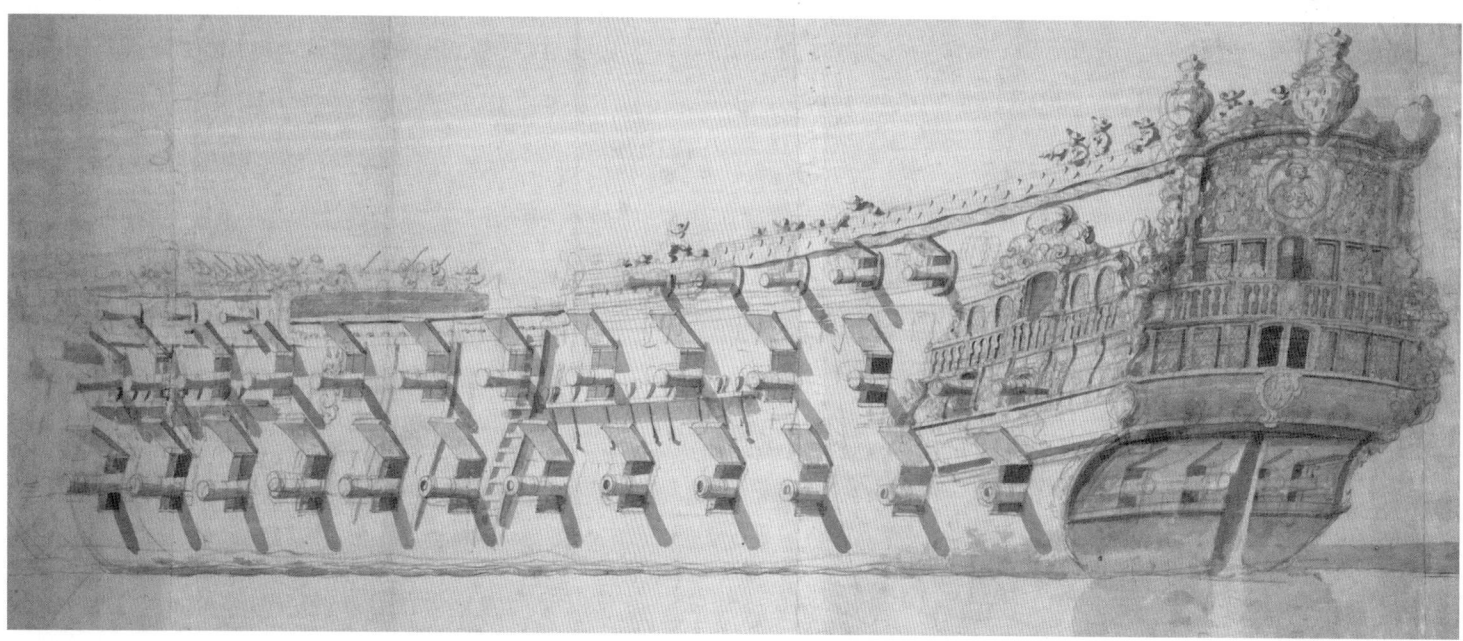

ÎLE DE FRANCE. 70 (later 76, then 84) guns. Designed and built by Louis Audibert. Like the *Henri* above, this ship was described by the French as a three-decker, but was effectively a two-decker with a partially-armed third deck divided by an unarmed waist, and functioning as a forecastle and quarterdeck. The LD was pierced for thirteen pairs of guns (excluding the unarmed chase ports), and the 2nd tier for a similar number. Extra 8pdr guns were added in the waist on the third deck around 1689–91 to turn this into a complete third gun deck. The LD was pierced for thirteen pairs of guns (excluding the unarmed chase ports). Rated as a 60-gun 2nd Rank in 1669 while building, but completed as a 70-gun 1st Rank.

    Dimensions & tons: 141ft 6in, 116ft 0in x 39ft 8in x 19ft 6in (45.96, 37.68 x 12.89 x 6.3m). 1,700 tons. Draught 20ft (6.50m). Men: originally 450 (66/234/150), +5 officers; by 1676 500 (86/274/140), +9 officers.

    Guns: 70 from 1671: LD 12 x 24pdrs + 14 x 18pdrs; MD 14 x 18pdrs + 12 x 12pdrs; UD (aft) 12 x 8pdrs, (fwd) 6 x 8pdrs. 4 x 4pdrs were added on the poop by 1676, to make a 74-gun ship, and a further 2 x 4pdrs by 1679. 80 guns in 1690, 84 from 1691.

Île de France Toulon Dyd.
    K: 9.1667. L: 16.2.1669. C: 7.1670. Renamed *Lys* 24.6.1671. Took part in Battles of Augusta 22.4.1676 (as flagship of LG Guillaume, Marquis d'Alméras) and Palermo 1.6.1676. Condemned at Toulon 2.1691 and BU.

PARIS. 70, later 80 guns. Designed and built by Jean Serrin. Like the *Henri* and *Île de France* above, this was described by the French as a three-decker, but was effectively a two-decker with a partially-armed third deck divided by an unarmed waist, and functioning as a forecastle and quarterdeck. The LD was pierced for thirteen pairs of guns (excluding the unarmed chase ports), and the 2nd tier for a similar number. Named as *Paris* in February 1668. Rated as a 60-gun 2nd Rank in 1669 while building, but completed as a 70-gun 1st Rank. The QD was extended forward in 1679 at Brest, allowing two more pairs of guns to be mounted.

    Dimensions & tons: 143ft 0in, 127ft 0in x 42ft 0in x 20ft 0in (46.45, 41.25 x 13.64 x 6.50m). 1,700 tons. Draught 20/21½ft (6.50/6.98m). 1,700 tons. Men: originally 450 (66/234/150), +5 officers; by 1676, 500 (86/274/140), +9 officers.

    Guns: 70 from 1671: LD 12 x 24pdrs + 14 x 18pdrs; MD 14 x 18pdrs + 12 x 12pdrs; UD (aft) 12 x 8pdrs + (fwd) 6 x 8pdrs. 6 x 4pdrs were added on the poop by 1674, turning this into a 76-gun ship. 80 guns from 1679, then 76 from 1688, and 80 from 1690.

Paris Toulon Dyd.
    K: 9.1667. L: 12.3.1669. C: 9.1670. Renamed *Royale Thérèse* 24.6.1671. Took part in the Battle of Texel 21.8.1673 (as flagship of CdE Damien, Marquis de Martel). Sank from neglect in early 1690, then hulked at Brest by Order of 3.10.1690, and condemned in same year.

ROYAL DUC. 104 guns. The third *vaisseau du premier rang extraordinaire*, designed and built by Laurent Hubac. A full three-decker, with three complete gun decks and an armed forecastle and quarterdeck. Pierced for fifteen pairs of LD gunports (excluding the unarmed chase ports), which each had a width of 32in, and were spaced 6ft 7in apart. Her forecastle was ordered removed on 28 June 1670.

    Dimensions & tons: 155ft 0in, 140ft 0in x 42ft 0in x 19ft 6in (50.35, 45.48 x 13.64 x 6.33m). 1,900 tons. Draught 20ft/22ft 10in

Another Van de Velde drawing from 1673, this one depicting *Reine* (originally called *Royal Duc*), the flagship of *Vice-amiral* Jean, Comte d'Estrées (1624–1707), who commanded the French squadron in the Anglo-French fleet at the Battles of Schooneveldt and Texel that year. With three complete gundecks, the ship was a genuine three-decker, and the drawing confirms the lower deck battery of fifteen guns a side, not counting the forward chase port which was unarmed most of the time. Like most three-deckers, there were also four stern chase ports on the lower deck, similarly unarmed (although sometimes shown armed by artistic licence). Above them, the middle deck ended in a false balcony, while at the upper deck level was an open gallery which was continued in the open quarter galleries. Unlike the *Royal Louis* and *Soleil Royal*, she had no armed poop deck, but she did mount a fourth tier of 6pdrs on both forecastle and quarterdeck. Her stern carving shows the influence of Mediterranean figures, with large statues of Fames on either side supporting the coat of arms of France and Navarre. (National Maritime Museum, London PZ7269)

(6.50/7.15m). Men: 750 (150/420/180) in 1669, +9 officers; 700 (96/374/230) in 1671, +8 officers; 800 (109/428/263) in 1673, +8 officers; 700 (110/250/230) from 1675, +9 officers.

Guns: 104 from 1669 (all bronze except the iron 36pdrs): LD 16 x 36pdrs + 14 x 24pdrs; MD 30 x 18pdrs; UD 26 x 8pdrs; QD 10 x 6pdrs; Fc 8 x 6pdrs. Reduced to 100 guns by 1688.

Royal Duc Brest Dyd.

K: 10.1667. L: 12.1668. C: 3.1669. Renamed *Reine* 24.6.1671. Took part in Battles of Schooneveldt 7 & 14.6.1673 and of Texel 21.8.1673 (all as flagship of Vice-Am. Jean, Comte d'Estrées). Condemned 2.4.1688 at Brest and BU 5.1688.

COURONNE. 82, later 76 guns. Designed and built by Laurent Hubac as a 76-gun ship with a partially-armed upper deck, but completed with three complete batteries like *Monarque*. Pierced for thirteen pairs of LD guns (excluding the unarmed chase ports). Rebuilt from March 1686 to 1687 at Brest (during which further UD guns were removed) and re-classed as a 2nd Rank ship in 1687. Briefly restored to the 1st Rank in 1690, reduced to the 2nd Rank in 1691, and finally restored to the 1st Rank in 1706.

Dimensions & tons: 143ft 0in, 120ft 0in x 38ft 6in x 18ft 0in (46.45, 38.93 x 12.51 x 5.85m). 1,500 tons. Draught 20/22½ft (6.50/7.31m). Men: 550 (92/300/158), +9 officers.

Guns: 82 from 1669: LD 12 x 24pdrs +14 x 18pdrs; MD 14 x 18pdrs +12 x 12pdrs; UD 26 x 8pdrs; poop 4 x 4pdrs. 80 guns from 1675 (with 2 x 8pdrs removed). 76 guns from 1691 (68 peace): LD 10 x 36pdrs + 14 x 24pdrs; MD 26 x 18pdrs; UD 22 x 8pdrs; poop 4 x 4pdrs. From 1698 the LD had 16 x 36pdrs + 10 x 24pdrs and the UD had 20 x 8pdrs, but from 1704 the 76 comprised LD 26 x 24pdrs; MD 26 x 18pdrs; UD 24 x 8pdrs; poop nil.

Couronne Brest Dyd.

K: late 1667. L: 18.2.1669. C: 1669. Took part in Battles of Lagos 28.6.1693 and of Vélez-Málaga 24.8.1704. Scuttled at Toulon in 7.1707, but refloated. Sold 1712 at Toulon to BU.

SCEPTRE. 80, later 84 guns. Designed and built by Laurent Coulomb as a 76-gun ship with a partially-armed upper deck, but completed with three entire batteries like *Monarque* and *Couronne*. Pierced for thirteen pairs of LD guns (excluding the chase ports). Named on 1 February 1669. Rebuilt at Toulon from January 1680 until January 1681.

Dimensions & tons: 148ft 0in, 122ft 0in x 42ft 0in x 19ft 0in (48.08, 39.63 x 13.64 x 6.17m). 1,600 tons. Draught 20ft (6.50m). Men: 600 (100/303/197), +9 officers.

Guns: 80 from 1671: LD 12 x 24pdrs +14 x 18pdrs; MD 14 x 18pdrs +12 x 12pdrs; UD 22 x 8pdrs; poop 6 x 4pdrs. 84 from 1674, with UD increased to 26 x 8pdrs. 76 guns from 1679, 80 in 1690 and 84 from 1691.

Sceptre Toulon Dyd.

K: 4.1668. L: 11.2.1670. C: end 1671. Took part in Battles of the Lipari Islands 11.2.1675 (as flagship of *Général des galères* Louis-Victor de Rochechouart, Duc de Vivonne), of Stromboli 12.2.1676 and Augusta 22.4.1676 (both as flagship of CdE Anne Hilarion de Costentin, Comte de Tourville), and of Palermo 31.5.1676 (again as flagship of the Duc de Vivonne, but with Tourville as CdE as well). Found 10.1688 to need reconstruction, condemned 2.1691 at Toulon, renamed *Sceptre Vieux* 5.1691, and BU 6.1692.

SOLEIL ROYAL. 106, later 110 guns. The fourth *vaisseau du premier rang extraordinaire*, designed and built by Laurent Hubac. Ordered in 1669 as *Grand Henri*, but renamed *Royal Soleil*, then *Soleil Royal* on 6 December 1669. A full three-decker, with three complete gun decks and an armed forecastle, quarterdeck and poop. Pierced for fifteen pairs of LD guns (excluding the foremost pair or chase ports, which were never armed, closest to the separate hawse ports). The LD gunport width was 32in, and the separation between these gunports was 7ft 2in. Her actual total of 106 guns was well below her notional rating (between 1669 and 1677) of 120 guns.

Taken to pieces and underwent a total rebuilding from the keel up in 1689 by Étienne Hubac at Brest; the potential number of guns was reduced to 110, but the actual number carried was 98 in July 1690 at Beachy Head. The LD now carried 28 guns, a mixture of 36pdrs and monstrous 48pdrs. The latter proved so unwieldy to operate that Tourville (whose flagship she was) had her 8 x 48pdrs replaced by an equal number of 36pdrs before the Battle of Barfleur. This rebuilding involved some of the most lavish decoration available, designed by Jean Bérain and executed by some of the leading woodcarvers and sculptors of the day, and intended to advertise the magnificence of the *Roi Soleil*.

Dimensions & tons: 164ft 6in, 142ft 0in x 44ft 6in x 21ft 0in (53.44, 46.13 x 14.46 x 6.82m). Draught 23½ft (7.63m). 2,400/2,500 tons. Men: 850 (118/466/266), later 900 (122/496/282), +9 officers.

Guns (106 from 1669): LD 16 x 36pdrs + 14 x 24pdrs; MD 30 x 18pdrs; UD 26 x 8pdrs; QD 10 x 6pdrs; Fc 6 x 6pdrs; poop 4 x 4pdrs. 108 guns from 1688, then 110 from 1690: LD 8 x 48pdrs + 20 x 36pdrs (but see note above); MD 30 x 18pdrs; UD 28 x 12pdrs; QD 14 x 6pdrs; Fc 6 x 6pdrs; poop 4 x 4pdrs. 104 guns in 5.1692 (actual): LD 28 x 36pdrs; MD 30 x 18pdrs; UD 30 x 12pdrs; QD/Fc 12 x 6pdrs; poop 4 x 4pdrs.

Soleil Royal Brest Dyd.

K: 12.1668. L: 13.12.1669. C: 8.1670. Rebuilt at Brest from 1688 to early 1690. Took part in Battles of Beachy Head 10.7.1690 and Barfleur 29.5.1692 (both times as flagship of Vice-Am. Anne Hilarion de Costentin, Comte de Tourville), then burnt by fireship HMS *Blaze* at Cherbourg 1.6.1692.

On 7 March 1669, Colbert additionally took over the portfolio of Secretary of State for the Navy, and brought to completion his major expansion program designed to bring France up to the first rank of naval powers. The initial rating system was set up by the *Règlement* of 4 July 1670, and provided that 1st Rank ships should have three complete gun decks (with the upper deck not cut at the waist) and mount from 70 to 120 guns. Nine ships were designated as 1st Rank at this time – the *Vendôme*, *Saint Philippe*, *Royal Louis*, *Dauphine Royal*, *Henri*, *Monarque*, *Royal Duc*, *Couronne* and *Soleil Royal* (the last still building), although it should be noted that, exceptionally, the *Vendôme* carried just 64 guns. Also on order – but unstarted – at this date was a tenth ship, the *Courageux* (later *Magnanime*).

MAGNANIME. 70 (later 76, then 84) guns. Designed by Rodolphe Gédéon but built by Charles Audibert, pierced for thirteen pairs of LD guns (excluding the unarmed chase ports). Begun as *Courageux* (so named on 21 February 1670), but renamed on 24 June 1671. One of only two ships of the line to be built and launched at Marseille, she then had to be completed at Toulon Dyd. Rebuilt at Toulon from July 1679 to November 1681. Built with a partially armed third deck, whose waist was fitted with extra 8pdrs around 1690 at Toulon to give her three full gun decks. Reduced to the 2nd Rank in 1703 after Lagos, then reconstructed again at Brest 1703–4, by Alexandre Gobert following the 'méthode du Sieur Gobert' (i.e. with iron knees for the deck), emerging as 1,400 tons with 147ft (47.75m) length.

Dimensions & tons: 144ft 0in, 121ft 0in x 44ft 0in x 20ft 0in. (46.78, 39.31 x 14.29 x 6.50m) 1,550 tons. Draught 20ft/23ft

THE FIRST RANK

The *Soleil Royal*, flagship of the Comte de Tourville, with the large white Bourbon naval ensign, is shown as the centre of Anglo-Dutch attention at the Battle of Barfleur (29 May 1692 NS). Having seen no action during the Franco-Dutch War of 1672–78, this flagship of the *Ponant* (Atlantic) Fleet had been completely rebuilt from 1688 to early 1690 at Brest by Étienne Hubac, the son of her original constructor. At the centre of the battle, the 104-gun *Soleil Royal* faced three English First Rates – Russell's 100-gun *Britannia*, and the 96-gun *London* and *Saint Andrew*. Tourville managed to extricate his outnumbered fleet with credit from this battle, but it was dispersed and many of its largest ships were later destroyed by boat attacks and fireships at Cherbourg and La Hougue, including the mighty *Soleil Royal*, which blew up 'with a frightful roar'. This oil painting by Ludolph Backhuysen, although executed shortly after the events it depicts, takes many liberties with circumstances of the battle, notably in ignoring the fog. Nor is the depiction of the ships very convincing, and his *Soleil Royal* is more generic than a real portrait. In fact, the gilded carvings on the magnificent stern-piece were discreetly masked with pearl-grey paint. (National Maritime Museum, London BHC0331)

(6.50/7.47m). Men: initially 450 (66/234/150), +5 officers; by 1675, 450 (83/230/137), +9 officers; in 1676, 500 (86/274/140), + 9 officers; from 1691, 550 men (89/304/157, as 84-gun ship).

Guns: 70 from 1671, then 76 from 1676: LD 12 x 24pdrs + 14 x 18pdrs; MD 14 x 18pdrs + 12 x 12pdrs; UD (aft) 12 x 8pdrs + (fwd) 6 x 8pdrs; poop 6 x 4pdrs. 80 guns from 1690, then 84 from 1691. 80 in war from 1696 (76 peace): LD 24 x 36pdrs; MD 26 x 18pdrs; UD 24 x 8pdrs; poop 6 x 4pdrs.

Magnanime Marseille.
K: 7.1670. L: 30.8.1673. To Toulon 10.1673. C: 1675 at Toulon. Took part in Battle of Lagos 28.6.1693. Lent as a privateer to LG André, Marquis de Nesmond as part of a squadron of five vessels 1695. At Battle of Vélez-Málaga on 24.8.1704 (as flagship of CdE Jean Bernard de Saint-Jean, Baron de Pointis). Driven ashore and burnt (with *Lys*) by her crew at Marbella 21.3.1705 to avoid capture by Vice-Adm Sir John Leake's squadron.

In early 1671 the number was briefly increased to sixteen 1st Rank (including the *Courageux/Magnanime* on the stocks at Marseille) by the upgrading of three ships which had been previously classed as 2nd Rank – the *Île de France*, *Paris* and *Sceptre* – and the launch of three new ships – the *Madame*, *Rubis* and *Joli*. Of these sixteen ships, ten were renamed on 24 June 1671: the *Vendôme* became the *Victorieux* (although she was condemned a few weeks after), the *Dauphin Royal* became the *Royal Dauphin*, the *Henri* became the *Souverain*, the *Île de France* became the *Lis*, the *Paris* became the *Royale Thérèse*, the *Royal Duc* became the *Reine* and the *Courageux* became the *Magnanime*, while the new *Madame*, *Rubis* and *Joli* became the *Pompeux*, *Florissant* and *Henri*. However, by the start of 1672 the last three had been moved to the 2nd Rank (and are detailed in Chapter 2), along with the *Saint Philippe*, while the older *Vendôme/Victorieux* had been hulked, reducing the number to eleven.

After a few years during which only one further order (*Victorieux*) was placed, construction resumed in 1675 with one new 1st Rank ship (*Souverain*) being built. This was the only new 1st Rank ship over the following fourteen years, and she never entered service, but three other ships built as 2nd Rank in this period were subsequently re-classed as 1st Rank – the *Grand* in 1687 and the *Magnifique* and *Conquérant* in 1690 (see Chapter 2 for these ships).

Increasingly a number of shipwrights, notably those at Rochefort, led by Blaise Pangalo (of Neapolitan origin and originally named Biaggio Pangalo but known in France as *Maître* Blaise) and strongly supported by Tourville, called for three-deckers to be built with a longer hull, able to carry a full third battery as well as to carry the requisite top hamper to allow improved sailing. In particular, they called for no further three-deckers with less than 80 guns, and for future 80-gun ships to have a length of around 158.5ft (51.5m). These proposals were opposed by the more conservative Brest shipwrights, led by Laurent Hubac, and the latter's views were accepted by Colbert and subsequently upheld by his son, Seignelay.

VICTORIEUX. 108, later 100 guns. Designed and built by François Pomet, she was a full three-decker, pierced for fifteen pairs of LD gunports (excluding the unarmed chase or hawse ports at the bow). Ordered on 26 December 1672 as a 50-gun ship like *Intrépide* with the

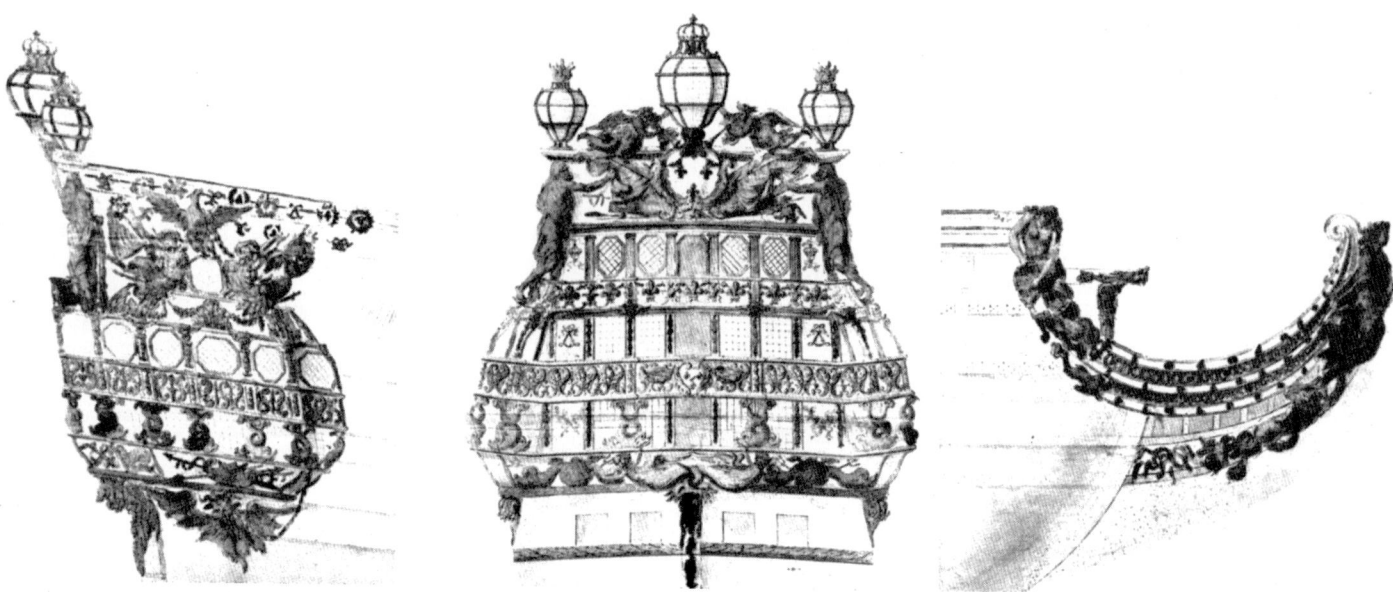

The decorative work – quarter galleries, stern and bow – of the *Victorieux*, 108 guns, laid down in 1673 at Rochefort. The carved work was probably designed by Claude Buirette, the master sculptor at the Rochefort arsenal, as it differs in style from the artists associated with the Court who were the usual choice for ships of the 1st Rank. Buirette's continued use of large figurative work was falling out of favour with Charles Le Brun, who was overseer of the master carvers, but the Rochefort Dockyard continued to use the more flamboyant style of baroque for some time to come. There are three stern galleries of which the lowest, on the middle deck, appears open but was actually enclosed according to the specification for the *Victorieux*'s carpentry. Above this, the gallery on the upper deck was for the Admiral while that on the quarterdeck level was for the Captain. (*Souvenirs de Marine*, Plate 146)

temporary name *Douteux*, she was renamed *Victorieux* 28 November 1673 when she was officially laid down, though construction may not have begun in earnest until 1675. The fifth *vaisseau du premier rang extraordinaire* to be ordered, her hull was completed on the ways in April 1677 but lacked its decoration, the proposed scheme being too cumbersome. At this time the Minister approved Pomet's request to add a forecastle and Pomet may have made other alterations. Construction was completed in 1679 and the ship was evidently launched around that time.

Victorieux had, however, been built of poor quality timber that Rochefort had been compelled to buy in around 1670 from agents of Mme de Montpensier. This timber deteriorated rapidly in storage and when exposed on the building slip. (*Orgueilleux* and *Superbe* were also built completely of this wood and suffered similarly from it while *Frédéric* was about half rebuilt with it.) By 1681 the hull planking of *Victorieux* at the waterline was rotten, but the Council of Construction at Rochefort determined that the arsenal could not repair such a large vessel because it lacked a large dock and the current in the river was too fast, so it was proposed instead to replace only the planking, give her a 'half-hull' to protect her in the winter, and keep her in condition to be sent to another port in the 'good' months. In late 1684 the Council estimated that much of her hull including some of her main timbers needed replacement at an estimated cost of over 160,000 *livres,* and in July 1685 the Intendant at Rochefort, Pierre Arnoul, decided that she had to be broken up even though she had never gone to sea. She would never have carried more than 100 guns, if she received any ordnance at all.

Dimensions & tons: 166ft 0in, 135ft 0in x 43ft (45ft outside planking) x 19ft 6in (53.92, 43.85 x 13.97/14.62 x 6.33m). 2,000 tons. Draught 20ft/21ft (6.50/6.82m). Men: orig 700 (110/360/230), later 800 (113/435/252), +9 officers.

Guns: Nominally 108 in 1676: LD 16 x 36pdrs + 14 x 24pdrs; MD 30 x 18pdrs; UD 30 x 12pdrs; QD 10 x 6pdrs; Fc 8 x 6pdrs. Reduced to 100 guns from 1677.

Victorieux Rochefort Dyd.
K: 28.11.1673. L: 1679? C: not commissioned. Condemned 7.1685 at Rochefort and BU.

SOUVERAIN. 80 (later 84) guns. Designed and built by Laurent Hubac. Built as *Admirable*, but renamed on 28 June 1678 (exchanging names with the original *Souverain*). Pierced for thirteen pairs of LD guns (excluding the unarmed chase ports). Originally had three complete decks of 26 guns, plus 2 (later 6) guns on the QD, but by 1696 a pair was removed from the UD and another pair from the QD. Underwent rebuilding at Brest from 1688 to January 1689.

Dimensions & tons: 148ft 0in, 123ft 0in x 38ft 3in x 18ft 6in (48.08, 39.96 x 12.425 x 6.01m). 1,450 tons (1,500 tons from 1687, then 1,600 from 1688). Draught 20ft/23ft (6.50/7.47m). Men: originally 500 (86/274/140) as 80-gun ship, then 560 (90/304/166) as 84-gun ship; +9 officers.

Guns: 80 in 1679–80: LD 12 x 24pdrs + 14 x 18pdrs; MD 14 x 18pdrs + 12 x 12pdrs; UD 24 x 8pdrs; poop 4 x 4pdrs. 84 guns from 1691. 80 in war from 1696 (76 peace): LD 26 x 36pdrs; MD 26 x 18pdrs; UD 24 x 8pdrs; QD 4 x 4pdrs.

Souverain Brest Dyd.
K: 4.1677. L: 1678. C: 12.1678. Took part in Battles of Beachy Head 10.7.1690 (as flagship of CdE André, Marquis de Nesmond), of Barfleur 29.5.1692 (as flagship of CdE Joseph Andrault, Marquis de Langeron), and of Lagos 28.6.1693, followed by the Great Armament at Toulon. Ordered to be sold 24.2.1706 at Brest and sold for BU 7.4.1706.

No new 1st Rank ships were built during the 1680s (although the 80-gun *Grand* of 1680 was raised from the 2nd Rank to the 1st during 1687, with her ordnance increased to 88 guns) until the 1688 invasion of England by William of Orange, which Louis XIV perceived as a declaration of war against France. He determined to expand his battlefleet to enable it to overpower the now allied English and Dutch navies, and this led to orders being placed for new three-deckers, all of 80 guns or more and armed with complete batteries of 36pdrs on their LDs, as well as numbers of lesser battlefleet units. He gave his naval and military support to the deposed James II's invasion of Ireland in March 1689 to muster Irish Catholic strength for the struggle to recover his kingdom. Subsequently the Battle of Bantry Bay (in May 1689) led to the formal declaration of war between the two states.

(C) Vessels acquired from 15 April 1689

By the start of 1689, following the re-classing of the *Grand* as a 1st Rank ship, all the nine 1st Rank ships extant were three-deckers – comprising the *Soleil Royal* (108 guns), *Royal Louis* (104), *Royal Dauphin* (104), *Grand* (88), *Souverain* (80), *Sceptre* (76), *Royale Thérèse* (76), *Lys* (76) and *Magnanime* (76). A tenth ship, the *Reine* (100) had recently been BU during 1688. During the course of 1690, the *Royale Thérèse* was removed from the List, while the seven existing or newbuilding 2nd Rank ships were raised to the 1st Rank – the *Saint Philippe*, *Magnifique* and *Conquérant* (now each with 84 guns); and the *Couronne*, *Triomphant*, *Tonnant* and *Fier* (each with 76 guns), although the latter four ships reverted to 2nd Rank by the end of 1691. The *Sceptre*, *Lys* and *Magnanime* were each raised from 76 to 84 guns. The new 84-gun category reflected the decision to provide fully-armed continuous UDs on ships which had previously been only partially armed on that deck (often divided in the waist). Coupled with the addition of the first units of the new construction program – *Intrépide*, *Monarque*, *Victorieux*, *Orgueilleux*, *Admirable* and *Foudroyant*, all laid down in 1689 or 1690 – this brought the total to twenty-one vessels by 1 January 1691.

Between 1689 (the outbreak of war against the English and Dutch) and 1695, twenty-five new three-deckers were built, all classed as 1st Rank, and all with a completely armed upper deck (with no waist gap in the guns). This phenomenal effort meant that, even after the losses in ships burnt at Cherbourg and La Hougue in 1692, the battlefleet was considerably stronger by 1695 than it was in early 1692. All guns supplied for these were bronze (the 2nd and 3rd Rank ships carried a mix of bronze and iron guns).

The new construction were essentially two groups. The first comprised the eighteen ships pierced with fourteen gunports per side on the lower deck (fitted with 28 x 36pdrs), which also carried 30 x 18pdrs on the middle deck, 28 x 12pdrs on the upper deck and 10 x 6pdrs on the quarterdeck. Five of the post-1692 vessels – *Soleil Royal*, *Merveilleux*, *Admirable* (ii), *Terrible* and *Foudroyant*, all somewhat longer than the others – were built with a forecastle on which they carried another 4 or 6 x 6pdrs, making them 104-gun ships; the other thirteen had no forecastle. An eighteenth ship (*Royal Louis*) was actually pierced with fifteen gunports per side, and briefly carried 48pdrs on this deck in lieu of 36pdrs. By 1692 the first pair of the LD gunports (the 'chase' ports) were no longer being pierced. The second group, comprising six ships, were pierced with just thirteen gunports per side, and mounted 26 x 36pdrs on this deck (the exception, *Admirable* of 1691, had 6 x 48pdrs and 18 x 36pdrs), with 28 x 18pdrs on the middle deck, 24 x 12pdrs on the upper deck and 6 x 4pdrs on the *gaillards*. Again, these were without forecastles.

Four of these twenty-five (as well as earlier three-deckers) were destroyed at La Hougue and Cherbourg in early June 1692, and their names were promptly reassigned to replacements under construction.

INTRÉPIDE. 82, later 84 guns. Designed and built by Honoré Malet. Pierced for fourteen guns per side on the LD (excluding the chase ports). Ordered as 2nd Rank, to have had a divided third tier, but raised to the 1st Rank in early 1690 when extra 8pdrs were added on the UD while under construction. From 1690 all 1st Rank ships would have three complete gun decks (until the appearance of the 80-gun two-decker in the 1740s).

    Dimensions & tons: 151ft 0in, 130ft 0in x 42ft 10in x 18ft 4in (49.05, 42.23 x 13.91 x 5.96m) 1,500 tons. Draught 19ft /20½ft (6.17/6.66 m). Men: 550 in war, 400 peace, +9 officers.

    Guns: 82 in war (78 peace): LD 28 x 36pdrs; MD 26 x 18pdrs; UD 24 x 8pdrs (26 x 8pdrs from 1706); poop 4 x 4pdrs.

Intrépide Rochefort Dyd.
    K: 4.1689. L: 3.1690. C: 5.1690. Took part in the Battle of Beachy Head 10.7.1690 (as flagship of LG Jean Gabaret), and the Battle of Lagos (attack on the Smyrna convoy) on 28.6.1693. Lent as a privateer to CV Bernard Renau d'Élissagaray as part of a squadron of four vessels 1696. Took part in the Battle of Vélez-Málaga on 24.8.1704 (as flagship of CdE Jean-Baptiste Ducasse). Scuttled at Toulon in 7.1707, but refloated. Condemned 6.1717 at Toulon and hulked; BU 1724.

MONARQUE. 90 guns. Designed and built by Blaise Pangalo. Ordered in 1689, named *Saint Esprit* on 24 September but renamed *Monarque* on 1 June 1690. Pierced for fourteen guns per side on the LD (excluding the chase ports). Ordered as 2nd Rank, but raised to the 1st Rank in 1690. In July 1690 she conducted satisfactory trials of four 48pdr bronze cannon while fitting out at Toulon, and in mid-1691 she may have tested four 64pdr *canons-bombes* at Brest. Rebuilt at Brest from June to December 1694.

    Dimensions & tons: 155ft 0in x 44ft 0in x 19ft 6in (50.35 x 14.29 x 6.33m). 1,900 tons. Draught 22½/24ft (7.31/7.80m). Men: 700 in war, 650 peace, +9 officers.

    Guns: 90 in war (84 peace): LD 28 x 36pdrs; MD 28 x 18pdrs; UD 28 x 8pdrs (26 from 1698); QD 6 x 6pdrs. 84 from 1704 (84 in war, 72 peace): LD 24 x 24pdrs; MD 26 x 18pdrs; UD 26 x 8pdrs; QD 8 x 6pdrs.

Monarque Brest Dyd.
    K: 10.11.1689. L: 24.5.1690. C: late 1690. Took part in the Battle of Barfleur 29.5.1692 (as flagship of CdE André, Marquis de Nesmond). Lent as a privateer to the now LG André, Marquis de Nesmond, as part of a squadron of six to eleven vessels, 1696. Took part in the Battle of Vélez-Málaga on 24.8.1704. Scuttled at Toulon 7.1707 to avoid the British bombardment, but refloated and returned to service. Condemned late 1716 at Toulon and BU 1717.

VICTORIEUX. 94, later 88 guns. Designed and built by Honoré Malet. Pierced for thirteen pairs of gunports on the LD (excluding the unarmed chase ports). Ordered in October 1689. Following Seignelay's death, Malet determined to increase the length of three-deckers towards the 158ft advocated by Tourville and Pangalo. At one point the ship was given 4 x 64pdr *canons-bombes* on the LD but in 1705 CdE Pierre Guérusseau Du Magnou asked to have these replaced by 2 x 36pdrs.

    Dimensions & tons: 156ft 0in x 43ft 4in x 18ft 0in (50.67 x 14.08 x 5.85m) 1,650 tons. Draught 21/21½ft (6.82 / 6.98m). Men: 700 in war, 600 peace, +9 officers.

    Guns: 94 in war (80 peace): LD 26 x 36pdrs (28 from 1707, presumably using chase ports); MD 28 x 18pdrs; UD 26 x 8pdrs (28 from 1715); QD 10 x 6pdrs (8 from 1715); poop 4 x 4pdrs (removed 1706).

Victorieux Rochefort Dyd.
    K: 4.1690. L: 1.1691. C: 4.1691. Took part in Battle of Lagos 28.6.1693. Condemned 1717 at Rochefort and raséed; BU 1719.

ORGUEILLEUX. 88, later 90 guns. Designed and built by Laurent Coulomb. Pierced for fourteen pairs of gunports on the LD (excluding the unarmed chase ports); each measured 34in width (and 30in height), and they were separated by 7ft 1in (2.3m) sections of hull. The fifteen pairs of MD gunports measured 30in width by 28in height, and the thirteen pairs of UD gunports measured 28in width by 26in height. Three pairs of gunports for 6pdr guns in the stern measured 20in width and 18in height. Named on 24 September 1689; ordered in October 1689.

Dimensions & tons: 153ft 0in, 125ft 0in x 43ft 0in x 19ft 3in (49.70, 40.60 x 13.97 x 6.25 m). 1,600 tons. Draught 21/23ft (6.82/7.47m). Men: 650 (104/334/212) in war, 400 peace, +9 officers.

Guns: 88 in 1691. 90 in war in 1696 (82 peace): LD 28 x 36pdrs; MD 30 x 18pdrs; UD 26 x 8pdrs; QD 6 x 6pdrs. From 1704: LD 26 x 36pdrs; MD 30 x 18pdrs; UD 26 x 8pdrs; QD 8 x 6pdrs.

Orgueilleux Lorient.
K: 6.1690. L: 29.3.1691. C: 5.1691. Took part in Battles of Barfleur 29.5.1692 (as flagship of LG Jean Gabaret), Lagos 28.6.1693 (as flagship of CdE Joseph Andrault, Marquis de Langeron) and Vélez-Málaga 24.8.1704. Scuttled at Toulon in 7.1707, but refloated. Condemned 11.3.1713 at Toulon and BU by order of 1.12.1715 (completed by August 1716).

FOUDROYANT Class. 90/86 guns. Designed and built by Blaise Pangalo, these three-deckers were built without a forecastle, and pierced for fourteen pairs of LD ports (excluding the chase ports). *Foudroyant* was ordered in January 1690 and named on 9 July, while *Merveilleux* was ordered in February 1691 and named on 13 May. These two ships were lost at La Hougue barely a year after construction, and replacements of the same names were built by Pangalo at Brest (see below), although this latter pair were fitted with forecastles.

Dimensions & tons: 157ft 0in, 136ft 0in x 44ft 0in x 20ft 0in (51.00, 44.18 x 14.29 x 6.50m). 1,600 tons. Draught 21ft (6.82m). Men: 560 (90/304/166), +9 officers.

Guns: 90 in war: LD 28 x 36pdrs; MD 28 x 18pdrs; UD 24 x 8pdrs; QD 10 x 6pdrs. (*Merveilleux* had only 26 LD and 26 MD guns). *Foudroyant* was listed with 84 guns in 1691–92 while *Merveilleux* had 80 in 1692.

Foudroyant Brest Dyd.
K: 7.1690. L: 5.3.1691. C: 6.1691. Took part in Battle of Barfleur 29.5.1792 (as flagship of CdE Ferdinand, Comte de Relingue), then burnt by fireship at La Hougue 2.6.1692.

Merveilleux Brest Dyd.
K: 7.5.1691. L: 19.11.1691. C: 4.1692. Took part in Battle of Barfleur 29.5.1792 (as flagship of LG Charles-François Davy, Marquis d'Amfreville), then burnt by fireship at La Hougue 2.6.1692.

The Battle of Vélez-Málaga in August 1704 involved most of France's 1st Rank ships in the Mediterranean, some seventeen vessels. While no ships were lost of either side, the strategic outcome was that the English retained control of newly-occupied Gibraltar, and the French Mediterranean fleet was effectively confined to Toulon. In this anonymous engraving from the middle of the eighteenth century, most are unidentified, but the *Fier* (numbered 2) is shown at the moment her poop was blown up by a shell (presumably from a bomb vessel – which could only have been sheer luck); number 4, in the right foreground, shows the *Tonnant* forced out of the line, while 5 (top right) indicates the damaged fleet flagship *Foudroyant* towed out of action by a galley. (Beverley R Robinson Collection, Annapolis 51.7.85)

ADMIRABLE. 84 guns. Designed and built by Laurent Coulomb. Originally ordered to the same design as *Orgueilleux*, but modified during construction and probably only pierced for thirteen pairs of gunports on the LD (excluding the unarmed chase ports), and seemingly only twelve pairs were armed in order to accommodate the weight of 48pdrs on that deck. Named on 24 September 1689 and ordered in October 1689.

>Dimensions & tons: 151ft 6in, 125ft 0in x 43ft 0in x 19ft 3in (49.21, 40.60 x 13.97 x 6.25 m). 1,600 tons. Draught 21/23ft (6.82/7.47m). Men: 550 (89/304/157) in war, 400 peace, +9 officers.
>
>Guns: 84 in war: LD 6 x 48pdrs + 18 x 36pdrs; MD 28 x 18pdrs; UD 24 x 8pdrs; QD 6 x 6pdrs.

Admirable Lorient Dyd.
>K: 9.1690. L: 10.9.1691. C: 3.1692. Took part in Battle of Barfleur 29.5.1692, then run ashore and burnt by boats from English ships at Cherbourg 1.6.1692, after a failed attempt by fireship HMS *Hound*.

SCEPTRE Class. 84 guns. Designed and built by François Coulomb. Pierced for thirteen pairs of gunports on the LD (excluding the unarmed chase ports); each measured 35in width (and 32½in height), and they were seperated by 7ft 3in (2.35m) sections of hull. The fourteen pairs of MD ports measured 32½in width by 30½in height, and the thirteen pairs of UD ports measured 26in width by 24in height. Three pairs of ports in the stern measured 20in width and 18in height. Ordered on 30 April 1691 (contract for *Sceptre*) and named on 13 May (both). At the request of Pointis, a small forecastle was added for the campaign of Cartagena.

>Dimensions & tons: (as ordered) 152ft 0in, 130ft 6in x 43ft 0in x 19ft 6in (49.38, 42.39 x 27.74 x 6.40m). (as built) 153ft 0in, 131ft 6in x 44ft 0in x 20ft 4in (49.70, 42.72 x 14.29 x 6.60m). 1,800 tons. Draught 23ft (7.47m). Men: 650 in war, 500 peace, +12 officers.
>
>Guns: 84 in war (78 peace): LD 26 x 36pdrs; MD 28 x 18pdrs; UD 24 x 8pdrs (26 from 1704); QD 6 x 4pdrs (6 x 6pdrs from 1699, 8 x 6pdrs from 1704).

Sceptre Toulon Dyd.
>K: 3.5.1691. L: 10.11.1691. C: 3.1692. Lent as a privateer to CdE Jean Bernard de Saint-Jean, Baron de Pointis 1696–97; took part in the capture of Cartagena de Indias 5.5.1697. Took part in the Battle of Vélez-Málaga on 24.8.1704. Scuttled at Toulon in 7.1707, but refloated. Condemned 18.12.1717 at Toulon, and ordered to be BU 12.1.1718.

Lys Toulon Dyd.
>K: 11.5.1691. L: 17.12.1691. C: 2.1692. Lent as a privateer to LG André, Marquis de Nesmond, as part of a squadron of five vessels, 1695–96. Took part in the Battle of Vélez-Málaga on 24.8.1704. Driven ashore and burnt (with *Magnanime*) by her crew at Marbella 21.3.1705 to avoid capture by Vice-Adm Sir John Leake's squadron.

FORMIDABLE. 90 guns. Designed and built by Étienne Hubac. Pierced for fourteen pairs of gunports on the LD (excluding the unarmed chase ports). Ordered in February 1691 and named on 13 May 1691.

>Dimensions & tons: 157ft 0in, 136ft 0in x 44ft 0in x 20ft 0in. (51.00, 44.18 x 14.29 x 6.50m) 1,800 tons. Draught 22/23¾ft (7.15/7.39m). Men: 700 in war, 660 peace, +13 officers.
>
>Guns: 90 in war (86 peace): LD 28 x 36pdrs; MD 28 x 18pdrs; UD 26 x 8pdrs (28 from 1706); QD 8 x 6pdrs (10 x 6pdrs from 1707).

Formidable Brest Dyd.
>K: 5.1691. L: 4.12.1691. C: 5.1692. Took part in Battle of Lagos 28.6.1693. Sold at Brest 1713 and BU 1714.

FULMINANT. 98 guns. Designed and built by Pierre Masson. Pierced for fourteen pairs of gunports on the LD (the redundant chase ports were never pierced). This ship, and its near-sister *Ambitieux*, were conceived in line with Tourville's (and Pangalo's) concept of 1680 to build 80-gun three-deckers with a length of 158ft and 42ft breadth. In 1690 Masson chose to put Tourville's project into effect, retaining the original dimensions, but over-gunning raised the firepower to over 90 guns to the detriment of the ship's sailing qualities.

>Dimensions & tons: 158ft 0in, 135ft 0in x 42ft 0in x 19ft 6in. (51.32, 43.85 x 13.64 x 6.33m) 1,800/3,686 tons. Draught 20/23ft (6.50/7.47m). Men: 750 in war, 700 peace, +12 officers.
>
>Guns: 98 in war (88 peace): LD 28 x 36pdrs; MD 30 x 18pdrs; UD 26 x 8pdrs (from 1707, 28 x 12pdrs); QD 12 x 6pdrs (from 1707, 10 x 6pdrs); poop 2 x 4pdrs.

Fulminant Rochefort Dyd.
>K: 7.1691. L: 12.1691. C: 5.1692. Badly hogged by 1715, condemned 1717 at Rochefort, and BU 1719.

AMBITIEUX. 92 guns. Designed and built by Honoré Malet, but virtually a sister to the *Fulminant* although widened 2.5ft by girdling at the insistence of its designated commander, Villette-Mursay, destroying any sailing qualities it might have had. Pierced for fourteen pairs of gunports on the LD (the redundant chase ports were never pierced).

>Dimensions & tons: 158ft 0in, 135ft 0in x 44ft 6in x 20ft 0in. (51.32, 43.85 x 14.46 x 6.50m) 1,600 tons. Draught 20ft (6.50m). Men: 850 war, 650 peace, +16 officers.
>
>Guns: 92 in war (88 peace): LD 28 x 36pdrs; MD 28 x 18pdrs; UD 26 x 12pdrs or 8pdrs; QD 10 x 6pdrs.

Ambitieux Rochefort Dyd.
>K: 7.1691. L: 12.1691. C: 4.1692. Took part in Battle of Barfleur 29.5.1692 (as flagship of LG Philippe Le Valois, Marquis de Villette-Mursay), then burnt by fireship at La Hougue 2.6.1692.

VAINQUEUR. 84 guns. Designed and built by Laurent Coulomb and Pierre Coulomb, but proved a mediocre sailer. Pierced for thirteen pairs of gunports on the LD.

>Dimensions & tons: 150ft 0in, 125ft 0in x 43ft 0in x 19ft 0in (48.73, 40.60 x 13.97 x 6.17m) 1,600 tons. Draught 22/23½ft (7.15/7.63m). Men: initially 550 (93/289/168), +7 officers; by 1696 – 630in war, 500 peace.
>
>Guns: 84 in war (76 peace): LD 26 x 36pdrs; MD 28 (or 26) x 18pdrs; UD 24 (or 26) x 8pdrs; QD 6 x 6pdrs.

Vainqueur Port Louis, near Lorient.
>K: 8.1691. L: 24.2.1692. C: 5.1692. Took part in the Battles of Lagos 28.6.1693 (under CdE Alain Emmanuel, Marquis de Coëtlogon) and of Vélez-Málaga on 24.8.1704 (as flagship of CdE Louis Alphonse Ignace, Bailli de Lorraine, who was killed in this battle). Scuttled at Toulon in 7.1707, but refloated. Condemned and hulked 6.1717 at Toulon; sank from neglect 1721 but refloated 1.9.1722 and BU.

ROYAL LOUIS. 110 guns. Designed and built by François Coulomb to replace the *Royal Louis* of 1669, which had become unserviceable by 1691. The largest and longest three-decker of the Sun King's navy, with the heaviest armament including massive 48pdrs (= 51.83 English pounds) on the lower deck. The order for thirty of the immense 48pdr guns (each of 10ft length and 8,000 *livres* weight) was placed with René Landouillette de Logivière, master gunmaker of the Toulon Foundry in October 1692, but the last of this calibre were not completed until 1698.

The lower deck was pierced for fifteen gunports per side on the lower deck (excluding the chase port, which was not cut through, to avoid weakening the hawsepieces); these ports measured 37in width (and 34in height), and were separated by 7ft 5in (2.41m) of hull. The prestigious name was assigned on 7 April 1692. It took part in Tourville's 'great commissioning' at Toulon in 1693 (as flagship of Vice-Am. Jean, Comte d'Estrées) but saw virtually no service until decommissioned in 1716. D'Estrées had the 48pdrs replaced with 36pdrs soon after commissioning as he felt the 48pdrs were too heavy and cumbersome; the guns were placed in a shore battery at Brest but continued to be assigned in theory to the ship for her whole career. Rebuilt at Brest in 1704–5.

   Dimensions & tons: 174ft 0in, 147ft 0in x 48ft 0in x 23ft 0in (56.52, 47.75 x 15.59 x 7.47m). By 1726 the length was increased by warping to 175ft 7in (57.04m). 2,600/3,928 tons. Draught 21/26ft (6.82/8.45m). Men: 1,050 in war, 990 peace.

   Guns: 110 in war (106 peace): LD 30 x 48pdrs; MD 32 x 18pdrs; UD 28 x 12pdrs; QD 10 x 6pdrs; Fc 6 x 6pdrs; poop 4 x 4pdrs. The 48pdrs were replaced with 36pdrs in 1693, and the 6pdrs and 4pdrs were later replaced by 8pdrs and 6pdrs respectively.

Royal Louis Toulon Dyd.
   K: 9.4.1692. L: 22.9.1692. C: 5.1693. Proposed for condemnation 1704 but the Minister ordered her refitted. Brest noted in 1715 that she was usable only in summertime and her upperworks were beginning to rot. Condemned 1723 at Brest and BU there 1727.

Following the Battle off Barfleur on 29 May 1692, three three-decker ships (the 1st Rank *Soleil Royal* and *Admirable*, and the 2nd Rank *Triomphant*, all three with battle damage) were sent by Tourville into Cherbourg, were they were beached; here they were attacked by English warships on 1 June. This attack was beaten off, but on 2 June three British fireships and some boats were employed and the French trio destroyed. Another twelve ships sailed into the roadstead at La Hougue and beached; here they were attacked by British long-boats and fireships, and all twelve were likewise burnt, six (the 1st Rank *Ambitieux*, *Merveilleux*, *Foudroyant*, *Magnifique*, and *Saint Philippe*, and the 2nd Rank *Terrible*) during the morning of 2 June off the islet of Tatihou, and the other six (the 2nd Rank *Bourbon*, *Fier* and *Tonnant* and the 3rd Rank *Saint Louis*, *Fort* and *Gaillard*) on the following morning while sheltering behind the Crocq de Quinéville sandbank. Notably, two further 3rd Rank ships (*Assuré* and *Sage* of LG Victor Marie, Comte d'Estrées's squadron) had been lost at Ceuta just a few weeks earlier, on passage from Toulon to join Tourville's Atlantic Fleet at Brest, with the loss of 317 men.

Following this disaster, with the King's assent, Louis, Marquis de Pontchartrain, Secretary of State for the Navy and Minister of Finance, began immediately to organize the replacement of these heavy losses and decided to act, even before he had received a full report about the disaster. As early as 4 June he ordered Hubert Desclouzeaux, the *intendant* at Brest, to have the two 2nd Rank ships recently ordered enlarged and converted into two 1st Rank ships. In an eight page letter he confirmed the construction of more '*gros vaisseaux*' to replace the losses, each vessel taking the name of a 1st Rank predecessor lost on 1 or 2 June. Similar directives were send to the *intendants* in the other ports. Between June and September 1692, six 1st Rank ships were laid down – *Magnifique*, *Foudroyant*, *Ambitieux*, *Merveilleux*, *Admirable* and *Terrible* – and five 2nd Rank – *Bourbon*, *Saint Louis*, *Éole*, *Prompt* and *Fort* (see Chapter 2). All these ships were launched by the end of February 1693 and all were commissioned before summer 1693.

Two more 1st Rank ships were started in December 1692 – *Tonnant* and *Saint Philippe* – and a final three during 1693 – *Triomphant*, *Soleil Royal* and *Fier*. All of them, except the last, were commissioned in 1694; these also were given the names of 1st or 2nd Rank ships lost at Cherbourg and La Hougue. During the same period five 3rd Rank ships were launched – *Mignon*, *Bon*, *Gaillard*, *Fougueux* and *Téméraire* (see Chapter 3) – two of them being built for *armement mixte en course* (privateering) on the request of private partners who advanced the cost of the construction. One 5th Rank ship was also launched at this time (*Volontaire* – see Chapter 5).

Thus in two years, from June 1692 to June 1694, the battlefleet was reconstituted. As the vessels lost (with the exceptions of those built since 1689) were in general mostly of lesser firepower than their replacements, by 1694 the *armée navale* was significantly stronger than before 1692: it

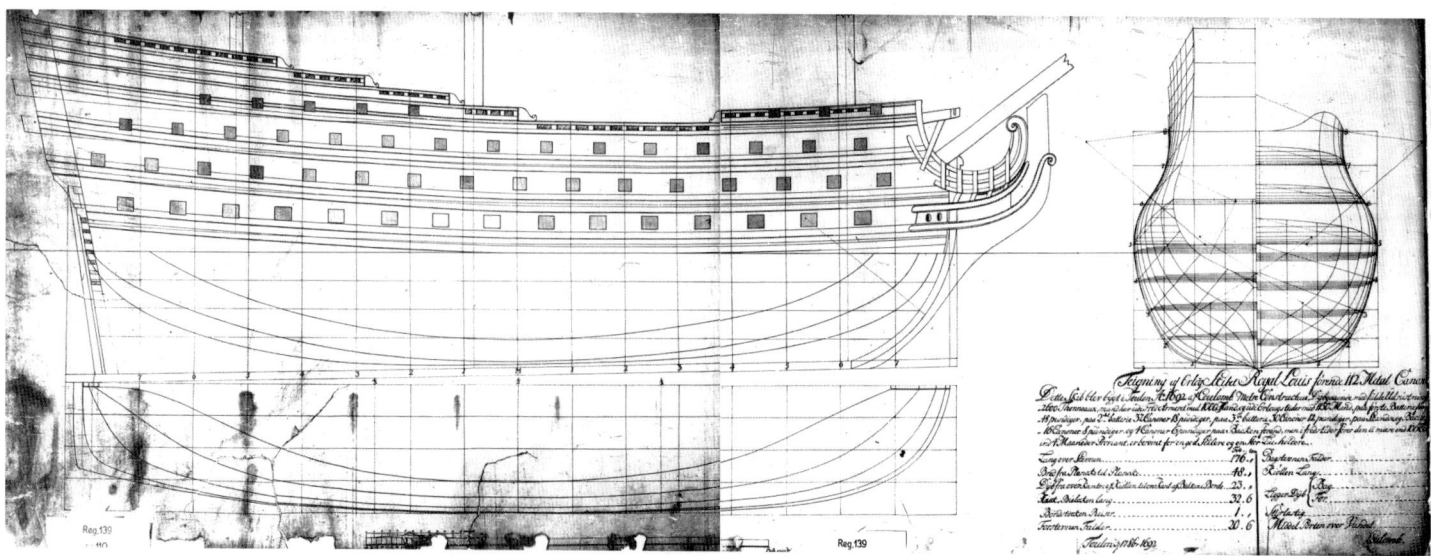

A rather battered Danish copy of the original sheer plan of the *Royal Louis*; the details given in the rubric confirm this to be the 1692 110-gun ship. The draught includes no provision for the 4pdr guns on the poop, but the *États abrégés* confirm these were carried, so presumably were added on completion, but were not carried in peacetime (after 1712 the 4pdrs were replaced by 6pdrs, and the 6pdrs on the quarterdeck by 8pdrs); the *dunette* was 39ft in length, extending forward to enclose the mizzen mast. The furthest aft of the fifteen ports on the upper deck were never armed, in order to improve the accommodation, so only fourteen pairs of 12pdrs were carried on that deck. The lower deck initially carried a battery of massive 48pdrs, but her commander quickly had them replaced by more manageable 36pdrs. By June 1716 she was lying disarmed at Brest, where she had been based since 1703 as flagship of the *Ponant* Fleet. (Rigsarkivet, Copenhagen)

was larger (four more 1st Rank ships), younger (none of its ships was older than two years) and more powerful (when completed, *Royal Louis* received a LD battery of 30 x 48pdrs, and for the 1693 campaign the old 2nd Rank *Pompeux* received 8 x 60pdr *canons-bombes* on her LD).

Although many follow Alfred Thayer Mahan in claiming that it was this disaster – this *contre-temps* as Louis XIV used to call it – that caused the French Navy to abandon a battlefleet strategy (*la guerre d'escadres*) in preference for commerce raiding (*la guerre de course*), the figures given above show that construction of 1st Rank and 2nd Rank vessels actually accelerated after June 1692. Indeed, this immense effort made to restore the French Navy in its former splendour has no equivalent in its history. In 1693 Tourville, the new *Maréchal de France*, had at his disposal the best fleet ever. Louis XIV, however, had in the meantime renounced his effort to restore James II to the English throne, ending the requirement for a large fleet in his grand strategy. In addition, the bad winter of 1693–94 and the unprecedented economic crisis left him with no money to maintain vessels for which he now had no use. His best option was to lend some of the vessels that he could not otherwise maintain for operation as privateers by private individuals. This greatly accelerated the program of *armements mixtes en course* – the use of vessels of the King's navy, including units of the battlefleet, for such privateering, which had begun on a small scale in 1688.

MAGNIFIQUE. 86 guns. Designed and built by Honoré Malet. A replacement for the ship of the same name burnt at La Hougue. Pierced for thirteen pairs of gunports on the LD.

Dimensions & tons: 154ft 0in x 44ft 6in x 19ft 0in (50.03 x 14.46 x 6.17m). 1,560 tons. Draught 21/22ft (6.82/7.15m). Men: 600 in war, 550 peace, +9–12 officers.

Guns: 86 in war (80 peace): LD 26 x 36pdrs; MD 28 x 18pdrs; UD 26 x 12pdrs; QD 6 (later 8) x 6pdrs.

Magnifique Rochefort Dyd.
K: 6.1692. L: 23.11.1692. C: 5.1693. Took part in the Battles of Lagos 28.6.1693 and Vélez-Málaga on 24.8.1704 (as flagship of CdE Jean de Belle-Isle-Érard, who was killed in the battle). Scuttled at Toulon in 7.1707; refloated, but condemned 11.3.1713 at Toulon; ordered BU 30.8.1715 and BU there 23.8.1716 to 11.4.1717.

SOLEIL ROYAL. 104 guns. Designed and built by Étienne Hubac. Ordered 8.6.1692 and named *Foudroyant* 21.6.1692 to replace the namesake burnt at La Hougue in June 1692. When Louis XIV ordered another 1st Rank to be named *Soleil Royal*, Étienne Hubac begged that this name be given to the ship he was building because the previous one lost at La Hougue had been built by his own father, *Maître* Laurent, between 1668 and 1670, and – as she had been rebuilt from the keel up by himself in 1689 – he still possessed *les gabarits* (the moulds). The King agreed on 1 March 1693 to Hubac's proposal (see *Foudroyant* below). Pierced for fourteen pairs of LD gunports (the fifteenth chase or hawse port was never pierced), and built with an armed forecastle.

Dimensions & tons: 170ft 0in x 46ft 0in x 22ft 0in (55.22 x 14.94 x 7.15m). 2,400 tons. Draught 23/24½ft (7.47/7.96m). Men: 900 in war, 810 peace, +17 officers; 950 from 1694, +17 officers.

Guns: 104 in war (96 peace): LD 28 x 36pdrs; MD 30 x 18pdrs; UD 28 x 12pdrs; QD 12 x 6pdrs; Fc 6 x 6pdrs.

Soleil Royal Brest Dyd.
K: 6.1692. L: 24.12.1692. C: 4.1693. Took part in the Battles of Lagos 28.6.1693, and of Vélez-Málaga on 24.8.1704 (as flagship of LG Joseph Andrault, Marquis de Langeron). Scuttled at Toulon in 7.1707; refloated, but judged unfit for service 14.10.1713, and ordered to be sold 1.11.1713, she was BU in 1714.

AMBITIEUX. 92 guns. Designed and begun by Honoré Malet, completed after Malet's death by Jean Guichard. A replacement for the first ship of this name (burnt at La Hougue in June 1692). Pierced for fourteen pairs of LD guns. From 1705 she was raised to 96 guns by the addition of an extra pair of 8pdrs on the UD, and an extra pair of 6pdrs on the QD; she briefly received 4 x 100pdrs, replaced by 4 x 36pdrs.

Dimensions & tons: 155ft 0in x 45ft 4in x 20ft 2in (50.35 x 14.73 x 6.52m). 1,650 tons. Draught 21½/24½ft (6.98/7.96m). Men: 850 in war, 650 peace, +?11 officers.

Guns: 92 in war (88 peace): LD 28 x 36pdrs; MD 28 x 18pdrs; UD 26 x 8pdrs (28 from 1706); QD 10 x 6pdrs (12 from 1707); Fc nil.

Ambitieux Rochefort Dyd.
K: 6.1692. L: 5.12.1692. C: 5.1693. Took part in Battle of Lagos 28.6.1693. Sold and BU at Brest 1713.

MERVEILLEUX. 100, later 98 guns. Designed and built by Blaise Pangalo. Pierced for fourteen pairs of LD guns, and – in a departure from earlier practice – built with a forecastle. Ordered 8 June 1692 and named 21 June as a replacement for the first ship of this name (burnt at La Hougue in June 1692). She was later reduced to 98 guns by the removal of a pair of 6pdrs from the *gaillards*.

Dimensions & tons: 163ft 9in, 140ft 0in x 45ft 0in x 19ft 0in (53.19, 45.48 x 14.62 x 6.17m). 2,200 tons. Draught 24ft (7.80m). Men: 800 in war, 720 peace, +13 officers.

Guns: 100 in 1693 (see above). 98 from 1696 in war (92 peace): LD 28 x 36pdrs; MD 28 x 18pdrs; UD 28 x 8pdrs; QD 10 x 6pdrs; Fc 4 x 6pdrs.

Merveilleux Brest Dyd
K: 6.1692. L: 20.11.1692. C: 4.1693. Took part in Battle of Lagos 28.6.1693. BU at Brest 1713.

ADMIRABLE. 96 guns. Designed and built by Laurent Coulomb. This was a replacement for the previous ship of the same name (burnt at Cherbourg in June 1692). Pierced for fourteen pairs of LD guns. Unlike her predecessor, she was built with a forecastle.

Dimensions & tons: 160ft 0in, 134ft 0in x 45ft 6in x 21ft 0in (51.97, 43.53 x 14.78 x 6.82m). 2,000 tons. Draught 22ft/23½ft (7.15/7.63m). Men: 725 in war, 550 peace, +11 officers.

Guns: 96 in war (88 peace): LD 28 x 36pdrs; MD 30 x 18pdrs; UD 28 x 8pdrs (26 x 12pdrs from 1699, 24 x 12pdrs from 1704); QD 10 x 6pdrs (6 from 1699).

Admirable Port Louis, near Lorient.
K: 7.1692. L: 23.12.1692. C: 3.1693. Took part in the Battles of Lagos 28.6.1693 and of Vélez-Málaga on 24.8.1704 (as flagship of CdE Jacques Cadot, Comte de Sébeville). Scuttled at Toulon in 7.1707; refloated, but condemned 11.3.1713 at Toulon and BU (by Orders of 30.8.1715 and 1.12.1715) in 6/8.1716.

TERRIBLE. 100, later 104 guns. Designed and built by Blaise Pangalo; ordered 19 July 1692 and named 27 August, again taking the name of a ship burnt at La Hougue. The lower deck was pierced for fourteen pairs of 36pdr guns (the fifteenth, chase or hawse, port was never pierced), and she had an armed forecastle. From 1705 she was raised to 104 guns by the addition of an extra pair of 18pdrs on the MD, and an extra pair of 6pdrs on the QD; the 8pdrs on her UD were also replaced with 12pdrs at this time.

Dimensions & tons: 165ft 0in x 45ft 0in x 19ft 0in (53.60 x 14.62 x 6.17m). 2,200 tons. Draught 23ft/24ft (7.47/7.80m). Men: 800 in war, 720 peace, +14 officers.

Guns: 100 in war (92 peace): LD 28 x 36pdrs; MD 28 x 18pdrs; UD 28 x 8pdrs; QD 10 x 6pdrs; Fc 6 x 6pdrs. 104 from 1706 (104 in war, 90 peace): LD 28 x 36pdrs; MD 30 x 18pdrs; UD

28 x 12pdrs; QD 12 x 6pdrs; Fc 6 x 6pdrs.

Terrible Brest Dyd.
K: 8.1692. L: 21.2.1693. C: 5.1693. Took part in the Battles of Lagos 28.6.1693 (as flagship of LG Louis Francois de Rousselet, Marquis de Châteaurenault) and of Vélez-Málaga on 24.8.1704 (as flagship of LG Ferdinand, Comte de Relingue, who was killed in the battle). Scuttled at Toulon in 7.1707; refloated, but condemned 18.8.1714 and sold.

TONNANT Class. 90 guns. Designed and built by François Coulomb. Pierced for fourteen LD guns per side (with no fifteenth or chase pair of gunports pierced), and completed without forecastle. Ordered and begun in 1692, and both named on 20 January 1693 for ships burnt at La Hougue in June 1692. *Saint Philippe* underwent rebuilding from 2.1699 to 1700, and *Tonnant* from November 1701 to January 1702, both at Toulon. Unlike the majority of the *Levant* Fleet, which was scuttled in the port of Toulon in July 1707 to avoid the British bombardment, these two ships were undergoing refits in the nearby basin of Le Mourillon, and were sailed to counter the British attack; they were both then used as floating batteries during the siege by the fleet of Adm Sir Clowdisley Shovell in July and August 1707.

Dimensions & tons: 158ft 0in, 134ft 0in x 44ft 6in x 20ft 6in (51.32, 43.53 x 14.46 x 6.66m). 1,750 tons. Draught 23ft (7.47m). Men: *Tonnant* 725 in war, 850 peace; *Saint Philippe* 750 in war, 870 peace; each + 10/13 officers.

Guns: 90 in war (82 peace): LD 28 x 36pdrs; MD 30 x 18pdrs; UD 26 x 12pdrs (28 in *Saint Philippe* from 1706?); QD 6 x 6pdrs.

Tonnant Toulon Dyd.
K: 12.1692. L: 9.1693. C: 12.1693. Took part in the Battle of Vélez-Málaga on 24.8.1704 (as flagship of LG Alain Emmanuel, Comte de Coëtlogon). Converted to a floating battery during the siege of Toulon (see note above). Damaged by fire 1707, grounded 1708 to avoid sinking. Condemned 7.4.1710 and sold by order of 28.5.1710.

Saint Philippe Toulon Dyd.
K: 12.1692. L: 10.1693. C: 12.1693. Took part in the Battle of Vélez-Málaga on 24.8.1704 (as flagship of LG Louis Le Roux, Marquis d'Infreville de Saint Aubin). Converted to a floating battery during the siege of Toulon (see note above). Unserviceable 11.3.1713, condemned 18.8.1714 and BU.

TRIOMPHANT. 94 guns. Designed and built by Laurent Coulomb. A near-sister to the *Admirable*, and like her built as a replacement for the previous ship of the same name burnt at Cherbourg in June 1692. Pierced for fourteen pairs of LD guns (the chase port was not pierced). Unlike her predecessor, built with a forecastle.

Dimensions & tons: 161ft 4in, 134ft 0in x 45ft 8in x 21ft 8in (52.29, 43.53 x 14.66 x 7.04m). 1,900 tons. Draught 22ft/23½ft (7.15/7.63m). Men: 750 in war, 580 peace, +11 officers.

Guns: 94 in war (82 peace): LD 28 x 36pdrs; MD 30 x 18pdrs; UD 28 x 8pdrs (26 x 12pdrs from 1699, 24 x 12pdrs from 1704); QD 8 x 6pdrs (6 from 1699).

Triomphant Port Louis, near Lorient
K: 2.1693. L: 1.10.1693. C: 1694. Took part in the Battle of Vélez-Málaga on 24.8.1704 (as flagship of LG François-René de Betz, Comte de La Harteloire). Scuttled at Toulon in 7.1707; refloated by 10.1707; condemned and hulked at Toulon 6.1717; sank from neglect 1721 and completed BU there by 28.2.1726.

FOUDROYANT. 104 guns. Designed and built by Blaise Pangalo, as a slightly enlarged version of the *Terrible*. Ordered 20 January 1693 under the name *Soleil Royal* to replace the ship of that name burnt at Cherbourg, but she and the ship then launched and completing as *Foudroyant* exchanged names on 1 March 1693 prior to her keel being laid down. Pierced for fourteen pairs of LD gunports (like most post-1692 ships, the fifteenth chase port was never pierced), and she had an armed forecastle. A significant design innovation saw the heel of the bowsprit, which had traditionally always been sited on the LD of three-deckers, being moved up to the MD on this vessel; consideration was given to retro-fitting this change to other three-deckers (notably to the *Fier*), but the cost was estimated to be prohibitive.

Dimensions & tons: 166ft 0in x 46ft 0in x 21ft 6in (53.92 x 14.94 x 6.98m). 2,200 tons. Draught 23ft/26ft (7.47/8.45 m). Men: 900 in war, 800 peace, +12/15 officers.

Lines plan of the 90-gun *Tonnant* and *Saint Philippe* of 1693, traced by László Veres from *Souvenirs de Marine*, Plate 263. *Vice-amiral* Pâris, who compiled this remarkable collection of plans and drawings, reconstructed the head and figure, which was missing from the original. These ships each had a broadside of 948 *livres* on completion (or 464 kg, equal to 1,023 English lbs).

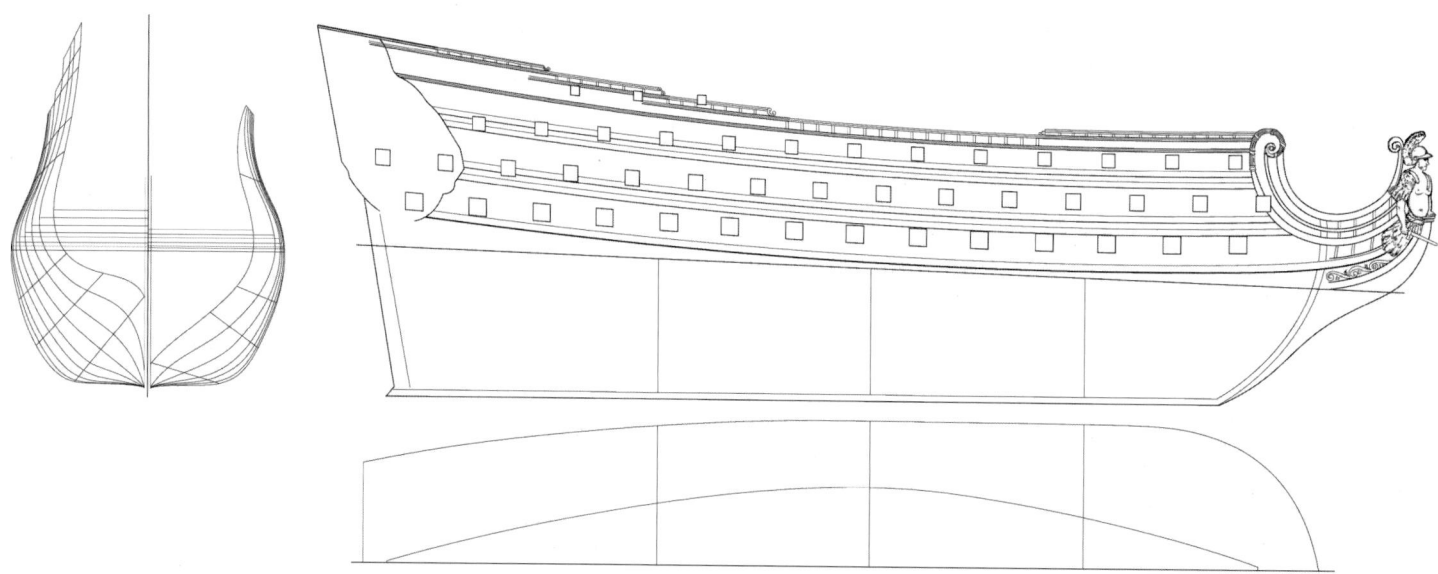

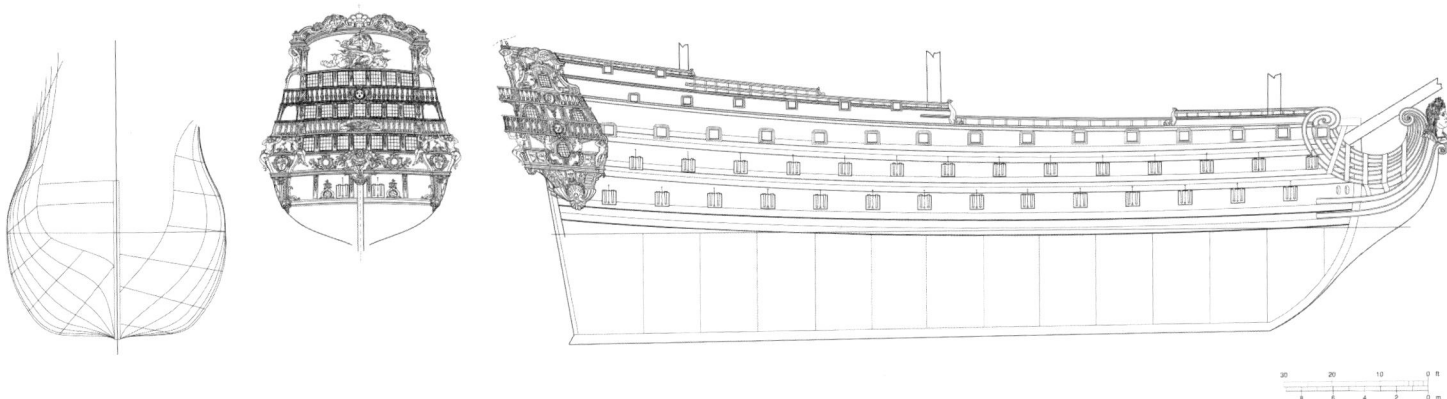

The 104-gun *Foudroyant* of 1693, reconstructed by László Veres from a sheer plan and decorative details in the Rigsarkivet, Copenhagen. With fourteen 36pdrs, fifteen 18pdrs, fourteen 12pdrs and nine 6pdrs on each side, her broadside amounted to 996 *livres* (or 487½ kg, equal to 1,075 English lbs). Badly damaged in action off Vélez-Málaga in 1707, and then suffering the ignominy of being submerged at Toulon three months later, she never returned to active service and was taken to pieces in 1714. There is some doubt about the identification of this plan. The draught shows no armed forecastle (which the 1693 *Foudroyant* certainly had), but does include gunports for two pairs of 4pdrs on the the poop, which *Foudroyant* did not carry. This plan may be an early conceptual design for the vessel.

Guns: 104 in war (94 peace): LD 28 x 36pdrs; MD 30 x 18pdrs; UD 28 x 12pdrs (30 from 1706); QD 12 x 6pdrs; Fc 6 x 6pdrs. 2 x 6pdrs were removed in 1706, when 2 extra UD guns were fitted.

Foudroyant Brest Dyd
   K: 4.1693. L: 14.11.1693. C: 1694. In 1701 flagship of LG Philippe Le Valois, Marquis de Villette-Mursay; in 1702 flagship of LG Ferdinand, Comte de Relingue, then flagship of *Vice-amiral* Victor Marie, Comte d'Estrées. Took part in the Battle of Vélez-Málaga on 24.8.1704 (as flagship of *Amiral de France* Louis-Alexandre de Bourbon, Comte de Toulouse). Scuttled at Toulon on 29.7.1707; refloated but condemned 11.3.1713 at Toulon, sold by order of 1.11.1713 and BU 1714.

FIER. 90, later 94 guns. Designed and built by Honoré Malet and Pierre Masson jointly. Pierced for thirteen pairs of LD guns, and built with no forecastle.

Dimensions & tons: (as ordered) 155ft 0in x 45ft 6in x 19ft 6in (50.35 x 14.78 x 6.33m). 1,700 tons. (as built) 158ft 0in x 46ft 10in x 19ft 6in (51.32 x 15.21 x 6.33m). 1,750 tons. Draught 21½ft/22½ft (6.98/7.31m). Men: 700 in war, 600 peace, +18 officers.

Guns: 90 in war (84 peace): LD 26 x 36pdrs (28 from 1706); MD 28 x 18pdrs; UD 26 x 8pdrs (28 from 1706); QD 10 x 6pdrs.

Fier Rochefort Dyd.
   K: 1693. L: 1694. C: 1695. Took part in Battle of Vélez-Málaga 24.8.1704 (as flagship of LG Philippe Le Valois, Marquis de Villette-Mursay). Scuttled at Toulon on 29.7.1707; refloated but condemned 11.3.1713 and sold by order of 1.11.1713.

After 1693 no further three-deckers were ordered for over thirty years. This was partly attributable to the financial crisis that beset the French government at this time, but also a change in priorities which gave the army preference at the expense of the battlefleet. By 1694 France had won the building race, achieving parity with the combined English and Dutch navies; had the losses at Cherbourg and La Hougue been avoided (*i.e.* if Louis XIV not sent his battlefleet out to combat the numerically superior Allied fleet in May 1692), France would undoubtedly have had a clear superiority in battlefleet numbers over the allied maritime powers by 1694. The strategic move from having a fleet in being (a *guerre d'escadres*) to a war on trade (a *guerre de course*) determined a major shift in the conduct of war and the use of the navy for the rest of Louis's reign, when privateering using naval vessels loaned to a variety of partnerships became the predominant naval activity.

In July 1707 twelve of the newer 1st Rank ships were among some forty-four ships deliberately scuttled at Toulon to avoid the attack by bomb vessels during the siege of that port by Sir Clowdisley Shovell's fleet. Sixteen of the Navy's twenty-two 1st Rank ships were at Toulon at this time; the only exceptions were the four at Brest (*Royal Louis, Merveilleux, Ambitieux* and *Formidable*) and two at Rochefort (*Fulminant* and *Victorieux*). Of the sixteen, the *Saint Philippe* and *Tonnant* were undergoing refits and were deployed to defend the port, while the *Conquérant* was under reconstruction into a 2nd Rank ship. The twelve newer ships were the *Intrépide, Monarque, Orgueilleux, Sceptre, Vainqueur, Soleil Royal, Admirable, Magnifique, Terrible, Triomphant, Foudroyant* and *Fier*; an older 1st Rank – the *Couronne* – was also scuttled. Most of the scuttled ships were refloated about October 1707, but some ten to fourteen ships of the line (including two-deckers of 50 guns or more) were 'subtracted permanently from the navy's rolls' (*see* Jean Meirat, 'Le Siège de Toulon en 1707', in *Neptunia* no 71; Summer 1963).

(D) Three-decked vessels acquired from 1 September 1715

Following the close of the war and the death of Louis XIV, the battlefleet was rapidly run down, with many of the remaining three-deckers being disposed of by 1715. Following the dismissal of Jérôme de Pontchartrain as Secretary of State for the Navy on 1 October 1715, a *Conseil de marine* was set up by the *Amiral de France* (Louis-Alexandre de Bourbon, Comte de Toulouse), directed by his two *Vice-amiraux* (Victor Marie, *Maréchal* and *Duc* d'Estrées and Alain Emmanuel, Comte de Coëtlogon, for the *Ponant* and *Levant* Fleets respectively), which ran the Navy for the next three years.

Nevertheless, there nominally remained eleven 1st Rank ships at the end of 1715, survivors of the 1689–94 building spree. All of these were three-deckers, almost all with a principal battery of 36pdrs (the sole exception was the *Monarque* which from 1704 had only 24pdrs on its LD) and all had a second battery of 18pdrs. The *Royal Louis, Triomphant, Vanqueur, Monarque* and *Intrépide* were all noted as in need of rebuilding, while the *Magnifique* was already condemned (since March 1713) and the

Orgueilleux and *Admirable* had been ordered (on 1 December 1715) to be broken up.

A year later the number was officially down to five – *Royal Louis*, *Sceptre*, and the soon-to-be-dismantled *Magnifique*, *Orgueilleux* and *Admirable* – and by the end of 1717 there were just four (the *Sceptre* had been condemned on 18 December, and would be ordered to be taken to pieces in January 1718). The *Royal Louis* (disarmed since 1716) lasted until condemned in 1723 and was broken up in 1727; no further three-deckers were attempted until 1723, and even then results were deplorable, no successful ship being achieved until the 1760s. After two short-term Secretaries in the five years from 1718, the appointment of Jean-Frédéric Phélypeaux, Comte de Maurepas (and son of Jérôme de Pontchartrain), began a term of office which lasted to his dismissal in 1749.

FOUDROYANT. A 110-gun ship designed and built by Laurent Hélie, but never put to sea.

Dimensions & tons: 173ft 10in, 153ft 0in x 47ft 0in x 22ft 10in (56.47, 49.70 x 15.27 x 7.42 m). By 1736 her length had been remeasured and she was several feet shorter!) 2,400/3,700 tons. Draught 21ft 4in/24ft (6.93/7.80 m). Men: 1,150 in war, 1,000 peace.

Guns (110 in war, 106 peace): LD 30 x 48pdrs; MD 32 x 18pdrs; UD 28 x 12pdrs; QD/Fc 16 x 8pdrs (+ 4 x 6pdrs on poop).

Foudroyant Brest Dyd.
K: 1.1723. L: 4.1724. C: 1725. Condemned at Brest 1742, BU ordered 3.4.1742, and BU 1742-43.

ROYAL LOUIS. A 118/124-gun ship designed and built by Blaise Ollivier. At 12ft more than the *Foudroyant*, this was the longest French warship yet built, and she had an extra pair of LD guns, similarly an extra pair on the MD, and three extra pairs on the UD. She was nearly completed, and would have been launched in 1743, but was burnt on the stocks on 25 December 1742 in an act of arson at the Brest dockyard, attributed to a Spanish worker Sr. Pontleau, who was condemned and executed; the fire started ashore in nearby buildings and spread to the ship.

Dimensions & tons: 185ft 0in, 167ft 8in x 50ft 8in x 22ft 2in (60.10, 54.46 x 16.46 x 7.20 m). 3,000/4,834 tons. Draught 23¼/24¾ft (7.55/8.04m). Men (intended): 1,200, +18 officers.

Guns: (intended 118 in war, 112 peace) LD 32 x 36pdrs; MD 34 x 18pdrs; UD 34 x 12pdrs; QD/Fc 18 x 8pdrs.

Royal Louis Brest Dyd.
K: 13.3.1740. Destroyed on the stocks 25.12.1742.

ROYAL LOUIS. 116-gun ship designed by Jacques-Luc Coulomb and built by Laurent Coulomb, and named on 22 May 1757. On completion, she was found to be unstable, leading to a decision on 20 November 1762 to remove the UD battery. A decade after her completion, she had deteriorated so badly that she was deemed irreparable and was taken to pieces without having seen any service.

Dimensions & tons: 190ft 0in, 171ft 6in x 51ft 6in x 24ft 6in (61.72, 55.71 x 16.73 x 7.96m). 3,000/4,732 tons. Draught 24ft 5in/25ft 8in (7.93/8.34m). Men: 1,320, +18 officers.

Guns: (as built) LD 32 x 36pdrs; MD 34 x 24pdrs; UD 34 x 12pdrs or 18pdrs; QD 10 x 8pdrs; Fc 6 x 8pdrs

Royal Louis Brest Dyd.
K: 6.1757. L: 5.1759. C: 7.1762. Docked for inspection 8.1771, condemned 9.1772 and BU 1773.

VILLE DE PARIS. Built as a 90-gun ship to a design by François-Guillaume Clairain-Deslauriers. Originally named as *Impétueux* on 10 September 1755, but not ordered until 29 May 1757, and little work took place on her during the Seven Years' War. Following the War, she

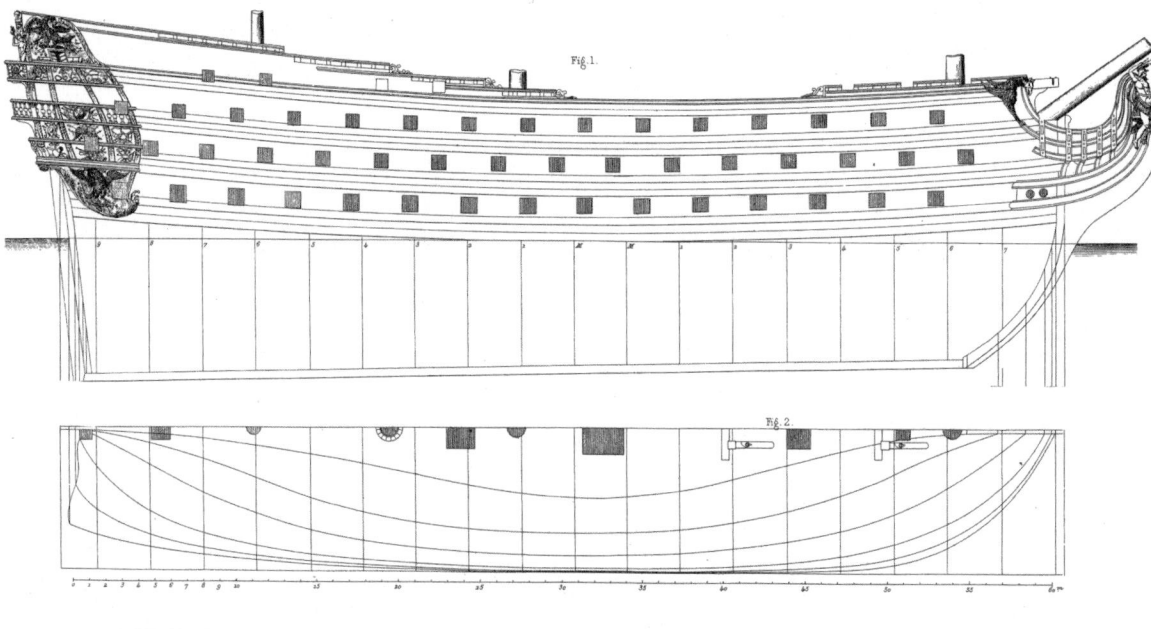

The *Foudroyant* of 1724. This 110-gun ship, the first three-decker to be built for the Navy since 1695, never sailed from Brest, and on 3 April 1742 she was ordered to be broken up; the demolition began on 2 May 1742 and continued into the following year. On the advice of René Duguay-Trouin, Maurepas and the French government built no other three-deckers until 1740, and the *Royal Louis* begun in the latter year was destroyed by fire while still on the stocks. It was not until the start of the Seven Years' War that the Government acceded to pressure from senior naval officers to construct any three-deckers, chiefly for reasons of prestige. (*Souvenirs de Marine*, Plate 148)

THE FIRST RANK

An oil painting by Thomas Whitcombe of the Battle of the Saintes, 12 April 1782, with Comte de Grasse's flagship the 104-gun *Ville de Paris* in the foreground, in close action with *Barfleur*, 98 guns, flying the flag of Sir Samuel Hood. Although captured during the battle, the French flagship was wrecked before she could reach a British port, so it is unclear what reference Whitcombe used for the appearance of the *Ville de Paris*. She had originally been built as a 90-gun ship at Rochefort between August 1757 and May 1764, but during repairs at Brest in 1778–79, the waist was filled in to create a continuous third deck, with a new quarterdeck and forecastle constructed above and fourteen 12pdrs and 6pdrs added to her ordnance. (National Maritime Museum, London, detail from BHC0446)

was funded as a gift to Louis XV by the Municipality of Paris as part of Choiseul's efforts to secure outside funding for new construction, and was renamed *Ville de Paris* in January 1762. Smaller than the contemporary *Royal Louis* and actually shorter and smaller than the 80s built from 1762 on, this ship was in many way closer to the 80-gun two-deckers than to the three-deckers. She was built as a flush-decked three-decker (*i.e.* lacking a forecastle and with a small quarterdeck like some of the 'three-deckers' of the late seventeenth century and with her UD only pierced for fourteen pairs of 12pdrs), but over the winter of 1778–79, a substantive forecastle, enlarged QD and *dunette* were added at Brest, she

A model thought to represent the 112-gun ship to be named *Sans Pareil* that was planned but never begun in Brest in 1760. The decision in 1758 to order several three-deckers, a major reversal of policy by Secretary of the Navy Claude-Louis d'Espinchal, Marquis de Massiac, had a detrimental effect upon naval construction, as the dockyards were starved of finance and artisans. (*Souvenirs de Marine*, Plate 100)

was coppered, and a further two pairs of UD guns added, together with 10 guns added to the new *gaillards* to increase her firepower to 104 guns.

Dimensions & tons: 177ft 0in, 144ft 0in x 48ft 6in x 23ft 0in (57.50, 46.78 x 15.75 x 7.47m). 2,000/4,222 tons. Draught 21/23½ft (6.82/7.63m). Men: 1,090, +6/25 officers.

Guns: (as built) LD 30 x 36pdrs; MD 32 x 24pdrs; UD 28 x 12pdrs. From 1779 had 4 x 12pdrs added to UD, 6 x 6pdrs added to Fc and 4 x 6pdrs to QD.

Ville de Paris Rochefort Dyd.

K: 8.1757. L: 19.1.1764. C: 28.5.1764. Took part in 3rd Battle of Ushant 27.7.1778 (as flagship of CdE Luc Urbain de Bouexic, Comte de Guichen). After refit in Brest she sailed back to the West Indies in March 1781, and took part in Battles of the Chesapeake 5.9.1781, of St Kitts 25.1.1782 and of the Saintes 12.4.1782 (all as flagship of LG François Joseph Paul, Comte de Grasse). Captured by the British at the Battle of the Saintes, but wrecked off Newfoundland en route to the UK on 19.9.1782.

The construction of three-deckers was controversial during the Seven Years' War. The influence of tradition and desire for prestige caused naval officers and dockyard officials to advocate them, but their only function was as flagships in major fleet actions which were not expected to occur during this war, the 80-gun two-deckers assuming this role in smaller actions. Nonetheless Rochefort began reserving timber for three-deckers in 1757 and naval officers successfully persuaded the Navy secretary, François Marie Peyrenc de Moras, to resume ordering them. Orders were placed at Rochefort (*Impétueux*) and Brest (*Royal Louis*). However, in 1759 a new Navy secretary, Nicolas-René Berryer, Comte de La Ferrière, withheld the funds needed to complete these two ships (already under construction) due to shortages of finance, and both were cancelled in 1760.

Three more 1st Rank ships of over 100 guns (and one of 90 guns) were planned during the Seven Years' War. Two were ordered at Toulon in the same month (May 1757) as the *Royal Louis* at Brest and the *Impétueux* (later *Ville de Paris*) at Rochefort. The larger, to a 114-gun design by Joseph Véronique-Charles Chapelle, was named *Majestueux* on 29 May and would have been pierced for sixteen pairs of 36pdrs on the LD, with seventeen pairs of 24pdrs on the MD and the same number of 12pdrs on the UD, with fourteen 8pdrs on the *gaillards*. The slightly smaller *Indomptable* was ordered to a 112-gun design by Joseph-Marie-Blaise Coulomb; with one less pair of guns on the LD and similarly one pair less on the MD, she would have carried just 30 guns on the UD but twenty on the *gaillards*. Toulon planned to begin work on the two in the spring of 1758 and acquired some timber for them. However, in February 1759 Berryer stopped the construction at Toulon, the financial and military situations by then making their construction out of the question, and both orders were cancelled during 1760 due to shortages both of finance and of suitable timber.

The other two ships were ordered at Brest. The first – the 90-gun three-decker – was also ordered in May 1757 to a design by Luc Coulomb, and was named *Médiateur* on 22 May. She was cancelled for similar reasons during 1760. In 1760 it was intended to order another 112-gun ship at Brest, to a design similar to the *Indomptable*, but with sixteen guns (*vice* twenty) on the *gaillards*. This design would have measured 174ft, 156ft x 51ft (56.52, 50.675 x 16.57m), like the *Indomptable*; this ship would have been named *Sans Pareil*, but the order was never placed, and was abandoned when the other ships were cancelled during 1760.

BRETAGNE. 100 (later 110) guns. Three-decker ordered in 1764 to be built at Lorient to a design by Antoine Groignard, this ship was begun there in late 1764, but work ceased in January 1765 when the order was transferred to Brest. Her cost was funded as a gift to Louis XV by the *États de Bretagne* (the Provincial High Court of Brittany), as part of Choiseul's efforts to secure finance from outside the State coffers. She

A lines plan of the 110-gun *Bretagne*, redrawn by László Veres from a copy in the Danish Orlogsvaerftet, Copenhagen. Designed by Antoine Groignard, she was first begun at Lorient, where timber was assembled, but in January 1765 the order was transferred to Brest. The frames were taken down at Lorient and sent by sea to Brest, where the keel was re-laid on 10 June in a dock. She was two-thirds rebuilt at Brest between 1775 and 1777, when a new forecastle was added. Under a new name (*Révolutionnaire*) she formed part of *Contre-amiral* Louis Thomas Villaret-Joyeuse's fleet which sailed from Brest on 16 May 1794 and encountered Lord Howe's fleet on 28 May. The *Révolutionnaire* was severely damaged in the action which commenced on that day, and lost nearly 400 men as well as much of her top hamper; she had to be towed into Rochefort for repairs and was thus not present during the main action on the Glorious First of June. She moved from Rochefort to Brest in August, and was disarmed, and in early 1796 was condemned and taken to pieces.

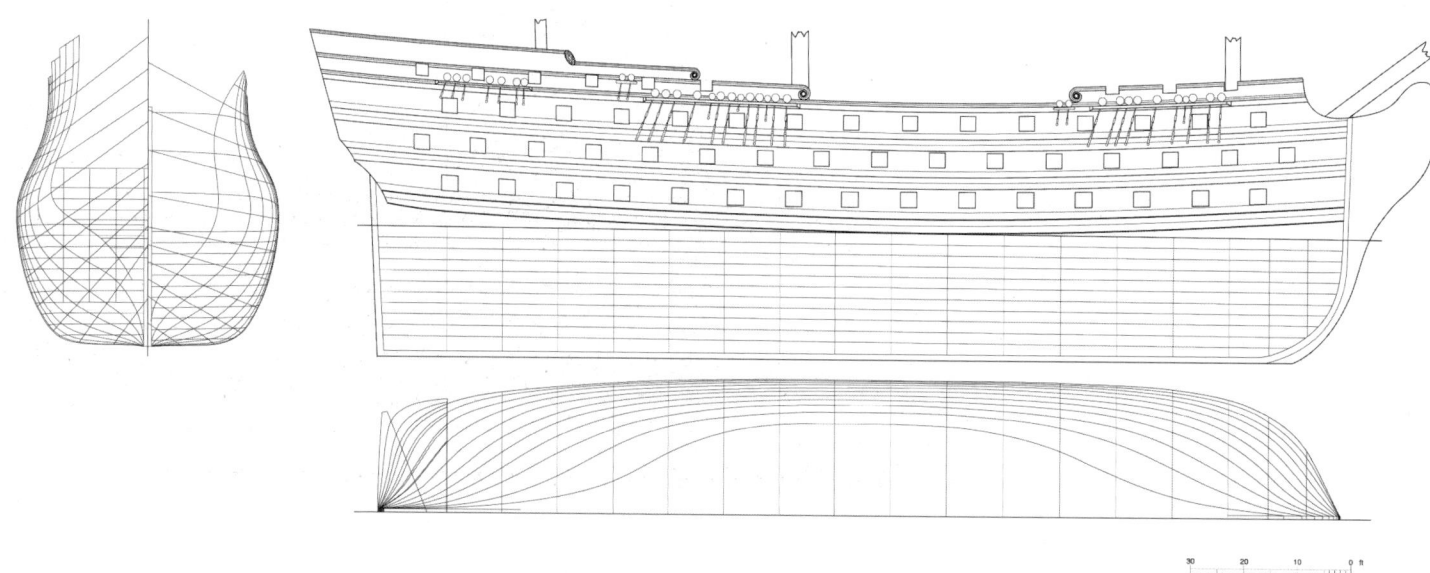

was completed at Brest with 100 guns (including just 6 x 8pdrs on the QD, and with no forecastle), but underwent a 2/3rds reconstruction in 1777, with two decks fully rebuilt and a new forecastle added, and was re-armed in 1781, with 16 x 6pdrs added on the *gaillards* in lieu of the 8pdrs to bring her up to 110 guns; she was coppered at Brest in March 1781, and re-coppered at Brest in May to July 1786.

    Dimensions & tons: 186ft 0in, 165ft 0in x 50ft 0in x 24ft 6in (60.42, 53.60 x 16.24 x 7.96 m). 2,600/4,666 tons. Draught 22½ft/24¾ft (7.31/8.04m). Men: 1,200 in war, 1,140 peace, + 10/19 officers.

    Guns: LD 30 x 36pdrs; MD 32 x 24pdrs; UD 32 x 12pdrs; QD 6 x 8pdrs (10 x 6pdrs from 1781); Fc 6 x 6pdrs from 1781. Nominally now of 110 guns, in fact she additionally carried 4 x 4pdrs on her *dunette*.

Bretagne Brest Dyd.

    K: 10.6.1765. L: 24.5.1766. C: 9.1767. Took part in 3rd Battle of Ushant 27.7.1778 (as flagship of LG Louis Guillouet, Comte d'Orvilliers). Renamed *Révolutionnaire* in October 1793, she was severely damaged in action on 28 May 1794, and in 1796 she was condemned and BU at Brest 1–5.1796.

On 1 December 1773 the Navy decided to rebuild Coulomb's *Royal Louis* of 1759 at Brest. She was listed as a vessel of 110 guns and 3,000 tons but the project was deferred from year to year until 1778, when Guignace's *Royal Louis* (below) was ordered instead.

INVINCIBLE. 100 (later 110) guns. Three-decker designed by François-Guillaume Clairain-Deslauriers and built by Jean-Denis Chevillard. Originally built as a 92-gun ship, with no forecastle and without guns on her QD, the QD 8pdrs were added in 1781 and a forecastle added and armed in 1784. Rebuilt at Brest from November 1793 to April 1795.

    Dimensions & tons: 184ft 0in, 167ft 0in x 50ft 0in x 24ft 6in (59.77, 54.25 x 16.24 x 7.96 m). 2,400/4,670 tons. Draught 23½/25½ft (7.63/8.28m). Men: 1,055–1,150.

    Guns: LD 30 x 36pdrs; MD 32 x 24pdrs; UD 30 x 12pdrs; QD 8 x 8pdrs from 1781, 2 more 8pdrs and 6 x 36pdr *obusiers* were added in 1785; Fc 6 x 8pdrs (from 1785). 2 more 12pdrs were added in 1794 and 2 *obusiers* removed.

Invincible Rochefort Dyd.

    K: 2.1779. L: 20.3.1780. C: 5.1780. Rebuilt and coppered at Brest in 1794. Re-armed there 9.1800–7.1802, but disarmed on 11.3.1807 and condemned on 6.1.1808 in accordance with Napoléon's 1803 edict, before being BU to 12.1808.

ROYAL LOUIS. 104 (later 110) guns. Three-decker designed by Léon-Michel Guignace. Her keel was laid in No 3 dry dock at Brest in March 1778 and the ship was named on 4 December 1778. Unlike the other three-deckers of this era, she was completed as a 110-gun ship, including the 8pdrs on the *gaillards*. Her original 48pdrs on the LD were transferred to *Majesteux* in December 1782.

    Dimensions & tons: 186ft 0in, 164ft 0in x 50ft 0in x 24ft 6in (60.42, 53.27 x 16.24 x 7.96m). 2,400/4,835 tons. Draught 24/26½ft (7.80/8.61m). Men: 1,055–1,150.

    Guns: LD 30 x 48pdrs (replaced by 36pdrs in 12.1782); MD 32 x

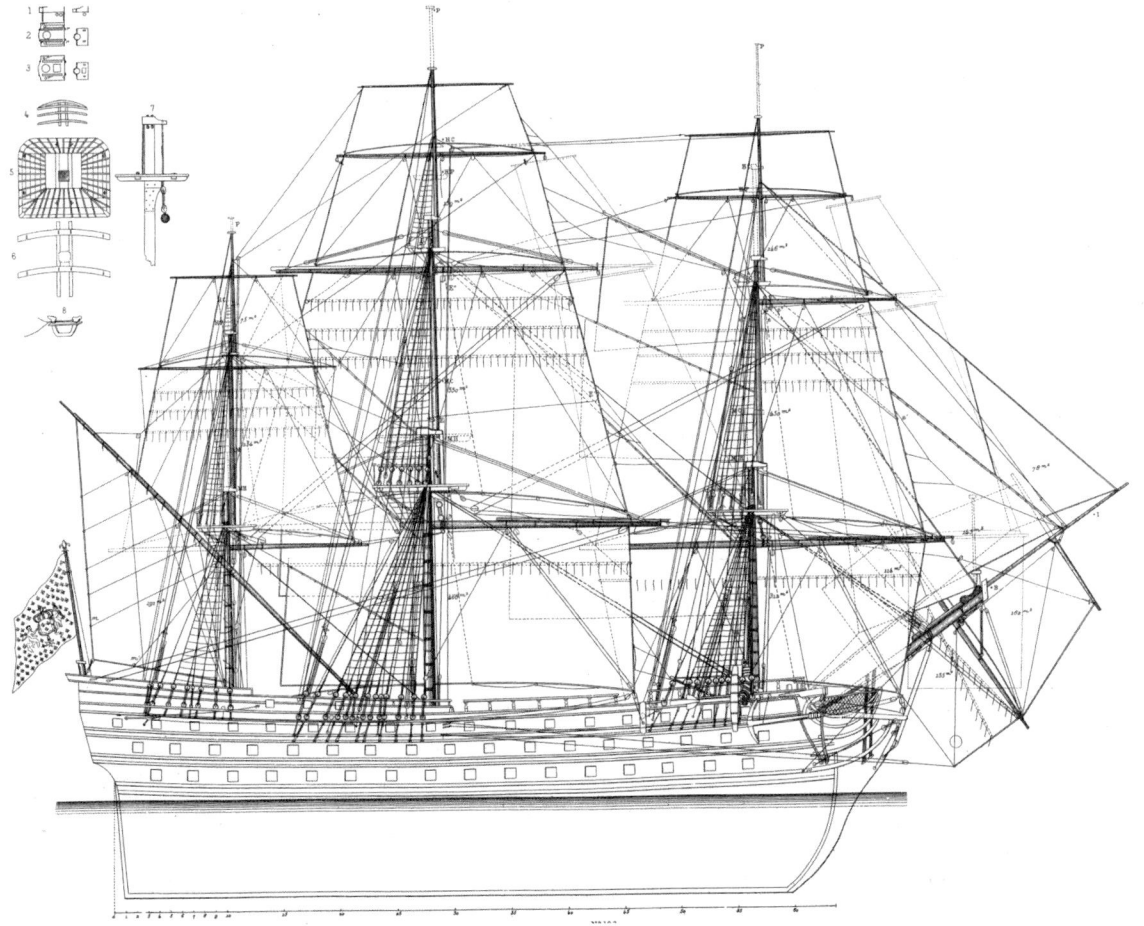

The sail plan of the 110-gun *Royal Louis* of 1759, as reconstructed by *Vice-amiral* Pâris. According to a note on the plate, the ship was 'built by M Coulomb at Toulon to the plans of the previous *Royal Louis* by J B Ollivier' (the plan is wrongly dated 1780, the ship was built at Brest not Toulon, and the dimensions are somewhat larger than Ollivier's design, so Pâris is far from infallible). The accompanying lines plan is annotated '*levé sur le vaisseau même à Brest dans une des formes de Pontaniou, par ordre de Mr le Comte d'Estaing, le 25 7bre 1772*' [taken off the ship herself at Brest in one of the docks at Pontaniou by order of Comte d'Estaing on 25 September], when the ship had just been condemned. It shows three full gundecks, so demonstrating that the 1762 order to remove the UD battery did not mean cutting down the ship. (*Souvenirs de Marine*, Plate 103)

24pdrs; UD 32 x 12pdrs; QD 6 x 8pdrs; Fc 6 x 8pdrs. 4 more 8pdrs were added on the QD in 1786, but 4 x 36pdr *obusiers* replaced them in 1794.

Royal Louis   Brest Dyd.
  K: 8.3.1778. L: 20.3.1780. C: 6.1780. Renamed *Républicain* 29.9.1792; reconstructed at Brest from 4.1793 to 4.1794, but then badly damaged at Battle of 13 Prairial (Glorious First of June, 1794 – as flagship of *Contre-amiral* Joseph Marie Nielly); wrecked off Brest 24.12.1794 (10 men drowned).

TERRIBLE Class. 94 (later 110) guns. Three-deckers designed and built by Joseph-Marie-Blaise Coulomb. As with the *Invincible*, they were completed as 94-gun ships, with the forecastle added subsequently – and 8pdrs mounted here and on the QD. The *Terrible* was ordered on 23 October 1778 and named on 4 December; her keel was first laid in April 1779 but (finding the site too small) was taken up and re-laid on 8 August. The *Majestueux* was ordered on 20 April 1780 and named on 16 June; she was experimentally fitted with 30 x 48pdrs on the LD in December 1782, but her original armament (identical to that in *Terrible*) was reinstated in February 1783.

  Dimensions & tons: 186ft 8in, 169ft 0in x 50ft 0in x 25ft 0in (60.64, 54.90 x 16.24 x 8.12m). 2,500/4,700 tons. Draught 23/24½ft (7.47/7.96m). Men: 1,055–1,150.
  Guns: LD 30 x 36pdrs; MD 32 x 24pdrs; UD 32 x 12pdrs; QD 10 x 8pdrs; Fc 6 x 8pdrs. (4 x 36pdr *obusiers* replaced 4 x 8pdrs in 1793). *Majestueux* from 12.1782 to 2.1783 had LD 30 x 48pdrs; MD 6 x 36pdrs + 26 x 24pdrs; UD 2 x 18pdrs + 30 x 12pdrs; QD 10 x 8pdrs; Fc 6 x 8pdrs.

Terrible   Toulon Dyd.
  K: 8.8.1779. L: 27.1.1780. C: 5.1780. Damaged at Battle of 13 Prairial (Glorious 1st of June, 1794 – as flagship of *Contre-amiral* François Joseph Bouvet). Disarmed at Brest 11.1801. Condemned 1802 at Brest and BU 8.1804 (by Order of 4.5.1804) in accordance with Napoléon's 1803 edict (see below).

Majestueux   Toulon Dyd.
  K: 5.7.1780. L: 17.11.1780. C: 4.2.1781. Renamed *Républicain* in 1797, becoming flagship of the fleet at Brest; repaired there in dock 1799–1800; condemned 1803 (her name transferred to the *République Française*) and disarmed 5.1807. BU 10.1808.

Although the Rank (*Rang*) system had fallen into temporary disfavour by the 1780s, the three-deckers still constituted a distinct group within the French Navy, serving as the flagships of the battlefleet. As at 1783 five three-deckers remained in the French Navy: the older *Bretagne* (of 1766), and four newer vessels which had all been launched in 1780. Each carried 94 guns on their three complete gun decks (*Invincible* had 2 fewer), including a principal battery of 30 guns (of 36 or 48 French pounds) on the lower deck, and all acquired a small number of lesser guns (8pdrs) on the *gaillards*, so that by 1786 each carried 110 guns in total. In June 1803 Napoléon was to rule that any ship of the line needing a refit of 18/24ths or more should not be repaired but should instead be taken to pieces. This ruling was to affect all three of these pre-1783 three-deckers which had survived into the Napoleonic War.

At least another three 110-gun ships (and two even larger vessels of 116 guns) were projected in 1782, but were cancelled in or about February 1783. One of these, to have been built by Joseph-Marie-Blaise Coulomb at Toulon, would have been similar to the *Terrible* and *Majestueux*; funded by the Bordeaux Chamber of Commerce, this was provisionally named *Commerce de Bordeaux*. Another, to have been named *Généralités* (also known as *circonscriptions financières* or financial districts), would have been built at Rochefort by François-Guillaume Clairain-Deslauriers, and may have been intended as similar to *Invincible*. The third, to have been funded by the Lyon Chamber of Commerce, would have borne the name *Commerce de Lyon*.

The two 116-gun ships were ordered in August 1782 to a design by Antoine Groignard, one to have been named *Commerce de Marseille* or *États de Bourgogne* (from the title of the Provincial High Court of Burgundy) and the other *Ville de Paris* or *Commerce de la Ville de Paris*, funded by the Marseille Chamber of Commerce and by the *Six Corps* of the Paris merchants respectively. They were suspended in February 1783 and the project cancelled at the close of that year. However, the pair were eventually re-ordered on 30 September 1785 to an amended 118-gun design by Jacques-Noël Sané, begun in 1786 and were finally completed in 1790 as the first two units of the *Commerce de Marseille* class – the name ship of the class at Toulon and the *États de Bourgogne* (originally called *Ville de Paris*) at Brest – see 1786–1861 volume for full details.

(E) 80-gun two-decked vessels (*Vaisseaux de 80*) acquired from 1740

All 80-gun ships prior to 1700 had been three-deckers, and none were built in the first four decades of the new century, but in 1740 the first of a series of two-decker 80s was begun. At the start of hostilities against Britain in 1744, this ship (*Tonnant*) was the only French warship with more than 74 guns, but more were begun from 1748 onwards. All had thirty 36pdr guns on the lower deck, and thirty-two guns (18pdrs or 24pdrs) on the upper deck, while eighteen guns (mostly 8pdrs) were fitted on the *gaillards*. Thirteen ships were built in the period to 1785 (one of which was rebuilt after a fire).

These ships were ambiguously classed in French official records, being usually defined as '*premier rang*' but in 1766 the earlier *Tonnant*, *Duc de Bourgogne*, and *Orient* (all with 18pdrs on the UD) were classed as '*second rang, premier ordre*' while the later *Languedoc*, *Saint Esprit*, and *Couronne* were '*premier rang, second ordre*'. We chose to class all of them here with the 1st Rank ships, as France built virtually no three-deckers for most of the eighteenth century, and in lieu of these deployed the 80-gun two-deckers as their principal capital ships. The original type with 18pdrs on the UD mustered a broadside of 900 *livres*, while the later substitution of 24pdrs on the UD raised this to 996 *livres* (or 1,075 English pounds), significantly greater than the standard French 74-gun ship's 838 *livres* (904 pounds), which was in turn greater than the 818-pound broadside of the British three-decked Second Rates of 90 guns, and not incomparable with the 1,140-pound broadside of the largest British three-decked First Rates of 100 guns.

TONNANT. 80 guns. Designed and built by François Coulomb Jnr. Named on 12 June 1740. The longest two-decker built for France up to this date, and the first to be pierced for fifteen pairs of lower deck guns. With this ship, the guns on the *gaillards* were initially only 6pdrs, although all subsequent 80-gun ships were to mount 8pdrs here. Refitted 1755–56 at Brest and 1770–71 at Toulon.

  Dimensions & tons: 168ft 0in, 154ft 0in x 46ft 0in x 22ft 3in (54.57, 50.03 x 14.94 x 7.47m). 1,700/3,400 tons. Draught 20ft/23½ft (6.50/7.63m). Men: originally 780, +6 officers; later 800, +7/16 officers.
  Guns (80 in war, 74 peace): LD 30 x 36pdrs; UD 32 x 18pdrs; QD 10 x 6pdrs; Fc 8 x 6pdrs. Re-armed 1764–65 at Toulon with 24pdrs and 8pdrs replacing the UD 18pdrs and *gaillards* 6pdrs.

Tonnant   Toulon Dyd.
  K: 18.10.1740. L: 17.11.1743. C: 6.1744. Damaged in action 25.10.1747 against Hawke's squadron at Battle of Finisterre (as

THE FIRST RANK

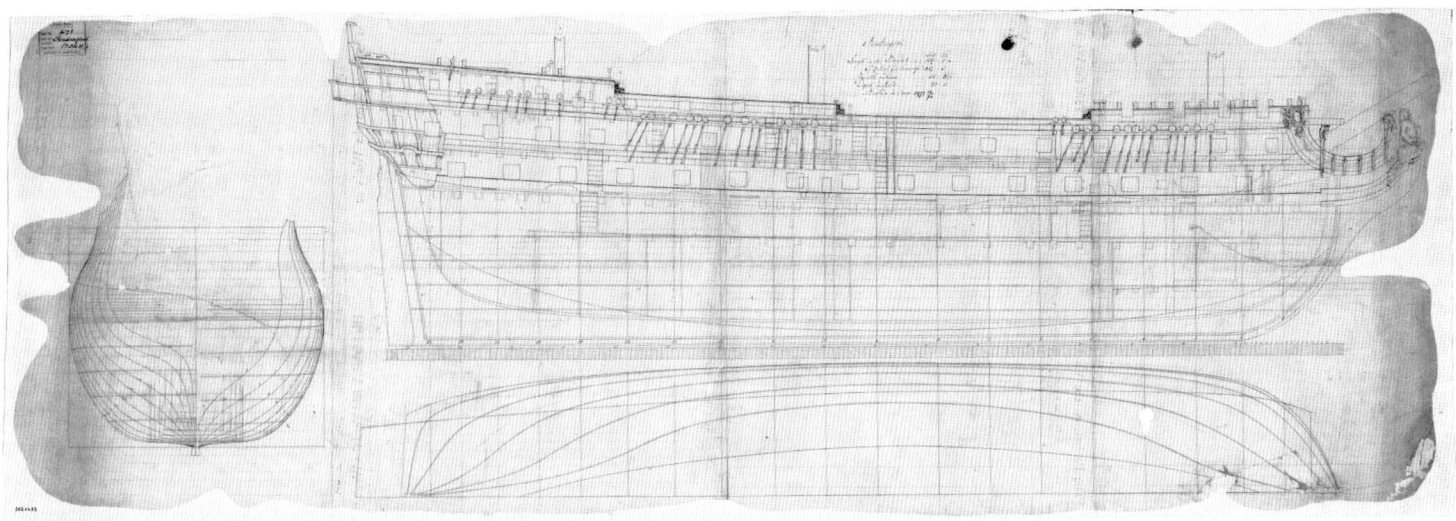

Admiralty draught of the 80-gun *Foudroyant* of 1750. She took part in the recapture on Minorca on 18 April 1756, sailing from Toulon eight days earlier as part of La Galissonniere's squadron of eleven ships of the line and six frigates, escorting 200 transports with 12,000 troops. Although undated, the French decorative detail suggest that it represents the ship as captured in February 1758 by Osborn's squadron off Cartagena. The draught has undergone paper conservation, but the area of the drawing itself is unaffected. (National Maritime Museum, London J2488)

flagship of CdE Henri-François Des Herbiers, Marquis de l'Éstenduère); repaired at Brest. Took part in the Battle of Quiberon Bay 20.11.1759 (as flagship of CdE Joseph de Bauffremont-Courtenay, Prince de Listenois et du Saint Empire). Took part in d'Estaing's 1778–79 campaign in the Caribbean (as flagship of CdE Pierre-Claude de Haudeneau, Comte de Breugnon). Condemned 4.1780 at Rochefort, and BU there 11.1780.

FOUDROYANT. 80 guns. Designed and built by François Coulomb Jnr. Ordered on 18 December 1747, and named on 3 January 1748. Her capture in 1758 was aided by a mutiny among the French crew.
   Dimensions & tons: 177ft 0in, 152ft 0in x 47ft 6in x 22ft 6in (57.50, 49.38 x 15.43 x 7.31m). 1,966/3,281 tons. Draught 21½ft/23ft (6.98/7.47m). Men: 800, +11/14 officers.
   Guns: LD 30 x 36pdrs; UD 32 x 18pdrs; QD 10 x 8pdrs; Fc 8 x 8pdrs.

Foudroyant Toulon Dyd.
   K: 29.8.1748. L: 18.12.1750. C: 4.1751. Took part in Battle of Minorca 20.5.1756 (as flagship of CdE Roland-Michel Barrin, Marquis de La Galissonière). Captured 28.2.1758 off Cartagena (Osborn's Action) as flagship of CdE Michel-Ange Duquesne, Marquis de Menneville, by HM Ships *Monmouth*, *Swiftsure* and *Hampton Court*, becoming HMS *Foudroyant*; BU at Plymouth 9.1787.

SOLEIL ROYAL. 80 guns. Designed and built by Jacques-Luc Coulomb. Ordered on 19 January 1748, and named on 1 March 1748. At 5ft longer than his brother's contemporary *Foudroyant*, this was the first two-decker French warship to exceed 180ft in length, and the first to carry more than 1,000 men. Uniquely among early 80-gun ships, the UD ordnance provided was 24pdrs (this did not become standard for 80-gun ships until 1765).
   Dimensions & tons: 182ft 0in, 174ft 2in x 48ft 0in x 23ft 0in (59.12,

Admiralty draught of the 80-gun *Formidable* of 1751. As it is undated it is unclear if this represents the ship as taken in Quiberon Bay in November 1759, where she gallantly but vainly tried to protect the rear of the Marquis de Conflans's squadron (CdE Du Verger was among more than 200 of her complement killed during the savage battering by HMS *Resolution*), but the shape of the stern galleries and topside details suggest the original French appearance. The draught has suffered from careless folding over the centuries and is now almost in two pieces, although the missing information is negligible. (National Maritime Museum, London J8110)

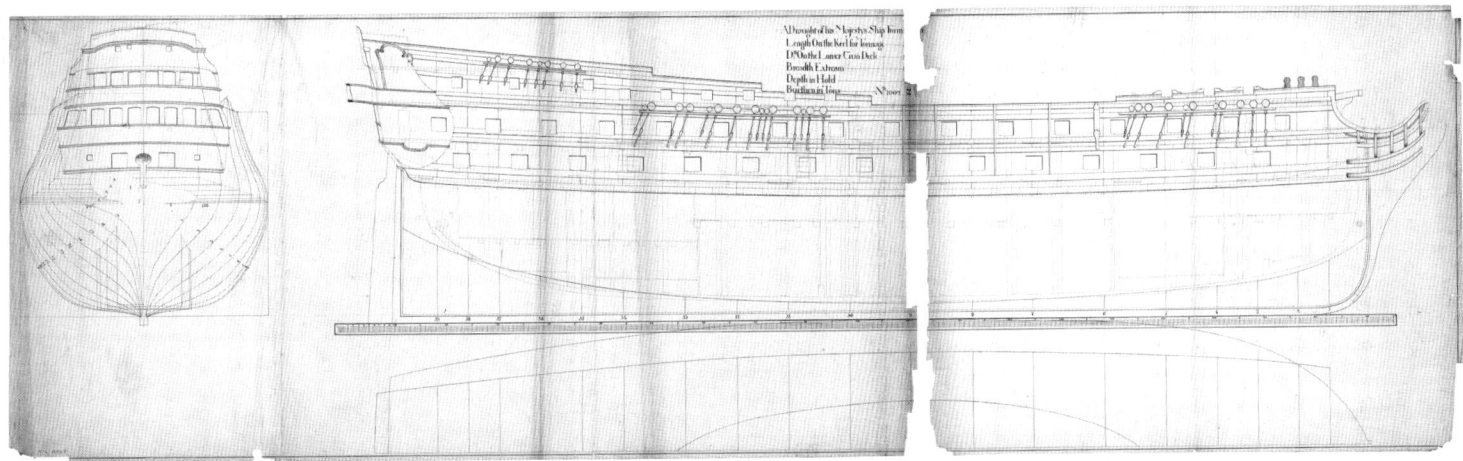

56.58 x 15.59 x 7.47m). Her overall dimensions as built were 183ft 2in x 48ft 6in x 23ft 3in (59.50 x 15.75 x 7.55m). 2,200/3,800 tons. Draught 20½ft/23½ft (6.66/7.63m). Men: 1,000, +14 officers.
Guns: LD 30 x 36pdrs; UD 32 x 24pdrs; QD 12 x 8pdrs; Fc 6 x 8pdrs.

Soleil Royal Brest Dyd.
K: 3.1748. L: 30.6.1749. C: 4.1750. Driven ashore and destroyed in action at Battle of Quiberon Bay 20.11.1759 (as flagship of Vice-Am. Hubert de Brienne, Marquis de Conflans).

FORMIDABLE. 80 guns. Designed and built by Jacques-Luc Coulomb. Ordered on 25 December 1748 and named on 13 January 1749.
Dimensions & tons: 178ft 0in, 168ft 6in x 44ft 10in x 21ft 10in (57.82, 54.74 x 14.56 x 7.09m). 1,800/3,400 tons. Draught unknown. Men: 800, +8/14 officers.
Guns: LD 30 x 36pdrs; UD 32 x 18pdrs; QD 12 x 8pdrs; Fc 6 x 8pdrs.

Formidable Brest
K: 20.1.1749. L: 6.1751. C: 12.1752. Comm: 6.4.1755. Captured at the Battle of Quiberon Bay 20.11.1759 (as flagship of CdE Louis de Saint André Du Verger), becoming HMS *Formidable*; BU 1767–68 at Plymouth.

DUC DE BOURGOGNE. 80 guns. Designed by François-Guillaume Clairain-Deslauriers and built by Antoine Groignard. This vessel was ordered and begun under the name *Brave*, but was renamed at her launch to celebrate the birth of the heir to the French throne.
Dimensions & tons: 174ft 0in, 152ft 6in x 44ft 6in x 22ft 6in (56.52, 49.54 x 14.46 x 7.31m). 1,800/3,400 tons. Draught 20½ft/22ft (6.66/7.15m). Men: 850, +8/14 officers.
Guns: LD 30 x 36pdrs; UD 32 x 18pdrs; QD 12 x 8pdrs; Fc 6 x 8pdrs.

Duc de Bourgogne Rochefort Dyd.
K: 1.1749. L: 20.10.1751. C: 12.1752. Intended to but failed to take part in 3rd Battle of Ushant 27.7.1778 (as flag of CdE Étienne-Pierre, Vicomte de Rochechouart). Sailed 2.5.1780 from Brest as flagship of CdE Charles-Henri-Louis Arsac de Ternay, leading troop convoy to America. Took part in Battles of Cape Henry 16.3.1781, St Kitts 25/26.1.1782 and the Saintes 12.4.1782. Renamed *Peuple* 9.1792, then *Caton* 2.1794. Condemned 2.1798 at Brest, and BU 1800–1801.

OCÉAN. 80 guns. Designed and built by Antoine Groignard for the *Foudroyant*. The master shipwright entrusted with the construction was Joseph Veronique-Charles Chapelle. Named on 2 July 1751.
Dimensions & tons: 175ft 0in, 154ft 0in x 48ft 0in x 23ft 0in (56.85, 50.03 x 15.59 x 7.47m). 1,900/3,300 tons. Draught unknown. Men: 800, +8/14 officers.
Guns: LD 30 x 36pdrs; UD 32 x 18pdrs; QD 12 x 8pdrs; Fc 6 x 8pdrs.

Océan Toulon Dyd.
K: 29.5.1753. L: 20.6.1756. C: 11.1756. Ran aground in Almadora Bay during Battle off Lagos 19.8.1759 (as flagship of LG Jean-François de Bertet de Sabran, Comte de La Clue), then burnt by HMS *America*.

ORIENT. 80 guns. Designed and built by Antoine Groignard for the *Compagnie des Indes* at their Lorient shipyard as their largest-ever warship, but purchased for the French Navy in May 1759. Rebuilt by Jean Geoffroy in 1765–66 at Brest as a 74-gun ship of 1,650 tons, with one pair of guns removed from each deck, and re-classed as a 2nd Rank; refitted again at Brest 1777–78.
Dimensions & tons: 174ft 0in, 159ft 0in x 44ft 0in x 20ft 6in (56.52, 51.65 x 14.29 x 6.66m). 1,800/3,000 tons. Draught 19ft 10in/21ft 0in (6.44/6.82m). Men: 750/850, +7/14 officers. 650 in war, 440 peace after 1766.
Guns: LD 30 x 36pdrs; UD 32 x 18pdrs; QD 12 x 8pdrs; Fc 6 x 8pdrs.

Orient Lorient Dyd.
K: 4.1756. L: 9.10.1756. C: 8.1757. Took part in Battle of Quiberon Bay 20.11.1759, then as flagship of CdE Joseph-Marie Budes, Seigneur de Guébriant. Took part in 3rd Battle of Ushant 27.7.1778 (as flag of CdE Charles Jean, Comte d'Hector). Participated in Battles of Sadras 17.2.1782, Providien (Trincomalee) 12.4.1782, Negapatam 6.7.1782 and Trincomalee 3.9.1782, then wrecked off Trincomalee 8.9.1782.

The stern decoration of the *Océan*, 80 guns, of 1756. Although it is still rather sculptural, the decorative scheme is very restrained by the standards of the Sun King's navy half a century earlier. The *Océan*, part of the Mediterranean Fleet, sailed from Toulon on 5 August 1759 as Comte de La Clue's flagship with eleven other ships of the line (and three frigates), intended to join up with the Brest squadron to prepare for an invasion of England, but on 19 August was intercepted by Admiral Boscawen's fleet off Lagos, Portugal; she sought refuge in Almadora Bay, where she grounded and was burnt by the British. (*Souvenirs de Marine*, Plate 146)

The British Navy rated these powerful 80-gun capital ships as equivalent to their own three-decked 90s (the French 80's broadside was 10 per cent greater by weight than the English 90's). Nevertheless, the French had lost four of these ships in action during 1758 and 1759, and two new vessels were put in hand as the war ended, as part of the *Don des vaisseaux*, a national subscription effort initiated by Choiseul to rebuild the Navy after such heavy losses. Choiseul argued that no more three-deckers should be built, and that instead larger 80-gun two-deckers should be constructed capable of carrying 24pdrs on their UDs.

THE FIRST RANK

SAINT ESPRIT. 80 guns. Designed and built by Joseph-Louis Ollivier. Construction was funded by the Order of the Holy Spirit (*Ordre du Saint Esprit*), and she was ordered on 11 January 1762 and named on 20 January. The first 80-gun ship, apart from the *Soleil Royal*, to exceed 180ft in length and to have 24pdrs on her upper deck; henceforth, this calibre would be standard on that deck of the 80s. Reconstructed 1777–78 at Brest, then again from December 1782 to May 1783 at Brest.
- Dimensions & tons: 184ft 0in, 168ft 0in x 48ft 6in x 23ft 2in (59.77, 54.57 x 15.75 x 7.53m). 2,050/3,800 tons. Draught 21ft 2in/24ft (6.88/7.80m). Men: 850 in war, 575 peace, +5/14 officers.
- Guns: LD 30 x 36pdrs; UD 32 x 24pdrs; QD 12 x 8pdrs; Fc 6 x 8pdrs, + 6 *pierriers* (swivel guns). From 1778 the QD/Fc carried 22 x 8pdrs, altered 1780 to 20 x 12pdrs, but original 18 x 8pdrs restored in 1782.

Saint Esprit Brest Dyd.
- K: 5.1762. L: 12.10.1765. C: 1766. Took part in 3rd Battle of Ushant 27.7.1778 (as flag of LG Louis-Philippe d'Orléans, Duc de Chartres), Battle of Fort Royal 29.4.1781, and Battle of the Chesapeake 5.9.1781. Renamed *Scipion* in 2.1794 and commissioned at Brest (under CV Huguet); took part in the Battle of 13 Prairial ('Glorious First of June') 1794. Foundered near Brest in a storm 26.1.1795 (with *Neuf Thermidor* and other ships).

LANGUEDOC. 80 guns. Designed and built by Joseph-Marie-Blaise Coulomb. Ordered and named on 9 December 1761, and funded by the *États du Languedoc* (the Provincial High Court of Languedoc). The largest two-decker yet, her QD was originally only pierced for five pairs of guns, allowing the sides of the *dunette* to be unpierced when built. Reconstructed 1775–76 at Toulon, then again 12.1782–7.1783 at Brest, and again in 1792 (by Jacques-Noel Sané).
- Dimensions & tons: 188ft 0in, 168ft 0in x 48ft 6in x 23ft 2in (61.07, 54.57 x 15.75 x 7.53m). 2,100/3,850 tons. Draught 21ft 4in/22ft 7in (6.93/7.34m). Men: 850, +12/14 officers.
- Guns: LD 30 x 36pdrs; UD 32 x 24pdrs; QD 10 x 12pdrs; Fc 8 x 12pdrs. 2 more 24pdrs added and 26 x 8pdrs replaced all 12pdrs in 4.1778 at Toulon, but in 1783 at Brest the extra 2 x 24pdrs were removed and the *gaillards* carried 12 x 12pdrs, 8 x 8pdrs and 4 x 4pdrs, giving her 86 guns in total.

Languedoc Toulon Dyd.

The 80-gun *Languedoc* was Comte d'Estaing's flagship for the expeditionary force France sent to support the American revolutionaries in 1778, sailing from Toulon for the Delaware on 14 April. With the fleet was the artist Pierre Ozanne, who was to record the events of the campaign in North America and the West Indies. His watercolour shown here depicts the *Languedoc*, which had been dismasted in a storm on 12 August (her bowsprit had also been carried away, and her rudder broken, rendering her unmanageable), under attack by the British 50-gun *Renown* on the evening of the following day. When all seemed lost, the helpless French flagship was rescued by other ships of d'Estaing's fleet the next day.

- K: 5.1762. L: 14.5.1766. C: 11.1767. Sailed 13.4.1778 for North America (as flagship of *Vice-amiral* Jean-Baptiste-Charles-Henri d'Hector, Comte d'Estaing); took part in Battle of St Lucia 14.12.1778. Took part in Battles of Fort Royal 29.4.1781, of the Chesapeake 5.9.1781 (as flagship of CdE Francois-Aymar, Comte de Monteil), of St Kitts 25/26.1.1782 and of the Saintes 4.1782. Handed over to Anglo-Spanish forces by French Royalists at the occupation of Toulon 29.8.1793; left by them at the evacuation of that port on 18.12.1793, and recovered by the French. Renamed *Anti-Fédéraliste* 21.4.1794, then *Victoire* 8.3.1795. and took part in Battle of Cape Noli 14.3.1795. Grounded at Cadiz 12.1795, but refloated. Condemned 2.1798 and BU at Brest 1799.

COURONNE. 80 guns. Designed and built by Antoine Groignard, and similar to the *Saint Esprit*. Substantially (2/3rds) reconstructed in 1777.
- Dimensions & tons: 183ft 0in, 168ft 6in x 46ft 0in x 23ft 0in (59.45, 54.74 x 14.94 x 7.37m). 1,745/3,770 tons. Draught 20¾ft/22½ft (m). Men: 850, +12/14 officers.
- Guns: LD 30 x 36pdrs; UD 32 x 24pdrs; QD 12 x 8pdrs; Fc 6 x 8pdrs.

Couronne Brest Dyd.
- K: 8.1766. L: 5.1768. C: 1768. Took part in 3rd Battle of Ushant 27.7.1778 (as flag of LG Louis-Charles de Besné, Comte du Chaffault). Burnt by accident at Brest Dyd in 4.1781, but refloated and rebuilt (see below).

AUGUSTE. 80 guns. Designed and built by Léon-Michel Guignace. Named on 20 February 1778. Actually an 84-gun ship, having 22 x 8pdrs on her *gaillards*.

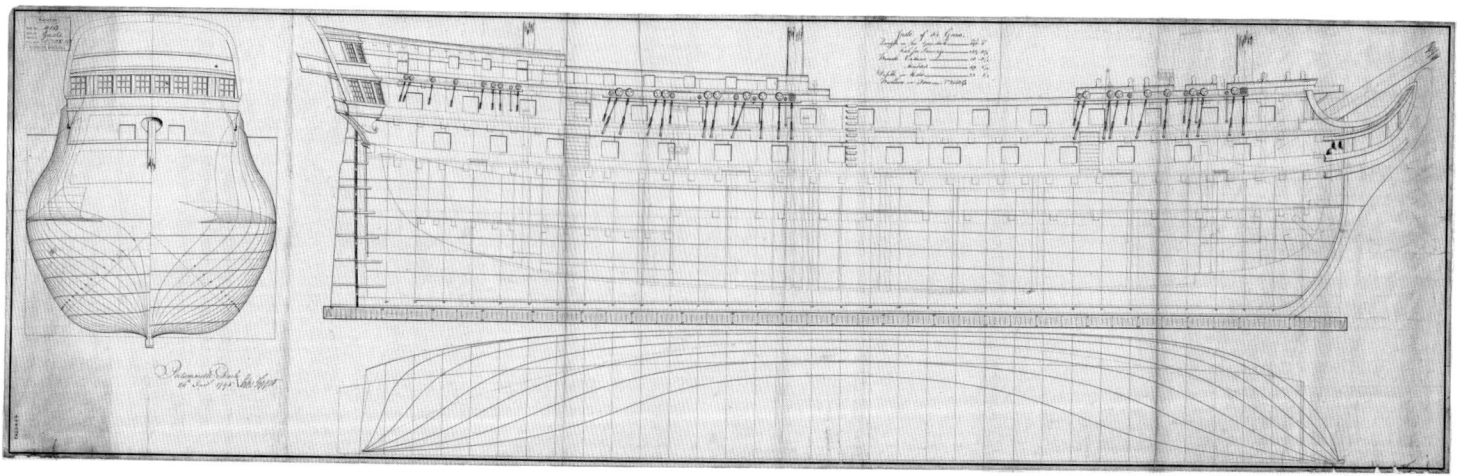

Admiralty draught of the *Juste* (ex-*Deux Frères*) as captured in 1794. Based on all the guns the ship was carrying at the time, she is described as an 84-gun ship, although this includes the four 36pdr *obusiers* added to her upperworks the year before she was taken. The forecastle has ports for three pairs of 8pdrs, and the quarterdeck for six pairs (all forward of the *dunette*); there are a further two pairs of gunports in the *dunette* itself, but these carried no ordnance until the *obusiers* were installed in 1793. (National Maritime Museum, London J7772)

Dimensions & tons: 186ft 0in, 171ft 0in x 46ft 0in x 23ft (60.42, 55.55 x 14.94 x 7.37m). 1,900/3,700 tons. Draught 21ft/24ft (6.82/7.80m). Men: 839, +13/17 officers.

Guns: LD 30 x 36pdrs; UD 32 x 24pdrs; QD 14 x 8pdrs; Fc 8 x 8pdrs (by 1793, these 22 x 8pdrs had been replaced by 18 x 12pdrs and 6 x 36pdr *obusiers*).

Auguste Brest Dyd.
K: 12.1777. L: 18.9.1778. C: 1.1779. Took part in Battle of the Chesapeake 5.9.1781 and in Battle of St Kitts 25/26.1.1782 (both as flagship of CdE Louis-Antoine de Bougainville). Renamed *Jacobin* 3.1793. Took part in Battle of 13 Prairial ('Glorious First of June') 1794, then renamed *Neuf Thermidor* 12.1794. Foundered near Brest in a storm 31.1.1795.

TRIOMPHANT. 80 guns. Designed and built by Joseph-Marie-Blaise Coulomb. Ordered on 29 November 1777 and named on 20 February 1778. Rebuilt at Toulon from 1791 to August 1793.

Dimensions & tons: 183ft 10in, 164ft 0in x 48ft 0in x 23ft 9in (59.72, 53.27 x 15.59 x 7.71m) 1,950/3,720 tons. Draught 22ft 4in/24ft (7.25/7.80m). Men: 839, +13/17 officers.

Guns: LD 30 x 36pdrs; UD 32 x 24pdrs; QD 10 x 8pdrs; Fc 8 x 8pdrs.

Triomphant Toulon Dyd.
K: 3.1778. L: 31.3.1779. C: 6.1779. Took part in Battle of the Saintes 12.4.1782. Handed over to Anglo-Spanish forces at Toulon on 29.8.1793, then burnt at evacuation of that port 18.12.1793; remains raised 1805 and BU.

COURONNE. 80 guns. Designed and rebuilt by Antoine Groignard. A rebuilding of the *Couronne* of 1768, following its virtual destruction by fire. By 1794, an extra 4 x 8pdrs had been fitted and subsequently replaced by 4 x 36pdr *obusiers*.

Dimensions & tons: 190ft 6in, 168ft 6in x 46ft 0in x 23ft 0in (61.88, 54.74 x 14.94 x 7.47m) 1,900/3,800 tons. Draught 22½ft/24ft (7.31/7.80m). Men: 839, +13/17 officers.

Guns: LD 30 x 36pdrs; UD 32 x 24pdrs; QD 14 x 8pdrs; Fc 8 x 8pdrs (by 1794, 18 x 12pdrs & 4 x 36pdr *obusiers* had replaced the 8pdrs).

Couronne Brest Dyd
K: 5.1781. L: 19.9.1781. C: 10.1781. Took part in Battle of St Kitts 25/26.1.1782. Renamed *Ça Ira* on 29.9.1792. Captured by Hotham's fleet at Battle of Cape Noli 13.3.1795. Burnt at Corsica by accident 11.4.1796.

DEUX FRÈRES. 80 guns. Designed by Antoine Groignard and built by Jacques-Augustin Lamothe. A modification of Groignard's design for the *Couronne* of 1766, and the quarterdeck and *dunette* sides were pierced for eight pairs of guns, although only six pairs were carried. Named on 20 July 1782 after the brothers of Louis XVI (the Comte de Provence and Comte d'Artois), who funded the construction.

Dimensions & tons: 184ft 0in, 174ft 0in x 46ft 6in x 23ft 0in (59.77, 56.52 x 15.105 x 7.47m) 1,900/3,800 tons. Draught 21½ft/23½ft (6.98/7.63m). Men: 839, +13/17 officers.

Guns: LD 30 x 36pdrs; UD 32 x 24pdrs; QD 12 x 8pdrs; Fc 6 x 8pdrs. 4 x 36pdr *obusiers* added in 1793.

Deux Frères Brest Dyd.
K: 7.1782. L: 13 or 17.9.1784. C: 1785. Renamed *Juste* on 29.9.1792, then rearmed at Brest 6.1793. Captured by the British Navy at the Battle of 13 Prairial ('Glorious First of June') 1.6.1794, becoming HMS *Juste*. Laid up 4.1802 at Plymouth; BU there 2.1811.

During 1782 a further 80-gun ship, to have been named *Monarque*, was projected and would have been laid down at Rochefort during 1783, but was cancelled in February 1783. After 1786, a series of 80-gun ships (the *Tonnant* Class) to a common design by Jacques-Noël Sané were produced (see our 1786–1861 volume for construction from 1786). These were the most effective two-deckers of their age; they carried the same number of guns as the *Triomphant* and *Deux Frères* (although with 12pdrs *vice* 8pdrs on the *gaillards*), supplemented by six 36pdr *obusiers*; in fact, they had sixteen LD gunports per side, but only fifteen were routinely provided with 36pdr guns. Twelve were initially projected in 1786; five of these were ordered and built between 1787 and 1793; six more were ordered in January 1794, but only the first three of the latter were named and built.

2 The Second Rank

(Vaisseaux du second rang)
with 68 to 78 guns after 1715

The French Navy's 2nd Rank warships formed and remained the bulk of the effective membership of the battlefleet, although the 3rd Rank ships remained more numerous until the mid-eighteenth century. The composition of the rank changed considerably during the Colbert era, and continued to do so until the early years of the next century. Initially it comprised ships with between 50 and 64 guns. These were all nominally three-deckers without a forecastle, with the third deck interrupted (*coupé*) in the waist, and sometimes with a (removable) centreline gangway or 'flying bridge' between the fore and aft sections of the third deck, but they are better understood as two-deckers with the ends of the broken third tier effectively forming a forecastle and quarterdeck. As nominal three-deckers these ships would have had the arrangement of accommodations in the stern prescribed for three-deckers, which was more ample that that allowed for two-deckers.

The *Règlement* of 4 July 1670 defined the 2nd Rank of *vaisseaux* as comprising ships with between 56 and 70 guns. Another *Règlement* on 22 March 1671 specified that future vessels with fewer than 70 guns would have only two decks. In practice the 2nd Rank included, as of the mid-1670s, two-deckers and older nominal three-deckers of 1,050 to 1,500 tons that carried from 60 to 78 guns. However, by the early 1690s the 60-gun ships had mainly been relegated to the 3rd Rank, and by about 1730 the 64-gun ships had gradually followed them, so that the 2nd Rank was exclusively composed of 68 to 74-gun ships, all of these now being two-deckers with thirteen pairs of 36pdrs on the lower deck and fourteen pairs of 18pdrs on the upper deck. From 1735 this became a minimum of 74 guns, with fourteen pairs of 36pdrs on the lower deck and fifteen pairs of 18pdrs on the upper deck, while a larger group was introduced into the 1st Rank with 80 guns.

To compensate for the near total lack of contemporary data on ship armaments prior to 1696, we have in Sections (A) and (B) provided estimated armaments based on the governing directives and the known characteristics of all of the individual ships. This issue is discussed in greater detail in the Introduction.

In 1680 or early 1681 an 'establishment total' of twenty-six 2nd Rank ships was set, a 'target' level which was maintained until after 1715 (except in 1688, when it was raised to 28, and in 1689, when it was reduced to 24). In January 1681 there were actually twenty-one 2nd Rank ships in the fleet (down from a peak of twenty-seven in 1676) – nine in the Brest Department, five at Rochefort, and seven at Toulon. This number was only gradually added to, and it was 1691 before the target of twenty-six was reached. Numbers declined in the early eighteenth century, and did not reach the same level until the 1760s, by which time all 2nd Rank ships were 74-gun two-deckers.

(A) Vessels in service as at 9 March 1661

Only two warships notionally armed with 60 guns were built prior to 1661, although by the late 1660s each had only 56 guns – these were the *Reine* of 1647 and the *Saint Louis* of 1658. They were nominally three-deckers with the third deck interrupted in the waist, but they are better viewed as two-deckers with the ends of the broken 3rd deck functioning as a forecastle and quarterdeck. Each was pierced for twelve pairs of LD guns – excluding the unarmed chase port – with eleven pairs of 12pdrs on the deck above. The third tier by the late 1660s comprised two pairs of 6pdrs forwards of the waist, and three pairs aft of it. Both ships had only 48 guns by 1671, and were moved to the 3rd Rank under the 1670 Regulation, and so are to be found in Chapter 3.

(B) Vessels acquired from 9 March 1661

When the French rating system was established under Colbert in 1669 and 1670, the 2nd Rank was formed from those ships carrying between 56 and 70 guns. The 4 July 1670 *Règlement* directed that such ships should have three 'full' gun decks (although the third deck in practice was only partially armed), with a short QD and no forecastle. They were essentially two-deckers with the ends of the broken third deck functioning as a forecastle and quarterdeck, the latter surmounted by a poop. Generally, they retained this layout until the end of the 1680s. Eleven ships provisionally rated as 2nd Rank in 1669 – the *Reine* and *Saint Louis* and nine later ships – were re-classed as 3rd Rank in 1670, and (like many others) were renamed; they are covered in Chapter 3. After the late 1680s no further three-deckers were built with fewer than 78 guns, so subsequent construction of 2nd Rank ships was entirely of two-deckers.

BOURBON. 66, later 64 guns. Designed and built by Jean-Pierre Brun. Nominally a three-decker, pierced for twelve pairs of LD gunports (excluding the chase ports), and with the forward and aft part of the upper deck connected by an unarmed section in the waist. Reduced to 3rd Rank in 1670, but restored to 2nd Rank in 1671. Reconstructed at Toulon from 1680 to September 1681.

Dimensions & tons: 137ft 6in x 34ft 6in x 16ft 0in (44.67 x 11.21 x 5.20m). 1,050 tons. Draught 17ft (5.52m). Men: 450 (70/260/120) in 1669, + 6 officers; 400 (60/206/34) in 1671, +5 officers.

Guns: 66 by 1669 and 60 from 1671. 64 from 1672: LD 10 x 24pdrs + 14 x 18pdrs; MD 24 x 12pdrs; UD 16 x 6pdrs. Reduced to 60 guns from 1674, but restored to 64 from 1677.

Bourbon Soubise.
K: 1665. L: 22.11.1665. C: 3.1666. Took part in the expedition to Candia 6.1669. Renamed *Éclatant* 24.6.1671. Took part in the Battles of Stromboli 8.1.1676, Augusta 22.4.1676 and Palermo 31.5.1676. Struck at Toulon 1684.

PRINCE. 64, later 70 guns. Designed and built by Laurent Hubac. Nominally a three-decker, similar to *Bourbon* above, pierced for twelve pairs of LD gunports (excluding the chase ports), and with the forward and aft part of the upper deck connected by an unarmed section in the waist. Classed as 2nd Rank in 1669, and retained that Rank throughout her life.

Dimensions & tons: 137ft 6in x 34ft 6in x 16ft 0in (44.67 x 11.21 x 5.20m). 1,200 tons. Draught 16ft/19½ft (5.20/6.33m). Men: in 1669, 450 (70/260/120), +6 officers; in 1671, 400 (60/206/134), +5 officers.

Guns: 64 by 1669. 66 from 1676: LD 10 x 24pdrs + 14 x 18pdrs; MD 24 x 12pdrs; UD 14 x 6pdrs; poop 4 x 4pdrs. Increased to 70 guns from 1679.

Prince Brest Dyd.
K: 5.1665. L: 4.1666. C: 12.1666. Commissioned: 4.1669. Renamed *Sans Pareil* 24.6.1671. Took part in Battles of Solebay 7.6.1672, Schoonevledt 7.6.1673, Walcheren 14.6.1673, Texel 21.8.1673, Stromboli 8.1.1676 and Augusta 22.4.1676 (both as flagship of CdE Louis Gabaret), and Palermo 31.5.1676. Lost in a storm on the Breton coast 21.10.1679 (78 survivors).

DANISH-BUILT. 64, later 72 then 60 guns. In 1665 three ships were ordered by Colbert from Denmark, although only two were actually delivered. Each was completed with a decked-over waist as in the Dutch-built ships below (turning them into flush three-deckers, albeit without guns on the third deck amidships), but the midships portion of this deck was removed upon arrival in France. The larger of these, *Frédéric*, was pierced for thirteen pairs of gunports on the lower deck (excluding the unarmed chase ports); she was partly rebuilt at Rochefort in summer 1670, turning her into a two-decker with the former 3rd deck becoming a QD and forecastle. The smaller of these, originally named *Grand Danois* but renamed *Sophie* before delivery to France, was classed as 3rd Rank in 1671, and is included in Chapter 3.

Dimensions & tons: 139ft 0in, 114ft 6in x 35ft 2in x 13ft 9in (45.15, 37.19 x 11.42 x 4.47m). 1,100 tons. Draught 17ft (5.52m). Men 450 (70/260/120), + 6 officers; from 1671, 400 (60/206/134), + 5 officers.

Guns: 64 by 1669. 72 from 1674: LD 12 x 24pdrs + 14 x 18pdrs; MD 26 x 12pdrs; UD (aft) 10 x 6pdrs + (fwd) 6 x 6pdrs; poop 4 x 4pdrs. 60 guns from 1676.

Frédéric Mathias, Copenhagen.
K: 8.1665. L: early 1666. C: 12.1666. Renamed *Admirable* 24.6.1671. Took part in Battle of Solebay 7.6.1672. BU 1677.

PRINCESSE. 60, later 64 guns. Designed and built by Jean-Pierre Brun. Pierced for twelve pairs of LD guns (excluding the chase ports), and with the forward and aft part of the upper deck connected by an unarmed section in the waist. Relegated to 3rd Rank in 1670, but

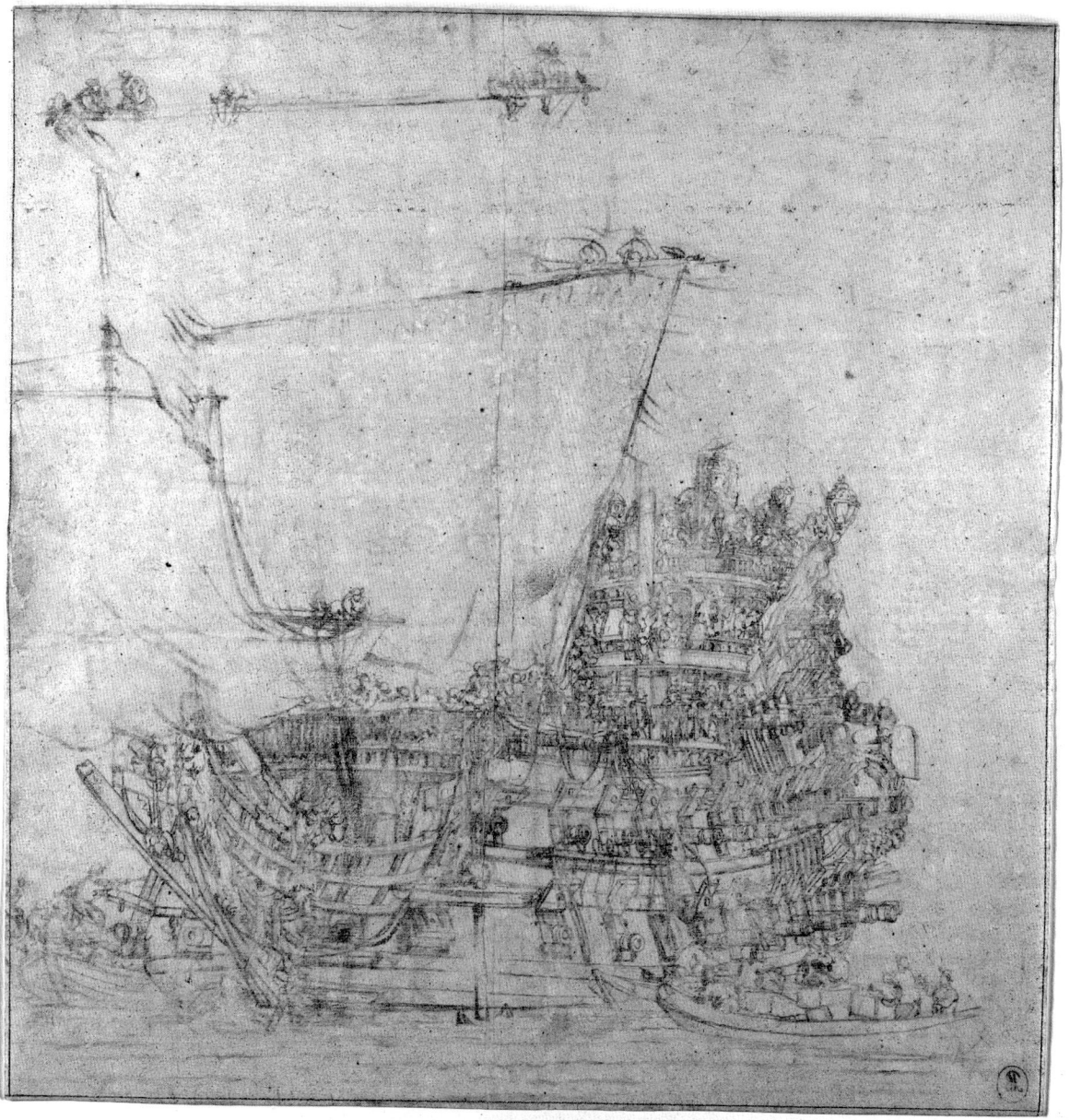

A Van de Velde drawing of a Danish two-decker, thought to be one of the two built in Denmark for France in 1666. With thirteen gunports on the lower deck, it probably represents the *Frédéric*, the larger of the two. Although the angle makes it difficult to see, the waist is decked over – suggested by the positions of some of the crew – but there are no guns between the forecastle and quarterdeck. This ship, renamed *Admirable* in 1671, had a short life, in spite of being virtually rebuilt at Rochefort in 1670, as much decayed wood was employed in her reconstruction there. (Museum Boijmans Van Beuningen, Rotterdam MB 1866-T 439)

A Van de Velde drawing of one of the six French 2nd Rank ships built in the Netherlands in 1666. The decorative scheme is typically Dutch, but the taffrail carries the arms of France and Navarre. As no guns are shown in the lower deck ports, it is not obvious that this battery comprised a mixture of 24pdrs and 18pdrs. (National Maritime Museum, London PY3881)

restored to 2nd Rank in 1671; reduced again to the 3rd Rank in 1677–78, and rebuilt at Toulon from October 1678 to February 1681, then raised again to the 2nd Rank in 1687.

  Dimensions & tons: 137ft 0in x 34ft 6in x 16ft 0in (44.50 x 11.21 x 5.20m). 1,100 tons. Draught 16ft (5.20m). Men: 450 (70/260/120), +6 officers; by 1671, 400 (60/206/134), +5 officers; by 1671, 400 (81/200/119), +9 officers.

  Guns: 60 by 1669. 64 from 1679: LD 10 x 24pdrs + 14 x 18pdrs; MD 24 x 12pdrs; UD (aft) 12 x 6pdrs + (fwd) 4 x 6pdrs.

Princesse Soubise.

  K: 12.1665. L: 5.1667. C: 5.1667. Took part in expedition to Candia 1669. Renamed *Triomphant* 24.6.1671 and *Constant* 28.6.1678. Struck and relegated to hulk 1690 (called *Vieux Constant*); not mentioned after 1704.

DUTCH-BUILT Group. 66, later 72 guns. In early 1666 the French shipyards were not yet ready to begin the construction of the numerous new ships of the line which Colbert needed urgently, so he arranged for the construction of eight three-deckers of 1,200 tons each, to be built in Amsterdam and Zaandam. The order was placed on 19 March 1666 with various Dutch builders believed to be as shown below (the contract negotiated through De Werf), although the orders for the final pair (never begun) were later rescinded. The six ships sailed from Amsterdam on 5 May 1667 (although all still required further work); they had problems traversing the shallows, and then had to wait off Texel for the arrival of the two Danish-built ships (*Frédéric* and *Sophie*) to join them.

The Treaty of Breda was concluded on 31 July 1667, and the squadron (accompanied by eight other French warships) left the Marsdiep on 12 August for France. These large vessels were pierced for 74 guns, with thirteen pairs on the LD (not including the chase ports), the same on the MD, nine pairs on the UD, and two pairs on the poop. Following Dutch practice the beams for the third deck went all the way across the ship even in the unarmed waist, making them full three-deckers as built. Each carried the arms of France and Navarre on its taffrail. The *Saint Louis* (ex-*Normand*) underwent rebuilding at Rochefort in 1673, and *Conquérant* at Toulon in 1677–78, while *Illustre* (ex *Neptune*) had two periods of rebuilding at Brest in 1683 and 1689–90.

  Dimensions & tons: 140ft 0in, 118ft 0in x 36ft 0in x 14ft 0in (45.48, 38.33 x 11.69 x 4.55m); *Courtisan* and *Intrépide* 143ft (46.45m) length; *Neptune* 137ft, 118ft x 37ft x 14ft 3in (44.50, 38.33 x 12.02 x 4.63m). 1,200 tons. Draught 17ft (5.52m). Men: 450 in 1669 (70/260/120), +6 officers. 400 by 1671 (60/206/134), 5 officers.

  Guns: 66 by 1669 and 64 from 1671. 72 from 1674: LD 12 x 24pdrs + 14 x 18pdrs; MD 26 x 12pdrs; UD (aft) 10 x 6pdrs + (fwd) 6 x 6pdrs; poop 4 x 4pdrs. *Conquérant* and *Illustre* (ex-*Neptune*) had 70 guns from 1679, and *Illustre* (the longest-lasting of the six) then had 64 from 1688, 74 from 1690, and 68 from 1696: LD 24 x 24pdrs; MD 26 x 12pdrs; UD (aft) 8 x 6pdrs + (fwd) 6 x 6pdrs; poop 4 x 4pdrs.

Conquérant Hendrik Dirckszoon Sluijck, Zaandam.

  K: 4.1666. L: 11.1666. C: 6.1667. Took part in Battles of Solebay 7.6.1672, Schooneveld 7 & 14.6.1673, and Texel 21.8.1673. Rebuilt at Toulon 1677–78. Wrecked 21.10.1679 in a storm off Ushant.

Courtisan Cornelis de Raffe, Amsterdam.

K: 4.1666. L: 12.1666. C: 6.1667. In expedition to Candia (Crete) 6.1669 (as flagship of LG Damien, Marquis de Martel. Renamed *Magnifique* 24.6.1671. Took part in the Battles of Stromboli 8.1.1676, Augusta 22.4.1676 and Palermo 3.6.1676. Hulked 1680–82.

Invincible Cornelis Michiels, Amsterdam.
K: 4.1666. L: 12.1666. C: 6.1667. Took part in Battles of Solebay 7.6.1672, Schooneveld 7 & 14.6.1673, and Texel 21.8.1673. Deleted 1681.

Normand Cornelis Michiels, Amsterdam.
K: 4.1666. L: 12.1666. C: 7.1667. Renamed *Saint Louis* 24.6.1671. Rebuilt at Rochefort in 1673. Condemned 1679 at La Rochelle and BU 1680.

Intrépide Hendrik Dirckszoon Sluijck, Zaandam.
K: 4.1666. L: 12.1666. C: 8.1667. Renamed *Grand* 24.6.1671. Took part in Battles of Solebay 7.6.1672, Schooneveld 7 & 14.6.1673, and Texel 21.8.1673. Deleted 1678.

Neptune Jan Hendrik Cardinaal, Amsterdam.
K: 4.1666. L: 12.1666. C: 9.1667. Renamed *Illustre* 24.6.1671. Took part in Battles of Solebay 7.6.1672, Schooneveld 7 & 14.6.1673, and Texel 21.8.1673. Rebuilt at Brest in 1683 and again in 1689–90. Struck at Rochefort 1698.

CHARENTE. 66 guns. Designed and built by Jean Laure. A nominal three-decker (with the third deck continuous but lacking guns and ports amidships, so that the fore and aft portions served as forecastle and QD respectively). Pierced for twelve pairs of LD guns (excluding the unarmed chase ports). She underwent major repairs at Martinique in December 1677.
  Dimensions & tons: 150ft 0in x 38ft 0in x ? (48.73 x 12.34m). 1,100 tons. Draught 18ft/19½ft (5.85/6.33m). Men: 400 (60/206/134), +5/9 officers.
  Guns: 66 from 1669, then 64 from 1671. 66 from 1677: LD 10 x 24pdrs + 14 x 18pdrs; MD 24 x 12pdrs; UD (aft) 8 x 6pdrs + (fwd) 6 x 6pdrs; poop 4 x 4pdrs.

Charente Rochefort Dyd.
K: 6.1666. L: 2.1669. C: end 1669. Renamed *Belliqueux* 24.6.1671. She was intended to be renamed *Courtisan* 28.6.1678, but had already been wrecked on the Îles d'Aves (in the Caribbean) 11.5.1678 with other ships of Vice-Am. Jean, Comte d'Estrées's squadron.

FORT. 66, later 76 guns. Designed and built by Jean Guichard. A nominal three-decker, similar to the *Charente* in construction, pierced for twelve pairs of LD guns (excluding the unarmed chase ports).
  Dimensions & tons: 146ft 0in, 120ft 0in x 37ft 0in x ? (47.43, 38.98 x 12.02m). 1,300/1,450 tons. Draught 19ft/20½ft (6.17/6.66m). Men: 425 (65/220/140), +5 officers.
  Guns: 66 from 1669. 68 from 1671: LD 10 x 24pdrs + 14 x 18pdrs; MD 24 x 12pdrs; UD (aft) 12 x 6pdrs + (fwd) 4 x 6pdrs; poop 4 x 4pdrs. 76 guns from 1679, 64 from 1688, and 76 from 1690.

Fort Rochefort Dyd.
K: 1668. L: 11.4.1669. C: 9.1670. Renamed *Foudroyant* 24.6.1671. Took part in Battles of Solebay 7.6.1672, Schooneveld 7 & 14.6.1673 and Texel 21.8.1673. Condemned 9.1690 at Brest and BU.

MADAME. 70, later 74 guns. Designed and built by Jean Guérouard, with sculpture designed by Pierre Puget. Named on 1 February 1669. A nominal three-decker, pierced for thirteen pairs of LD guns (excluding the chase ports). Classed as 1st Rank in 1671, but reduced to 2nd Rank later the same year. Underwent rebuilding at Toulon in 1679. For the 1693 campaign she received 8 x 60pdrs on her LD.
  Dimensions & tons: 143ft 0in x 40ft 0in x 17ft 0in (46.45 x 12.99 x 5.52m). 1,450 tons. Draught 18ft/21ft (5.85/6.82m). Men: 450 (66/234/150), +5 officers.
  Guns: 70 from 1671: LD 12 x 24pdrs + 14 x 18pdrs; MD 14 x 18pdrs + 12 x 12pdrs; UD (aft) 12 x 8pdrs + (fwd) 6 x 8pdrs. 72 guns from 1674, 70 again from 1679, and 74 from 1691. 68 (in war or peace) from 1696: LD 20 x 24pdrs; MD 24 x 18pdrs; UD 20 x 8pdrs; poop 4 x 4pdrs.

Madame Toulon Dyd.
K: 6.1668. L: 28.2.1670. C: end 1671. Renamed *Pompeux* 24.6.1671. Took part in Battles of Texel 21.8.1673, Pharo (Messina) 2.1.1675, Lipari Islands 11.2.1675, Stromboli 8.1.1676, Augusta 22.4.1676 and Palermo 31.5.1676 (last five under CV Jean-Baptiste de Valbelle). Condemned and hulked at Toulon 4.1696, sold 2.1709.

ROYALE THÉRÈSE. 68, later 76 guns. Designed and built by Rodolphe Gédéon. A nominal three-decker, pierced for twelve pairs of LD guns (excluding the chase ports). Named on 1 February 1669.
  Dimensions & tons: 142ft 0in, 116ft 0in x 39ft 0in x 17ft 0in (46.13, 37.68 x 12.67 x 5.52m). 1,400 tons. Draught 19ft (6.17m). Men: 450 (83/230/137), +5 officers.
  Guns: 68 from 1671: LD 10 x 24pdrs + 14 x 18pdrs: MD 24 x 12pdrs; UD 16 x 6pdrs; poop 4 x 4pdrs. 70 guns from 1673 and 72 from 1674. 76 from 1677.

Royale Thérèse Toulon Dyd.
K: 6.1668. L: 4.3.1670. C: 1671. Renamed *Saint Esprit* 24.6.1671. Took part in Battles of the Lipari Islands 11.2.1675, Stromboli 8.1.1676, Augusta 22.4.1676 and Palermo 2.6.1676, and in attack on Algiers 23.7.1682 (flag of LG Abraham Duquesne in all five cases). Condemned 1689 at Toulon, and sale ordered 24.9.1689; foundered 1691, remains sold 1692.

FLORISSANT Class. 70 guns, later 76 (*Florissant*) or 80 (*Henri*). Designed and built by Rodolphe Gédéon, lengthened versions of the *Royal Thérèse*. Pierced for thirteen pairs of LD guns (excluding the chase ports). These two ships were ordered at the end of 1667 and were named *Rubis* and *Joli* on 1 February 1669, but were renamed *Florissant* ('flourishing') and *Henri* respectively on 24 June 1671. Both were initially classed as 1st Rank in the re-classifications of 1671 but reduced to the 2nd Rank in the same year. They were both rebuilt at Toulon in 1677, and *Florissant* underwent a second reconstruction there in 1680–81.
  Dimensions & tons: 146ft 0in, 116ft 0in x 39ft 0in x 17ft 0in. (47.43, 37.68 x 12.67 x 5.52m) 1,400 tons. Draught 18ft /20ft (5.85/6.50m). Men: 450 (66/234/150), +5 officers.
  Guns: 70 from 1671: LD 12 x 24pdrs + 14 x 18pdrs; MD 14 x 18pdrs + 12 x 12pdrs; UD (aft) 12 x 8pdrs + (fwd) 6 x 8pds. Subsequently, *Henri* had 74 guns from 1676 and 80 from 1679, while *Florissant* had 74 guns from 1676, 72 from 1679, 70 from 1682, 72 from 1687 and 76 from 1690.

Florissant Toulon Dyd.
K: 3.1669. L: 15.10.1670. C: 1671. Took part in the Battles of Beachy Head 10.7.1690 and Lagos 28.6.1693. Condemned 3.1696 at Toulon and became breakwater; BU after 1700.

Henri Toulon Dyd.
K: 4.1669. L: 2.10.1670. C: 1671. Sold 6.1687 at Toulon and BU.

FRANÇOIS. 62, later 66 guns. Designed and built by Laurent Hubac,

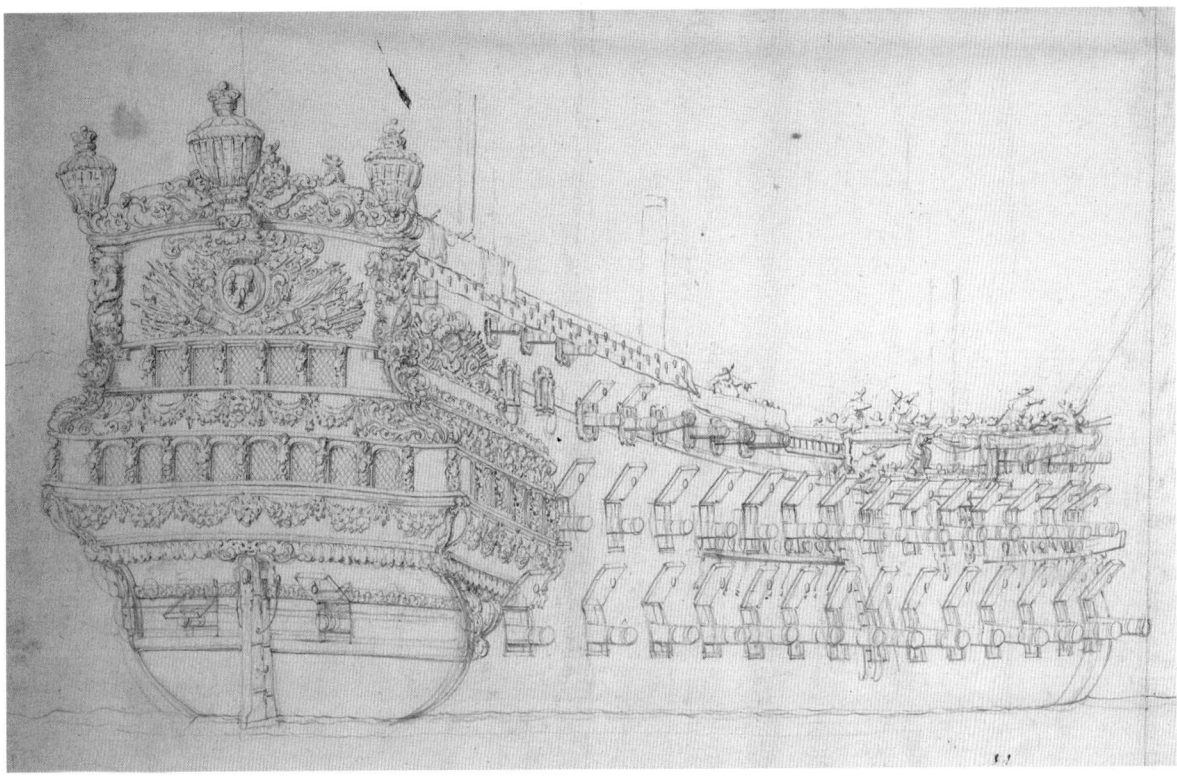

A Van de Velde drawing of *Orgueilleux*, one of a pair of unusually large two-deckers with a lower deck battery of 28 guns launched in 1671. This is sometimes identified as *Superbe*, her sister ship, but she was not present in 1673 when Van de Velde had his only opportunity to draw any French ships of this generation. Both ships suffered from the poor quality timber employed in their construction at Rochefort. (National Maritime Museum, London PY9358)

the first of three essentially similar vessels. Pierced for twelve pairs of LD ports (excluding the chase ports), and with four gunports on the stern counter. Ordered on 4 October 1668 and named on 17 May 1669.

Dimensions & tons: 136ft 0in, 116ft 0in x 37ft 0in x 16ft 0in (44.18, 37.68 x 12.02 x 5.20m). 1,100 tons. Draught 18ft (5.85m). Men: 400 in war (60/206/134), +5 officers.

Guns: 62 from 1671. 64 from 1672: LD 10 x 24pdrs + 14 x 18pdrs; MD 24 x 12pdrs; UD (aft) 10 x 6pdrs + (fwd) 6 x 6pdrs. 66 guns from 1674, then 60 from 1676.

François (Français) Brest Dyd.
K: 11.1668. L: 25.10.1669. C: 8.1670. Renamed *Glorieux* 24.6.1671. Took part in the Battles of Solebay 7.6.1672, Schooneveld 7 & 14.6.1673, and Texel 21.8.1673. Took part in attack on Cayenne 17.12.1676 (as flagship of Vice-Am. Jean, Comte d'Estrées), then burnt in action against the Dutch 56-gun *Huis te Kruiningen* (which also was destroyed) in Battle of Tobago 3.3.1677.

SUPERBE Class. 68, later 76 guns. Designed and built by François Pomet. Pierced for fourteen pairs of LD ports (excluding the chase ports). The first ship was named on 17 May 1669 as *Faucon* and the second on 21 February 1670 as *Vermandois* (named after Louis de Bourbon-Vendôme, Comte de Vermandois, legitimised son of Louis XIV and *Amiral de France*); however, the two were renamed as *Orgueilleux* ('proud') and *Superbe* respectively on 24 June 1671. They were completed as two-deckers of unusual length (151ft overall), and in 1673 it was felt that more ordnance should be added. Thus, on Colbert's instructions, the *Superbe* was taken back into Rochefort Dyd and a partially-armed third deck added between forecastle and quarterdeck, making her a nominal three-decker. The *Orgueilleux* was then modified in the same way.

Dimensions & tons: 146ft 0in, 122ft 0in x 39ft 0in x 18ft 0in (47.43, 39.63 x 12.67 x 5.85m). 1,400 tons. Draught 19ft/20ft (6.17/6.50m). Men: 450 in war (66/234/150), + 5 officers.

Guns: 68 from 1671, then 70 from 1673: LD 14 x 24pdrs + 14 x 18pdrs; UD 14 x 18pdrs + 12 x 12pdrs; QD 10 x 8pdrs; Fc 6 x 8pdrs. 76 from 1674 after reconstruction: LD unchanged; MD (formerly UD) unchanged; UD (formerly QD/Fc) 16 x 8pdrs; poop 6 x 4pdrs. *Orgueilleux* reduced to 74 guns in 1685.

Superbe Rochefort Dyd.
K: 5.1670. L: 6.1671. C: 4.1672. Took part in Battle of Solebay 7.6.1672 (as flagship of CdE Marquis de Treillebois de la Rabesnières, who was killed in this battle). Condemned 1687 and BU at Rochefort.

Orgueilleux Rochefort Dyd.
K: 5.1669. L: 9.1671. C: 10.1672. Took part in Battles of Schooneveld 7 & 14.6.1673 (as flagship of CdE François-Bénédict de Rouxel, Marquis de Grancey), and Texel 21.8.1673. Condemned 1688, BU at Rochefort.

When the French rating system was established in 1669, the 2nd Rank was formed from those ships carrying from 56 to 68 guns (although the elderly 64-gun *Vendôme* was placed in the 1st Rank); it comprised the smaller nominal three-decked vessels, and the formal Regulation issued on 4 July 1670 defined the Rank accordingly; while that Regulation placed the upper limit at 70 guns, in practice the only two 70-gun ships at that date (*Saint Philippe* and *Henri*) had been classed with the 1st Rank. The ships established as 2nd Rank in 1669 had between 50 guns and 66 guns. There were two divisions as regards manning. The twelve largest ships each had 6 commissioned officers and 450 men – the latter comprising 70 petty officers, 260 sailors and 120 soldiers belonging to the *compagnies franches de la marine* (marines). This group comprised the *Bourbon, Conquérant, Courtisan, Invincible, Normand, Intrépide, Neptune, Charente* and *Fort* – each with 66 guns; *Prince* and *Frédéric* with 64 guns; and *Princesse* with 60 guns). The eleven smaller ships each had 5 commissioned officers and 400 men – the latter comprising 60 petty officers, 230 sailors and 110 soldiers. The smaller group consisted of the *Sophie, Paris, Île de France* and *Lys* with 60 guns; *Navarre, Breton* and *Rochefort* with 56 guns; *Royale* and *Diamant* with 54 guns; and the older *Saint Louis* with 52 guns and *Reine* with 50 guns.

TERRIBLE. 68, later 70 guns. Designed and built by Laurent Hubac, enlarged from the *François* design, with a notably longer keel. Pierced for twelve pairs of LD guns (excluding chase ports). Named on 21 February 1670.

Dimensions & tons: 140ft 0in, 125ft 0in x 37ft 6in x 17ft 0in (45.48, 40.60 x 12.18 x 5.52m). 1,300 tons. Draught 18½ft (6.01m). Men: 450 in war (66/234/150), + 5 officers.

Guns: 68 from 1671: LD 10 x 24pdrs + 14 x 18pdrs; MD 24 x 12pdrs; UD (aft) 10 x 6pdrs + (fwd) 6 x 6pdrs; poop 4 x 4pdrs. 70 guns from 1673.

Terrible Brest Dyd.
K: 10.1669. L: 19.9.1670. C: early 1671. Took part in the Battles of Solebay 7.6.1672 (as flagship of LG Abraham Duquesne), Schooneveldt 7 & 14.6.1673 (as flagship of CdE Hector Des Ardens) and Texel 21.8.1673 (still Des Ardens's flag). Wrecked on the Îles Aves (in the Caribbean) on 11.5.1678 with other ships of Vice-Am. Jean, Comte d'Estrées's squadron, while *en route* to Curaçao.

TONNANT. 68, later 66 guns. Designed and built by Laurent Hubac, also a development from the *François* design. Pierced for twelve pairs of LD guns (excluding chase ports). Named on 21 February 1670.

Dimensions & tons: 137ft 6in, 118ft 6in x 36ft 8in x 17ft 0in (44.67, 38.49 x 11.91 x 5.52m). 1,200 tons. Draught 17ft/18ft (5.52/5.85m). Men: 400 in war (60/206/134), + 5 officers.

Guns: 68 from 1671: LD 10 x 24pdrs + 14 x 18pdrs; MD 24 x 12pdrs; UD (aft) 10 x 6pdrs + (fwd) 6 x 6pdrs; poop 4 x 4pdrs. 64 guns from 1672, then 66 guns from 1675.

Tonnant Brest Dyd.
K: 10.1669. L: 19.9.1670. C: 6.1671. Took part in the Battles of Solebay 7.6.1672, Schooneveldt 7 & 14.6.1673 and Texel 21.8.1673. Wrecked on the Îles Aves (in the Caribbean) on 11.5.1678 with other ships of *Vice-amiral* Jean, Comte d'Estrées's squadron, while *en route* to Curaçao.

The 12 March 1671 adjustment to the rating system, which specified that future vessels with fewer than 70 guns would have only two decks, saw the 2nd Rank list shortened to sixteen ships, with six ships of 68 guns and 425 men added to the Rank; these comprised the *Vermandois* and *Faucon* (to be renamed *Superbe* and *Orgueilleux*) building at Rochefort, *Royal Thérèse* (to become *Saint Esprit*) at Toulon, *Terrible* and *Tonnant* at Brest, plus the re-graded *Fort* (now *Foudroyant*) at Rochefort.

The six Dutch-built ships and the *Charente* dropped to 64 guns (and 400 men), joining the *Frédéric*, while the *Prince* and the new *François* were classed as 62 guns and 400 men; all were based at Rochefort except for the *Courtisan* at Toulon and the *François* at Brest. The ships of 60 or fewer guns were all reduced to the 3rd Rank (except for *Paris* and *Île de France*, which were both re-armed as 70-gun ships and raised to the 1st Rank). In addition, many of these ships were renamed on 24 June 1671 (see under individual entries and in Appendix H). Six months later on 1 January 1672, the list jumped quantitatively back to twenty-two ships,

A Van de Velde drawing probably depicting *Terrible*, flagship of Hector Des Ardens, the second-in-command at the two battles of Schoonevelt. The artist annotated the drawing 'The square rear-admiral [a reference to the second-in-command's flag] being damaged, the World's Wonder took her place.' For unknown reasons, this was the nickname of *Royale Thérèse*, so this drawing was assumed to represent this ship, which indeed took over as flagship of the second-in-command for the subsequent Texel battle. However, *Royale Thérèse* was very different in appearance (see Chapter 1) so the artist's note must refer to the previous second-in-command, the *Terrible*. (National Maritime Museum, London PZ7270)

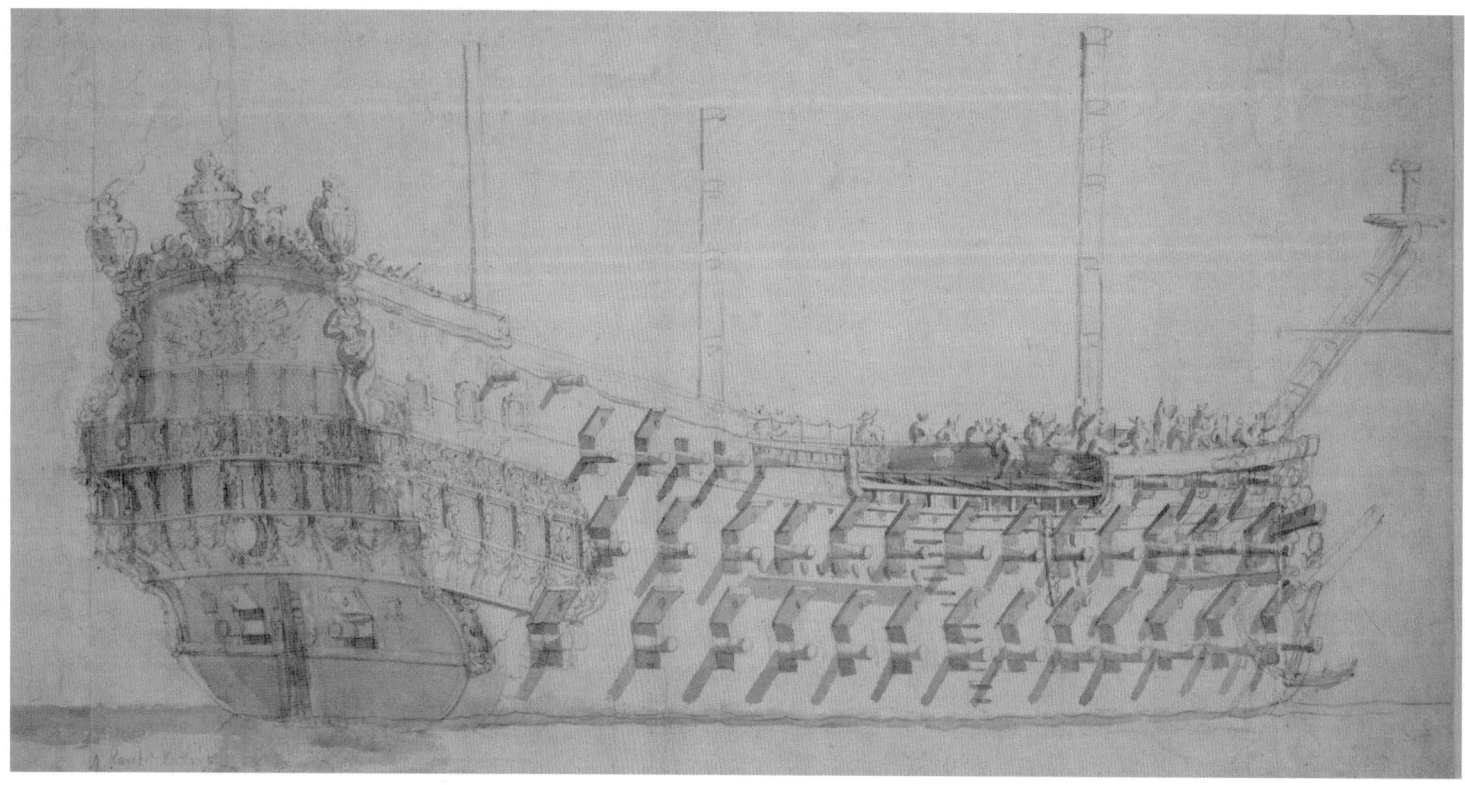

comprising thirteen ships of 64 guns and 400 men, five ships of 68 guns and 425 men, and four ships of 70 guns and 450 men.

CONSTANT Class. 74, later 76 guns. Designed and built by Laurent Hubac. These were the first of five 70/76-gun nominal three-deckers built at Brest to Hubac's designs and pierced for thirteen pairs of LD guns (excluding the chase ports). The first ship was begun in 1674 as *Brave*, but was renamed soon after launching – the names *Constant* and *Courtisan* was allocated on 26 June 1675. Both ships were renamed on 28 June 1678 as shown below. They were reconstructed at Brest in 1687–88 and 1689–90 respectively. *Triomphant* was re-classed as 1st Rank in 1690, but reverted to 2nd Rank in 1691.

Dimensions & tons: 143ft 6in, 120ft 0in x 38ft 0in x 18ft in (46.61, 38.98 x 12.34 x 5.85m) 1,350 tons. Draught 18ft/19ft (5.85/6.17 m). Men: 400/500, +9 officers.

Guns: 74 from 1676: LD 12 x 24pdrs + 14 x 18pdrs; MD 14 x 18pdrs + 12 x 12pdrs; UD 18 x 8pdrs; poop 4 x 4pdrs. 76 guns from 1679, 74 again from 1688, and 76 from 1691. 76 in war from 1696 (70 peace): LD 16 x 36pdrs + 10 x 24pdrs; MD 26 x 18pdrs; UD 20 x 8pdrs; poop 4 x 4pdrs.

Constant Brest Dyd.
K: 5.1674. L: 20.6.1675. C: 1676. Renamed *Triomphant* 28.6.1678. Took part in Battles of Beachy Head 10.7.1690 and Barfleur 29.5.1692. Burnt by fireship HMS *Wolf* at Cherbourg 1.6.1692.

Courtisan Brest Dyd.
K: 5.1674. L: 28.6.1676. C: 16/7. Renamed *Belliqueux* 28.6.1678. Took part in Battle of Beachy Head 10.7.1690. Condemned 1.1706 at Brest and to be BU by Order 19.9.1708.

GLORIEUX. 60, later 64 guns. Designed and built by Laurent Hubac, as a replacement for the previous *Glorieux* (ex- *François* of 1669), which had been destroyed off Tobago on 3 March 1677. This vessel initiated a new group of ships smaller than the 70/76-gun type, and pierced for just twelve pairs of LD guns (excluding the chase ports), with a spacing of 7¼ft between the LD gunports (themselves 32in wide). Like the 70/76-gun type she was nominally a three-decker without a forecastle but is better understood as a two-decker with the ends of the broken third deck functioning as a forecastle and quarterdeck. While built as a 2nd Rank ship, she was reduced to the 3rd Rank in 1700, but reinstated as 2nd Rank in 1702–3, then reconstructed during 1705 at Brest and reduced again to 3rd Rank in 1706.

Another seven ships would be built to a similar pattern during the 1680s – see the *Ardent, Bourbon, Furieux, Content, Sérieux, Courtisan* and *Henri* below, and most served until well into the eighteenth century. However, their twelve pairs of LD guns meant they were not able to mount more than 66 guns in total (the slightly longer *Henri* was an exception), and they were mostly reduced to the 3rd Rank later in their careers.

Dimensions & tons: 138ft 6in, 120ft 0in x 37ft 0in x 17ft 0in (44.99, 38.98 x 12.02 x 5.52m). 1,100 tons. Draught 18ft/22ft (5.85/7.15m). Men: 400/380, +7/9 officers.

Guns: 60 from 1679: LD 10 x 24pdrs + 14 x 18pdrs; MD 24 x 12pdrs; UD (aft) 8 x 6pdrs + (fwd) 4 x 6pdrs. 54 guns from 1687, 62 from 1688, then 64 from 1691. 64 in war from 1696 (54 peace): LD 24 x 24pdrs; MD 26 x 12pdrs; UD (aft) 10 x 6pdrs + (fwd) 4 x 6pdrs; occasionally poop 2 x 4pdrs.

Glorieux Brest Dyd.
K: 2.1678. L: 2.1679. C: 1679. Took part in Battles of Beachy Head 10.7.1690 and Lagos 28.6.1693 (the latter under CV Jean Bart). Lent as a privateer to CV Henri-Louis, Marquis de Chavagnac, and CV Pierre Le Moyne d'Iberville, as part of a squadron of ten vessels, for operations in the West Indies 1705–6. Lent as a privateer to CdE Jean-Baptiste Ducasse, as part of a squadron of seven vessels, in support of the Spanish Navy escorting galleons in 1707. Lent as a privateer to CV René Duguay-Trouin, as part of a squadron of thirteen vessels 1711–12; took part in the capture of Rio de Janeiro on 22.9.1711. Struck early 1717 at Brest, and BU 1719.

FURIEUX. 70 guns. A new 70-gun ship of this name was ordered in November 1678 to be built at Toulon (the existing 3rd Rank *Furieux* had been renamed *Brillant* on 28 June 1678), but the order was cancelled in 1680. However, the order was reinstated in 1684 (see below).

TERRIBLE. 72, later 76 guns. Designed and built by Laurent Hubac, a replacement for the previous ship of this name lost in 1678, and seemingly an intermediate step between the *Constant* Class and the *Tonnant* Class. Pierced for thirteen pairs of LD guns (excluding the chase ports).

Dimensions & tons: 142ft 0in, 120ft 0in x 38ft 0in x 17ft 6in. (46.13, 38.98 x 12.34 x 5.68m). 1,300 tons. Draught 18ft /19ft (5.85/6.17m). Men: 9 officers, 490 men.

Guns: 72 from 1680, then 74 from 1687: LD 12 x 24pdrs + 14 x 18pdrs; MD 14 x 18pdrs + 12 x 12pdrs; UD (aft) 12 x 6pdrs + (fwd) 6 x 6pdrs; poop 4 x 4pdrs (2 more added from 1691).

Terrible Brest Dyd.
K: 6.1679. L: 1680. C: 12.1680. Took part in Battles of Beachy Head 10.7.1690 (where her gun-room was destroyed by a mortar, causing 95 deaths) and of Barfleur 29.5.1692. Burnt by fireship at La Hougue 2.6.1692.

GRAND. 70, later 88 guns. Designed and built by Honoré Malet, ordered 17 July 1679. Pierced for thirteen pairs of LD guns (excluding the chase ports). Completed as a 70-gun 2nd Rank, but raised to an 80-gun 1st Rank in 1687. In 1706 raséed by one deck at Brest to 72 guns and re-classed as 2nd Rank.

Dimensions & tons: 156ft 0in, 130ft 0in x 40ft 0in x 18ft 6in (50.675, 42.23 x 12.99 x 6.01m). 1,600 tons. Draught 20ft/22ft (6.50/7.15 m). Men: 630 (500 as 72-gun ship), +9 officers.

Guns: 70 from 1680: LD 12 x 24pdrs + 14 x 18pdrs; MD 14 x 18pdrs + 12 x 12pdrs; UD 18 x 8pdrs. 80 from 1687: LD & MD unchanged; UD now 24 x 8pdrs; poop 4 x 4pdrs. 88 from 1688 and 86 from 1691. 84 in war from 1696 (78 in peace): LD 26 x 36pdrs; MD 26 x 18pdrs; UD 24 x 8pdrs; QD/Fc 8 x 6pdrs. As 72-gun from 1707 had LD 26 x 36pdrs; MD 28 x 18pdrs; UD 16 x 8pdrs; poop 2 x 4pdrs.

Grand Rochefort Dyd.
K: 8.1679. L: 10.1680. C: 7.1681. Took part in Battles of Beachy Head 10.7.1690 (as flagship of LG Victor Marie, Comte d'Estrées), Barfleur 29.5.1692 (as flagship of CdE François Panetié) and Lagos 28.6.1693. Lent as a privateer to CdE Jean-Baptiste Ducasse, as part of a squadron of seven vessels, in support of the Spanish Navy escorting galleons 1707. Condemned 6.1716 at Brest and BU there 1717.

ARDENT. 64 guns. Designed by Étienne Salicon. Originally planned as a 50-gun 3rd Rank ship of 800 tons similar to Salicon's *Arrogant* and *Brave* (and listed as such until 1686), she was structurally more like the *Glorieux* of 1678 (see above), and pierced for twelve pairs of LD guns (excluding the chase ports). She was re-classed as 2nd Rank in 1690, reduced to 3rd Rank in 1700, and back to 2nd Rank in 1702–3. Refitted 1697 at Brest.

The bombardment of Genoa in 1684, an anonymous, undated engraving but one claiming extraordinary precision in its timing: between one and two o'clock in the afternoon of 24 May. The careful representation of the various ship-types in the French fleet is convincing, so the depiction of Duquesne's flagship *Ardent* in the centre may be a portrait and not a generic image. The *Ardent* took part in many of the battles of Louis XIV's fleet – notably as Châteaurenault's flagship at the action in Bantry Bay in 1689 – before she was captured by the Dutch in March 1705 off Gibraltar. (Beverley R Robinson Collection, Annapolis 51.7.69)

Dimensions & tons: 142ft 0in, 114ft 0in x 36ft 0in x 16ft 0in (46.13, 37.03 x 11.69 x 5.20m). 1,100 tons. Draught 17½ft/19ft (5.68/6.17m). Men: 380.
Guns: 66 from 1687: LD 10 x 24pdrs + 14 x 18pdrs; MD 24 x 12pdrs; UD 14 x 6pdrs; poop 4 x 4pdrs. 64 in war from 1696 (54 peace): LD 24 x 24pdrs; MD 26 x 12pdrs; UD 14 x 6pdrs.

Ardent Le Havre.
K: 4 1680. L: 21.11.1680. C: 4.1682. Took part in Bombardment of Genoa 18-28.5.1684 (as flagship of LG Abraham Duquesne), in the attack on Tripoli in June 1685 (as flagship of *Vice-amiral* Jean, Comte d'Estrées) and in the Battles of Bantry Bay 11.5.1689 (as flagship of LG Louis François de Rousselet, Comte de Châteaurenault), Beachy Head 10.7.1690, Lagos 28.6.1693 and Vélez-Málaga 24.8.1704. Captured 21.3.1705 by the Dutch *Overijssel* at the Battle of Marbella, then wrecked 4.1705.

TONNANT Class. 70, later 76 guns. Designed and built by Laurent Hubac (the last of his 70-gun ships), although – following his death on 14 June 1682 – the *Fier* was completed by his son Étienne. Pierced for thirteen pairs of LD guns (excluding the chase ports). The last nominal three-deckers to be built as 2nd Rank, with a mixed LD battery of 24pdrs and 18pdrs. Both re-classed as 1st Rank in 1690, but reverted to 2nd Rank in 1691.
Dimensions & tons: 145ft 0in, 124ft 0in x 39ft 0in x 18ft 0in (47.10, 40.28 x 12.67 x 5.85m). 1,350 tons. Draught 19ft (6.17 m). Men: 9 officers, 490 men.
Guns: 70 from 1682: LD 12 x 24pdrs + 14 x 18pdrs; MD 14 x 18pdrs + 12 x 12pdrs; UD (aft) 12 x 8pdrs + (fwd) 6 x 8pdrs. 74 from 1688 with 4 x 4pdrs added on poop, and a third pair added from 1691.

Tonnant Brest Dyd.
K: 5.1680. L: 8.1681. C: 1682. Took part in Battles of Beachy Head 10.7.1690 (as flagship of CdE Marquis de Laporte) and Barfleur 29.5.1692, then burnt by fireship at La Hougue 3.6.1692.

Fier Brest Dyd.
K: 5.1681. L: end 1682. C: 6.1684. Took part in Battles of Beachy Head 10.7.1690 (as flagship of CdE Ferdinand, Comte de Relingue) and Barfleur 29.5.1692, then burnt by fireship at La Hougue 3.6.1692.

BOURBON. 62, later 64 guns. Designed and built by Honoré Malet. Originally planned as a 50-gun 3rd Rank ship of 800 tons similar to Salicon's *Ardent* (and listed as such until 1687), she was structurally like the *Glorieux* of 1678 (see above), she was raised from the 3rd to the 2nd Rank in 1687. Pierced for 12 pairs of LD guns (excluding the chase

THE SECOND RANK

An anonymous oil painting in the style of Van de Velde showing the boat attack on the French ships embayed off La Hougue on 2 June (NS) 1692. The listing ship with her topsails still set being fired (at centre of the middle ground) is presumably intended to be the *Terrible*, which was run aground on Tatihou island before being boarded and burnt. Among the twelve major ships destroyed in this action were four other 2nd Rank ships – *Tonnant*, *Fier*, *Bourbon* and *Gaillard* – as well as the *Magnifique*, which had been promoted to 1st Rank by this time. (National Maritime Museum, London BHC0335)

ports). Originally named *Entreprenant*, but renamed 1679 before being laid down.

   Dimensions & tons: 140ft 0in, 118ft 0in x 35ft 0in x 17ft 3in (45.48, 38.33 x 11.37 x 5.60m). 1,100 tons. Draught 16ft/18ft (5.20/5.85m). Men: 380.
   Guns: 62 from 1688: LD 10 x 24pdrs + 14 x 18pdrs; MD 24 x 12pdrs; UD 14 x 6pdrs. 64 guns from 1691.

Bourbon Rochefort Dyd.
   K: 1681. L: 1683. C: 3.1684. Took part in the Battles of Beachy Head 10.7.1690 and Barfleur 29.5.1692, then burnt at La Hougue 3.6.1692.

In 1680 the new LG Anne Hilarion de Costentin, Chevalier de Tourville, urged that the ideal 2nd Rank ship should be a three-decker of 80 guns, having a length of some 158ft; he was supported in this scheme by Blaise Pangalo. For the 3rd Rank the two proposed a two-decker of 66 guns and some 148ft length; this type would be pierced for thirteen pairs of 24pdrs on the lower deck, with 18pdrs on the upper deck. These two-deckers were to become the model for the 2nd Rank ships from 1686 onwards, albeit carrying a combination of bronze 24pdrs and iron 18pdrs on their lower deck. Construction of smaller three-deckers tapered off in the 1680s; one 72-gun ship (*Magnifique* – see below) and one 64-gun ship (*Furieux*) were ordered in 1683, three more 64s were ordered in 1686 (*Content*, *Sérieux* and *Courtisan*) and another 64 in 1687 (*Henri*). Two larger new 2nd Rank ships were begun at Toulon and one at Rochefort in the early summer of 1686, while 1687 saw another two 2nd Rank ships started at Toulon and one at Dunkirk. However, these new ships were mainly replacements for lost or discarded vessels, and did not significantly increase force levels.

MAGNIFIQUE. 72, later 84 guns. Designed and built by François Chapelle and named in January 1684. Pierced for thirteen pairs of LD guns (excluding the chase ports). A three-decker, possibly intended as an 84-gun 1st Rank, and probably built with a complete third deck, but this deck was initially armed without guns in the waist, and she was completed as a 72-gun 2nd Rank. Re-classed as an 84-gun 1st Rank during 1690, when extra 8pdrs were added amidships to give a complete third battery.

   Dimensions & tons: 142ft 0in, 116ft 0in x 39ft 0in x 17ft 0in (46.13, 37.68 x 12.67 x 5.52 m). 1,500 tons. Draught 17ft /21½ft (5.52 / 6.98 m). Men: 9 officers, 550 men.

Guns: 72 from 1686: LD 12 x 24pdrs + 14 x 18pdrs; MD 14 x 18pdrs + 12 x 12pdrs; UD (aft) 10 x 8pdrs + (fwd) 6 x 8pdrs; poop 4 x 4pdrs. 84 from 1691: LD & MD unchanged; UD 26 x 8pdrs; poop 6 x 4pdrs.

Magnifique Toulon Dyd.
K: 10.1683. L: 12.4.1685. C: 12.1685. Took part in the Battles of Beachy Head 10.7.1690 (as flagship of LG Charles-François Davy, Marquis d'Amfreville) and of Barfleur 29.5.1692, then burnt by fireship at La Hougue 2.6.1692.

FURIEUX. 70, later 62 guns. Designed and built by Blaise Pangalo. Structurally like the *Glorieux* of 1678 (see above), she was pierced for twelve pairs of LD guns (excluding the chase ports). Reduced from the 2nd Rank to the 3rd Rank in 1687, but rebuilt at Brest during 1699 and raised again to the 2nd Rank in 1702–3, then reverted to the 3rd Rank in 1706.

Dimensions & tons: 140ft 0in x 36ft 0in x 17ft 1in (45.48 x 11.69 x 5.55m). 1,000 tons. Draught 18ft/19½ft (5.85/6.33m). Men: 350 in war, 300 peace, + 7 officers.

Guns: 70 from 1686. 60 from 1688: LD 6 x 24pdrs + 18 x 18pdrs; UD 24 x 12pdrs; QD 8 x 4pdrs; Fc 4 x 4pdrs. 60 from 1696 in war (50 peace): LD 24 x 24pdrs; UD 26 x 12pdrs (24 from 1706); QD/Fc 10 x 6pdrs (12 from 1699 to 1706).

Furieux Brest Dyd.
K: 2.1684. L: 23.10.1684. C: 5.1685. Took part in Battle of Bantry Bay 11.5.1689. Lent as a privateer to CdE Jean Bernard de Saint-Jean, Baron de Pointis, as part of a squadron of fourteen vessels, 1696–97; took part in the capture of Cartagena de Indias 5.5.1697. Lent as a privateer to CV René Duguay-Trouin, as part of a squadron of three vessels, 1703. Took part in Battle of Vélez-Málaga 24.8.1704. Scuttled at Toulon in 7.1707 but refloated 11.1707. Hulked 1720 at Toulon, sank there from neglect 1721, ordered BU 10.1.1724, salvage and BU completed 1727.

CONTENT. 64, later 66 guns. Designed and built by Blaise Pangalo. Structurally like the *Glorieux* of 1678 (see above), she was pierced for twelve pairs of LD guns (excluding the chase ports). Named as *Courtisan* on 25 May 1686, contracted on 20 June 1686, and renamed *Content* on 2 July. Initially classed as 3rd Rank, but raised to 2nd Rank in 1690.

Dimensions & tons: 139ft 0in, 112ft 0in x 37ft 6in x 16ft 6in (45.15, 36.38 x 12.18 x 5.36m). 1,100 tons. Draught 17ft/19ft (5.52/6.17m). Men: 380, +7 officers.

Guns: 64 from 1687: LD 10 x 24pdrs + 14 x 18pdrs; MD 24 x 12pdrs; UD (aft) 10 x 6pdrs + (fwd) 6 x 6pdrs. 66 guns from 1688.

Content Toulon Dyd.
K: 5.1686. L: 23.12.1686. C: 4.1687. Took part in the Battle of Beachy Head 10.7.1690, Barfleur 29.6.1692 and Lagos 28.6.1693. Captured by HM Ships *Carlisle* and *Newcastle* of Pettigrew's squadron in Action off Cape Bon 18.1.1695, becoming HMS *Content Prize*; hulked 7.1703 at Lisbon, and sold there 21.5.1708.

SÉRIEUX. 64 guns. Designed and built by Laurent Coulomb. Originally planned as a 58-gun 3rd Rank ship of 900 tons (and listed as such until 1687), she was structurally like the *Glorieux* of 1678 (see above), pierced for twelve pairs of LD guns (excluding the chase ports). Ordered and named as *Sérieux* on 25 May 1686. Raised from the 3rd to the 2nd Rank before completion in 1687, but returned to the 3rd Rank in 1698; again raised to 2nd Rank in 1702–3, then reduced to 3rd Rank in 1706.

Dimensions & tons: 139ft 0in, 114ft 0in x 37ft 6in x 15ft 8in (45.15, 37.03 x 12.18 x 5.09m). 1,050 tons. Draught 16ft/19ft (5.20/6.17m). Men: 380, +7 officers.

Guns: 64 from 1688: LD 10 x 24pdrs + 14 x 18pdrs; MD 24 x 12pdrs; UD (aft) 10 x 6pdrs + (fwd) 6 x 6pdrs. 64 in war from 1696 (56 peace): LD 24 x 18pdrs; MD 26 x 12pdrs; UD 14 x 6pdrs (12 from 1699). 58 from 1706 (52 peace): LD 22 x 24pdrs; UD 26 x 12pdrs; UD 10 x 6pdrs.

Sérieux Toulon Dyd.
K: 6.1686. L: 11.1.1687. C: 4.1687. Renamed *Croissant* in 1688, but restored to *Sérieux* a year later. Took part in the Battles of Beachy Head 10.7.1690, Barfleur 29.5.1692 and Lagos 28.6.1693. Scuttled at Toulon in 7.1707 but refloated. Condemned 6.1717 at Toulon, and BU 1718.

COURTISAN. 64 guns. Designed and built by Honoré Malet. Structurally like the *Glorieux* of 1678 (see above), she was pierced for twelve pairs of LD guns (excluding the chase ports). Raised from the 3rd to the 2nd Rank in 1687.

Dimensions & tons: 144ft 0in x 37ft 6in x 17ft 11in (46.78 x 12.18 x 5.82m). 1,140 tons. Draught 18ft/19ft (5.85/6.17m). Men: 380, +8 officers.

Guns: 64 from 1687: LD 10 x 24pdrs + 14 x 18pdrs; MD 24 x 12pdrs; UD (aft) 10 x 6pdrs + (fwd) 6 x 6pdrs. 64 in war from 1696 (58 peace): LD 24 x 24pdrs; MD 26 x 12pdrs; UD 14 x 6pdrs.

Courtisan Rochefort Dyd.
K: 7.1686. L: 10.1686. C: 1.1687. Took part in the Battles of Beachy Head 10.7.1690, Barfleur 29.6.1692 and Lagos 28.6.1693. Participated in operations at Nova Scotia under LG André, Marquis de Nesmond, in a squadron of twenty-three vessels, 1697. Burnt by accident near Rochefort 5.1702.

HENRI. 68, later 70 guns. Designed and built by Hendryck Houwens. Structurally like the *Glorieux* of 1678 (see above), she was pierced for twelve pairs of LD guns (excluding the chase ports). Reduced to 3rd Rank in 1701, restored to 2nd Rank in 1702–3.

Dimensions & tons: 144ft 0in x 38ft 3in x 16ft 2in (46.78 x 12.43 x 5.25m). 1,100 tons. Draught 18ft/20½ft (5.85/6.66m). Men: 400, +9 officers.

Guns: 68 from 1689: LD 10 x 24pdrs + 14 x 18pdrs; MD 24 x 12pdrs; UD (aft) 10 x 6pdrs + (fwd) 6 x 6pdrs; poop 4 x 4pdrs. 70 guns from 1691, then 64 in war from 1696 (58 peace): LD 24 x 24pdrs; MD 26 x 12pdrs; UD 14 x 6pdrs. Listed with LD 26 x 24pdrs and UD 12 x 6pdrs in 1698, then reverted to 1696 armament in 1700.

Henri Dunkirk.
K: 1687. L: 13.8.1688. C: 5.1689. Took part in Battles of Beachy Head 10.7.1690, Barfleur 29.5.1692, Lagos 28.6.1693 and Vélez-Málaga 24.8.1704. Scuttled at Toulon in 7.1707, but refloated. Hulked at Toulon 8.1726. Sank there from neglect but refloated. Ordered to be BU 11.1.1735.

ÉCLATANT. 70, later 68 guns. Designed and built by Laurent Coulomb. The first two-decker to be pierced for thirteen pairs of LD guns.

Dimensions & tons: 143ft 0in, 117ft 0in x 39ft 0in x 17ft 3in (46.45, 38.01 x 12.67 x 5.60m). 1,300 tons. Draught 17½ft/20ft (5.68/6.50m). Men 400 (81/200/119), +5 officers; from 1690, 500 (84/276/140), +9 officers; then from 1691, 450 (81/232/137), 430 peace, +9 officers.

Guns: 70 from 1688: LD 12 x 24pdrs + 14 x 18pdrs; UD 14 x 18pdrs + 12 x 12pdrs; QD 8 x 8pdrs; Fc 6 x 8pdrs; poop 4 x 4pdrs. 68 in war from 1696 (62 peace): LD 26 x 24pdrs; UD 28 x 12pdrs; QD 8 x 6pdrs; Fc 6 x 6pdrs. From 1706, 2 fewer 6pdrs and occasionally 2 x 4pdrs restored.

Éclatant Toulon Dyd.
K: 6.1687. L: 28.6.1688. C: 1688. Took part in the Battles of Beachy Head 10.7.1690 and Vélez-Málaga 24.8.1704. Lent as a privateer to CFL René Duguay-Trouin, as part of a squadron of three vessels, 1703. Scuttled at Toulon in 7.1707 but refloated. Lent in 1711 (with *Fendant* and *Adélaïde*) as a privateer to Antoine Crozat, Marquis du Châtel, Director of the *Compagnie des Indes Orientales*. Foundered with all hands 3.1713 in the Indian Ocean with *Fendant* and a prize, *Charbon Anglais*.

CONQUÉRANT. 76, later 84 guns. Designed and built by Blaise Pangalo. Contracted on 23 May 1687. Also pierced for thirteen pairs of LD guns (excluding the chase ports), but this somewhat larger ship was built with a third deck, albeit this was not armed in the waist until 1690. Completed as a 76-gun 2nd Rank, but like *Magnifique* she was re-classed as an 84-gun 1st Rank during 1690.

Dimensions & tons: 146ft 6in x 41ft 0in x 18ft 0in (50.675 x 12.99 x 6.01m). 1,600 tons. Draught 20ft /22ft (6.50/7.15m). Men: 450 (83/230/137), +9 officers while building, then raised to 600 (99/304/197) after completion; 550 (89/304/157) by 1691.

Guns: 76 from 1689: LD 12 x 24pdrs + 14 x 18pdrs; MD 14 x 18pdrs + 12 x 12pdrs; UD 18 x 8pdrs; poop 6 x 4pdrs. 84 from 1691: 8 x 8pdrs added in UD waist. 80 in war from 1696 (72 peace): LD 10 x 36pdrs + 16 x 24pdrs; MD 28 x 18pdrs; UD 22 x 6pdrs; poop 4 x 4pdrs.

Conquérant Toulon Dyd.
K: 6.1687. L: 10.8.1688. C: 4.1689. Took part in Battles of Beachy Head 10.7.1690 (as flagship of LG Philippe de Valois, Marquis de Villette-Mursay), Barfleur 29.5.1692 and Lagos 28.6.1693. Rebuilt as a 2nd Rank at Toulon by François Chapelle from March 1707 until relaunched in February 1712 (see below).

(C) Vessels acquired from 15 April 1689

At the start of 1689, there were twenty-one ships of the 2nd Rank, ranging between 62 and 78 guns, including the *Henri* and *Conquérant*, still completing. There was one ship with 78 guns (*Saint Philippe*), two with 76 guns (*Saint Esprit* and *Conquérant*), five with 74 guns (*Terrible*, *Triomphant*, *Belliqueux*, *Tonnant* and *Fier*), two with 72 guns (*Florissant* and *Magnifique*), three with 70 guns (*Couronne*, *Pompeux* and *Éclatant*), one of 68 guns (*Henri*), five of 64 guns (*Illustre*, *Constant*, *Foudroyant*, *Sérieux* and *Courtisan*) and two of 62 guns (*Glorieux* and *Bourbon*). One of these ships (*Couronne*) had a complement of 550 men (92/300/158), five (*Saint Philippe*, *Saint Esprit*, *Pompeux*, *Florissant* and *Conquérant*) each had a complement of 450 (83/230/137), and the other fifteen each had a complement of 400 (81/200/119); each in addition now had 9 (commissioned) officers.

AIMABLE. 70 guns. Designed and built by Pierre Masson. A two-decker, initially listed while building as 3rd Rank, but was raised to the 2nd Rank during 1690. Enlarged dimensions recorded by 1698, indicating possible girdling before that year.

Dimensions & tons: 144ft 0in, 126ft 0in x 38ft 0in x 17ft 6in (46.78, 40.93 x 12.34 x 5.68m). By 1698 measured 145ft x 39½ft x 16½ft (47.10 x 12.83 x 5.36m). 1,200 tons. Draught 19¼ft/21ft (6.25/6.82m). Men: 350 (67/189/94) in 1690, +7 officers; 400 (79/202/119) from 1691, +9 officers; by 1696, 430 in war, 340 peace, +9 officers.

Guns: 70 in war (64 in peace): LD 26 x 24pdrs; UD 28 x 18pdrs (from 1709, 12pdrs); 16 x 6pdrs (from 1710, 14 x 6pdrs).

Aimable Rochefort Dyd.
K: 4.1689. L: 3.1690. C: 5.1690. Took part in Battles of Beachy Head 10.7.1690, Barfleur 29.5.1692 and Lagos 28.6.1693. Lent as a privateer to LG André, Marquis de Nesmond, as part of a squadron of six to eleven vessels, 1696. Participated in operations at Nova Scotia under LG André, Marquis de Nesmond, in a squadron of twenty-three vessels, 1697. Lent as a privateer to CdE Michel de Chabert, as part of a squadron of two vessels, in support of the Spanish Navy for a voyage to Lima 1707. Sold at Lorient 5.1714 and burnt there by accident 9.1715.

BRILLANT. 64 guns. Designed and built by Étienne Salicon, with sculpture by Jean Berain. The first of the 64-gun two-decked 2nd Rank ships, pierced for twelve pairs of LD gunports (excluding the unarmed chase ports forwards); also had 4 stern chase gunports at that level. Initially listed while building as 3rd Rank, but was raised to the 2nd Rank during 1690. Refitted 1706–8 at Brest, and reduced to 3rd Rank in 1706.

Dimensions & tons: 138ft 0in x 37ft 6in x 16ft 0in (44.83 x 12.18 x 5.20m). 950 tons. Draught 18½ft/20½ft (6.01/6.66m). Men: 380 in war, 350 peace, +7 officers.

Guns: 64 in war (56 peace): LD 24 x 24pdrs; UD 26 x 12pdrs; QD 8 x 6pdrs; Fc 6 x 6pdrs. From 1698 had 26 x 24pdrs, 26 x 12pdrs and 12 x 6pdrs, but 2 x 6pdrs were added from 1707 and 2 x 24pdrs removed from 1715.

Brillant Le Havre.
K: 6.1689. L: 1.1690. C: 3.1690. Took part in Battles of Beachy Head 10.7.1690, Barfleur 29.5.1692 and Lagos 28.6.1693. Lent as a privateer to CV Henri-Louis, Marquis de Chavagnac, and CV Pierre Le Moyne d'Iberville, as part of a squadron of ten vessels, for operations in the West Indies 1705–6. Lent as a privateer to CV René Duguay-Trouin (1711–12); took part in the capture of Rio de Janeiro on 22.9.1711. Condemned at Brest 1719.

SUPERBE Class. 70, later 68 guns. Designed and built by François Coulomb at Toulon. This first pair were named and ordered on 24 September 1689 and contracted on 26 December 1689. Pierced for thirteen pairs of LD guns (excluding the unarmed chase ports).

Dimensions & tons: 143ft 0in, 117ft 0in x 39ft 0in x 17ft 6in (45.45, 38.01 x 12.67 x 5.68m). 1,200 tons. Draught 17½ft/19–21ft (5.68/6.17–6.82m). Men: 450 (81/232/137) in 1692, +6 officers.

Guns: 70 in war (62 peace): LD 26 x 24pdrs; UD 28 x 18pdrs (12pdrs in *Superbe* from 1698); QD 10 x 6pdrs (2 x 6pdrs were removed by 1696); Fc 6 x 6pdrs.

Superbe Toulon Dyd.
K: 7.1689. L: 3.1690. C: 2.1691. Captured by the Dutch at Vigo 23.10.1702 and burnt.

Invincible Toulon Dyd.
K: 7.1689. L: 4.1690. C: 2.1691. Lent as a privateer to LG André, Marquis de Nesmond, as part of a squadron of six to eleven vessels, 1696. Took part in Battle of Vélez-Málaga 24.8.1704. Scuttled at Toulon in 7.1707 but refloated. Condemned 17.12.1727 and hulked at Toulon; BU (by Order of 31.8.1743) completed there 8.3.1748.

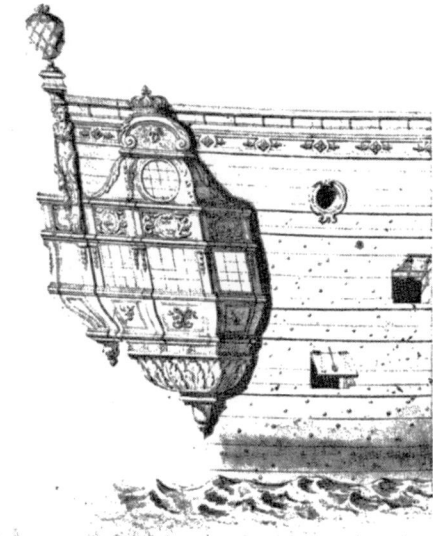

The head and stern decoration of the *Brillant* of 1690, drawn by Jean Bérain, one of the greatest of a highly talented group of artists working on the ships of Louis XIV's navy. His influence was evident, particularly in the shape of the quarter galleries (which were entirely closed), well into the eighteenth century. As overseer Bérain designed the scheme, but the actual carved work was carried out by Philippe Caffieri. This drawing was officially requested shortly before the death in 1690 of Charles Lebrun, who was responsible for oversight of all the decorative works on Louis's Navy; Bérain was appointed his successor upon his death. (*Souvenirs de Marine*, Plate 148)

Modified *SUPERBE* Class. 68 guns (listed with 70s while building). Designed and built by François Coulomb at Toulon. With the design slightly widened (by a foot) and deepened (by 4 inches) from the preceding pair, and carrying one fewer pair of 6pdrs, this second pair was adjudicated on 12 November 1689, contracted on 16 April 1690, and named on 9 August 1690.

Dimensions & tons: 143ft 0in, 117ft 0in x 40ft 0in x 17ft 10in (46.45, 38.01 x 12.99 x 5.79m). 1,200 tons. Draught 17½ft/19–21ft (5.68/6.17–6.82m). Men: 450 (81/232/137) in 1692, +6 officers.

Guns: 68 in war (62 peace): LD 26 x 24pdrs; UD 28 x 18pdrs (replaced by 12pdrs in *Heureux* from 1698 to 1704, and in *Constant* from 1707); QD 8 x 6pdrs; Fc 6 x 6pdrs.

Constant Toulon Dyd.
K: 3.1690. L: 28.11.1690. C: 3.1691. Took part in Battle of Vélez-Málaga 24.8.1704. Docked for major repairs at Rochefort 1707, struck 1712 and BU 1714.

Heureux Toulon Dyd.
K: 4.1690. L: 11.1690. C: 3.1691. Took part in Battles of Santa Marta 30.8.1702 (as flagship of CdE Jean-Baptiste Ducasse) and of Vélez-Málaga 24.8.1704. Lent as a privateer to LG André, Marquis de Nesmond, as part of a squadron of six to eleven vessels, 1696. Participated in operations at Nova Scotia under LG André, Marquis de Nesmond, in a squadron of twenty-three vessels, 1697. Scuttled at Toulon in 7.1707 but refloated. Struck at Lorient 1709 and lent for mercantile and privateering service to EV Nicolas Du Buisson de Varenne, 2.1710; captured 2/3.1710 by the British.

GAILLARD. 64 guns. Designed and built by Étienne Salicon. A stretched version of the *Brillant*, pierced for thirteen pairs of LD guns. Listed as a 3rd Rank ship during her brief career but comparable with the 2nd Rank *Laurier* and *Sirène*.

Dimensions & tons: 141ft 0in, 121ft 0in x 37ft 3in x 17ft 0in (45.80, 39.31 x 12.10 x 5.52m). 1,000 tons. Draught 15½ft/18½ft (5.035/6.01m). Men: 350 (67/189/94), +7 officers.

Guns: 64 in war from 1691: LD 26 x 24pdrs; UD 28 x 12pdrs; QD 10 x 6pdrs; Fc nil.

Gaillard Le Havre.
K: 5.1690. L: 12.1690. C: 3.1691. Took part in Battle of Barfleur on 29.5.1692, then grounded and burnt by fireships at La Hougue 3.6.1692.

***LAURIER* Class.** 64 guns. Designed and built by Pierre Masson, although Masson was directed by Seignelay to use Laurent Coulomb's templates in lieu of his own; however, this does not appear to have happened, due to the difficult requirements for construction at Bayonne, whose harbour entrance was restricted by a sandbank. Pierced for twelve pairs of LD gunports (excluding the chase ports), but with only twelve pairs of UD gunports, so that the thirteenth pair of 12pdrs had to be placed through the quarter gallery, restricting the space in the wardroom. Both ships were reduced to 60-gun 3rd Rank ships in 1696–97 with the removal of 4 x 6pdrs; *Sirène* then reduced to 56 guns (by a further 4 x 6pdrs) in 1699.

Dimensions & tons: (*Laurier*) 136ft 0in, 116ft 6in x 36ft 6in x 16ft 6in (44.18, 37.84 x 11.86 x 5.36m). 900/1,810 tons. Draught 17½ft/19ft (5.68/6.17m). Men: 350 (67/189/94) in war, later 380 in war, 350 peace, + 7 officers. (*Sirène*) 137ft 0in, 116ft 6in x 37ft 4in x 16ft 6in (44.50, 37.84 x 12.13 x 5.36m). 985 tons. Draught 18ft/18½ft (5.85/6.01m). Men: 350 (67/189/94) in war, later 380 in war, 320 peace, + 7 officers.

Guns: 64 in war (56 peace): LD 24 x 24pdrs; UD 26 x 12pdrs; QD 10 x 6pdrs; Fc 4 x 6pdrs. *Laurier* reduced in 1698 to 10 x 24pdrs + 14 x 18pdrs (14 x 12pdrs from 1701) on the LD and 10 x 6pdrs on the QD/Fc. *Sirène* reduced in 1697 to 6 x 6pdrs on the QD/Fc, followed in 1704 by *Laurier*.

Laurier Bayonne.
K: 3.1690. L: 12.1690. C: 4.1691. Took part in Battle of Barfleur 29.5.1692. Struck 1704 and hulked at Toulon; ordered to be sold 27.4.1707. Scuttled at Toulon in 7.1707 but refloated.

Sirène Bayonne.
K: 3.1690. L: 14.1.1691. C: 5.1691. Took part in Battles of Barfleur 29.5.1692, Lagos 28.6.1693. Lent as a privateer to CV François Colbert de Saint Mars, as part of a squadron of four vessels, 1696.

Took part in Battle of Vigo 22.10.1702, where burnt and ran ashore, then captured by the Dutch and destroyed in situ.

SAINT ESPRIT. 76, later 74 guns. Designed and built by Jean Guichard. A two-decker, pierced for thirteen pairs of LD guns (and had no chase ports cut through). The longest French two-decker to this date, and the first to carry 36pdrs as part of her LD ordnance, although these were replaced by 24pdrs in 1704–5. Ordered in October 1689, and named in June 1690.
 Dimensions & tons: 151ft 9in x 40ft 1in x 17ft 2in (49.29 x 13.02 x 5.58m). 1,200/1,380 tons. Draught 19ft/19¼ft (6.17/6.25m). Men: 490 in war, 400 peace.
 Guns: 76 in war (68 peace): LD 18 x 36pdrs + 8 x 24pdrs (from 1706, 26 x 24pdrs); UD 28 x 18pdrs; QD/Fc 18 x 6pdrs (2 removed from 1706); poop 4 x 4pdrs.

Saint Esprit Rochefort.
 K: 4.1690. L: early 1691. C: 6.1691. Took part in the Battles of Barfleur 29.5.1692, Lagos 28.6.1693 and of Vélez-Málaga on 24.8.1704. Scuttled at Toulon in 1707, but refloated. Ordered hulked at Toulon 25.5.1716 and condemned 6.1716. Intended to become a careening hulk there 6.1717, but instead ordered BU 10.8.1717 and BU after 1718.

ÉCUEIL. 66 guns. Designed by Bernard Renau d'Élissagaray using his theory of elliptical lines and built by René Levasseur. Two-decker, pierced for twelve pairs of LD guns (and had no chase ports); and unusually had fourteen pairs of UD gunports, requiring an extra pair cut into the quarter gallery. Raised from the 3rd Rank to the 2nd Rank in 1692 soon after completion; reverted to 3rd Rank in 1700 but raised again to 2nd Rank in 1702–3, then dropped again to 3rd Rank in 1706.
 Dimensions & tons: 137ft 6in, 120ft 0in x 37ft 6in x 17ft 0in (44.67, 38.98 x 12.18 x 5.52m). 1,000 tons. Draught 18½ft/19ft (6.01/6.17m). Men: 380 in war, 300 peace, +7 officers.
 Guns: 66 in war (60 peace): LD 24 x 24pdrs; UD 28 x 12pdrs; QD/Fc 14 x 6pdrs.

Écueil Dunkirk.
 K: 9.1690. L: 3.1691. C: 6.1691. Took part in Battles of Lagos 28.6.1693 and Vélez-Málaga 24.8.1704. Scuttled at Toulon in 7.1707, raised but not maintained and run aground 1708 to prevent sinking. Struck 1709, condemned 7.4.1710, and sold by Order of 28.5.1710.

JUSTE. 64 guns. Designed by Étienne Salicon; completed after his death on 2 December 1691 by Philippe Cochois. Two-decker, pierced for thirteen pairs of LD guns (and had no chase ports). She was initially reported as a longer ship, her measurements in 1696 and 1698 being quoted as 149ft 0in x 37ft 6in x 15ft 6in (48.40 x 12.18 x 5.035m) and 1,200 tons with a draught of 15ft/18½ft (4.87/6.01m), but this data seems suspect. During 1698 she was re-classed as a 3rd Rank, but reverted to the 2nd Rank in 1702-03.
 Dimensions & tons (as recorded from 1699): 138ft 0in x 37ft 0in x 16ft 0in (44.83 x 12.02 x 5.20m). 1,000 tons. Draught 19½ft (6.33m). Men: 350 (67/189/94), + 7 officers; by 1696, 380 in war, 300 peace.
 Guns: 64 in war (58 peace): LD 26 x 24pdrs; UD 28 x 12pdrs; QD/Fc 10 x 6pdrs. 62 guns in war from 1699 (54 peace) – 2 fewer 12pdrs. 66 guns in war from 1706 (50 peace): LD 26 x 24pdrs; UD 26 x 12pdrs; QD 8 x 6pdrs; Fc 6 x 6pdrs. 64 in war from 1707 (50 peace) – 2 fewer 12pdrs.

Juste Le Havre.
 K: 7.1691. L: 20.12.1691. C: 3.1692. Took part in Battle of Lagos 28.6.1693. Participated in operations at Nova Scotia under LG André, Marquis de Nesmond, in a squadron of twenty-three vessels, 1697. Lent as a privateer to Beaubriant-L'Évêque from St Malo, with *Alcyon* in 1702, then with *Hasardeux* in 1703. Lent as a privateer to CV Henri-Louis, Marquis de Chavagnac, and CV Pierre Le Moyne d'Iberville, as part of a squadron of ten vessels, for operations in the West Indies 1705–6. Condemned at Rochefort in early 1717 and BU 1719.

BIZARRE. 68 guns. Designed and built by Félix Arnaud. A two-decker, pierced for thirteen pairs of LD guns (and had no chase ports). Reduced to the 3rd Rank in 1700 but restored to 2nd Rank in 1701.
 Dimensions & tons: 145ft 4in, 124ft 6in x 39ft 6in x 16ft 8in (47.21, 40.44 x 12.83 x 5.41m). 1,100 tons. Draught 18ft (5.85m). Men: 400 in war, 320 peace.
 Guns: 68 in war (62 peace): LD 26 x 24pdrs; UD 28 x 12pdrs; QD 8 x 6pdrs; Fc 6 x 6pdrs.

Bizarre Bayonne.
 K: 5.1691. L: autumn 1692. C: 5.1693. Took part in Battle of Lagos 28.6.1693. Participated in operations at Nova Scotia under LG André, Marquis de Nesmond, in a squadron of twenty-three vessels, 1697. Hauled out in 1704 and rebuilt at Toulon by Chapelle. Scuttled at Toulon in 7.1707, but refloated. Unserviceable 1718 at Toulon, sank from neglect 1721, condemned 10.1.1724 and ordered BU, refloated 14.7.1727, and completed BU 31.12.1727.

With the heavy losses incurred at Cherbourg and La Hougue in June 1692 (including five 2nd Rank ships), there was firstly an increase in building 1st and 2nd Rank battlefleet units to replace the losses. Two 2nd Rank ships on order at Brest were re-ordered as 1st Rank three-deckers (these became the *Foudroyant* – renamed *Soleil Royal* in March 1693 – and *Merveilleux*). The losses were replaced, but in a volte-face by Louis XIV, after 1694 France concentrated on building smaller vessels for the *guerre de course*. Three-decker construction ceased entirely (see Chapter 1), and a more restricted program of 70-gun two-deckers was put in hand.
 Of the thirteen 64-gun ships existing in 1696 – *Ardent* (1682), *Courtisan* (1687), *Sérieux* (1686), *Parfait* (1671), *Glorieux* (1672), *Brillant* (1690), *Sirène* (1690), *Laurier* (1691), *Juste* (1691), *Henri* (1687), *Content* (1695), *Saint Louis* (1692) and *Éole* (1693) – several were downgraded to the 3rd Rank. *Sirène* and *Laurier* were reduced to 60-gun 3rd Rank by 1698, *Juste*, *Sérieux*, *Saint Louis* and *Éole* by 1699, *Oriflamme* and *Henri* by 1702. Of later 62-gun ships, the *Toulouse* and *Achille* were re-classed as 3rd Rank in 1706, and the *Oriflamme* in 1708.

BOURBON. 68 guns. Designed and built by Francois Coulomb as a replacement for the ship of the same name destroyed at La Hougue on 3 June 1692. Contracted 19 June 1692 and ships named 1 July 1692. A two-decker, pierced for thirteen pairs of LD guns (with no chase ports).
 Dimensions & tons: 140ft 0in, 114ft 0in x 39ft 4in x 18ft 0in (45.48, 37.03 x 12.78 x 5.85m). 1,100/1,200 tons. Draught 20ft (6.50m). Men: 450 in war, 350 peace, +8 officers.
 Guns: 68 in war (62 peace): LD 26 x 24pdrs; UD 28 x 12pdrs; QD 8 x 6pdrs; Fc 6 x 6pdrs.

Bourbon Toulon Dyd.
 K: 6.1692. L: 17.11.1692. C: 13.2.1693. In the West Indies under CV Des Augiers 1696. Captured by the Dutch *Zeven Provincien* at Vigo 10.1702, and burnt by them a week later.

SAINT LOUIS Class. 64 guns. Designed by Joseph Andrault, Marquis de Langeron, 1692, and built by Philippe Cochois and Pierre Chaillé

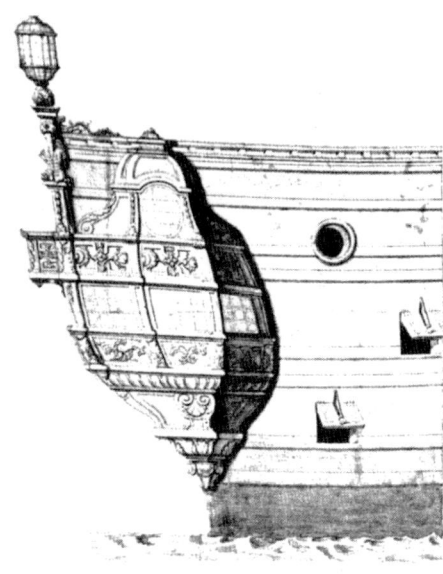

The decorative work of the *Saint Louis*, a two-decked 64-gun ship of 1692, derived from the *Brillant*. It bears all the hallmarks of Jean Bérain's work. In line with the 1673 Regulation, the stern had only one gallery at the level of the stateroom on the quarterdeck. (*Souvenirs de Marine*, Plate 147)

respectively. Two-deckers, pierced for twelve pairs of LD guns (with no chase ports). Both were reduced from the 2nd Rank to the 3rd Rank in 1698, then restored to the 2nd Rank in 1702-03 but demoted again to the 3rd Rank in 1706.

Dimensions & tons: 136ft 0in, 117ft 6in x 37ft 6in x 17ft 0in (44.18, 38.17 x 12.18 x 5.52m). 1,000 tons. Draught 17¾ft/20ft (5.77/6.50m). Men: 380 in war, 300 peace, +7/9 officers

Guns: 64 in war (56 peace): LD 24 x 24pdrs; UD 26 x 12pdrs; QD 8 x 6pdrs; Fc 6 x 6pdrs. Both ships were reduced to 58 guns by around 1705, *Éole* losing 2 x 12pdrs from the UD and 4 x 6pdrs from the *gaillards*, while *Saint Louis* lost 6 x 6pdrs from the *gaillards*.

Saint Louis Le Havre.
K: 6.1692. L: 10.12.1692. C: 2.1693. Lent as a privateer to CdE Jean Bernard de Saint-Jean, Baron de Pointis, as part of a squadron of fourteen vessels, 1696-97; took part in attack on Cartagena 5.1697. Took part in Battle of Vélez-Málaga 24.8.1704. Scuttled at Toulon in 7.1707, raised but not maintained and run aground 1708 to prevent sinking. Condemned 1709, refloated 1712 and sold to BU 1712 with *Couronne* and *Content*.

Éole Le Havre.
K: 7.1692. L: 23.2.1693. C: 5.1693. Took part in Battle of Vélez-Málaga 24.8.1704. Scuttled at Toulon in 7.1707, raised but not maintained and run aground 1708 to prevent sinking. Struck 1709, condemned 7.4.1710, ordered sold 28.5.1710.

The oldest draught of a French prize in the Admiralty collection is this sheer and half-breadth of *Prompt*, captured on 22 October 1702 at Vigo. Although commissioned as HMS *Prompt Prize* four days later, and sailed to Chatham, where she was registered as an English Third Rate in January 1703, she lasted only four months before being taken to pieces 'to apply her timbers to wharfing'. (National Maritime Museum, London J6132)

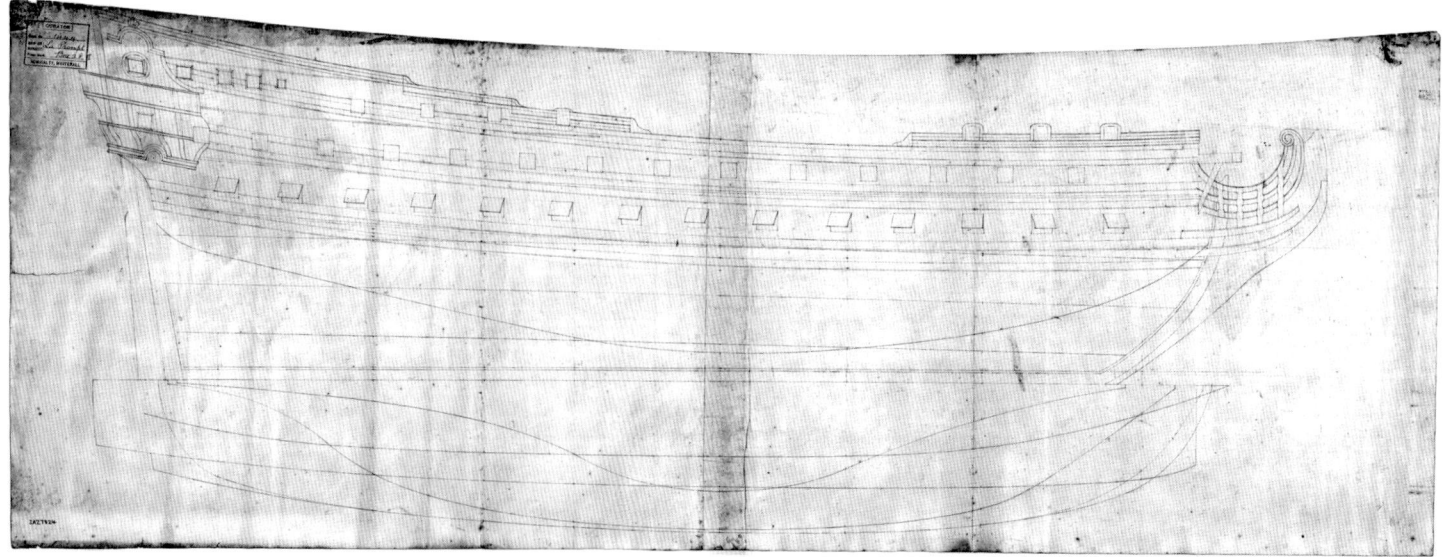

PROMPT. 70, later 76 guns. Designed and built by René Levasseur. A two-decker, originally pierced for fourteen pairs of LD guns (and had no chase ports). She was substantially rebuilt at Brest during 1698, emerging with a reported length of 9ft less (the figures are suspect), and with one fewer pair of guns on each of the LD and UD, but with increased numbers of guns on the *gaillards*.

> Dimensions & tons: (as built) 154ft x 40ft x 15ft 8in (50.03 x 12.99 x 5.09m). 1,200 tons. Draught 22ft (7.15m). Men: 500 in war, 380 peace, +10 officers. As rebuilt 1698: 145ft 0in, 125ft 0in x 40ft 0in x 16ft 6in (47.10, 40.60 x 12.99 x 5.36m). 1,200 tons. Men: 520 in war, 450 peace, +10 officers. Draught 21ft (6.82m).
> Guns: 70 in war from 1693 (62 peace): LD 28 x 24pdrs; UD 30 x 18pdrs; QD/Fc 12 x 6pdrs. 76 in war from 1698 (64 peace): LD 12 x 36pdrs + 14 x 24pdrs; UD 28 x 12pdrs; QD 12 x 6pdrs; Fc 6 x 6pdrs; poop 4 x 4pdrs.

Prompt Dunkirk.
> K: 9.1692. L: 25.12.1692. C: 3.1693. Took part in Battle of Lagos 28.6.1693. Captured by Edward Hopsonn's squadron at Vigo 22.10.1702, becoming HMS *Prompt Prize* four days later; condemned 20.5.1703 and BU 6.1703 at Chatham.

FORT. 68, later 70 guns. Designed and built by Pierre Masson. A two-decker, pierced for thirteen pairs of LD guns (and had no chase ports). She was initially recorded as a longer ship, her measurements in 1696 and 1698 being recorded as 152ft x 41ft x 18ft (49.38 x 13.32 x 5.85m), and 1,400 tons, but like the *Prompt* this data seems suspect.

> Dimensions & tons: 142ft 0in x 41ft 0in x 17ft 9in (46.13 x 13.32 x 5.77m). 1,200 tons. Draught 20ft/20½ft (6.50/6.66m). Men: 450 in war, 350 peace, +7/9 officers.
> Guns: 68 in war (62 peace): LD 26 x 24pdrs; UD 28 x 18pdrs (replaced by 12pdrs from 1699); QD/Fc 14 x 6pdrs (2 more added from 1699).

Fort Rochefort Dyd.
> K: 7.1692. L: 2.1693. C: 5.1693. Took part in Battle of Lagos 28.6.1693. Lent as a privateer to LG André, Marquis de Nesmond, as part of a squadron of six to eleven vessels, 1696. Lent as a privateer to CdE Jean Bernard de Saint-Jean, Baron de Pointis, as part of a squadron of fourteen vessels; took part in attack on Cartagena 5.1697. Burnt at Vigo to avoid capture by the English Navy 22.10.1702.

CONTENT. 64, later 60 guns. Designed and built by François Coulomb. A two-decker, pierced for twelve pairs of LD guns (with no chase ports). Re-classed as 3rd Rank in 1698 (when 4 x 6pdrs were removed from the *gaillards*), but restored to 2nd Rank in 1702–3. Refitted as a 54-gun ship at Toulon from February 1703 to 1704, and reduced to 3rd Rank again in 1706. She appears to be identical in structure to Coulomb's 3rd Rank ships, albeit slightly larger.

> Dimensions & tons: 140ft 0in, 113ft 0in x 37ft 10in x 16ft 10in (45.48, 37.71 x 12.29 x 5.47m). 1,000/1,050 tons. Draught 18ft/18½ (5.85/6.01m). Men: 380 in war, 300 peace, +8 officers.
> Guns (64 in war, 56 peace): LD 24 x 24pdrs; UD 26 x 18pdrs; QD 10 x 6pdrs; Fc 4 x 6pdrs. In 1698 the 18pdrs were replaced by 12pdrs. 54 from 1704: LD 24 x 24pdrs; UD 22 x 12pdrs; QD/Fc 8 x 4pdrs.

Content Toulon Dyd.
> K: 5.1695. L: 9.1695. C: 1.1696. Took part in Battle of Vélez-Málaga 24.8.1704. Scuttled at Toulon in 7.1707 but refloated. Condemned at Toulon 15.12.1710, ordered sold 24.12.1710, in too poor condition to be refitted 1712 and sold at auction with *Couronne* and *Saint Louis*.

Ex-ENGLISH PRIZE (1695). 70 guns. The English Third Rate *Hope* was captured by Duguay-Trouin in *François*, which was sent to reinforce LG André, Marquis de Nesmond's squadron on 26 April 1695 off the Lizard. The *Amiral de France* awarded the prize to the King rather than to the privateers.

> Dimensions & tons (French re-measurements): 143ft 6in, 114ft 0in x 38ft 0in x 14ft 6in (46.61, 37.03 x 12.34 x 4.71m). 1,125 tons. Draught 19ft/20ft (6.17/6.50m). Men: 430 in war, 300 peace, +6/8 officers; by 1700, 400 in war, 266 peace.
> Guns: 70 in war (64 peace): LD 26 x 24pdrs; UD 28 x 12pdrs; QD 12 x 6pdrs. 64 in war (60 peace) by 1698: LD 24 x 24pdrs; UD 26 x 12pdrs; QD/Fc 14 x 6pdrs.

Espérance d'Angleterre Robert Castle, Deptford.
> Ordered: 3.1678. L: 1678. Lent as a privateer to CV Bernard Renau d'Élissagaray, as part of a squadron of four vessels for operations in the West Indies, 1696. Burnt to avoid capture at the Battle of Vigo 22.10.1702.

FERME. 66, later 70 guns. Designed and built by Honoré Malet and Pierre Masson. A two-decker, pierced for thirteen pairs of LD guns. Ordered as 3rd Rank, but raised to the 2nd Rank in 1700.

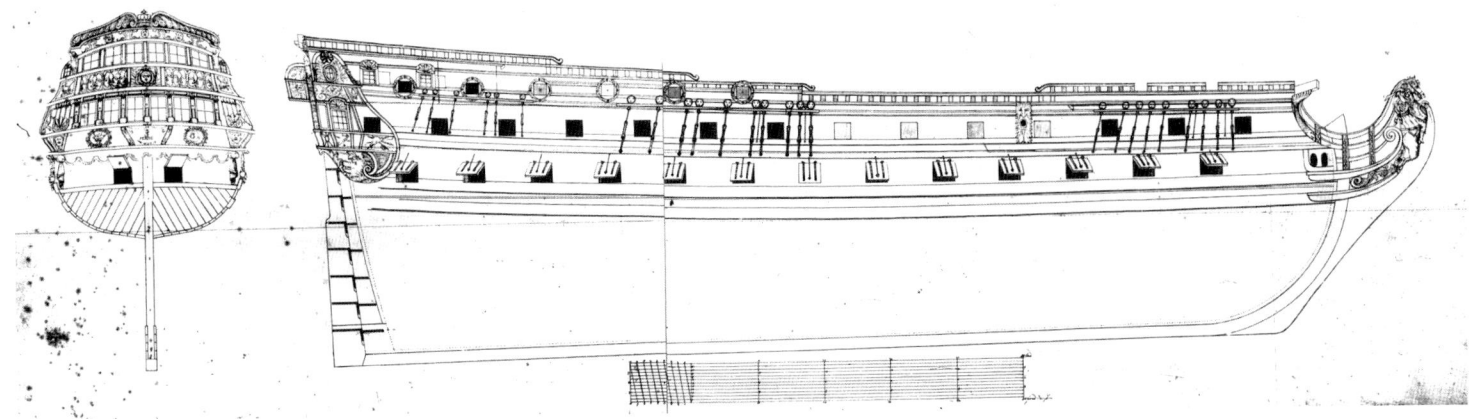

A draught of the 70-gun *Ferme* preserved in the Danish archives. It has far more detail than was usual on French official draughts, so appears to be a Danish drawing (the scale is in Danish feet), but whether it was taken off the ship or copied from another draught is unknown. As the ship was captured by the English in 1702, one possibility is that it was copied from a since-lost Admiralty draught of the ship as taken at Vigo – there are many plans of English origin from this period in the Danish archives, some original and others redrawn. Prior to her capture, she was sent to protect the Spanish galleon trade at Havana, where the LG Marquis de Nesmond had died aboard of yellow fever on 11 June 1702. (Rigsarkivet, Copenhagen)

One of a series of French etchings depicting the exploits of the great corsairs of the War of the Spanish Succession. Here Duguay-Trouin's flagship, the 60-gun *Achille* escapes from a pursuing English squadron, having captured the *Bristol*, 50 guns, on 5 May 1709 (NS). The British ship was recaptured the following day in a sinking condition and later foundered, but although Duguay-Trouin escaped, he lost the *Gloire* (see Chapter 4), shown far right with much damage aloft. (National Maritime Museum, London, detail from PU5209)

Dimensions & tons: 147ft 4in, 130ft 0in x 40ft 9in x 16ft 6in (47.86, 42.23 x 13.24 x 5.36m). 1,300 tons. Draught 17ft/19½ft (m). Men: 400 in war, 370 peace, +7/8 officers.
Guns: 66 in war (46 peace): LD 26 x 24pdrs; UD 28 x 12pdrs; QD 6 x 6pdrs; Fc 6 x 6pdrs. 4 x 4pdrs added later on poop.

Ferme Rochefort Dyd.
K: 1698. L: 1700. C: 6.1700. Captured by the English Navy at Vigo on 22.10.1702, becoming HMS *Ferme*; sold 11.1713.

PARFAIT. 72 guns. Designed and built by François Coulomb, and longer than any previous 2nd Rank ship, this 1699-ordered ship – a two-decker, pierced for thirteen pairs of LD guns (with no chase ports), and with an armed QD, forecastle and poop – set the precedent for all the 70-gun and 74-gun ships for the first third of the eighteenth century with their principal batteries of 36pdrs (although in *Parfait* 24pdrs were substituted in 1704 for her original 36pdrs on the LD).

Dimensions & tons: 152ft 0in, 125ft 0in x 42ft 0in x 19ft 6in. (49.4 x 13.6 x 7.1 m) 1,400 tons. Draught 21ft/22ft (m). Men: 500 in war, 400 peace, +9 officers.
Guns: 72 in war (62 peace): LD 26 x 36pdrs; UD 28 x 12pdrs; QD 6 x 6pdrs; Fc 6 x 6pdrs; poop 6 x 4pdrs. After completion 2 more LD and 2 more QD guns were added in 1702. From 1704: LD 26 x 24pdrs; UD 28 x 18pdrs; QD 12 x 6pdrs; Fc 6 x 6pdrs.

Parfait Toulon Dyd.
K: 3.1700. L: 14.3.1701. C: 30.5.1701. Took part in Battle of Vélez-Málaga 24.8.1704. Scuttled at Toulon 7.1707, but refloated. Hulked 5.1722 at Toulon; struck 1723, ordered BU 6.2.1726 and sold to BU 20.7.1726.

ORIFLAMME Class. 62 guns. Designed and built by François Coulomb. These were two-deckers, pierced for twelve pairs of LD guns (with no chase ports). *Oriflamme* contracted on 31 March 1703, and both named on 12 May. Initially classed as 2nd Rank, they were re-classed as 3rd Rank in 1706 and 1708 respectively.

Dimensions & tons: 140ft 0in, 115ft 0in x 38ft 0in x 17ft 6in (45.48, 37.36 x 12.34 x 5.68m). 918/1,050 tons. Draught 19ft/20ft (6.17/6.50m). Men: 380 in war, 300 peace, +5/9 officers.
Guns: 62 in war (56 peace): LD 24 x 24pdrs (*Oriflamme*: 18pdrs from 1707, 24pdrs restored 1715); UD 26 x 12pdrs; QD 8 x 6pdrs; Fc 4 x 6pdrs (*Oriflamme* carried these 4 x 6pdrs on a poop deck). 2 x 6pdrs were removed in *Oriflamme* in 1707.

Toulouse Toulon Dyd.
K: 4.1703. L: 8.12.1703. C: 5.1704. Took part in Battle of Vélez-Málaga 24.8.1704. Scuttled at Toulon in 7.1707, but refloated. Captured by HM Ships *Stirling Castle* and *Hampton Court* off Mahon 2.12.1711.

Oriflamme Toulon Dyd.
K: 4.1703. L: 15.1.1704. C: 2.6.1704. Took part in Battle of Vélez-Málaga 24.8.1704. Lent as a privateer under CdE Michel de Chabert, as part of a squadron of two to four vessels, in support of the Spanish Navy and for a voyage to Lima 1707. Lent as a privateer to CFL Jean-François Du Clerc, as part of a squadron of four vessels for operations on the Brazilian coast, 1709–10. Raséed and hulked at Rochefort 1722; BU 1727.

ACHILLE. 64, later 62 guns. Designed and built by Blaise Pangalo. A two-decker, pierced for twelve pairs of LD guns. This ship was ordered on 9 July 1704, and was named on 24 September. Reduced to 3rd Rank in 1706. She was reconstructed in 1713–14 at Brest by Étienne Hubac, and again in 1725.

Dimensions & tons: 142ft 0in x 38ft 0in x 18ft 6in (46.13 x 12.34 x 6.01m). 1,000 tons. Draught 21ft/21½ft (6.82/6.98m). Men: 400 in war, 360 peace, +8 officers.

Guns: 64 in war (54 peace): LD 24 x 24pdrs; UD 26 x 12pdrs; QD 10 x 6pdrs (2 x 6pdrs removed between 1715 and 1723); Fc 4 x 6pdrs.

Achille Brest Dyd.
  K: 8.1704. L: 23.2.1705. C: 1705. Lent for privateering to CV Des Augiers, as part of a squadron of three vessels for a campaign in the West Indies, 1705–6. Lent to CV René Duguay-Trouin, as part of a squadron of five to seven vessels, 1707–9. Lent again as a privateer to Duguay-Trouin, now as part of a squadron of thirteen vessels, 1711–12; took part in the Capture of Rio de Janeiro 9.1711. Took part in Barailh's squadron in expedition to Danzig 5–8.1734. Condemned 1741 at Brest and BU in 2.1743.

The preceding three 62/64-gun ships were the last of this gun-rating to be built as 2nd Rank vessels, and were re-classed to the 3rd Rank shortly after entering service. From mid-1703, a series of six 72/76-gun 2nd Rank ships were built (including one rebuilding), and no lesser-armed vessels of this rank were built subsequently (except for the replacement *Toulouse* of 1714). Each was pierced for thirteen pairs of LD ports, and while the *Neptune* and rebuilt *Conquérant* carried 24pdrs on that deck, the others mounted all 36pdrs. Their UD battery comprised 16 bronze and 12 iron 12pdrs (later replaced by 18pdrs), while the standard armament on the *gaillards* was 18 bronze 6pdrs (later replaced by 8pdrs), often with 4 bronze 4pdrs on the poop. Like the *Parfait* of 1701 (see above), all these ships were at least 150ft in length and about 1,400 tons.

NEPTUNE. 72 guns. Designed and built by François Coulomb, a development of his *Parfait* design. A two-decker, pierced for thirteen pairs of LD guns (and had no chase ports). Named on 12 May 1703.

Dimensions & tons: 152ft 0in, 126ft 0in x 42ft 0in x 19ft 9in (49.38, 40.93 x 13.64 x 6.42m). 1,400 tons. Draught 22ft (7.15m). Men: 500 in war, 400 peace, +9 officers.

Guns (76 intended): LD 12 x 36pdrs + 14 x 24pdrs; UD 28 x 12pdrs; QD 12 x 6pdrs; Fc 6 x 6pdrs; poop 4 x 4pdrs. 72 in war from 1704 (62 peace): LD 26 x 24pdrs; UD 28 x 18pdrs; QD 12 x 6pdrs; Fc 6 x 6pdrs.

Neptune Toulon Dyd.
  K: 7.1703. L: 27.8.1704. C: 12.1704. Comm: 2.1.1705. Scuttled at Toulon in 7.1707, but refloated.
  Wrecked at night on 3.2.1713 off La Guaira (Venezuela), wreck abandoned 6.2.1713.

SAINT MICHEL. 70 guns. Designed and built by Alexandre Gobert. A two-decker, pierced for thirteen pairs of LD guns (and had no chase ports). She was the first French major warship built according to the 'method of Sieur Gobert' which included the replacement of wooden knees for the deck with iron ones to reinforce the structure of the hull, the replacement of the tiller with a wheel for steering, and the improvement of the pumps, especially those in the hold. She was the first two-decker to be completed with and retain a complete 36pdr LD battery. Her first captain, CV Jacques-François de Robec, Baron de Pallières, wrote '*c'est un des plus beau vaisseaux que l'on puisse monter*'.

Dimensions & tons: 153ft 6in x 41ft 0in x 21ft 0in (51.3 x 13.8 x 6.1m). 1,400 tons. Draught 21ft/23ft (6.82/7.47m). Men: 500 in war, 450 peace.

Guns: 70 in war (60 peace): LD 26 x 36pdrs; UD 28 x 18pdrs; QD/Fc 16 x 8pdrs. Also carried 4 x 4pdrs on poop from 1715.

Saint Michel Port Louis, near Lorient.
  K: 6.1705. L: 1.2.1706. C: 9.1706. Lent as a privateer to CV René Duguay-Trouin, as part of a squadron of five to seven vessels, 1708. Lent as a privateer to LG Jean-Baptiste Ducasse, as part of a squadron of three vessels in support of the Spanish Navy in the West Indies, 1711. Struck early 1717 at Brest, and BU 1719.

LYS. 72 guns. Designed and built by Blaise Pangalo. A two-decker, pierced for thirteen pairs of LD guns (and had no chase ports). Ordered on 21 October 1705. This ship, and the similar *Magnanime* below, took the names of the two larger French ships lost at Marbella on 21 March 1705.

Dimensions & tons: 150ft 0in x 41ft 0in x 20ft 6in (48.73 x 13.32 x 6.66m). 1,400 tons. Draught 21ft/21½ft (6.82/6.98m). Men: 500 in war, 450 peace.

Guns: 72 in war (64 peace): LD 26 x 36pdrs; UD 28 x 18pdrs; QD/Fc 14 x 8pdrs; poop 4 x 4pdrs.

Lys Brest Dyd.
  K: 1.1706. L: 6.1706. C: 9.1706. Lent as a privateer to CV René Duguay-Trouin, as part of a squadron of five to seven vessels, 1707–9. Sailed 9.6.1711 from La Rochelle as flagship of Duguay-Trouin leading a squadron of 17 ships on an attack on Rio de Janeiro on 22.9.1711; departed Rio 13.10.1711, arriving at Brest 6.1.1712. Rebuilt 1725–26 at Brest by Blaise Ollivier. Condemned there 1745 and BU 1747.

MAGNANIME. 72 guns. Designed and built by Étienne Hubac. A two-decker, pierced for thirteen pairs of LD guns (with no chase ports). Ordered on 21 October 1705 and named on 3 February 1706.

Dimensions & tons: 150ft 0in x 41ft 0in x 20ft 0in (48.73 x 13.32 x 6.50m). 1,400 tons. Draught 21ft (6.82m). Men: 500 in war, 450 peace.

Guns: 72 in war (64 peace): LD 26 x 36pdrs; UD 28 x 18pdrs; QD/Fc 16 x 8pdrs; poop 2 x 4pdrs.

Magnanime Brest Dyd.
  K: 3.1706. L: 6.10.1706. C: early 1707. Lent as a privateer under CdE Jean-Baptiste Ducasse, as part of a squadron of four vessels in support of the Spanish Navy for escorting galleons, 1707. Lent as a privateer to CV René Duguay-Trouin, as part of a squadron of thirteen vessels, 1711–12; took part in the capture of Rio de Janeiro on 22.9.1711. Wrecked 29.1.1712 in a storm off the Azores (600 drowned and 600,000 *livres* of gold & silver lost). See comments in Chapter 3 concerning the 3rd Rank ships *Jason* and *Auguste* of 1704.

POMPEUX. 72 guns. Designed and built by Pierre Masson, with decorative work designed by Thomas Buirette. A two-decker, pierced for thirteen pairs of LD guns (and had no chase ports). This ship was never brought into service, and remained at Rochefort throughout her life.

Dimensions & tons: 153ft 6in x 44ft 4in x 18ft 3in (49.86 x 14.40 x 5.93m). 1,380/1,400 tons. Draught 21ft/21½ft (6.82/6.98m). Men: 550 in war, 350 peace.

Guns: 72 in war (68 peace): LD 26 x 36pdrs; UD 28 x 18pdrs; QD 8 x 8pdrs; Fc 6 x 8pdrs; poop 4 x 4pdrs.

Pompeux Rochefort Dyd.
  K: 1706. L: 8.1707. C: 1708. Cut down to a single deck and struck at Rochefort in 1718, and BU in 1719.

CONQUÉRANT. 70 guns. Designed and rebuilt by François Chapelle. A rebuilding of the Pangalo-designed three-decked ship of 1688, reduced to a two-decker, pierced for thirteen pairs of LD guns (and had no chase ports). She was not commissioned until 1728, when she received 36pdrs on the LD instead of the planned 24pdrs.

Dimensions & tons: 150ft 0in x 41ft 0in x 18ft 0in (48.73 x 13.32 x 5.85m). 1,400 tons. In 1728 became 148ft 0in x 42ft 6in x 18ft 6in (48.08 x 13.81 x 6.04m); 1,300 tons. Draught 20ft (6.50m). Men: 500 in war, 400 peace.

Guns: 70 in war (60 peace): LD intended 26 x 24pdrs (replaced by 36pdrs in 1728); UD 28 x 18pdrs; QD/Fc 16 x 6pdrs (14 x 6pdrs from 1728).

Conquérant Toulon Dyd.
K: 1707. L: 2.1712. C: 1712. Condemned at Rochefort 1743 and BU.

Ex-BRITISH PRIZES (1704–1707). Three British two-decker Third Rates of 70 guns and one three-decker of 80 guns were captured by the French during the War of the Spanish Succession, and all were added to the French Navy without any change in name. The 'brand-new' *Elizabeth* was captured on 22 November 1704 off the Isles of Scilly by CFL René Duguay-Trouin's squadron. The *Grafton* and *Hampton Court* were captured on 13 May 1707 off Brighton by Claude de Forbin's squadron. All three ships had been rebuilt from earlier British vessels of 1678–79; these were added to the *Marine Royale* initially as 2nd Rank, although *Élisabeth* and *Grafton* were reduced to 3rd Rank in 1708 and 1712–14 respectively. The 80-gun *Cumberland* was captured off Brittany on 21 October 1707 by CV René Duguay-Trouin's *Lys* while defending her Lisbon-bound convoy against CdE Forbin's and CV Duguay Trouin's squadrons; added to the French Navy at Brest on 28 October. Dimensions below are as re-measured (in French units). *Élisabeth* was reconstructed 1713–14 at Brest (by Étienne Hubac), and *Grafton* in 1722–23, also at Brest, and later at Toulon in the first half of 1728.

Élisabeth Portsmouth Dyd (constructor, Elias Waffe).
Ordered 25.2.1699. L: 3.9.1704.

Dimensions & tons: 147ft 0in, 112ft 7in x 38ft 0in x 16ft 6in (47.75, 36.57 x 12.34 x 5.36m). 1,100 tons. Draught 18ft/19½ft (5.85/6.33m). Men: 420 in war, 380 peace, +7 officers.

Guns: 72 in war (60 peace): LD 24 x 24pdrs; UD 28 x 12pdrs; QD/Fc 16 x 6pdrs; poop 4 x 3pdrs. From 1715 (French guns): LD 26 x 24pdrs; UD 26 x 12pdrs; QD/Fc 14 x 6pdrs.

Lent as a privateer to CV Des Augiers, as part of a squadron of three vessels for a campaign in the West Indies, 1705–6. Lent as a privateer under CdE Jean-Baptiste Ducasse, as part of a squadron of seven vessels in support of the Spanish Navy for escorting galleons 1707. Struck *c.*1720 at Brest and BU.

Grafton John & Richard Wells, Rotherhithe.
Ordered 1699. L: 27.8.1700.

Dimensions & tons: 145ft 0in, 113ft 3in x 38ft 0in x 17ft 0in (47.10, 36.79 x 12.34 x 5.52m). 1,000 tons. Draught 15ft 8in/19ft (5.09/6.17m). Men: 500 in war, 430 peace, +11 officers.

Guns: 68 in war (60 peace): LD 26 x 24pdrs; UD 26 x 18pdrs; QD 12 x 6pdrs; poop 4 x 3pdrs (all British calibres). 66 guns from 1715: LD 26 x 24pdrs (24 from 1734); UD 28 x 12pdrs (26 from 1729); QD 12 x 6pdrs (14 from 1741).

Lent as a privateer to provisional CV Cornil Sauss, as part of a squadron of six vessels 1711-12. Took part in bombardment of Tunis and Tripoli on 20-26.7.1728. Condemned 1744 at Brest and BU.

Hampton Court Henry Johnson, Blackwall.
Ordered 27.9.1699. L: 22.5.1701.

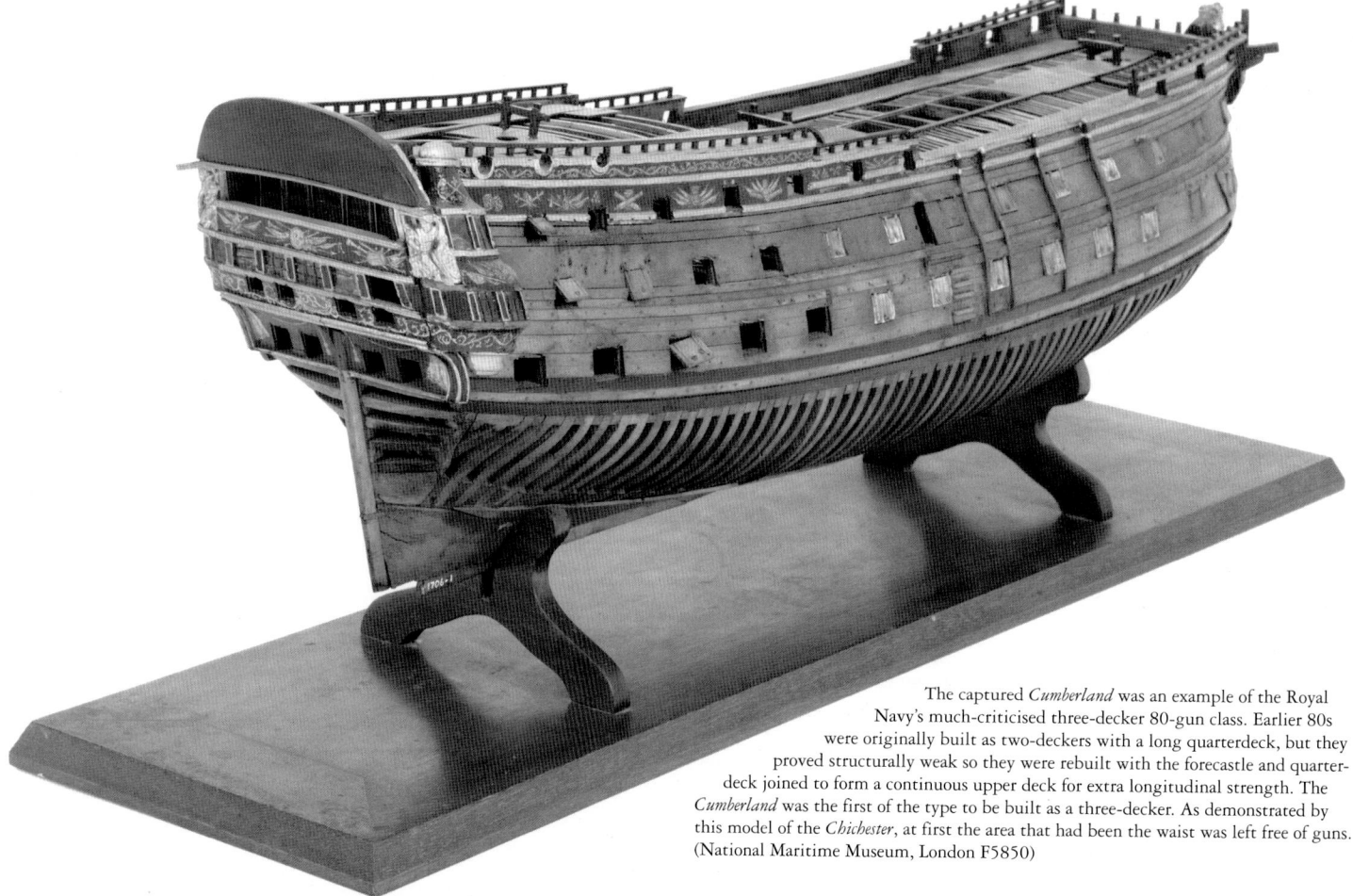

The captured *Cumberland* was an example of the Royal Navy's much-criticised three-decker 80-gun class. Earlier 80s were originally built as two-deckers with a long quarterdeck, but they proved structurally weak so they were rebuilt with the forecastle and quarter-deck joined to form a continuous upper deck for extra longitudinal strength. The *Cumberland* was the first of the type to be built as a three-decker. As demonstrated by this model of the *Chichester*, at first the area that had been the waist was left free of guns. (National Maritime Museum, London F5850)

Dimensions & tons: 145ft 6in, 113ft 10in x 38ft 4in x 15ft 0in (47.26, 36.98 x 12.45 x 4.87m). 800 tons. Draught 18ft 4in/18ft 8in (5.96/6.06m). Men: 550 in war, 500 peace, +12 officers.
Guns: 64 in war (60 peace): LD 24 x 24pdrs; UD 26 x 12pdrs; QD/Fc 10 x 6pdrs; poop 4 x 3pdrs (all British calibres).
Sold 1712 at Dunkirk to the Spanish Navy, becoming their *Capitaine*; renamed *Nuestra Señora del Carmen* (72 guns), then *Capitana de Galeones*; foundered 1715.

Cumberland Mrs Anne Wyatt & John Button, Bursledon.
Contract of 4.5.1694. L: 12.11.1695.
Dimensions & tons: 150ft 0in, 131ft 0in x 38ft 0in x 18ft 0in (48.73, 42.55 x 12.34 x 5.85m). 1,300 tons. Draught 20ft (6.50m). Men: 550 in war, 500 peace.
Guns: 84 in war (70 peace): LD 26 x (British) 24pdrs; MD 28 x 18pdrs; UD 24 x 6pdrs; poop 6 x 4pdrs.
Cut down from three- to two-decker in 1715, and sold at Genoa 5.1715 to the Spanish Navy, becoming their 72-gun *Principe de Asturias*. Retaken by the British at Battle of Cape Passaro 22.8.1718, and sold to the Austrians, becoming the Austrian Navy's *San Carlos*, then *San Carlo* in the Neapolitan Navy; discarded 1733.

Another 70-gun ship was ordered at Lorient in January 1706, and would have been named *Redoutable*; however, this order was cancelled a month or two later.

Eight of the navy's twenty 2nd Rank ships were at Toulon during the attack in July 1707 by Sir Clowdisley Shovell's besieging fleet – the *Henri*, *Éclatant*, *Invincible*, *Heureux*, *Bizarre*, *Saint Esprit*, *Parfait* and *Neptune*. All were submerged (scuttled) in the harbour on Louis's orders to prevent their being destroyed by the bombardment, but all were refloated about October 1707.

After 1707, there were no further additions to the 2nd Rank for more than a decade. By 1715, classification had settled down, and the 2ème Rang now included only eleven surviving two-decker ships of 64–74 guns – the *Grand*, *Henri*, *Invincible*, *Saint Esprit*, *Juste* and *Bizarre* of the pre-1692 vessels, and the more recent *Parfait*, *Saint Michel*, *Lys*, *Pompeux* and (rebuilt) *Conquérant*. The *Henri*, *Invincible*, *Saint Esprit*, *Juste*, *Bizarre*, *Parfait* and *Conquérant* each had a main battery of twenty-six 24pdrs (twenty-four only in *Henri*), while the *Grand*, *Saint Michel*, *Lys* and *Pompeux* each carried twenty-six 36pdrs in their main batteries and twenty-eight 18pdrs in their second battery, an ordnance which would remain standard until the longer *Terrible* was built in the mid-1730s.

After 1715, all new 2nd Rank ships would be of at least 74 guns (the exception would be the *Aimable* of 1725, which had a 24pdr main battery and omitted the 4 x 4pdr poop guns carried by the others). By 1736, all 74s would carry 74 guns except for the (by then) elderly *Lys* and *Conquérant*, the latter now having a LD battery of 36pdrs.

(D) 74-gun two-decked vessels (*Vaisseaux de 74*) acquired from 1 September 1715

The ninety 74-gun ships built or begun between 1719 and 1785 fall into two groups in regards to ordnance layout. In the earliest twelve vessels (to 1735) the former 70-gun format was simply altered by the addition of four small (4pdr) guns added to the roof of the roundhouse or poop (*dunette*); these ships all had a length of between 152 and 155½ feet. The first two, built at Brest, seemingly were not actually fitted with ordnance – the *Bourbon* not until 1739, and the *Sceptre* never – the guns listed below remaining theoretical. In addition to these twelve, a single 70-gun ship (the *Aimable*) was built without the 4pdrs, and with only 24pdrs in its main battery, as mentioned above.

In the subsequent seventy-eight vessels (including the first twelve *Téméraire* Class ships of the Sané-Borda program), a longer hull (apart from François Coulomb Jnr's two ships of 1739 and 1747, all the others were over 160 feet in length) allowed an additional pair of gunports to be inserted on the lower deck and another pair on the upper deck, and the four 4pdrs were deleted. This layout was maintained for a half-century with no significant enlargement. After 1785, the same standard armament was to continue in further units of the Sané-designed *Téméraire* Class.

SCEPTRE. 74 guns. Designed and built to an Étienne Hubac design, drawn in 1719 and approved in April 1720 by the *Conseil de Marine*. She was not commissioned before Hubac refitted her afloat in 1736 and probably never saw sea service.
Dimensions & tons: 152ft 0in, 134ft 0in x 42ft 0in x 21ft 0in (49.37, 43.53 x 13.64 x 6.82m). 1,500/2,500 tons. Draught 22½ft (7.31m). Men: 550 in war, 500 peace, +6 officers.
Guns: 74 in war (66 peace): LD 26 x 36pdrs; UD 28 x 18pdrs; QD 10 x 8pdrs; Fc 6 x 8pdrs; poop 4 x 4pdrs.
Sceptre Brest Dyd.
K: 7.1719. L: 7.1720. C: 1721. Struck at Brest 1745 and BU.

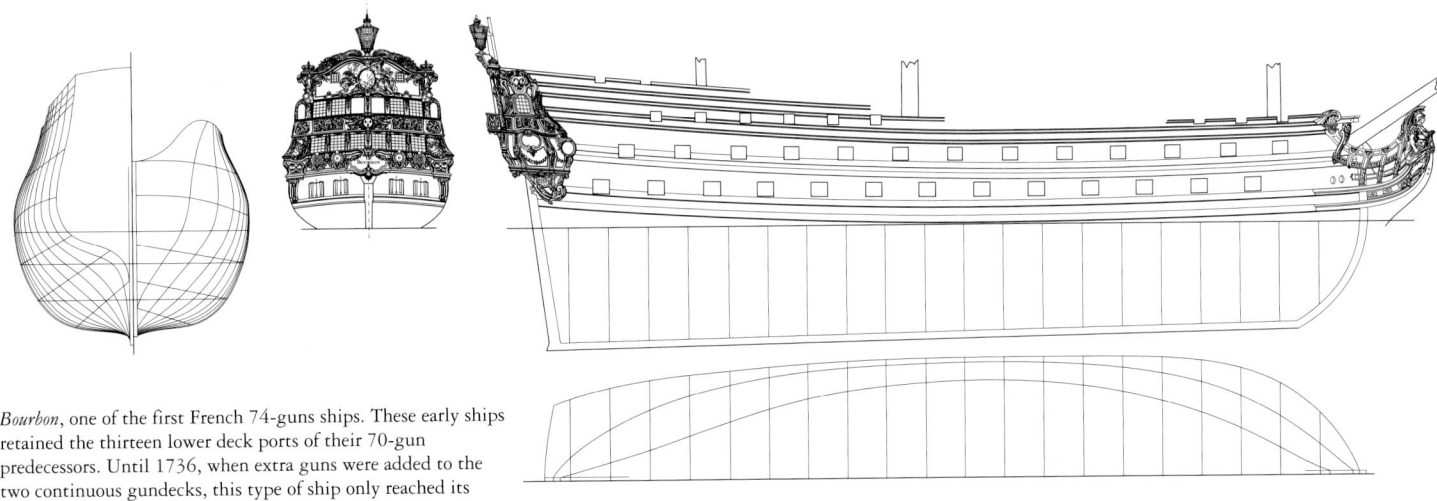

Bourbon, one of the first French 74-guns ships. These early ships retained the thirteen lower deck ports of their 70-gun predecessors. Until 1736, when extra guns were added to the two continuous gundecks, this type of ship only reached its nominal rating of 74 guns by counting in four small guns mounted on the poop. Drawing by László Veres based on the original plan in the Service Historique de la Marine, Vincennes.

BOURBON. 74 guns. Designed and built to a Laurent Hélie design, drawn in 1719 and similarly approved in April 1720. Almost identical with Hubac's *Sceptre*, but 2ft longer on the keel. Reconstructed in a dock by Hélie in 1734 at Brest, saw first sea service in 1739.

Dimensions & tons: 152ft 0in, 136ft 0in x 42ft 0in x 21ft 0in (49.37, 44.18 x 13.64 x 6.82m). 1,500/2,500 tons. Draught 22½ft (7.31m). Men: 550 in war, 500 peace, +6 officers.

Guns: 74 in war (66 peace): LD 26 x 36pdrs; UD 28 x 18pdrs; QD 10 x 8pdrs; Fc 6 x 8pdrs; poop 4 x 4pdrs.

Bourbon Brest Dyd.
K: 7.1719. L: 9.1720. C: 1721. Developed leaks returning from the Antilles and sank 10 leagues off Cape Finisterre 12.4.1741 (517 drowned, with 24 survivors).

SAINT PHILIPPE. 74 guns. Designed by Pierre Masson, dated 8 July 1720, and begun by him, but completed by Blaise Ollivier following Masson's death later in 1720. A sister, to have been named *Tonnant*, was also ordered in 1720 to be built to the same design at Rochefort, but was cancelled in the same year. By 1729 it was recorded that *Saint Philippe* needed a major reconstruction, and this was carried out by Julien Geslain at Rochefort in 1731–32.

Dimensions & tons: 152ft 4in, 136ft 10in x 43ft 4in x 18ft 5in (49.48, 44.45 x 14.08 x 5.98 m). 1,469/2,441 tons. Draught 21¼/22½ft (6.90/7.31m). Men: 550 in war, 500 peace, +6 officers.

Guns: 74 in war (66 peace): LD 26 x 36pdrs; UD 28 x 18pdrs; QD 10 x 8pdrs; Fc 6 x 8pdrs; poop 4 x 4pdrs.

Saint Philippe Rochefort Dyd.
K: 5.1720. L: 1722. C: 1723. Condemned 1745 at Brest and BU 1746.

DUC D'ORLÉANS Class. A quartet of 74-gun ships were built at Toulon to this René Levasseur design of 1719. The first two were named 12 July 1719; *Ferme* was ordered on 26 July 1719. Unusually, pierced for only two pairs of Fc guns, so carried six pairs on the QD. The 6pdrs on the *gaillards* were sometimes listed as 8pdrs. *Duc d'Orléans* underwent reconstruction at Toulon from 1731 to 1737.

Dimensions & tons: 152ft 0in, 136ft 8in x 43ft 4in x 18ft 0in (49.38, 44.39 x 14.08 x 5.85m). 1,400/2,500 tons. Draught 21ft/22ft (6.82/7.15m). Men: 550 in war, 400 peace, +6 officers.

Guns: 74 in war (60 peace): LD 26 x 36pdrs; UD 28 x 18pdrs; QD 12 x 6pdrs; Fc 4 x 6pdrs; poop 4 x 4pdrs.

Duc d'Orléans Toulon Dyd.
K: 8.1720. L: 13.8.1722. C: 1723. Had not yet sailed in 1729, was very rotten and was repaired at Toulon in 1731–37 but potential commanders refused her as she was hogged by 28 inches and her lower battery was too close to the water. Took part in Battle of Toulon 22.2.1744. Hulked 1748 at Toulon, and sold 16.8.1766.

Phénix Toulon Dyd.
K: 8.1720. L: 17.3.1723. C: 1723. In 1733 was rotten and 'completely hogged' without ever having been to sea. Condemned and hulked at Toulon 1.1736. Ordered BU 30.10 1750, BU 1751.

Ferme Toulon Dyd.
K: 30.12.1722. L: 11.11.1723. C: 1724. Took part in Battle of Toulon 22.2.1744. Ordered converted to a careening hulk at Toulon 23.5.1755.

Espérance Toulon Dyd.
K: 4.1723. L: 8.8.1724. C: 1.9.1725. Took part in Battle of Toulon 22.2.1744 (as flagship of CdE Pierre Gabaret, who died on board). Fitted in Spring 1755 as a 22-gun *flûte* at Brest, but captured and burnt by HM Ships *Oxford*, *Revenge* and *Buckingham* off Newfoundland 11.11.1755.

An engraving published in 1750 showing three of the prizes taken by Hawke's squadron off Cape Finisterre on 25 October (NS) 1747. The *Neptune* is in the centre, with *Terrible* on her starboard side, and *Severn* (see Chapter 4) moored separately to port. The delineation of the stern carvings is careful and detailed, the ex-British *Severn* being distinctly different from the two French-built ships. (National Maritime Museum, London PY9598)

NEPTUNE. 74 guns. Designed and built by Laurent Hélie in 1723, a development from his *Bourbon* design.

    Dimensions & tons: 154ft 6in, 135ft 0in x 42ft 0in x 21ft 0in (50.19, 43.85 x 13.64 x 6.82m). 1,500/2,500 tons. Draught 17½ft/22½ft (5.68/7.31m). Men: 550 in war, 500 peace, +6 officers.

    Guns: 74 in war (66 peace): LD 26 x 36pdrs; UD 28 x 18pdrs; QD 10 x 8pdrs; Fc 6 x 8pdrs; poop 4 x 4pdrs.

Neptune Brest Dyd.

    K: 2.1723. L: 11.1723. C: 1724. Took part in 2nd Battle off Cape Finisterre 25.10.1747, when captured by HMS *Yarmouth* of Hawke's squadron, then burnt as was too damaged to be sailed to England.

SAINT ESPRIT. 74 guns. Designed and built by Blaise Coulomb, 1724. Named 6 September 1724. The 6pdrs on the *gaillards* were sometimes listed as 8pdrs.

    Dimensions & tons: 154ft 0in x 44ft 6in x 20ft 1in (50.03 x 14.46 x 6.85m). 1,400/2,500 tons. Draught 17ft 10in/21ft (5.79/6.82m). Men: 550 in war, 480 peace, +6 officers.

    Guns: 74 in war (60 peace): LD 26 x 36pdrs; UD 28 x 18pdrs; QD 12 x 6pdrs; Fc 4 x 6pdrs; poop 4 x 4pdrs.

Saint Esprit Toulon Dyd.

    K: 1.1724. L: 9.1.1726. C: 4.1728. Took part in Battle of Toulon 22.2.1744. Hulked at Brest 1749; BU 1761.

JUSTE. 74, later 70 guns. Designed and built by Julien Geslain, 1724. Note that in this ship the 6pdrs on the *gaillards* were superseded by 8pdrs. Was slightly damaged in the fire at Brest on 25 December 1742 that destroyed the new 1st Rank *Royal Louis*.

    Dimensions & tons: 152ft 4in x 43ft 4in x 18ft 9in (49.48 x 14.08 x 6.09m). 1,492/2,500 tons. Draught 19½ft/ 22ft 4in (6.33/7.25m). Men: 500 in war, 400 peace, +6 officers.

    Guns: 74 in war (66 peace): LD 26 x 36pdrs; UD 28 x 18pdrs; QD 10 x 8pdrs; Fc 6 x 8pdrs; poop 4 x 4pdrs. In 1751–52 refit, the 36pdrs were replaced by 24pdrs, while the 4pdrs were removed.

Juste Rochefort Dyd.

    K: 1724. L: 9.1725. C: 1726. Refitted at Brest in 1741 and at Rochefort in 1751. Wrecked off St Nazaire following the Battle of Quiberon Bay 20.11.1759 (with 487 killed or drowned).

AIMABLE. 70 guns. Designed and built by Laurent Hélie, 1725. The smallest of the post-1715 70-gun ships (she did not have 4pdrs on the poop), the only 2nd Rank ship of this era shorter than 150ft, and the only one completed with a 24pdr main battery.

    Dimensions & tons: 147ft 0in x 38ft 6in x 19ft 3in (47.75 x 12.51 x 6.25m). 1,100/2,100 tons. Draught 21½ft (6.98m). Men: 460 in war, 410 peace, +6 officers.

    Guns: 70 in war (62 peace): LD 26 x 24pdrs; UD 28 x 12pdrs; QD 10 x 6pdrs; Fc 6 x 6pdrs.

Aimable Brest Dyd.

    K: 1.1725. L: 8.1725. C: 1726. Condemned at Brest in late 1735 and BU there in 1736.

After a gap of ten years, two more 74-gun ships were built at Brest – these were the last to be pierced for only thirteen pairs of LD guns, and were followed in the next year's program by a significantly extended design built at Toulon.

SUPERBE. 74, later 70 guns. Designed and built by Jean-Marie Hélie, 1735. Reconstructed by Hélie at Brest from 1747 to 1748 (re-launched 26 July 1748).

    Dimensions & tons: 152ft 6in, 133ft 0in x 42ft 8in x 21ft 0in (49.54, 43.20 x 13.86 x 6.82m). 1,500/2,501 tons. Draught 19½/22½ft (6.33/7.31m). Men: 550 in war, 500 peace, +6 officers.

    Guns: 74 in war (66 peace): LD 26 x 36pdrs; UD 28 x 18pdrs; QD 10 x 8pdrs; Fc 6 x 8pdrs; poop 4 x 4pdrs. In 1748 refit, the 36pdrs were replaced by 24pdrs, while the 4pdrs were removed.

Superbe Brest Dyd.

    K: 11.1735. L: 27.6.1738. C: 5.1740. Capsized and foundered during Battle of Quiberon Bay 20.11.1759 after opening her LD ports (with 636 killed or drowned).

DAUPHIN ROYAL. 74, later 70 guns. Designed and built by Blaise Ollivier, 1735. Named on 10 October 1738. Reconstructed in 1751 and again in 1771 at Brest.

    Dimensions & tons: 155ft 10in, 137ft 0in x 42ft 4in x 20ft 6in (50.62, 44.50 x 13.75 x 6.66m). 1,400/2,608 tons. Draught 18ft 10in / 20ft 4in (6.12/6.605m). Men: 550 in war, 500 peace, +6 officers.

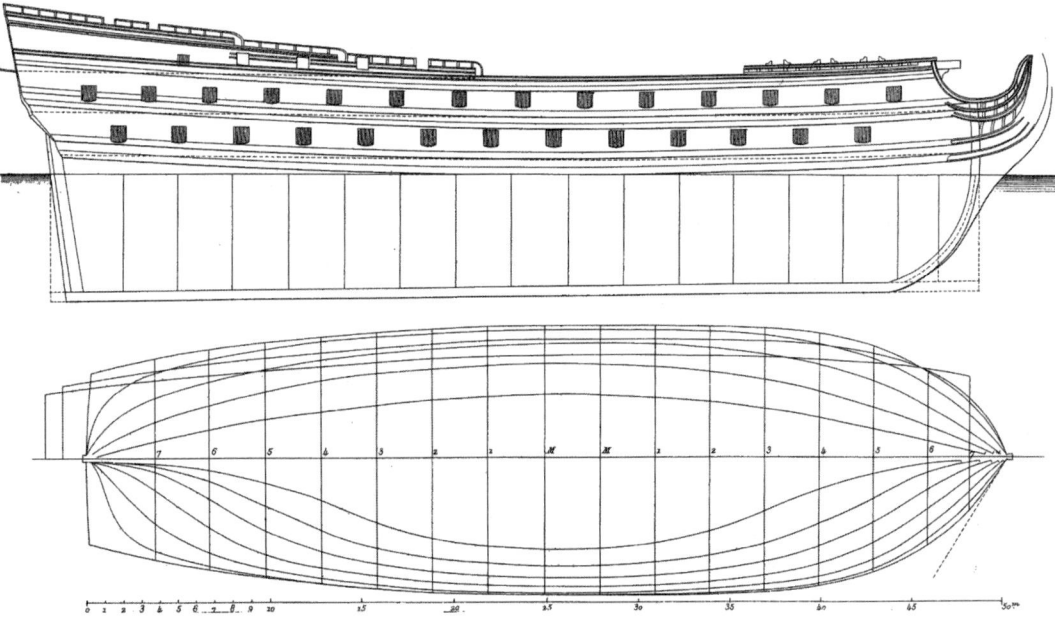

Sheer and lines plan of the *Dauphin Royal* of 1738, one of the early 74-gun ships with only thirteen lower deck gunports. According to *Vice-amiral* Pâris, this was copied from an eighteenth century original. (*Souvenirs de Marine*, Plate 248)

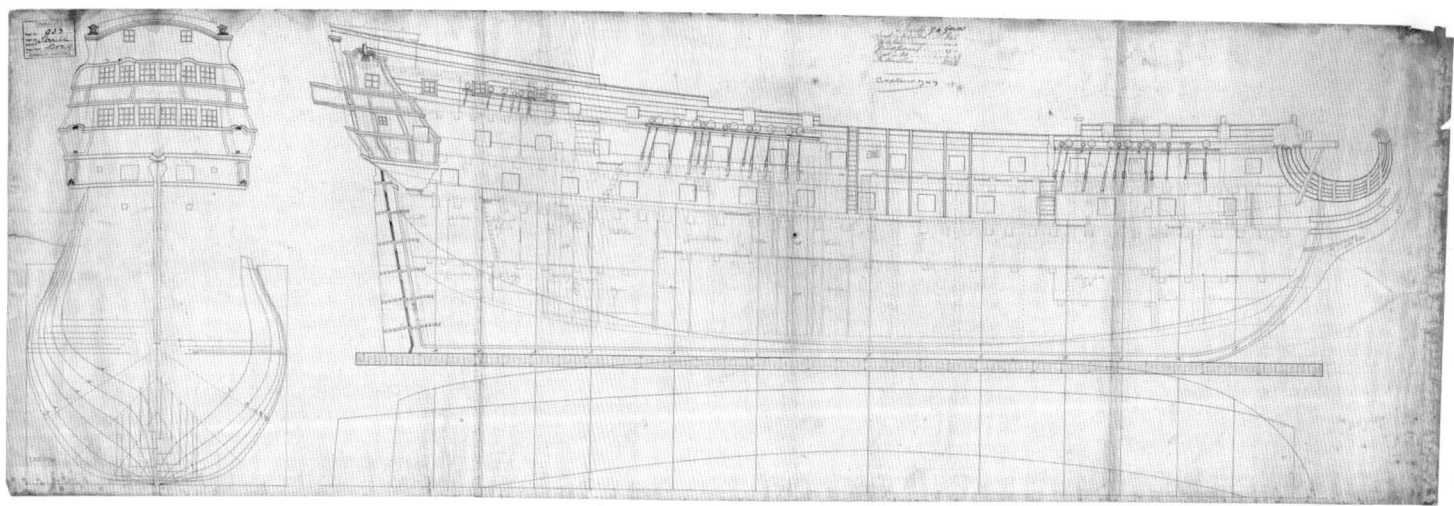

Guns: 74 in war (66 peace); LD 26 x 36pdrs; UD 28 x 18pdrs; QD 10 x 8pdrs; Fc 6 x 8pdrs; poop 4 x 4pdrs. In 1751 refit, the 4pdrs were removed, while the 36pdrs may have later been replaced by 24pdrs.

Dauphin Royal Brest Dyd.
K: 11.1735. L: 13.10.1738. C: 10.1740. Took part in Battles of Quiberon Bay 20.11.1759 and of St Kitts 25/26.1.1782. Condemned 9.1783 and hulked; sold 6.1787 to BU.

TERRIBLE. 74 guns. Designed and built by François Coulomb Jnr. Named on 16 April 1737. This ship significantly modified the existing 74-gun concept with a longer hull; extra pairs of guns were added to each of the LD and UD batteries, initially raising the number of guns to 78 in wartime (70 in peace), but in 1744 the small poop guns were

Admiralty draught of the *Terrible*, the first of the new style French 74s with fourteen gunports on the lower deck. Note that in order to make room on the upper deck for fifteen ports, one has to be cut through the quarter gallery. The ship appears to be drawn substantially as captured. (National Maritime Museum, London J3118)

deleted (as ineffective). This ordnance layout was to become the standard pattern for all French 74-gun ships for the next half century; it provided for the French 74 a broadside of 838 *livres* (or 904 English pounds), significantly greater than the British (Common Class) 74-gun ship's 781 pounds, and actually greater than the 842-pound broadside of the British three-decked Second Rates of 90 guns.

Dimensions & tons: 156ft 0in, 131ft 0in x 44ft 4in x 21ft 0in (50.67, 42.55 x 14.40 x 6.82m). 1,500/2,800 tons. Draught

Invincible in Royal Navy service, a grey wash drawing by John Hood, who was clerk to Sir John Bentley during his command of the ship from 1749 to 1752. Highly regarded by the British, *Invincible* directly inspired the first big 74-gun ships in the Royal Navy, *Valiant* and *Triumph*. (National Maritime Museum, London PU8491)

19ft/21ft (6.17/6.82m). Men: 620 in war, 550 peace, +6/19 officers.

Guns: 74 in war (70 peace): LD 28 x 36pdrs; UD 30 x 18pdrs; QD 10 x 8pdrs; Fc 6 x 8pdrs.

Terrible Toulon Dyd.

K: 11.1736. L: 19.12.1739. C: 1740. Took part in the Battle of Toulon 22.2.1744 (as flagship of LG Charles-Élisée Court de La Bruyère), then in 2nd Battle off Cape Finisterre 25.10.1747, when captured by Hawke's squadron, and added to the RN as HMS *Terrible*. BU at Chatham completed 16.2.1763.

INVINCIBLE. 74 guns. Designed and built by Pierre Morineau (the nephew of Pierre Masson). After her acquisition by the British, she served as the model for British 74s.

Dimensions & tons: 162ft 0in, 150ft 6in x 44ft 2in x 21ft 4in (52.62, 48.89 x 14.35 x 6.93m). 1,500/2,961 tons. Draught 21ft 8in (7.04m). Men: 700 in war, 600 peace, +6 officers.

Guns: 74 in war (70 peace): LD 28 x 36pdrs; UD 30 x 18pdrs; QD 10 x 8pdrs; Fc 6 x 8pdrs.

Invincible Rochefort Dyd.

K: 5.1741. L: 21.10.1744. C: 1.1745. Took part in 1st Battle off Cape Finisterre 14.5.1747, when captured by Anson's squadron, and added to the RN as HMS *Invincible*. Wrecked off Portsmouth (in RN service) 19.2.1758.

MAGNANIME. 74 guns. Designed and built by Blaise Geslain. This alternative design to Morineau's featured a similar improvement in the ordnance in an even larger hull.

Dimensions & tons: 165ft 0in, 153ft 6in x 44ft 6in x 22ft 0in (53.60, 49.86 x 14.46 x 7.15m). 1,600/2,900 tons. Draught 22ft/22½ft (7.15/7.31m). Men: 700 in war, 600 peace, +6 officers.

Guns: 74 in war (70 peace): LD 28 x 36pdrs; UD 30 x 18pdrs; QD 10 x 8pdrs; Fc 6 x 8pdrs.

Magnanime Rochefort Dyd.

K: 5.1741. L: 22.11.1744. C: 1.1745. Captured by British *Nottingham* and *Portland* off Ushant 12.1.1748, and added to the British Navy as HMS *Magnanime*. BU at Portsmouth 4.1775.

Ex-BRITISH PRIZE (1744). 68 guns. The first of four 70-gun ships ordered in 1741 for the British Navy under the 1741 Establishment, but re-ordered under the 1743 Establishment of Guns as 64-gun ships with 32pdrs, 18pdrs and 9pdrs replacing the previous 24pdrs, 12pdrs and 6pdrs respectively. To carry the additional weight, six of the smaller guns on the QD and Fc were deleted. The *Northumberland* (originally ordered on 20 September 1739) was captured within six months of her completion by the 64-gun *Mars* and 60-gun *Content* off Ushant on 19 May 1744. She was initially rated in the 3rd Rank, but was normally listed as 2nd Rank after 1752.

Dimensions & tons (French measurements): 149ft 0in, 129ft 0in x 40ft 6in x 19ft 0in (48.40, 41.90 x 13.16 x 6.17m). 1,150/2,273 tons. Draught 18ft 8in/19ft 7in (6.06/6.36m). Men: 520 in war, 480 peace, +6/11 officers.

Guns: 68 in war (62 peace): LD 26 x 32pdrs; UD 28 x 18/16pdrs; QD/Fc 14 x 8pdrs.

Northumberland Woolwich Dyd.

K: 16.10.1740. L: 7.10.1743. C: 21.11.1743. Rebuilt by Léon-Michel Guignace at Brest in 1757–59. Took part in Battle of Quiberon Bay 20.11.1759. Rebuilt again at Rochefort 1762. Renamed *Atlas* 1.1776. Condemned at Brest 1.1779, then fitted in 6.1780 as a 1,350-ton *flûte* with 26 guns at Brest. Wrecked on Ushant 21.1.1781.

CONQUÉRANT. 74 guns. Designed and built by François Coulomb Jnr. Ordered on 5 March 1743 and named on 4 December 1743. Built of poorly seasoned wood, reported as rotten in 1750.

Dimensions & tons: 157ft 0in, 135ft 6in x 43ft 0in x 21ft 0in (51.00, 44.02 x 13.97 x 6.82m). 1,500/2,700 tons. Draught 19½ft/22ft (6.33/7.15m). Men: 600, 6 officers.

Guns: 74 in war (70 peace): LD 28 x 36pdrs; UD 30 x 18pdrs; QD 10 x 8pdrs; Fc 6 x 8pdrs.

Conquérant Toulon Dyd.

K: 2.1745. L: 10.3.1746. C: 1.1747. Needed repairs by early 1755, so was not used throughout the Seven Years' War. Rebuilt by Joseph-Louis Ollivier at Brest 17.3.1764–29.11.1765 (see below).

Admiralty draught of *Magnanime* as taken off at Plymouth, 29 June 1757, at the conclusion of a five-year Great Repair. The ship was thoroughly refitted to British requirements, although the French-style stern decoration survived. The body plan shows the doubling applied below the waterline for what looks like stability reasons. Despite a very active career in the Royal Navy, the ship never acquired a reputation to rival *Invincible*'s. (National Maritime Museum, London J3619)

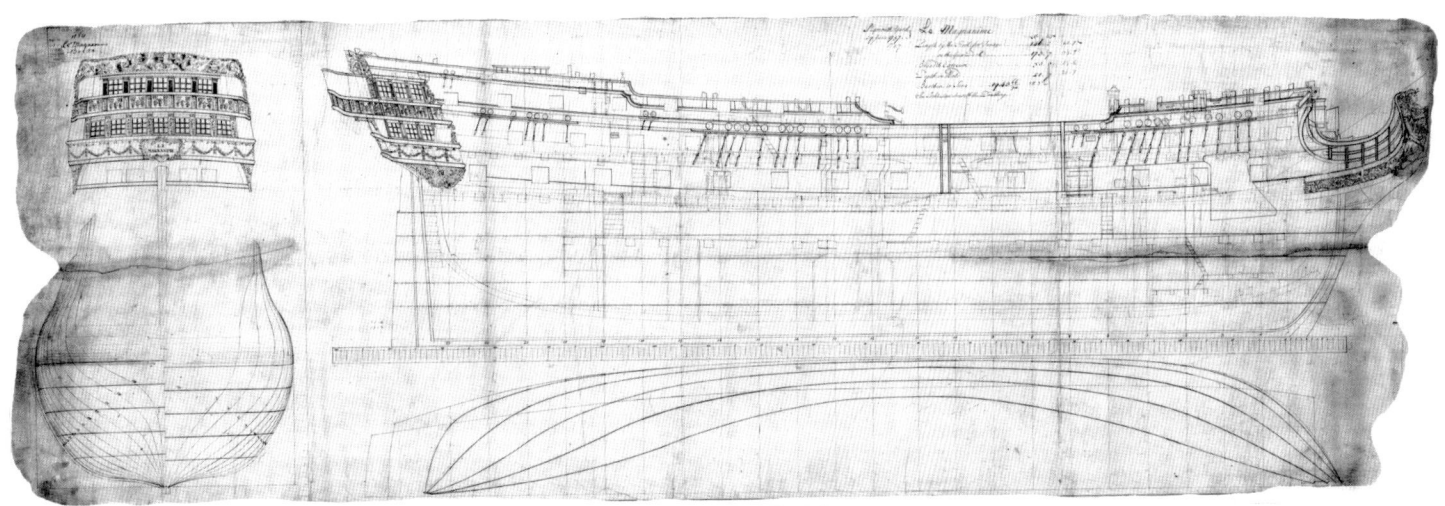

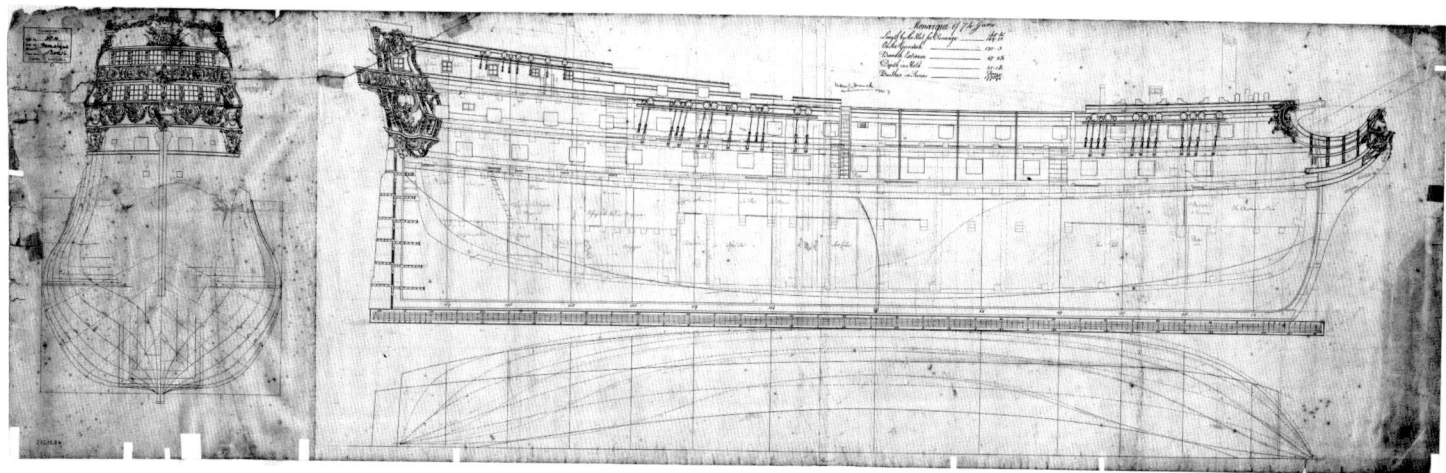

Admiralty draught of *Monarque* as captured. When taken by Hawke's squadron in October 1747, the ship was only a few months old. (National Maritime Museum, London J3202)

MONARQUE Class. 74 guns. Designed and begun by Blaise Ollivier. Ollivier died in October 1746, so these three ships were completed by Luc Coulomb. As of 1746 all three were also to have carried 4 x 4pdrs on the poop (as in *Terrible*) for a total of 78 guns in war, 74 in peace; but these were probably never mounted. *Intrépide* was the test-bed for an inclining experiment (the first ever recorded) performed May 1748 by François-Guillaume Clairain-Deslauriers; her GM (metacentric height) was found to be 5ft 7in (1.81m). *Intrépide* was rebuilt by Léon-Michel Guignace at Brest from 1758 to April 1759, and *Sceptre* by Jean Geoffroy at Brest from August 1761 to July 1762.

    Dimensions & tons: 166ft 0in, 157ft 0in x 43ft 6in x 20ft 6in (53.92, 51.00 x 14.13 x 6.66m). 1,500/2,718 tons. Draught 18¾ft/21ft (6.09/6.82m). Men: 734 in war, 650 peace, +6/10 officers.

    Guns: 74 in war (70 peace): LD 28 x 36pdrs; UD 30 x 18pdrs; QD 10 x 8pdrs; Fc 6 x 8pdrs.

Monarque Brest Dyd.
    K: 1.1745. L: 3.1747. C: 7.1747. Took part in 2nd Battle off Cape Finisterre 25.10.1747, when captured by Hawke's squadron, and added to the RN as HMS *Monarch*, sold at Woolwich 1760.

Intrépide Brest Dyd.
    K: 1.1745. L: 24.3.1747. C: 8.1747. Took part in 2nd Battle off Cape Finisterre 25.10.1747, in Battle of Quiberon Bay 20.11.1759, and in 3rd Battle of Ushant 27.7.1778. Burnt off Cape Français 22.7.1781 when a barrel of local rum caught fire.

Sceptre Brest Dyd.
    K: 1.1745. L: 21.6.1747. C: 12.1747. Hulked at Brest 1.1779.

MAGNIFIQUE Class. 74 guns. Designed and built by Jacques-Luc Coulomb; the *Guerrier* was named on 18 September 1750 and completed by Joseph-Marie-Blaise Coulomb. *Magnifique* was reconstructed at Brest by Pierre Salinoc from 1756 to December 1757; she was reconstructed there again in 1772–73. *Guerrier* was reconstructed at Toulon from June 1766 to July 1770 and again in 1775–76 and 1785–86.

    Dimensions & tons: 165ft 0in, ?157ft 0in x 43ft 0in x 20ft 4in (53.60, ?51.00 x 13.97 x 6.61m). 1,455/2,700 tons. Draught 19ft/20ft 5in (6.17/6.63m). Men: 750 in war, 660 peace, +6/12 officers.

    Guns: 74 in war (70 peace): LD 28 x 36pdrs; UD 30 x 18pdrs; QD 10 x 8pdrs; Fc 6 x 8pdrs.

Magnifique Brest Dyd.
    K: 1747. L: 7.3.1749. C: 7.1750. Took part in the Battle of Quiberon Bay 20.11.1759, in 3rd Battle of Ushant 27.7.1778, and Battle of the Saintes 21.4.1782. Wrecked in Boston harbour 10.8.1782 (the sole American ship of the line was then given to France by the Continental Congress as a replacement).

Entreprenant Brest Dyd.
    K: 1750. L: 19.10.1751. C: 12.1752. Set on fire by British mortar fire at Louisbourg 21.7.1758 and blew up.

Guerrier Toulon Dyd.
    K: 10.1750. L: 7.9.1753. C: early 1754. Took part in the Action off Minorca 20.5.1756 and in the Battle of Lagos 18.8.1759. Handed over to Anglo-Spanish forces at Toulon 8.1793, but retaken by the French at the evacuation of that port in 12.1793, and restored to service in 9.1794. Captured by Nelson's fleet at Aboukir 2.8.1798 and burnt.

COURONNE. 74 guns. Designed and begun by Blaise Geslain, and completed by Pierre Morineau after Geslain died in September 1748.

    Dimensions & tons: 167ft 0in, 153ft 6in x 44ft 0in x 22ft 7in (54.25, 49.86 x 14.29 x 7.34m). 1,360/2,760 tons. Draught 20ft/22ft (6.50/7.15m). Men: 680, +6/13 officers.

    Guns: 74 in war (70 peace): LD 28 x 36pdrs; UD 30 x 18pdrs; QD 10 x 8pdrs; Fc 6 x 8pdrs.

Couronne Rochefort
    K: 5.1748. L: 1749. C: 8.1750. Took part in the Action off Minorca 20.5.1756 (as flagship of CdE Jean-François de Bertet de la Clue-Sabran). Condemned 5.1766 at Brest and BU there; replaced by a new 80-gun ship of the same name.

TÉMÉRAIRE. 74 guns. Designed by François Coulomb Jnr and built by Pierre-Blaise Coulomb. Ordered on 18 December 1747 and named on 3 January 1748.

    Dimensions & tons: 161ft 9in x 43ft 6in x 21ft 0in (52.54 x 14.13 x 6.50m). 1,580/2,800 tons. Draught 19ft (6.17m). Men: 680, +6/13 officers.

    Guns: 74 in war (70 peace): LD 28 x 36pdrs; UD 30 x 18pdrs; QD 10 x 8pdrs; Fc 6 x 8pdrs.

Téméraire Toulon Dyd.
    K: 8.1748. L: 24.12.1749. C: 1750. Took part in the Battle off Minorca 20.5.1756 and the Battle of Lagos 18.8.1759; sought refuge under the Portuguese guns 19.8.1759 but was captured by HMS *Warspite*, becoming HMS *Temeraire*; hulked 1783, then sold 6.1784 to BU

THE SECOND RANK

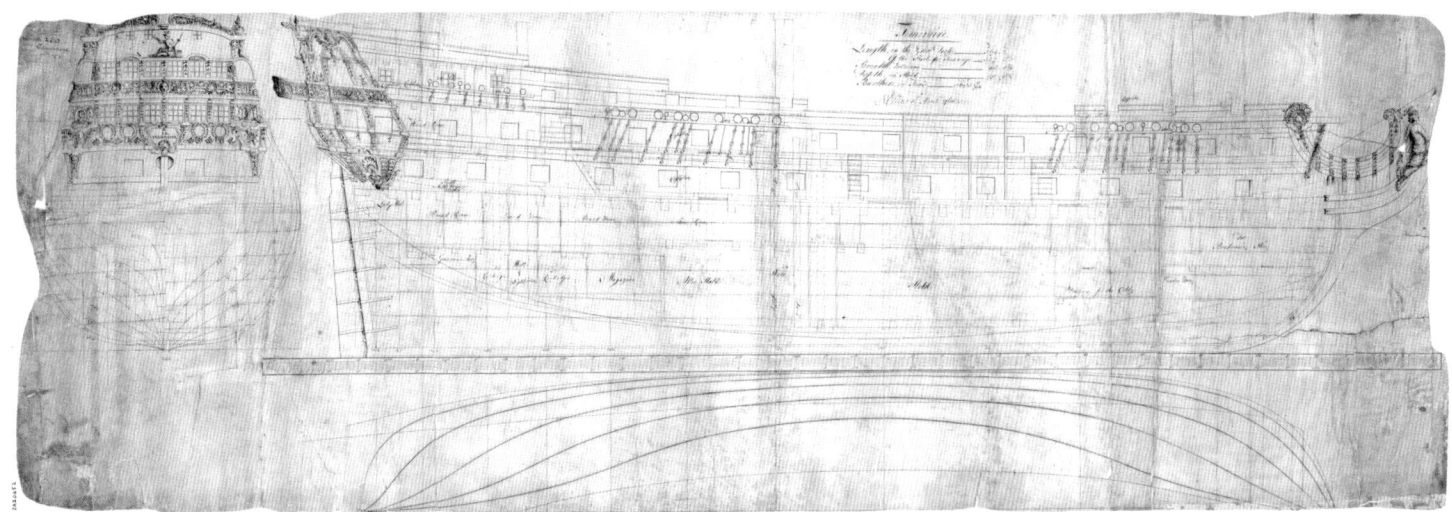

Admiralty draught of *Temeraire*, dated 5 March 1760, produced as part of the survey of the captured ship. The order to purchase the ship for British service followed on 19 March. At this period, the 'as captured' plans often included fairly detailed renditions of the ship's decorative works, as in this example. (National Maritime Museum, London J2385)

FLORISSANT Class. 74 guns. Designed and built by Pierre Morineau.
  Dimensions & tons: 166ft 0in x 45ft 0in x 22ft 3in (53.92 x 14.62 x 7.23m). 1,500/2,790 tons. Draught 20½/22½ft (6.66/7.31m).
  Men: 715 in war, 650 peace, +6/12 officers.
  Guns: 74 in war (70 peace): LD 28 x 36pdrs; UD 30 x 18pdrs; QD 10 x 8pdrs; Fc 6 x 8pdrs.
Florissant Rochefort Dyd.
  K: 4.1748. L: 18.7.1750. C: 3.1751. Took part in Battle of Minorca 20.5.1756. Pursued by the British while returning from Martinique and took refuge at Cadiz 9.1759, in bad condition 9.1761, condemned there 9.1762.
Prudent Rochefort Dyd.
  K: 8.1751. L: 28.7.1753. C: 10.1754. Captured by boat action at Louisbourg 26.7.1758 while most of her crew was fighting ashore and burnt.

The destruction of the *Prudent* in Louisbourg harbour on 27 June 1758. The ship was captured by the crews of British boats, but being hard aground, could not be moved so was set on fire. The British were able to take away the 64-gun *Bienfaisant* on the right. Most of the crews of both ships were fighting ashore. Engraving after a painting by Richard Paton, published in February 1771. (Beverley R Robinson Collection, Annapolis 51.7.144)

REDOUTABLE. 74 guns. The final 74 to be designed by François Coulomb Jnr, lengthened from his *Téméraire* design; built by Noël Pomet following Coulomb's death. Ordered on 26 January 1749 and named on 17 June 1749.

  Dimensions & tons: 163ft 6in x 43ft 0in x 21ft 0in (53.11 x 13.97 x 6.50m). 1,580/2,800 tons. Draught 19ft (6.2m). Men: 680, +6/13 officers.

  Guns: 74 in war (70 peace): LD 28 x 36pdrs; UD 30 x 18pdrs; QD 10 x 8pdrs; Fc 6 x 8pdrs.

Redoutable Toulon Dyd.

  K: 12.1749. L: 5.5.1752. C: 1.1753. Took part in the Battle off Minorca 20.5.1756 (as flagship of CdE Pierre-André, Commandeur de Glandevès-Castellet) and the Battle of Lagos 18.8.1759; sought refuge under the Portuguese guns 19.8.1759 but was then burnt by the British.

ALGONKIN. 72 guns. Designed and built by René-Nicolas Levasseur. France's first (and only) attempt to build a 2nd Rank ship in Canada, but she was only armed with 24pdrs (*vice* 36pdrs) and 12pdrs (*vice* 18pdrs). Comments made upon her arrival at Brest (in November 1753) were that her gunports were too small and situated too close together.

  Dimensions & tons: 160ft 0in, 135ft 0in x 44ft 0in x 22ft 0in (51.97, 43.85 x 14.29 x 7.15m). 1,400/2,700 tons. Draught unknown.

  Guns: LD 28 x 24pdrs; UD 30 x 12pdrs; QD/Fc 14 x 8pdrs.

Algonkin Quebec.

  K: 10.1750. L: 3.7.1753. C: 9.1753. Condemned 1758 at Brest and hulked there. Not mentioned after 1784 but not BU until 1815.

PALMIER Class. 74 guns. Designed and built by Joseph Véronique-Charles Chapelle.

  Dimensions & tons: 163ft 8in, 144ft 5in x 43ft 0in x 20ft 6in (53.17, 46.91 x 13.97 x 6.66m). 1,500/2,800 tons. Draught 19½ft/21ft (6.33/6.82m). Men: 715 war, 650 in peace, +6/10 officers.

  Guns: LD 28 x 36pdrs; UD 30 x 18pdrs; QD 10 x 8pdrs; Fc 6 x 8pdrs.

Palmier Brest Dyd.

  K: 11.1750. L: 21.7.1752. C: 10.1752. Ordered rebuilt 23.6.1766 at Brest on the proportions of *Conquerant* because her timbers were so rotten that it was not possible to save any for a refit. (see below).

Héros Brest Dyd.

  K: 11.1750. L: 1.9.1752. C: 10.1752. Took part in Battle of Quiberon Bay 20.11.1759, where grounded at Croisic and was burnt by the British 21.11.1759.

COURAGEUX. 74 guns. Designed and built by Jean Geoffroy.

  Dimensions & tons: 163ft 0in x 44ft 0in x 20ft 0in (52.95 x 14.29 x 6.50m). 1,500/2,800 tons. Draught 19ft/21ft (6.17/6.82m). Men: 600 in war, 550 peace, +6 officers.

  Guns: LD 28 x 36pdrs; UD 30 x 18pdrs; QD 10 x 8pdrs; Fc 6 x 8pdrs.

Courageux Brest Dyd.

  K: 4.1751. L: 11.10.1753. C: 1754. Captured by HMS *Bellona* off Vigo 14.8.1761, becoming HMS *Courageous*. Wrecked near Gibraltar 12.1796.

DÉFENSEUR. 74 guns. Designed and built by Pierre Salinoc.

  Dimensions & tons: 164ft 0in x 44ft 0in x 21ft 0in (53.27 x 14.29 x 6.82m). 1,500/2,800 tons. Draught 19ft/22ft (6.17/7.15m). Men: 600 in war, 550 peace, +6 officers.

  Guns: LD 28 x 36pdrs; UD 30 x 18pdrs; QD 10 x 8pdrs; Fc 6 x 8pdrs.

Défenseur Brest Dyd.

  K: 6.1752. L: 6.3.1754. C: 10.1754. Out of service 1773 at Brest, and in 1775 a rebuilding was projected (see below) but not effected; not mentioned after 1778.

HECTOR. 74 guns. Designed and begun by Pierre-Blaise Coulomb, the *Hector* was named on 2 July 1751. After he died on 21 December 1753, building of the *Hector* was completed by his nephew Joseph-Marie-Blaise Coulomb, who later built *Centaure* to a derivative of this design. Largely (50 per cent) rebuilt at Toulon 1766–68.

  Dimensions & tons: 164ft 0in, 145ft 6in x 43ft 0in x 20ft 6in (53.27, 47.26 x 13.97 x 6.66m). 1,450/2,800 tons. Draught 19ft 11in/21ft 11in (6.47/7.12m). Men: 620 (later 734), +6/10 officers.

  Guns: LD 28 x 36pdrs; UD 30 x 18pdrs; QD 10 x 8pdrs; Fc 6 x 8pdrs.

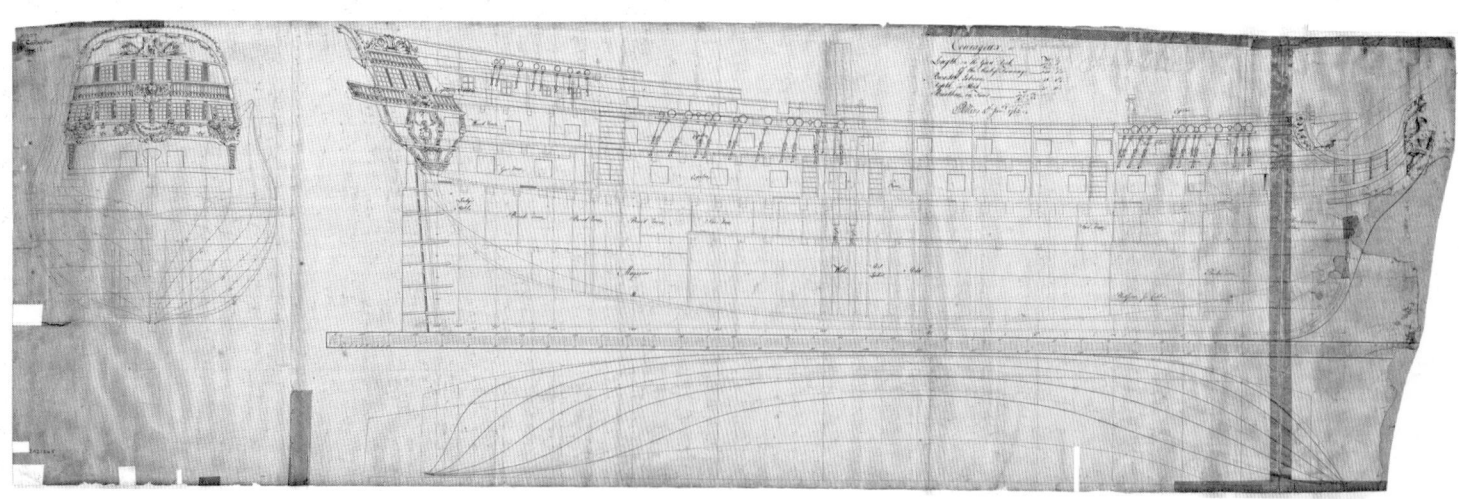

Admiralty draught of the *Courageux*, dated 4 January 1762. The usual practice with important prizes was to carry out a thorough survey which concluded with taking off the lines and producing a draught showing the ship as captured. This formed the basis of the Admiralty decision on whether or not to purchase the ship for Royal Navy service. *Courageux* proved to be a very highly regarded ship, her hull form providing inspiration for some British designs for half a century. This frequent recourse to the original draught may explain its present poor condition. (National Maritime Museum, London J3199)

THE SECOND RANK

Hector Toulon Dyd.
  K: 7.1752. L: 23.7.1755. C: 5.1756. Took part in Battle of the Chesapeake 5.9.1781, St Kitts 25/26.1.1782, and the Saintes 12.4.1782, when captured by HM Ships *Canada* and *Alcide* of Rodney's fleet, then in action 5.9.1782 against frigates *Aigle* and *Gloire*. Abandoned in sinking condition off Newfoundland 3.10.1782.

GLORIEUX. 74 guns. Designed and built by François-Guillaume Clairain-Deslauriers.
  Dimensions & tons: 164ft 0in x 43ft 0in x 20ft 7in (53.27 x 13.97 x 6.69m). 1,500/2,765 tons. Draught 19½ft/21½ft (6.33/6.98m). Men: 734 (later 750) +6 officers.
  Guns: LD 28 x 36pdrs; UD 30 x 18pdrs; QD 10 x 8pdrs; Fc 6 x 8pdrs.
Glorieux Rochefort Dyd.
  K: 7.1753. L: 10.8.1756. C: 11.1756. Took part in Battle of Quiberon Bay 20.11.1759, 3rd Battle of Ushant 27.7.1778, at Battles of Chesapeake 5.9.1781, of St Kitts 25/26.1.1782 and finally of the Saintes 12.4.1782, where captured by Rodney's fleet, becoming HMS *Glorieux*; foundered 18.9.1782 in a hurricane with all hands off Newfoundland.

DIADÈME Class. 74 guns. Designed and built by Jacques-Luc Coulomb (brother of Pierre-Blaise). All named 10 September 1755. *Minotaure* was partly rebuilt at Brest during 1766 by Joseph-Louis Ollivier, and *Diadème* by Jean Geoffroy from 1766 to 1767.
  Dimensions & tons: 168ft 0in x 43ft 6in x 20ft 6in (54.57 x 14.13 x 6.66m). 1,500/2,800 tons. Draught 19½ft/21ft (6.33/6.82m). Men: 734 (later 750), +6/9 officers.
  Guns: LD 28 x 36pdrs; UD 30 x 18pdrs; QD 10 x 8pdrs; Fc 6 x 8pdrs. *Brutus* in 1794: LD 28 x 36pdrs; QD/Fc 14 x 18pdrs.
Diadème Brest Dyd.
  K: 9.1755. L: 26.6.1756. C: 11.1756. Took part in 3rd Battle of Ushant 27.7.1778, and in Battles of the Chesapeake 5.9.1781, St Kitts 25/26.1.1782 and the Saintes 12.4.1782. Renamed *Brutus* 29.9.1792, and raséed from 12.1793 to 5.1794 to a 42-gun ship. BU 1797 at Brest.
Zodiaque Brest Dyd.
  K: 10.1755. L: 19.11.1756. C: 2.1757. Took part in 3rd Battle of Ushant 27.7.1778. Sold 1784.

Minotaure Brest Dyd.
  K: 4.1756. L: 4.1757. C: 2.1758. Floating battery at St Domingue 7.1781. Hulked 1785 at Brest (by order of 31.7.1782) and sold there to BU 6.1787.

SOUVERAIN Class. 74 guns. Designed and built by Noël Pomet. Named on 25 October 1755 and 10 September 1755 (the latter relayed by ministerial despatch of 24 October) respectively. *Souverain* was reconstructed at Toulon from 26 September 1778 to 25 June 1779.
  Dimensions & tons: 164ft 0in x 43ft 6in x 21ft 6in (53.27 x 14.13 x 6.98m). 1,536/2,800 tons. Draught 19ft/22ft (6.17/7.15m). Men: 715 in war, 650 peace, +6/12 officers.
  Guns: LD 28 x 36pdrs; UD 30 x 18pdrs; QD 10 x 8pdrs; Fc 6 x 8pdrs.
Souverain Toulon Dyd.
  K: 11.1755. L: 6.6.1757. C: 11.1757. Took part in Battle of Lagos 8.1759. Tool part in Battles of Chesapeake 5.9.1781, St Kitts 25/26.1.1782 and the Saintes 12.4.1782. Renamed *Peuple Souverain* 9.1792. Refitted at Toulon 6.1794 to 2.1795; handed over to Anglo-Spanish forces at Toulon in 8.1793, but restored to France at the evacuation of that city in 12.1793. Captured by Nelson's squadron at Aboukir 1.8.1798, becoming HMS *Guerrier*; hulked at Gibraltar 1799 until BU in 1810.
Protecteur Toulon Dyd.
  K: 29.5.1757. L: 21.5.1760. C: 4.1762. Hulked as hospital ship at Rochefort 1784.

CENTAURE. 74 guns. Designed and built by Joseph-Marie-Blaise Coulomb, to a design derived from and almost identical with the *Hector* of 1751 (the dimensions were precisely the same). Named 25 October 1755.

Admiralty draught of the *Centaure* as captured. It is endorsed 'Purchased 7 Jan 1760' and 'was then about 6 months launched' – the ship had actually been in service nearly two years so was clearly in very good condition. Built by Joseph-Marie-Blaise Coulomb, who was named as *Constructeur* at Toulon in the month of her launch, a post he retained until 1786, although the title was redesignated as *Ingénieur-constructeur* in April 1765. Her original plan of 1755, conserved in the archives at Toulon, is for one of the six orders for 74-gun ships that Jean-Baptiste de Machault, the Secretary of the Navy approved and signed that autumn. (National Maritime Museum, London J2607)

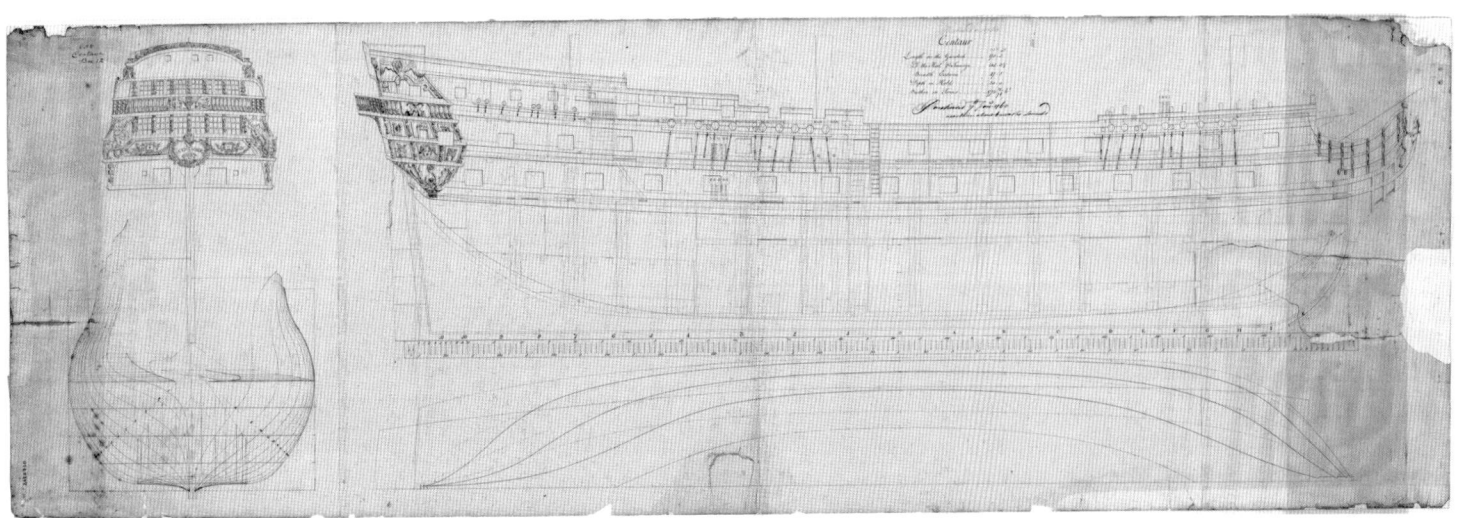

Dimensions & tons: 164ft 0in, 145ft 6in x 43ft 0in x 20ft 6in (53.27, 47.26 x 13.97 x 6.66m). 1,450/2,800 tons. Draught 19ft 11in/21ft 11in (6.47/7.12m). Men: 620 (later 734), +6/10 officers.

Guns: LD 28 x 36pdrs; UD 30 x 18pdrs; QD 10 x 8pdrs; Fc 6 x 8pdrs.

Centaure Toulon Dyd.
K: 2.1756. L: 17.3.1757. C: 10.1757. Captured by Boscawen's fleet at the Battle of Lagos 18.8.1759, becoming HMS *Centaur*; foundered off Newfoundland 24.9.1782.

THÉSÉE. 74 guns. Designed and built by Pierre Salinoc (or possibly Jean Geoffroy).

Dimensions & tons: 164ft 0in, 146ft 0in x 44ft 0in x 22ft 0in (53.27, 47.43 x 14.29 x 7.15m). 1,500/2,800 tons. Draught 19ft/22ft (6.17/7.15m). Men: 734 in war, 650 peace, +6/12 officers.

Guns: LD 28 x 36pdrs; UD 30 x 18pdrs; QD 10 x 8pdrs; Fc 6 x 8pdrs.

Thésée Brest Dyd.
K: 5.1757. L: 28.1.1759. C: 5.1759. Capsized and foundered at Battle of Quiberon Bay 20.11.1759, due to failure to close the LD ports; barely 20 survivors.

ROBUSTE. 74 guns. Designed by Antoine Groignard, and named 25 September 1755; built by the *Compagnie des Indes* at its Lorient dockyard for the French Navy. The order replaced one for a 64-gun 3rd Rank of the same name, which had been ordered at Brest Dyd on 10 September 1755, but was moved to Lorient in December 1756 (see Chapter 3).

Dimensions & tons: 175ft 0in x 44ft 4in x 21ft 10in (56.85 x 14.40 x 7.09m). 1,600/3,000 tons. Draught 20ft/21½ft (6.50/6.98m). Men: 715 in war, 650 peace, +6/12 officers.

Guns: LD 28 x 36pdrs; UD 30 x 18pdrs; QD 10 x 8pdrs; Fc 6 x 8pdrs.

Robuste Lorient Dyd.
K: 10.1757. L: 2.9.1758. C: 4.1759. Took part in Battle of Quiberon Bay 20.11.1759, and in 3rd Battle of Ushant 27.7.1778 (as flagship of CdE François-Joseph Paul, Comte de Grasse). Condemned 1783 at Brest and BU there 1784.

ORION. 74 guns. A ship to a design (dated June 1757) by Pierre Morineau, to have been built by his nephew François-Guillaume Clairain-Deslauriers, was ordered from Rochefort Dyd in May 1757 and named on 29 May 1757. She would have measured 166ft, 152ft x 45ft x 21ft 10½in (53.92, 48.73 x 14.62 x 7.11m) and 1,500/3,011 tons, and carried the standard 74-gun ordnance of this date. With her were ordered *Astronome* (below), *Résolu* (64) and the frigate *Revêche*. In 1760 all of these orders were cancelled on account of shortage of both money and suitable timber.

ASTRONOME. 70 guns. A ship to a smaller design by François-Guillaume Clairain-Deslauriers, was ordered from Rochefort Dyd and named at the same time as the *Orion*. Her intended characteristics are set out below. In 1760 the order – like that for the *Orion* – was cancelled on account of shortage of both money and suitable timber.

Dimensions & tons: 153ft 0in, 138ft 0in x 42ft 0in x 21ft 0in (49.70, 44.83 x 13.64 x 6.82m). .../2,300 tons. Draught 18ft/19¼ft (5.85/6.25m).

Guns: LD 28 x 24pdrs; UD 30 x 18pdrs; QD/Fc 12 x 8pdrs.

Ex-TURKISH PURCHASE. 74 guns. This ship was originally the Ottoman *Osmanli Tac*, built in Instanbul. She was captured in September 1760 by escaping slaves at Cos, and purchased in August 1761 by France as *Couronne Ottomane*, becoming the Maltese *San Salvadore* in January 1762 and eventually restored to the Ottomans as *Sultane*. No technical details known except that she carried LD 28 guns, UD 30 guns and *gaillards* 16 guns.

DILIGENT Class. 74 guns. Designed by Antoine Groignard (a modified version of the *Robuste* design) and built by the *Compagnie des Indes* in the Caudan expansion of its Lorient dockyard. The *Diligent* was funded by the *Régisseurs des Postes*. The second ship was funded by the *Six Corps* of the merchants of Paris. Her only sea service was probably her transit from Lorient to Brest in 1763.

Dimensions & tons: 176ft 0in x 43ft 0in x 20ft 6in (57.17 x 13.97 x 6.66m). 1,600/3,000 tons. Draught 19½ft/21ft (6.33/6.82m). Men: 715 in war, 650 peace, +6/12 officers.

Guns: LD 28 x 36pdrs; UD 30 x 18pdrs; QD 10 x 8pdrs; Fc 6 x 8pdrs.

Diligent Lorient-Caudan.
K: 4.1762. L: 11.1762. C: 8.1763. Condemned 21.6.1779 at Brest and BU there 11.1779.

Six Corps Lorient-Caudan.
K: 4.1762. L: 29.12.1762. C: 9.1763. Condemned 21.6.1779 at Brest and BU there 11.1779.

CITOYEN Class. 74 guns. Designed by Joseph-Louis Ollivier. The first ship was funded by the Army Bankers (*Banquiers et Trésoriers Généraux de l'Armée*), and was named *Cimeterre* in May 1757; renamed *Citoyen* 20 January 1762; originally planned launching was 10 August 1764, but she stuck on the ways at that attempt. The *Conquérant* was a rebuilding from 17 March 1764 (in the basin at Brest) of the 74-gun ship launched in 1746 (see above) to the design of the *Citoyen*. The *Palmier* was likewise rebuilt from 23 June 1766 (in a basin at Pontaniou, Brest) by Ollivier from the 74-gun ship launched in 1752, while the *Actif* was rebuilt in the same location from the remains of the previous 64-gun *Actif* of 1752 (see next chapter). *Palmier* and *Actif* were reconstructed again at Brest in 1776 and 1774 respectively.

Dimensions & tons: 169ft 6in x 43ft 0in x 20ft 9in (55.06 x 13.97 x 6.74m). 1,500/3,000 tons. Draught 19½ft/21ft (6.33/6.82m). Men: 715 in war, 650 peace, +6/12 officers.

Guns: LD 28 x 36pdrs; UD 30 x 18pdrs; QD 10 x 8pdrs; Fc 6 x 8pdrs.

Citoyen Brest Dyd.
K: 7.1761. L: 27.8.1764. C: 12.1764. Took part in Battles of the Chesapeake 5.9.1781, of St Kitts 25/26.1.1782 and of the Saintes 12.4.1782. BU ordered 1790, last mentioned 3.1791.

Conquérant Brest Dyd.
K: 1.1765. L: 29.11.1765. C: 12.1765. Took part in 3rd Battle of Ushant 27.7.1778 (as flagship of CdE François-Aymar, Baron de Monteil), in Battle off Cape Henry 16.3.1781, and in Battles of St Kitts 25/26.1.1782 and the Saintes 12.4.1782. Captured by Nelson's fleet at Aboukir 2.8.1798, becoming HMS *Conquerant* (hospital ship). BU 1803.

Palmier Brest Dyd.
K: 5.1766. L: 12.1766. C: 12.1766. Took part in 3rd Battle of Ushant 27.7.1778 and in in Battles of the Chesapeake 5.9.1781, St Kitts 25/26.1.1782 and the Saintes 12.4.1782. Wrecked in a storm off Bermuda 24.10.1782.

Actif Brest Dyd.
K: 4.1767. L: 5.10.1767. C: 4.1768. Took part in 3rd Battle of Ushant 27.7.1778. Sold 1784 to BU.

ZÉLÉ. 74 guns. Designed and built by Joseph-Marie-Blaise Coulomb, and funded by the *Receveurs Généraux des Finances* (Tax-collectors).

Named on 9 December 1761. Work was suspended in July 1762 due to shortage of labour, but later resumed.

Dimensions: 170ft 6in, 151ft 6in x 43ft 6in x 20ft 9in (55.39, 49.21 x 14.13 x 6.74m). 1,500/2,900 tons. Draught 19½ft/20ft 8in (6.33/6.71m). Men: 715 in war, 650 peace, +6/12 officers.

Guns: LD 28 x 36pdrs; UD 30 x 18pdrs; QD 10 x 8pdrs; Fc 6 x 8pdrs.

Zélé Toulon Dyd.
K: 2.1762. L: 1.7.1763. C: 1764. Took part in Battles of the Chesapeake 5.9.1781 and St Kitts 25/26.1.1782. Ordered BU 12.11.1804, then ordered hulked 8.1.1805 at Brest, renamed *Réserve*, entered dock to BU 1.5.1806.

BOURGOGNE. 74 guns. Designed by Noël Pomet, and funded by the *États de Bourgogne* (Burgundy Estates); ordered and named on 16 January 1762 (originally to have been of 80 guns). Reconstructed (2/3rds) from August 1777 to October 1778 at Toulon.

Dimensions & tons: 168ft 0in, 146ft 0in x 43ft 6in x 21ft 6in (54.57, 47.43 x 14.13 x 6.98m). 1,550/2,900 tons. Draught 20½ft/23ft (6.66/7.47m). Men: 715 in war, 650 peace, +6/12 officers.

Guns: LD 28 x 36pdrs; UD 30 x 18pdrs; QD 10 x 8pdrs; Fc 6 x 8pdrs.

Bourgogne Toulon Dyd.
K: 31.1.1762. L: 26.6.1766. C: 11.1767. Took part in Battles of the Chesapeake 5.9.1781, St Kitts 25/26.1.1782 and the Saintes 12.4.1782. Wrecked 4.2.1783 on the Venezuelan coast near Curaçao, with 900 of Rochambeau's troops from America on board, of whom 100 were lost.

MARSEILLAIS. 74 guns. Designed by Joseph-Marie-Blaise Coulomb, and built by Joseph Véronique-Charles Chapelle, she was funded by the City of Marseille; ordered in 1761 and named 16 January 1762, but construction was delayed through shortage of timber. Her figurehead was sculpted by Pierre Audibert. Reconstructed (2/3rds) from 1772 to 1776 at Toulon.

Dimensions & tons: 168ft 0in, 146ft 6in x 43ft 6in x 21ft 0in (54.57, 47.59 x 14.13 x 6.82m). 1,550/2,900 tons. Draught 19½ft/20ft 8in (6.33/6.71m). Men: 715 in war, 650 peace, +6/12 officers.

Guns: LD 28 x 36pdrs; UD 30 x 18pdrs; QD 10 x 8pdrs; Fc 6 x 8pdrs. In 1793, 4 x 36pdr carronades were added to the *gaillards* armament.

Marseillais (Marseillois) Toulon Dyd.
K: 2.1763. L: 16.7.1766. C: 11.1767. Took part in Battles of the Chesapeake 5.9.1781, St Kitts 25/26.1.1782 and the Saintes 12.4.1782. Renamed *Vengeur du Peuple* 2.1794. Surrendered following action with HMS *Brunswick* during Battle of 'Glorious First of June' 1794 and then sank, with 391 dead and 270 survivors.

The 80-gun *Orient* of 1756–57 (see Chapter 1) was rebuilt by Jean Geoffroy in 1765–66 at Brest as a 74-gun ship of 1,650 tons, with one pair of guns removed from each level, and was re-classed as a 2nd Rank.

CÉSAR Class. 74 guns. Designed and built by Joseph-Marie-Blaise Coulomb, as a modification of his *Zélé* design, with a longer keel. *César* was ordered in 1767 and named on 10 March 1767. A second ship to this design was ordered from Toulon in December 1769, but no name was issued, and that order was cancelled in March 1770. Instead, *Destin* was ordered on 7 February 1770 and named on 20 March.

Dimensions: 168ft 6in, 157ft 6in x 43ft 6in x 20ft 9in (54.74, 51.16 x 14.13 x 6.74m). 1,500/2,900 tons. Draught 19½ft/20ft 8in (6.33/6.71m). Men: 715 in war (later 734), 650 peace, +6/12 officers.

Guns: LD 28 x 36pdrs; UD 30 x 18pdrs; QD 10 x 8pdrs; Fc 6 x 8pdrs.

César Toulon Dyd.
K: 7.1767. L: 3.8.1768. C: 11.1768. Took part in Battles of the Chesapeake 5.9.1781, St Kitts 25/26.1.1782 and of the Saintes 12.4.1782, where captured by HMS *Centaur* but blew up immediately after.

Destin Toulon Dyd.
K: 4.1770. L: 21.10.1777. C: 6.1778. Took part in Battles of the Chesapeake 5.9.1781, St Kitts 25/26.1.1782 and the Saintes 12.4.1782. Handed over to Anglo-Spanish forces at the occupation of Toulon 8.1793, but burnt by the British on the evacuation of that port 18.12.1793.

BIEN AIMÉ Class. 74 guns. Designed and built by Antoine Groignard for the *Compagnie des Indes*, but purchased 1769 while under construction by Le Frété-Bernard, following the 'nationalisation' of the former *Compagnie* shipyard at Lorient.

Lines plan of the 74-gun *Bien Aimé* and *Victoire* of 1769–70, drawn by László Veres from a Danish copy of the original plans in the Orlogsvaerftet, Copenhagen. French design draughts traditionally omitted all but the essential lines – even the outline of the quarter galleries – because external decorative details were the subject of separate drawings. This practice dates from Louis XIV's time, when the naval architecture of the ship and its decorative scheme were the responsibilities of different individuals.

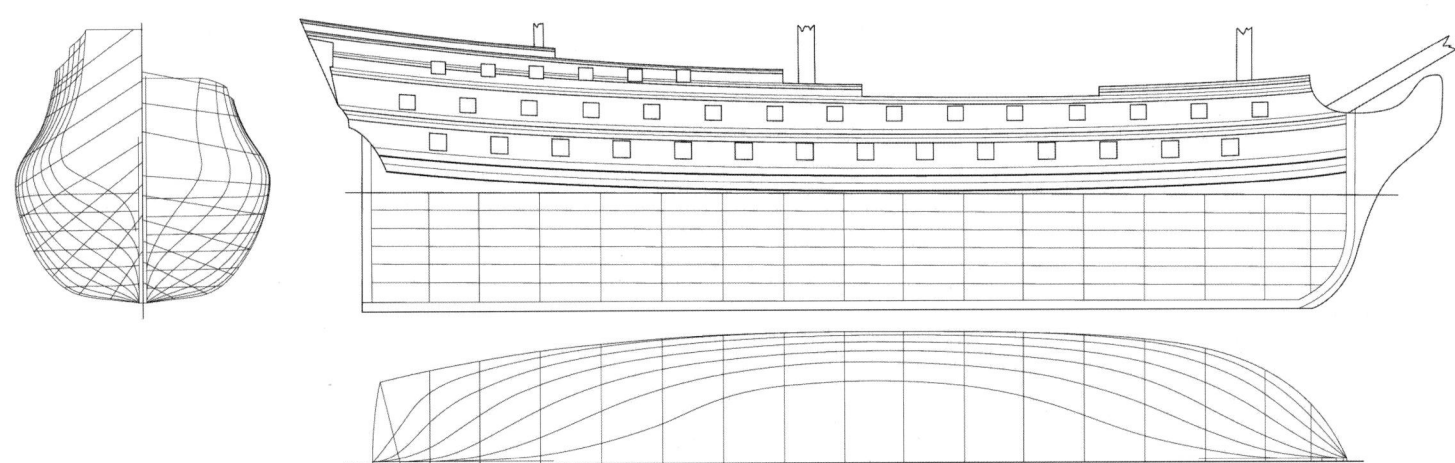

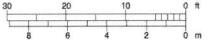

Dimensions: 170ft 0in, 160ft 0in x 43ft 6in x 21ft 5in (55.22, 51.97 x 14.13 x 6.96m). 1,500/2,884 tons. Draught 20ft/21ft 2in (6.50/6.88m). Men: 715 in war (later 734), 650 peace, +6/12 officers.

Guns: LD 28 x 36pdrs; UD 30 x 18pdrs; QD 10 x 8pdrs; Fc 6 x 8pdrs.

Bien Aimé Lorient.
K: 3.1768. L: 22.3.1769. C: 11.1769. Took part in 3rd Battle of Ushant 27.7.1778. Condemned 1783 at Brest.

Victoire Lorient.
K: 8.1768. L: 4.10.1770. C: early 1771. Took part in Action off Dominica 17.4.1780 and Battle of the Chesapeake 5.9.1781. Condemned 7.1792 at Brest and BU 1793.

FENDANT. Designed by Antoine Groignard, with a reduced length compared with his *Bien Aimé* Class. Built at Rochefort by Jean-Denis Chevillard. Refitted at Rochefort from February to March 1778.

Dimensions: 164ft 0in, 150ft 0in x 44ft 0in x 22ft 0in (53.27, 48.73 x 14.29 x 7.15m). 1,500/2,884 tons. Draught 20½ft/22½ft (6.66/7.31m). Men: 715 in war (later 734), 650 peace, +12/17 officers.

Guns: LD 28 x 36pdrs; UD 30 x 18pdrs; QD 10 x 8pdrs; Fc 6 x 8pdrs.

Fendant Rochfort Dyd.
K: 5.1772. L: 11.11.1776. C: 2.1777. Took part in 3rd Battle of Ushant 27.7.1778, and in Battle of Cuddalore 20.6.1783 as part of Suffren's squadron. Condemned at Île-de-France (Mauritius) 10.1785 as 'completely decayed'.

Orders for further 74s ceased in the early 1770s, but resumed again following the American Declaration of Independence as France prepared for war in support of the insurrectionists. The rebuilding of one 74-gun ship projected in 1775 was cancelled, but twenty-nine new ships were ordered between late 1777 and June of 1782, and a further five in 1784–85.

DÉFENSEUR. 74 guns. This vessel of 1754 (see above) was intended in May 1775 to be rebuilt to a design by Joseph-Louis Ollivier, but the scheme was abandoned in October with no work having begun, and the ship was BU.

Dimensions & tons: 170ft 0in, 152ft 0in x 43ft 6in x 20ft 0in (55.23, 49.38 x 14.13 x 6.50m). 1,500/3,099 tons.

Guns: LD 28 x 36pdrs; UD 30 x 18pdrs; QD 10 x 8pdrs; Fc 6 x 8pdrs.

NEPTUNE. 74 guns. A one-off design by Pierre-Augustin Lamothe in 1778, one of the first two new 74s to be ordered after a gap of some five years, and named on 20 February 1778.

Dimensions & tons: 168ft 6in, 146ft 6in x 44ft 0in x 22ft 0in (54.74, 47.59 x 14.29 x 7.15m). 1,500/2,856 tons. Draught 19½/20½ft (6.33/6.66m). Men: 734 in war, 650 peace, +12/17 officers.

Guns: LD 28 x 36pdrs; UD 30 x 18pdrs; QD 10 x 8pdrs; Fc 6 x 8pdrs. From 1793 carried 20 x 8pdrs +4 x 36pdr *obusiers* on the *gaillards*.

Neptune Brest Dyd.
K: 12.1777. L: 20.8.1778. C: 16.9.1778. Took part in Action off Cape Henry 16.3.1781 and in Battles of the Saintes 12.4.1782 and of 13 Prairial ('Glorious First of June') 1794. Wrecked in a storm off the north coast of Brittany 28.1.1795.

ANNIBAL Class. Jacques-Noël Sané's original design, dated 24 November 1777, was for a ship of 166ft length and 2,793 tons displacement, with a freeboard (height of LD sills above the waterline at normal load) of 5½ft. The *Annibal* was named on 20 February 1778, at the same time as the *Neptune*. Sané's amended plan for her was dated 10 January 1779. His plan for her near-sister *Northumberland*, which was a foot longer and 26 tons more in displacement than the *Annibal's* dimensions quoted below, was dated 3 March 1780. Both ships had a freeboard of 5ft. They were both captured by Howe's fleet at the battle on the Glorious First of June 1794 off Ushant, and were briefly commissioned into the British Navy before being taken to pieces.

Dimensions & tons: 168ft 0in, 151ft 6in x 44ft 0in x 21ft 6in (54.57, 49.21 x 14.29 x 6.98m). 1,478/2,939 tons. Draught 20ft 2in/22ft 2in (6.55/7.20m). Men: 734 in war, 690 peace, +12/17 officers.

Guns: LD 28 x 36pdrs; UD 30 x 18pdrs; QD 10 x 8pdrs; Fc 6 x 8pdrs. In 1793, 4 x 36pdr *obusiers* were added.

Annibal Brest Dyd.

Admiralty draught of the *Achille*, taken off at Plymouth Yard in August 1795. As the *Annibal* the ship had given long and arduous service in the East Indies, which had left her in poor condition, so she was not taken into British service. *Achille* was broken up early the following year. The draught shows an early example of the elegant stern with its horseshoe-shaped taffrail favoured by Sané, a more restrained classically-influenced design that finally broke with the more 'architectural' forms of earlier decades. (National Maritime Museum, London J2641)

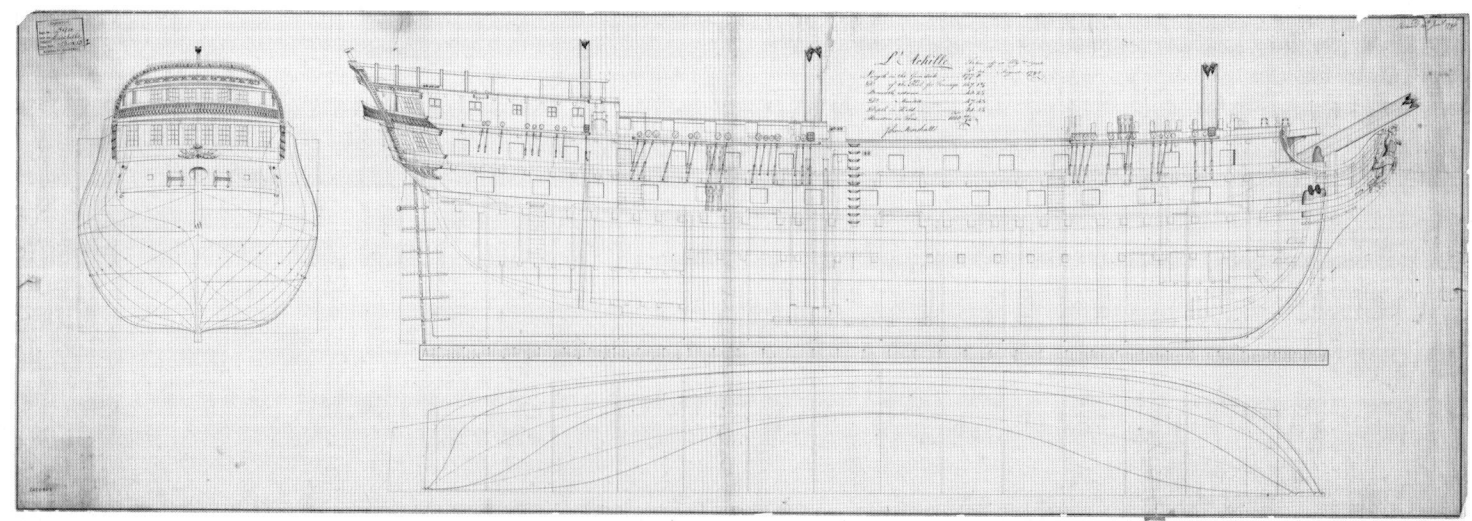

K: 12.1777. L: 5.10.1778. C: 1.1779. Took part in Battles of Porto Praya 16.4.1781, Sadras 17.2.1782, Providien (Trincomalee) 12.4.1782, Negapatam 3.7.1782, Trincomalee 3.9.1782 and Cuddalore 20.6.1783 as part of Suffren's squadron. Renamed *Achille* 21.1.1786. Took part in Battle of 13 Prairial ('Glorious First of June') 1794, where dismasted and captured (with 36 men killed) by HMS *Ramilles*, becoming HMS *Achille*; BU at Plymouth 2.1796.

Northumberland Brest Dyd.
K: 24.2.1779. L: 3.5.1780. C: 7.1780. Took part in Battles of the Chesapeake 5.9.1781, St Kitts 25/26.1.1782, the Saintes 12.4.1782 and of 13 Prairial ('Glorious First of June') 1794; dismasted and captured at the last of these (with 60 men killed), becoming HMS *Northumberland*; BU at Plymouth 11.1795.

SCIPION Class. François-Guillaume Clairain-Deslauriers design, 1778. The design of these ships was found to lack stability, and a further pair of orders placed at this port were considerably lengthened (see *Argonaute* Class below). All three were 'girdled' (sheathed) with 32cm of pine at Rochefort from March to May 1779 to overcome their instability.

Dimensions & tons: 165ft 6in, ?155ft 0in x 43ft 6in x 21ft 6in (53.76, ?50.35 x 14.13 x 6.98m). 1,424/2,943 tons. Draught 20ft 2in/22ft 6in (6.55/7.31m). Men: 662/750.

Guns: LD 28 x 36pdrs; UD 30 x 18pdrs; QD 10 x 8pdrs; Fc 6 x 8pdrs.

Scipion Rochefort Dyd.
K: 10.4.1778. L: 19.9.1778. C: 2.1779. Took part in the Battle of the Chesapeake 5.9.1781 and the Saintes 12.4.1782. Wrecked in Samana Bay (St Domingue) 19.10.1782.

Hercule Rochefort Dyd.
K: 1.4.1778. L: 5.10.1778. C: 2.1779. Took part in the Battles of the Chesapeake 5.9.1781, St Kitts 25/26.1.1782 and the Saintes 12.4.1782. Raséed 2.1794–6.1794, and renamed *Hydre* 5.1795. Condemned 1797 and BU 1799.

Pluton Rochefort Dyd (*Constructeur*, Henri Chevillard)
K: 10.4.1778. L: 5.11.1778. C: 2.1779. Took part in the Battles of the Chesapeake 5.9.1781, St Kitts 25/26.1.1782 and the Saintes 12.4.1782. Intended rasée in 1794 was cancelled. Renamed *Dugommier* 17.12.1797. Condemned at Brest and ordered BU 7.1.1805.

HÉROS. A one-off design by Joseph-Marie-Blaise Coulomb, the *ingénieur-constructeur en chef* at Toulon from 1768; ordered on 29 November 1777 and named on 20 February 1778. Achieved fame as Suffren's flagship during the campaigns in the Indian Ocean from 1781 to 1783.

Dimensions: 169ft 0in, 149ft 0in x 43ft 6in x 21ft 0in (54.90, 48.40 x 14.13 x 6.82m). 1,500/2,800 tons. Draught 19 6in/21ft (6.33/6.82m). Men: 707/750.

Guns: LD 28 x 36pdrs; UD 30 x 18pdrs; QD 10 x 8pdrs; Fc 6 x 8pdrs.

Héros Toulon Dyd.
K: 10.5.1778. L: 30.12.1778. C: 5.1779. Took part in Battles of Porto Praya 16.4.1781, then of Sadras 17.2.1782, Providien (Trincomalee) 12.4.1782, Negapatam 3.7.1782, Trincomalee 3.9.1782 and Cuddalore (Gondelour) 20.6.1783, all as flagship of CdE Pierre André de Suffren's squadron. Handed over to the Anglo-Spanish forces at Toulon 8.1793, and burnt 18.12.1794 by the Allies at the evacuation of that port; remains raised and BU 1806.

The Battle of Providien (12 April 1782), focusing on the hard-fought engagement between the flagships, the French *Héros*, 74 and HMS *Monmouth*, 64, which was almost totally dismasted during the fighting. Engraving after a painting by Dominic Serres, published in October 1786. (Beverley R Robinson Collection, Annapolis 51.7.227)

MAGNANIME Class. Designed and built by Jean-Denis Chevillard.
Dimensions & tons: 171ft 3in, ?160ft 0in x 44ft 0in x 22ft 0in (55.63, ?51.97 x 14.29 x 7.15m). 1,500/2,950 tons. Draught 19/21ft (6.17/6.82m). Men: 660/750.
Guns: LD 28 x 36pdrs; UD 30 x 18pdrs; QD 10 x 8pdrs; Fc 6 x 8pdrs.

Magnanime Rochefort Dyd.
K: 10.1778. L: 27.8.1779. C: 12.1779. Took part in the Battles of the Chesapeake 5.9.1781, St Kitts 25/26.1.1782 and the Saintes 12.4.1782. Struck at Brest 1792 and BU there 1793.

Illustre Rochefort Dyd.
K: 8.1779. L: 23.2.1781. C: 3.1781. Took part in Battles of Trincomalee 3.9.1782 and Cuddalore 20.6.1783 as part of Suffren's squadron. Renamed *Mucius Scévola* 1.1791, shortened to *Scévola* 2.1794 and raséed 8.1793–2.1794. Wrecked in a storm 30.12.1796 during the attempted invasion of Ireland.

ARGONAUTE Class. This François-Guillaume Clairain-Deslauriers design, with length extended by 4½ft from his *Scipion* design of 1778, and broader by 6in to improve stability, was approved in June 1779. The designer died at Rochefort on 10 October 1780, and his work was completed by Jean-Denis Chevillard, who was appointed his successor as *ingénieur-constructeur en chef* at that dockyard in July 1781. Both ships were raséed at Brest in 1793–94 to become heavy frigates (see 1786–1861 volume for revised ordnance).
Dimensions & tons: 170ft 0in, 159ft 0in x 44ft 0in x 22ft 0in (55.22, 51.65 x 14.29 x 7.15). Draught 21ft/22¾ft (6.82/7.39m). Men: 658/751.
Guns: LD 28 x 36pdrs; UD 30 x 18pdrs; QD 10 x 8pdrs; Fc 6 x 8pdrs.

Argonaute Rochefort Dyd.
K: 8.1779. L: 5.6.1781. C: 12.1781. Took part in Battle of Cuddalore 20.6.1783 as part of Suffren's squadron. Raséed 12.1793-5.1794 and renamed *Flibustier* 6.1794. Disarmed 12.1795 and later BU.

Brave Rochefort Dyd.
K: 10.1779. L: 6.6.1781. C: 11.1781. Took part in Battle of the Saintes 12.4.1782. Hulked 1.1798 at Brest, and later BU.

SCEPTRE. A one-off design by Pierre-Augustin Lamothe in 1778, modified (and slightly enlarged, although GD length was shortened) from his design for the *Neptune*. Reconstructed 1787 at Brest, then 2.1795–2.1796 at Lorient.

Dimensions & tons: 166ft 6in, 151ft 0in x 44ft 3in x 21ft 6in. (54.09, 49.05 x 14.37 x 6.98 m) 1,585/2,996 tons. Draught 20ft 4in/22ft 4in (6.61/7.25 m) Men: 734 in war, 690 peace, +10/17 officers.
Guns: LD 28 x 36pdrs; UD 30 x 18pdrs; QD 10 x 8pdrs; Fc 6 x 8pdrs. From 1793 carried 20 x 8pdrs +4 x 36pdr *obusiers* on the *gaillards*.

Sceptre Brest Dyd.
K: 25.5.1780. L: 21.9.1780. C: 10.1780 (built and commissioned in 105 days). Took part in Battles of the Chesapeake 5.9.1781, St Kitts 25/26.1.1782 and the Saintes 12.4.1782. Renamed *Convention* 29.9.1792 and *Marengo* 8.1800. Took part in Battle of 13 Prairial ('Glorious First of June') 1794. Condemned 8.4.1803; ordered BU 9.11.1803, provisionally used as prison and raséed 11.1803 as a prison hospital. BU begun 31.12.1811.

PÉGASE Class. Antoine Groignard design, 1781. All six were ordered during the first half of 1781 and were named on 13 July 1781. The design lacked stability and the *Pégase* had to be girdled after completion. The name-ship of the class was captured by the British Navy just two months after her completion; the other five ships were all at Toulon in August 1793 when that port was handed over by French Royalists to the occupying Anglo-Spanish forces, and they were seized by the British Navy. When French Republican forces forced the evacuation of the Allies in December, the *Puissant* was sailed to England, and the *Liberté* (ex-*Dictateur*) and *Suffisant* were destroyed during the evacuation of the port; the remaining pair were recovered by the French Navy.
Dimensions & tons: 170ft 0in, 161ft 0in x 44ft 0in x 21ft 9in. (55.22, 52.30 x 14.29 x 7.07 m) 1,515/3,000 tons. Draught 19ft 6in/21ft (6.33/6.82 m). Men: 734 in war, 690 peace, +10/17 officers.
Guns: LD 28 x 36pdrs; UD 30 x 18pdrs; QD 10 x 8pdrs; Fc 6 x 8pdrs.

Pégase Brest Dyd.
K: 6.1781. L: 5.10.1781. C: 2.1782. Captured in the Bay of Biscay (with 80 men killed) by HMS *Foudroyant* of Barrington's squadron

Admiralty draught of the *Pégase*, taken off at Portsmouth Yard 27 June 1782 following her capture two months earlier. It was originally intended to commission the ship for active service as the draught shows proposed alterations to follow British practice, but she was employed as a guardship and then in various harbour roles until broken up at the end of the Napoleonic Wars. (National Maritime Museum, London J7692)

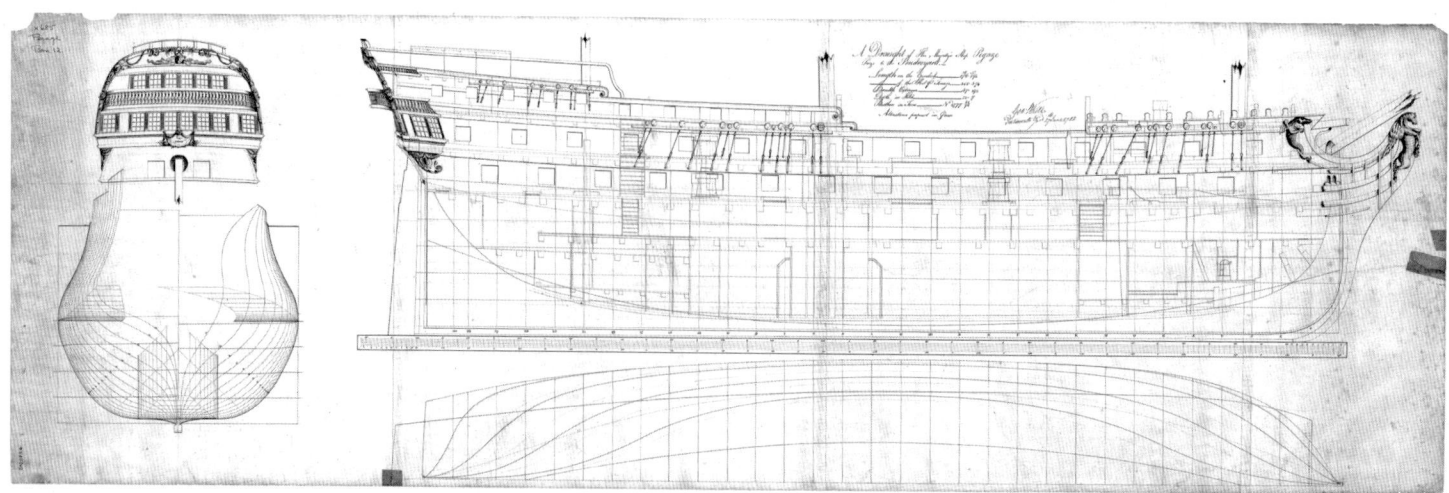

21.4.1782, becoming HMS *Pegase*; hulked 1794 at Plymouth and BU 1815.

Dictateur Toulon Dyd.
  K: 7.1781. L: 16.2.1782. C: 6.1782. Renamed *Liberté* 9.1792. Handed over to the Anglo-Spanish forces at Toulon on 29.8.1793, then burnt there at the evacuation 18.12.1793; refloated 1805 then BU 1808.

Suffisant Toulon Dyd.
  K: 7.1781. L: 6.3.1782. C: 8.1782. Handed over to the Anglo-Spanish forces at Toulon on 29.8.1793, then burnt there at the evacuation 18.12.1793; refloated 1805 then BU 1806.

Puissant Lorient Dyd (*Constructeur*, Charles Segondat-Duvernet).
  K: 8.1781. L: 13.3.1782. C: 6.1782. Handed over to the Anglo-Spanish forces at Toulon 29.8.1793, and removed to Britain on evacuation of that port; sold 7.1816.

Alcide Rochefort Dyd.
  K: 7.1781. L: 25.5.1782. C: 1.1783. Took part in Hotham's Action off the Hyères, where captured by HMS *Cumberland*, but caught fire and burnt off Fréjus 18.7.1795 (316 died).

Censeur Rochefort Dyd.
  K: 8.1781. L: 24.7.1782. C: 10.1783. Took part in Battle of Cape Noli, where captured by Hotham's squadron 14.3.1795; retaken 7.10.1795 by de Richery's squadron off Cape St Vincent. Condemned at Cadiz and sold to Spain 6.1799 in exchange for the Spanish *San Sebastián*, which became the French *Alliance*.

French losses of 74s during the war years 1780–1782 amounted to eight ships – the *Intrépide*, *Orient*, *Palmier* and *Magnifique* by natural causes in 1781–82 and the *Glorieux*, *Hector*, *César*, and *Pégase* in combat in 1782. With the end of hostilities, France began the task of replacing the lost vessels, with eleven new 74s ordered during 1782 and another five following the peace treaty.

CENTAURE Class. Designed and built by Joseph-Marie-Blaise Coulomb, original plan dated 28 March 1782. A development of Groignard's 1768 design for the *Victoire*, as amended by Coulomb.
  Guns: LD 28 x 36pdrs; UD 30 x 18pdrs; QD 10 x 8pdrs; Fc 6 x 8pdrs.

(i) First pair – ordered 15 February 1782 and named 13 April 1782.
  Dimensions & tons: 168ft 0in, 150ft 6in x 44ft 0in x 21ft 9in (54.57, 48.73 x 14.29 x 7.07m). 1,530/3,010 tons. Draught 20½ft/21ft 8in (6.66/7.04m). Men: 703-723.

Centaure Toulon Dyd.
  K: 12.5.1782. L: 7.11.1782. C: 12.1782. Handed over to the Anglo-Spanish forces at Toulon on 29.8.1793, then burnt there at the evacuation 18.12.1793; refloated 1805 then BU 1806.

Heureux Toulon Dyd.
  K: 12.5.1782. L: 19.12.1782. C: 4.1783. Captured at Aboukir 2.8.1798 by the British, then burnt 29.8.1798.

(ii) Second pair – ordered 1 June 1782 and named 21 August 1782.
  Dimensions & tons: 173ft 3in, 156ft 0in x 43ft 7in x 22ft 0in (56.28, 50.67 x 14.16 x 7.34m). 1,550/3,100 tons. Draught 20ft 6in/22ft 8in (6.66/7.37m).

Séduisant Toulon Dyd.
  K: 8.1782. L: 5.7.1783. C: 1783. Renamed *Pelletier* 28.9.1793, but reverted to *Séduisant* 30.5.1795. Took part in Battle of Glorious First of June 1.6.1794. Wrecked 16.12.1796 in the passage of the Raz de Sein upon sailing from Brest for Hoche's expedition to Ireland.

Mercure Toulon Dyd.
  K: 8.1782. L: 4.8.1783. C: 1783. Captured at Aboukir 2.8.1798 by HMS *Alexander*, then burnt 30.8.1798.

TÉMÉRAIRE Class. Designed by Jacques-Noël Sané, adopted in May 1782. From the middle of 1782 until the end of the Napoleonic era, all French 74s were built to this standard Sané design (including a few experimental variations to the basic draught). Some 120 vessels to this design (including derivatives) were eventually to be ordered between 1782 and 1813, of which the following twelve were ordered before 1786.
  Dimensions & tons: 172ft 0in (170ft 8in wl), 155ft 0in x 44ft 6in (45ft 10in wl) x 22ft 0in. (55.87, 50.35 x 14.46 x 7.15m) 1,537/3,069 tons. Draught 19ft 10in/22ft (6.44/7.15m). Men (1786): 690 in war, 495 peace, +12 officers, comprising a *capitaine de vaisseau* (to command), a *capitaine de frégate* (as second-in-command), 5 *lieutenants* and 5 *enseignes*.
  Guns: (original) LD 28 x 36pdrs; UD 30 x 18pdrs; QD 10 x 8pdrs (plus 4 x 36pdr *obusiers* after 1787); Fc 6 x 8pdrs. (*Patriote*, 1810): LD 28 x 36pdrs; UD 30 x 18pdrs; QD/Fc 12 x 8pdrs, 10 x 36pdr carronades.

(i) 1782 Orders. One ship was ordered on 15 February 1782 at Lorient and two at Rochefort, and all three were named on 13 April; two more were ordered at Brest and named on 1 June (Sané was *constructeur* of this pair), while another two were ordered at Lorient on 1 June and named on 21 August. Four were begun in May (including the name-ship of the class) and July; the other three were not begun until 1784. An eighth 74 to this design, to be named *Thésée*, was projected in 1782 at Rochefort, but was cancelled in February 1783, to be re-ordered in October 1787.

Téméraire Brest Dyd.
  K: 5.1782. L: 17.12.1782. C: 7.1783. Took part in Battle of 13 Prairial ('Glorious First of June') 1794. Condemned at Brest 9.11.1802, BU ordered 29.11.1802, BU 1803.

Superbe Brest Dyd.
  K: 7.1782. L: 11.11.1784. C: 1785. Lost by accident with all hands off Brest 30.1.1795.

Audacieux Lorient Dyd (*Constructeur*, Charles Segondat-Duvernet)
  K: 8.7.1782. L: 28.10.1784. C: 1785. Condemned at Brest 9.11.1802, BU ordered 29.11.1802. BU 2-3.1803.

Généreux Rochefort Dyd (*Constructeur*, Henri Chevillard).
  K: 24.7.1782. L: 21.6 or 7.1785. C: 10.1785. Took part in Battle of Cape Noli ('Hotham's Action') 13.3.1795, in Hotham's subsequent Action off the Hyères 13.7.1795, and in Battle of Aboukir ('the Nile') 1.8.1798. Captured 18.2.1800 south of Sicily by the British, became HMS *Genereux*. Prison hulk 1805, BU 2.1816.

Orion Rochefort Dyd (*Constructeurs*, Pierre Train and Joseph Niou)
  K: 10.1784. L: 18.4.1787. C: 1788. Frame made at Bayonne, construction delayed by lack of carpenters. Renamed *Mucius Scaevola* 11.1793, then *Mucius* 30.11.1793. Took part in Battle of 13 Prairial ('Glorious First of June') 1794, in Battle of Île de Groix 23.6.1795 ('Bridport's Action') and in Hoche's expedition to Ireland 12.1796. Condemned 13.10.1803, BU completed 8.4.1804.

Fougueux Lorient Dyd (*Constructeur*, Charles Segondat-Duvernet)
  (Work begun 8.1782, but stopped 1.11.1783, and parts put into storage until put back on the ways in 11.1784.) K: 11.1784. L: 19.9.1785. C: 12.1785. Took part in Hoche's expedition to Ireland 12.1796. Captured by boarding at Trafalgar 21.10.1805, but abandoned by the British in the ensuing storm and went ashore 28.10.1805 on the Santi Petri reefs to the east of Cadiz.

Borée Lorient Dyd. (*Constructeur*, Charles Segondat-Duvernet)
  K: 11.1784. L: 17.11.1785. C: 8.1787. Renamed *Ça Ira* 4.1794, then *Agricola* 6.1794; raséed as a heavy frigate 4–7.1794. Hospital hulk at Rochefort 4.1796, and BU there 1803.

(ii) 1784–85 Orders. A second batch of five was ordered in 1784–85. The pair ordered at Toulon were known simply as *Vaisseau No.1* and *Vaisseau No.2* until named *Commerce de Bordeaux* and *Commerce de Marseille* respectively on 23 January and 27 January 1786 – funded by donations from the Bordeaux and Marseille merchants respectively; the second name was amended to *Lys* on 17 July 1786. *Patriote* and *Léopard* at Brest (again with Sané as *constructeur*) and *Ferme* (also at Brest, but constructed by Lamothe) were named on 28 January 1786.

Commerce de Bordeaux Toulon Dyd.
  K: 9.1784. L: 15.9.1785. C: ?1786. Renamed *Bonnet Rouge* 12.1793, then *Timoléon* 2.1794. Took part in Battle of Cape Noli ('Hotham's Action') 13.3.1795. Burnt by her crew at the Battle of Aboukir ('the Nile') 2.8.1798 to avoid capture.

Lys Toulon Dyd.
  K: 9.1784. L: 7.10.1785 C: 9.1787. Renamed *Tricolore* 6.10.1792. Handed over to Anglo-Spanish forces at Toulon 8.1793, and burnt during the evacuation of that port 18.12.1793; raised and BU 1807.

Patriote Brest Dyd.
  K: 10.1784. L: 3.10.1785. C: 4.1786. Handed over to Anglo-Spanish forces at Toulon 8.1793, returned to the French 9.1793 to evacuate 1,400 counter-revolutionary sailors. Took part in Battle of 13 Prairial ('Glorious First of June') 1794, and in Hoche's expedition to Ireland 12.1796. Damaged by high winds 19.8.1806 and put in at Annapolis on 29.8.1806. Condemned 5.1820 at Rochefort, conversion to mooring hulk approved 16.1.1821, conversion completed 2.4.1821 and designated *Ponton No.4*. Grounded 9.1830, BU 1832–33.

Ferme Brest Dyd (*Constructeur*, Pierre-Augustin Lamothe).
  K: 12.1784. L: 16.9.1785. C: 1.1786. Renamed *Phocion* 10.1792. Handed over to the Spanish at Trinidad 11.1.1793 by her pro-Royalist crew; added to the Spanish Navy 1794; BU at La Guairá 1808.

Léopard Brest Dyd.
  K: 15.11.1785. L: 22.6.1787. C: 7.1787. Grounded in bad weather off Cagliari 17 2.1793 and burnt two days later to avoid capture.

AMERICA. Following the loss of the French 74-gun *Magnifique* on 10 August 1782 (see above), the American Congress on 3 September 1782 presented the *America* (the sole ship of the line built for the American Continental Navy during the war) to France as a replacement. For details of this ship's American origins and design see the 1786–1861 volume in this series. Note that the American specifications given below for *America*, cited by the historian Robert W. Neeser from an unknown source, differ from those on a draught for a 74-gun ship (not necessarily *America*) by her designer, Joshua Humphrey, which were (American units) 180ft, 166ft x 49ft x 19ft (54.86, 50.60 x 14.94 x 5.79m) with a draught of 21ft/24ft 6in (6.40/7.47m).

Magnifique's commander, Jean-Baptiste de Macarty-Macteigne, took charge of *America* immediately after her launch, placed the guns salvaged from *Magnifique* on board, and sailed *America* to France in June 1783. The French described her as 'very long, very wide, with little depth of hull and a lot of tumblehome'. On 20 August 1786 Castries reported to Louis XVI that a careful inspection of *America* at Brest on 11 August had shown that the ship, although only four years old and carefully built, was entirely rotten. Consequently he recommended that the King order the demolition of the ship and the construction of another 74 under the same name, a recommendation that Louis approved (this replacement was built at Brest in 1787–89 as a *Téméraire* Class ship).

  Dimensions & tons (French units): 172ft 0in, 153ft 0in x 47ft 4in x 21ft 0in (55.87, 49.70 x 15.38 x 6.82m). 1,500/3,000 tons. Men: 690, +13/17 officers.
  Guns: (ex-*Magnifique*) LD 28 x 36pdrs; UD 30 x 18pdrs; QD 10 x 8pdrs; Fc 6 x 8pdrs.

America James K. Hackett, Portsmouth, N.H.
  K: 5.1777. L: 5.11.1782. C: 6.1783. Given to France 3.9.1782. Struck 20.8.1786 and BU.

At the end of the period, the new 1786 Program for new construction drafted by Borda (and approved by Castries) included the construction of sixty new 74s, all to be built to Sané's draught for the *Téméraire* Class.

3 The Third Rank

(Vaisseaux du troisième rang)
with 56 to 66 guns after 1715

The 3rd Rank included the smallest units of the battlefleet – those ships able to take their place in the line of battle. Initially defined under the *Règlement* of 4 July 1670 as comprising ships with between 40 and 50 guns, in practice this Rank subsequently included ships with from 48 to 60 guns (ships of 850 to 1,100 tons), which can be seen to compose of two different groups: the first with a mix of 24pdrs and 18pdrs on the lower deck, from which the 64-gun ships of the eighteenth century would evolve; and the second with a mix of 18pdrs and 12pdrs on the lower deck, from which the 50-gun ships of the eighteenth century would evolve. There were a number of exceptions to this, as a few were armed with single-calibre LD batteries, and after the mid-1690s this became the standard pattern, with 3rd Rank ships carrying either a 24pdr or an 18pdr LD battery on the lower deck. Finally this crystallised into two groups – the larger ships of 60–64 guns (with 24pdrs), and those of 50–56 guns (with 18pdrs).

As with the 1st and 2nd Ranks, the 3rd Rank until 1689 contained a mixture of ships defined as two-deckers and three-deckers. However, the latter should be understood as not having a continuous battery of guns on their third tier, and in that sense equated more to the two-decker types in the English and Dutch Navies. While we have defined the armaments of such ships as though they were carried on three full decks – LD, MD and UD – in practice the MD should be better considered as the UD of a two-decker, while the UD actually equated to the forecastle and QD of a two-decker.

This situation was altered by successive regulations. Firstly, the *Règlement* of 4 July 1670 stipulated that ships of 50 guns and below should in future only be built as two-deckers. This was quickly extended with the *Règlement* of 22 March 1671 which provided that in future ships of below 70 guns should be constructed as two-deckers. This entailed the removal of the light structure on some ships linking (across the waist) the separate fore and aft sections of the third deck, often a fairly straightforward process transforming the fore part into a forecastle and the aft part into a quarterdeck.

The 3rd Rank was the largest ship type to be equipped with oars and pierced with oar-ports (fifteen pairs in the case of 3rd Rank ships). In his *Mémoires*, LG René Duguay-Trouin explained how useful they were for *Jason* and *Auguste* when they were engaged by Byng's squadron off Ushant in 1705. Oars were mainly made at the Bayonne Dyd from pine-wood brought from the Pyrenees.

To compensate for the near total lack of contemporary data on actual ship armaments prior to 1696, we have in Sections (A) and (B) provided estimated armaments based on the governing directives and the known characteristics of all of the individual ships. This issue is discussed in greater detail in the Introduction.

The 1660s saw a major increase in the number of 3rd Rank vessels (as they would be rated from 1670) and the growth continued in the early 1670s, so that this contingent then formed the largest section of the fleet numerically. This was almost entirely made up of the 56-gun type, the smallest of the nominal three-deckers forming the French fleet; these typically carried a mixture of calibres on the lower and middle decks. The normal pattern was twelve 18pdrs (of bronze) and ten 12pdrs (4 bronze and 6 iron) on the LD, twelve 12pdrs (bronze) and eight 8pdrs (iron) on the MD, with ten 6pdrs (iron) on the UD – of which six 6pdrs were aft of and four forward of the unarmed waist; however, there were variations, dependent on the supply available in the dockyards, and sometimes upon the whim of the commander. Most carried two or four iron 4pdrs on the QD.

In 1680 or early 1681 an 'establishment total' of forty 3rd Rank ships was set. In January 1681 there were thirty-six 3rd Rank ships in the fleet – ten in the Brest Department, four at Rochefort, two at Le Havre, and twenty for the *Levant* Fleet at Toulon. The establishment level for 3rd Rank ships was decreased to 38 ships in 1688 and to 36 in 1689, but was restored to 40 in 1690 and remained at that level until after 1715. The actual number extent would be maintained or even exceeded until about 1710, when like other Ranks it suffered from the general decline in the Navy.

(A) Vessels in service as at 9 March 1661

When Colbert assumed control of the Navy in 1661, the 3rd Rank of *vaisseaux* comprised (at least in name) ships carrying between 30 and 40 guns. However, by 1669 these were reduced to the 4th Rank, and by the start of 1671 the 3rd Rank comprised ships of 48 to 60 guns. This section is thus limited to the five vessels begun before 1661 which were (or, in the case of the *Brézé* below, would have been, if surviving to 1670) classed as 3rd Rank under the 1670 re-classification; all five belonged to what may best be termed the '56-gun type', although there were variations from this figure with the precise number of guns that individual vessels carried.

Three smaller vessels which were classed as 3rd Rank in 1669 but were re-rated as 4th Rank in 1670 (the *Soleil* of 1642, *Mazarin* of 1647 and *Hercule* of 1657 – renamed *Hercule*, *Bon* and *Marquis* respectively in June 1671) will be found in Chapter 4, as is the *Anna* of 1650, which similarly became a 3rd Rank in 1669 but was hulked before the 1670 re-classing took effect. The ships below – and those following in Section (B) – while nominally three-deckers, in practice had just two complete gun decks, with a third tier above that was armed fore and aft, but with an unarmed waist. Thus – as with the previous chapters – we have described the three levels as LD, MD and UD, with the UD guns separated into those aft and forward of the waist. Please see a fuller discussion of this issue in our Introduction to this volume.

REINE. 56, later 48 guns. Designed and built by Rodolphe Gédéon. Nominally a three-decked ship, pierced for twelve pairs of LD gunports (excluding the unarmed chase ports), and with the forward and aft part of the upper deck separated in the waist. Ordered 12 March 1645 and named in March 1647. Reconstructed at Brouage from 1660 to 1661. Classed as 2nd Rank in 1669, but reduced to 3rd Rank in 1670.

> Dimensions & tons: 134ft 0in x 34ft 0in x 16ft 0in (43.53 x 11.04 x 5.20m). 1,000 tons. Draught 17ft/18ft (5.52/5.85m). Men: 400 (60/230/110), +5 officers as 2nd Rank; in 1671, 350 (55/180/115) as 3rd Rank, +5 officers.
>
> Guns: 56 in 1666: LD 6 x 24pdrs + 18 x 18pdrs; MD 22 x 12pdrs; UD (aft) 6 x 6pdrs + (fwd) 4 x 6pdrs. 50 guns by 1669 (with just 4 x 6pdrs remaining), then 48 from 1671 (with 2 x 12pdrs removed).

Reine Toulon Dyd.
K: 3.1646. L: 9.2.1647. Comm: 8.1647 as flagship of the *Levant* Fleet. C: 6.1648. From 3.1650 (to 4.1652) flagship of CdE Jean-Paul de Saumeur (known as 'Chevalier Paul'). Took part in Battle of Cherchell 24.8.1665 (under CV Hector Des Ardens). Renamed *Brave* 24.6.1671. Took part in Battle of Solebay 7.6.1672 (under CV Jean-Baptiste de Valbelle). Condemned 1673 at Brest and sold to BU there 24.2.1674.

When France intervened in a revolt against Spanish rule in Sicily, the Dutch, who were also at war with the French, sent a squadron under the formidable Admiral Michiel de Ruyter to co-operate with the Spanish fleet in the Mediterranean. The Battle of Augusta, fought on 22 April 1676 (NS), was a tactical draw, but de Ruyter was severely wounded, losing a leg, and died shortly after. This Dutch engraving by Bastiaan Stoopendael is keyed and numbered, but lists the commanding officers rather than the ship names. The French fleet under Duquesne comprised 29 ships of the line (backed by 8 fireships and 5 frigates) facing the allied forces of 17 Dutch and about 11 Spanish ships of the line (plus 5 Dutch fireships), but it included many relatively small ships – 13 of the 3rd Rank (with between 50 and 56 guns) and 6 of the 4th Rank. The 3rd Rank ships involved were the *Agréable, Fidèle, Aimable, Fortuné, Vermandois, Prudent, Sage, Téméraire, Vaillant, Apollon, Aquilon, Heureux* and *Assuré*. (Beverley R Robinson Collection, Annapolis 51.7.63).

BRÉZÉ. 56 guns. Designed and built by Rodolphe Gédéon. Another nominal three-decker, pierced to carry eleven guns per side on the lower deck (excluding the unarmed chase ports). Initially with the *Levant* Fleet (where she served at the blockade of Barcelona in 1652), but in 1659 transferred to the *Ponant* Fleet. Named in honour of Admiral Jean-Armand de Maillé, Marquis de Brézé (1619-1646), Richelieu's nephew and his successor as *Grand-Maître, Chef et Surintendant de la Navigation et Commerce de France*, who had died in battle in 1646.

Dimensions & tons: dimensions unknown, but probably similar to the *César* below. 900 tons. Men: 350 in war, +5 officers.
Guns: 56 in 1665: LD 12 x 18pdrs + 10 x 12pdrs; MD 12 x 12pdrs + 8 x 8pdrs; UD (aft) 6 x 6pdrs + (fwd) 4 x 6pdrs; QD 4 x 4pdrs.

Brézé Toulon Dyd.
K: 4.1646. L: 9.10.1647. C: 4.1648. Wrecked 25.11.1665 between the Trousses and Île d'Aix (at the mouth of the Charente).

CÉSAR. 52, later 56 guns. Designed and built by Laurent Hubac. The Brest equivalent of the *Brézé*, similarly pierced to carry eleven guns per side on the lower deck. Probably named for César de Bourbon, Duc de Vendôme (1594–1665), who was the legitimised son of Henri IV and

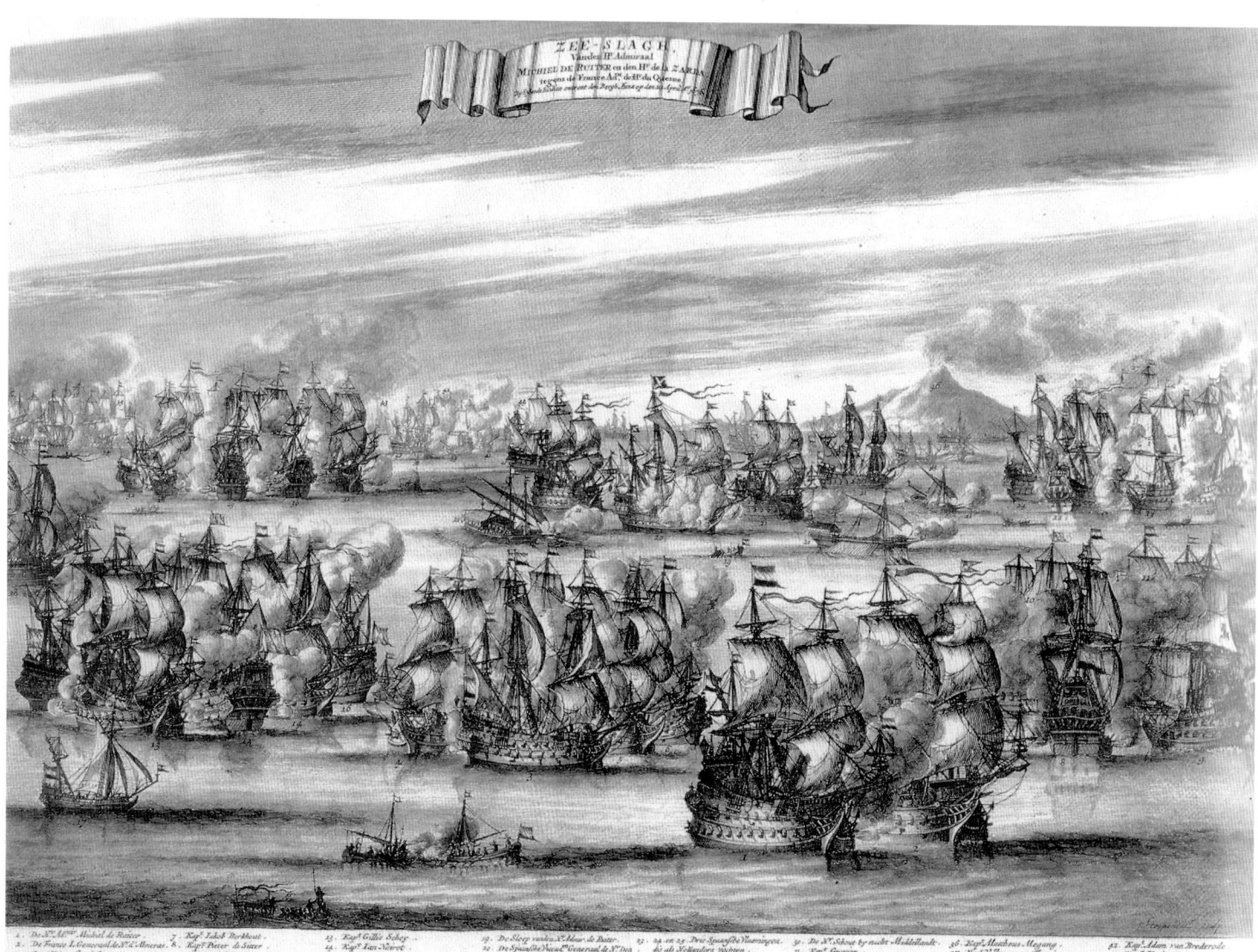

THE THIRD RANK

became *Grand-Maître de la Navigation* in 1650. Classed as a 3rd Rank ship in 1669, and remained so in the 1670 re-classification and thereafter.

Dimensions & tons: 127ft 0in x 33ft 6in x ? (41.25 x 10.88 x ?m). 850 tons. Draught 15½ft (5.035m). Men: 300/330, +5 officers.

Guns: Originally 56. 52 in 1666: LD 12 x 18pdrs + 10 x 12pdrs; MD 12 x 12pdrs + 8 x 8pdrs; UD (aft) 6 x 6pdrs + (fwd) 4 x 6pdrs; QD nil (originally 4 x 4pdrs). Reduced to 50 guns by 1669 and 48 from 1671.

César Brest Dyd.
K: 1646. L: 1648. C: 1650. Took part in Battle of Perthuis d'Antioche 9.8.1652. Renamed *Rubis* 24.6.1671. Took part in Battle of Solebay 7.6.1672. Struck 1673 at Brest, and sold 8.9.1673 to BU.

SAINT LOUIS. 56, later 48 guns. Designed and built by Jean Laure. Structurally similar to the *Reine* above, with twelve pairs of LD guns. Classed as 2nd Rank in 1669, and reconstructed in 1670 at Rochefort, then reduced to 3rd Rank (with 48 guns).

Dimensions & tons: 140ft 0in, 110ft 0in x 31ft 6in x 14ft 6in (45.48, 35.73 x 10.23 x 4.71m). 950 tons. Draught 17ft/18½ft (5.52/6.01m). Men: 400 (60/230/110), +5 officers as 2nd Rank; in 1671, 300 (46/154/100) as 3rd Rank, +5 officers; 325 (50/168/107) from 1673, +5 officers.

Guns: Originally 60: LD 6 x 24pdrs + 18 x 18pdrs (may later have carried 22 x 24pdrs); MD 22 x 12pdrs; UD (aft) 6 x 6pdrs + (fwd) 4 x 6pdrs; QD 4 x 4pdrs. 56 in 1666 (less the 4pdrs), 52 by 1669, 48 from 1671, and 52 from 1673. 56 guns from 1675: LD 6 x 24pdrs + 18 x 18pdrs; MD 22 x 12pdrs; UD 10 x 6pdrs. 52 guns from 1689.

Saint Louis Brouage.
K: 9.1656. L: 3.7.1658. C: 1659. Renamed *Aimable* 24.6.1671. Took part in Battles of the Lipari Islands 11.2.1675, Stromboli 8.1.1676, Augusta 22.4.1676 and Palermo 2.6.1676. Removed from service 10.1688, struck 10.4.1689 at Toulon and BU 1690.

ROYALE (or **FRÉGATE ROYALE**). 56 guns. Designed and built by Laurent Hubac, pierced to carry eleven guns per side on the LD. Again, this was nominally a three-decker, but constructed with a third (or upper) deck with the forward and after portions separated by an unarmed waist. Initially classed in 1669 as 2nd Rank, but reduced to 3rd Rank in 1670.

Dimensions & tons: 133ft 0in x 33ft 6in x 15ft 0in (43.20 x 10.88 x 4.87m). 1,000 tons. Draught 18ft (5.85m). Men: 400 in war (60/230/110), +5 officers.

Guns: 56 in 1666: LD 12 x 18pdrs + 10 x 12pdrs; MD 12 x 12pdrs + 8 x 8pdrs; UD (aft) 6 x 6pdrs + (fwd) 4 x 6pdrs; QD 4 x 4pdrs. 54 by 1669 (2 x 4pdrs removed). 52 guns from 1671, 54 from 1674, and 56 from 1676.

Royale Brest Dyd.
K: 4.1660. L: 2.1661. C: 11.1661. Took part in bombardment of Bougie (Algeria) 21.7.1664 and in Battles of La Goulette 2/3.3.1665 (as flagship of François de Vendôme, Duc de Beaufort) and Cherchell 24.8.1665. Renamed *Ferme* 24.6.1671. Re-classed as a hulk 13.12.1675. Condemned 5.1676 at Toulon.

(B) Vessels acquired from 9 March 1661

The early ships of this group generally followed the format of the *César* of 1648 and *Royale* of 1661, pierced for eleven pairs of guns on the LD (excluding a twelfth pair in the chase position which did not usually have guns) which was a mix of 18pdrs and 12pdrs, with a mix of 12pdrs and 8pdrs on the deck above, and what was nominally a third deck separated the waist into what was effectively a quarterdeck and forecastle at that level. To convey the French formal terminology of 'three-decker' we have described this tier as 'upper deck' (or *3ᵉ pont*) rather than QD and Fc. The *Dauphin*, *Diamant*, *Thérèse*, *Trident*, *Fleuron* and *Comte* followed this pattern, along with the *Vaillant* and *Téméraire* at the end of the decade. Later ships of this group were constructed as two-deckers – the *Wallon*, *Louvre*, *Oriflamme*, *Brave*, *Brillant*, *Heureux*, and *Saint Michel*; these were followed by the *Fendant*, *Bon*, *Maure* and *Hercule*.

Slightly larger were the ships pierced for an additional pair of LD guns – following the lines of the *Reine* of 1645 and *Saint Louis* of 1656. Sixteen more ships followed this pattern, from the *Rubis* of 1664 and *Navarre* of 1666 to *Brave* (originally *Incertain*) of 1672; in principle, they were to carry of LD mix of 24pdrs and 18pdrs, compared with the 18pdrs and 12pdrs of the smaller type, but in practice many of then carried nothing larger than 18pdrs. All of these were nominally three-deckers, with the third deck interrupted in the waist. Almost all of these ships of both groups had a change of name in June 1671; for those completed by then we have used their original names.

TRIOMPHE. 42, later 48, then 44 guns. Designed and built by Laurent Hubac under the name *Chalain* or *Grand Chalain* to a private order for Nicolas Fouquet (then Louis XIV's *Surintendant* of Finance). Following Fouquet's downfall in 1661, the ship was confiscated by the Crown in September 1661 and added to the Navy, being renamed *Triomphe* in October 1663. Originally classed as 3rd Rank in 1669, she was moved to the 4th Rank in 1670, but was restored to the 3rd Rank in 1671.

Dimensions & tons: dimensions unknown. 800 tons. Men: 300 (45/175/80) in 1669, 270 (42/138/90) in 1671, +5 officers.

Guns: 42 in 1661, 44 by 1669 and 38 from 1671. 48 from 1672: LD 12 x 18pdrs + 10 x 12pdrs; MD 12 x 12pdrs + 8 x 8pdrs; UD (aft) 6 x 6pdrs.

Triomphe Concarneau.
K: 1657. L: 1657. C: 1660. Renamed *Courageux* 24.6.1671 (in theory, but in practice she remained *Triomphe* until her disposal). Out of service at San Thomé (India) 8.1672, her guns removed ashore for the port's defences; BU there probably in 1673 or 1674.

RUBIS. 60, later 64 guns. Designed and built by Laurent Hubac, the first of three similar ships of this type by him. Three-decker, pierced for twelve pairs of LD gunports (excluding the unarmed chase ports), and with the forward and aft part of the upper deck separated in the waist. Essentially similar in design to the *Reine* and *Saint Louis* (see Chapter 2), this ship would undoubtedly have been re-classed as a 2nd Rank in 1669 and a 3rd Rank in July 1670 (as her half-sisters were) if she had not been captured in 1666. It should be noted that in English service from 1666 she carried three full tiers of guns, demonstrating that it was practical to convert such ships into complete three-deckers.

Dimensions & tons: 135ft 0in, 113ft 0in x 35ft 0in x 16ft 0in (43.85, 36.71 x 11.37 x 5.20m). 900 tons. Draught 17½ft (5.68m). Men: 350, +5/9 officers.

Guns (60): LD 6 x 24pdrs + 18 x 18pdrs (may later have carried 22 x 24pdrs); MD 22 x 12pdrs; UD (aft) 6 x 6pdrs + (fwd) 4 x 6pdrs; poop 4 x 4pdrs. Later raised to 64 guns. When taken she carried 40 bronze guns, 14 iron guns, and six *pedreros* (lightweight anti-personnel cannon mounted on stocks, called *pierriers* by the French and *swivels* by the English), according to the journal of her captor, Adm Sir Thomas Allin.

Rubis Brest Dyd.
  K: early 1662. L: 11.1664. C: 1.1665. Taken by HMS *Royal James* under Adm Sir Thomas Allin with the assistance of the *Foresight* and *Adventure* on 28.9.1666 off Dungeness and added to the British Navy as HMS *French Ruby*; hulked at Portsmouth 1.1686, and BU later.

DIAMANT. 54, later 56 guns. Designed and built by Laurent Hubac. Nominally a three-decker, with the forward and aft portions of the UD separated in the waist. Pierced for eleven pairs of LD guns (excluding the unarmed chase ports). Initially classed in 1669 as 2nd Rank, but reduced to 3rd Rank in 1670.
  Dimensions & tons: 136ft 0in x 35ft 0in x 16ft 0in (44.18 x 11.37 x 5.20m). 1,000 tons. Draught 17½ft (5.68m). Men: 450 in 1666, then 400 (60/230/110) in 1669, +5 officers; 350 (55/180/115) in 1671, +5 officers.
  Guns: 54 by 1669. 56 from 1673: LD 12 x 18pdrs + 10 x 12pdrs; MD 12 x 12pdrs + 8 x 8pdrs; UD (aft) 6 x 6pdrs + (fwd) 4 x 6pdrs; poop 4 x 4pdrs.
Diamant Brest Dyd.
  K: 1662. L: 12.1664. C: 8.1665. Took part in Battle of Texel 21.8.1673. BU 1685.

DAUPHIN. 56, later 54 guns. Designed by Rodolphe Gédéon and built by François Pomet. Nominally a three-decker, with the forward and aft portions of the UD separated in the waist. Pierced for eleven pairs of LD guns (excluding the unarmed chase ports). Reconstructed at Toulon from November 1681 to early 1682.
  Dimensions & tons: 132ft 6in, 105ft 0in x 33ft 0in x 15ft 6in (43.04, 34.11 x 10.72 x 5.035m). 900 tons. Draught 15ft/17½ft (4.87/5.68m). Men: 350 (50/200/100), +5 (later 7) officers.
  Guns: 56 in 1666, 50 by 1669, 48 from 1671, and 50 from 1673. 54 from 1676: LD 12 x 18pdrs + 10 x 12pdrs; MD 12 x 12pdrs + 8 x 8pdrs; UD 8 x 6pdrs; poop 4 x 4pdrs. 52 in war from 1696 (46 peace) LD 22 x 18pdrs; MD 24 x 12pdrs; UD (aft) 6 x 6pdrs.
Dauphin Toulon Dyd.
  K: 7.1662. L: 3.1664. C: 8.1664. Took part in Battle of Cherchell 24.8.1665. Renamed *Vermandois* 24.6.1671. Took part in Battles of Augusta 22.4.1676 and Palermo 31.5.1676. Renamed *Vigilant* 28.6.1678. Took part in Bombardment of Genoa 18-28.5.1684, in Battle of Beachy Head 10.7.1690, and in Lagos campaign 1693. Sold 2.1700 to BU at Toulon.

THÉRÈSE. 60 guns. Designed and built by François Pomet. Nominally a three-decker, with the forward and aft portions of the UD separated in the waist. Pierced for eleven guns per side on the LD (excluding the chase ports). Construction was delayed during 1663 due to shortage of timber. Named in April 1663.
  Dimensions & tons: 127ft 0in x 32ft 0in x 15ft 0in (41.25 x 10.39 x 4.87m). 850 tons. Men: 350 (50/200/100), +5 officers.
  Guns: 60 in 1666: LD 12 x 18pdrs + 10 x 12pdrs; MD 12 x 12pdrs + 10 x 8pdrs; UD (aft) 8 x 6pdrs + (fwd) 4 x 6pdrs; poop 4 x 4pdrs.

Another engraved panorama by Bastiaan Stoopendael, this one representing the Battle of the Texel (21 August 1673) between the Dutch and an Anglo-French fleet attempting to land troops on the beaches of Camperdown. The viewpoint is between the shore and the Dutch line, with most of the fighting in the foreground involving the English centre and rear squadrons under Prince Rupert and Sir Edward Spragge respectively. The French squadron under the Comte d'Estrées, which formed the van squadron, was forced out of the action early on and appears on the horizon in this view. The French line of around thirty ships contained some of the largest ships of the Atlantic fleet, but it also included some seventeen 3rd Rank ships – *Diamant, Excellent, Fier, Fortuné, Assuré, Téméraire, Vaillant, Aimable, Sage, Prince, Aquilon, Bourbon, Duc, Précieux, Maure, Oriflamme,* and *Bon.* (Beverley R Robinson Collection, Annapolis 51.7.57)

Thérèse Toulon Dyd.
> K: 7.1662. L: 13.3.1665. C: 12.1665. Blew up by accident off Candia (Crete) 24.7.1669, with just 7 survivors, while bombarding Ottoman forces ashore with the rest of the French fleet, which withdrew after her loss.

NAVARRE. 56, later 54 guns. Designed and built by Jean-Pierre Brun. Nominally a three-decker, with the forward and aft portions of the UD separated in the waist. Pierced for twelve guns per side on the LD (excluding the chase ports). Initially classed in 1669 as 2nd Rank, but reduced to 3rd Rank in 1670.
> Dimensions & tons: 137ft 0in x 34ft 6in x 16ft 0in (44.50 x 11.21 x 5.20m). 950 tons. Men: 350 (55/180/115) in war, +5 officers.
> Guns: 56 by 1669: LD 6 x 24pdrs + 18 x 18pdrs; MD 22 x 12pdrs; UD (aft) 6 x 6pdrs + (fwd) 4 x 6pdrs. 54 guns from 1671.

Navarre Tonnay-Charente.
> K: 4.1665. L: 6.1666. C: 1.1667. Nominally renamed *Constant* 24.6.1671, but in practice this was never effective prior to her loss. Wrecked off India in 6.1673.

TRIDENT. 44 later 54 guns. Designed and built by Laurent Hubac. Another nominal three-decker, with the forward and aft portions of the UD separated in the waist. Pierced for eleven pairs of LD guns (excluding the unarmed chase ports). Underwent reconstruction at Toulon during 1688.
> Dimensions & tons: 127ft 0in x 32ft 0in x 15ft 6in (41.25 x 10.39 x 5.035m). 850 tons. Draught 16ft/18ft (5.20/5.85m). Men: 300 (46/154/100) in war, +5 officers.
> Guns: 44 by 1669, 48 from 1671 and 50 from 1674. 52 in 1676: LD 12 x 18pdrs + 10 x 12pdrs; MD 12 x 12pdrs + 8 x 8pdrs; UD (aft) 6 x 6pdrs + (fwd) 4 x 6pdrs. 54 from 1691, then 50 in war from 1696 (44 peace): LD 14 x 18pdrs + 8 x 12pdrs; MD 22 x 8pdrs; UD 6 x 6pdrs.

Trident Brest Dyd.
> K: 5.1665. L: 1.1666. C: 4.1666. Renamed *Aquilon* 24.6.1671. Took part in Battles of Texel 21.8.1673, Stromboli 8.1.1676, Augusta 22.4.1676 and Palermo 31.5.1676 and in bombardment of Genoa 18–28.5.1684. Condemned 8.1697 at Toulon.

BRETON. 56 guns. Designed and built by Laurent Hubac, and similar to *Rubis*. Another nominal three-decker, with the forward and aft portions of the UD separated in the waist. Pierced to carry twelve pairs of LD guns (excluding the unarmed chase ports). Initially classed in 1669 as 2nd Rank, but reduced to 3rd Rank in 1670.
> Dimensions & tons: 135ft 0in, 113ft 0in x 34ft 0in x 16ft 0in (43.85, 36.71 x 11.04 x 5.20m). 900 tons. Draught 17½ft (5.68m). Men: 350, +5/7 officers.
> Guns: 56 by 1669: LD 6 x 24pdrs + 18 x 18pdrs; MD 22 x 12pdrs; UD (aft) 6 x 6pdrs + (fwd) 4 x 6pdrs. 48 guns from 1671, then restored to 56 from 1674.

Breton Brest Dyd.
> K: 5.1665. L: 8.2.1666. C: 4.1666. Nominally renamed *Courtisan* 24.6.1671, but in practice this was never effective prior to her loss. Wrecked 1.5.1674 on the Coromandel Coast (with 75 drowned).

FLEURON. 48, later 50 guns. Designed and built by Laurent Hubac, effectively a sister ship to the *Trident*. Another nominal three-decker, with the forward and aft portions of the UD separated in the waist. Pierced to carry eleven pairs of LD guns (excluding the unarmed chase ports). Rebuilt at Toulon from February 1675 to May 1676, and again from May 1680 to March 1681.
> Dimensions & tons: 127ft 0in x 32ft 0in x 15ft 6in (41.25 x 10.39 x 5.035m). 850 tons. Men: 300, +5/7 officers.
> Guns: 48 by 1669, then 50 from 1673: LD 12 x 18pdrs + 10 x 12pdrs; MD 12 x 12pdrs + 8 x 8pdrs; UD 8 x 6pdrs. 48 guns again from 1677.

Fleuron Brest Dyd.
> K: 7.1665. L: early 1668. C: 5.1669. Took part in Bombardments of Algiers 26.6.1683 and of Genoa 18–28.5.1684. Condemned 1688 at Toulon.

COMTE. 50, later 60 guns. Designed and begun by Jean Nissard, but completed by Rodolphe Gédéon following Nissard's death in 1666. Another nominal three-decker, with the forward and aft portions of the UD separated in the waist. Pierced to carry eleven pairs of LD guns (excluding the unarmed chase ports). Originally named *Vivonne* when ordered, but renamed *Comte* on 3 November 1665 (still named in honour of the Comte de Vivonne). Reconstructed from November 1681 to early 1682 at Toulon.
> Dimensions & tons: 123ft 0in, 112ft 0in x 37ft 0in x 14ft 0in (39.96, 36.38 x 12.02 x 4.55m). 950 tons. Draught 15ft/15½ft (4.87/5.035m). Men: 350 in war (50/200/100), by 1671 300 (46/154/100), +5/7 officers.
> Guns: 50 by 1669, then 52 from 1673 and 54 from 1675. 56 from 1677: LD 12 x 18pdrs + 10 x 12pdrs; MD 12 x 12pdrs + 8 x 8pdrs; UD (aft) 6 x 6pdrs + (fwd) 4 x 6pdrs; poop 4 x 4pdrs. 58 guns from 1679, 60 from 1690.

Comte Toulon Dyd.
> K: 8.1665. L: 15.1.1667. C: 5.1667. Renamed *Prudent* 24.6.1671. Took part in the Battles of Pharo (Messina) 2.1.1675, Lipari Islands 11.2.1675, Stromboli 8.1.1676, Augusta 22.4.1676 and Palermo 31.5.1676. Took part in Bombardment of Algiers 26.6.1683 (as flagship of CdE Henri Cauchon de Lhéry) and in Battle of Beachy Head 10.7.1690. Hulked 5.1695 at Toulon and condemned 1696.

DANISH-BUILT. 60, later 56 guns. The smaller of two ships built to a 1665 order by Colbert from Denmark (see Chapter 2 for this). Completed with a decked-over waist, but this was removed upon arrival in France. Pierced for twelve pairs of LD ports (excluding the chase ports), she was originally named *Grand Danois*, but was renamed *Sophie* before delivery to France; she was raséed at Rochefort from March to July 1670, and re-classed as 3rd Rank in 1670.
> Dimensions & tons: 133ft 4in, 108ft 0in x 33ft 9in x 13ft 0in (43.31, 35.08 x 10.96 x 4.22m). 1,000 tons. Draught 16ft/17ft (5.20/5.52m). Men 400 (60/230/110), + 5 officers; from 1671, 350 (55/180/115), + 5 officers.
> Guns: 60 by 1669, reduced to 54 in 1671. 56 from 1673: LD 10 x 24pdrs + 14 x 18pdrs; MD 24 x 12pdrs; UD 8 x 6pdrs.

Sophie Mathias, Copenhagen.
> K: 8.1665. L: early 1666. C: 12.1666. Renamed *Fort* 24.6.1671. Took part in Battle of Solebay 7.6.1672. BU 1677.

ROUEN. 52 guns. Designed and built by Jean Esnault for the *Compagnie des Indes Orientales*, and purchased on the stocks in February 1668 for the Navy (along with the 44-gun *Le Havre*). Pierced to carry eleven pairs of LD guns (excluding the unarmed chase ports).
> Dimensions & tons: dimensions unknown. 850 tons. Men: 280/300, +5 officers.
> Guns: 52 by 1669: LD 22 x 12pdrs; UD 22 x 6pdrs; QD 8 x 4pdrs.

Rouen Le Havre.
> K: 12.1665. L: 11.9.1668. C: 11.1669. Wrecked in a storm 17.1.1670 on a rock near Le Havre.

LYS. 60 guns. Designed and built by Laurent Hubac, and similar to *Breton* and *Rubis*. Pierced to carry twelve pairs of LD guns (excluding the unarmed chase ports). Initially classed in 1669 as 2nd Rank, but reduced to 3rd Rank in 1670. Rebuilt at Toulon from February 1680 to January 1682.

    Dimensions & tons: 134ft 0in x 33ft 3in x 16ft 0in (43.53 x 10.80 x 5.20m). 950 tons. Draught 17ft (5.52m). Men: 350 (55/180/115) in war, +5/7 officers.

    Guns: 60 by 1669: LD 6 x 24pdrs + 18 x 18pdrs (may have later carried 22 x 18pdrs); MD 22 x 12pdrs; UD (aft) 6 x 6pdrs + (fwd) 4 x 6pdrs; poop 4 x 4pdrs. 54 guns from 1671, then 56 from 1674, and 60 again from 1677.

Lys Brest Dyd.
    K: 3.1666. L: Spring 1667. C: 1668. Renamed *Assuré* 24.6.1671. Took part in Battles of Stromboli 8.1.1676, Augusta 22.4.1676 and Palermo 31.5.1676 and in Bombardments of Algiers 23.7.1682 and of Genoa 18–28.5.1684. Condemned 1689 at Toulon and sold by Order of 10.4.1689.

FIER. 56, later 60 guns. Designed by Jean Laure and constructed by François Pomet. Pierced to carry twelve pairs of LD guns (excluding the unarmed chase ports). Initially named *Alsace* on 17 May 1669, but renamed *Fier* on 24 June 1671. Raised to the 2nd Rank in 1675, but reverted to 3rd Rank in 1677–78.

    Dimensions & tons: 140ft 0in, 112ft 0in x 35ft 6in x 17ft 0in (45.48, 36.38 x 11.53 x 5.52m). 1,050 tons. Draught 16ft/19½ft (5.20/6.33m). Men: 350 (55/180/115, then 68/188/94), +5 officers; 320 (65/180/75) in 1690; then from 1692 330 in war (67/179/84), + 7 officers.

    Guns: 56 from 1671. 60 from 1674: LD 6 x 24pdrs + 18 x 18pdrs; UD 24 x 12pdrs; QD 8 x 4pdrs; Fc 4 x 4pdrs.

Fier Rochefort Dyd.
    K: 8.1668. L: 4.10.1670. C: 1671. Took part in Battles of Texel 21.8.1673 and Palermo 31.5.1676. Renamed *Ferme* 28.6.1678. Grounded by accident 11.1689 on the Fillettes (a reef in the Brest narrows), but was salved and repaired 12.1689 to 5.1690 at Brest. Took part in Battle of Beachy Head 10.7.1690. Hulked at Toulon 5.1695, condemned 1696 and BU before 1700.

WALLON. 48, later 50 guns. Designed and built by Laurent Hubac. Another nominal three-decker, with the forward and aft portions of the UD separated in the waist. Pierced to carry eleven pairs of LD guns (excluding the unarmed chase ports). Ordered in 1668 and named *Wallon* on 17 May 1669. Reconstructed at Brest during 1684. Reduced to 4th Rank in 1687, but reverted to 3rd Rank in 1690.

    Dimensions & tons: 122ft 6in, 102ft 0in x 33ft 0in x 15ft 0in (39.79, 33.13 x 10.72 x 4.87m). 750 tons. Draught 15½ft (5.035m). Men: 270 (42/138/90) in 1671, 300 (46/154/100) by 1672, +5 (later 7) officers.

    Guns: 48 from 1671, then 50 from 1674: LD 12 x 18pdrs + 10 x 12pdrs; MD 12 x 12pdrs + 8 x 8pdrs; UD (aft) 6 x 6pdrs + (fwd) 2 x 6pdrs.

Wallon Brest Dyd.
    K: 11.1668. L: 30.8.1669. C: 4.1670. Renamed *Duc* 24.6.1671. Took part in Battles of Texel 21.8.1673 and of Bantry Bay 11.5.1689. Condemned at Lorient 9.1691.

ROCHEFORT. 56 guns. Designed and built by François Pomet. Another nominal three-decker, with the forward and aft portions of the UD separated in the waist. Pierced to carry twelve pairs of LD guns (excluding the unarmed chase ports). Initially classed in 1669 as 2nd Rank, but reduced to 3rd Rank in 1670. Rebuilt at Brest from July 1684 to 1686.

    Dimensions & tons: 132ft 0in, 107ft 0in x 35ft 0in x 14ft 8in (42.88, 34.76 x 11.37 x 4.76m). 950 tons. Draught 16ft/18½ft (5.20/6.01m). Men: 300 in war (46/154/100), +5 officers; 320 (65/180/75) in 1690, then from 1692 330 in war (67/179/84), + 7 officers.

    Guns: (56): LD 6 x 24pdrs + 18 x 18pdrs; MD 22 x 12pdrs; UD (aft) 6 x 6pdrs + (fwd) 4 x 6pdrs. Reduced to 50 guns from 1671, then raised to 54 from 1676, down to 52 from 1679, and back to 56 from 1690.

Rochefort Rochefort Dyd.
    K: end 1668. L: 5.1669. C: 4.1670. Renamed *Sage* 24.6.1671. Took part in Battles of Solebay 7.6.1672, Texel 21.8.1673, Pharo (Messina) 2.1.1675, Lipari Islands 11.2.1675, Palermo 31.5.1676 and Bantry Bay 11.5.1689. Wrecked (along with *Assuré*) while part of LG Victor Marie d'Estrées's squadron at Ceuta in a storm 19.4.1692.

BRAVE. 48, later 54 guns. Probably designed and built by François Pomet. Ordered in 1668. Pierced to carry eleven pairs of LD guns (excluding the unarmed chase ports) and seemingly the first true two-decker 3rd Rank to be built.

    Dimensions & tons: 131ft 0in, 110ft 1in x 35ft 0in x 16ft 0in (42.55, 35.76 x 11.37 x 5.20m). 900 tons. Draught 19½ft (6.33m). Men: 300, +5/7 officers.

    Guns: 48 from 1671, then 50 from 1673; 54 from 1674: LD 12 x 18pdrs + 10 x 12pdrs; UD 12 x 12pdrs + 8 x 8pdrs; QD 8 x 6pdrs; Fc 4 x 4pdrs.

Brave Rochefort Dyd.
    K: end 1668. L: 3.1670. C: 7.1670. Renamed *Prince* 24.6.1671. Took part in the Battle of Texel 21.8.1673. Wrecked on the Îles Aves (in the Caribbean) 11.5.1678, with other ships of *Vice-amiral* Jean, Comte d'Estrées's squadron.

As at 1 September 1669, there were twenty-five ships comprising the 3rd Rank – all with 5 commissioned officers and between 250 and 350 men. These comprised: *Comte*, *Dauphin* and *César*, with 50 guns and 350 men (50/200/100); the *Fleuron* of 48 guns, the *Brave* of 46 guns and *Mazarin* of 40 guns, each with 340 men (50/195/95); the *Galant* of 44 guns and *Rouen* of 52 guns, each with 325 men (50/190/85); the *Triomphe* of 44 guns and 300 men (45/175/80); the *Hercule* and *Anna* of 40 guns, the *Soleil* of 38 guns and *Trident* of 44 guns, each with 275 men (50/150/75); and twelve ships each with 250 men (45/135/70) – the *Toulon*, *Cheval Marin* and *Sirène* (44 guns each); *Duc* (42 guns); *Provençal*, *Dunkerquois*, *Flamand* and *Havre* (40 guns each); *Tigre*, *Mercœur*, *Beaufort* and *Jules* (36 guns each).

However, all of the last twelve, as well as the elderly *Mazarin*, *Galant*, *Triomphe*, *Hercule* and *Soleil*, were re-classed as 4th Rank in the re-organisation of 1671, and details on all these will be found in Chapter 4. Conversely, the 3rd Rank acquired 27 vessels which in 1669 had either not existed – *Furieux*, *Fier*, *Fidèle*, *Glorieux*, *Navarrois*, *Alsace*, *Maure*, *Indien*, *Ardent*, *Émerillon*, *Anjou*, *Oriflamme*, *Louvre*, *Wallon*, *Brillant* and *Heureux* – or had been classed as 2nd Rank – *Bourbon*, *Princesse*, *Sophie*, *Reine*, *Diamant*, *Lys*, *Navarre*, *Royale*, *Rochefort*, *Saint Louis* and *Breton* – so that the total within the 3rd Rank at 1 July 1671 had reached thirty-three vessels.

FORTUNÉ. 54, later 56 guns. Designed by François Pomet and constructed by Pomet and Jean Guichard, with twelve ports per side (excluding the chase ports) on the lower deck for the usual mix of

The Sicilian revolt against Spanish rule broke out in Messina, and in January 1675 the Spanish blockade of the port was broken by a French squadron comprising the 72-gun *Pompeux* (Valbelle's flagship), and the 3rd Rank *Fortuné*, *Agréable*, *Prudent*, *Téméraire* and *Sage*. Engraving of the approach of the French fleet by Johan Corvinus, published about 1700. (Beverley R Robinson Collection, Annapolis 51.7.60)

24pdrs and 18pdrs. Initially named *Émerillon* on 17 May 1669, but renamed *Fortuné* on 24 June 1671 (4 days after launching). Rebuilt at Toulon during 1680.

   Dimensions & tons: 134ft 0in, 108ft 0in x 36ft 0in x 16ft 0in (43.53, 35.08 x 11.69 x 5.20m). 1,000 tons. Draught 16ft/19½ft (5.20/6.33m). Men: 350 (55/180/115, later 68/188/94), +5 (later 7) officers.

   Guns: 54 from 1671, then 56 from 1673: LD 6 x 24pdrs + 18 x 18pdrs (may later have carried 22 x 24pdrs); UD 24 x 12pdrs; QD 8 x 4pdrs. 4 guns removed 1676.

Fortuné Rochefort Dyd.
   K: 5.1669. L: 20.6.1671. C: 11.1672. Took part in Battles of Schooneveldt 7 & 14.6.1673, Texel 21.8.1673, Pharo (Messina) 2.1.1675, Lipari Islands 11.2.1675 and Palermo 31.5.1676, and in bombardment of Genoa 18–28.5.1684. Condemned 1688 at Toulon.

BOURBON Class. 54, later 56 guns. Designed and built by Laurent Hubac, with eleven ports per side (excluding the chase ports) on the lower deck for 18pdrs. Nominally built as three-deckers, with the forward and aft portions of the UD separated in the waist. Named as *Louvre* and *Oriflamme* on 21 February 1670, but the former was renamed *Bourbon* on 24 June 1671. *Oriflamme* was rebuilt at Brest from August 1684 to September 1685, and reduced to 4th Rank in 1687.

   Dimensions & tons: 123ft 0in, 108ft 0in x 33ft 0in x 15ft 0in

(39.96, 35.08 x 10.72 x 4.87m). 800 tons. Draught 16ft (5.20m). Men: 300 (46/154/100, later 65/160/75), +5 (later 7) officers.

Guns: 48 from 1671. 50 from 1674: LD 12 x 18pdrs + 10 x 12pdrs; UD 12 x 12pdrs + 8 x 8pdrs; UD (aft) 4 x 4pdrs + (fwd) 4 x 6pdrs. *Oriflamme* had 48 guns from 1688 and 50 from 1691.

Bourbon Brest Dyd.
  K: 9.1669. L: 29.4.1670. C: 8.1670. Took part in Battle of Texel 21.8.1673. Wrecked on Îles Aves (in the Caribbean) 11/12.5.1678 with other ships of *Vice-amiral* Jean, Comte d'Estrées's squadron.

Oriflamme Brest Dyd.
  K: 12.1669. L: 1.11.1670. C: 6.1671. Took part in the Battles of Solebay 7.6.1672, Schooneveld 7 & 14.6.1673 and Texel 21.8.1673. Refitted at Brest 1684. Wrecked on the coast of Brittany 2.1691 while returning from Martinique, with all 256 hands lost.

EXCELLENT. 56, later 60 guns. Designed by François Pomet, with gun arrangement as in the *Fortuné*. Initially named *Navarrois* (or *Navarrais*) on 17 May 1669, but renamed *Excellent* in Colbert's mass renamings of 24 June 1671.

  Dimensions & tons: 136ft 0in, 108ft 0in x 37ft 0in x 16ft 0in (44.18, 35.08 x 12.02 x 5.20m). 1,050 tons. Draught 17ft/19½ft (5.52/6.33m). Men: 350 (55/180/115, later 68/188/94), +5 (later 7) officers.

  Guns: 56 from 1671, then 60 from 1674: LD 6 x 24pdrs + 18 x 18pdrs (may later have carried 22 x 24pdrs); UD 24 x 12pdrs; QD 8 x 4pdrs; Fc 4 x 4pdrs.

Excellent Rochefort Dyd.
  K: 4.11.1669. L: 27.11.1670. C: 1671. Took part in Battle of Texel 21.8.1673. Badly damaged by grounding 4.1674 in the Charente; refloated and taken to Soubise where found unrepairable, and BU by order of 14.9.1675.

A 3rd Rank ship of 50 guns to be built at Rochefort was named *Aquilon* on 21 February 1670, but the project was abandoned before the name was reassigned to the former *Triton* in June 1671.

FURIEUX. 56, later 58 guns. Designed and built by Rodolph Gédéon. A two-decker, pierced for twelve pairs of LD guns (excluding the unarmed chase ports). Named as *Furieux* on 21 February 1670. Moved to the 2nd Rank with 60 guns in 1673 but reverted to the 3rd Rank and 56 guns in 1674.

  Dimensions & tons: 132ft 0in x 39ft 3in x 19ft 0in (42.88 x 12.75 x 6.17m). 1,000 tons. Draught 17ft (5.52m). Men: 350 in war, 300 peace, +5/7 officers.

  Guns: 56 from 1671, then 58 from 1679: LD 6 x 24pdrs + 18 x 18pdrs (possibly later had 24 x 18pdrs); UD 24 x 12pdrs; QD/Fc 10 x 4pdrs.

Furieux Toulon Dyd.
  K: 3.1670. L: 15.4.1671. C: 6.1672. Renamed *Brillant* 28.6.1678. Condemned 6.1687 at Toulon; sold 8.1687 and BU 1688 or 1689.

FIDÈLE Class. 56, later 62 guns. Designed and built by Laurent Coulomb. Two-deckers, pierced for twelve pairs of LD guns (excluding the unarmed chase ports). Named as *Fidèle* and *Glorieux* on 21 February 1670, but the second ship was renamed *Agréable* on 24 June 1671. *Agréable* was rebuilt at Brest 1697–98, later reconstructed 1705–6 at Lorient.

  Dimensions & tons: 133ft 0in, 106ft 0in x 37ft 0in x 18ft 0in (43.20, 34.43 x 12.02 x 5.85m). 1,000 tons. Draught 17ft/19½ft (5.52/6.33m). Men: 350 (68/188/94), +7 officers.

  Guns: 56 from 1671: LD 6 x 24pdrs + 18 x 18pdrs: UD 24 x 12pdrs; QD 8 x 4pdrs. *Agréable* had 60 from 1677, then 56 in war from 1696 (50 peace): LD 22 x 24pdrs (2 more added 1699); UD 24 x 12pdrs (2 more added 1698); QD 6 x 6pdrs (2 more added 1698); Fc 4 x 6pdrs. Reduced to 50 guns in 1702, 52 in 1706–7, and then reverted to previous 62-gun armament,

Fidèle Toulon Dyd.
  K: 6.5.1670. L: 1.7.1671. C: end 1671. Took part in Battles of the Lipari Islands 11.2.1675, Augusta 22.4.1676 and Palermo 3.6.1676. Wrecked 11.1676 off Porto Vecchio, Corsica.

Agréable Toulon Dyd.
  K: 6.5.1670. L: 14.6.1671. C: end 1671. Took part in Battles of Pharo (Messina) 2.1.1675, Lipari Islands 11.2.1675 and of Palermo 31.5.1676, and in Bombardment of Tripoli 22.6.1685 (as flagship of LG Anne Hilarion de Costentin, Comte de Tourville). Lent (with *Mutine*) as a privateer under CV Châteaumorant, for escorting to India the mercantile *Étoile d'Orient*, *Perle d'Orient*, *Phélypeaux* and *Saint Louis* of the *Compagnie des Indes Orientales* in

The head and stern decoration of the 56-gun *Agréable*, launched in 1671, but rebuilt at Brest in 1697–98. It is known that Jean Bérain devised a new decorative scheme for the refitted ship, and this drawing very probably represents that design. (*Souvenirs de Marine*, Plate 147)

1692–94. Lent again as a privateer, now under CV Robecq, Baron de Pallière, for escorting to India the mercantile *Aurore* and *Saint Louis* of the *Compagnie des Indes Orientales* in 1704–5. Lent (with *Apollon*) as a privateer under CV Joseph, Baron d'Oroigne, in support of the Spanish squadron of Don Andrés de Paz in 1707. Hulked 1711 at Brest: condemned there 1715 and BU 1717.

MAURE Class. 48, later 58 guns. Ordered on 23 December 1669 as 4th Rank ships of 42 guns, but moved to 3rd Rank by end of 1672, and eventually carried 56 guns. Pierced for eleven ports per side (excluding the chase ports) on the lower deck. Designed by Joseph Saboulin, and built by Jean Hontabat. Named as *Artois* and *Grâces* respectively on 21 February 1670, but renamed *Maure* (sometimes written *More*) and *Fendant* on 24 June 1671 while building. The first ship was actually ready for launch in June 1672, but the position of the builders' yard was such that an arch of a bridge had to be demolished (by order of 12 August 1672) in order that the ship could put into the water; the second ship was much delayed in construction (to Colbert's expressed wrath!) and both ships had to be completed at Rochefort.

    Dimensions & tons: 122ft 0in, 100ft 0in x 36ft 0in x 17ft 6in (39.63, 32.48 x 22.69 x 5.68m). 881 tons. Draught 16ft/17ft (5.20/5.52m); *Fendant* was 1ft deeper. Men: 300 (46/154/100), +5 officers; later 330 (67/179/84), +6 officers.

    Guns: 48 from 1673, then 50 (*Fendant*) and 60 (*Maure*) from 1674. Both 56 from 1676: LD 12 x 18pdrs + 10 x 12pdrs; UD 12 x 12pdrs + 8 x 8pdrs; QD 6 x 6pdrs; QD 4 x 6pdrs; poop 4 x 4pdrs. *Fendant* had 54 guns from 1677, 50 from 1688, 48 from 1689 and 54 from 1691; *Maure* had 52 guns from 1679.

Maure Bayonne.
    K: Spring 1670. L: 29.8.1672. C: 4.1673 (at Rochefort Dyd). Took part in Battle of Texel 21.8.1673. Renamed *Content* 28.6.1678. Grounded in a storm on the Morbihan coast 22.10.1679; refloated 1.1680 and repaired at Auray then at Nantes. Took part in Battle of Beachy Head 10.7.1690. Hulked at Rochefort in late 1685.

Fendant Bayonne.
    K: Spring 1670. L: 29.8.1672. C: 3.1676 (at Rochefort Dyd). Took part in attack on Cayenne 17.12.1676, and in Battles of Tobago 3.3.1677, Bantry Bay 11.5.1689 and Beachy Head 10.7.1690. Lent as a privateer under CV Jacques Dandenne, for escorting to India the mercantile *Écueil*, *Florissant* and *Lonray*, of the *Compagnie des Indes Orientales* in 1692–94. Hulked at Lorient 4.1694, but in 2.1702 became a floating battery at nearby Port Louis.

INTRÉPIDE. 48, later 56 guns. Designed by François Pomet and built by Honoré Malet. A two-decker, pierced to carry twelve pairs of LD guns (excluding the unarmed chase ports). Ordered and named on 21 February 1670 as *Saint Esprit*, but renamed on 24 June 1671.

    Dimensions & tons: 135ft 0in, 102ft 0in x 34ft 0in x 16ft 0in (43.85, 33.13 x 11.04 x 5.20m). 900 tons. Draught 15ft/17ft (4.87/5.52m). Men: 300 (65/160/75), +7 officers.

    Guns: 48 from 1672 and 50 from 1674 (while still incomplete). 56 from 1676: LD 6 x 24pdrs + 18 x 18pdrs (may later have had 24 x 24pdrs); UD 24 x 12pdrs; QD 8 x 4pdrs.

Intrépide Rochefort Dyd.
    K: 6.1670. L: 7.1671. C: 6.1676. Grounded in the Charente River while leaving Rochefort 7.1676. Took part in attack on Cayenne 17.12.1676, then subsequently holed and run aground in action with the Dutch *Beschermer* and captured by the Dutch at the Battle of Tobago 3.3.1677, and added to Amsterdam Admiralty under same name; repurchased by French Navy at Amsterdam 11.3.1679. Became sheer hulk at Le Havre 11.1686.

SAINT MICHEL. 56, later 60 then 64 guns. Designed and built by Louis Audibert. A two-decker, pierced for twelve pairs of LD guns (excluding the unarmed chase ports), and with forecastle and QD. Ordered and named on 21 February 1670 as *Fier*, but renamed on 24 June 1671. Classed as 3rd Rank in 1670, but raised to 2nd Rank in 1673. Transferred to Toulon for completion 10.1673.

    Dimensions & tons: 137ft 0in, 107ft 0in x 39ft 0in x 18ft 0in (44.50, 34.76 x 12.67 x 5.85m). 1,100 tons. Draught 18ft (5.85m). Men: 400 in war (60/206/134), + 9 officers.

    Guns: 56 from 1671: LD 6 x 24pdrs + 18 x 18pdrs; UD 24 x 12pdrs; QD/Fc 8 x 4pdrs. 60 from 1674, then 64 from 1677.

Saint Michel Marseille.
    K: 7.1670. L: 8.1673. C: 6.1674 at Toulon Dyd. Took part in Battles of the Lipari Islands 11.2.1675, Stromboli 8.1.1676, Augusta 22.4.1676 and Palermo 2.6.1676 (flag of CdE Raymond Louis de Crevant, Marquis de Preuilly d'Humières for all four). Hulked at Toulon by order of 10.9.1685, and BU 1687.

PRÉCIEUX Class. 48, later 54 guns. Designed and built by contract by Barthélémy Tortel. Nominally built as three-deckers, pierced to carry eleven pairs of LD guns (excluding the unarmed chase ports), but probably converted to two-deckers during or soon after construction. Ordered on 21 June 1669, named on 21 February 1670 as *Brillant* and *Heureux*, but the first ship was renamed *Précieux* on 24 June 1671 while still under construction. The *Heureux* was rebuilt at Toulon from July 1679 to April 1680.

    Dimensions & tons: 124ft 0in, 100ft 0in x 36ft 0in (40.28, 32.48 x 11.69m). 800 tons. Draught 17ft/18ft (5.52/5.85m). Men: 300 (46/154/100), +5 officers.

    Guns: 48 from 1672. *Heureux* 50 from 1674, then 52 from 1675: LD 12 x 18pdrs + 10 x 12pdrs; MD 12 x 12pdrs + 8 x 8pdrs; UD (aft) 6 x 6pdrs + (fwd) 4 x 6pdrs. *Précieux* 54 from 1674: same but UD 8 x 6pdrs; poop 4 x 4pdrs.

Précieux Barthélémy Tortel, Le Havre.
    K: 7.1670. L: 15.12.1671. C: 4.1673. Took part in Battles of Schooneveld 7 & 14.6.1673 and of Texel 21.8.1673. Took part in attack on Cayenne 17.12.1676, then run aground and captured by the Dutch at the Battle of Tobago 3.3.1677, and added to Amsterdam Admiralty under same name; retaken 12.1677 at Tobago. Condemned there 1.1678 and burnt.

Heureux Barthélémy Tortel, Le Havre.
    K: 8.1670. L: 3.10.1671. C: 4.1672. Took part in the Battles of Solebay 7.6.1672, the Lipari Islands 11.2.1675, Stromboli 8.1.1676, Augusta 22.4.1676 and Palermo 31.5.1676. Hulked 7.1690 at Brest; BU after 1693.

APOLLON. 44, later 60 guns. Designed and built by François Pomet as a 4th Rank two-decker, and pierced for eleven pairs of LD guns (excluding the chase ports). Originally named as *Saint Michel*, but renamed *Apollon* on 24 June 1671. Raised from 4th Rank to 3rd Rank in 1673 with 56 guns, then 52 from 1675, then reduced to 4th Rank again in 1687 but was rebuilt at Toulon during 1688 and reinstated with the 3rd Rank in the same year.

    Dimensions & tons: 127ft 0in, 102ft 0in x 34ft 0in x 16ft 0in (41.25, 33.13 x 11.04 x 5.20m). 850 tons. Draught 16ft/18ft 4in (5.20/5.96m). Men: 330 in war; 260 peace, +5/7 officers.

    Guns: 44 from 1672. 52 from 1675: LD 12 x 18pdrs + 10 x 12pdrs; MD 12 x 12pdrs + 8 x 8pdrs; UD 10 x 6pdrs. 50 guns from 1677 and 54 from 1689. 54 in war from 1696 (50 peace): LD 22 x 18pdrs; UD 24 x 12pdrs; QD 8 x 6pdrs. 60 from 1699: LD 14 x 24pdrs + 10 x 18pdrs; UD 24 x 8pdrs; QD/Fc 12 x 6pdrs. In

1707 reverted to the 1696 armament but with 8 x 4pdrs on the QD.
Apollon Rochefort Dyd.
K: 8.1670. L: 8.1671. C: 12.1672. Took part in the Battles of Schooneveldt 7 & 14.6.1673, Texel 21.8.1673, the Lipari Islands 11.2.1675, Stromboli 8.1.1676, and Augusta 22.4.1676. Renamed *Hardi* 28.6.1678. Took part in Battle of Beachy Head 10.7.1690. Struck 1709 at Brest.

VAILLANT Class. 50, later 54 guns. Designed and built by Laurent Hubac. Nominally built as three-deckers, pierced for eleven pairs of LD guns (excluding the chase ports) with a mixed LD battery of 18pdrs and 12pdrs. Ordered 19 July 1670 and named on 27 July as *Anjou* and *Ardent*, the two ships were renamed *Vaillant* and *Téméraire* respectively on 24 June 1671 soon after launching. *Vaillant* was rebuilt at Toulon from April 1680 to February 1681, and *Téméraire* in the same location during 1687–88.

Dimensions & tons: 127ft 6in, 114ft 0in x 33ft 8in x 15ft 6in (41.42, 37.03 x 10.94 x 5.035m). 900 tons. Draught 16ft/16½ft (5.20/5.36m). Men: 300 (65/160/75), later 350.

Guns: *Vaillant* had 50 guns while *Téméraire* had 54 from 1671; both had 52 from 1673. 54 guns in both from 1675: LD 12 x 18pdrs + 10 x 12pdrs; MD 12 x 12pdrs + 8 x 8pdrs; UD 8 x 6pdrs; poop 4 x 4pdrs. *Téméraire* had 48 guns from 1677, 50 from 1688, and 56 from 1691.

Vaillant Brest Dyd.
K: 9.1670. L: 25.5.1671. C 4.1672. Took part in Battles of Solebay 28.5.1672, Schooneveldt 7 & 14.6.1673, Texel 21.8.1673, Stromboli 11.2.1675, Alicudi 8.1.1676 and Palermo 2.6.1676, Bombardment of Algiers 1682 and of Genoa 18–28.5.1684, and Battle of Beachy Head 10.7.1690. Condemned 1690 at Rochefort and BU 1691.

Téméraire Brest Dyd.
K: 9.1670. L: 25.5.1671. 24.6.1671. C 4.1672. Took part in Battles of Schooneveldt 7 & 14.6.1673, Texel 21.8.1673, Pharo (Messina) 2.1.1675, Lipari Islands 11.2.1675 and Palermo 2.6.1676, Beachy Head 10.7.1690 and Lagos 28.6.1693. Captured 9.12.1694 by HMS *Montagu* off Kinsale and burnt.

PARFAIT. 54, later 60 then 64 guns. Designed and built by François Chapelle. A two-decker, pierced for twelve pairs of guns on the LD (excluding the unarmed chase ports), and with forecastle and QD. Ordered and named on 21 February 1670 as the *Indien*, but renamed on 24 June 1671 prior to launch. Raised to the 2nd Rank in 1675, but reverted to the 3rd Rank in 1677–78 and underwent rebuilding at Toulon in late 1679; again raised to the 2nd Rank in 1692–95, but reverted to the 3rd Rank in 1698.

Dimensions & tons: 138ft 0in, 122ft 0in x 38ft 6in x 17ft 1in (44.83, 39.63, 12.51 x 5.55m). 1,050 tons. Draught 17ft/21ft (5.52/6.82m). Men: 350 in war, 300 peace, +5/7 officers.

Guns: 54 from 1671 (while building) then 56 from 1673: LD 6 x 24pdrs + 18 x 18pdrs; UD 24 x 12pdrs; QD 8 x 4pdrs. 60 guns from 1676, then 64 in war from 1696 (58 peace): LD 24 x 24pdrs; UD 26 x 12pdrs; QD 10 x 6pdrs (8 x 12pdrs from 1699); Fc 4 x 6pdrs.

Parfait Toulon Dyd.
K: 20.10.1670. L: 31.7.1671. C: 6.1672. Took part in the Sicilian Campaign 1675–76, in the Battles of Stromboli 11.2.1675, Stromboli (or Alicudi Island) 8.1.1676 and Palermo 2.6.1676, and in the bombardment of Genoa 18–28.5.1684. Also took part in Battles of Beachy Head 10.7.1690 and Lagos 28.6.1693. Struck 1698 and condemned 4.1699 at Toulon.

FOUGUEUX. 54, later 60 guns. Designed and built by Jean Guérouard. A two-decker, pierced for twelve pairs of LD guns (excluding the chase ports). Ordered and named on 21 February 1670 as the *Maure*, but renamed on 24 June 1671 prior to launch.

Dimensions & tons: 138ft 0in x 38ft 0in x 17ft 0in (44.83 x 12.34 x 5.52m). 1,000 tons. Draught 16ft/17ft (5.20/5.51m). Men: 350 in war, 300 peace, +5/7 officers.

Guns: 54 from 1671 (while building) then 56 from 1673. 60 from 1677: LD 6 x 24pdrs + 18 x 18pdrs; UD 24 x 12pdrs; QD 8 x4pdrs; Fc 4 x 4pdrs.

Fougueux Toulon Dyd.
K: 20.10.1670. L: 15.8.1671. C: 6.1672. Took part in Battle of Beachy Head 10.7.1690. Grounded 25.3.1691 in the Charente (on the Vergeroux Rock); unable to be refloated, she was lost on 1.4.1691.

BON. 48, later 56 guns. Designed by Laurent Hubac, and built by Jean Hontabat and Joseph Saboulin. A two-decker, pierced for eleven pairs of LD guns (excluding the unarmed chase ports). Named on 30 May 1672 (following launch).

Dimensions & tons: 127ft 6in, 114ft 0in x 34ft 0in x 15ft 6in (41.42, 37.03 x 11.04 x 5.035m). 800 tons. Draught 16½ft (5.36m). Men: 330 (67/179/84) in war, 280 peace, +5/7 officers.

Guns: 48 from 1672, then 54 from 1674: LD 12 x 18pdrs + 10 x 12pdrs; UD 12 x 12pdrs + 8 x 8pdrs; QD 8 x 6pdrs; Fc 4 x 4pdrs. 56 from 1691, probably with 2 more QD guns.

Bon Brest Dyd.
K: 5.1671. L: 25.5.1672. C: 9.1672. Took part in Battles of Schooneveld 7 & 14.6.1673, of Texel 21.8.1673 and of Ushant 17.3.1678 against Dutch (Evertsen's) squadron. Took part in Battle of Beachy Head 10.7.1690. Sailed from Toulon in 4.1692 as part of LG Victor Marie, Comte d'Estrées's squadron to join Tourville's fleet at Brest, but condemned on arrival at Brest and BU there at end 1692.

BRAVE. 48, later 56 guns. Designed and built by Hendryck Houwens. Provisionally named *Incertain* on 7 August 1671, but was given the permanent name of *Brave* in 1674 (2 years after her launching!). A two-decker, pierced for twelve pairs of LD guns (excluding the unarmed chase ports).

Dimensions & tons: 140ft 0in x 37ft 6in x ? (45.48 x 12.18m). 900 tons. Draught 14ft/17ft (4.55/5.52m). Men: 300 (65/160/75) in war, later 350, +7 officers.

Guns: 48 from 1672, then 50 from 1674. 56 from 1675: LD 6 x 24pdrs + 18 x 18pdrs; UD 24 x 12pdrs; QD 8 x 4pdrs.

Brave Dunkirk.
K: 5.1671. L: 22.9.1672. C: 8.1675? Condemned 9.6.1681 at Brest.

By 1 January 1672, further adjustments had added to the total which now comprised thirty-five vessels of between 56 and 48 guns. There were six vessels of 56 guns apiece (*Furieux, Saint Michel, Excellent, Fidèle, Agréable* and *Fier*); eight vessels of 54 guns apiece (*Fort, Diamant, Fougueux, Parfait, Fortuné, Assuré, Constant* and *Téméraire*); the 52-gun *Vaillant*; three vessels of 50 guns apiece (*Ferme, Prudent* and *Courtisan*); and seventeen vessels of 48 guns each (*Brave, Sage, Aimable, Vermandois, Prince, Fleuron, Oriflamme, Aquilon, Bourbon, Duc, Bon, Précieux, Heureux, Intrépide, Courageux, Rubis* and one unnamed newbuilding ship – which eventually became the new *Brave* – at Dunkirk). The first sixteen of these, plus the old *Brave*, had 360 men (and 5 officers) each, the others 300 men apiece. Apart from the elderly *Brave* at Brest, all were built in or after 1660, but after these there was a brief pause until fresh orders were placed in 1673.

In July 1684 the 48-gun *Bon* (under CV Comte de Relingue) was becalmed off Elba, when she was surrounded and attacked by thirty-six Spanish, Neapolitan, Genoese and Sicilian galleys. These adopted classic galley tactics, forming a semi-circle with their forward-firing guns pointing at the target, twelve astern and the remainder off the bow where the *Bon* had few guns that could fire back. The *Bon* lost 90 men killed. Eventually, using sweeps, the French ship brought her broadside to bear, which made it too dangerous for the galleys to close in, and a five-hour battle ensued. When a breeze sprang up, giving the ship power of manoeuvre, the galleys had to withdraw. For many naval historians this action is highly significant, marking the point at which the broadside-armed ship of the line finally triumphed over the age-old technology and tactics of the galley. This is *Vice-amiral* Pâris's depiction of the action. (*Souvenirs de Marine*, Plate 126)

Ex-SPANISH PRIZES (1672–1674). A Spanish Netherlands vessel probably named *San Cosimo* was captured off Gibraltar in late 1672 by Châteaurenault's squadron and added to the *Marine Royale* as *Rubis* on 28 November 1673 (she was briefly called *Saint Cosme*). The Spanish *San Pedro* was taken in 1674 by the *Magnifique* (with Vivonne's squadron off Catalonia); she was initially named *Saint Pierre* before being renamed *Constant* on 10 December 1674.

Rubis Builder unknown.
Dimensions & tons: dimensions unknown. 800 tons.
Guns: 50 from 1674 (could not carry large-calibre guns)
Condemned 5.1677 at Rochefort and sold by Order of 15.7.1677 to the *Compagnie des Indes Orientales*.

Constant Barcelona
Dimensions & tons: dimensions unknown. 850 tons.
Guns: 50 (including twelve pairs of LD guns, could not carry large-calibre guns)
Built in 1662 by Audibert. Formally renamed *Arc en Ciel* 6.1675 but continued to be called *Constant* until struck in November 1676.

HERCULE. 52 guns. Designed and built by Laurent Hubac. A two-decker, pierced for eleven pairs of LD guns (excluding the unarmed chase ports. Ordered on 3 February 1673 and named on 28 November 1673.
Dimensions & tons: 123ft 0in x 32ft 6in x 14ft 6in (39.96 x 10.56 x 4.71m). 800 tons. Draught 15½ft (5.035m). Men: 300 (65/160/75) in war, +7 officers.
Guns: 52 from 1674: LD 12 x 18pdrs + 10 x 12pdrs; MD 12 x 12pdrs + 8 x 8pdrs; UD (aft) 6 x 6pdrs + (fwd) 4 x 6pdrs.

Hercule Brest Dyd.
K: 2.1673. L: 10.1673. C: 7.1674. Nominally renamed *Arrogant* 28.6.1678, but had already been wrecked 11.5.1678 on the Îles Aves (in the Caribbean), with other ships of *Vice-amiral* Jean, Comte d'Estrées's squadron.

ÉCUEIL. 50, later 60 guns. Designed and built by Laurent Coulomb. A two-decker, pierced for twelve pairs of LD guns (excluding the unarmed chase ports). Ordered on 9 August 1673 and named on 28 November 1673. Her launch was originally scheduled for December 1677 but had to be postponed. Reconstructed 1687–88 at Brest.
Dimensions & tons: 136ft 0in, 110ft 0in x 37ft 1in x 16ft 0in (44.18, 35.73 x 12.05 x 5.20m). 900 tons. Draught 16ft (5.20m). Men: 350 (67/189/94) in war, 300 peace, +7 officers.
Guns: 50 intended during construction, then 56 from 1679: LD 6 x

24pdrs + 18 x 18pdrs; UD 24 x 12pdrs; QD 8 x 4pdrs. 60 guns from 1691.

Écueil Toulon Dyd.
K: 6.1674. L: 14.4.1678. Renamed *Fort* 21.7.1678. C: 1679. Took part in Battles of Bantry Bay 11.5.1689, Beachy Head 10.7.1690 and Barfleur 29.5.1692, then burnt by the British at La Hougue 2.6.1692.

EXCELLENT. 50, later 68 guns. Designed and built by Honoré Malet. Pierced for twelve pairs of LD guns (excluding the unarmed chase ports). Ordered and named on 11 December 1676, in theory being a rebuilding of the *Excellent* of 1670 with materials from her and the *Admirable* (ex *Frédéric*) of 1666. Her building was interrupted in order to build the *Gaillarde* and *Favorite* (*frégates légères*).
Dimensions & tons: 138ft 0in, 115ft 0in x 37ft 0in x 16ft 0in (44.82, 37.36 x 12.02 x 5.19m). 900 tons. Draught 17½ft/18½ft (5.68/6.01m). Men: 350 (67/189/94) in war, 300 peace, + 7 officers.
Guns: 50 from 1679. 60 from 1687: LD 6 x 24pdrs + 18 x 18pdrs; UD 24 x 12pdrs; QD 8 x 4pdrs; Fc 4 x 4pdrs. 60 in war from 1696 (40 peace): LD 24 x 24pdrs; UD 24 x 12pdrs; QD/Fc 12 x 6pdrs. 68 from 1706: LD 26 x 24pdrs; UD 28 x 12pdrs; QD/Fc 12 x 6pdrs + 2 x 4pdrs.

Excellent Rochefort Dyd.
K: 6.1677. L: 1679. C: 4.1680. Took part in Battles of Bantry Bay 11.5.1789, Beachy Head 10.7.1690, Barfleur 29.5.1692 and Lagos 28.6.1693. Lent as a privateer to CV François Colbert de Saint Mars, as part of a squadron of four vessels, 1696. Participated in operations at Nova Scotia under LG André, Marquis de Nesmond, in a squadron of twenty-three vessels 1697. Took part in Battle of Véléz-Malaga 24.8.1704. Scuttled at Toulon in 7.1707, raised but not maintained and run aground 1708 to prevent sinking. Condemned 15.12.1710 and sold by Order of 24.12.1710.

COURAGEUX. 50, later 60 guns. Designed and built by François Pomet, but virtually a sister ship to the *Excellent*. Originally named on 28 November 1673, to start building in 1674, but not begun until 1677 and name re-awarded 11 December 1676. Pierced for twelve pairs of LD guns (excluding the unarmed chase ports). Underwent reconstruction at Brest 1683–84.
Dimensions & tons: 136ft 0in, 115ft 0in x 35ft 6in x 16ft 0in (44.18, 37.36 x 11.53 x 5.19m). 900 tons. Draught 17½ft/19ft (5.68/6.17m). Men: 350 in war, 280 peace, + 7 officers.
Guns: 50 from 1679 and 56 from 1687. 60 from 1690: LD 6 x 24pdrs + 18 x 18pdrs; UD 24 x 12pdrs; QD 8 x 4pdrs; Fc 4 x 4pdrs. 58 in war from 1698 (50 peace): LD 14 x 24pdrs + 10 x 18pdrs; UD 24 x 12pdrs (8pdrs from 1699); QD/Fc 10 x 6pdrs.

Courageux Rochefort Dyd.
K: 10.1677. L: 18.12.1679. C: 1680. Took part in Battles of Bantry Bay 11.5.1689 (as flagship of CdE Job Forant), Beachy Head 10.7.1690, Barfleur 29.5.1692 and Lagos 28.6.1693. Struck 1705 at Brest.

Ex-DUTCH PRIZE (1677). The Dutch East India Company *Berchermer* (or *Bescherming*), built at Amsterdam in 1666, was acquired by the Amsterdam Admiralty and refitted at Amsterdam in 1676. She was captured by *Vice-amiral* Jean d'Estrées's squadron on 10 December 1677 prior to the capture of the island of Tobago and was renamed *Défenseur* (the French version of her Dutch name). The dimensions below are Dutch measurements converted to French feet.
Dimensions & tons: 123ft 6in x 34ft 10in x 12ft 2in (40.12 x 11.31 x 3.95m). Tons unknown. Men: 200
Guns: 54.

Défenseur Amsterdam
Remained in the Caribbean after captured, wrecked with other ships of *Vice-amiral* Jean, Comte d'Estrées's squadron on the Îles Aves on 11.5.1678.

ENTREPRENANT. 50, later 60 guns. Designed and built by Jean-Pierre Brun, and pierced for twelve pairs of LD guns (excluding the unarmed chase ports). Ordered and named as *Rubis* on 20 January 1678, her construction was inspected on 31 May 1679 by Seignelay, and she was renamed *Entreprenant* on 20 March 1680. Louis XIV also visited the ship on 28 July 1680, at Dunkirk. She underwent a two-third reconstruction at Toulon from October 1701 to March 1703 by François Chapelle, prolonging her life to a total of 60 years.
Dimensions & tons: 129ft 0in, 114ft 0in x 35ft 0in x 16ft 0in (41.90, 37.03 x 11.37 x 5.20m). 800? tons. Draught 15½ft/18½ft (5.035/6.01m). Men: 350 in war, 280 peace, +7 officers.
Guns: 50 from 1679. 60 from 1687: LD 6 x 24pdrs + 18 x 18pdrs; UD 24 x 12pdrs; QD 8 x 4pdrs; Fc 4 x 4pdrs. 58 in war from 1696 (50 peace): LD 8 x 24pdrs + 16 x 18pdrs; UD 24 x 12pdrs; QD/Fc 8 x 6pdrs; Fc 2 x 6pdrs. 58 from 1704: LD 10 x 24pdrs + 14 x 18pdrs; UD 26 x 12pdrs; QD/Fc 8 x 6pdrs.

Entreprenant Brest Dyd.
K: 2.1678. L: 3.1680. C: 3.1680? Took part in Battles of Bantry Bay 11.5.1689 and Beachy Head 10.7.1690. Scuttled at Toulon in 7.1707 but refloated. Condemned 1718 at Toulon, and was instructed on 6.3.1720 to convert to a careening hulk; sheer (i.e. masting) hulk 1722. Sold by Order of 13.8.1738.

A 3rd Rank ship of 60 guns was ordered in November 1678 at Toulon, and was assigned the name *Courtisan* following the loss of the 2nd Rank ship of that name on the Îles d'Aves in June, but the order was cancelled in 1680. In February 1683 a new 56-gun 3rd Rate to bear the name *Courtisan* was ordered to be built at Brest, but the order was cancelled later that year or in 1684.

PRÉCIEUX. 50, later 58 guns. Designed and built by Étienne Salicon. Two-decker, pierced for twelve pairs of LD guns (excluding the unarmed chase ports). Two 3rd Rank ships, one to be named *Intrépide* and the other *Précieux*, were projected in 1678 for construction at Rochefort after the loss of the previous ships of those names in the Battle of Tobago, but the plan was abandoned in the same year; instead, the new *Précieux* was ordered from Le Havre early in 1679 while the captured *Intrépide* was bought back from the Dutch. *Précieux* was listed as a 900-ton ship with 56 guns in 1680 and as an 800-ton ship with 50 guns from 1681.
Dimensions & tons: 134ft 0in, 110ft 0in x 33ft 0in x 15ft 0in (43.53, 35.73 x 10.72 x 4.87m). 800 tons. Draught 16ft (5.20m). Men: 330 (67/179/84), later 350 in war, 300 peace, +7 officers.
Guns: 50 from 1681, 56 from 1686, and 54 from 1688. 58 from 1691: LD 6 x 24pdrs + 18 x 18pdrs; UD 24 x 12pdrs; QD 10 x 4pdrs.

Précieux Le Havre.
K: 3.1679. L: 5.10.1679. C: 3.1680. Took part in Battles of Bantry Bay 11.5.1689 and Beachy Head 10.7.1690. Present at Battle of Lagos 28.6.1693, then struck in 1694.

PRINCE. 54, later 60 guns. Designed and built by Jean-Pierre Brun. Two-decker, pierced for twelve pairs of LD guns (excluding the unarmed chase ports). Rebuilt at Lorient 1692–93, and at Rochefort 1703–4.
Dimensions & tons: 131ft 0in, 116ft 0in x 36ft 10in x 16ft 0in (42.55, 37.68 x 11.96 x 5.20m). 850 tons. Draught 15½ft/18½ft (5.035/6.01m). Men: 350 in war, 280 peace, +7 officers.

Guns: 54 from 1680. 60 from 1688: LD 6 x 24pdrs + 18 x 18pdrs; UD 24 x 12pdrs; QD 8 x 4pdrs; Fc 4 x 4pdrs. 56 in war from 1696 (50 peace): LD 10 x 24pdrs + 14 x 18pdrs; UD 24 x 12pdrs; QD 8 x 6pdrs. 58 from 1706: LD 24 x 24pdrs; UD 26 x 12pdrs; QD/Fc 8 x 6pdrs.

Prince Brest Dyd.
  K: 6.1679. L: 1680. C: 6.1682. Took part in Battle of Beachy Head 10.7.1690. Present at Battle of Lagos 28.6.1693. Lent as a privateer to CV Henri-Louis, Marquis de Chavagnac, and CV Pierre Le Moyne d'Iberville, as part of a squadron of ten vessels, for operations in the West Indies, 1705–6. Condemned 1717 at Rochefort.

ARROGANT Class. 50, later 60 guns. Designed by Jacques Doley and built by Étienne Salicon. Two-deckers, pierced for twelve pairs of LD guns (excluding the unarmed chase ports). The *Arrogant* was originally ordered in early 1680 to be built as a 3rd Rank ship at Rochefort, but in July 1681 the order was transferred to Le Havre, where Doley's design was assisted by Renau; this was the first ship whose design was modified on ellipsographic lines.

  Dimensions & tons: 132ft 0in, 113ft 0in x 35ft 6in x 16ft 6in (42.88, 36.71 x 11.53 x 5.36m). 900 tons. Draught 16ft/18ft (5.20/5.85m). Men: 350in war, 300 peace, +7 officers.

  Guns: 50 from 1682. 60 from 1686 in *Brave* and 1688 in *Arrogant*: LD 6 x 24pdrs + 18 x 18pdrs; UD 24 x 12pdrs; QD 8 x 4pdrs; Fc 4 x 4pdrs. 58 in war from 1696 (50 peace): LD in *Arrogant* 10 x 24pdrs + 14 x 18pdrs and in *Brave* 6 x 24pdrs + 18 x 18pdrs; UD 24 x 12pdrs; QD/Fc 10 x 6pdrs. *Arrogant* from 1699 (58) LD 24 x 24pdrs; UD 24 x 12pdrs; QD/Fc 10 x 6pdrs. 58 from 1702: LD 24 x 24pdrs; UD 26 x 12pdrs; QD/Fc 8 x 6pdrs.

Arrogant Le Havre.
  K: 8.1681. L: 6.5.1682. C: 12.1682. Took part in Battles of Bantry Bay 11.5.1689, and Vélez-Málaga 24.8.1704. Captured 21.3.1705 by Vice-Adm John Leake's squadron off Gibraltar, becoming HMS *Arrogant*; wrecked with loss of all hands 15.1.1709.

Brave Le Havre.
  K: 6.1682. L: 7.6.1683. C: 10.1683. Took part in Battles of Beachy Head 10.7.1690 and Barfleur 29.5.1692. Present at Battle of Lagos 28.6.1693. Struck 1697.

APOLLON. 50, later 62 guns. Designed by Joseph Andrault, Marquis de Langeron, utilising the elliptical lines developed by Bernard Renau d'Élissagaray; and built by Étienne Hubac and Blaise Pangalo. Pierced for twelve pairs of LD guns (excluding chase ports).

  Dimensions & tons: 133ft 0in x 35ft 6in x 16ft 6in (43.20 x 11.53 x 5.36m). 900 tons. Draught 16ft/18ft (5.20/5.85m). Men: 300 (65/160/75), +7 officers.

  Guns: 50 from 1683. 56 from 1687: LD 6 x 24pdrs + 18 x 18pdrs; UD 24 x 12pdrs; QD 8 x 4pdrs. 60 from 1690, 58 from 1696. 56 from 1698 in war (36? peace): LD 12 x 24pdrs + 12 x 18pdrs; UD 24 x 12pdrs; QD 8 x 6pdrs. 62 from 1707: LD 24 x 24pdrs; UD 26 x 12pdrs; QD 8 x 6pdrs; Fc 4 x 6pdrs. 56 from 1710: LD 22 x 24/18pdrs; UD 24 x 12pdrs; QD/Fc 10 x 6pdrs.

Apollon Brest Dyd.
  K: 5.1682. L: 1.1683. C: 4.1683. Took part in the Battles of Bantry Bay 11.5.1689 and Beachy Head 10.7.1690. Lent as a privateer to CdE Jean Bernard de Saint-Jean, Baron de Pointis, as part of a squadron of fourteen vessels, 1696–97; took part in the capture of Cartagena de Indias 5.5.1697. Lent as a privateer to CV Henri-Louis, Marquis de Chavagnac, and CV Pierre Le Moyne d'Iberville, as part of a squadron of ten vessels, for operations in the West Indies 1705–6. Lent (with *Agréable*) as a privateer under CV Joseph, Baron d'Oroigne, in support of the Spanish squadron of Don Andrés de Pez, 1707. Struck 6.1716 and hulked at Port Louis; the hulk was handed over in 8.1719 to the *Compagnie des Indes* at Lorient.

VERMANDOIS. 60, later 62 guns. Designed and built by Étienne Hubac. Pierced to carry twelve pairs of LD guns (excluding chase ports). Reduced from the 2nd Rank to the 3rd Rank in 1687; rebuilt at Brest from November 1699 to March 1701, then raised again to the 2nd Rank in 1702-3, but reverted to the 3rd Rank in 1706.

  Dimensions & tons: 136ft 0in x 36ft 6in x 16ft 0in (44.18 x 11.86 x 5.20m). 1,000 tons. Draught 17ft/19ft (5.52/6.17m). Men: 350 in war, 280 peace, +7 officers.

  Guns: 60 from 1686: LD 6 x 24pdrs + 18 x 18pdrs; UD 24 x 12pdrs; QD 8 x 4pdrs; Fc 4 x 4pdrs. 62 from 1696 in war (54 peace): LD 24 x 24pdrs; UD 26 x 12pdrs (24 from 1706); QD/Fc 10 x 6pdrs (10 in 1698, 12 from 1699).

Vermandois Brest Dyd.
  K: 1.1684. L: 1.4.1684. C: 1684. Took part in Battles of Bantry Bay 11.5.1689, Beachy Head 10.7.1690 and Lagos 28.6.1693. Lent as a privateer to CdE Jean Bernard de Saint-Jean, Baron de Pointis, as part of a squadron of fourteen vessels, 1696-97; took part in the capture of Cartagena de Indias 5.5.1697. Took part in Battle of Vélez-Málaga 24.8.1704. Scuttled at Toulon in 7.1707, but refloated. Hulked 5.1716 at Toulon, sheer hulk there 6.1717, sank from neglect 1721, raised and BU 1727 (by Order of 10.1.1724).

Ex-GENOESE PRIZE (1684). The Genoese *San Giacomo* was captured on April 1684 and added to the French Navy as the *Saint Jacques* (under which name she took part in the Bombardment of Genoa in May 1684), but was quickly renamed *Saint Louis* in June. Initially rated as 2nd Rank, but moved to 3rd Rank 1687.

  Dimensions & tons: dimensions unknown. 900 tons. Draught 17ft/19ft (5.52/6.17m). Men: 350 in war, 280 peace, +7 officers.

  Guns: 56 in 1684; 60 from 1686, 58 from 1687, then 60 again from 1690.

Saint Louis Genoa.
  L: 1681. Took part in Battles of Beachy Head 10.7.1690 and Barfleur 29.5.1692, then burnt by British at La Hougue 2.6.1692.

MARQUIS. 58, later 60 guns. Designed and built by Laurent Coulomb. Pierced for twelve pairs of LD guns (excluding the unarmed chase ports). Ordered in May 1684.

  Dimensions & tons: 135ft 0in, 113ft 0in x 37ft 6in x 16ft 0in (43.85, 36.71 x 12.18 x 5.20m). 900/1,595 tons. Draught 16ft/18ft (5.20/5.85m). Men: 350 in war, 280 peace, +7 officers.

  Guns: 58 from 1686. 60 from 1691: LD 6 x 24pdrs + 18 x 18pdrs; UD 24 x 12pdrs; QD 8 x 4pdrs; Fc 4 x 4pdrs. 60 in war from 1696 (50 peace): LD 24 x 18pdrs; UD 26 x 12pdrs; QD/Fc 10 x 6pdrs (8 from 1705).

Marquis Toulon Dyd.
  K: 5.1684. L: 4.3.1685. C: 12.1685. Took part in Battles of Beachy Head 10.7.1690, Barfleur 29.6.1692, Lagos (in Reserve) 28.6.1693 and Vélez-Málaga 24.8.1704. Captured by the Dutch *Veere* 21.3.1705 off Marbella; wrecked 4.1705.

SANS PAREIL. 60, later 58 guns. A two-decker, designed by Jacques Doley (enlarged from *Arrogant* design) and built by Étienne Salicon. Pierced for twelve pairs of LD guns (excluding chase ports). Reduced from the 2nd to 3rd Rank in 1687.

Dimensions & tons: 133ft 0in, 118ft 0in x 35ft 0in x 17ft 0in (43.20, 38.33 x 11.37 x 5.52m). 1,000 tons. Draught 17ft/19ft (5.52/6.17m). Men: 350 in war, 280 peace, +7 officers.

Guns: 60 from 1686: LD 6 x 24pdrs + 18 x 18pdrs; UD 24 x 12pdrs; QD 8 x 4pdrs; Fc 4 x 4pdrs. 58 in war from 1696 (50 peace): LD 24 x 24pdrs; UD 24 x 12pdrs; QD/Fc 10 x 6pdrs.

Sans Pareil Le Havre.
K: 7.1684. L: end 1685. C: 4.1686. Took part in Battles of Beachy Head 10.7.1690, Barfleur 29.5.1692 and Lagos 28.6.1693. Struck at Rochefort 1698.

MODÉRÉ. 60, later 52 guns. A two-decker, designed and built by Hendryck Houwens. Pierced for eleven pairs of LD guns (excluding the chase ports).

Dimensions & tons: 126ft 8in x 33ft 8in x 15ft 4in (41.15 x 10.94 x 4.98m). 800 tons. Draught 16ft/19ft (5.20/6.17m). Men: 300 (65/160/75), later 350 in war, 280 peace, +7 officers.

Guns: 60 from 1686: LD 12 x 18pdrs + 10 x 12pdrs; UD 12 x 12pdrs + 8 x 8pdrs; QD 6 x 6pdrs; Fc 4 x 6pdrs. 50 from 1687, then 52 from 1696 in war (44 peace): LD 22 x 18pdrs; UD 24 x 8pdrs; QD 6 x 6pdrs. 52 from 1699: LD 12 x 18pdrs + 10 x 12pdrs; UD 24 x 8pdrs; QD 6 x 4pdrs.

Modéré Dunkirk.
K: 8.1684. L: 1685. C: 5.1686? Took part in Battle of Bantry Bay 11.5.1689. Present at Battle of Lagos 28.6.1693. Lent as a

A plan of the siege of Toulon in August 1707 (book illustration published in 1759). Although ultimately unsuccessful in taking the town, the Allied bombardment was very damaging to the French Navy. The 3rd Rank *Sage* was sunk by the fire of British bomb vessels, and the *Fortuné* was so severely damaged that she had to be condemned immediately after the siege, while 22 other 3rd Rank ships were among the 44 vessels intentionally scuttled to avoid a similar fate, including *Diamant*, *Fleuron* and *Fendant*. The scuttled ships were raised once the siege was over, but few were ever returned to active service. (Beverley R Robinson Collection, Annapolis 51.7.97)

privateer to LG André, Marquis de Nesmond, as part of a squadron of six to eleven vessels, 1696. Captured 23.10.1702 by Anglo-Dutch forces at Vigo, becoming HMS *Moderate*; hulked at Portsmouth 1712 and sold 12.1713.

DIAMANT. 58, later 60 guns. A two-decker, designed and built by Hendryck ('Endricq') Houwens. Pierced for twelve pairs of LD guns (excluding the unarmed chase ports). Rebuilt at Brest from late 1701 to early 1702.

>Dimensions & tons: 128ft 0in x 35ft 2in x 16ft 3in (41.58 x 11.42 x 5.28m). 800 tons. Draught 17ft/19ft (5.20/6.17m). Men: 300 (65/160/75), later 350 in war, 280 peace, +7 officers.
>
>Guns: 58 from 1687 and 54 from 1688. 60 from 1690: LD 6 x 24pdrs + 18 x 18pdrs; UD 24 x 12pdrs; QD 8 x 4pdrs; Fc 4 x 4pdrs. 52 in war from 1696 (46 peace): LD 12 x 24pdrs + 12 x 18pdrs; UD 24 x 12pdrs; QD 4 x 6pdrs. 58 from 1698: LD 14 x 24pdrs + 10 x 18pdrs (24 x 18pdrs from 1706); UD 24 x 12pdrs (22 x 8pdrs between 1699 and 1704); QD/Fc 10 x 6pdrs.

Diamant Dunkirk.
>K: 10.1684. L: 2.1687. C: 7.1687. Took part in Battle of Bantry Bay 11.5.1689, where her poop was destroyed in a munitions explosion; repaired at Brest. Took part in Battles of Beachy Head 10.7.1690 and Barfleur 29.5.1692; at Battle of Lagos (in Reserve) 28.6.1693. Took part in Battle of Vélez-Málaga 24.8.1704. Damaged (upper deck burnt) by the fire of English bomb vessels at Toulon 8.1707, then scuttled to avoid further bombardment, but refloated about 10.1707 and repaired. Aground at Toulon from 1716 to 1724 for lack of maintenance. BU at Toulon 8.2.1724–15.1.1725 by Order of 10.1.1724.

SAINT MICHEL. 58, later 60 guns. A two-decker, designed and built by Étienne Salicon, probably derived from his *Sans Pareil* design. Pierced for twelve pairs of LD guns; there were no chase ports cut through, an early example of the elimination of this outmoded feature which became normal practice by *c*.1700. As usual, gunports were 32in wide, and were spaced 7ft 2in apart, so that there was now an uncut (and thus structurally strengthened) section of 17ft in this ship from the stem to the most forward LD gunport. Rebuilt at Brest during 1699, and raised from the 3rd Rank to 2nd Rank in 1702-3.

>Dimensions & tons: 135ft 0in, 118ft 0in x 35ft 6in x 16ft 6in (43.85, 38.33 x 11.53 x 5.36m). 1,000 tons. Draught 18¾ft/20½ft (6.09/6.66m). Men: 350 (67/189/94); by 1696, 380 in war, 300 peace, +7 officers.
>
>Guns: 58 from 1687, then 56 from 1688. 60 from 1690: LD 6 x 24pdrs + 18 x 18pdrs; UD 24 x 12pdrs; QD 8 x 4pdrs; Fc 4 x 4pdrs. 58 in war (50 peace) from 1696: LD 24 x 24pdrs; UD 26 x 12pdrs; QD 8 x 6pdrs; Fc nil. 60 in war (52 peace) from 1698, when 2 x 12pdrs were removed from the UD and 4 x 6pdrs added to the Fc.

Saint Michel Le Havre.
>K: 4.1686. L: 14.12.1686. C: 7.1687. Took part in Battles of Bantry Bay 11.5.1689 (as flagship of CdE Louis Gabaret), Beachy Head 10.7.1690 and Barfleur 29.5.1692. Present at Battle of Lagos 28.6.1693. Lent as a privateer to CdE Jean Bernard de Saint-Jean, Baron de Pointis, as part of a squadron of fourteen vessels, 1696-97; took part in the capture of Cartagena de Indias 5.5.1697. Grounded in the Baie de Trépassés (near Pointe du Raz) and lost 1.5.1704.

FORTUNÉ Class. 56, later 60 guns. With war brewing against the English and Dutch, these were additions to the *Flotte du Levant* which replaced the ships of the same names that had been condemned in 1688. Two-deckers, designed by Laurent Coulomb, and built by Laurent and his son François Coulomb respectively. Pierced for eleven pairs of LD guns (excluding the chase ports). Contracted on 14 August 1688, and named on 4 October. *Fortuné* underwent rebuilding at Toulon from January to March 1699.

>Dimensions & tons: 132ft 0in, 108ft 0in x 36ft 0in x 16ft 2in (42.88, 35.08 x 11.69 x 5.25m). 900 tons. Draught *Fortuné* 16ft/18ft (5.20/5.85m). *Fleuron* 17ft/17ft 4in (5.52/5.63m). Men: 350 in war, 280 peace, +7 officers.
>
>Guns: 56 from 1689 (incomplete), 60 from 1690, then (*Fleuron* only) reduced to 58 from 1691. *Fortuné* from 1696: 52 in war (50 peace): LD 8 x 24pdrs +14 x 18pdrs; UD 24 x 12pdrs; QD/Fc 6 x 6pdrs (8 from 1698). *Fleuron* from 1696 and *Fortuné* from 1699: 56 in war (48 peace): LD 8 x 24pdrs +16 x 18pdrs; UD 24 x 12pdrs; QD/Fc 8 x 6pdrs. *Fleuron* from 1704 (52 guns): LD 22 x 18pdrs; UD 24 x 12pdrs; QD 6 x 6pdrs (*Fortuné* same but 2 extra 6pdrs).

Fortuné Toulon Dyd.
>K: 9.1688. L: 16.7.1689. C: 2.1690. Took part in the Battles of Beachy Head 10.7.1690 and Lagos 28.6.1693. Lent as a privateer to Locquet de Granville from St Malo under the command of Beaubriant-L'Évêque, 1694–95. Lent as a privateer to LG André, Marquis de Nesmond, as part of a squadron of six to eleven vessels, 1696. Took part in the Battle of Vélez-Málaga 24.8.1704. Burnt 21.8.1707 in Toulon harbour by incendiary fire from British bomb vessels and condemned.

Fleuron Toulon Dyd.
>K: 10.1688. L: 21.7.1689. C: end 1689. Took part in Battles of Beachy Head 10.7.1690 and Barfleur 29.5.1692. Participated in operations at Nova Scotia under LG André, Marquis de Nesmond, in a squadron of twenty-three vessels 1697. Took part in the Battle of Vélez-Málaga 24.8.1704. Scuttled in Toulon harbour 7.1707 to avoid incendiary fire from British bomb vessels, but refloated 11.1707 and refitted. Hulked at Toulon 1715, struck in 1719 beached on 26.9.1722 to BU.

(C) Vessels acquired from 15 April 1689

At the start of 1689 the 3rd Rank comprised thirty-seven vessels, including the *Fortuné* and *Fleuron* still under construction; two were of 66 guns each (*Ardent* and *Content*), thirteen were of 60 guns each (*Assuré, Ferme, Agréable, Fougueux, Parfait, Entreprenant, Excellent, Prince, Arrogant, Brave, Vermandois, Furieux* and *Sans Pareil*), three had 58 guns each (*Prudent, Saint Louis* and *Marquis*), six had 56 guns each (*Fort, Courageux, Apollon, Saint Michel, Fortuné* and *Fleuron*), six had 54 guns each (*Vigilant, Vaillant, Bon, Hardi, Précieux* and *Diamant*), four had 52 guns each (*Aimable, Aquilon, Sage* and *Heureux*), two were of 50 guns (*Téméraire* and *Modéré*) and one was of 48 guns (*Fendant*). Thirteen ships had a complement of 350 men (68/188/94) while twenty-four had a complement of 300 men (65/160/75); each in addition had 7 (commissioned) officers.

Ex-DUTCH PRIZES (1688–90). Three ships of 46/54 guns were captured from the Dutch Navy during the early part of the War of the League of Augsburg and added to the French Navy. The *Moriaans Hoofd* (built in 1679–80) was captured off Stromboli on 20 September 1688, and was first named *Teste de More*, but acquired the name *Brusque* on 27 March 1689. The elderly *Amsterdam* (built in 1653) was captured about May 1689 and was first added under the same name, but was renamed

Vaillant in 1690. The *Catharina* (built in 1685) was captured in October 1690 and was initially added under the francophonic equivalent *Catherine*, but was renamed *Envieux* in 1691. *Brusque* was increased from the 4th Rank in 1690 while *Envieux* may have been re-classed to the 3rd Rank from the *flûte Catherine* in 1691. *Brusque* and *Envieux* were present at Battle of Lagos 28.6.1693. Four further ships were captured in 1692–94, but are listed in the next section.

Brusque Amsterdam
   Dimensions & tons: 115ft 0in x 31ft 0in x 12ft 3in (37.36 x 10.07 x 3.98m). 600 tons. Draught 14ft/17½ft (4.55/5.68m). Men: 300 in war (64/161/75), 240 peace, +7 officers.
   Guns: 46 from 1689, and 50 from 1691 in war (44 peace): LD 22 x 18pdrs; UD 24 x 8pdrs; QD 4 x 4pdrs.
   Struck 1697.

Vaillant Amsterdam
   Dimensions & tons: 122ft 0in x 30ft 0in x 12ft 2in (39.63 x 9.75 x 3.95m). 700 tons. Men: 300 in war.
   Guns: 54 from 1691.
   Struck 1692.

Envieux Amsterdam
   Dimensions & tons: 110ft 0in x 31ft 0in x 10ft 2in (m). 700 tons. Draught 14ft/14½ft (m). Men: 280, +4 officers.
   Guns: 50 in war (44 peace): LD 20 x 12pdrs; UD 20 x 8pdrs; QD 10 x 6pdrs.
   Participated in operations at Nova Scotia and Hudson Bay under CV Le Moyne d'Iberville, in a squadron of four vessels 1696–97. Struck 1699 at Rochefort; probably sold for commerce.

A new series of vessels was begun after mid-1689. The new *Ordonnance* brought in by Louis XIV on 15 April of that year (comprising 405 pages) set out a new structure for the Navy. Following the start of the War of the League of Augsburg (called in Britain 'King William's War'), and especially following the early death on 3 November 1690 of the 39-year-old Marquis de Seignelay, the French Minister for the Navy and Colbert's son and successor (thus bringing to an end the Colbert era), construction began of a new fleet with a greater emphasis on the smaller *vaisseaux* of the 3rd Rank. The 1689 *Ordonnance* ideally envisaged that future 3rd Rank ships should be of 60 guns, and their LD ordnance should be pierced for eleven pairs of guns, continuing to be a mixed-calibre battery, which would comprise 6 x 24pdrs (bronze) and 16 x 18pdrs (iron); the UD should mount twelve pairs of 12pdrs (14 bronze and 10 iron), and the QD and forecastle should carry 10 x 6pdrs (bronze), with the armament completed by 4 x 4pdrs (iron) on the poop. Five ships were built and fitted with mixed-calibre LD batteries, although the actual mix varied from ship to ship.

ASSURÉ. 60 guns. Designed and built by Hendryck Houwens. Pierced for twelve pairs of LD gunports (excluding the chase ports).
   Dimensions & tons: dimensions unknown. 800 tons. Draught 17ft/17½ft (5.52/5.68m). Men: 350 (67/189/94) in war, 280 peace, +7 officers.
   Guns: 60 in war (50 peace): LD 10 x 24pdrs + 14 x 18pdrs; UD 26 x 12pdrs; QD 8 x 6pdrs.

Assuré Dunkirk.
   K: 7.1689. L: 12.1689. C: 5.1690. Wrecked (along with *Sage*) while part of LG Victor Marie, Comte d'Estrées's squadron at Ceuta in a storm 19.4.1692.

ENTENDU. 58 guns. Designed and built by René Levasseur. Pierced for twelve pairs of LD gunports (excluding the chase ports), fitted with a mixture of 24pdrs and 18pdrs on that deck.
   Dimensions & tons: 136ft 0in x 35ft 8in x 16ft 6in (44.18 x 11.59 x 5.36m). 900 tons. Draught 16½ft/19½ft (5.36/6.33m). Men: 350 (67/189/94) in war, 280 peace, +7 officers.
   Guns: 58 in war (50 peace): LD 10 x 24pdrs + 14 x 18pdrs; UD 26 x 12pdrs; QD 8 x 6pdrs (10 from 1699).

Entendu Dunkirk.
   K: 9.1690. L: 2.1691. C: 5.1691. Took part in Battle of Barfleur 29.5.1692, then wrecked at Le Havre (broke her back) but salved. Present at Battle of Lagos 28.6.1693. Struck at Rochefort 1701.

CAPABLE. 58 guns. Designed and built by René Levasseur. Pierced for twelve pairs of LD gunports (excluding the chase ports), this was armed like the *Entendu* with a mixture of 24pdrs and 18pdrs on that deck.
   Dimensions & tons: 131ft 0in x 35ft 6in x 14ft 8in (42.55 x 11.53 x 4.76m). 850 tons. Draught 19ft (6.17m). Men: 350, +7 officers.
   Guns: 58 in war (50 peace): LD 10 x 24pdrs + 14 x 18pdrs (24 x 24pdrs from 1699); UD 26 x 12pdrs; QD 8 x 6pdrs.

Capable Dunkirk.
   K: 1.1692. L: 9.1692. C: 2.1693. Took part in Battle of Lagos 28.6.1693. Participated in operations in Nova Scotia under LG André, Marquis de Nesmond, in a squadron of twenty-three vessels 1697. Condemned and BU at Brest 1.1706.

INDIEN. 52 guns. Designed and built by Pierre Coulomb. Pierced for twelve pairs of LD gunports (excluding the chase ports), this was armed like the *Entendu* with a mixture of 24pdrs and 18pdrs on that deck, although with fewer 24pdrs and more 18pdrs.
   Dimensions & tons: 127ft 0in, 100ft 0in x 34ft 0in x 15ft 9in (41.25, 32.48 x 11.04 x 5.12m). 800/850 tons. Draught 18ft/19ft (5.85/6.17m). Men: 330-340 in war, +7/9 officers.
   Guns: 52 in war (46 peace): LD 6 x 24pdrs + 18 x 18pdrs; UD 24 x 12pdrs; QD 4 x 6pdrs. 56 from 1698/9: LD 14 x 24pdrs + 10 x 18pdrs; UD 22 x 8pdrs; QD/Fc 10 x 6pdrs.

Indien Lorient.
   K: 5.1692. L: 22.10.1692. C: 2.1693. Present at the Battle of Lagos 28.6.1693. Lent as a privateer to CV Des Augiers, as part of a squadron of four vessels, for escorting to India the mercantile *Marchand des Indes*, *Perle d'Orient*, *Pontchartrain* and *Princesse de Savoie* of the *Compagnie des Indes Orientales* in 1697–98; lost by grounding at Negrais (Burma) 1698.

In April 1692 orders were placed for three 60-gun 3rd Rank ships, two to be built at Brest (named as *Duc* and *Fougueux*) and one at Rochefort (*Oriflamme*). Orders for a 50-gun ship at Rochefort (*Mignon*) and seven fireships (two each at Brest, Lorient and Rochefort, and one at Toulon) were issued at the same time, but all of these ships were cancelled in June 1692. The 60-gun ships were probably intended to have been of mixed LD batteries as specified in the 1689 Ordonnance, but in their place three 50-gun ships (with 18pdr batteries) were ordered in 1694 – *Oriflamme* at Bayonne (renamed *Gaillard*) in 1693, and *Fougueux* and *Téméraire* in 1694 at Brest (see below).

BON. 56 guns. Designed to dimensions and elliptical lines specified by Bernard Renau d'Élissagaray with the intention of employing her for privateering, and built by Jean-Pierre Brun. Ordered on 6 May 1693 and named on 15 August although the name had been in use since May. Pierced for twelve pairs of LD gunports (the chase ports were probably never cut through), this was armed like the *Entendu* with a mixture of 24pdrs and 18pdrs on that deck. Reconstructed during 1697 at Rochefort including sheathing the underwater hull in lead.

Dimensions & tons: 132ft 0in x 33ft 8in x 14ft 0in (42.88 x 10.94 x 4.55m). 750 tons. Draught 16ft/17ft (5.20/5.52m). Men: 330 in war, 260 peace, +7/8 officers.

Guns: 56 in war (50 peace): LD 8 x 24pdrs + 16 x 18pdrs; UD 24 x 8pdrs; QD 8 x 4pdrs. 54 from 1698/9: LD 10 x 24pdrs + 14 x 8pdrs; UD 24 x 12pdrs; QD/Fc 6 x 6pdrs. 52 from 1701: LD 24 x 18pdrs; UD 24 x 8pdrs; QD/Fc 4 x 4pdrs.

Bon Brest Dyd.
K: 6.1693. L: 17.8.1693. C: 3.1694. Lent as a privateer to CV Bernard Renau d'Élissagaray 1693, and captured the HEICo 64-gun *Berkeley Castle* off the Isles of Scilly. Lent as a privateer under CV Des Augiers, as part of a squadron of four vessels, for escorting to India the mercantile *Marchand des Indes*, *Perle d'Orient*, *Pontchartrain* and *Princesse de Savoie* of the *Compagnie des Indes Orientales* in 1697-98. Struck 1703 at Lorient.

Ex-DUTCH PRIZES (1693). The Dutch 64-gun ships *Zeelandia* (built in 1685) and *Wapen van Medemblik* (built in 1689) were captured off Lagos by Gabaret (commanding the van of Tourville's fleet) on 27 June 1693 while defending the Smyrna convoy, and added to the French Navy. Both were raised from the 3rd Rank to 2nd Rank in 1702–3, but were restored to 3rd Rank in 1706.

Zélande Amsterdam.
Dimensions & tons: 126ft 8in x 34ft 6in x 14ft 0in (41.15 x 11.20 x 4.55m). 818 tons. Draught 16ft/17½ft (5.20/5.68m). Men: 350 in war, 320 peace, +7/10 officers.

Guns: 60 in war (52 peace): LD 12 x 24pdrs + 12 x 18pdrs (24 x 24pdrs from 1701); UD 24 x 12pdrs; QD/Fc 12 x 6pdrs.

Lent as a privateer under CV Guillaume d'Aché, Comte de Serquigy, as part of a squadron of three vessels, for escorting to India the mercantile *Florissant*, *Lonray* and *Pontchartrain*, of the *Compagnie des Indes Orientales* in 1695–98, then lent to CV Des Augiers, as part of a squadron of three vessels, for escorting to India the mercantile *Marchand des Indes*, *Perle d'Orient*, *Pontchartrain* and *Princesse de Savoie*, of the *Compagnie des Indes Orientales* in 1697–1700. Took part in Battle of Vélez-Málaga 24.8.1704. Scuttled at Toulon in 7.1707, but refloated. Condemned 6.6.1708 and hulked 26.6.1708 at Toulon.

Ville de Médemblick Medemblick, North Holland.
Dimensions & tons: 122ft 0in x 37ft 0in x 12ft 0in (39.63 x 12.02 x 3.90m). 746 tons. Draught 15ft/16ft (4.87/5.20m). Men: 350 in war, 320 peace, +8 officers.

Guns: 62 in war (50 peace): LD 24 x 24pdrs; UD 24 x 12pdrs; QD/Fc 14 x 6pdrs. 50 from 1699: LD 20 x 18pdrs; UD 22 x 8pdrs; QD/Fc 8 x 6pdrs. 52 from 1708: LD 22 x 18pdrs; UD 24 x 8pdrs; QD/Fc 6 x 6pdrs.

Lent for privateering to CV Guillaume d'Aché, Comte de Serquigy, as part of a squadron of three vessels, for escorting to India the mercantile *Florissant*, *Lonray* and *Pontchartrain*, of the *Compagnie des Indes Orientales* in 1695–98. Lent as a privateer to François Saupin, Sieur du Rocher (a wood merchant at Brest, and Director of the *Compagnie de l'Asiento*) 1704. Struck at Rochefort 1712.

After 1694, no longer were there mixed batteries of guns of differing calibre on the same deck (although sometimes there remained mixes of bronze and iron guns). The new 3rd Rank ships were built with a LD battery either entirely of 24pdrs or entirely of 18pdrs. The larger type of 3rd Rank was generally of between 135ft and 142ft in length, and had twelve pairs of LD gunports (the additional chase ports were increasingly deleted, although in some vessels they persisted until about 1700, after which they were no longer cut through) in which 24pdrs were carried.

The smaller type was generally of between 120ft and 138ft in length, and had either twelve or eleven pairs of LD gunports (again, excluding any chase ports) in which 18pdrs were carried. As this bifurcation soon became established, the two groups are listed separately in the remainder of the Section.

24pdr-armed type

These ships were the direct ancestors of the 60-gun and 64-gun ships of the eighteenth century. The first of these was begun in 1692, and four ships of this type were built for the French Navy (as well as two similar ships for the Knights of Malta) between 1695 and 1705, while a final unit was built from 1712 as a replacement for a lost vessel. All were pierced for twelve pairs of LD guns. As well as the primary battery of 24 x 24pdrs (usually 12 of these were iron guns and 12 bronze) on the lower deck, they usually carried 26 x 12pdrs on the upper deck (usually 16 iron and 10 bronze), and carried a number of bronze 6pdrs on the quarterdeck and forecastle.

PHÉNIX. 60 guns. The first of five 60-gun ships to be designed and built for the French Navy at Toulon by François Coulomb, who had replaced his father Laurent there. Named on 7 April 1692 with labour contract concluded 28 May, she was originally planned to be 126ft in length (102 ft keel) and have 50 guns, but in June 1692 the design was stretched by 9ft to allow extra guns to be mounted. Rebuilt at Rochefort from 1707 to 1710.

Dimensions & tons: 135ft 0in, 111ft 0in x 37ft 8in x 17ft 6in (43.85, 36.06 x 12.24 x 5.68m). 1,050 tons. Draught 20ft (6.50m). Men: 350-380.

Guns: 60 in war (50 peace): LD 24 x 24pdrs; UD 26 x 12pdrs; QD/Fc 10 x 6pdrs (12 from 1707) (+ 5 x 10in mortars).

Phénix Toulon Dyd.
K: 3.1692. L: 7.10.1692. C: 12.2.1693. Lent as a privateer to CV Bernard Renau d'Élissagaray, as part of a squadron of four vessels, for operations in the West Indies, 1696. Lent as a privateer to CV Henri-Louis, Marquis de Chavagnac, and CV Pierre Le Moyne d'Iberville, as part of a squadron of ten vessels, for operations in the West Indies, 1705–6. Struck 1712 at Rochefort and BU 1714.

TRIDENT. 60, later 56 guns. Designed by François Coulomb. An improved version of the *Phénix*. Rebuilt at Toulon from December 1703 to 1704.

Dimensions & tons: 136ft 0in, 111ft 0in x 37ft 6in x 16ft 6in (44.18, 36.06 x 12.18 x 5.36m). 950/1,000 tons. Draught 17ft/18ft (5.52/5.85m). Men: 350.

Guns: 60 in war (54 peace): LD 24 x 24pdrs; UD 26 x 18pdrs (12pdrs from 1699); QD/Fc 10 x 6pdrs. From refit of 12.1703 carried LD 24 x 18pdrs; UD 26 x 12pdrs; QD 6 x 4pdrs.

Trident Toulon Dyd.
K: 5.1695. L: 8.1695. C: 1.1696. Took part in Battle of Vélez-Málaga 24.8.1704. Scuttled at Toulon in 7.1707 but refloated. Condemned 6.1717 at Toulon; struck 10.1718 and BU 1720.

ASSURÉ Class. 60 guns. Designed by François Coulomb, with decorative work by Jean Bérain; two were named on 6 January 1697, the first replacing the ship of the same name lost in 1692, and the second replacing the earlier ship hulked in 1695. Although longer than the *Trident*, these were likewise pierced for just twelve pairs of LD guns. With this pair, no further orders for battlefleet units were placed until after the outbreak of the War of the Spanish Succession.

Dimensions & tons: 140ft 0in, 114ft 0in x 37ft 10in x 16ft 10in

(45.48, 37.03 x 12.29 x 5.47m). 1,000/1,050 tons. Draught 18ft (5.85m). Men: 390.

Guns: 60 in war (56 peace): LD 24 x 24pdrs; UD 26 x 12pdrs; QD 10 x 6pdrs.

Assuré Toulon Dyd.

K: 12.1696. L: 1697. C: 1.1698. Captured by the British Navy at Vigo 23.10.1702, becoming HMS *Assurance*; BU 1812.

Prudent Toulon Dyd.

K: 12.1696. L: 31.8.1697. C: 1.1698. Burnt at Vigo to avoid capture 23.10.1702.

With the conclusion of the Nine Years' War, no further ships of this class were built for France until 1703. However, on 31 March 1700 the Grand Master of the Order of Saint John (the Knights of Malta) proposed the introduction of sailing warships into their force (hitherto composed of galleys), and this was authorised by Pope Clement XI on 15 April 1701. As Malta lacked facilities to build large sailing warships at that time, orders were placed in France for the initial two 3rd Rank ships. The two – the flagship *San Giovanni Battista* and the slightly smaller *San Giacomo* – were designed and laid down at Toulon by François Coulomb and his son Blaise on 26 April 1702. Commissioned in 1704, and similar in design to Coulomb's 24pdr-armed ships for the French Navy, each carried 64 guns and a complement of 380 men (+12 officers), and served until 1716 and 1718 respectively.

FIDÈLE. 58 guns. Designed and built by Philippe Cochois. Pierced for twelve pairs of LD guns.

Dimensions & tons: 136ft 0in, 120ft 0in x 38ft 2in x 15ft 8in (44.18, 38.98 x 12.40 x 5.09m). 800 tons. Draught 17½ft/19½ft (5.68/6.33m). Men: 380 in war, 300 peace, +8 officers.

Guns: 58 in war (50 peace): LD 24 x 24pdrs; UD 26 x 12pdrs; QD 6 x 6pdrs; Fc 2 x 6pdrs. From 1707 carried 18pdrs instead of 24pdrs on the LD, 2 fewer UD guns and 2 more QD guns.

Fidèle Le Havre.

K: 6.1703. L: 1.1704. C: 1704. Took part in the Battle of Beachy Head 10.7.1690, and present at the Battle of Lagos 28.6.1693. Lent as a privateer to CV Henri-Louis, Marquis de Chavagnac, and CV Pierre Le Moyne d'Iberville, as part of a squadron of ten vessels, for operations in the West Indies, 1705–6. Lent as a privateer to CV René Duguay-Trouin, as part of a squadron of thirteen vessels 1711–12; took part in the Capture of Rio de Janeiro 9.1711. Wrecked on the return journey in a storm off the Azores 29.1.1712 with all crew (480 aboard) lost.

During 1705–6 most of the remaining 2nd Rank ships with fewer than 64 guns were re-classed to the 3rd Rank (as well as some 64-gun ships); the last of this type, *Oriflamme*, followed in 1708.

In July 1707 ten of the Navy's 24pdr-armed 3rd Rank ships were at Toulon during the siege of that port by Sir Clowdisley Shovell's fleet – the *Excellent, Vermandois, Furieux, Sérieux, Écueil, Saint Louis, Éole, Zélande, Content* and *Toulouse*. There were also two 3rd Rank ships with mixed LD batteries of 24pdrs and 18pdrs – *Laurier* and *Entreprenant*. All were scuttled on Louis's orders on 29 July to avoid the bombardment, and all were refloated in about October, but the *Laurier* (which had been hulked since 1704) was immediately condemned.

TOULOUSE. 62 guns. Designed and built by François Coulomb, and named 22 October 1712 (to replace the ship of the same name captured in 1711). Pierced for twelve pairs of LD guns.

Dimensions & tons: 141ft 0in x 38ft 4in x 17ft 6in (45.80 x 12.45 x 5.68m). 1,050 tons. Draught 18ft/19ft 5in (5.85/6.31m). Men: 380 in war, 320 peace, +8 officers.

Guns: 62 in war (54 peace): LD 24 x 24pdrs; UD 26 x 12pdrs; QD/Fc 12 x 6pdrs.

Toulouse Toulon Dyd.

K: 1.1712. L: late 1714. C: 5.1716. Took part in Battle of Toulon 22.2.1744. Condemned 1750 (order to be BU 30.10.1750) and hulked 1751 at Toulon; not mentioned after 1755.

18pdr-armed type

These ships provided the ancestors of the 50-gun ships of the eighteenth century. Some twenty-three ships of this type were built between 1690 and 1710, while others were captured from the English and Dutch navies. The building of some was specifically funded by various individuals and partnerships so that they could be employed for privateering. As well as the primary battery of 22 or 24 x 18pdrs (usually 8 of these were iron guns and 14 bronze), they generally carried 24 or 26 x 8pdrs on the upper deck (usually 12 iron and 12 bronze), and some carried a number of bronze 6pdrs or 4pdrs on the quarterdeck (with none on the forecastle). Many survivors of this type were eventually re-classed as 4th Rank.

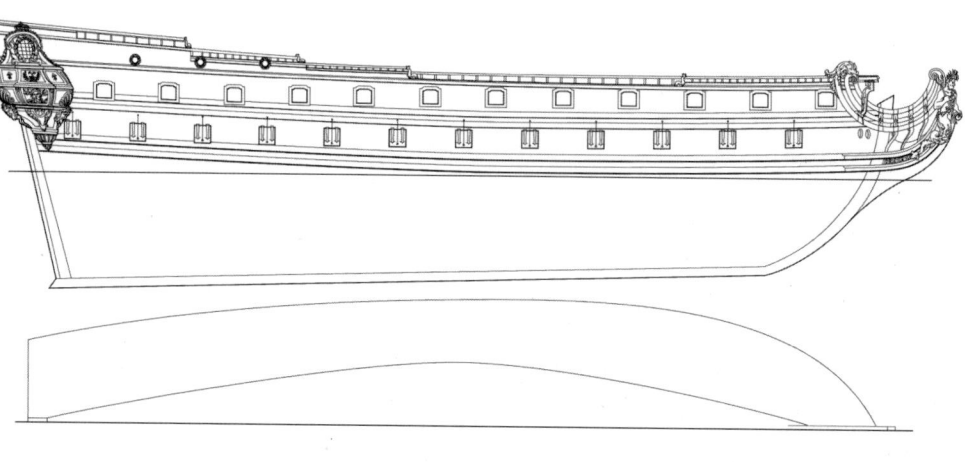

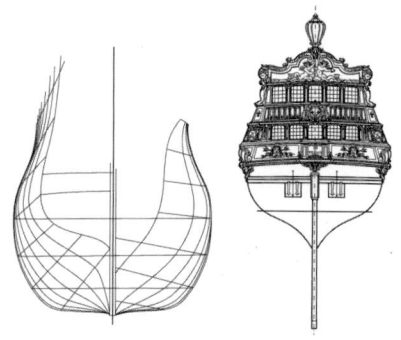

Lines and decoration plan of the 60-gun *Trident* of 1695 produced by László Veres based on four original plans in the Rigsarkivet, Copenhagen. She was part of Comte d'Estrées's squadron at the Bombardment of Barcelona in 1697, and later that summer – in company with the *Sérieux* – she cruised among the Greek islands in the campaign against the Mediterranean corsairs. Her original 24pdr main guns were replaced by 18pdrs during a major refit at Toulon in 1704.

PERLE. 52 guns. Designed and built by René Levasseur. Pierced for eleven pairs of LD guns. Rebuilt at Toulon 1701–2.
  Dimensions & tons: 126ft 0in, 100ft 0in x 35ft 0in x 16ft 0in (40.93, 32.48 x 11.37 x 5.20m). 800 tons. Draught 16½ft/19ft (5.36/6.17m). Men: 300, +7 officers.
  Guns: 52 in war (46 peace): LD 22 x 18pdrs; UD 24 x 8pdrs; QD 6 x 6pdrs (4pdrs from 1704); Fc nil
Perle Dunkirk.
  K: 7.1690. L: 12.1690. C: 4.1691. Took part in the Battle of Barfleur 29.5.1692, and present at the Battle of Lagos 28.6.1693. Lent as a privateer to LG André, Marquis de Nesmond, as part of a squadron of six to eleven vessels, 1696. Took part in the Battle of Vélez-Málaga 24.8.1704. Scuttled at Toulon in 7.1707, but refloated. Wrecked at Tenedos 1710.

Ex-BRITISH PRIZES (1691). The English Fourth Rates *Mary Rose* and *Happy Return*, originally built under the Protectorate as the *Maidstone* and *Winsby* (building details below) and renamed in 1660, were captured by the French – the former on 22 July 1691 off Portugal by the *Constant*, and the latter on 14 November 1691 off Dunkirk. Both were added to the *Marine Royale* (the former initially called *Marie-Rose* until renamed 9 June 1692) and their details (with French re-measurements) are given below. The similar *Constant Warwick* was captured at the same time as the *Mary Rose*, but seemingly was not added to the French Navy. The English Fourth Rate *Jersey* (building details below) was captured by French warships off Dominica on 28 December 1691 and also added to the *Marine Royale* as a 3rd Rank ship; she was reduced to the 4th Rank in 1700, restored to the 3rd Rank in 1706, and reduced again in 1708.
Vaillant John Mundy, Woodbridge.
  Ord: 12.1652. L: 11.1653.
  Dimensions & tons: 118ft 0in, 95ft 9in x 32ft 8in x 12ft 7in (38.33, 31.10 x 10.61 x 4.09m). 800 tons. Draught 15ft (4.87m). Men: 300 in war, 240 peace, +7 officers.
  Guns: 50 in war (44 peace): LD 22 x 18pdrs; UD 22 x 8pdrs; QD 6 x 4pdrs.
  Present at Battle of Lagos 28.6.1693. Lost 12.1698 off Cyprus.
Heureux Retour Edmund Edgar, Great Yarmouth.
  Ord: 12.1652. L: 21.2.1654.
  Dimensions & tons: 125ft 0in, 97ft 7in x 30ft 0in x 14ft 0in (40.60, 31.70 x 9.75 x 4.55m). 800 tons. Draught 16½ft (5.36m). Men: 270 in war (50/145/75), 200 peace, +6 officers.
  Guns: 46 in war (40 peace): LD 20 x 18pdrs; UD 22 x 8pdrs; QD/Fc 4 x 4pdrs. 46 from 1704: LD 22 x 16pdrs; UD 22 x 8pdrs; QD/Fc 2 x 4pdrs.
  Re-classed as 4th Rank by 1696, returned to 3rd Rank in 1701. Present at the Battle of Lagos 28.6.1693. Scuttled at Toulon in 7.1707, but refloated. Retaken by HMS *Burford* 5.1708, but not re-added to British Navy.
Jerzé (Gerzé, Gerzey) Starling, Woodbridge.
  Ord: 4.1665. L: 1666.
  Dimensions & tons (French measurements): 105ft 0in, 82ft 7in x 26ft 6in x 11ft 0in (42.9 x 10.9 x 3.9m). 400 tons. Draught 14ft (4.3m). Men: 380 in war, 230 peace, +? officers.
  Guns: 48 in war (42 peace): LD 24 x 18pdrs; UD 20 x 6pdrs; QD 6 x 6pdrs. 46 from 1699: LD 20 x 12pdrs; UD 20 x 8pdrs; QD 6 x 6pdrs (6 x 4pdrs from 1701). 40 from 1708: LD 18 x 12pdrs; UD 20 x 8pdrs; QD 2 x 4pdrs. 42 from 1715: LD 20 x 12pdrs; UD 18 x 8pdrs; QD 4 x 3pdrs.
  Lent as a privateer to CV Marc-Antoine de Saint-Pol Hécourt, as part of a squadron of six vessels 1704. Lent as a privateer to Jacques Cassard from Nantes, 1708. Struck 1716 at Brest and sold 1717.

***PÉLICAN* Class** (50 guns). Designed and built by Félix Arnaud. Pierced for eleven pairs of LD guns (excluding the chase ports). *Mignon* probably replaced a 3rd Rank ship of the same name ordered at Rochefort in April 1692 but cancelled in June; she underwent reconstruction at Dunkirk from October 1696 to May 1697. Later, in a flurry of re-classifications, she was reduced to the 4th Rank in 1700, raised again in 1701, reduced again in 1702–3, increased in 1704–5 and finally reduced in 1706.
  Dimensions & tons: 118ft 0in x 32ft 6in x 12ft 6in (38.33 x 10.56 x 4.06m). 500 tons. Draught 14ft/16ft (4.55/5.20m). Men: 280 in war, 230 peace.

A Van de Velde drawing of the *Happy Return*, probably executed about 1678. When captured and taken into French service in 1691, the ship was already nearly forty years old, but survived a further seventeen years until recaptured in 1708. (National Maritime Museum, London PZ7576)

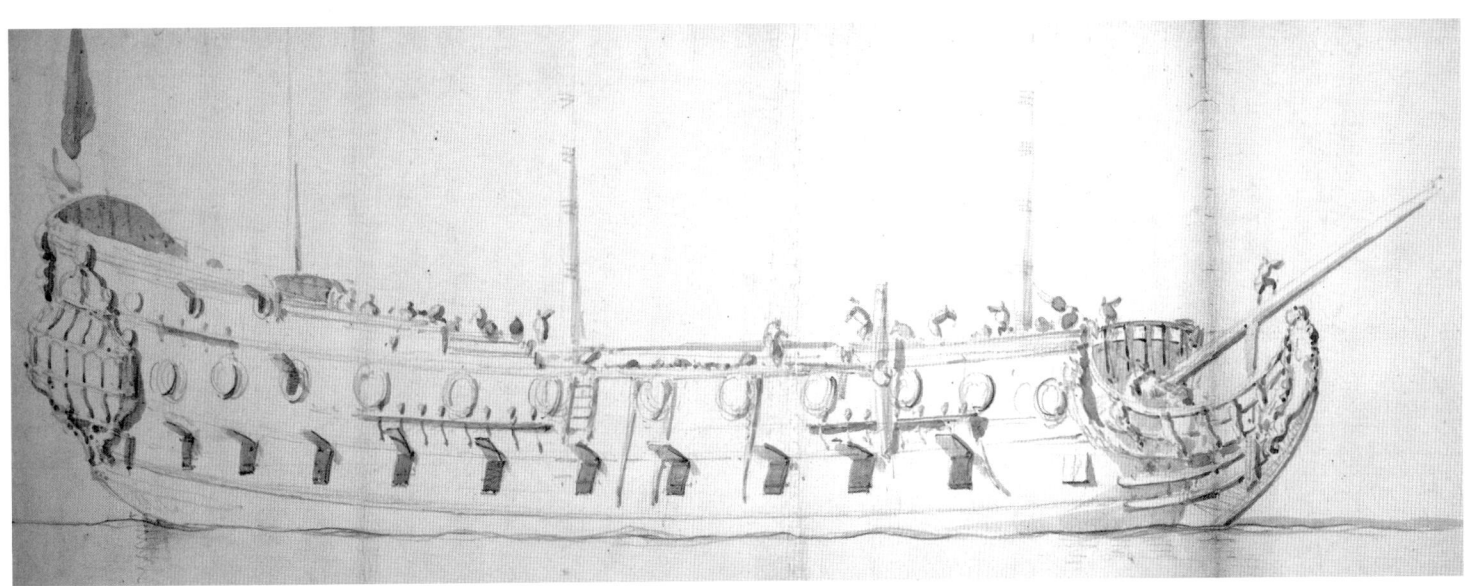

Guns: 50 in war (44 peace): *Pélican* LD 22 x 12pdrs; UD 20 x 8pdrs; QD 8 x 4pdrs; Fc nil. *Mignon* LD 10 x 18pdrs + 12 x 12pdrs (20 x 12pdrs from 1699); UD 22 x 8pdrs; QD 6 x 6pdrs (4pdrs from 1699); Fc nil.

Pélican Bayonne.
K: 4.1692. L: early 1693. C: 5.1693. Grounded by accident when leaving Bayonne 5.1693, but refloated. Lent as a privateer to LG André, Marquis de Nesmond, as part of a squadron of four vessels 1695. Participated in operations in Nova Scotia and Hudson Bay under CV Pierre Le Moyne d'Iberville, in a squadron of four vessels 1696-97. Wrecked off Fort Nelson (in Hudson's Bay) 5.9.1697.

Mignon Bayonne.
K: 7.1692. L: Spring 1693. C: 7.1693. Lent as a privateer to the *Compagnie de l'Asiento* 1706–9. Escaped capture at Bastimentos, near Puerto Bello (see *Coventry* in Chapter 4) 4.1709. Sold at Cartegena de Indias (in the Caribbean) 1709 in poor condition.

Ex-SPANISH PRIZE (1692). The (probably Dutch-built) Spanish *San Juan* of 50 guns were captured on 7 August 1692 and added to the French Navy.

Dimensions & tons: 118ft 0in x 34ft 0in x 15ft 0in (38.33 x 11.04 x 4.87m). 800 tons. Draught 15ft (4.87m). Men: 300 in war, 240 peace.

The *Stad-en-lande* drawn by the younger Van de Velde during a visit to the Netherlands in 1686. The identity of the ship is confirmed by the artist's annotation, bottom left. The ship had been built by Jan van Rheenen at Amsterdam in 1682 and hired by the Friesland Admiralty in 1691. Captured by Jean Bart's squadron's 44-gun *Mignon* on 29 June 1694; in the same action Bart's flagship, the *Glorieux*, captured the Friesland Admiralty's *Prins Friso* (then mounting 74 guns), while the smaller *Zeerijp* (40 guns) struck to the *Fortuné*. The *Stad-en-lande* was pierced for twelve pairs of LD guns, but in French service only carried eleven pairs of 18pdrs on this deck. (Museum Boijmans Van Beuningen, Rotterdam MB 1866-T 264)

Guns: 50 in war (44 peace): LD 22 x 18pdrs; UD 22 x 12pdrs; QD 6 x 6pdrs.

Saint Jean d'Espagne Holland.
K: 1683. C: 1684. Present at the Battle of Lagos 28.6.1693. Struck at Toulon 7.1696 and BU 1697.

Ex-DUTCH PRIZES (1692–94). Three more ships of 50/54 guns were captured – all from the Friesland Admiralty – during the middle part of the War of the League of Augsburg and added to the French Navy. The *Castricum* (built in 1686) was captured on 21 August 1692, and the *Prins Friso* and *Stad-en-lande* (built in 1693 and 1682 respectively) were taken by Jean Bart on 29 June 1694 off Texel. *Castricum* and *Stad-en-lande* were originally built for the Amsterdam Admiralty, and had been hired by Friesland in 1691.

Castricum Amsterdam.
Dimensions & tons: 123ft 0in x 32ft 0in x 12ft 7in (39.96 x 10.39 x 4.09m). 675/750 tons. Draught 15½ft/17½ft (5.035/5.68m). Men: 330, +6/8 officers.
Guns: 52 in war (46 peace): LD 22 x 18pdrs; UD 22 x 8pdrs; QD 8 x 4pdrs.
Present at Battle of Lagos 28.6.1693. Lent as a privateer under CV Des Augiers, as part of a squadron of four vessels, for escorting to India the mercantile *Marchand des Indes*, *Perle d'Orient*, *Pontchartrain* and *Princesse de Savoie* of the *Compagnie des Indes Orientales* in 1697–1700. BU 1701 at Lorient.

Prince de Frise Harlingen.
Dimensions & tons: 117ft 0in x 32ft 0in x 13ft 5in (38.01 x 10.39 x 4.36m). 590 tons. Men: 350 in war, 240 peace.
Guns: 54 in war (50 peace): LD 16 x 18pdrs + 8 x 12pdrs; UD 24 x 8pdrs; QD 6 x 4pdrs.
Sold 1703 at Rochefort.

Stadenland Amsterdam.
Dimensions & tons: 120ft 0in x 31ft 0in x 13ft 6in (38.98 x 10.07 x

4.39m). 600 tons. Draught 13ft 6in (4.39m). Men: 300 in war, 240 peace.
Guns: 52 in war (44 peace): LD 22 x 18pdrs; UD 22 x 8pdrs; QD 8 x 4pdrs.
Condemned 1.1702 at Dunkirk.

GAILLARD. 54 guns. Designed and built by Félix Arnaud. Pierced for twelve pairs of LD guns. Ordered as *Oriflamme*, but renamed in December 1693; she may have replaced the 3rd Rank *Oriflamme* of 60 guns ordered at Rochefort in April 1692 and cancelled two months later.
Dimensions & tons: 132ft 0in x 35ft 0in x 13ft 9in (42.88 x 11.37 x 4.47m). 680 tons. Draught 15½ft/17ft (5.035/5.52m). Men: 330/300, +7 officers.
Guns: 54 in war (50 peace): LD 24 x 18pdrs; UD 24 x 8pdrs (12pdrs from 1707); QD 6 x 4pdrs (4 from 1699).
Gaillard Bayonne,
K: 6.1693. L: 13.10.1693. C: 4.1694. Lent as a privateering to CV Bernard Renau d'Élissagaray, as part of a squadron of four vessels, for operations in the West Indies, 1696. Took part in Battle of Vélez-Málaga 24.8.1704. Scuttled at Toulon in 7.1707, but refloated. Sold at Toulon for commerce 1709; as merchant (carrying only 38 guns), captured 13.5.1710 by HMS *Suffolk* off Italy.

FOUGUEUX. 50 guns. Designed and built by Blaise Pangalo for privateering at the request of LG André, Marquis de Nesmond, who funded the cost of construction. Pierced for twelve pairs of LD guns. She probably replaced the 3rd Rank *Fougueux* of 60 guns ordered at Brest in April 1692 and cancelled two months later.
Dimensions & tons: 135ft 0in x 35ft 0in x 16ft 0in (43.85 x 11.37 x 5.20m). 750 tons. Draught 19ft (6.17m). Men: 330, +7 officers.
Guns: 50 in war (48 peace): LD 24 x 18pdrs; UD 26 x 8pdrs; QD nil.
Fougueux Brest Dyd.
K: 1694. L: 14.5.1695. C: 1695. Lent as a privateer to LG André, Marquis de Nesmond, as part of a squadron of six vessels, 1695–96. Lent (illegally by Hubert Desclouzeaux, *intendant* at Brest) as a privateer to René Duguay-Trouin from St Malo, 1696. Captured 10.12.1696 by HM Ships *Weymouth* and *Dover*, but struck a rock during the action, probably in an attempt to avoid capture, and foundered soon after with all hands.

TÉMÉRAIRE. 50, later 54 guns. Designed and built by Étienne Hubac for privateering at the request of LG André, Marquis de Nesmond, who funded the cost of construction. Pierced for twelve pairs of LD guns (with no chase ports). She probably replaced the 3rd Rank *Duc* of 60 guns ordered at Brest in April 1692 and cancelled two months later. Rebuilt at Toulon in 1705–6.
Dimensions & tons: 136ft 0in x 35ft 6in x 16ft 0in (44.18 x 11.53 x 5.20m). 850 tons. Draught 16ft/16½ft (5.20/5.36m). Men: 330 in war, 320 peace.
Guns: 50 in war (48 peace): LD 24 x 18pdrs; UD 26 x 8pdrs; QD/Fc nil. 54 from 1699: LD 10 x 24pdrs + 14 x 8pdrs; UD 26 x 12pdrs; QD/Fc 4 x 4pdrs. 50 from 1704: LD 24 x 18pdrs; UD 22 x 12pdrs; QD 4 x 4pdrs.
Téméraire Brest Dyd.
K: 1694. L: 6.1695. C: 1695. Lent as a privateer to LG André, Marquis de Nesmond, as part of a squadron of six vessels, 1695–96. Participated in operations at Nova Scotia under LG André, Marquis de Nesmond, in a squadron of twenty-three vessels 1697. Scuttled at Toulon in July 1707 to avoid the English bombardment, but refloated in November and restored to service. Hulked at Toulon by Order of 6.3.1720; sank from neglect 1721, refloated 11.1722 and BU 1722–27 by Order of 15.11.1722.

SOLIDE. 50 guns. Designed and built by Blaise Pangalo for privateering at the request of François Saupin, Sieur du Rocher (a wood merchant at Brest), and CV Jacques Dandenne, who funded the cost of construction 1695–97. Ordered on 26 May 1695 and named on 27 June. Pierced for 12 pairs of LD guns (with no chase ports).
Dimensions & tons: 137ft 0in x 35ft 6in x 16ft 0in (44.50 x 11.53 x 5.20m). 800 tons. Draught 19ft (6.17m). Men: 330, +6/10 officers.
Guns: 50 in war (46 peace): LD 24 x 18pdrs; UD 26 x 8pdrs; QD/Fc nil.
Solide Brest Dyd.
K: 5.1695. L: 10.9.1695. C: 2.1696. Lent as a privateer, as part of a squadron of four vessels under CV Jacques Dandenne, 1695–97. Burnt by the English at the Battle of Vigo 23.10.1702.

MERCURE. 50 guns. Designed and built by Étienne Hubac for privateering at the request of François Saupin, Sieur du Rocher (a wood merchant at Brest), and CV Jacques Dandenne, who funded the cost of construction. Ordered in April 1696 and named on 12 June. Pierced for twelve pairs of LD guns. Rebuilt at Brest in 1711–12 and again in 1719.
Dimensions & tons: 136ft 0in x 35ft 6in x 16ft 0in (44.18 x 11.53 x 5.20m). 800/850 tons. Draught 16½ft/18½ft (5.36/6.01m). Men: 350, + 5 officers.
Guns: 50 in war (46 peace): LD 24 x 18pdrs; UD 26 x 8pdrs; QD nil (2 x 4pdrs in 1704). 2 x 4pdrs. Re-armed 1712 with LD 24 x 24pdrs, UD 26 x 12pdrs; QD/Fc 10 x 6pdrs.
Mercure Brest Dyd.
K: 6.1696. L: 7.12.1696. C: 1697. Lent as a privateer, as part of a squadron of four vessels under CV Jacques Dandenne, 1695–97. Took part in the Battle of Vélez-Málaga 24.8.1704. Scuttled at Toulon in 7.1707 but refloated. Lent for commerce and privateering to Louis François Mouffle de Champigny, Director of the *Compagnie des Indes Orientales*, under command of CV Hervé René Du Coudray Guymont, with *Jason* and *Vénus* 1711–16. Became a hospital ship 1746 for the expedition to Louisbourg. Captured 14.8.1746 by HMS *Namur* in the North Atlantic.

HASARDEUX. 50 guns. Designed and built by Pierre Coulomb. Pierced for twelve pairs of LD guns. Elevated from 4th to 3rd Rank in 1701.
Dimensions & tons: 128ft 0in x 35ft 6in x 14ft 0in (41.58 x 11.53 x 4.55m). 725 tons. Draught 17ft/17½ft (5.52/5.68m). Men: 350 in war, + 5 officers.
Guns: 50 in war: LD 22 x 18pdrs; UD 22 x 12pdrs; QD 6 x 6pdrs.
Hasardeux Port Louis, near Lorient Dyd.
K: 3.1699. L: 8.1699. C: 2.1701. Lent (with *Juste*) as a privateer to Beaubriant-L'Évêque from St Malo, 1703. Captured by HM Ships *Oxford*, *Warspite* and *Lichfield* in the Channel 2.11.1703, becoming HMS *Hazardous*; wrecked 30.11.1706 off Selsey Bill.

ORIFLAMME. 64 guns. Designed and built by François Coulomb. Named on 1 January 1698, and contracted on 14 February 1699. Pierced for just twelve pairs of LD guns, this two-decker was unusual among 64-gun ships in having 18pdrs *vice* 24pdrs in her LD battery (she was probably initially designed to mount 24pdrs), and 6pdrs in the poop battery which probably replaced the QD of the 66-gun three-deckers.

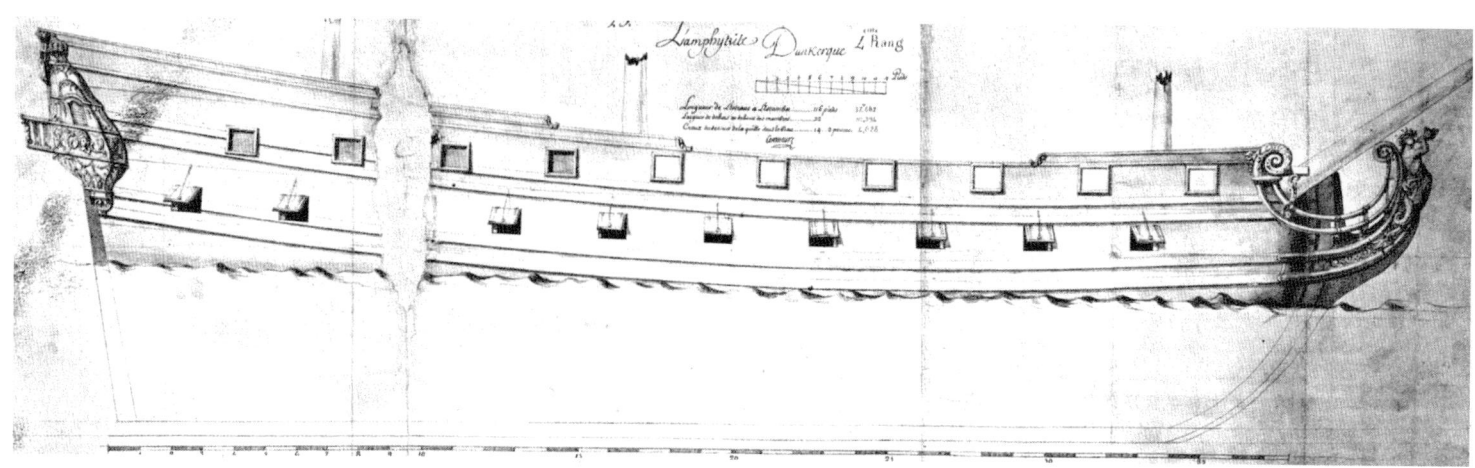

A copy of the original sheer draught of *Amphitrite* (52 guns, launched 1700), as reproduced by *Vice-amiral* Pâris. This somewhat 'pictorial' style of plan was common, especially for smaller *vaisseaux*, until the French draughting style became more standardised in the later eighteenth century. (*Souvenirs de Marine*, Plate 276)

Dimensions & tons: 140ft 0in, 115ft 0in x 38ft 0in x 17ft 0in (45.48, 37.36 x 12.34 x 5.52m). 1,000 tons. Draught 18ft/19ft (5.85/6.17m). Men: 380 in war, 300 peace, +7/9 officers.

Guns: 64 in war (56 peace): LD 24 x 18pdrs; UD 26 x 12pdrs; QD 10 x 6pdrs; poop 4 x 6pdrs.

Oriflamme Toulon Dyd.
K: 3.1699. L: 31.10.1699. C: 5.1700. Burnt at the Battle of Vigo 20.10.1702 to avoid capture (replaced by a 24pdr-armed ship, taking the same name).

AMPHITRITE. 52 guns. Designed and built by René Levasseur. Re-classed as 4th Rank between 1712 and 1714, but rebuilt at Brest from early 1717 to late 1718.

Dimensions & tons: 120ft 0in, 102ft 0in x 34ft 10in x 13ft 4in (38.98, 33.13 x 11.32 x 4.33m). 550 tons. Draught 15½ft/17ft (5.035/5.52m). Men: 300 in war, 250 peace, +5/7 officers.

Guns: 52 in war (44 peace): LD 22 x 18pdrs; UD 22 x 8pdrs; QD 8 x 4pdrs. 48 from 1707: LD 22 x 12pdrs; UD 22 x 8pdrs (reduced to 20 x 8pdrs from 1715); QD 4 x 4pdrs.

Amphitrite Dunkirk.
K: 1699. L: 10.1700. C: 4.1701. Lent as a privateer to CV Marc-Antoine de Saint-Pol Hécourt, as part of a squadron of six vessels 1704. To avoid confusion between the old 4th Rank *Amphitrite* (sold to the *Compagnie de Chine* in 1.1698 and temporarily re-acquired by the French Navy in early 1704) and the new Dunkirk-built 3rd Rank *Amphitrite*, the former was nicknamed the '*Amphitrite de Chine*' and the latter as the '*Amphitrite de Dunkerque*', then, wisely, was renamed *Protée* 3.1705 (a new *Amphitrite* was being built). Lent as a privateer to provisional CV Cornil Sauss, as part of a squadron on six vessels 1711–12. Struck at Brest 1722.

FENDANT. 58, later 56 guns. Designed and built by Philippe Cochois. Pierced for twelve pairs of LD guns, plus thirteen pairs on the UD and four pairs on the QD. Raised to the 2nd Rank in 1702–3, reverted to the 3rd Rank in 1706.

Dimensions & tons: 137ft 0in, 117ft 6in x 37ft 4in x 17ft 0in (44.8 x 11.9 x 5.8m). 900 tons. Draught 18ft/20ft (6.5m). Men: 350 in war, 300 peace, +4/8 officers.

Guns: 58 in war (46 peace): LD 24 x 18pdrs; UD 26 x 8pdrs (24 x 12pdrs from 1706); QD/Fc 8 x 6pdrs

Fendant Le Havre.
K: 4.1701. L: 18.10.1701. C: 3.1702 at Dunkirk. Took part in the Battle of Vélez-Málaga 24.8.1704. Scuttled at Toulon to avoid the British bombardment 1707, but then refloated. Lent (with *Éclatant* and *Adélaïde*) as a privateer to Antoine Crozat, Marquis du Châtel, Director of the *Compagnie des Indes Orientales*, 1711; sailed from Toulon for the East Indies but disappeared with all hands (along with *Éclatant*) in the Indian Ocean 3.1713.

SAGE. 54, later 56 guns. Designed and built by Pierre Coulomb. Ordered on 22 April 1701.

Dimensions & tons: 131ft 0in x 36ft 6in x 14ft 0in (42.2 x 11.9 x 4.4m). 770 tons. Draught 18ft/18½ft (5.8m). Men: 330 in war, 280 peace, +6/8 officers.

Guns: 54 in war: LD 24 x 18pdrs; UD 24 x 12pdrs (26 from 1706); QD/Fc 6 x 6pdrs.

Sage Port Louis, near Lorient.
K: 4.1701. L: 28.11.1701. C: 5.1702. Took part in Battle of Vélez-Málaga 24.8.1704. Burnt during the British bombardment of Toulon 21.8.1707 (hulk ordered to be sold 5.10.1707).

ACQUIRED (1701–1703). The origin, former identity, and construction years of these Dutch and Flemish ships are unknown. They may have been purchased.

Pélican Holland
Acquired c.1701
Dimensions & tons: 120ft 0in x 31ft 0in x 12ft 6in (38.98 x 10.07 x 4.06m). 600 tons. Draught 15½ft (5.04m). Men: 250 in war, 150 peace.

Guns: 58 in war (38 peace): LD 26 x 18pdrs; UD 24 x 12pdrs; QD/Fc 8 x 6pdrs. 46 from 1704: LD 6 x 18pdrs + 14 x 12pdrs; UD 20 x 8pdrs; QD 6 x 6pdrs. 48 from 1706: LD 20 x 12pdrs; UD 22 x 8pdrs; QD 6 x 4pdrs.

Struck 1706 at Rochefort.

Aquilon Ostende
Acquired c.1702–3
Dimensions & tons: 115ft 6in x 31ft 6in x 11ft 6in (37.52 x 10.23 x 3.74m). 600 tons. Draught 15¾ft (5.12m). Men: 200 in war, 150 peace.

Guns: 48 in war (34 peace): LD 22 x 12pdrs; UD 24 x 8pdrs; QD/Fc 10 x 4pdrs.

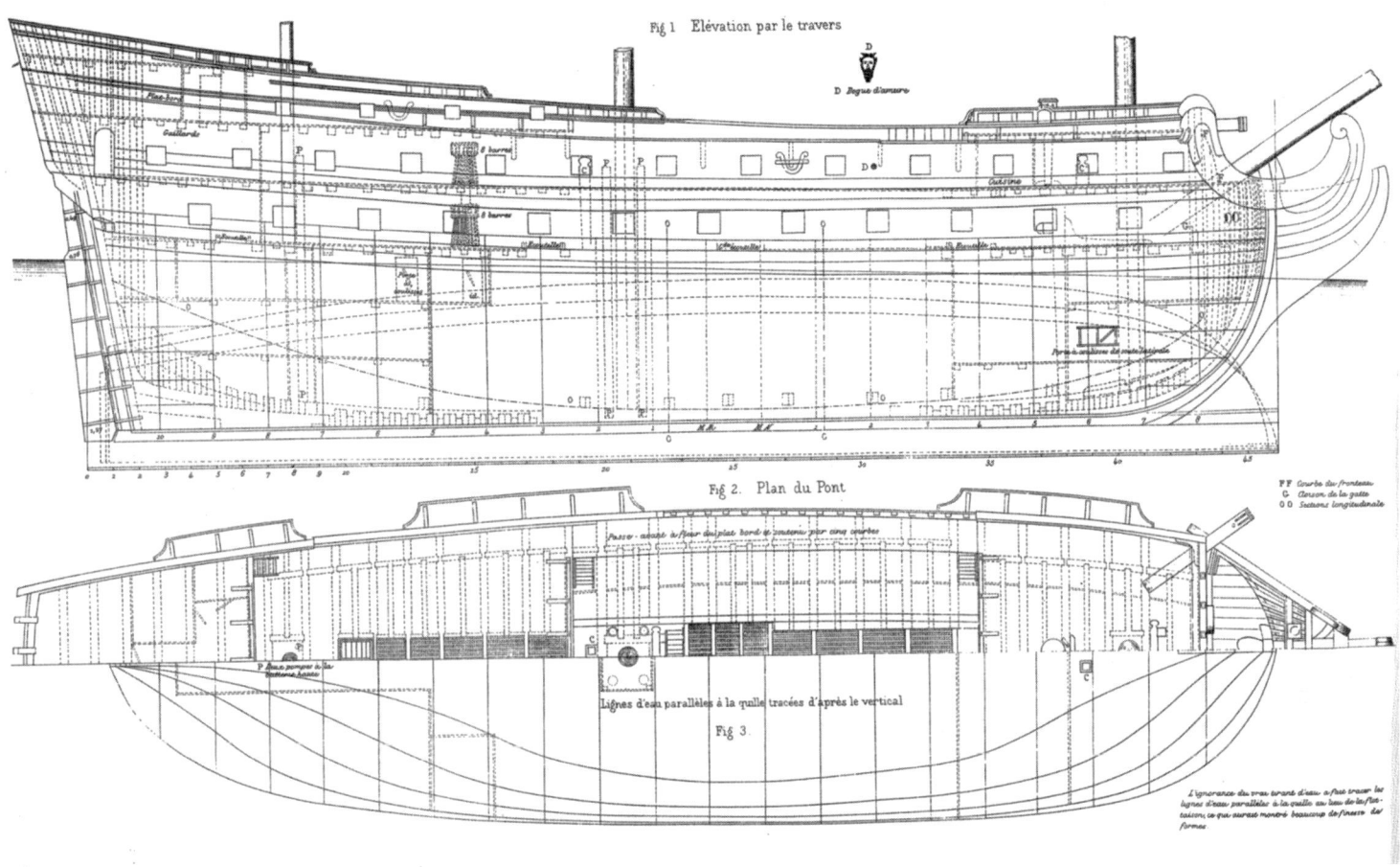

A reconstruction by *Vice-amiral* Pâris of a '60-gun ship' traced from an original plan, with details added from two unrigged models. In the accompanying sail plan, the ship is identified as *Fendant*, and the basic specification agrees with the 58-gun ship of 1702. (*Souvenirs de Marine*, Plate 139)

Lent as a privateer to François Saupin, Sieur du Rocher (a timber merchant at Brest, and Director of the *Compagnie de l'Asiento*) 1704–5. Condemned 1707 at Rochefort and BU.

Ex-DUTCH PRIZES (1702–1703). The Dutch *Wapen van Hoorn* or *Eenhorn* (built in 1682) was captured in July 1702 and became the French *Licorne*. The Dutch *Gaasterland* (built by Hendrik Cardinaal in 1688–90) and *Beschermer* (or *Schermer*, built in 1690) were taken on 22 May 1703 while escorting a convoy and their names were rendered in French as *Caterlan* and *Beschermer*, although the name of the latter was also rendered *Bechermel* and translated as *Défenseur*. *Licorne* was reduced from the 3rd to the 4th Rank in 1708 and restored to the 3rd Rank between 1712 and 1714 although only a hulk.

Licorne Enkhuizen.
  Dimensions & tons: 117ft 0in x 31ft 0in x 13ft 3in (38.01 x 10.07 x 4.30m). 560 tons. Draught 15½ft (5.04m). Men: 300 in war, 250 peace
  Guns: 52 in war (44 peace): LD 22 x 12pdrs; UD 24 x 8pdrs; QD/Fc 6 x 4pdrs (10 from 1708)
  Hulk at Brest 1706, BU 1720.

Caterlan Amsterdam
  Dimensions & tons: 118ft 0in x 30ft 9in x 11ft 10in (38.33 x 9.99 x 3.84m). 690 tons. Draught 14ft (4.55m). Men: 280 in war, 200 peace
  Guns: 48 in war (36 peace): LD 20 x 12pdrs; UD 20 x 8pdrs; QD/Fc 8 x 4pdrs.
  Struck 1704 at Toulon.

Beschermer Amsterdam
  Dimensions & tons: 114ft 0in x 30ft 8in x 11ft 0in (37.03 x 9.96 x 3.57m). 550 tons. Draught 13ft (4.22m). Men: 250 in war, 180 peace
  Guns: 48 in war (36 peace): LD 20 x 12pdrs; UD 20 x 8pdrs; QD/Fc 8 x 4pdrs.
  Struck 1704, probably sold at Toulon.

TRITON. 52 guns. Designed and built by Antoine Tassy. Pierced for twelve pair of LD guns.
  Dimensions & tons: 127ft 0in x 35ft 0in x 14ft 3in (41.25 x 11.37 x 4.63m). 600 tons. Draught 16½ft/17½ft (5.36/5.68m). Men: 300 in war, 250 peace, +5/7 officers.
  Guns: 52 in war (48 peace): LD 24 x 18pdrs; UD 24 x 8pdrs; QD 4 x 4pdrs. 52 from 1708: LD 22 x 18pdrs; UD 24 x 8pdrs; QD 6 x 4pdrs (returned to 4 x 4pdrs from 1715).

Triton Bayonne.
  K: late 1702. L: 1703. C: 6.1705. Lent to Sieur Courtois, of Dunkirk, for transportation between his town and Brest, under LV Saint-Clair, 1704. With a squadron of six of the King's vessels under CV Marc-Antoine de Saint-Pol Hécourt, captured the (non-naval) *Marlborough Galley* and *Tiger Galley*, 1705. Lent as a privateer in support of the Spanish Navy, 1707 and 1709. Grounded by accident at Martinique early 1720 but refloated; condemned 4.1720 and sold there 5.1720 to BU.

Ex-BRITISH PRIZES (1703–1705). Four English Fourth Rates of a 130-foot type ordered in 1694 and 1695 were captured by the French in 1703-5. The *Salisbury* was captured by a French squadron off Orford Ness on 10 April 1703; the *Coventry* was taken by a squadron of French privateers off the Isles of Scilly 24 July 1704; the *Pendennis* was taken by the French *Salisbury* and *Triton* off the Dogger Bank on 20 October 1705 while defending a convoy; and the *Blackwall* was captured by the French *Protée* off Dogger Bank on 31 October 1705. All four were added to the French Navy, but the *Coventry* – added as a 4th Rank ship – will be found in Chapter 4. The other three became 3rd Rank ships, the *Salisbury* with her name unchanged, while the *Pendennis* had her name rendered as *Pindenize*. and the *Blackwall* had her name first rendered as *Blekoualle*, and from 1709 as *Blakoual*. *Blakoual* was reduced to the 4th Rank between 1712 and 1714. Note that the '-16pdrs' and '7pdrs' below indicate retained English 18pdr and 9pdr guns (*Blakoual* was re-armed with French equivalent guns).

Salisbury Richard and James Herring, Bailey's Hard.
  Ord: 24.12.1695. L: 18.4.1698.
  Dimensions & tons (French measurements): 125ft 0in x 32ft 4in x 13ft 0in (40.60 x 10.50 x 4.22m). 450 tons. Draught 14½ft (4.71m).
  Guns: 52 in war (44 peace): LD 22 x 12pdrs; UD 24 x 8pdrs; QD 6 x 4pdrs.
  Lent as a privateer to CV Marc-Antoine de Saint-Pol Hécourt, as part of a squadron of six vessels, 1704. Part of CdE Claude, Comte de Forbin's squadron 1706–7. Retaken by HMS *Leopard* 15.3.1708 and renamed *Salisbury Prize* (as a new *Salisbury* was under construction). BU 1739.

Pindenize. Robert & John Castle, Deptford.
  Ordered 18.11.1694. L: 15.10.1695.
  Dimensions & tons (French measurements): 124ft 0in x 32ft 4in x 12ft 6in (40.28 x 10.50 x 4.06m). 450 tons. Draught 15ft 4in (4.98m). Men: 300 in war.
  Guns: 54 in war (44 peace): LD 22 x 16pdrs; UD 24 x 7pdrs; QD 8 x 4pdrs.
  Sold 1706 at Dunkirk.

Blakoual Henry Johnson, Blackwall.
  Ord: 4.1695. L: 1696. C: 1697.
  Dimensions & tons (French measurements): 127ft 0in x 32ft 6in x 12ft 6in (41.25 x 10.56 x 4.06m). 460 tons. Draught 15½ft (5.04m). Men: 300 in 1706; 350 in war, 200 peace from 1707.
  Guns: 54 in war (44 peace): 22 x 16pdrs; 24 x 7pdrs; QD 8 x 4pdrs. 52 from 1715: LD 22 x 12pdrs; UD 22 x 8pdrs (6pdrs from 1717); QD 8 x 4pdrs.
  Part of CdE Claude, Comte de Forbin's squadron 1706-07, then under CV Jean Alexandre Le Voye, in the Chevalier de Tourouvre's squadron in 1708. Retaken 3.1708 by the British, but captured again later that year. Lent as a privateer to provisional CV Cornil Sauss, as part of a squadron of six vessels 1711-12. Struck 1720 at Brest.

RUBIS. 56 guns. Designed and built by Pierre Coulomb, initially ordered as a privateer but acquired for the King's service. Pierced for twelve pairs of LD guns. Rebuilt at Toulon in 1716.
  Dimensions & tons: 141ft x 37ft 8in x 15ft 0in (45.80 x 12.24 x 4.87m). 800 tons. Draught 17ft/17½ft (5.52/5.68m). Men: 330 in war, 280 peace, +7/9 officers.
  Guns: 56 in war (50 peace): LD 24 x 18pdrs; UD 26 x 8pdrs; QD 6 x 6pdrs.

Rubis Port Louis, near Lorient.
  K: 9.1703. L: 21.1.1704. C: 4.1704. Took part in Battle of Vélez-Málaga 24.8.1704. Scuttled at Toulon in 7.1707, but refloated. Condemned 6.1717 at Toulon and ordered hulked 10.8.1717. Sank from neglect 8.1718 but refloated 1719 and ordered converted to careening hulk 6.3.1720; condemned 10.11.1729 and ordered to BU 26.11.1729.

JASON. 54 guns. Designed and built by Blaise Pangalo. Ordered 2 January 1704, specifically to meet the requirements for privateering of CFL René Duguay-Trouin, who funded the cost of construction. Reconstructed at Brest in 1711–12 (by Julien Geslain).
  Dimensions & tons: 136ft 0in, 116ft 0in x 36ft 0in x 17ft 0in (44.18, 37.68 x 11.69 x 5.52m). 800 tons. Draught 19ft (6.17m). Men: 350 in war, 300 peace, +7/10 officers.

A French etching depicting the very successful attack on a large convoy bound for Portugal by the joint squadrons of Duguay-Trouin and Forbin in October 1707. Of the convoy's five escorts, which included two 80-guns ships, only one escaped. Here the *Jason* (second from left, marked 'D') engages the *Chester*, 50, while astern *Lys* and *Gloire* tackle the 80-gun *Cumberland*; both British ships were captured. Further off, *Maure* and *Achille* attack *Ruby*, 50 and *Royal Oak*, 76. The other 80-gun ship, *Devonshire* (shown far left, marked 'a'), later blew up in action, and only a badly damaged *Royal Oak* escaped. (National Maritime Museum, London, detail from PU5206)

Guns: 54 in war (48 peace): LD 24 x 18pdrs; UD 26 x 8pdrs; QD 4 x 4pdrs (8 from 1715).

Jason Brest Dyd.
K: 1.1704. L: 2.5.1704. C: 7.1704. Lent as a privateer to CFL René Duguay-Trouin, as part of a squadron of four vessels,1704–5. Taken back into the King's service (as well as *Hercule*, and with *Paon* added), and placed under (the now CV) Duguay-Trouin for the defence of Cadiz, 1706. Lent anew as a privateer to CV Duguay-Trouin, as part of a squadron of six to ten vessels, 1707–9. Lent as a privateer to Louis François Mouffle de Champigny, Director of the *Compagnie des Indes Orientales*, under CV Hervé René Du Coudray Guymont, with *Vénus* and *Mercure* 1711–16. Struck at Brest 1720.

AUGUSTE. 54 guns. Designed and built by Étienne Hubac. Ordered on 2 January 1704, specifically to meet the requirements for privateering of CFL René Duguay-Trouin, who funded the cost of construction, and was named in the same month. Very similar to *Jason*, the *Auguste* was a swift sailer, but with the fore part of the hull too narrow, in heavy seas she plunged deep; Duguay-Trouin saw therein the reasons for her capture. Hubac was admonished, but nevertheless, when the 2nd Rank *Lys* and *Magnanime* were built in 1706, the same faults appeared in *Magnanime*, and when the latter was lost in 1712, Duguay-Trouin again blamed Hubac's design.

Dimensions & tons: 137ft 0in, 115ft 0in x 36ft 6in x 16ft 0in (44.50, 37.36 x 11.86 x 5.20m). 800 tons. Draught 15ft/18ft (4.87/5.85m). Men: 400 in war, 320 in peace, +10 officers.

Guns: 54 in war (48 peace): LD 24 x 18pdrs; UD 26 x 8pdrs; QD 4 x 4pdrs.

Auguste Brest Dyd.
K: 1.1704. L: 3.5.1704. C: 7.1704. Lent as a privateer to CFL René Duguay-Trouin, as part of a squadron of four vessels, 1704–5. Captured by HM Ships *Chatham* and *Medway* (of George Byng's fleet) 19.8.1705, becoming HMS *August*; wrecked 21.11.1716 on Anholt Island while en route home from the Baltic.

HERCULE. 56, later 60 guns. Designed and built by Desjumeaux, specifically to meet the requirements for privateering of EV Charles de Ruis Embito da La Chesnardière, who funded the cost of construction. Reconstructed at Brest in 1713–14 (by Laurent Hélie), 1722–23 and 1734–35.

Dimensions & tons: 136ft 0in x 37ft 3in x 16ft 0in (44.18 x 12.10 x 5.20m). 760 tons. Draught 17ft 8in/19½ft (5.74/6.33m). Men: 350 in war, 300 peace, +6 officers.

Guns: 56 in war (?50 peace): LD 24 x 18pdrs; UD 26 x 8pdrs; QD 6 x 6pdrs. 60 in war from 1708 (52 peace): LD 24 x 24pdrs; UD 26 x 12pdrs; QD 6 x 6pdrs; Fc 4 x 6pdrs.

Hercule Port Louis, near Lorient.
K: 3.1705. L: 22.6.1705. C: 9.1705. Lent as a privateer to EV Charles de Ruis Embito da La Chesnardière, 1705, but was quickly taken back into the King's service and – added to *Jason* and *Paon* – served under CV René Duguay-Trouin for the defence of Cadiz 1706. Lent as a privateer to CdE Jean-Baptiste Ducasse, as part of a squadron of seven vessels in support of the Spanish Navy for escorting galleons, 1707. Lent again to (the now LG) Ducasse, as part of a squadron of three vessels in support of the Spanish Navy in the West Indies, 1711. Condemned and hulked 1741 at Brest; BU there 1746.

MARS. 54 guns. Designed and built by René Levasseur. Pierced for twelve pairs of LD guns.

Dimensions & tons: 134ft 0in x 36ft 6in x 14ft 9in (43.53 x 11.86 x 4.79m). 700 tons. Draught 16½ft/18ft (5.36/5.85m). Men: 380 in war, 250 peace.

Guns: 54 in war (50 peace): LD 24 x 18pdrs; UD 26 x 8pdrs; QD 4 x 4pdrs.

Mars Dunkirk.
K: 6.1705. L: 12.1705. C: 4.1796. Part of CdE Claude, Comte de Forbin's squadron 1706–7, then under CV Jean Alexandre Le Voye, in the Chevalier de Tourouvre's squadron in 1708. Lent as a privateer to CV René Duguay-Trouin, as part of a squadron of thirteen vessels, 1711–12; took part in the Capture of Rio de Janeiro 9.1711. Out of service 1719; condemned 1721 at Brest and BU.

DAUPHINE. 60 guns. Designed and built by Philippe Cochois for privateering at the request of LV Louis-François Gouyon de Miniac, who funded the cost of construction.

Dimensions & tons: 138ft 0in, 120ft 0in x 38ft 0in x 16ft 0in (44.83, 38.98 x 12.34 x 5.20m). 900 tons. Draught 17½ft/19½ft (5.68/6.33m). Men: 350-380.

Guns: 60 in war (52 peace): LD 24 x 18pdrs; UD 26 x 8pdrs (12pdrs from 1710); QD 6 x 6pdrs; Fc 4 x 6pdrs.

Dauphine Le Havre.
K: 10.1705. L: 23.3.1706. C: 5.1706. Lent as a privateer to LV Louis-François Gouyon de Miniac 1706–9 for the original partnership; then lent as a privateer to CV René Duguay-Trouin under CFL Pierre Aubert de Courserac 1709–11. Lent for commerce and privateering 1711–12. Hulked at Brest 1717; BU there 1721.

BOURBON. 54 guns. Designed and built by Laurent Hélie and Alain Donard, and rated at 50 guns while building. She was built following the '*méthode du Sieur Gobert*', the extra cost of the iron knees under the deck being reduced by fitting her with the ones salvaged from the *Magnanime* (burnt on 31 March 1705 near Marbella, Spain).

Dimensions & tons: dimensions unknown. 700 tons. Draught 17½ft/19½ft (5.68/6.33m). Men: 375 in war, 300 peace.

Guns: 54 in war: LD 24 x 18pdrs; UD 26 x 8pdrs or 12pdrs; QD 4 x ?4pdrs.

Bourbon Lorient Dyd.
K: 2.1706. L: 26.6.1706. C: 12.1706. Captured 16.3.1707 by Dutch frigates off Belle-Île, becoming privateer *Gekronde Burg*; wrecked 12.1710.

Ex-DUTCH PRIZES (1706). A Dutch-built ship built in 1690, possibly named *Hamburg Staadt* (but probably not a naval vessel) was captured in July 1706 and added to the French Navy as *Ville de Hambourg* (also rendered as *Ville d'Hombourg*). She had 56 gunports, but only 38 guns were carried in French service. A second vessel, the *Hardenbroek*, built by Hendrik Cardinaal at Amsterdam in 1698 or 1699 for the Amsterdam Admiralty, was captured on 2 October 1706 but was quickly retaken.

Ville de Hambourg Holland.
Dimensions & tons: 126ft 0in x 32ft 0in x 11ft 0in (40.93 x 10.39 x 3.57m). 733 tons. Draught 17ft (5.52m). Men: 300 in war, 250 peace, +1 officer.

Guns: 38 in war: LD 14 x 12pdrs; UD 10 x 8pdrs + 10 x 6pdrs; QD 4 x 6pdrs.

Sold *c.*1709 at Port Louis to the *Compagnie de l'Asiento*, which had been using her since at least 1707.

Hardenbroek Amsterdam
Dimensions & tons (in Amsterdam feet of 283mm): 139ft x 37½ft x 14¾ft. *c.*770 tons. Men: 240.

Guns (Dutch): LD 22 x 18pdrs; UD 22 x 8pdrs; QD 8 x 4pdrs.
Retaken by the Dutch 11/12.1706. (Another *Hardenbroek*, built at Rotterdam for the Maas Admiralty in 1708, was captured by Dunkirk privateers on 11.11.1709 but saw no service for the French Navy and was sold to Russia in 1712, renamed *Esperans*.)

AUGUSTE. 54 guns. The last of seven 3rd Rank ships to be designed and built by René Levasseur; named to replace the *Auguste* of 1704, which had been captured in 1705. Built for privateering by a group of private citizens from Dunkirk, who funded the cost of construction.
Dimensions & tons: 128ft 0in, 118ft 0in x 36ft 0in x 14ft 9in (41.58, 38.33 x 11.69 x 4.79m). 800 tons. Draught 17ft/18ft (5.52/5.85m). Men: 370 in war, 250 peace.
Guns: 54 in war (50 peace): LD 24 x 18pdrs; UD 26 x 8pdrs; QD 4 x 4pdrs. From 1714 two 8pdrs were removed and four more 4pdrs added.
Auguste Dunkirk.
K: 12.1706. L: 21.9.1707. C: 3.1708. Lent as a privateer to a group of private citizens from Dunkirk, 1708. Lent as a privateer to provisional CV Cornil Sauss, as part of a squadron of six vessels 1711–12. Struck at Brest 1720.

In July 1707 there were twelve of the Navy's 18pdr-armed 3rd Rank ships at Toulon during the siege of that port by Sir Clowdisley Shovell's fleet – the *Diamant*, *Fortuné*, *Fleuron*, *Perle*, *Heureux Retour*, *Gaillard*, *Téméraire*, *Trident*, *Mercure*, *Fendant*, *Sage* and *Rubis*. The *Sage* and *Fortuné* were left afloat; the *Sage* was set afire during the bombardment and destroyed, while the *Fortuné* was damaged and was condemned immediately following the siege. All the others were scuttled on Louis's orders on 29 July to avoid the bombardment, and all were refloated in about October.

SUPERBE. 56 guns. Designed and built by Pierre Coulomb, and rated at 50 guns while building. Built for privateering at the request of Thomas-Auguste Miniac, Sieur de La Moinerie (+ partners from Dunkirk), who funded the cost of construction. Named on 5 September 1708.
Dimensions & tons: 136ft 0in x 37ft 0in x 14ft 0in (44.18 x 12.02 x 4.55m). 730 tons. Draught 17ft (5.52m). Men: 350 in war, 300 peace.
Guns: LD 24 x 18pdrs; UD 4 x 12pdrs + 22 x 8pdrs; QD 6 x 6pdrs.
Superbe Port Louis, near Lorient.
K: 8.1708. L: 12.12.1708. C: 3.1709. Lent as a privateer under the command of Thomas-Auguste Miniac, Sieur de La Mointerie, from St Malo, 1708–10. Captured by HMS *Kent* 10.8.1710, becoming HMS *Superb*; rebuilt 1721 at Woolwich, deleted 1732.

Ex-BRITISH PRIZES (1709–1710). 60 guns. These two British Fourth Rates were captured, the first by *Lys* and *Achille* on 26 October 1709 while escorting a convoy off Cape Clear (Ireland), and the second by *Parfait*, *Phénix* and *Sirène* off Toulon on 8 January 1710. Both added to the French Navy but seemingly never re-armed with French ordnance, the calibres quoted below being British ones.
Gloucester John Burchett, Rotherhithe.
Ordered 17.3.1708. L: 25.7.1709.
Dimensions & tons: 140ft 0in x 34ft 9in x 15ft 0in (45.48 x 11.29 x 4.87m). 900 tons.
Guns (British): LD 24 x 18pdrs; UD 26 x 9pdrs; QD 10 x 6pdrs.
Sold 1711 as a privateer at St Malo. Resold 1716 to Spain as *Conquistador*; in Spanish service until 1738.
Pembroke Edward Snelgove, Limehouse.
Ordered 8.1.1694. L: 22.11.1695.
Dimensions & tons: dimensions unknown. 900 tons.
Guns (British): LD 24 x 18pdrs; UD 26 x 9pdrs; QD 10 x 6pdrs.
Retaken 22.3.1711 off La Spezia but foundered same day.

At 1 September 1715 the 3rd Rank comprised twenty-four vessels. Thirteen of these mounted 24pdr guns on their LDs – the *Glorieux* (1678), *Furieux* (1684), *Vermandois* (1685), *Sérieux* (1688), *Brillant* (1689), *Mercure* (1697), *Oriflamme* (1703), *Achille* (1705), *Hercule* (1705), *Dauphine* (1706) and *Toulouse* (1714), plus the ex-British prizes *Élisabeth* and *Grafton* (see details in Chapter 2). Nine more mounted 18pdr guns of their LDs – the *Prince* (1682), *Diamant* (1687), *Trident* (1695), *Jason* (1704), *Rubis* (1704), *Auguste* (1707), *Mars* (1705), *Triton* (1705), and *Téméraire* (1706). The final two still carried mixed LD batteries of 24pdrs and 18pdrs – *Entreprenant* (1680, but rebuilt 1702) and *Apollon* (1683).

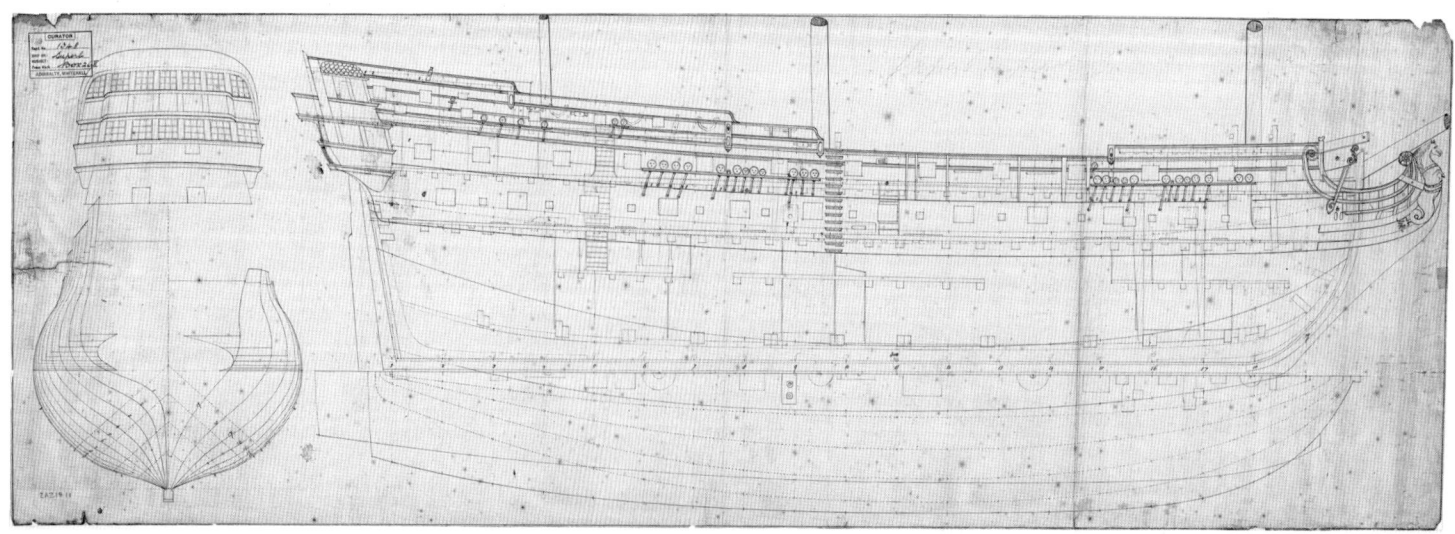

Admiralty draught of the 56-gun *Superbe*, undated but presumably as captured. This large ship was designed and built specifically for the *guerre de course* (meeting criteria laid down by the great privateer Duguay-Trouin himself). These priorities are manifest in the very sharp hull form and the row of oar ports on the lower deck. These latter allowed the ship in light winds to creep up on mercantile victims or, conversely, to escape from more powerful warships. Although the ship was fast in ideal conditions, Duguay-Trouin thought the hull was too fine forward, which cause the ship to plunge into a head sea, impeding her sailing. (National Maritime Museum, London J4012)

(D) 24pdr- and 36pdr-armed vessels acquired from 1 September 1715

By September 1715 the 3rd Rank was composed of two distinct streams: the first, described in this Section, comprised ships with 60–64 guns (overwhelmingly with a lower deck battery of twenty-four 24pdr guns, although sometimes a mix of 24pdrs and 18pdrs, and an upper deck battery of twenty-six 12pdr guns, with some variations); the second, treated in Section (E) below, comprised the numerically few ships of between 50 and 56 guns (generally with a lower deck battery of 18pdr guns). Most variations related to the ordnance on the *gaillards*.

The origins of the 60/64-gun ship can be found in the early 1660s, and the type remained a constant presence for over a century. They continued to carry a lower deck battery of twenty-four 24pdrs, and an upper deck almost always with twenty-six 12pdrs, until the 1730s when – commencing with the *Éole* of 1733 – space was provided for an additional pair of guns on the lower deck, and – with the *Borée* of 1734 – space was provided for an additional pair of guns on the upper deck as well, and within a decade this became the new standard armament, with ten guns (6pdrs) remaining to the *gaillards*.

While no new ships of this type were built for France before 1720, a similar vessel was built for the Order of Saint John (the Knights of Malta) at Toulon in 1717. Given the close ties between the Knights and the French Navy in this era, we detail below the construction data for this vessel, which replaced the original *San Giovanni Battista* (see above) in 1718 as the squadron flagship and took her name.

Two somewhat smaller 50-gun ships were built for France with a 24pdr battery: these were the *Amphion* (1748) and *Sagittaire* (1759), and are included in this section chronologically.

SAN GIOVANNI BATTISTA. 64 guns. Built for and operated by the Order of Saint John, as a replacement for the ship of the same name built in 1702–4. In February 1717 François Coulomb's son Blaise, accompanied by his own two sons, arrived in Malta to oversee shipbuilding activity there, and train local shipwrights in ship design and construction. They remained there for ten years, constructing four 3rd Rank ships for the Knights, of which the *San Giovanni Battista* was the replacement flagship. Pierced for thirteen pairs of LD guns, and fourteen pairs on the UD.

The other three ships were all built by Blaise and his sons in the French Creek at Malta. They comprised the somewhat smaller *San Giorgio* (completed 1719), *San Vicenzo* (1720) and *San Antonio di Padua* (1727).

Dimensions & tons: 142ft 0in, 116ft 0in x 39ft 4in x 18ft 0in (46.31, 37.83 x 12.83 x 5.87m). Draught (aft) 12½ft (4.08m). Men: 440, +14 officers.

San Giovanni Battista Toulon Dyd.
K: 1.9.1717. L: 16.4.1718. In service with the Order until 1765.

ÉCLATANT. 62, later 64 guns. Designed and built by Julien Geslain.
Dimensions & tons: 140ft 0in, 124ft 0in x 38ft 0in x 18ft 6in (45.48, 40.28 x 12.34 x 6.01m). 950/1,900 tons. Draught 19ft/21ft (6.17/6.82m). Men: 450 in war, 400 peace, +6 officers.
Guns: 62 in war (56 peace): LD 24 x 24pdrs; UD 26 x 12pdrs; QD 8 x 6pdrs (an extra 2 x 6pdrs were added in 1729); Fc 4 x 6pdrs.

Éclatant Brest Dyd.
K: 1720. L: 1.4.1721. C: 1722. Hulked 1745 at Brest; BU 1764.

SOLIDE. 62, later 64 guns. Designed and built by René Levasseur; ordered 26 July 1719 and plan dated 15 December 1719.
Dimensions & tons: 142ft 0in, 126ft 0in x 39ft 2in x 19ft 0in (46.13, 40.93 x 12.72 x 6.17m). 1,050/2,000 tons. Draught 18ft/19ft (5.85/6.17m). Men: 450 in war, 400 peace, +6 officers.
Guns: 62 in war (54 peace): LD 24 x 24pdrs; UD 26 x 12pdrs; QD 8 x 6pdrs (an extra 2 x 6pdrs were added in 1729); Fc 4 x 6pdrs. Listed with 6 x 8pdrs and 8 x 4pdrs on the QD and Fc in 1746.

Solide Toulon Dyd.
K: 8.1720. L: 14.11.1722. C: 3.1724. Hulked 10.1750 at Toulon; ordered sold 12.2.1770 as totally rotten, sold 10.8.1771 and BU.

SAINT LOUIS Class. 62, later 64 guns. Designed by Pierre Masson. Masson died in 1720 and these vessels were built by Joseph Ollivier and Julien Geslain respectively. Reconstructed in 1731–32 and 1742 respectively at Rochefort.
Dimensions & tons: 140ft 8in, ?125ft 0in x 39ft 2in x 19ft 0in (45.69, ?40.60 x 12.72 x 6.17m). 1,000/1,787 tons. Draught 19ft/21ft (6.17/6.82m). Men: 450 in war, 400 peace, +6 officers.
Guns: 62 in war (54 peace): LD 24 x 24pdrs; UD 26 x 12pdrs; QD 8 x 6pdrs (an extra 2 x 6pdrs were added in *Ardent* from 1729 and in *Saint Louis* from 1739); Fc 4 x 6pdrs.

Saint Louis Rochefort Dyd.
K: 12.1720. L: 1.1723. C: 1724. Condemned 1745 at Rochefort and hulked; BU 1748 at Brest.

Ardent Rochefort Dyd.
K: 5.1721. L: 1723. C: 1724. Grounded in Quiberon Bay 7.11.1746, and then captured and burnt by the British.

ÉLISABETH. 64 guns. Designed and built by Laurent Hélie, similar to *Éclatant* but with a slightly longer keel; plan dated 7 April 1722. She was listed with 26 x 24pdrs on the LD while under construction but was completed with 24.
Dimensions & tons: 140ft 0in, 125ft 0in x 38ft 0in x 18ft 6in (45.48, 40.60 x 12.34 x 6.01m). 950/1,900 tons. Draught 19ft/21ft (6.17/6.82m). Men: 450 in war, 400 peace, +6 officers.
Guns: 64 in war (56 peace): LD 24 x 24pdrs; UD 26 x 12pdrs; QD 10 x 6pdrs; Fc 4 x 6pdrs.

Élisabeth Brest Dyd.
K: 4.1722. L: 11.1722. C: 12.1724. Severely damaged in single-ship action with HMS *Lion* off Audierne on 20.7.1745 (with 65 killed and 136 wounded), and repaired at Brest. Hulked 1748 at Rochefort; burnt by accident 1756.

LÉOPARD. 62 guns. Designed and built by Blaise Coulomb. Named 2 December 1726. Underwent rebuilding at Toulon 1738–39, and at Rochefort in 1746.
Dimensions & tons: 143ft 0in x 41ft 2in x 18ft 6in (46.45 x 13.37 x 6.01m). 1,100/1,950 tons. Draught 17ft/19½ft (5.52/6.33m). Men: 450 in war, 400 peace, +6 officers.
Guns: 62 in war (54 peace): LD 24 x 24pdrs; UD 26 x 12pdrs; QD 8 x 6pdrs; Fc 4 x 6pdrs.

Léopard Toulon Dyd.
K: 12.1726. L: 29.11.1727. C: 5.1728. Condemned and burnt at Quebec 1757 after an epidemic.

TRITON. 60 guns. Designed and built by Laurent Hélie. Reconstructed in 1733 by CV Raymond Renault, Comte de Radouay, in accordance with Pierre Bouguer's proposals to reduce mast heights and widen yardarms; in order to decrease the displacement of the ship (whose freeboard was too low), the ship was reduced to 48 guns. In 1740 this ship was re-armed with 60 guns but with 18pdrs on the LD (*vice* her original 24pdrs) and 8pdrs on the UD (replacing her original 12pdrs).
Dimensions & tons: 136ft 6in, 118ft 0in x 36ft 6in x 17ft 0in

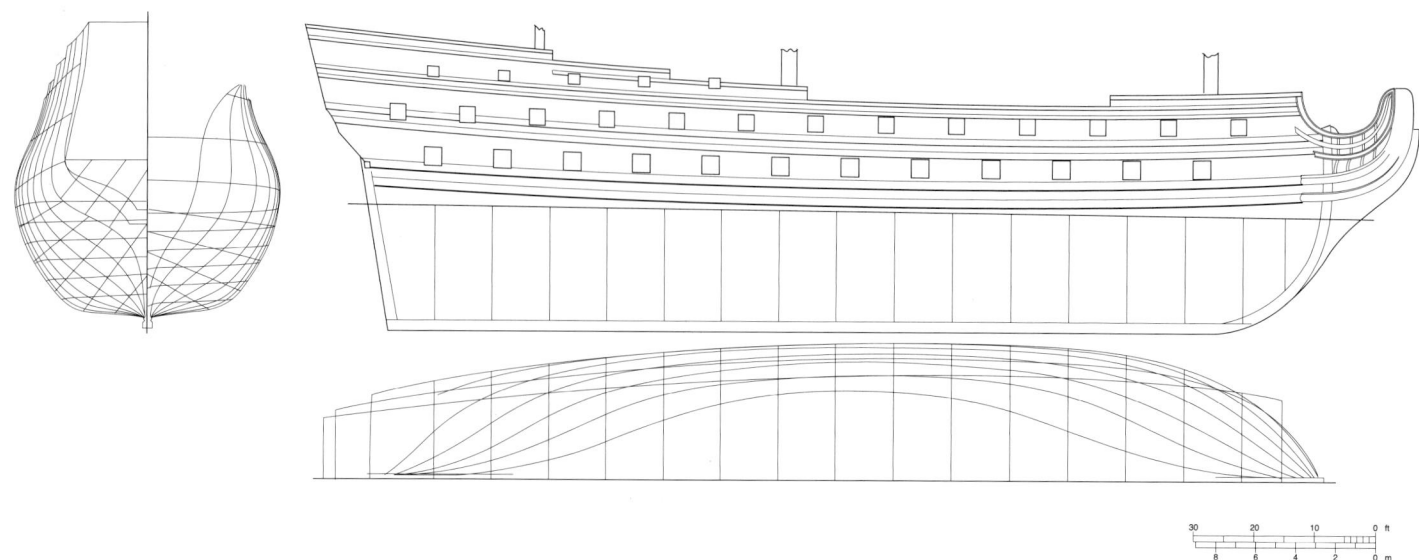

Lines plan of the 64-gun *Fleuron*, drawn by László Veres after an original in *Vice-amiral* Pâris's *Souvenirs de Marine*, Plate 249, itself traced from an original in the collection of Henri Ollivier, '*Capitaine de frégate*, descendant of the engineers of that name (including the ship's designer, Blaise Ollivier) and of their cousin Coulomb.'

(44.34, 38.33 x 11.86 x 5.52m). 850/1,500 tons. Draught 17½ft/18½ft (5.68/6.01m). Men: 400 in war, 350 peace, + 6 officers.

Guns: 60 in war (54 peace): LD 24 x 24pdrs; UD 26 x 12pdrs; QD 6 x 6pdrs; Fc 4 x 6pdrs. Re-armed 1740 with LD 24 x 18pdrs; UD 26 x 8pdrs; QD 6 x 6pdrs; Fc 4 x 6pdrs.

Triton Brest Dyd.
K: 6.1727. L: 11.4.1728. C: 3.1730. Condemned 1745 at Brest and BU.

FLEURON. 64 guns. Designed by Blaise Ollivier (plan dated 20 June 1729) and built by Joseph Ollivier; ordered 5 April 1729. The designer had proposed a length of 148ft for 3rd Rank vessels 'of the 1st Order' (pierced for thirteen pairs of LD guns to give a total of 68 guns altogether) and 144ft for those 'of the 2nd Order' (pierced for twelve pairs of LD guns to give a total of 64 guns altogether). The *Fleuron* was built to the smaller model, but it was to be the larger (albeit with 4 fewer guns on the QD to retain the total at 64 guns) that provided the concept of expansion that produced the classic layout. Her hull was constructed with diagonal planking to improve longitudinal strength; this experiment was not repeated due to high costs and difficulties in construction. On her first cruise twelve of her 24pdrs were bronze.

Dimensions & tons: 144ft 0in, 127ft 8in x 39ft 4in x 18ft 2in (46.78, 41.47 x 12.78 x 5.90m). 950/1,924 tons. Draught 15½ft/18ft (5.035/5.85m). Men: 450 in war, 400 peace, +6 officers.

Guns: 64 in war (56 peace): LD 24 x 24pdrs; UD 26 x 12pdrs; QD 10 x 6pdrs; Fc 4 x 6pdrs.

Fleuron Brest Dyd.
K: 20.6.1729. L: 29.4.1730. C: 20.2.1732. Took part in CV Jean André. Marquis de Barailh's squadron in expedition to Danzig 5–8.1734. Burnt by accident (then blew up) at Brest 2.2.1745.

ÉOLE. 64 guns. Designed and built by Blaise Coulomb. Named on 4 August 1731. This vessel introduced a thirteenth pair of 24pdrs on the LD, but retained the same number of UD guns.

Dimensions & tons: 144ft 6in, ?120ft 6in x 41ft 3in x 19ft 0in (46.94, ?39.14 x 13.40 x 6.17m). 1,058/2,000 tons. Draught 20ft/20¾ft (6.50/6.74m). Men: 440 in war, 400 peace, +6 officers.

Guns: 64 in war (60 peace): LD 26 x 24pdrs; UD 26 x 12pdrs; QD 8 x 6pdrs; Fc 4 x 6pdrs.

Éole Toulon Dyd.
K: 1731. L: 30.12.1733. C: 5.1734. Took part in Battle of Toulon 22.2.1744. Wrecked on the Île d'Aix 31.5.1745.

BORÉE. 62 guns. Designed by Francois Coulomb Jnr. Named on 26 July 1734. With the added length, space was provided for an additional pair of guns on *both* decks, and within a decade this became the new standard armament, with ten guns (6pdrs) remaining to the QD and forecastle.

Dimensions & tons: 148ft 6in, ?120ft 6in x 40ft 4in x 19ft 4in (48.24 x 13.10 x 6.28m). 1,150/2,000 tons. Draught 18½ft/20¼ft (6.01/6.58m). Men: 400 in war, 340 peace, +6 officers.

Guns: 62 in war (60 peace): LD 26 x 24pdrs; UD 28 x 12pdrs; QD 8 x 6pdrs; Fc nil. Listed with 12 x 6pdrs on the QD and Fc in 1746.

Borée Toulon Dyd.
K: 1.1734. L: 22.12.1734. C: 8.1735. Took part in Battle of Toulon 22.2.1744. Wrecked 12.12.1746 on Turk's Bank off Lorient, wreck sold 1747.

SÉRIEUX. 64 guns. Designed and begun by René Boyer (who died on 31 March 1740), then completed by Pierre-Blaise Coulomb. Ordered 6 February 1738, and named on 16 October.

Dimensions & tons: 145ft 0in, 130ft 0in x 40ft 0in x 19ft 4in (47.10, 42.23 x 12.99 x 6.28m). 1,058/c.2,000 tons. Draught 20ft/20¾ft (6.50/6.74m). Men: 400 (later 460) in war, 340 (later 410) peace, +6 officers.

Guns: 64 in war (60 peace): LD 26 x 24pdrs; UD 28 x 12pdrs; QD 6 x 6pdrs; Fc 4 x 6pdrs.

Sérieux Toulon Dyd.
K: 4.10.1738. L: 26.10.1740. C: 5.1741. Took part in Battle of Toulon 22.2.1744, and in 1st Battle off Cape Finisterre 14.5.1747 (as flagship of CdE Jacques-Pierre de Taffanel, Marquis de La Jonquière), when captured (with *Invincible*) by Anson's squadron, becoming HMS *Intrepid*; BU at Chatham 1765.

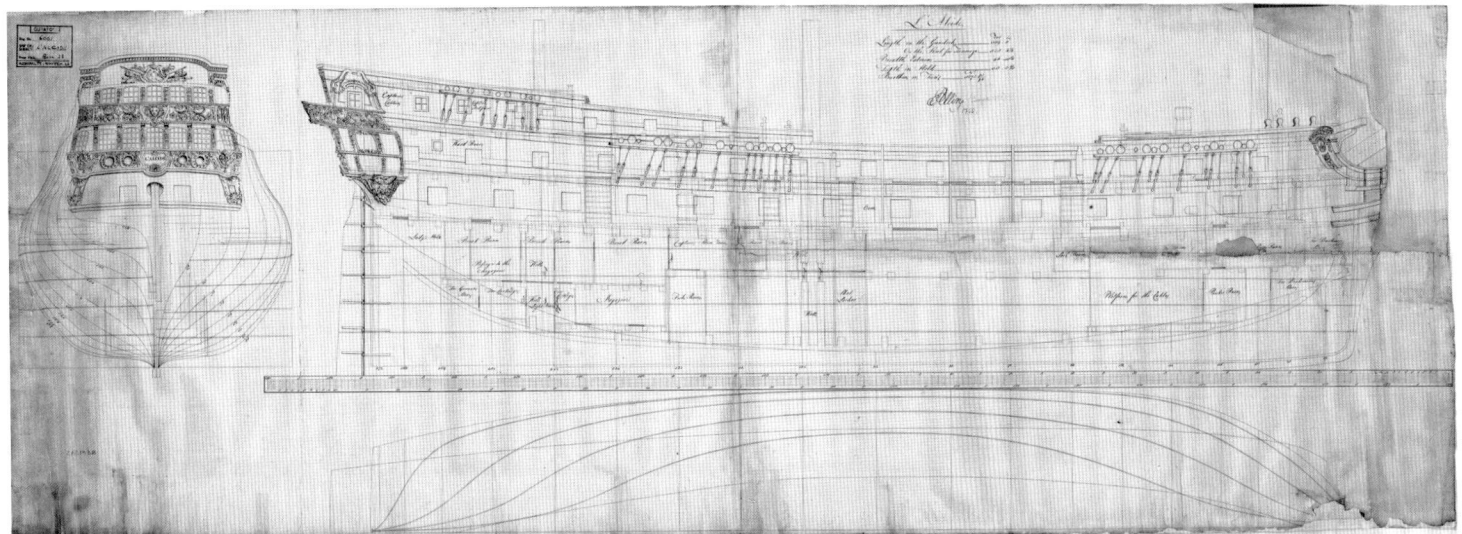

Admiralty draught of the 64-gun *Alcide*, undated but signed by 'Allin' – as Joseph Allin, the Surveyor of the Navy, was replaced in 1755, this must be Edward Allin who was Master Shipwright at Portsmouth, where the ship was surveyed early in 1757. (National Maritime Museum, London J3124)

MARS Class. 64 guns. Designed and built by Blaise Ollivier. The first ship was ordered in December 1738, and may first have been intended to be called *Aimable*; the second was ordered in February 1741 and named in October. *Alcide* was rebuilt at Brest between May 1752 and November 1753.

Dimensions & tons: 149ft 0in, 147ft 0in x 40ft 6in x 19ft 0in (48.4 x 13.8 x 5.9m). 1,100/2,000 tons. Draught 19ft/24ft (6.2m). Men: 460 in war, 410 peace, +6 officers.

Guns: 64 in war (58 peace): LD 26 x 24pdrs; UD 28 x 12pdrs; QD 8 x 6pdrs; Fc 2 x 6pdrs.

Mars Brest Dyd.
K: 1.1739. L: 5.1740. C: 4.1741. Captured by HMS *Nottingham* off Cape Clear 11.10.1746, becoming HMS *Mars*; wrecked at entrance to Halifax harbour 24.7.1755.

Alcide Brest Dyd.
K: 3.1742. L: 6.12.1743. C: 1744. Captured (with *Lys*) by HM Ships *Dunkirk* and *Torbay* of Boscawen's squadron 8.6.1755, becoming HMS *Alcide*; sold at Portsmouth 27.5.1772.

SAINT MICHEL Class. 64 guns. Designed by Jean-Marie Hélie. This was one of the last designs to have just twelve pairs of 24pdrs on the LD; other than the *Fier* of the same period, all future 64s would have thirteen pairs of LD gunports (and consequently fewer QD guns), and the *Saint Michel* was reduced to a 60-gun ship in 1762 when two pairs of 6pdrs were removed. She underwent reconstruction five time: at Brest in 1751–52, at Rochefort in 1759 and again in 1761–62, and at Brest in 1770–71 and 1776–77.

Dimensions & tons: 143ft 6in, 130ft 6in x 38ft 6in x 18ft 9in (46.61, 42.39 x 12.51 x 6.09m). 1,242/2,150 tons. Draught 17ft/19½ft (5.52/6.33m). Men: 450 in war, 400 peace, +6 officers.

Guns: 64 in war (58 peace): LD 24 x 24pdrs; UD 26 x 12pdrs; QD 10 x 6pdrs (reduced to 6 x 6pdrs in 1762); Fc 4 x 6pdrs.

Saint Michel Brest Dyd.
K: 11.1739. L: 1.1741. C: 5.1741. Took part (as a member of CdE Pierre-André Suffren de Saint-Tropez's squadron) in the Battles of Trincomalee 3.9.1782 and Cuddalore 20.6.1783. Struck in 1786.

Transferred to the *Compagnie des Indes* at Lorient for commerce in 5.1787, but never used by them and probably hulked.

Vigilant Brest Dyd.
K: 3.1742. L: 11.5.1744. C: 12.1744. Captured off Louisbourg on 19.5.1745 by HM Ships *Superb*, *Eltham* and *Mermaid*, becoming HMS *Vigilant*; sold at Chatham 11.12.1759.

TRIDENT. 64 guns. Designed and built by Pierre-Blaise Coulomb, and named 23 October 1740. Possibly to same design as *Sérieux*, although with a shorter keel.

Dimensions & tons: 145ft 0in, 122ft 0in x 40ft 0in x 19ft 3in (47.10, 39.63 x 12.99 x 6.25m). 1,150/c.2000 tons. Draught 19½ft/20ft (6.33/6.50m). Men: 400 (later 460) in war, 340 (later 410) peace, +6 officers.

Guns: 64 in war (60 peace): LD 26 x 24pdrs; UD 28 x 12pdrs; QD 6 x 6pdrs; Fc 4 x 6pdrs.

Trident Toulon Dyd.
K: 10.1740. L: 13.9.1742. C: 12.1742. Took part in Battle of Toulon 22.2.1744, and in 2nd Battle of Cape Finisterre 25.10.1747, where captured by Hawke's squadron, becoming HMS *Trident*; sold 3.1763.

PODER. 60 guns. This Spanish vessel, purchased by the Spanish Navy in 1740, was briefly in French hands at the close of the Battle of Toulon on 22 February 1744. Dismasted, she was captured by the British (HMS *Berwick*), but being unable to move, the *Poder* and the British prize crew were retaken by the French, but the ship had to be burnt by them to prevent a further recapture. No technical details are relevant.

LYS Class. 64 guns. Designed and built by Jacques-Luc Coulomb. *Dragon* was rebuilt at Brest in 1757–58.

Dimensions & tons: 149ft 0in, 143ft 6in x 40ft 0in x 19ft 0in (48.40, 46.61 x 12.99 x 6.17m). 1,100/2,100 tons. Draught 18ft/19½ft (5.85/6.33m). Men: 500 in war, 460 peace, +6 officers.

Guns: 64 in war (60 peace): LD 26 x 24pdrs; UD 28 x 12pdrs; QD 6 x 6pdrs; Fc 4 x 6pdrs.

Lys Brest Dyd.
K: 1.1745. L: 10.9.1746. C: 1.1747. After sailing from Brest 3.5.1755 when armed *en flûte*, captured by HM Ships *Defiance* and *Fougueux* (see below) of Boscawen's squadron off Newfoundland 8.6.1755, but not added to British Navy.

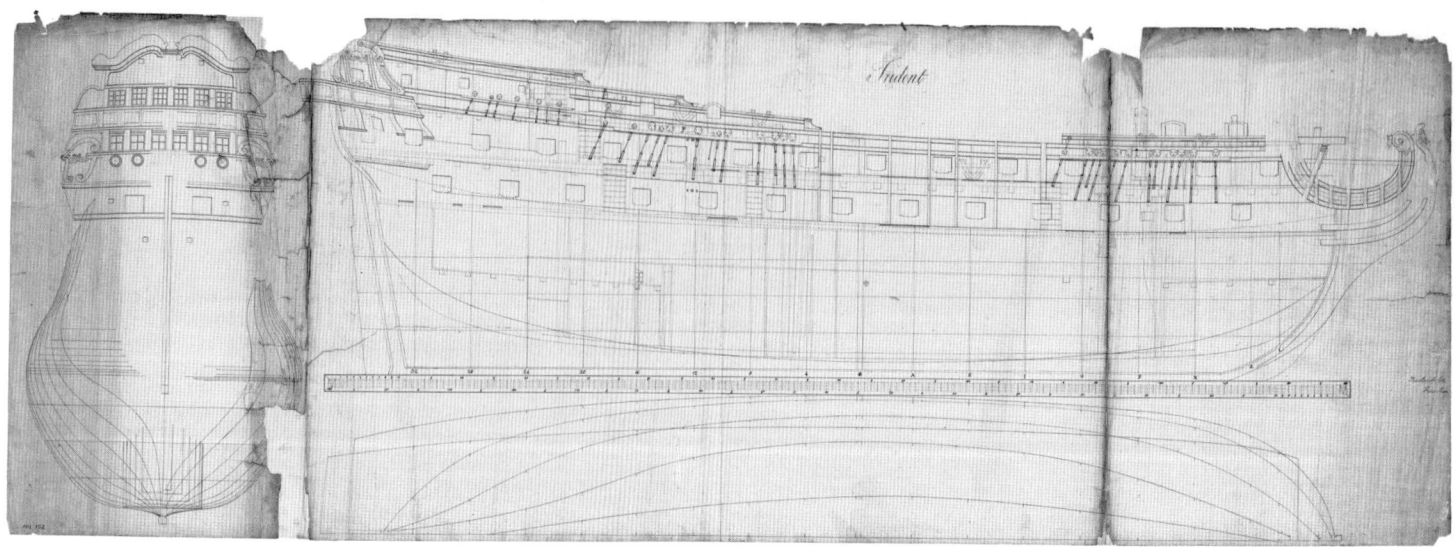

Admiralty draught of the 64-gun *Trident*. Besides the name, there is no other annotation or date. The draught probably derived from the survey of the ship at Portsmouth in 1748. The ship was five years old when captured in 1747. (National Maritime Museum, London J8258)

Fougueux Brest Dyd.
　K: 1.1745. L: 3.1747. C: 7.1747. Took part in 2nd Battle of Cape Finisterre 25.10.1747, where captured by HMS *Kent* of Hawke's squadron, becoming HMS *Fougueux*; BU at Portsmouth 5.1759.

Dragon Brest Dyd.
　K: 1.1745. L: 16.9.1747. C: 1.1748. Took part in the Battle of Quiberon Bay 20.11.1759. Wrecked off Cape Français (St Domingue) 17.3.1762.

CONTENT Class. 64 guns. Designed by Joseph Véronique-Charles Chapelle, who built the first ship, which was ordered 9 November 1745, contracted on 8 January 1746 and named 11 March 1746; the second ship to the same plan (but built by François Chapelle) was ordered on 18 December 1747 and named on 3 January 1748.

　Dimensions & tons: 146ft 0in, 130ft 0in x 40ft 0in x 19ft 0in (47.43, 42.23 x 12.99 x 6.17m). 1,180/2,100 tons. Men: 560 in war, 440 peace, +6/11 officers.

　Guns: LD 26 x 24pdrs; UD 28 x 12pdrs; QD 8 x 6pdrs; Fc 2 x 6pdrs.

Content Toulon Dyd.
　K: 1.1746. L: 11.2.1747. C: 12.1747. Took part in the Battle off Minorca 20.5.1756. Condemned 1.1770 and became careening hulk at Toulon 1772, where burnt by the Anglo-Spanish occupying forces in 12.1793.

Orphée Toulon Dyd.
　K: 1.1748. L: 10.5.1749. C: 1750. Took part in the Battle off Minorca 20.5.1756. Captured 28.2.1758 by HM Ships *Revenge* and *Berwick* off Cartagena (Osborn's Action).

TRITON. 64 guns. Ordered on 9 November 1745 to a design by François Coulomb Jnr, and named on 11 March 1746. Rebuilt at Rochefort from early 1775 to November 1776; disarmed at Toulon in April 1783, she was loaned for commerce (to the *Compagnie des Indes orientales et de la Chine*) from that September until August 1785.

　Dimensions & tons: 149ft 6in, 126ft 3in x 40ft 6in x 19ft 2in (48.56, 41.01 x 13.16 x 6.23m). 1,242/2,150 tons. Draught 18ft 2in/21ft (5.90/6.82m). Men: 480-560, +9/12 officers.

　Guns: LD 26 x 24pdrs; UD 28 x 12pdrs; QD 6 x 6pdrs; Fc 4 x 6pdrs.

Triton Toulon Dyd.
　K: 1.1746. L: 4.8.1747. C: 12.1747. Took part in the Battle off Minorca 20.5.1756. Hulked as a guardship at Cherbourg in 1786. Aground there in 1790, sold for commercial use 1791, and BU at Cherbourg in 1794.

SAINT LAURENT Class. 60 guns. Designed by René-Nicolas Levasseur, these were the largest warships to be built in Canada for the French Navy (except for the 72-gun *Algonkin* in 1753). They were constructed of poor quality timber, and the *Saint Laurent* had a short life, while the second ship broke apart while being launched and was BU in situ.

　Dimensions & tons: 145ft 0in, 128ft 0in x 39ft 4in x 18ft 8in (47.10, 41.58 x 12.78 x 6.06m). 1,000/1,900 tons. Draught 19¾ft (6.42m). Men: 430, +6 officers.

　Guns (conjectural): LD 26 x 24pdrs; UD 28 x 12pdrs; QD 6 x 6pdrs.

Saint Laurent Quebec.
　K: 9.1746. L: 13.6.1748. C: 10.1748. Arrived at Toulon from Brest 19.10.1750, offered for sale 8.8.1752, ordered BU 12.10.1752 as she could not be sold, hulked at Toulon in early 1753, condemned 10.1753 and BU 1753–54.

Orignal Quebec.
　K: 10.1748. L: 2.9.1750. Not completed.

ACHILLE. 64 guns. Designed and built by Pierre-Blaise Coulomb. Ordered 9 November 1745 and named 11 March 1746.

　Dimensions & tons: 145ft 0in x 38ft 6in x ? (47.10 x 12.51 x ?m). 1,200/2,000 tons. Men: 480 in war, 320 peace, +9/12 officers.

　Guns: LD 26 x 24pdrs; UD 28 x 12pdrs; QD 6 x 6pdrs; Fc 4 x 6pdrs.

Achille Toulon Dyd.
　K: 12.1746. L: 15.11.1747. C: 1.1748. Captured by HMS *Thunderer* 17.7.1761 off Cadiz, but not added to British Navy.

PROTÉE Class. 64 guns. Designed and built by François-Guillaume Clairain-Deslauriers. *Protée* was reconstructed at Brest in 1757–58.

　Dimensions & tons: 154ft 0in x 40ft 6in x 19ft 4in (50.03 x 1316 x 6.28m). 1,300/2,200 tons. Draught 17ft 7in/19½ft (5.71/6.33m). Men: 480 in war, 320 peace, +8/9 officers.

THE THIRD RANK

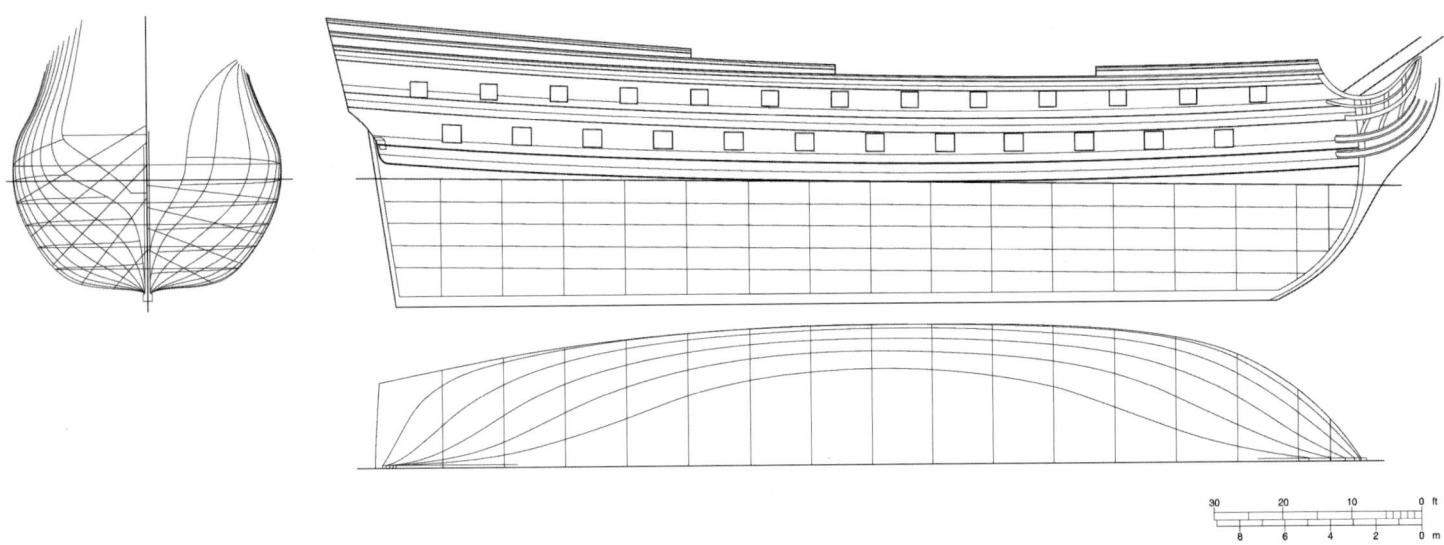

Lines plan of the 50-gun *Amphion* of 1749, drawn by László Veres after a Danish copy of the original in the Orlogsvaerftet, Copenhagen. This ship was unusual for a 50 in carrying a main battery of 24pdrs rather than the usual 18pdrs, hence her initial classification as a 3rd Rank ship.

Guns: LD 26 x 24pdrs; UD 28 x 12pdrs; QD 6 x 6pdrs; Fc 4 x 6pdrs.
Protée Brest Dyd.
K: 1746. L: 1.12.1748. C: 8.1750. Condemned 11.1770 at Brest and BU 1771 by order of 23.6.1771.
Hercule Brest Dyd.
K: 1746. L: 15.2.1749. C: 8.1750. Hulked 12.1756 at Port Mahon (Minorca); struck and sold there 4.1761.

By the mid-eighteenth century ships with only 18pdrs on the LD were regarded as relatively useless in that they could not stand in the line of battle, but Navy Secretary Antoine-Louis Rouillé, Comte de Jouy, authorised the construction of 50-gun ships to use up stocks of timber in the dockyards. The new *Amphion*, begun under Maurepas's time in office, was larger than the old 50s and was designed for 24pdrs in the main battery instead of 18pdrs.

AMPHION. 50 guns. Designed and built by Jacques-Luc Coulomb. The first of only two 50-gun ships to carry a 24pdr main battery, she was ordered on 19 January 1748 and named on 1 March. Reduced to 4th Rank by 1753, when she was two-thirds rebuilt at Rochefort (to March 1764); restored to 3rd Rank in 1766; later rebuilt again at Brest 1769–71 and reverted to 4th Rank in 1772. Rebuilt again at Brest 1775–76.
Dimensions & tons: 145ft 0in, 127ft 0in x 39ft 0in x 18ft 0in (47.10, 41.25 x 12.67 x 5.85m). 900/1,740 tons. Draught 16½ft/17ft 4in (5.36/5.63m). Men: 470 in war, 400 peace, +5/10 officers.
Guns: LD 24 x 24pdrs; UD 26 x 12pdrs; QD 6 x 6pdrs added.
Amphion Brest Dyd.
K: 3.1748. L: 28.7.1749. C: 1750. Took part in 3rd Battle of Ushant 27.7.1778, and in Action off Monti Christi 20.3.1780. Condemned 1787 at Rochefort and BU.

HARDI Class. 64 guns. Two ships designed and built at Rochefort by Pierre Morineau. *Hardi* underwent reconstruction at Rochefort in 1762–64, and again at Toulon from late 1768 to 1772.
Dimensions & tons: 149ft 0in x 40ft 6in x 20ft 9in (48.40 x 13.16 x 6.74m). 1,100/2,100 tons. Draught 19ft/20ft 2in (6.17/6.55m). Men: 520, +8/11 officers.
Guns: LD 26 x 24pdrs; UD 28 x 12pdrs; QD 6 x 6pdrs; Fc 4 x 6pdrs.
Hardi Rochefort Dyd.
K: 1748. L: 1750. C: 4.1751. Converted to a *flûte* in 1782. Took part (as a member of of CdE Pierre-André Suffren de Saint-Tropez's squadron) in the Battle of Cuddalore 20.6.1783. Hulked 1786 at Toulon; floating prison there 1791; not mentioned after 5.1798. Reduced to a floating prison at Toulon in 1786, became a hulk there in 1788 and a floating prison hulk in 1791. Struck in 5.1798.
Inflexible Rochefort Dyd.
K: 1751. L: 1752. C: 4.1755. Damaged in Battle of Quiberon Bay 20.11.1759. Further damaged by a gale in the Vilaine, condemned 8.1760 and BU 1763.

ILLUSTRE Class. 64 guns. Designed and built by Pierre Salinoc. *Illustre* was ordered 25 December 1748, and named on 13 January 1749.
Dimensions & tons: 150ft 0in, 131ft 6in x 40ft 8in x 20ft 4in (48.73, 42.72 x 13.21 x 6.605m). 1,100/2,150 tons. Draught 17ft/20ft (5.52/6.50m). Men: 500, +6/8 officers.
Guns: LD 26 x 24pdrs; UD 28 x 12pdrs; QD 6 x 6pdrs; Fc 4 x 6pdrs.
Illustre Brest Dyd.
K: 1.1749. L: 1750. C: 3.1751. Irreparably damaged off Île de France 1.1760 in a hurricane. Condemned 10.1761 and BU there.
Actif Brest Dyd.
K: 1750. L: 15.12.1752. C: 5.1754. Struck 12.1766 at Brest and BU 1767.

OPINIÂTRE. 64 guns. Designed and built by Jean Geoffroy; ordered 25 December 1748, named on 13 January 1749.
Dimensions & tons: 150ft 0in x 40ft 4in x 19ft 5in (48.73 x 13.10 x 6.31m). 1,100/2,150 tons. Draught 17ft/18¾ft (5.52/6.09m). Men: 500, +6/8 officers.
Guns: LD 26 x 24pdrs; UD 28 x 12pdrs; QD 6 x 6pdrs; Fc 4 x 6pdrs.
Opiniâtre Brest Dyd.
K: 1.1749. L: 8.1750. C: 4.1751. Anchors failed to hold during a storm, and wrecked 1.1758 at Plougastel, while leaving the Brest roadstead in a storm.

***LION* Class.** 64 guns. Two ships designed and built at Toulon by Pierre-Blaise Coulomb. *Lion* was ordered on 26 January 1749 and both were named on 17 June. *Lion* underwent a 2/3rds reconstruction at Toulon from mid-1765 to late 1768.

    Dimensions & tons: 150ft 0in, 134ft 0in x 40ft 6in x 19ft 6in (48.73, 43.53 x 13.16 x 6.33m). 1,100/2,084 tons. Draught 17¾/21½ft (5.77/6.98m). Men: 560 in war, 480 peace, +9/12 officers.

    Guns: LD 26 x 24pdrs; UD 28 x 12pdrs; QD 6 x 6pdrs; Fc 4 x 6pdrs.

Lion Toulon Dyd.
    K: 7.1749. L: 22.5.1751. C: 1752. Took part in the Battle off Minorca 20.5.1756. Hulked at Toulon 12.1783. Sold there 8.1785.

Sage Toulon Dyd.
    K: 12.1749. L: 29.12.1751. C: 1752. Took part in the Battle off Minorca 20.5.1756. Loaned for privateering off St Domingue and then New England in 1760–61. Reconstruction abandoned, condemned at Brest 10.1767 and BU there 1768.

BIZARRE. 64 guns. Designed and built by Jacques-Luc Coulomb. She underwent reconstruction at Rochefort in early 1768, and again in 1778 at Brest, being widened by 6in (16cm).

    Dimensions & tons: 153ft 0in, 135ft 0in x 40ft 10in x 19ft 0in (49.70, 43.85 x 13.26 x 6.17m). 1,100/2,200 tons. Draught 18/19½ft (5.85/6.33m). Men: 560 in war, 480 peace, +9 officers.

    Guns: LD 26 x 24pdrs; UD 28 x 12pdrs; QD 6 x 6pdrs; Fc 4 x 6pdrs.

Bizarre Brest Dyd.
    K: 12.1749. L: 9.1751. C: 3.1753. Took part in the Battle of Quiberon Bay 20.11.1759. Grounded and lost at Gondelour (Ceylon) 4.10.1782.

ÉVEILLÉ. 64 guns. Designed and built by Antoine Groignard, and ordered 1750.

    Dimensions & tons: 153ft 0in, 137ft 4in x 40ft 8in x 19ft 6in (49.70, 55.61 x 13.21 x 6.33m). 1,200/2,200 tons. Draught 18ft 2in/20ft 4in (5.90/6.605m). Men: 560 in war, 480 peace, +9 officers.

    Guns: LD 26 x 24pdrs; UD 28 x 12pdrs; QD 6 x 6pdrs; Fc 4 x 6pdrs.

Éveillé Rochefort Dyd.
    K: 1.1752. L: 12.1752. C: 1753. Took part in the Battle of Quiberon Bay 20.11.1759. Condemned 11.1770 at Brest and BU 1772 by order of 23.6.1771.

CAPRICIEUX. 64 guns. Designed and built by François-Guillaume Clairain-Deslauriers.

    Dimensions & tons: 150ft 0in, 134ft 0in x 40ft 2in x 19ft 3in (48.73, 43.63 x 13.05 x 6.25m). 1,100/2,200 tons. Men: 560 in war, 480 peace, +9 officers.

    Guns: LD 26 x 24pdrs; UD 28 x 12pdrs; QD 6 x 6pdrs; Fc 4 x 6pdrs.

Capricieux Rochefort Dyd.
    K: 1.1752. L: 13.9.1753. C: 1754. Burnt during attack by the British Navy 21.7.1758 at the siege of Louisbourg.

BIENFAISANT. 64 guns. Designed and built by Mathurin-Louis Geoffroy.

    Dimensions & tons: 150ft 0in x 40ft 8in x 20ft 0in (48.73 x 13.21 x 6.50m). 1,100/2,200 tons. Draught 17/20ft (5.52/6.50m). Men: 500.

    Guns: LD 26 x 24pdrs; UD 28 x 12pdrs; QD 6 x 6pdrs; Fc 4 x 6pdrs.

Bienfaisant Brest Dyd.
    K: late 1752. L: 13.10.1754. C: 2.1756. Captured by boat action at the siege of Louisbourg 26.7.1758 while most of her crew was fighting ashore, becoming HMS *Bienfaisant*; became hulk at Plymouth; BU 11.1814.

***SPHINX* Class.** 64 guns. Designed and built by Pierre Salinoc. *Sphinx* was ordered in 1752, and *Belliqueux* to the same design in August 1755, the latter being named on 10 September.

    Dimensions & tons: 150ft 0in, 135ft 0in x 40ft 6in x 20ft 0in (48.73, 43.85 x 13.16 x 6.50m). 1,200/2,200 tons. Draught 19ft 11in/21ft 5in (6.47/6.96m). Men: 560 in war, 480 peace, +11 officers.

    Guns: LD 26 x 24pdrs; UD 28 x 12pdrs; QD 6 x 6pdrs; Fc 4 x 6pdrs.

Sphinx Brest Dyd.
    K: late 1752. L: 20.8.1755. C: 2.1756. Took part in the Battle of Quiberon Bay 20.11.1759. Rebuilt at Brest 1.1775–12.1776 (see below)

Belliqueux Brest Dyd.
    K: 9.1755. L: 8.1756. C: 12.1756. Captured by HMS *Antelope* off

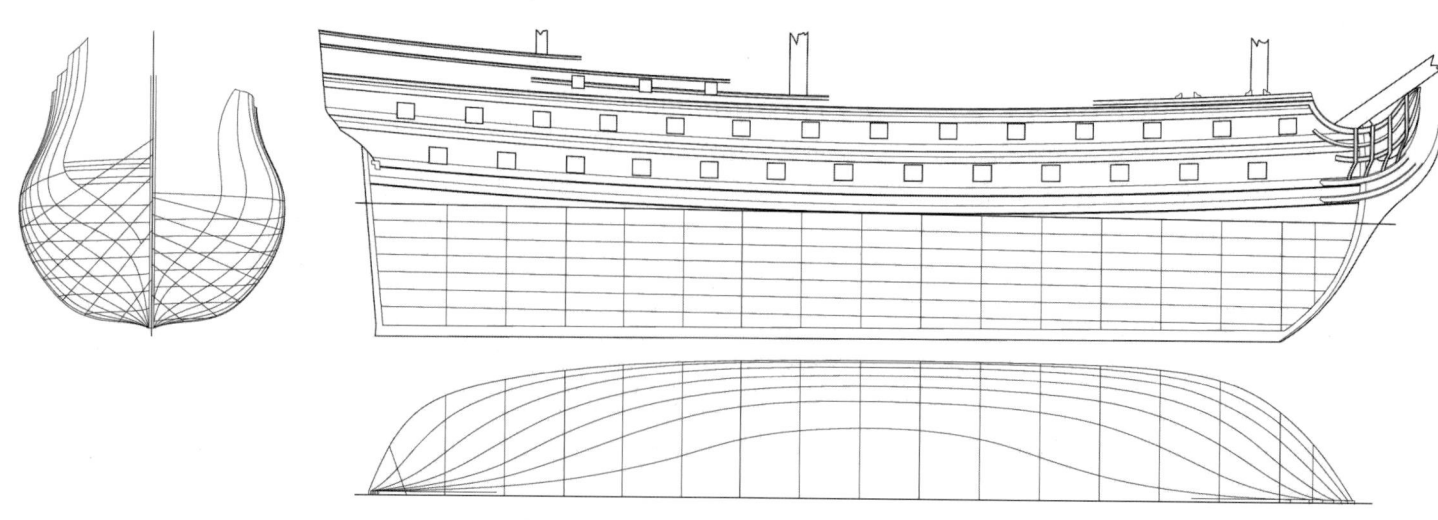

Lines plan of the *Capricieux*, a 64-gun ship of 1753, drawn by László Veres after a Danish copy of the original in the Orlogsvaerftet, Copenhagen. The *Capricieux* and another 64, *Célèbre*, were destroyed by fire in Louisbourg harbour when the 74-gun *Entreprenant* was set alight and blew up on 21 July 1758 during Boscawen's siege of the port.

THE THIRD RANK   145

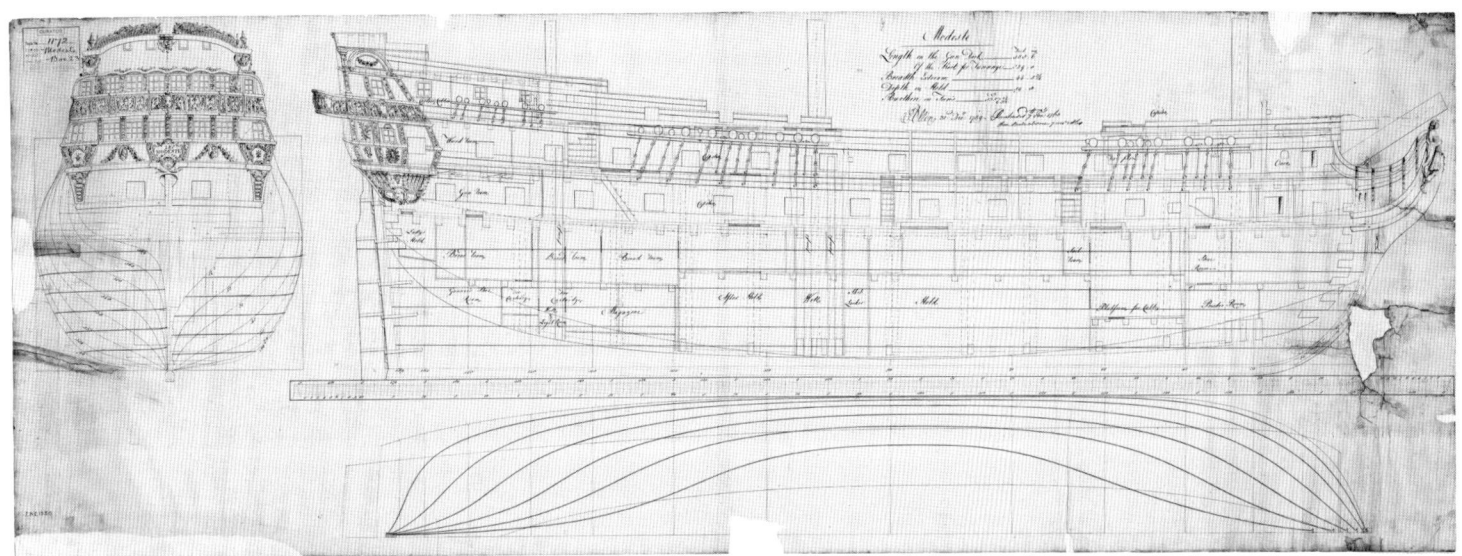

Admiralty draught of the 64-gun *Modeste*, dated 31 December 1759. It is annotated 'Purchased Jan 1760 then built about 7 months', an accurate assessment for a ship completed in May 1759. (National Maritime Museum, London J2658)

Ilfracombe (in the Bristol Channel) 31.10.1758, becoming HMS *Belliqueux*; BU 9.1772.

VAILLANT Class. 64 guns. Designed and built by Noël Pomet. Named on 27 July 1752 and 10 September 1755 respectively. *Vaillant* was rebuilt at Lorient in 1764, and then at Toulon in 1770–71 (1/2) and 1775 (2/3rds).
    Dimensions & tons: 151ft 0in, 127ft 9in x 40ft 6in x 19ft 8in (49.05, 41.50 x 13.16 x 6.39m). *Modeste*'s keel length was 3¼ft longer at 131ft (42.55m). 1,150/2,200 tons. Draught 18ft/20ft (5.85/6.50m). Men: 560 in war, 480 peace, +9/11 officers.
    Guns: LD 26 x 24pdrs; UD 28 x 12pdrs; QD 6 x 6pdrs; Fc 4 x 6pdrs.
Vaillant Toulon Dyd.
    K: 11.1752. L: 1.10.1755. C: 6.1756. Leased to the *Compagnie des Indes* 12.1760 to 12.1763. Took part in Battle of the Chesapeake 5.9.1781. Hulked 1783 at Rochefort; sheer (for masting) hulk 1792.
Modeste Toulon Dyd.
    K: 4.1756. L: 12.2.1759. C: 5.1759. Captured 19.8.1759 by Boscawen's squadron at Battle of Lagos, becoming HMS *Modeste*; hulked 1778 and BU 1800.

RAISONNABLE. 64 guns. Designed and built by Pierre Morineau; ordered in February 1754 and named on 31 March.
    Dimensions & tons: 152ft 0in, 138ft 6in x 40ft 0in x 20ft 4in (49.38, 44.99 x 12.99 x 6.605m). ?/2,200 tons. Men: 620 in war.
    Guns: LD 26 x 24pdrs; UD 28 x 12pdrs; QD 6 x 6pdrs; Fc 4 x 6pdrs.
Raisonnable Rochefort Dyd.
    K: 6.1754. L: 11.1756. C: 12.1757. Captured 29.5.1758 (with 61 men killed) by HM Ships *Dorsetshire* and *Achille* off Bec du Raz, becoming HMS *Raisonnable*; wrecked 7.1.1762 off Martinique.

ROBUSTE Class. 64 guns. Two ships were ordered in August 1755 to be built at Brest Dyd to a design by Antoine Groignard, and were named as *Robuste* and *Solitaire*. In December 1756 the two ships were cancelled and the orders moved to the *Compagnie des Indes* shipyard at

Admiralty draught of the 64-gun *Raisonnable*, undated but probably drawn during the survey of the ship in July 1758. As it was all hand-made, paper in the eighteenth century was expensive, so there was pressure to economise. This draught was drawn on the back of printed Progress forms – issued to the dockyards in large quantities – and the imprint of the letterpress shows through above the ship image. (National Maritime Museum, London J3127)

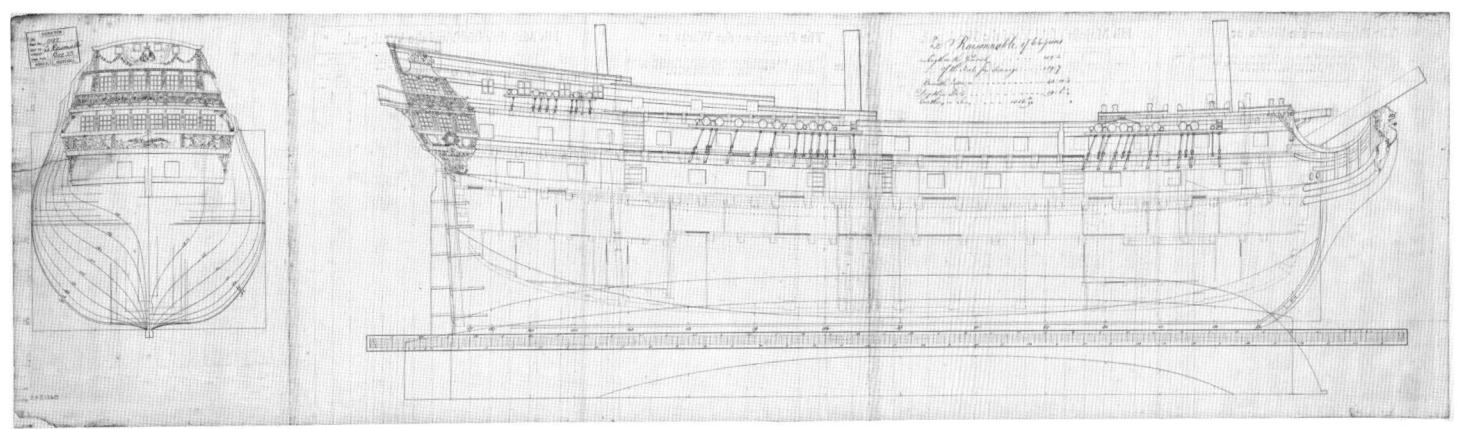

Lorient, the *Robuste* now to be a 74-gun 2nd Rank (see Chapter 2) and the *Solitaire* as a 64 (see below for the unchanged design details).

CÉLÈBRE. 64 guns. Designed and built by Pierre Salinoc, and named 10 September 1755.

Dimensions & tons: approx 150ft 0in x 40ft 6in (48.73 x 13.16m). 1,200 tons. Draught 20ft (6.50m). Men: 560 in war, 480 peace, +9/11 officers.

Guns: LD 26 x 24pdrs; UD 28 x 12pdrs; QD 6 x 6pdrs; Fc 4 x 6pdrs.

Célèbre Brest Dyd.
K: 9.1755. L: 2.1757. C: 5.1757. Burnt during attack by the British Navy 21.7.1758 at the siege of Louisbourg.

Ex-BRITISH PRIZES (1756-1758). 60 guns. The British Fourth Rate *Warwick* was captured by *Prudente*, *Atalante* and *Zéphyr* off Martinique on 11 March 1756 and added to the French Navy. The British Fourth Rate *Greenwich* was captured on 17 March 1757 by *Éveillé* (64) and *Diadème* (74) off St Domingue (Cape Cabron). As for most other captured British Navy ships, the dimensions cited here are from French sources.

Warwick Plymouth Dyd (Master Shipwright Pierson Lock).
Dimensions & tons: 139ft 0in x 38ft 10in x 15ft 10in (45.15 x 12.61 x 5.14m). 1,000/1,650 tons. Draught 17¾ft/18ft 7in (5.77/6.04m). Men: 400.
Guns (British): LD 24 x 24pdrs; UD 26 x 9pdrs; QD 10 x 6pdrs.
Ordered: 14.3.1727. K: 1.4.1730. L: 25.10.1733. C: 27.8.1734. Loaned to the *Compagnie des Indes* 1760, and armed *en flûte* (34 guns only); recaptured 24.1.1761 in the Mediterranean by HMS *Minerva* and BU.

Greenwich Moody Janverin, Lepe (in the Solent)
Dimensions & tons: 139ft 0in x 38ft 9in x 16ft 6in (45.15 x 12.59 x 5.36m). 1,500 tons displacement. Draught 16½ft (5.36m)
Guns (British): LD 22 x 24pdrs; UD 22 x 12pdrs; QD 6 x 6pdrs.
Ordered: 3.10.1745. K: 11.1745. L: 19.3.1748. C: 26.3.1748. Put into French service at St Domingue, arrived at Brest 12.1757. Wrecked in a squall 14.1.1758 with *Outarde* (*flûte*) on Kermorvan Isle near Plougastel in the Brest roadstead.

BRILLANT. 64 guns. Designed and built by Jacques-Luc Coulomb and Joseph-Louis Ollivier. Built for the *Compagnie des Indes* on one of the three new slipways at Caudan across the river from the Lorient dockyard. Sold to the King in November 1758 after a cruise to Quebec in which she captured a small prize for the Company. First launch attempt failed 14 September 1757. Her sister-ship *Fortuné* (launched 4 weeks earlier from the same shipyard) remained in *Compagnie des Indes* service until wrecked in South Africa in September 1763.

Dimensions & tons: 156ft 0in, 148ft 0in x 41ft 0in x 20ft 0in (50.67, 48.08 x 13.32 x 6.50m). 1,250/2,250 tons. Draught 19ft/19½ft (6.17/6.33m). Men: 560 in war, 480 peace, +11 officers.

Guns: LD 26 x 24pdrs; UD 28 x 12pdrs; QD 6 x 6pdrs; Fc 4 x 6pdrs.

Brillant Lorient–Caudan.
K: 1.4.1756. L: 27.9.1757. C: 11.1758. Took part in the Battle of Quiberon Bay 20.11.1759. Condemned at Brest 11.1770, and BU by order of 23.6.1771.

FANTASQUE Class. 64 guns. A slight modification to the *Lion* Class of 1749, with a one-foot increase in length. Two ships were ordered to this design at the outbreak of the Seven Years' War; *Fantasque* was named 25 October 1755 and *Altier* on 29 May 1757. *Fantasque* was 2/3rds rebuilt at Toulon in 1765–68 and again in 1777.

Dimensions & tons: 151ft 0in, 134ft 0in x 40ft 6in x 19ft 6in (49.05, 43.53 x 13.16 x 6.33m). 1,100/2,084 tons. Draught 17¾/21½ft (5.77/6.98m). Men: 480 in war, 320 peace, +9/12 officers.

Guns: LD 26 x 24pdrs; UD 28 x 12pdrs; QD 6 x 6pdrs; Fc 4 x 6pdrs.

Fantasque Toulon Dyd (*Constructeur*, Joseph Véronique-Charles Chapelle).
K: 7.1757. L: 10.5.1758. C: 5.1759. Became a hospital ship 2.5.1780 for the movement of Rochambeau's troops from Brest to America, then a transport 5.1781; grounded at Newport (Rhode Island) in a storm 10.1781, but refloated. Condemned at Lorient 3.1784, then then sent to Fort-Royal (Martinique) and hulked there 11.1784.

Altier Toulon Dyd (*Constructeur*, Joseph-Marie-Blaise Coulomb).
K: 7.1758. L: 23.3.1760. C: 4.1762. Condemned at Toulon 11.1770 and sold 1772 for commercial service.

SOLITAIRE. 64 guns. Designed by Antoine Groignard. Ordered in August 1755, initially for construction at Brest Dyd, but on 10 September she was named and construction shifted to the main dockyard of the *Compagnie des Indes* at Lorient.

Dimensions & tons: 165ft 0in x 41ft 0in x 20ft 6in (53.60 x 13.32 x 6.66m). 1,250/2,300 tons. Men: 480 in war, 320 peace, +11 officers.

Guns: LD 26 x 24pdrs; UD 28 x 12pdrs; QD 6 x 6pdrs; Fc 4 x 6pdrs.

Solitaire Lorient Dyd.
K: 10.1757. L: 30.11.1758. C: 4.1759. Took part in the Battle of Quiberon Bay 20.11.1759. Struck and ordered BU 23.6.1771, BU at Brest between July and September.

Two 64-gun ships were ordered in May 1757 and in 1758, but were cancelled in 1760 due to shortage of funds as well as of suitable timber. The first, to have been named *Résolu*, was awarded to Rochefort Dyd and named on 29 May 1757; she would have measured 148ft x 41ft 6in x 20ft 4in (48.08 x 13.48 x 6.61m). The second, to have been named *Alcyon*, would have been built at Brest Dyd. Both would have carried the standard 64-gun ordnance; but by 1759 the master constructors in the dockyards were already planning for future 64s to carry 18pdrs (*vice* 12pdrs) in their UD batteries.

In 1759 Toulon Dyd also reported that it had on hand only enough non-appropriated timber to build a 50-gun ship, and that since the wood was four to five years old it had to be used or wasted. The construction of a 50-gun ship was therefore authorised on the model of the *Amphion* with a 24pdr main battery. At this time 50-gun ships were still considered useful in the eastern Mediterranean, and by 1762 the Navy had moved all its remaining 50s to Toulon.

SAGITTAIRE. 50 guns. Designed and built by Joseph-Marie-Blaise Coulomb, she was named on 18 October 1759. The launch in August 1761 was supervised by Joseph Véronique-Charles Chapelle, as Coulomb was away in Malta. She was probably built as a 4th Rank ship, but was raised to 3rd Rank in 1766 and then reverted to 4th Rank in 1772. One of only two 50-gun ships to carry a 24pdr main battery (the first being *Amphion*), but these guns were replaced by 18pdrs at Toulon in 1780.

Dimensions & tons: 147ft 0in x 39ft 4in x 18ft 6in (47.75 x 12.78 x 6.01m). 1,000/1,800 tons. Draught 17ft/18ft 2in (5.52/5.90m). Men: 400 in war (280 peace); later 460/430, +7/8 officers.

Guns: LD 24 x 24pdrs (reduced to 18pdrs in 1781); UD 26 x 12pdrs; QD 4 x 6pdrs added.

Sagittaire Toulon Dyd.
K: 1.1760. L: 8.8.1761. C: 3.1762. Lent to the *Compagnie des Indes*

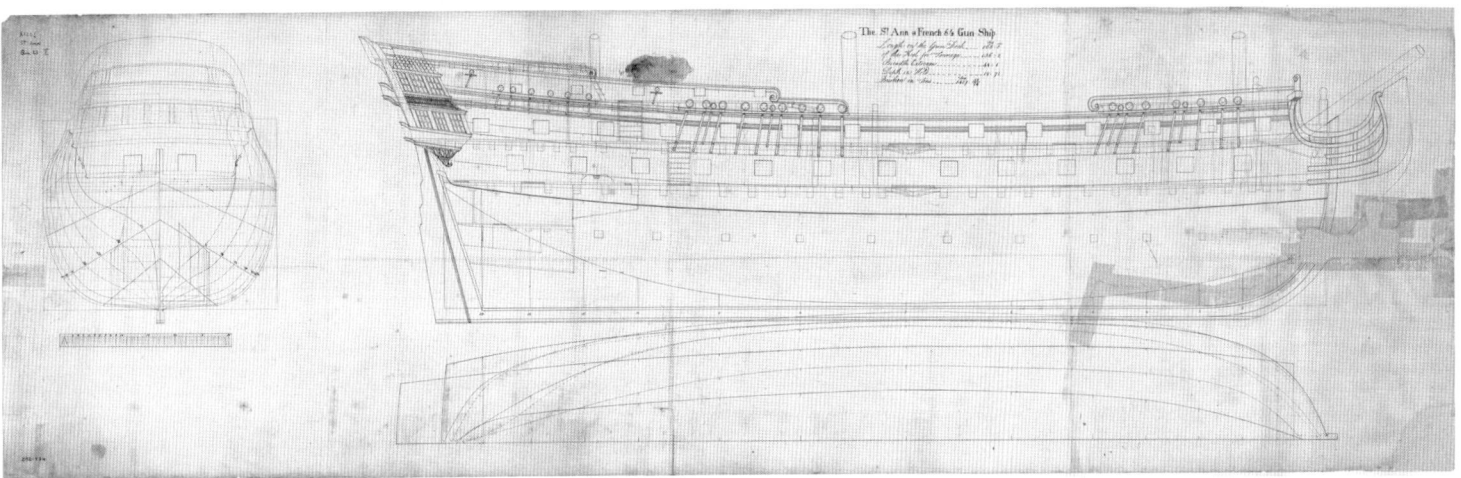

Admiralty draught of the *Sainte Anne*, undated but presumably as captured since the label describes her as 'a French 64-gun ship'. Built in Genoa, the hull form of this ship could never be mistaken for a French design; indeed, she closely resembles British ships of the previous generation in body plan and steeply raked sternpost. However, the stern galleries and topside detail are so distinctly English that it raises suspicions that the draught represents the ship after the 6-month refit at Woolwich in the first half of 1762. (National Maritime Museum, London J3615)

orientales et de la Chine for commerce 9.1783 to 8.1785. Condemned 1786 at Lorient, and hulked there 4.1788; sold for commerce about 1790.

Ex-GENOESE PURCHASES (1760). Following a proposal by Charles-Louis Merle, Comte de Beauchamps (France's ambassador at Lisbon), four 64-gun ships of Genoese construction were purchased, the first at Lisbon in February 1760 and three sister ships from their Genoese owner during 1760. The purchase was reportedly financed discretely by Portugal in response to French claims over the destruction of La Clue's squadron in Portuguese waters following the Battle of Lagos. Designed and built by Ange-Marie Rati. However, these ships were built of fir, rather than oak, and so were not durable. They acted as supply vessels initially, before commissioning as 3rd Rank ships. The first three were loaned out by the Navy for commerce or privateering in 1760, the *Sainte Anne* being captured in this role, and the other two nearly taken also. *Saint François de Paule* similarly operated as a privateer during the latter half of 1762.

Dimensions & tons: 155ft 3in x 41ft 3in x 18ft 5in (50.44 x 13.40 x 5.98m). 1,150/2,200 tons. Draught 18½ft (6.01m). Men: 480 in war (320 peace); later 560 war, +9 officers.
Guns: LD 26 x 24pdrs; UD 28 x 18pdrs or 12pdrs; QD/Fc 10 x 8pdrs or 6pdrs.

Sainte Anne Genoa.
K: 1754. L: 1756. C: 1759. Captured (while armed *en flûte* with just 40 guns) 5.6.1761 by HMS *Centaur* off St Domingue, becoming HMS *Sainte Anne*; sold 10.1784 at Plymouth.

Notre Dame du Rosaire Genoa.
K: 1754. L: 1757. C: 1760. Renamed *Hazard* 24.6.1762. Condemned 11.1770 at Toulon, hulked there in 1771.

Vierge de Santé Genoa.
K: 1754. L: 1759. C: 1760. Renamed *Rencontre* 24.6.1762. Condemned 11.1769 at Brest and BU.

Saint François de Paule Genoa.
K: 1755. L: 1759. C: 1761. Renamed *Aventurier* 16.4.1764. Condemned 11.1770 at Toulon and sold 1772.

Soon after Choiseul's appointment as Secretary of the Navy in October 1761, some 16 million *livres* was raised for the Navy by donations from a variety of public and private bodies and individual, allowing for another seventeen ships of the line to be funded. Besides four 1st Rank ships – *Bretagne*, *Impétueux* (later renamed *Ville de Paris*), *Languedoc* and *Saint Esprit* – and six 2nd Rank 74s – *Cimeterre* (later renamed *Citoyen*), *Bourgogne*, *Diligent*, *Six Corps*, *Zélé* and *Marseillais*) – this program included three 3rd Rank 64s – *Entêté* (later renamed *Union*), the original *Union* (later renamed *Provence*), and *Artésien* – and four 56s – *Bordelais*, *Ferme*, *Utile* and *Flamand*.

UNION (64 guns). Designed and built by Jean Geoffroy. Ordered in August 1755, and funded by public subscription. Originally named *Entêté* on 10 September, she was to have been renamed *Orion* on 1 March 1762, but instead was renamed *Union* on 17 March, taking over the name which was first allotted to the 64 scheduled to be built at Toulon.

Dimensions & tons: 156ft 0in x 40ft 6in x 20ft 0in (50.67 x 13.16 x 6.50m). 1,087/2,250 tons. Draught 18ft/19½ft (5.85/6.44m). Men: 480 in war (320 peace); later 560 in war, 480 peace, +9 officers.
Guns: LD 26 x 24pdrs. UD 26 x 12pdrs; QD/Fc 10 x 6pdrs.

Union Brest Dyd.
K: 1761. L: 11.1763. C: 5.1764. Converted to a hospital ship in 1778, but wrecked in the Atlantic in February 1782.

BORDELAIS Class. 56 guns. In 1761 Choiseul summoned to Paris the naval constructor Antoine Groignard, then stationed at Bordeaux, to instruct him to design four ships of the line carrying 36pdrs and 18pdrs for use in the shallow waters around Dunkirk. Choiseul also recruited donors for all four ships. The *Bordelais* was funded ('offered to the King') by the *Parlement* and City of Bordeaux, the *Ferme* and *Utile* by the *Fermiers Généraux* and the *Flamand* by the *États de Flandre*. A contract was awarded on 3 November 1761 to Sieur Risteau representing the *Compagnie des Indes* to manage the construction 'with economy' of four 56-gun ships at the *Chantiers du Roi* at Bordeaux after plans by Groignard. Built by *sous-constructeur* Léon-Michel Guignace, these were probably the largest ships of the line that could be built at Bordeaux, as the Garonne River was too shallow for 74-gun ships to reach the city.

Originally listed (with *Sagittaire*) in the 4th Rank with 50 guns, these ships emerged as 56-gunners with 36pdrs on the LD and 18pdrs on the UD. Not fitting into any standard category, they were first moved to the 3rd Rank in 1764 (presumably because of their number of guns), then to the 2nd Rank in 1768 (presumably because of their 36pdrs), and then back to the 3rd Rank in 1771. All four were based permanently at

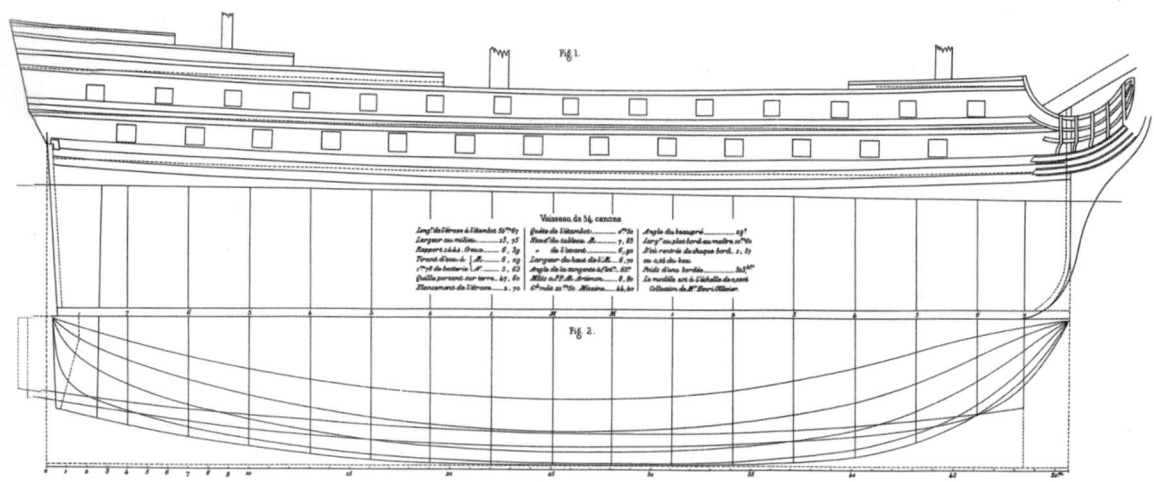

This unnamed plan in *Vice-amiral* Pâris's work can be identified from the details provided as one of the *Bordelais* class, an unusual 56-gun design of relatively shallow draught, armed with 36pdrs on the lower deck and 18pdrs on the upper deck, to give a broadside of 684 *livres* compared with the 510 *livres* of the current 64s. Intended for use in the restricted waters around Dunkirk, they were also the largest that could be launched into the shallow river at Bordeaux.(*Souvenirs de Marine*, Plate 250)

Rochefort throughout their lives; *Ferme* was rebuilt there in 1769, *Bordelais* and *Flamand* in 1770–71 there, and *Utile* began a similar reconstruction there in April 1771 but was swiftly condemned. After the sale of *Ferme* in 1774, the last two survivors, now with 24pdrs in their main battery, were reduced to the 4th Rank in 1776, completing the circle.

    Dimensions & tons: 156ft 0in, 146ft 6in x 42ft 4in x 19ft 8in (50.675, 47.59 x 13.75 x 6.39m). 1,100/2,005 tons. Draught 18ft 2in/19½ft (5.90/6.33m). Men: 480 in war (320 peace); later 560 in war, 500 peace.

    Guns: LD 24 x 36pdrs; UD 26 x 18pdrs; QD/Fc 6 x 6pdrs (8pdrs in *Ferme* in 1764). *Bordelais* and *Flamand* re-armed from 1776: LD 24 x 24pdrs; UD 26 x 12pdrs; QD/Fc 6 x 6pdrs.

Bordelais (Bordelois) Bordeaux.
    K: 7.1762. L: 26.4.1763. C: 7.1763. Hulked at Lorient and struck 5.1779. Purchased 10.1779 and rebuilt as a frigate, renamed *Artois* (rebuilding funded by the *États d'Artois*) – see Chapter 4.

Ferme Bordeaux.
    K: 8.1762. L: 10.10.1763. C: 12.1763. Sold to the Ottoman Sultan 8.1774.

Utile Bordeaux.
    K: 5.1763. L: 14.8.1764. C: 12.1764. Condemned 12.1771 at Rochefort and converted to a sheer hulk there by 1773. Possibly replaced and deleted in 1792.

Flamand Bordeaux.
    K: 10.1763. L: 11.5.1765. C: 7.1765. Sold to the Ottoman Sultan *c*.7.1774, but refused by him as the price was deemed too high (she brought home the crew of *Ferme* which was accepted). Careened at Île de France in 1779 and possibly in 1783–84. Took part (as a member of Suffren's squadron) in all the actions off India in 1782–83. Condemned at Rochefort in 1785–86 and struck.

PROVENCE. 64 guns. Designed and built by Jean-François Gauthier. Funded by the *États de Provence*. Originally named *Union* in February 1762, but quickly renamed *Provence* on 17 March. Rebuilt (2/3rds) at Toulon from 1771–75, and at Brest from June to September 1782.

    Dimensions & tons: 153ft 0in, 136ft 0in x 40ft 6in x 19ft 8in (49.70, 44.18 x 13.16 x 5.39m). 1,150/2,320 tons. Draught 19ft 1in/21ft 4in (6.20/6.93m). Men: 480 in war (320 peace); later 550, +9/10 officers.

    Guns: LD 26 x 24pdrs; UD 28 x 12pdrs; QD 6 x 6pdrs; Fc 4 x 6pdrs.

Provence Toulon Dyd.
    K: 5.1763. L: 29.4.1763. C: 6.1763. Took part in Action off Cape Henry 16.3.1781. Disarmed 3.6.1782 at Brest, and lent to the *Compagnie des Indes orientales et de la Chine* 12.1783–8.1785. Struck 1785 at Rochefort and BU there 1786.

ARTÉSIEN Class. 64 guns. Five ships designed and built by Joseph-Louis Ollivier. The *Artésien* was funded by the *États d'Artois* in 1761 and ordered in 1762. The *Roland* and *Alexandre* were ordered to the same design on 29 January 1770 and named on 25 February, and two further ships were built a year later; the older *Sphinx* of 1755 was rebuilt by Ollivier at Brest in 1775–76 to the same design. *Artésien* underwent rebuilding at Rochefort in 1776–77, and *Protée* at Brest (to one half) in 1778–79.

    Dimensions & tons: 154ft 6in, 141ft 0in x 40ft 6in x 20ft 0in (50.19, 45.80 x 13.16 x 6.50 m). 1,200/2,084 tons. Draught 17ft/18ft 10in (5.52/6.12m). Men: 480 in war (320 peace); later 570-590, +9 officers.

    Guns: LD 26 x 24pdrs; UD 28 x 12pdrs; QD 6 x 6pdrs; Fc 4 x 6pdrs.

Artésien Brest Dyd.
    K: 3.4.1764. L: 7.3.1765. C: 5.1765. Took part in 3rd Battle of Ushant 27.7.1778, in the Battle of Porto Praya 16.4.1781 and (as a member of of CdE Pierre-André Suffren de Saint-Tropez's squadron) in all the actions off India in 1782–83. Condemned 2.1785 at Rochefort and used as sheer hulk.

Roland Brest Dyd.
    K: 22.1.1770. L: 14.2.1771. C: 9.1771. Took part in 3rd Battle of Ushant 27.7.1778. Burnt by accident (with *Zéphyr*) at Brest 28.2.1779.

Alexandre Brest Dyd.
    K: 22.1.1770. L: 28.2.1771. C: 8.1771. Took part in 3rd Battle of Ushant 27.7.1778. Reduced to 28-gun *flûte* 1782 (later 24-gun), and taken by HMS *Mediator* 12.12.1782.

Protée Brest Dyd.
    K: 2.1771. L: 10.11.1772. C: 8.1773. Taken 24.2.1780 by HM Ships *Resolution* and *Bedford* off Madeira.

Éveillé Brest Dyd.
    K: 2.1771. L: 10.12.1772. C: 8.1773. Took part in 3rd Battle of Ushant 27.7.1778 and in Action off Cape Henry 16.3.1781, then in Battles of St Kitts 25/26.1.1782 and the Saintes 12.4.1782. Condemned 1786 at Rochefort and struck 1787.

VENGEUR. 64 guns. Designed and built by Antoine Groignard for the *Compagnie des Indes*, and purchased by the Navy in July 1765. Rebuilt at Brest in 1765–66, and again (to 2/3rds) from 1776 to March 1778.

THE THIRD RANK

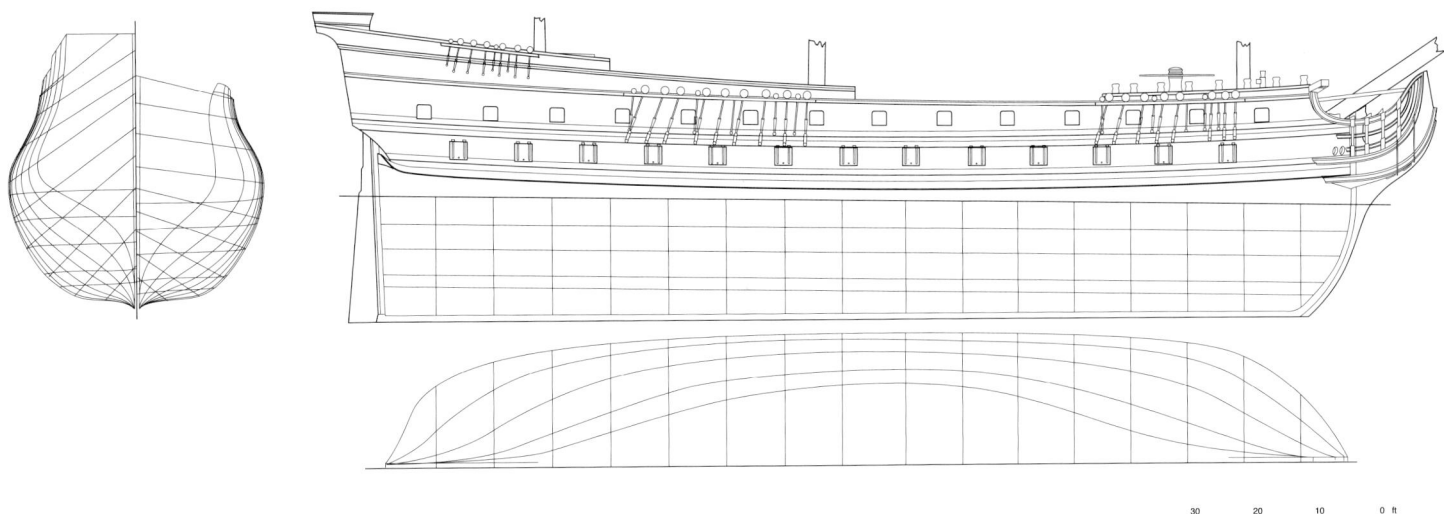

Lines plan of the 64-gun *Vengeur*, drawn by László Veres after a draught in the Rigsarkivet, Copenhagen. The Danish plan is heavily annotated in French so is probably an original rather than a copy. In Denmark trainee naval constructors were encouraged to carry out study tours of foreign dockyards and wherever possible to bring back examples of ship plans. This is why the most varied, if not the largest, collection of ship plans from the sailing era is to be found, not in London, Paris or Amsterdam, but in Copenhagen.

Dimensions & tons: 162ft 0in, ?150ft 0in x 41ft 6in x 21ft 0in (52.62 x 13.48 x 6.82m). 1,250/2,350 tons. Draught 19¼ft/20¾ft (6.25/6.74m). Men: 560-580, +9 officers.

Guns: LD 26 x 24pdrs; UD 28 x 12pdrs; QD/Fc 10 x 6pdrs.

Vengeur Lorient-Caudan.
K: 5.1756. L: 25.10.1756. C: 2.1757. Took part in 3rd Battle of Ushant 27.7.1778, in the Battle of Porto Praya 16.4.1781 and (as a member of Suffren's squadron) in all the actions off India in 1782–83. Condemned 2.1784 at Île de France (Mauritius), and sold for commerce 4.1784; wrecked off Île Bourbon (Réunion) 3.1785.

BRILLANT. 64 guns. Designed by Antoine Groignard, and built by Groignard and Jean-François Étienne.

Dimensions & tons: 157ft 0in, 142ft 0in x 40ft 6in x 20ft 0in (51.00, 46.13 x 13.16 x 6.50m). 1,200/2,300 tons. Draught 18¾/19¾ft (6.09/6.42m). Men: 580 in war, 489 peace, +9 officers.

Guns: LD 26 x 24pdrs; UD 28 x 12pdrs; QD 6 x 6pdrs; Fc 4 x 6pdrs.

Brillant Brest Dyd.
K: 11.1772. L: 9.1774. C: 12.1774. Took part (as a member of Suffren's squadron) in all the actions off India in 1782-83. Hulked as guard ship at Cherbourg 9.1787; condemned 9.1795 and BU there 1797.

SOLITAIRE Class. 64 guns. Designed and built by Antoine Groignard.

Dimensions & tons: 154ft 0in, 142ft 0in x 41ft 0in x 20ft 6in (50.03, 46.13 x 13.32 x 6.66m). 1,090/2,200 tons. Draught 19ft/20ft (6.17/6.50m). Men: 580 in war, 491 peace, +9 officers.

Guns: LD 26 x 24pdrs; UD 28 x 12pdrs; QD 6 x 6pdrs; Fc 4 x 6pdrs.

Solitaire Brest Dyd.
K: 12.1773. L: 22.10.1774. C: 3.1776. Took part in 3rd Battle of Ushant 27.7.1778, and in Battle of the Chesapeake 5.9.1781. Captured by the British in the Antilles 12.1782.

Réfléchi Rochefort Dyd.
K: 5.1772. L: 25.11.1776. C: 2.1777. Took part in 3rd Battle of Ushant 27.7.1778, and in Battles of the Chesapeake 5.9.1781, St Kitts 25/26.1.1782 and the Saintes 12.4.1782. Hulked at Brest 11.1788, raséed in 1793 and renamed *Turot*; not mentioned thereafter.

SPHINX. 64 guns. This vessel had been originally built in 1752–56 at Brest by Pierre Salinoc (see above), but was 75 per cent rebuilt there in 1775–76 to a new design by Jacques-Noël Sané. She took part in all the actions off India in 1782–83, and was refitted in 1784 on returning home.

Dimensions & tons: 151ft 0in, 135ft 0in x 41ft 0in x 20ft 6in (49.05, 43.85 x 13.32 x 6.66m). 1,200/2,200 tons. Draught 19ft 11in/21ft 5in (6.47/6.96m). Men: 560 in war, 491 peace, +11 officers.

Guns: LD 26 x 24pdrs; UD 28 x 12pdrs; QD 6 x 6pdrs; Fc 4 x 6pdrs.

Sphinx Brest Dyd (*Constructeur*, Joseph-Louis Ollivier).
K: 1.1775. L: 9.12.1776. C: 1777. Took part in 3rd Battle of Ushant 27.7.1778, in the Battle of Porto Praya 16.4.1781 and (as a member of of CdE Pierre-André Suffren de Saint-Tropez's squadron) in all the actions off India in 1782–83. Hulked as floating battery at Rochefort 5.1793, disarmed 1.1802.

CATON Class. 64 guns. Designed and built by Joseph-Marie-Blaise Coulomb. A two-ship class of 64s was ordered on 7 February 1770 to be built at Toulon, and these were named *Caton* and *Bélier* on 25 February. On 20 March the order for *Bélier* was replaced by one for a 74-gun ship, to which the name *Destin* was awarded (see previous chapter). Work on both was begun in April, but a shortage of timber meant that construction of both ships was deferred. The order for the second 64-gun ship was reinstated on 29 November 1777, and the new name *Jason* was assigned on 20 February 1778. Both vessels were captured by the British in April 1782 in the Mona Passage off Puerto Rico and added to the British Navy.

Dimensions & tons: 156ft 0in, 139ft 0in x 40ft 6in x 19ft 8in (50.67, 45.15 x 13.16 x 6.39m). 1,100/2,300 tons. Draught 17ft 11in/19ft 1in (5.82/6.20m). Men: 589 in war, 540 peace, +11 officers.

Guns: LD 26 x 24pdrs; UD 28 x 12pdrs; QD 6 x 6pdrs; Fc 4 x 6pdrs.

Caton Toulon Dyd.
K: 4.1770. L: 5.7.1777. C: 5.1778. Took part in Battles of the

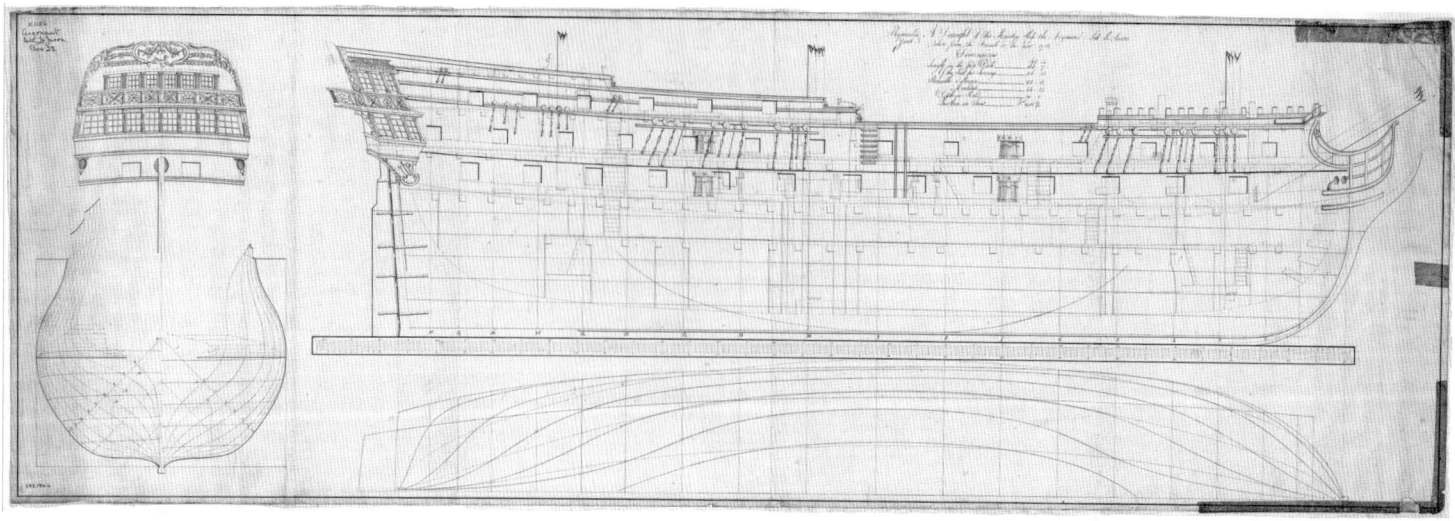

Admiralty draught of the 64-gun *Argonaut* 'late *Le Jason*', endorsed Plymouth Yard but undated. It shows an entirely British style of internal arrangements, with characteristic drumhead capstans and chain pumps prominently visible, so most probably dates from the fitting out in April–September 1793. (National Maritime Museum, London J3948)

Chesapeake 5.9.1781, St Kitts 25/26.1.1782 and the Saintes 12.4.1782. Captured by HMS *Valiant* of Hood's squadron on 19 April 1782 in the Mona Passage off Puerto Rico and added to the British Navy as HMS *Caton*.

Jason Toulon Dyd.
   K: 24.5.1778. L: 13.2.1779. C: 21.6.1779. Took part in Action off Cape Henry 16.3.1781, and in Battles of St Kitts 25/26.1.1782 and the Saintes 12.4.1782. Captured by HMS *Valiant* of Hood's squadron on 19 April 1782 in the Mona Passage off Puerto Rico and added to the British Navy as HMS *Argonaut*.

INDIEN Class. 64 guns. This group of vessels had been originally ordered by the *Compagnie des Indes* in the late 1760s and early 1770s to a design by Antoine Groignard and Gilles Cambry; all the vessels were built at Lorient-Caudan, a set of three slipways on the opposite shore of the Scorff River immediately upstream from the main dockyard that had been in use since 1755. The three earliest ships, *Actionnaire* (the prototype, was about 2ft shorter than the others), *Indien* and *Mars*, were acquired by the Navy in April–July 1770 following Louis XV's revoking of the Company's monopolies.

   Dimensions & tons: 157ft 6in, 148ft 0in x 40ft 6in x 17ft 6in (51.16, 48.08 x 13.16 x 5.68m) except *Actionnaire* lengt6h 155ft 6in, 146ft 0in (50.51, 47.43m) only. 1,300/2,250 tons. Draught 20/21ft (6.50/6.82m). Men: 580 in war, 560 peace, +9 officers.
   Guns: LD 26 x 24pdrs; UD 28 x 12pdrs; QD/Fc 10 x 6pdrs.

Actionnaire Lorient–Caudan.
   K: 6.1767. L: 22.12.1767. C: 3.1768. Purchased by the Navy 4.1770. Captured 20.4.1782 by HMS *Foudroyant* (of Barrington's squadron) on sailing from Brest.

Indien Lorient–Caudan.
   K: 1.1768. L: 30.7.1768. C: 1.1769. Purchased by the Navy 4.1770. Took part in 3rd Battle of Ushant 27.7.1778. Condemned 1783 at Toulon and sold 1784.

Mars Lorient–Caudan.
   K: 10.1768. L: 17.8.1769. C: 3.1770. Purchased by the Navy 7.1770. Burnt by accident at Île de France 19.11.1773.

A second trio were built in the mid-1770s at Lorient-Caudan by François Caro, all to the same design as the earlier group. Built for commercial operators, they were used as merchantmen until 1778, but then the *Sévère* and *Maréchal de Broglie* (the latter renamed *Ajax* on 13 August 1779), were purchased by the Navy in November 1778 and April 1779 respectively as part of the war preparations, while the *Superbe* was sold in 1779 to Austria; these were the last 64-gun ships (other than prizes) to be added to the French Navy.

Maréchal de Broglie Lorient–Caudan.
   K: 12.1772. L: 14.1.1774. C: 3.1774. Renamed *Ajax* 13.8.1779. Took part in of CdE Pierre-André Suffren de Saint-Tropez's squadron in all battles off India 1782–83 (except Negapatam, when absent due to damage). Struck in 1786, but reinstated as a floating battery at Verdon 6.1795. BU after 3.1801.

Superbe Lorient–Caudan.
   K: 12.1772. L: 11.3.1774. C: 3.1774. Sold 1779 to Austria as *Prince de Kaunitz*, but leased back by the French Navy at Toulon in 5.1782; struck 1783.

Sévère Lorient–Caudan.
   K: 12.1773. L: 17.1.1775. C: 3.1775. Took part in of CdE Pierre-André Suffren de Saint-Tropez's squadron in all battles off India 1782–83. Wrecked 26.1.1784 in Table Bay, South Africa.

Ex-BRITISH PRIZE (1779). 62 guns. The British Third Rate *Ardent*, built to a 1761 design by Thomas Slade, was captured by *Junon*, *Gentille*, *Gloire* and *Bellone* (of LG Louis Guillouet, Comte d'Orvilliers's squadron) off Plymouth on 17 August 1779 and added to the French Navy.

   Dimensions & tons (in French re-measurement): 154ft 0in, 138ft 6in x 41ft 7in x 20ft 0in (50.03, 44.99 x 13.51 x 6.50m). 1,250/2,200 tons. Draught 20ft 0in (5.77/6.50m). Men: 589.
   Guns (British): LD 24 x 24pdrs; UD 26 x 18pdrs; QD/Fc 12 x 9pdrs.

Ardent Hugh Blaydes, Hessle, Hull.
   Ordered: 16.12.1761. K: 15.1.1762. L: 13.8.1764. C: 31.8.1764. Took part in the Battles of St Kitts 25/26.1.1782 and of the Saintes 12.4.1782, then retaken by Rodney's fleet 14.4.1782. Renamed HMS *Tiger* 28.8.1783; sold at Plymouth 10.6.1784 to BU.

New construction of the type ceased in the 1770s, as the battlefleet concentrated on the more effective 74-gun type. Two new 64s were projected in 1782 – the *Oriflamme* and *Breton* (both to have been begun at Brest in 1783) – but these were cancelled in February 1783. Subsequent acquisitions of 64-gun ships after 1786 were only by capture of existing enemy vessels during the next few decades.

The capture of the 64-gun HMS *Ardent* on 17 August was the sole tangible result of the domination of Channel waters by the vast Franco-Spanish fleet in the summer of 1779. In this anonymous hand-coloured French engraving, *Ardent* is in the centre with the French frigates *Gentille* and *Junon* to the right and left. (Beverley R Robinson Collection, Annapolis 51.7.185)

Ex-BRITISH PRIZE (1782). 52 guns. The 50-gun two-decker HMS *Hannibal* of the *Portland* Class was built to a design by John Williams. She was captured off Sumatra on 21 January 1782 by the *Héros* and *Artésien*, and added to the French Navy under the name *Annibal* (or *Petit Annibal*, to distinguish her from the 74-gun *Annibal* of 1779).

Dimensions & tons (as re-measured by French): 139ft 6in, 126ft 0in x 37ft 4in x 18ft 0in (45.315, 40.93 x 12.13 x 5.85m). 800/1,600 tons. Draught 17.25ft.19ft (5.60/6.17m). Men: 280.

Guns: LD 22 x 24pdrs; UD 24 x 12pdrs (2 more than in British service); QD 4 x 6pdrs; Fc 2 x 6pdrs.

Annibal Henry Adams, Bucklers Hard.
Ordered 24.5.1776 (contract 17.6.1776). K: 7.1776. L: 26.12.1779. C: 22.2.1780 at Portsmouth Dyd. Struck at Rochefort 1787, and became a careening hulk there 1792.

(E) 18pdr-armed vessels acquired from 1 September 1715

By 1715 the 3rd Rank had clearly split into two groups (labelled by Blaise Coulomb as '*Premier Ordre*' and '*Second Ordre*'). The latter comprised those ships with a main battery of 18pdrs, generally pierced for eleven or twelve pairs of this calibre on the lower deck. Relatively few of these were added after 1715, as the 18pdr gun's effectiveness was seen as inadequate for the battlefleet, and construction focused on the larger 24pdr-armed 3rd Rank ships – see Section (D) above. However, the re-arming in 1740 of the *Triton* moved that vessel from the 24pdr to the 18pdr category. Differences in the overall number of guns generally reflected the provision or otherwise of 6pdr or 4pdr guns on the QD – with these not counted, almost all these ships had 50 guns in the two batteries. Two 50-gun ships built with 24pdrs, *Amphion* (1748) and *Sagittaire* (1759), are listed in Section (D) above.

CONTENT. 56, later 60 guns. Designed and built by Pierre Coulomb.
Dimensions & tons: 136ft 0in, 121ft 0in x 37ft 6in x 17ft 0in (44.18, 39.31 x 12.18 x 5.52m). 950 tons. Draught 16½ft/18½ft (5.36/6.01m). Men: 380 in war, 350 peace, +6 officers.

Guns: 56 in war (50 peace): LD 24 x 18pdrs; UD 26 x 12pdrs; QD/Fc 6 x 6pdrs (10 from 1729).

Content Port Louis, near Lorient.
K: 7.1716. L: 3.1717. C: 11.1717. Captured (with *Mars*) HMS *Northumberland* off Ushant 19.5.1744. Sold to the *Compagnie des Indes* 5.1747 for commerce; hulked at Île de France (Mauritius) 3.1749.

BRILLANT. 56, later 58 guns. Designed and built by Laurent Hélie.
Dimensions & tons: 135ft 0in x 35ft 0in x 16ft 2in (43.95 x 11.37 x 5.25m). 800/1,098 tons. Draught 17½ft/18ft (5.68/5.85m). Men: 350/330, +5 officers.

Guns: 56 in war (50 peace): LD 24 x 18pdrs; UD 26 x 12pdrs (replaced by 8pdrs in 1741); QD/Fc 6 x 6pdrs (8 from 1741).

Brillant Brest Dyd.
K: 2.1724. L: 10.1724. C: 1725. Took part in CV Jean André, Marquis de Barailh's squadron in expedition to Danzig 5-8.1734. Hulked 1745 at Brest, and BU 1748.

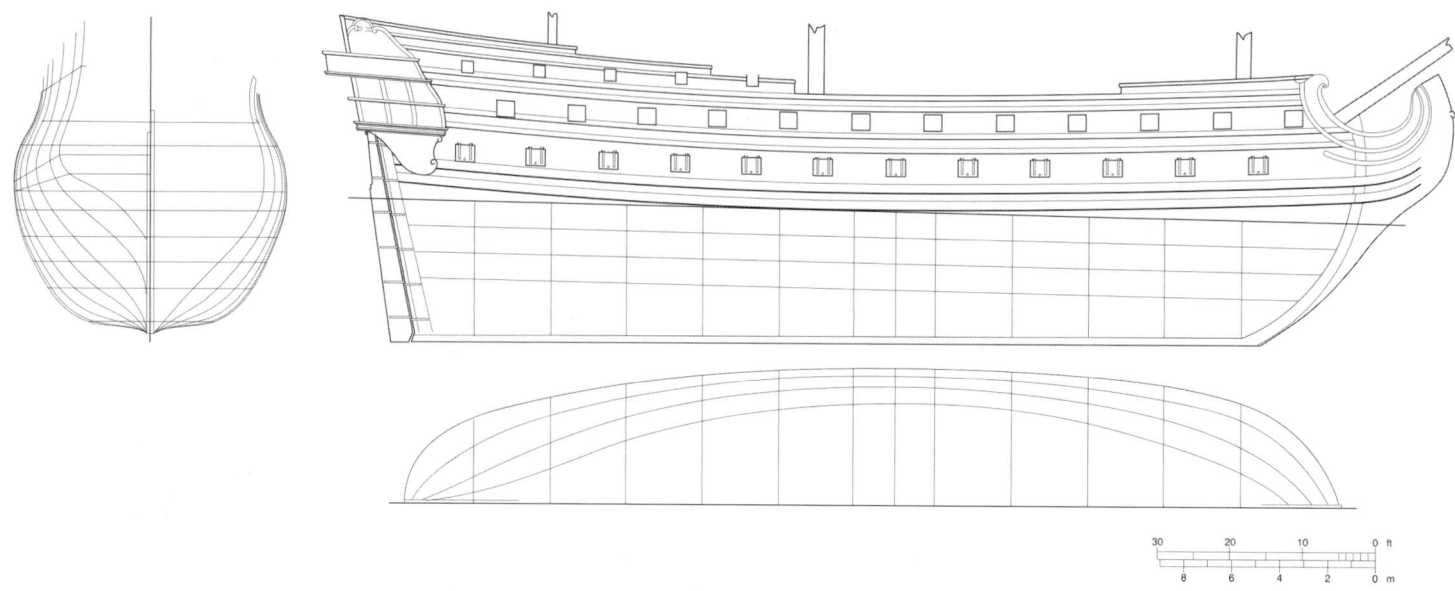

A drawing by László Veres based on a Danish original in the Orlogsvaerftet, Copenhagen of a French 58-gun ship built at Toulon in 1727. In dimensions and armament, the ship is a close fit for *Heureux*, which must have had an extra pair of gunports added on the upper deck when purchased for the Navy in 1730.

HEUREUX. 60 guns. Designed by Pierre Sterein, and built as mercantile *Comte de Morville*; purchased for the French Navy in October 1730 and renamed 27 November.

Dimensions & tons: 137ft 6in x 38ft 6in x 19ft 0in (44.67 x 12.51 x 6.17m). 1,000/1,800 tons. Draught 19ft 2in (6.23m). Men: 380 (later 420) in war, 300 peace, +5 officers.

Guns: 60 in war (54 peace): LD 24 x 18pdrs; UD 26 x 12pdrs; QD/Fc 10 x 6pdrs. As *flûte*, had 20 x 8pdrs only.

Heureux Toulon–La Ponché Rimade.
K: 1726. L: 1730. C: 5.1731. Converted to a *flûte* at Rochefort 12.1750–4.1751. Hulked 1755; allegedly sold 2.12.1760, but apparently not sold; condemned 1768 at Rochefort.

DIAMANT. 50 guns. Designed and built by François Coulomb Jnr. Named on 27 March 1730. Reduced to the 4th Rank between 1743 and 1746. This vessel never carried guns on her QD or forecastle.

Dimensions & tons: 136ft 6in, 113ft 6in x 37ft 0in x 17ft 6in (44.34, 36.87 x 12.02 x 5.68m). 830 tons. Draught 18ft/18ft 4in (5.85/5.96m). Men: 330 in war, 250 peace, +5/9 officers.

Guns: 50 in war (40 peace): LD 24 x 18pdrs; UD 26 x 8pdrs; QD/Fc nil.

Diamant Toulon Dyd.
K: 1.1730. L: 4.9.1733. C: 5.1734. Took part in Battle off Cape Sicié 22.2.1744. Captured off Cape Ortegal 14.5.1747, becoming HMS *Isis*; sold at Chatham 7.1767.

APOLLON. 56 guns. Designed and built by Pierre Morineau. Rebuilt 1750–51 at Brest; reduced to 4th Rank by 1752.

Dimensions & tons: 132ft 6in, 118ft 0in x 36ft 4in x 17ft 11in (43.04, 38.33 x 11.80 x 5.82m). 800/1,528 tons. Draught 16ft/18ft (5.20/5.85m). Men: 340 in war, 240 peace, +5/7 officers; as *flûte*, 167, +8 officers.

Guns: 56 in war (50 peace): LD 22 x 18pdrs; UD 24 x 8pdrs; QD/Fc 10 x 4pdrs.

Apollon Rochefort Dyd.
K: 8.1738. L: 1740. C: 1741. Captured HMS *Anglesea* 29.3.1745. Converted to a *flûte* 1758. Burnt and scuttled at Louisbourg to block the channel 28.6.1758.

CARIBOU. 52 guns. Designed and built (with poor quality timber) by René-Nicolas Levasseur.

Dimensions & tons: 129ft 0in, 115ft 0in x 35ft 0in x 16ft 6in (41.90, 37.36 x 11.37 x 5.36m). 850/1,200 tons. Draught 15ft 10in/17ft 4in (5.14/5.63m). Men: 300 in war, 200 peace, +5 officers.

Guns: 52 in war (46 peace): LD 22 x 18pdrs; UD 24 x 8pdrs; QD 6 x 4pdrs.

Caribou Quebec.
K: 6.1742. L: 13.5.1744. C: 7.1744. Raséed at Brest in early 1748. Hulked 1749 and condemned 1757 at Brest.

ORIFLAMME. 56, later 50 guns. Designed and built by Pierre-Blaise Coulomb. Ordered on 16 February 1743 and named on 10 March. By 1752 reduced to 4th Rank. Rebuilt at Toulon from August 1756 to July 1757.

Dimensions & tons: 135ft 0in, 118ft 5in x 37ft 0in x 17ft 9in (43.85, 38.47 x 12.02 x 5.77m). 1,000/1,600 tons. Draught 18½ft (6.01m). Men: 380 in war, 300 peace, +5/10 officers.

Guns: 56 in war (50 peace): LD 24 x 18pdrs; UD 26 x 8pdrs; QD 6 x 4pdrs (removed 1757); Fc nil.

Oriflamme Toulon Dyd.
K: 4.1743. L: 30.10.1744. C: 12.1744. Driven ashore in action with HM Ships *Monarch* and *Montagu* off Cartagena on 28.2.1758 (Osborn's Action), but refloated and salved. Converted to a *flûte* in Spring 1761, with 40 guns. Captured by HMS *Isis* off Cape Trafalgar 1.4.1761, but not added to the British Navy.

ARC EN CIEL. 56, later 50 guns. Designed and built by Pierre Morineau. By 1752 reduced to 4th Rank.

Dimensions & tons: 135ft 0in x 37ft 0in x 18ft 9in (43.85 x 12.02 x 6.09m). 800/1,500 tons. Draught 17ft/19ft 4in (5.52/6.28m). Men: 380 in war, 300 peace, +5 officers.

Guns: 56 in war (50 peace): LD 24 x 18pdrs; UD 26 x 8pdrs; QD 6 x 4pdrs (removed by 1756).

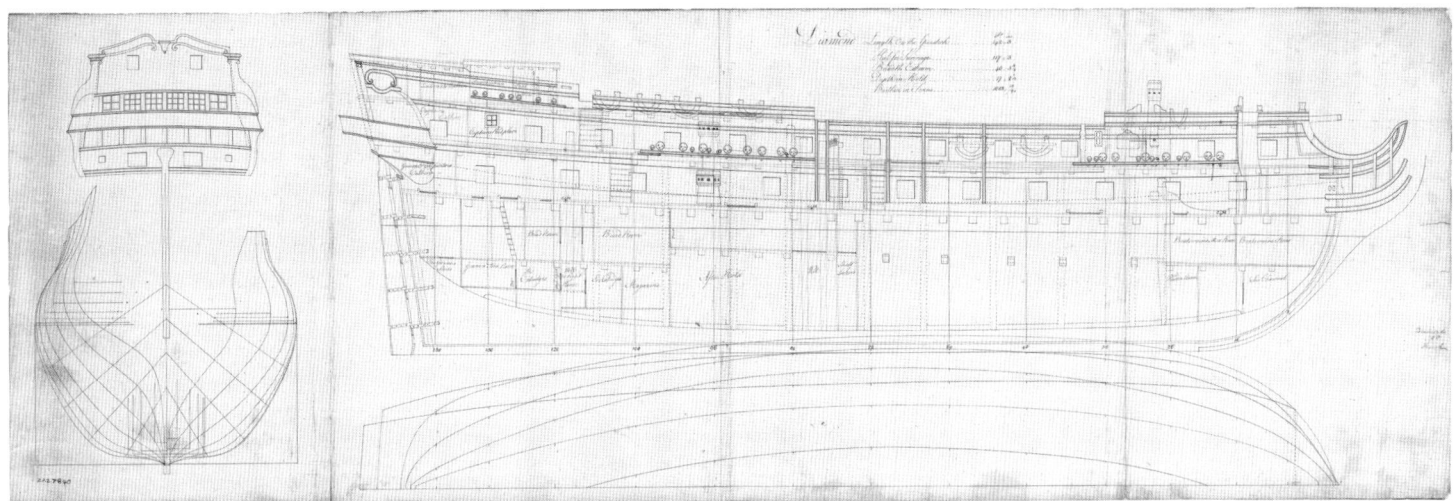

Admiralty draught of the 50-gun *Diamant*. It is undated, but labelled '*Diamond*' (she was renamed *Isis* in British service), and all the internal arrangements are French, so the plan must represent the ship as captured in 1747. (National Maritime Museum, London J3549)

Arc en Ciel Bayonne.
 K: 1744. L: 1745. C: 4.1746. Converted to a *flûte* in late 1755, with *c*.20 guns. Captured by HM Ships *Lichfield* and *Norwich* off Louisbourg on 12.6.1756; sold 6.9.1759 at Chatham.

The *Oriflamme* and *Arc en Ciel* were the last 56-gun ships built by the French (apart from the much bigger 36pdr-armed *Bordelais* Class of 1761). With their 18pdr main batteries they no longer had the firepower to stand in the line of battle, and – with *Apollon* – they were reduced to 50-gun 4th Rank ships, and considered as heavy frigates. However, being designed for the battlefleet, they lacked the endurance for cruising overseas, particularly in the Caribbean. The 50-gun and 60-gun ships with 18pdrs on the LD were similarly considered no longer adequate for the line of battle; only two more 50s (both begun in 1748) were completed; and of the 60s, the relatively new *Fier* was reduced to 50 guns in 1750, the very elderly *Toulouse* (of 1714) was hulked at Toulon and the 20-year-old *Heureux* was converted into a *flûte*.

FIER. 60, later 50 guns. Designed and built by Joseph Véronique-Charles Chapelle. Named on 5 May 1745. The last 60-gun ship ordered by the French. In 1756 reduced to 50 guns, and re-classed as 4th Rank. Rebuilt at Rochefort (to 2/3rds) from April 1768 to April 1769. Briefly moved back to the 3rd Rank in 1771 when an attempt was made to abolish the 4th Rank.
 Dimensions & tons: 143ft 3in, 120ft 9in x 38ft 6in x 17ft 8in (46.53, 39.22 x 12.51 x 5.74m). 880/1,750 tons. Draught 17ft 2in/19ft (5.58/6.17m). Men: 500 in war, 430 peace, +9 officers.
 Guns: 60 in war (54 peace): LD 24 x 18pdrs; UD 26 x 12pdrs; QD/Fc 10 x 6pdrs (removed 1756).
Fier Toulon Dyd.
 K: 4.1745. L: 1.12.1745. C: 5.1746. Took part in Battle of Minorca 20.5.1756 and in 3rd Battle of Ushant 27.7.1778. Converted to a *flûte* 10.1780. Struck and sold for commerce 5.1782.

AIGLE. 50 guns. Designed and built by Pierre Morineau. This vessel had a forecastle, quarterdeck and poop, but was not designed to have guns on her *gaillards* and never carried guns there. By 1752 reduced to 4th Rank.
 Dimensions & tons: 140ft 0in x 37ft 6in x 18ft 7in (45.48 x 12.18 x 6.04m). 900/1,611 tons. Draught 17ft/19¼ft (5.52/6.25m). Men: 400, +5/7 officers.
 Guns: LD 24 x 18pdrs; UD 26 x 12pdrs; QD/Fc nil.
Aigle Rochefort Dyd.
 K: 1.1748. L: 1750. C: 4.1751. Armed four times between 1752 and 1757, but converted to a *flûte* 8.1758. Wrecked in the Strait of Belle Isle in 1765 near Mécatina, Canada, then burnt.

HIPPOPOTAME. 50 guns. Designed and built by François Coulomb Jnr. Ordered on 18 December 1747 and named on 1.3.1748. By 1752 reduced to 4th Rank. Rebuilt at Toulon from August 1755 to March 1756, at Rochefort from 1765 to September 1766, and again there from May to November 1777. Briefly moved back to the 3rd Rank in 1771 when an attempt was made to abolish the 4th Rank.
 Dimensions & tons: 141ft 9in, 120ft? x 38ft 6in x 17ft 11in (46.05, *c*.39.00 x 12.51 x 5.82m). 900/1,611 tons. Draught 16ft 1in/19ft 5in (5.52/6.31m). Men: 400 (later 450) in war, 350 peace, +5/10 officers.
 Guns: LD 24 x 18pdrs; UD 26 x 12pdrs; QD/Fc nil.
Hippopotame Toulon Dyd.
 K: 2.1748. L: 5.7.1749. C: 4.1750. Took part in the Battle off Minorca 20.5.1756. Sold to the playwright Pierre-Augustin Caron de Beaumarchais 4.1777 and renamed *Fier Rodrigue*; employed in running arms to the American rebels. Requisitioned 5.1779 in the Caribbean to reinforce *Vice-amiral* Charles-Henri-Théodat, Comte d'Estaing's fleet. Became hospital ship at Charleston 8.1779. Condemned 3.1782 and BU at Rochefort 1784.

ARTÉSIENNE Class. Two new 50-gun ships – to be named *Artésienne* and *Ferme* – were ordered in December 1761 and March 1762 to be built at Dunkirk to a design by Jean-Joseph Ginoux. They were to be funded by donations from the *États d'Artois* and the *Fermiers Généraux* respectively. The first was begun at Dunkirk in March 1762, but in June the order was cancelled and instead a 64-gun ship (*Artésien*) was to be built at Brest; the second ship, *Ferme*, was not begun, and instead the order was transferred to Bordeaux, becoming a 56-gun ship of the same name.

The 50-gun ship was not abandoned totally, although no further vessels were built. In December 1768 (20 years after the *Hippopotame* was built) Jacques-Noël Sané, then a sub-constructor at Brest, produced a fresh design for a 50-gun ship of 1,700 tons (disp.) but carrying an identical armament to the *Hippopotame*. It would have measured 148ft 6in x 38ft 0in x 18ft 4in (48.24 x 12.34 x 5.96m), with a freeboard (height of LD sills above waterline) of 4ft 9in (1.54m). In February 1769 Joseph-Marie-Blaise Coulomb, as Chief Constructor at Toulon, produced a similar design with identical dimensions and armament. However, neither design was adopted and no ship ordered or named.

PONDICHÉRY. 56 guns. Designed by Gilles Cambry and built by Cambry and François Caro for the *Compagnie des Indes*. Purchased for the Navy on 4 October 1769, on the liquidation of that Company.

Dimensions & tons: 149ft 5in, 129ft 9in x 38ft 2in x 14ft 6in (48.54, 42.15 x 12.40 x 4.71m). 900/1,500 tons. Draught 17ft (5.52m). Men: 430.

Guns: to have carried LD 28? x 18pdrs and UD 28 x 8pdrs, but appears she was never armed on LD.

Pondichéry Lorient, Cie des Indes Dyd.
K: 8.1768. L: 17.6.1769. C: 12.1769. Sold for commerce 8.1771 and renamed *Gualbert*. Repurchased by the Navy 12.1778; hulked 7.1782 at Lorient, but not mentioned after 1791.

DUC DE PENTHIÈVRE **Class.** 56 guns. Designed by Antoine Groignard and built by Gilles Cambry for the *Compagnie des Indes*. Purchased for the Navy in November and October 1769 respectively, on the liquidation of that Company.

Dimensions & tons: 145ft 0in, 126ft 0in x 36ft 8in x 15ft 0in (47.10, 40.93 x 11.91 x 4.87m). 900/1,500 tons. 16¾ft/17½ft (5.44/5.68m). Men: unknown.

Guns: Probably intended to have been as *Pondichéry* but never armed by the French Navy.

Duc de Penthièvre Lorient, Cie des Indes Dyd.
K: 7.1763. L: 20.12.1763. C: 2.1764. Sold for commerce 8.1771.

Duc de Duras Lorient, Cie des Indes Dyd.
K: 4.1765. L: 28.11.1765. C: 1.1766. Sold for commerce 9.1771. Repurchased by the Navy at Nantes 12.1778 and given to the American John Paul Jones 2.1779 as a privateer, and renamed *Bonhomme Richard*. Refitted at Lorient 1–5.1779, and armed with 42 guns (6 x 18pdrs, 28 x 12pdrs and 8 x 9pdrs) and 380 men 31.8.1779. Sunk in action with HMS *Serapis* 29.9.1779 (with 116 killed).

Ex-BRITISH PRIZE (1779). 50 guns. The British Fourth Rate two-decker HMS *Experiment* was built to a John William design, approved on 9 November 1772. Initially intended to mount 24pdrs on her LD, but instead completed with 12pdrs on both decks. She was captured by *Sagittaire* off the American coast on 24 September 1779 and added to the French Navy. Classed as an 18pdr *frégate* in January 1787 (although apparently always retained 12pdrs on both decks), then re-classed as a 12pdr *frégate* in June 1794, and as a horse transport in December 1797.

Dimensions & tons (French re-measurement): 136ft 0in, 121ft 0in x 36ft 0in x 17ft 0in (44.18, 39.31 x 11.69 x 5.52m). 700/1,400 tons. Draught 16ft/17ft (5.20/5.52m). Men: 450.

Guns: LD 20 x 12pdrs; UD 22 x 12pdrs; QD 6 x 6pdrs; Fc 2 x 6pdrs. Only 4 x 6pdrs in 1794, and as horse-transport only had 4 x 12pdrs + 8 x 6pdrs.

Expériment Henry Adams & John Barnard, Deptford.
Ordered 9.11.1772. K: 12.1772. L: 23.8.1774. C: 26.8.1775 at Deptford Dyd. Struck 7.1800, and hulked 23.8.1802 at Rochefort.

Ex-BRITISH PRIZES (1779–1783). 44 guns. Three British 44-gun ships of the twenty-ship *Roebuck* Class, specially designed by Thomas Slade for service in the shallow coastal waters off North America, were captured by the French during the 1779–1783 period. The *Serapis* was captured on 23 September 1779 off Flamborough Head by the American 42-gun privateer *Bonhomme Richard* (see *Duc de Duras* above for her origins); John Paul Jones handed her over to the French Navy in December 1779. The *Romulus* was captured on 19 February 1781 off the Chesapeake by the *Éveillé* and two frigates (*Gentille* and *Surveillante*), and the *Argo* was captured on 17 February 1783 off Tortola by *Nymphe* and *Amphitrite*, although retaken two days later by HMS *Invincible*.

Dimensions & tons: 135ft 0in x 35ft 6in (43.85 x 11.53m). 700/1,350 tons. Draught 16ft (5.20m). Men: 400.

Guns: LD 20 x 18pdrs; UD 22 x 9pdrs; QD nil; Fc 2 x 6pdrs. In French service, *Serapis* was re-armed with 24 x 24pdrs, 22 x 18pdrs and 6 x 6pdrs.

Serapis Randall & Co, Rotherhithe.
Ordered 11.2.1778. K: 3.3.1778. L: 4.3.1779. C: 6.5.1779 at Deptford Dyd. Burnt by accident off Ste Marie, Madagascar 7.1781.

Romulus Henry Adams, Bucklers Hard.
Ordered 14.5.1776. K: 7.1776. L: 17.12.1777. C: 7.4.1778 at Portsmouth Dyd. Renamed *Résolution* 6.11.1784, then *Reine* 1.1787 but reverted to *Résolution* 3.1787; Put out of service with cyclone damage 12.1788 and hulked at Mauritius 6.1789.

Argo John Baker & Co, Howden Pans, Newcastle.
Ordered 26.2.1779. K: 18.8.1779. L: 8.6.1781. C: 15.10.1781 at Chatham Dyd. Recaptured 19.2.1783 by HMS *Invincible*. Sold 11.1.1816 at Sheerness.

4 The Fourth Rank

(Vaisseaux de quatrième rang) with 40 to 54 guns after 1715, sometimes described as Frigates of the 1st Order (*Frégates du 1er ordre*), and 12pdr-armed and larger frigates after 1747

The 4th Rank of ships included those vessels which were normally not for inclusion in the battlefleet, but whose primary purposes were escort and patrol (the British equivalent term was 'convoys and cruising'). Like the larger *vaisseaux*, those built or acquired before 1689 were armed with a mixed battery on the lower deck, but in general this mixture comprised 12pdr and 8pdr guns compared with the 24pdrs, 18pdrs and 12pdrs on the higher Ranks – a level of force which mitigated against them standing in the line of battle, although on occasion individual 4th Rank ships found themselves in that situation. A *Règlement* of 4 July 1670 defined the 4th Rank as ships with between 30 and 40 guns, but in practice it included – as at 1 January 1672 – ships of 550 to 750 tons which carried between 36 and 44 guns. By the early 1680s the upper limit had extended to 48 guns, and in 1689 it was 50 guns. The *Règlement* of 5 October 1674 allowed the leasing of naval vessels for privateering but limited it to ships of the 5th Rank and smaller types. The *Règlement* of 5 December 1691 extended it to ships armed with up to 44 guns, which meant including much of the 4th Rank.

In 1680 or early 1681 an 'establishment level' of twenty-six 4th Rank ships was set – this being the actual number of 4th Rank ships on the List in January 1681. This level was retained until 1688, when it was raised to thirty-three vessels, but this dropped back to thirty vessels in 1689 and returned to twenty-six vessels in 1690, at which level it stayed until after 1715. The actual number in the 4th Rank varied over that quarter-century, but rarely rose above twenty vessels.

For almost a century, up until the 1730s, the larger 4th Rank ships, often called '*frégates-vaisseaux*', were two-decked vessels, almost always with a lower deck battery of 12pdrs, and an upper deck battery of 8pdrs, and often with smaller guns (4pdrs) on the *gaillards*. After 1748, a new type of single-deck frigate, armed with an upper deck battery of 12pdrs, was introduced and soon after became the most usual type of cruiser; these are detailed in Section (E) of this chapter.

In 1769–70, when the mercantile *Compagnie des Indes* was declared bankrupt, many of its ships were purchased by the Navy, and ten 56-gun two-deckers with 12pdrs on the lower deck were briefly added; these saw no actual naval service and were quickly disposed of, but are covered in Section (F) below. Finally, larger single-deck frigates mounting an upper deck battery of 18pdrs rather than 12pdrs were introduced from 1778 onwards, and these are to be found in Section (G).

To compensate for the nearly total lack of contemporary data on individual ship armaments prior to 1696, we have provided, where actual guns are not recorded, estimated armaments in Sections (A) and (B) based on the governing directives and the known characteristics of the individual ships. This issue is discussed in greater detail in the Introduction.

(A) Vessels in service as at 9 March 1661

For vessels removed from the Navy prior to 1671 (when the parameters of the '4th Rank' were set), the qualification for inclusion hereunder is whether they would have fallen within the contemporary 36- to 44-gun limits if they had survived to 1671. In fact, only the 36-gun *Françoise* and *Infante* of those originating from before 1661 and classed as 4th Rank in 1669 remained so under the revised criteria of 1670.

CARDINAL. 30 guns, later 42. The survivor (along with *Triomphe* and *Faucon* in the next Chapter) of six ships ordered from Dutch builders on 13 January 1637.
  Dimensions & tons: 100ft 0in keel x 32ft 0in (32.48 keel x 10.39m). 600 tons. Draught 13ft (4.22m). Men: 245, +6 officers.
  Guns: Originally (and in 1646) 30 guns – 18 bronze and 12 iron. By 1661 had 42 guns.
Cardinal Amsterdam.
  K: 4.1637. L: 2.1638. C: 6.1638. Took part in Battles of Guétaria 22.8.1638, Orbitello 14.6.1646 and Castellammare 21-22.12.1647. Ineffective by 5.1661, when condemned at Toulon, and BU 1662.

LUNE Class. 36 to 40 guns. In 1638 a decision was taken by Richelieu to create a specialised shipyard for warship-building in France, and a site on the Île d'Indret on the Loire near Nantes was swiftly developed, the *Lune* and *Soleil* being the first major vessels built there – although few warships were to be built at Indret thereafter. During the 1670s and 1680s, this island was the site where young Protestants were educated to become naval officers should they later convert to Catholicism. Following the *Édit* of Fontainebleau, 18 October 1685, revoking the *Édit* of Nantes, the *Académie d'Indret* closed on 5 January 1686.

The *Lune* and *Soleil* were designed by Deviot, and constructed by Jean de Werth (real name Jan Gron). Pierced for eleven pairs of LD guns. In the early 1640s, 40 guns was a respectable ordnance, and both vessels served as squadron flagships early in their career, but by the 1660s these vessels were no longer fit for front-line service. Details below apply to *Soleil*; *Lune* was believed to be identical. Both ships were part of the *Levant* Fleet; *Lune* was reconstructed 1660–61 at Toulon, and *Soleil* from March to June 1665, also at Toulon. *Soleil* was initially classed as 3rd Rank in 1669, but was classed as 4th Rank from 4 August 1670.
  Dimensions & tons: 117ft 0in x 29ft 6in x 12ft 0in (38.01 x 9.58 x 3.90m). 700 tons. Draught 13ft (4.22m). Men: 275 (50/150/75), +5 officers.
  Guns: originally 36 to 46, of which 36 bronze: LD 4 x 18pdrs + 18 x 12pdrs; UD 10 x 8pdrs + 6 x 7pdrs or 5pdrs. *Soleil* 38 guns by 1669, 36 from 1671: LD 22 x 12pdrs; UD 14 x 8pdrs.
Lune Indret.
  K: 1640. L: 1641. C: 1642. Took part in Battles of Orbitello 14.6.1646 (as flag of Vice-Adm Louis Foucault de Saint-Germain-Beaupré, Comte du Daugnon) and Castellammare 21-22.12.1647. Took part in Battle of Perthuis d'Antioche 8.8.1652, in support of *Fronde* rebels against Louis XIV. Sailed 9.11.1664 from Toulon for the Hyères Islands while carrying troops of the 1st Regiment of Picardy, but a half-hour after sailing she suddenly broke apart at the head and sank 'like a marble' (only 60 survivors out of over 600 aboard). Wreck discovered by accident on 15 May 1993.
Soleil Indret.
  K: 1640. L: 1642. C: 7.1643. Took part in Battles of Orbitello 14.6.1646 (as flag of CdE Marquis de Montigny) and

Castellammare 21-22.12.1647. Took part in the Battle of Barcelona 1655. Renamed *Hercule* 24.6.1671, then *Marquis* 17.7.1671. Condemned 28.6.1672 at Brest and sold to break up 8.1672.

MAZARIN. 48 guns, then 42 from 1671. Designed and built by Laurent Hubac. Pierced for eleven pairs of LD guns. Initially rated at 48 guns, but actually armed in April 1666 with 40 guns under Duquesne. Classed as a 3rd Rank under the 1669 proposals, but moved to 4th Rank in 1670 accompanying her reconstruction at Rochefort from July 1670 to February 1671, when she was altered to 42 guns.

Dimensions & tons: dimensions unknown. 750 tons. Men: originally 340 (50/195/95); 250 in 1669, +5 officers.

Guns: Originally 48, 40 from 1666. 42 from 1671: LD 22 x 12pdrs; UD 20 x 8pdrs.

Mazarin Brest Dyd.
K: 1646. L: early 1647. C: 1647. Took part in Battle of Castellammare 21-22.12.1647 (as flagship of CdE de Montade). Renamed *Bon* on 24.6.1671. Wrecked 12.1671 on Île de la Tortue.

ÉMINENT. 36 to 46 guns. Four warships were purchased by CdE Abraham Duquesne from Sweden on 1 March 1647 including the Swedish *Smaalands Lejon*, which had been built in 1634–35 on the same slipway from which the *Vasa* had been launched. She was initially called *Lion de Smaaland*, but was renamed *Éminent* in August 1647. Of the other three ships, the *Régine* (ex-Swedish *Regina*) is found below; the largest (*Jupiter*) was condemned in June 1658 and BU at Brouage, while the *Chasseur* (ex-Swedish *Jagaren*) was condemned in 1660 and BU at Toulon.

Dimensions & tons: 122ft 0in x 30ft 0in x 12ft 0in (39.63 x 9.745 x 3.90m). 690 tons. Men: 250.

Guns: 36/40/46.

Éminent Stockholm (Blasieholmen).
L: 1634. C: 1635. Took part in Battle of Castellammare 21–22.12.1647. Condemned 5.1661 at Toulon and BU.

RÉGINE. 32, later 38 guns. Another of the four warships were purchased by Abraham Duquesne from Sweden on 1 March 1647 was the Swedish *Regina* which the French renamed *Régine*.

Dimensions & tons: 117ft 6in x 29ft 6in x 11ft 3in (38.17 x 9.58 x 3.65m). 560/950 tons. Men: 200–230.

Guns: 32 to 38 guns.

Régine Sweden.
K: 1643. L: 1644. C: 9.1644. Took part in Battle of Castellammare 21-22.12.1647. Employed *en flûte* in 1648. Captured (along with similar *Chasseur*) by Michiel de Ruyter's Dutch squadron in the Mediterranean 28.2.1657, and renamed *Koningen* in Dutch service, but returned to the French at Toulon on 20.6.1657. Condemned 1667 at Toulon and struck.

ANNA. 46, later 40 guns. Built in 1649–50 as the Swedish *Sankt Anna*, this vessel was given as a gift by Sweden's Queen Christina to the French Regent (Anne d'Autriche) in 1650. Originally classed as 3rd Rank in 1669, but then as 4th Rank from 1670.

Dimensions & tons: 115ft 2in x 26ft 0in x 11ft 0in (37.41 x 8.45 x 3.57m). 650 tons. Draught 12ft (3.90m). Men: originally 340; 275 (50/150/75) in 1669, +5 officers.

Guns: originally 42–46, then 40 from 1666.

Anna Skeppsholmen, Stockholm.
L: 1649. C: 1650. Re-armed as a 10-gun *flûte* 1665. Hulked at Rochefort 8.1670. Not mentioned after 1675 until sold 1678 to BU.

FRANÇOISE. 32 to 36 guns. Designed and built by Tanguy. Pierced for ten pairs of LD guns. Classed as 4th Rank in 1669, and remained so in 1670. Reconstructed at Brest in 1671, when the poop and the *gaillards* were removed.

Dimensions & tons: 100ft 0in x 26ft 0in x 11ft 0in (32.48 x 8.45 x 3.57m). 550 tons. Draught 14ft (4.55m). Men: 230, + 5 officers.

Guns: originally 32 to 36. 32 in 1665: 12 x 12pdrs + 2 x 10pdrs + 14 x 8pdrs + 4 x 6pdrs. 36 from 1669: LD 10 x 12pdrs + 10 x 8pdrs; UD 16 x 6pdrs.

Françoise Tanguy, St Malo.
K: 1655. L: late 1656. C: 1657. Commanded by Chevalier de Châteauneuf 1665–67. Renamed *Éole* 24.6.1671. Took part in Battle of Solebay 7.6.1672. Condemned 2.1673 at Le Havre; scuttled there 12.1673 and BU 1674.

HERCULE. 36 to 40 guns. Designed by Georges Carteret and Laurent Hubac. Pierced for eleven pairs of LD guns. Reconstructed from March to June 1665 at Toulon. Initially classed as 3rd Rank in 1669, then re-classed as 4th Rank in 1670.

A contemporary engraving of the *Smålands Lejon* in Swedish service. This ship was sold to the French in 1647 and eventually renamed *Éminent*.

THE FOURTH RANK

Dimensions & tons: 120ft 0in, 92ft 0in x 30ft 0in x 12ft 0in (38.98, 29.89 x 9.75 x 3.90m). 750 tons. Draught 15ft (4.87m). Men: 300/250, + 5 officers.

Guns: originally 40 to 46. 36 in 1665: 14 x 12pdrs + 8 x 8pdrs + 8 x 6pdrs + 6 others. 40 by 1669: LD 20 x 12pdrs; UD 20 x 8pdrs. 38 from 1671.

Hercule Brest Dyd

K: 1655. L: 1655. C: 2.1660. Took part in attack on Djidjelli (Algeria) 7.1664, and in Battle of Cherchell 24.8.1665. Renamed *Marquis* 24.6.1671 but restored to *Hercule* 23 days later. Condemned 28.6.1672 at Brest and BU 1673.

INFANTE. 34 to 36 guns. Designed and built by Laurent Hubac. Pierced for eleven pairs of LD guns. Rebuilt in 1669 at Rochefort, and rated as 4th Rank in 1669 and remained so in 1670.

Dimensions & tons: 120ft 0in, 96ft 0in x 30ft 0in x 13ft 6in (38.98, 31.18 x 9.75 x 4.39m). 600 tons. Men: 230 in 1669 (35/130/65), then 220 in 1671 (34/120/66), +5 officers.

Guns: originally 36. 34 in 1669, then 36 from 1671: LD 22 x 12pdrs; UD 14 x 8pdrs.

Infante Brest Dyd.

K: 4.1660. L: 6.1661. C: 10.1661. Renamed *Écueil* 24.6.1671. Converted to a fireship 3.1672 at Rochefort. Wrecked off the north coast of Puerto Rico 25.2.1673.

(B) Vessels acquired from 9 March 1661

JULES. 36, later 38 guns. Designed and built by Rodolphe Gédéon. Pierced for ten pairs of LD guns (excluding the chase ports). Originally classed as 3rd Rank in 1669, but then as 4th Rank from 4 August 1670.

Dimensions & tons: 113ft 0in, ?95ft x 26ft 0in x 12ft 1in (38.71, ?30.86 x 8.45 x 3.93m). 700 tons. Draught 13ft (4.22m). Men: 250 (40/126/84) from 1669, +5 officers.

Guns: originally 38 (LD 18 bronze, UD 20 iron). 24 in 1665: 2 x 18pdrs +2 x 12pdrs + 16 x 8pdrs + 2 x 6pdrs + 2 x 4pdrs. 36 by 1669, then 38 by 1673: LD 10 x 12pdrs + 10 x 8pdrs; UD 18 x 6pdrs.

Jules Toulon Dyd.

K: early 1661. L: 7.1661. C: 11.1661. Renamed *Indien* 24.6.1671, but in practice this never became effective prior to her loss. Wrecked 5.1673 at the entrance of the River Tagus.

BEAUFORT Class. 36 guns. Designed and built by Rodolphe Gédéon. Pierced for eleven pairs of LD guns. Ordered 1660 as *Mancini* and *Mercœur*, but the former was renamed *Beaufort* in 1662 before completion. The two were named after the sons of César de Bourbon-Vendôme (the *Grand-Maître de la Navigation*): François, Duc de Beaufort (who in 1665 was to succeed his father as *Grand-Maître*) and Louis, Duc de Mercœur. In 1669 these were originally classed as 3rd Rank ships, like *Jules*, with 36 guns and 250 (45/135/70) men and 5 officers), but under the *Règlement* of 4 August 1670 they became 4th Rank ships with the data set out below. They were reduced to the 5th Rank in 1676, but restored to 4th Rank in 1677–78.

Dimensions & tons: 116ft 0in, 90ft 0in x 25ft 8in x 12ft 2in (37.68, 29.24 x 8.34 x 3.95m). 600 tons. Men: 220 (34/120/66), + 5 officers; raised to 230 (34/120/76) in 1673; reduced to 200 (45/95/60), +5/6 officers in 1676.

Guns: originally 36. *Mercœur* 32 in 1665: LD 2 x 20pdrs + 6 x 16pdrs x 10 x 12pdrs; UD 14 x 8pdrs. 36 guns by 1669: LD 22 x 12pdrs; UD 14 x 8pdrs. Both had 38 guns from 1676.

Beaufort Toulon Dyd.

K: early 1661. L: 15.5.1662. C: 12.1662. Renamed *Neptune* 24.6.1671, then *Maure* 10.1.1679. Struck 1686.

Mercœur Toulon Dyd.

K: early 1661. L: 6.1661. C: 11.1662. Took part in Battle of La Goulette 2/3.3.1665. Renamed *Trident* 24.6.1671. Took part in Battles of Augusta 22.4.1676 and of Palermo 31.5.1676. Condemned at Toulon 1686.

CHEVAL MARIN. 44, later 46 guns. Designed and built by Laurent Coulomb. Pierced for eleven pairs of LD guns. Originally named *Prince* in June 1664 but renamed in April 1665 while building. First classed as 3rd Rank in 1669, but then as 4th Rank from July 1670. Rebuilt at Toulon from September 1687 to August 1688, at Brest from 1702 to March 1703 (by Alexandre Gobert) and at Toulon again in 1718.

Dimensions & tons: 122ft, 97ft x 32ft 5in x 14ft 3in (39.63, 29.25 x 10.6 x 4.63m). 700 tons. Men: 250 (45/135/70) in 1669, +5-6 officers, 250–260 ratings.

Guns: 44 by 1669, then 46 from 1676: LD 22 x 12pdrs, UD 20 x 8pdrs; QD 4 x 4pdrs. 44 in war from 1696 (40 peace): LD 20 x 12pdrs (18 x 18pdrs from 1706): UD 20 x 8pdrs; QD 4 x 4pdrs.

Cheval Marin 'Toulon' (actually built at La Ciotat)

K: 24.7.1664. L: 6.1666. C: 25.9.1666. Took part in Bombardments of Algiers in 23.7–5.9.1682 and 26.6–18.81683, and of Tripoli 22–26.6.1685, and in Battle of Beachy Head 10.7.1690. Employed in 1696 (for the King's service) under CV Des Augiers as part of a squadron of nine vessels transporting settlers and young women ('for marrying') to the West Indies. Probably scuttled at Toulon in 7.1707, but refloated. Deleted 10.11.1727. Condemned and hulked 12.7.1728 at Toulon, BU by Order of 11.5.1729.

SIRÈNE. 44, later 46 guns. Designed and built by François Pomet. Pierced for eleven pairs of LD guns. Ordered as *Monarque*, but renamed in April 1665 on the stocks. Originally classed as 3rd Rank in 1669, then as 4th Rank from 1670. Reconstructed in early 1681 at Toulon.

Dimensions & tons: 122ft 0in, 98ft 0in x 29ft 6in x 14ft 0in (39.63, 29.25 x 8.45 x 3.93 m). 750 tons. Draught 15ft (4.87m). Men: 250 (45/135/70) in 1669, +5/6 officers.

Guns: 44 by 1669. 46 from 1676: LD 22 x 12pdrs; UD 20 x 8pdrs; QD 4 x 4pdrs.

Sirène Toulon Dyd.

K: 8.1664. L: 6.1666. C: 25.9.1666. Wrecked 16.1.1684 off Formentera.

DUC. 42, later 44 guns. Designed and built by Laurent Hubac. Pierced for eleven pairs of LD guns. Classed as 3rd Rank in 1669 and as 4th Rank from 1670.

Dimensions & tons: 120ft 0in, 98ft 0in x 30ft 0in x 14ft 0in (38.98, 31.83 x 9.745 x 4.55m). 700 tons. Men: 250 (40/126/84) +5 officers, later 250 (48/134/68), +6 officers.

Guns: originally LD 10 x 12pdrs + 12 x 8pdrs; UD 20 x 6pdrs (later 4 x 4pdrs added on the *gaillards*). 42 by 1669: LD 22 x 12pdrs; UD 20 x 8pdrs. 44 from 1675.

Duc Brest Dyd.

K: 9.1664. L: 1666. C: 11.1666. Renamed *Comte* 24.6.1671. Took part in Battles of Schoonevelt 7 & 14.6.1673. Wrecked 25.12.1677 in the Mediterranean (60 men lost).

TIGRE. 36, later 44 guns. Designed and built by Jean Guichard. Pierced for ten pairs of LD guns. Classed as 3rd Rank in 1669, then 4th

Rank from 1670. Reduced to the 5th Rank in 1687.
   Dimensions & tons: 120ft 0in, 98ft 0in x 30ft 8in x 14ft 0in (38.98, 31.83 x 9.96 x 4.55m). 550 tons. Draught 15ft (4.87m). Men: 220/200, +5/6 officers.
   Guns: 36 by 1669. 40 from 1675: LD 20 x 12pdrs; UD 20 x 8pdrs. Possibly later had QD 4 x 4pdrs added.

Tigre Soubise.
   K: 1.1665. L: 11.1666. C: 2.1667. Condemned and hulked at Brest 12.6.1689; BU 9.1697.

DUNKERQUOIS. 40, later 44 guns. Designed and built by Debast. Classed as 3rd Rank in 1669, then 4th Rank from 1670.
   Dimensions & tons: dimensions unknown. 750 tons. Draught 14ft (4.55m). Men: 250 (40/126/84), + 5 officers.
   Guns: 40 by 1669, then 44 from 1671

Dunkerquois Dunkirk.
   K: 3.1665. L: early 1667. C: 12.1667. Renamed *Brusque* 24.6.1671. Took part in Battles of Augusta 22.4.1676 and Palermo 31.5.1676. Condemned 13.2.1688 at Toulon, and hulked (not mentioned after 1693).

FLAMAND. 40 guns. Designed and built by Hendryck Houwens. Classed as 3rd Rank in 1669, then 4th Rank from 1670.
   Dimensions & tons: dimensions unknown. 650 tons. Draught 14ft. Men: 230 (34/120/76), + 5 officers.
   Guns: 40 by 1669.

Flamand Dunkirk.
   K: 3.1665. L: 1667. C: 4.1668. Renamed *Arc en Ciel* 24.6.1671, but in practice this was never effective prior to her loss. Captured by the Dutch 11.1673 at Balassor.

TOULON. 42, later 48 guns. Designed and built by Charles Audibert. Classed as 3rd Rank in 1669, then 4th Rank from 1670. Raised to the 3rd rank in 1677–78, restored to the 4th rank in 1687, raised again to the 3rd rank in 1691.
   Dimensions & tons: dimensions unknown. 750 tons. Draught 15ft/16ft. Men: 250 (40/126/84), + 5 officers.
   Guns: 42 by 1669, 44 from 1671, 48 from 1677 and 50 from 1691.

Toulon Toulon Dyd.
   K: 9.1665. L: 2.1667. C: 5.1667. Renamed *Joli* 24.6.1671, then *Fidèle* 28.6.1678. Took part in Battle of Beachy Head 10.7.1690. Out of service at Toulon 1695 (hulked), and condemned 1696.

PROVENÇAL. 40, later 48 guns. Designed by Rodolphe Gédéon and built by Barthélemy Tortel. Pierced for ten guns per side on the LD. Classed as 3rd Rank in 1669, then 4th Rank from 1670. Raised to the 3rd rank in 1677–78, but reverted to the 4th rank in 1687.
   Dimensions & tons: 116ft 0in x 33ft 0in x 15ft 0in (37.68 x 10.72 x 4.87m). 750 tons. Draught 15ft. Men: 250 (40/126/84), + 5 officers.
   Guns: 40 in 1669, then 44 from 1671: LD 10 x 12pdrs + 10 x 8pdrs; UD 20 x 6pdrs; QD 4 x 4pdrs. 48 from 1677.

The Battle of Augusta (22 April 1676) in a French engraving by Le Clerc published about 1705. This birds-eye view shows the French attacking the combined Dutch-Spanish fleet off the Sicilian port. In the foreground one of the ships will be the *Brusque* (originally called *Dunkerquois*) of 40 guns. This was the battle in which the great Michiel de Ruyter was mortally wounded. (Beverley R Robinson Collection, Annapolis 51.7.62)

Provençal Toulon Dyd.
K: 9.1665. L: 3.1667. C: 7.1667. In expedition to Candia 1669. Renamed *Mignon* 24.6.1671. Took part in Battles of Stromboli 8.1.1676, Augusta 22.4.1676 and Palermo 31.5.1676. Renamed *Capable* 28.6.1678. Took part in Battle of Bantry Bay 11.5.1689. Struck at end 1690 at Le Havre, and BU in 1691.

LE HAVRE. 36, later 44 guns. Designed and built by Jean Esnault for the *Compagnie des Indes Orientales*, and purchased on the stocks in February 1668 for the Navy (along with the 52-gun *Rouen*). Pierced to carry nine pairs of LD guns (excluding the chase ports). Classed as 3rd Rank in 1669 and as 4th Rank from 1670.
  Dimensions & tons: dimensions unknown. 600 tons. Men: 5–6 officers, 200–230 ratings.
  Guns: 40 from 1669, 36 from 1671, 38 from 1674 and 40 from 1675. 44 (probably) from 1677: LD 18 x 12pdrs, UD 18 x 8pdrs, QD/Fc 8 x 4pdrs.

Le Havre Le Havre.
K: 5.1666. L: 8.1669. C: 12.1669. Renamed *Alcyon* 24.6.1671. Took part in Battle of Solebay 7.6.1672. Grounded on the Îles Aves (in the Caribbean) on 11.5.1678, with other ships of *Vice-amiral* Jean, Comte d'Estrées's squadron, but was refloated. Condemned 1686, not recorded after 1696.

GALANT (or *Galland*). 44, later 46 guns. Designed and built by Laurent Hubac. Pierced for ten pairs of LD guns. Classed as 3rd Rank in 1669 and as 4th Rank from 1670. Raised to 3rd Rank in 1677–78, restored to 4th Rank in 1687.
  Dimensions & tons: 118ft 0in, 104ft 0in x 32ft 0in x 14ft 6in (38.33, 33.78 x 10.39 x 4.71m). 700 tons. Draught 15ft/17ft (4.87/5.52m). Men: 250 (40/126/84), +5/6 officers.
  Guns: 44 from 1669: LD 20 x 12pdrs; UD 20 x 8pdrs; QD 4 x 4pdrs. 40 guns from 1671, 42 from 1672, 44 from 1673 and 46 from 1674.

Galant Dunkirk
K: 9.1666. L: early 1668. C: 4.1669. Took part in Battles of Solebay 7.6.1672 and Tobago 3.3.1677. Renamed *Opiniâtre* 28.6.1678. Condemned 1688 at Brest, and BU 1689.

In March 1669, Colbert additionally took over the portfolio of Secretary of State for the Navy, and launched a major expansion program designed to bring France up to the first rank of naval powers. When the new Rank system for classing warships was constituted by decree on 1 December 1669, the 4th Rank initially comprised twenty-one two-decked ships of between 30 and 36 guns, ranged between 350 and 550 tons, but on 22 March 1671 the limits were raised to those between 36 and 44 guns, and now comprised twenty-five ships, ranged between 600 and 800 tons. There were seven ships each of 750 tons, with 44 guns and 250 men (*Dunkerquois*, *Toulon*, *Cheval Marin*, *Sirène*, *Provençal*, *Assuré* and *Constant*), four with 42 guns (*Mazarin*, *Duc*, *Grâces* and *Artois*), four with 40 guns (*Saint Antoine de Gênes*, *Flamand*, *Galant* and *Basque*), two with 38 guns (*Hercule* and *Triomphe*) and eight with 36 guns (*Soleil*, *Jules*, *Françoise*, *Mercœur*, *Infante*, *Tigre*, *Le Havre* and *Beaufort*). Thus, in 1671 the former 4th Rank vessels all were moved to the newly-created 5th Rank (see next Chapter) with the sole exception of the 36-gun *Françoise* and the *Infante* (the latter raised from 34 to 36 guns) while 23 other vessels were moved from the 3rd Rank to the 4th Rank.

PURCHASED VESSEL (1669). The Portuguese-built *São Antonio*, which had become a Genoese ship in 1667 (belonging to the Marquis de Centurion) was purchased for the French Navy in November 1669 and renamed *Saint Antoine de Gênes* (occasionally listed as *Saint Antoine du Portugal*). Classed in the 4th Rank in 1670 but reduced to the 5th Rank in 1671. Rebuilt at Toulon April to August 1674.
  Dimensions & tons: dimensions unknown. 600 tons. Draught 11½ft/15ft (3.74/4.87m). Men: 230 (34/120/76), +5 officers.
  Guns: 40 from 1669, 34 from 1672, 36 from 1676, and 40 from 1677.

Saint Antoine de Gênes Lisbon.
K: 1663. L: 13.6.1665. C: 9.1665. Renamed *Léger* in 24.6.1671. Condemned 3.1678 at Toulon; BU c.1.1679.

BASQUE. 40, later 44 guns. Designed by Joseph Saboulin for the *Compagnie des Indes Orientales*, and purchased for the Navy while building in August 1670 (named on 17 August). Pierced for ten pairs of LD guns. Reduced to the 5th Rank in 1687, when reconstructed at Brest, then restored to the 4th Rank in 1690.
  Dimensions & tons: ?120ft, 100ft x ?30ft x ?15ft (39 x 9.7 x 4.9 m). 700 tons (only 480 from 1678). Men: 250 (48/134/68), + 6 officers; from 200 (45/95/60), + 6 officers.
  Guns: 40 from 1671. 44 from 1676: LD 20 x 12pdrs; UD 20 x 8pdrs; QD 4 x 4pdrs. Reverted to 40 guns from 1679 (without the 4pdrs).

Basque Bayonne
K: 6.1669. L: 1.1.1671. C: 6.1671.
  Renamed *Brillant* 24.6.1671, then *Triton* 28.6.1678. Lent to the *Compagnie du Sénégal* 1689. Deleted late 1694 at Martinique.

FRANÇOIS Class. 44, later 48 guns. Designed and built by Hendryck Houwens, both ships were ordered on 7 September 1669 and named *Assuré* and *Constant* on 21 February 1670, but were renamed on 24 June 1671 prior to entering service. Pierced for ten pairs of LD guns. *Oiseau* was rebuilt in 1680 (at Dunkirk or Brest) and again 1684–85 (at Brest).
  Dimensions & tons: approx. 120ft, 96ft x 30ft x ? (m). 700 tons. Men: 250 (40/126/84), + 5 officers; from 1675 – 250 (48/134/68), + 6 officers.
  Guns: 44 from 1671: LD 20 x 12pdrs; UD 20 x 8pdrs; QD 4 x 4pdrs. 46 from 1675 and 48 from 1679. *Oiseau*: 40 guns from 1688 and 46 from 1690.

François Dunkirk
K: 3.1670. L: 12.1670. C: 6.1671. Out of service 8.1685 at Brest. Condemned 27.9.1686 at Brest and BU.

Oiseau Dunkirk
K: 3.1670. L: 12.1670. C: 6.1671. Sailed on second voyage to Siam in 1685-86 of CV Vaudricourt de L'Aulnay and LV Claude, Chevalier de Forbin-Gardannes, with *Gaillard* and *Normande*. Took part in Battle of Bantry Bay 11.5.1689. Lent, under CV Abraham, Marquis Duquesne-Guitton, to the *Compagnie des Indes Orientales* 1.1690. Out of service 6.1692 at Port Louis. Sold to BU 12.1693.

ARTOIS Class. 42 guns. Designed by Joseph Saboulin and first ordered as the 42-gun 4th Rank *Artois* and *Grâces*, these two were subsequently built as 54-gun 3rd Rank, renamed *Maure* and *Fendant*, and are found in Chapter 3.

ENTENDU Class. 40, later 46 guns. Designed and built by Hendryck Houwens, ordered 27 August 1671 as fireships with 12 guns (see Chapter 8) and originally named *Fâcheux* and *Brutal* in 1672, but re-classed as 5th Rank in 1673 and then as 4th Rank in 1674 and renamed *Entendu* and *Croissant* respectively on 31 January 1675. Pierced for ten pairs of LD guns. *Croissant* was raised to the 4th Rank with the new *Entendu* (ex-*Dauphin*, see below) in 1675 and restored to 5th Rank in 1687.

Dimensions & tons: approx. 120ft, 96ft x 30ft (38.98, 31.18 x 9.745m). 500 tons. Draught 12ft/13ft (3.90/4.22m). Men: 200 (45/95/60), +5/6 officers.

Guns: 30 in 1674. 40 from 1675: LD 10 x 12pdrs + 8 x 8pdrs; UD 16 x 6pdrs; QD 6 x 4pdrs. *Croissant* later reported as 46: LD 20 x 12pdrs; UD 20 x 8pdrs, QD/Fc 6 x 4pdrs.

Entendu Dunkirk.
K: 12.1671. L: 11.1673. C: 10.1674. Burnt by accident off the Kent coast 22.2.1675 by her crew (annoyed at receiving wine instead of beer ration).

Croissant Dunkirk.
K: 12.1671. L: 11.1673. C: 11.1674. Out of service 6.1692. Sold to BU 12.1693.

MARQUIS. 42, later 46 guns. Designed and built by Laurent Hubac. Ordered on 1 July 1672 and named *Attendant* in November 1672, but renamed *Marquis* on 26 December. Pierced for eleven guns per side on the LD.

Dimensions & tons: 118ft 0in, 104ft 0in x 32ft 0in x 14ft 6in (38.33, 33.78 x 10.39 x 4.71m). 750 tons. Draught 15ft (4.87m). Men: 250, +5/6 officers.

Guns: 42 from 1673, 44 from 1674. 46 from 1675: LD 22 x 12pdrs; UD 20 x 8pdrs; QD 4 x 4pdrs.

Marquis Brest Dyd.
K: 8/9.1672. L: 3.1673. C: 5.1673. Destroyed in explosion (with all 250 men lost) during combat at Tobago with Dutch *Leyden* on 3.3.1677.

ÉTOILE. 34, later 40 guns. Designed and built as a fireship by Pierre Malet and Benjamin Chaillé, and originally named on 26 December 1672 as *Actif*, but re-classed as a 4th Rank ship in 1675 and renamed *Étoile* 6 December 1675. Pierced for ten pairs of LD guns. Reduced to 5th Rank in 1692–95.

Dimensions & tons: 105ft 0in, 80ft 0in x 32ft 0in x 14ft 0in (34.11, 25.99 x 10.39 x 4.55m).

Guns: 30 from 1674, 34 from 1675; 40 from 1676, 38 from 1679, and 40 from 1688. 36 in war from 1696 (30 peace): LD 18 x 12pdrs; UD 18 x 8pdrs.

Étoile Rochefort Dyd.
K: 1.1673. L: 9.1673. C: 1674. Took part in the Bombardments of Algiers 23.7.1682 and 26.6.1683. Struck 1697 at Toulon, and given to the *Compagnie des Indes Orientales*.

ÉOLE. 38, later 46 guns. Designed and built by François Chapelle. Pierced for ten pairs of LD guns. Ordered as *Changeant*, but renamed at launch. Rebuilt 1688 at Toulon. If she became the fireship *Caché* in 1693 (see note below), she would have measured 130ft 0in x 33ft 0in x 15ft 4in (42.23 x 10.72 x 4.98m) with a draught of 17ft (5.52m).

Dimensions & tons: dimensions unknown (but see above). 600 tons. Draught 14ft/15ft (4.55/4.87m). Men: 250 (48/134/68) in 1675, 200 (45/95/60) in 1676, + 6 officers.

Guns: 44 from 1674, 38 from 1675; 40 from 1676. 44 from 1677: LD 10 x 12pdrs + 10 x 8pdrs; UD 20 x 6pdrs; QD 4 x 4pdrs. 46 guns from 1691.

Éole Toulon Dyd.
K: 4.1673. L: 17.11.1673. C: 1674. Took part in Battle of Beachy Head 10.7.1690. Re-classed as a *flûte* and renamed *Arche de Noé* in 2.1692. Struck in 1693, but possibly became fireship *Caché*, in service to 1696 (although this may have been the following vessel).

INDIEN. 38, later 50 guns. Designed and built by Laurent Coulomb. Ordered as *Anonyme*, but renamed at launch. Pierced for ten pairs of guns on the LD.

Dimensions & tons: 127ft 0in, 101ft 0in x 33ft 0in x 15ft 0in (41.20, 32.81 x 10.72 x 4.87m). 600 tons. Draught 14ft/15ft. Men: 250, +6 officers.

Guns: 44 from 1674, 38 from 1675 and 40 from 1676. 44 guns from 1677: LD 10 x 12pdrs + 10 x 8pdrs; UD 20 x 6pdrs; QD 4 x 4pdrs. 50 guns from 1690, then 8 only from 1696 as fireship: 8 x 8pdrs.

Indien Toulon Dyd.
K: 4.1673. L: 21.11.1673. C: 1674. Took part in Bombardment of Genoa 18–28.5.1684, and in Battle of Beachy Head 10.7.1690. Struck at Rochefort 1691. Converted to *flûte* 4.1692, renamed *Concorde*; probably became fireship in 1693, renamed *Caché*, in service to 1696 (see above).

A 4th Rank ship of 40 guns to be built at Brest and named *Entendu* was ordered in July 1673, abandoned in 1674, reinstated in April 1675 (although the name in the meantime had been reassigned to a former fireship – see above), and was finally abandoned later in 1675.

FAUCON. 34, later 40 guns. Designed and built by Jean Guichard. Pierced for ten pairs of LD guns. Ordered 14 July 1673 and named on 13 August as *Inconnu*, but renamed *Faucon* on 28 November; sometimes called *Faucon Français* from 1694 until 1703, to distinguish her from *Faucon Anglais* (prize of 1694). Originally 5th Rank, increased to the 4th Rank in 1675.

Dimensions & tons: 115ft 0in, 96ft 0in x 29ft 0in x 13ft 0in (37.36, 31.18 x 9.42 x 4.22m). 450 tons. Draught 14ft/15ft (4.55/4.87m). Men: 230/200, +6 officers.

Guns: 34 from 1675. 40 from 1676: LD 10 x 12pdrs + 10 x 8pdrs; UD 20 x 6pdrs. 44 guns from 1677, then 40 again from 1688 (34 peace): LD 6 x 12pdrs + 12 x 8pdrs; UD 18 x 6pdrs; QD 4 x 4pdrs. From 1699 to 1708 the LD battery was reduced to just the 12 x 8pdrs, while the UD had 18 or 20 x 6pdrs and the QD sometimes 4 x 4pdrs.

Faucon Rochefort Dyd.
K: 8.1673. L: 1674. C: 1674. Took part in Battles of Bantry Bay 11.5.1689 and Beachy Head 10.7.1690. Lent as a privateer to CV Guillaume Aché, Comte de Serquigny, as part of a squadron of three vessels, for escorting to India the mercantile *Florissant*, *Lonray* and *Pontchartrain*, of the *Compagnie des Indes Orientales* 1695–96. Struck 1705 but reinstated on the List 1706. Lent as a privateer to the *Compagnie de l'Asiento* 1705. Condemned 7.1708 to be BU at Lorient.

HASARDEUX. 34, later 44 guns. Designed and built by Honoré Malet. Pierced for ten pairs of LD guns. Ordered 14 July 1673 and named on 13 August. Originally rated as 5th Rank, but raised to 4th Rank in 1675.

Dimensions & tons: 115ft 0in, 96ft 0in x 26ft 0in x 13ft 0in (37.36, 31.18 x 9.42 x 4.22m). 500 tons. Draught 13ft/15ft (4.22/4.87m). Men: 200 (45/95/60), +6 officers.

Guns: 34 from 1674, then 40 from 1676. 44 from 1677: LD 10 x 12pdrs + 10 x 8pdrs; UD 20 x 6pdrs; QD 4 x 4pdrs. Reduced to 38 guns from 1688 and 40 from 1690.

Hasardeux Rochefort Dyd.
K: 8.1673. L: 1674. C: 1674. Lent as a privateer to CFL Jean-Baptiste Ducasse, as part of a squadron of four vessels, for operations against Surinam, 1688. Wrecked off St Domingue 4.1695.

A *Règlement* of 10 February 1674 nominally provided for new 4th Rank vessels (*frégates-vaisseaux*) to carry a recommended armament of 40 guns, comprising 10 x 12pdrs (6 iron and 4 bronze guns) and 10 x 8pdrs (all iron) on their LD, and 18 x 6pdrs (12 iron and 6 bronze) on their UD, with 2 x 4pdrs (iron) on the QD. While the *Règlement* itself did not suggest dimensions for these vessels, a contemporary source (Dassié) stated that the typical dimensions for this Rank were 120ft length x 30ft breadth x 15ft depth in hold (38.98 x 9.745 x 4.87m).

LAURIER. 44 guns. This vessel, and the *Arc en Ciel* below, were originally ordered as 12-gun *frégates légères* of 120 tons in 1671 (see Chapter 6), but the instructions were cancelled in 1673, and instead these two vessels were begun in the following year as 5th Rank (later 4th Rank in 1676) ships. At first planned for 30 guns (in 1675), then 38 in 1676 and 40 from 1679. The first was designed and built by François Chapelle; ordered as *Serpente*, but renamed *Ferme* in January 1678, then *Laurier* in June 1678. Pierced for ten guns per side on the LD.

  Dimensions & tons: 115ft 0in, 96ft 0in x 32ft 0in x 13ft 6in (37.36, 31.18 x 10.39 x 4.39m). 500 tons. Draught 13ft/14ft (4.22/4.55m). Men: 250/200, +6 officers.
  Guns: 40 from 1679: LD 10 x 12pdrs + 10 x 8pdrs; UD 20 x 6pdrs.

Laurier Toulon Dyd.
  K: 6.1674. L: 29.1.1678. C: 6.1679. Condemned 1690 at Toulon; sold 4.1692 to a shipowner at St Malo.

ARC EN CIEL. 40, later 50 guns. Designed and built by Charles Audibert. See comments about 1671 order as a *frégate légère* above. Ordered as *Rieuse*, but renamed *Arc en Ciel* in December 1676. Pierced for ten guns per side on the LD. Raised from the 4th to the 3rd Rank in 1691, but restored to 4th Rank in 1692–95.

  Dimensions & tons: 115ft 0in, 96ft 0in x 32ft 0in x 13ft 6in (37.36, 31.18 x 10.39 x 4.39m). 500 tons. Draught 14ft/17ft (4.55/5.52m). Men: 280/200, +6 officers.
  Guns: 40 from 1679: LD 10 x 12pdrs + 10 x 8pdrs; UD 20 x 6pdrs. 44 from 1688 and 50 from 1690. 46 in war from 1696 (40 peace): LD 20 x 18pdrs; UD 22 x 8pdrs; QD 4 x 4pdrs.

Arc en Ciel Toulon Dyd.
  K: 6.1674. L: 31.3.1678. C: 8.1678. Took part in Battles of Bantry Bay 11.5.1689 and Beachy Head 10.7.1690. Struck 1698 at Toulon, and probably BU 1699.

ENTENDU. 40 guns. Purchased in February 1675 as *Dauphin*, and renamed in March following loss of earlier *Entendu* in February (see above). Originally classed as 5th Rank, but increased to 4th Rank later in 1675.

  Dimensions & tons: 111ft 0in, 92ft 0in x 34ft 0in x ? (36.06, 29.89 x 11.04m). 400 tons. Draught 14ft/16½ft (4.55/5.36m). Men: 200 (44/96/60), +6 officers.
  Guns: 40 from 1675 (probably armed as per the *Règlement* of 10 February 1674).

Entendu St Malo (purchased)
  K: 1664. L: 1665. C: 2.1666. Struck 1690, but used as a *flûte* at Toulon; condemned there 4.1692 and sold.

Ex-SPANISH PRIZE (1675). The Spanish *Nuestra Señora del Pueblo* was captured by de Vivonne's fleet at the Battle of the Lipari Islands (off Sicily) on 15 February 1675 and taken into French naval service as *Madona del Popolo*.

  Dimensions & tons: dimensions unknown. 400 tons. Men: 200.
  Guns: 40, 42 or 44 depending on the source.

Madona del Popolo Spain.

Built 1673–74. Her guns were landed by the French at Augusta (Sicily) in August 1675. She was retaken by the Spanish in January 1676 off Sicily, and was still in Spanish service in 1686.

COMTE. 40, later 44 guns. Designed and built by Jean-Pierre Brun. Pierced for ten pairs of LD guns. Ordered as *Fidèle*, but renamed *Comte* in April 1677.

  Dimensions & tons: 112ft 0in, 98ft 0in x 29ft 6in x 14ft 0in (39.02, 31.83 x 9.58 x 4.55m). 450 tons. Draught 14ft/15ft (4.55/4.87m). Men: 230 in war, 200 peace, +6 officers.
  Guns: 40 from 1679: LD 10 x 12pdrs + 10 x 8pdrs; UD 18 x 6pdrs; QD 2 x 4pdrs. 38 in 8.1692: LD 18 x 8pdrs; UD 18 x 6pdrs. Re-armed 1696: 44 in war (38 peace): LD 20 x 12pdrs; UD 20 x 6pdrs; QD 4 x 4pdrs.

Comte Brest Dyd.
  K: 3.1677. L: 11.1677. C: 3.1678. Took part in the Battle of Beachy Head 10.7.1690. Lent as a privateer to the Marquis de Seignelay (Secretary of State for the Navy) and CV Ferdinand, Comte de Relingue 1688–89. Struck 1698 at Dunkirk.

NEPTUNE. 40, later 50 guns. Designed and built by Laurent Hubac. Ordered and named as *Maure*, but renamed January 1679 before completing. Pierced for eleven pairs of LD guns. Girdled/sheathed around 1681. Classed as 4th Rank until 1691, when raised to 3rd Rank.

  Dimensions & tons: 114ft 0in, 100ft 0in x 30ft 0in x 14ft 0in (37.03, 32.48 x 9.75 x 4.55m). 600 tons. Draught 15½ft/17½ft (5.035/5.68m). Men: 200 (45/95/60) in 1679, +6 officers; 250 in 1690 (47/135/68), then 280 from 1691 (50/155/75), then 300 in war (240 peace) in 1696, +6 officers.
  Guns: 40 from 1679, then 44 from 1680: LD 12 x 18pdrs + 10 x 12pdrs; UD 22 x 8pdrs. 40 again from 1688, then 50 in war from 1690 (44 peace): as 1680 with 6 x 6pdrs added on the *gaillards*. LD 22 x 18pdrs from 1696.

Neptune Brest Dyd.
  K: 1.1678. L: 20.8.1678. C: 5.1679. Took part in the Battles of

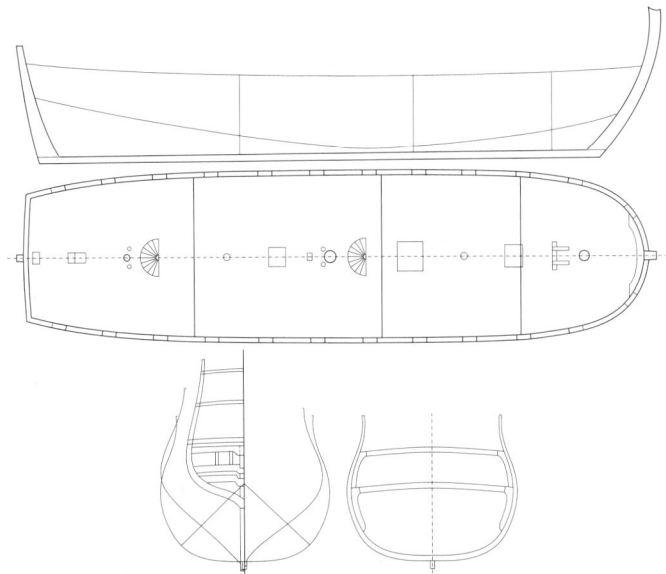

Neptune of 1678, a ship variously listed as 4th and then 3rd Rank, mounting 40 and later 50 guns. This is an early attempt to graphically represent the underwater shape of a ship by lines, from which the familiar modern sheer plan was to develop. This drawing was first published in the nineteenth century in *Souvenirs de Marine* from which this tracing was produced by László Veres.

Bantry Bay 11.5.1689 and Beachy Head 10.7.1690. Condemned 1702 at Toulon.

ÉCUEIL. 40 guns. Designed and built by Étienne Salicon. Pierced for ten pairs of LD guns. Ordered in early 1678 and named on 11 April as *Lion*, but renamed *Marin* on 28 June and then *Écueil* on 22 July. A second ship which was built following her (*Léger*) was somewhat smaller, and is listed separately below.

Dimensions & tons: 117ft 6in, 102ft 0in x 29ft 6in x 11ft 6in (38.17, 33.13 x 9.58 x 3.74m). 500 tons. Draught 14ft (4.55m). Men: 250 in war, 200 peace, +6 officers.

Guns: 40 from 1679: LD 20 x 12pdrs; UD 20 x 8pdrs. 44 from 1687 (4 x 4pdrs added on QD).

Écueil Le Havre.
K: 5.1678. L: 2.11.1678. C: 12.1678. Sold to the *Compagnie des Indes Orientales* 9.1689 under order of 1.10.1688; BU at Chandanagore 1699.

LÉGER. 40, later 44 guns. Designed and built by Étienne Salicon immediately after *Écueil* above. Pierced for ten pairs of LD guns.

Dimensions & tons: 114ft 0in, 100ft 0in x 28ft 6in x 12ft 6in (37.03, 32.48 x 9.26 x 4.06m). 410 tons. Draught 12½ft (4.06m). Men: 250 in war, 200 peace, +6 officers.

Guns: 40 from 1680, then 44 from 1690: LD 10 x 12pdrs + 10 x 8pdrs; UD 20 x 6pdrs; QD 4 x 4pdrs (removed by 1691).

Léger Le Havre.
K: 6.1679. L: 3.11.1679. C: 3.1680. Took part in Battles of Bantry Bay 11.5.1689 and Beachy Head 10.7.1690. Condemned and hulked at Rochefort 1695; not mentioned after 1696.

A 4th Rank ship of 46 guns, to be named *Capricieux*, was ordered in 1681 to be built at Rochefort but the order was cancelled in 1682.

In 1683 the 4th Rank consisted mainly of ships between 40 and 46 guns (although the 38-gun *Étoile* and the 36-gun *Maure* and *Trident* also remained classed as 4th Rank). Apart from these three exceptions, the Rank comprised twenty-two ships at the start of 1683 – two of 48 guns (*François** and *Oiseau**), two of 46 (*Cheval Marin** and *Sirène**), seven of 44 (*Alcyon*, *Brusque**, *Éole*, *Faucon*, *Hasardeux*, *Indien* and *Neptune*), one of 42 (*Bizarre*) and ten of 40 (*Arc en Ciel*, *Aventurier*, *Comte*, *Croissant*, *Écueil**, *Entendu**, *Laurier*, *Léger**, *Tigre* and *Triton*). Each of the twenty-five ships had 6 officers in addition to a wartime complement of 200 men – except the eight asterisked above, which had 250 men each, and the *Aventurier* and *Bizarre* with just 150 each.

SOLIDE Class. 40, later 46 guns. Designed and built by Hendryck Houwens. Pierced for ten pairs of LD guns. Initially named *Railleuse* and *Trompeuse* respectively, but renamed as below in February 1683 prior to keel laying.

Dimensions & tons: 118ft 0in x 32ft 0in x 14ft 0in (38.33 x 10.39 x 4.55m). 600 tons. Draught 15ft/17½ft (4.87/5.68m). Men: 250 (48/134/68) in war, 210 peace, +6 officers.

Guns: 40 from 1686, then 44 from 1687: LD 10 x 12pdrs + 10 x 8pdrs; UD 20 x 6pdrs; QD 4 x 4pdrs, 46 in war in *Emporté* from 1696 (40 peace): LD 20 x 12pdrs; UD 22 x 8pdrs; QD 4 x 4pdrs. 42 from 1698 (2 x 6pdrs & 2 x 4pdrs removed).

Solide Dunkirk.
K: 4.1683. L: 6.11.1683. C: 4.1684. Took part in the Battle of Beachy Head 10.7.1690. Wrecked 8.1694 on the Île de la Tortue.

Emporté Dunkirk.
K: 4.1683. L: 20.11.1683. C: 4.1684. Took part in the Battle of Bantry Bay 11.5.1689. Lent as a privateer to CV François Colbert de Saint Mars, as part of a squadron of four vessels, 1696. Condemned 9.1704 at Léogane (St Domingue).

GAILLARD. 36, later 48 guns. Designed and built by Étienne Salicon. Pierced for ten pairs of LD guns. Initially 5th Rank, but re-classed as 4th Rank in 1687.

Dimensions & tons: 120ft 8in x 32ft 6in x 15ft 0in (39.20 x 10.56 x 4.87m). 600 tons. Draught 15ft (4.87m). Men: 250, +6 officers.

Guns: 36 from 1686, then 44 from 1687: LD 10 x 12pdrs + 10 x 8pdrs; UD 20 x 6pdrs; QD 4 x 4pdrs. 48 guns from 1688.

Gaillard Le Havre.
K: 7.1683. L: 17.11.1684. C: 4.1685. Sailed on second voyage to Siam in 1685–86 of CV Vaudricourt de L'Aulnay and LV Claude, Chevalier de Forbin-Gardannes, with *Oiseau* and *Normande*. Sold 9.1689 at Brest under order of 1.10.1688 to the *Compagnie des Indes Orientales*; lost 6.1699 at Balassor.

FRANÇOIS. 40, later 52 guns. Designed and built by Étienne Salicon. Pierced for eleven pairs of LD guns, seemingly an enlarged version of the *Gaillard*. Re-classed as 3rd Rank from 1691, then restored to 4th Rank in c.1713.

Dimensions & tons: 125ft 6in x 33ft 0in x 15ft 0in (40.77 x 10.72 x 4.87m). 700 tons. Draught 15ft/17ft (4.87/5.52m). Men: 280, +6 officers.

Guns: 40 from 1688, then 50 from 1691: LD 12 x 18pdrs + 10 x 12pdrs; UD 22 x 8pdrs; QD 6 x 4pdrs. 52 in war from 1696 (50 peace): LD 10 x 18pdrs + 12 x 12pdrs; UD 24 x 8pdrs; QD 6 x 4pdrs (only 4 from 1698). LD guns reported as 22 x 12pdrs from 1699–1700. Reportedly LD guns were 22 x 18pdrs from 1729.

François (Français) Le Havre.
K: 4.1687. L: 20.12.1687. C: 4.1688. Took part in the Battles of Bantry Bay 11.5.1689 and Beachy Head 10.7.1690. Lent as a privateer to René Duguay-Trouin, from St Malo, 1694–95. Lent as a privateer to LG André, Marquis de Nesmond, as part of a squadron of six to eleven vessels, 1696. Refitted 1708–9 at Rochefort. BU (by Order of 2.10.1735) at Rochefort 1736.

TRIDENT. 44, later 50 guns. Designed and built by Laurent Coulomb. Pierced for eleven pairs of LD guns. Contract awarded on 18 August 1687 and ship named on 1 September. Raised to 3rd Rank in 1690. This ship (and the similar *Maure*, below) replaced the ships of the same name (originally called *Mercœur* and *Beaufort*, built 1662 – see above) which had been condemned in 1686.

Dimensions & tons: 125ft 0in, 100ft 0in x 33ft 0in x 14ft 6in (40.60, 32.48 x 10.72 x 4.71m). 700 tons. Draught 15ft/15½ft (4.87/5.035m). Men: 250 (48/134/68) in 1689, +6 officers; 300 (64/161/75) in 1690, +7 officers.

Guns: 44 from 1688: LD 12 x 18pdrs + 10 x 12pdrs; UD 22 x 8pdrs. 50 from 1692 (2 more 8pdrs, and 4 x 6pdrs on QD).

Trident Toulon Dyd.
K: 8.1687. L: 22.6.1688. C: 9.1688. Took part in the Battle of Beachy Head 10.7.1690, and present at the Battle of Lagos 28.6.1693. Captured by HM Ships *Falmouth* and *Adventure* of Captain James Killigrew's squadron in Action off Cape Bon on 18.1.1695, becoming HMS *Trident Prize*; sunk as a breakwater at Harwich 14.1.1701.

MAURE. 44, later 54 guns. Designed and built by Blaise Pangalo. Pierced for eleven pairs of LD guns. Contract awarded on 18 August 1687 and ship named on 1 September. Raised to 3rd Rank in 1690.

Dimensions & tons: 127ft 0in x 34ft 0in x 15ft 0in (41.25 x 11.04 x 4.87m). 750 tons. Draught 15ft/18ft (4.875.85m). Men: 250 (48/134/68) in 1689, +6 officers; 300 (64/161/75) in 1690, +7 officers.

Guns: 44 from 1688: LD 12 x 18pdrs + 10 x 12pdrs; UD 22 x 8pdrs. 54 from 1691, then 50 in war from 1696 (44 peace): LD 22 x 18pdrs; UD 22 x 12pdrs; QD 6 x 6pdrs. 54 from 1699: LD 22 x 18pdrs; UD 24 x 8pdrs; QD 8 x 6pdrs (replaced by 4 x 4pdrs from 1707).

Maure Toulon Dyd.
K: 8.1687. L: 8.1688. C: 10.1688. Took part in the Battle of Beachy Head 10.7.1690. Lent as a privateer to Sieur François de Beauvais (called Beauvais-Le Fer) from St Malo 1707–8; then lent as a privateer to CV René Duguay-Trouin, as part of a squadron of five to nine vessels, 1708–9; then lent for commerce and privateering to CV Louis Gabriel Du Coudray-Guimont, 1709. Captured by HM Ships *Warspite* and *Breda* 13.12.1710, becoming HMS *Moor*. Sunk as a breakwater at Plymouth 7.3.1716.

Ex-DUTCH PRIZE (1688). A Dutch commercial vessel – possibly named *Triompantelijk* or *Zegervierend* – was captured in December 1688 and taken into French naval service as *Triomphant*.

Dimensions & tons: dimensions unknown. 600 tons.
Guns: 40 in 1689, including 12pdrs on the LD.

Triomphant Holland.
Refitted at Dunkirk 4–5.1689, but judged unusable for war in 6.1689. She may have been briefly in commission, but did not appear in any French official fleet list.

ALCYON. 40, later 42 guns. Designed and begun by Hendryck Houwens; completed by his son Jean-Nicolas after his death. Pierced for ten pairs of LD guns. Built as 5th Rank, but raised to 4th Rank in 1690; reduced to 5th Rank again in 1700, but restored to 4th Rank in 1702–3.

Dimensions & tons: 107ft 0in x 28ft 0in x 13ft 0in (34.76 x 9.10 x 4.22m). 350 tons. Draught 14ft 10in/15¾ft (4.82/5.12m). Men: 150 (35/78/37) in 1690, +6 officers; 200 in 1691 (44/96/60) in war (150 peace), +6 officers.

Guns: 44 in 1690, then 40 from 1691: LD 10 x 12pdrs + 10 x 8pdrs; UD 18 x 6pdrs; QD 2 x 4pdrs. 40 in war from 1696 (34 peace): LD 20 x 12pdrs; UD 20 x 6pdrs; QD nil. 42 from 1699: LD 18 x 8pdrs; UD 20 x 6pdrs; QD 4 x 4pdrs (removed 1704). 38 from 1710: LD 18 x 12pdrs; UD 20 x 6pdrs; QD nil.

Alcyon Dunkirk.
K: 1.1689. L: 7.1689. C: 11.1689. Took part in the Battle of Beachy Head 10.7.1690. Lent as a privateer to LG André, Marquis de Nesmond, as part of a squadron of five vessels, 1695, Lent as a privateer to Beaubriant-L'Évêque, of St Malo (with *Juste*), 1702. Condemned at Lorient 1717 and BU there 3.1718.

(C) Vessels acquired from 15 April 1689

At the start of 1689 the 4th Rank comprised twenty-five ships with between 40 and 48 guns, in addition to the 50-gun *Duc*, 38-gun *Hasardeux* and 34-gun *Prompt*, which lay outside these formal limits. In addition, the new *Alcyon* was ordered but not yet begun at Dunkirk. Notably during 1689 the new *Trident* and *Maure*, which had a mix of 18pdrs and 12pdrs on the LD, were raised from 44 to 58 guns, so that in 1690 they were moved to the 3rd Rank. The similarly-armed *Neptune* of 1678 and the new *François* followed them into the 3rd Rank in 1691.

The great Navy *Ordonnance* issued on 15 April 1689 amended the 1674 establishment for 4th Rank ships, adding 4 x 18pdrs (bronze) to their LD, which retained 16 of the 12pdrs (iron) but no longer included 8pdrs. They also were to carry 20 x 8pdrs (12 iron and 8 bronze) on the UD, and 4 x 4pdrs (bronze) on the QD. The prescribed dimensions were set at 120ft length x 32½ft breadth x 14½ft depth in hold (38.98 x 10.56 x 4.71m). Like previous *Règlements*, this directive was generally ignored by the *constructeurs* in the dockyards.

The width of LD gunports was set at 2ft 4in (0.76m) and these ports were to be separated by a distance of 7ft 3in (2.355m). From this the ideal length of a 4th Rank ship with 11 pairs of LD ports could be determined (in theory) to vary from 111ft 8in (36.27m) to 126ft (40.93m); a variant with one fewer pair of LD ports would be between 102¾ft (33.38m) and 117¼ft (38.09m), while a variant with one more pair of ports would be between 121½ft (39.47m) and 135ft (43.85m).

ADROIT. 44 guns. Designed and built by Étienne Salicon. Pierced for eleven pairs of guns on the LD. Initially classed in the 5th Rank with just 36 guns but increased to the 4th Rank with 44 guns between 1692 and 1695.

Dimensions & tons: 114ft 0in, 102ft 0in x 31ft 6in x 12ft 6in (35.73, 33.13 x 9.26 x 3.90m). 500 tons. Draught 11ft/14½ft (3.57/4.71m). Men: 150 in war, 130 peace (34/66/30) + 6 officers.

Guns: 44 in war from 1696 (36 peace): LD 22 x 12pdrs; UD 22 x 8pdrs. 42 from 1699: LD 20 x 12pdrs; UD 18 x 6pdrs; QD 4 x 4pdrs.

Adroit Le Havre.
K: 7.1690. L: 20.1.1691. C: 8.1691. Destroyed in action with Dutch *Chateau d'Anvers* when the latter blew up off the Orkney Is. 22.6.1703 (224 killed).

POLI Class. 40 guns. Designed by Honoré Malet, and begun around July 1689; built by Malet and Pierre Masson. Pierced for ten pairs of guns on the LD. When completed, these were initially classed as 5th Rank, with just 34 guns and of 400 tons, but by 1696 they were 4th Rank ships with 40 guns, noted as 'good sailers', with data as set out below. The survivor *Poli* was reduced again to 36 guns in 1701.

Dimensions & tons: 110ft 0in x 28ft 6in x 12ft 0in (35.73 x 9.26 x 3.90m). 500 tons. Draught 11ft/14½ft (3.57/4.71m). Men: 150 in war, 130 peace (34/66/30) + 6 officers.

Guns: 40 in war from 1696 (36 peace): LD 20 x 12pdrs (replaced by 8pdrs during 1698); UD 20 x 6pdrs. 40 in both from 1699: LD 20 x 8pdrs; UD 20 x 6pdrs. 36 in *Poli* from 1701: LD 16 x 8pdrs; UD 20 x 6pdrs.

Poli Rochefort Dyd.
K: 3.1690. L: 8.1691. C: 12.1691. Leased to the *Compagnie de Guinée* in 1697, and employed as a slaver from 1701. Transferred to the *Compagnie du Sénégal* in 1708, but a planned refit at Rochefort from 1709 to 1712 was never completed, and she was struck there (between 1712 and 1714) and BU in 1717.

Opiniâtre Rochefort Dyd.
K: 3.1690. L: 7.1691. C: 8.1691. Struck 1699 at Rochefort, and transferred to the *Compagnie Royale de St Domingue* for service as a slaver.

Ex-SPANISH PRIZE (1691–1692). 40 guns. The Spanish (Netherlands) privateer *Carlos II* was captured by the French in late 1691 or 1692 and added to the French Navy.

Dimensions & tons: 102ft 0in x 28ft 0in (33.13 x 9.10m). 450 tons. Draught 15ft (4.87m). Men: 200 (44/96/60), +6 officers.

Guns: 40 (Spanish ordnance, not known to have been replaced)

Charles II Ostend.
K: 1679. C: 9.1680. Grounded 10.1693 by accident off Dunkirk and seemingly unrepaired. Struck there 1694.

Ex-DUTCH PRIZE (1692). 48/50 guns. The Dutch *Maria-Elizabeth* was captured in August 1692 and taken into French naval service as *Marie-Élisabeth*.
   Dimensions & tons (Dutch measurements converted to French units): 113ft 3in x 29ft 7in x 12ft 2in (36.79 x 9.62 x 3.96m). 400 tons.
   Guns: 48/50.
Marie-Élisabeth Amsterdam
   Built 1685. Took part in Battle of Lagos 28.6.1693. Became a *flûte* in 1693, hulk at Toulon in 1695, sold 1.1697.

VOLONTAIRE. 40 guns. Designed and built by François Coulomb. Pierced for ten pairs of guns on the LD.
   Dimensions & tons: 108ft 0in, 85ft 0in x 30ft 0in x 12ft 6in (36.40, 27.61 x 9.75 x 4.06m). 450 tons. Draught c.14ft (4.55m). Men: 200 in war, +5 officers.
   Guns: 44 in war (38 peace): LD 18 x 12pdrs; UD 18 x 6pdrs; QD 4 x 4pdrs. 36 from 1701: LD 18 x 12pdrs; UD 18 x 6pdrs.
Volontaire Toulon Dyd.
   K: late 1692. L: 1693. C: 1693. Wrecked at St Tropez 3.1695.

Ex-ENGLISH PRIZE (1694). The English Fifth Rate *Falcon* was captured by four French warships (*Solide*, *Téméraire*, *Envieux* and a corvette) off Jamaica on 11 May 1694 and added to the *Marine Royale*.
   Dimensions & tons (French measurements): 105ft 0in, 82ft 7in x 26ft 6in x 11ft 0in (34.11, 26.83 x 8.61 x 3.57m). 330 tons. Draught 14ft (4.55m). Men: 230 in war, 160 peace, +7 officers.
   Guns: 48 in war (40 peace): LD 10 x 12pdrs + 10 x 8pdrs; UD 22 x 6pdrs; QD 6 x 4pdrs. 44 from 1708: LD 20 x 8pdrs; UD 20 x 6pdrs; QD 4 x 4pdrs.
Faucon Anglais Woolwich Dyd.
   Ord: 4.1665. L: 1666. Lent as a privateer to CV Jean-Baptiste, Comte de Gennes and Seigneur d'Oyac as part of a squadron of six vessels, 1695–97. Struck 1698 at Rochefort but reappeared on the list in 1699 as a larger 3rd Rank ship of 125ft, 700 tons, and 50 or 54 guns. Remained in the 3rd Rank after her reported dimensions were reduced in 1704 back to those shown above. Lent as a privateer to Gilles Petit for the *Compagnie des Indes Orientales*, 1706–7. Struck in 1708 at Rochefort and ceded to the *Compagnie de l'Asiento* (the French holder of the monopoly for transporting slaves to the Spanish colonies).

Ex-ENGLISH PRIZE (1695). 42 guns. The English Fourth Rate *Nonsuch*, designed by Anthony Deane and built in 1668, was captured on 14 January 1695 off the Isles of Scilly by René Duguay-Trouin's *François*, and taken into French service as a privateer under the same name.
   Dimensions & tons (French measurements): 82ft 10in (keel) x 26ft 0in x 10ft 2in (26.91 keel x 8.45 x 3.30m). Draught 12ft 2in (3.95m). 360 tons. Men: 260 in war, 200 peace.
   Guns (37): 18 x 10pdrs, 17 x 6pdrs, 2 x 4pdrs (these probably being her English 9pdrs, 5¼pdrs, and 3pdrs). 42 in French service.
Nonsuch Portsmouth Dyd.
   Built 1668 and modified 1669. Renamed *Sans Pareil* and armed as a true privateer with 42 guns by René Duguay-Trouin from St Malo, 1696–97. Badly damaged in combat 3.1697 and retired to Lorient. Last mentioned 1697.

MUTINE. 40 guns. Designed by François Brun 'following the system of Petit Renau' (Bernard Renau d'Élissagaray), and built as a privateer at the request of LG André, Marquis de Nesmond, who funded the cost of construction. Pierced for ten pairs of guns on the LD.
   Dimensions & tons: 120ft 0in x 30ft 0in x 15ft 0in (38.98 x 9.75 x 4.87m). 500 tons. Draught 14ft/15ft 8in (4.55/5.09m). Men: 250 in war, 230 peace, + 5 officers.
   Guns: 40 in war (36 peace): LD 20 x 12pdrs; UD 20 x 6pdrs.
Mutine Brest Dyd.
   K: early 1695. L: 28.5.1695. C: 3.1696. Lent as a privateer to LG André, Marquis de Nesmond, as part of a squadron of five vessels, 1695–96; then lent as a privateer to CdE Jean Bernard de Saint-Jean, Baron de Pointis, as part of a squadron of fourteen vessels 1696-98; took part in the capture of Cartagena de Indias 5.5.1697. Lent anew as a privateer to CV de La Roque and CFL de Saint-Vandrille (with *Hermione*), for operations in the Gulf of Guinea 1702–3. Chartered by the King (with *Agréable*) to escort to India the mercantile *Aurore* and *Saint Louis*, ships belonging to the *Compagnie des Indes Orientales*, 1704–5. Wrecked 4.1707 at La Corogne.

VOLONTAIRE. 44 guns, later 36. Designed and built by François Coulomb, and named 30 October 1693; a replacement for Coulomb's 1693-launched ship of the same name, which had been wrecked in March 1695 at St Tropez. Pierced for ten pairs of guns on the LD.
   Dimensions & tons: 112ft 0in, 88ft 0in x 30ft 6in x 12ft 10in (36.38, 28.59 x 9.91 x 4.17m). 480 tons. Draught 14ft/14½ft (4.55/4.71m). Men: 240 in war, 220 peace, + 5 officers.
   Guns: 44 in war (38 peace): LD 20 x 12pdrs; UD 20 x 6pdrs; QD 4 x 4pdrs. 36 in war from 1701 (30 peace): LD 18 x 12pdrs; UD 18 x 6pdrs.
Volontaire Toulon Dyd.
   K: 5.1695. L: 8.1695. C: 3.1696. Captured by the Dutch at Vigo 22.10.1702, then burnt.

AMPHITRITE. 42 guns. Designed and built by Pierre Masson. Pierced for eleven pairs of guns on the LD.
   Dimensions & tons: 122ft 0in x 32ft 0in x 12ft 6in (39.63 x 10.39 x 4.06m). 550 tons. Draught 13½ft/15½ft (4.39/5.04m). Men: 250 in war, 200 peace, + 5 officers.
   Guns: 40 in war in 1706 (34 peace): LD 22 x 12pdrs; UD 16 x 6pdrs; QD 2 x 4pdrs. 42 from 1708: LD 20 x 12pdrs; UD 22 x 8pdrs.
Amphitrite Rochefort Dyd.
   K: 1696. L: 1696. C: 1697. Sold to the *Compagnie de la Chine* in 1.1698, she was reacquired by the Navy in 1.1704; she was then known as the '*Amphitrite de Chine*' (as there was a new 3rd Rate *Amphitrite* built by René Levasseur in Dunkirk Dyd in 1699), before being sold to François Saupin, Sieur Du Rocher (a timber merchant in Brest), as Director of the *Compagnie de l'Asiento*, for which she was employed as a slaver from 1704. Burnt by accident at Buenos Aires 7.1713. The other *Amphitrite* (identified as the '*Amphitrite de Dunkerque*'), was renamed *Protée* in 3.1705.

AVENANT. 42 guns. Designed by Blaise Pangalo. This was a former 16-gun *flûte* (launched July 1671 at Toulon) which was rebuilt as a 4th Rank ship by Pangalo. Pierced for eleven pairs of LD guns.
   Dimensions & tons: 109ft 0in x 27ft 6in x 13ft 0in (35.41 x 8.93 x 4.22m). 400 tons. Draught 16ft (5.20m). Men: 250 in war, 230 peace, + 5 officers.
   Guns: 42 in war (36 peace): LD 18 x 12pdrs; UD 18 x 6pdrs; QD 6 x 4pdrs. 42 from 1699: LD 10 x 12pdrs + 12 x 8pdrs; UD 20 x 6pdrs.

THE FOURTH RANK

The decorative works of *Amphitrite*, 42-gun ship of 1697. This ship had barely a year's service with the Navy before being sold to the Sieurs Jourdan, and in March 1698 was fitted out at Port Louis for a commercial voyage to Canton, China, from which she returned in August 1700. A second voyage resulted from a fresh contract between the Sieurs Jourdan and the *Compagnie des Indes*. She returned to Nantes in August 1703 (leased by the *Compagnie de la Chine*) and was reacquired for the Navy in January 1704. She was now generally referred to as the '*Amphitrite de Chine*' to distinguish her from another *Amphitrite*, a 3rd Rank ship built at Dunkirk in 1699 for the Navy. On 15 August of that year she was part of René Duguay-Trouin's squadron at the capture of HMS *Falmouth* to the southwest of the Isles of Scilly. Sold in 1709 to the *Compagnie de l'Asiento*, she sailed from La Rochelle on 18 February on a slaving voyage, disembarking 298 slaves at Buenos Aires on 9 December. She made another slaving cruise from La Rochelle in January 1712, arriving in November at Buenos Aires again, but was accidentally burnt there in July 1713. (*Souvenirs de Marine*, Plate 149)

Avenant Brest Dyd.
  K: 2.1696. L: 11.1696. C: 10.1696. Lent as a privateer to the Marquis de Seignelay, who funded it for 2/3, as part of a squadron of three to four under CV Jacques Dandenne 1689–90. Lent as a privateer to CdE Jean Bernard de Saint-Jean, Baron de Pointis, as part of a squadron of fourteen vessels, 1696–97; took part in the capture of Cartagena de Indias 5.5.1697. Chartered by the *Compagnie de l'Asiento* in 2.1704 as a slaver; burnt by accident at Cape Lopez (Gabon) 8.12.1704, with some 460 slaves burnt to death.

Ex-SPANISH PRIZES (1696–1697). A Spanish galleon called by the French *Sainte Croix* or *Sainte Croix Galion* and built in 1693 was taken in the Caribbean in 1696. This ship was probably named *Santa Cruz* and may have been the *Urca de Cartagena* of 36 guns taken in June 1696. She was initially classed in the 3rd Rank and was reduced to the 4th Rank during 1698. Another Spanish galleon, *Santo Christo de Maracaibo*, belonging to the Armadilla de Barlovente, was captured in January 1697 in the Caribbean by *Bourbon* of CV Des Augiers's squadron and taken into French naval service as *Christ*, and left behind to be used by Pointis.

Sainte Croix Central America (probably Cartagena)
  Dimensions & tons: 120ft 0in x 34ft 0in x 13ft 6in (38.98 x 11.04 x 4.39m); 925 tons; Draught 21ft (6.82m). Men: 300 in war, 200 peace.
  Guns: 40 in war (26 peace): LD 22 x 12pdrs; UD 18 x 8pdrs
  Struck at Rochefort 1699. Possibly sold to the Spanish since a 36-gun galleon named *Santa Cruz* was lost at Vigo in 10.1702.

The British Admiralty's systematic collecting of plans taken off captured ships is well recorded from the early eighteenth century, but they also caused block models to be made as a form of three-dimensional draught. These did not require the same familiarity with drawing conventions so could be more easily understood by laymen, and as a practice may even pre-date the formal collection of plans. This block model represents the *Triton*, a French 4th Rank ship captured at Vigo in 1702. The ship's fine lines are apparent even in a two-dimensional photograph. (National Maritime Museum, London L2398)

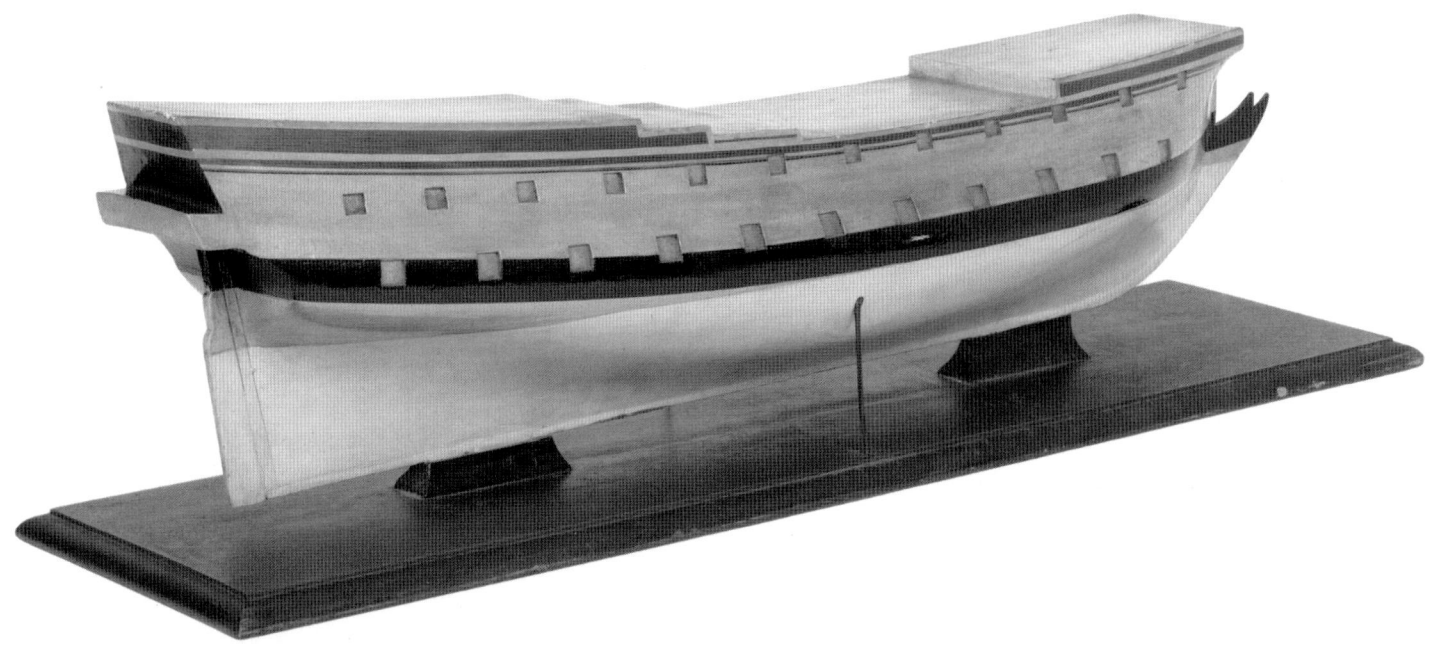

Christ (Chrisot) Central America
Dimensions & tons: unknown. Men: 220.
Guns: 44
Added to his squadron of fourteen vessels by CdE Jean Bernard de Saint-Jean, Baron de Pointis; took part in the capture of Cartagena de Indias 5.5.1697. Captured by the Dutch 6.1697 near Cartagena and probably returned or resold to the Spanish. Captured by the British 10.1702 at Vigo and renamed *Monmouth's Prize*. Wrecked 11.1702 on a reef while departing Vigo.

TRITON. 40, later 44 guns. Designed and built by Blaise Pangalo. Pierced for ten pairs of LD guns. Ordered April 1696 and named on 12 June.
Dimensions & tons: 123ft 0in x 31ft 6in x 14ft 0in (39.96 x 10.23 x 4.55m). 500 tons. Draught 16ft/16½ft (5.20/5.36m). Men: 250 in war, 230 peace, +5/7 officers.
Guns: 40 in war in 1698 (36 peace): LD 20 x 12pdrs; UD 20 x 6pdrs. 4 x 3pdrs added to QD from 1699.
Triton Brest Dyd.
K: 7.1696. L: 1.1697. C: 1697. Lent as a privateer to François Saupin (wood merchant in Brest) under CV Jacques Dandenne, as part of a squadron of four vessels, 1697. Captured by the British at Vigo 22.10.1702, becoming HMS *Triton*; sold 1709.

DAUPHINE. 42, later 40 guns. Designed by Pierre Chaillé, and built by Philippe Cochois. Pierced for eleven pairs of LD guns.
Dimensions & tons: 121ft 0in, 103ft 0in x 33ft 0in x 13ft 0in (39.31, 33.46 x 10.72 x 4.22m). 500 tons. Draught 12ft/14ft (3.90/4.55m). Men: 250 in war, 230 peace, +6 officers.
Guns: 42 in war in 1698 (30 peace): LD 22 x 12pdrs; UD 20 x 6pdrs. Reduced by 2 x 12pdrs from 1699.
Dauphine Le Havre.
K: 8.1696. L: 9.1.1697. C: 1697. Burnt at Vigo 23.10.1702 by her own crew to avoid capture by Anglo-Dutch forces.

THÉTIS. 44 guns. Designed and built by Honoré Malet. Pierced for eleven pairs of LD guns.
Dimensions & tons: 122ft 0in x 33ft 0in x 12ft 6in (39.63 x 10.72 x 4.06m). 550 tons. Draught 14½ft/15½ft (4.71/5.035m). Men: 200 in war, 150 peace, + 5/6 officers.
Guns: 44 in war (30 peace): LD 22 x 12pdrs; UD 22 x 6pdrs.

Thétis Rochefort Dyd.
K: 1696. L: 1697. C: 1697. Captured (along with the *flûtes Gloutonne*, *Éléphant*, and *Jean et Jacques* that she was escorting) 25.2.1705 off Cape Finisterre by HMS *Exeter* of Byng's squadron.

RENOMMÉE. 48 guns. Designed by Antoine Tassy. Pierced for eleven pairs of LD guns.
Dimensions & tons: 120ft 0in x 32ft 0in x 14ft 6in (38.98 x 10.39 x 4.71m). 550 tons. Draught 15½ft/16ft (5.035/5.20m). Men: 250 in war, 200 peace, + 5 officers.
Guns: 48 in war (40 peace): LD 22 x 12pdrs; UD 22 x 8pdrs; QD 4 x 6pdrs or 4pdrs. Reported in 1701–2 with LD 10 x 18pdrs + 12 x 8pdrs, UD 12 x 6pdrs + 10 x 4pdrs; later with LD 22 x 12pdrs, UD 22 x 6pdrs, QD 4 x 4pdrs; and from 1708 with LD 22 x 12pdrs; UD 20 x 8pdrs; QD 6 x 4pdrs.
Renommée Bayonne.
K: 1697. L: early 1698. C: 6.1698. Struck 1712.

ADÉLAÏDE. 44 guns. Designed and built by François Coulomb. Named 1.1.1698. Pierced for ten pairs of LD guns.
Dimensions & tons: 115ft 0in, 90ft 0in x 30ft 6in x 13ft 5in (37.36, 29.24 x 9.91 x 4.36m). 400 tons. Draught 14ft/14ft 4in (4.55/4.66m). Men: 220 in war, 180 peace, + 6 officers.
Guns: 44 in war (30 peace): LD 20 x 12pdrs; UD 20 x 6pdrs; QD 4 x 4pdrs. In 1704 reduced to 36 guns (LD 18 x 12pdrs, UD 18 x 6pdrs).
Adélaïde Toulon Dyd.
K: 12.1697. L: 10.1.1699. C: 1699. Scuttled at Toulon in 7.1707 but refloated 11.1707. Chartered between 1708 and 1714 to the *Compagnie du Cap Nègre* (to resupply Spain with grain), the *Compagnie des Indes Orientales*, and the *Compagnie de l'Asiento* (for the slave trade). Wrecked in a hurricane off Cap Corrientes (Cuba) 10.10.1714 (with 78 dead). Wreck discovered 2003.

MAUREPAS. 46 guns. Designed and built by François Le Brun. Pierced for eleven pairs of LD guns. Initially named *Hasardeux*, but renamed in June 1698 while on the stocks and transferred to the *Compagnie des Indes Orientales*.
Dimensions & tons: 123ft 0in x 32ft 0in x 13ft 6in (39.96 x 10.39 x 4.39m). 600 tons. Men: 350/180.
Guns: 46 in war: LD 20 x 12pdrs; UD 22 x 6pdrs; QD 4 x 4pdrs.

The decorative works of *Renommée*, 48-gun ship of 1698. (*Souvenirs de Marine*, Plate 148)

Maurepas Port Louis, near Lorient Dyd.
   K: 1.1698. L: 10.1698. C: 1.1699. Re-purchased by the Navy from the *Compagnie des Indes Orientales* in early 1703. Chartered by the King under LV Fontenay to escort to India that company's *Pondichéry*, 1703–4. Sold back to the Company in 1705.

HÉROS. 46 guns. Designed and built by Pierre Coulomb for the *Compagnie des Indes Orientales*, but purchased by the Navy in June 1702, and probably completed by Desjumeaux. Pierced for ten pairs of LD guns. Initially 4th Rank, but moved to 3rd Rank in 1704–5, then to 4th Rank in 1708. Rebuilt at Rochefort 1721–22, to 3rd Rank in 1736–7, and to 4th Rank in 1738.
   Dimensions & tons: 121ft 0in x 34ft 0in x 13ft 10in (39.31 x 11.04 x 4.49m). 700 tons. Draught 17ft/17½ft (5.52/5/68m). Men: 280 in war, 186 peace.
   Guns: 46 in war (30 peace): LD 20 x 12pdrs; UD 20 x 8pdrs; QD 6 x 4pdrs. 42 from 1709: LD 4 x 18pdrs + 10 x 12pdrs; UD 22 x 8pdrs; QD 6 x 2pdrs. 46 from 1715: LD 20 x 18pdrs; UD 20 x 8pdrs; QD 6 x 6pdrs. 50 from 1729: LD 20 x 18pdrs; UD 22 x 8pdrs; QD 8 (later 4) x 4pdrs.
Héros Port Louis, near Lorient Dyd.
   K: 3.1700. L: 24.11.1700. C: 9.1702. Condemned 1740 at Rochefort

PURCHASED VESSELS (1701). Two mercantile ships were purchased in 1701 from the *Compagnie de la Mer du Sud* (South Sea Company) and fitted as 4th Rank ships and attached to Rochefort. The first was British-built (in *c*.1698) while the second had been built in Bayonne by Félix Arnaud in 1692.
Indien England
   Dimensions & tons (1709): 121ft 0in x 31ft 0in x 12ft 0in (39.31 x 10.07 x 3.90m). 466 tons. Draught 15ft/16ft (4.87/5.20m). Men: 240 in war, 160 peace, +4/7 officers.
   Guns: 40 in war (26 peace): LD 20 x 12pdrs; UD 20 x 8pdrs. 46 from 1704: LD 20 x 12pdrs; UD 20 x 6pdrs; QD 6 x 4pdrs (4 from 1708). 44 from 1715: LD 22 x 12pdrs; UD 22 x 6pdrs.
   Struck 1719 at Rochefort.
Africain Bayonne.
   Dimensions & tons (1708): 115ft 0in x 30ft 0in x 11ft 6in (37.36 x 9.75 x 3.74m). 450 tons. Draught 5ft/15½ft (4.87/5.04m). Men: 250 in war, 166 peace, +4/6 officers.
   Guns: 42 in war (28 peace): LD 10 x 12pdrs + 12 x 8pdrs; UD 20 x 6pdrs. 46 from 1704: LD 20 x 12pdrs; UD 20 x 6pdrs; QD 6 x 4pdrs. 42 from 1715: LD 22 x 12pdrs; UD 20 x 6pdrs.
   Struck 1723 at Rochefort and hulked.

DRYADE. 46 guns. Designed and built by Philippe Cochois for privateering at the request of Gratton and Ruotte, citizens of Le Havre, who funded the cost of the construction. Pierced for eleven pairs of LD guns. Raised from 5th to 3rd Rank in 1704–5, then reduced to 4th Rank in 1706.
   Dimensions & tons: 118ft 0in x 30ft 4in x 12ft 6in (38.33 x 9.85 x 4.06m). 423 tons. Draught 13ft/15ft (4.22/4.87m). Men: 280 in war, 200? peace, +4 officers.
   Guns: 46 in war: LD 4 x 12pdrs + 18 x 8pdrs; UD 20 x 6pdrs; QD 4 x 3pdrs. From 1705 had LD 22 x 8pdrs, UD 22 x 6pdrs.
Dryade Le Havre.
   K: 7.1702. L: 21.10.1702. C: 12.1702. Lent as a privateer to Gratton and Ruotte, 1702–5. Lent as a privateer to CGA Nicolas de Lambert 1706; part of CdE Claude, Comte de Forbin's squadron 1706–7. Lent for privateering to citizens of Le Havre 1707–9; captured 10.1709 by the British (with 15 killed) but not taken into the RN.

SYLVIE. 40 guns. Designed and built by François Coulomb; ordered as a commercial vessel, but purchased for the Navy in October 1703 while on the stocks. Pierced for eleven pairs of LD guns.
   Dimensions & tons: 120ft 0in, 99ft 0in x 32ft 0in x 15ft 0in (38.98, 44.82 x 10.39 x 4.87m). 400 tons. Draught 14ft (4.55m). Men: 250 (in war), +4 officers.
   Guns: 40 in war (34 peace): LD 22 x 12pdrs; UD 16 x 6pdrs; QD 2 x 4pdrs.
Sylvie Toulon Dyd.
   K: 1701. L: 30.11.1703. C: 1.1704. Renamed *Princesse* 9.4.1704. Sold for commercial service 1706.

PARFAITE Class. 40 guns. Designed and built by François Coulomb. Pierced for eleven pairs of LD guns. Both ships were probably scuttled at Toulon in July 1707 to avoid the bombardment by British bomb vessels, and were then refloated in November.
   Dimensions & tons: 120ft 0in, 99ft 0in x 32ft 4in x 15ft 0in (38.98, 32.16 x 10.50 x 4.87m). 400 tons. Draught 14ft/16ft (4.55/5.20m). Men: 250 in war, 200 peace.
   Guns: 40 in war (34 peace): LD 22 x 12pdrs; UD 16 x 6pdrs; QD 2 x 4pdrs.
Parfaite Toulon Dyd.
   K: 10.1703. L: 29.9.1704. C: 11.1704. Probably scuttled at Toulon in 7.1707, but refloated. Wrecked 29.11.1718 in Famagusta Bay (Cyprus).
Vestale Toulon Dyd.
   K: 1704. L: 1705. C: 1705. Probably scuttled at Toulon in 7.1707, but refloated. Sold 1725 at Toulon (by Order of 6.2.1725), but sale cancelled. Became a careening hulk by Order of 15.5.1729. BU by Order of 26.6.1739.

GRIFFON. 44, later 50 guns. Designed by Blaise Pangalo, and built by Pierre Coulomb for privateering, at the request of CFL Robert de Fondelin, who funded the cost of the construction. Pierced for eleven pairs of LD guns. Briefly in the 3rd Rank *c*.1736–38.
   Dimensions & tons: 124ft 6in x 33ft 0in x 14ft 6in (40.44 x 10.72 x 4.71m). 500 tons. Draught 15ft/16ft 8in (4.87/5.41m). Men: 280 in war, 250 peace.
   Guns: 44 in war (36 peace): LD 22 x 12pdrs; UD 22 x 6pdrs (24 from 1729). 4 x 4pdrs added on the QD in 1715.
Griffon Port Louis, near Lorient Dyd.
   K: 9.1704. L: 10.1.1705. C: 3.1705. Lent as a privateer to CFL Robert de Fondelin, 1705, then lent as a privateer to CV Des Augiers, as part of a squadron of three vessels, for a campaign in the West Indies, 1705–6. Lent as a privateer to LG Jean-Baptiste Ducasse, as part of a squadron of three vessels in support of the Spanish Navy in the West Indies, 1711. Lent to Antoine Crozat, Marquis de Châtel, Director of the *Compagnie de l'Asiento*, 1712. Captured by the British off Cap Finisterre on 19.8.1712, but returned to France at end of hostilities in 1713. Loaned to the *Compagnie des Indes* in 8.1741. Condemned late 1744 at Brest, and BU 1748.

THÉTIS. 44 guns. Designed and built by Blaise Pangalo and his son Joseph, for privateering, at the request of Jacques Du Val d'Éspréménil, a citizen of Le Havre, who funded the cost of the construction. Pierced for eleven pairs of LD guns. Named 6 May 1705.
   Dimensions & tons: 117ft 0in x 30ft 0in x 14ft 0in (38.01 x 9.75 x 4.55m). 500 tons. Draught 15ft (4.87m). Men: 220 in war.
   Guns: 44 in war (38 peace): LD 20 x 12pdrs; UD 22 x 6pdrs; QD 2 x 4pdrs.

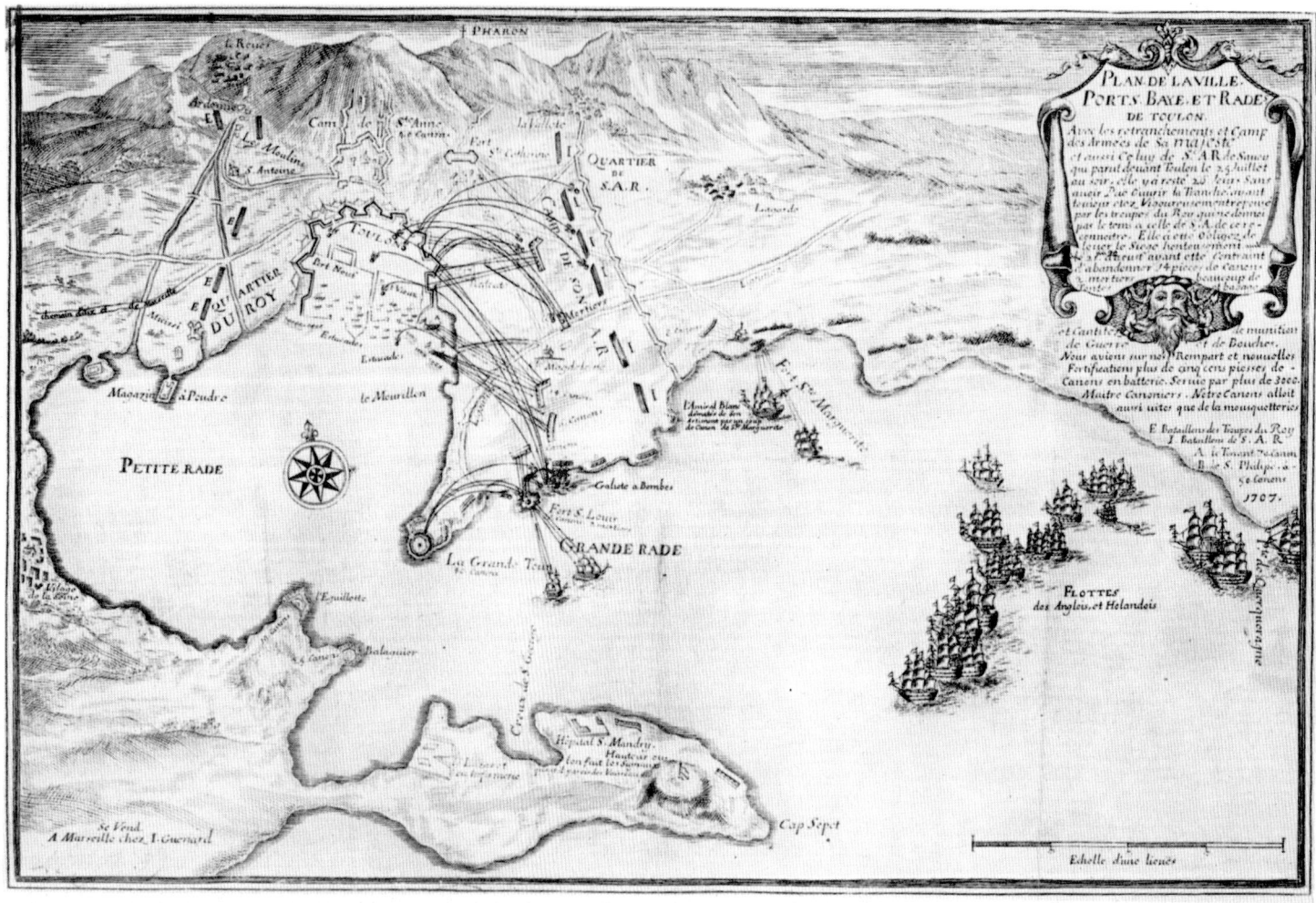

A contemporary French map of the siege of Toulon in 1707, showing arcs of fire of the besieging forces. Ships huddled together in the Old Port made a potentially easy target for mortar fire, so many of the ships were deliberately scuttled to reduce the risk of destruction by fire. Among these were probably the 4th Rank *Cheval Marin*, *Rozendal*, *Adélaïde*, *Parfaite* and *Vestale*; however, all five were restored to service after the siege.

Thétis Brest Dyd.

  K: early 1705. L: 20.6.1705. C: late 1705. Lent as a privateer to Jacques Du Val d'Esprémenil, 1705–6. Captured by HM Ships *Windsor* and *Weymouth* off Boston on 6.5.1711, but not added to British Navy.

Ex-BRITISH PRIZES (1704). The English Fourth Rate *Falmouth* of a 123-foot type (British measurement) ordered in 1690 and 1692 was captured by René Duguay-Trouin's squadron off the Isles of Scilly on 15 August 1704. The English Fourth Rate *Coventry* of a 130-foot type ordered in 1694 and 1695 was taken by a squadron of French privateers off the Isles of Scilly 4 August 1704. Both were added to the French Navy as 4th Rank ships with their names unchanged. Three similar ships built to the same specification as the *Coventry* (*Salisbury*, *Pendennis* and *Blackwall*) were captured by the French in 1703 and 1705, but were added as 3rd Rank ships and so will be found in Chapter 3.

Falmouth Edward Snelgrove, Limehouse

  Ordered 1.1.1692. L: 25.6.1693.

  Dimensions & tons (British measurements in French feet): 116ft 4in, 95ft 3in x 31ft 7in (37.79, 33.18 x 10.26m). 500 tons (French).

  Guns: 48 in war: probably LD 22 x 12pdrs; UD 22 x 6pdrs; QD 4 x shorter 6pdrs.

  Sold for merchant service at Brest 1.1706. Grounded near Buenos Aires 9.1706 with nearly all of her crew dead of illness and privation. Burned by the Spanish 2.1707.

Coventry Deptford Dyd.

  Ordered 16.11.1693. L: 20.4.1695.

  Dimensions & tons (French measurements): 124ft 0in x 32ft 0in x 11ft 6in (40.28 x 10.39 x 3.74m). 520 tons. Draught 16ft (5.20m). Men: 250 in war, 200 peace.

  Guns: 50 in war (46 peace): LD 22 x 16pdrs; UD 20 x 7pdrs (22 from 1708); QD 8 x 4pdrs (6 from 1707).

  Lent to the *Compagnie de l'Asiento* 1706. While she was at Basimentos (near Puerto Bello) with *Mignon* (see Chapter 3), she was retaken by HMS *Portland* 17.5.1709 (while carrying 20,000 pieces-of-eight) and BU 1709.

Ex-DUTCH PRIZES (1703–1705). Two Dutch 40-gun ships were captured during this period, the *Rotterdam* (built in 1695) in May 1703 and the *Mercurius* (built in 1692) in 1705.

Rotterdam Rotterdam.

  Dimensions & tons: 108ft 4in x 29ft 3in x 10ft 2in (35.19 x 9.50 x 3.30m). 450 tons. Draught 11ft (3.57m). Men: 200 in war, 150 peace.

  Guns: 40 in war (30 peace): LD 18 x 12pdrs; UD 18 x 6pdrs; QD 4 x 4pdrs.

In service 1704 as a *flûte* with 12 guns. Struck 1706 at Toulon.
Mercure Zeeland.
  Dimensions & tons: unknown
  Guns: 40/42
  Captured by the British in January 1707 while on loan as a privateer.

ATALANTE Class. 42, later 44 guns. Designed and built by Philippe Cochois. Pierced for eleven pairs of LD guns.
  Dimensions & tons: 116ft 0in x 31ft 0in x 12ft 0in (37.68 x 10.07 x 3.90m). 388 tons. Draught 15ft (4.87m). Men: 250 in war, 140 peace.
  Guns: 42 in war (36 peace): LD 22 x 8pdrs; UD 20 x 6pdrs. 44 guns from 1709 (est.): LD 12 x 12pdrs + 10 x 8pdrs; UD 8 x 8pdrs + 10 x 6pdrs; QD 4 x 4pdrs. 40 from 1715: LD 22 x 8pdrs; UD 18 x 6pdrs.
Atalante Le Havre.
  K: 4.1706. L: 2.1707. C: 5.1707. Lent as a privateer to CdE Jean-Baptiste Ducasse, as part of a squadron of seven vessels, in support of the Spanish Navy for escorting galleons, 1707. Lent as a privateer to CFL Jean-François Du Clerc, as part of a squadron of four vessels, for operations off the Brazilian coast, 1709–10. Hulked at Rochefort from 1723, later condemned and BU by 1733.
Diane Le Havre.
  K: 4.1706. L: 2.1707. C: 5.1707. Lent as a privateer to CdE Jean-Baptiste Ducasse, as part of a squadron of seven vessels, in support of the Spanish Navy for escorting galleons, 1707. Lent as a privateer to CFL Jean-François Du Clerc, as part of a squadron of four vessels, for operations off the Brazilian coast, 1709–10. Struck 1711.

AMAZONE. 40 guns. Designed and built by Blaise Pangalo, for privateering at the request of CV René Duguay-Trouin, who funded the cost of construction. Originally a *frégate légère*, but re-classed as 4th Rank in 1708; briefly classed as 3rd Rank from c.1736–38. A *demi-batterie* type, pierced for four pairs of LD guns and thirteen UD pairs.
  Dimensions & tons: 118ft 0in x 31ft 6in x 13ft 0in (38.33 x 10.23 x 4.22m). 450 tons. Draught 15ft/16½ft (4.55m). Men: 230 in war, 200 peace.
  Guns: 40 in war (36 peace): LD 6 x 12pdrs; UD 26 x 8pdrs; QD 8 x 4pdrs. From 1714 an extra pair of 12pdrs was added on LD.
Amazone Toulon Dyd.
  K: 9.1706. L: 16.4.1707. C: 10.1707. Lent as a privateer to CV René Duguay-Trouin, for all his operations 1707-12; took part in the capture of Rio de Janeiro 9.1711. Hulked 1741 at Brest, and taken to pieces 1748.

GLOIRE. 38 guns. Designed by Laurent Hélie, and built by Hélie and Alain Donnard, according to the '*méthode du Sieur Gobert*', for privateering, at the request of CV René Duguay-Trouin, who funded the cost of construction. A *demi-batterie* type, pierced for five pairs of LD guns and twelve UD pairs.
  Dimensions & tons: 120ft 0in, 106ft 0in x 32ft 6in x 12ft 0in (38.98, 34.43 x 10.56 x 3.90m). 500 tons. Draught 14ft/14½ft (4.55/4.71m). Men: 210 in war, 130 peace, + 5 officers.
  Guns: 38 in war (34 peace): LD 10 x 12pdrs; UD 24 x 8pdrs; QD 4 x 4pdrs.
Gloire Lorient Dyd.
  K: 29.1.1707. L: 18.4.1707. C: 6.1707. Lent as a privateer to CV René Duguay-Trouin, as part of a squadron of six vessels, 1707–9. Captured 6.5.1709 by HMS *Chester* in the Channel, becoming HMS *Sweepstakes*; sold 6.1716.

ARGONAUTE. 42, later 50 guns. Designed and built by Blaise Pangalo for privateering at the request of *Brigadier des gardes de la marine* Emmanuel Auguste de Cahideuc, Comte Du Bois de La Motte, future *Vice-amiral* and holder of the Grand-Cross of the *Ordre du Saint-Esprit* (1762), who funded the cost of construction. Pierced for eleven pairs of LD guns.
  Dimensions & tons: 120ft 0in x 32ft 0in x 15ft 3in (38.98 x 10.39 x 4.95m). 500 tons. Draught 17ft/17½ft (5.52/5.68m). Men: 270 in war, 230 peace.
  Guns: 42 in war (40 peace): LD 16 x 12pdrs; UD 22 x 8pdrs; QD 4 x 4pdrs. 50 guns from 1715: LD 16 x 12pdrs + 4 x 8pdrs; UD 22 x 8pdrs; QD 8 x 4pdrs.
Argonaute Toulon Dyd.
  K: 9.1708. L: 14.11.1708. C: 12.1708. Lent as a privateer to EV

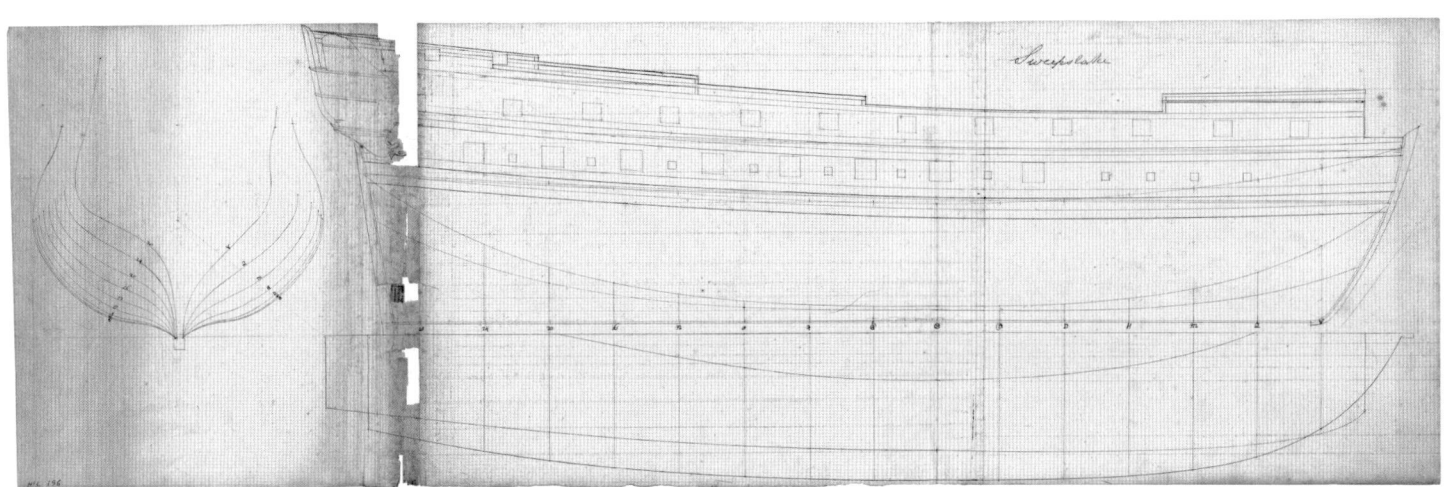

Admiralty draught of the *Sweepstakes*, ex-French *Gloire* captured in 1709. It is one of the oldest surviving plans of a French prize, although the drawing itself is undated. In *Souvenirs de Marine Vice-amiral* Pâris reproduces a plan of this ship with only three pairs of gunports on the lower deck, right aft, so presumably as designed. Under Duguay-Trouin's command she would have needed at least five pairs for her known LD armament, while in British service she had eight (as shown in this draught), so it was clearly easy – and a great temptation – to increase the guns on the lower deck of *demi-batterie* ships. (National Maritime Museum, London J8262)

Emmanuel Auguste de Cahideuc, Comte Du Bois de La Motte. Lent as a privateer to CV Duguay-Trouin, as part of a squadron of thirteen vessels, 1711–12; took part in the Capture of Rio de Janeiro 9.1711. Condemned 12.1720 and hulked until 1745. BU 1.1746.

In July 1707 five ships then in the Navy's 4th Rank were at Toulon during the siege of that port by Sir Clowdisley Shovell's fleet – the *Cheval Marin, Adélaïde, Parfaite, Vestale* and *Rozendal*. All were probably scuttled on Louis's orders on 29 July to prevent their being destroyed by the bombardment and then refloated in around October or November.

In September 1715 there remained eleven ships of the 4th Rank – *Héros, François, Cheval Marin, Alcyon, Protée* (ex-*Amphitrite*), *Parfaite, Vestale, Griffon, Amazone, Atalante* and *Argonaute* – plus the ex-mercantile purchases *Indien* and *Africain*, and the ex-British prizes *Jerzé* (ex-HMS *Jersey*) and *Blakoual* (ex-HMS *Blackwall*), the last two having originally been added as 3rd Rank ships. All carried a primary battery of 12pdr guns on the lower deck, apart from the *Héros* and *Cheval Marin*, which carried 18pdrs, and the *Atalante*, which had only 8pdrs.

(D) Vessels acquired from 1 September 1715

No new 4th Rank ships were added after 1708, and the postwar Navy was run down. When construction resumed in 1721, eight ships were built during the 1720s, the first pair taking the names of earlier ships recently deleted. Two of the eight (*Tigre* and *Alcyon*) had main batteries of 18pdrs, while the other six had 12pdr batteries. All were pierced for eleven pairs of LD guns, apart from the *Néréide* of 1724 (ten pairs). After 1730, only three more 4th Rank ships were built (plus one rebuilding) with 12pdr LD batteries, but six other vessels were built as '*demi-batterie*' type, *i.e.* having only a partial battery on the LD but a complete battery of lesser guns on the UD. All had been lost or withdrawn from service by 1760, but from 1748 a new type of single-decked cruiser with a battery of 12pdrs was introduced – see Section (E).

A detailed and annotated internal profile of the *Néréide*, 42 guns, drawn by Blaise Ollivier in early 1724, as reproduced by *Vice-amiral* Pâris in his *Souvenirs de Marine*. In this elaborate drawing the young Blaise documented his design for the largest ship both designed and built by himself and his father Joseph during their stay at Rochefort in 1720–1724. The profile shows unusual structural features like the diagonal ceiling in the hold, while the accompanying transverse section (not reproduced here) shows iron plate knees. Blaise's technical creativity continued with the diagonal planking in his 64-gun *Fleuron* of 1729. (*Souvenirs de Marine*, Plate 261)

***ARGONAUTE* Class.** 46 guns. Designed and built by Laurent Hélie, with decoration by master-sculptor François-Charles Caffiéri. While the design length was 122ft (as reported below), the *Argonaute* by 1741 actually measured 120ft 6in (39.14m) and the *Parfaite* 121ft 10in (39.58m).

Dimensions & tons: 122ft 0in x 32ft 0in x 15ft 0in (39.63 x 10.39 x 4.87m). 500/1,050 tons. Draught 16ft (5.2m). Men: 270 in war, 240 peace, +5 officers.

Guns: 46 in war (40 peace): LD 22 x 12pdrs; UD 24 x 6pdrs; QD nil.

Argonaute Brest Dyd.
K: 1721. L: 7.1722. C: 1.1723. Carried Stanislas Leczinski (claimant to Polish throne) to Danzig during 1733. Hulked 1741 at Brest, but re-armed 1743. Converted to 28-gun fireship at Brest 4.1746. Hulked 1.1748 at Brest, and BU 1762.

Parfaite Brest Dyd.
K: 1722. L: 1.1723. C: 1723. Converted to fireship at Brest 4.1746. Burnt by accident at Chibouctou 10.1746.

***NÉRÉIDE*.** 42 guns. Designed and built by Blaise Ollivier (as *sous-constructeur* at Rochefort from January 1721, his father Joseph being *constructeur* here since the previous month). Pierced for ten pairs of LD guns, and eleven pairs on the UD, with no guns on the *gaillards*. Reconstructed 1733 at Rochefort by Julien Geslain.

Dimensions & tons: 122ft 0in, 108ft 0in x 33ft 8in x 13ft 2in (39.63, 35.08 x 10.94 x 4.28m). 540/1,100 tons. Draught 15/17½ft (4.87/5.68m). Men: 260 in war, 230 peace, +5 officers.

Guns: 42 in war (40 peace): LD 20 x 12pdrs; UD 22 x 6pdrs; QD nil.

Néréide (*Nereïde*) Rochefort Dyd.
K: 1722. L: 24.3.1724. C: 11.1724. Condemned at Rochefort 1743 and BU.

***JASON*.** 50, later 52 guns. Designed and built by Jacques Poirier. Rebuilt 1744–45 at Rochefort.

Dimensions & tons: 126ft 6in, 107ft 6in x 34ft 0in x 15ft 4in (41.09, 34.92 x 11.04 x 4.98m). 600/1,150 tons. Draught 15½ft/17½ft (5.035/5.68m). Men: 300 in war, 250 peace, +5 officers.

Guns: 50 in war (44 peace): LD 22 x 12pdrs; UD 24 x 8pdrs; QD 4 x 4pdrs (6 x 4pdrs later). In 1740, re-armed with 22 x 18pdrs, 24 x 6pdrs and 6 x 4pdrs, but in 1745 restored to original guns (but with QD retaining 6 x 4pdrs).

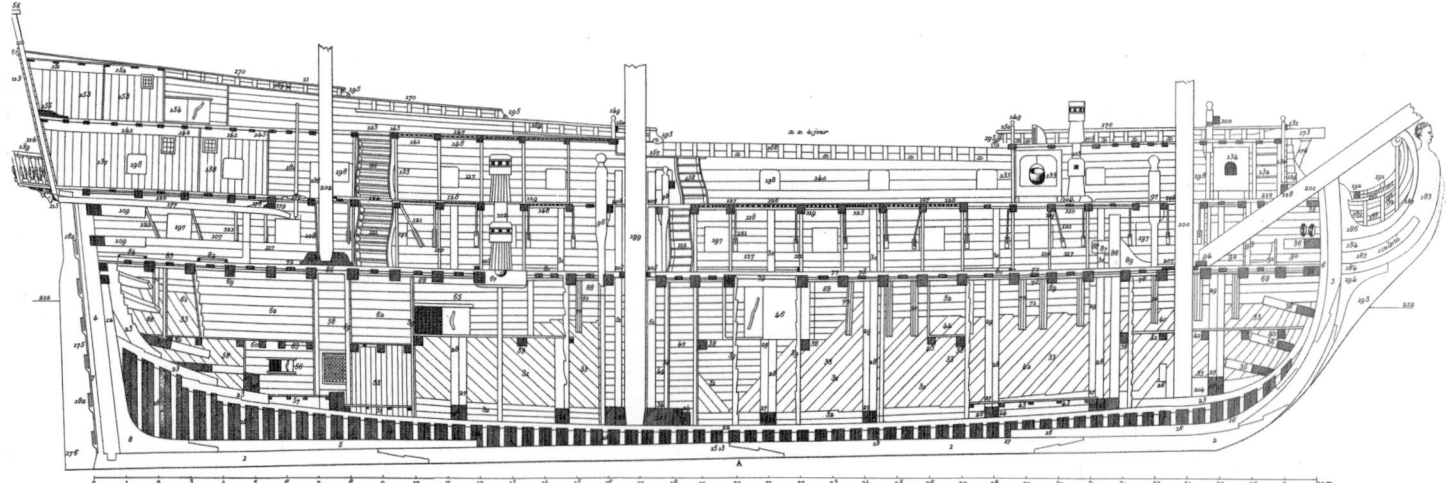

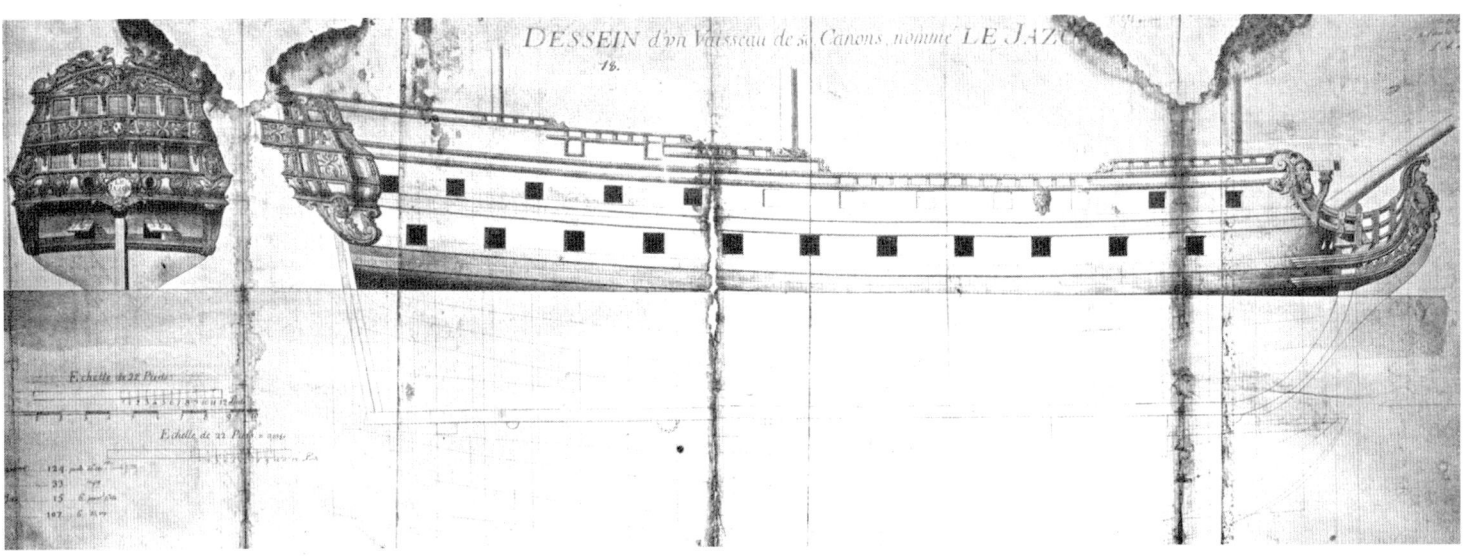

The original draught of the *Jason*, 50 guns, of 1724. Another of the 'pictorial' style plans, like the *Amphitrite* reproduced in Chapter 3, and likewise published by *Vice-amiral* Pâris. Following her reconstruction at Brest in 1744–45, she was re-armed at Rochefort in December 1746 for the account of the *Compagnie des Indes*. (*Souvenirs de Marine*, Plate 276)

Jason Le Havre.
  K: 4.1723. L: 1724. C: 8.1724. Captured by Anson's squadron at Battle off Cape Ortegal 14.5.1747, becoming HMS *Jason*; sold 3.1762.

TIGRE. 50 guns. Designed and built by Blaise Coulomb, this vessel was ordered on 19 August 1722 and named on 25 June 1723. Rebuilt at Lorient from September 1747 to June 1748.
  Dimensions & tons: 131ft 0in x 37ft 10in x 16ft 6in (42.55 x 12.29 x 5.36). 700/1,109 tons. Draught 14ft 1in/17¼ft (4.57/5.60m). Men: 340 in war, 300 peace, +5/9 officers.
  Guns: 50 in war (40 peace): LD 22 x 18pdrs; UD 24 x 8pdrs; QD 4 x 4pdrs.
Tigre Toulon Dyd.
  K: 5.6.1723. L: 19.10.1724. C: 3.1725. Took part in Battle of Toulon 22.2.1744. Condemned 1754 and BU at Québec.

GLOIRE. 46 guns. Designed and built by Jacques Poirier.
  Dimensions & tons: 122ft 0in x 32ft 6in x 15ft 6in (39.63 x 10.56 x 5.035m). 500/1,100 tons. Draught 16ft/17½ft (5.20/5.68m). Men: 270 in war, 240 peace, + 5 officers.
  Guns: 46 in war (40 peace): LD 22 x 12pdrs; UD 24 x 6pdrs; QD nil.
Gloire Le Havre.
  K: 4.1724. L: 5.1725. C: 1727. Took part in expeditionary force to Danzig in 1733–34 and with *Fleuron* captured the Russian frigate *Mittau* (below) 6.1734. Rebuilt 1736–42 at Brest (see below).

ALCYON. 50 guns. Designed and built by René Levasseur. Named 6 September 1724 (name often rendered *Alcion*).
  Dimensions & tons: 132ft 0in x 36ft 4in x 18ft 0in (42.88 x 11.80 x 5.85m). 760/1,300 tons. Draught 16ft/18ft 7in (5.20/6.04m). Men 360 in war, 300 peace, +5/9 officers.
  Guns: 50 in war (40 peace): LD 24 x 18pdrs; UD 22 x 8pdrs; QD 4 x 4pdrs.

Alcyon Toulon Dyd.
  K: 3.1725. L: 14.3.1726. C: 4.1727. Burnt in action with HM Ships *Hussard* and *Dolphin* in the Atlantic 23.11.1759, all hands lost.

RUBIS. 50, later 54 guns. Designed by Jacques Poirier or Julien Geslain.
  Dimensions & tons: 131ft 0in, 117ft 0in x 35ft 6in x 15ft 0in (42.55, 38.01 x 11.53 x 4.87m). 751/1,200 tons. Draught 17ft/17½ft (5.52/5.68m). Men: 295 in war, 225 peace, +5 officers.
  Guns: 50 in war (44 peace): LD 22 x 12pdrs (18pdrs from 1734); UD 24 x 8pdrs; QD 4 x 4pdrs (8 from 1741, 6 from 1746).
Rubis Le Havre.
  K: 5.1728. L: 18.11.1728. C: 3.1729. Captured in Battle off Cape Ortegal by Anson's squadron 14.5.1747 while in use as a 26-gun *flûte*, becoming HMS *Rubis*; BU 1748.

AQUILON. 42, later 48 guns. Designed and built by Jean-Armand Levasseur, and ordered in 1731 as a 40-gun frigate, she was named on 16 July 1731. Two-decked ships with 44 guns or less were listed as frigates by the late 1740s while those credited with 46 or more were listed in the 4th Rank.
  Dimensions & tons: 127ft 0in x 35ft 0in x 17ft 0in (41.25 x 11.37 x 5.52m). 660/1,200 tons. Draught 16ft/18ft (5.20/5.85m). Men: 250 in war, 200 peace, +5/9 officers.
  Guns: 42 in war (30 peace): LD 22 x 12pdrs; UD 20 x 6pdrs. 48 guns from 1739: LD 24 x 12pdrs; UD 24 x 6pdrs (replaced by 8pdrs in 1747). 46 guns by 1746 (2 x 12pdrs removed).
Aquilon Toulon Dyd.
  K: 7.1731. L: 24.11.1733. C: 4.1734. Wrecked 14.5.1757 in Audierne Bay while avoiding pursuit.

Ex-RUSSIAN PRIZE (1734). While having fewer than the 40 guns usually deemed the minimum for a two-decked frigate, the Russian *Mitau*, briefly captured in 1734, falls into this category. Built as a one-off design by G. A. Okunev and I. S. Ramburg, this vessel probably carried the ordnance set out below (no definitive record exists). En route from Kronstadt to Danzig in 1734, she was intercepted by a French squadron under CV Jean-André, Marquis de Barrailh in June 1734, but was very quickly exchanged for 2,100 French troops, captured by the Russians at Danzig.
  Dimensions & tons (converted from Russian data): 113ft 11in x 29ft

An engraving published in 1750 showing three of the prizes from Anson's victory off Cape Ortegal in May 1747. On the left is the *Rubis*, 54 guns, with the stern view of *Jason*, 52 to the right, and *Diamant*, 50 between them. *Diamant*, carrying 24pdrs in her main battery, was classed as a 3rd Rank, while the *Rubis* (normally with 18pdrs, but armed en flûte at this time) and the *Jason* and *Gloire* (the latter not shown here) with 12pdrs were 4th Rank ships. The careful rendition of the decorative details suggests that the artist had actually seen the ships – by no means always the case with eighteenth century published prints. (National Maritime Museum, London PZ5886)

5in x 14ft 3in (37.00 x 9.56 x 4.63m). Tons unknown. Men: 100.
Guns (probable): LD 20 x 12pdrs; UD 12 x 6pdrs (Russian 1723 Establishment).

Mittau St Petersburg.
K: 23.12.1731. L: 28.5.1733. C: 1733. Captured 6.1734 in the Baltic; returned to Russia 9.1734 at Copenhagen in exchange for captured French troops, following the end of the Danzig conflict of 1733–35.

GLOIRE. 44 guns. Designed by Pierre Morineau. A rebuilding of Poirier's vessel of 1725.
Dimensions & tons: 124ft 0in x 33ft 6in x 12ft 6in (40.28 x 10.88 x 4.06m). 600 tons. Draught 16½ft (5.36m). Men: 280 in war, 200 peace, + 5 officers
Guns: 44 in war (40 peace): LD 22 x 12pdrs; UD 22 x 8pdrs.

Gloire Le Havre.
K: 1736. L: 1742. C: 1742. Captured by HMS *Prince George* of Anson's squadron at Battle of Cape Ortegal 14.5.1747, becoming HMS *Glory*. Sold 15.3.1763.

AUGUSTE. 52 guns. Designed and built by Jean Geoffroy.
Dimension & tons: 128ft 10in x 34ft 6in x 15ft 0in (41.85 x 11.21 x 4.87m). 650/1,277 tons. Draught 13¾ft/15¼ft (4.47/4.95m). Men: 320 in war, 250 peace, +5 officers.
Guns: 52 in war (46 peace): LD 22 x 12pdrs; UD 24 x 8pdrs; QD 6 x 4pdrs.

Auguste Brest Dyd.
   K: 1739. L: 1.1741. C: 5.1741. Captured 9.2.1746 by HMS *Portland*, becoming HMS *Portland's Prize*; sold 5.1749.

ATALANTE. 32 guns. *Demi-batterie* type, designed and built by Joseph Véronique-Charles Chapelle. Actually classed as a *frégate légère* in view of her reduced number of guns.
   Dimensions & tons: 115ft 0in x 30ft 10in x 14ft 0in (37.36 x 10.02 x 4.55m). 441/850 tons. Draught 14¼ft/15½ft (4.63/5.035m). Men: 200 in war, 160 peace, +4/6 officers.
   Guns: 32 in war (24 peace): LD 10 x 12pdrs; UD 22 x 8pdrs.
Atalante Toulon Dyd.
   K: 11.1740. L: 16.3.1741. C: 6.1741. Re-armed as a *flûte* 3.1759, with just 12 x 8pdrs. Burnt 16.5.1760 in the St Laurence in action with HM Ships *Diana* and *Lowestoft*.

At the start of 1739 the 4th Rank comprised twelve ships – *Héros* 1701, *Griffon* (1705), *Amazone* (1707), *Parfaite* (1722), *Argonaute* (1722), *Jason* (1724), *Tigre* (1724), *Alcyon* (1724), *Gloire* (1726), *Aquilon* (1733), *Néréide* (1733) and *Rubis* (1737). At the start of 1742 and of 1743 the 4th Rank comprised eleven ships – those extent in 1739 with the removal of the *Héros* and *Amazone*, but with the addition of the new *Auguste* (1739).

AURORE. 46 guns. Designed (in October 1742) and built by Pierre Morineau. France's last 12pdr-armed two-decker, subsequent ships carrying this calibre as their battery ordnance being either *demi-batterie* (with a small number of LD weapons) or true frigates with no gunports on their LD. In his manuscript *Repertoir de construction* Morineau describes a design very similar to *Aurore* but with 8pdrs on the UD and a variant, evidently a *demi-batterie*, with 14 x 12pdrs and 26 x 8pdrs.
   Dimensions & tons: 129ft 0in, 116ft 0in x 35ft 0in x 16ft 6in (43.51, 37.68 x 11.37 x 5.36m). 600/1,200 tons. Draught 14ft 5in/17ft (4.68/5.52m). Men: 320 in war, 270 peace, +5/8 officers.
   Guns: 46 in war (40 peace): LD 22 x 12pdrs; UD 24 x 6pdrs; QD nil.
Aurore Rochefort Dyd.
   K: 11.1742. L: 3.4.1745. C: 1745. Hulked at Brest 10.1748; struck 1753.

DIANE. 28 guns. *Demi-batterie* type, designed and built by François Coulomb Jnr. Named 4 December 1743.
   Dimensions & tons: 115ft 0in x 30ft 4in x 13ft 8in (37.36 x 9.85 x 4.44m). 436/900 tons. Draught 13¾ft/15¼ft (4.47/4.95m). Men: 300, +4 officers.
   Guns: 28 in war (20 peace): LD 4 x 12pdrs; UD 22 x 8pdrs; QD 2 x 4pdrs.
Diane Toulon Dyd.
   K: 12.1743. L: 19.12.1744. C: 4.1745. Captured (while armed *en flûte*, with 20 guns and 105 men) by HMS *Boreas* 4.1758 off the American coast, but not added to the British Navy.

ÉTOILE. 46 guns. *Demi-batterie* type, designed and built by Pierre Chaillé, Jnr. Rated as a 50-gun *frégate légère* with 30 x 12pdrs in 1746; however, this appears to be an incorrect record as the ship was only long enough to carry 26 guns on the UD, and was reported elsewhere with 46 guns.
   Dimensions & tons: 128ft 6in, 115ft 0in x 37ft 0in x 13ft 6in (41.74, 37.36 x 12.02 x 4.39m). 650/1,200 tons. Draught 15ft/17ft (4.87/5.52m). Men: 250, +5 officers.
   Guns: 46 in war: LD 8 x 18pdrs; UD 26 x 12pdrs, QD/Fc 12 x4pdrs.
Étoile Le Havre.
   K: 11.1744. L: 4.1745. C: 8.1745. Burnt off Cape Ortegal to avoid capture by Anson's squadron 14.5.1747.

Ex-BRITISH PRIZE (1745). The British 40-gun (Fifth Rate) *Anglesea* was captured on 8 April 1745 off Kinsale by the 54-gun *Apollon* and added to the French Navy. She was usually listed as a frigate of 44 guns or less but was sometimes shown in the 1750s as a ship of the 4th Rank with 50 or 52 guns.
   Dimensions & tons: 121ft 8in, 107ft 0in x 33ft 6in x 16ft 0in (39.52, 34.76 x 10.88 x 5.20m). 600/1,100 tons. Draught 15½ft/17½ft (5.035/5.68m). Men: 250, +5 officers.
   Guns: LD 20 x 18pdrs; UD 20 x 9pdrs; QD 4 x 6pdrs.
Anglesea Hugh Blaydes, Hull.
   Ordered 28.9.1741. K: 11.1741. L: 3.11.1742. C: 6.2.1743. Condemned 1753 at Brest and hulked; still extent in 1771.

Ex-BRITISH PRIZE (1746). The British 50-gun (Fourth Rate) *Severn* was captured on 29 October 1746 in the Channel by *Terrible* and *Neptune* (of Conflans's squadron) and added to the French Navy.
   Dimensions & tons: 130ft 0in, 111ft 0in x 36ft 0in x 14ft 10in (42.23, 36.06 x 22.69 x 4.82m). 600/1,100 tons. Draught 15½ft/16ft (5.035/5.20m). Men: ?
   Guns: LD 20 x 12pdrs; UD 22 x 6pdrs; QD 6 x 6pdrs.
Severn Henry Johnson, Blackwall.
   Ordered 13.5.1734. K: 10.2.1735. L: 28.3.1739. C: 23.9.1739. Recaptured off Cape Finisterre by HMS *Devonshire* of Hawke's fleet 25.10.1747, but not restored to British service.

Ex-BRITISH PRIZE (1746). The British 32-gun privateer frigate *Pearl* was captured on 22 July 1746 in the Mediterranean by the *Fier* and *Flore*, and added to the French Navy as *Perle*. Her specifications are unknown, although she may previously have been the RN frigate *Pearl* (20 x 12pdrs, 20 x 6pdrs), which was rebuilt at Deptford in 1726 and sold out of the service in June 1744. She was recaptured in January 1748 by the British near Martinique.

JUNON. 44 guns. *Demi-batterie* type, designed and built by Pierre Chaillé, Jnr. On 19 December 1746 the naval minister ordered Mathieu de Clieu de Derchigny, the *Intendant* at Le Havre, to have Chaillé build two new frigates there during 1747, one to be of 24 guns (with a 6pdr battery) and the other of 30 guns (with a battery of 8pdrs). He was to build the first to the lines of his *Émeraude* of 1744, and on 30 December the minister approved building the second to the lines of Chaillé's *Embuscade* of 1745 (see Chapter 5 for details of both these 8pdr-armed ships). The royal order naming the two ships *Junon* and *Favorite* respectively was forwarded to Le Havre on 30 January 1747.
   As built *Junon* bore no resemblance to *Émeraude* and emerged as a large *demi-batterie* ship much closer in concept to Chaillé's *Étoile* of 1745. In September 1747 CV Louis-Roger Franssure de Villers, who assisted Derchigny, observed to Chaillé that *Junon* was built strongly enough to carry 18pdrs instead of 12pdrs, and in January 1748 he assessed her as capable of carrying 42 guns including thirty 18pdrs (of which two were aft in the gun room) and twelve 6pdrs on the *gaillards* (eight aft and four forward). A rather different armament primarily of 12pdrs was ultimately fitted. Described by a critic as 'shaped like a fish, full forward and thin aft', she drew an excessive seven feet more aft than forward when launched and had to offload her guns and stores to get out of the shallow basin at Le Havre. Her commander's first impressions of her sailing qualities were favourable, and both she and *Favorite* were retained for overseas service after the end of the War of the Austrian Succession while most other ships were decommissioned. *Junon* was listed as a frigate with 44 guns when completed and thereafter usually with 40 guns, though she was listed as a 46-gun 4th Rank ship in 1752 and as a 50-gun 4th Rank in 1754 and 1756.

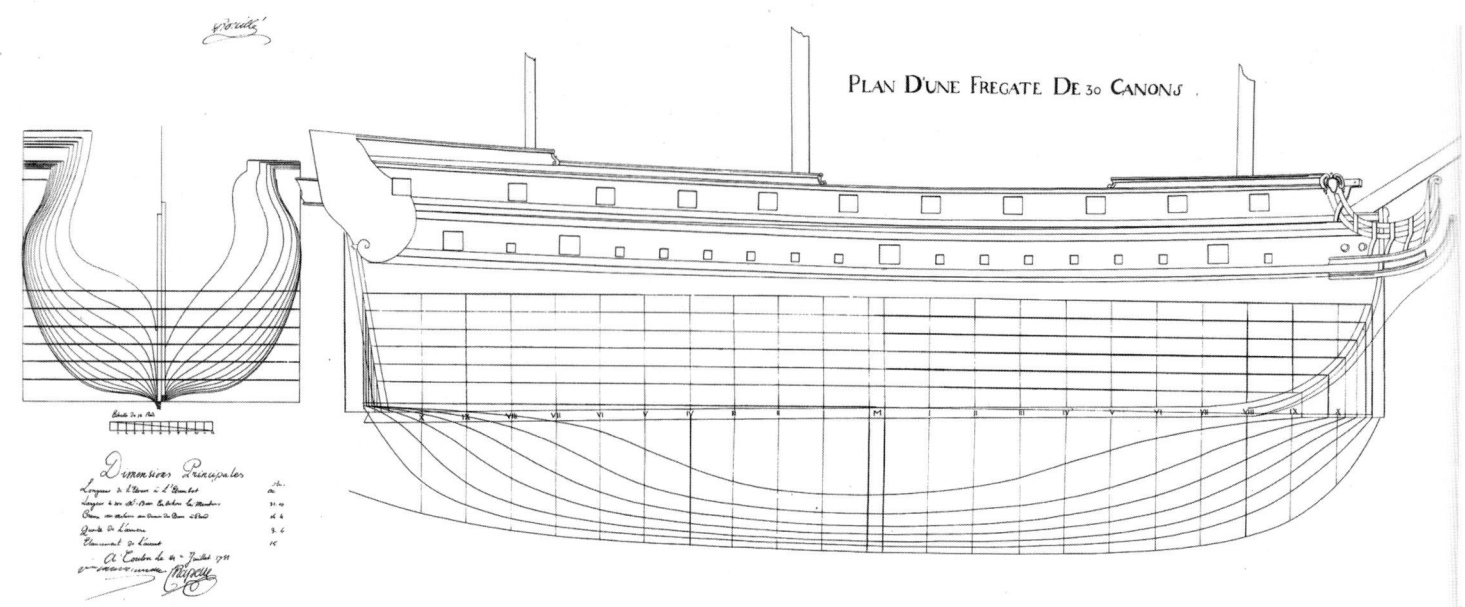

Lines plan of the *Rose* (30 guns) of 1752, drawn in July 1751, one of the last *demi-batterie* type frigates in the French Navy. The nearest British equivalents were 24-gun Sixth Rates, whose construction had been abandoned about 1748 in favour of frigate-form ships. These had carried two or four 9pdrs on the lower deck aft, compared with the eight 12pdrs in the *Rose*. The height of the lower sills of the *Rose*'s gunports on this deck above the waterline was only 3¾ft, restricting the employment of her 12pdrs in anything but the calmest seas. Original from the Toulon Archives.

Dimensions & tons: 137ft 4in x 37ft 6in x 16ft 6in (44.61 x 12.18 x 5.36m). 780/1,300 tons. Draught 17½ft (5.68m). Men: 300 in war, 250 peace, +5/8 officers.
Guns: LD 6 x 18pdrs; UD 28 x 12pdrs, QD/Fc 10 x 6pdrs.
Junon Le Havre.
K: 1.1747. L: 2.12.1747. C: 3.1748. Departed Le Havre for Brest 12.5.1748. Cruised to the Caribbean with *Favorite* in 1749. Arrived at Toulon on 19.10.1750, took part in the Tripoli campaign of 4–9.1752, and was part of La Galissonnière's squadron in April 1756 sent to occupy Minorca, being present at the Battle of Minorca on 20.5.1756. Severely damaged 2.1.1757 by striking a rock while entering Port Mahon in bad weather, condemned as unfit for sea 19.1.1757. Decommissioned and hulked there 27.1.1757, and sold at end of that year.

ROSE. 30 guns. *Demi-batterie* type, designed and built by Joseph Véronique-Charles Chapelle. Named 11 June 1750. Her 12pdr gunports were distributed with one pair forward, a second pair amidships, and two pairs aft, with 14 pairs of rowports also on the LD.
Dimensions & tons: 120ft 4in, 101ft 6in x 31ft 10in x 14ft 4in (39.09, 32.97 x 10.34 x 4.66m). 290/750 tons. Draught 12½ft/14ft 5in (4.06/4.68m). Men: 240 in war, 210 peace, +5/9 officers.
Guns: LD 8 x 12pdrs; UD 22 x 8pdrs; QD/Fc nil.
Rose Toulon Dyd.
K: 17.8.1751. L: 22.10.1752. C: 5.1754. Part of La Galissonnière's squadron in April 1756 sent to occupy Minorca and present at the Battle of Minorca on 20.5.1756. Grounded on the coast of Malta 30.6.1758 after combat with HMS *Thames*, and burnt to avoid capture.

ABÉNAKISE Class. 38 guns. *Demi-batterie* type, designed and built by René-Nicolas Levasseur. Following her capture by the British, *Abénakise*'s conversion to meet British requirement resulted in the removal of her 18pdrs (with the LD gunports permanently sealed, thus becoming a 'true' frigate). Her hull lines served as a model for the design of two types of British frigates.
Dimensions & tons: 139ft 0in, 126ft 0in x 36ft 0in x 14ft 3in (45.15, 40.93 x 11.69 x 4.63m). 650/1,200 tons. Men: 260, +5 officers.
Guns: LD 8 x 18pdrs; UD 28 x 12pdrs; QD 2 x 6pdrs.
Abénakise Québec
K: 7.1753. L: 6.1756. C: 11.1756. Captured by HMS *Unicorn* off Brest 23.11.1757, becoming HMS *Aurora*; BU 4.1763.
Québec Québec
K: 6.1756. Never launched, suspended 10.1758 and destroyed on the stocks at Québec by the RN when they attacked that town in 9.1759.

FORTUNE. 26 guns. This frigate was designed by Jean-André Couturier who owned her. She languished incomplete afloat at Marseille from 1757 until the naval minister ordered her purchase on 28 August 1762. The purchase followed in September. She had the hull dimensions of a 54-gun two-decker but her entire armament was on the LD in small gunports; the UD had only small ports for oars.
Dimensions & tons: 135ft 9in, 124ft 9in x 34ft 3in x 16ft 6in (44.10, 40.52 x 11.13 x 5.36m). 600/1,100 tons. Men: 150, +8 officers (as *flûte*)
Guns: LD 26 x 12pdrs; UD nil.
Fortune Marseille
K: 1756. L: 11.1757. C: 1.3.1763. Converted to a *flûte* at Rochefort during 1766 and renamed *Ambulante* 2.8.1766. Sailed 23.11.1766 for Port Louis, Île de France, and wrecked there 29.2.1772 during a typhoon.

(E) 12pdr-armed frigates (*Frégates de 12*) acquired from 1747

With the achievement of the 8pdr-armed 'true' frigate in the early 1740s (see Chapter 5), it was inevitable that thoughts would turn swiftly to the practicalities of enlarging the concept to create frigates with a heavier battery. The 12pdr-armed 'true' frigates, built from 1747 onwards, were the successors to the *Frégates du Premier Ordre* covered in the preceding section, which had generally carried a battery of 12pdrs on their lower decks and a second battery of 6pdrs or 8pdrs on the deck above. With the primary battery removed to the upper deck, the former gun deck could be sealed and lowered to the waterline, providing improved accommodation for the crew while giving the primary guns a freeboard large enough that their ports could be opened and the guns used even in heavy weather.

In his treatise written following the building of the 8pdr-armed *Médée*, Blaise Ollivier had conceived of a frigate carrying thirty 12pdrs in a single battery, with a length of 127ft (41.25m); the fifteen gunports per side would need to be 2ft 4in (0.76m) wide, and separated by 5ft 10in (1.89m) between ports. The concept was put into practice in 1747 with the building of the first 12pdr-armed frigate, entrusted to Chaillé at Le Havre. A second was awarded to Morineau at Rochefort (Ollivier had died in 1746). However, the first was built with fourteen pairs of guns in its battery, while the second had just thirteen ports per side, allowing a separation of 6ft 4in (2.06m) between gunports. Independently, in 1748 Joseph Véronique-Charles Chapelle at Toulon had advocated a 12pdr-armed frigate with twelve ports per side, and one was ordered in early 1749 – the only 12pdr frigate to be built with this arrangement.

FAVORITE. 38 guns. Designed by Pierre Chaillé, Jnr, and originally ordered 19 December 1746 as a 30-gun frigate with an 8pdr battery, to have been of similar design to *Embuscade* (see note under *demi-batterie* frigate *Junon* above). Built simultaneously with *Junon* (see above), *Favorite* turned out to be a bit longer and narrower than *Embuscade* but was probably otherwise similar. In January 1748 she was assessed as easily able to carry twenty-eight 12pdrs and at least eight or ten 6pdrs on the gaillards (which were pierced for twelve), essentially the armament that she received. The British similarly rearmed *Embuscade* with 12pdrs after capturing her in April 1746, resulting in a very successful ship.

Dimensions & tons: 127ft 0in x 33ft 0in x 14ft 0in (41.25 x 10.72 x 4.55m). 500–600/1,100 tons. Draught 16ft (5.20m). Men: 200 (peace), +5 officers.

Guns: UD 28 x 12pdrs; QD/Fc 10 x 4pdrs.

Favorite Le Havre.
K: 1.1747. L: 18.9.1747. C: 1.1748. Departed Le Havre for Brest 4.5.1748. Cruised to the Caribbean with *Junon* in 1749 and to St Domingue between November 1750 and October 1751. Returned to Brest with CE Hubert de Brienne, Comte de Conflans and his entourage as passengers and with a crew decimated by yellow fever. Off most lists of frigates after 1752, reduced to a barracks hulk at Brest by 1757, last mentioned 1.1771.

HERMIONE. 26 guns. Designed and built by Pierre Morineau with no openings on the LD (except two set into the stern counter to let some light into the gunroom), this order inaugurated the classic 12pdr-armed frigate which remained the dominant type for a half-century. Morineau's manuscript *Repertoir de construction* also contains a variant of this design that had 17 rowports per side on the unarmed LD, requiring raising both decks about a foot and a half (0.49m) to get the oarports 30in (0.81m) above the waterline.

Dimensions & tons: 127ft 6in, 119ft 0in x 33ft 8in x 13ft 8in (41.42, 38.66 x 10.94 x 4.44m). 640/1,100 tons. Draught 14ft 2in/16ft 8in (4.60/5.41m). Men: 286 in war, 220 peace, +7 officers.

Guns: UD 26 x 12pdrs, QD nil (later fitted with 2 x 6pdrs, replaced 1758 by 4 x 4pdrs).

Hermione Rochefort Dyd.
K: 1748. L: 28.4.1749. C: 8.1750. Captured by HMS *Unicorn* 23.11.1757 in the Atlantic, and added to the British Navy as HMS *Unicorn's Prize*; retaken 1758 and reverted to *Hermione*, but taken by the British again in 8.1759 although not re-added to British Navy.

GRACIEUSE. 24 guns. Designed and built by Joseph Véronique-Charles Chapelle. Named on 21 April 1749. This design retained an unarmed LD for accommodation, but – unlike the *Hermione* – this level was pierced for eleven rowports per side. Rebuilt 1770–71 at Toulon.

One of the first French 12pdr-armed 'true' frigates, *Hermione*, 26 guns, launched in 1749 (an earlier frigate, the *Favorite* of 1747, also had all its 12pdrs on the upper deck but had originally been ordered to carry 8pdrs). Drawing by László Veres after an original in the Rigsarkivet, Copenhagen. By eliminating all the apertures on the lower deck, the freeboard (height of the lower sills of the centre gunports above the waterline) was 7ft, enabling all her guns to be fought in any ordinary sea state while minimising the windage of the hull. Originally she carried no secondary guns on her gaillards, but these were added later. Proportionally, the ship has a much deeper hull than became the norm for later French frigates, suggesting a concern to ensure the longitudinal girder strength of the ship.

Confusingly, the French *Compagnie des Indes* also built and operated a frigate of the same name at the same time, built at Lorient-Caudan by Nicolas Leveque and launched on 30 November 1754. Pierced to mount 22 guns (6pdrs), she was only carrying 14 when captured off Pondicherry in October 1750 by the boats of HMS *Southsea Castle*.

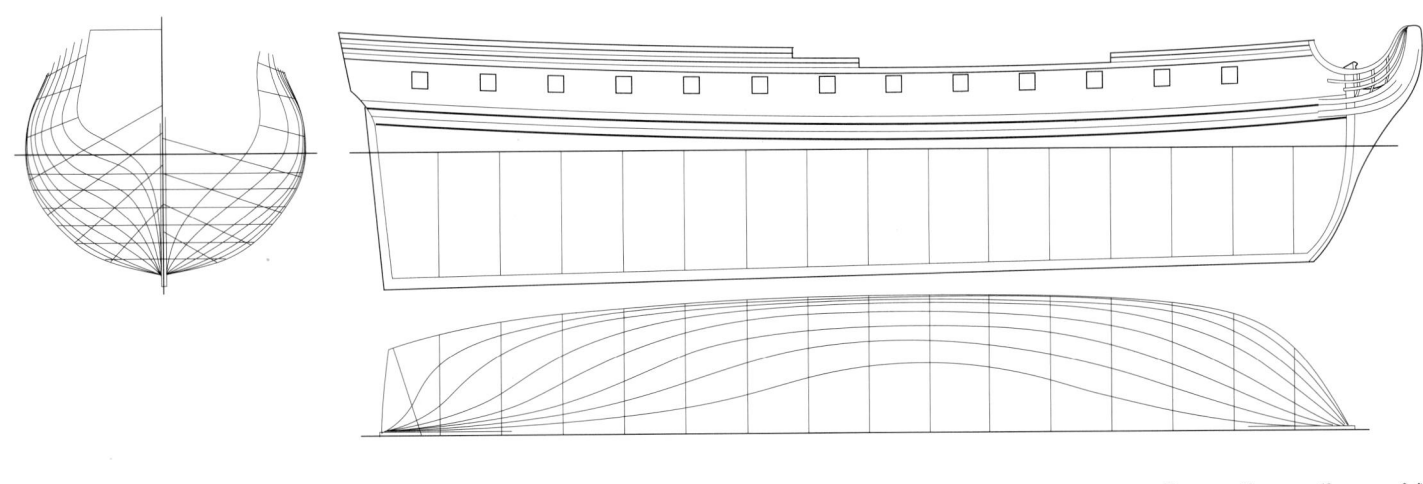

Dimensions & tons: 124ft 0in, 108ft 0in x 32ft 8in x 16ft 6in (41.25, 35.08 x 10.61 x 5.36m). 550/980 tons. Draught 14ft 4in/15ft 3in (4.66/5.28m). Men: 210/230, +8/9 officers.

Guns: UD 24 (later 26) x 12pdrs, QD/Fc nil. The 12pdrs were replaced by 8pdrs in 1779 at Toulon.

Gracieuse Toulon Dyd.
K: 5.1749. L: 23.4.1750. C: 3.1751. Part of La Galissonnière's squadron in April 1756 sent to occupy Minorca and present at the Battle of Minorca on 20.5.1756. Sold 2.1781 at Marseille, and chartered in 1782–83 as a troop transport to the Caribbean.

Following the above three prototypes, no further 12pdr-armed frigates were begun until the outbreak of the Seven Years' War, when three much bigger vessels (to carry fifteen pairs of battery guns) were begun at Le Havre. A further 12pdr-armed frigate was purchased on the stocks, but no further large frigates were ordered during the war.

DANAÉ. 40 guns. Designed and built by Jean-Joseph Ginoux. The first of the larger 12pdr-armed frigates, with fifteen pairs of UD gunports.

Dimensions & tons: 141ft 0in, 128ft 0in x 35ft 6in x 11ft 0in (45.80, 41.58 x 11.53 x 3.57m). 600/1,150 tons. Draught 13ft/15ft (4.22/4.87m). Men: 350.

Guns: UD 30 x 12pdrs; QD 8 x 6pdrs; Fc 2 x 6pdrs.

Danaé Le Havre.
K: 3.1756. L: 13.9.1756. C: 5.1757. Captured by HM Ships *Southampton* and *Melampus* off Dunkirk 28.3.1759, becoming HMS *Danae*; BU at Chatham 14.6.1771.

HÉBÉ Class. 36 guns. Designed and built by Jean-Joseph Ginoux, and pierced for fifteen pairs of UD guns. While designed to carry a 12pdr battery (including one pair of 18pdrs), the *Hébé* was completed with a much lighter armament, presumably as structural weaknesses were discovered. Another frigate named *Danaé*, probably to the same design, was ordered on 10 May 1762 along with two corvettes from Sieur Le Clerc at Le Havre. The contract was cancelled in June 1762 because the Minister found the price to be too high. It was reinstated in August 1762 but cancelled around November 1762.

Dimensions & tons: 144ft 6in x 34ft 6in x 14ft 11in (46.94 x 11.21 x 4.85m). 950/1,300 tons. Draught 16ft/16ft 4in (5.20/5.31m). Men: 300 in war, 250 peace.

Guns: (design) UD 2 x 18pdrs + 28 x 12pdrs; QD 6 x 6pdrs. (actual) UD 2 x 12pdrs + 28 x 8pdrs; QD 8 x 4pdrs.

Hébé Le Havre.
K: 9.1756. L: 7.6.1757. C: 2.1758. Grounded in the Canaries 9.1763; refloated but condemned and BU at Tenerife.

Harmonie Le Havre.
K: 9.1756. L: 8.6.1757. C: 3.1758. Leased at Dunkirk for commerce for an expedition to the West Indies, but wrecked 12.1760 while departing from Dunkirk.

An unnamed 40-gun frigate was ordered in early 1758 at Bayonne to plans by the Chevalier De Grassy. The order was postponed on 24 June 1758 for lack of funds, then cancelled.

CHIMÈRE. 32, later 26 guns. Designed by Joseph-Marie-Blaise Coulomb as a privateer (ordered 18 October 1756 by the Marseille Chamber of Commerce) and purchased by the Navy on 10 October 1757 while building; named on same day. Reconstructed 1775 at Toulon.

Dimensions & tons: 136ft 0in x 35ft 8in x 17ft 10in (44.18 x 11.59 x 5.79m). 610/1,200 tons. Draught 13½ft/14½ft (4.39/4.71m). Men: 240 in war, 180 peace, + 4/7 officers; later 190 war, 130 peace.

Guns: UD 26 x 12pdrs, QD 6 x 6pdrs (removed later).

Chimère Toulon Dyd.
K: 1.1757. L: 6.2.1758. C: 7.1758. Loaned for commerce 1780, sheathed with nails 8.1780, and sold 8.1783.

TERPSICHORE. 30 guns. Designed by Antoine Groignard (he had previously built a similar large frigate with 30 x 12pdrs at Lorient for the French East India Co – the *Sylphide* of 1756), and built by Jean-Hyacinthe Raffeau. Named on 22 December 1762. Pierced for 30 guns on the UD, originally with no armament on the *gaillards*. Rebuilt at Rochefort from December 1770 to early 1772.

Admiralty draught of the *Danaé* as captured in March 1759, a ship that created a lot of technical interest among British naval officers. The size of the ship, and its odd *dunette* or poop cabin, cast doubt on whether it should be regarded as a frigate (the draught describes it as a 'French ship of war'); the structural strength of such a long ship was also a matter of concern and, unusually, the draught also lists the dimensions of the principal scantlings. (National Maritime Museum, London J5312)

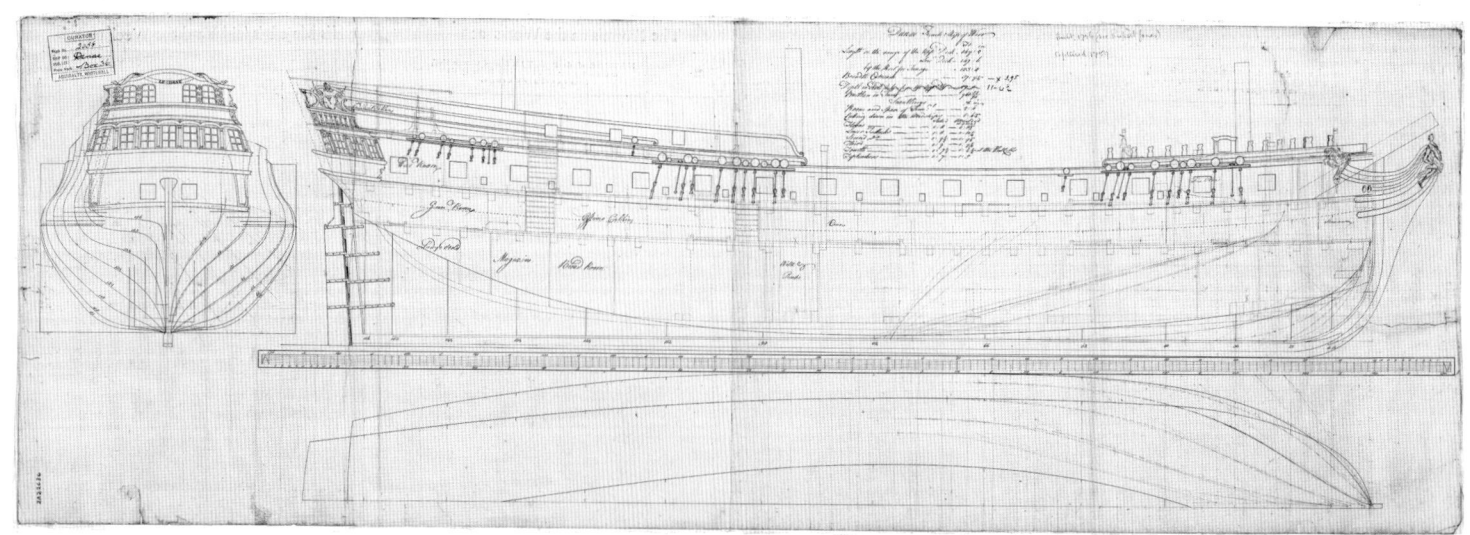

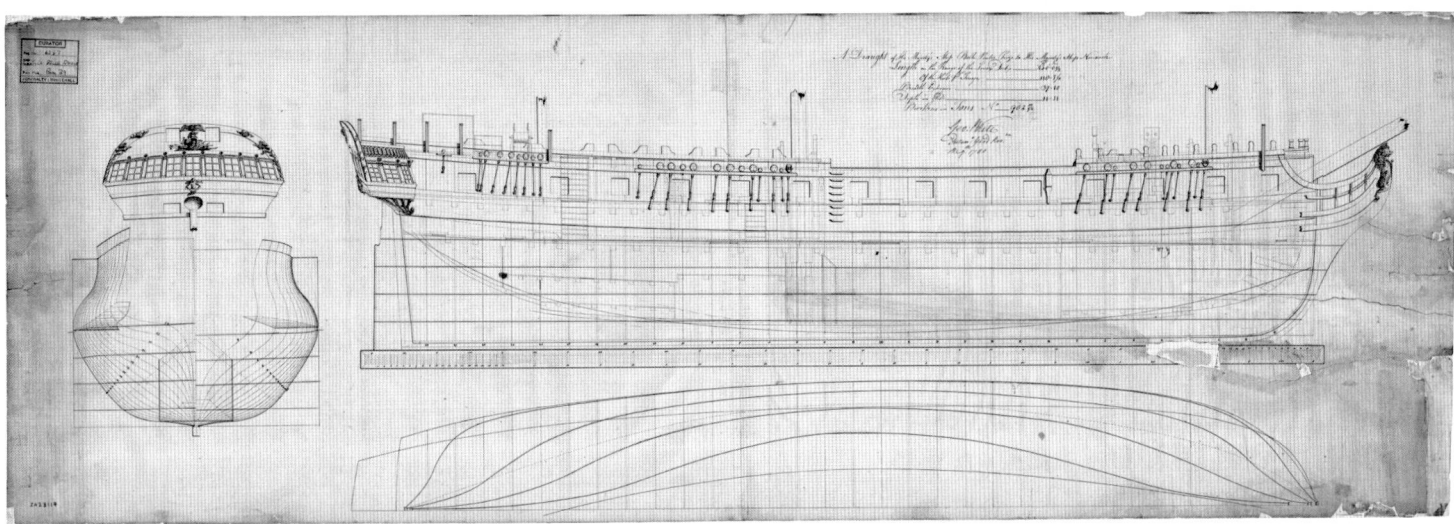

Admiralty draught of the *Belle Poule* as captured, dated Portsmouth Yard 9 November 1780. The body plan shows an exaggerated example of the typical French hull form of a narrow floor, two-turn bilge and acute tumblehome. The ship also demonstrates an extreme attempt to reduce windage, by removing any barricades or rails from the *gaillards* – originally the ship carried no guns on the superstructure, so the lack of protection mattered less, but as captured the ship mounted six 6pdrs firing over the low chocks (necessary as foundations to the breeching rings) visible on the draught; their crews must have been horribly exposed, even to small arms fire, in action. (National Maritime Museum, London J6627)

Dimensions & tons: 140ft 10in x 34ft 2in x 17ft 4in (45.75 x 11.10 x 5.63m). 600/1,000 tons. Draught 15ft (4.87m). Men: 220 (later 270) in war, 150 peace, +7 officers.

Guns: UD 30 x 12pdrs; QD nil (later 6 x 4pdrs later added).

Terpsichore Indret (near Nantes).
  K: 7.1762. L: 10.8.1763. C: 12.1763. Condemned 8.1783 at Brest, and sold 3.1787.

SULTANE. 26 (later 32) guns. Designed and built by Jean-Baptiste Doumet-Revest. Named 16 April 1764. Rebuilt at Toulon from August 1783 to 1784.

Dimensions & tons: 130ft 0in x 34ft 0in x 17ft 4in (42.23 x 11.04 x 5.63m). 650/1,100 tons. Draught 14ft/15ft (4.55/4.87m). Men: 240 (later 262) in war, 180 peace, + 7/8 officers.

Guns: UD 26 x 12pdrs; QD/Fc nil (later 6 x 6pdrs added).

Sultane Toulon.
  K: 3.1764. L: 28.6.1765. C: 5.1766. Floating hospital at Toulon 9.1792. Handed over to the British at Toulon 8.1794 and burnt at their evacuation 18.12.1793.

INFIDÈLE Class. 26/32 guns. Designed by Jean-Joseph Ginoux, and built in pairs at Le Havre; the first pair were named on 21 November 1764, the second pair on 24 July 1765, and the third pair on 28 March 1766; a fourth order was placed in October 1766 (two frigates to be named *Flore* and *Zéphyr*), and two further frigates to this design were intended, but in December 1766 the construction of further frigates at Le Havre was suspended (until 1785) due to the mediocre performance of the earlier ships of this design, and the orders for *Flore* and *Zéphyr* were moved to Brest, where they were built to other designs with 8pdr batteries. *Inconstante* was rebuilt at Brest from December 1775 to May 1776, and *Blanche* from 1776 until early 1779.

Dimensions & tons: 130ft 0in x 34ft 0in x 17ft 0in (42.23 x 11.04 x 5.52m). 600/1,100 tons. Draught 15ft 1in/15ft 7in (4.90/5.06m). Men: 180/240, +7 officers.

Guns: UD 26 x 12pdrs; QD/Fc nil (later possibly 6 x 6pdrs added).

Infidèle Le Havre.
  K: 10.1764. L: 6.1765. C: 9.1765. Became pontoon at Brest 1777, BU there 1783.

Légère Le Havre.
  K: 10.1764. L: 6.1765. C: 9.1765. Struck 1777, but reinstated in 1780; grounded and burnt by the British.

Sincère Le Havre.
  K: 6.1765. L: 12.3.1766. C: 10.1766. Sold at Brest 1777.

Inconstante Le Havre.
  K: 6.1765. L: 26.3.1766. C: 10.1766. Burnt by accident off St Domingue 7.1781.

Blanche Le Havre.
  K: 6.1766. L: 20.10.1766. C: 1.1768. Taken by the British 22.12.1779 off Guadeloupe, became HMS *Blanche*; lost in a cyclone 11.10.1780 in the East Indies.

Enjouée Le Havre.
  K: 6.1766. L: 4.11.1766. C: 1.1768. Became pontoon at Brest 1777, BU there 1783.

DÉDAIGNEUSE Class. 26/32 guns. Designed and built by Léon-Michel Guignace at the Chantier du Roi in Bordeaux; the design was much praised as being superior to the contemporary *Infidèle* Class. The first pair were named on 12 January 1765. The third ship was originally named on 21 March 1766 as *Impérieuse*, but was renamed *Amphitrite* in February 1767 while on the stocks; the fourth ship was named on 31 March.

Dimensions & tons: 132ft 6in, 119ft 0in x 34ft 6in x 17ft 6in (43.04, 38.66 x 11.21 x 5.68m). 620/1,150 tons. Draught 14ft/15ft (4.55/4.87m). Men: 185/220 (later 260), + 7/8 officers.

Guns: UD 26 x 12pdrs; QD/Fc nil (later possibly 6 x 6pdrs added).

Dédaigneuse Bordeaux.
  K: 3.1765. L: 12.4.1766. C: 9.1766. Converted to *flûte* 5.1780, then to pontoon at Rochefort 5.1783. Sold 1784.

Belle Poule Bordeaux.
  K: 3.1765. L: 18.11.1766. C: early 1767. Deployed to Indian Ocean for hydrographic services 1772–76 (under Cmdt. Jacques-Raymond de Grenier). Transported Benjamin Franklin from Brest to America in 1.1778. Single-ship action 17.6.1778 against HMS *Arethusa*. Taken by HMS *Nonsuch* off Ile d'Yeu 16.7.1780.

Amphitrite Bordeaux.
   K: 11.1766. L: 26.10.1768. C: 9.1769. Wrecked 22.1.1791 off the coast of Brittany (or on 30.4.1791).

Tourterelle Bordeaux.
   K: 12.1766. L: 18.9.1770. C: 11.1770. Condemned at Brest 3.1783.

BOUDEUSE. 26 (later 32) guns. Designed and built by Jean-Hyacinthe Raffeau; a much smaller design than elsewhere. Named on 6 June 1765. Refitted at Brest 1775–76.
   Dimensions & tons: 125ft 0in, 118ft 0in x 32ft 8in x 16ft 6in (40.60, 37.36 x 10.61 x 5.36m). 510–580/960–1,030 tons. Draught 13ft 5in/13ft 10in (4.36/4.49m). Men: 240 in war, 180 peace, +7/12 officers.
   Guns: UD 26 x 12pdrs; QD/Fc 6 x 6pdrs. 2 x 36pdr carronades added 5.1794.

Boudeuse Indret (Nantes).
   K: 5.1765. L: 25/26.3.1766. C: 10.1766. Refitted at Brest 1776–78. Under Louis-Antoine de Bougainville, this frigate completed France's first circumnavigation of the world between 15.11.1766 and 16.3.1769 (accompanied by the *flûte Étoile*). Taken by British at Toulon 8.1793, but retaken by French 12.1793; refitted early 1794 at Toulon; condemned and BU 7.1800 at La Valette.

ENGAGEANTE. 26 (later 32) guns, designed and built by Jean-François Étienne. Ordered 18 August 1765 and named 28 March 1766. Refitted at Rochefort 1779–80.
   Dimensions & tons: 134ft 0in, 120ft 0in x 35ft 5in x 17ft 10in (43.53, 38.98 x 11.50 x 5.79m). 600/1,010 tons. Draught 13½/14½ft (4.39/4.71m). Men: 190 (later 250).
   Guns: UD 26 x 12pdrs; QD 6 x 6pdrs (4 x 36pdr *obusiers* added in 1794).

Engageante Toulon Dyd.
   K: 10.1765. L: 14.11.1766. C: 4.1768. Captured by HMS *Concord* in the Channel on 23.4.1794, becoming HMS *Engageante*; hospital ship 7.1794; BU at Plymouth 5.1811.

COQUETTE. 26 guns. A smaller 12pdr frigate was ordered at Toulon in February 1766 – to have been designed and built by Joseph Véronique-Charles Chapelle. However, in May 1768 the order was amended to provide for an 8pdr-armed frigate instead, and this in turn was cancelled finally in 1769 without the keel being laid.
   Dimensions & tons: 132ft 0in x 35ft 4in x 17ft 10in (42.88 x 11.48 x 5.79m).

Lengthened BOUDEUSE Class. 34 guns. Modified design by Jean-Hyacinthe Raffeau, stretched by 5ft from the *Boudeuse* to carry a fourteenth pair of 12pdrs. Named on 6 May 1766. A further order was also placed in 1766 for two 8pdr frigates (named as *Amour* and *Psyché*) to be built to Raffeau's design at Nantes, but in the event the orders were first moved in 1767 to Brest and subsequently cancelled in 1769.
   Dimensions & tons: 130ft 0in x 33ft 0in x 16ft 6in (42.23 x 10.72 x 5.36m). 600/1,050 tons. Draught 13ft 5in/14ft 2in. Men: 190/200/250, +7 officers.
   Guns: UD 28 x 12pdrs; QD 6 x 6pdrs.

Indiscrète Indret.
   K: 3.1766. L: 14.3.1767. C: 8.1767. Converted to *flûte* 4.1780. Condemned 3.1784 at the Cape.

Sensible Indret.
   K: 3.1766. L: 15.3.1767. C: 8.1767. Converted to *flûte* 4.1780, then became a careening pontoon at Lorient 11.1780. Disposed of in 1789.

AURORE. 32 (originally 26) guns, designed and built by Jean-Denis Chevillard. Ordered in early 1766 and named *Envieuse* on 31 March, but renamed *Aurore* in February 1767. Refitted at Toulon 1777–78 and 1784–85.
   Dimensions & tons: 128ft 0in x 33ft 4in x 17ft 0in (41.58 x 10.83 x 5.52m). 600/1,100 tons. Draught 14ft 5in/15ft 4in (4.68/4.98m). Men: 190 (later 250).
   Guns: UD 26 x 12pdrs; QD 6 x 6pdrs.

Aurore Rochefort Dyd.
   K: 9.1766. L: 23.11.1768. C: 1769. Handed over to the British at Toulon on 29.8.1793 and removed by them on evacuation of that port on 18.12.1793, becoming HMS *Aurora*; hulked as prison ship at Gibraltar 1799, and BU there in 1803.

ATALANTE. 32 guns, designed by Jacques-Luc Coulomb as a modified (broadened) version of his *Chimère* of 1758.
   Dimensions & tons: 137ft 0in, 122ft 0in x 35ft 7in x 17ft 11in (44.50, 39.63 x 11.56 x 5.82m). 611/1,140 tons. Draught 13½/14½ft (4.39/4.71m). Men: 220 (later 260), +7 officers.
   Guns: UD 26 x 12pdrs; QD 6 x 6pdrs.

Atalante Toulon Dyd.
   K: 4.1767. L: 1.5.1768. C: 3.1769. Captured by HMS *Swiftsure* off Cork on 6.5.1794, becoming HMS *Espion*; floating battery 1798, then troop transport 1799; wrecked on the Goodwins 16.11.1799.

RENOMMÉE. 30 guns, designed and built by Antoine Groignard. The last of the long-hulled 12pdr frigates to carry a battery of 30 guns, with no provision for secondary armament on the *gaillards*. The height of the gunport sills above the waterline amidships (the 'freeboard') was 6½ft (2.11m).
   Dimensions & tons: 145ft 0in x 34ft 0in x 17ft 8in (46.70 x 11.21 x 5.68m). 600/1,170 tons. Draught 14ft 1in/15½ft (4.57/5.04m). Men: 220 (later 270), +7 officers.
   Guns: UD 30 x 12pdrs; QD nil (on occasion up to 10 x 8pdrs added).

Renommée Brest.
   K: 9.1766. L: 22.8.1767. C: end 1767. Damaged by grounding off Brest 4.1776, but refloated and repaired. Condemned 8.1783 at Brest.

TRITON. 26 to 32 guns. Designed and built by Antoine Groignard for the *Compagnie des Indes*. Ordered purchased for the Navy in April 1770, purchased in October 1771 upon her return from a commercial voyage to the Indian Ocean.
   Dimensions & tons: 130ft 0in, 118ft 0in x 34ft 0in x 12ft 0in (42.23, 38.33 x 11.04 x 3.90m). 600/1,100 tons. Draught 16ft (5.20m). Men: 180/240, +7 officers.
   Guns: UD 26 x 12pdrs; QD/Fc nil or 6 x 6pdrs.

Triton Lorient, Cie des Indes Dyd.
   K: 12.1768. L: 17.10.1769. C: 3.1770. Fitted as a *flûte* and renamed *Cybèle* 7.1779. though the name change took effect only upon her return from St Domingue. Wrecked in America 12.1782.

After 1768, no further 12pdr-armed frigates were begun for the French Navy until after the death of Louis XV in 1774. A new series of 12pdr frigates, built to designs from several contributors, were ordered from early 1777 on, and nearly sixty were built during the following ten years. Many of these were designed and built with fourteen pairs of gunports on the UD, but rarely carried more than the thirteen pairs of guns with which they were actually rated. The nine frigates ordered at St Malo were first given numbers – Nos.1 (*Résolue*), 2 (*Gentille*), 3

The epic battle between the French frigate *Surveillante* and the British *Quebec* on 6 October 1779 was a popular subject for marine artists, this engraving being based on a painting by the well-known painter Robert Dodd. The ships fought one-another to a standstill over four hours, but *Quebec* then caught fire and after burning furiously for a further four hours, blew up and sank. Neither captain survived the action. To add to the heroic nature of the encounter, despite the crippled state of the *Surveillante*, the French made gallant and strenuous efforts to save as many survivors as possible from the stricken British frigate. (Beverley R Robinson Collection, Annapolis 51.7.199)

(*Amazone*), 4 (*Prudente*), 5 (*Gloire*), 6 (*Bellone*), 7 (*Médée*), 8 (*Minerve*, later *Diane*) and 9 (*Néréide*) – and names were not assigned until late in 1777 or early 1778.

IPHIGÉNIE Class. 32 guns. Designed by Léon-Michel Guignace. Two ships built at Lorient by Gilles Cambry and seven by contracts at St Malo (the latter known simply as Nos 1–7 respectively until October 1777 – for the first four – or early 1778 – for the last three), by various builders. *Bellone* was rebuilt during 1787, *Surveillante* from October 1788 to July 1789, *Gentille* from 1793 to April 1794, *Gloire* from 1793 to August 1794, and *Amazone* at Brest from October 1794 to June 1795 – all at Brest.

Dimensions & tons: 134ft 0in, ?120ft 0in x 34ft 6in x 17ft 6in (43.53, 38.98 x 11.21 x 5.68 m). Draught 14/15ft (4.55/4.87m).
Men: 270–278, +9/10 officers.
Guns: UD 26 x 12pdrs; QD 6 x 6pdrs.

Iphigénie Lorient Dyd.
K: 2.1777. L: 16.10.1777. C: 3.1778. Captured by the British at Toulon 29.8.1793, burnt at evacuation of Toulon 12.1793 but recovered by France and repaired. Captured by Spanish squadron 10.2.1795 off Formentera, becoming Spanish *Ifigena*.

Surveillante Lorient Dyd.
K: 8.1777. L: 26.3.1778. C: 5.1778. Single-ship action off Ushant 6.10.1779 resulting in destruction of frigate HMS *Quebec*. Burnt in Bantry Bay during expedition to Ireland 1.1797.

Résolue St Malo (*Constructeur*, Lemarchand)
K: 4.1777. L: 16.3.1778. C: 4.1778. Seized off Tellicherry by HM Ships *Phoenix* and *Perseverance* 11.1791, but restored to France, Captured by HMS *Melampus* in the Irish Sea 14.10.1798, becoming HMS *Resolue*, but never commissioned (used as a receiving ship); BU at Portsmouth 8.1811.

Gentille St Malo (*Constructeur*, Beaugeard de Segrey)
K: 7.1777. L: 18.6.1778. C: 8.1778. Captured by HM Ships *Hannibal* and *Robust* in the Channel 11.4.1795, becoming HMS *Gentille*; sold 9.1802 at Portsmouth.

Amazone St Malo (*Constructeurs*, Guillemant Depeches and Fromy Dupuy)
K: 8.1777. L: 11.5.1778. C: 7.1778. Captured by HMS *Santa Margarita* 28.7.1782, but retaken the next day; wrecked 1.1797 on the Penmarcks.

Prudente St Malo (*Constructeur*, Marion Brillantais)
K: 8.1777. L: 3.1778. C: 7.1778. Captured by the British at St Domingue 22.6.1779.

Gloire St Malo (*Constructeurs*, Guillemant Depeches and Fromy Dupuy)
K: 1.1778. L: 9.7.1778. C: 1.10.1778. Captured by HMS *Astraea* in the Channel 10.4.1795, becoming HMS *Gloire*; sold 24.3.1802 at Deptford.

Bellone St Malo
K: 1.1778. L: 22.8.1778. C: 2.1779. Captured by HM Ships *Melampus* and *Ethalion* in the Irish Sea 12.10.1798, becoming HMS *Proserpine*; sold 27.8.1806.

Médée St Malo
K: 1.1778. L: 20.9.1778. C: 2.1779. Captured by HEICo *Exeter* and

Bombay off Rio de Janeiro 4.7.1800, becoming HMS *Medee* but never commissioned (used as a prison ship); sold 1805.

CHARMANTE Class. 32 guns. Designed and built by Jean-Denis Chevillard. This design was revived in 1785 when three more (*Gracieuse*, *Inconstante* and *Hélène*) were built at Rochefort.

Dimensions & tons: 136ft 0in, 121ft 9in x 34ft 6in x 17ft 6in (44.18, 39.55 x 11.21 x 5.68m). 535/1,089 tons. Draught 15ft 3in/16ft 7in (4.95/5.39m). Men: 270 in wartime/188 in peace.
Guns: UD 26 x 12pdrs; QD 6 x 6pdrs.

Charmante Rochefort Dyd.
K: 4.1777. L: 30.8.1777. C: 1.1778. Wrecked in the approaches to the River Seine 24.3.1780, with just 83 survivors.

Junon Rochefort Dyd.
K: 9.1777. L: 3.1778. C: 5.1778. Took part in the Battle off Ushant 27.7.1778. Wrecked on the Île St Marcouf (by St Vincent) in a hurricane 11.10.1780.

NYMPHE Class. 32 guns. Designed and built by Pierre-Augustin Lamothe. Named on 11 April 1777, 29 September 1777 and 4 December 1778 respectively (the third was initially intended to be built at St Malo).

Dimensions & tons: 135ft 0in, 119ft 0in x 34ft 6in x 17ft 6in (43.85, 38.65 x 11.21 x 5.68 m). Draught 15¾/16½ft (5.12/5.36m). Men: 280, +9/10 officers.
Guns: UD 26 x 12pdrs; QD 6 x 6pdrs.

Nymphe Brest Dyd.
K: 4.1777. L: 18.8.1777. C: 11.1777. Captured by HMS *Flora* off Ushant 10.8.1780, becoming HMS *Nymphe*; wrecked 18.12.1810 off Dunbar in the Firth of Forth.

Andromaque Brest Dyd.
K: 8.1777. L: 24.12.1777. C: 4.1778. Run ashore to avoid capture by Warren's squadron 22.8.1796 and burnt.

Astrée Brest Dyd.
K: 8.1779. L: 16.5.1780. C: 7.1780. Lost 5.1795 in the Atlantic, cause unknown.

SIBYLLE Class. 32 guns. Designed by Jacques-Noël Sané, who built the prototype (named *Sibylle* 11 April 1777) at Brest. Four were built a year later by contract, two at St Malo (by Geoffroy) and two at Nantes (by Jean-Jacques Maistral), and all were named on 4 December 1778 (the *Diane* was originally called *Minerve* until December 1778 while on the stocks). *Néréide* was rebuilt at Rochefort from March 1793 to November 1794.

Dimensions & tons: 135ft 2in, 120ft 6in x 34ft 6in x 17ft 6in (43.91, 39.14 x 11.21 x 5.68m). 600/1,082 tons. Draught 14½/16½ft (4.71/5.36m). Men: 255–260, + 9/10 officers.
Guns: UD 26 x 12pdrs; QD 6 x 6pdrs.

Sibylle Brest Dyd.
K: 4.1777. L: 1.9.1777. C: 11.1777. Took part in Battle of Ushant 7.1778. Captured by HMS *Centurion* off the American coast 22.2.1783; sold to BU at London 1784.

Diane St Malo.
K: 3.1778. L: 18.1.1779. C: 4.1779. Upset in a storm and lost with all hands at St Lucia 17.3.1780.

Néréide St Malo.
K: 10.1778. L: 31.5.1779. C: 8.1779. Captured by HMS *Phoebe* off the Isles of Scilly 20.12.1797, becoming HMS *Nereide*. Retaken 28.8.1810 by Duperré's squadron at the Battle of Grand Port (Île de France), but retaken again by the British 4.12.1810 in the capitulation of Île de France, and sold there for BU 1.3.1816.

Fine Nantes.
K: 10.1778. L: 11.8.1779. C: 10.1779. Wrecked 3.1794 in Chesapeake Bay.

Émeraude Nantes.
K: 12.1778. L: 25.10.1779. C: 12.1779. Condemned 1797 at Brest and BU.

CONCORDE Class. 32 guns. Designed and built by Henri Chevillard, all three built at Rochefort. *Courageuse* was rebuilt in 1783 at Rochefort, and in 1794 at Toulon; *Hermione* in 1788–89 at Rochefort.

Dimensions & tons: 136ft 0in, 111ft 6in x 34ft 6in x 17ft 8in (44.18, 36.22 x 11.21 x 5.74m). 550/1,100 tons. Draught

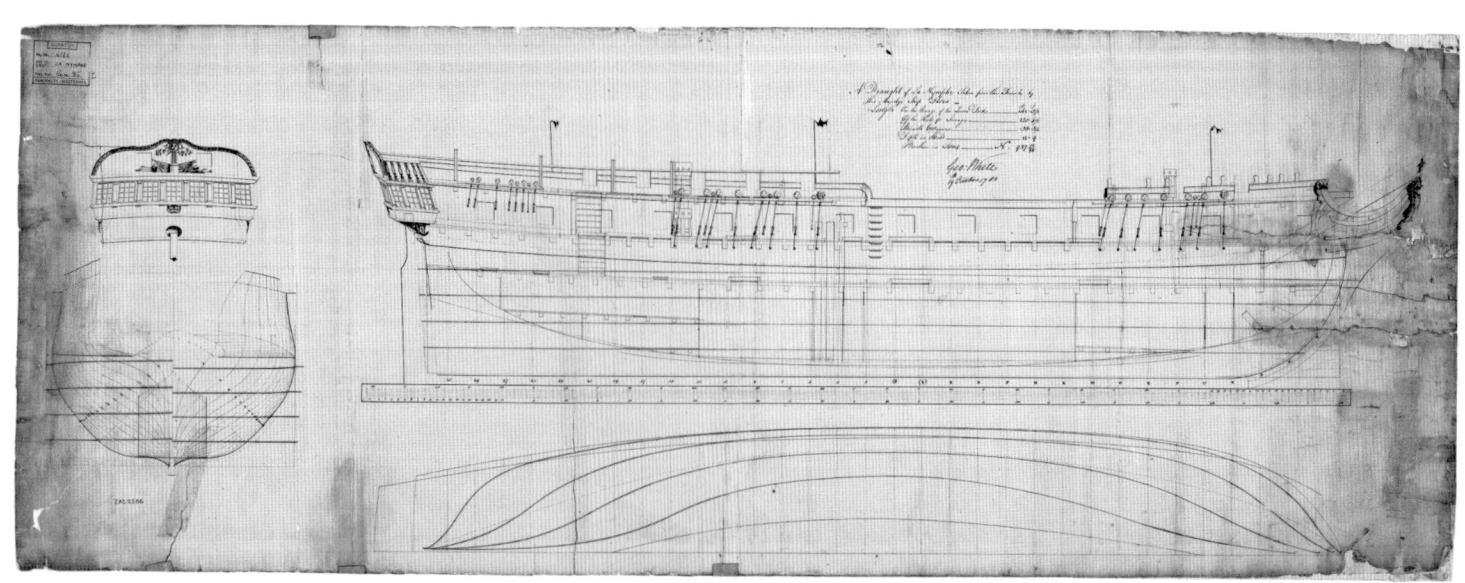

Admiralty draught of the *Nymphe*, signed by George White (of Portsmouth Yard), 19 October 1780. By this time the ship had been in dockyard hands for nearly six weeks so it is possible that the quarterdeck barricades were added by the British – they were common in the Royal Navy by this date – but there are no other obvious alterations to French features visible on the draught. (National Maritime Museum, London J5388)

THE FOURTH RANK

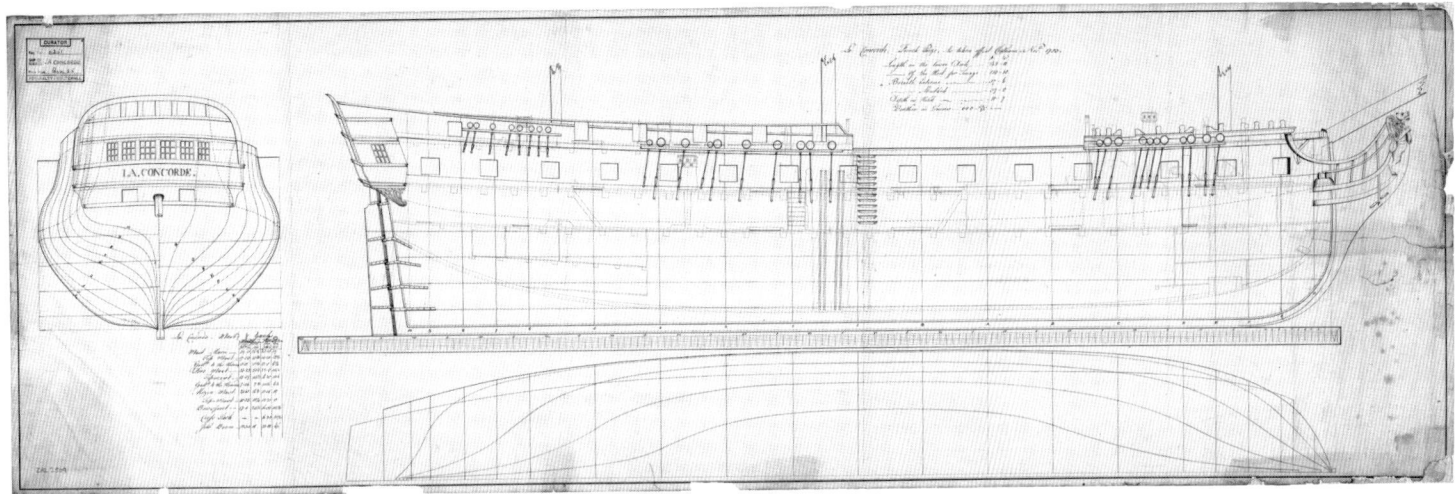

Admiralty draught of the *Concorde*, 'As taken off at Chatham – Nov 1783'. The ship had been captured in the Caribbean in February of that year, so this was probably as early as a survey in Britain could be undertaken. The draught records the ship's mast and spar dimensions, which reinforces the probability that this plan represents the ship as captured. (National Maritime Museum, London J5325)

13½/14¾ft (4.38/4.79m). Men: 270–290, +10/12 officers.
Guns: UD 26 x 12pdrs (*Concorde*, 28 x 18pdrs); QD 6 x 6pdrs.

Concorde Rochefort Dyd.
  K: 4.1777. L: 3.9.1777. C: 1.1778. Carried correspondence between Rochambeau and De Grasse, June to August 1781, which ensured that the French-American army and French Navy would surround and defeat Cornwallis at Yorktown in October. Captured by HMS *Magnificent* in the Caribbean 15.2.1783, becoming HMS *Concorde*; sold at Deptford 21.2.1811.

Courageuse Rochefort Dyd.
  K: 9.1777. L: 28.2.1778. C: 4.1778. Taken by HMS *Centaur* off Toulon 18.6.1799, becoming HMS *Courageux* (note change in gender!); used as a prison or receiving ship at Malta; BU 1802.

Hermione Rochefort Dyd.
  K: 3.1778. L: 28.4.1779. C: 6.1779. Sailed 21.3.1780 from Rochefort (with General Gilbert du Motier, Marquis de Lafayette, aboard) to Boston, arriving 28.4.1780 (a replica of this ship departed Île d'Aix for America on 18.4.2015, 235 years later). Wrecked 20.9.1793 near the Pointe de Croisic by a coastal pilot while escorting a convoy from the Loire to Brest.

FORTUNÉE. 32 guns. Designed and built by Pierre-Alexandre-Laurent Forfait (the first frigate to be built by him).
  Dimensions & tons: 136ft 3in x 34ft 8in x 17ft 7in (44.26 x 11.26 x 5.71m). 600/1,120 tons. Draught 17½ft (5.68)m. Men: 270, +9 officers.
  Guns: UD 26 x 12pdrs; QD 6 x 6pdrs.

Fortunée Brest Dyd.
  K: 8.1777. L: 26.12.1777. C: 3.1778. Captured by HMS *Suffolk* in the Leeward Islands 22.12.1779 and became HMS *Fortunee*; prison hulk 10.1785; BU 1800.

MAGICIENNE Class. 32 guns. Designed and built by Joseph-Marie-Blaise Coulomb. All ships to this design were built at Toulon, the first two being ordered on 7 February 1777 and named on 9 May; two more were ordered on 28 August and 23 October 1778, and these were named on 4 December of that year; another pair were ordered on 20 April 1780 and named on 16 June, and a seventh was begun in 1781. *Lutine* fitted with the support structure to carry a bomb bed in the hold, where one or two mortars were installed in September 1792. Two more were begun in February 1785, and a further three ships were built at Toulon from 1786 on (*Sensible*, *Topaze* and *Artémise* – see 1786–1861 volume).
  Dimensions & tons: 136ft 0in, 119ft 0in x 34ft 6in x 17ft 10in (44.18, 38.66 x 11.21 x 5.79 m). Draught 15/16ft (4.87/5.20m). Men: 265–285.
  Guns: UD 26 x 12pdrs; QD 6 x 6pdrs.

Magicienne Toulon Dyd.
  K: 3.1777. L: 1.8.1778. C: 10.1778. Captured by HMS *Chatham* off Boston on 2.7.1781, becoming HMS *Magicienne*; grounded and burnt to prevent recapture at Mauritius 24.8.1810.

Précieuse Toulon Dyd.
  K: 6.8.1777. L: 22.8.1778. C: 11.1778. Condemned 10.1814 and BU 1816 at Brest.

Sérieuse Toulon Dyd
  K: 3.1779. L: 28.8.1779. C: 10.1779. Sunk by Nelson's fleet at Aboukir Bay 1.8.1798.

Lutine Toulon Dyd.
  K: 3.1779. L: 11.9.1779. C: 11.1779. Handed over to the British at Toulon 29.8.1793.

Vestale Toulon Dyd.
  K: 5.1780. L: 14.10.1780. C: 2.1781. Captured by HMS *Terpsichore* off Cadiz 12.12.1796, but retaken same day by her own crew; taken again by HMS *Clyde* off Bordeaux 19.8.1799, and used as a floating battery.

Alceste Toulon Dyd.
  K: 5.1780. L: 28.10.1780. C: 2.1781. Captured by the British at Toulon 29.8.1793, and transferred to the Sardinian Navy, but retaken by *Boudeuse* 10.6.1794; taken again by HMS *Bellona* off Toulon 18.6.1799.

Iris Toulon Dyd.
  K: 5.1781. L: 29.10.1781. C: 2.1782. Captured by the British at Toulon 29.8.1793, burnt at evacuation of Toulon 12.1793.

Réunion Toulon Dyd.
  K: 2.1785. L: 23.2.1786. C: 1.1787. Captured by HMS *Crescent* off Barfleur 20.10.1793, becoming HMS *Reunion*; wrecked in the Swin 7.12.1796.

Modeste Toulon Dyd.

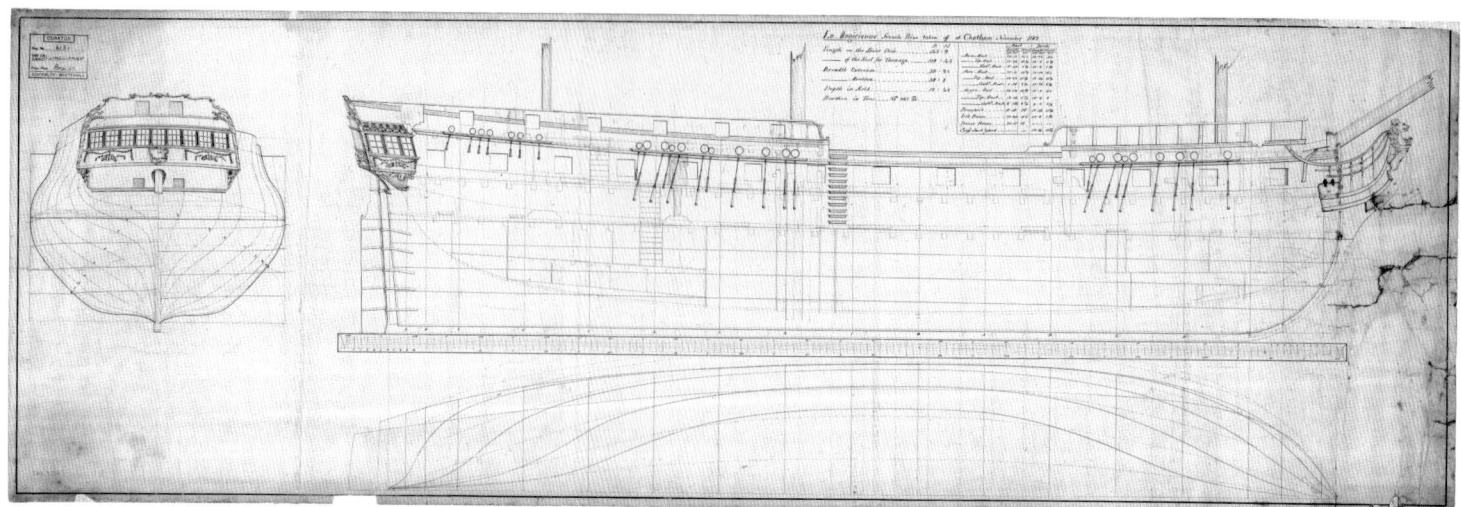

Admiralty draught of *Magicienne*, taken off at Chatham November 1783. The ship had been on foreign service since her capture off Boston (Mass) in September 1781, so this would have been the first opportunity to carry out a survey. In most respects the ship is as captured, but the quarterdeck barricades and forecastle rails look like British modifications – note in particular the extra-large gunports with the notched sills right forward and right aft that were probably intended for early-model carronades, at that time the monopoly of the British. (National Maritime Museum, London J6647)

K: 2.1785. L: 18.3.1786. C: 1.1787. Captured by HM Ships *Bedford* and *Captain* at Genoa 7.10.1793, becoming HMS *Modeste*. Re-armed in British service with 26 x 18pdrs *vice* 12pdrs. To Trinity House 1803–5. BU 6.1814 at Deptford.

GALATÉE Class. 32 guns, designed and built by Raymond-Antoine Haran. The third unit was ordered in early 1782 and named on 13 April 1782. A fourth ship ordered at Rochefort in 1782 may have been intended to be to this design; named *Favorite*, she was laid down in March 1783, but was cancelled in June with one-eighth of construction done. Three more were built to this design at Rochefort during the 1790s (see 1786–1861 volume). *Galatée* underwent reconstruction at Brest from February to August 1793.

Dimensions & tons: 137ft 0in, 124ft 0in x 34ft 6in x 17ft 6in (44.50, 40.28 x 11.21 x 5.72 m). 600/1,150 tons. Draught 14ft 8in/16ft (4.76/5.20m). Men: 280 (later 322).

Guns: UD 26 x 12pdrs; QD 6 x 6pdrs.

Railleuse Bordeaux
K: 11.1777. L: 11.8.1779. C: 2.1780. Refitted 1783 at Rochefort. Struck 1797 at Rochefort, and sold 17.1.1798 becoming privateer *Égyptienne*, captured 3.1804 by HMS *Hippomenes* in the West Indies, becoming HMS *Antigua*; became prison ship at Antigua, deleted 1816.

Galatée Rochefort
K: 3.1778. L: 28.6.1779. C: 9.1779. Wrecked 23.4.1795 on the Penmarcks.

Fleur de Lys Rochefort
K: 1.1783. L: 2.12.1785. C: 1786. Renamed *Pique* 6.1792. Captured by HMS *Blanche* off Guadeloupe 6.1.1795.

CÉRÈS Class. 32 guns. Designed and built by Charles-Étienne Bombelle. Similar to Chevillard's *Concorde* Class of 1777.

Dimensions & tons: 136ft 0in, 123ft 0in x 34ft 6in x 17ft 6in (44.18, 39.96 x 11.21 x 5.72 m). 564/1,100 tons. Draught 13ft 9in/15ft 4in (4.47/4.98m). Men: 270.

Guns: UD 26 x 12pdrs; QD 6 x 6pdrs.

Cérès Rochefort Dyd.
K: 5.1779. L: 24.11.1779. C: 1.1780. Struck at Rochefort 7.1787 and BU there.

Fée Rochefort Dyd.
K: 5.1779. L: 19.4.1780. C: 7.1780. Struck at Rochefort 5.1789 and BU there 1790.

CAPRICIEUSE Class. 34 guns. Designed and built by Charles Segondat-Duvernet. The first pair were ordered in 1778 and named on 4 December; these carried fourteen pairs of guns in their UD battery. The lead ship to this design – original *Capricieuse* – was burnt by the British in 1780, and another ship to the same design was ordered in 1785 and given the same name on 28 January 1786, but while still having fourteen pairs of gunports, she only carried 26 UD guns on the UD. A fourth ship to this design (*Prudente*) was ordered in 1789 (see 1786–1861 volume).

Dimensions & tons: 136ft 0in x 34ft 6in x 17ft 6in (44.18 x 11.21 x 5.68 m). 600/1,100 tons. Draught unknown. Men: 270.

Guns: UD 28 x 12pdrs (*Prudente* 26 x 12pdrs); QD 6 x 6pdrs + 2 x 36pdr *obusiers*.

Capricieuse (i) Lorient
K: 8.1778. L: 23.12.1779. C: 6.1780. Burnt in action by HM Ships *Prudente* and *Licorne* off Cape Finisterre 5.7.1780.

Friponne Lorient
K: 12.1778. L: 20.3.1780. C: 6.1780. Handed over to the Anglo-Spanish forces at Toulon in 8.1793, but restored to France in 12.1793. Struck at Brest 12.1796.

Capricieuse (ii) Lorient
K: 9.1785. L: 20.11.1786. C: 9.1787. Wrecked 10.1788 but salved and repaired. Wrecked 1.1800 off Lorient.

VÉNUS Class. 32 guns, designed by Jacques-Noël Sané, and built by Geoffroy and Benjamin Dubois. A modification of his *Sibylle* design of the previous year. While only carrying thirteen pairs of 12pdrs, these ships had fourteen pairs of UD gunports. From 1783 to 1793, the *Cléopâtre* carried 18pdrs *vice* 12pdrs, but the 12pdrs were reinstalled in 1793.

Dimensions & tons: 137ft 11in, 124ft 0in x 34ft 7in x 17ft 9in (44.80, 40.28 x 11.23 x 5.77 m). 600/1,082 tons. Draught

15/16ft (4.87/5.20m). Men: 270, +10 officers.
Guns: UD 26 x 12pdrs; QD 6 x 6pdrs (10 x 6pdrs in 1793).

Vénus St Malo.
K: 4.1779. L: 6.3.1780. C: 6.1780. Wrecked on the Glénans Rocks (off the south coast of Finisterre) 8.1781.

Cléopâtre St Malo.
K: 1780. L: 19.8.1781. C: 12.1781. Captured off Guernsey by HMS *Nymphe* 19.6.1793, becoming HMS *Oiseau*; prison hulk 1810, then sold 9.1816 to BU.

Ex-BRITISH PRIZES (1778–1781). Four British Fifth Rates (with 26 x 12pdr British guns on the UD and 6 x 6pdrs on the QD/Fc) were captured during the American War. The *Minerva* was captured on 22 August 1778 off the north of St Domingue by the French *Concorde*, the *Montreal* on 4 May 1779 off Gibraltar by *Bourgogne* and *Victoire*; the *Richmond* on 8 September 1781 by *Bourgogne* and *Aigrette* in the Chesapeake, and the *Iris* on 11 September 1781 by *Diligente* and *Cléopâtre*, also in the Chesapeake. The original names of three were slightly changed in French hands, with *Minerva* being altered to *Minerve*, *Montreal* to *Montréal*, and *Richmond* (probably) to *Richemont*. The fourth ship, *Iris*, was originally the American *Hancock*, captured on 8 July 1777 by HM Ships *Rainbow* and *Victor*. All are listed below, with re-measurements in French units. Two of them – *Montréal* and *Richemont* – were re-armed with French 12pdrs and – listed as 26-gun frigates (the French normally excluded QD/Fc guns from the official count) – remained in the French Navy until 1793.

Minerve Quallett, Rotherhithe.
K: 6.1756. L: 17.1.1759. C: 3.1759.
Dimensions & tons: 120ft 0in, 108ft 0in x 32ft 6in x 17ft 0in (38.98, 35.08 x 10.56 x 5.52m). 550/1,020 tons. Draught 14ft/15ft (4.55/4.87m). Men: 300.
Retaken 4.1.1781 by HM Ships *Courageous* and *Valiant* off Ushant, becoming HMS *Recovery*; sold 12.1784.

Montréal Sheerness Dyd.
K: 26.4.1760. L: 15.9.1761. C: 10.10.1761.
Dimensions & tons: 121ft 0in, 106ft 0in x 33ft 0in x 15ft 9in (39.31, 34.43 x 10.72 x 5.12m). 550/1,000 tons. Draught 14ft/16½ft (4.55/5.36m). Men: 220 in war, 150 peace, +10 officers.
Hulked 4.1793 at Toulon, becoming powder magazine 8.1793; captured by the Anglo-Spanish forces at the occupation of Toulon, then destroyed by the British at the evacuation of that port on 18.12.1793.

Richemont John Buxton, Deptford.
K: 4.1756. L: 12.11.1757. C: 7.12.1757.
Dimensions & tons: 123ft 6in, 105ft 9in x 32ft 2in x 17ft 0in (40.12, 34.35 x 10.45 x 5.52m). 550/1,000 tons. Draught 14ft/15ft (4.55/4.87m). Men: 220 in war, 150 peace, +10 officers.
Grounded and burnt off San Pietro, Sardinia 25.5.1793 to avoid capture by the Spanish.

Iris Jonathan Greenleaf, Newbury Port, Mass.
K: 3.1776. L: 1776. C: 1777.
Dimensions & tons: 130ft 0in, 116ft 0in x 32ft 0in x 16ft 0in (42.69, 37.68 x 10.39 x 5.25m). 600/1,100 tons. Draught 15ft/16ft 1in (4.87/5.22m). Men: ?
Sold 3.1784 at Rochefort, becoming the slaver *Iris* until summer 1785.

ESPÉRANCE. 32 guns. This 12-pdr frigate building at Bordeaux was purchased on the slip in 1779.
Dimensions & tons: 127ft 0in x 32ft 10in (41.25 x 10.66m). 550/1,050 tons.
Guns: UD 26 x 12pdrs; QD/Fc 6 x 6pdrs.

Espérance Bordeaux.
K: 1778 or early 1779. L: late 1779. C: 2.1780. Captured 9.1780 by HMS *Pearl* becoming HMS *Clinton*. Became a transport 1783, sold by the RN 7.1784.

CYBÈLE. A 12pdr-armed frigate was ordered in January 1782 to be built by Deslandes at Granville, with a 26-gun main battery. This may have been intended to bear the name *Cybèle*, but no design details are available. The order was cancelled in February 1783.

FLORE AMÉRICAINE. 32 guns. This purchased vessel was originally the French 8pdr-armed frigate *Vestale* of 1756 which had been captured

Admiralty draught of the *Iris*, dated Plymouth Yard 21 October 1779 but taken off the previous June. The ship had been the *Hancock* of the Continental Navy captured from the Americans on 8 July 1777, but whatever work was carried out on the ship in the interim did not include altering the decorative scheme – the taffrail still sports the rattlesnake emblem with its 'Don't tread on me' motto adopted by the rebels in the early stages of the struggle for independence. On 11 September 1781 she was captured in the Chesapeake by *Diligente* and *Cléopâtre*, and used to transport troops from Annapolis to the James River for the siege of Yorktown. Sailing from Boston to the Loire at the end of 1782, she was disarmed at Rochefort preparatory to being refitted, but found to be in too poor a state. (National Maritime Museum, London J5880)

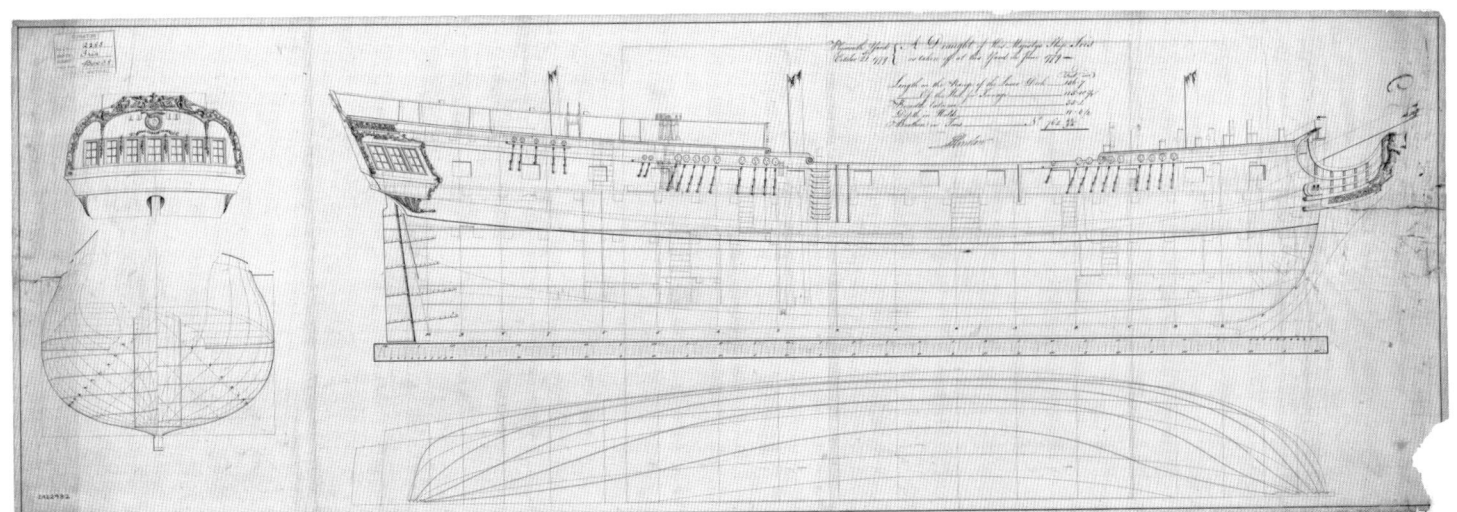

by HMS *Unicorn* off the Penmarcks on 8.1.1761, renamed *Flora*, and re-armed with a 12pdr main battery. She was scuttled and partly burnt at the evacuation of Rhode Island on 5 August 1778 to prevent her capture by the French, but was refloated by the Americans in early 1783, repaired and brought to Bordeaux, where the French Navy repurchased her in September 1784.

> Dimensions & tons: 126ft 6in, 113ft 0in x 32ft 2in x 16ft 4in (41.09, 36.71 x 10.45 x 5.31 m). 411/900 tons. Draught 14/15ft (4.55/4.87m). Men: 171-184, +10 officers.
>
> Guns (1784): UD 26 x 12pdrs; QD/Fc 6 x 6pdrs. The 12pdrs were replaced by 26 x 8pdrs in 1788. When re-acquired in 1793, she was re-armed with 26 x 8pdrs and 8 x 6pdrs.

Flore Américaine Le Havre

> K: 9.1755. L: 3.1756. C: 7.1756. Repurchased 9.1784 from the Americans as *Flore Américaine* (there already being an 8pdr-armed *Flore* in French service). Refitted 1–5.1786. Renamed *Flore* 1787, re-rated as a corvette 1788 and re-armed with 8pdr guns again. Struck and hulked at Rochefort 2.1789, being disarmed in 1791. Sold 4.7.1792, renamed *Citoyenne Française* 4.1793 and commissioned as a Bordeaux privateer in 5.1793. Requisitioned by the French Navy in 8.1793 but returned to former owners in 12.1795 and resumed her career as a privateer. Captured as *Flore* by HM Ships *Anson* and *Phaeton* in the Channel 6.9.1798 but not added to the RN.

FÉLICITÉ Class. 32 guns. Design by Pierre-Alexandre Forfait, as approved by Léon-Michel Guignace. The design was probably very similar to Forfait's earlier *Fortunée* of 1777, which had been lost to the British in 1779. They carried 19,209 sq.ft of sail. Although only 6 x 6pdr guns were carried on the *gaillards*, there were ports for 14 guns there. Two more ships of this class were built after 1785: *Fidèle* (1789) and *Fortunée* (1791) as were many others of similar designs.

> Dimensions & tons: 136ft 0in, 119ft 0in x 34ft 8in x 17ft 9in (44.18, 38.66 x 11.26 x 5.77 m) 600/1,140 tons. Draught 16ft 2in / 17ft 4in (5.25/5.63 m). Men: 261, +10 officers.
>
> Guns: UD 26 x 12pdrs; QD/Fc 6 x 6pdrs.

Félicité Brest Dyd.

> K: 1.1.1785. L: 4.8.1785. C: 28.8.1785. Captured by HM Ships *Latona* and *Cherub* in the Caribbean 18.6.1809; sold to Haitian King Christophe 7.1809, becoming Haitian *Améthyste*; taken by Haitian rebels 1811 and renamed *Heureuse Révolution*; captured again by HMS *Southampton* 3.2.1812, resuming original name, then returned to Christophe's government as *Améthyste*; sold 1818.

Calypso Brest Dyd.

> K: 4.7.1785. L: 2.12.1785. C: 1.1786. Her Royalist crew 'emigrated' (*i.e.* defected) in her to Trinidad and handed her over to the Spaniards there in 1.1793.

Thus, at the start of 1786 there were forty-three 12pdr-armed frigates in service or building; nineteen of these were under the Brest Naval Département (excluding the *Capricieuse* on the stocks), fourteen under Toulon (including the *Réunion* and *Modeste* on the stocks), and ten under Rochefort (including the *Fleur de Lys* still completing).

(F) 12pdr-armed vessels (two-deckers) acquired in 1770

During 1769 and 1770, thirteen small two-deckers, all built at Lorient for the *Compagnie des Indes*, were purchased by the French Navy from the Company. Three acquired in late 1769 mounted a principal battery of 18pdrs, and are listed in Chapter 3. The other ten below – acquired from the Company during 1770 following the liquidation of its assets – originally carried 12pdrs on the LD and 8pdrs on the UD but did not carry any guns at the time of sale to the Navy or during their brief period in naval hands. All (except *Berryer*) appeared briefly on the Navy List at Lorient at the start of September 1771 but were not employed as naval vessels.

CONDÉ. 56 guns. Designed and built by Nicolas Levesque. Purchased by the Navy in April 1770.

> Dimensions & tons: 132ft 0in, 117ft 0in x 36ft 0in x 16ft 0in (42.88, 38.01 x 11.69 x 5.20m). 850/1,400 tons. Draught 19ft (6.17m).

Condé Lorient, Cie des Indes Dyd.

> K: 10.1752. L: 30.8.1753. C: 12.1753. Hulked at Lorient 1773.

PAIX. 56 guns. Originally one of a class of three ships designed and built at Lorient by Gilles Cambry, this ship was originally named *Duc de Penthièvre* but was captured by the British on 26 December 1756, and was renamed *Paix* on being re-acquired by the *Compagnie des Indes* at the end of 1762. Purchased by the Navy in April 1770. Her original sisters *Seychelles* and *Moras* had been wrecked in 1760 and 1761 respectively at Île de France.

> Dimensions & tons: 132ft 0in, 115ft 3in x 36ft 0in x 16ft 0in (42.88, 37.44 x 11.69 x 5.20m). 900/1,400 tons. Draught 18ft (5.85m).

Paix Lorient, Cie des Indes Dyd.

> K: 9.1753. L: 25.5.1754. C: 9.1754. Hulked at Lorient 1772, and BU *c*.1780.

COMTE D'ARGENSON. 56 guns. Designed and built by Nicolas Levesque. Purchased by the Navy in April 1770.

> Dimensions & tons: 141ft 0in, 125ft 0in x 36ft 0in x 16ft 0in (45.80, 40.60 x 11.69 x 5.20m). 900/1,500 tons. Draught 19ft (6.17m).

Comte d'Argenson Lorient, Cie des Indes Dyd.

> K: 7.1755. L: 3.7.1757. C: 11.1757. Condemned 5.1770 at Lorient and removed from service 9.1771.

MASSIAC. 56 guns. Designed and built by Antoine Groignard. Purchased by the Navy in April 1770.

> Dimensions & tons: 140ft 0in, 126ft 0in x 35ft 0in x 15ft 6in (45.48, 40.93 x 11.49 x 5.035m). 900/1,450 tons. Draught 16½ft/17ft (5.41/5.52m).

Massiac Lorient, Cie des Indes Dyd.

> K: 5.1758. L: 30.12.1758. C: 2.1759. Sold for commercial service 10.1771.

BERRYER. 56 guns. Designed by Antoine Groignard, but built by Nicolas Levesque. Reconstructed from August to November 1767 at Lorient. Purchased by the Navy in April 1770 while lying at Île de France.

> Dimensions & tons: 145ft 7in, 125ft 6in x 35ft 0in x 15ft 6in (47.29, 40.77 x 11.37 x 5.035m). 900/1,500 tons. Draught 16ft (5.20m).

Berryer Lorient, Cie des Indes Dyd.

> K: 3.1759. L: 20.10.1759. C: 2.1760. LV Yves-Joseph de Kerguelen-Trémarec sailed in her in May 1771 from Port Louis on an expedition to find the postulated southern continent in the Indian Ocean, but upon arrival at Île de France transferred his expedition to the *flûte Fortune* and the *gabarre Gros Ventre* because he felt

Berryer, a merchant ship, was not suited to handle the hazardous southern seas.

BERTIN Class. 56 guns. Designed by Antoine Groignard. Reconstructed from July 1768 (until December 1768 and February 1769 respectively) at Lorient. Both purchased by the Navy in July 1770.
 Dimensions & tons: 145ft 0in, 126ft 0in x 36ft 0in x 15ft 0in (47.10, 40.93 x 11.69 x 4.87m). 900/1,500 tons. Draught 16ft/17½ft (5.20/5.68m).
 Guns: pierced for 56 guns, but actually carried 4 x 12pdrs and 20 x 8pdrs in mercantile service.
Bertin Lorient, Cie des Indes Dyd.
 K: 4.1761. L: 29.9.1761. C: 3.1762. Out of service at Lorient 9.1771; sold 7.1773.
Duc de Choiseul Lorient, Cie des Indes Dyd.
 K: 4.1761. L: 13.10.1761. C: 2.1762. Out of service at Lorient 9.1771; sailed 6.1772 to Île de France as hulk.

BEAUMONT Class. 56 guns. Designed by Antoine Groignard (modified from his *Bertin* design) and built by François Caro. Reconstructed from July 1768 (until November 1768 and August 1769 respectively) at Lorient. Purchased by the Navy in July and June 1770 respectively.
 Dimensions & tons: 145ft 4in, 126ft 4in x 37ft 0in x 14ft 6in (47.21, 41.04 x 12.02 x 4.71m). 900/1,600 tons. Draught 17ft/18ft (5.52/5.85m).
 Guns: pierced for 56 guns, but actually carried 2 x 12pdrs and 20 x 8pdrs in mercantile service.
Beaumont Lorient, Cie des Indes Dyd.
 K: 3.1762. L: 19.8.1762. C: 12.1762. Sold for commerce 5.1772.
Villevault Lorient, Cie des Indes Dyd.
 K: 3.1762. L: 7.9.1762. C: 12.1762. Sold for commerce 1.1771, but returned to Navy 7.1771; sold again 5.1774.

DAUPHIN. 56 guns. Designed by Antoine Groignard and built by Gilles Cambry. Purchased by the Navy in July 1770.
 Dimensions & tons: 147ft 8in, 130ft 0in x 36ft 8in x 15ft 0in (47.97, 42.23 x 11.91 x 4.87m). 900/1,500 tons. Draught 17½ft (5.68m).
Dauphin Lorient, Cie des Indes Dyd.
 K: 3.1766. L: 4.10.1766. C: 12.1766. Sold for commerce 3.1771. Leased back by the French Navy 3.1780 and captured by HMS *Argo* in the Caribbean 23.10.1782.

(G) 18pdr-armed frigates (*Frégates de 18*) and heavier frigates acquired from 1772

While the standard primary armament of the frigate before 1779 was the 12-pounder gun, in late 1778 Britain developed designs for 'heavy' frigates with a main battery of either 26 or 28 x 18-pounder guns (plus a number of smaller guns on the *gaillards*). The idea of building 18pdr-armed frigates underwent a long gestation; in June 1757 a Capt Shirley submitted a scheme to the British Navy for a 'super-frigate' measuring 146 x 37 (British) feet, carrying 28 x 18pdrs on the UD and 12 x 9pdrs or 6pdrs on the superstructure.

In France, the Brest Assistant *Constructeur* Pierre-Augustin Lamothe took a similar plan to Louis XV on 22 November 1762, with a design for a frigate of 145 x 37 (French) feet, to carry 30 x 18pdrs and 20 x 8pdrs, outclassing not only all existing frigates but also the two-decker 50-gun ship types. His timing was inauspicious, but in January 1769 the undeterred Lamothe took a modified version to his superiors. This followed a request from the Navy secretariat in 1768 for new designs for a 50-gun two-decker, armed with 24pdr guns on its lower deck. Again, Lamothe was turned down, but in November Joseph-Marie-Blaise Coulomb revived the idea, suggesting that such a vessel be built for trade protection, to carry 26 x 18pdrs and 10 x 8pdrs in wartime, but only fitted with 12pdrs in peacetime so as to not unnecessarily strain the hull structure. Nevertheless, no action followed at this time.

Meanwhile, LV Jacques Boux in 1770 propounded the idea of a 24pdr-armed frigate, with the suggestion that six of this type could be stationed in the Indian Ocean to disrupt British trade to the Orient in the event of a further war; two ships were built to this plan, but these were soon re-armed with 18pdrs. Following the British adoption of the 18pdr-armed type, France finally took the plunge in 1781; the early designs with 26 guns in their main battery soon gave way to those with 28 guns. From 1786 the standard designs of Jacques-Noël Sané became predominant and – while other classes of frigate were contributed by other designers – Sané designs were used for the vast majority of frigates built thereafter up to 1814.

POURVOYEUSE Class. A pair of very large 38-gun frigates were designed by Jacques Boux in early 1772 and named on 6 February 1772. They were originally planned to carry 26 x 24pdr guns as their primary armament, although during construction these were quickly replaced by 18pdrs. They were both built by Pierre Train at Lorient to Boux's plan (with certain modifications made by Léon-Michel Guignace). They served during the Anglo-French War of 1778–82 in the Indian Ocean operations, as part of the squadron of Pierre-André de Suffren. Intended for long-distance operations, able to carry provisions for a crew of 350 men for up to a year, they were misleadingly re-classed as *flûtes* as there was no peacetime cruising role envisaged for these expensive-to-operate vessels. Boux intended them to replace 50-gun two-deckers.
 Dimensions & tons: 154 ft 0in, 139ft 0in x 38ft 0in x 16ft 5in (50.025, 45.15 x 12.34 x 5.33 m). 840/1,928 tons. Draught 19ft/19½ft (6.17/6.33m). Men: 320, + 7 officers.
 Guns (as completed): UD 26 x 18pdrs; QD 8 x 8pdrs; Fc 4 x 8pdrs.
Pourvoyeuse Lorient Dyd.
 K: 3.1772. L: 10.11.1772. C: 1773. In the Indies 1777 to 1783. Refitted about 1783 at Ile-de-France. Deleted 1786 at Brest.
Consolante Lorient Dyd.
 K: 4.1772. L: 26.6.1775. C: 3.1776. Refitted 11–12.1781 at Ile-de-France, and 7/10.1783 at Trincomalee. Hulked 1784 at Brest but listed into 1786; BU 11.1804.

FLÛTES FRÉGATÉES. In early 1777 the American Commissioners in France contracted with Jacques Boux, 'one of the ablest sea officers of France', to 'superintend the building of 'two ships of war, of a particular construction, which though not of half the cost, shall be superior in force and utility to ships of 64 guns.' According to a contemporary draught the ships had a single gun deck (*i.e* constructed as large frigates, although built with the lines of a 74-gun ship) with fourteen ports per side, and with a forecastle and a long quarterdeck with additional ports (four pairs on the QD and three pairs on the forecastle) and a spar deck connecting the two. A development from Boux's *Pourvoyeuse* Class, to conceal their ownership and destination the ships were built in the name of a private firm, the *Maison Fizeau*. Only one of these frigates, named *Indien*, was laid down at Amsterdam in 1777 (although a second, *Tigre*, followed later). They were intended to carry French 24pdr guns, but in the event *Indien* mounted Swedish-made 36pdrs (the Swedish pound weight was 86.7 per cent of the French *livre*), making her the most

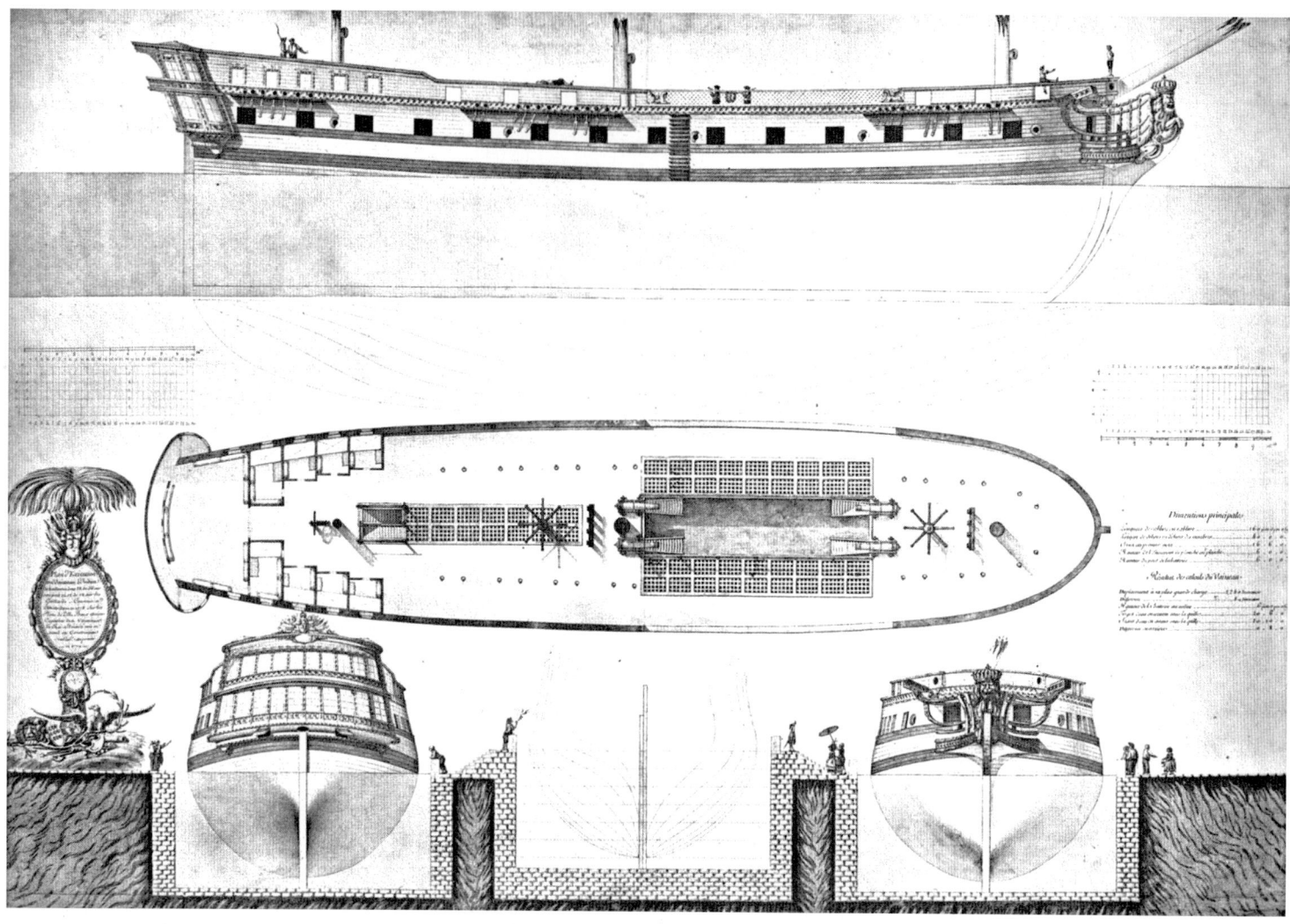

A drawing of *Indien* reproduced by *Vice-amiral* Pâris from a coloured copy in the Ollivier family collection. Originally ordered for the American Continental Navy, the ship was a radical attempt to produce a frigate-style ship with the firepower of a ship of the line, in many way prefiguring the spar-decked frigates of the *Constitution* type built for the US Navy after independence. Significantly, Joshua Humphries, the greatest advocate of these big frigates, owned a copy of the lines of *Indien,* although there is no close resemblance between the hull forms of his designs and the French ship. The influence was probably more conceptual – an unusually big, heavily armed but fine-lined frigate. Easily the most powerful warship to serve in the American interest during the War of Independence, she was acquired by the South Carolina State Navy and renamed *South Carolina*; she carried a battlefleet-quality ordnance of twenty-eight Swedish 36pdrs and ten 12pdrs, plus six lesser guns. John Paul Jones had hoped to command her, but in the event the ship was captained by Commander Alexander Gillon, who had arranged her acquisition from the Chevalier de Luxembourg, and manoeuvred her in stages from Amsterdam to the open sea. Without a home port or government to base her on (Charleston had been occupied by British forces since May 1780), she refitted at Corunna and then at Santa Cruz de Tenerife before crossing the Atlantic to the Bahamas and subsequently to Havana. She was captured by the British 58-gun *Diomede* and two 32-gun frigates (*Astraea* and *Quebec*) off Delaware in December 1782. (*Souvenirs de Marine*, Plate 277)

powerfully-armed frigate to that date. The Americans were unable to fit out and man such large ships in a neutral port and sold them to Louis XVI who, in turn, lent them to Anne Paul Sigismund de Montmorency, the Chevalier de Luxembourg, with an option to purchase after three years.

In May 1780 Luxembourg leased *Indien* for three years to Commodore Alexander Gillon of the South Carolina State Navy for use as a frigate for one quarter of her prize money; she was renamed *South Carolina*. American designer Joshua Humphries copied her lines which he later used in devising the frigates USS *Constitution* and *Constellation*. Although the French Navy had its own ships with the same names, *Indien* and *Tigre* were inscribed in 1780 and 1781 in official fleet lists entitled *Forces Navales* following *Serapis* and *Sagittaire* as *flûtes frégatées* (frigate-built *flûtes*). The combination of a heavy armament and great length caused *Indien* to hog and she was considered by her British captors to be a weakly built ship.

- Dimensions & tons: 160ft 0in, 149ft 0in x 40ft 0in x 16ft 6in (51.97, 48.40 x 12.99 x 5.36m). 1,260/2,240 tons. Draught 20ft 6in/20ft 10in (6.66/6.77m). Men: 131/570, +8 officers.
- Guns (from *Forces Navales*): UD 28 x 36pdrs; QD/Fc 12 x 8pdrs; (as *South Carolina*): UD 28 x 36pdrs; QD 10 x 12pdrs; Fc 2 x 9pdrs; 4 smaller.

Indien Amsterdam.
- K: spring 1777. L: 11.1777. C: 4.1778. Renamed *South Carolina* 1779. Delayed by the shallow water of the Texel, *Indien* only got to sea in 8.1781. Arriving at Havana in 1.1782 Gillon joined a successful Spanish assault on the Bahamas in 5.1782. The ship refitted at Philadelphia over the summer while Luxembourg replaced Gillon with another commander. *Indien* left Philadelphia

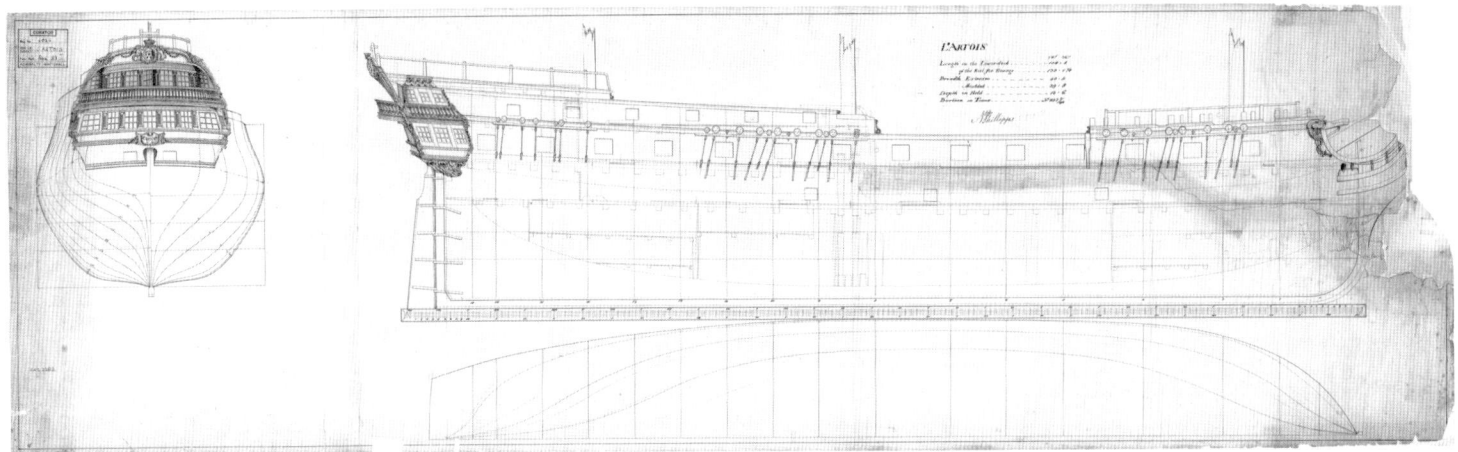

Admiralty draught of the *Artois*, undated. Although some of the larger French frigates of the mid-century were built with a small cabin or *dunette* on the quarterdeck, *Artois* has two complete tiers of stern galleries, complete with open balcony – features retained when the ship was converted from the 56-gun ship of the line *Bordelais*. The 'frigate' layout was achieved by disarming the lower gundeck and blocking up the ports, although three pairs of small loading ports were inserted on that deck, each abreast one of the lower deck hatches. (National Maritime Museum, London J5590)

in 12.1782 but was captured on 19.12.1782 off the Delaware Capes by HM Ships *Diomede*, *Astraea* and *Quebec* after an 18-hour chase and a two-hour fight. Subsequently, in 1783 at the war's end, she evacuated Hanoverian troops from New York to Deal (Kent) and thence proceeded to the Indian Ocean (her ship's bell was unearthed during the Second World War at a jute mill near Calcutta).

Tigre Amsterdam.
  K: 10.1778. L: 10.1779. C: 3.1780. To commercial use 9.1781, last mentioned 5.1782 arriving at Bordeaux.

ARTOIS. 40 guns. Provided by the Charles-Philippe de Bourbon, Comte d'Artois (Louis XV's youngest brother and the future Charles X), converted from the 56-gun *Bordelais* built at Bordeaux in 1762–63 (see Chapter 3), which had been hulked at Lorient in May 1779. Renamed *Artois* (or *États d'Artois*), she was rebuilt there by Arnous as a frigate with funds provided by the Comte at his own expense.
  Dimensions & tons: 152ft 0in, 144ft 0in x 37ft 10in x 18ft 0in (49.38, 46.78 x 12.29 x 5.85m). 1,100/2,000 tons. Draught 16ft/17ft 4in (5.20/5.63m). Men: 460.
  Guns: UD 28 x 18pdrs; QD/Fc 12 x 8pdrs.
Artois Lorient Dyd.
  K: 1.1780. L: 1.1780. C: 5.1780. Captured by HMS *Romney* 1.7.1780, becoming HMS *Artois*; sold 2.1786.

AIGLE. 32 (later 36–40) guns. Designed by Jacques-Noël Sané, built at Chantiers Dujardin as a privateer. Purchased in April 1783 for the Navy by Clamart.
  Dimensions & tons: 138ft 10in x 35ft 10in x 17ft 10in (45.10 x 11.64 x 5.79m). 650/1,200 tons. Draught 15ft/16ft (4.87/5.20m). Men: 350, +10 officers.
  Guns: UD 26 x 18pdrs; QD/Fc 6 (later 10–14) x 8pdrs.
Aigle St Malo.
  K: 1779. L: 11.2.1780. C: 3.1781. Grounded 12.9.1782 in the Delaware, then captured 14.9.1782 by Keith's squadron, becoming HMS *Aigle*; wrecked 19.7.1798 at Cape Farina (Morocco).

DANAÉ. 36 (later 42) guns. Designed and built by Charles Segondat-Duvernet, although originally begun to the lines of the 12pdr-armed *Capricieuse* Class. On completion, the 18pdrs proved too heavy for the construction, and were replaced by 12pdrs during a refit at Brest in early 1784.
  Dimensions & tons: 140ft length (45.48m); other dimensions unknown. /00 tons. Men: 261, +10 officers (as a 12pdr-armed ship).
  Guns: UD 26 x 18pdrs; QD/Fc 10 x 8pdrs. Re-armed 1785 with 26 x 12pdrs and 6 x 8pdrs. At end 1793 a fourteenth pair of UD 12pdrs was added, and the *gaillards* fitted with 10 x 6pdrs + 4 x 36pdr *obusiers*.
Danaé Lorient Dyd.
  K: 9.1781. L: 27.5.1782. C: 10.1782. Deleted 1795 at Brest (not mentioned after 1.1796).

HÉBÉ Class. 34 (later 40–42) guns. Designed by Jacques-Noël Sané. Four were begun between 1781 and 1784. A further two to the same design (*Sibylle* and *Carmagnole*) were begun in 1790 and 1792 (see 1786–1861 volume); these later ships carried an additional pair of 18pdrs, and *Dryade* and *Proserpine* were fitted similarly by 1794. The name-ship was captured by the British a month after completion, and her lines copied; from this both France and Britain developed the design further, so that it became the basis of numerous ships in both navies.
  Dimensions & tons: 142ft 6in, 129ft 0in x 36ft 8in x 19ft 0in (46.29, 41.90 x 11.91 x 6.17m). 700/1,350 tons. Draught 16ft/17ft (5.20/5.52m). Men: 350 in war, 315 peace, +10/11 officers.
  Guns: UD 26 x 18pdrs; QD/Fc 8 x 8pdrs initially (by the time *Proserpine* was launched, the standard ordnance on the *gaillards* comprised 10 x 8pdrs + 4 x 36pdr *obusiers*).
Vénus Brest Dyd.
  K: 11.1781. L: 14.7.1782. C: 10.1782. Wrecked in a storm in the Indian Ocean 31.12.1788.
Hébé St Malo.
  K: 12.1781. L: 25.6.1782. C: 8.1782. Captured by HMS *Rainbow* in the Channel 4.9.1782, becoming HMS *Hebe*; renamed HMS *Blonde* 1804; BU 1811.
Dryade St Malo.
  K: 1782. L: 3.2.1783. C: 4.1783. Hulked at Brest 1796, then BU by Order of 16.10.1801.

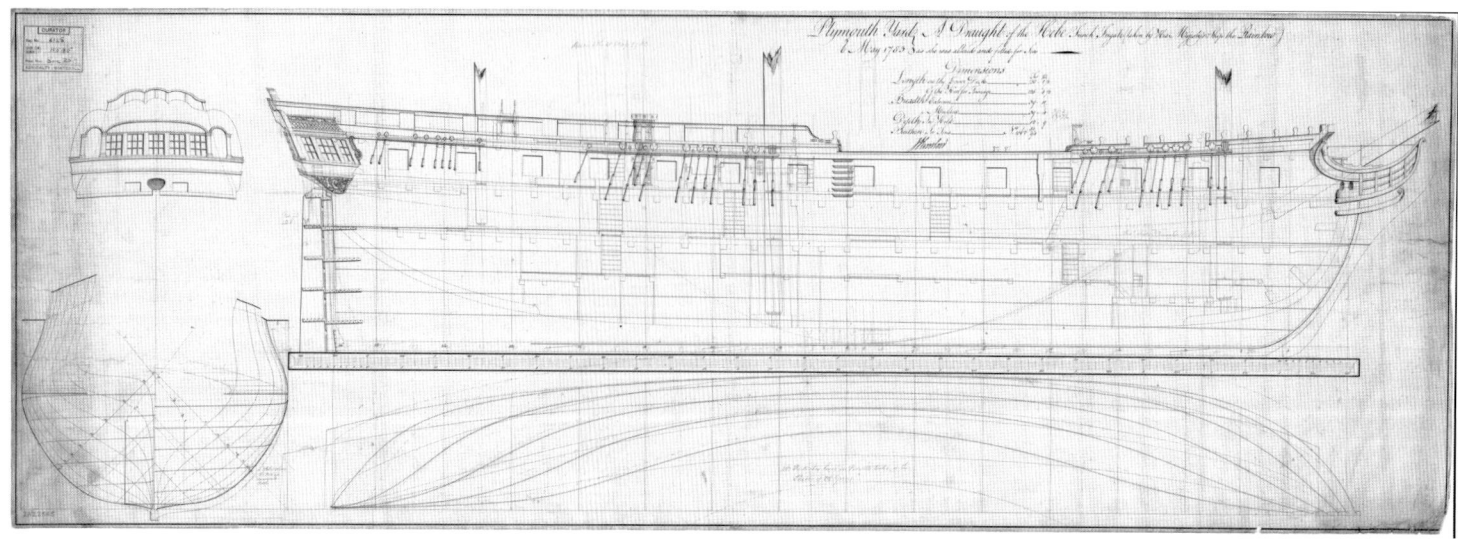

Admiralty draught of the *Hebe* 'as she was altered and fitted for sea', Plymouth Yard 6 May 1783. This ship was the first in a long line of generally similar frigates to Sané's design, which employed a less exaggerated form of the characteristic French midship section. The underwater shape also found favour with the ship's captors, inspiring the British *Leda* class 38s built in large numbers throughout the Napoleonic Wars and beyond. (National Maritime Museum, London J5333)

Proserpine Brest Dyd.
  K: 12.1784. L: 25.6.1785. C: 8.1795. Captured by HMS *Dryad* off Cape Clear (Ireland) 13.6.1796, becoming HMS *Amelia*; BU at Deptford 12.1816.

NYMPHE Class. 34 (later 40–44) guns. Designed by Pierre-Augustin Lamothe, Jnr. The prototype was built as a replacement for his father's 12pdr-armed frigate of the same name, which had been captured in August 1780, and was named on 5 December 1781. A second ship to this design was begun in September 1785 (although not formally ordered until 4 November 1786) and was named *Thétis* on 2 September 1787. Two further ships to the same design (*Cybèle* and *Concorde*) were begun at Brest in 1788 and 1790 (see 1786–1861 volume); these last two ships carried an additional pair of 18pdrs, and *Thétis* was retro-fitted similarly by 1794. *Thétis* was rebuilt at Rochefort from October 1802 to September 1803.
  Dimensions & tons: 144ft 5in x 36ft 8in x 19ft 3in (46.91 x 11.91 x 5.25m). 744/1,423 tons. Draught 15ft 10in/18ft (5.14/5.85m). Men: 360 in war, 315 peace, + 10/11 officers.
  Guns: UD 26 x 18pdrs; QD/Fc 8 x 8pdrs (by 1794, the standard ordnance on the *gaillards* comprised 10 x 8pdrs + 4 x 36pdr *obusiers*).
Nymphe Brest Dyd.
  K: 12.1781. L: 30.5.1782. C: 8.1782. Wrecked in action at Noirmoutier 30.12.1793.
Thétis Brest Dyd.
  K: 9.1785. L: 16.6.1788. C: 10.1788. Captured off Lorient by HMS *Amethyst* 10.11.1808, becoming HMS *Brune*; hulked 1816 and BU 1838.

MINERVE Class. 34 (later 40) guns. Designed and built by Joseph-Marie-Blaise Coulomb. Two were ordered on 30 October 1781 and named on 28 November, and a third was ordered in November 1785. A further two to the same design (*Melpomene* and *Perle*) were begun at Toulon in 1786–89 (see 1786–1861 volume); the last two ships carried an additional pair of 18pdrs, and *Perle*'s design was lengthened slightly. A sixth ship to a further lengthened version of the design was ordered in 1791, and was given the name *Minerve* after the class prototype was captured in 1794.
  Dimensions & tons: 142ft 0in, 128ft 0in x 36ft 0in x 18ft 9in (46.13, 41.58 x 11.69 x 6.09m). 700/1,330 tons. Draught 16¼ft/16ft 10in (5.28/5.47m). Men: 314, +10/11 officers.
  Guns: UD 26 x 18pdrs; QD/Fc 8 x 8pdrs (by 1794, the standard ordnance on the *gaillards* comprised 10 x 8pdrs + 4 x 36pdr *obusiers*).
Minerve Toulon Dyd.
  K: 1.1782. L: 31.7.1782. C: 10.1782. Captured by the British at the seizure of San Fiorenzo (Saint-Florent, Corsica) 19.2.1794, becoming HMS *San Fiorenzo*; troopship 1810, then receiving ship 1812. BU at Deptford 9.1837.
Junon Toulon Dyd.
  K: 2.1782. L: 14.8.1782. C: 2.1783. Captured by HMS *Bellona* off Toulon 18.6.1799, becoming HMS *Princess Charlotte*; renamed HMS *Andromache* 1.1812. BU at Deptford 1828.
Impérieuse Toulon Dyd.
  K: 2.1786. L: 11.7.1787. C: 5.1788. Chased by British ships of the line into La Spezia 12.10.1793, where captured by HMS *Captain*, becoming HMS *Impérieuse*. Renamed HMS *Unite* 3.9.1803. Hospital hulk 1836, BU 1858.

MÉDUSE Class. 36 (later 40–44) guns. Designed and built by Charles Segondat-Duvernet, as lengthened versions of his *Danaé*. The prototype was ordered on 15 February 1782 and named on 13 April; a second ship was ordered in late 1784 and named on 18 February 1785. The design was re-used for another single ship ordered in 1787 (*Uranie*, to a somewhat lengthened design to carry 28 guns *vice* 26), as well as another probable derivative (*Vertu*) in 1793, and was revived for four more ships in 1803–5 (see 1786–1861 volume).
  Dimensions & tons: 143ft 6in, 131ft 0in x 37ft 0in x 19ft 0in (46.61, 42.55 x 12.02 x 6.17m). 700/1,370 tons. Draught 15ft 10in/16½ft (5.14/5.36m). Men: 314, +10/11 officers.
  Guns: UD 26 x 18pdrs; QD/Fc 10 x 8pdrs. In 1788, 4 x 16pdr 'carronades' were added to *Méduse*, which was re-armed in 1794 with UD 28 x 18pdrs; QD/Fc 12 x 8pdrs + 4 x 36pdr *obusiers*.
Méduse Lorient Dyd.
  K: 6.1782. L: 18.11.1782. C: 3.1783. Burnt by accident in the Atlantic 3.12.1796.

THE FOURTH RANK

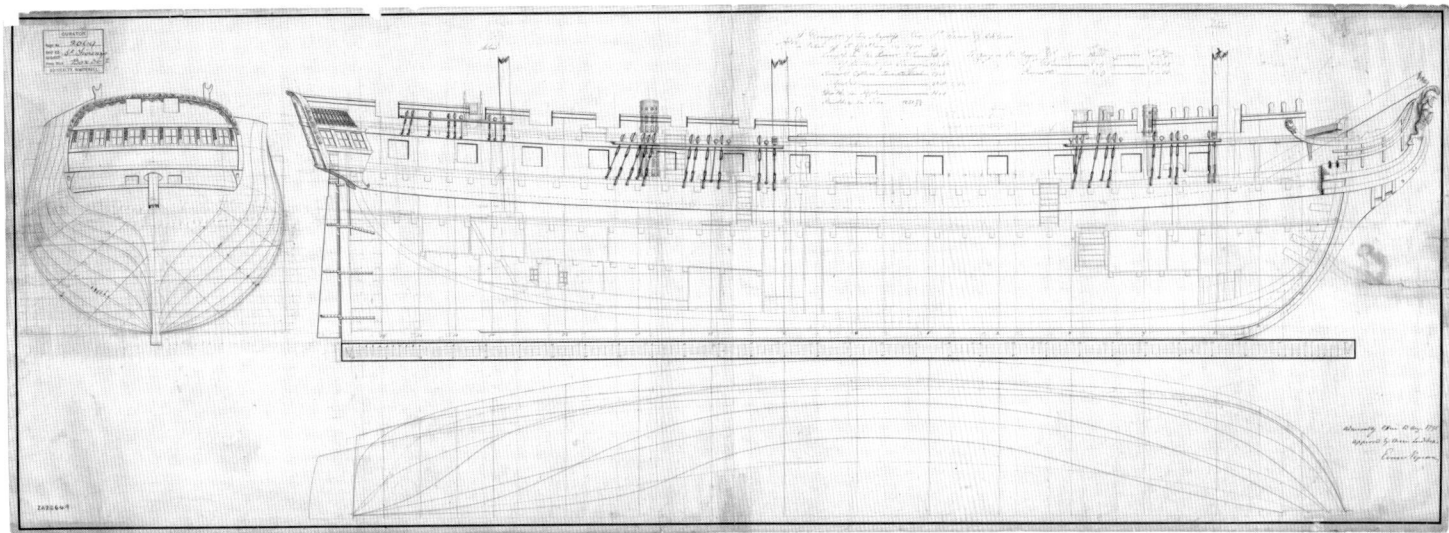

Admiralty draught of the *San Fiorenzo* 'as taken off at Chatham in 1795'. The ship has not been altered much from her original incarnation as the French *Minerve*, although the barricades have been modified to accept 32pdr carronades outside the line of the shrouds; the smaller ports are for 9pdr long guns, which could fire through the shrouds because their muzzle-flash was less of a danger. (National Maritime Museum, London J5204)

Didon Lorient Dyd.
   K: 1.1785. L: 20.8.1785. C: 3.1787. Grounded by accident and burnt 9.1792 in the West Indies, although other sources suggest she was renamed *Royaliste* in 10.1792 and handed over by her pro-monarchist crew to the Spanish at Trinidad (later fate unknown).

POMONE. 32 (later 40–44) guns. A one-off design by Baron Charles-Étienne Bombelle, with gunports designed to take 26 x 24pdrs on the UD and 6 x 8pdrs on the *gaillards*; named on 13 April 1782, and built by Hubert Pennevert and Henri Chevillard. She is listed in 1786 as carrying 18pdrs in her UD battery, so it is possible that she was completed with 18pdrs instead of the designed 24pdrs, but this long vessel, when captured by the British, was certainly carrying 24pdrs at the time, and so became the British Navy's prototype 24pdr-armed frigate (although she was re-armed with 18pdrs in British service during 1799).
   Dimensions & tons: 150ft 0in x 37ft 6in x 18ft 4in (48.73 x 12.18 x 5.96m). 700/1,400 tons. Draught 15ft/15ft 10in (4.87/5.13m). Men: 314, +10/11 officers.
   Guns: UD 26 x 24pdrs (see note above); QD/Fc 6 x 8pdrs (re-armed 1794 with 12 x 8pdrs + 4 x 36pdr *obusiers*).
Pomone Rochefort Dyd.
   K: 20.2.1783. L: 16.11.1785. C: 5.1787. Taken by HM Ships *Flora* and *Arethusa* of Warren's squadron off Île Bas 23.4.1794, becoming HMS *Pomone*; BU at Portsmouth 12.1802.

PÉNÉLOPE. 36 guns. A one-off design by Pierre-Augustin Lamothe (or possibly by Jacques-Noël Sané), ordered on 30 September 1785, named on 28 January 1786 and built by Pierre-Élisabeth Rolland. After her construction began, it was delayed for a while, but later resumed.
   Dimensions & tons: dimensions unknown. 700 tons. Men: 314, +10/11 officers.
   Guns: UD 26 x 18pdrs; QD/Fc 10 x 8pdrs.
Pénélope Brest Dyd.
   K: 28.11.1785. L: 12.7.1787. C: 7.1787. Wrecked in False Bay (South Africa) 10.1788.

Thus, at the start of 1786 there were ten 18pdr-armed frigates in service or building, including seven under the Brest Naval *Département* (including the *Proserpine* and *Didon* on the stocks), the Coulomb-designed *Minerve* and *Junon* at Toulon, and one completing at Rochefort (*Pomone*). Others were under construction, and the 1786 Program for new construction provided for a substantial increase in this type, with another twenty 18pdr-armed frigates to be built.

5 The Fifth Rank

(Vaisseaux du cinquième rang), sometimes described as Frigates of the 2nd Order (Frégates du 2e ordre) and 8pdr-armed frigates after 1740

These small two-deckers lacked the structural strength and the firepower to stand in the line of battle, but were useful to serve as cruisers, for patrol and escort purposes or to interdict the commerce of France's wartime opponents. The concept proved inadequate, however, as these ships had their LD gunports too close to the waterline, which inhibited their combatant abilities in rough weather, and much of their role moved to the single-decked *frégates légères*.

The initial division into Ranks under Colbert's orders in 1669 did not include a 5th Rank, and vessels with as few as 24 guns were included in the 4th Rank. This system was refined in 1670, however, and vessels with between 24 and 34 guns were placed in a new 5th Rank. In 1680 or early 1681 an 'establishment total' of sixteen 5th Rank *frégates-vaisseaux* was set and this was retained as a standard until after 1715 (except for two years – in 1688 when it was raised to twenty-two ships, and 1689 when it was reduced to eighteen before returning to sixteen the following year.) In January 1681 the navy actually had 20 ships of the 5th Rank and the numbers extant varied up to twenty-four (in 1705), but thereafter declined rapidly due to wartime losses.

By 1689 the rating structure had been altered and was more confused, with the 5th Rank including three vessels of 40 guns, although two years later the upper limit was clearly fixed at a maximum of 36 guns. The last 5th Rank two-deckers designed and built for the French Navy were launched in 1699 (see Section (B) below), and the category in practice ceased to exist when the last one on the List (the hulked former prize *Ludlow*) was moved to the 4th Rank between 1723 and 1729. No further 5th Rank ships appeared in the annual fleet lists.

Many of the 5th Rank two-deckers, however, had carried 8pdr guns as their main (LD) battery, and their role in the Navy was effectively taken by the new type of single-deck frigates armed with a battery of 8pdrs, which were the inheritors of the *frégates légères*, and which entered the fleet beginning with the *Médée* in 1740; all these appear in Section (E) of this chapter.

To compensate for the near total absence of contemporary data on ship armaments prior to 1696, we have in Sections (A) and (B) provided estimated armaments based on the governing directives and the known characteristics of all of the individual ships. This issue is discussed in greater detail in the Introduction.

(A) Vessels in service at 9 March 1661

In March 1661 the French Navy possessed a number of cruising vessels of between 24 and 34 guns, some dating back to the 1630s. The majority of these needed replacement – indeed, among those at Toulon several were discarded in May 1661.

Ex-DUTCH PURCHASES (1638). 30 guns. In 1637 the French Navy purchased six new vessels which were built in Amsterdam; all were laid down in 1637, launched in February 1638 and completed in June 1638. One of these – the *Cardinal* – was of 42–46 guns and is found in the previous chapter. Three more – the 26-gun *Triton*, the 34-gun *Victoire* and the 34-gun *Vierge* – were lost in 1652, 1654 and 1660 respectively, leaving the two listed below, both of which were condemned in May 1661 at Toulon and BU.

Triomphe Amsterdam
  Dimensions & tons: dimensions unknown. 600 tons. Men: 215, +5 officers.
  Guns: 30.
Faucon Amsterdam
  Dimensions & tons: dimensions unknown. 400 tons. Men: 190, +5 officers.
  Guns: 26.

DAUPHIN. 24 guns. Designed and built by Rollin.
  Dimensions & tons: 80ft 0in x 21ft 6in (25.99 x 6.98m). 400 tons. Men: 185, +5 officers.
  Guns: 24.
Dauphin Le Havre.
  K: 1637. L: 17.3.1638. C: 7.1638. Condemned 5.1661 at Toulon and BU.

SOURDIS. 34 guns. Named after Henri d'Escoubleau de Sourdis, Archbishop of Bordeaux and C-in-C of naval operations during the Thirty Years' War, against Spain, Sweden and the Empire.
  Dimensions & tons: dimensions unknown. 600 tons. Men: 225/240, +5 officers.
  Guns (34): LD 18 x 8pdrs; UD 16 x 6pdrs.
Sourdis Toulon Dyd.
  K: 1640. L: 1641. C: 1643. Condemned 3.5.1661 at Toulon and BU.

TIGRE. 30 guns. Designed and built by Jean de Werth (real name, Jan Gron). Her sister *Léopard* (similarly built 1640–44 by him at Indret) was lost in April 1651 when the crew mutinied and handed over the ship to the Spanish at San Lucar.
  Dimensions & tons: dimensions unknown. 300 tons. Men: 170, +5 officers.
  Guns: 28 in 1644; 30 by 1661.
Tigre Indret.
  K: 1640. L: 1642. C: 1644. Sank 23.9.1664 off Cap de la Casse, Sardinia (64 drowned. 58 survived).

DRAGON. 42, later 34 guns. Designed and built by Laurent Hubac. Reconstructed March–June 1665 at Toulon, then in November 1666 to April 1667 at Dieppe. Originally classed as 4th Rank in 1669, but moved to 5th Rank in 1670.
  Dimensions & tons: 112ft 0in x 30ft 0in x 12ft 2in (36.38 x 9.75 x 3.95m). 550 tons. Draught 14ft (4.55m). Men: 225, +5 officers.
  Guns: 42 originally, reduced to 34 in 1669: LD 20 x 8pdrs; UD 6 x 6pdrs + 8 x 4pdrs.
Dragon Brest Dyd.
  K: 1646. L: 1646. C: 1647. Hulked 1674 at Brest. Sold there 7.1684.

ELBEUF. 30 guns. Designed and built by Michel Richot at Elbeuf, a river port on the Seine, about 20 kilometres upstream from Rouen. Two other orders for similar 400-ton vessels of 26 guns each were placed with Richot in August 1646, but these were never built or even named.

Reported with 20 guns on the LD (so pierced for ten pairs) and 10 on the UD.

Dimensions & tons: 96ft 6in x 24ft 0in x 9ft 8in (31.35 x 7.80 x 3.14m). 400 tons. Draught 10ft (3.25m). Men: 190, +?5 officers.

Guns: 29 in 1665: 1 x 12pdr, 10 x 8pdrs, 12 x 6pdrs, 2 x 5pdrs; 4 x 4pdrs; 16 guns as fireship from 9.1669.

Elbeuf Elbeuf.

K: 4.1646. L: 9.1646. C: 10.1646 at Le Havre. Converted to fireship 9.1669. Hulked at Toulon end 1670. Called *Boeuf* from 1688; not mentioned after 1693.

Ex-SPANISH PRIZE (1651). 30 guns. The Spanish privateer *Santa Ana* was captured in 1651, and taken into French naval service as *Saint Anne*. She was often called *La Galéasse* (presumably a description of her type). Before 1661 the French added a forecastle.

Dimensions & tons: dimensions unknown. 250/300 tons. Men: 285.

Guns: 24-30.

Sainte Anne Vizcaya.

Built 1646. Took part in Battle of Pertuis d'Antioche 9.8.1652. Disarmed at Toulon 21.8.1663, and BU there in 1664.

Ex-SPANISH PRIZE (1654). The Spanish Netherlands *San Antonio* was captured in March 1654 in the North Sea, and put into French service under the name *Saint Antoine* (or *Saint Antoine d'Espagne*) with 38 guns.

Dimensions & tons: 94ft 0in x 22ft 0in x 10ft 0in (30.53 x 7.15 x 3.25m). 350/500 tons. Draught 11ft 8in (3.79m). Men: 350, 4 officers; 200 by 1666; 25, +1 officer as fireship.

Guns: 38, 30 by 1666, 4 as fireship.

Saint Antoine Amsterdam.

Built 1650. Part of Duc de Beaufort's squadron in 1666 for operations against North African ports. Converted to fireship (200 tons, 4 guns) 1668. Leased 1670 for commerce, but wrecked 9.1670 on the Hoc rock off Le Havre.

VICTOIRE. 26 guns. Designed and built by Jean-Pierre Brun (the nephew of Laurent Hubac).

Dimensions & tons: 82ft 7in keel x 27ft 3in x 10ft 9in (36.84 keel x 8.85 x 3.49m). 400 tons. Men: 250 in war, 200 peace.

Guns: A document entitled 'An inventory and appraisement of the frigatt *Victoria* of Rochelle' and dated 1.6.1666 in the UK archives (Kew, SP29/158, f.17) states her armament at the time of capture was 26 guns, specifically 2 x 16pdrs (bronze), 6 x 12pdrs (2 bronze & 4 iron), 6 x 8pdrs (iron), 8 x 6pdrs (iron) and 4 x 5pdrs (bronze). The English retained the French guns and added 6 sakers (5¼pdrs) and 2 falcons (2½pdrs) at Plymouth to fit her as a 34-gun Fifth Rate.

Victoire Soubise (near Rochefort).

K: 9.1656. L: 18.6.1658. C: 11.1658. Captured by HM Ships *Resolution* and *Oxford* off Lisbon 18.4.1666, becoming HMS *French Victory*; taken by the Dutch 15.5.1672 off North Foreland and not subsequently recorded.

FLEUR DE LYS. 30 guns. Designed and built by Georges Carteret.

Dimensions & tons: dimensions unknown. 400 tons.

Guns: 30: LD 16 x 8pdrs; UD 14 x 6pdrs.

Fleur de Lys Brest Dyd.

K: 1657. L: 1659. C: 2.1660. Wrecked on Verdin Rock (near La Rochelle) 20.1.1662.

NOTRE DAME. 28, later 36 guns. Former *Notre Dame du Ciel*, purchased 1661.

Dimensions & tons: 105ft 0in x 24ft 0in x 11ft 4in (34.11 x 7.80 x 3.68m). 400 tons. Draught 14ft (4.55m). Men: 230, +5 officers.

Guns: 28 in 1665 (2 x 16pdrs + 8 x 12pdrs + 4 x 8pdrs; 8 x 5pdrs + 6 others), later 30 then 36.

Notre Dame Nice.

K: 1656. C: 1658. Took part in Battle of Cherchell 24.8.1665. Hulked 1670 at Toulon; not mentioned after 1675.

(B) Vessels acquired from 9 March 1661

ÉCUREUIL. 34 guns. Designed and built by Laurent Hubac as the *Grand Écureuil* to a private order for Nicolas Fouquet (Louis XIV's *Surintendant des Finances*); she was named after Fouquet's patronymic which, at that period, meant 'squirrel'. Following his downfall in 1661, the ship was confiscated by the Crown in September 1661 and added to the Navy with the name shortened to *Écureuil*. Classed as 4th Rank in 1669, then as 5th Rank from 1670.

Dimensions & tons: 104ft 0in, 85ft 0in x 26ft 0in x 12ft 0in (33.78, 27.61 x 8.45 x 3.90m). 500 tons. Draught 14ft (4.55m). Men: 200 (34/100/66), +5 officers.

Guns: 34 by 1669.

Écureuil Toulon Dyd.

K: 6.1658. L: 1659. C: 4.1660. Took part in Battle of La Goulette 2/3.3.1665. Renamed *Orage* 24.6.1671. Removed from service and struck at Toulon 4.1675, but reinstated as a fireship 12.1675 and probably renamed *Éclair*. Expended at Battle of Palermo 3.6.1676.

SAINT SÉBASTIEN. 30 guns. Like *Écureuil*, designed and built by Laurent Hubac for Nicolas Fouquet, and similarly confiscated by the Crown in September 1661 and added to the Navy. Classed as 4th Rank in 1669, then as 5th Rank from July 1670.

Dimensions & tons: dimensions unknown. 350 tons. Men: 150 in 1669 (25/85/40); 120 in 1671 (20/60/40), +5 officers.

Guns: 30 by 1669, then 28 from 1671.

Saint Sébastien Brest Dyd.

K: 1656. L: 1657. C: 6.1658. Renamed *Faucon* 24.6.1671. Wreckd at Terceira 6.1673.

PURCHASED VESSEL (1662). 24 guns. The mercantile *Saint André* (possibly Swedish-built), of c.400 tons, was purchased in February 1662 and added to the French Navy, renamed *Terron*. She was transferred to the *Compagnie des Indies Orientales* in September 1665.

Ex-ALGERINE PRIZES (1663–1665). Five Barbary Coast warships were captured during the mid-1660s. The Algerian *Tric*, built in 1658, was captured on 6 June 1663 by *Soleil* off Collo (Algeria) and became the French Navy's *Perle*. The Algerian *Nejma*, built in 1657–61, was captured in October 1664 and became the French *Étoile*. Three Algerian vessels were captured at the Battle of Cherchell on 24 August 1665: the *Chems*, built in 1656–58, became the French *Soleil d'Afrique*; the *Hillell*, built in 1661–62, became the French *Croissant d'Afrique*; and the *Nekhla*, built in 1654–56, became the French *Palmier*. All five ships were classed as 4th Rank in 1669, then as 5th Rank from 1670.

Perle Algiers.

Dimensions & tons: 105ft 0in x 28ft 10in x 13ft 0in (34.11 x 9.37 x 4.22m). 450 tons. Draught 12ft/13ft (3.90/4.22m). Men: 200, +5 officers.

Guns: 30 in 1669: 16 x 10pdrs; 4 x 8pdrs; 10 x 5pdrs. 32 from 1671, then 34 from 1675.

Took part in Battles of La Goulette 2/3.3.1665 and Cherchell

Even without the formal declaration of war, there was an almost permanent state of hostility between European maritime powers and the so-called Barbary States of North Africa. This anonymous engraving celebrates an early victory for Louis XIV's navy, the capture of three such corsair vessels in the Straits of Gibraltar in December 1643. The powerful French squadron was commanded by Armand de Maillé, Duc de Brézé; earlier in the same year, his fleet also defeated Spanish squadrons on 30 June (off Gibraltar, taking six vessels) and 3 September (at Cartagena). Beverley R Robinson Collection, Annapolis 51.7.27)

24.8.1665. Converted to fireship 6.1674. Condemned 1675 at Toulon; sold there 11.1676 and BU.

Étoile Algiers.
   Dimensions & tons: 104ft 0in x 28ft 0in x 13ft 0in (33.78 x 9.10 x 4.22m). 450 tons. Draught 12ft/14ft (3.90/4.55m). Men: 200, +5 officers.
   Guns: 38 initially, 36 by 1669, 32 from 1671, and 34 from 1675. 16 guns as *flûte*.
   Took part in Battle of La Goulette 2/3.3.1665. Converted to *flûte* 1675, and renamed *Bretonne* 12.1675. Struck 1678 at Toulon and BU.

Soleil d'Afrique Algiers.
   Dimensions & tons: 106ft 0in x 25ft 8in x 10ft 6in (34.43 x 8.34 x 3.41m). 450 tons. Draught 12ft/13ft (3.90/4.22m). Men: 200, +5 officers.
   Guns: 30 by 1669, 32 from 1671, and 30 from 1675.
   Converted to fireship 6.1674. Out of service 4.1675 at Toulon; sold there 11.1676 and BU.

Croissant d'Afrique Cherchell, Algeria.
   Dimensions & tons: 104ft 0in x 26ft 0in x 10ft 9in (33.78 x 8.45 x 3.49m). 450 tons. Draught 15ft (4.87m). Men: 200, +5 officers.
   Guns: 30 by 1669, then 32 from 1671: 2 x 16pdrs; 4 x 8pdrs; 7 x 7pdrs + 13 x 6pdrs; 6 x 4pdrs; 1 x 3pdr + 3 swivels. 12 guns from 1675 as fireship.
   Converted to fireship 1674. Renamed *Fâcheux* 1.1675, but condemned and BU at Brest same year.

Palmier Algiers.
   Dimensions & tons: 93ft 0in x 24ft 0in x 9ft 6in (30.21 x 7.80 x 3.09m). 400 tons. Men: 180, +5 officers.
   Guns: 24 by 1669: 14 x 6pdrs; 4 x 5pdrs; 2 x 4pdrs; 2 x 3pdrs, +2 swivels. 12 guns in 1672 as fireship.
   Renamed *Actif* 24.6.1671, and converted to fireship. Condemned 8.1672, sold and BU.

HIRONDELLE. 28–34 guns. Designed and built by Hendryck Houwens. Classed as 4th Rank in 1669 and 5th Rank from 1670.
    Dimensions & tons: dimensions unknown. 450 tons. Draught 12½ft/15ft (4.06/4.87m). Men: 180 (34/90/58) in war, 150 peace, +5 officers.
    Guns: 30 by 1669, 28 from 1671, 32 from 1674, 34 from 1675 and 30 from 1676.
Hirondelle Dunkirk.
    K: 8.1663. L: 7.11.1664. C: 4.1665. Struck 1679 at Rochefort.

HERMINE. 34 guns. Designed and built by Hendryck Houwens. Classed as 4th Rank in 1669 and 5th Rank from 1670, but raised to 4th Rank again in 1677–78.
    Dimensions & tons: dimensions unknown. 500 tons. Draught 14ft/15ft (4.55/4.87m). Men: 200 (34/100/66) in war, 150 peace, +5/6 officers.
    Guns: 32 by 1669, then 34 from 1671: LD 22 x 12pdrs; UD 12 smaller. 30 from 1676 and 40 from 1677.
Hermine Dunkirk.
    K: 8.1663. L: 19.11.1664. C: 1665. Renamed *Capricieux* 24.6.1671. Hulked 10.1680 at Le Havre; BU 1686.

SAINT CHARLES. 34 guns. Ordered for the *Compagnie des Indes Orientales*, but purchased for the Navy in July 1666 while on the stocks. She was named either *Saint Charles* or *Grand Charles*, and was classed as 4th Rank in 1669, but would have been included in the 5th Rank if not lost in early 1670.
    Dimensions & tons: dimensions unknown. 550 tons. Men: 230 (35/130/65) in war, +5 officers.
    Guns: 34 by 1669.
Saint Charles Bayonne.
    K: 1665. L: 8.1666. C: 11.1666. Wrecked 1.1670 en route to Canada, her crew saved by *Lion d'Or*.

LIGOURNOIS. 24, later 32 guns. Another Barbary Coast prize, captured at Tunis in August or November 1665 (but originally built in Tuscany in 1658), and added to the French Navy 29 April 1666 on the instruction of the Duc de Beaufort. Classed as 4th Rank in 1669, then as 5th Rank from 1670.
    Dimensions & tons: dimensions unknown. 400 tons. Men: 110 (32/128/60) in 1669, 150 (25/75/50) in 1671, +5 officers.
    Guns: 24 by 1669, then 28 from 1672 and 32 from 1673.
Ligournois Livorno.
    Renamed *Émerillon* 24.6.1671. Converted to fireship 4.1672, and expended against the Dutch at the Battle of Solebay 7.6.1672.

LION ROUGE. 24, later 32 guns. Originally built in England as the Ottoman vessel *al-Assad al-Ahmar* and captured in 1665 (probably on the Barbary Coast). On capture named *Grand Anglais* but quickly renamed *Lion Rouge*. Classed as 4th Rank in 1669, then as 5th Rank from 1670.
    Dimensions & tons: 100ft 0in x 23ft 6in x 11ft 6in (32.48 x 7.63 x 3.74m). 450 tons. Draught 13ft (4.22m). Men: 220 (32/128/60) in 1669, 170 (30/90/50) in 1671, +5 officers.
    Guns: 24 in 1669, 28 in 1671, 30 in 1672, 32 in 1673.
Lion Rouge England.
    Built 1656. Renamed *Entendu* 24.6.1671. Converted (by Order of 4.1.1673) to fireship (400 tons, 24 guns) 3.1673, and present at the Battle of Schooneveldt 7.6.1673. Burnt 26.2.1675 on the English coast.

PURCHASED VESSELS (1666). All except *Vierge* (already a *flûte*) were classed as 4th Rank in 1669, but as 5th Rank from 1670.
Saint Joseph La Ciotat (designed and built by Laurent Coulomb).
    Dimensions & tons: 100ft 3in, 77ft 0in x 28ft 0in x 12ft 6in (32.57, 25.01 x 9.10 x 4.06m). 400 tons. Draught 12ft/13ft (3.90/4.22m). Men: 220 in war (32/128/60) in 1669, 170 30/90/50) in 1671, +5 officers.
    Guns: 30 from 1669, then 28 from 1671 and 32 from 1677.
    K: 1661. C: 1664. Purchased 12.2.1666. Renamed *Dur* 24.6.1671, then *Poli* 28.6.1678. Condemned 2.1691; sold 4.1692 and BU.
Ville de Rouen Brest Dyd.
    Dimensions & tons: 108ft 0in, 88ft 2in x 25ft 1in x 11ft 1in (35.08, 28.64 x 8.15 x 3.60m). 400 tons. Draught 14ft (4.55m). Men: 230 in war (35/130/65) in 1669, 200 (34/100/66) in 1671, +5 officers.
    Guns: 32 from 1669, then 34 from 1671.
    K: 1659. C: 1662. Purchased at Toulon 12.4.1666. Renamed *Hasardeux* 24.6.1671. Converted to fireship 5.1673 and expended against the Dutch at 1st Battle of Schooneveldt 7.6.1673.
Vierge Hoorn.
    Dimensions & tons: 98ft 0in x 23ft 0in x 12ft 0in (31.83 x 7.47 x 3.90m). 400 tons. Draught 12ft/14ft (3.90/4.55m). Men: 250 in war, 200 peace, +5 officers. 40 (8/32/0) as *flûte*, +2 officers.
    Guns: originally 34; as *flûte* in 1669, 8 only, then 12 from 1671 and 16 from 1676.
    K: 1656. C: ?1656. Purchased 12.4.1666 at Toulon (from French East India Co.). Renamed *Profond* 24.6.1671. Re-classed as *flûte* 1669. Struck at Toulon 10.1678.
Sauveur Brest Dyd (designed and built by Laurent Hubac).
    Dimensions & tons: 100ft 1in, 89ft 2in x 27ft 1in x 12ft 0in (32.51, 28.96 x 8.80 x 3.90m). 550 tons. Draught 14ft/15ft (4.55/4.87m). Men: 230 in war (35/130/65) in 1669, 200 (34/100/66) in 1671, +5 officers.
    Guns: 32 from 1669, then 34 from 1671 and 36 from 1676.
    K: 1660. L: 1662. C: 1663. Purchased 12.4.1666 at Toulon. Renamed *Lion* 24.6.1671, then *Grand Ponton* 11.1676 when became a sheer (*i.e.* masting) hulk at Le Havre. Removed from use 7.1686 and BU.
Lion d'Or Marseille (designed and built by Jean Étienne).
    Dimensions & tons: 90ft 0in x 23ft 0in x 9ft 1in (29.24 x 7.47 x 2.95m). 350 tons. Draught 11ft (3.57m). Men: 220 in 1669 (32/128/60), then 120 in 1671 (20/60/40), +5 officers.
    Guns: 24 from 1669, then 28 from 1671.
    K: 1660. C: 1661. Purchased 1666. Renamed *Vigilant* 24.6.1671. Struck at Rochefort 8.1673.

BAYONNAIS. 34 guns. Former merchant vessel *Saint Jean*, designed by Joseph Saboulin and built by Jean Hontabat for the *Compagnie des Indes Orientales*; purchased for the Navy in September 1667 and renamed *Bayonnais* or *Saint Jean de Bayonne*. Classed as 4th Rank in 1669 but as 5th Rank from 1670.
    Dimensions & tons: dimensions unknown. 500 tons. Draught 14ft (4.55m). Men: 230 in war (35/130/65) in 1669, 200 (34/100/66) in 1671, or 170 peace, +5 officers.
    Guns: 32 by 1669, then 34 from 1671 and 32 from 1675.
Bayonnais (Bayonnois) Bayonne.
    K: 1666. L: 1666 or 1667. C: 5.1667. Sailed 3.1670 for the East Indies with the Persia Squadron of Jacob Blanquet de la Haye. Renamed *Adroit* 24 June 1671 but continued to be called *Bayonnais* or *Saint Jean de Bayonne* until run ashore and lost at Tranquebar (a Danish fort in southeast India) 11.1673.

Ex-GENOESE PURCHASES (1669). The 500-ton vessels *San Augustino* and *Princepessa*, both belonging to the Marquis de Centurion, were purchased at Toulon in December 1669 by order of Colbert (together with the *Frégate du Portugal*) and renamed *Saint Augustin de Gênes* and *Princesse de Gênes* respectively. They were classed as 5th Rank from 1670.

Saint Augustin de Gênes Holland
Dimensions & tons: dimensions unknown. Men: 200 (34/100/66) +5 officers.
Guns: 34
Built 1658–60. Renamed *Palmier* 24.6.1671. Rebuilt at Toulon 1674, but struck 1.1676 and hulked at Messina, where she was abandoned to the Spanish 3.1678

Princesse de Gênes Genoa
Dimensions & tons: dimensions unknown. 200 (34/100/66) +5 officers.
Guns: 34
Built 1663–65. Renamed *Prompt* 24.6.1671. Re-classed as 4th Rank 1687 but reverted to 5th Rank 1690; struck 1691 (either lost or sold during a voyage to the Levant)

LES JEUX. 28 guns. Designed and built by Jean Guichard. Pierced for ten pairs of LD guns.
Dimensions & tons: 106ft 0in, 84ft 0in x 25ft 0in x 12ft 0in (34.43, 27.29 x 8.12 x 3.90m). 350 tons. Draught 14ft/14½ft (4.55/4.71m). Men: 120 (20/60/40) in 1671, + 5 officers; from 1672, 150 (25/75/50), +5 officers.
Guns: 28 from 1670, then 30 from 1675. 36 from 1676: LD 20 x 8pdrs; UD 6 x 6pdrs + 12 x 4pdrs. 40 from 1677.

Les Jeux Rochefort Dyd.
K: end 1669. L: 25.7.1670. C: 3.1671. Took part in successful repulse of Dutch attack (by Michiel de Ruyter) on Fort Royal (Martinique) 20.7.1674, and in Battle of Tobago 3.3.1677. Sold at Rochefort early 1687 to *Compagnie des Indes Orientales*.

TROMPEUSE Class. 28 guns. Designed and built by Rodolphe Gédéon. Pierced for nine pairs of LD guns. Ordered in late 1668, and named on 21 February 1670. *Mercure* (ex-*Trompeuse*) was rebuilt at Toulon in 1689.
Dimensions & tons: 101ft 8in x 26ft 0in x ?ft 0in (33.03 x 8.45m). 350 tons. Draught 12ft (3.90m). Men: 150 (25/75/50), +5 officers.
Guns: 28 from 1671; LD 18 x 8pdrs; UD 10 x 6pdrs. 20 from 1677 (from 1679 for *Gaillard*). 32 from 1689 in *Mercure*.

Bouffonne Toulon Dyd.
K: 12.1669. L: 29.6.1670. C: 12.1670. Renamed *Drôle* 24.6.1671, then *Gaillard* 28.6.1678. Wrecked off Le Havre 7.1682.

Trompeuse Toulon Dyd.
K: 12.1669. L: 6.7.1670. C: 12.1670. Renamed *Triton* 24.6.1671, then *Mercure* 28.6.1678. Took part in Bombardment of Genoa in 5.1684. Struck 1690 at Toulon. May possibly have been captured by the English and then recaptured by the French and taken into Brest, see the *Mercure* of 1690 below.

TOURBILLON Class. 28 guns. Designed and built by Laurent Hubac. Pierced for nine pairs of LD guns. Ordered on 21 December 1669 as 'frigates able to serve as fireships', and named on 21 February 1670.
Dimensions & tons: 90ft 0in, 78ft 0in x 24ft 0in x 11ft 0in (29.24, 25.34 x 7.80 x 3.57m). 300/350 tons. Draught 12ft (3.90m). Men: 120 (20/60/40), + 5 officers.
Guns: 28 from 1671: LD 18 x 8pdrs; UD 10 x 6pdrs. 30 guns in *Pétillant* from 1691.

Laurier Brest Dyd.
K: 2.1670. L: 27.5.1670. C: 8.1670. Probably lost off the coast of French Guiana 7.1677.

Tourbillon Brest Dyd.
K: 2.1670. L: 28.5.1670. C: 8.1670. Renamed *Pétillant* 28.6.1678. Converted to fireship 1693. Struck at Toulon *c*.1694.

ÉVEILLÉ. 24, later 28 guns. Designed and built by Hendryck Houwens. Ordered in early 1670, and named *Dur* on 27 July 1670, but renamed *Éveillé* on 24 June 1671. Pierced for ten pairs of LD guns. Reduced to a *frégate légère* in 1685 and renamed, and reconstructed 1686–87 at Brest.
Dimensions & tons: 108ft 0in, 96ft 0in x 26ft 0in x 13ft 6in (35.08, 31.18 x 8.45 x 4.39m). 300/350 tons. Draught 11ft/12½ft (3.57/4.06m). Men: 120 (20/60/40), + 5 officers.
Guns: 24 from 1671, then 28 from 1672: LD 20 x 8pdrs; UD 8 x 4pdrs. 22 from 1676, then 24 from 1679, and 20 from 1688.

Éveillé Dunkirk.
K: 1670. L: 2.1671. C: 6.1671. Renamed *Bien Aimée* 1685 when re-classed as *frégate légère*. Lent as a privateer to the Marquis de Seignelay, Secretary of State for the Navy, who funded it for 2/3, as part of a squadron of three to four under CV Jacques Dandenne 1689–90. Struck (possibly became a fireship) *c*.1693.

CANADIEN. 36 guns. The first warship to be built in North America, constructed by an unnamed master shipwright sent from Rochefort for the purpose. Her life was short (certainly in comparison with the five-year period of putting her into service), an indication of the inferior quality timber available locally.
Dimensions & tons: dimensions unknown. 500 tons. Men: 200, +6 officers.
Guns: 36 in 1677.

Canadien Quebec.
K: 6.1670. L: 10.1673. C: 1675. Renamed *Lion* 20.11.1676. Condemned and ordered to be sold or BU 4.6.1677 at Rochefort.

In theory, the Regulation of 4 August 1670 provided for the 5th Rank to consist of two-decked vessels carrying between 24 and 34 guns. However, in practice the list of vessels as at 1 January 1671 contained twenty-nine vessels of 300 to 550 tons, with between 24 and 34 guns. These comprised ten ships of 34 guns (*Dragon*, *Écureuil*, *Hermine*, *Ville de Rouen*, *Sauveur*, *Bayonnais*, *Saint Augustin de Gênes*, *Princesse de Gênes*, *Galante* and *Mignonne*), four of 32 guns (*Perle*, *Étoile*, *Soleil d'Afrique* and *Croissant*), twelve of 28 guns (*Hirondelle*, *Lion Rouge*, *Saint Sébastien*, *Saint Joseph*, *Lion d'Or*, *Jeux*, *Bouffonne*, *Trompeuse*, *Laurier*, *Tourbillon*, *Victoire* and *Périlleux*) and three of 24 guns (*Ligournois*, *Palmier* and *Dur*). Apart from the newly-ordered *Victoire*, *Périlleux*, *Galante* and *Mignonne* (see below), and the ten built since 1669 (listed above from *Les Jeux* to *Éveillé*), all had featured in the previous List (at September 1669) as 4th Rank.

ARROGANT Class. 28 guns, designed and built by Laurent Hubac. Pierced for nine pairs of LD guns. Ordered on 29 May 1670, and named on 27 July 1670 as *Victoire* and *Périlleux*, but renamed as *Arrogant* and *Hardi* on 24 June 1671 prior to completion.
Dimensions & tons: 98ft 0in, 86ft 0in x 24ft 0in x 12ft 0in (31.83, 27.94 x 7.80 x 3.90m). 350/450 tons. Draught 14ft/14½ft (4.55/4.71m). Men: 120 (20/60/40) in 1671, + 5 officers; from 1672, 170 (30/90/50), +5 officers; *Arrogant* in 1673, 200 in war (34/100/66), + 5/6 officers.
Guns: 28 from 1671: LD 18 x 8pdrs; UD 10 x 6pdrs. 32 guns from 1672. *Hardi*/*Joli* 34 guns from 1675, then 36 from 1691.

Arrogant Brest Dyd.
K: 9.1670. L: 15.3.1671. C: 7.1671. Converted to a fireship 6.1673, and expended at the Battle of Texel 21.8.1673.

Hardi Brest Dyd.
K: 9.1670. L: 15.3.1671. C: 7.1671. Took part in Battle of Solebay 7.6.1672. Renamed *Joli* 28.6.1678. Wrecked 1692 off Terra Nova.

AVENTURIER Class. 34, later 40 guns, designed and built by Louis Audibert. Probably pierced for ten pairs of LD guns. First named on 10 October 1670 as *Galante* and *Mignonne*, they were renamed *Aventurier* and *Bizarre* on 24 June 1671 while on the stocks. Both were raised from the 5th to the 4th Rank in 1677–78, but *Aventurier* was restored to the 5th Rank in 1692–95, while *Bizarre* was re-classed as a *flûte*. *Bizarre* was rebuilt at Toulon from 1680 to April 1681.

Dimensions & tons: 105ft 0in, 85ft 0in x 32ft 0in x 14ft 0in (34.11, 27.61 x 10.39 x 4.55m). 500 tons. Draught 12ft/14ft (3.90/4.55m). Men: 200 (34/100/66), + 5 officers; from 1675, 150 (35/78/37), + 6 officers.

Guns: 34 from 1673. *Bizarre* had 42 guns from 1677: LD 20 x 12pdrs; UD 18 x 8pdrs; QD 4 x 4pdrs. 44 from 1691. *Aventurier* had 40 guns from 1679. 36 guns in war from 1696 (30 peace): LD 16 x 12pdrs; UD 16 x 8pdrs; QD 4 x 4pdrs.

Aventurier Marseille.
K: 8.1670. L: 11.1671. C: 5.1673. Took part in the Bombardment of Tripoli 22.6.1685. Reconstructed 1688 at Toulon. Struck 1697, probably at Toulon.

Bizarre Marseille.
K: 8.1670. L: 29.8.1672. C: 8.1673. Took part in the Bombardments of Algiers 26.6.1683, Genoa 18–28.5.1684, and Tripoli 22.6.1685, and in Battle of Lagos 28.6.1693. Renamed *Colosse* 2.1692, and re-classed as 20-gun *flûte*. Struck 1694, and sold for commerce at Dunkirk, renamed *Concorde*.

ÉMERILLON. 34 guns, designed and built by Laurent Hubac. Pierced for nine pairs of LD guns. Ordered on 7 November 1670, named *Actif* on 30 May 1672, and completed in June for coast guard duties. Renamed *Émerillon* on 7 January 1673 and refitted for escort duties at Brest. Rebuilt 1683 at Rochefort.

Dimensions & tons: 98ft 0in, 86ft 0in x 24ft 0in x 12ft 0in (31.83, 27.94 x 7.80 x 3.90m). 350 tons. Draught 12ft/14ft (3.90/4.55m). Men: 200 (45/96/60) in war, 150 peace, +6 officers.

Guns: 32 from 1674. 34 from 1675: LD 18 x 8pdrs; UD 16 x 6pdrs. 26 guns from 1677, then 34 from 1688 and 36 from 1690.

Émerillon Brest Dyd.
K: 3.1671. L: 4.1672. C: 6.1672. Grounded accidentally at Martinique 8.1691, but refloated. Struck 1694 (probably captured by the English).

Eight purpose-built 300-ton fireships were ordered during 1671, each intended to carry 12 guns and 40 men (8/32/–), plus 1 officer. These comprised the *Fâcheux* and *Brutal* at Dunkirk, the *Entreprenant* and *Fin* at Rochefort, the *Déguisé* and *Périlleux* at Brest, and the *Dangereux* and *Incommode* at Toulon. The first three of these were converted to 5th Rank *frégates* in 1673 (although the Dunkirk pair were then raised to 4th Rank in 1675 – see Chapter 4) and renamed. Another two fireships were ordered later – the *Éclair* at Rochefort in 1672 and the *Caché* at Brest in 1673, and these were also converted to 5th Rank *frégates*.

VIGILANT. 28 guns. Designed and built by Jean Guichard as a 12-gun fireship. Ordered as *Entreprenant* on 9 August 1671 (along with her sister *Fin*) and completed in 1672, but on 24 February 1673 it was ordered that she be fitted as a 5th Rank ship and she was renamed *Vigilant* on the same date.

Dimensions & tons: 99ft 0in, 80ft 0in x 27ft 10in x 11ft 2in (32.16, 25.99 x 9.04 x 3.63m). 350 tons. Draught 13½ft/14ft 7in (4.39/4.74m). Men: 150 (25/75/50), +5 officers.

Guns: 28 from 1673, then 30 from 1675, 36 from 1690 and 40 from 1691.

Vigilant Rochefort Dyd.
K: 9.1671. L: 1.1672. C: 5.1672. Renamed *Mignon* 26.6.1678, and then *Coche* 2.1692 when re-classed as an 18-gun *flûte* (with 4 x 8pdrs and 14 x 6pdrs; 45 men); condemned at Toulon 1704.

SOLEIL D'AFRIQUE. 32 guns, designed and built by Abraham Aubier (or Aubin), Jean Guichard and/or Pierre Mallet. Ordered and named *Éclair* on 26 December 1672 as a fireship with 12 guns and completed in 1673, but renamed *Soleil d'Afrique* 6.12.1675 and re-rated and re-armed as 5th Rank in 1675. Rebuilt 1687 at Brest.

Dimensions & tons: 95ft 0in, 80ft 0in x 28ft 2in x 12ft 4in (30.86, 25.99 x 9.15 x 4.01m). 300 tons. Draught 13½ft/14ft (4.39/4.55m). Men: 150 (35/78/37), +6 officers.

Guns: 34 from 1675, then 30 from 1676 and 32 from 1679. As reconverted to fireship 1695: 6 x 4pdrs only, then 8 x 6pdrs from 1704.

Soleil d'Afrique Rochefort Dyd.
K: 12.1672. L: 28.5.1673. C: 8.1673. Renamed *Lion* 26.8.1678. Took part in campaign in Ireland 1689. Lent, under CV Abraham, Marquis Duquesne-Guitton, with *Dragon* and *Oiseau*, to escort to India the mercantile *Écueil*, *Florissant* and *Gaillard* from the *Compagnie des Indes Orientales* 1689–91. Re-converted to a fireship 1695. Probably scuttled at Toulon in 7.1707, but refloated. Condemned 15.12.1710 at Toulon, and ordered to be sold 9 days later.

ARROGANT Class. 32 guns, designed and built by Laurent Hubac. Ordered 3 February 1673 as fireships, to carry 12 guns, and named the next day as *Caché* and *Entreprenant*, but modified as *frégates-vaisseaux* during construction, renamed *Arrogant* and *Dragon* respectively on 28 November 1673 after launching and re-classed as 5th Rank. Pierced for eight pairs of LD guns. *Dragon* underwent rebuilding in 1681–82 and again in 1689 at Brest.

Dimensions & tons: 92ft 6in, 80ft 0in x 24ft 6in x 12ft 0in (30.05, 25.99 x 7.96 x 3.90m). 300/350 tons. Draught 12ft/13½ft (3.90/4.39m). Men: 150 (35/78/37), + 6 officers.

Guns: 34 from 1674, then 30 from 1679. *Dragon* had 32 in war from 1696 (26 peace): LD 16 x 8pdrs; UD 16 x 4pdrs (6pdrs in 1708).

Arrogant Brest Dyd.
K: 5.1673. L: 10.1673. C: 11.1674. Renamed *Galant* 28.6.1678. Wrecked 3.1684 off the Portuguese coast.

Dragon Brest Dyd.
K: 5.1673. L: 10.1673. C: 1674. Lent, under CV Abraham, Marquis Duquesne-Guitton, with *Oiseau et Lion*, to escort to India *Écueil*, *Florissant* and *Gaillard* from the *Compagnie des Indes Orientales* 1689–91. Re-classed as 200-ton *flûte* 1709. Condemned at Rochefort 1712.

The new *Règlement* of 10 February 1674 assigned to ships of the 5th Rank an armament of 30 guns; this comprised a mixed battery of 4 (bronze) 12pdrs and 12 (iron) 8pdrs on their LDs, and an UD battery of 14 x 6pdrs (4 to be bronze and 10 iron). There were, however, many exceptions to this allocation, and in practice extra 8pdrs seem to have been fitted instead of the 12pdrs. Ideal dimensions for such 5th Rank ships were not included in the *Règlements*, but in 1677 F. Dassié (in his *L'Architecture Navale*, the first French treatise on naval architecture) stated that typical dimensions for this Rank would be 108ft x 27ft x 13½ft (35.08 x 8.77 x 4.385m).

PURCHASED VESSEL (1674). The former privateer *Dauphin* (or *Dauphin de Bayonne*), was purchased for the Navy in April 1674. She was built by Honoré Malet.

Dimensions & tons: 106ft 0in, 84ft 0in x 23ft 0in x 12ft 0in (34.43, 27.29 x 7.47 x 3.90m). 350 tons. Draught 11ft/13ft (3.57/4.22m). Men: in 1675, 120 (33/60/27), +6 officers; by 1688, 150 (35/78/37), +6 officers.

Guns: 28 from 1675, then 32 from 1677.

Dauphin Bayonne (or Rochefort?)
K: 1667. L/C: 1670. Renamed *Perle* 6.12.1675. Struck in the Caribbean 1690.

Ex-SPANISH PRIZE (1675). The former Spanish *San Antonio* was captured around July 1675 by *Brillant* and added to the French Navy under the name *Orage* (after briefly being called *Saint Antoine*) on 6 December 1675.

Dimensions & tons: dimensions unknown. 250 tons (100 as fireship). Men: 120 (33/60/27) +6 officers (30 men +2 officers as fireship)
Guns: 24 (4 as fireship)

Orage Bilbao
Built in 1673 (probably by Juan de Olaeta) although also listed as built in Flanders. Captured by the Dutch in May 1676 but retaken by the French in June. Refitted from 1677 to May 1678, then re-classed as a fireship and renamed *Lion* on 28 June 1678, resuming the name *Orage* at the end of that year. Converted to a 4-gun fireship from 1679, but condemned in 1680.

PALMIER Class. 36-gun type. First named *Favorite* and *Gracieuse* in September 1676, but renamed *Palmier* and *Adroit* respectively on 11 December 1676 (*Favorite* was earlier renamed *Soleil d'Afrique* in October 1676). Designed and built by Benjamin Chaillé, who died 12 June 1677. The work on *Adroit* was continued by his son Pierre for a month, and then completed from 13 July by Élie Guichard. Both ships probably pierced for ten pairs of LD guns. On 24 January 1681 *Adroit* was ordered used for experiments at Dunkirk with mortars as part of the development of *galiotes à mortiers* by Renau d'Élissagaray. *Palmier* was rebuilt at Brest in 1687–88, and at Rochefort in 1700–1; she was raised from the 5th Rank to 4th Rank in 1698, but reverted to 5th Rank in 1708.

Dimensions & tons: 114ft 0in, 100ft 0in x 27ft 0in x 11ft 0in (37.03, 32.48 x 8.77 x 3.57m). 300 tons. Draught *Palmier* 11ft/13¾ft (3.57/4.47m), *Adroit* 12½ft/14ft (4.06/4.55m). Men: 150 (35/78/37), +6 officers.

Guns: 36 from 1677: LD 20 x 8pdrs; UD 6 x 6pdrs + 10 x 4pdrs. *Palmier* had 36 from 1696 in war (30 peace): LD 18 x 8pdrs; UD 18 x 6pdrs. From 1699, *Palmier* had 20 x 12pdrs and 20 x 6pdrs, then from 1706 10 x 8pdrs + 20 x 6pdrs.

Palmier Le Havre.
K: 4.1676. L: 23.12.1676. C: 5.1677. Lent as a privateer to the Marquis de Seignelay, with *Comte* and *Mutine*, under CV Ferdinand

This pen and wash drawing, signed by Chabert *le cadet* and probably dating from the last quarter of the seventeenth century, does not exactly match the known characteristics of any French warship of that period. Given its armament, it is tempting to describe it as a 5th Rank ship, but in layout it appears to be closest to several classes of large *frégates légères* built with 24 to 28 guns between 1675 and 1681 (see Chapter 6). It probably gives a good impression of the appearance of those ships, but none of these had more than nine pairs of armed ports in the battery while all had more guns on the *gaillards*. The absence of rowports in these careful drawings rules out the otherwise possible *Gracieuse* and *Bien Aimée* of 1672. The extreme height of the gunports and the presence of a single raft-port low in the stern indicate that the frigate is two-decked with the battery on the UD, and indeed she bears a closer resemblance to the 'true' frigates of the 1740s than to any ships of Louis XIV's navy. (After an original in the Musée de la Marine, Paris)

de Relingue, who shared the funding 1688–89. It was the first 'armement mixte' arrangement organised by Seigneley (the war having not yet been declared). *Palmier* was then under the command of CV François René de Betz de La Harteloire, future LG (1705) and Grand-Cross of the *Ordre du Saint Esprit* (1724). Took part in operations at Nova Scotia and Hudson Bay under CV Pierre Le Moyne d'Iberville, in a squadron of four vessels, 1696–98. Ordered sold 27.4.1707 at Toulon as unserviceable, scuttled there 7.1707 but refloated, sale order confirmed 25.9.1709.

Adroit Le Havre.
K: 5.1676. L: 15.7.1677. C: 1.1678. Captured by two Dutch vessels off St Domingue 1.1689.

MARQUIS. 28 guns. Designed and built by Laurent Hubac. Pierced for ten pairs of LD guns. Ordered in early 1678 and named on 28 June as *Laurier*, but renamed in December 1678 while still on the stocks.

Dimensions & tons: 108ft 0in, 96ft 0in x 26ft 0in x 13ft 0in (35.08, 31.18 x 8.45 x 4.22m). 250 tons. Men: 150 (35/78/37), +6 officers.

Guns: 28 from 1679: LD 20 x 8pdrs; UD 8 x 6pdrs.

Marquis Brest Dyd.
K: early 1678. L: 1679. C: 1680. Wrecked 1684 off Brest (on the rock thereafter known as 'La Marquise').

HERCULE. 30 guns. Designed and built by Laurent Hubac, and seemingly an enlarged version of his *Marquis* above. Pierced for ten pairs of LD guns. Named on 28 June 1678. Rebuilt at Brest from November 1693 to February 1694.

Dimensions & tons: 112ft 0in, 96ft 0in x 26ft 10in x 13ft 6in (36.38, 31.18 x 8.72 x 4.39m). 250/420 tons. Draught 12½ft/15ft (4.06/4.87m). Men: 150 (35/78/37), +6 officers.

Guns: 30 from 1679: LD 20 x 8pdrs; UD 10 x 6pdrs. 30 in war from 1696 (28 peace): unchanged.

Hercule Brest Dyd.
K: 4.1678. L: 1679. C: 4.1680. Lent as a privateer to the Marquis de Seigneley, who funded it for 2/3, as part of a squadron of three to four under CV Jacques Dandenne 1689–90. Lent as a privateer to Louis d'Oger, Marquis de Cavoye, under the command of René Duguay-Trouin from St Malo who shared the funding 1693. Took part in Battle of Vélez-Malaga 24.8.1704. With the *Croissant* (ex-*Sérieux*) and *Oiseau* (see below) and the *frégate légère Sibylle*, deliberately beached and burnt 9.11.1704 to avoid capture by Vice-Adm Sir John Leake's squadron off Gibraltar.

From July 1678 to the start of 1680, Colbert – disappointed at the slow pace of naval construction – ordered Toulon, Brest and Rochefort to experiment with pre-fabricated material to increase efficiency. The following three vessels indicate how sophisticated the process of prefabrication had become in the principal dockyards in order that the numbers of cruisers could be quickly augmented at short notice; designs were drawn and stocks of prepared frames were cut to those designs and stored in anticipation of orders. There was keen competition between the *constructeurs* to see how quickly they could complete the process of keel-laying – Hubac attempted to compete with Coulomb's record of seven hours, but failed. Both *Ponant* dockyards fell well short of Toulon's standard.

MARIN. 28 guns. Designed by Honoré Malet, and built by Honoré and Pierre Malet. Probably pierced for ten pairs of LD guns. Ordered in December 1678, prefabricated and laid on slip 23/24 May 1679 (in 33 hours).

Dimensions & tons: 110ft 0in, 96ft 0in x 24ft 0in x 12ft 0in (35.73, 31.18 x 7.80 x 3.90m). 250 tons. Draught 10ft/13½ft (3.25/4.39m). Men: 160 in war, 140 peace, +6 officers.

Guns: 28 from 1680: LD 20 x 8pdrs; UD 8 x 6pdrs. 30 guns from 1691 – still 30 in war in 1696 (28 peace): LD 20 x 8pdrs; UD 6 x 6pdrs; QD 4 x 4pdrs. Re-armed 1699 with LD 18 x 6pdrs + UD 12 x 4pdrs (8 x 4pdrs in 1700), then 1701 with 34 guns: 22 x 6pdrs + 12 x 4pdrs. LD guns replaced by 12pdrs in 1702 and 8pdrs in 1704, while UD guns were replaced by 6pdrs in 1702 and finally 10 x 4pdrs in 1704.

Marin Rochefort Dyd.
K: 5.1679. L: 7.1679. C: 4.1680. Lent as a privateer to the deposed King James II, under command of Richard Giraldin Jnr, from St Malo, 1695. Lent as a privateer to CdE Jean Bernard de Saint-Jean, Baron de Pointis, as part of a squadron of fourteen vessels, 1696–97; took part in the capture of Cartagena de Indias 5.5.1697. Exploration of the mouths of the Mississippi (under CV Pierre Le Moyne d'Iberville) 1699. Struck 1703, and leased to the *Compagnie de l'Asiento* as a slaver 2.1704. Condemned 5.1705 at La Guaira (Venezuela).

SÉRIEUX. 36 guns. Designed and built by Laurent Coulomb, and pierced for ten pairs of LD guns. Ordered in August 1678, prefabricated in April to June 1679 and laid down on the 13 July in a seven-hour period; she was then taken down and re-laid, and launched in the presence of the Marquis de Seigneley, Secretary of State for the Navy. Built as *Royale* (or *Frégate Royale*), but soon after completion was renamed *Sérieux*. Ordered in 1679 as 5th Rank, re-classed as 4th Rank in 1680, and reverted to 5th Rank in 1682. A similar design was prepared by François Coulomb in 1683 to train shipwrights at Toulon; this was not actually built (but is fully documented by Jean-Claude Lemineur in his monograph *Vaisseau de 5^e Rang Le François*).

Dimensions & tons: 103ft 0in, 86ft 0in x 25ft 0in x 13ft 0in (33.46, 27.94 x 8.12 x 4.22m). 300/350 tons. Draught 12ft/12½ft (3.90/4.06m). Men: 200 (45/95/60), +6 officers; by 1687, 150 (35/78/37) in war, 120 (33/60/27) peace, +6 officers.

Guns: 40 from 1680, then 38 from 1683: LD 20 x 8pdrs; UD 6 x 6pdrs + 12 x 4pdrs. 30 guns from 1687 – still 30 in war in 1696 (22 peace): LD 18 x 8pdrs; UD 12 x 4pdrs. 38 from 1699: LD 20 x 8pdrs (6pdrs in 1704); UD 18 x 4pdrs (16 in 1704).

Sérieux Toulon Dyd.
K: 7.1679. L: 6.11.1679. C: 12.1679. Renamed *Croissant* 1.6.1690 (as a new 2nd Rank *Sérieux* was being built). Like the *Hercule* (see above), she was deliberately beached and burnt 9.11.1704 to avoid capture by Vice-Adm Sir John Leake's squadron off Gibraltar.

HIRONDELLE. 28 guns. Designed and built by Laurent Hubac. Pierced for ten pairs of LD guns. Ordered in December 1678, the component parts were prefabricated (as with *Royale* above) with a view to assembling the keel on one day in the presence of Louis XIV. In fact, they were laid down over the 4/5 July 1679 in a 22-hour period, but had to be taken up and re-laid later.

Dimensions & tons: 108ft 0in, 96ft 0in x 26ft 10in x 13ft 6in (35.08, 31.18 x 8.72 x 4.39m). 250 tons. Draught 12½ft (4.06m). Men: 120 (33/60/27), +6 officers.

Guns: 28 from 1680: LD 20 x 8pdrs; UD 8 x 6pdrs.

Hirondelle Brest Dyd.
K: 4.7.1679. L: 11.1679. C: 12.1679. Struck 1687 at Toulon.

SOLEIL D'AFRIQUE. 28 guns. Designed and built by Pierre Malet. Pierced for ten pairs of LD guns. Rebuilt at Rochefort in 1690–91.

Dimensions & tons: 110ft 0in, 96ft 0in x 24ft 0in x 12ft 0in (35.73, 31.18 x 7.80 x 3.90m). 330 tons. Draught 10½ft (3.41m). Men: 150 (35/78/37), +6 officers.

Guns: 28 from 1682: LD 20 x 8pdrs; UD 8 x 6pdrs. 30 guns from 1688, then 32 from 1696 in war (30 peace): LD 20 x 8pdrs; UD 12 x 4pdrs.

Soleil d'Afrique Rochefort Dyd.
K: 1680. L: 1681. C: 1682. Lent as a privateer to CFL Jean-Baptiste Ducasse, as part of a squadron of four vessels, for operations against Surinam 1688. Lent as a privateer to CV Jean-Baptiste, Comte de Gennes, Seigneur d'Oyac, as part of a squadron of six vessels, 1695–97. Struck 1698 at Rochefort.

For most of the 1680s, very few further ships were added to the 5th Rank; in fact, no new ships of this Rank were ordered until 1688, with the outbreak of the War of the League of Augsburg (or Nine Years' War) against the English and Dutch. The 21 ships of this Rank in 1682 were in general retained until the end of the decade.

ÉVEILLÉ. 28, later 32 guns. Constructed by Étienne Hubac in 1685, probably converted from the *flûte Fourgon* (of 1679 – see Chapter 9), repurchased from the Spanish at Cadiz in 1685.

Dimensions & tons: 90ft 0in, 73ft 6in x 24ft 0in x 11ft 0in (29.24, 23.88 x 7.80 x 3.57m). 250 tons. Draught 11½ft/12ft (3.74/3.90m). Men: 120 (33/60/27), +5/6 officers.

Guns: 28 from 1686, 30 from 1691, then 6 only (6 x 6pdrs) from 1696 as a fireship. 32 guns in war from 1699 (20 peace): LD 16 x 8pdrs; UD 16 x 4pdrs. In 1702 the 4pdrs were replaced by 16 x 6pdrs.

Éveillé Brest Dyd.
Captured by HM Ships *Lively*, *Foresight* and *Mordaunt* 4.8.1689, becoming HMS *Lively Prize*; retaken by a French squadron off the Isles of Scilly 14.10.1689. Lent as a privateer to Sieur Bréal, from St Malo, and CB Jacques Macquerel de Boisougé 1692. Converted to fireship 1.1694. Took part in operations at Nova Scotia under LG André, Marquis de Nesmond, in a squadron of twenty-three vessels 1697. Re-classed back to 5th Rank in 1701 after 1699 re-arming, but expended as a fireship at Vigo 22.10.1702.

Ex-ALGERIAN PRIZES (1687). The Algerian *Sameche*, built in 1667–69, was captured in July 1687 and became the French *Soleil d'Alger* while the Algerian *Thalatha Warda al-Dhabe*, built in 1680–85, was captured in October 1687 and became the French *Trois Roses*, soon renamed *Hirondelle*. *Hirondelle* was reconstructed at Toulon in 1698–99.

Soleil d'Alger Algiers.
Dimensions & tons: dimensions unknown. 350 tons. Men: 200 in war, 150 peace, +6 officers.
Guns: 36 from 1689.
Renamed *Galant* 11.1688. Returned by Louis XIV to the Dey of Algiers 12.1689 (in accord with Treaty of 25.9.1689).

Trois Roses Algiers.
Dimensions & tons: 104ft 0in x 30ft 2in x 13ft 2in (33.78 x 9.80 x 4.28m). 300 tons. Draught 12ft/14ft (3.90/4.55m). Men: 150, +6 officers.
Guns: 32 from 1689. 36 in war from 1696 (28 peace): LD 18 x 12pdrs or 8pdrs; UD 18 x 6pdrs or 4pdrs.
Renamed *Hirondelle* 11.1688. Rebuilt at Toulon by Chapelle in 1699 (see below).

GAILLARDE Class. 34 guns. Designed and built by Pierre Masson, and originally classed as *frégates légères*, even though their size and ordnance indicated that they should always have been included in the 5th Rank, and indeed they were so re-classed in 1692–95. Pierced for ten pairs of LD guns.

Dimensions & tons: 108ft 0in x 28ft 4in x 12ft 6in (35.08 x 9.20 x 4.06m). 350 tons. Draught 12½ft/14ft (4.06/4.55m); *Gaillarde* had a foot extra draught. Men: 130 (34/70/26) in 1690, then 140

A Van de Velde drawing identified as the *Play Prize*, ex-French *Les Jeux* of 1688–89. She was probably typical of the small frigates that had been built at Dunkirk (as well as the ports of the Spanish Netherlands) since the early 1600s, primarily for privateering. Besides eight guns on the lower deck broadside, there is an unarmed bow chase port right forward; the position of the men amidships suggests that either the armed forecastle (with its chase guns) and quarterdeck formed a single upper deck or there are gangways across the waist, but the gun battery there was separated fore and aft whatever the layout of the deck. There are also four small guns at a higher level aft that might be regarded as a poop or quarterdeck, depending on how the deck below is defined. (National Maritime Museum, London PY1898)

(25/73/42) from 1691, + 5 officers.

Guns: 34 from 1690: LD 20 x 8pdrs; UD 6 x 6pdrs + 8 x 4pdrs. 32 in war from 1696 (30 peace): LD 20 x 8pdrs; UD 12 x 4pdrs (12 x 6pdrs in both from 1699, then 2 x 6pdrs + 10 x 4pdrs). 32 guns in *Gaillarde* from 1708 (LD 14 x 8pdrs, UD 18 x 6pdrs), then 36 from 1709: UD 16 x 8pdrs; UD 18 x 6pdrs (plus 8 x 4pdrs from 1710).

Gaillarde Rochefort Dyd.
K: 1687. L: 6.1689. C: 1690. Lent as a privateer to the Marquis de Seignelay, who funded it for 2/3, as part of a squadron of three to four under CV Jacques Dandenne 1689–90. Lent as a privateer to LG André, Marquis de Nesmond, as part of a squadron of four to five vessels, 1695. Lent as a privateer to François Saupin, Sieur Du Rocher, a wood merchant in Brest, under CV Jacques Dandenne, as part of a squadron of two to four vessels, 1696. Lent again as a privateer to François Saupin, now also Director of the *Compagnie de l'Asiento*, 1702-05. Captured by HMS *Orford* 2.10.1708, becoming HMS *Orford Prize*; retaken by two French 30-gun privateers off Lundy 6.6.1709 and restored to original name. Condemned 6.1712 and sold 7.1712 at Le Havre, becoming the Spanish *Santo Francisco de Paolo* in c.1714.

Badine Rochefort Dyd.
K: 1688. L: 6.1689. C: 1.1690. Sailed in the King's service to the West Indies in 1696 under CV Des Augiers as part of a squadron of nine vessels carrying to the West Indies settlers and young marriageable women. Lent as a privateer to François Saupin, Sieur Du Rocher, (a timber merchant in Brest and Director of the *Compagnie de l'Asiento*), 1702-5. Wrecked off Cartagena (Colombia) 3.1705, with just 9 survivors.

LES JEUX. 30 guns. Designed and built by Hendryck Houwens. Pierced for eight pairs of LD guns.
Dimensions & tons: 95ft 0in x 26ft 0in (30.86 x 8.45m). 230 tons. Draught 12½ft (4.06m). Men: 120, +6 officers.
Guns: 30 from 1689: LD 16 x 8pdrs; UD (aft) 6 x 6pdrs + (fwd) 4 x 6pdrs; QD 4 x 4pdrs (as drawn by Van de Velde, who also shows two additional 6pdrs in chase ports on the forecastle).

Les Jeux Dunkirk.
K: 5.1688. L: 8.1.1689. C: 2.1689. Under command of CFL Jean Bart, she was captured, along with *Railleuse* (commanded by LV Claude de Forbin-Gardanne), by HM Ships *Nonsuch* and *Tiger* 22.5.1689, becoming HMS *Play Prize*. Both captains escaped back to France 5.6.1689. Scuttled as a breakwater at Sheerness 8.1697.

CAPRICIEUX Class. 34, later 36/40 guns. Designed and built by Hendryck Houwens. Pierced for ten pairs of LD guns.
Dimensions & tons: 110ft 0in, 99ft 0in x 30ft 0in x 13ft 7in (35.73, 32.16 x 9.75 x 4.41m). 300 tons. Draught 12ft/15½ft (3.90/5.04m). Men: 150, +6 officers.
Guns: 34 in 1690 in *Capricieux*: LD 20 x 8pdrs; UD 6 x 6pdrs + 8 x 4pdrs; 36 in *Capricieux* from 1691. 40 in *Opiniâtre* in 1690.

Capricieux Dunkirk.
K: 1.1689. L: 7.1689. C: 11.1689. Wrecked in the North Sea 1.1690.

Opiniâtre Dunkirk.
K: 3.1689. L: 9.1689. C: 11.1689. Lent as a privateer to the deposed King James II, under command of Sieur Marin, from St Malo, 1695. Probably captured by HMS *Saint Albans* off Rame Head 28.7.1690.

(C) Vessels acquired from 15 April 1689

At the start of 1689 the 5th Rank comprised twenty-two vessels each carrying between 28 and 40 guns: there were three vessels of 40 guns each (*Tigre*, *Croissant* and *Triton*), three of 36 guns each (*Adroit*, *Palmier* and the ex-Algerine *Galant*), two of 34 guns each (*Joli* and *Émerillon*), five of 32 guns each (*Poli*, *Mercure*, *Perle*, *Lion* and the ex-Algerine *Hirondelle*), six of 30 guns each (*Soleil d'Afrique*, *Sérieux*, *Mignon*, *Dragon*, *Hercule* and *Les Jeux*) and three of 28 guns each (*Marin*, *Pétillant* and *Éveillé*). Fourteen of these carried a complement of 150 men (35/78/37) and 6 officers; five (*Palmier*, *Mignon*, *Dragon*, *Hercule* and *Les Jeux*) had a complement of 120 men (33/60/27) and 6 officers, and three (*Lion*, *Pétillant* and *Éveillé*) had a complement of 100 men (20/54/26) and 5 officers.

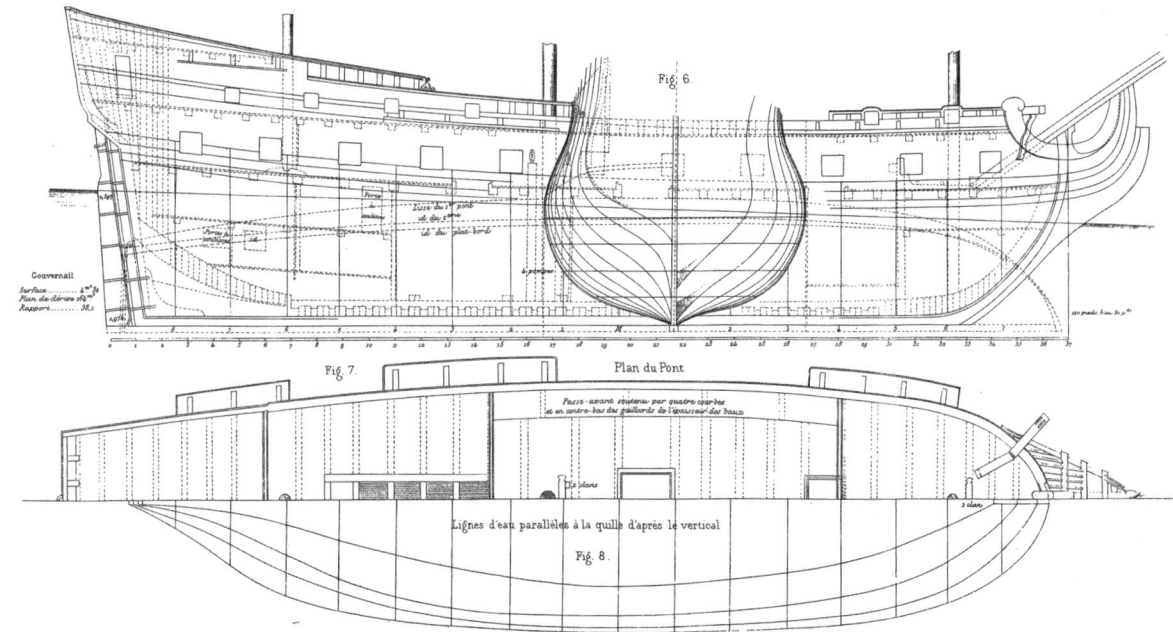

Vice-amiral Pâris's plan of *Capricieux*, 34 guns of 1689, based on a contemporary model. The drawing shows one extra pair of lower deck gunports and one pair too few on the *gaillards* but the dimensions of the model are a close fit. (*Souvenirs de Marine*, Plate 140)

The great Navy Ordinance of 15 April 1689 significantly amended the parameters of the 5th Rank, which now covered vessels with two batteries of between 30 and 36 guns (although some exceptions remained). New vessels of this Rank were ideally to be of 36 guns (with the main battery being 8pdrs) and meet the following specification:

- Dimensions & tons: 110ft 0in x 27ft 6in x 14ft 0in (35.73 x 8.93 x 4.55m). 300 tons.
- Guns: LD 18 x 8pdrs (6 being bronze and 12 being iron); UD 6 x 6pdrs (bronze) and 12 x 4pdrs (iron).
- The width of LD gunports was set at 2ft (0.65m) and these ports were to be separated by a distance of 7ft 2in (2.33m). From this the ideal length of a ship with nine pairs of LD ports could be determined (in theory) to be 99ft 3in (32.24m); a variant with one fewer pair of LD ports would be 90ft 1in (29.26m), while a variant with one more pair of ports would be 108ft 5in (35.22m).

LES JEUX Class. 36 guns. Designed and built by Hendryck Houwens. Pierced for nine pairs of LD guns. *Tigre* was rebuilt in 1696–97 and later in 1705, both times at Dunkirk. Until 1698 the dimensions and tonnage were given as first shown below, but in 1699 the significantly reduced figures were recorded.

- Dimensions & tons: until 1698: 114ft 0in x 27ft 0in x 12ft 6in (37.03 x 8.77 x 4.06m). 300 tons. Draught 14½ft (4.71m). Men: 150 (35/78/37), +6 officers. From 1699: 100ft 0in x 26ft 8in x 8ft 6in (32.48 x 8.66 x 2.76). 245 tons. Draught 12ft/14ft (3.90/4.55m). Men: 160 in war (100 peace), +6 officers.
- Guns: 36 in war (30 peace): LD 18 x 6pdrs; UD 18 x 4pdrs. 28 from 1708 (in *Tigre*): LD 14 x 6pdrs; UD 14 x 4pdrs (16 x 4pdrs from 1710).

Les Jeux Dunkirk.
  K: 6.1689. L: 11.1689. C: 1.1690. Lent as a privateer to LGA Nicolas Claude de Lambert 1704. Captured by HM Ships *Tartar* and *Adventure* 10.7.1706, becoming HMS *Child's Play*; wrecked 30.8.1707 in a hurricane at Palmetto Point, St Kitts in the Caribbean.

Tigre Dunkirk.
  K: 7.1689. L: 12.1689. C: 7.1690. Sold at Dunkirk 1713. This may have been the frigate purchased in 1714 by the Spanish Navy and in service under the same name, which was captured by Byng's fleet off Cape Passaro 21.8.1718.

CURIEUX. 24 guns. This small vessel was formerly the *Fin*, constructed in Malta by Sieur Bouvier using the remains of the frigate *Bien Aimée*. It was confiscated by the King in November 1690 to settle a debt, and renamed *Curieux* on 10 December.

- Dimensions & tons: dimensions unknown. 180 tons. Draught 9ft (2.92m). Men: 90, +6 officers.
- Guns: 24 from 1691.

Curieux Valetta, Malta.
  K: 1688. L: 6.1689. C: 8.1689. Sold 4.1692 at Toulon to the Genoese.

Ex-ENGLISH PRIZE (1690). 30 guns. A merchant vessel or privateer captured from the English and assigned to Brest, formerly named *Mercury* or *Mercurius*, although may possibly have been originally the 5th Rank *Mercure* (ex-*Trompeuse*) of 1670 (see above).

- Dimensions & tons: dimensions unknown. 300 tons. Men: 120, +6 officers (30 men + 1 officer as *flûte*),
- Guns: 30 from 1691; 6 as *flûte* from 1692.

Mercure England.
  Renamed *Économe* and re-rated as *flûte* 3.1692. Fitted as a hospital ship, but burnt 6.1692 at La Hougue by the Anglo-Dutch forces.

CAPRICIEUX Class. 36 guns. Two new 5th Rank ships were ordered in July 1690 to be built at Dunkirk by Hendryck Houwens. These would have been of 400 tons, with a draught of 13ft (4.22m), and to have had 150 men and 6 officers. The names *Capricieux* (replacing the ship lost in January) and *Galant* were assigned, but in 1691 they were cancelled.

AIGLE Class. 36 guns. Probably designed by Pierre Masson; built by Félix Arnaud. Pierced for ten (or possibly eleven) pairs of LD guns. *Aigle* reconstructed and re-armed at Rochefort from 1709 to June 1711. A poor sailer, she received a sheathing of wood to improve her stability.

- Dimensions & tons: 111ft 0in, ?94ft 0in x 27ft 6in x 12ft 6in (36.06, ?30.59 x 8.93 x 4.06m). 300 tons. Draught 13ft/14ft (4.22/4.55m). Men: 150 (35/78/37) in war, 120 peace, +6 officers.

Contemporary drawing of the decorative work of the 36-gun *Aigle* of 1692, as reproduced by *Vice-amiral* Pâris. (*Souvenirs de Marine*, Plate 149)

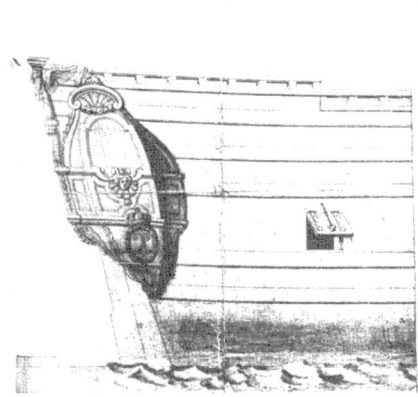
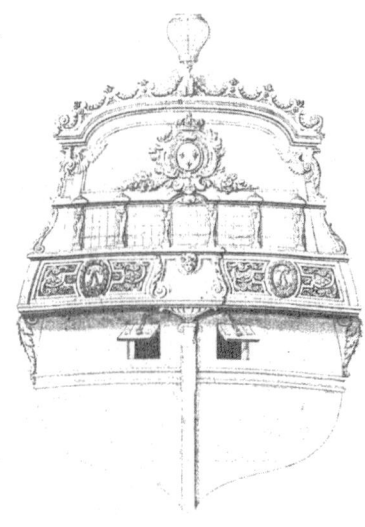
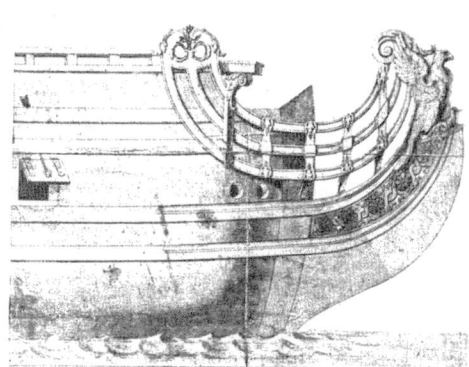

Guns: 36 in war (30 peace): LD 20 x 8pdrs; UD 16 x 6pdrs (in 1696–98 *Aigle* is listed with 22 x 8pdrs and 14 x 6pdrs; it is unclear if the extra 2 x 8pdrs occupied UD gunports). 34 in *Aigle* from 1699: LD 18 x 8pdrs; UD 16 x 6pdrs (*Favori* had LD 20 x 8pdrs & UD 10 x 6pdrs). 38 in *Aigle* after 1710: LD 20 x 8pdrs; UD 18 x 6pdrs.

Aigle Bayonne.
  K: 5.1691. L: early 1692. C: 4.1692. Sailed in the King's service to the West Indies in 1696 under CV Des Augiers as part of a squadron of nine vessels carrying to the West Indies settlers and young marriageable women. Lent as a privateer to CV Duguay-Trouin, as part of a squadron of thirteen vessels 1711–12; took part in the Capture of Rio de Janeiro 9.1711. She sailed under Sieur de La Mar de Caen, from St Malo, with provisional rank of LV, and came back, loaded with sugar, under CGA Thébault de La Rufinière. As *Fidèle* was in poor condition, her captain choose to find shelter at Cayenne, where his brother was governor; she foundered there at anchor 2.1712, without loss of life and part of the sugar retrieved was later sent to Brest.

Favori Bayonne.
  K: 1691. L: early 1692. C: 4.1692. Sailed in the King's service to the West Indies in 1696 under CV Des Augiers as part of a squadron of nine vessels carrying to the West Indies settlers and young marriageable women. Lent as a privateer to CV Des Augiers, as part of a squadron of four vessels 1696. Lent as a privateer to CdE Jean Bernard de Saint-Jean, Baron de Pointis, fitted as a *flûte* as part of a squadron of fourteen vessels, 1696–97; took part in the capture of Cartagena de Indias 5.5.1697. Became a fireship 1701, and expended at Vigo against the Anglo-Dutch forces 23.10.1702.

The *frégate légère Fée* of 1676 (see Chapter 6), which had been sold in 1685, was reacquired in 1690 by confiscation, renamed *Jalouse*, and was re-classed as a 5th Rank ship between 1692 and 1695. She was condemned as such in 1698.

MUTINE. 34 guns. Originally ordered in April 1692 as fireship *Mutin*, to a design by Pierre Coulomb (see Chapter 8), and begun at Lorient on 2 May 1692, but the order was cancelled in June and the vessel dismantled, the pieces being stored. She was set up again on the stocks in the following February as the 5th Rank *Mutine*, redesigned and built by Pierre Coulomb.
  Dimensions & tons: dimensions unknown. 400 tons.
  Guns: 34 – probably LD 18 x 8pdrs; UD 16 x 6pdrs.

Mutine Lorient Dyd.
  K: 2.1693. L: 7.1693. C: 9.1693. Renamed *Sphère* 9.1693. Employed as a privateer at St Malo in 1694, then as a coast guard ship in 1694–95. Struck at Port Louis 1695.

Ex-DUTCH PRIZES (1694). 30–32 guns. Two ships – *Weesp* and *Zeerijp* (both built in 1692) – were taken from the Dutch at the time of Adm Lord John Berkeley's attempt to land a force at Camaret Bay on 18 June 1694 during the War of the League of Augsburg, and added as 5th Rank. *Zeripsée* was refitted at Dunkirk from 1695 to February 1696.

Weeps (*Wesp*) Amsterdam.
  Dimensions & tons: 99ft 0in x 27ft 4in x 9ft 4in (32.16 x 8.88 x 3.03m). 280 tons. Draught 11½ft/13ft (3.74/4.22m). Men: 150, +1/3 officers.
  Guns: 32 in war (26 peace): LD 14 x 8pdrs; UD 14 x 4pdrs; QD 4 x 3pdrs.
  Operations at Nova Scotia and Hudson Bay under CV Pierre Le Moyne d'Iberville, in a squadron of four vessels 1696–97. Sold 1705 at Plaisance (Newfoundland).

Zeripsée Amsterdam.
  Dimensions & tons: 96ft 0in x 26ft 9in x 9ft 0in (31.18 x 8.69 x 2.92m). 250 tons. Draught 12ft (3.90m). Men: 150, +1 officer.
  Guns: 30 in war (20 peace): LD 14 x 8pdrs; UD 14 x 4pdrs; QD 2 x 2pdrs.
  Struck 1705 at Rochefort.

The fireship *Lutin* was re-classed as a 5th Rank ship in 1694 and was last mentioned in 1697. She is listed in Chapter 8.

OISEAU. 30 guns. Designed and built by Étienne Hubac as a privateer at the request of François Saupin, Sieur Du Rocher (and a timber merchant in Brest), and CV Jacques Dandenne. Pierced for ten pairs of guns on the LD. Ordered 26 May 1695 and named 27 June.
  Dimensions & tons: 112ft 0in x 28ft 0in x 13ft 6in (36.38 x 9.10 x 4.39m). 300 tons. Draught 14ft (4.55m). Men: 170 in war, 150 peace/180, +3/6 officers.
  Guns: 30 in war (26 peace): LD 20 x 8pdrs; UD 10 x 6pdrs (12 x 6pdrs from 1701).

Oiseau Brest Dyd.
  K: 6.1695. L: 9.1695. C: 2.1696. Lent as a privateer to François Saupin, Sieur Du Rocher (see above), under CV Jacques Dandenne, as part of a squadron from two to four vessels 1696–97. Burnt to avoid capture off Gibraltar 9.11.1704.

During late 1695 three unusual warships were begun in French yards – the *Martiale* at Le Havre, the *Bellone* at Brest and the *Foudroyante* at Lorient. Described as *frégate-bombardiers* ('bomb-frigates') and each to a different design, and mounting an UD battery of 8pdrs but also fitted with 2 x 12in mortars, they were initially classed with the bomb vessels (and their details appear in Chapter 7), but during 1698 the *Martiale* and *Bellone* were re-classed as 5th Rank (the *Foudroyante* had already been lost to the English) and their mortars were removed.

HIRONDELLE. 36 guns. Reconstruction by François Chapelle of ex-Algerian prize captured in October 1687 (see above).
  Dimensions & tons: 104ft 0in x 30ft 2in x 13ft 2in (33.78 x 9.80 x 4.28m). 350 tons. Draught 14ft (4.55m). Men: 150, +4 officers.
  Guns: 36 in war (28 peace): LD 18 x 8pdrs; UD 18 x 6pdrs (reduced to 12 x 6pdrs in 1703).

Hirondelle Toulon Dyd.
  K: 1.1699. L: 22.3.1699. She was then hauled back onto the stocks and restarted in 4.1699 and re-L: 19.3.1700. Leased to *Compagnie de l'Asiento* 11.1702 and wrecked in 1703 or 1704, probably off Buenos Aires, with 325 lost.

HÉROÏNE. 38 guns. Designed and built by Antoine Tassy. Pierced for ten pairs of LD guns. Built as 4th Rank, but re-classed to 5th Rank in 1700.
  Dimensions & tons: 116ft 0in x 31ft 6in x 14ft 6in (37.68 x 10.23 x 4.71m). 600 tons. Draught 14½ft/15½ft (4.71/5.04m). Men: 250/200, +5 officers.
  Guns: 38 in war (30 peace): LD 20 x 8pdrs; UD 18 x 6pdrs.

Héroïne Bayonne.
  K: Spring 1699. L: Autumn 1699. C: 1700. Wrecked 1701 or 1702.

HERMIONE. 30 guns. Designed and built by Étienne Hubac. Ordered in May 1699, and named on 29 May while already laid down. *Demi-batterie* type, with fewer guns on the LD.
  Dimensions & tons: 115ft 0in x 29ft 0in x 13ft 6in (37.36 x 9.42 x

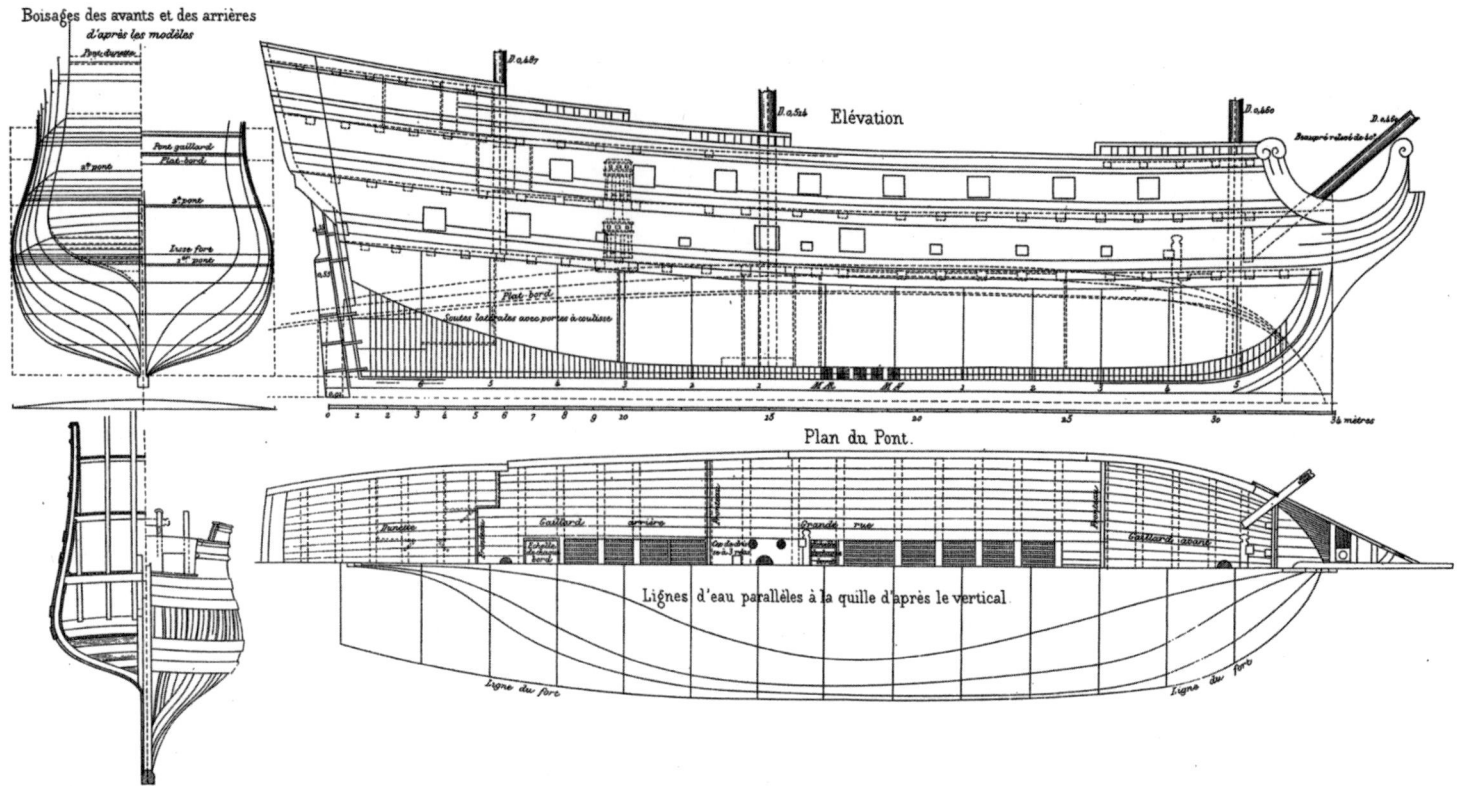

An unidentified *demi-batterie* 5th Rank ship reconstructed by *Vice-amiral* Pâris from two contemporary models. The scale of the models makes this ship slightly smaller than *Hermione*, but it gives a good impression of the appearance of the type. With the addition of two pairs of gunports on the upper deck (for which there is plenty of space aft), this ship could accommodate the known armament of *Hermione* in 1702. (*Souvenirs de Marine*, Plate 141)

4.39m). 300/445 tons. Draught 14ft/15ft (4.55/4.87m). Men: 200/170, +6 officers.

Guns: 30 in war (26 peace): LD 10 x 12pdrs; UD 20 x 6pdrs. 28 from 1702: LD 8 x 8pdrs; UD 20 x 6pdrs (2 x 6pdrs removed 1703).

Hermione Brest Dyd.
K: 5.1699. L: 23.9.1699. C: 1700. Lent as a privateer to CV de La Roque and CFL de Saint-Vandrille, with *Mutine*, for operations in the Gulf of Guinea 1702–3. Lost 4.1705.

MÉDUSE. 30 guns. Designed and built by Blaise Pangalo. Near-sister to *Hermione*; the two were the final two-decker 5th Rank ships to be built for the French Navy, but were built with only partially-armed LDs. Ordered in May 1699, and named on 29 May. Re-classed as a *frégate légère* in 1704–5, but restored to 5th Rank in 1708.

Dimensions & tons: 115ft 0in x 30ft 0in x 14ft 0in (37.36 x 9.75 x 4.55m). 350 tons. Draught 14ft/15½ft (4.55/5.04m). Men: 200/170, +4/7 officers.

Guns: 30 in war (26 peace): LD 8 x 12pdrs; UD 22 x 6pdrs. 28 from 1704: LD 6 x 8pdrs; UD 22 x 6pdrs.

Méduse Brest Dyd.
K: 5.1699. L: 23.9.1699. C: 1700. Condemned 3.1713 at Martinique and perhaps wrecked.

The *frégate légère Milfort* (see Chapter 6), was promoted to the 5th Rank in 1701. Formerly the British *Milford*, she was reportedly condemned at Dunkirk *c*.1702 but was still on the list in 1704.

Ex-DUTCH PRIZES (1703). 30–34 guns. Three ships were taken from the Dutch in 1703 – *Waakzaamheid* (in March), *Rozendaal* (on 22.5.1703 by *Éole* off Cape Rocca) and *Zaamslagh* (in July) – and added as 5th Rank. They had been built in 1702, 1692, and 1687 respectively. *Rozendal* was moved to the 4th Rank in 1706, but restored to the 5th Rank in 1710–11.

Vigilance Flushing.
Dimensions & tons: 98ft 0in x 26ft 0in x 12ft 0in (31.83 x 8.45 x 3.90m). 300 tons. Draught 14ft (4.55m). Men: 150.
Guns: 32 in war (24 peace): LD 20 x 8pdrs; UD 12 x 4pdrs.
Struck 1712 at Toulon.

Rozendal Rotterdam
Dimensions & tons: 108ft 0in x 29ft 0in x 9ft 2in (35.08 x 9.42 x 2.98m). 400 tons. Draught 10ft (3.25m). Men: 180, +4 officers.
Guns: 34 in war (24 peace): LD 10 x 12pdrs; UD 20 x 6pdrs; QD 4 x 4pdrs.
Probably scuttled at Toulon in 7.1707, but refloated. Sold by Order of 14.8.1709, but not struck until 1712 at Toulon.

Samslaack Holland.
Dimensions & tons: 96ft 6in, 86ft 0in x 27ft 0in x 10ft 4in (31.35, 27.94 x 8.77 x 3.36m). 300 tons. Draught 10¾ft/13¾ft (3.49/4.47m). Men: 140.
Guns: 30 in war (24 peace): LD 16 x 16pdrs; UD 14 x 3pdrs. 6 x 6pdrs as fireship from 1706. 34 from 1708: LD 14 x 8pdrs; UD 16 x 6pdr; QD 4 x 3pdrs. 28 from 1715: LD 14 x 6pdrs; UD 14 x 4pdrs.
Lent in 1704 as a privateer to François Saupin, Sieur Du Rocher (a timber merchant in Brest and Director of the *Compagnie de l'Asiento*). Struck early 1717 at Rochefort; not mentioned after 1720.

VÉNUS. 32 guns. Designed and built by Antoine Tassy, and purchased for the French Navy while building. Based at Port Louis, initially for escort duties. By 1707 reduced to 20 guns (20 x 6pdrs) in war, 10 peace, and 120 men. After being salvaged from a grounding *c*.1706 she was repaired and re-armed with just 20 guns, but was later criticised for weak scantlings.

Dimensions & tons: 94ft 6in x 25ft 8in x 9ft 0in (30.70 x 8.34 x 2.92m). 230 tons. Draught 12ft/12½ft (3.90/4.06m). Men: 180 in war, 150 peace, + 4/6 officers.

Guns: 32 in war (24 peace): LD 18 x 8pdrs; UD 14 x 6pdrs. 20 from 1707: 20 x 6pdrs. 18 from 1708: 18 x 4pdrs only (reduced to 16 x 4pdrs from 1715).

Vénus Bayonne.

K: 1703. L: 1704. C: 1705. Lent as a privateer to Louis François Mouffle de Champigny (Director of the *Compagnie des Indes Orientales*), under CV Hervé René Du Coudray Guymont, with *Jason* and *Mercure* 1711–16. Returned to Port Louis 1715, then employed from 1720 in hydrographic survey in Indian Ocean. Condemned and struck at Brest 1722.

Ex-ENGLISH PRIZES (1703–1705). Four English 32-gun Fifth Rates were acquired by the French in 1703–5. The 32-gun *Ludlow* was captured 28 January 1703 by the French *Adroit* in the Thames Estuary; the 32-gun *Milford*, captured on 17 January 1697 by five French privateers, was purchased for the French Navy in 1703; the 32-gun *Fowey*, captured on 12 August 1704 by seven French privateers off Isles of Scilly, was promptly acquired for the Navy; finally the 32-gun *Sorlings* was captured on 31 October 1705 by *Jersey* and others in the same engagement off the Dogger Bank in which the larger HM Ships *Blackwall* and *Pendennis* were taken (see Chapter 3). Note change of spellings on acquisition. All were of the *demi-batterie* type, optimised for cruising duties but able to employ oars when needed for inshore assault operations, with a part-armed LD and a complete UD battery. Their launch dates below are of British (Julian) calendar. All were attached to the Brest Département, except *Sorlingue* which was attached to Dunkirk. *Ludlow*, the last survivor and already hulked, was moved from the 5th Rank to the 4th Rank between 1723 and 1729 when the 5th Rank was abolished.

Ludlow Mrs Anne Mundy, Woodbridge.

K: 1698. L: 12.9.1690. C: 1690.

Dimensions & tons: 100ft 0in x 25ft 4in x 10ft 6in (32.48 x 8.23 x 3.41m). 250 tons. Draught 11½ft/12½ft (3.74/4.06m). Men: 180/150, +6 officers.

Guns: 30 in war (26 peace): LD 8 x 8pdrs; UD 16 x 4pdrs; QD 6 x 2pdrs. 30 from 1708: LD 8 x 8pdrs; UD 20 x 6pdrs; QD 2 x 4pdrs.

Hulked at Rochefort 1719; not mentioned after 1729.

Milfort William Hubbard, Ipswich.

K: 1694. L: 6.3.1695. C: 1695.

Dimensions & tons: 103ft 0in x 26ft 3in x 11ft 0in (33.46 x 8.53 x 3.57m). 250 tons. Draught 13ft/13¼ft (4.22/4.30m). Men: 170/150, +3/4 officers.

Guns: 32 in war (26 peace): LD 8 x 12pdrs; UD 20 x 8pdrs; QD 4 x 4pdrs. 28 from 1715: LD 4 x 8pdrs; UD 18 x 8pdrs; QD 6 x 4pdrs.

Lent as a privateer to CV Marc-Antoine de Saint-Pol Hécourt, as part of a squadron of six vessels, 1704. Lent as a privateer to CV Henri-Louis, Marquis de Chavagnac, and CV Pierre Le Moyne d'Iberville, as part of a squadron of ten vessels, for operations in the West Indies 1705–6. Lent as a privateer to *lieutenant de port* Tayran, first for wheat supply in 1709, then for commerce and privateering in the West Indies in 1711–12. Hulked 5.1717 at Brest, and BU 1720.

Fouey Thomas Burgess & William Briggs, Shoreham.

K: 1695. L: 7.5.1696. C: 1696.

Dimensions & tons: 104ft 0in x 26ft 0in x 10ft 0in (33.78 x 8.45 x 3.25m). 250 tons. Draught 12ft/12½ft (3.90/4.06m). Men: 160/150, +4/5 officers.

Guns: 30 in war (26 peace): LD 4 x 12pdrs; UD 20 x 6pdrs; QD 6 x 3pdrs.

Used on coast guard duty in the Channel and the North Sea. Hulked 1713 at Brest, and BU 1720.

Sorlingue Richard Barrett, Shoreham.

K: 1693. L: 19.3.1694. C: 1694.

Dimensions & tons: 100ft 0in x 26ft 0in x 10ft 0in (32.38 x 8.45 x 3.25m). 250 tons. Draught 13ft (4.22m). Men: 180, +3/5 officers.

Guns: 32 in war (26 peace): LD 4 x 8pdrs; UD 22 x 6pdrs; QD 6 x 3pdrs (in war).

Lent as a privateer to La Brosse, from Dunkirk, 1709–11. Retaken 2.1711 by the British but not re-added to British Navy.

JUNON. 36 guns. Designed and built by Philippe Cochois as a privateer for Sieur Bataille, but seized for the Navy in April 1709 while building, and named on 29 May. Restored to Sieur Bataille in December 1709, so never served in French Navy. No further details known.

Junon Le Havre.

K: 2.1709. L: 4.12.1709. C: 1710. Believed sold by Sieur Bataille and became Spanish *Juno*.

(D) Vessels acquired from 1 September 1715

By the close of 1715 the 5th Rank had shrunk to five vessels – the *Bellone*, *Vénus* and three ex-British prizes (*Ludlow*, *Milfort* and *Fouey*). No further additions were made to this group, and by 1729 the Rank was extinct (the last to be struck was the *Ludlow*, which had been hulked in 1719). Their role re-emerged in the 1740s with the new 8pdr-armed frigates. Two *frégates légères* were built in 1727–28 with 8pdr batteries (the *Astrée* and *demi-batterie Flore* – for which see Chapter 6) but otherwise no vessels with 8pdr batteries were built until the 'true frigate' type appeared with the *Médée* and *Volage* of 1740.

Interestingly, however, writing in 1735, Blaise Ollivier proposed a new definition of the 5th Rank. He restricted the 4th Rank to ships of between 50 and 56 guns, all of which would be two-deckers carrying a LD battery of 18pdrs. His 5th Rank covered ships of up to 46 guns, split into three 'Orders'. His 1st Order would be two-deckers carrying between 42 and 46 guns, and would be between 120ft and 122ft in length. His 2nd Order would be *demi-batterie* ships of 36 guns, carrying a complete upper deck battery of 6pdrs (pierced for ten, eleven or twelve pairs of gunports on this deck) and a partial lower deck battery of 8pdrs or 12pdrs (pierced for four or six pairs of gunports at this level); ships with fewer than the maximum number of LD and UD gunports listed in this proposal would have two or three pairs of gunports on the quarterdeck for 4pdrs to bring them up to 36 guns; they would be between 115ft and 118ft in length. Ollivier's 3rd Order would mount between 24 and 30 guns, and would be between 104ft and 108ft in length; they might have either one deck or be of the *demi-batterie* type, carrying either 6pdrs or 8pdrs as their principal battery. However, his theoretical structure does not appear to have been adopted in practice.

(E) 8pdr-armed frigates (*frégates de 8*) acquired from 1740

These 8-pdr ships were the earliest 'true' frigates; the prototypes were rated as *frégates légères* until 1746 (see Chapter 6). Most carried thirteen

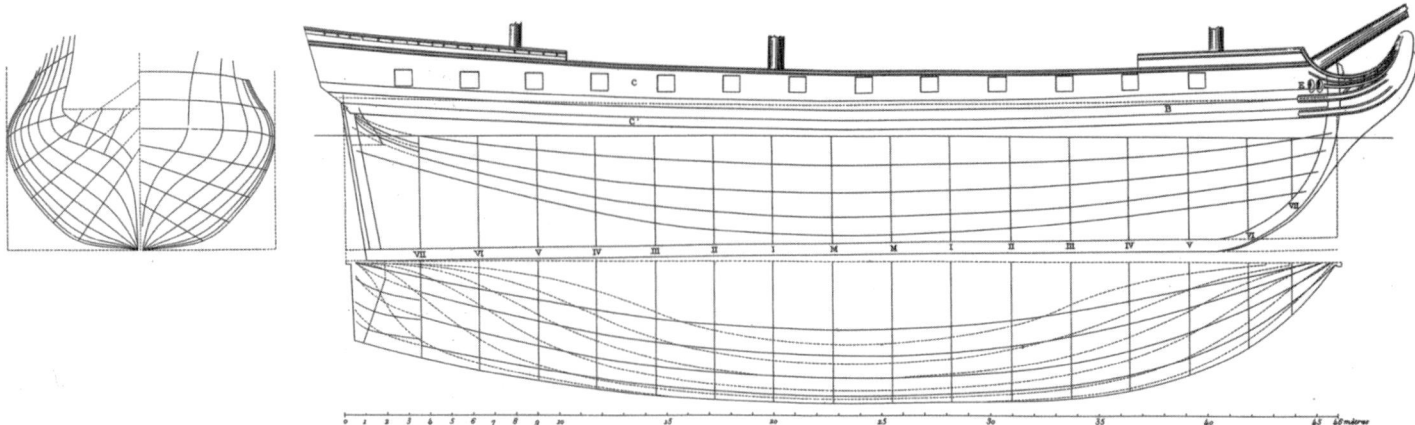

pairs of 8pdrs on the upper deck, although a few early vessels had only ten or twelve pairs. The prototypes had unarmed *gaillards* (quarterdecks and forecastles), but later vessels were built generally with a varying number (usually 4 or 6) of 4pdrs on the *gaillards*; these secondary weapons fluctuated over time. The complement included 4 commissioned officers (7 in the later ships). Altogether some forty-six 8pdr frigates were constructed for the French Navy between 1740 and 1776, when the last of this rating were launched; the vast majority were built during the 1750s, after which production declined. The above total includes three constructed for the *Compagnie des Indes*, but excludes several built as privateers or captured from the enemy.

Lines plan of *Médée* of 1741, a long, low ship with no guns on the upperworks. The contrast in silhouette between the new frigate-form ships and their two-decked predecessors is marked. The much-reduced height of topside made for more weatherly sailers, while the freeboard of the main battery was actually greater at 5ft 2in (1.68m) than that usually found in two-decked cruisers, so the ships could be fought in heavier seas. Thus the frigate offered both improved sailing qualities and more effective fighting power. In creating this design, Blaise Ollivier adopted the concepts originated by Pierre Bouguer. (*Souvenirs de Marine*, Plate 258)

MÉDÉE. 26-gun type, designed and built by Blaise Ollivier. Often seen as the first 'true' frigate, with no ports to the lower deck, which was effectively a light platform (the structural deck being the one above) at the level of the waterline, with headroom reduced to *c*.4ft. The unarmed forecastle and quarterdeck had no barricades, removing topside weight and height to reduce windage. She was substantially a development from the large *frégate légère Astrée* of 1727 (which Blaise Ollivier had designed in conjunction with his father Joseph), with the remaining side openings to the LD omitted.

Dimensions & tons: 114ft 6in, 98ft 0in x 30ft 6in x 14ft 4in (37.19, 31.83 x 9.94 x 4.66m). 380/840 tons. Draught 13ft/14ft (4.22/4.55m). Men: 200 in war, 180 peace, +4 officers.
Guns: 26 in war (20 peace): UD 26 x 8pdrs, QD/Fc nil.

Médée Brest Dyd.
K: 9.1740. L: 2.1741. C: 1741. Taken by HMS *Dreadnought* 15.4.1744 and added to the RN as HMS *Medea*, but sold 1745 and became privateer *Boscawen*.

VOLAGE. 24-gun type, designed and built by Pierre Morineau. His contemporary equivalent to the *Médée*. Designs in Morineau's manuscript *Repertoir de construction* that match this ship and his very similar *Friponne* of 1747 (see below) had a complete *faux pont* (lightweight orlop deck) at waterline level under the battery deck; designs matching his larger *Hermione* of 1749 – described in the previous chapter – had a second full deck in place of the orlop. The only LD openings in the 24-gun ships were a single pair in the stern counter to let some daylight into the orlop.

Dimensions & tons: 112ft 0in x 31ft 4in x 13ft 6in (36.38 x 10.18 x 4.39m). 480/800 tons. Draught 13¾ft/14¾ft (4.49/4.79m). Men: 215 in war, 180 peace, +4/7 officers.
Guns: 24 in war and peace: UD 24 x 8pdrs (reduced in 1746 to 22 guns), QD/Fc nil.

Volage Rochefort Dyd.
K: 9.1740. L: 1.4.1741. C: 6.1741. Taken by HMS *Stirling Castle* off Cape St Martin (Spain) 15.4.1746, recaptured the next day by *Oriflamme* but hulked at Marseille 10.1748 and BU there 1753.

AMPHITRITE Class. 30-gun type, designed and built by Venard at Bayonne. *Mégère* was rebuilt at Brest in summer 1750.
Dimensions & tons: 116ft 0in, 99ft 0in x 31ft 8in x 16ft 0in (37.68, 32.16 x 10.29 x 5.20m). 490/920 tons. Draught 13½ft/14½ft (4.39/4.74m). Men: 220 in war, 200 peace, +4 officers.
Guns: UD 26 x 8pdrs; QD 4 x 4pdrs.

Amphitrite Bayonne.
K: 12.1743. L: 1744. C: 11.1744. Wrecked off Puerto Rico 7.1745.

Mégère Bayonne.
K: 1.1744. L: 12.1744. C: 5.1745. Leased for commerce from 9.1750 to 7.1752. Condemned at Rochefort 1753.

FINE Class. 28-gun type, designed and built by Pierre Chaillé, Jnr.
Dimensions & tons: 118ft 0in, 87ft 0in x 31ft 8in x 16ft 0in (38.33, 28.26 x 10.29 x 5.20m). 480/900 tons. Draught 13½ft/15ft (4.39/4.87m). Men: 220 in war, 150 peace, + 4/8 officers.
Guns: UD 24 x 8pdrs; QD 4 x 4pdrs.

Fine Le Havre.
K: 2.1744. L: 27.5.1744. C: 8.1744. Grounded and wrecked off Montrose (Scotland) 12.1745 in action with HMS *Milford* (during the Jacobite uprising).

Émeraude Le Havre.
K: 2.1744. L: 10.6.1744. C: 8.1744. Captured 21.9.1757 off Brest by HMS *Southampton*, and became HMS *Emerald*; BU 11.1761 at Portsmouth.

SIRÈNE Class. 30-gun type. Designed by Blaise Ollivier, and built by Jacques-Luc Coulomb and François-Guillaume Clairain-Deslauriers respectively. Unlike Ollivier's prototype *Médée*, these carried light guns (4pdrs) on the QD. *Renommée* was reputedly the fastest frigate of her day,

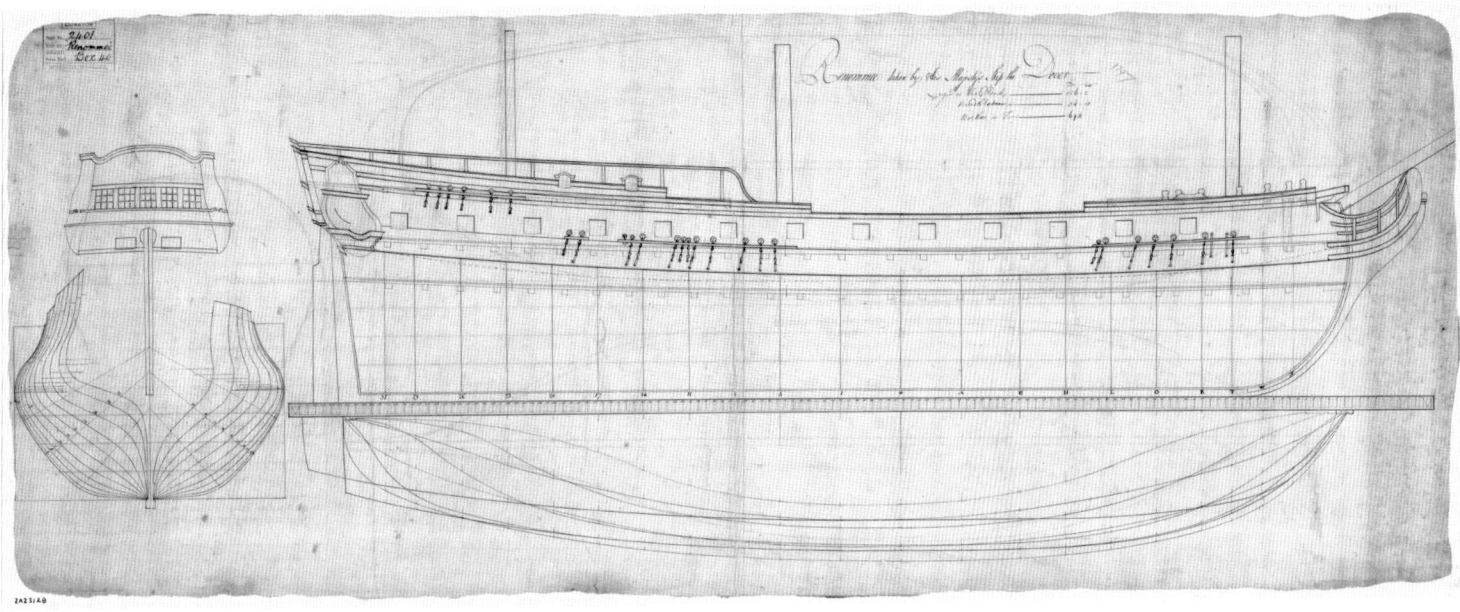

Admiralty draught of *Renommée*, undated but as captured. The ship was highly regarded by the Royal Navy and, unlike many other lightly built French prizes, was thought worthy of an extensive and expensive rebuilding in 1757–58. (National Maritime Museum, London J6630)

but in British hands the lightly-built ship was substantially rebuilt and lost much of her sailing qualities. *Sirène* underwent rebuilding at Brest in 1757.

Dimensions & tons: 118ft 0in, 100ft 0in x 31ft 8in x 16ft 0in (38.33, 32.48 x 10.29 x 5.20m). 520/952 tons. Draught 13¼ft/14½ft (4.30/4.74m). Men: 220 in war, 180 peace, +4 officers.

Guns: UD 26 x 8pdrs; QD 4 x 4pdrs.

Sirène Brest Dyd.
K: 3.1744. L: 24.9.1744. C: 11.1744. Captured near Jamaica by HMS *Boreas* on 18.10.1760, but not added to the British Navy.

Renommée Brest Dyd.
K: 5.1744. L: 19.12.1744. C: 1.1745. Captured by HMS *Dover* off Ushant on 24.9.1747, becoming HMS *Fame*, renamed HMS *Renown* 9.1749; BU at Woolwich 5.1771.

EMBUSCADE. 38 guns. Designed by Pierre Chaillé, Jnr. The largest frigate-built prize captured by the British during the War of the

Admiralty draught of the ex-French *Embuscade*, undated but showing signs of haste and unfinished details (the decorative work around the stern and quarter galleries is only vaguely sketched in pencil). The intense interest this ship generated among its captors is reflected in the fact that this is one of three surviving sheer draughts of the ship in the Admiralty Collection, only one of which is finished to the usual draughting standard. The main purpose of this quickly-executed plan is to be found in the lines of the half-breadth, which are the basis for the calculation of the underwater volume of the hull and a comparison with an (unidentified) vessel. *Embuscade* was surveyed at Plymouth, where the Master Shipwright, Benjamin Slade, was in regular contact with Admiral Anson on the subject of improved cruiser design, so this draught is probably part of Slade's campaign. (National Maritime Museum, London J5470)

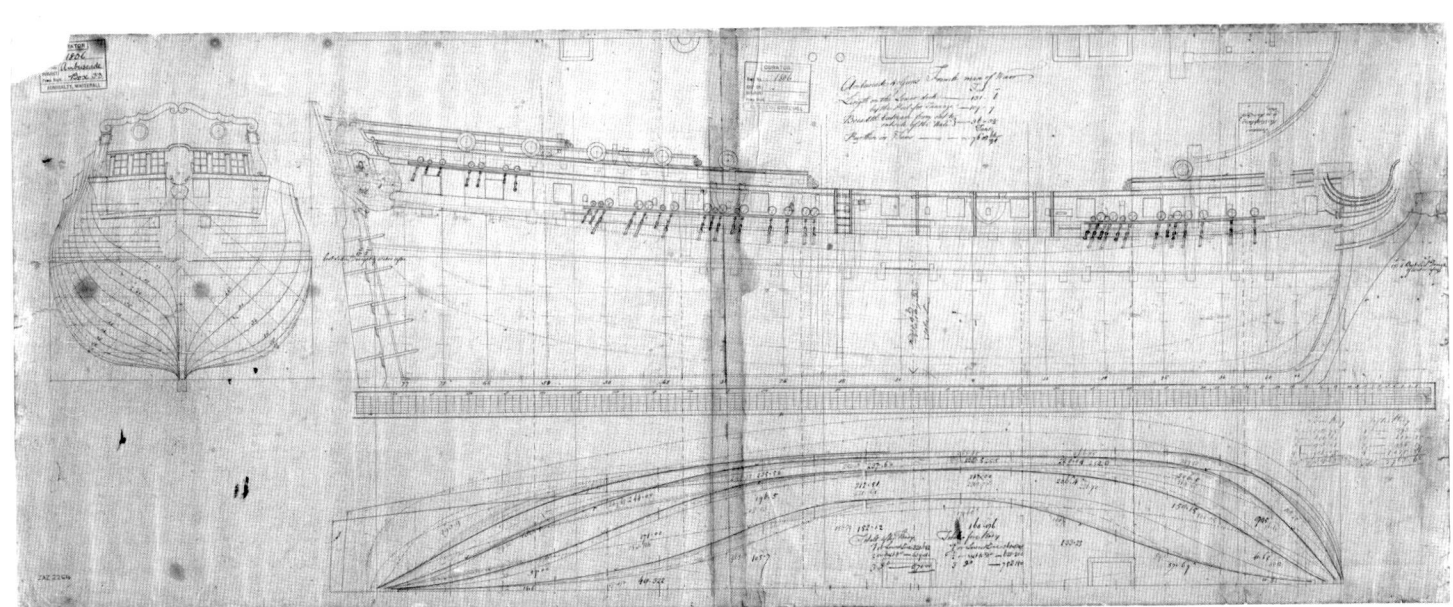

Austrian Succession, she was as big as 44-gun British two-deckers and, when rearmed with 12pdrs in place of her French 8pdrs, proved the worth of the large single-decked frigate to Vice-Adm Anson, who considered her his most effective cruiser.

> Dimensions & tons: 122ft 9in, 110ft 0in x 35ft 9in x 16ft 6in (39.87, 35.73 x 11.61 x 5.36m). 450/1,090 tons. Draught 14ft 4in/16ft 1in (4.66/5.22m). Men: 180, +5 officers.
> Guns: UD 26 x 8pdrs; QD 10 x 4pdrs; Fc 2 x 4pdrs.

Embuscade Le Havre
> K: 11.1744. L: 19.3.1745. C: 7.1745. Captured 21.4.1746 by HMS *Defiance* in the Channel, becoming HMS *Ambuscade* (40). Sold 9.2.1762 by the RN to private adventurers who used her in 1762 in an attack on Spanish settlements in the La Plata River.

CASTOR Type. 8pdr-armed type, designed and built at Quebec by René-Nicolas Levasseur. Data is for *Castor*, but *Martre* is believed to be similar.

> Dimensions & tons: 118ft 6in x 31ft 3in x 13ft 2in (38.49 x 10.15 x 4.28m). 500 tons. Draught 14ft (4.55m). Men: 200, +4 officers.
> Guns: 26 x 8pdrs (*Martre* reported to carry only 20 x 6pdrs and 4 x 4pdrs).

Castor Quebec.
> K: 6.1744. L: 16.5.1745. C: 10.1745. Captured off Cape Finisterre 30.10.1747 by HMS *Hampshire*, but not added to British Navy owing to the poor quality Canadian timber.

Martre Quebec.
> K: 5.1745. L: 6.6.1746. C: 1.1747. Struck and hulked at Rochefort early 1753; not mentioned after 4.1757.

A British newspaper reported in June 1745 that 'His majesty's ship the *Blandford*, of twenty guns, captain Dodd commander, has had the misfortune to fall in with a French squadron of seven sail, between Lisbon and Gibraltar, and was sent to Brest. The captain was threatened with being hanged if he did not discover to the commodore whether there was any English squadron at sea. This he very bravely refused to comply with.' This report has been repeated in some modern histories, but there is no other record of this capture and the series of British records for this ship for 1745–46 is unbroken. The report of *Blandford*'s 1745 capture probably originated in unfounded press rumours. Ironically, *Blandford* was taken by the French under somewhat similar circumstances in August 1755 off Ushant as a diplomatic protest and then released, see below.

Ex-BRITISH PRIVATEERS (1746). The Liverpool privateer *Rover* was captured on 4 March 1746 and was added to the French Navy under the same name. Notwithstanding her (alleged) 8pdr guns, she may equally be rated with the corvettes. The British Sixth Rate frigate *Dursley Galley* had been designed and built by Richard Stacey at Deptford to Torrington's original concept of the galley-frigate, with oarports and presumably a loading port (but no gunports) on the LD; sold out of RN service on 21 February 1745, she had become a privateer, was captured on 8 May 1746.

Rover Liverpool.
> Dimensions & tons: 90ft 9in x 24ft 0in x 9ft 9in (29.50 x 7.80 x 3.17m). 240/400 tons. Draught 14½ft (4.71m). Men: 130, +4 officers.
> Guns: UD 16 x 8pdrs; QD 6 smaller.
> Struck at Rochefort 1749

Dursley Galley Deptford Dyd.
> Dimensions & tons: 104ft 0in x 27ft 0in x 12ft 6in (33.78 x 8.77 x 4.06m). 300/500 tons. Draught 11ft 6in/13ft 8in (3.74/4.44m).

> Men: 180, +4/7 officers.
> Guns: UD 22 x 8pdrs (oarports on the LD).
> Ordered: 14.3.1718. L: 13.2.1719. C: 8.3.1719. Taken out of service 5.1748 at Brest and struck.

FRIPONNE. 24-gun type, a development from the *Volage* with an extra two feet in the stern; designed and built by Pierre Morineau.

> Dimensions & tons: 115ft 0in, 104ft 6in x 31ft 8in x 16ft 10in (37.36, 33.95 x 10.29 x 5.47m). 400/856 tons. Draught 14ft/15ft (4.55/4.87m). Men: 198/180, +4-7 officers.
> Guns: 24 in war (24 peace): UD 24 x 8pdrs; QD nil.

Friponne Rochefort Dyd.
> K: 1.1747. L: 1747. C: 1747. Condemned 10.1761 at Rochefort; sold 1762 as a Bordeaux privateer, renamed *Duchesse de Choiseul*.

FIDÈLE. 30-gun type, designed and built by Blaise Geslain.

> Dimensions & tons: 119ft 0in x 31ft 0in x 17ft 7in (38.66 x 10.07 x 5.71m). 500/900 tons. Draught 15¼ft/16¾ft (4.93/5.47m). Men: 206/185, +4 officers.
> Guns: 30 in war (24 peace): UD 24/26 x 8pdrs; QD 4 x 4pdrs.

Fidèle Rochefort Dyd.
> K: 1747. L: 1.1748. C: 1748. Scuttled and burnt to block the entrance to Louisbourg harbour 28.6.1758.

MARÉCHAL DE SAXE. 24 guns. This frigate which had been built for privateering was purchased at St Malo in February 1748 for 120,000 *livres*.

> Dimensions & tons: 100ft 0in x 27ft 0in x 14ft 0in (32.48 x 8.77 x 4.55m). 750 tons. Men: 120, +4 officers.
> Guns: 24, calibre unknown.

Maréchal de Saxe Morlaix
> Built 1747. Condemned 6.1752, placed on sale 8.8.1752, ordered BU 12.10.1752 as she could not find a buyer but instead hulked at Toulon, then BU 1755.

TOPAZE Class. 24-gun type, pierced for twelve pairs of UD gunports. *Topaze* was designed and built by Jean-Joseph Ginoux, and the design was probably adapted for the other two, which were built by Mathurin-Louis Geoffroy. *Héroïne* was named on 30 November 1751. None of the thee was armed until 1753 or later. *Topaze* was rebuilt in 1761–62.

> Dimensions & tons: 114ft 0in x 30ft 0in x 15ft 0in (37.03 x 9.75 x 4.87m). 450/800 tons. Draught 13½ft/14½ft (4.39/4.71m). Men: 219 in war, 180 peace, +5/10 officers.
> Guns: UD 24 x 8pdrs; QD 4 x 4pdrs.

Topaze Brest Dyd.
> K: 1749. L: 30.10.1750. C: 4.1751. Part of La Galissonnière's squadron in April 1756 sent to occupy Minorca and present at the Battle of Minorca on 20.5.1756. Condemned 1773 at Toulon, and struck 1775.

Thétis Brest Dyd.
> K: 10.1751. L: 17.11.1751. C: 1752. Condemned 1777 at Brest and struck.

Héroïne Brest Dyd.
> K: 1.1752. L: 20.12.1752. C: 9.1753. Ordered 1.6.1766 to be raséed to become guard ship at Brest.

NYMPHE. 20-gun type. Designed and built by Antoine Groignard.

> Dimensions & tons: 114ft 0in, 108ft 0in x 29ft 0in x 15ft 0in (37.03, 35.08 x 9.42 x 4.87m). 450/710 tons. Draught 12½ft/13¼ft (4.06/4.30m). Men: 180, + 5/8 officers.
> Guns: UD 20 x 8pdrs; QD nil.

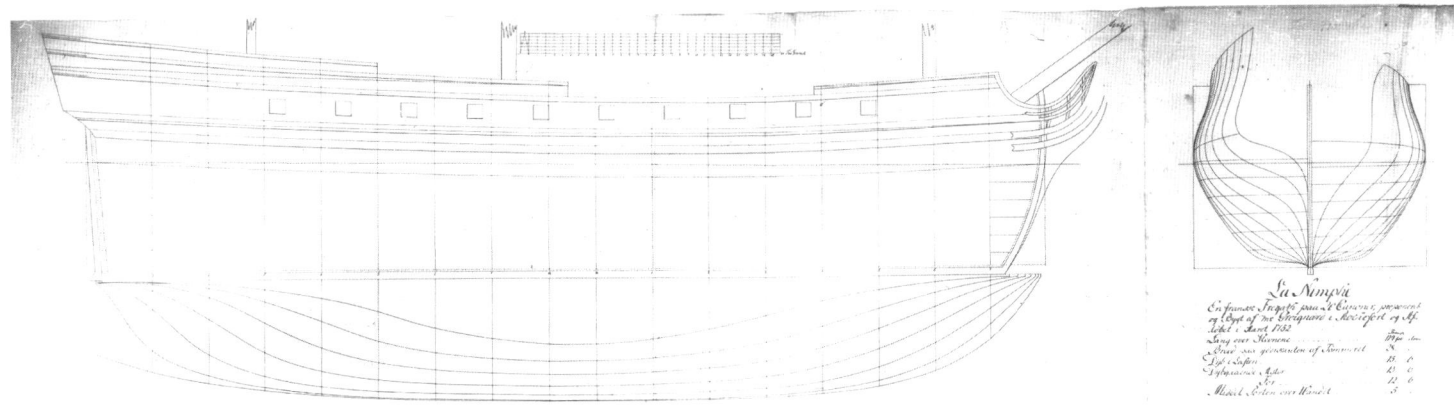

A Danish draught of the 20-gun *Nymphe*. With the same paucity of detail to be found on standard French design plans, this is almost certainly a straight copy of the original, although Danish draughting convention put the body plan to the right. With only ten ports a side, the ship's battery is concentrated amidships, allowing very fine lines forward and aft. (Rigsarkivet, Copenhagen)

Nymphe Rochefort Dyd.
   K: 2.1751. L: 1.1752. C: 11.1752. Part of La Galissonnière's squadron in April 1756 sent to occupy Minorca and present at the Battle of Minorca on 20.5.1756. Driven ashore by HMS *Hampton Court* and burnt at Minorca 20.6.1757 to avoid capture.

COMÈTE Class. 30 guns. Designed and built by Joseph-Louis Ollivier. *Comète* was named on 20 December 1752; *Concorde* was ordered in December.1753, and named on 24 May 1754.
   Dimensions & tons: 120ft 0in, 107ft 0in x 31ft 8in x 16ft 3in (38.98, 34.76 x 10.29 x 5.28m). 520/900 tons. Draught 13¼ft/14ft 7in (4.30/4.74m). Men: 200, +9 officers.
   Guns: UD 26 x 8pdrs; QD 4 x 4pdrs.
Comète Brest Dyd.
   K: 1752. L: 20.12.1752. C: 8.1753. Captured 16.3.1761 by HMS *Bedford* off Ushant, but bought back by the French Navy 4.1763, then repaired in 1764 at Cayenne. Condemned 20.9.1767 and struck.

Fleur de Lys Brest Dyd.
   K: 1.3.1753. L: 6.6.1754. C: 11.1754. Grounded 18.10.1760 off St Domingue, and burnt to avoid capture.
Concorde Brest Dyd.
   K: 5.1754. L: 15.11.1755. C: 3.1756. Wrecked off Port Navalo 9.1756.

ROSE. 24 guns. Design by François Chapelle, for building at Toulon. Named *Rose* on 11 June 1750, but not built to this draught (instead, a *demi-batterie* ship was built with the same name at Toulon by Joseph Véronique-Charles Chapelle 1751–54, with 8 x 12pdrs and 22 x 8pdrs; see Chapter 4).
   Dimensions & tons: 114ft 0in x 32ft 8in x 16ft 4in (37.03 x 10.61 x 5.31m). 290/750 tons.
   Guns: UD 24 x 8pdrs; QD nil.

AMÉTHYSTE. 30 guns. Designed and built by Mathurin-Louis Geoffroy, and named on 7 January 1753.

Danish draught of the *Comète*, 30 guns of 1752. The specification describes the ship as 'proposed to be built' so is presumably a copy of the design draught. It shows the quarterdeck gun positions, so the secondary armament was part of the original requirement. (Rigsarkivet, Copenhagen)

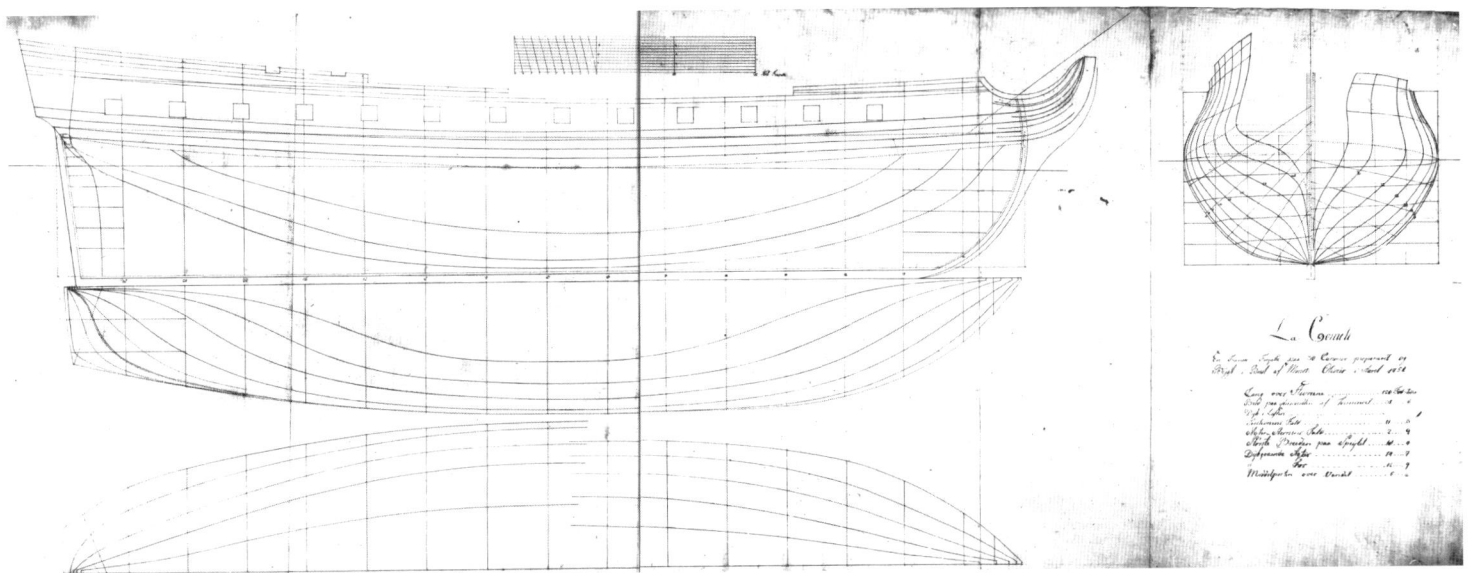

Dimensions & tons: 120ft 6in, 105ft 0in x 32ft 0in x 16ft 3in (39.14, 34.11 x 10.39 x 5.28m). 526/868 tons. Draught 12ft/13ft 10in (3.90/4.49m). Men: 180.
Guns: UD 26 x 8pdrs; QD 4 x 4pdrs.

Améthyste Brest Dyd.
K: 1.3.1753. L: 3.6.1754. C: 11.1754. Condemned 2.1763 at Léogane and hulked at St Louis (St Domingue) 1763. Struck 1771.

VALEUR. 20 guns. Designed and built by François-Guillaume Clairain-Deslauriers.
Dimensions & tons: 112ft 0in x 30ft 6in x 10ft 2in (36.38 x 9.91 x 3.30m). 450/700 tons. Draught 11ft/12ft 1in (3.57/3.93m). Men: 160.
Guns: UD 20 x 8pdrs; QD 4 x 4pdrs added later.

Valeur Rochefort Dyd.
K: 3.1754. L: 29.10.1754. C: 5.1755. Captured by HMS *Lively* off St Domingue 18.10.1759, becoming HMS *Valeur*; sold 1.1764.

PLÉIADE. 32 guns. Designed and built by Joseph-Marie-Blaise Coulomb. Ordered in January 1753 (named on 7 January). Reconstructed in February–May 1779 at Toulon, then undertook hydrography duties in Aboukir Bay.
Dimensions & tons: 120ft 0in, 105ft 0in x 29ft 10in x 15ft 10in (38.98, 34.11 x 9.69 x 5.14m). 478/860 tons. Draught 13ft 4in/14ft 8in (4.33/4.76m). Men: 200 in war (later 225), 180 peace, +7/9 officers.
Guns: UD 26 x 8pdrs; QD 6 x 4pdrs added.

Pléiade Toulon Dyd.
K: 4.1754. L: 17.11.1755. C: 4.1756. Condemned 27.7.1786 at Toulon and sold in 1787.

BLONDE Class. 32 guns. Designed by Jean-Joseph Ginoux. The first two were ordered in January 1753 (named on 7 January), but not begun until 20 months later. *Aigrette* and *Vestale* were present at the Battle of Quiberon Bay 20.11.1759. All were captured by the British in 1760–61 except *Aigrette*, which was rebuilt at Rochefort in 1764–65.
Dimensions & tons: 127ft 0in, 113ft 0in x 32ft 0in x 16ft 0in (41.25, 36.71 x 10.39 x 5.20m). 480/880 tons. Draught 13ft 2in/13ft 9in (4.28/4.47m). Men: 190–202 in war (130-147 peace), +7 officers.
Guns: UD 26 x 8pdrs; QD 6 x 4pdrs.

Blonde Le Havre.
K: 9.1754. L: 23.8.1755. C: 3.1756. Captured 28.2.1760 by HM Ships *Aeolus*, *Pallas* and *Brilliant* off the Isle of Man, becoming HMS *Blonde*. Wrecked off Cape Sable 10.5.1782.

Brune Le Havre.
K: 9.1754. L: 23.8.1755. C: 3.1756. Captured by HM Ships *Venus* and *Juno* in the Atlantic 30.1.1761, becoming HMS *Brune*. Sold 2.10.1792.

Aigrette Le Havre.
K: 9.1755. L: 3.1756. C: 7.1756. Condemned 10.1789 at Brest and struck.

Vestale Le Havre.
K: 9.1755. L: 3.1756. C: 7.1756. Captured by HMS *Unicorn* off Rhode Island 8.1.1761, becoming HMS *Flora*.

Félicité Le Havre.
K: 3.1756. L: 23.8.1756. C: 5.1757. Captured by HMS *Richmond* off the Hague 23.1.1761 and burnt.

MINERVE Class. 30 guns. Designed by Jacques-Luc Coulomb and built by Joseph-Marie-Blaise Coulomb. Ordered on 17 February 1754 and 3 March 1754; both named on 24 May 1754.
Dimensions & tons: 120ft 0in x 31ft 8in x 16ft 4in (38.98 x 10.29 x 5.31m). 500/900 tons. Men: 240, +6/7 officers.
Guns: UD 26 x 8pdrs; QD 4 x 4pdrs.

Minerve Toulon Dyd.
K: 5.1754. L: 15.2.1756. C: 7.1756. Wrecked in a storm off Villefranche 27.10.1762.

Oiseau Toulon Dyd.
K: 6.1754. L: 25.4.1757. C: 7.1757. Captured off Spain by HMS *Brune* 23.10.1762, but not added to the British Navy.

LICORNE Class. 32 guns. Designed by Jean Geoffroy. The first two were ordered in December 1753 and named on 24 May 1754.
Dimensions & tons: 120ft 6in x 31ft 10in x 16ft 10in (39.14 x 10.34 x 5.47m). 550/950 tons. Draught 14ft 7in/15ft 5in (4.74/5.01m).

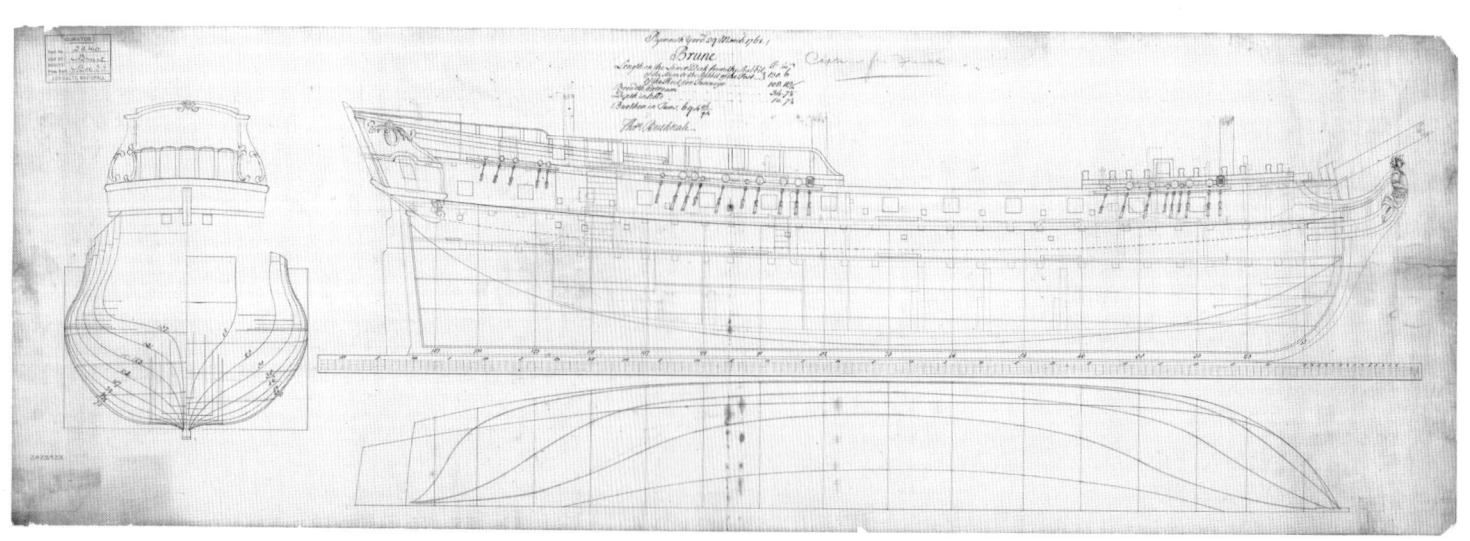

Admiralty draught of *Brune*, dated Plymouth Yard 29 March 1761. The ship is as captured, and includes the small *dunette* on the quarterdeck that many French frigates carried at this period. The draught shows a number of small openings in the broadside, which includes what seems to be a full set of sweep ports between the gunports on the upper deck and half a dozen small scuttles on the lower deck, presumably for ventilation or light. (National Maritime Museum, London J5849)

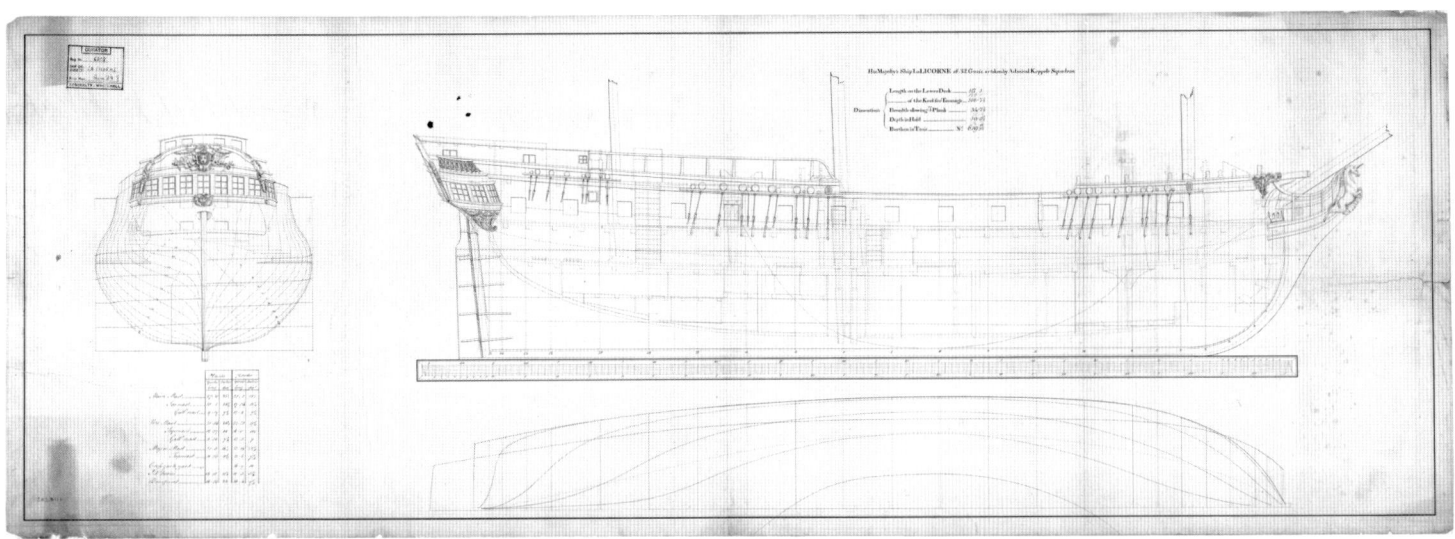

Admiralty draught of *Licorne*, 'as taken by Admiral Keppel's Squadron'. As with most of these 8pdr-armed frigates, the main battery was replaced by 12pdrs in British service, but it was rapidly decided that these were too heavy for the ship and were replaced by 9pdrs in November 1778. (National Maritime Museum, London J6626)

Men: 190 in war, 130 peace, +7 officers.
Guns: UD 26 x 8pdrs; QD 4 x 4pdrs; Fc 2 x 4pdrs.
Licorne Brest Dyd.
  K: 5.1754. L: 12.1755. C: 3.1756. Captured 18.6.1778 off northern Brittany by HMS *America*, becoming HMS *Unicorn*; sold at Deptford 2.12.1783.
Sauvage Brest Dyd.
  K: 12.9.1754. L: 3.1.1756. C: 3.1756. Wrecked on the coast of Poitou 3.1759.
Hermine Bayonne.
  K: 1756. L: 5.1757. C: 9.1757. Lost, presumed wrecked off Vigo 12.1761.
Opale Bayonne.
  K: 1756. L: 5.1757. C: 10.1757. Wrecked off Mangane Island, St Domingue 23.7.1762.

Ex-BRITISH PRIZE (1755). The British Sixth Rate *Blandford* was taken in August 1755 in peacetime as a diplomatic protest. See above for an alleged capture of the same ship in 1745.

Dimensions & tons: 105ft 0in, 90ft 0in x 28ft 6in x 9ft 6in (34.11, 29.24 x 9.26 x 3.09m). 550 tons displacement. Draught 11ft/12ft (3.57/3.90m).
Guns: UD 20 x 9pdrs; QD 4 x 6pdrs.
Blandford Thomas West, Deptford. Ordered: 27.12.1740.
  K: ?3.12.1740. L: 2.10.1741. C: 8.12.1741. Taken 13.8.1755 by the frigate *Fleur de Lys* and a squadron of five other ships west of Ushant in reprisal for the capture in peacetime on 8.6.1755 of *Alcide* (64) and *Lis* (64). Taken to Nantes and then Brest, but released 20.9.1755 in the hope that the British would return the French ships, which they did not do. Sold by the UK 20.12.1763.

BELLONE. 32 guns. Designed and built by François-Guillaume Clairain-Deslauriers.

Admiralty draught of *Bellone* (in a different hand – 'changed to the *Repulse*'). Although the ship had twenty-eight ports, in British service she carried the standard twenty-six 12pdrs of Royal Navy 32-gun ships. (National Maritime Museum, London J6619)

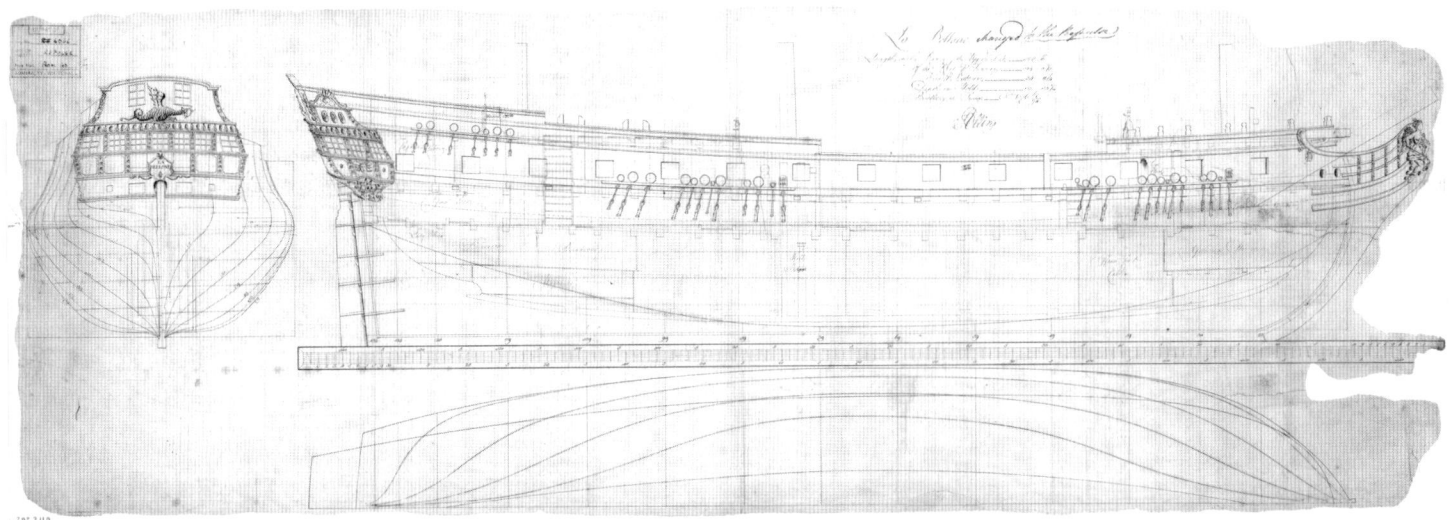

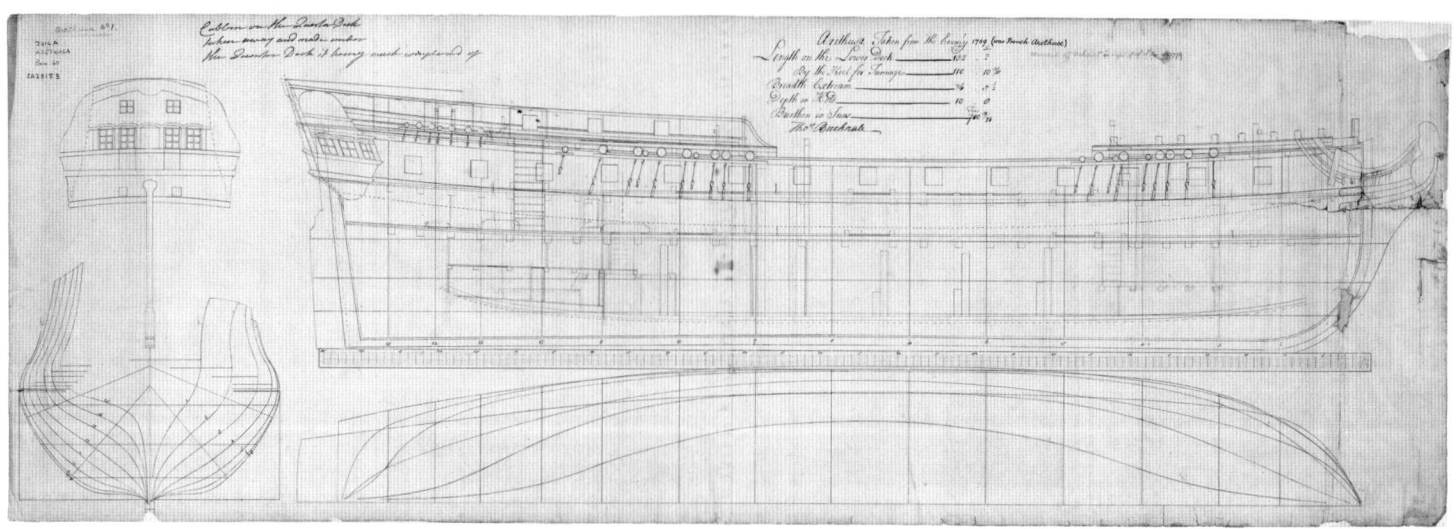

Admiralty draught of the *Arethusa*, 'Taken from the Enemy 1759 [actually 1758] (was French *Aréthuse*)'. A later hand notes 'Cabbin on the Quarter Deck taken away and made under the Quarter Deck it being much complained of.' Although built as a privateer, the ship was designed by Jean-Joseph Ginoux who had constructed many of the King's frigates at Le Havre, and *Aréthuse* was similar in every important respect to his work for the French Navy, specifically to the five frigates of the *Blonde* Class he had built from 1754 to 1757 (compare the draught of *Brune* on an earlier page). (National Maritime Museum, London J6580)

Dimensions & tons: 121ft 0in, 109ft 0in x 32ft 3in x 15ft 6in (39.31, 35.41 x 10.48 x 5.035m). 500/870 tons. Draught 13¼ft/14½ft (4.30/4.71m).
Guns: UD 28 x 8pdrs; QD 4 x 4pdrs.
Bellone Rochefort Dyd.
K: 1755. L: 9.1757. C: 4.1758. Captured in the Atlantic by HMS *Vestal* 21.2.1759, and became HMS *Repulse*; lost (presumed foundered with all hands) off Bermuda 12.1776.

HÉBÉ Class. 36 guns. Designed and built by Jean-Joseph Ginoux, these long frigates (pierced for fifteen pairs of UD guns) were planned to carry 2 x 18pdrs + 28 x 12pdrs, although structural weakness resulted in the *Hébé* being re-armed with 2 x 12pdrs + 26 x 8pdrs (plus 8 x 4pdrs on the *gaillards*); accordingly, they will be found in Chapter 4.

BOUFFONNE Class. 32-gun type. Designed by Jean-Joseph Ginoux. Begun at Caen in May 1757 by De Jouvencourt, but construction was stopped in October 1757 when it was realised that the canal from Caen to the sea was inadequate; the frames were taken to Le Havre where Ginoux re-laid the keels in January 1758.
Dimensions & tons: 124ft 0in x 32ft 0in x 16ft 4in (40.28 x 10.39 x 5.31m). 550/900 tons. Draught 10ft 10in/14½ft (3.52/4.71m). Men: 230 in war, 170 peace.
Guns: UD 26 x 8pdrs; QD 6 x 4pdrs or 6pdrs.
Bouffonne Le Havre.
K: 10.1757. L: 30.6.1758. C: 3.1759. Captured 17.7.1761 by HM Ships *Thetis*, *Modeste* and *Favourite* off Cadiz, but not added to the British Navy.
Malicieuse Le Havre.
K: 10.1757. L: 3.7.1758. C: 3.1759. Condemned 1777 at Brest and BU.

ARÉTHUSE. 36 guns. Designed and built by Jean-Joseph Ginoux as a privateer, under the name *Pèlerine*, and purchased for the Navy in December 1757, being renamed on 21 January 1758.
Dimensions & tons: 127ft 0in, 111ft 0in x 32ft 4in x 10ft 0in (41.25, 36.06 x 10.50 x 3.25m). 540/900 tons. Draught 14ft/14½ft (4.55/4.71m). Men: 245, +7 officers.
Guns: LD 4 x 12pdrs + 24 x 8pdrs; QD 8 x 4pdrs.
Aréthuse Le Havre.
K: 1.1757. L: 12.1757. C: 12.1757. Captured by HM Ships *Venus*, *Thames* and *Chatham* off Audierne Bay 18.5.1758, becoming HMS *Arethusa*; wrecked 19.3.1779.

Further 8pdr-armed frigates were ordered or planned over the next few years but not built due to budgetary issues. A 20-gun vessel was named as *Revêche* in 1755 and ordered at Rochefort in May 1757, but by January 1758 had not been laid down and was cancelled in 1760. Two 24-gun frigates, named as *Planète* and *Réussite*, were planned in 1758 but the orders were cancelled in 1760, along with orders for further frigates placed in 1758 – *Méfiance*, *Surprise*, *Naïade* and *Daphné*. All these were believed to have been intended to carry 8pdr batteries. Instead, the Navy purchased a number of 8pdr-armed privateers, either recently built or nearing completion.

VICTOIRE. This *vaisseau* of 40/48 guns was captured in November 1757 and was wrecked in December 1757 on the Pointe St Marc, 'one league from La Rochelle'. She was still there in January 1758 and was struck later that year. When lost she was probably manned *en flûte* by 44 men and 1 officer. Her other specifications, including her armament, are unknown. She is sometimes identified as HMS *Tartar's Prize* (ex-privateer *Marie-Victoire* from Le Havre), a 24-gun ship that sailed on 24 October 1757 from the UK for the Mediterranean and served there until lost on 2 March 1760, but they are probably different ships.

ÉCHO. 30 guns. The newbuilding privateer *Maréchal de Richelieu* was purchased at Nantes in December 1757 for the French Navy while still on the stocks, and was renamed on 21 January 1758 prior to completion.
Dimensions & tons: 113ft 0in x 30ft 6in x 9ft 4in (36.71 x 9.91 x 3.03m). 400/700 tons.
Guns: UD 24 x 8pdrs; QD 6 x 4pdrs.
Écho Nantes.
K: 1757. L: 1.1758. C: 3.1758. Captured off Louisbourg by HMS *Juno* 28.8.1758, becoming HMS *Echo*; sold 5.6.1770.

THE FIFTH RANK

Ex-BRITISH PRIZE (1758). The 24-gun British privateer *Tigre* (36 guns of unknown calibre including 12 *pierriers*) was captured on 4 March 1758 by the frigate *Rose* in the Mediterranenan. She was recaptured by the British in January 1762. No specifications are available.

The French 64-gun ship *Triton* and a frigate captured a British vessel named *Deal Castle* in June 1758 and took her into Malta. She has been mis-identified as the Sixth Rate HMS *Deal Castle*, but was in fact a 400-ton, 22-gun British privateer commanded by Richard Harman that was granted a letter of marque in July 1756. She was retaken by HMS *Cerberus* and taken into Jamaica in 1761, she was then stated to have been in the Leghorn trade.

Ex-BRITISH NAVAL PRIZE (1758). The British Sixth Rate *Winchelsea* was captured on 10 October 1758 by *Bizarre* (60) and *Mignonne* (28) southwest of Ireland while escorting a convoy; 44 merchant ships from the convoy were also captured.
  Dimensions & tons: 104ft 0in, 90ft 0in x 29ft 0in x 10ft 0in (m). 600 tons displacement. Draught 12ft/13ft (m).
  Guns (British): 20 x 9pdrs, 4 small.
Winchelsea Limehouse
  Retaken by the Bristol privateer *Duke of Cornwall* 27 October 1758 (17 days after her capture). BU completed 8.1761 at Portsmouth.

ENTREPRISE. A frigate of this name was put into service at Toulon on 18 January 1759. Her crew consisted of 158 men and 5 officers. She returned to Toulon in May 1759, was placed out of service, and was not further mentioned. Her origins, fate, and other specifications, including her armament, are unknown.

ZÉNOBIE. 24 guns. Designed and built by Jean-Philippe Bonvoisin as the frigate *Maréchal d'Estrées* for the *Compagnie des Indes*, who sold her in May 1759 to the French Navy while still building.
  Dimensions & tons: 114ft 0in x 30ft 0in x 16ft 0in (37.03 x 9.745 x 5.20m). 500 tons. Men: unknown.
  Guns: UD 24 x 8pdrs; QD nil.
Zénobie Le Havre.
  K: 1756. L: 1759. C: 6.1759. Sold for commerce 1.1762, and wrecked 11.1762 off Portland with all hands.

DILIGENTE. 26 guns. Designed by Jacques-Luc Coulomb, built by Joseph-Louis Ollivier for the *Compagnie des Indes*, who sold her in September 1761 to the French Navy. She was the first ship built at Lorient-Caudan, three slipways added in 1755 across the river from the main dockyard.
  Dimensions & tons: 122ft 0in, 105ft 0in x 31ft 8in x 16ft 0in (39.63, 34.11 x 10.29 x 5.20m). 470/1,000 tons. Draught 13½/14½ft (4.39/4.71m). Men: 200/180.
  Guns: UD 26 x 8pdrs; QD (sometimes) 6 x 4pdrs.
Diligente Lorient-Caudan.
  K: 12.1755. L: 28.4.1756. C: 12.1756. Wrecked off Cape Henry, Virginia 1.1782.

FOLLE. 34 guns. Designed and built by Pierre-Augustin Lamothe, Snr, as a privateer (provisionally named *Conscience*), but was purchased by the French Navy in November 1761.
  Dimensions & tons: 120ft 0in x 34ft 6in x 16ft 0in (38.98 x 11.21 x 5.20m). 500/1,000 tons. Draught 13ft 4in/14ft (4.33/4.55m). Men: 230 in war, 190 peace, + 7 officers.
  Guns: UD 26 x 8pdrs; QD 6 x 4pdrs.
Folle Nantes.
  K: 1759. L: 1761. C: 4.1762. Captured 10.1762, but restored to France 5.1763 and served as a privateer until 24.5.1765. Used for fishery protection from 2.1767 until struck in 1780 and BU at Toulon

Following the Seven Years' War, just five more 8pdr frigates were begun during the 1760s, with a final pair laid down in the mid-1770s, as preference moved to the use of 12pdr-armed frigates. Subsequent acquisitions of 8pdr ships were only by purchase or capture.

DANAÉ. 26 guns. Designed by Antoine Groignard, and built by Jean-Hyacinthe Raffeau. Named *Comète* 22.12.1762, renamed *Danaé* when the previous *Comète* was bought back from the British.
  Dimensions & tons: 124ft 0in x 32ft 0in x 16ft 0in (40.28 x 10.39 x 5.20m). 550/800 tons. Draught 12ft 8in/13ft 4in (4.11/4.33m).

Admiralty draught of *Danaé* as captured, dated Plymouth Yard 24 August 1779. The gunport right forward in the eyes of the ship was a chase port and not regularly armed. (National Maritime Museum, London J5918)

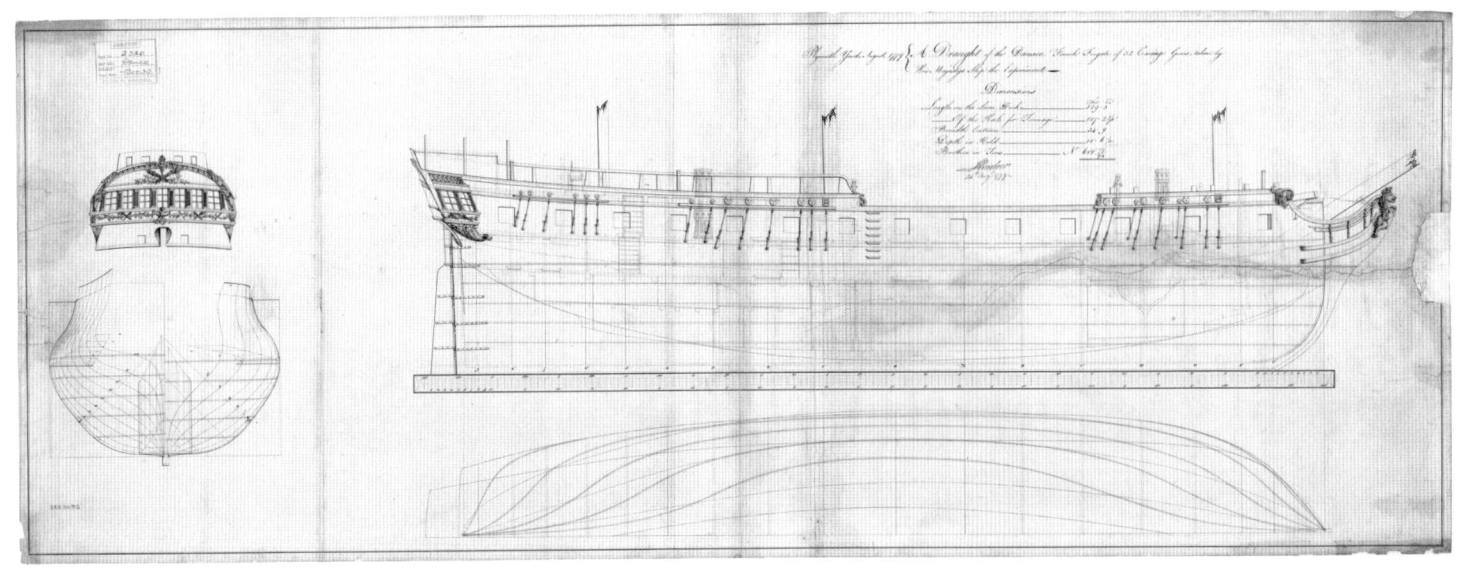

Men: 190 in war, 130 peace, + 7 officers.
Guns: UD 26 x 8pdrs; QD/Fc nil (later 6 x 4pdrs added).
Danaé Indret (Nantes).
K: 9.1762. L: 22.10.1763. C: 5.1764. Captured in Cancale Bay by HMS *Experiment* and her consorts 13.5.1779 and added to the British Navy as HMS *Danae*; sold 10.1797 at Woolwich.

Ex-BRITISH PRIZE (1762). The British Sixth Rate *Hussar* stranded off Cap François, St Domingue, on 23 May 1762 and was taken by the French who rendered her name as *Hussard*. She was built of softwood (fir).
Dimensions & tons: 114ft 0in x 32ft 0in x 9ft 7in (37.03 x 10.39 x 3.11m). 700 tons displacement.
Guns: 24 x 9pdrs, 4 x 3pdrs.
Hussard Chatham Dyd. (built by John Lock)
Ordered: 18.4.1757. K: 3.5.1757. L: 23.7.1757. C: 17.8.1757. Listed as wrecked in the Antilles 5.1762 (probably not salvaged after capture).

MIGNONNE. 30 (later 32) guns. A single ship to a one-off design by Jean-Baptiste Doumet-Revest. A *Mignonne* had been projected in 1762 but was never ordered. This one was ordered on 5 August 1765 and originally named *Précieuse* on 31 March 1766, her name being changed to *Mignonne* on 16 February 1767. A second ship was ordered in January 1766 and named as *Étoile*, with a slightly altered plan approved on 31 May, but was cancelled in 1767.
Dimensions & tons: 122ft 2in, 108ft 0in x 32ft 0in x 15ft 9in (39.68, 35.08 x 10.39 x 5.12m). 500/880 tons. Draught 13/14ft (4.22/4.55m). Men: 200 in war, 150 peace, +7 officers.
Guns: UD 26 x 8pdrs; QD 4 x 4pdrs (6 x 4pdrs from 1789).
Mignonne Toulon Dyd. (*Constructeur*, Claude Saucillon).
K: 10.1765. L: 26.4.1767. C: 7.1768. Raséed to a corvette at Toulon in 1794, but captured (in poor condition) by Adm Hood's squadron at the surrender of Calvi on 10.8.1794, becoming HMS *Mignonne*; burnt 7.1797 at Port-Ferrajo.

ÉTOILE. 26 guns. An order for an 8pdr-armed frigate – to be named *Étoile* – was placed at Toulon in January 1766 with Jean-Baptiste Doumet-Revest, whose design of 26 April 1766 was approved on 31 May (see below for dimensions). However, this order was cancelled in 1767. A second 8pdr frigate was ordered in February 1766, to have been named *Fine* (design and intended builder unknown), but this was cancelled in 1769 without being laid down, as was the case with a third vessel, the *Coquette*, originally ordered in February 1766 as a 12pdr frigate, but from May 1768 modified to carry 8pdrs instead.
Dimensions & tons: 120ft 0in, 110ft 0in x 32 ft 0in x 15ft 9in (38.98, 35.73 x 10.39 x 5.12m). ..../820 tons. Draught 13ft/14½ft (4.22/4.71m).

ZÉPHYR. 32 guns, designed and built by Joseph-Louis Olliver. This frigate was originally ordered in October 1766 to be built with 12pdr guns to a Ginoux design at Le Havre, but the order (now for an 8pdr type) was moved to Brest in December 1766.
Dimensions & tons: 126ft 0in, 119ft 0in x 32ft 4in x 16ft 5in (40.93, 38.66 x 10.50 x 5.33m). 540/950 tons. Draught 10ft 7in (3.44m). Men: 230/170, +7 officers.
Guns: UD 26 x 8pdrs; QD 6 x 4pdrs.
Zéphyr Brest Dyd.
K: 10.1767. L: 23.10.1768. C: 1769. Burned by accident at Brest 2.1779.

FLORE. 26 guns. Probably designed by Nicolas Ozanne, but built by Antoine Groignard. Like the *Zéphyr*, this frigate was originally ordered in October 1766 to be built with 12pdr guns to a Ginoux design at Le Havre, but the order (now for an 8pdr type) was moved to Brest in December 1766.
Dimensions & tons: 126ft 0in, 117ft 0in x 32ft 6in x 16ft 4in (40.93, 38.01 x 10.56 x 5.31m). 540/950 tons. Draught 13ft 5in/14ft (4.36/4.55m). Men: 230/190, +4/7 officers.

An unusual profile draught of *Mignonne* from the Danish archives. Despite its provenance, all the annotation is in French, and must post-date the building of the ship as it quotes the launch date. The labelling mostly concerns the functions of the internal spaces and cabins: the *dunette* on the quarterdeck, for example, accommodated cabins for the Captain and Second Captain right aft, with cabins for the Master and Pilot forward of them. This was a curious feature, entirely at odds with the design philosophy of minimising windage by keeping down topside height, but it gave the officers responsible for conning the ship rapid access to the quarterdeck. It was very unpopular in the Royal Navy, which usually removed it from French prize frigates as quickly as possible. (Rigsarkivet, Copenhagen)

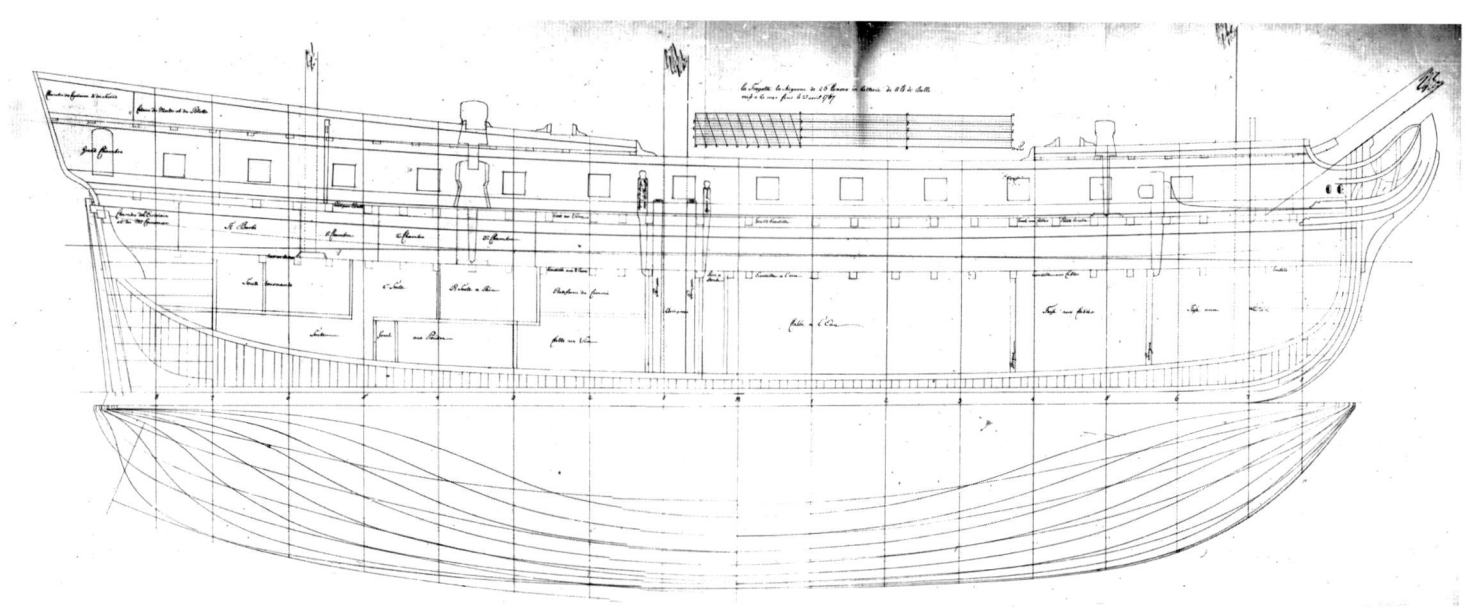

THE FIFTH RANK

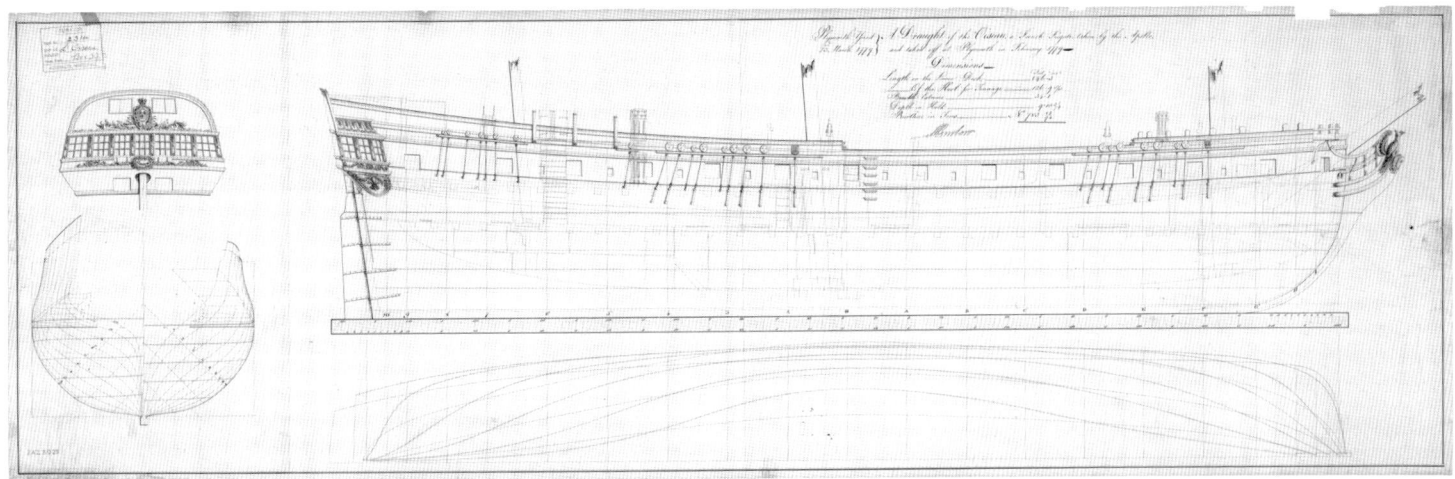

Admiralty draught of the *Oiseau*, dated Plymouth Yard, 23 March 1779. In terms of proportions, the hulls of French frigates were usually longer and shallower than their British equivalents, but this ship was an extreme example, having been designed specifically to obtain high speed. The midship section is actually less exaggerated and more rounded than the classic French form, and the hull lines are not unusually fine, the designer relying on length to obtain the desired speed (in naval architecture, all other characteristics remaining the same, the longer hull will be faster). Unfortunately, there are no known sailing quality reports on the ship in French or British sources, but it is likely that the ship met the pure speed requirement, although the shallow hull would have made her leewardly, and the great length would slow her tacking and wearing. (National Maritime Museum, London J5916)

Guns: UD 26 x 8pdrs; QD nil (6 x 4pdrs added later).
Flore Brest Dyd.
K: 2.1768. L: 11.11.1768. C: 1769. Undertook scientific voyage in 1771–72 (to the Canaries, Gorée, the West Indies, Iceland and Denmark) to validate instruments and chronometers designed to evaluate latitudes and longitudes (under CV Verdun de La Crenne, with LV Charles de Borda aboard). Condemned 1785 at Toulon and sold 1787.

OISEAU Class. 26 guns. Designed by François-Guillaume Clairain-Deslauriers. In late 1766 orders were issued to Léon-Michel Guignace to build two new 8pdr frigates – *Oiseau* and *Nymphe* – to this design at Bayonne. In November-December 1766 Clairain-Deslauriers proposed to build at Rochefort a 135-foot frigate with high speed, and in 1767 the orders for both of these frigates were moved there.
Dimensions & tons: 137ft 0in x 31ft 0in x 15ft 0in (33.50 x 10.07 x 4.87m). 485/950 tons. Draught 12½ft/13ft 10in (3.24m). Men: 200/180, + 7 officers.
Guns: UD 26 x 8pdrs; QD nil (6 x 4pdrs added later).
Oiseau Rochefort Dyd.
K: end 1767. L: 11.1.1769. C: 11.1770. Captured 31.1.1779 by HMS *Apollo* in the Channel, becoming HMS *Oiseau*; sold 6.1783.
Nymphe Rochefort Dyd.
Order deferred and then cancelled 1769.

AMOUR Class. In 1766 two frigates with 26 x 8pdrs named *Amour* and *Psyché* were ordered at Nantes, possibly from Jean-Hyacinthe Rafeau. The order was transferred to Brest in February 1767, then deferred, and finally cancelled in 1769.

ALCMÈNE. 32 guns. In 1772 the Marquis de Boynes (the Navy Minister) instructed Antoine Groignard to prepare a standard plan for all future 26-gun 8pdr frigates; ironically only two more were ever built to naval orders. Designed by Antoine Groignard, and built by Jean-Baptiste Doumet-Revest. Unlike earlier 8pdr frigates, these two had open stern galleries. The first was named on 27 September 1772. In RN use after capture, *Alcmène* was re-armed with 9pdrs *vice* French 8pdrs.
Dimensions & tons: 124ft 0in, 115ft 0in x 32ft 0in x 17ft 0in (40.28, 37.36 x 10.39 x 5.52m). 500/966 tons. Draughts 13¾ft/14ft 10in (4.47/4.82m). Men: 224–239.
Guns: UD 26 x 8pdrs; QD 2 x 4pdrs; Fc 4 x 4pdrs.
Alcmène Toulon Dyd.
K: 5.1773. L: 14.6.1774. C: 9.1774. Captured 20.10.1779 by HMS *Proserpine* off Martinique; sold 8.1784.

AIMABLE. 32 guns. Designed by Antoine Groignard, a slight enlargement from the *Alcmène*. Named on 5 May 1775. In RN use after her capture, *Aimable* was re-armed with British 12pdrs *vice* the French 12pdrs with which she had been re-armed in 1781.
Dimensions & tons: 126ft 2in, c.117ft 0in x 33ft 3in x 17ft 2in (40.98, c.38.00 x 10.80 x 5.58m). 500/960 tons. Draughts 14ft/15ft 2in (4.55/4.93m). Men: 224–239.
Guns: UD 26 x 8pdrs (replaced by 12pdrs in 1781); QD 2 x 4pdrs; Fc 4 x 4pdrs.
Aimable Toulon Dyd.
K: 1775. L: 20.7.1776. C: 9.1776. Captured 19.4.1782 by HMS *Magnificent* of Hood's squadron in the Mona Strait, becoming HMS *Aimable*; BU 5.1814.

PALLAS. 32 guns. The former privateer *Prince de Conti*, designed and built by Léon-Michel Guignace, then purchased for the French Navy in September 1777 at St Malo, rebuilt there from September 1777 to January 1778 and renamed.
Dimensions & tons: 120ft 0in x 33ft 0in (38.98 x 10.72m). 575/940 tons.
Guns: UD 26 x 8pdrs; QD 4 x 4pdrs.
Pallas St Malo.
K: 4.1773. L: 1773. C: 10.1773. Captured by HMS *Victory* in the Channel on 19.6.1778, becoming HMS *Inconstant*; renamed HMS *Convert*, and sold at Woolwich 28.11.1782 to BU.

Ex-BRITISH PRIZES (1778–1783). During the American Revolutionary War, the French captured and put into service the following nine British 9pdr frigates (excluding one former ship sloop, *Barboude*, which carried 6pdr guns and is thus included in Chapter 10 with the corvettes, although the French Navy classed her as a frigate).

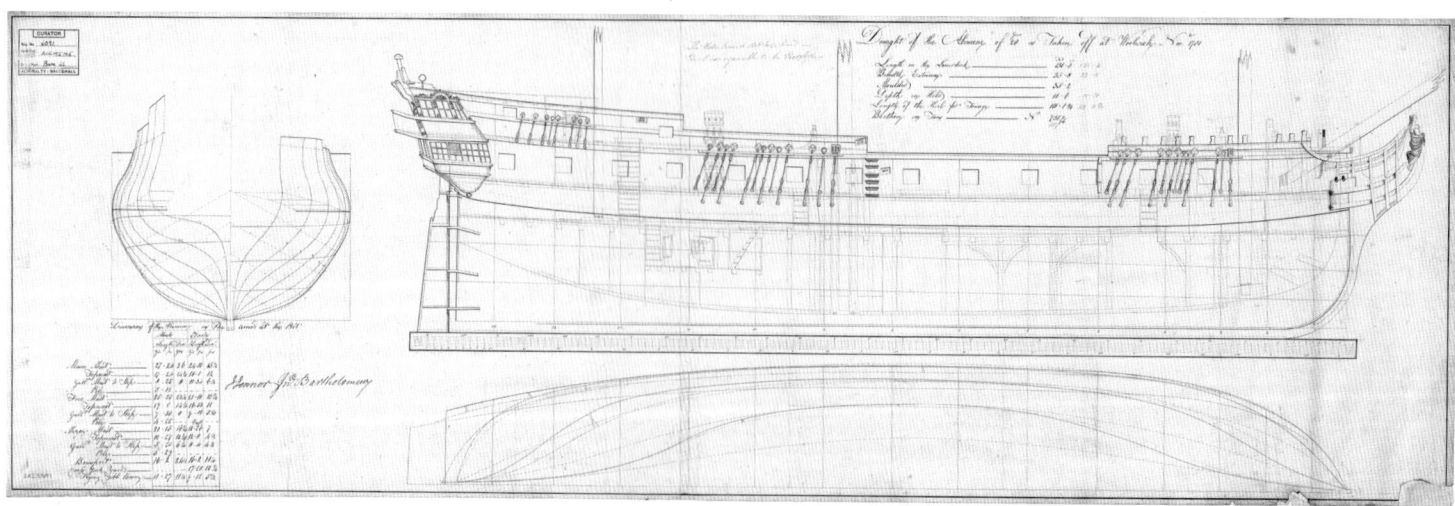

Admiralty draught of *Alcmène* 'as Taken off at Woolwich Nov 1781'. The ship was captured in the West Indies in 1779 but did not reach a British dockyard until 1781, so the appearance is probably as taken – indeed, the draught is annotated 'Dimensions of the Alcmene as she arrived at this port'. The most curious feature of what was intended to be a standard design was the expansion of the *dunette* cabins into a full-blown poop, complete with a second tier of quarter galleries and an open balcony. To thus compromise the sailing qualities of the ship for the comfort of her officers is an odd priority in a fighting ship. (National Maritime Museum, London J6315)

Most retained their British guns in French service (French 8pdrs and British 9pdrs were virtually the same calibre). Dimensions given below are in French units (feet and inches), following re-measurement by the captors.

British *GIBRALTAR* Class. Seven 20-gun Sixth Rates were built to this 1753 design by Thomas Slade, of which the *Lively* was captured off Ushant by the *Iphigénie* on 9 July 1778.

Dimensions & tons: 105ft 0in, 93ft 0in x 28ft 6in x 13ft 6in (34.11, 30.21 x 9.26 x 4.39m). 350/600 tons. Draught 11ft/13ft 8in (3.57/4.44m).

Guns: UD 22 x 9pdrs; QD 2 x 4pdrs.

Lively Moody Janverin, Bursledon-on-Hamble.
Ord: 20.5.1755. K: 6.1755. L: 10.8.1756. C: 17.10.1756 at Portsmouth Dyd. Retaken 29.7.1781 by HMS *Perseverance* in the Channel, but then laid up at Plymouth until sold there on 11.3.1784.

British *COVENTRY* Class. Thirteen 28-gun Sixth Rates were built (excluding five more which were constructed of fir) to this 1756 design by Thomas Slade, of which three were captured during 1778–83. The *Active* was captured on 1 September 1778 by *Charmante* and *Dédaigneuse* off St Domingue; the *Guadeloupe* was salved and added by the French on 19 October 1781, after being scuttled by the British in the York River (Virginia) on 10 October; and the *Coventry* was captured by Suffren's squadron off Ganjam in the Bay of Bengal on 12 January 1783.

Dimensions & tons: 116ft 0in, 100ft 0in x 31ft 8in x 15ft 0in (37.68, 32.48 x 10.29 x 4.87m). 450/850 tons. Draught 13½ft/15ft 4in (4.39/4.98m). Men: 210 in war, 150 peace, +11 officers.

Guns: *Active* UD 24 x 9pdrs (2 more added 1780); QD nil. In 1793 re-armed with French guns: UD 24 x 8pdrs; QD 4 x 4pdrs. *Guadeloupe* UD 24 x 9pdrs; QD 4 x 6pdrs. In 1784 re-armed with French guns: UD 29 x 8pdrs; QD 5 smaller. *Coventry* UD 22 x 9pdrs; QD/Fc 6 x 3pdrs.

Active Thomas Stanton & Co, Rotherhithe.
Ord: 6.5.1757. K: 13.6.1757. L: 11.1.1758. C: 2.3.1758 at Deptford Dyd. Redesignated as a corvette 1.1789. Condemned 11.1794 at Brest.

Guadeloupe Plymouth Dyd.
Ord: 29.6.1758. K: 8.5.1759. L: 5.12.1763. C: 11.6.1764. Ordered 8.7.1786 to be BU at Rochefort, but this was not carried out. Seized by Jervis's squadron 4.1794 on the capture of (the island of) Guadeloupe, but not added to British Navy.

Coventry Henry Adams, Buckler's Hard.
Ord: 13.4.1756. K: 31.5.1756. L: 30.5.1757. C: 31.7.1757 at Portsmouth Dyd. Disarmed at Brest 1.1785 and BU.

British *ENTERPRISE* Class. Twenty-eight 28-gun Sixth Rates were built (and one more cancelled) to this 1770 design by John Williams, of which two were captured during 1778 and 1781. The *Fox* was captured on 11 September 1778 by the *Junon* off Brest, and the *Crescent* by the *Friponne* and *Gloire* on 19 June 1781 (having been earlier in French hands on 30 May 1781 for a few hours).

Dimensions & tons: 116ft 0in, 104ft 0in x 31ft 6in x 17ft 0in (37.68, 33.78 x 10.23 x 5.52m). 450/850 tons. Draught 14ft/15ft (4.55/4.87m). Men: 210 in war, 130 peace.

Guns: UD 24 x 9pdrs; QD 4 x 3pdrs.

Fox Thomas Raymond, Northam (Southampton).
Ord: 25.12.1770. K: 5.1771. L: 2.9.1773. C: 12.2.1776 at Portsmouth Dyd. Wrecked 3.4.1779 off Quiberon.

Crescent James Martin Hilhouse, Bristol.
Ord: 19.7.1777. K: 19.8.1777. L: 3.1779. C: 30.6.1779 at Plymouth Dyd. Wrecked 1.1786 off St Domingue.

British *SPHINX* Class. Ten 20-gun Sixth Rates were built to this 1773 design by John Williams, of which three were captured by French frigates during 1779–80. The *Ariel* was captured on 10 September 1779 by the *Amazone* off Georgia, the *Sphinx* was captured on 29 September 1779 by the *Amphitrite* off Martinique, and the *Unicorn* was captured on 4 September 1780 by the *Andromaque* off Tortuga.

Dimensions & tons: 105ft 0in, 93ft 0in x 28ft 2in x 11ft 0in (34.11, 30.21 x 9.15 x 3.57m). 350/650 tons. Draught 13ft/14½ft (4.22/4.71m). Men: 210 in war, 130 peace.

Guns: UD 20 x 9pdrs; QD 4 x 4pdrs; Fc 2 x 4pdrs.

Ariel John Perry & Co, Blackwall.
Ord: 3.7.1776. K: 7.1776. L: 7.7.1777. C: 12.8.1777 at Woolwich Dyd. Lent by France to the (American) Continental Navy from

The capture of HMS *Fox*, a 28-gun Sixth Rate, by the 32-gun *Junon* off Ushant on 11 September 1778 [wrongly dated November on the print]. An engraving by François Dequevauviller after a 1788 painting by CV Auguste-Louis de Rossel de Cercy, one of a series of thirty-six depictions of naval actions from this war executed by this former naval captain at the instigation of Louis XVI. The *Fox* was dismasted and surrendered following a gruelling 3½-hour exchange. (Beverley R Robinson Collection, Annapolis 51.7.141)

10.1780 to 6.1781. Redesignated as a corvette 1.1789. Burnt on the Scheldt 24.3.1793 during the evacuation of Antwerp by the French.

Sphinx Portsmouth Dyd.
   Ord: 15.4.1773. K: 11.1773. L: 25.10.1775. C: 29.12.1775. Retaken by HMS *Proserpine* 29.12.1779 in the West Indies, and resumed British service until BU 1811 at Portsmouth.

Licorne John Randall & Co, Rotherhithe.
   Ord: 30.10.1775. K: 11.1775. L: 23.3.1776. C: 25.5.1776 at Woolwich Dyd. Retaken by HMS *Resource* 20.4.1781 in the West Indies, and resumed British service under her original name until BU 8.1787 at Deptford.

COMTESSE Class. 20-gun type. On 4 August 1780 Sartine approved the acquisition of two 260-ton Dunkirk privateers, the *Comte d'Artois* and *Comte de Provence*, armed with 20 x 8pdrs and built in the previous year by Étienne Daniel Denys and his first cousin Jacques. Pourrat et Cie. had acquired them from Jean Baptiste Carpeau de Maricourt on 26 February 1780, and they had previously been placed in service by R. Coppens, Cailliez and Coffyn (as 400-ton ships) under the names *Prince de Robecq* and *Rohan Soubise* (Denys had previously built three smaller Dunkirk privateers, the 150-ton *Comtesse d'Artois* and *Comtesse de Provence* in 1778 and the 120-ton *Chaulieu* in 1779). The French Navy placed these two larger ships into service as commerce raiders, reverting to their original names.
   Dimensions & tons: 107ft 0in x 26ft 4in (34.76 x 8.55m). 300/550 tons. Men: 200/160, + 3 officers.
   Guns: UD 20 x 8pdrs; QD 2 (*Robecq*) or 4 (*Rohan Soubise*) x 6pdr *obusiers*.

Rohan Soubise Étienne Daniel & Jacques Denys, Dunkirk.
   K: 4.1779. L: 10.1779. C: 4.1780. Captured 27.4.1781 by HM Ships *Proselyte* and *Repulse*, but not added to British Navy.

Robecq Étienne Daniel & Jacques Denys, Dunkirk.
   K: 4.1779. L: 10.1779. C: 4.1780. Captured 30.6.1782 by HMS *Ariadne*, briefly becoming HMS *Robecque*; not put into service by the British, and sold 5.6.1783 at Plymouth.

MESNY. The slaver *Mesny* of 300 tons, originally built at St Malo in 1763, was hired by the Navy from June to December 1779 prior to being purchased in October 1780 without change of name. She was employed by the Navy as a training frigate, manned by 42 men (+4 officers) as well as 390 trainees in December 1780, then 470 trainees in February 1781. She was wrecked on the Carolles rocks off Granville in February 1781, with no casualties. No details are available of dimensions or armament.

MARQUISE DE LA FAYETTE. 30 guns. The privateer frigate *Marquise de La Fayette* was built 1778 at Bayonne by Descande. She was captured by a British privateer at the start of 1780 but was retaken by the *Gentille* in May 1780 and was then purchased by the French Navy in November 1780 without change of name.
   Dimensions & tons: dimensions unknown. 400 tons.
   Guns: UD 26 x 8pdrs; QD 4 x 4pdrs. Re-armed *en flûte* in 1781

Marquise de La Fayette Bayonne
   L: 17.11.1778. Probably wrecked late 1783 off St Domingue.

6 Light Frigates

(Frégates légères)

French *frégates légères* (light frigates) were unranked vessels, as the classification system stopped at the 5th Rank, although occasionally vessels built as *frégates légères* were re-classified as 5th Rank (and vice versa). The early vessels were termed 'advice frigates' (*frégates d'avis*), a term which indicates their earliest role. However, from about 1670 the term *frégate légère* was employed, to distinguish them from the two-decker *frégates-vaisseaux* of the 4th and 5th Ranks; in general, they carried their guns on a single upper deck (apart from small guns on the *gaillards*). With few exceptions, their main batteries were composed of 6pdr or 4pdr guns, although a very few mounted 8pdrs, and some of the latter were small two-deckers.

Under the *Règlement* of 4 July 1670, *frégates légères* were expected to carry between 8 and 16 guns (although a few carried only 4 or 6 in mid-1671). However, by 1675 eight vessels carried more than this, and by 1683 the category included vessels from 10 to 22 guns; by 1690, a minimum armament of 14 guns was required to distinguish the *frégate légère* from the smaller combatants such as the corvette or *barque longue* (which are found in Chapter 10), and in practice the category comprised vessels of up to 28 guns, and exceptionally vessels of up to 34 guns.

(A) Frigates in service at 9 March 1661

ÉMINENTE. The sole light frigate in service at the start of 1661 was the Dunkirk frigate *Éminente* (sometimes called *Frégate de Dunkerque* or simply *Dunkerquois*), which had been captured in June 1658. She was of 200 tons, and carried 24 guns and a complement of 200 men. In theory, she would have been classed as a 5th Rank ship, but was never included in that category. She was removed from service at La Rochelle in October 1666.

(B) Frigates acquired from 9 March 1661

SAINTE ANNE. 12 guns. Originally built in 1653–55 and purchased in 1660 in Holland for Nicolas Fouchet as *Sainte Anne de Biscaye*, Following his downfall in early 1661, the ship was confiscated in September 1661 by the Crown and added to the Navy with the name shortened to *Sainte Anne*.
    Dimensions & tons: 80ft 0in x 19ft 0in x 9ft 0in (25.99 x 6.17 x 2.92m). 120 tons. Draught 10½ft (3.41m). Men: 120 in war, 90 peace, +3 officers.
    Guns (from 1669): 6 x 6pdrs; 6 x 3pdrs, +12 swivels.
Sainte Anne Holland.
    K: 1653. L: ? C: 1655. Grounded on the coast in early 1670 and BU.

BELLE-ÎLE. 10 guns. A small frigate belonging to Nicolas Fouquet, and named after the island off the south coast of Brittany which was Fouquet's personal stronghold. Like the *Sainte Anne*, she was confiscated by the Crown in September 1661 after Fouquet was dismissed from office and imprisoned in 1661.
    Dimensions & tons: dimensions unknown. 80 tons (100 in 1669).
    Men: 60 (12/30/18) in 1669, +3 officers; 40 (8/20/12) in 1671, +2 officers.
    Guns: 10.
Belle-Île Rochefort.
    K: early 1661. L: 1663. C: 1665. Renamed *Fée* 24.6.1671. Struck in 1674 at Rochefort.

PETITE FRÉGATE DE BREST. Designed and built by Laurent Hubac at Brest, this vessel was of 50 tons, but no other details are recorded.
    K: 1663. L: 1.1664. C: 2.1664. Struck *c.*1668.

POSTILLON. 8 guns. Built by Imbert at Marseille. A *mémoire* on her construction dated 14 February 1665 stated that her function was to carry news and for that reason she was named *le Postillon Royal*. She was

The work of the Dutch artists Willem van de Velde, father and son, offer the single most important visual source of information on seventeenth century small craft, and indeed shipping in general. The Elder in particular was a prolific sketcher of all sorts of ships and boats, but unfortunately few of his subjects can be identified or even dated accurately. This small Dutch frigate, thought to have been drawn around 1665 by his son, is probably a close approximation to a vessel like the *Sainte Anne*. Despite their diminutive size, they carried a full ship rig, although there was no square topsail on the mizzen. (National Maritime Museum, London PY1777)

to have seven pairs of oars and was to be completed within four months 'more beautiful than the model'. Her crew was to consist of 12 petty officers including a surgeon, a captain and a lieutenant, plus 36 good sailors for a total of 50. The dimensions and armament specified in this *mémoire* are shown below. She was listed with 50 tons, 6 guns, and 30 men when last mentioned in May 1669.

> Dimensions & tons: 50ft 0in x 18ft 0in x 11ft 0in (16.24 x 5.85 x 3.57m). 60 tons. Men: 48, +2 officers.
> Guns: 8 x 8pdrs, +8 *pierriers* (swivels).

Postillon Marseille.
> K: 3.1665. L: 27.8.1665. C: 12.1665. Armed at Toulon and sailed 29.4.1666 for a campaign on the Atlantic coast. Disarmed at Toulon 29.10.1666. Classed as ineffective by 5.6.1668. Not mentioned after 5.1669 (and might perhaps have been ceded to the *Compagnie des Indes Orientales* even earlier).

AVENTURE. Probably purchased in April 1665 as the English-built *Adventure*, this 130-ton vessel carried 14 guns but no other details are recorded. She was struck in March 1666.

ADRIATIQUE. 14-gun frigate of 130 tons, launched 1663 in London and purchased there for Louis XIV on 30 April 1665. Renamed *Dunkerquoise* soon after purchase, she was lost (overset by a strong wind) on 21 September 1665.

MORINE. 6 guns. Ex-pirate vessel built in 1658 or 1660 at Dunkirk, and seized from the pirate Morin Le Bailleul (after whom she was named) in August 1665; he was hung on 12 October 1665.

> Dimensions & tons: dimensions unknown. 30 tons (60 in 1669).
> Men: 30 (6/14/10) in 1669, +3 officers; 2 officers in 1671.
> Guns: 6 (reduced to 4 from 1671).

Morine Dunkirk.
> Renamed *Surprenante* 24.6.1671. Condemned 25.7.1673 at Brest and BU 1674.

AURORE. 8 guns. Designed and built by Laurent Hubac.
> Dimensions & tons: dimensions unknown. 80 tons. Men: 40 (10/20/12) in 1669, +3 officers; 30 (8/13/10) in 1671, +2 officers.
> Guns: 8 (reduced to 6 from 1671).

Aurore Brest Dyd.
> K: 9.1665. L: 11.1665. C: 11.1665. Renamed *Sibylle* 24.6.1671. Struck 1675 at Rochefort.

NOTRE DAME DES ANGES. 16 guns. Sometimes listed as *Reyne des Anges*, this small frigate was purchased for Louis XIV on 20 February 1666.

> Dimensions & tons: dimensions unknown. 150 tons. Men: 80 (15/40/25) in 1669, +3 officers; 60 (12/30/18) in 1671, +2 officers.
> Guns: 16 (reduced to 14 from 1671).

Notre Dame des Anges Dunkirk.
> K: 3.1665. L: 6.1665. C: 8.1665. Seized by the Spanish at Ostend 1.1667, but restored to France 2.1667. Ordered to be disarmed 30.6.1668, but renamed *Subtile* 24.6.1671. Refitted as a fireship at Le Havre in July 1673. Struck 1674.

PURCHASED FRIGATE (1666). Designed and built by Laurent Hubac in 1659, this vessel (*Infante* or *Petite Infante*) was purchased for the Navy in May 1666 at Toulon.

> Dimensions & tons: 76ft 5in x 19ft 0in x 10ft 0in (24.82 x 6.17 x 3.25m). 100/200 tons. Draught 10ft/12ft (3.25/3.90m). Men: 50 (14/21/15), +5 officers.
> Guns: 16 by 1669, 10 from 1671, 12 from 1672, 10 from 1675, and 14 from 1677.

Petite Infante St Malo.
> Renamed *Légère* 24.6.1671. Listed in 1677 as a '*vieux bâtiment donné à fret*', and struck at Rochefort 1678.

DILIGENTE. 16, later 12 guns. Designed and built by Laurent Hubac.
> Dimensions & tons: 80ft 0in x 19ft 0in (25.99 x 6.17m). 120 tons. Men: 50, +2/3 officers.
> Guns: 16; reduced to 12 by 1669.

Diligente Brest Dyd.
> K: early 1666. L: 1666. C: 12.1666. Removed from service at Pondicherry 4.1674 and BU there.

SAINTE CATHERINE. 8–10 guns. Ordered from the Dutch during 2nd Anglo-Dutch War. Listed in May 1669 as a galiote.
> Dimensions & tons: 55ft 0in keel x 15ft 0in x 7ft 6in (17.87 x 4.87 x 2.44m). 80 tons. Draught 8ft/9ft. Men: 50 (14/21/15) in war, 40 peace, +2/3 officers.
> Guns: 8 (5.1669).

Sainte Catherine Amsterdam,
> K: 4.1666. L: 11.1666. C: 9.1667. Ceded to the privateer Moïse Vauclin in the West Indies 5.1669; not mentioned after 3.1670.

SAINT JEAN. 6 (later 10) guns. Ordered from the Dutch during 2nd Anglo-Dutch War. Listed in May 1669 as a galiote.
> Dimensions & tons: 55ft 0in keel x 15ft 0in x 7ft 6in (17.87 x 4.87 x 2.44m). 60 tons (80 in 5.1669 and 1683). Draught 8ft/9ft (2.60/2.92m). Men: in 1669, 30 (6/14/10), + 3 officers; in 1683, 50 (14/21/15) in war, 40 peace, +2/5 officers.
> Guns: 8 by 1669, 6 from 1671, 11 from 1672, 10 from 1673, and 6 from 1679.

Saint Jean Amsterdam.
> K: 4.1666. L: 11.1666. C: 9.1667. Renamed *Gentille* 24.6.1671. Captured by the Spanish 7.1684.

CHRISTINE. 8 (later 10) guns. Ordered from the Dutch during 2nd Anglo-Dutch War.
> Dimensions & tons: dimensions unknown. 60 tons (100 in 1679). Draught 9ft (2.92m). Men: in 1669, 30 (6/14/10), + 3 officers; in 1679, 28 (9/19/–), +2 officers.
> Guns: 8 by 1669; 6 from 1671, 10 from 1672, 8 from 1677.

Christine Amsterdam.
> K: 1666. L: late 1666. C: 1667. Renamed *Sans Peur* 24.6.1671. Rigged as a hoy in 1677, as munitions carrier. Re-rated as a *barque longue* in 1677–78. Hulked 10.1680 at Le Havre, and sold there 9.1681.

Ex-ENGLISH PRIZE (1667). An English vessel built at Bristol in 1656 or 1660 was captured by *Étoile d'Afrique* in March 1667 and renamed *Saint Pierre*. She was listed in September 1669 as a 200-ton *flûte* with six guns but by 1671 had become a 60-ton *frégate légère*.
> Dimensions & tons: 60 tons. Men: 30 (6/14/10), +2 officers.
> Guns: 6 from 1671.

Saint Pierre Bristol
> Renamed *Moqueuse* 24.6.1671. Wrecked in Audierne Bay 1672; struck and BU 1673.

Ex-SPANISH PRIZE (1667). 10 guns. The Spanish frigate *Fuenterrabia*, probably built in 1655, was captured by the French in

1667, with the name changed to *Fontarabie*.
  Dimensions & tons: 50ft 0in x 12ft 0in x 5ft 6in (16.24 x 3.90 x 1.79m). 80 tons. Men: 50 in war, 40 peace, +2 officers.
  Guns: 8/10.
Fontarabie Spain.
  Renamed *Biscayenne*, then *Folle* 24.6.1671. Condemned 1673 at Rochefort.

DIEPPOISE Class. 12 guns. Ordered in November 1667.
  Dimensions & tons: dimensions unknown. 120 tons. Men: 60 (12/30/18) in 1671, +3 officers; from 1671, 50 in war (10/24/16), 40 peace, + 2 officers.
  Guns (both): 12 from 1669, then 14 from 1675.
Dieppoise Dieppe.
  K: 11.1667. L: 4.1668. C: 5.1668. Renamed *Lutine* 24.6.1671. For sale 3.1675 at Le Havre, struck 1675.
Gaillarde Dieppe.
  K: 12.1667. L: 4.1668. C: 5.1668. Classed as a *bâtiment de charge* (cargo ship) 11.1675, then converted to fireship 5.1677. Renamed *Inconnu* 5.1678, then *Incommode* 28.6.1678. BU 6.1681.

MADELEINE. 8 guns. Designed and built by Benjamin Chaillé.
  Dimensions & tons: dimensions unknown. 80 tons (60 tons by 1673). Men: 40 (8/20/12) in 1669, +3 officers; 30 (8/14/10) in 1671, + 2 officers.
  Guns: 8; reduced to 6 from 1671.
Madeleine Rochefort Dyd.
  K: end 1667. L: 1668. C: 1668. Renamed *Belle* 24.6.1671. Struck at Rochefort 1673, and BU 1674.

When the new rating system was introduced under Colbert in September 1669, there were just fourteen vessels, with up to 16 guns, which were excluded from the defined *Rangs* and classed as *frégates* (later described as *frégates légères*). These comprised the *Infante de Sainte Marie* and *Notre Dame des Anges* (of 16 guns each); the *Sainte Anne*, *Diligente*, *Dieppoise* and *Gaillarde* (of 12 guns); the *Belle-Île* (10 guns); the *Biscayenne*, *Aurore* and *Madeleine* (of 8 guns); the 'galleys' *Christine* and *Saint Jean* (also of 8 guns); the *Morine* (6 guns); and a tiny vessel of 30 tons named *Laurier* (with just 2 guns, 25 men +1 officer), of which nothing further is recorded.

In mid-1671 there were twenty-two vessels, with between 6 and 18 guns. These comprised the newly-built *Dangereux*, *Embuscade* and *Hameçon* (of 18 guns each); the *Friponne*, *Maligne*, *Mutine* – all three also newly-built –and the older *Notre Dame des Anges** (of 14 guns each); the *Dieppoise**, *Gaillarde*, *Diligente* and *Bretonne** (of 12 guns each); the *Normande*, *Petite Infante**, *Belle-Île** and *Fontarabie** (of 10 guns each); the *Madeleine**, *Aurore**, *Marguerite* and *Saint Pierre* (of 6 guns each); the galleys *Christine** and *Saint Jean** (also of 6 guns each); and the small *Morine** (now with just 4 guns). However, on 24 June 1671 the names of eleven *frégates légères* were altered, and those affected are indicated by asterisks in the previous sentence (see Appendix 'C' for details). Just six months later, the total had grown to thirty vessels, still ranging from 6 to 18 guns, and that number was still the same (albeit with additions matching deletions) a further year on at the start of 1673.

EMBUSCADE Class. 18 guns, designed and built by Jean Tortel. Named on 27 July 1670.
  Dimensions & tons: 95ft 0in, 84ft 0in x 24ft 0in x 10ft 0in (30.86, 27.29 x 7.80 x 3.25m). 200 tons. Draught 12ft (3.90m). Men: 60 (12/30/18), +2 officers.
  Guns: 18 from 1671, 16 from 1677 in *Embuscade* and 14 in *Bouffonne*.
Embuscade Le Havre.
  K: early 1670. L: 21.7.1670. C: 8.1670. Re-classed as fireship 1677, renamed *Dangereux* briefly but resumed original name. Sold 1678 at Rochefort.
Dangereux Le Havre.
  K: 11.1670. L: 10.3.1671. C: 1671. Renamed *Bouffonne* 24.6.1671. Re-classed as fireship 5.1677. Renamed *Dangereux* again 5.1678. Struck *c*.1681.

HAMEÇON. 18 guns. Built by Hendryck Houwens, probably to *Embuscade* design, and likewise named on 27 July 1670.
  Dimensions & tons: 95ft 0in x 24ft 0in x 10ft 0in (30.86 x 7.80 x 3.25m). 200 tons. Men: 60 (12/30/18), +2 officers.
  Guns: 18.
Hameçon Dunkirk.
  K: early 1670. L: 8.1670. C: 2.1671. Renamed *Trompeuse* 24.6.1671. Wrecked off Normandy 9.1674.

FRIPONNE Class. 14, later 16 guns. Designed and built by Honoré Malet, with the *Maligne* built by Jean Guichard. The second ship was first ordered under the name *Lutine*, but the name was changed to *Mutine* on 17 August 1670, when all three were formally named. *Friponne* was reconstructed in November 1676 with a light 'bridge' added and tonnage raised to 180; then mounted 22 guns. *Maligne* was also reconstructed as 180 tons at Le Havre in August 1677 and fitted with 24 guns, but these were reduced to 18 in 1688 and then 12 in 1691.
  Dimensions & tons: 80ft 0in, 66ft 0in x 21ft 0in x 10ft 0in (25.99, 21.44 x 6.82 x 3.25m). 150 tons. Draught 9ft/10ft (2.92/3.25m). Men: 60 (12/30/18), +2 officers; by 1675 had 50 (14/21/15), +5 officers, but *Friponne* has original 60 men by 1677 (still 5 officers).
  Guns: 14 from 1671, all increased to 16 from 1675, 22 in *Friponne* and 24 in *Maligne* from 1676, 16 in *Friponne* from 1677, 20 in *Friponne* and 18 in *Maligne* from 1688, and 10 or 12 (4 x 6pdrs + 8 x 4pdrs) in *Maligne* from 1691.
Friponne Rochefort.
  K: 7.1670. L: 11.1670. C: 3.1671. Captured by the English 12.1690.
Mutine Rochefort.
  K: 7.1670. L: 11.1670. C: 3.1671. Captured by Ostend privateer *Saint Sébastien* off Bayonne 6.1675.
Maligne Rochefort.
  K: 7.1670. L: 12.1670. C: 5.1671. Converted to a fireship 10.7.1670, armed accordingly in 4.1692, and expended 1693.

BRETONNE. 12 guns. Designed and built by Laurent Hubac. Ordered 16 August 1670 and named on 10 October.
  Dimensions & tons: 80ft 0in x 21ft 0in (25.99 x 6.82m). 120 tons. Draught 9½ft (3.09m). Men: 50 (10/24/16), +2 officers.
  Guns: 12 from 1671, 22 from 1674.
Bretonne Brest Dyd.
  K: 9.1670. L: 4.11.1670. C: early 1671. Renamed *Tempête* 24.6.1671. Became coast guard 1675, but captured by Spanish privateer 7.1675.

NORMANDE. 10 guns. Designed and built by Laurent Hubac alongside *Bretonne*. Ordered 16 August 1670 and named on 10 October.
  Dimensions & tons: 70ft 0in x 19ft 0in (22.74 x 6.17m). 100 tons. Draught 8ft/10ft (2.60m). Men: 40 (8/20/12), +2 officers.
  Guns: 10 from 1671, 12 from 1672, 18 from 1674, 14 from 1679, 4 as a *flûte* 1691.

LIGHT FRIGATES

Normande Brest Dyd.
   K: 9.1670. L: 5.11.1670. C: early 1671. Renamed *Aurore* 24.6.1671. Became *patache Volante* 1688, then a *flûte* 1.1691. Renamed *Abondante* 2.1692, possibly burned at La Hougue 6.1692.

In 1671 four 12-gun *frégates légères* of 120 tons each were to have been begun at Toulon; they were named as *Sorcière*, *Serpente*, *Rieuse* and *Mignonne*, but in 1673 these plans were abandoned, and instead *Serpente* and *Rieuse* were to be built at Toulon as 30-gun *frégates légères* of 500 tons – ordered on 9 September, with names confirmed on 28 November 1672. They were projected in 1674 as *frégates à rames* of 300 tons and 24 guns like the *Bien Aimée* class, below, and were altered in 1675 firstly to 38 guns, and later to 46-gun 4th Rank 'rowing-frigates' of 550 tons (although they were renamed *Ferme* and *Arc en Ciel* in 1676) – see Chapter 4 – while the *Mignonne* was built instead at Dunkirk as a small 10-gun frigate, and the *Sorcière* was not built.

RAILLEUSE. 10 guns. Designed and built by Laurent Hubac. Ordered on 9 January 1671 as a ketch (*caiche*), and originally simply called *Caiche Neuve*, but renamed *Railleuse* on 24 June 1671 when rated *frégate légère*. Still listed by Brest as a *cache* (*caiche*) or ketch in 1674.
   Dimensions & tons: 60ft 0in, 50ft 0in x 18ft 6in x 8ft 0in (19.49, 16.24 x 6.01 x 2.60m). 80/120 tons. Draught 9ft (2.92m). Men: 50 in war (14/21/15), +5 officers; 40 peace (8/20/12), +2 officers.
   Guns: 10 from 1672; 8 from 1676.
Railleuse Brest Dyd.
   K: 4.1671. L: 1.6.1671. C: 2.1672. Present at Battle of Solebay 7.6.1672, as tender. Condemned at Toulon 8.1681, and sold the following month.

FAVORITE. 10 guns. Begun in 1670 under the name of *Petite Royale*, but renamed *Jolie* in 1671 then *Favorite* on 24 June 1671.
   Dimensions & tons: dimensions unknown. 80 tons. Men: 50 in war (10/24/16), 40 peace (8/20/12), +2 officers.
   Guns: 10.
Favorite Rochefort Dyd.
   K: 5.1671. L: end 1671. C: 9.1672. Burnt off the Poitou coast 1674.

BIEN AIMÉE Class. 8 (later 18/24) guns. Designed by François Chapelle, who built the *Bien Aimée*; dimensions given below relate to this ship, with *Gracieuse* believed to be to same design but actually built by Laurent Coulomb. Both ordered 24 April 1671 and named in October 1671. Designed primarily for propulsion by oars, and listed in 1674 as rowing frigates (*frègates à rames*) for coast guard service.
   Dimensions & tons: 105ft 0in, 83ft 0in x 27ft 0in x 13ft 4in (34.11, 26.96 x 8.77 x 4.33m). 300 tons. Draught 10ft (3.25m). Men: 150 in war (25/75/50 in 1672, 35/78/37 in 1683), 120 peace, + 5 (later 6 officers).
   Guns: 8 from 1672, 24 from 1674, 20 in *Bien Aimée* from 1676.
Gracieuse Toulon Dyd.
   K: 10.1671. L: 10.3.1672. C: 9.1672. Captured by ten Spanish galleys off Sicily 7.1675, then taken into Reggio where she was burnt (along with more than a dozen Spanish ships and most of the town) in the same month by a fireship (*Incommode*) sent into the port by Tourville.
Bien Aimée Toulon Dyd.
   K: 10.1671. L: 13.3.1672. C: 9.1672. Struck 1685 at Toulon and sold 12.1687, being BU 1688 at Malta.

JOLIE. 6 (later 10) guns. This former fireship, built in 1668 or 1669 as *Marguerite*, was re-classed as a *frégate légère* in 1670 and renamed *Jolie* on 24 June 1671.
   Dimensions & tons: dimensions unknown. 100 tons (80 in 1673). Men: 25 as fireship (5/20/–), then as frigate 50 (10/24/16), +2 officers.
   Guns: 4 as fireship; 6 from 1671 as frigate, then 10 from 1672.
Jolie builder unknown.
   Submerged at Le Havre in 12.1672, then struck 1674 and sold.

MIGNONNE. 10 guns. Designed and built by Hendryck Houwens.
   Dimensions & tons: dimensions uncertain. 60 tons. Men: 50 (10/24/16, later 14/21/15), +2 officers.
   Guns: 12 from 1672, 10 from 1673 and 8 from 1675. 10 from 1677: 10 x 4pdrs; probably replaced by 2 x 6pdrs, 6 x 4pdrs and 2 x ?3pdrs.
Mignonne Dunkirk.
   K: 1672. L: 4.1673. C: 6.1673. Wrecked off Nieuport 1.1682, but refloated 2.1682. Struck 1694, possibly at Brest.

Ex-DUTCH PRIZES (1673–1674). Four vessels were captured from the Dutch in 1673 and 1674, and added as *frégates légères*, each with a crew of 50 men (14/21/15) and 5 officers. The first, a *caiche*, was captured in March 1673 and was initially renamed *Chat* in 1673, but was renamed *Trompeuse* in 1674. The second, built in 1672 and also captured during 1673, was initially renamed *Prise de la Preille* (named after her captor's commander) but was renamed *Surprenante* on 10 December 1674. The third vessel, built in 1670 and captured in June 1674 by the *Éveillé*, was initially renamed *Prise de Montortié* (after her captor's commander) but was renamed *Favorite* on 10 December 1674. The fourth vessel, built in Zeeland in 1672, was captured in December 1674; she was renamed *Moqueuse* on 10 December 1674.
Trompeuse
   Dimensions & tons: 50 tons, draught 7ft (2.27m)
   Guns: 6 from 1675: 4 x 4pdrs + 2 x 3pdrs
   Sold at Le Havre in March 1675.
Surprenante
   Dimensions & tons: 60 tons, draught 8ft (2.60m). As *barque longue*: 40 tons, draught 6ft (1.95m). Men as *barque longue*: 28 (9/19/–) + 2 officers
   Guns: 6. 4 guns as *barque longue*
   Re-classed as a *barque longue* during 1675. Sold at Dunkirk 1676.
Favorite
   Dimensions & tons: 100 tons, draught 10ft (3.25m)
   Guns: 10 from 1675, 12 from 1676
   Recaptured in May 1676.
Moqueuse
   Dimensions & tons: 60 tons, draught 8ft (2.60m)
   Guns: 6 from 1675
   Struck at Brest early 1676.

Ex-SPANISH PRIZES (1673–1674). Three vessels were captured from the Spanish in 1673 and 1674 and added as *frégates légères*, each with a crew of 50 men (14/21/15) and 5 officers. The first, originally a French vessel (built in Granville in 1672), was captured in October 1673 by Chammartin and was initially renamed *Toison d'Or* in 1673, but renamed *Subtile* in 1674. The second, built in (Spanish) Sardinia as *Nuestra Señora de los Angeles*, was captured in April 1674 and was first renamed *Notre Dame des Anges* in 1674, but was renamed *Favorite* in December 1676. The third, built in Ostend in 1670, was captured on the dike at La Rochelle in December 1674 and was renamed *Folle*.
Subtile
   Dimensions & tons: 80 tons, draught 10ft (3.25m)
   Guns: 8 from 1675

A drawing by the younger Van de Velde of a small Dutch frigate from about 1665, rather like the *Favorite* captured in 1674. Omitting the masting in the drawing better reveals the hull details – a single deck with five or possibly six gunports, a short quarterdeck and a forecastle platform. Most of the small cruisers in the navies of northern Europe were similar in basic layout. (National Maritime Museum, London PY1778)

Condemned in 1675 and sold in October at Le Havre.;
Favorite
  Dimensions & tons: 100 tons, draught 9ft (2.92m)
  Guns: 4 from 1677
  Condemned at Toulon in 1678.
Folle
  Dimensions & tons: 100 tons, draught 12ft (3.90m)
  Guns: 10 from 1675.
  Captured by a Dutch privateer in July 1676.

PURCHASED VESSEL (1674). The French privateer *Sainte Thérèse*, built at La Ciotat (near Marseille), was purchased in February 1674 and renamed *Gracieuse* in December 1676.
  Dimensions & tons: 80 tons, with a draught of 8ft (2.60m); by 1686, 100 tons and 9ft (2.92m). Men: 50 (14/21/15) + 5 officers.
  Guns: 2 from 1677, 6 from 1679.
Gracieuse La Ciotat
  Based at Toulon until condemned there in 1687.

Following the separate peace treaty signed between England and the Dutch at Westminster on 19 February 1673 the now isolated French had to strengthen all their forces to fight on alone, so a program was begun to augment the light frigate element of the French Navy. Two 24-gun vessels were ordered in early 1675, and a larger order was placed on 6 December 1675.

TROMPEUSE Class. 24 guns, designed and built by Benjamin Chaillé. Ordered and named on 1 March 1675.
  Dimensions & tons: 88ft 0in, 72ft 0in x 22ft 0in x 11ft 6in (28.59, 23.39 x 7.15 x 3.74m). 200 tons. Draught 8½ft/12ft (2.76/3.90m). Men: 100, +5 officers.
  Guns: 24 from 1676: UD 18 x 8pdrs; *dunette* (poop) 6 x 6pdrs. 10 guns in *Jolie* from 1691.

Trompeuse Le Havre.
  K: 3.1675. L: 4.9.1675. C: 10.1675. Leased for commerce 3.1681; attacked and burnt (as a pirate) by the English at St Thomas (Virgin Is) 7.1683.
Jolie Le Havre.
  K: 3.1675. L: 19.9.1675. C: 10.1675. Lent as a privateer in 1688–89 to the Marquis de Seignelay (Secretary of State for the Navy) and Sieur Languillet at Brest; in campaign in Ireland 1689. Lent as a privateer to the deposed King James II, under command of Andrew White in 1690. Converted to fireship 1691; wrecked near Granville 10.1692.

PURCHASED VESSEL (1675). This experimental armoured vessel, built by Henri d'Estival at Brouage in 1664 (original name unknown) and rebuilt at Bayonne in 1668, was purchased for the French Navy in August 1675 and renamed *Mutine* on 30 August, but was found unsuitable for service and swiftly struck.
  Dimensions & tons: 104ft 0in x 25ft 0in (33.78 x 8.12m). tonnage unknown.
  Guns: 4 (2 fwd. and 2 aft).
Mutine Brouage
  K: early 1664. C: 6.1664. Struck at end 1675 at Rochefort.

GAILLARDE Class. 18 guns. 6pdr type, designed and built by Hendryck Houwens. Ordered on 6 December 1675 (along with several other pairs of *frégates légères*, in demand to meet the needs for additional escorts with the new circumstances relating to the Franco-Dutch War, and named on 10 January 1676.
  Dimensions & tons: 83ft 0in, 70ft 0in x 22ft 0in x 9ft 0in (26.96, 22.74 x 7.15 x 2.92m). 120 tons. Draught 9½ft/11ft (3.09/3.57m). Men: 50 (14/21/15), +5 officers.
  Guns: 16 in *Sorcière* and 12 in *Lutine/Vipère* from 1677, 14 in *Vipère* from 1679, 24 in *Sorcière* and 20 in *Vipère* from 1687. 14 in war in *Vipère* from 1696 (10 peace): 14 x 6pdrs (add 4 x 3pdrs from 1699).
Gaillarde Dunkirk.
  K: 12.1675. L: 12.5.1676. C: 7.1676. Renamed *Sorcière* 11.12.1676. Not mentioned after 1695.
Lutine Dunkirk.
  K: 12.1675. L: 6.1676. C: 11.1676. Renamed *Vipère* 28.6.1678. Lent

as a privateer in 1689 to LV Claude, Chevalier de Forbin-Gardanne. Wrecked 1.1703 in the Adour.

TEMPÊTE. 28 guns. Designed and begun by Joseph Saboulin; completed by Étienne Salicon. Ordered on 6 December 1675, and named on 10 January 1676.
  Dimensions & tons: 104ft 0in, 84ft 0in x 24ft 0in x 12ft 0in (33.78, 27.29 x 7.80 x 3.90m). 300 tons. Draught 11ft/12ft (3.47/3.90m). Men: 130 (34/70/26), +5 officers.
  Guns: 28 from 1677: LD 18 x 8pdrs; UD 10 x 4pdrs.
Tempête Rochefort Dyd.
  K: 1.1676. L: 5.1676. C: 7.1676. Struck 1690 at Brest.

DILIGENTE. 28 guns. Designed and built by Jean Guichard. Ordered on 6 December 1675, and named on 10 January 1676.
  Dimensions & tons: 98ft 0in, 83ft 0in x 24ft 0in x 11ft 0in (31.83, 26.96 x 7.80 x 3.57m). 300 tons. Draught 10½ft/11ft (3.41/3.57m). Men: 130 (34/70/26), +5 officers.
  Guns: 26 from 1677. 28 from 1688: LD 18 x 8pdrs; UD 10 x 4pdrs.
Diligente Rochefort Dyd.
  K: 1.1676. L: 1676. C: 12.1676. Grounded in action off St Domingue 6.1690, but refloated. Struck 1691 at Rochefort.

SUBTILE Class. 10 guns. Designed by Laurent Hubac, and built by Jean-Pierre Brun and Étienne Hubac. Ordered on 6 December 1675, and probably named on 2 May 1676.
  Dimensions & tons: 70ft 0in, 60ft 0in x 17ft 0in x 8ft 0in (22.74, 19.49 x 5.52 x 2.60m). 75 tons. Draught 7½ft/8ft (2.44/2.60m). Men: 50, +5 officers.
  Guns: 10 x 4pdrs.
Moqueuse Brest Dyd.
  K: 2.1676. L: 4.1676. C: 5.1676. Took part in Bombardment of Algiers 6–7.1683. Sold 29.10.1685 at Toulon (probably to Algiers).
Subtile Brest Dyd.
  K: 2.1676. L: 4.1676. C: 5.1676. Renamed *Pressante* 28.6.1678. Lent as a privateer in 1688 (recipient unknown), then in 1689 to LFL Imbert. Condemned 8.1695 at St Domingue, becoming privateer; wrecked 1696.

FÉE Class. 28 guns. 8pdr type, designed by Laurent Hubac, and ordered 6 December 1675. Named 16 May 1676. Built by Hubac and Jean-Pierre Brun respectively. Both ships were described in 1677 as 'with very fine hull lines, and promising much' and in 1679 as 'good under sail and suited for commerce raiding'. The *Jalouse* (ex-*Fée*) was re-classed as a 5th Rank between 1692 and 1695.
  Dimensions & tons: 103ft 0in, 92ft 0in x 25ft 6in x 12ft 6in (44.46, 29.89 x 8.28 x 4.06m). 300 tons. Draught 11ft/13½ft (3.57/4.39m). Men: 130 (34/70/26), +6 officers.
  Guns: 28 from 1677: LD 14 x 8pdrs; UD 14 x 4pdrs. *Jalouse* from 1696 as a 5th Rank ship (30 in war, 20 peace): LD 14 x 8pdrs; UD 16 x 4pdrs.
Fée Brest Dyd.
  K: 2.1676. L: 8.1676. C: 9.1676. Sold 16.2.1685 at Toulon, but reacquired 1690 by confiscation and renamed *Jalouse* 10.12.1690; condemned 1698 at Toulon.
Mutine Brest Dyd.
  K: 2.1676. L: 8.1676. C: 1677. Lent as a privateer in 1688–89 to the Marquis de Seignelay (with *Comte* and *Palmier*) under the command of CV Ferdinand de Relingue, who shared the funding. These were the first *armements mixtes* (operation of the King's ships under loan by private interests at their expense) organised by Seignelay; in campaign in Ireland 1689. Wrecked off Cape Bon in a storm 2.1694.

In January 1676 a frigate of 250 tons and 20–22 tons – to be named *Belle* – was ordered to be built at Rochefort by Benjamin Chaillé. The order was cancelled in March 1676, Chaillé having been sent to Le Havre.

Ex-SPANISH PRIZE (1676). The Spanish Netherlands vessel *Nuestra Señora de Loretto* was captured in 1676 and added to the French Navy under the name *Belle*, using the name of the ship ordered at Rochefort and cancelled in March.
  Dimensions & tons: dimensions unknown. 80 tons. Draught 8ft/9ft (2.60/2.92m). Men: 50 (14/21/15), +5 officers.
  Guns: 4 to 8.
Belle Ostend (probably)
  Condemned 1678, probably at Toulon.

During 1676 the *barque longue Folle* (ex-*Corvette*) was re-classed as a *frégate légère*, reverting to a *barque longue* in 1677 or 1678. Two small prizes, *Surprenante* and *Sibylle*, first appeared on the list as *frégates légères* in January 1677 but became *barques longues* later that year or in 1678.

ARMES DE FRANCE. A 100-ton *frégate légère* with 6 guns built in Genoa was captured c.2.1677, possibly from Tripoli, and named *Armes de France*. She was wrecked in November 1678 at Port Vendres.

SERPENTE. 26 guns. Designed and built by Hendryck Houwens. Named 11 June 1677.
  Dimensions & tons: dimensions unknown. 140 tons (190 from 1687). Draught 11½ft/12ft (3.74/3.90m). Men: 110 (20/60/30), +5 officers.
  Guns: 26 from 1679: probably 16 x 6pdrs; 10 x 4pdrs. 24 guns from 1691.
Serpente Dunkirk.
  K: 6.1677. L: 23.6.1678. C: 4.1679. Struck 1691 at Dunkirk.

BADINE Class. 10 guns. Designed and built by Hendryck Houwens, and named on 28 June 1678.
  Dimensions & tons: dimensions unknown. 100 tons. Men: 50 (14/21/15), +5 officers.
  Guns: 10 from 1679: 10 x 4pdrs.
Badine Dunkirk.
  K: 3.1678. L: 6.7.1678. C: 10.1678. Struck 1684 at Dunkirk.
Charmante Dunkirk.
  K: 3.1678. L: 6.7.1678. C: 10.1678. Struck 1684 at Dunkirk.

BOUFFONNE. 18 guns (later 26). Designed by Laurent Hubac, and built by Jean-Pierre Brun. Named 28 June 1678.
  Dimensions & tons: 86ft 0in x 24ft 0in x 9ft 6in (27.94 x 7.80 x 3.09m). 150 tons. Draught 12ft (3.90m). Men: 80 (16/38/26), +5 officers.
  Guns: 18 from 1680 and 10 from 1691. 26 in war from 1696 (20 peace): LD 16 x 8pdrs; UD 10 x 4pdrs
Bouffonne Brest Dyd.
  K: 1678. L: 1678. C: 1678. Lent as a privateer in 1689–90 to the Marquis de Seignelay, who provided two-thirds of the funding, as part of a squadron of three to four vessels under CV Jacques Dandenne. Struck 12.1696 at Rochefort.

FAVORITE Class. 12 guns (later 26). Designed and built by François Pomet. Both named 28 June 1678 while already building at Rochefort. *Gaillarde* was lengthened 12ft by Blaise Pangalo at Rochefort in 1680 and *Favorite* may have been too. In 1680 *Favorite* was listed as a 260-ton ship with 22 guns and *Gaillarde* was a 100-ton ship with 12 guns. *Gaillarde* continued to be listed through 1686 as a 100-ton ship but both had 12 guns from 1681. A list of ships at Rochefort dated 15 July 1682 shows both as 300-ton ships with 30 guns, *Favorite* with a length of 100ft (88ft on the keel) and *Gaillarde* with 96ft (80ft).
  Dimensions & tons: 91ft 0in x 25ft 4in x 11ft 0in (29.56 x 8.23 x 3.57m). 260 tons. Draught 14ft (4.55m).
  Guns: 12 from 1681, 28 in *Favorite* and 26 in *Gaillarde* from 1687, 10 in *Séditieux* in 1691 as fireship. *Séditieux* from 1696 (26 in war, 20 peace): LD 18 x 6pdrs; UD 8 x 4pdrs.
Favorite Rochefort Dyd.
  K 5.1678. L: 11.1678. C: 4.1679. Lent as a privateer in 1689–90 to the Marquis de Seignelay, sailed under LV Jean de Montségur. Lent as a privateer in 1692–93 to Louis d'Oger, Marquis de Cavoye, under CB Gaspard de Russy, an arrangement organized by the elder brother of René Duguay-Trouin. Captured by three Flushing pirate vessels 8.1694 in the Mediterranean.
Gaillarde Rochefort Dyd.
  K 5.1678. L: 11.1678. C: 4.1679. Struck 1688 at Rochefort and hulked. Restored to service as a fireship 1690, renamed *Gaillard* 1690, then *Séditieux* 1.1691. Re-classed as a *frégate légère* 1695, and lent as a privateer in 1695–97 to CV Jean-Baptiste, Comte de Gennes, Seigneur d'Oyac, as part of a squadron of six vessels. Struck 1698.

In 1679 two *frégates légères* of 20 or 24 guns and 160 tons each were ordered from Henryck Houwens, to be built at Dunkirk. They were to be named *Embuscade* and *Légère*. The orders were cancelled in January 1680, reinstated in May 1680, and finally cancelled a month later; however, two larger new vessels bearing the same names were begun – one at Le Havre in August 1680 and one at Brest in 1682. Another *frégate légère*, to be named *Railleuse* and to be of 30 guns was ordered in November 1682 from Houwens, but this order was cancelled at the start of 1683 and the name given instead to a second-hand vessel purchased in September.

EMBUSCADE. 28 guns, designed and built by Étienne Salicon. Originally to be named *Royale*, and stated in 1682 to be of 150 tons and to carry 10 guns and 100 men (20/54/26) +5 officers. The order for this ship may have replaced an order of June 1679 at Le Havre for a 20-gun frigate that was named *Gracieuse* on 6 October 1679, although that name was already in use.
  Dimensions & tons: 98ft 0in x 25ft 2in x 10ft 6in (31.83 x 8.18 x 3.41m). 300 tons. Draught 12½ft (4.06m). Men: 130 in war, 80 peace.
  Guns: 10 from 1683, 20 from 1687, 28 from 1688, and 10 from 1691. 28 in war from 1696 (20 peace): UD 18 x 8pdrs; QD 10 x 4pdrs.
Embuscade Le Havre.
  K: 8.1680. L: 23.12.1681. C: 2.1682. Struck at Rochefort 1698.

LÉGÈRE. 24 guns, designed and built by Blaise Pangalo.
  Dimensions & tons: 98ft 0in x 25ft 0in x 10ft 4in (31.83 x 8.12 x 3.36m). 250 tons. Draught 10½ft/12ft (3.41/3.90m). Men: initially 100 (20/54/26), + 5 officers; from 1692, 110 (22/55/33), + 5 officers.
  Guns: 24 from 1683, 26 from 1691.

Légère Brest Dyd.
  K: 6.1682. L: 12.1682. C: 3.1683. Captured 6.1693 by HMS *Dover*, becoming HMS *Dover's Prize* and used as hulk at Plymouth; wrecked in a storm in Plymouth Sound 4.1.1690.

RAILLEUSE. 24 guns, designed and built by Hendryck Houwens in 1676–77 as the mercantile *Dauphin*, purchased for the Navy in September 1683 and renamed.
  Dimensions & tons: 82ft 0in keel x 23ft 0in x 10ft 0in (26.64 x 7.47 x 3.25m). 170/250 tons. Draught 10½ft/11½ft (3.41/3.74m). Men: 100 in war, 80 peace, +5 officers; from 1686 120 men (33/60/27), +6 officers.
  Guns: 24 from 1686, 22 from 1687 and 16 from 1688.
Railleuse Dunkirk.
  K: 1676. L: 1677. C: 12.1677. From 9.1688 served as privateer commanded by CV Claude de Forbin-Gardanne. While escorting a convoy between Dunkirk and Brest in company with *Les Jeux* under CFL Jean Bart, both vessels were captured 22.5.1689 by HM Ships *Nonsuch* and *Tiger* off Cherbourg, *Railleuse* becoming HMS *Swift Prize*; both captains escaped custody on 5.6.1689; sunk as a breakwater at Portsmouth 4.5.1695.

Ex-ALGERINE PRIZE (1683). An Algerian vessel was taken in June 1683 and renamed *Caravelle*. She completed a refit at Toulon in December 1683 and was renamed *Trompeuse* in March 1684. She had a crew of 30 men and was pierced with a total of fourteen gunports. She was given by the King to the Dey of Algiers in April 1685.

Ex-PRUSSIAN PRIZE (1685). A Brandenburg vessel named *Morian* was captured in February 1685 and listed by the Navy as *Morian* or *Morien*.
  Dimensions & tons: dimensions unknown. 70ft x 19ft
  Guns: 12 or 16.
Morian or Morien Kolberg
  Built 1679–1680. Confirmed as a legitimate prize by a judgment of 12 August 1685 but returned to Brandenburg January 1687 by order of the king. Considered to be unserviceable at the time of her return.

The 5th Rank ship *Éveillé* (ex-*Dur*) was renamed *Bien Aimée* and re-classed as a *frégate légère* in 1685. She was struck as such *c*.1693.

Ex-ALGERINE PRIZE (1687). The Algerian caravelle *Tinine Dahabia* was captured by CdE Charles-François Davy Du Péron, Marquis d'Amfreville's squadron in August 1687 and initially sold at Toulon on 16 November 1687 for commerce under the name *Dragon d'Or*, but was reacquired for the Navy on 27 November as a 16-gun *frégate légère*, and was renamed *Moqueuse* in November 1688.
  Dimensions & tons: dimensions unknown. 120 tons. Draught 8ft (2.60m). Men: 70 in war, 60 peace, +5 officers.
  Guns: 16 from 1689.
Moqueuse unknown
  Built 1680. Handed over to the Dey of Algiers 2.1691, as result of Article 6 of the Treaty of 25.9.1689.

GENTILLE Class. 16 guns. Designed and built by Pierre Chaillé.
  Dimensions & tons: 85ft 0in, 71ft 0in x 19ft 0in x 7ft 0in (27.61, 23.06 x 6.17 x 2.27m). 80 tons. Draught 8ft/9ft (2.60/2.92m). Men (80 in war, 60 peace): 60/70, +5 officers.
  Guns: 14 from 1689. 16 in war from 1696 (12 peace): 16 x 4pdrs.
Gentille Le Havre.

K: 11.1688. L: 4.1689. C: 5.1689. Struck 12.1697 at Le Havre, and sold 2.1698.

Gracieuse Le Havre.
K: 11.1688. L: 4.1689. C: 5.1689. Sailed in the King's service to the West Indies in 1696 under CV Des Augiers as part of a squadron of nine vessels carrying to the West Indies settlers and young marriageable women. Left (with *Serpente*) to Jean-Baptiste Ducasse, governor of St Domingue; both ships became *frégates flibustières* 2.1697; joined CdE Jean Bernard de Saint-Jean, Baron de Pointis's squadron and took part in the capture of Cartagena de Indias 5.5.1697; captured by the Dutch 11.1697.

TROMPEUSE Class. 12 guns. Designed and built by Hendryck Houwens.
Dimensions & tons: 70ft 0in x 21ft 0in x 10ft 0in (22.74 x 6.82 x 3.25m). 80 tons. Draught 8ft/10ft (2.0/3.25m). Men: 60 in war (17/25/18), 40 peace, +3 officers.
Guns: 12 from 1689: 12 x 4pdrs. *Fée* from 1696 (10 in war, 8 peace): 10 x 4pdrs; from 1698: 14 x 4pdrs.

Charmante Dunkirk
K: 12.1688. L: 3.1689. C: 5.1689. Burnt by accident 1692.

Fée Dunkirk
K: 12.1688. L: 3.1689. C: 5.1689. Struck 1703.

Trompeuse Dunkirk
K: 12.1688. L: 3.1689. C: 5.1689. Lent as a privateer in 1695 to the deposed King James II, with command given to CFL Sir Peter Nagle (Secretary to James II). Struck 1696.

MÉCHANTE Class. Designed by Étienne Hubac, and built by Jean-Pierre Brun and Laurent Hélie respectively. Both ordered on 9 February 1689 and named on 21 May. These were initially classed as *barques longues* from completion, the survivor *Méchante* was classed as a *frégate légère* between 1692 and 1695 (the *Bayonnaise* would doubtless have followed suit, but for her early loss). They were listed as 25-ton vessels in 1690 and *Méchante* was listed at 50 tons in 1691–92; her 1696 specifications are below. The *Émeraude* Class below were very similar and may have been to same design. From the 1670s to early 1690s vessels with at least 70ft in length and 10 guns were *frégates légères* while smaller ships with fewer guns were *barques longues*.
Dimensions & tons: 70ft 0in, 60ft 0in x 17ft 0in x 7ft 6in (22.74, 19.49 x 5.52 x 2.44m). 60 tons. Draught 8ft/10ft (2.60/3.25m). Men: 50, +5 officers.
Guns: 10 in war (8 peace): 10 x 4pdrs.

Méchante Brest Dyd.
K: 2.1689. L: 7.5.1689. C: 6.1689. Took part in campaign in Ireland, 1690. Survey of the mouth of the river at Limerick. Struck 1698 at Brest, sold 1699.

Bayonnaise Brest Dyd.
K: 2.1689. L: 8.5.1689. C: 6.1689. Sometimes nicknamed *Noix*. Took part in campaign in Ireland, 1690. Survey of Galway Bay. Sunk 4.1691 by the English in Dublin Bay.

(C) Frigates acquired from 15 April 1689

By the start of 1689, the *frégate légère* category covered vessels of between 10 and 28 guns (the newbuilding *Gaillarde* and *Badine* of 34 guns were exceptions until re-classed as 5th Rank), being either two-decked ships with no guns carried on the lower deck, or single-decked ships with a single battery of, typically, 6pdr guns; they often also carried a few 4pdr guns on the QD. The smallest *frégates légères* mounted only a battery of 4pdrs, but they carried ten or more while the largest *barques longues* carried, at least initially, eight or fewer.

The deliberate strategic move towards a *guerre de course* in the 1690s saw a vast expansion in the ranks of frigates of all types, and of *frégates légères* in particular, procured by the Crown as well as private enterprise (many of these naval vessels, while owned by the King (*i.e.* part of the Navy) were actually funded by privateering 'firms'). Many of these naval vessels were made available to privateering consortia during the decade with the King sharing in the profits.

Ex-SCOTTISH PRIZES (1689). Merchant vessels *Pelican* and *Janet* leased in April 1689 by the Scots Navy to serve as coast guard vessels. Captured by three French frigates on 20 July 1689 and added as *Pélican* and *Jeannette*.

Pélican Glasgow.
Dimensions & tons: dimensions unknown. 200 tons. Men: 120.
Guns: 18/20.
Captured by the English Navy 1690, becoming HMS *Pelican Prize*, 8-gun fireship.

Jeannette Glasgow.
Dimensions & tons: 88ft 0in x 23ft 4in x 10ft 0in (28.59 x 7.58 x 3.25m). 100/200 tons. Draught 9ft/13ft (2.92/4.22m). Men: 120 in war, 80 peace.
Guns: 10 in 1691 as *flûte*. 12 in war from 1696 as fireship (12 peace): 12 x 6pdrs. 4 from 1701 as a *frégate légère*: 4 x 4pdrs (6 from 1702); 6 from 1708: 6 x 3pdrs.
Converted to 10-gun *flûte* 1.1691, renamed *Normande*. Lent as a privateer in 1691 to the deposed King James II. Converted to 6-gun fireship 1694, renamed *Enflammé*. Re-classed as a *frégate légère* 1700 and as fireship 1702–3. Struck at Toulon 1709, then captured 5.1710.

Ex-ENGLISH NAVAL PRIZE (1689). 22 (later 18) guns. Former English ketch-rigged bomb vessel (classed as Fifth Rate) *Firedrake*, designed and built by Fisher Harding, and captured by a French squadron on 22 November 1689 in the Channel. Hubert Desclouzeaux, the naval intendant at Brest, was amazed at this 'strange frigate' which had – in addition to the expected artillery of such a ship (8 minions, 2 falconets and some patereros) – two 'bizarre pieces' (cushee pieces) and two mortars of 12.25 inches that were extraordinary light for their size. Classed as a *frégate légère* in the French Navy, she was initially renamed *Canard de Feu* but was renamed *Tempête* on 3 July 1690.
Dimensions & tons (as re-measured in French units): 78ft 0in x 23ft 6in x 10ft 0in (25.34 x 7.63 x 3.25m). 170 (130 in 1691)/200 tons. Draught 11ft/13ft (3.57/4.22m). Men: 120 (23/61/36) in war, +5 officers; from 1696, 80 in war, 65 peace; from 1699, 95 in war, 30 peace.
Guns: 28 in 1691. 22 in war from 1696 (20 peace): UD 16 x 6pdrs; QD 6 x 4pdrs (one pair of 6pdrs and one pair of 4pdrs were removed by 1699).

Tempête Deptford Dyd.
Ordered 4.12.1687. L: 23.6.1688. Converted to a *patache* in 1712. Hulked 1713 at Port Louis and sold there 6.1726 to BU.

YACK. 16 guns. Similar to the *Méchante* and *Émeraude* classes, but designed by CV Bernard Renau d'Élissagaray and built by Jean-Pierre Brun (although also attributed to Blaise Pangalo). Ordered in November 1689 by Tourville. The name means 'yacht'.
Dimensions & tons: 70ft 0in x 17ft 0in x 7ft 0in (22.74 x 5.52 x 2.27m). 60 tons. Draught 10ft (3.25m). Men: 70 in war, 60 peace.
Guns: 16 in war (12 peace): UD 12 x 4pdrs; QD 4 x 2pdrs.

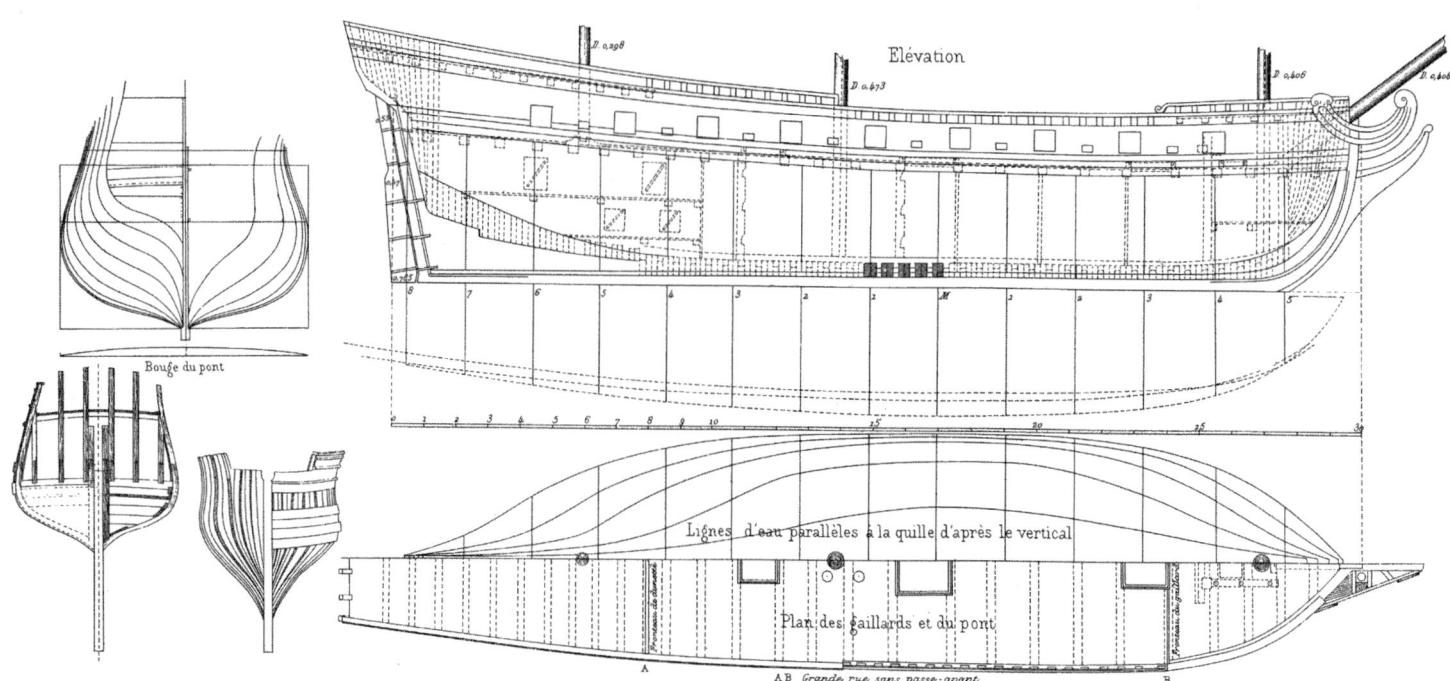

This reconstruction by *Vice-amiral* Pâris of a small frigate is based on a contemporary model. It is described as of 16 guns, but has gunports for 18. Scaled up, it is too large for *Gentille* of 1689 but is a closer fit to *Aurore* and *Railleuse* of 1690, although it would be necessary to find space for two more guns. Even if not an exact representation of either candidate, it probably bears a general resemblance to the larger light frigates of the 1690s. The single deck configuration of this small cruiser is clearly shown. (*Souvenirs de Marine*, Plate 141)

Yack (Jack) Brest Dyd.
  K: 11.1689. L: 27.3.1690. C: 7.1690. Condemned and sold 11.1697 at Le Havre.

AURORE Class. 20 guns. Designed and built by Hendryck Houwens.
  Dimensions & tons: 88ft 0in x 23ft 6in x 9ft 6in (28.59 x 7.63 x 3.09m). 160 tons. Draught 11ft/12ft (3.57/3.90m). Men: 90 (20/43/27), +5 officers.
  Guns: 20 from 1690: 20 x 6pdrs. *Railleuse* reduced to 18 x 6pdrs from 1691, and then 16 in war (12 peace) from 1696, but restored to 18 from 1699.
Aurore Dunkirk
  K: end 1689. L: 1690. C: 12.1690. Captured by the English 19.8.1697.
Railleuse Dunkirk
  K: end 1689. L: 1690. C: 12.1690. Lent as a privateer in 1702 to CFL René Duguay-Trouin (with *Bellone*). Burnt with *Joyeuse* by three English vessels at Avranches 5.8.1703.

Ex-SPANISH PRIZE (1691). This Spanish Netherlands privateer (original name unknown), designed and built in 1688 by LeFevre at Ostend, was captured in January 1691, and renamed *Chasse*. She was unusually small for a *frégate légère*, and would normally be considered as a *barque longue* or corvette.
  Dimensions & tons: 55ft 0in x 17ft 0in x 6ft 6in (17.87 x 5.52 x 2.11m). 40 tons. Draught 8ft (2.6m). Men: 45 in war (16/19/10), 12 peace, + 4 officers.
  Guns: 10 in 1692. 8 in war from 1696 (6 peace): UD 8 x 4pdrs, +2 swivels.
Chasse Ostend
  Built 1688. Struck 11.1697 at Le Havre, and BU 1702.

Ex-DUTCH PRIZE (1691–92). A Dutch vessel, *Charles Duc*, with design attributed to Honoré Malet and built either at Flushing or in St Malo, was captured in early 1691, and renamed *Friponne*. The Dutch *Pauw*, built at Amsterdam in 1676, was captured in November 1692 and named *Paon*.
Friponne Flushing or St Malo
  Dimensions & tons: 78ft 0in x 20ft 0in x 9ft 0in (25.3 x 6.5 x 2.9). 200 tons. Draught 9ft (2.9m). Men: initially 90 (20/43/27), +5 officers; from 1696, 120 in war, 80 peace.
  Guns: 18 from 1691, then 16 in war from 1692 (12 peace): UD 8 x 8pdrs; QD 8 x 6pdrs.
  Converted to a fireship 6–8.1691 (with 66 men + 2 officers). Struck 1696 or 1697 at Toulon.
Paon Amsterdam
  Dimensions & tons: 75ft 0in x 19ft 2in x 8ft 6in. 120 tons.
  Guns: 18.
  Sold in 1693 or early 1694 at Dunkirk for use as a privateer.

ÉMERAUDE Class. 10 guns. Designed by Philippe Cochois and built by Jean-Nicolas Houwens. Ordered 1 June 1691 and named on 29 July. However, their origins are confused, as when first listed in 1692 *Émeraude* was described as a 50-ton *barque longue* (with 8 guns) under construction at Dunkirk by Cochois, while *Choquante* was said to be an 80-ton *frégate légère* (of 12 guns) being built at Brest by Laurent Hélie and similar to the *Bonne*, below. Both were then recorded in 1696 and 1698 as 60-ton *frégates légères* (with 10 guns) built at Brest Dyd by Jean-Pierre Brun, and were very similar to the *Méchante* class previously built there by Brun and Hélie. In 1700 both were re-classed as corvettes or *barques longues*.
  Dimensions & tons: 70ft 0in x 17ft 0in x 7ft 6in (22.74 x 5.52 x 2.44m). 60 tons. Draught 7½ft/10ft (2.44/3.25m). Men: 50 in war, 40 peace, +2 officers.

Plate from Guéroult du Pas's work of 1710 showing a small 10-gun frigate. The size of the crew gives an accurate impression of just how small these vessels were – they possessed the rig and profile of a large warship, complete with head and quarter gallery, but simply scaled down. It is easy to see how such a ship straddled the divide between *barque longue* and *frégate légère* as the *Joyeuse* did in the 1690s.

Guns: 8 in *Émeraude* and 12 in *Choquante* from 1692. Both 10 in war from 1696 (8 peace): 10 x 4pdrs.

Émeraude Dunkirk.
  K: 1691. L: 1.1692. C: 2.1692. Burnt at Vigo 10.1702.
Choquante Dunkirk.
  K: 7.1691. L: 1.1692. C: 4.1692. Burnt at Vigo 10.1702.

BONNE. 12 guns. Designed and built by François Le Brun.
  Dimensions & tons: 70ft 0in x 17ft 9in x 6ft 6in (22.74 x 5.77 x 2.11m). 80 tons. Draught 8½ft (2.76m). Men: 60 in war, 20 peace, +2 officers.
  Guns: 12 from 1692. 12 in war from 1696 (10 peace): 12 x 4pdrs.
Bonne Brest Dyd.
  K: 7.1691. L: 1.1692. C: 4.1692. Sold at Lorient in early 1707.

JOYEUSE. 10 guns. Designed by Étienne Salicon as a *barque longue* but re-classed as a *frégate légère* between 1692 and 1695.
  Dimensions & tons: 70ft 0in, 58ft 0in x 17ft 6in x 6ft 6in (22.74, 18.84 x 5.68 x 2.11m). 60 tons. Draught 7½ft/8ft (2.44/2.63m). Men: 50/70 + 2/5 officers.
  Guns: 10 from 1692: 10 x 4pdrs. 10 in war from 1696 (6 peace): 10 x 4pdrs (12 from 1699).
Joyeuse Le Havre
  K: 7.1691. L: 11.1691. C: 12.1691. Captured 1694 by the English and renamed *Joyful*, but retaken in 1694 or 1695 and reincorporated in the Navy under her original name. Captured 8.1702 by the English and became a merchant ship, recaptured 3.1709 by the French and struck.

SERPENTE. 14 guns. Designed and built by CV Bernard Renau d'Élissagaray, employing his concepts of elliptical lines Ordered as *Yack* (a name meaning 'yacht'), but renamed at launch.
  Dimensions & tons: dimensions unknown.
  Guns: 14 from 1692: 14 x 6pdrs.

Serpente Le Havre.
  K: 10.1691. L: 20.1.1692. C: 2.1692. Wrecked off Dunkirk 11.1692.

In October 1691 two larger *frégates légères* of 34 guns were ordered to be built at Le Havre to a design by Pierre Chaillé; they were intended to be named *Autruche* and *Moqueuse*, but the orders were cancelled in June 1692. If completed, they would presumably have been re-classed as 5th Rank.

NAÏADE. 12 guns. Designed and built by Jean-Nicolas Houwens.
  Dimensions & tons: dimensions unknown. 120 tons. Draught 10½ft (3.41m). Men: 70 in 1692 (20/50/–), 40, +5 officers.
  Guns: 12 from 1692.
Naïade Dunkirk.
  K: 12.1691. L: 2.1692. C: 4.1692. Present at Battle of Texel 29.6.1694. Struck 1695 at Dunkirk.

AUDACIEUSE. 12 guns. Designed and built by Jean-Nicolas Houwens.
  Dimensions & tons: 72ft 0in x 20ft 0in x 8ft 6in (23.38 x 6.50 x 2.76m). 90 tons. Draught 11ft (3.57m). Men: 70 in 1692 (20/50/–), by 1696 80 in war, 50 peace, +5 officers.
  Guns: 12 from 1692. 12 in war from 1696 (12 peace): 4 x 6pdrs + 8 x 4pdrs. From 1699 carried 16 x 6pdrs, then from 1701 had 6 x 6pdrs + 8 x 4pdrs; finally from 1704 had 14 x 6pdrs.
Audacieuse Dunkirk.
  K: 12.1691. L: 2.1692. C: 4.1692. Wrecked at Cherbourg 9.1706. Refloated 10.1706, but condemned 11.1706 and sold.

SUFFISANTE. 12 guns. Designed and built by René Levasseur.
  Dimensions & tons: dimensions unknown. 100 tons. Draught 9ft (2.92m). Men: 70 (20/50/–), +5 officers.
  Guns: 12 from 1692. 12 in war from 1696: UD 12 x 4pdrs (estimated).

Suffisante Dunkirk.
K: 12.1691. L: 2.1692. C: 4.1692. Struck 1695.

DILIGENTE. 34 guns. Designed by Étienne Salicon and built by Pierre Chaillé.
Dimensions & tons: 112ft 0in x 30ft 0in (36.38 x 9.75m). 400 tons. Draught 13ft (4.22m). Men: 150 (35/78/37), +5 officers.
Guns: 34 from 1692: 20 x 8pdrs; 14 x 4pdrs.
Diligente Le Havre.
K: 1.1692. L: 19.7.1692. C: 10.1692. Lent as a privateer in 1694 to *Vice-amiral* Anne Hilarion de Costentin, Comte de Tourville, and placed under the command of René Duguay-Touin of St Malo, who shared the funding. Captured (with Duguay-Trouin aboard) by HM Ships *Monck*, *Mary*, *Dunkirk*, *Ruby*, *Dragon* and *Adventure* 12.5.1694 (Duguay-Trouin escaped captivity on 30.6.1694); sold 1698.

JOLIE. 12 guns. Called *Bayonne* until November 1692. This vessel was called a privateer by the English.
Dimensions & tons: 62ft 0in, 52ft 4in x 18ft 3in x 8ft 6in (20.14, 17.0 x 5.93 x 2.76m). 80 tons. Men: 60.
Guns: 12 (*Bayonne*), 10 (*Jolie*)
Jolie Bayonne (probably)
K: spring 1692. L: 1692. C: 8.1692. Captured 6.1693 by HMS *Southampton* at Lagos, becoming HMS *Jolly Prize*. Sold 25.11.1698.

HÉROÏNE. 20 guns. Ordered in May 1692 and named on 30 July.
Dimensions & tons: 70ft 0in x 20ft 10in x 9ft 2in (22.74 x 6.77 x 2.98m). 120 tons. Men: 70, +5? officers
Guns: 14/16 guns.
Héroïne Brest Dyd.
K: 6.1692. L: 29.7.1692. C: 9.1692. Captured 7.1694 off Gibraltar by HMS *Essex*, becoming HMS *Essex Prize*. Sold 1.10.1702 at Deptford.

HEUREUSE. A private vessel built in 1692 at Dieppe by David Chauvel, and purchased for the Navy in November 1692; she was captured by the Dutch in early 1693.

SERPENTE. 16 guns. Designed by Étienne Salicon and probably built by Jean-Pierre Brun.
Dimensions & tons: 71ft 0in x 20ft 0in x 7ft 6in (23.06 x 6.50 x 2.44m). 100 tons. Draught 9½ft (3.09m). Men: 80 in war, 60 peace.
Guns: 16 in war (12 peace): UD 16 x 4pdrs.
Serpente Le Havre.
K: 12.1692. L: 3.1693. C: 1693. Sailed in the King's service to the West Indies in 1696 as part of a squadron of nine vessels under CV Des Augiers, carrying settlers and young marriageable women. Left (with *Gracieuse*) to Jean-Baptiste Ducasse, Governor of St Domingue, both ships became *frégates flibustières*, and joined CdE Jean Bernard de Saint-Jean, Baron de Pointis's squadron; took part in the capture of Cartagena de Indias 5.5.1697. Struck 1696 and BU at Léogane at end 1697.

AURORE. 18 guns. Probably built by Jean-Nicolas Houwens.
Dimensions & tons: 93ft 0in, 80ft 0in x 25ft 0in (30.21, 25.99 x 8.12m).
Guns: 18 x 6pdrs.
Aurore Dunkirk
K: End 1692. L: 4.1693. C: 5.1693. Wrecked 1694.

GUERRIÈRE. A *frégate légère* of unknown characteristics (probably similar to *Jolie* below, although this may be a misreporting of the same vessel) built at Bayonne in 1692–93, probably by Félix Arnaud, brought into service in April 1693 with a complement of 60 men (50 in peace), and wrecked in the same month with all hands lost on the bar at the mouth of the River Adour, when first leaving Bayonne.

JOLIE. 16 guns. Designed and built by Félix Arnaud.
Dimensions & tons: 80ft 0in x 20ft 0in x 9ft 6in (25.99 x 6.50 x 3.09m). 100 tons (125 tons in 1701). Draught 10ft (3.25m). Men: 100 in war, 60 peace.
Guns: 16 in war (12 peace): UD 16 x 6pdrs. 14 from 1699: 8 x 6pdrs + 6 x 4pdrs (8 x 4pdrs from 1701).
Jolie Bayonne.
K: early 1693. L: 6.1693. C: 7.1693. Lent as a privateer in 1695 to the deposed King of England, James II, under command of Andrew White. Wrecked 11.1702 at the mouth of the River Adour with survivors from Vigo, 200 men lost.

HAUTAINE. 12 guns. Designed and built by Jean-Nicolas Houwens.
Dimensions & tons: 64ft 0in, 55ft 0in x 18ft 0in x 8ft 0in (20.79, 17.87 x 5.85 x 2.60m). 60 tons. Draught 6½ft/7ft (2.11/2.27m). Men: 55 in war, 45 peace, +? officers; as corvette 50 in war, 30 peace.
Guns: 10 in war (8 peace): 6 x 4pdrs, 4 x 2pdrs. 8 from 1698: 8 x 4pdrs (12 from 1699).
Hautaine Dunkirk.
K: 2.1693. L: 5.1693. C: 8.1693. Re-classed as a corvette or *barque longue* in 1696–97. Condemned 6.1702 at Dunkirk and sold.

Ex-PRUSSIAN PRIZE (1693). A '*Frégate du Brandebourg*' named *Salamander* was captured in 1693 and renamed *Salamandre*. She was rebuilt at Rochefort from 1693 to 5.1694 by Pierre Malet.
Dimensions & tons: 81fr 0in x 23ft 0in x 9ft 6in. 150/160 tons. Draught 11ft/11ft 8in. Men: 100 +4 officers.
Guns: 22 in war (20 peace): 6 x 6pdrs; 16 x 4pdrs.
Salamandre Pillau
Built 1683–84. Renamed *Atalante* 3.1696. Struck at Rochefort 1704 or 1705.

Ex-ENGLISH NAVAL PRIZES (1693–1696). The English ketch *Harp* was captured by two French privateers on 27 June 1693 and became the French navy's *Harpe*. The English Fifth Rate *Milford* was taken by a French squadron of four ships off Orfordness on 11 December 1693 and was taken into the navy as the *frégate légère* *Milfort* or *Milford*. The English Sixth Rate *Newport* was taken 15 July 1696 by French warships in the Bay of Fundy and became the French *Nieuport*.
Harpe John Frame, Scarborough
Dimensions & tons: dimensions unknown. 94 tons (bm).
Guns: 10 (in English service)
Taken by enemies 9.1695.
Milfort Woolwich Dyd.
Dimensions & tons: 103ft 0in x 26ft 3in x 11ft 0in (33.46 x 8.53 x 3.57m). 250 tons. Draught 13ft (4.22m). Men: 170 in war, 150 peace.
Guns: 22 in war (18 peace): 4 x 12pdrs; 18 x 8pdrs. 32 from 1698: 22 x 8pdrs; 10 x 2pdrs. 32 from 1699: 2 x 8pdrs; 20 x 6pdrs (8pdrs from 1702?); 10 x 2pdrs. 30 from 1704: 14 x 8pdrs; 12 x 4pdrs; 4 x 2pdrs.
Promoted to the 5th rank in 1701. Reportedly condemned at Dunkirk c.1702 but was still on the list in 1704, and served to

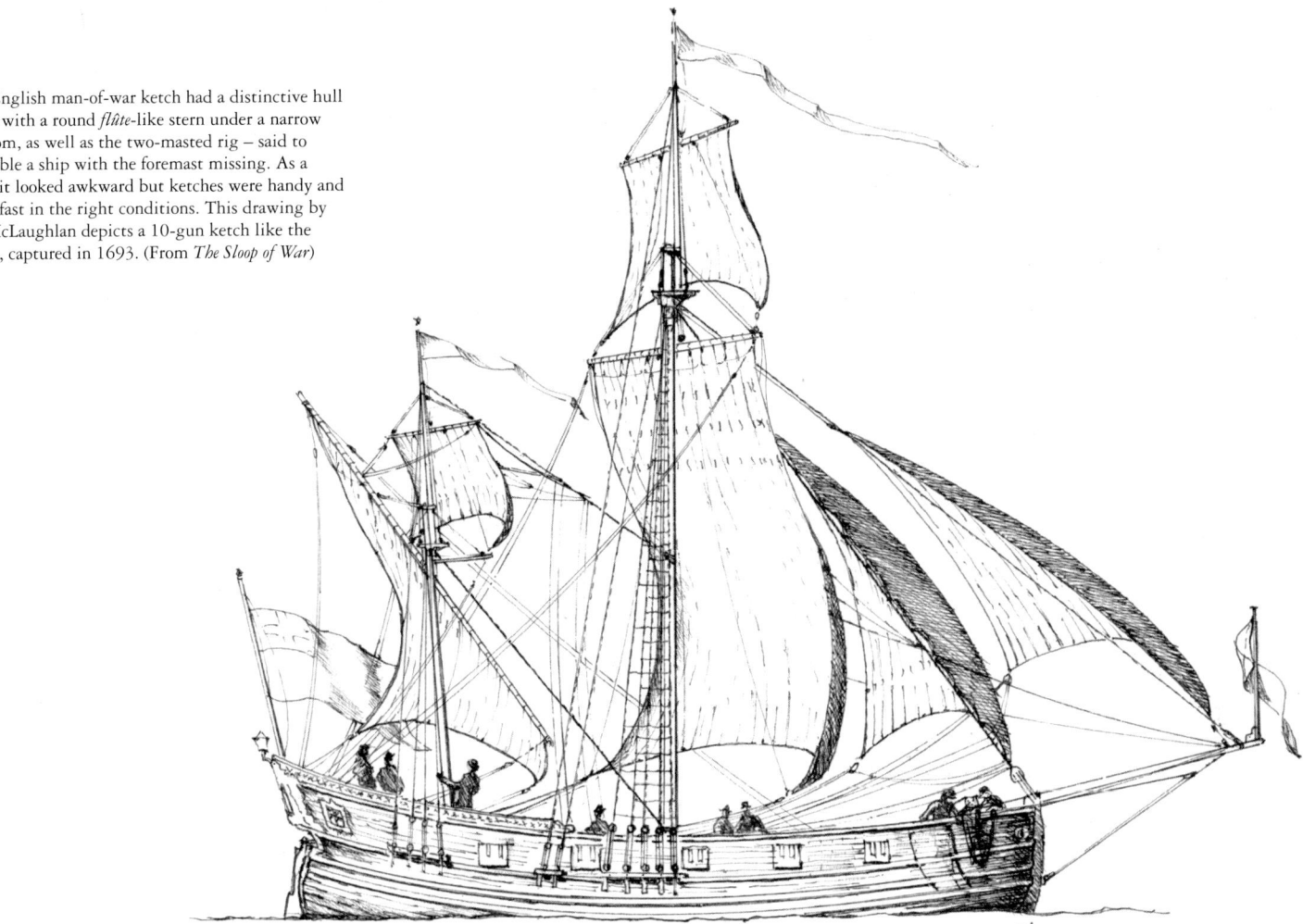

The English man-of-war ketch had a distinctive hull form, with a round *flûte*-like stern under a narrow transom, as well as the two-masted rig – said to resemble a ship with the foremast missing. As a type, it looked awkward but ketches were handy and often fast in the right conditions. This drawing by Ian McLaughlan depicts a 10-gun ketch like the *Harpe*, captured in 1693. (From *The Sloop of War*)

protect ships carrying grain to Brest in 1709.

Nieuport Portsmouth Dyd.
  Dimensions & tons: 88ft 0in x 22ft 0in x 7ft 6in (28.59 x 7.15 x 2.44m). 110 tons. 10½ft (3.41m). Men: 120 in war, 80 peace.
  Guns: 24 in war (16 peace): 20 x 6pdrs; 4 x 3pdrs. 18 from 1706: 18 x 6pdrs.
  Struck 11.1697 at Le Havre and sold.

Ex-ENGLISH PRIZE (1694). An English merchantman or privateer – possibly named *Three Daggers* – was captured in 1694 and renamed *Trois Poignards*.
  Dimensions & tons: 64ft 0in x 17ft 6in x 7ft 0in (20.79 x 5.68 x 2.27m). 70 tons. Draught 9ft (2.92m). Men: 60 in war, 20 peace.
  Guns: 14 in war (6 peace): 14 x 4pdrs.
Trois Poignards England?
  Built 1692. Struck 11.1697 at Le Havre and sold.

Ex-SPANISH PRIZE (1694). 16 guns. This vessel, possibly named *Creciente*, was taken in 1694 and renamed *Croissant d'Espagne*.
  Dimensions & tons: 71ft 0in x 20ft 0in x 7ft 0in (23.06 x 6.50 x 2.27m). 90 tons. Draught 9ft (2.92m). Men: 100 in war, 80 peace.
  Guns: 16 in war (12 peace): 12 x 4pdrs; 4 x 2pdrs.
Croissant d'Espagne Ostend
  Struck at Rochefort 1696 or 1697.

ENTREPRENANTE. 22 guns. This vessel was acquired between 1693 and 1695. She was designed by Barthe and built at Bayonne.
  Dimensions & tons: 90ft 0in x 24ft 0in x 9ft 0in (29.24 x 7.80 x 2.92m). 200 tons. Draught 11ft (3.57m). Men: 120 in war, 70 peace.
  Guns: 22 in war (18 peace): 18 x 6pdrs; 4 x 4pdrs.
Entreprenante Bayonne
  Built 1691–1692. Burned at Vigo 10.1702.

ÉCUREUIL. A *frégate légère* with this name was in service at Brest in December 1694 but was lent as a privateer in January 1695 to LG Victor Marie, Comte d'Estrées (with command given to EV Michel de Bellisle). Struck later in 1695. No further details of her are known.

HÉROÏNE Class. 20 guns. Both ships designed and built by Laurent Hélie and Blaise Pangalo for privateering at the request of François Saupin, Sieur Du Rocher (a timber merchant in Brest) and CV Jacques Dandenne, who funded the construction. Ordered and named on 4 April 1695.
  Dimensions & tons: 90ft 0in x 24ft 0in x 11ft 6in (29.24 x 7.80 x 3.74m). 170 tons. Draught 11ft/12½ft (3.57/4.06m). Men: 110 in war, 95 peace; *Galatée* later 120 in war, 80 peace, +?2 officers.
  Guns: 20 in war (16 peace): LD 20 x 8pdrs. 20 from 1699: 20 x 4pdrs. 18 from 1704: 2 x 6pdrs, 16 x 4pdrs.
Héroïne Brest Dyd.
  K: 4.1696. L: 30.5.1696. C: 6.1696. Lent as a privateer in 1696 to François Saupin, Sieur Du Rocher, under the command of CV Jacques Dandenne as part of a squadron of three to five ships. Captured 1697 by the Spanish at Papachim.

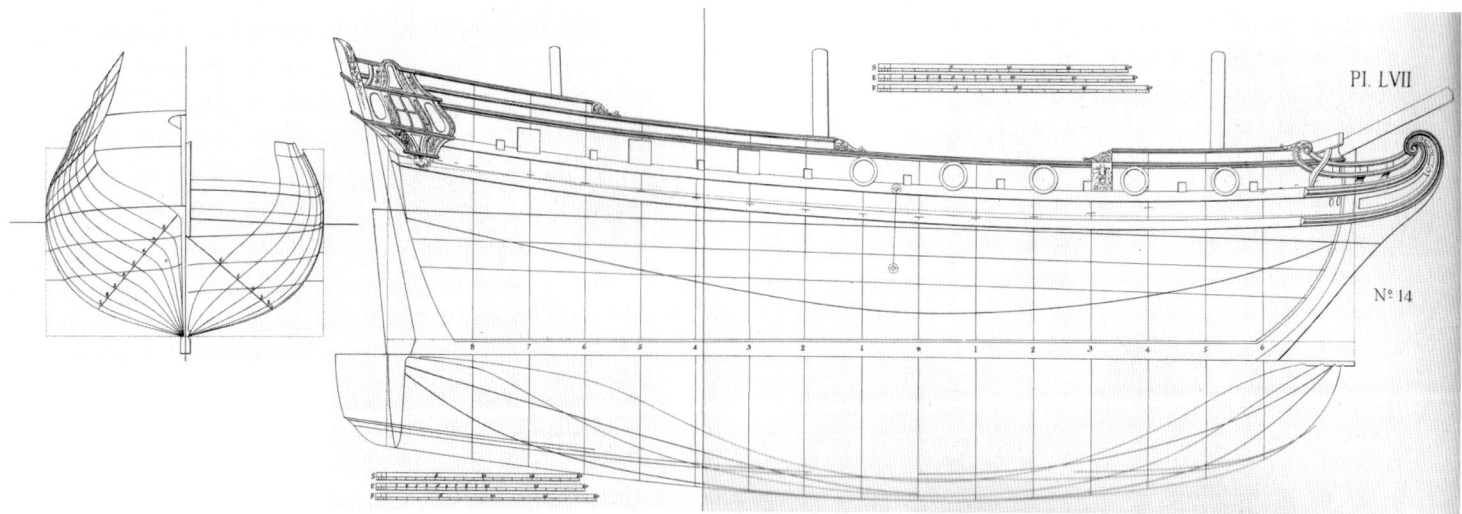

This drawing of the privateer *Neptunus* is taken from *Architectura Navalis Mercatoria*, the famous work of 1768 by Fredrik Henrik af Chapman, the Swede often considered the first true naval architect. It is significant in Chapman's career, being the first draught he ever attempted (at the age of 10), but as redrawn for publication the vessel is described as Flemish, 'built in Ostend at the end of the last century: an especially good sailer'. It is a good example of the kind of fast-sailing privateer that was the speciality of the Spanish Netherlands for much of the seventeenth century, a number of which including a *Neptun* were captured by the French Navy in the 1690s.

Galatée (Galathée) Brest Dyd.
K: 4.1696. L: 13.8.1696. C: 9.1696. Lent as a privateer in 1696 to LG André, Marquis de Nesmond, as part of a squadron of six to eleven vessels; then lent as a privateer in 1697 to François Saupin, Sieur Du Rocher, under the command of CV Jacques Dandenne as part of a squadron of three to five ships. Captured 19.5.1708 by the British.

NAÏADE Group. 20 guns, designed and built by Blaise Pangalo. Both ordered (and named) on 21 March 1696, and launched in second half of May. The second was somewhat larger than the first. Curiously, the *Naïade* was initially armed with 8pdr guns on the upper deck (soon exchanged for 4pdrs), while the *Néréide* mounted 6pdrs (most of which were also eventually exchanged for 4pdrs).

Dimensions & tons: *Néréide* 80ft 0in x 20ft 0in x 9ft 6in (25.99 x 6.50 x 3.09m). 100 tons. Draught 9ft/11ft (2.92/3.57m). *Néréide* 84ft 0in x 22ft 0in x 10ft 6in (27.29 x 7.15 x 3.41m). 150 tons. Draught 9ft/11½ft (2.92/3.74m). Men: 110 in war, 95 peace.
Guns: 20 in war: (16 peace): initially (1698) UD 20 x 8pdrs (*Naïade*) or 6pdrs (*Néréide*). By 1699 *Naïade* had all 8pdrs replaced by 4pdrs and may have been reduced to 16 guns. By 1704 *Néréide* had 4 x 6pdrs replaced by 4pdrs, and by 1706 was altered to 2 x 6pdrs + 20 x 4pdrs.

Naïade (Nayade) Brest Dyd.
K: 4.1696. L: 5.1696. C: 6.1696. Struck 1705 at Dunkirk.

Néréide (Nereïde) Brest Dyd.
K: 4.1696. L: 5.1696. C: 6.1696. Lent as a privateer in 1696 to LG André, Marquis de Nesmond, as part of a squadron of six to eleven vessels. Struck 1712 or 1713 at Rochefort.

Ex-PRIVATEERS (1696–1697). A vessel built at Ostend in 1690–91 was probably either the Spanish privateer *San Paulo* or the Jersey privateer *Saint Paul* when taken by the French in September 1696 and renamed *Saint Paul d'Ostende*. The Spanish *Armas de Velasco*, built in Majorca and probably a privateer, was captured in September 1696 and briefly became the French *Armes de Velasque*. Another vessel built at Flushing or Amsterdam was either the English or Dutch privateer *Neptun* when taken by the French in April 1697 and renamed *Neptune*.

Saint Paul d'Ostende Ostend
Dimensions & tons: 66ft 0in x 18ft 6in x 7ft 0in (21.44 x 6.01 x 2.27m). 100 tons. Draught 9ft (2.92m). Men: 70 in war, 25 peace.
Guns: 16 in war (10 peace): 4 x 4pdrs; 10 x 3pdrs, 2 x 2pdrs. 14 from 1702: 12 x 3pdrs, 2 x 2pdrs.
Lent as a privateer in 1702 to EV Jacques, Chevalier Dailly. Struck at Port Louis 1704.

Armes de Velasque
Dimensions & tons: unknown. Men: 100 + 7 officers
Guns: unknown
Sold 10.1697 at Toulon.

Neptune Flushing or Amsterdam
Dimensions & tons: 72ft 0in x 21ft 0in x 8ft 6in (23.39 x 6.82 x 2.76m). 120 tons. Draught 11ft (3.57m). Men: 80 in war, 52 peace.
Guns: 14 in war (8 peace): 14 x 4pdrs.
Condemned at Rochefort 1698, BU 1699.

AURORE (i). 24 guns. Little information is available on this ship; she may have been a prize.
Dimensions & tons: unknown.
Guns: 24 (according to the English)

Aurore Rochefort.
K: 1696/7. L: 1696/7. C: 1697. Captured by the English off Olonne (on the Vendée coast) 7.1697.

AURORE (ii). 22 guns. Designed and built by Philippe Cochois.
Dimensions & tons: 92ft 0in, 81ft 0in x 24ft 6in x 8ft 6in (29.89, 26.31 x 7.96 x 3.6m). 220 tons. Draught 10ft (3.25m). Men: 100 in war, +5 officers.
Guns: 22 in war (14 peace): 18 x 6pdrs; 4 x 4pdrs. 18 from 1704: 18 x 6pdrs only. 18 from 1709: 12 x 6pdrs + 6 x 4pdrs, but restored to 18 x 6pdrs from 1715.

Aurore Le Havre.
K: 5.1697. L: 3.8.1697. C: 8.1697. Leased in 10.1705 to 1706 to the *Compagnie Royale de St Domingue*, and in 1707 to the *Compagnie de la Mer du Sud*. Briefly re-classed as a *flûte* in 1708. Condemned 1720 at Rochefort.

LIGHT FRIGATES

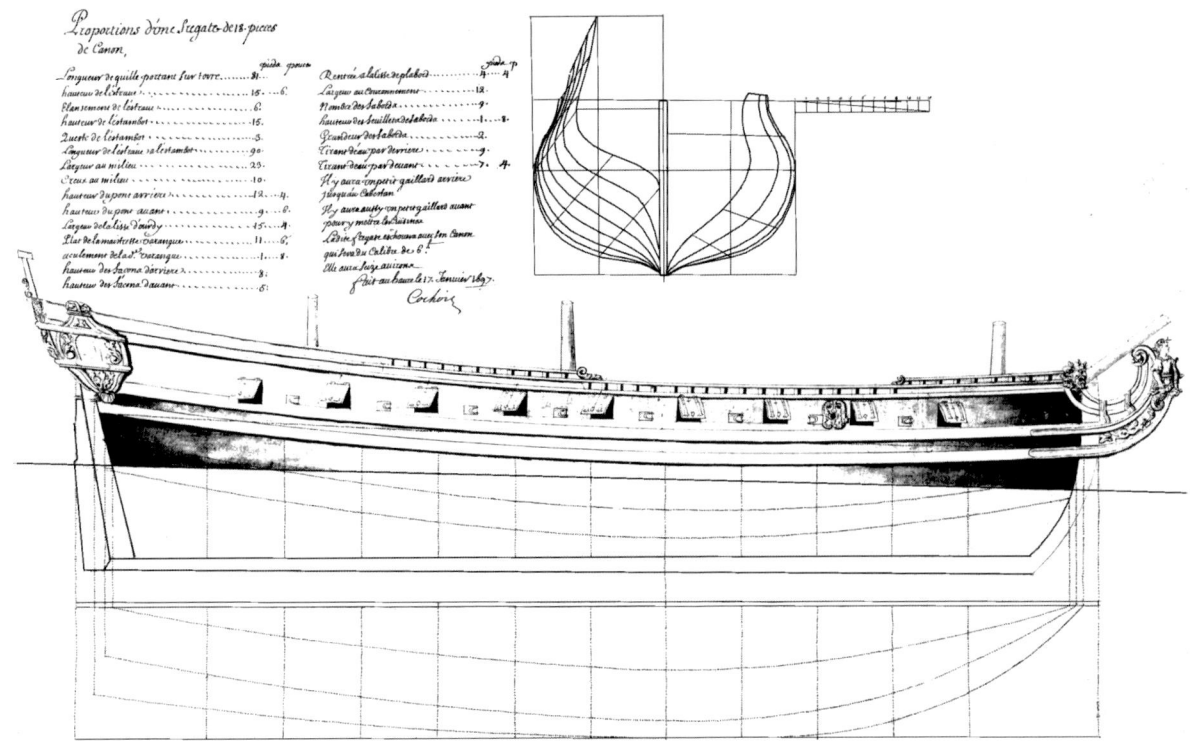

A drawing of an unidentified 18-gun frigate dated 17 January 1697 and signed by [Philippe] Cochois. The dimensions are very close to the known details of the *Aurore* built in that year and in his modelling monograph on that ship Jean-Claude Lemineur confidently based his reconstruction on this draught. Apart from the nine pairs of gunports on the upper deck, *Aurore* also carried two pairs of guns on the quarterdeck. (After an original in the Musée de la Marine, Paris)

With the close of the Nine Years War in 1697, no further light frigates were ordered by the French until late in 1701. However, the bomb vessel *Salamandre* was classed as a *frégate légère* from 1698 to 1704 or 1705 and the fireship *Fourbe* was re-classed as a *frégate légère* during 1701 only to be wrecked in January 1703.

GRACIEUSE. 16 guns. Designed and built by Philippe Cochois.
  Dimensions & tons: 84ft 0in x 21ft 9in x 9ft 0in (27.29 x 7.07 x 2.92m). 120 tons. Draught 9ft 4in (3.03m). Men: 80 in war.
  Guns (16 in war, 12 peace): 16 x 4pdrs.
Guns: 16 in war (12 peace): 16 x 4pdrs.
Gracieuse Le Havre.
  K: 10.1701. L: 16.1.1702. C: 3.1702. Captured 29.5.1702 by HMS *Rochester*, becoming HMS *Rochester Prize*. Sold 4.1712.

GENTILLE (i). 12 guns. Designed and built by Jean Guéroult.
  Dimensions & tons: 72ft 0in x 19ft 0in x 8ft 0in (23.39 x 6.17 x 2.60m). 100 tons. Draught 8½ft (2.76m).
  Men: 70 in war, 45 peace. Guns (12 in war, 8 peace): 12 x 4pdrs.
Guns: 12 in war (8 peace): 12 x 4pdrs.
Gentille Dieppe.
  K: 10.1701. L: 5.1702. C: 6.1702. Sold 6.1702 at Dieppe to the *Compagnie de l'Asiento*.

NYMPHE. 26 guns. Designed and built by Philippe Cochois for privateering at the request of CB Michel de Bellisle, who funded the construction.
  Dimensions & tons: 98ft 0in x 24ft 9in x 12ft 0in (31.83 x 8.04 x 3.90m). 200 tons. Draught 11ft 10in/13ft (3.84/4.22m). Men: 130 in war, 100 peace, +3/5 officers.
  Guns: 26 in war (20 peace): UD 20 x 6pdrs; QD 6 x 4pdrs. 22 from 1709: UD 18 x 6pdrs (20 again from 1715), QD 4 x 4pdrs.

A Danish draught of the *Nymphe* of 1702. The accompanying legend (not reproduced here) in Danish identifies the ship, the designer (Cochois) and the place of build (Le Havre). (Rigsarkivet, Copenhagen)

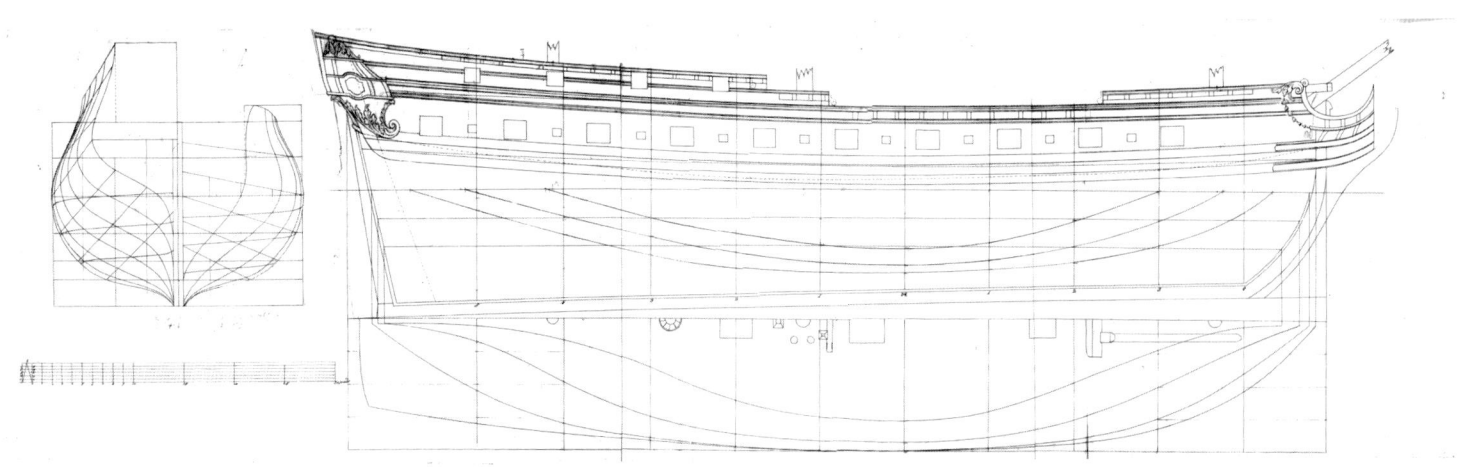

Nymphe Le Havre.
> K: 3.1702. L: 26.5.1702. C: 6.1702. Lent as a privateer in 1702–5 to CB Michel de Bellisle, then lent as a privateer in 1705–6 to CV Henri-Louis, Marquis de Chavagnac, and CV Pierre Le Moyne d'Iberville, as part of a squadron of ten vessels, for operations in the West Indies. Struck 1719 at Rochefort.

Ex-DUTCH PRIZES (1702–1703). With the renewal of war in 1702, five vessels captured from the Dutch were added to the French Navy. The *Vier Broers* (built 1696–97) was captured in April 1702 and renamed *Quatre Frères*. Two more vessels (identity unknown), captured in April 1703, were renamed *Flessingoise* and *Cavalier de Flessingue*. A larger vessel – the *Wolfswinkell* – captured in June 1703, was renamed *Boutique de Loux* (or *Boutine de Loux*) and carried a 6pdr battery. Another Dutch ship, built in 1691 and also captured in 1703, was renamed *Sirène*.

Quatre Frères Flushing.
> Dimensions & tons: 75ft 0in x 21ft 8in x 10ft 0in (24.36 x 7.04 x 3.25m). 110 tons. Draught 9½ft (3.09m). Men: 80 in war, 60 peace; in 1709, 120 in war, 25 peace.
> Guns: 14 in war (12 peace): UD 14 x 4pdrs.
> Struck at Le Havre 1709.

Flessingoise Flushing.
> Dimensions & tons: 68ft 0in x 19ft 0in x 9ft 0in (22.09 x 6.17 x 2.92m). 100 tons. Draught 9½ft (3.09m). Men: 60 in war, 50 peace.
> Guns: 14 in war (10 peace): UD 14 x 4pdrs.
> Captured by an enemy 1706; taken again by *Aimable* 11.1706 but not restored to service.

Cavalier de Flessingue Flushing.
> Dimensions & tons: 73ft 0in x 21ft 4in x 8ft 3in (23.71 x 6.93 x 2.68m). 110 tons. Draught 10ft (3.25m). Men: 100 in war, 50 peace, +4 officers.
> Guns: 18 in war: UD 14 x 4pdrs + 4 x 3pdrs.
> Used to protect ships carrying grain imports to Lorient 1709. Carried alcohol to Brittany 1711–12. Name shortened to *Cavalier* 1713. Struck at Port Louis 1717.

Boutique de Loux Holland.
> Dimensions & tons: 88ft 0in x 24ft 0in x 8ft 6in (28.59 x 7.80 x 2.76m). 150 tons. Draught 10ft (3.25m). Men: 100 in war, 50 peace.
> Guns: 24 in war (20 peace): UD 16 x 6pdrs; QD 8 x 2pdrs.
> Sold at Dunkirk 6.1705.

Sirène Holland.
> Dimensions & tons: 80ft 0in x 21ft 6in x 10ft 6in (25.99 x 6.98 x 3.41m). 150 tons. Draught 11ft (3.57m). Men: 90 in war, 40 peace; in 1712, 120 in war, 45 peace.
> Guns: 18 in war (12 peace): UD 2 x 6pdrs + 16 x 4pdrs (20 from 1706).
> Struck at Rochefort 1712.

GENTILLE (ii). Designed and built by Philippe Cochois.
> Dimensions & tons: 93ft 0in, 81ft 0in x 24ft 8in x 10ft 9in (30.21, 26.31 x 8.01 x 3.49m). 150 tons. Draught 10ft/11½ft (3.25/3.74m). Men: 100 in war, 70 peace.
> Guns: 18 in war (14 peace): 18 x 6pdrs.

Gentille Le Havre.
> K: 6.1702. L: 13.8.1702. C: 10.1702. Captured 20.8.1708 by a Flemish frigate.

JOYEUSE. Designed and built by Philippe Cochois.
> Dimensions & tons: dimensions unknown. 110 tons. Men: 100 in war, ?90 peace.
> Guns: 14 x 4pdrs.

Joyeuse Le Havre.
> K: 8.1702. L: 21.10.1702. C: 11.1702. Burnt at Avranches during an English raid 8.1703.

CHASSE. Designed and built by Pierre Chaillé.
> Dimensions & tons: 86ft 0in x 21ft 8in x 7ft 9in (28.24 x 7.12 x 2.55m). 100/110 tons. Draught 9ft/9½ft (2.92/3.09m) Men: 90/100.
> Guns: 14 in war (12 peace): 14 x 4pdrs.

Chasse Le Havre.
> K: 8.1702. L: 8.11.1702. C: 1.1703. Lent as a privateer to associate bankers Samuel Bernard, Comte de Goubert, and Jean Nicolas; sailed under LV Jacques Gratton and later Van Émeric. Ceded 12.1709 to Sieur Maguire of Rouen, but captured by the British (crew freed 1.1710).

LÉOPOLD. An Austrian vessel, *Leopoldus*, was captured in 1702 in the Mediterranean and was commissioned by the French as *Léopold*. She was put on sale at Toulon in March 1703.

EMBUSCADE. 32 guns. Designed and built by Philippe Cochois or Pierre Chaillé.
> Dimensions & tons: 101ft 0in x 26ft 8in x 9ft 8in (32.81 x 8.66 x 3.14m). 200 tons. Draught 13½ft (4.39m). Men: 200.
> Guns: 30 in war (18 peace): 22 x 6pdrs; 8 x 4pdrs (2 more 4pdrs added from 1707).

Embuscade Le Havre.
> K: 1703. L: 1704. C: 1704. Lent as a privateer to Tanqueray 1704–7. Captured by the English 5.1707.

DAUPHINE. Designed and built by Philippe Cochois for privateering, at the request of Jacques Du Val Espréménil, a citizen of Le Havre, who funded the construction.
> Dimensions & tons: 102ft 0in x 27ft 4in x 11ft 6in (33.13 x 8.88 x 3.74m). 180 tons. Draught 13ft (4.22m). Men: 180 in war, 90 peace.
> Guns: 28 in war (22 peace): UD 22 x 8pdrs; QD 6 x 4pdrs.

Dauphine Le Havre.
> K: 5.1703. L: 26.8.1703. C: 10.1703. Lent as a privateer in 1703–4 to Jacques Du Val Espréménil, under the command of Du Bocage. Wrecked 11.12.1704 on entering St Malo, on an underwater rock known as La Natière, while escorting in the captured (non-naval) prize *Dragon*. Raised 1.1705.

ÉTOILE. 30 guns. Designed and built by Philippe Cochois.
> Dimensions & tons: 107ft 0in x 27ft 8in x 12ft 0in (34.76 x 8.99 x 3.90m). 200 tons. Draught 13½ft (4.39m). Men: 200 in war, 100 peace.
> Guns: 30 in war (22 peace): UD 22 x 8pdrs; QD 8 x 4pdrs.

Étoile Le Havre.
> K: 8.1703. L: 25.10.1703. C: 11.1703. Captured 10.11.1704 off Gibraltar by HMS *Swallow*, becoming HMS *Swallow Prize*; wrecked 29.7.1711 off Ajaccio.

ANDROMÈDE. 12 guns. Designed and built by Pierre Masson.
> Dimensions & tons: 75ft 0in x 19ft 0in x 9ft 6in (24.36 x 6.17 x 3.09m). 100 tons. Draught 9ft (2.92m). Men: 70 in war, 25 (40 in 1708) peace, +2 officers.
> Guns: 12 in war (8 peace): UD 12 x 4pdrs.

Andromède Rochefort Dyd.
> K: 1703. L: 2.1704 C: 4.1704. Damaged by the British

bombardment of Toulon on 21.8.1707, and not repaired; removed from service 4.1.1709 and sold by Order of 22.1.1709.

SIBYLLE. 12 guns. Designed and built by Pierre Masson, near-sister to *Andromède*.
Dimensions & tons: 74ft 0in x 19ft 6in x 9ft 0in (24.04 x 6.33 x 2.92m). 100 tons. Draught 12ft (3.90m). Men: 70 in war, 25 peace, +2 officers.
Guns: 12 in war (8 peace): UD 12 x 4pdrs.
Sibylle Rochefort Dyd.
K: 1703. L: early 1704. C: 7.1704. Grounded near Gibraltar 9.11.1704 in action with an English squadron and burnt to avoid capture (as were *Oiseau*, *Hercule* and *Croissant*).

MÉDÉE. 16 guns. Designed and built by René Levasseur.
Dimensions & tons: 86ft 0in x 24ft 0in x 10ft 3in (27.94 x 7.80 x 3.33m). 150 tons. Draught 12ft (3.90m). Men: 100 in war, 90 peace, +2/4 officers.
Guns: 16 in war (12 peace): UD 16 x 6pdrs.
Médée Dunkirk.
K: 12.1703. L: 5.4.1704. C: 5.1704. Lent as a privateer in 1704 to CV Marc-Antoine de Saint-Pol Hécourt, as part of a squadron of six vessels. Captured 10.1708 by the British, but not added to British Navy.

HÉROÏNE. 20 guns. Designed and built by René Levasseur alongside his *Médée*.
Dimensions & tons: 88ft 0in x 24ft 8in x 8ft 9in (28.59 x 8.01 x 2.84m). 150 tons. Draught 11ft (3.57m). Men: 100 in war (130 in 1708), 60 peace, +4 officers.
Guns: 20 in war (16 peace): UD 18 x 6pdrs; QD 2 x 2pdrs.
Héroïne Dunkirk.
K: 12.1703. L: 12.4.1704. C: 5.1704. Lent as a privateer in 1704 to CV Marc-Antoine de Saint-Pol Hécourt, as part of a squadron of six vessels. Captured and burnt by Zeelanders 1.1708.

VALEUR. 24 guns. Designed and built by Laurent Helié for privateering, at the request of CV René Duguay-Trouin, who funded the construction. Ordered and named in January 1704.
Dimensions & tons: 98ft 0in x 25ft 8in x 11ft 0in (31.83 x 8.34 x 3.57m). 300 tons. Men: 150 in war, 70 peace, +3/4 officers.
Guns: 24 in war (18 peace): UD 18 x 6pdrs; QD 6 x 2pdrs.
Valeur Brest Dyd.
K: 1.1704. L: 21.3.1704. C: 6.1704. Lent as a privateer to CV René Duguay-Trouin, as part of a squadron of four vessels, under the command of his younger brother Nicolas Trouin, who died 19.12.1704 from wounds received in fighting a Flushing privateer. Then under command of LV de Saint-Auban she was captured by HMS *Worcester* 15.5.1705, becoming HMS *Valeur*. Seized 6.9.1710 by French boats in Newfoundland but recovered 13.12.1710 by HMS *Essex*. BU 1718 at Deptford.

VICTOIRE. 26 (later 34) guns. Designed and built by René Levasseur.
Dimensions & tons: 100ft 0in x 26ft 10in x 10ft 0in (32.48 x 8.72 x 3.25m). 250 tons (from 1716, 280 tons). Draught 12½ft (4.06m). Men: 150 in war, 80 (120 from 1736) peace, +4/5 officers.
Guns: 26 in war (20 peace): UD 20 x 8pdrs (6pdrs from 1712); QD 6 x 4pdrs; from 1729, 22 x 6pdrs + 12 x 4pdrs.
Victoire Dunkirk.
K: 4.1704. L: 9.1704. C: 12.1704. Lent as a privateer in 1709–11 to citizens of Dunkirk, under Batteman. Carried alcohol in Brittany 1711–12. Rebuilt at Rochefort 1736–37 by Blaise Geslain, then condemned and BU there 1743.

FORTUNE. 22 (later 22) guns. Designed and built by René Levasseur alongside his *Victoire*.
Dimensions & tons: 88ft 0in x 24ft 8in x 8ft 9in (28.59 x 8.01 x 2.84m). 150 tons (from 1717, 200 tons). Draught 11ft (3.57m). Men: 100 in war, 60 peace, +2/3 officers; from 1723, 150 in war, 80 peace.
Guns: 20 in war (16 peace): UD 18 x 6pdrs; QD 2 x 2pdrs; from 1715, UD 18 x 4pdrs, QD 4 x 3pdrs.
Fortune Dunkirk.
K: 4.1704. L: 9.1704. C: 12.1704. Lent as a privateer in 1705 to Pierre Alexandre Jazier, Seigneur de La Garde, Director of Victualling at Brest and husband of the elder sister of the Trouin brothers; sailed under Philippe Plet, Sieur de Saint-Jean. Later lent as a privateer in 1709 to citizens of Dunkirk, and then to (provisional) CV Cornil Sauss in 1711 as part of a squadron of six vessels. Converted to a *patache* 6.1726 at Lorient; struck there 1728.

DIANE. 28 guns. Designed and built by Pierre Coulomb for privateering, according to the 'méthode du Sieur Gobert', at the request of LV Vaujoux, who funded the construction.
Dimensions & tons: unknown
Guns: 28
Diane Lorient.
K: 8.1704. L: 11.1704. C: 12.1704. Wrecked on the Île de Sein 2.1705 or 6.1705, 140 lost.

The 5th Rank two-decker *Méduse* was re-classed as a *frégate légère* in 1704–5 but reverted to the 5th Rank in 1708.

A *frégate légère* named *Entreprenante* of unknown origin was lent as a privateer to Sieur Du Hérobose at Le Havre; she took three vessels of which two are recorded in the judgments of the *Amiral de France*, and was then captured by the British; 94 men from 'one *Entreprenante*' were repatriated in September and December 1705.

Ex-DUTCH PRIZE (1705). Probably the Zeeland Admiralty's *Pauw* (both the Dutch and French names mean 'Peacock'), built in 1702 and captured 8.1705 at Flushing by CV René Duguay-Trouin.
Dimensions & tons: 74ft 0in x 24ft 0in x 9ft 6in (24.04 x 7.80 x 3.09m). 150 tons. Draught 11ft (3.57m). Men 100 in war, 50 peace, +?5 officers.
Guns: 18 in war (14 peace): 16 x 4pdrs; 2 x 3pdrs.
Paon Flushing.
L & C: 1702. Used by CV René Duguay-Trouin in 1706 to reinforce *Jason* and *Hercule* in the defence of Cadiz. Lent for commerce and privateering in 1711 to Sieur Du Tourbian Monot. Rebuilt and enlarged in 1711–12 at Brest, see below.

BICHE. 20 guns. Designed by Governor Jacques Brouillan
Dimensions & tons: unknown. Men: 60 + 1 officer
Guns: 20
Biche Port Royal (Acadia).
K: 5.1704. L: 1706. C: 5.1707. Commissioned as a privateer 1708. This was probably the frigate that was captured by HMS *Medway* on 5.9.1709 and renamed *Hind* (6th Rate, 190 tons, 78ft 0in x 23ft 6in British measurements). Wrecked 10.12.1711 at Dublin..

ZÉPHYR. 24 guns. Designed and built by René Levasseur. The name *Zéphyr* was originally assigned to a 4th Rank ship of 40 guns that was projected in January 1706 for construction at Dunkirk but this project was abandoned and the name was reassigned to this *frégate légère* that was already on the slip.

    Dimensions & tons: 90ft 0in x 25ft 6in x 10ft 0in (29.24 x 8.28 x 3.25m). 200 tons. Draught 12ft (3.90m). Men: 150 in war, 70 peace, +3/4 officers.

    Guns: 24 in war (18 peace): UD 18 x 6pdrs; QD 6 x 2pdrs (3pdrs from 1710).

Zéphyr Dunkirk.
    K: 12.1705. L: 1706. C: 1706. Lent as a privateer to citizens of Dunkirk, under *Brigadier des gardes de la Marine* Des Blanques, initially operating independently 1708–9, then with a squadron of six vessels (under provisional CV Cornil Sauss), 1710–12. Wrecked near Calais 1713.

NAÏADE. 28 guns. Purchased 1706 at St Malo. The name *Naïade* was originally assigned to a 34-gun *frégate légère* that was projected in January 1706 to be built at Brest but that project was abandoned and the name was reassigned to this purchased frigate.

    Dimensions & tons: 86ft 0in x 22ft 6in x 8ft 0in (27.94 x 7.31 x 2.60m). 130/200 tons. Draught 10½ft (3.41m). Men: 130 in war, 60 peace, +2 officers; from 1710, 120 in war, 50 peace.

    Guns: 28 in war (20 peace): LD 4 x 6pdrs; UD 20 x 4pdrs; QD 4 x 2pdrs. From 1709, the 2pdrs and 2 x 4pdrs were removed leaving just 22 guns.

Naïade St Malo.
    Struck at Dunkirk 1710.

HERMIONE. Two-decked type, designed and built by Desjumeaux.
    Dimensions & tons: 113ft 9in x 30ft 11in x 10ft 9in (36.95 x 10.04 x 3.49m). 400 tons. Draught 14½ft/15½ft (4.71/5.04m). Men: 210 in war, 150 peace, +5 officers.

    Guns: 34 in war (30 peace): LD 22 x 8pdrs; UD 12 x 6pdrs.

Hermione Bayonne.
    K: 5.1706. L: 10.1706. C: 12.1706. Wrecked in the Caribbean 2.1707.

VALEUR. Two-decked type, designed and built by Desjumeaux, similar to but slightly larger than the *Hermione*.

    Dimensions & tons: 114ft 0in x 31ft 0in x 11ft 8in (37.03 x 10.07 x 3.79m). 410/478 tons. Draught 14½ft/15½ft (4.71/5.04m). Men: 210 in war, 150 peace, +5 officers.

    Guns: 34 in war (30 peace): LD 22 x 8pdrs; UD 12 x 6pdrs. From 1712 an additional 8 x 6pdrs were mounted, giving her 42 guns.

Valeur Bayonne.
    K: 5.1706. L: 11.1707. C: 3.1708. Lent as a privateer in 1709–10 to CFL Jean-François Du Clerc, as part of a squadron of four vessels for operations off the Brazilian coast. Struck at Rochefort 1719–20.

Blaise Pangalo's 40-gun two-decker *Amazone* was initially listed as a *frégate légère* in 1707 and 1708 but was re-classed more appropriately as a 4th Rank ship later in 1708 less than a year after her completion. She is listed in Chapter 4.

ASTRÉE. *Demi-batterie* type, designed and built by Blaise Pangalo for privateering at the request of CV René Duguay-Trouin, who funded the construction.

    Dimensions & tons: 94ft 0in x 26ft 0in x 10ft 4in (30.53 x 8.45 x 3.36m). 250 tons. Draught 12ft/13ft (3.90/4.22m). Men: 140 in war, 110 peace, +5 officers.

    Guns: 24 in war (20 peace): LD 4 x 6pdrs; UD 20 x 4pdrs. 26 from 1715: LD 6 x 6pdrs; UD 20 x 6pdrs.

Astrée Brest Dyd.
    K: 12.1706. L: 3.5.1707. C: 6.1707. Lent as a privateer to CV René Duguay-Trouin in 1707–9, as part of a squadron on six vessels; then lent as a privateer/slaver to the *Compagnie de l'Asiento* 1709. Lent again as a privateer in 1711–12 to CV René Duguay-Trouin, as part of a squadron of thirteen vessels; took part in the capture of Rio de Janeiro 9.1711. Lost at Barcelona 1.1719.

Ex-BRITISH MERCHANT PRIZES (1705–1707). Three British merchant vessels were added into the French Navy. The East Indiaman *Upton Galley* (built 1701) was captured in 1705 and added as *Upton*. The merchantman *Haston* was captured in early 1707 and added under the same name, and the *Jean Galley* was taken in April 1707 and added as *Sphère d'Angleterre*.

Upton England.
    Dimensions & tons: 86ft 6in x 24ft 0in x 9ft 10in (28.10 x 7.80 x 3.19m). 150 tons. Draught 9ft (2.92m). Men: 80 in war, 40 peace.
    Guns: 20 in war (18 peace): UD 16 x 4pdrs; QD 4 x 2pdrs.
    Captured by the Dutch 6.1706.

Haston England.
    Dimensions & tons: 70ft 0in x 18ft 9in x 8ft 8in (22.74 x 6.09 x 2.82m). 150 tons. Men: 100 in war, 40 peace.
    Guns: 6 in war (4 peace): 6 x 4pdrs.
    Struck at Toulon 1708.

Sphère d'Angleterre Jersey.
    Dimensions & tons: 71ft 6in x 20ft 6in x 7ft 6in (23.23 x 6.66 x 2.44m). 129 tons. Draught 9ft (2.92m). Men: 80 in war, 70 peace, +2/3 officers.
    Guns: 16 in war (12 peace); 16 x 3pdrs (replaced from 1715 by 14 x 4pdrs).
    Name shortened to *Sphère* in early 1717. On harbour service as a storeship (*gabarre pontée*) 1737 at Rochefort but again listed as a *frégate légère* in 1738. Removed from service 1.1741.

Ex-BRITISH NAVAL PRIZES (1706–1707). 24 guns. Two British Sixth Rates were captured and added into the French Navy. The *Squirrel* was captured by six French privateers off the Goodwins on 18 July 1706 and added as *Écureuil* (an earlier *Squirrel*, built in 1703, was similarly captured by five French privateers off Hythe on 1 October 1703, but does not seem to have been commissioned by the French Navy). Her half-sister *Nightingale* was captured by six French privateer galleys off Harwich on 6 September 1707 and added as *Rossignol*.

Écureuil Portsmouth Dyd.
    Dimensions & tons: 92ft 0in x 23ft 0in x 9ft 0in (29.89 x 7.47 x 2.92m). 130/260 tons. Draught 10½ft/11½ft (3.41/3.74m). Men: 100 in war (120 by 1709), 50 peace.
    Guns: 26 in war: UD 20 x 6pdrs; QD 6 x 3pdrs.
    L: 10.1704. Employed in CdE Claude, Comte de Forbin's attempt on Scotland in 1707–8, but recaptured and then foundered 25.3.1708. Note the *Écureuil* lent as a privateer in 1709–10 to citizens of Dunkirk (under the command of Louis Le Mel) was a different vessel.

Rossignol Chatham Dyd.
    Dimensions & tons: 91ft 0in x 23ft 0in x 10ft 0in (29.56 x 7.47 x 3.25m). 150/251 tons. Draught 9ft (2.92m). Men: 180 in war.
    Guns: 24 in war: UD 24 x 6pdrs; QD 4 x 4pdrs.
    L: 16.12.1702. Employed in CdE Claude, Comte de Forbin's attempt

LIGHT FRIGATES

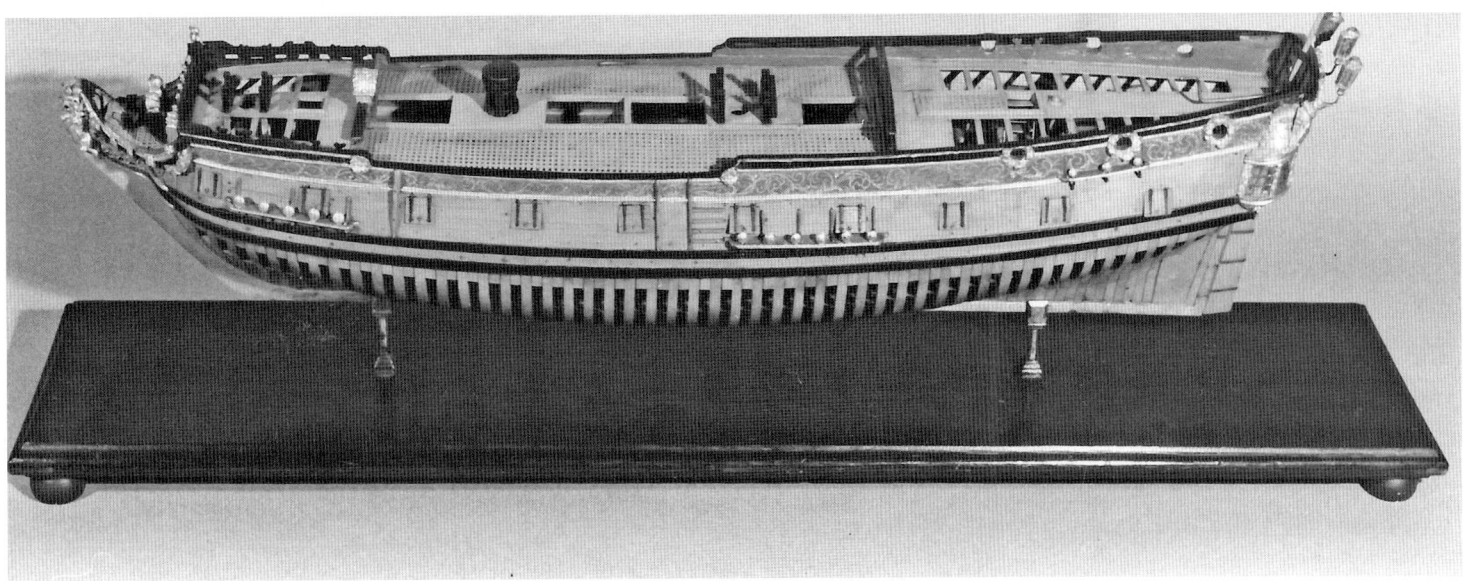

During Louis XIV's naval wars the British Navy suffered heavily in single-ship and squadron actions as a result of boarding. This tactic was encouraged by large French crews, which gave even privateers a good chance of success against small warships. So seriously was the problem perceived in Britain that specific countermeasures were introduced in the design of cruisers, chief of which was a spar deck over the main battery. This was intended to prevent a boarding party gaining easy access to the upper deck, allowing the gun crews to keep firing while the hand-to-hand combat went on over their heads. This model, now in the Thomson collection in the Art Gallery of Ontario, shows the feature clearly, and probably represents the *Nightingale* of 1702. The questionable efficacy of this measure can be judged by the fact that the ship was captured by six privateer galleys (large rowing boats rather than Mediterranean-style war galleys), a fate repeating that of her sister *Squirrel*.

on Scotland in 1707–8, and recaptured on her way back 10.1.1708 off Dunkirk by HMS *Ludlow Castle*, and renamed HMS *Fox* in same month; BU 3.1724 at Deptford.

FLORE. 4pdr-armed type, designed and built by Philippe Cochois.
  Dimensions & tons: 71ft 0in x 19ft 6in x 7ft 6in (23.06 x 6.33 x 2.44m). 90 tons. Draught 8ft/8½ft (2.60/2.76m). Men: 110 in war, 110 peace, +5 officers.
  Guns: 10 in war (6 peace): UD 10 x 4pdrs.
Flore Le Havre.
  K: 12.1707. L: 20.3.1708. C: 6.1708. Employed (with *Amarante*) to protect ships carrying grain to Le Havre in 1709. Struck 1724 at Brest.

AMARANTE. 4pdr-armed type, designed and built by Philippe Cochois alongside the *Flore*.
  Dimensions & tons: 75ft 0in x 21ft 0in x 7ft 6in (24.36 x 6.82 x 2.44m). 100 tons. Draught 9ft (2.92m). Men: 120 in war, 110 peace, +5 officers.
  Guns: 14 in war (6 peace): UD 14 x 4pdrs. From 1710 carried one fewer pair of 4pdrs, leaving 12 guns.
Amarante Le Havre.
  K: 12.1707. L: 20.3.1708. C: 6.1708. Employed (with *Flore*) to protect ships carrying grain to Le Havre in 1709. Struck 1724 at Brest.

HERMIONE. Designed by Desjumeaux, the third of the 34-gun vessels built by him at Bayonne, and a replacement for the previous vessel of the same name, lost in 1707.
  Dimensions & tons: 120ft 0in x 30ft 0in x 13ft 2in (38.98 x 9.75 x 4.28m). 450 tons. Men: 230 in war, 150 peace.
  Guns: 34 in war (30 peace): LD 22 x 8pdrs; UD 12 x 6pdrs.
Hermione Bayonne.
  K: early 1708. L: 1708. C: end 1709. Sold 6.1710 for commerce; recovered in 1713, and in 3–6.1714 served with the naval squadron off Barcelona, then transferred to the Spanish Navy as *Hermiona* (and burned by the British at Messina 9.1719).

GALATÉE. 6pdr-armed type, designed and built by Philippe Cochois. Named 28 June 1708 while building.
  Dimensions & tons: 106ft 0in x 28ft 0in x 11ft 0in (34.43 x 9.10 x 3.57m). 150 tons. Draught 13ft/14ft (4.22/4.55m). Men: 220 in war, 120 peace, +2 officers.
  Guns: 28 in war (22 peace): LD 22 x 6pdrs; QD 6 x 4pdrs (replaced 1710 by 12 x 3pdrs).
Galatée Le Havre.
  K: 5.1708. L: 16.8.1708. C: 10.1708. Captured by the British in the Caribbean 2.1712.

VOLANTE or **FREGATE DU ROI.** This vessel was purchased at St Domingue for the King's service in about May 1708 and was wrecked there in the following July. No details are recorded.

Ex-BRITISH PRIZE (1709). 4pdr-armed type. A small English vessel of unknown identity (not naval) was fitted as a *frégate légère* after capture in 1709 and renamed *René*.
  Dimensions & tons: 77ft 0in x 21ft 0in x 10ft 6in (25.01 x 6.82 x 3.41m). 100 tons. Draught 11ft (3.57m). Men: 60 in war, 50 peace, +4 officers.
  Guns: 10 in war (8 peace): UD 8 x 4pdrs; QD 2 x 3pdrs.
René unknown
  Employed to transport alcohol in Brittany 1711–12. Struck in 1713 at Brest.

ACIS. This 'small frigate' was begun at Brest 1710 and launched in January 1711. She capsized and sank on 28 January 1711 during her first day of sailing trials after completing construction. Her commander,

EV de La Boularderie, had invited local notables aboard for the day, and after a pleasant cruise with a light breeze the ship was returning to her moorings in the evening when her lights disappeared. Most on board were drowned. A commentator felt that the loss could only be attributed to a complete lack of stability. No technical details of the ship have been found.

AMITIÉ and ***MERCURE VOLANTE***. Two vessels were recorded in 1710 and 1711 as *frégates légères*, but their origins and other details are unknown. One was the *Amitié*, put into service at Le Havre in October 1710; she was lent as a privateer to citizens of Le Havre and placed under the command of LFL Louis Chauval de Jonval, who was killed in combat when she was captured by the Flemish in 1711. The other was the *Mercure Volante*, listed as commissioned at Toulon in March 1711 but not further reported. She may have become the fireship *Aigle Volant*.

PAON. 24/18 guns. The *Paon* captured from the Dutch in 1705 (see above) was reconstructed and enlarged in 1711–12 at Brest, then in 1720 at Rochefort. She had originally been good under sail but was mediocre as rebuilt.

 Dimensions & tons: 86ft 0in, 74ft 0in x 23ft 7in x 9ft 6in (27.94, 24.04 x 7.66 x 3.09m). 197 tons. Draught 10½ft/12½ft (3.41/4.06m). Men 120, +5 officers.

 Guns: 24 in war (18 peace): 18 x 6pdrs, 6 x 3pdrs (3pdrs removed by 1715). 16 from 1729: 16 x 6pdrs.

Paon Flushing, rebuilt at Brest
 Hulked 1735 as guard ship at Rochefort. BU 1744.

Ex-BRITISH PRIZE (1711). 4pdr-armed type. The *Concord*, an English vessel of unknown identity (not naval), was captured by *Élisabeth* and *Hampton* of CV Gilles Des Nos, Comte de Champmeslin's squadron in 1711, fitted as a *frégate légère* for the King's service and renamed *Concorde*.

 Dimensions & tons: 97ft 0in x 23ft 0in x 12ft 0in (31.51 x 7.475 x 3.90m). 250/400 tons. Draught 12½ft (4.06m). Men: 130 in war, 100 peace, +5 officers.

 Guns: 14 in war and peace: 14 x 4pdrs.

Concorde unknown
 Handed over to CV René Duguay-Trouin 1711. Under command of his cousin Nicolas Pradel de Daniel, she was loaded with barrels of water to support the squadron sailing to South America. When the force left Rio de Janeiro, *Concorde* was fitted as a *flûte*, and in company with a Portuguese prize, *Notre Dame de l'Incarnation*, loaded with merchandise for trade and sent to the South Sea. After deployment to the Pacific, she was converted to a slaver and used for commerce until sold in 1713 in Chile or Peru. She was re-acquired by the French in November 1716, then sold again in March 1717. She was then acquired in November 1717 by the piratical Edward Teach, becoming his notorious *Queen Anne's Revenge*.

COSSE D'ANGÉLIQUE. 4pdr-armed type, designed and built by Philippe Cochois (who died in office on 5 March 1715, having designed and built a number of *frégates légères* at Le Havre over 20 years). Her original name was also rendered as *Cosse de l'Angélique*.

 Dimensions & tons: 79ft 0in x 22ft 6in x 9ft 0in (25.67 x 7.31 x 2.92m). 133 tons. Draught 10ft (3.25m).

 Men: 130 in war, 80 peace, +5 officers.

 Guns: 16 in war (8 peace): UD 16 x 4pdrs.

Cosse d'Angélique Le Havre.
 K: 7.1714. L: 1715. C: 8.1717. Name shortened to *Angélique* in early 1718. Sold at Brest 9.1718.

(D) 6pdr-armed *frégates légères* acquired from 1 September 1715

As at September 1715, the French Navy included thirteen vessels listed as *frégates légères*. These comprised nine built in France – the *Aurore* (launched in 1697), *Nymphe* (1702), *Fortune* (1704), *Victoire* (1704), *Flore* (1707), *Astrée* (1707), *Valeur* (1707), *Amarante* (1708) and *Cosse d'Angélique* (1715) – and four taken from the British and Dutch – the *Nieuport* (taken in 1696), *Cavalier de Flessingue* (1703), *Paon* (1705) and *Sphère d'Angleterre* (1707). Details of all thirteen appear in the previous section.

Six of them – the *Fortune*, *Flore*, *Amarante*, *Cosse d'Angélique*, *Cavalier de Flessingue* and *Sphère d'Angleterre* – were armed with 4pdr batteries and, while listed above, should thus be better considered as 'corvettes', while the two-decked *Valeur* mounted 8pdrs in her battery; the other six were 6pdr-armed frigates. The *Nieuport* and *Cavalier de Flessingue* were struck before the end of 1716, the *Cosse d'Angélique* during 1717, and the *Aurore*, *Nymphe*, *Astrée* and *Valeur* within the next six years.

The construction of *frégates légères* restarted in 1722 with three vessels constructed by Jacques Poirier at Le Havre, followed by two 8pdr-armed vessels in 1727 at Toulon and Brest. In principle, the classification of *frégates légères* continued until 1746. However, in order to cover the development of 8pdr-armed 'true' frigates from their origin in 1740 with the *Médée*, those ships originally rated as *frégates légères* with 8pdr batteries built from 1740 onwards have been included in Chapter 5; similarly, the post-1715 *frégates légères* with 4pdr batteries have been included with the corvettes in Chapter 6, as this was the category with which they effectively merged.

THÉTIS. *Frégate légère* of 26 (including 20 x 6pdr) guns, designed by René Levasseur and built by Jacques Poirier at Le Havre in the 1720s. Also built by Jacques Poirier alongside the *Thétis* was a smaller vessel, *Méduse*, also listed as a *frégate légère*; however, she was built of deficient material and was taken to pieces in a little more than four years; a replacement was built in 1727 and given the same name; however both vessels were only armed with 4pdrs, and usually considered as corvettes, and both are included in Chapter 10.

 Dimensions & tons: 101ft 0in x 27ft 6in x 10ft 6in (32.81 x 8.93 x 3.41m). 350/500 tons. Draught 13½/15ft (4.4/4.9m). Men: 170 in war, 100 peace, +4 officers.

 Guns: 26 in war (20 peace): UD 20 x 6pdrs; QD 6 x 4pdrs.

Thétis Le Havre.
 K: 3.1722. L: 9.1722. C: 11.1722. Condemned at Toulon 27.10.1729 and BU 1730 by Order of 14.11.1729.

VÉNUS. A slightly enlarged version of the *Thétis*, a *frégate légère* of 26 (20 x 6pdr) guns, designed by René Levasseur and built by Jacques Poirier in the 1720s. The two were the only 6pdr-armed frigates to be built between 1707 and 1740 apart from the 18-gun *Gazelle*.

 Dimensions & tons: 101ft 9in x 27ft 7in x 11ft 9in (33.05 x 8.96 x 3.82m). 350/540 tons. Draught 14/15ft (4.5/4.9m). Men: 170 in war, 100 peace, +4 officers.

 Guns: 26 in war (20 peace): UD 20 x 6pdrs; QD 6 x 4pdrs.

Vénus Le Havre.
 K: 12.1722. L: 10.1723. C: 1.1724. Refitted at Martinique 7.1727–9.1727 while cruising on private account 2.1727–7.1728. Wrecked off Île de Batz 5.1745, decommissioned 6.1745.

Later in this decade, Poirier also built three larger two-decked vessels at Le Havre – *Jason*, *Gloire* and *Rubis* – but these 4th Rank ships appear in Chapter 4.

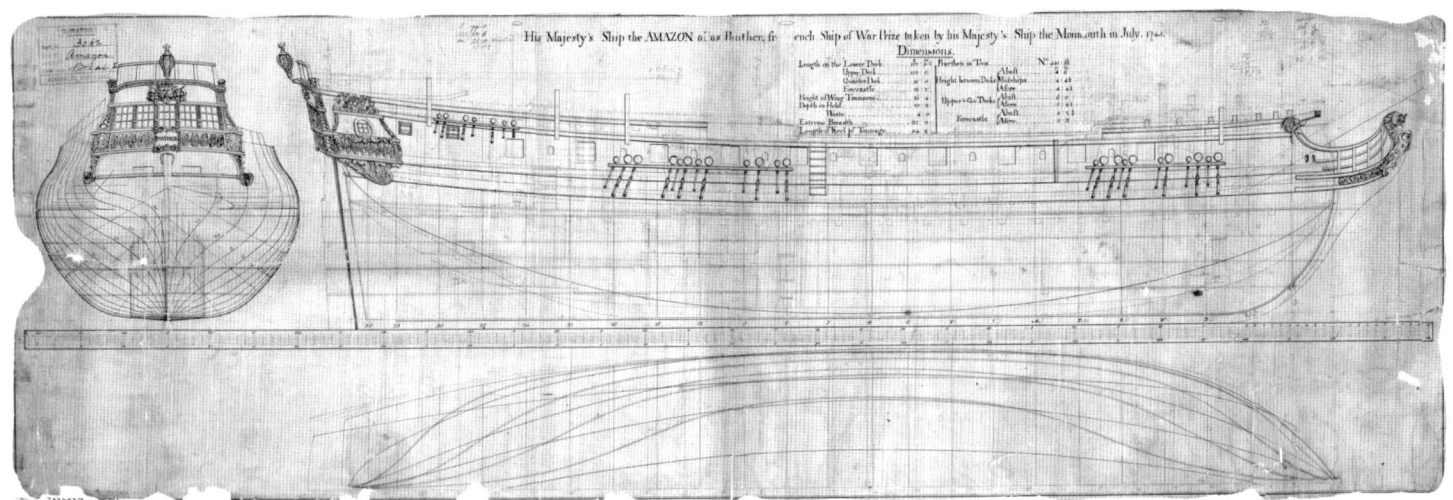

Admiralty draught of *Amazon*, ex-*Panthère*, undated but as captured, with some proposed alterations in pencil. The new frigate-form produced a lower and more weatherly hull, but in the smallest ships it had a major disadvantage in the restricted height between decks – in this ship barely 4½ feet – which made for uncomfortable conditions for the crew. Nevertheless, the underwater hull form was immensely influential in the British Navy, forming the basis for many different types and classes over the next half-century. Significantly, the hull form was not an extreme example of French design practice, lacking hollow in the garboards and a steeply rising floor. (National Maritime Museum, London J4236)

GAZELLE. 6pdr-armed type, designed and built by Jacques Poirier. Used as a test vehicle by the designer Pierre Bourger to evaluate his concept of devising the metacentre of a vessel.

Dimensions & tons: 90ft 0in x 25ft 6in x 11ft 0in (29.24 x 8.28 x 3.57m). 150/386 tons. Draught 12ft/13½ft (3.90/4.39m). Men 130 in war, 100 peace.

Guns: 18 in war (14 peace): UD 18 x 6pdrs; QD nil.

Gazelle Le Havre.

K: 5.1732. L: 9–10.1733. C: 1.1734. Hulked at Brest 1745 and BU 1748.

Three small *frégates légères* armed with 4pdr guns, the *Levrette*, *Fée* and *Vipère*, were built at Rochefort around 1734. Like the *Méduse* mentioned above, these are included in Chapter 10. Two similar vessels, the *Naïade* and *Dryade*, were built at the same time at Le Havre and classed as corvettes; of these *Dryade* was listed as a *frégate légère* from 1739 to 1743.

VICTOIRE. Rebuilding of the frigate of 1704 (see Section C above) by Blaise Geslain.

Dimensions & tons: 100ft 0in x 27ft 0in x 10ft 11in (32.48 x 8.77 x 3.55m). 280/500 tons. Draught 12ft/13ft (3.90/4.22m). Men 160 in war, 120 peace.

Guns: 34 in war (24 peace): UD 22 x 6pdrs; QD 12 x 4pdrs. The 4pdrs were not listed after 1739, when she may also have carried only 20 x 6pdrs.

Victoire Rochefort Dyd.

K: 1736. L: 1737. C: 1.1737. Condemned 1743 at Rochefort and BU.

SUBTILE. 6pdr-armed type, designed and building commenced by Jacques Poirier (who died in November 1740 soon after the ship was begun); completed by Venard.

Dimensions & tons: 102ft 0in x 28ft 0in x 12ft 6in (33.13 x 9.10 x 4.06m). 320/600 tons. Draught 14ft (4.55m). Men: 150 in war (later 200), 80 peace, +4 officers.

Guns: 20 in war and peace: UD 20 x 6pdrs; QD nil.

Subtile Le Havre.

K: 9.1740. L: 7.1741. C: 10.1741. Captured 19.11.1746 by HMS *Portland*, but not added to British Navy; deleted 3.1747.

PANTHÈRE. 6pdr-armed type, designed and built by Jacques-Luc Coulomb. Ordered on 2.1743 and named on 3.1743. Almost the first of the new frigate-form ships to be captured by the British (the 8pdr-armed *Médée* had been taken in 1744), her low weatherly hull and fast lines were copied by the British designers for many years, but *Panthère* herself proved too wet and lightly built until she underwent refits in 1748 and 1753.

Dimensions & tons: 108ft 0in, 96ft 0in x 28ft 6in x 14ft 2in (35.08, 31.18 x 9.26 x 4.60m). 400/694 tons. Draught 10½ft/11ft 10in (3.41/3.84m). Men: probably as *Galatée* Class (180 in war, 140 peace, +4/5 officers).

Guns: 26 in war (20 peace): UD 20 x 6pdrs; QD 4 x 4pdrs.

Panthère Brest Dyd.

K: 4.1743. L: 2.1744. C: 5.1744. Captured by HMS *Monmouth* in the Channel 6.4.1745, becoming HMS *Amazon* 24.8.1745 (4.9.1745 New Style); sold 10.1763.

GALATÉE Class. 6pdr-armed type, designed by Jean Geoffroy, and built by Pierre Salinoc and Mathurin-Louis Geoffroy respectively. Almost the final frigates to be built with a 6pdr battery. The pair formed a flying squadron in 1747 to protect the coast, where together they captured on 21 June 1747 the East Indiaman *Duke of Cumberland*; this ship was added to the French Navy as the frigate *Cumberland* (see below).

Dimensions & tons: 110ft 0in x 29ft 0in x 14ft 6in (35.73 x 9.42 x 4.71m). 380/700 tons. Draught 11¼ft/13ft (3.63/4.22m). Men: 180 in war, 140 peace, +4/5 officers.

Guns: 24 in war (20 peace): UD 24 x 6pdrs.

Galatée Brest Dyd.

K: 2.1744. L: 13.9.1744. C: 4.1745. Captured by HM Ships *Essex* and *Pluto* off the Gironde 7.4.1758, but not added to British Navy.

Mutine Brest Dyd.

K: 3.1744. L: 16.10.1744. C: 3.1745. Damaged in collision with *Raisonnable* (64) while escorting a convoy to Canada 3.1758,

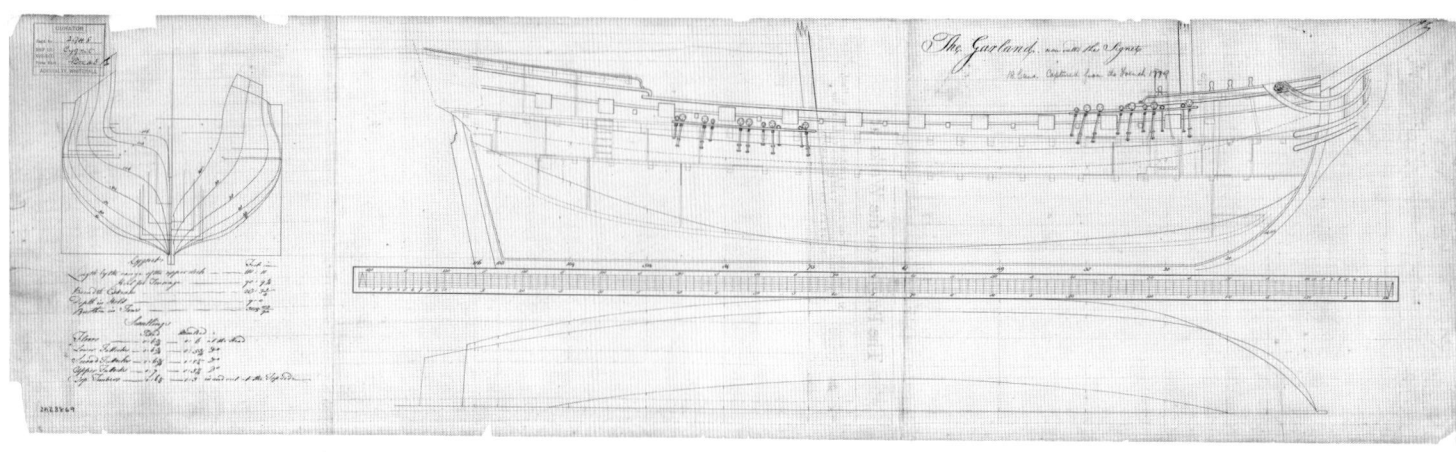

Admiralty draught of 'The *Garland* [*Guirlande*], now called the *Signet* [*Cygnet*]'. The basic scantlings of this ship, built to serve at the Île d'Aix, are listed but not any spar dimensions so it is unclear what sort of two-masted rig the ship carried. In Royal Navy service *Cygnet* became a sloop, although she had been rated a frigate. This latter designation may have been a reflection of the complete unarmed lower deck. The very sharp lines, with the steep deadrise in the midship section, suggest a design aiming at very high speed. (National Maritime Museum, London J4161)

diverted to Martinique where she was declared unrepairable 5.1758 and sent back to Rochefort.

Only six small frigates with 6pdr guns were added after 1746, as construction was concentrated on frigates with 8pdr and (from 1748) 12pdr guns. Following the Seven Years' War, a royal decision in 1763 introduced the calibre of 6pdr guns to the ranks of the corvette; further frigate-type vessels of this calibre will thus be found in Chapter 10.

GUIRLANDE. Small 6pdr-armed type, designed and built by Pierre Salinoc as a two-masted vessel to serve at the Île d'Aix, but rated as a *frégate*.
Dimensions & tons: 105ft 0in, 83ft 6in x 26ft 8in x 8ft 6in (34.11, 27.12 x 8.66 x 2.76m). /500 tons. Men: 195 in war, 170 peace, +9/12 officers.
Guns: UD 18 x 6pdrs; QD 4 x 4pdrs.
Guirlande Brest Dyd.
K: 2.1756. L: 1.1757. C: 2.1757. Captured by HM Ships *Rochester* and *Renown* off Alderney in the Channel Islands 29.6.1758, becoming HMS *Cygnet* (rated sloop); sold 26.7.1768 in South Carolina.

TERPSICHORE. 6pdr-armed type, built by Jacques & Daniel Denys for commerce, but purchased on the stocks in February 1758 by the French Navy.
Dimensions & tons: 110ft 0in x 29ft 0in x 13ft 5in (35.73 x 9.42 x 4.36m). 300/600 tons. Men: 100 in war.
Guns: UD 22 x 6pdrs; QD 6 x 3pdrs.
Terpsichore Dunkirk.
K: 1757. L: 6.1758. C: 10.1758. Captured by HM Ships *Aeolus*, *Pallas* and *Brilliant* off the Isle of Man 28.2.1760, becoming HMS *Terpsichore*; sold 4.11.1766 at Deptford.

GUIRLANDE. 26 guns. This 6pdr-armed small frigate was built at Nantes as a privateer and purchased by the Navy in November 1761.
Dimensions & tons: unknown.
Guns: 26 (22 on the UD and 4 on the QD);
Guirlande Nantes.
K: 1759. L: 1760. C: 1762. Captured 18.8.1762 by HM Ships *Rochester* and *Maidstone* off Alderney (in the Channel Islands), but not added to British Navy.

ÉTOURDIE. 20 guns. Like *Guirlande*, above, this 6pdr-armed small frigate was built at Nantes as a privateer and purchased by the Navy in November 1761.
Dimensions & tons: 107ft 0in x 26ft 0in x 13ft 4in (34.76 x 8.45 x 4.33m). 320/550 tons. Draught 10¼ft/11¾ft (3.33/3.82m). Men: 120 in war, 100 peace, +7 officers.
Guns: 20: UD 16 x 6pdrs; QD 4 x 6pdrs or 4pdrs.
Étourdie Nantes.
K: early 1761. L: 1.1762. C: 2.1762. Re-classed as a corvette 5.1768. Wrecked 1.1783 off the Île de Sein.

Ex-BRITISH PRIVATEER (1762). The small frigate, effectively a corvette (and so re-classed in May 1768), changed hands several times, and it is uncertain whether she was originally built in Britain or France, but was probably built at St Malo in 1754. As the 26-gun British privateer *Biche*, she was (re?)captured in October 1762 and put into service with the French Navy under the same name.
Dimensions & tons: 102ft 0in x 26ft 0in (33.13 x 8.45m). 290 tons. Men: 140 in war, 120 peace.
Guns: UD 22 x 6pdrs; QD 4 x 4pdrs.
Biche St Malo (probably)
Condemned and struck at Brest in 1774.

BAYONNAISE. 6pdr-armed type, built by Pierre & Dominique Gassies. Funded by the City of Bayonne (the only frigate to be funded under Choiseul's *Don des vaisseaux* initiative) and built at a cost of 95,600 *livres*, but employed as a training ship, and re-armed with just 6 guns.
Dimensions & tons: 100ft 0in, 91ft 0in x 27ft 0in (32.48, 29.56 x 8.77m). 310/550 tons. Draught 11ft (3.57m). Men: unknown.
Guns: UD 22 x 6pdrs; QD 2 x 4pdrs.
Bayonnaise (Bayonnoise) Bayonne.
K: 1762. L: 4.1764. C: 7.1764. Wrecked at St Domingue 8.1765.

(E) 8pdr- and 12pdr-armed *frégates légères* acquired from 1 September 1715

At the start of September 1715, the *Valeur* was the only *frégate légère* armed with 8pdrs. A modest number of additions were made, often with 'demi-batterie' ships carrying a few 8pdrs or 12pdrs on the LD, with a full battery of lighter weapons on the UD, but the type declined with the introduction of the 'true' frigates carrying a complete battery of 8pdrs or 12pdrs on the UD, and with no guns (or ports) on the LD. These new types are covered in Chapters 5 and 4.

ZÉPHYR. *Demi-batterie* type, with 12pdrs on the LD. Designed and built by François Coulomb Jnr. Contracted on 20 May 1727 and named (*Zéphire*) 6.7.1728. Also listed as *Zéphir*.

Dimensions & tons: 115ft 0in x 30ft 6in x 14ft 4in (37.36 x 9.91 x 4.66m). 412/650 tons. Draught 14ft 8in/15½ft (4.76/5.04m). Men: 200 in war, 130 peace, +4/6 officers.

Guns: 28 in war (22 peace): LD 4 x 12pdrs (4 more added from 1746); UD 22 x 8pdrs; QD 2 x 4pdrs.

Zéphyr Toulon Dyd.
K: 6.1727. L: 16.11.1728. C: 15.1.1729. Reconstructed 1754 at Rochefort. Captured 9.1762 off Brest by the British, but not added to RN.

ASTRÉE. 8pdr-armed type, designed and built by Blaise Ollivier and his father, Joseph Ollivier. To a considerable extent, this vessel was the forerunner of the classic 8pdr-armed frigate, with its main battery on the upper deck and with an unarmed lower deck.

Dimensions & tons: 109ft 0in x 29ft 0in x 13ft 0in (35.41 x 8.42 x 4.22m). 412/650 tons. Draught 13ft 10in (4.49m) aft. Men: 190 in war, 160 peace, +4/5 officers.

Guns: 30 in war (22 peace): UD 22 x 8pdrs; QD 8 x 4pdrs.

Astrée Brest Dyd.
K: 7.1727. L: 1.1728. C: 4.1728. Condemned 1741 at Brest, and BU 2.1743.

FLORE. *Demi-batterie* type, with 8pdrs on the LD. Designed and built by Pierre-Blaise Coulomb. Contracted on 20.5.1727 and named on 6.7.1728.

Dimensions & tons: 105ft 0in x 29ft 8in x 13ft 0in (34.11 x 9.64 x 4.22m). 395/750 tons. Draught 13ft/14ft (4.22/4.55m). Men: 200 in war, 130 peace, +4/6 officers.

Guns: 26 in war (18 peace): LD 4 x 8pdrs; UD 22 x 6pdrs.

Flore Toulon Dyd.
K: 7.1727. L: 28.11.1728. C: 1.1729. Hulked 4.1753 at Marseille; condemned 11.1754 and sold commercially 12.1759 or 11.1761, taken by the British 1762.

In September 1740 two new 8pdr-armed *frégates légères* were laid down at Brest and Rochefort. These were of a new type which dispensed with any ordnance on the lower deck; indeed they had no openings at all on this level, which was consequently able to lower the deck to approximately sea level, with a much reduced side profile (and thus improved sailing qualities). These two vessels – Blaise Ollivier's *Médée* and Morineau's *Volage* – initiated the development of the 'true' frigate; the term *frégate légère* was dropped by the close of the decade, and therefore these two vessels and their successors in the 1740s (of which the *Fine*, *Émeraude* and *Embuscade* at Le Havre, the *Sirène* and *Renommée* at Brest, the *Amphitrite* and *Mégère* at Bayonne, the *Friponne* and *Fidèle* at Rochefort, and the *Castor* at Quebec, were all originally classed as *frégates légères*) will be found in Chapter 5, as logical successors to the 5th Rank *frégate-vaisseau*. The *demi-batterie Atalante* and *Diane* in Chapter 4 were also initially classed as *frégates légères*.

EX-BRITISH NAVAL PRIZES (1744). Two British 24-gun Sixth Rates were captured by CE François-César de Vimeur de Rochambeau's squadron during 1744 – the *Seaford* on 27 June off the Tagus and the *Solebay* on 17 August (by the *Saint Michel*) off Cape St Vincent. The former was used as a privateer until she was recaptured in August of the same year. These were two of a dozen Sixth Rates built to the British 1733 Establishment, nominally to a design by Jacob Acworth; they had two widely-spaced pairs of gunports on the lower deck, as well as a 20-gun battery on the upper deck.

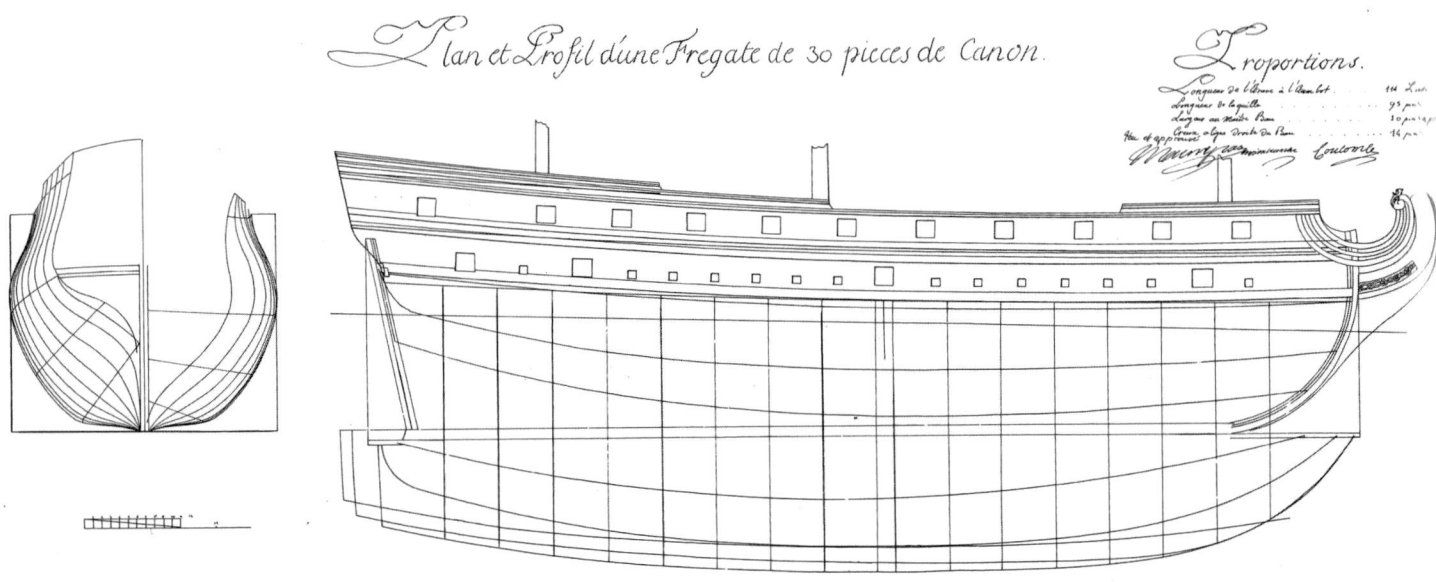

Design draught of the *Pomone*, 30 guns, of 1749. Something of a throwback, this final *demi-batterie* ship was similar in concept to British 24-gun Sixth Rates, which had been much criticised since the early 1740s when the new frigate form had become public knowledge and whose construction was suspended in 1748. It is perhaps more than coincidence that the type was abandoned by the two navies at almost exactly the same time. The small openings in the lower deck are rowing ports. (Toulon Archives)

Dimensions & tons (as re-measured in French units): 104ft 0in, 90ft 0in x 28ft 6in x 10ft 3in (33.78, 29.24 x 9.26 x 3.33m). 250/600 tons. Draught 12ft/13ft (3.90/4.22m). Men: 220 in war, +4/7 officers.

Guns (British): LD 2 x 8pdrs; UD 20 x 8pdrs; QD 6 x 6pdrs.

Seaford Daniel Stow & Benjamin Bartlett, Shoreham.
Ordered 10.6.1740. K: 30.6.1740. L: 6.4.1741. C: 8.7.1741. Retaken 24.8.1744; BU at Woolwich (by Order of 18.7.1754) completed 7.8.1754.

Solebay Digory Veale, Plymouth (by contract).
Ordered 30.6.1740. K: 11.7.1740. L: 20.7.1742. C: 19.8.1742. Retaken by Bristol privateer *Alexander* 20.4.1746; sold at Woolwich 15.3.1763 for commerce.

Ex-BRITISH MERCANTILE PRIZE (1744). The British *Caesar Augustus* was captured in December 1744.

Dimensions & tons: 102ft 0in x 24ft 6in x 11ft 4in (33.13 x 7.96 x 3.68m). 280/530 tons. Draught 13ft (4.22m). Men: 150 in war, +4 officers.

Guns: 30 in war (22 peace): UD 22 x 8pdrs (by 1748, 22 x 4pdrs replaced the 8pdrs); QD 8 x 4pdrs.

César-Auguste Britain.
Condemned 1748 at Brest.

Ex-BRITISH PRIVATEER (1745). The British privateer frigate *Dutchess Theresa* was captured in April 1745.

Dimensions & tons: 81ft 6in x 23ft 0in x 11ft 6in (26.47 x 7.47 x 4.74m). 275/400 tons.

Guns: 20 in war: 4 x 5pdrs; 16 x 4pdrs.

Duchesse Thérèse Britain?
Struck 1747 at Toulon without having been recommissioned by the French.

Ex-BRITISH PRIZE (1747). This was the former East Indiaman *Duke of Cumberland*, mentioned above as captured by *Galatée* and *Mutine* – see Section (D) – on 21 June 1747.

Dimensions & tons: 102ft 0in x 26ft 0in x 13ft 0in (33.13 x 8.45 x 4.22m). 250/550 tons. Draught 11¼ft/13½ft (3.59/4.39m). Men: 180 in war, 110 peace, +4 officers.

Guns: UD 20 x 6pdrs or 8pdrs; QD 4 x 4pdrs or 3pdrs

Cumberland Britain.
L: 1744. Struck 3.1758 at Brest, sold for commerce and renamed *Mars* (lost in the following year).

POMONE. The last *demi-batterie* ship to be ordered in France, and the final *frégate légère* to carry 8pdrs on the LD. Designed and built by François Coulomb Jnr. Ordered on 18 December 1747 and named on 3 January 1748.

Dimensions & tons: 114ft 0in, 95ft 0in x 30ft 4in x 14ft 0in (37.03, 30.86 x 9.85 x 4.55m). 500 tons. Draught 13ft 2in/14ft 2in (4.28/4.60m). Men: 220 in war, 160 peace, +4/8 officers.

Guns: 30 in war: LD 8 x 8pdrs; UD 22 x 6pdrs.

Pomone Toulon Dyd.
K: 1.1748. L: 28.1.1749. C: 1750. Burnt 16.5.1760 after running aground in the St Lawrence to avoid capture by the British.

7 Bomb Vessels and other Coastal Warfare Craft

(Galiotes à mortiers, Galiotes à bombes, Prames, Chaloupes-canonnières, etc)

This chapter groups together vessels whose principal role lay in attack on or the defence of coastal positions. It includes vessels whose primary weapons were sea-based mortars for bombardment of land-based facilities (such as bomb vessels as well as the mortar-carrying *prames* of the Seven Years' War), and smaller craft whose function revolved around coastal encounters, such as gunboats (*chaloupes-canonnières*). These all shared a common feature of being designed to operate in shallow waters or even in inshore locations such as estuaries and bays.

BOMB VESSELS

The idea of using large mortars at sea for high-trajectory bombardment of shore targets originated with CV Bernard Renau d'Élissagaray, a naval officer, engineer and a scientific designer (his concepts were actively supported by Sébastien Le Prestre de Vauban) of Basque origin known as 'Petit Renau' on account of his small stature, who was later appointed in 1691 as the first and only *ingénieur général de la Marine*. His first purpose-built bomb vessels in 1681–82 provided the French Navy with a broad-beamed and stable weapons platform. These vessels, of which five were built initially (with another pair following) were of smaller size than any ranked vessel, but much sturdier construction, based on the Dutch galiote without any upper decks – there was only a platform or false deck built on the keel, in which hollow spaces were formed for receiving the mortars 'as in beds', the beds being a thick layer of earth laid upon a thick timber framework, the whole to absorb the recoil of the mortars. They were rigged as ketches, with no foremast and with a tall mainmast positioned amidships in order to allow unobstructed fire over the bows from the twin mortars, which were mounted side by side, and fixed both in traverse and with high elevation.

The mortars were first tried out in the frigate *Adroit* (then undergoing work at Dunkirk). The French designated these vessels until about 1703 as *galiotes à mortiers*, then usually as *galiotes à bombes*, or simply as *bombardes*. Projecting explosive-packed 'shells', they were considered such a significant innovation that they were added to the official structure of the Navy during 1683, the King fixing their authorised strength at the existing seven units, although an additional three were ordered in the same year.

Their main strategic use was intended to be against the corsair bases of the Barbary coast, particularly Algiers, and the first operation, in July 1682, employed the original five bomb vessels in a squadron also comprising eleven vessels, fifteen galleys, three fireships and support ships, commanded by LG Abraham Duquesne and LG Anne Hilarion de Costentin, Comte de Tourville. The initial firing on 28 July, by the *Foudroyante*, proved disastrous as the projectiles all fell into the sea; in a second attempt by the *Cruelle* – commanded by LV Jean Bernard de Saint-Jean, Baron de Pointis with Petit Renau aboard – a fire ignited aboard and almost caused the vessel's loss. Greater success was achieved in a renewed attempt during the night of 30 August, with 114 projectiles launched into the city. A further night operation on 4/5 September, was equally successful, but poor weather caused Duquesne to retire to Toulon soon after.

After wintering at Toulon, a second attack was made by Duquesne on 26 June 1683 with an enlarged squadron comprising seventeen ships of the line and three frigates, plus seven bomb vessels – Pointis was in command of *Menaçante* – and numerous smaller craft. Beginning at 1am, 90 bombs were launched at Algiers, with a further deluge of 127 bombs during the following night. In retaliation, the Dey ordered Father Jean Le Vacher, the French consul, to be tied at the muzzle of a large gun known as *Baba Mersoug* (the Lucky Father) and fired it. The gun was seized when Algiers was captured in 1830 and now stands as a memorial column in Brest dockyard. Further bombardment by the squadron took place on 21 July and 18 August, after which Duquesne, now short of projectiles (10,200 had been launched), retired to Toulon, leaving Tourville to maintain the blockade for several more weeks.

During 1684, the new weapon was deployed against the Republic of Genoa, officially because Genoa was supporting Spain against France in the brief War of the Reunions but also because Genoa was a commercial and political rival to France in the Mediterranean. A fleet under Tourville (Duquesne, although present, having declined to command the naval forces) attacked the city and port of Genoa on 18 May, with thirteen warships and all ten of the bomb vessels; a bombardment was continued until 28 May, launching 3,000 bombs and destroying three-quarters of the city. Promoted *capitaine de galiote et d'artillerie* and *commissaire ordinaire de l'artillerie*, Pointis, then Tourville's adviser, was wounded.

A new operation was mounted in June 1685, this time against the town of Tripoli, a major base of the Barbary Corsairs. This operation, under the command of *Vice-amiral* Jean, Comte d'Estrées, saw a bombardment commence at 10pm on 22 June, with the fire from five bomb vessels directed by Tourville. Over 500 bombs were launched against the town during that night, with more following the next night. A third attack on Algiers took place in June 1688, again under the command of d'Estrées, employing all ten existing bomb vessels; over the course of 16 days, over 20,000 bombs were launched against the city by the bomb vessels.

By now the new concept was being copied by the English Navy, which built its own prototype bomb vessels in 1687. They may initially have intended to use their bomb ketches in combat against vessels, as indicated by the presence of *Firedrake* under the command of Cdr John Leake, the son of the Master Gunner of England, at the Battle of Bantry Bay, in 1689. In an attempt to increase firepower, the French fitted a new design of 18in mortar into two vessels in May 1688, able to launch 500-pound projectiles, but these proved too powerful for the structures and were removed on 6 July.

(B) Vessels acquired from 9 March 1661

***FOUDROYANTE* Class**. *Galiotes à mortiers*, ordered in late 1681. Designed by 'Petit' Renau (who was moved to Dunkirk in January 1682 for the purpose) and built by Hendryck Houwens. They both departed Dunkirk 26 May 1682 (with the three *Brûlante* class) for Brest and then to Algiers, which they bombarded from 28 July. The mortars for this class were first tested on the hoy *Dunkerquoise* (see Chapter 13).

Dimensions & tons: 70ft 0in, 60ft 0in x 24ft 0in x 11ft 6in (22.74,

In 1682 Edmund Dummer, a rising star among English shipwrights who was to become Surveyor of the Navy in 1692, was sent on an industrial espionage mission to the Mediterranean. At Toulon in 1683 he was eyewitness to the preparations by the French to attack Algiers using their new weapons system, the ship-mounted mortar. He understood the full significance of what he had seen, so went to great lengths to obtain details of the *galiotes à mortiers* and the methods of employment. This cutaway is one of the illustrations from his report, *A Voyage into the Mediterranean Seas*, subsequently sumptuously bound and now in the King's Library collection of the British Library.

19.49 x 7.80 x 3.74m). 120 tons. Draught 10ft (3.25m). Men: 40 (15/25/–), +3 officers.

Guns: 4 x 8pdrs, plus 2 x 12in mortars.

Foudroyante Dunkirk.
K: 1.1682. L: 23.2.1682. C: 4.1682. Took part in Bombardments of Algiers 28.7.1682 and 26.6.1683, of Genoa 18–28.5.1684. Hulked at Toulon 1695, and name transferred to a newbuilding *frégate-bombardière*. Sale ordered 24.12.1710.

Bombarde Dunkirk.
K: 1.1682. L: 23.2.1682. C: 4.1682. Took part in Bombardments of Algiers 28.7.1682 and 26.6.1683, of Genoa 18–28.5.1684., and of Tripoli on 22–25.6.1685. Hulked at Toulon 1695. Condemned 15.12.1710, and sale ordered 24.12.1710.

BRÛLANTE Class. *Galiotes à mortiers*, ordered 18 February 1682. Designed and built by Étienne Salicon. They were all sent from Le Havre to Dunkirk on completion, and departed thence 26 May (with *Foudroyante* and *Bombarde*) for Brest and then to Algiers, which they bombarded from 28 July. They were subsequently based at Toulon, with the similar bomb vessels built at that Dyd. The first two returned to Algiers for the bombardment which took place there from 26 June 1683, and all three took part in the Bombardment of Genoa on 18–28 May 1684; *Menaçante* took part in the bombardment of Tripoli on 22–25 June 1685.

Dimensions & tons: 70ft 0in, 63ft 0in x 24ft 0in x 9ft 0in (22.74, 20.46 x 7.80 x 2.92m). 120 tons. Draught 10/11ft (3.25/3.57m). Men: 40 (15/25/–), +3 officers.

Guns: 4 x 8pdrs, plus 2 x 12in mortars.

Brûlante Le Havre.
K: 2.1682. L: 16.3.1682. C: 4.1682. Hulked at Toulon 1695. Sale ordered 28.9.1712.

Cruelle Le Havre.
K: 2.1682. L: 21.3.1682. C: 4.1682. Hulked at Toulon 1695. Sale ordered 28.9.1712.

Menaçante Le Havre.
K: 2.1682. L: 20.3.1682. C: 4.1682. Hulked at Toulon 1695. Sold 7.8.1711.

FULMINANTE Class. *Galiotes à mortiers*. Designed and built by Laurent Coulomb. Both took part in the 2nd Bombardment of Algiers from 26 June 1683, in the Bombardment of Genoa 18–28 May 1684, and *Fulminante* in the Bombardment of Tripoli on 22–25 June 1685.

Dimensions & tons: 75ft 7in, 64ft 0in x 25ft 0in x 10ft 0in (24.55, 20.79 x 14.87 x 3.25m). 140/150 tons. Draught 11ft 0in/11½ft (33.57/3.74m). Men: 39–45 (naval).

Guns: 4 x 6pdrs, plus 2 x 12in mortars.

Fulminante Toulon Dyd.
K: 12.1682. L: 2.1683. C: 4.1683. Out of service at Toulon 3.1713 and condemned 11.1713.

Ardente Toulon Dyd.
K: 12.1682. L: 2.1683. C: 4.1683. Hulked 1714 at Toulon.

Modified *FULMINANTE* Class. *Galiotes à mortiers*. Slightly modified from the *Fulminante* design, drawn and built by Laurent Coulomb. Named in February 1684. *Belliqueuse* was slightly different. Following their completion, all three took part in the Bombardment of Genoa 18–28 May 1684; *Éclatante* and *Terrible* took part in the bombardment of Tripoli on 22–25 June 1685; both were fitted experimentally with an 18in mortar from May to July 1688.

Dimensions & tons: 77ft 0in, 65ft 0in x 25ft 0in x 11ft 0in (25.01 x 8.12 x 2.92m), except *Belliqueuse* 78ft 0in x 24ft 0in x 10ft 0in (25.34 x 7.89 x 3.25m). 140/250 tons. Draught 11ft (3.57m), except *Belliqueuse* 11½ft (3.74m). Men: 39–45 (naval).

Guns: 6 x 4pdrs (mounted under the QD), plus 2 x 12in mortars.

Éclatante Toulon Dyd.
K: 12.1683. L: 16.3.1684. C: 4.1684. Lent as a privateer in 1696–97 to CdE Jean Bernard de Saint-Jean, Baron de Pointis, used as a *galiote à mortiers* in a squadron of fourteen vessels, and took part in the capture of Cartagena de Indias 5.5.1697. No longer seaworthy she was abandoned, officially scuttled but more likely sold.

Terrible Toulon Dyd.
K: 12.1683. L: 20.3.1684. C: 4.1684. Struck 1697 at Brest.

Belliqueuse Toulon Dyd.
K: 12.1683. L: 21.3.1684. C: 5.1684. Out of service at Brest 1.1710, condemned 1.1712.

Another of the illustrations from Dummer report, a plan showing the basic layout of the vessel and the details of the mortars, which were cast into a fixed bed, so they could be neither elevated nor traversed. The detail of the forward section seems to show the mortars toed-inwards, but this is just an exaggeration of the perspective: the mortars were parallel to the keel, positioned abreast on either side of the centreline, and were aimed simply by pointing the ship at the target. The six defensive guns under the quarterdeck suggests the subject is a Modified *Fulminante* Class *galiote*, but these had not been built at the time of Dummer's visit, so either he gained access to plans or the earlier bombs in fact had six gunports despite the established armament of four.

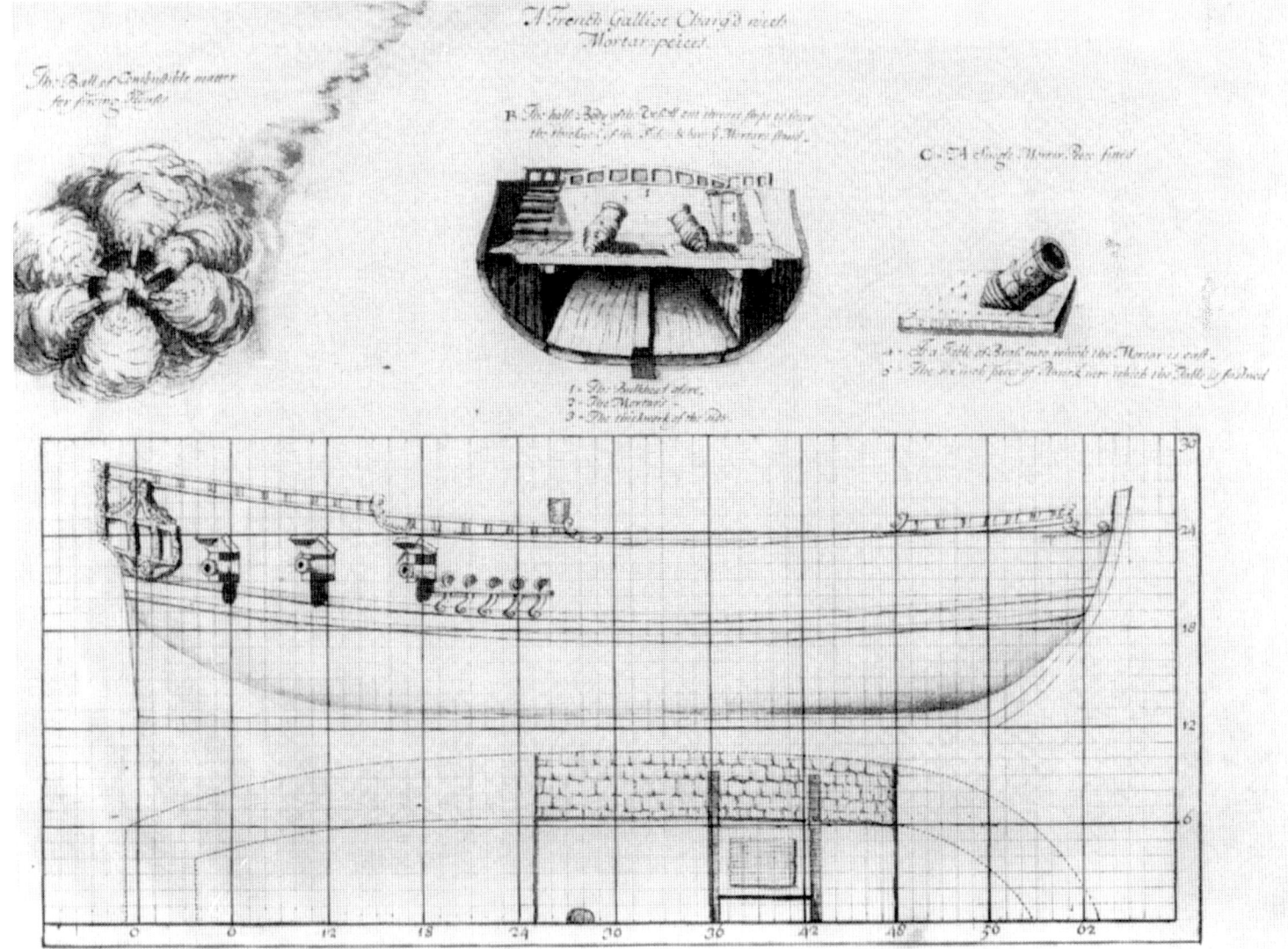

(C) Vessels acquired from 15 April 1689

In 1695 three larger vessels were ordered, to carry a full battery of 8pdrs as well as two mortars. One was captured shortly after completion; but a slightly smaller vessel was built at Toulon in 1696 along similar lines. During 1698 the first two were re-classed as 5th Rank vessels and the smaller vessel (*Salamandre*) as a light frigate.

MARTIALE. *Galiote à mortiers*, or *frégate-bombardière*. Designed and built by Philippe Cochois. A specification of this ship signed by Cochois on 30 April 1695 (when she was probably ordered) shows that at that time she was called a *frégate du 5e rang et du deuxième ordre* and that her quarterdeck was 45ft long, her forecastle 18ft long, and her poop 8ft long. She was designed with 22 gunports in the 1st battery, measuring 2ft 2in square and 6ft 6in apart, plus 4 ports in the 2nd battery that were 1ft 8in square and 6ft 10in apart. As completed she carried additional guns in the 2nd battery. The 1695 document shows no structural features relating to mortars; these may have been added before or during construction. Her masting plan as of 2 December 1695 consisted of the usual three-masted ship rig; she was then still a *frégate* but was listed as a *galiote à mortiers* in the January 1696 *État abrégé*. Re-classed to a 5th Rank ship during 1698, reverted to a *galiote à mortiers* in 1700.

Dimensions & tons: 95ft 0in, 84ft 0in x 27ft 0in x 8ft 0in (30.86, 27.29 x 8.77 x 2.60m). 150/250 tons. Draught 9½ft/10ft (3.09/3.25m). Men: 150 in war, 100 peace in 1696; 180 in war, 150 peace in 1698 (naval).

Guns: 30 in war (22 peace): UD 22 x 8pdrs; QD 8 x 4pdrs. 28 from 1699: UD 12 x 8pdrs + 10 x 6pdrs; QD 6 x 4pdrs (3pdrs from 1701); plus 2 mortars.

Martiale Le Havre.
K: 10.1695. L: 2.1696. C: 4.1696. Refitted as a 5th Rank ship and lent as a privateer in 1702–3 to EV François Du Censiff (then Sieur Du Hérobose) and then to CB Jacques Cochart. Captured 9.8.1703 by HMS *Lichfield* 'by her own fault' according to Louis, Comte de Pontchartrain, Secretary of State of the Navy. Became HMS *Litchfield Prize*; lost 8.12.1703 on the coast of Sussex but salved and put back into service on Newfoundland convoys, finally sold on 4.11.1706, for £150.

FOUDROYANTE. *Galiote à mortiers*, or *frégate-bombardière*. Designed and built by François Le Brun employing Renau's concepts with the use of elliptical lines in the design. Probably rigged as *Martiale*.

Dimensions & tons: 114ft 0in x 28ft 6in x 13ft 3in (37.03 x 9.26 x 4.30m). ?/445 tons. Draught 12ft 9in (4.14m). Men: 150 (naval).

Guns: 30 in war (8 peace): 20 x 8pdrs, + 10 x 4pdrs; plus 2 x 12in mortars.

Foudroyante Port Louis (Lorient)
K: 11.1695. L: 15.2.1696. C: 4.1696. Captured 5.1696, becoming HMS *Thunderbolt*; hulked 1699 and BU 1731 at Plymouth.

BELLONE. *Galiote à mortiers*, or *frégate-bombardière*. Designed and built by Blaise Pangalo. Probably rigged as *Martiale*. Re-classed from a *galiote à mortiers* to a 5th Rank ship in 1698.

Dimensions & tons: 112ft 0in x 28ft 0in x 12ft 7in (36.38 x 9.10 x 4.09m). 340 tons. Draught 13½ft/14½ft (4.39/4.71m). Men: 180 in war (150 peace), +3/6 officers.

Guns: 30 in war (26 peace): 20 x 8pdrs + 10 x 6pdrs; plus 2 x 12in mortars. 36 guns from 1707 (another 6 x 6pdrs added). 38 from 1715: LD 18 x 12pdrs; UD 20 x 6pdrs.

Bellone Brest Dyd.
K: 11.1695. L: 1.1696. C: 3.1696. Refitted as a 5th Rank ship and lent as a privateer in 1696 to LG André, marquis de Nesmond as part of a squadron of six vessels. Lent as a privateer in 1702 with *Railleuse* to CFL René Duguay-Trouin. Lent as a privateer in 1711–12 to CV René Duguay-Trouin as part of a squadron of thirteen vessels and fitted as *galiote à mortiers*, took part in the Capture of Rio de Janeiro 9.1711. Leased to the *Compagnie de l'Asiento* in 1713 for service as a slaver, but not so employed and instead leased to the Duc d'Antin in 1714 as a transport. Condemned end 1715 at Brest. Hulked 1719 at Brest and BU 1741.

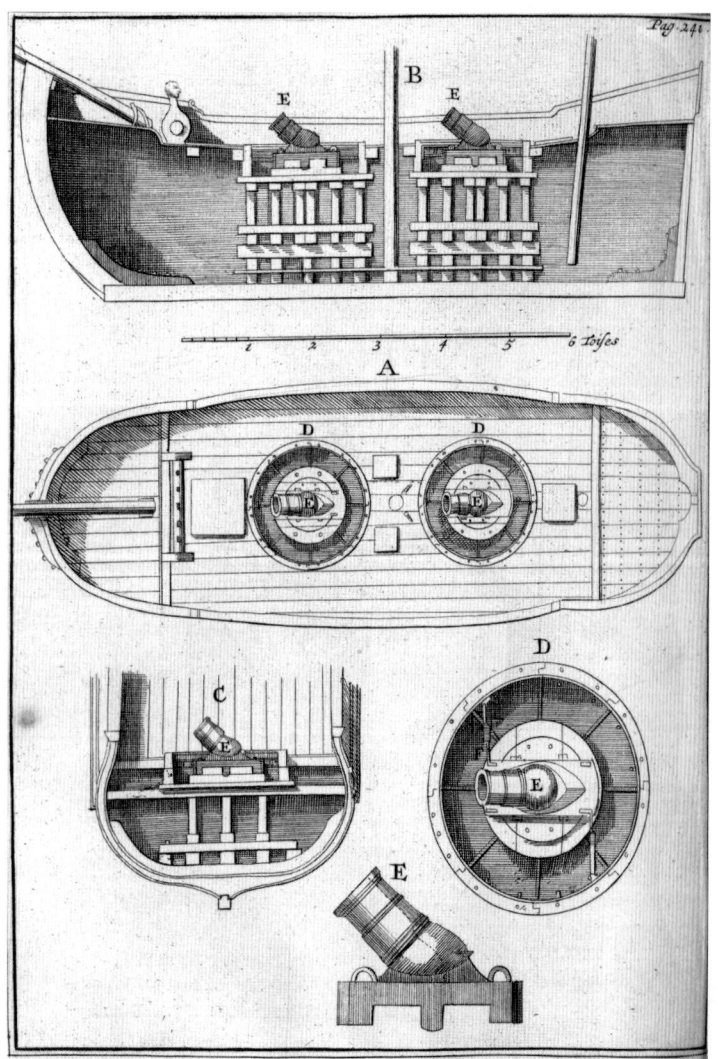

Although invented in France, the bomb vessel's subsequent development was largely English, including the introduction of elevating and traversing mortars on the centreline rather than abreast and, eventually, more seaworthy ship-rigged versions. This drawing is taken from a French treatise, *Mémoires d'Artillerie* by Pierre Suriry de Saint Remy published in 1698, and almost certainly depicts the *Tonnerre*, captured in 1696. Built the previous year as HMS *Thunder*, the vessel shows the first English improvement to the original concept in the form of swivelling mortars (although at this stage they were still of fixed elevation). These developments were a response to the difficulties of operating bomb vessels in the strongly tidal waters of northern Europe – in the almost tideless Mediterranean where the *galiotes* were first employed, it was possible to keep the bomb vessel facing its target with simple moorings, but the first English attacks on the French coast quickly proved that accurate attacks could only be made at slack water. The traversing mortars were intended to allow them to bear on the target while bomb vessel was moored to best stem the tide. (National Maritime Museum, London L2922)

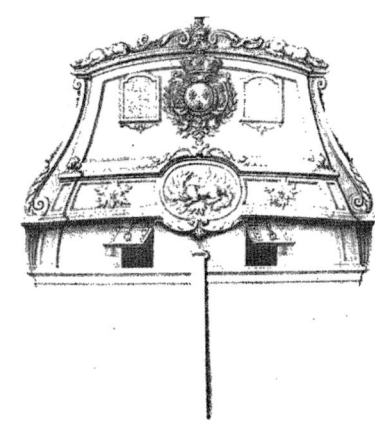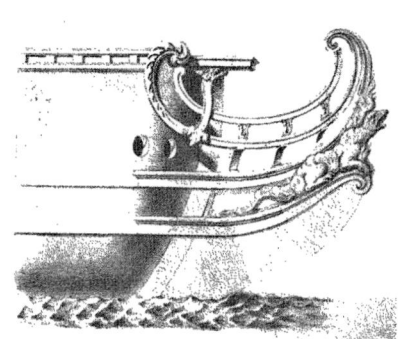

The decorative works of the *Salamandre* of 1696. In Louis XIV's navy even the more utilitarian vessels were thought worthy of carved works, but as a *frégate bombardière* the *Salamandre* was a cut above the usual run of *galiotes à mortiers*. (*Souvenirs de Marine*, Plate 147)

Ex-ENGLISH NAVAL PRIZE (1696). *Galiote à mortiers*. The English bomb vessel HMS *Thunder* was captured by two French privateers off the Dutch coast on 16 April 1696 and added to the French Navy.

Dimensions & tons (as re-measured in French units): 69ft 0in x 24ft 0in x 10ft 0in (22.41 x 7.80 x 3.25m). 80 tons. Draught 8ft (2.60m). Men: 55 in war, 35 peace

Guns: 4 x 2pdrs, + 2 x 12in mortars.

Tonnerre Snelgrove, Limehouse.

Ordered 9.1.1695. K: 1691. L: 13.4.1691. Condemned 1713.

SALAMANDRE. *Galiote à mortiers*, designed by François Coulomb as a *frégate bombardière*. Named on 20 March 1696. Re-classed as a *frégate légère* in 1698, reverted to a *galiote à bombes* in 1704–5.

Dimensions & tons: 95ft 0in, 77ft 6in x 27ft 6in x 12ft 0in (30.86, 25.175 x 8.93 x 3.90). 200 tons. Draught 9½ft/13ft (3.09/4.22m). Men: 100 (naval)

Guns: 20 in war (12 peace) 16 x 12pdrs (6pdrs from 1704), + 4 x 4pdrs; plus 2 mortars.

Salamandre Toulon Dyd.

K: 3.1696. L: 10.1696. C: 12.1696. Out of service 16.1.1709, and sold 26.6.1709 at Toulon.

PROSERPINE. *Galiote à mortiers*, designed by François Coulomb.

Dimensions & tons: 76ft 9in, 65ft 0in x 26ft 0in x 10ft 4in (24.93, 21.11 x 8.45 x 3.25m). 160 tons. Draught 12ft (3.90m)

Guns: 6 x 6pdrs, plus 2 x 12in mortars.

Proserpine Toulon Dyd.

K: 3.1696. L: 10.1696. C: 1697. Condemned 16.1.1717 at Toulon, sold 17.3.1717 and BU 1720.

VULCAIN. *Galiote à mortiers*, designed by François Coulomb, slightly lengthened from the *Proserpine* design.

Dimensions & tons: 78ft 9in, 65ft 0in x 26ft 0in x 10ft 4in (25.58, 21.11 x 8.45 x 3.25m). 170 tons. Draught 12ft (3.90m). Men:

Guns: 6 x 6pdrs, plus 2 x 12in mortars.

Vulcain Toulon Dyd.

K: 3.1696. L: 10.1696. C: 1697. Condemned 23.11.1713 at Toulon, and sold to the Spanish Navy 1715.

Of the bomb vessels existing in 1689, one – *Éclatante* – was employed in 1697 in an attack on the Spanish Caribbean port of Cartagena de Indias, as part of the fleet commanded by CdE Jean Bernard de Saint-Jean, Baron de Pointis. For the transit she received a temporary foremast and its rigging, which was labour intensive and required many sailors to handle. This operation, the closing action of the War of the League of Augsburg, amounted to a raid on the wealthy Caribbean city. For this operation Pointis purchased four 50-ton *traversiers d'Aunis* named *Ester*, *Marie-Anne*, *Saint Pierre* and *Saint Louis* at Port-des-Barques at the mouth of the Charente to be used as landing craft and coastal bomb vessels. Armed with one small mortar and one *pierrier*, they were sailed to the Caribbean by civilian crews comprising a skipper, a *maître de barque*, and three men. On completion of the operation, three *traversiers* were abandoned, officially scuttled but more likely sold. Retained as in better condition, *Saint Louis* was captured on the 9 June by HMS *Warwick*, in company with a *flûte* serving as a hospital ship, the *Maison de Ville d'Amsterdam*, which had an epidemic on board that spread to her captors. Each owner was paid 8,050 *livres* as compensation of the loss of his ship.

Ex-ENGLISH NAVAL PRIZE (1706). *Galiote à mortiers*. The English bomb vessel HMS *Comet* was captured by three French privateers off Dunkirk on 21 October 1706 and added to the French Navy.

Dimensions & tons (as re-measured in French units): 62ft 0in, 56ft 0in x 21ft 9in x 9ft 5in (20.14, 18.19 x 7.07 x 3.06m). 80 tons. Draught unknown.

Guns: 4 x 2pdrs, + 2 x 12in mortars.

Comète Henry Johnson, Blackwall.

Ordered 9.1.1695. K: 1695. L: 23.4.1695. Struck 1709.

Two *traversiers* were purchased at La Rochelle in 1711 for use as bomb vessels by CV Duguay-Trouin for his raid on Rio de Janeiro. They carried one 9-inch mortar or '*deux petits mortiers*' (according to Duguay-Trouin's *Mémoires*) and, under command of a *maître entretenu*, were manned, *Françoise* by 11 sailors and 8 soldiers, and *Patient* by 12 sailors and 10 soldiers. Both *traversiers* were sold in November 1711 before the return voyage to France, one to Sieur Du Bocage, a former French privateer, regarded as a traitor as now serving the King of Portugal.

(D) Vessels acquired from 1 September 1715

Although less frequently deployed after 1715, the bomb vessels saw more operations against ports in North Africa – at Tripoli in 1728 (where 1,752 bombs were expended), at Salé and Larache in Morocco during 1765 (which witnessed 366 and 442 bombs expended respectively), and at Bizerte and Sousse in Tunisia during 1770 (146 and 469 bombs respectively).

This contemporary engraving by Claude Randon shows the main features of French *galiotes à mortiers* of the 1690s. The ketch sail plan minimized the amount of rigging that needed to be dismantled before the mortars could be brought into action. As described by Dummer, 'To defend themselves from galleys they have a half deck and three good pieces of cannon on each side, and in case of other shots between wind and water there is 4 feet thickness of timber, whose heads remain bare and uncovered, evenly cut off with the deck between bulkhead and bulkhead.' Given their initial deployment in the Mediterranean, it is logical that the galley would be seen as the main threat to a stationary bomb vessel.

ARDENTE Class. *Galiotes à bombes*. The first two were ordered on 25 July 1724, with their construction awarded to Sieur Serpolet, but they were built by François Chapelle and François Coulomb Jnr respectively; both named 14 July 1726. A third vessel was approved on 20 May 1727, ordered on 3 September, and built by François Coulomb Jnr; named on 25 December 1727. All three were employed in the attack on Tripoli during July 1728, as part of the squadron under CdE Étienne Nicolas de Grandpré.

BOMB VESSELS AND OTHER COASTAL WARFARE CRAFT

France built very few bomb vessels after 1700. They were only ever useful in wartime, and even then could only be deployed where sea control was assured, for the French a situation that rarely applied in any conflict with a major European sea power, so their use was largely confined to operations against north African states. As a result, there was little development in the design of French *galiotes à bombes*, as demonstrated by this fine model of the *Salamandre* of 1754 by Dr Peter Schoeberl, based on Jean Boudriot's monograph on the vessel. The mortars were located side by side forward of the mainmast under the removable deck beams.

Dimensions & tons: 80ft 0in, 67ft 0in x 25ft 6in x 10ft 11in (25.99, 21.76 x 8.28 x 3.2m). 180/350 tons. Draught 9½ft/11ft (3.9m). Men: 50–70.

Guns: 8 x 6pdrs, + 2 x 12in mortars.

Ardente Toulon Dyd.
  K: 1725. L: 23.7.1726. C: 4.1728. Hulked at Toulon in August 1745 and struck in 1757.

Tempête Toulon Dyd.
  K: 1725. L: 24.8.1726. C: 1727. Struck at Toulon 1786 and ordered to be sold 15.7.1786.

Foudroyante Toulon Dyd.
  K: 9.1727. L: 5.3.1728. C: 5.1728. Captured by a British privateer off Ushant while en route from Toulon to Brest in 2.1746.

SALAMANDRE Class (1734). *Galiotes à bombes*, ordered and named in March 1734. Designed and built by Blaise Ollivier.

  Dimensions & tons: 79ft 9in, 66ft 0in x 29ft 0in x 13ft 0in (25.91, 21.44 x 9.42 x 4.22m). 180/350 tons. Draught (aft) 11ft 2in (3.63m). Men: 60.

  Guns: 8 x 6pdrs, + 2 x 12in mortars.

Salamandre Brest Dyd.
  K: 3.1734. L: 12.1734. C: 1735. Condemned 1746 at Brest and BU 1750.

Tonnante Brest Dyd.
  K: 4.1734. L: 2.1735. C: 1735. Condemned 1746 at Brest and BU 1750.

SALAMANDRE Class (1754). *Galiotes à bombes*. *Salamandre* and *Etna* were ordered on 16 November 1752, the first designed by Joseph-Marie-Blaise Coulomb and the second by François Chapelle. A third order was placed in 1754, but was cancelled in 1756. *Salamander* and *Etna* were both deployed for the bombardments carried out in Morocco in 1765 and in Tunisia in 1770.

  Dimensions & tons: 81ft 0in, 68ft 0in x 25ft 0in x 11ft 2in (26.31, 22.09 x 8.12 x 3.63m). 180/350 tons. Draught 12ft (3.90m). Men: 74 in war, 60 peace, + 6 officers.

  Guns: 8 x 6pdrs, + 2 x 12in mortars.

Salamandre Toulon Dyd.
  K: 5.1753. L: 30.3.1754. C: 8.1754. Struck 1785 at Toulon (not mentioned after 1791).

Etna Toulon Dyd.
  K: 6.1753. L: 13.4.1754. C: 8.1754. Struck 1785 or 1786 at Toulon.

Fournaise Toulon Dyd.
  Ordered 1754, and named 28.7.1754, but cancelled 1756.

TERREUR Class. *Galiotes à bombes*, designed and built by Jacques-Luc Coulomb. Ordered early 1754 and named on 24 May 1754.

  Dimensions & tons: 87ft 4in, 78ft 0in x 25ft 4in x 11ft 2in (28.37, 25.34 x 8.23 x 3.59m). 240/380 tons.

  Guns: 8 x 6pdrs, + 2 x 12in mortars.

Terreur Brest Dyd.
  K: 5.1754. L: 18.9.1755. C: 1756. Struck 1762 at Brest.

Vésuve Brest Dyd.
  K: 5.1754. L: 18.9.1755. C: 1756. Struck 1762 at Brest.

PURCHASED VESSELS (1759). Two hoys (*heux*) purchased at Le Havre and converted to *galiotes à bombes*, each carrying an 8in mortar (no other guns), and a complement of 12 men (10 in *Aimable Mélanie*) plus 1

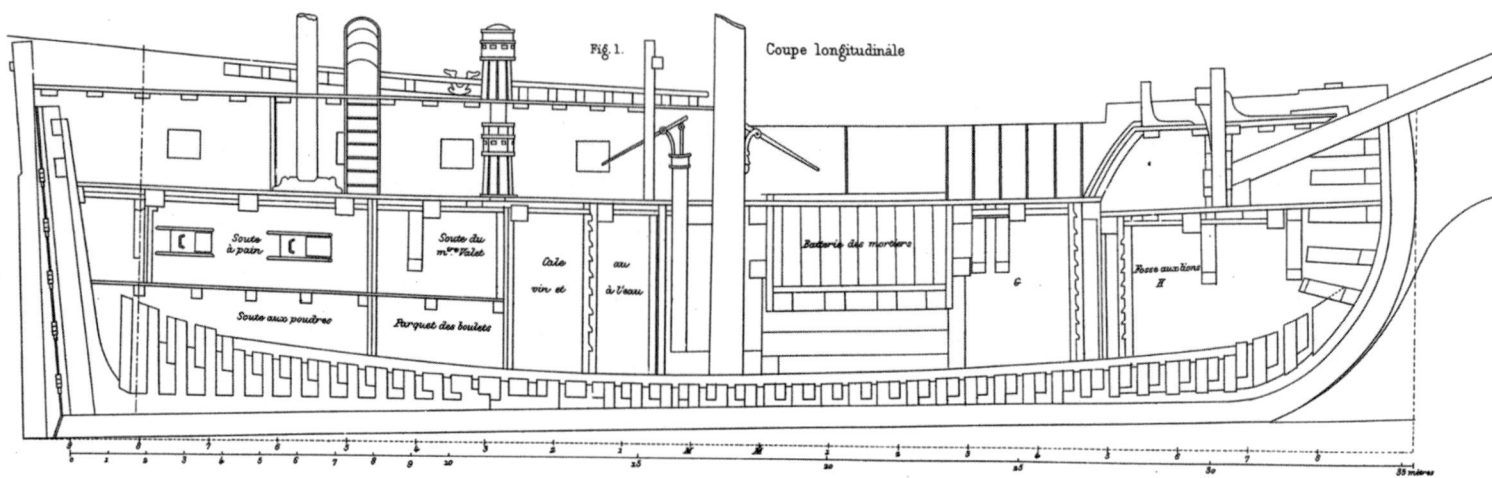

Vice-amiral Pâris's profile of the Bombelle design for the abortive *Tenare* Class of October 1778. Similar in layout to the *Salamandre*, this design shows that there had been no fundamental change in the layout and construction of French bomb vessels since their inception nearly a century earlier. (*Souvenirs de Marine*, Plate 246)

officer. The first was purchased in August 1759; the second was purchased in September. Following the war, they were converted to *gabarres* in September and November 1763 respectively; both were leased out in March 1764 and lost.

Notre Dame de Grâce Le Havre. Stranded near Plozevet 1764.
Aimable Mélanie Le Havre. Wrecked 7.1766.

TENARE Class. Two *galiotes à bombes* were projected in October 1778 to be laid down at Rochefort in 1779 to plans by Charles-Étienne Bombelle that were dated 5 October 1778. Construction was deferred from year to year until 1784 when the project was abandoned.

Dimensions & tons: 112ft 0in, 102ft 6in x 25ft 0in x 10ft 3in (36.38, 33.30 x 8.12 x 3.33m). 250/500 tons. Mean draught 9ft 8in (3.14m).

Guns: 8 x 6pdrs, + 2 x 12in mortars.

Tenare Rochefort Dyd.
Construction not begun.
Vésuve Rochefort Dyd.
Construction not begun.

PURCHASED VESSEL (1779). *Heureuse Marthe*, a 195-ton hoy from Le Havre built in 1775, was requisitioned in June 1779 for conversion to a *bombarde*. Antoine Groignard rebuilt her at Le Havre in June and July 1779 with 2 x 12-inch mortars. She was decommissioned at Le Havre on 28 November 1779 but was retained for the King's service in 1780.

PRAMS (*PRAMES*)

For the projected invasion of England mooted in 1759, orders were placed with builders at three different ports for a series of twelve heavily-armed *prames*, with an intended heavy armament of 36pdr long guns and carrying two 12in mortars for coastal bombardment (hence their inclusion in this chapter). These three-masted vessels resembled small low freeboard ships of the line in above-waterline appearance, and

A plan of the *Fortunée*, a 20-gun *prame* built in 1759, for a projected invasion of England. Redrawn by László Veres from an original French draught in the Danish archives. The vertical dashed lines indicate the position of the two 12in mortars. The prames of 1759 were rigged as *galiotes à bombes* with their two mortars abreast except for two that had ship rigs and that carried their mortars on the centreline. (Orlogsvaerftet, Copenhagen)

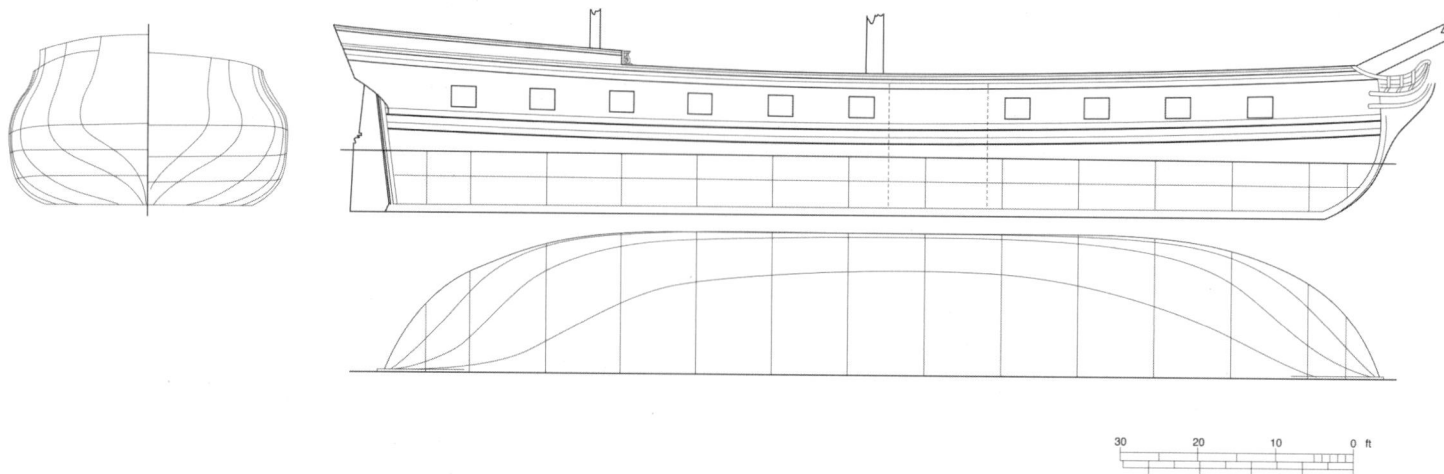

carried a main battery of those ships' heaviest guns, but they were essentially flat-bottomed vessels with three parallel keels, designed for amphibious operations. A further order for four similar *prames* was projected in June 1760 for construction by the sieurs Eustache at Rouen, but this project was abandoned in July 1760 before any work commenced and no names were assigned to these vessels.

(D) Vessels acquired from 1 September 1715

FORTUNÉE Class. *Prames*, ordered 1759, and all named 18 October 1759. Designed by Antoine Groignard and Gilles Cambry at Lorient.
Dimensions & tons: 133ft 0in, 121ft 0in x 37ft 0in x 8ft 1in (43.20, 39.31 x 12.02 x 2.63m). 362/1,087 tons. Draught 8ft 0in/9ft 4in (2.60/3.03m). Men: 150.
Guns: 20 x 36pdrs; also 2 x 12in mortars.
Fortunée Nantes
  K: 9.1759. L: 23.12.1759. C: 4.1760. Condemned 4.1768 at Rochefort, and BU there 8–9.1769.
Élisabeth Nantes
  K: 9.1759. L: 3.1.1760. C: 4.1760. Struck 1765 or 1766 at Rochefort. Not mentioned after 6.1783.
Charlotte Nantes
  K: 10.1759. L: 14.1.1760. C: 4.1760. Struck 1765 or 1766 at Bordeaux and became a sheer hulk.
Aglaé Nantes
  K: 10.1759. L: 22.2.1760. C: 5.1760. Struck 1765 or 1766 at Rochefort, and BU there 3–6.1767.
Monique Nantes
  K: 11.1759. L: 11.3.1760. C: 6.1760. Condemned 1765 or 1766 at Rochefort, and hulked there. Not mentioned after 9.1769.
Cunégonde Nantes
  K: 11.1759. L: 15.3.1760. C: 5.1760. Hulked 5.1766 at Rochefort, and BU there 1.1774.

LOUISE Class. *Prames*, ordered 1759, and all named 18 October 1759. Designed by François-Guillaume Clairin-Deslauriers.
Dimensions & tons: 131ft 0in x 37ft 0in x 9ft 0in (42.55 x 12.02 x 2.92m). 391/1,040 tons. Draught 8ft 0in/10ft 2in (2.60/3.30m). Men: 150.
Guns: 20 x 36pdrs (some also carried 6 smaller guns at times); also 2 x 12in mortars.
Louise Bordeaux.
  K: 10.1759. L: 5.1760. C: 7.1760. Struck at Rochefort 1765–66 and hulked 1778. Not mentioned after 6.1783.
Sophie Bordeaux.
  K: 10.1759. L: 17.6.1760. C: 4.1761. Probably BU 1767.
Batilde Bordeaux.
  K: 11.1759. L: ?10.1760. C: 7.1761. Hulked at Rochefort 4.1768. Listed in 1781 as protecting the river at Rochefort. Struck 8.1781.
Françoise Bordeaux.
  K: 11.1759. L: 10.1760. C: 5.1761. Hulked at Rochefort 4.1768 and used as *gabarre* 10.1777. Not mentioned after 6.1783.

THÉRÈSE Class. *Prames*, ordered 1759, and both named 18 October 1759. Designed by Joseph-Louis Ollivier and constructed by Pierre Tugghe at Dunkirk.
Dimensions & tons: 132ft 0in x 36ft 9in x 9ft 0in (42.88 x 11.94 x 2.92m). 300/1,000 tons. Men: 150.
Guns: 20 in 1765; 36 guns in 1767: 24 x 36pdrs, 12 x 12pdrs; also 2 x 12in mortars.

Thérèse Dunkirk.
  K: 10.1759. L: 24.9.1760. C: 7.1761. Hulked at Brest 1.1766 and BU 1783.
Christine Dunkirk.
  K: 10.1759. L: 23.11.1760. C: 7.1761. Hulked at Brest 1767 and BU 1783.

FLOATING BATTERIES

(D) Vessels acquired from 1 September 1715

DIABLE. Hexagonal floating battery without masts hastily built as the British approached Quebec. Designed by Captain Nicolas-Pierre Duclos-Guyot.
Dimensions & tons: unknown.
Guns: 6 x 24pdrs, 6 to 12 x 12pdrs.
Diable Quebec
  K: 5.1759. L: 27.6.1759. C: 6.1759. Lost 9.1759 at the capitulation of Quebec, probably broken up for use as firewood in the autumn of 1759.

Another floating battery was built at Quebec at the same time and for the same reason as *Diable* to a design by either Duclos-Guyot or René-Nicolas Levasseur. This unnamed craft was credited with 3 x 24pdr guns, was launched in 6.1759, and suffered the same fate as *Diable*.

GUNBOATS (*CHALOUPES-CANONNIÈRES*) AND MORTAR BOATS (*CHALOUPES-CARCASSIÈRES*)

Gun launches or gunboats called *chaloupes-canonnières* and similar craft armed with small mortars called *chaloupes-carcassières* were built by the French Navy for offensive use as bombardment craft in the English Channel and the Mediterranean and for defensive coastal use.

Chaloupes-canonnières were launches (*chaloupes*) that were larger than all other launches and that carried one and sometimes two 18pdr, 24pdr, or 36pdr guns forward and another aft. They were at least 50ft long, sometimes reaching 60ft, and were very handy under oars and under sail. They were excellent for defending a coast and supporting assaults by landing craft. They were also called *chaloupes à canon* and *chaloupes armées*.

Chaloupes-carcassières were larger than the largest launch or long-boat of a ship of the line and carried a small mortar. Designed to bombard a shore in support of a landing, they were typically about 40ft long, rigged with two masts, each with a lateen sail, and equipped with oars similarly to ships' boats. They were not embarked on ships but followed the fleet under sail or under tow by frigates. They were also called *chaloupes à mortier* and *chaloupes-bombardières*.

These specialized *chaloupes* were usually built in wartime and were generally disposed of promptly, either after the operation for which they had been built or following the conclusion of peace.

(B) Vessels acquired from 9 March 1661

TWO *CHALOUPES-CANONNIÈRES-GALIOTES*. These unnamed craft were built at Dunkirk, probably by Hendryck Houwens, at the

same time as the two hoys of the *Dunkerquoise* class (see Chapter 13). They may have carried 1 x 3pdr gun. They were built for the defence of the *fosse* (an offshore channel) at Mardick.
K: 3.1678, L: 15.5.1678. C: 5.1678. Fate unknown.

CHALOUPES No.1 TO No.7. *Chaloupes à canon* built at Toulon for use in an assault against Algiers. They were begun in 12.1682 and launched and completed in 3–4.1683. Four of them measured 36 tons and three 34 tons; all carried one gun. Two were wrecked 6.1783, one was captured 8.1683 off Algiers, and the other four were last mentioned in action at Algiers.

CHALOUPES No.8 TO No.16. *Chaloupes à mortier* or *chaloupes-carcassières* built at Toulon in 3–4.1684. They measured 36 tons and carried one mortar. They were last mentioned in 1691 at Toulon.

ONE CHALOUPE CANONNIÈRE. Built at Brest in 7–8.1684 with one gun in the bow. Her fate is unknown.

(C) Vessels acquired from 15 April 1689

EIGHT CHALOUPES CANONNIÈRES. These craft, perhaps designated *No.1* to *No.8*, were built at Le Havre in 4–5.1692. They carried 1 x 4pdr and were last mentioned in 6.1692 at Le Havre.

SIX CHALOUPES-CARCASSIÈRES. Built by Laurent Hélie at St Malo 1694 as copies of an English model. They carried one mortar, and their fate is unknown.

TWELVE CHALOUPES ARMÉES. These craft, probably unnamed, were built at Dunkirk and put into service in 8.1694 or 9.1694. Their crews consisted of 30 men each. They were removed from service at Dunkirk at the end of 1694 but in 4.1695 six of them were re-equipped as *chaloupes-canonnières*.

EIGHT BATEAUX-PLATS. These barges were built at Brest in 3.1694 by Sébastien Vauban for coastal defence use and each probably carried one mortar. They were last mentioned in 6.1694 at Bertheaume, at Le Conquet, and at the mouth of the Aulne, all defensive positions in the approaches to Brest.

AIMABLE Class. *Chaloupes-canonnières*. All built at Dunkirk in 4–5.1695. Three of these were sunk 8.1695 in combat with the British and Dutch at Dunkirk and were either replaced or restored to service.
Dimensions & tons: 4 tons. Men: 30 + 1 officer.
Guns: 1 x 3pdr or one *pierrier*.
Aimable, Aurore, Brusque, Comtesse, Coquette, Enjouée, Étoile, Fantasque, Fidèle, Fortunée, Mauresque, Pucelle: all last mentioned 9.1697 out of service at Dunkirk.
Sérieuse: last mentioned 1702 in service at Antwerp
Grondeuse, Perle: last mentioned 11.1708 at Dunkirk.
Impérieuse: handed over for commercial use 5.1708 at Dunkirk
Droite (or *Adroite*): handed over for commercial use in 1708 or 1709 at Dunkirk
Mignonne: handed over for commercial use *c*.1711 at Dunkirk

SIX CHALOUPES-BOMBARDIERES. Built at Toulon in 1695.
Dimensions & tons: 40ft 0in, 36ft 0in x 10ft 0in x 4ft 0in (12.99, 11.69 x 3.25 x 1.30m). Tons unknown.
Guns: 1 mortar

K: 4.1695. L: 4 to 14.5.1695. C: 22.5.1695. Last mentioned 7.1695 at Marseille.

EIGHT CHALOUPES-CANONNIÈRES or *double-chaloupes*. Put into service at St Malo 7.1695, these craft carried 1 x 4pdr and their fate is unknown.

FOUR CHALOUPES CANONNIÈRES or *chaloupes armés*. Put into service at St Malo 7.1695, these craft carried one small gun and their fate is unknown.

CANOT MAJOR. *Bateau canonnier*. Was in service at Dunkirk in 6.1697, removed from service there 9.1697.

(D) Vessels acquired from 1 September 1715

CHALOUPE-CARCASSIÈRE. Completed 10.1740 at Dunkirk. 10/11 men + 1 officer. 1 mortar. Removed from service 10.1741 at Dunkirk and last mentioned there 8.1742.

AMPHITRITE Class. *Chaloupes-carcassières* designed by Blaise Geslain and built at Le Havre. Until 9.1741 the first four were known as *Chaloupes-carcassières Nos. 1–4* respectively. They could mount 8 or 9 pairs of oars.
Dimensions & tons: Unknown. Men: 19 + 3 petty officers.
Guns: 1 mortar, probably replaced in 1742 with 1 x 4pdr + 2 *pierriers*.
Amphitrite Le Havre
K: 4.1741. L: 6.1741. C: 6.1741. Ex-*Chaloupe-Carcassière No.1*. Removed from service 11.1742 at Dunkirk, last mentioned 12.1742.
Galatée Le Havre
K: 4.1741. L: 6.1741. C: 6.1741. Ex-*Chaloupe-Carcassière No.2*. Removed from service 11.1742 at Dunkirk, last mentioned 12.1742.
Syrène Le Havre
K: 4.1741. L: 6.1741. C: 7.1741. Ex-*Chaloupe-Carcassière No.3*. Removed from service 11.1742 at Dunkirk, last mentioned 12.1742.
Thétis Le Havre
K: 6.1741. L: 8.1741. C: 8.1741. Ex-*Chaloupe-Carcassière No.4*. Last mentioned 1756 at Dunkirk.
Chaloupe-Carcassière No.5 Le Havre
Possibly begun in 6 or 7.1741 but not launched or completed.
Chaloupe-Carcassière No.6 Le Havre
Possibly begun in 6 or 7.1741 but not launched or completed.

FOUR CHALOUPES-CARCASSIÈRES. These craft, probably *No.1* to *No.4*, were built at Toulon in 1741 and carried 1 mortar each. They were used in 1742 as service craft (*chaloupes de servitude*).

DILIGENTE Class. *Chaloupes-carcassières* built at Brest.
Dimensions & tons: unknown
Guns: 1 mortar
Diligente Brest
Built 1746 and listed 1.1748 at Brest as a *chaloupe-carcassière*. At Brest 1758. Struck 1763.
Légère Brest
Built 1746 and listed 1.1748 at Brest as a *chaloupe-carcassière*. At Brest 1758. Struck 1763.

CARCASSIÈRE. *Chaloupe-carcassière* in service at Le Havre on 9.9.1759 under the command of a Captain Dessault and carrying one mortar. No other information.

ANGUILLE Class. *Chaloupes-canonnières* designed by Augustin Pic and built at Rochefort.
  Dimensions & tons: 62ft 0in x 14ft 2in x 4ft 8in (20.14 x 4.65 x 1.52m). 50 tons. Men:
  Guns: 1 x 24pdr + 12 *pierriers*.
Anguille Rochefort
  K: 1756. L: 1756. C: 6.1757. Hauled out 1768 at Rochefort, struck 12.1769.
Aventure Rochefort
  K: 1756. L: 1756. C: 6.1757. Ex-*Espérance* 1757. Last mentioned at Rochefort 1763, may have been sent to Gorée in 8.1763.

COULEUVRE Class. *Chaloupes-canonnières* built at Rochefort.
  Dimensions & tons: . Men: 55/97 + 1/4 officers.
  Guns: 1 x 24pdr + 1 *pierrier*
Couleuvre Rochefort.
  K: 1758. L: 1759. C: 1759. Out of service 1760. Sold 12.1763 at Brest.
Vive Rochefort.
  K: 1758. L: 1759. C: 1759. Careened 4.1760 at Vannes. Last mentioned 6.1763 in service in the Vilaine

VIPÈRE Class. *Chaloupes-canonnières*. These were probably the two *chaloupes-canonnières* built at St Malo in 1759 by Antoine Thévenard as indicated below, although they might have been built at Brest where they were put into service in July 1760; by 1762 both were reported there as in need of routine maintenance. They could pull 14 pairs of oars.
  Dimensions & tons: 46ft 10in x 13ft 0in x 6ft 6in (15.21 x 4.22 x 2.11m). 40 tons. Men: 44/64 + 1 officer.
  Guns: 1 x 12pdr in the bow.
Vipère St Malo.
  K: 1.1759. L: 4.1759. C: 5.1759. Condemned 1766 at Brest, BU there 9–11.1766.
Aspic St Malo.
  K: 1.1759. L: 4.1759. C: 5.1759. Condemned 1766 at Brest, BU there 9–11.1766.

SAUTERELLE Class. *Chaloupes-canonnières* designed by Jean-Denis Chevillard and built at Bordeaux.
  Specifications unknown.
Sauterelle Bordeaux.
  K: 4.1759. L: 6.1759. C: 6.1759. Last mentioned 10.1762 at Bordeaux, struck *c*.1763.
Flèche Bordeaux.
  K: 4.1759. L: 6.1759. C: 6.1759. Last mentioned 10.1762 at Bordeaux, struck *c*.1763.

ÉCLAIR Class. *Chaloupes-canonnières* designed by Antoine Groignard and built at Le Havre for the defence of that port. They could mount 11 pairs of oars. Out of service 11.1762 after the end of hostilities in the Seven Years' War.
  Dimensions & tons: 42ft 0in x 12ft 0in x 6ft 0in (13.64 x 3.90 x 1.95m). 40 tons. Draught 4ft (1.30m). Men: 60, + 1 officer.
  Guns: 1 x 24pdr.
Éclair Havre.
  K: 6.1759. L: 10.8.1759. C: 9.1759. Unserviceable 2.1768 and sold at Harfleur, BU there 1768.

Foudre Havre.
  K: 6.1759. L: 10.8.1759. C: 9.1759. Unserviceable 2.1768 and sold at Harfleur, BU there 1768.
Tempête Havre.
  K: 6.1759. L: 10.8.1759. C: 9.1759. Unserviceable 2.1768 and sold at Harfleur, BU there 1768.
Tonnerre Havre.
  K: 6.1759. L: 10.8.1759. C: 9.1759. Unserviceable 2.1768 and sold at Harfleur, BU there 1768.

NOVICE. *Chaloupe Canonnière* in service at Rochefort in 1759 and 1760. 84 men + 3 officers, 3 guns. Struck 8.1764 at Brest.

In 1761 there were two *chaloupes-canonnières* in the port at Brest, six at Rochefort of which two were in the Vilaine supporting one *prame*, and four in the Charente with three *prames*, six out of commission at Le Havre and two out of service at Gravelines, two in the port at Dunkirk supporting two *prames*, and two at Bordeaux with two *prames* for a total of 20 in the *Ponant*. There were also two at Toulon and two at Mahon. In 1766 there were two at Brest, five at Toulon, two at Rochefort, and six at Le Havre for a total of fifteen. Lists from 1768 and 1769 show only nine *chaloupes-canonnières* left in service: seven at Toulon and two at Rochefort.

FLAMANDE Class. *Chaloupes-canonnières* built at Dunkirk. In 1760 Daniel Denÿs was asked to design and build two *chaloupes-canonnières* with one 24pdr gun each to accompany the two *prames* then being built at Dunkirk by Jacques-Luc Ollivier – *Thérèse* and *Christine*. His design for them was returned approved by the Minister on 26 November 1760, the contract was signed on 17 December 1760, and the first was nearly ready to be launched on 18 March 1761. Denÿs was authorized to arm them with either a 24pdr or an 18pdr gun. The sliding mounting that allowed the transfer of the gun from the bow to the stern only permitted an 18pdr in the first but the Minister insisted on a 24pdr in the other.
  Dimensions & tons: dimensions unknown, 35 tons.
  Guns: 1 x 18pdr or 1 x 24pdrs. Replaced 1762 with 4 x 4pdrs.
Flamande Dunkirk.
  K: early 1761. L: 3–4.1761 C: 1761. Sold 9.1768 at Dunkirk.
Picarde Dunkirk.
  K: early 1761. L: 4–5.1761 C: 1761. Probably lost 5.1762 near Dunkirk.

LÉGÈRE Class. *Chaloupes-canonnières* designed by Jean-Joseph Ginoux and built at Le Havre. *Pallas* was 'poor under sail, being too long' and was never fully commissioned.
  Dimensions & tons: ?80 tons. Men: 60/90 + 1 officer
  Guns: 3 x 24pdrs (two forward and one aft) + 8 or 10 *pierriers*.
Légère Le Havre
  K: 3.1760. L: 10.4.1760. C: 5.1760. Ex-*Monsieur de Berville* 4.1760. Probably abandoned 2.1763 at Dunkirk and struck.
Victoire Le Havre
  K: 3.1760. L: 10.4.1760. C: 5.1760. Ex-*Duc d'Harcourt* 4.1760. Probably lost 5.1762 near Dunkirk.
Danaé Le Havre
  K: 3.1760. L: 12.4.1760. C: 5.1760. Ex-*Ville du Havre* 4.1760. Repaired 7.1761 at Le Havre, sold there 7.1768.
Pallas Le Havre
  K: 3.1760. L: 12.4.1760. C: 5.1760. Ex-*Monsieur de Beauvoir* 4.1760. Repaired 7.1761 at Le Havre, sold there 7.1768 and BU.

COQUETTE Class. Twenty-one *chaloupes-canonnières* were built at Lorient by the Arnous brothers on plans by Antoine Groignard. There were two types: five of the vessels (including *Badine*) were a smaller variant mounting two guns; the other sixteen (including *Coquette*) were a larger variant mounting three guns. The name *Fidèle* was also initially reported, but this is believed to be the unit that was renamed *Reine du Maroc*. In December 1762 *Coquette*, *Gracieuse*, *Constante* and *Psyché*, all with 3 guns, were at Brest ready to be put into service at the first order.

Dimensions & tons: Smaller variant: 65ft 0in x 13ft 6in (21.11 x 4.43m). 50 tons. Men: 56 + 1 officer

Larger variant: 76ft 0in x 16ft 0in (24.69 x 5.20m). 80 tons. Men: 66 + 1/3 officers.

Guns: Smaller variant: 2 x 24pdrs or 18pdrs. Larger variant: 3 x 24pdrs or 18pdrs.

Badine Lorient
K: 7.1761. L: 10.1761. C: 10.1761. Struck before 1766.

Coquette Lorient
K: 7.1761. L: 10.1761. C: 10.1761. Struck 8.1764 at Brest.

Capricieuse Lorient
K: 7.1761. L: 11.1761. C: 11.1761. Struck before 1766.

Fantasque Lorient
K: 7.1761. L: 11.1761. C: 12.1761. Struck before 1766.

Fringante Lorient
K: 7.1761. L: 11.1761. C: 12.1761. Struck before 1766.

Parfaite Lorient
K: 7.1761. L: 11.1761. C: 12.1761. Struck before 1766.

Pimpante Lorient
K: 7.1761. L: 11.1761. C: 12.1761. Struck before 1766.

Reine du Maroc Lorient
K: 7.1761. L: 11.1761. C: 12.1761. Struck before 1766.

Melanide Lorient
K: 7.1761. L: 11.1761. C: 12.1761. Last mentioned 9.1769 at Rochefort.

Adélaïde Lorient
K: 10.1761. L: 12.1761. C: 12.1761. Last mentioned 1.1763 out of service at Port Louis.

Agaçante Lorient
K: 10.1761. L: 1.1762. C: 2.1762. Last mentioned 12.1762 out of service at Port Louis.

Brave Lorient
K: 10.1761. L: 1.1762. C: 2.1762. Struck before 1766.

Charmante Lorient
K: 10.1761. L: 1.1762. C: 2.1762. Struck 8.1764 at Brest.

Constante Lorient
K: 10.1761. L: 1.1762. C: 2.1762. In service at Brest from 21.5.1762 to 20.10.1762, struck 8.1764 at Brest

Gracieuse Lorient
K: 10.1761. L: 1.1762. C: 2.1762. Struck 8.1764 at Brest.

Jolie Lorient
K: 10.1761. L: 1.1762. C: 2.1762. Careened 4.1763 at Vannes, last mentioned 6.1763 in service in the Vilaine.

Légère Lorient
K: 10.1761. L: 1.1762. C: 2.1762. Last mentioned 3.1764 upon arrival at Cayenne rigged as a snow.

Psyché Lorient
K: 10.1761. L: 1.1762. C: 2.1762. Struck 8.1764 at Brest.

Thérèse Lorient
K: 10.1761. L: 1.1762. C: 2.1762. Struck before 1766.

Victorieuse Lorient
K: 10.1761. L: 1.1762. C: 2.1762. Struck before 1766.

Volage Lorient
K: 10.1761. L: 1.1762. C: 2.1762. Last mentioned 9.1763 when out of service.

CÉSAR. *Chaloupe-canonnière* in service at Gorée 3.1765. Last mentioned 8.1765. Note that *Aventure*, ex-*Espérance* (1757, above) was sent to Gorée in 1763, although available records contain no indication that she and *César* were the same vessel.

VIOLENTE Class. *Chaloupes-canonnières* designed by Antoine Geoffroy and built at Brest. They could mount 20 pairs of oars. These two moved from Brest to their duty station at St Malo in 1779.

Dimensions & tons: 100ft 0in, 80ft 0in x 17ft 0in x 5ft 3in (32.48, 25.99 x 5.52 x 1.71m). 60/100 tons. Men: 42/60 + 1/3 officers.

Guns: 3 x 24pdrs originally, 1 x 24pdr only after 1781, then 2 x 24pdrs from 1792.

Violente Brest Dyd.
K: 3.1778. L: 21.5.1778. C: 8.1778. Repaired at Le Havre 1–3.1782. Condemned 2.1793 at Antwerp or lost in the Scheldt and struck.

Rusée Brest Dyd.
K: 3.1778. L: 20.5.1778. C: 8.1778. Repaired at Le Havre 1–3.1782. Condemned 2.1793 at Antwerp or lost in the Scheldt and struck.

LEVRETTE Class. *Chaloupes-canonnières* designed by Henri Chevillard the elder and built at St Malo. They were similar to the *Impudente* class, below.

Dimensions & tons: 60ft 6in x 13ft 2in x 5ft 6in (19.65 x 4.28 x 1.79m). 60 tons. Men: 60/65 + 2/4 officers.

Guns: 1 x 24pdr. *Levrette* was listed with 3 x 32pdrs while at Lorient from late 1781 to early 1783.

Levrette St Malo.
K: 4.1778. L: 6.1778. C: 7.1778. Struck 1785 or 1786 at St Malo.

Méfiante St Malo.
K: 4.1778. L: 6.1778. C: 7.1778. Sheathed in copper in 1783. Struck 1785 or 1786 at St Malo.

BRUYANTE Class. *Chaloupes-canonnières*. In July 1777 Daniel Denÿs submitted plans for a *chaloupe-canonnière* on the model of *Flamande* (1760) with one 24pdr gun. On 12 June 1778 the construction of *Couleuvre* and *Bruyante* was well advanced and they were expected to be launched around 17 July. In 1779 Sartine wanted to build two *chaloupes-canonnières* at Calais similar to those of Dunkirk and noted that it would suffice to place a new contract with Denÿs and that there would be no need for new plans. On 2 April 1779 the minister decided they would be built at Dunkirk and were to be ready by the end of May. On 22 May Denÿs reported they were well advanced, and they were launched before 18 June. The vessels carried 14 pairs of oars and were stationed at Le Havre.

Dimensions & tons: dimensions unknown, 35 tons.

Guns: 1 x 24pdr + 12 *pierriers* in the first two units.

Bruyante Dunkirk.
K: 5.1778. L: 10.7.1778. C: 8.1778. For sale 6.1783 at Le Havre, sold or struck 1784.

Couleuvre Dunkirk.
K: 5.1778. L: 11.7.1778. C: 8.1778. For sale 6.1783 at Le Havre, sold or struck 1784.

Cerbère Dunkirk.
K: 4.1779. L: 8.6.1779. C: 6.1779. Converted into a *gabarre* 1–2.1784 at Le Havre and sent to St Domingue, arriving 17.4.1784. Fate unknown.

Furieuse Dunkirk.
K: 4.1779. L: 9.6.1779. C: 6.1779. For sale 6.1783 at Le Havre, sold or struck 1784.

IMPUDENTE Class. *Chaloupes-canonnières* designed by Raymond-Antoine Haran and built in 1778–79, all at Rochefort, except *Lynx* at

BOMB VESSELS AND OTHER COASTAL WARFARE CRAFT

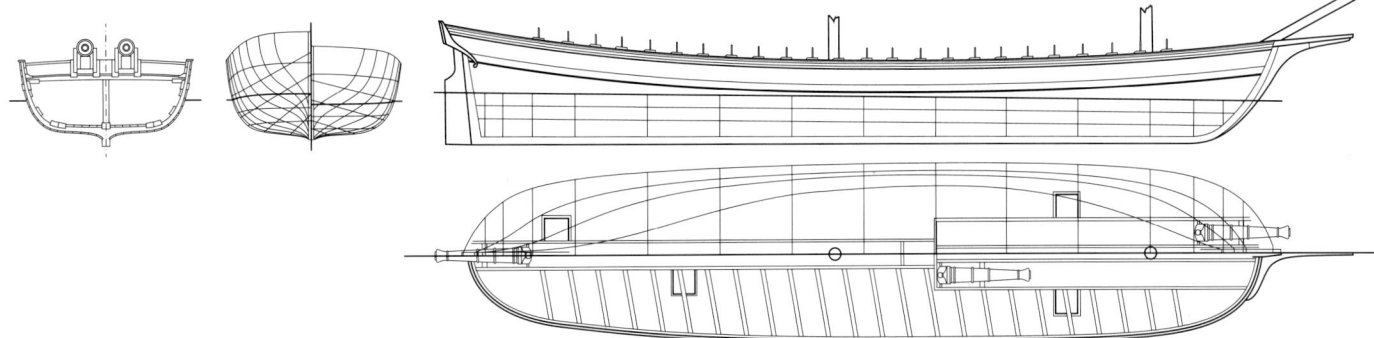

Plan of a French *chaloupe-canonnière* redrawn by László Veres from a French draught in the Danish archives. The original is known to have been taken to Denmark by the constructor F C H Hohlenberg in 1791, but the details identify it as one of the *Vautour* Class of 1779. Armament is listed as three 24pdrs, two forward and one aft; they were mounted on slides so they could be shifted nearer the centre of the boat to improve seakeeping when on passage. Although the boat could be sailed, its principal power of manoeuvre was provided by 24 pairs of oars. (Orlogsvaerftet, Copenhagen)

Bordeaux. They had 14 pairs of oars. All were stationed at Rochefort where as of late 1782 they were in use in the harbour and the roadstead.

Dimensions & tons: 60ft 0in, 53ft 0in x 16ft 6in x 6ft 0in (19.49, 17.22 x 5.36 x 1.95m). 42/80 tons. Draught 5ft 0in/5ft 8in (1.62/1.84m). Men: 38/50 + 1 officer; 77 + 3/4 officers in *Nantaise*.

Guns: 3 x 18pdrs (2 forward and 1 aft) + 8 *pierriers*. The class was listed in 1781 with 1 x 24pdr and *Embuscade* and *Cyclope* were listed in 1784 with this armament.

Impudente Rochefort Dyd.
K: 10.1778. L: 27.12.1778. C: 1.1779. For sale 5.1783 at Rochefort, sold 1784.

Mégère Rochefort Dyd.
K: 10.1778. L: 16.1.1779. C: 2.1779. Repaired 1785 or 1786 at Rochefort, then sent to Cherbourg. Renamed *Méridienne* 5.1795. Struck 1797 at Cherbourg.

Embuscade Rochefort Dyd.
K: 10.1778. L: 30.1.1779. C: 3.1779. Sold 7.1783 at Rochefort but still there 8.1784 and struck 1784. Name also rendered as *Ambuscade*.

Nantaise Rochefort Dyd.
K: 11.1778. L: 16.2.1779. C: 3.1779. Also listed as *Canonnière de Nantes* (in 1780) and as *Arrogante* (from 1781). Repaired 1784 at Rochefort and 1788 in Senegal (hull coppered). Struck 2.1792 at Rochefort and ordered BU 1.5.1792.

Panthère Rochefort Dyd.
K: 11.1778. L: 19.2.1779. C: 3.1779. For sale 8.1783 at Rochefort, sold and struck 1784.

Cyclope Rochefort Dyd.
K: 1.1779. L: 5.1779. C: 6.1779. For sale 8.1783 at Rochefort, sold and struck 8.1784.

Lynx Bordeaux.
K: 5.1779. L: 10.7.1779. C: 8.1779. Also listed in error as *Binks* or *Bincks*. Repaired 1785–1786 at Rochefort, then sent to Cherbourg. Struck 1797 at St Malo.

MARTINIQUE Class. *Chaloupes-canonnières*. A class of two vessels designed by Jean-Joseph Ginoux and built at Le Havre in 1779–80 in response to a request from Martinique. These were modified in 4–5.1780 at Le Havre by Antoine Groignard. They carried 20 pairs of oars and were schooner-rigged. Another pair was built at St Malo, probably to the same plans.

Dimensions & tons: 81ft 0in, 71ft 0in x 17ft 0in x 5ft 0in (26.31, 23.06 x 5.52 x 1.62m). 70/100 tons. Draught 4/5ft (1.30/1.62m). Men: 50/63 + 1/2 officers.

Guns: 3 x 24pdrs (2 forward and 1 aft) + 12 *pierriers*. *Sainte Lucie* from 1797: 1 x 24pdr, 2 x 18pdrs + 2 *pierriers*.

Martinique Le Havre.
K: 2.1779. L: 4.5.1779. C: 6.1779. Rebuilt 9.1791 to 5.1792 at Le Havre. Wrecked 10.1792 near Dunkirk.

Sainte Lucie Le Havre.
K: 2.1779. L: 4.5.1779. C: 6.1779. Rebuilt 9.1791 to 1792 at Le Havre and stationed 11–12.1792 in the mouth of the Scheldt. Captured there 20.3.1793 by Dutch boats, returned 6.1795. Decommissioned 3.1801 at Dunkirk, sold 12.1801.

Lionne St Malo.
K: 12.1779. L: 2.1780. C: 1780. Struck and sold 1784 at St Malo.

Querelleuse St Malo.
K: 12.1779. L: 5.1780. C: 6.1780. Struck and sold 1784 at St Malo.

VAUTOUR Class. *Chaloupes-canonnières*. *Vautour* was prefabricated at Nantes in early 1779 and sent to Lorient for assembly. The other two were prefabricated either at Nantes or at Rochefort between 4.1779 and 6.1779 and assembled at Cayenne by Sébastien Verdy (?).

Dimensions & tons: 80ft 0in x 17ft 0in x 5ft 0in (25.99 x 5.52 x 1.62m), 60 tons.

Guns: 3 x 24pdrs in *Vautour*, probably 3 guns in the others.

Vautour Lorient.
K: 4.1779. L: 10.6.1779. C: 6.1779. Sold 5.1783 to Sr. Arnous (the shipbuilder) at Lorient and struck.

Premier Bâtiment Cayenne.
K: 9.1779. L: 24.4.1780. C: 6.1780. Originally called *La Canonnière*, renamed 1781. Taken out of commission 1783 at Cayenne, last mentioned as a service craft at Cayenne 5.1785.

Second Bâtiment Cayenne.
K: 4.1780. L: 3.1781. C: 4.1781. Fate unknown.

VAILLANTE. *Chaland ponté* (decked lighter) completed at Cherbourg in 5.1780 as a *canonnière* (gunboat) armed with 1 x 24pdr. Struck 1782 or 1783 at Cherbourg.

SAGE. *Canonnière* (gunboat) of unknown origin in service in 1783 at Cherbourg. Last mentioned there at the end of 1783.

8 Fireships
(Brûlots)

The use of fireships in naval warfare (*i.e.* ships designed to be set alight and sailed into enemy fleets or harbours to cause conflagrations) goes back thousands of years, but was very prevalent during the sixteenth and seventeenth centuries. Between 1627 and 1661 the French Navy acquired over fifty vessels which it adapted for use as fireships, starting with four ships expended on 23 October 1628 against the English fleet off La Rochelle.

Fireships continued to be used successfully against enemy fleets during the middle part of the century – notably during the war against Spain (paticularly in August 1638 at Guétaria and in July 1640 at Cadiz) and against the Dutch in the 1670s. Numerous fireships were added, either by conversion or by purpose-built construction. However, by the 1690s their use against fleets at sea became less effective due to improved defensive tactics by the line of battle, although their use against ships in harbour or at anchor was to continue for another century. Against stationary vessels (as by the English at La Hougue in June 1692) it was found equally effective – and less costly in resource terms – to use warships' own boats, which could be fitted with grapples and firechains (to which combustibles could be attached) and rowed alongside the target vessel, with the combustibles fired before the boat would be safely withdrawn. The combustible material was not a constant concoction, but what the English termed 'wildfire', generally a mixture of priming powder, pitch, naptha, sulphur, resin, turpentine and flaxseed oil.

Whether purpose-built for the role or converted from mercantile purchases and prizes, fireships were adapted for their special role in a number of ways. Most had tween-deck spaces that could be loaded with considerable amounts of combustible materials, and they were fitted with large sallyports positioned aft on the lower deck through which the remaining members of the crew could escape into launches or other boats once the combustibles were properly ignited and the ship set on course for its intended target.

Unlike the gunport lids on conventional small warships, those on fireships were hinged at the bottom, so that they would not close themselves and would fall open once the retaining tackles burnt through, creating a draught throughout the ship; for similar reasons funnels were fitted through the upper deck to add to air circulation. Finally, to delay the time when the ship's top hamper (masts, spars and sails) would catch fire, the ships were fitted with cofferdams around the lower masts on each deck to prevent the fire reaching the masts too early.

The crew size of fireships was kept to a minimum because of the need to evacuate the vessel rapidly once it was fired. The standard complement of French naval fireships from 1669 to 1673 was 25 men (5 *officiers mariniers* or petty officers, 20 *matelots* or seamen, and no soldiers) plus 2 *officers principaux* or commissioned officers. The standard manning from 1675 to 1692 was 30 (10/20/–) men +2 officers. Significant exceptions are indicated in the individual entries below.

(A) Vessels in service as at 9 March 1661

While just over fifty fireships had been acquired or converted by the French in the period from 1627 to 1652, none remained in 1661. There was a single more recent acquisition dating from 1660 – the *Ussedon* (probably an ex-English prize).

USSEDON. This vessel, probably a captured English merchantman brought into Toulon *c.*1660, was described on a list of ships at Toulon on 3 May 1661 as old and able to serve only as a fireship, although her performance under sail might be too bad even for that. This defect would prevent a commercial sale and it was recommended that she be hulked because Toulon badly needed hulks for dockyard stores. She was duly hulked in late 1661 and was not mentioned after February 1666.

A list of the French Navy in September 1661 showed eight fireships in the Navy at that time while a list from 1662 showed four, but neither list named the vessels. These may have included the *flûtes Licorne, Espérance,* and *Tête Noire,* which were shown in the 3 May 1661 list as suitable only for use as fireships but had reverted to *flûtes* by 1662, and Fouquet's mercantile *Saint Nicolas*, which had been idle in the Seudre since September 1660 and was wrecked near La Rochelle in late February or early March 1662.

(B) Vessels acquired from 9 March 1661

ACQUIRED VESSELS (1661–1662). Two vessels were seized or purchased from French owners in 1661 and 1662 and fitted as fireships. One was expended as a fireship in battle in 1676.

Saint Antoine de Padoue. Built at Hoorn in 1659 (completed 11.1659) and purchased in Holland 1660 by Nicolas Fouquet (Louis XIV's Minister of Finance). Seized by the French monarchy 11.1661 following the dismissal and downfall of Fouquet and converted to a fireship. Not to be confused with the 5th Rate *Saint Antoine* of 1654 which was a fireship in 1668–70.
 Dimensions & tons: dimensions unknown. 200 tons (150 from 1672). Draught 8ft (2.60m).
 Guns: 16 gunports. 6 guns from 1671, 4 from 1676.
 Renamed *Ardent* 24.6.1671. Rebuilt 7.1674 to 4.1675 at Toulon. Expended at Battle of Palermo 2.6.1676.

Petit Hercule (or Gosse). Vessel *Hercule* from La Rochelle purchased at Brouage from Michel Gosse 2.1662 and rated as a fireship. 150 tons. Last mentioned 2.1666 as unserviceable at Toulon.

Ex-BARBARY COAST PRIZES (1663–1664). Three vessels were taken from the Arabs during the Duc de Vivonne's punitive expedition against Algerine corsairs. One ship, *Triton*, was captured on 12 April 1663 at La Goulette by the division of Chevalier Paul and fitted as a fireship in May 1663 at Cagliari, and two more were captured in April 1664 at Bougie by *Hercule* (36), *Cœur Doré* being fitted in June 1664 as a hospital ship. *Saint Augustin* was later called *Petit Saint Augustin* to distinguish her from the *flûte* of the same name captured from the Algerines in May 1664.

Triton. Merchant vessel from Olonne taken by Barbary corsairs. Struck 1667.

Saint Augustin or Petit Saint Augustin. Merchant vessel launched at

Genoa in 1654 and taken by the Barbary corsairs. 80 tons (150 from 1671). 4 guns (6 from 1671). Renamed *Éclair* 24.6.1671. Struck 8.1671 at Toulon.

Cœur Doré. Ex-Barbary *Khalb Dahbi*. Last mentioned 2.1666 as unserviceable.

Ex-ENGLISH MERCHANT PRIZES (1666). Two English merchantmen captured in 1666 and initially called *Petit Anglais* and *Grand Anglais* were fittted as fireships. One was expended in battle as a fireship in 1676. A previous *Grand Anglais* became the 5th Rank *Lion Rouge* in around 1665.

Guillaume. English vessel, probably named *William*, taken in early 1666 and initially referred to as *Petit Anglais* but renamed *Guillaume* later that year. 120 tons (150 from 1671). 4 guns (6 from 1671). Struck at Rochefort 3.1671.

Justice. English merchantman built *c*.1662, captured 5.1666, converted to a fireship, and called *Grand Anglais* until renamed *Justice* 1667. She may have been the *Good Hope* (34 guns, 272 tons, 101ft) that was hired by the Royal Navy in 1664 as a 4th Rate and taken by the Dutch 20.5.1665 while escorting a convoy from Hamburg.

Dimensions & tons: dimensions unknown. 400 tons (200 from 1671, 300 from 1673, and 160 in 1676). Draught: 9ft (2.92m). Men: 38 (8/30/), +2 officers; 30 (6/24/), +1 officer from 1672.

Guns: 16, 10 from 1669, 4 in 1676.

Renamed *Hameçon* 24.6.1671. Based at Toulon, rebuilt there 1674–76 (may have lost name briefly to the captured *Ruben*, below). Expended at the Battle of Palermo 2.6.1676.

PURCHASED AND ACQUIRED VESSELS (1665–1668). A mixed selection of vessels was acquired during the late 1660s, including some bought at Toulon for operations against the Barbary coast and some bought from the Dutch. Two were expended in minor actions in 1667 and 1671, one was lost in battle in 1673, and one was expended against an enemy fleet in 1676.

Saint Cyprien. Purchased at Toulon 1.1665 from Sieur Livry. 33 men in 1666, later 25. Took part in Battles of La Goulette 3.3.1665 and Cherchell 24.8.1665. Hull stove in 12.1667 while loading marble at Honfleur, condemned there and crew released 8.1.1668.

Malgue (Maligne?). Purchased 3.1665 at Dunkirk. 120 tons (150 from 1671). 4 guns (6 in 1671). Struck 3.1671 at Brest.

Bilbaut (Bilbaud). Built 1662 in Holland and purchased there 2.1666.

Dimensions & tons: dimensions unknown, 120 tons (150 from 1669, 200 from 1672). 25 men, 30 (6/24/), +1 officer from 1672.

Guns: 6, 10 from 1672, 4 from 1673.

Renamed *Inquiet* 24.6.1671. Condemned 1.1674 at Toulon, and sold to BU there 11.1676.

Although a limited number of fireships were purpose-built, the most cost-effective source of such weapons was either a superannuated warship or converted merchantman: this is an example of the latter (actually the *Thomas and Elizabeth*, but about the same size as the English prize *Good Hope* taken in 1666). In this drawing by Willem van de Velde the younger, the sallyport can be seen aft on the lower deck, just ahead of an open gunport. This deck would be where the combustibles and firing train would be fitted – a row of closed ports is indicated here, whereas the ship's defensive armament can be seen on the deck above. (National Maritime Museum, London PY1899)

Trois Rois. Built in Provence and purchased in early 1666. 100 tons (120 from 1669). 12 guns (4 from 1668). Thrown ashore late 1669, broke up and remains sold.

Roi David. Built in Provence and purchased in early 1666. 120 tons (150 from 1671). 28 men in 1666 (later 35). 4 guns (6 from 1671). Struck at Brest 3.1671.

Concorde. Vessel in service at Toulon 4.1666. 100 tons (150 from 1669). 12/20 guns (6 from 1669). Renamed *Fin* 24.6.1671. Wrecked while trying to burn shipping in port of Sousse 7/8.1671.

Vaillante (Vaillance). In service 6.1666 on the Charente. Last mentioned 10.1666 at Rochefort.

Cher Ami. In service 7.1666 at La Rochelle. Expended 7.1667 against the English at St Pierre de la Martinique. May have belonged to the *Compagnie des Indes Occidentales*.

Trinité (or Truite?). Built in Provence, acquired 1666. 120 tons (150 from 1671). 4 guns (6 from 1671). Struck 3.1671 at Rochefort.

Maréchal Phébus (or Phébus). Purchased 1666 at Toulon. 120 tons (150 from 1671). 6 guns. Condemned 5.1671 at Toulon and struck (her officers on 14.8.1671 called her a very poor sailer); sold 11.1676 and BU 1677.

Flambeau. Dutch vessel (possibly *Toorts*) built in Holland and purchased 11.1666. 200 tons (120 from 1669, 150 from 1671). 4 guns (6 from 1671). Renamed *Entreprenant* 24.6.1671. Last mentioned 7.1671.

Pèlerin (Pèllerin). Dutch vessel (possibly *Pelgrim*) purchased 1666 or 1667. This was probably the fireship called *Pélican* in 1667–1668. 120 tons (150 from 1671). 4 guns (6 from 1671). Struck 3.1671 at Brest.

Tigre. Dutch vessel (possibly *Tijger*) built 1662 and purchased in Holland 4 or 11.1667. 150 tons. 16 guns (6 from 1669). Renamed *Inconnu* 24.6.1671. Took part in both Battles of Schooneveldt 7 (under Capt. Rocuchon) & 14.6.1673, and was burnt by the Dutch at the 2nd Battle.

Phénix. Dutch vessel built in Holland and purchased there 5 or 11.1667. 120 tons (150 from 1669). 12 guns (6 from 1668). Unserviceable 5.4.1670 at Toulon and ordered BU.

Léopard. Purchased 12.1667. Last mentioned 1668.

Symbole. Dutch vessel (possibly *Symbol*) built in Holland in 1662–63 and purchased 1668. 120 tons (150 from 1671). Draught 8ft (2.60m). 4 guns (6 from 1671, 4 from 1676). Renamed *Impudent* 24.6.1671. Present (but not expended) at 1st Battle of Schooneveldt. Expended at Battle of Palermo 2.6.1676.

Additional vessels may have been acquired during the 1660s for which no records have survived. There were eighteen fireships on the list when the first ranking system was introduced in September 1669 (although fireships themselves were not ranked). This included two larger vessels of 400 tons, each with a crew of 38 men (8/30/–) and 2 officers – the 16-gun *Elbeuf* (originally a 26-gun *vaisseau* dating from 1646, converted to a fireship in September 1669) and the 10-gun *Justice* (a prize taken from the English in May 1666). The *Saint Antoine* (a former Spanish 38-gun ship converted in 1668) was recorded as being of 200 tons, with 4 guns and a complement of 25 men (5/20/–) and 1 officer, and there were fifteen others of 150 tons or less mentioned with an identical complement: *Bilbaud*, *Tigre*, *Phénix*, *Concorde* and *Phébus* (all five with 6 guns each); and *Marguerite*, *Flambeau*, *Roi David*, *Symbole*, *Pèlerin*, *Trois Rois*, *Trinité*, *Guillaume*, *Malgue* and *Petit Saint Augustin* (each with 4 guns). Most of these would undergo changes of name on 24 June 1671 if still extent then. By January 1671 the list was reduced to sixteen vessels. The *Elbeuf* was hulked at Toulon at the end of 1670, and the *Phénix*, *Marguerite* and *Trois Rois* deleted. Other than the *Justice* of 10 guns and 30 men (+2 officers) and the new purpose-built fireships, all other fireships were each rated at 6 guns and 20 men (+1 officer).

PURCHASED VESSELS (1670). Two vessels were purchased in 1670 that were constructed by the shipbuilder Daviaud at Libourne, upriver on the Dordogne. One, the existing *Auguste* – probably built in 1662 – was purchased at La Rochelle for service as a fireship, 'for which it was not found suitable'; the other was the *Sauvage*, newbuilt by Daviaud in 1670 for the *Compagnie des Indes Orientales*, which was initially classed as a *flûte* but by early 1672 was classed in the role in which she was lost a year later. *Sauvage* was praised by *Vice-amiral* Jean, Comte d'Estrées in January 1671 as the best sailer in his squadron. Both were renamed in June 1671, and were based at Rochefort.

Auguste Daviaud, Libourne.
  Dimensions & tons: dimensions unknown. 150 tons. Men: 25 (5/20/), +1 officer.
  Guns: 6.
  Built 1662. Renamed *Fanfaron* 24.6.1671. Rebuilt (cut down) at Rochefort 7-8.1671. Condemned at Rochefort 4.1673 and sold 7.1673, possibly to a privateer.

Sauvage Daviaud, Libourne.
  Dimensions & tons: dimensions unknown. 300 tons as *flûte*; 150 as fireship from 1672. Men: 30 (6/24/), +2 officers as *flûte*; 25 (5/20/), +1 officer as fireship from 1672.
  Guns: 10 as *flûte*, 6 as fireship from 1672.
  K: 1669. L: 1670. C: 7.1670. Renamed *Voilé* 24.6.1671. Took part in both Battles of Schooneveldt 7 & 14.6.1673 (under Capt. Chaboisseau), and was burnt by the Dutch at the 2nd Battle.

TROMPEUR Class. The first purpose-built fireships were begun in 1670, when a 200-ton vessel were ordered from the builder Daviaud at Libourne; this vessel was known by the name of its builder until 24 June 1671, when it was named *Trompeur*. Orders for two more ships of this class was placed with this builder. However, building of the *Déguisé* was moved to Brest on 20 February 1671 (see below). All three vessels were named on 24 June 1671, and all were expended against the Dutch fleet at the Battles of Schooneveldt.
  Dimensions & tons: 90ft 0in, 75ft 0in x 24ft 0in x 11ft 0in (or 12ft) (29.24, 24.36 x 7.80 x 3.57 or 3.90m). 200 tons (350 for *Serpent* in 1673). Men: 30 (6/24/), +1 officer; 35 (7/28/), +1 officer in *Serpent* in 1673.
  Guns: 6, 10 from 6.1671, 12 in *Serpent* from 1673.

Trompeur Libourne.
  K: 1670. L: 1.1671. C: 2.1671. Took part in d'Estrées's squadron at both Battles of Schooneveldt 7 & 14.6.1673 (Capt. du Rivau) and was burnt by the Dutch at the 2nd Battle.

Serpent Libourne.
  K: 2.1671. L: 10.1671. C: 12.1671. Took part in d'Estrées's squadron at both Battles of Schooneveldt 7 & 14.6.1673 (Capt. Saint-Michel) and was burnt by the Dutch at the 2nd Battle.

Eight purpose-built 300-ton fireships were ordered during 1671, each intended to carry 12 guns and 40 men (8/32/-), plus 1 officer. These were mainly constructed of fir, since durability was not seen as a requirement. The design of these evolved from the light frigate and the galley-frigate, the latter a type capable of being propelled either by sail or by oars, similar to the English galley-frigates such as the *Charles Galley* and *James Galley*. Their frigate-type hulls meant that they were fast sailing vessels, and rather than being expended as fireships the majority saw service in the frigate role.

The new ships comprised the *Fâcheux* and *Brutal* at Dunkirk, the

Entreprenant and *Fin* at Rochefort, the *Déguisé* and *Périlleux* at Brest, and the *Dangereux* and *Incommode* at Toulon. The first three of these were converted to frigates and renamed – the *Entreprenant* being renamed *Vigilant* (5th Rank) in 1673 and listed in Chapter 5, and the Dunkirk pair being renamed *Entendu* and *Croissant* (4th Rank) in 1674 and listed in Chapter 4.

FIN. Purpose-built fireship. Designed and built by Jean Guichard. Ordered on 9 August 1671, and named in September after the fireship expended at Sousse. Her sister *Entreprenant* was completed as a 5th Rank *frégate* (renamed *Vigilant*) as noted above.

    Dimensions & tons: 99ft 0in, 78ft 0in x 27ft 10in x 11ft 2in (32.16, 25.34 x 9.04 x 3.63m). 300 tons. Men: 40 (8/32/), +1 officer; 35 (7/28/), +1 officer in 1673.

    Guns: 12.

Fin Rochefort Dyd.
    K: 9.1671. L: 12.1671. C: 4.1672. Expended at Battle of Schooneveldt 7.6.1673.

DÉGUISÉ Class. Purpose-built fireships, designed and built by Laurent Hubac. The first two were ordered in 1671 (*Déguisé* was first ordered at Lilbourne, but the order was moved to Brest on 20 February 1671, while *Périlleux* was not ordered until 31 July). These two were named respectively *Déguisé* and *Incommode* on 24 June 1671, the latter soon exchanging names with the *Périlleux* at Toulon, below. *Périlleux* was briefly armed and manned for a short time as a 24-gun frigate in 1675.

    Dimensions & tons: 86ft 0in x 26ft 0in x 8ft 6in (27.94 x 8.45 x 2.76m). 300 tons (*Périlleux* 200 from 1675, 290 from 1679, and 200 from 1696). Draught 13ft (4.22m). Men: 40 (8/32/), +1 officer; 35 (7/28/), +1 officer from 1673; *Périlleux* 120 men (33/60/27), +6 officers in 1675, then 30 men).

    Guns: LD 6 x 4pdrs; UD 4 x 4pdrs + 2 x 3pdrs. *Périlleux*: 30 in 1674, 24 in 1675, 18 from 1676, 10 from 1679, and 6 from 1696.

Déguisé Brest Dyd.
    K: 7.1671. L: 18.12.1671. C: 4.1672. Expended at Battle of Schooneveldt 7.6.1673.

Périlleux Brest Dyd.
    K: 9.1671. L: 15.1.1672. C: 4.1672. Unserviceable 1.1696 at Port Louis; struck 1700 and condemned 1.1702 at Port Louis.

Caché Brest Dyd.
    K: 2.1673. L: 4.1673. C: 5.1673. Expended at Battle of Schooneveldt 7.6.1673.

DANGEREUX Class. Purpose-built fireships, designed and built by Rodolphe Gédéon. Ordered on 24 April 1671 and named respectively *Dangereux* and *Périlleux* on 24 June 1671, the latter soon exchanging names with the *Incommode* at Brest, above. (The confusion lingered, however, and from January 1672 to 1675 the Toulon ship was called *Incommode* at Versailles and *Périlleux* at Toulon.) Both were armed and manned as 20-gun frigates in 1674 for use in a squadron in the Strait of Gibraltar.

    Dimensions & tons: 81ft 0in (26.31m) on keel. 300/350 tons (200 from 1675). Draught 10ft (3.25m). Men: 40 (8/32/), +1 officer; 35 (7/28/), +1 officer from 1673; 120 (33/60/27), +6 officers in 1675, 30 men in 1676.

A two-decked configuration was preferred for fireships as this allowed the lower deck to be permanently fitted up as a fire-deck when in service without disturbing the running of the ship. However, the *brûlot* shown in this Claude Randon engraving seems to be single-decked – there is enough height of side for a lower deck, but no evidence of ports below the wales, and the sallyport is definitely on the upper deck. Given the degree of decorative work and the heavy armament, the ship probably depicts one of the purpose-built fireships that could also function as a frigate. However, the ship exhibits one of the other signs of a fireship, the grapnels at the yardarms; there is even one on the sprit top at the end of the bowsprit.

Guns: 12, 30 from 1674, 20 from 1675

Dangereux Toulon Dyd.
   K: 31.10.1671. L: 4.10.1672. C: 12.1672. Expended (under Cdt Durivau) at Battle of Palermo 2.6.1676.

Incommode Toulon Dyd.
   K: 3.11.1671. L: 26.9.1672. C: 12.1672. Expended at Reggio 7.1675 to destroy the captured *frégate légère Gracieuse*.

The 4th Rank *Écueil* (ex-*Infante*) was converted to a fireship in March 1672 at Rochefort and wrecked in February 1673. She is listed in Chapter 4.

Two 12-gun fireships were ordered at Rochefort, named on 26 December 1672 as *Actif* and *Éclair*, and completed in 1673–74. In early 1675 both were armed and manned as 34-gun frigates with 150 men (35/78/37) and 6 officers although still listed as fireships. *Actif* was re-classed as a 4th Rank ship in 1675 and renamed *Étoile* 6 December 1675 while *Éclair* was re-classed as 5th Rank in 1675 and renamed *Soleil d'Afrique*, also on 6 December 1675. They are listed in Chapters 4 and 5 respectively. Two 12-gun fireships were ordered 3 February 1673 at Brest and named the next day as *Caché* and *Entreprenant*, but were modified as *frégates-vaisseaux* during construction, renamed *Arrogant* and *Dragon* on 28 November 1673 after launching, and re-classed as 5th Rank ships (see Chapter 5). Two more fireships, *Trompeur* and *Inconnu*, were projected in 1673 to be built at Rochefort and were named on 28 November 1673, but the contract was cancelled in August 1674.

FANFARON. Purpose-built fireship, designed and built by Abraham Aubier. Originally ordered 1672 and named on 13 January 1673 as *Actif*, but renamed *Fanfaron* in April 1673 (taking the name of the purchased fireship, ex-*Auguste*, condemned in April). Briefly armed and manned as a 30-gun frigate in 1675.

   Dimensions & tons: 95ft 0in, 80ft 0in x 28ft 0in x 12ft 0in (30.86, 25.99 x 9.10 x 3.90m). 350 tons (300 from 1676, 290 from 1679). Draught 12ft/14ft (3.90/4.55m). Men: 150 (35/78/37), +6 officers in 1675, 30 men in 1676.
   Guns: 30, 24 from 1676, 10 from 1679.

Fanfaron Rochefort Dyd.
   K: 12.1672. L: 4.1673. C: 5.1673. Rebuilt 8.1685 at Brest (see below).

PURCHASED AND ACQUIRED VESSELS (1673–1676). The French Navy acquired fifteen merchantmen for use as fireships during the Franco-Dutch War: three in 1673, four in 1674, two in 1675, and six in 1676. Of these five were expended as fireships and another was sunk by the enemy before she could be expended.

Sauvage. Acquired 1673. Expended 8.1673 against the Dutch at the battle of Ostend.

Voilé. Purchased 8.1673, Built 1671 in England. Initially called *Anglois*, renamed 28.11.1673. 150 tons. Draught 9ft (2.92m). 12 guns (10 from 1675, 8 from 1676). Struck 1676 at Brest.

Caché. Purchased 8.1673. Built 1670 in England. Initially called *Anglois*, renamed 28.11.1673. 150 tons (100 in 1676–77). Draught 9ft (2.92m). 20 guns (10 from 1675, 4 from 1676, 10 from 1679). Struck 1681, last mentioned 1682 at Toulon. A fireship listed at Toulon as *Inconnu* on the 1.1.1677 fleet list may have been this vessel after she moved from Rochefort to Toulon in 1676.

Entreprenant. Merchant *Auguste* purchased 1.1674 and renamed 19.2.1674. Built 1663, perhaps in the Seudre. 200 tons (100 in 1679). Draught 9ft (2.92m). 30 guns (6 from 1675). Renamed *Étourdi* 26.8.1678. Struck 1681, probably at Toulon.

Serpent. Merchant *Lion d'Or* purchased 1.1674 and renamed 19.2.1674. Built 1664 at St Malo.
   Dimensions & tons: dimensions unknown. 200 tons (80 in 1676). Draught 10ft (8ft in 1676) (3.25/2.60m). Men: 120 (33/60/27), +6 officers in 1675, 30 men in 1676.
   Guns: 30 (20 from 1675, 4 from 1676).
   Briefly armed and manned as a 20-gun frigate in 1675. Struck 1676 at Rochefort.

Inconnu. Privateer *Couronne* built 1665, captured 1671, purchased 1.1674, and soon renamed. 150 tons. Draught 8ft (2.60m). 6 guns (4 from 1676). Expended 5.1676 against a Spanish ship off the coast of Calabria.

Inquiet. Merchant *Saint François* purchased 2.1674 and renamed 19.2.1674. Built 1665 at La Rochelle. 150 tons. Draught 8ft (2.60m). 10 guns (6 from 1675, 4 from 1676). Expended at Battle of Palermo 2.6.1676.

Notre Dame de Lumière. Purchased 11.1675. 80 tons. Draught 8ft (2.60m). 4 guns. Expended at Battle of Palermo 2.6.1676.

Actif. Merchant *Roi David* purchased 11.1675 and renamed 6.12.1675. Built 1668 in Holland. 130 tons (150 from 1676). Draught 8ft (2.60m). 4 guns. Sunk by the Dutch 8.1.1676 in the second Battle of Stromboli.

Hameçon. Merchant *Armes de France* acquired 4.1676 and renamed 8.1676. Built 1660 or 1666 at Marseille by Brochon. 200 tons. Draught 11ft (3.57m). 4 guns (12 from 1679). Struck 1681, probably at Toulon.

Actif. Merchant *Petit Vivonne* or *Vivonne* purchased 6.1676 and soon renamed. Built 1666 at Marseille by Brochon. 350 tons (200 from 1677). Draught 9ft (2.92m). 6 guns (4 from 1677). Expended 6.1678 before Barcelona.

Ardent. Merchant *Saint Louis* purchased 6.1676 and soon renamed. Built 1666 at Cassis by Honoré Dalais or Dallix. 350 tons (200 from 1677). Draught 10ft (3.25m). 4 guns (8 from 1679). Renamed *Espion* 28.6.1678. Burned 7.1683 before Algiers by Barbary captives imprisoned on board.

Inquiet. Merchant *Lion d'Or* purchased 6.1676 and soon renamed. Built 1666 at Toulon by Pierre Hubac or François Chapelle. 200 tons. Draught 10ft (3.25m). 4 guns (10 from 1679). Rebuilt 3–5.1681 at Toulon. Captured 11 or 12.1681 by Algerians, may have been renamed *Taiffa* or *Kalik*.

Serpent. Merchant *Dauphin* from Le Havre purchased 1676 and soon renamed. Built 1670. 90 tons. Draught 11ft (3.57m). 6 guns. Probably wrecked 7.1678 on Viequès (Crab) Island off Puerto Rico after escaping the loss of most of *Vice-amiral* Jean, Comte d'Estrées's squadron in the Îles Aves, although listed as condemned and BU at the end of 1678, probably at Rochefort.

Déguisé. Acquired 1676, built in England in 1664. 100 tons. Draught 8ft (2.60m). 4 guns. Struck 1678.

Ex-ENGLISH PRIZE (1672). In 1672 French forces in India attacked the Portuguese town of São Tomé, today within Madras. When the French squadron of Jacob Blanquet de La Haye arrived in June 1672 an English merchant vessel named *Ruby* belonging to 'Sieur Gersey' was lying in the roadstead. Acting on a hint from the English agent at Madras, who disliked Mr Jearsey, the French commander seized the ship in around August 1672 and eventually dispatched her to France. Upon arrival at Rochefort she was classed as a fireship and renamed *Ruben* or *Rubis*. She had probably been built at Madras in around 1669–70.

   Dimensions & tons: 70ft 0in, 56ft 0in x 20ft 0in x 9ft 0in (22.74, 18.19 x 6.50 x 2.92m). 100 tons (90 from 1676, 100 from 1688). Draught 8ft/11ft (2.60/3.57m).

Guns: 6 (4 in 1676).
Ruben (Rubis). Madras
  Renamed *Brutal* 1.1675 (may previously have been renamed *Hameçon* 19.2.1674). Struck 1693, may have been lost 6.1692 at La Hougue.

Five 5th Rank ships captured from the Algerians in 1663–65 were re-classed as fireships in 1672–74. These vessels were *Perle*, *Soleil d'Afrique*, *Croissant d'Afrique* (renamed *Fâcheux* in January 1675), *Actif*, and *Émerillon*. All were quickly deleted except for *Émerillon*, which was expended at Solebay on 7 June 1672. The 5th Rank *Entendu* (captured in 1665), and the 5th Rank *Hasardeux* (purchased in 1666) were converted to fireships in March and May 1673 and were present at the first Battle of Schoonevcldt on 7 June 1673, in which *Hasardeux* was expended against a Dutch division flagship, sinking her, while *Entendu* was not expended but was later burnt on the English coast. The 5th Rank *Arrogant* (newly built in 1671) was converted to a fireship in June 1673 and expended at the Battle of Texel on 21 August 1673. The 5th Rank *Écureuil* (seized in 1661) was converted to a fireship at Toulon in December 1675, probably renamed *Éclair*, and expended at Palermo on 3 June 1676. The 5th Rank *Orage* (ex-Spanish *San Antonio*, captured 1675) became a fireship in 1678 (being briefly renamed *Lion*) but was condemned in 1680. All of these vessels are listed in Chapter 5.

Ex-SPANISH PRIZES (1674–1676). Spain was an ally of the Dutch during the Franco-Dutch War, and the French Navy turned seven or eight captured Spanish vessels into fireships during the conflict. Three of these were expended as fireships or lost during fleet actions against the Spanish and Dutch in the Mediterranean in 1676.
Fin. Ex-Spanish *San Juan Bautista* captured 1674 and called *Saint Jean Baptiste* until renamed *Fin* 1674. Built 1664 at Brest. 150 tons. Draught 8ft (2.60m). 6 guns (4 from 1676). Burned 8.1.1676 to avoid capture in the second Battle of Stromboli.
Notre Dame des Carmes. Ex-Spanish *Madona de Carma* captured 2.1675. Built at Genoa. 120/200/250 tons. 10 guns (4 from 12.1675). Expended 8.1.1676 without success in the second Battle of Stromboli.
Ligournais (Ligournois). Captured 9.1675, ex-Spanish *Salvador*. Called *Salvador* until renamed 5.1676. Built at Castellammare. 120 tons. 4 guns. Expended at Battle of Palermo 2.6.1676.
Fin. Captured 7.1675 or 7.1676 at Messina, ex-Spanish *Nuestra Señora de Misericordia*. Called *Notre Dame de Miséricorde* or *Prise de Messine* until renamed *Fin* 1676. Built 1664 at Genoa. 150 tons (200 from 1679). Draught 8ft/10ft (2.60/3.25m). 10 guns. Rebuilt 7–8.1681. Struck 1686 at Toulon.
Notre Dame de Bon Voyage. Captured 7.1675, ex-Spanish *Nuestra Señora de Buen Viaje* or barque *Notre Dame* of 1673–74. 100 tons. Draught 8½ft (2.76m). 4 guns. Struck 12.1676 at Toulon, or may have become the fireship *Voilé* of 1676 (below).
Trompeur. Merchant *Saint Firmin*, a Spanish prize, acquired 1.1676 and renamed 2.1676. Built 1672 at St Malo. 120 tons. Draught 10ft (3.25m). 10 guns. Probably struck 1678 at Rochefort.
Saint Nazaire. Spanish vessel, possibly ex-*San Nazarro*, captured 11.1676. Built at Genoa. 100 tons. Draught 8ft (2.60m). 6 guns. Not carried on the fleet lists, probably being considered a *bâtiment interrompu* or a service craft. Repaired 10.1681 at Toulon, at Tetuan 12.1782, last mentioned 6.1683 at Toulon.
Voilé. Probably the *Paule* from Leghorn taken from the Spanish 12.1676, but may instead have been the *Notre Dame de Bon Voyage*, above, renamed. Called *Prise de Messine* until renamed *Voilé* 12.1676. 100 tons. Draught 8ft (2.60m). 6 guns. Rebuilt 6.1681 at Toulon. Struck 1684 or 1685 at Toulon.

Ex-DUTCH PRIZES (1674–1677). The French Navy converted two captured Dutch vessels into fireships during the Franco-Dutch War.
Déguisé. Dutch vessel captured 1674. Built 1664 in England. 80 tons (100 from 1675). Draught 8ft (2.60m). 6 guns (4 from 1676). Struck 1677 at Rochefort.
Déguisé. Dutch vessel captured 7.1677, called *Saint Benoît* (her Dutch name?) until renamed *Déguisé* 1678. Built 1670 in Holland. 120 tons (100 from 1688). Draught 10ft/12ft (3.25/3.90m). 10 guns (4 from 1688, 6 from 1691). Based at Brest 1682–92. Lent as a privateer in 1689–90 to CB Jacques Du Vignau. Struck 1693 at Toulon.

MISCELLANEOUS PRIZES (1676). Two or three additional vessels were captured in June 1676 during the Franco-Dutch War under uncertain circumstances and two became French fireships. The fireship *Éclair*, below, may have been the same vessel as the *flûte Soleil* (200 tons, 25 men, 4 guns, see Chapter 9), which was also listed as captured in June 1676, probably with the *Saint Rosaire*. The *Soleil* was lost at Palma, Sicily, in March 1678 to privateers from Flushing, and the *Impudent* and *Éclair* were struck from the French lists at about the same time.
Impudent. Ex-Tuscan *San Rosario* captured 6.1676 and called *Saint Rosaire* until renamed 12.1676. May have been built at Pisa or Leghorn. 80 tons (200 from 1677). Draught 8½ft/10ft (2.76/3.25m). 8 guns. Struck 5.1678 at Toulon.
Éclair. English-built vessel captured 1676 at Messina. Struck 1678 at Toulon.

On 21 June 1678, Louis XIV signed an ordinance aiming to stimulate the bravery and the combativeness of the fireships' captains. Those who succeeded in setting fire to an enemy vessel would receive 6,000 *livres* for an ordinary ship, 10,000 for the enemy Rear-Admiral's ship, 15,000 for the Vice-Admiral's, and 20,000 for the commanding Admiral's plus a commission as *capitaine de vaisseau*.

Ex-BARBARY COAST PRIZES (1681–1683). Louis XIV's navy bombarded Algiers twice, in 1682 and in 1683, to obtain from the Barbary pirates a favourable treaty and the liberation of Christian slaves. During the conflict three Barbary Coast vessels were captured and incorporated into the Navy as fireships. One of these may have been captured from the French by the Spanish in 1684 in the brief War of the Reunions, which also saw a punitive French bombardment of Genoa in which the other two captured Algerine fireships participated.
Inquiet. Ex-Tripolitanian *Europa* captured 12.1681 and called *Europa* or *Europe* until renamed *Inquiet* 2.1683. Previously a French merchantman possibly built in Majorca and captured by Tripolitanian corsairs. 6 guns. Struck 1684, possibly captured by the Spanish 7.1684.
Caché. Ex-Algerian *Mistara* (meaning 'rule') captured 11.1682 and called *Règle* or *Règle de l'Espérance* until renamed *Caché* 1.3.1684. Built 1662–63 in England.
  Dimensions & tons: 108ft 0in x 20ft 0in x 10ft 0in (35.08 x 6.50 x 3.25m). 250 tons (200 from 1688, 140 from 1691). Draught 12ft/9ft (3.90/2.92m).
  Guns: 10; in 11.1682 had 6 x 4pdrs, 2 x 3pdrs, 4 x 2pdrs, and 8 *pierriers*.
  Participated in the bombardment of Genoa 5.1684. Struck late 1692 at Toulon.
Hameçon. Captured late 1683 from the North Africans, previously the mercantile *Clément* and called *Clément* until renamed *Hameçon* 1.3.1684. Built 1676 at Saint Malo. 100 tons (130 from 1691).

Draught 9ft (2.92m). 12 guns (6 from 1688). Participated in the bombardment of Genoa 5.1684. Struck 1694 at Port Louis.

After a gap of some twelve years, the building of specialist fireships resumed in the Royal Dockyards. However, it is noticeable that none of the later purpose-built fireships were expended in that role, and they served mainly as small frigates in the patrol and escort *rôles*.

FÂCHEUX Class. Purpose-built fireships, designed by Laurent and François Coulomb and built under a contract dated 13 September 1684, possibly at Cassis. Both were armed and manned as frigates in 1698 (*Dangereux* in 1698–1701).
> Dimensions & tons: 85ft 0in, 73ft 0in x 23ft 0in x 9ft 6in (27.61, 23.71 x 7.47 x 3.09m). 200 tons. Draught 10½ft/12ft (3.41/3.90m). Men: 30 (10/20/) as fireship, later 45 in war and peace; 120 in *Fâcheux* and 80 in *Dangereux* as frigates in 1698.
> Guns: 6 in *Fâcheux*, 8 in *Dangereux*. 16 in both from 1688, 10 from 1689. 6 in war from 1691 and 1696 (6 peace): 6 x 4pdrs. 26 in *Fâcheux* in 1698: LD 16 x 8pdrs, UD 10 x 4pdrs. 14 in *Dangereux* in 1698-1701: 6 x 8pdrs, 8 x 4pdrs. Both then reverted to 6 x 4pdrs.

Fâcheux Toulon Dyd (by contract).
> K: 10.1684. L: 31.3.1685. C: 8.1685. Accepted 23.10.1685. Struck at Toulon 1704–05.

Dangereux Toulon Dyd (by contract).
> K: 10.1684. L: 1.4.1685. C: 8.1685. Delivered 20.10.1685. Operated off Nova Scotia in 1697 under LG André, Marquis de Nesmond, in a squadron of twenty-three vessels. Probably submerged at Toulon 7.1707 to evade mortar attacks and refloated 11.1707. Struck at Toulon 1709.

FANFARON Class. Purpose-built fireships, designed and built by Étienne Hubac. *Fanfaron* was a rebuilding of the vessel of 1673 above while *Espion* was named in June 1686 and ordered on 1 July 1686. *Espion* was armed as a frigate when completed.
> Dimensions & tons: 90ft 0in, 80ft 0in x 27ft 6in x 11ft 5in (29.24, 25.99 x 8.93 x 3.71m). 250 tons. Draught 12ft/13½ft (3.90/4.39m). Men: 30 (10/20/), +2 officers.
> Guns: 10 in *Fanfaron*, 28 in *Espion*. *Espion* reduced to 24 from 1688. *Fanfaron* had 6 from 1691 and 8 in war (8 peace) from 1696: 8 x 4pdrs

Fanfaron Brest Dyd.
> K: 8.1685. L: 1.1686. C: 4.1686. Lent as a privateer in 1688–89 (before war began) to Charles d'Adlbert d'Ailly, Duc de Chaulnes, Governor of Brittany, under command of LV Gilles François Des Blottières. Lent as a privateer in 1689–90 to the Marquis de Seignelay, Secretary of State for the Navy, as part of a squadron of three vessels under CV Jacques Dandenne. Captured 5.1697 by the Dutch while transporting about thirty 24pdr guns from Rochefort to Dunkirk.

Espion Brest Dyd.
> K: 9.8.1686. L: 1.3.1687. C: 4.1687. Ordered on 1.10.1688 to be sold at Brest to the *Compagnie des Indes Orientales* and renamed *Lonray*. She was lost leaving Surat in late 1696.

IMPUDENT. Purpose-built fireship designed and built by Blaise Pangalo and sometimes considered a sister of *Éclair*, below. She was named on 30 June 1686 and the contract for her construction was dated 29 July 1686.
> Dimensions & tons: 97ft 0in x 27ft 6in (31.51 x 8.93m). 300 tons. Draught 12ft (3.90m). Men: 30 (10/20/), +2 officers.

> Guns: 30, then 10 from 1689.

Impudent Toulon Dyd (by contract).
> K: 6.1686. L: 11.12.1686. C: 4.1687. Not listed after 1690, fate unknown.

ÉCLAIR. Purpose-built fireship designed and built by François Coulomb. She was named on 30 June 1686 and the contract for her construction was dated 29 July 1686. She was armed and manned as a frigate in 1698–1700.
> Dimensions & tons: 97ft 0in, 82ft 0in x 26ft 6in x 11ft 0in (31.51, 26.64 x 8.61 x 3.57m). 300 tons. Draught 13½ft (4.39m). Men: 30; 40 in 1691, 35 in 1692, 45 in war and peace in 1696, 150 as frigate in 1698–99.
> Guns: 30, 10 from 1689, 28 from 1691, 10 from 1692. 8 from 1696: 8 x 6pdrs. 28 guns from 1688 (LD 16 x 8pdrs, UD 12 x 4pdrs), but reverted to 8 x 6pdrs by 1701.

Éclair Toulon Dyd (by contract).
> K: 6.1686. L: 19.12.1686. C: 4.1667. Lent as a privateer in 12.1697 at Brest to Sieur Manet to carry a supply of grain from Port-Louis to Bayonne. Rebuilt 2–4.1701 at Toulon. Probably submerged at Toulon 7.1707 to evade mortar attacks and refloated 11.1707. Guard hulk at Toulon 1715, struck 20.10.1720, ordered BU 29.11.1721.

Ex-DUTCH PRIZES (1688). In the months leading up to the War of the League of Augsburg between France and a coalition including the Dutch Republic, Spain, and England, the French seized or otherwise acquired two Dutch merchantmen which they put in service as fireships. Both became naval *flûtes* in 1692 as did several more fireships acquired in 1689.

Incommode. Dutch vessel *Burg* or *Groot Dorp* seized 9.1688, classed as a fireship, and called *Bourg* until renamed *Incommode* 4.1689. Built 1684 at Amsterdam.
> Dimensions & tons: dimensions unknown. 260 tons (200 from 1691). Draught 10ft/12½ft (3.25/4.06m). Men: 30, +2 officers; 20, + 2 officers as *flûte*.
> Guns: 8, 16 as *flûte*.
> Re-classed as a 200-ton, 16-gun *flûte* and renamed *Dromadaire* 4.1692. Sold at Dunkirk 7.1693 for merchant service and renamed *Demoiselle Cecilia*. Seized by the Dutch during a port call at Amsterdam 6.1697.

Étourdi. Dutch vessel acquired or captured 1688. Built 1683 at Trever (Holland), designed by Geoffre.
> Dimensions & tons: 94ft 0in x 20ft 6in x 11ft 0in (30.53 x 6.66 x 3.57m). 190/195 tons (290 from 1696). Draught 12½ft (4.06m). Men: 30, +2 officers; 30 in war, 25 peace as *flûte*.
> Guns: 6. 10 in war (4 peace) from 1696 as *flûte*: 6 x 6pdrs, 4 x 4pdrs
> Re-classed as a 290-ton, 10-gun *flûte* and renamed *Écrevisse* 3.1692, name reverted to *Étourdi* 7.1692. Lent as a privateer in 1694 to Sieur Chaillou, a wood merchant at Brest, to carry timbers from the Vilaine/Loire area to Brest. Carried grain with *Mulet* and *Providence* from Port Louis to Bayonne 1697. Unserviceable at Brest 1700, *patache* (tender or advice boat) from 1704, unserviceable hulk 1710–12.

(C) Vessels acquired from 15 April 1689

At the start of 1689 the official list included ten fireships, six being dockyard-built and four acquired. The former comprised the four Toulon-built ships of 1685–86 (see above) and the Brest-built *Fanfaron* and older *Périlleux*; each carried 10 guns and a crew of 30 men (+1 officer). The remaining four were the *Caché, Hameçon, Brutal* and *Déguisé*. The numbers expanded rapidly – to twenty by the start of 1690 and then to thirty-six by the start of 1691, falling to thirty-one a year later.

PURCHASED VESSELS (1689–1691). The War of the League of Augsburg led to the acquisition by the French Navy of a large number of merchantmen for use as fireships, both by purchase and by capture. Between 1689 and 1691 (mostly in 1689) up to sixteen French merchantmen were acquired, although the circumstances of several of the acquisitions are unclear and several may have been converted from naval service craft. Only one of these vessels is known to have been expended as a fireship in a fleet action.

Terre-Neuvier. Vessel from Le Havre found abandoned 1.1689 and put into service 4.1689 as a fireship. Fate unknown.

Dur. Ex-*Ville de Marseille* purchased 4.1689 at Marseille, and renamed 21.5.1689. Built at Dunkirk in 1684. 200 tons. Draught 10ft (3.25m). 10 guns. Present (but not expended) at Battle of Beachy Head 10.7.1690, last mentioned 7.1690.

Boutefeu. Ex-*Diamant*, purchased 4.1689 at Marseille and renamed 21.5.1689. Built at La Ciotat in 1686 (probably by Louis Audibert);
Dimensions & tons: 85ft 0in x 25ft 6in x 11ft 6in (27.61 x 8.28 x 3.74m). 257 tons (250 from 1691). Draught 10½ft/13ft (3.41/4.22m). Men: 30; later 40 in war, 40 peace
Guns: 10, 6 from 1691. 6 in war (6 peace) from 1696: 6 x 6pdrs
Present (but not expended) at Battle of Beachy Head 10.7.1690. Struck 1697, probably at Toulon.

Insensé. Ex-*Saint Joseph*, purchased at Marseille 4.1689 and renamed 21.5.1689. Built at Marseille in 1681.
Dimensions & tons: 75ft 0in, 48ft 0in x 15ft 0in x 7ft 0in (24.36, 15.59 x 4.87 x 2.27m). 230 tons (130 from 1691). Draught 10½ft/12ft (3.41/3.90m).
Guns: 10, 6 from 1691.
Lent as a privateer in 1689–90 to the Marquis de Seignelay and *Vice-amiral* Anne Hilarion de Costentin, Comte de Tourville, under the command of CB de Nandy, and in company with *Extravagant*, below. Present (but not expended) at Battle of Beachy Head 10.7.1690. In Tourville's fleet during the 1691 *Campagne du large*, lost at La Hougue 2/3 June 1692 with *Enflammé*. Said to have become HMS *Wild* [*Prize*] but that ship was the French privateer *Farouche* captured 15.5.1692 by HMS *Centurion* in the Channel.

Extravagant. Ex-*Visitation*, purchased 4.1689 and renamed 21.5.1689. Built at La Ciotat 1687 by Pierre Martin.
Dimensions & tons: 90ft 0in x 24ft 0in x 11ft 0in (29.23 x 7.80 x 3.57m). 257 tons (250 from 1691). Draught 9½ft (3.09m).
Guns: 10, 6 from 1691.
Lent as a privateer in 1689–90 to the Marquis de Seignelay and *Vice-amiral* Anne Hilarion de Costentin, Comte de Tourville, under the command of CV François, chevalier de Venise, and in company with *Insensé*, above. Present (but not expended) at Battle of Beachy Head 10.7.1690. Captured by HMS *Saint Albans* 2.11.1691, becoming the fireship HMS *Extravagant* [*Prize*]; set alight by a French shot and burnt at the Battle of Barfleur 29.5.1692.

Marianne. Ex-*Marianne*, purchased 7.1689 at Rochefort with *Chesne Vert* (see *Farouche*, below) and the *flûte Providence* from Sieur Regnier of Rochefort. Built 1682.
Dimensions & tons: 76ft 0in x 22ft 6in x (24.69 x 7.31m). 200 tons.
Guns: 6.
Never appeared on the fleet list as *Marianne* and may have become the fireship *Inquiet* (below) in 1691. Alternatively she might have become the French privateer *Marianne* which was captured 6.2.1693 by HM Ships *York* and *Dover* and became the fireship HMS *Marianna* [*Prize*].

Espion. Ex-*Notre Dame de Grâce*, purchased late 1689 and renamed 28.1.1690. Built 1674 at Marseille by Barthelémy.
Dimensions & tons: 92ft 6in x 25ft 3in x 11ft 4in (30.05 x 8.20 x 3.68m). 300 tons (200 in 1691–92, 180 from 1699). Draught 12ft/13ft 10in (3.90/4.49m). Men: 30; later 35 in war, 35 peace
Guns: 6. 6 in war, (6 peace) from 1696: 6 x 4pdrs
Taken out of service 1700 and condemned 1702 at Toulon.

Trompeur. Ex-Spanish *Vierge de Grâce*, probably built 1673 in Holland, captured in 1689 by CV Jacques Dandenne's squadron of three vessels funded by the Marquis de Seignelay while loaded with fish oil and *morue blanche* (dried cod), then acquired for the King's service, converted to a fireship, and renamed *Trompeur* on 11.3.1690.
Dimensions & tons: dimensions unknown. 250 tons. Draught 13ft (4.22m).
Guns: 6
Last mentioned 5.1691 at Brest. May have been planned for conversion to a *flûte*, either the *Prodigue* or *Endormie* of 1692, although that project was soon cancelled.

Fleur de Blé. Either captured 1689 or converted from a Rochefort *chatte* (service craft). Used as a *flûte* in 1689 to transport arms and ammunition from Brest to Ireland. Captured 11.11.1689 by HMS *Dover* (42), purchased 9.12.1689 by the RN and renamed *Blade of Wheat* (150 tons, 10 guns). Driven from her moorings in a storm and wrecked 4.1.1690 in Mill Bay (Plymouth Sound).

Farouche. Acquired 1690, perhaps the *Chesne Vert* purchased 7.1689 at Rochefort or an old Rochefort service craft. Expended 10.7.1690 in the Battle of Beachy Head.

Actif. Acquired or converted 2.1690. Probably a Rochefort service craft (*chatte*?) converted to a fireship. Designed by Honoré Malet and built 1670 at Rochefort. 60 tons. Draught 8½ft (2.76m). 6 guns. Struck 5.1691, may have become service craft at Rochefort.

Inquiet. Acquired or converted 2.1690. Probably a Rochefort service craft (*chatte*?) converted to a fireship. Designed by Honoré Malet. Built 1675 at Rochefort. 60 tons. Draught 8½ft (2.76m). Men: 35 (11/24/), +2 officers. 10 guns. Struck 5.1691, may have become service craft at Rochefort.

Enflammé. Acquired or converted spring 1690. Probably a Rochefort service craft (*yack* or *gabarre*?) converted to a fireship. Designed by Honoré Malet. Built 1687 at Rochefort. 100 tons. Draught 9½ft (3.09m). 6 guns. Present in the Battle of Barfleur 29.5.1692, lost at La Hougue 2/3 June 1692 with *Insensé*.

Impudent. Ex-*Dauphin Couronné*, purchased 4.1690 and renamed 3.4.1690. Designed by Laurent Coulomb. Built 1675 at Marseille.
Dimensions & tons: 89ft 0in, 67ft 0in x 24ft 9in x 10ft 10in (28.91, 21.76 x 8.04 x 3.52m). 200 tons. Draught 11½ft (3.74m). Men: 40 (12/28/), +2 officers.
Guns: 10.
Grounded off Dunkirk 3.1691, refloated 7.1691, struck 1691.

Dur. Purchased 1690 at Toulon. Built 1675 at Saint Malo.
Dimensions & tons: 77ft 6in x 22ft 0in x 9ft 0in (25.18 x 7.15 x 2.92m). 150 tons (100 from 1696). Draught 11ft (3.57m). Men: 30; later 35 in war, 30 peace
Guns: 6. 6 in war (6 peace) from 1696: 6 x 4pdrs
Condemned 1698 at Brest, BU there 12.1699.

Inquiet. Purchased 1691. Built 1684 at Royan (near Rochefort) by Grozelier. May have been the fireship *Marianne* (above) of 1689. 120 tons. Draught 12ft (3.90m). Men: 28 (6/19/), +3 officers. 8 guns. Last mentioned 1692.

Ex-SPANISH PRIZE (1689). The merchantman *Cristina* from the Spanish Netherlands, one of France's opponents in the War of the League of Augsburg, was captured in 1689 by CV Jacques Dandenne's squadron of three vessels funded by the Marquis de Seignelay, then acquired for the King's service, converted to a fireship, and called *Christine* by the French until being renamed *Renard* on 11 March 1690. She was built in 1670 at Flushing. 120 tons; Draught 9ft (2.92m); 6 guns. She was used as a *flûte* in 1690 in the squadron of LG Charles François Davy Du Perron, Marquis d'Amfreville, during the Irish campaign. She blew up and was scuttled 7.1691 off Brest, being surrounded by four enemy ships.

Ex-DUTCH PRIZES (1689–1692). During the early part of the War of the League of Augsburg the French captured eight Dutch merchantmen that they converted into naval fireships. Of these one was expended in India in 1690 and a second may have been expended in the same year.

Orage. Ex-French cod fisherman *Ville de Caudebec*, designed by Étienne Salicon and built at Le Havre 1682. Captured by the Dutch 2.1689 while loaded with *morue verte* (salted cod), retaken three days later by *Mutine*, part of a squadron of three lent as privateers to the Marquis de Seignelay and CV Ferdinand, Comte de Relingue. Bought for 7,400 *livres* for the King's service, converted to a fireship, and renamed *Orage* 11 March 1690.

Dimensions & tons: 78ft 0in x 23ft 0in x 11ft 0in (25.34 x 7.47 x 3.57m). 150 tons (120/125 in 1698/99). Draught 12ft/12½ft (3.90/4.06m). Men: 30; later 35 in war, 30 peace.

Guns: 6. 6 in war (4 peace) from 1696: 6 x 4pdrs. 6 from 1698: 6 x 6pdrs.

Classed as *flûte* by 1696 (but unserviceable), reverted to fireship 1698 (but used as a *patache*), unserviceable 1700, guard hulk at Brest 1703, unserviceable 1710, and BU 1712.

Inconnu. Dutch vessel, name unknown, captured 1689. Built 1680 in Zeeland.

Dimensions & tons: 85ft 0in x 20ft 6in x 10ft 0in (27.61 x 6.66 x 3.25m). 230 tons (200 from 1691). Draught 12ft (3.90m). Men: 30; later 25 in war, 25 peace

Guns: 6. 6 in war (6 peace) from 1696: 6 x 4pdrs

Renamed *Paisible* 3.1692 when re-classed as a 200-ton *flûte*. Struck 1699 at Toulon.

Rusé. Dutch vessel *Soubreau* captured 1689 and renamed *Rusé* 11.3.1690. Built 1675 at Flushing.

Dimensions & tons: dimensions unknown. 120 tons. Draught 9ft (2.92m).

Guns: 6 guns.

Used as a *flûte* in the squadron of LG Charles François Davy Du Perron, Marquis d'Amfreville, during the Ireland campaign of 1690. Captured 1.6.1692 by HMS *Adventure* (40), becoming fireship HMS *Ruzee Prize*; burnt by accident 14.7.1692.

Dévorant. Dutch *Samaritaans*, built in Holland in 1674, was captured by CV Jacques Dandenne's squadron of three funded by the Marquis de Seignelay. Acquired for the King's service and converted to a fireship called *Samaritaine* until renamed *Dévorant* 11.3.1690.

Dimensions & tons: 85ft 6in x 24ft 6in x 10ft 0in (27.77 x 7.96 x 3.25m). 230 tons (220 in 1696-98). Draught 13½ft (4.39m). Men: 30; later 40 in war, 35 peace

Guns: 6. 6 in war (6 peace) from 1696: 6 x 6pdrs. 6 from 1698: 6 x 4pdrs.

Unserviceable at Brest 1700, guard hulk 1704. Condemned 11.1715, BU 1716.

Voilé. Captured 1689, possibly the Dutch *Wapen van Amsterdam* (36), built 1674-75 at Amsterdam and taken by the French in 1689. 280 tons (220 from 1691). Draught 10ft/12ft (3.25/3.90m). 6 guns. Renamed *Massue* 3.1692, when re-classed as a 200-ton *flûte*. Last mentioned 5.1693 at Brest.

Fin. Dutch vessel captured 1689. Built 1680 at Amsterdam. 260 tons (230 by 1691). Draught 12ft/13ft (3.90/4.22m). 6 guns. Last mentioned 1691, probably expended in 1690.

Brûlot du Capitaine d'Auberville. Probable Dutch vessel captured 8.1690 at Pondicherry and fitted as a fireship. 40 tons. Expended 8.1690 without success at Madras.

Corossol. Dutch *pinasse* possibly named *Curaçao* captured 2.1692. Built in Holland. 200 tons, 20 guns. Last mentioned 3.1693 at Port Louis.

Ex-ENGLISH PRIZES (1689–1692). During the early part of the War of the League of Augsburg the French also captured six or seven English merchantmen that they converted into naval fireships. Reflecting the low rate of expenditure of fireships during this war, none of these vessels were lost in action.

Drôle. English vessel *Sarah Elizabeth*, Built 1668 in England. Captured 6.1689 by CV Jacques Dandenne's squadron of three vessels funded by the Marquis de Seignelay. Acquired for the King's service and converted to a fireship called *Sarah-Elisabeth* until renamed *Drôle* 3.1690.

Dimensions & tons: dimensions unknown. 120 tons. Draught 8½ft (2.76m).

Guns: 6.

Used as a *flûte* in the squadron of LG Charles François Davy Du Perron, Marquis d'Amfreville, during the Ireland campaign of 1690. Condemned 1695.

Serpent. English vessel *Royal Jacques* vessel, built in 1672 in England. Captured 10.1690 by CV Jacques Dandenne's squadron of three vessels funded by the Marquis de Seignelay, then acquired for the King's service, converted to a fireship, and renamed *Serpent*.

Dimensions & tons: 88ft 0in x 23ft 0in x 7ft 8in (28.59 x 7.47 x 2.49m). 200 tons. Draught 14ft (4.55m).

Guns: 8. 14 in war (10 peace) from 1696 although 18 listed: LD 4 x 6pdrs, UD 6 x 6pdrs, 8 x 4pdrs

Condemned 1.1696 at Lorient.

Impertinent. English vessel *Marchand de Londres* probably built in 1683 at London, taken by the 4th Rank *Comte* (40) 1.1690, part of a squadron of three vessels lent as privateers to the Marquis de Seignelay and CV Ferdinand, Comte de Relingue. Acquired for the King's service, converted to a fireship, and renamed *Impertinent* 20.2.1690.

Dimensions & tons: 90ft 0in x 23ft 8in x 10ft 10in (29.24 x 7.69 x 3.52m). 200 tons (260 from 1698). Draught 12½ft (4.06m). Men: 30. In 1696: 40 in war, 40 peace. In 1698: 150 in war, 45 peace

Guns: 10. 6 in war (6 peace) from 1696: 6 x 6pdrs. 28 in war (8 peace) from 1698: LD 16 x 8pdrs, UD 12 x 4pdrs

Operated at Nova Scotia in 1697 under LG André, Marquis de Nesmond, in a squadron of twenty-three vessels. Armed and manned 1698 as a frigate. Struck 1.1699 at Toulon.

Ange. English vessel *Angel* captured 7.1691. Built in England.

Dimensions & tons: 95ft 0in x 23ft 0in or 25ft 0in x 11ft 6in (30.86 x 7.47 or 8.12 x 3.74m). 200 tons. Draught 12ft (3.90m). Men: 40–45 in war and peace

Guns: 6 in war (6 peace): 6 x 4pdrs. 16 from 1698: 8 x 8pdrs, 8 x 4pdrs

Rebuilt 6–7.1693 at Lorient. Struck 1698 at Brest, sold 1699.

Guillaume de Londres. English vessel *William* captured 10 or 11.1692. Built in England. Renamed *Guillaume* 6.1693. 45 men and 1 officer, 10 guns. Struck 1694.

Bon Succès. English vessel *Good Success* (?) captured 12.1692. Also called by the French *Bon Succès de Londres* and *Heureux Success*. Built 1678 at London.
   Dimensions & tons: 74ft 0in x 22ft 6in x 10ft 6in (24.04 x 7.31 x 3.41m). 150 tons (100 in 1696). Draught 13ft (4.22m). Men: 25 in war, 20 peace
   Guns: 8. From 1696: 6 in war (6 peace): 6 x 4pdrs
   Struck 12.1697 at Brest and placed on sale.

Ex-ENGLISH NAVAL PRIZES (1690–1691). The English merchantman *Olive Branch* was purchased in 1690 by the Royal Navy as a fireship and was captured 3.1690 by CV Jacques Dandenne's squadron of three vessels, which had been lent as privateers to the Marquis de Seignelay. Acquired for the King's service as a fireship called *Branche d'Olivier* before being renamed *Fin* on 3 July 1690. The 4th Rate *Constant Warwick* was captured off Portugal on 22 July 1691 by a French squadron while escorting a convoy to the West Indies and renamed *Chasseur*.
Fin England.
   Dimensions & tons: dimensions unknown. 260 tons (230 in 1692). Draught 12ft/13ft (3.90/4.22m).
   Guns: 6.
   Built 1670. Put on sale 12.1693 at Toulon.
Chasseur John Tippets at Portsmouth
   Dimensions & tons: 84ft 6in on keel x 26ft 5in x 11ft 3in (27.45 x 8.58 x 3.65m). 380 tons. Men: 50, +2 officers.

   Guns: 12/18 plus 6 *pierriers*.
   Ord: 3.1664. K: 8.1665. L: 21.6.1666. Grounded and burnt 5.1694 near Le Conquet to avoid capture by the English 5.1694. A mortar and 200 mortar shells were salvaged from the wreck.

VIOLENT Class. Purpose-built fireships, designed by Pierre Coulomb and built by Nicolas Chapelle and Joseph Pomet respectively. The contract for their construction was dated 6 April 1690 and the ships were named on 10 December 1690.
   Dimensions & tons: 87ft 0in, 72ft 0in x 24ft 0in x 10ft 4in (28.26, 23.39 x 7.80 x 3.36m). 180 tons (200 from 1696 in *Violent*, 250/260 in *Indiscret*, 200 from 1701 in *Indiscret*). Draught 9ft/13ft (2.92/4.22m). Men: 45 in war, 30 peace, +2 officers. In 1696: 45 in war and peace. *Indiscret* in 1698–1700: 100 in war, 40 peace. Later 40 in war and peace.
   Guns: 6 x 6pdrs (8 x 6pdrs in *Indiscret* from 1696). In a frigate role in 1698 *Indiscret* carried 20 guns (12 x 8pdrs + 8 x 4pdrs), soon reduced to 6 x 4pdrs. *Violent* carried 8 x 6pdrs from 1704.
Violent Toulon Dyd (by contract).
   K: 4.1690. L: 28.10.1690. C: 1.1691. Operated at Nova Scotia in 1697 under LG André, Marquis de Nesmond, in a squadron of twenty-three vessels. Probably submerged at Toulon 7.1707 to evade mortar attacks and refloated 11.1707. Condemned 1712 at Toulon.
Indiscret Toulon Dyd (by contract).
   K: 4.1690. L: 4.11.1690. C: 1.1691. Wrecked near Rochefort 3.1693, but raised and rebuilt there 4.1693. Armed and manned as a frigate 1698–1700. Operated at Nova Scotia in 1697 under LG André, Marquis de Nesmond, in a squadron of twenty-three vessels. Captured by the English at Vigo Bay 12.10.1702.

A vessel named *Fourbe* was listed in January 1691 with *Séditieux* (a former *frégate légère*, see chapter 6) as a 10-gun fireship at Rochefort with 2 officers and 40 men but with no other details. This may have reflected a plan to convert the *Friponne* from a *frégate légère* into a fireship, but *Friponne* was also listed in January 1691 as a frigate, although she had been captured in December 1690.

FOURBE Class. Purpose-built fireships, designed by Pierre Coulomb and built by Nicolas Chapelle and Joseph Pomet respectively. They were named on 29 July 1691 and the contract with Teisseire (an entrepreneur at Toulon) for their construction was dated 31 July 1691.
   Dimensions & tons: 92ft 0in x 25ft 0in x 10ft 6in (29.89 x 8.12 x 3.41m). 300 tons (260 from 1696, 200 by 1701). Draught 10ft/14ft (3.25/4.55m). Men: 35 (11/24/), +2 officers as fireships, 130 in war (100 peace) in *Fourbe* in 1696; 150 in war (20 peace) in *Lutin* in 1696 as a 5th Rank.
   Guns: 10. *Fourbe* had 26 in war (20 peace) from 1696: LD 12 x 6pdrs, UD 14 x 4pdrs; and 16 guns from 1700: 16 x 4pdrs. *Lutin* had 32 in war (24 peace) as 5th Rank in 1696: LD 16 x 8pdrs, UD 14 x 4pdrs.
Fourbe Toulon Dyd (by contract).
   K: 8.1691. L: 17.12.1691. C: 3.1692. Re-classed as *frégate légère* in 1701 (220 tons, 120 men). Used as a coast guard in the Channel as the beginning of the War of the Spanish Succession, ordered to stay as close to the coast as as she could, she came so close that she ran aground and was lost near Carteret 31.1.1703.

The small English two-decker *Constant Warwick*, seen in this drawing by Willem van de Velde the elder from about 1685, was captured in 1691 and converted into a fireship. (National Maritime Museum, London PY1877)

Lutin Toulon Dyd (by contract).
K: 8.1691. L: 1.1692. C: 3.1692. Re-classed as 5th Rank 1694. Grounded at Calais 3.1696 and not mentioned after 1697.

IMPUDENT Class. Ordered in April 1692, named on 7 April 1692, and designed by François Coulomb. *Impudent* was the last French naval vessel to be completed for the fireship role, although like all fireships built by the French Navy since 1684 and in contrast with many of those built in 1670–73 she was not expended in that capacity.
Dimensions & tons: as *Fourbe* Class above. Men: 150 in war (20 peace)
Guns: 32 in war (20 peace): LD 18 x 8pdrs, UD 14 x 6pdrs
Impudent Toulon Dyd.
K: 6.1692. L: early 1693. C: 5.1693. Often called *Imprudent*. Operated at Nova Scotia in 1697 under LG André, Marquis de Nesmond, in a squadron of twenty-three vessels. Sold 11.1698 to the *Compagnie Royale de St Domingue*.
Fantasque Toulon Dyd.
Not built; order cancelled 6.1692.

In addition to the two Toulon ships above, orders were placed in April 1692 for six other fireships – two each at Lorient (*Mutin* and *Trompeur*), Brest (*Inconnu* and *Renard*) and Rochefort (*Actif* and *Étourdi*). The Lorient pair were laid down – by Pierre Coulomb – in May 1692, but all six, together with the *Fantasque* above, were cancelled in June. At Lorient the *Trompeur* was broken up on the stocks but the *Mutin* was dismantled and her timbers were put into storage, she was again set up on the slip in February 1693 to become the 5th Rank *vaisseau Mutine*, later *Sphère* (see Chapter 5).

The twelve fireships ordered in 1690–92 were the last purpose-built fireships intended to be built for the French Navy. The English attack on the French warships at La Hougue on 2/3 June 1692, which resulted in the destruction of twelve major vessels (see Chapter 1), was carried out by ships' boats and other small craft; fireships had been sent in as well but were not needed, as the undefended ships could be boarded and set aflame by cheaper methods. The French Navy took the lesson on board, and ceased the expensive construction of purpose-built vessels.

PURCHASED VESSELS (1693).
Léopard. Purchased early 1693 for conversion to a fireship although sometimes called a *flûte*. 35 men, 8 guns. Condemned 1695.
Sainte Marie or *Esther-Marie*. Acquired 1693 at Toulon. Last mentioned 1694.

Ex-SPANISH PRIZE (1693). A vessel probably named *Ciudad de Cadiz* and built in Spain was captured in early 1693. Renamed *Ville de Cadiz*, she had 10 guns and 40 men in French service and was last mentioned in September 1693.

PRINCESSE ANNE DE DANEMARK. This vessel was either a merchant vessel from Hamburg named *Fürstin Ann von Danemark* that was captured in November 1693 or a Dutch ship captured on 14 September 1695.
Dimensions & tons: 57ft 0in x 17ft 0in x 7ft 6in (18.52 x 5.52 x 2.44m). 80 tons. Draught 9½ft (3.09m). Men: 25 in war, 25 peace
Guns: 6 in war (6 peace): 6 x 4pdrs.
Princesse Anne de Danemark England.
Sold 12.1697 at Brest.

Ex-ENGLISH NAVAL PRIZE (1695). HMS *Post Boy*, an advice boat, was captured 13 July 1695 in Lyme Bay by the French privateer *Facteur de Bristol* (a previous HMS *Post Boy*) while carrying despatches from the Channel Islands to Plymouth. She was added to the French Navy as the fireship *Facteur de Bristol*.
Dimensions & tons: 81ft 0in x 21ft 0in x 9ft 0in (26.31 x 6.82 x 2.92m). 180 tons. Draught 10½ft (3.41m). Men: 30 in war, 30 peace
Guns: 6 in war (6 peace): 6 x 4pdrs.
Facteur de Bristol William Stigant at Portsmouth Dyd
Ord: 3.10.1694. L: 1695. Struck 1698 at Toulon.

Another *Facteur de Bristol* was captured 25.8.1696 by CV Renau d'Élissagaray (Petit-Renau), a privateer from St Malo and was armed by him to reinforce the squadron of five King's vessels lent to him for privateering operations, for which he was financially associated with Yves Le Gac, Sieur de L'Armorique, former mayor of Brest 1691–93. The prize was initially adjudicated for 2,040 *livres* to Le Gac but Hubert de Champy Desclouzeaux, *intendant* at Brest, claimed the priority for the Crown; the ship was bought and converted in fireship 11.1696. She was lent as a privateer to Sieur Rhodon 1697 and was struck 1698 at Brest.

Ex–ENGLISH PRIZE (1696). A French merchantman built at Olonne around 1693 was captured by the English and named *St John* and was then captured in May 1696 by the French, becoming the French fireship *Saint Jean de Plymouth*.
Dimensions & tons: 63ft 0in x 20ft 0in x 9ft 0in (20.46 x 6.50 x 2.92m). 110 tons. Draught 10½ft (3.41m). Men: 30 in war, 25 peace
Guns: 6 in war (6 peace): 6 x 4pdrs.
Saint Jean de Plymouth Olonne
Unserviceable 1700 at Brest, used as a *patache* (tender or advice boat) from 1704. Captured 17.12.1704 by the English but recaptured 1705 by the French and resumed service as a *patache*. Struck 1712.

By the start of 1702 the number of fireships on the official List had fallen to eight – six being purpose-built (including one old and unserviceable), one (*Lion* ex-*Soleil d'Afrique*) converted from an old 5th Rank ship that had been begun as the fireship *Éclair*, and one old merchantman. The War of the Spanish Succession which began in that year led to the acquisition of only a handful of additional fireships and the construction of none. No French Navy fireships were expended as such during this war.

PURCHASED VESSELS (1702–1706). Four French merchant vessels were acquired for use as fireships during the War of the Spanish Succession
Espion. The mercantile *Cene* was purchased at Toulon in 1702 and was renamed *Espion* 22.8.1702. She was built at Toulon in 1698 by Thomas (?) Angalier.
Dimensions & tons: 86ft 8in x 24ft 9in x 10ft 6in (28.46 x 8.04 x 3.41m). 280 tons. Draught 14ft (4.55m). Men: 45 in war, 40 peace
Guns: 8 in war (8 peace): 8 x 6pdrs.
Probably submerged at Toulon 7.1707 to evade mortar attacks and refloated 11.1707. Struck 1709 at Toulon and handed over for commercial use. Run ashore on the Corsican coast in 1711 to avoid being captured by two British ships of the line.
Bourbon. The *Compagnie des Indes Orientales* ship *Bourbon* was built at St Malo between 1699 and 4.1701 and was purchased 10.1703 for use as a fireship.
Dimensions & tons: 85ft 0in x 22ft 8in x 9ft 3in (27.61 x 7.36 x 3.00m). 190 tons. Draught 12½ft (4.06m). Men: 45 in war, 45 peace

Guns: 6 in war: 6 x 4pdrs.

Renamed *Impudent* 1705. Struck 1708 at Port Louis but rebuilt at Lorient 1708–9 and returned to service 1709. Chartered 1.1713 for commercial use. Wrecked in 1715 while trying to ascend the frozen Loire.

Aigle Volant. Vessel built at La Ciotat and acquired 7.1704.

Dimensions & tons: 70ft 3in x 21ft 0in x 9ft 4in (22.82 x 6.82 x 3.03m). 200/180 tons. Draught 10ft (3.25m). Men: 40 in war, 40 peace

Guns: 6 in war (6 peace): 6 x 3pdrs.

Probably submerged at Toulon 7.1707 to evade mortar attacks and refloated 11.1707. Given 1712 by the King to Jacques Cassard. Captured 1712 by the British in the Atlantic.

Prince. Put into service 1706 at Toulon. Struck there 1706.

Ex-ENGLISH NAVAL PRIZE (1703). HMS *Aetna*, an English fireship, was captured by a French 40-gun privateer off Berry Head 28 April 1697 and renamed *Bonfaisant*. (French sources state that *Bonfaisant* was instead a captured Spanish ship built in Spain in 1695). She was purchased for the French Navy and renamed *Etna* (*Ethna*) 22 May 1703.

Dimensions & tons: 80ft 0in x 23ft 8in x 9ft 6in (25.99 x 7.69 x 3.09m). 200 tons. Draught 11ft (3.57m). Men: 40 in war, 30 peace

Guns: 6 in war (6 peace): 6 x 4pdrs.

By the middle of the eighteenth century, the employment of fireships in fleet actions had ceased, and their use was confined to situations in which the targets were restricted in manoeuvre, either within harbours or in other confined waters. Often the fireship attack was improvised, encouraged by a perceived opportunity presenting itself at short notice, and unless the results were spectacular (a very rare occurrence), the event often went unrecorded in mainstream history. One such incident was the capture of Port Louis (in present-day Haiti) by the squadron of Rear Admiral Charles Knowles in March 1748. Port Louis was at the head of a deep narrow channel, and the French defenders sent down a fireship against the English squadron, which forced the *Elizabeth* to be towed out of the path of the fireship, which then burnt itself out harmlessly (seen at bottom left). If it were not for this painting by Richard Paton, the inconsequential intervention of the fireship might have been entirely overlooked. (National Maritime Museum, London BHC0372)

Etna John Frame, Hessle (near Hull)

Ord: 25.9.1690. L: 19.3.1691. C: 3.5.1691. Guard hulk at Toulon 1705, unserviceable 1708, condemned 15.12.1710, ordered sold 24.12.1710.

Ex-DUTCH PRIZE (1708). The Dutch *Zeven Verenigde Provincen* from Flushing was captured in January 1708 and renamed *Sept Provinces*. Although scheduled to be converted to a fireship, she was instead armed with 28 guns and loaned as a privateer in 1708 and then struck at Toulon.

(D) Vessels acquired from 1 September 1715

The last fireships to be built for the French Navy were ordered in 1692, although seven of the eight ordered were quickly cancelled (see above). By 1715 the idea of using fireships in fleet actions had largely been abandoned, and the category of *brûlot* had disappeared from the fleet lists. However, the idea of employing burning ships as weapons in various contexts persisted, and during the eighteenth century there were occasions when circumstances prompted the ad hoc conversion of merchant vessels to fireships, the best-known example being the unsuccessful attempt on the British fleet at Quebec in 1759.

ACQUIRED VESSELS (1742–1743). Merchant vessels purchased or hired at Toulon and put into service as fireships.

Bellone. Acquired 5.1742. 200 tons, 42 men and 4 officers, 8 guns. Last mentioned 8.1744 going out of service at Toulon.

Saint Pierre. Brigantine acquired 5.1742. 200 tons, 47 men and 4 officers, 8 guns. Last mentioned 8.1744 going out of service at Toulon.

Vainqueur. Brigantine acquired 1743. 41 men and 3 officers, 8 guns. Last mentioned 7.1744 going out of service at Toulon.

ACQUIRED VESSELS (1747). Tartanes purchased or hired at Toulon and put into service as fireships.

Incendiaire. Acquired 4.1747. 4 tons. Probably taken out of service 6.1747.

The last significant French use of fireships was against the fleet of Admiral Sir Charles Saunders off Quebec on 28 June 1759. Eight fireships and two fire-rafts were deployed at night, but Saunders was fore-warned and boats of the fleet intercepted and diverted all the burning vessels from their targets. It made a dramatic subject for a marine artist, as demonstrated in this painting by Samuel Scott. (National Maritime Museum, London BHC0391)

Enflammée. Acquired 4.1747. 9 men and 5 petty officers. Probably taken out of service 6.1747.

REQUISITIONED VESSELS (1748). Three merchant ships, names unknown, were requisitioned at Cap François, St Domingue and placed in service as fireships in 1748. They seem to have been returned to their owners in August 1748.

ACQUIRED VESSELS (1756). Merchant ships purchased or hired at Toulon and put into service as fireships.
Union. Acquired 1756. 12 men and 2/5 officers. Last mentioned 11.1756 going out of service at Toulon.
Grand Adrien. Acquired 1756. 12 men and 2 officers. Last mentioned 11.1756 going out of service at Toulon.

ACQUIRED VESSEL (1758). The merchant ship *Princesse d'Angole*, possibly of 200 tons, was purchased or hired at Rochefort in 1758 and put into service as a fireship. She was last mentioned in 1758.

REQUISITIONED VESSELS (1759). Eight merchant vessels were appropriated in early 1759 at Quebec to be deployed as fireships against the blockading British fleet. These eight comprised the 400-ton *Américain*, 300-ton *Toison d'Or*, 230-ton *Charmante Rachel* and 110-ton *Bonne Amie* (or *Bonnes Amies*), all four being Bordeaux merchantmen; the 140-ton *Colibri* from Cadiz; the 120-ton *Rameau* of Quebec; and two other vessels of unknown tonnage – the *Ambassadeur* and *Amélie*. Each was manned by about 10 men (+1 officer) and deployed unsuccessfully in June 1759, all eight being fired and destroyed.

PURCHASED VESSELS (1762). During 1762 four Spanish snows (*senaults*) were purchased as Rochefort for use as fireships, although the precise mission for which they were intended has not been identified. They were not used in that role, and the three survivors were quickly re-classed as snows.
Grand Saint Louis. Purchased in 1762.
  Dimensions & tons: 62ft 6in x 19ft 8in (20.30 x 6.39m). 90 tons.
  Reconverted to a snow 2.1764. In bad condition at Rochefort 1766, ordered BU 3.6.1767, BU 1770.
Saint Jean Baptiste. Purchased in 1762.
  Dimensions & tons: unknown. 100 tons.
  Reconverted to a snow 2.1764. Struck 1767 at Rochefort.
Sainte Élisabeth or *Élisabeth.* Purchased in 1762.
  Dimensions & tons: unknown.
  Captured by Algerine pirates 7.1763.
Ville de Bilbao. Purchased 5.1762.
  Dimensions & tons: 62ft 6in x 19ft 8in (20.30 x 6.39m). 104 tons.
  Draught 10½/11½ft (3.41/3.74m). Men: 17, +1 officer. No guns.
  Reconverted to a snow 3.1763. Struck 6.1767 at Rochefort and BU.

ACQUIRED VESSELS (1778). Two merchant vessels were placed in service in July 1778 at St Malo as fireships.
Ménage. 500 tons. 30 men (+5 officers). Returned to service 5.1780 as a *gabarre* (storeship) with 20 guns and 29/55 men (+1/5 officers). Taken out of service 1782 or 3.1783 at Rochefort and struck.

Although fireships had ceased to have much tactical importance by the mid-eighteenth century, they continued to be treated as a conventional part of the naval order of battle in theoretical works. This engraving of a *brûlot* is taken from *Marine Militaire* by Nicolas-Marie Ozanne, published in 1762. The book contains a number of elaborate (and rather unrealistic) tactical scenarios in which fireships might be employed.

Érasme. 30 men (+4 officers). Captured in August 1778 by the British.

Ex-BRITISH PRIZES (1779). Two captured British merchantmen were adapted as fireships in May 1779 at Brest Dyd.

Dashwood. 200-ton, 20-gun merchant brig *Dashwood* from Falmouth captured 10.1778 by *Fier* (60) or *Roland* (64). Carried 24 men (+5 officers) as a fireship. Converted into a *gabarre* with 20 guns in 1780, struck 1782 or 1783.

London. Merchant ship *London* captured in January 1779. Carried 29 men (+4 officers) as a fireship. Converted into a *gabarre* with 27/35 men (+1/5 officers) in May 1780. Retaken by the British 12.1781, recaptured 4.1782 by Suffren's squadron. Left Ceylon for Île de France 4.1782, later fate unknown. Struck 1782 or 1783.

PULVÉRISEUR. Vessel of unknown origin (probably not the former *flûte Salomon* of 1762 as sometimes reported) acquired in August 1781 in India, fitted as a fireship in September–October 1781 at Trincomalee, Ceylon, and named *Pulvériseur* (or *Pulvérisateur*).

Dimensions & tons: dimensions unknown. 220 tons. Men: 80, +6/7 officers

Guns: 4 or 6 (?)

Pulvériseur Origin unknown.
Commanded by CB Villaret de Joyeuse. Re-rigged 7.1782 at Gondelour (Cuddalore) with the masts of the British prize *Yarmouth*. Removed from service 9.11.1782 in India, wrecked 1784.

The names *Boutefeu*, *Porc Épic*, and *Volcan* were reported for fireships in 1780 but the ships probably never existed. The fireship *Salamandre* of 1783 was originally the transport *Jeune Héloïse* which is listed in Chapter 13.

9 Storeships and Cargo Ships

(Flûtes and Gabarres)

In addition to its combatant warships, the French Navy contained large numbers of purpose-built and acquired transport vessels of various sizes and types, especially during wartime. The number of French transport ships was generally larger than that in the British Royal Navy, in part because the French Navy had to assume the functions that in Britain were carried out by the Transport Board (1690-1724) and in part because the French did not have the large merchant marine that the Royal Navy relied on to carry out many of its transportation and supply functions. Most of the larger French transports fell into two categories, *flûtes* and *gabarres*. These are discussed in separate sections below.

STORESHIPS (*FLÛTES*)

The word *flûtes* (*flustes*) was originally the French equivalent to the Dutch *fluijts* or *fluyts*. These were large Dutch merchant cargo vessels specially designed to carry the largest possible cargoes on long voyages with the smallest possible crews. They had rounded sterns and were of 300 tons or more. By 1680 the French Navy was using the term *flûte* to refer to all large cargo ships that served as supply or hospital vessels for a fleet or as troop transports, including both the Dutch type and conventional ships with square sterns. The British used the term storeships for vessels with these military functions.

Flûtes with round sterns ('Dutch *flûtes*') had hulls with a very flat floor, tall sterns that were as round as their bows, and topsides with exaggerated 'tumblehome' (concave in cross-section so that the maximum breadth of the hull near the waterline was nearly twice the width of the top deck. Originally designed to minimise taxation that was based on the breadth of a ship at deck level, this configuration gave them a very large cargo capacity. They had a standard ship rig, although the masts were shorter in proportion to the ship's size, allowing them to be sailed by small crews. In the 1730s they ranged from 200 to 800 tons in capacity and from 100 to 130ft in length between perpendiculars. A typical one measured 108ft between perpendiculars, 22ft in breadth, and 11ft in depth. The larger *flûtes* with round sterns had two complete decks plus a quarterdeck aft, with ports for up to six 6pdrs or 4pdrs per side on the upper deck or quarterdeck, all aft of the mainmast. Those of only 200 or 300 tons generally had no gunports. The French built *flûtes* of this type with a demi-battery on the lower deck aft of the mainmast and a complete battery on the upper deck. Most *flûtes* with round sterns had no forecastle.

Flûtes with square sterns had hulls and ship rigs very much like those of other large French war and merchant ships, in this case the term denoting the role rather than a hull design. After about 1715 the French Navy shifted from round to square sterns in its purpose-built *flûtes*. *Flûtes* with round sterns looked like vulnerable merchant vessels, inviting attack by all but the weakest of privateers, while those with square sterns looked like warships, deterring attack. *Flûtes* with square sterns could also be armed as warships in case of need, and their upper decks were wider, providing better accommodations for officers and crew

The main features of the Dutch *fluijt* or *fluyt* is clearly demonstrated by this drawing: the round stern topped by a very narrow taffrail, the capacious hull, and the extreme tumblehome that made the ship far narrower at deck level than waterline. This last characteristic was said to be a response to the Sound Dues, taxes levied on all ships entering the Baltic, which were based on the breadth of the ship at weather deck level. Trade with the Baltic area was hugely significant to the economy of the Netherlands, so this design gave the Dutch a big commercial advantage. The drawing shows a ship with 1642 on the taffrail, and may be an early work by Willem van de Velde the elder. (National Maritime Museum, London PY1712)

and more deck space for working the ship. Under the waterline they differed from warships in that, like merchant ships, they had fuller lines and the bow was less sharp; above the waterline they were similar in structure and appearance to frigates. In 1735 Blaise Ollivier described three types of *flûtes* with square sterns; while probably theoretical, these variants illustrate the diversity of the ships of this type. According to Ollivier *flûtes* of 120 to 125ft in length between perpendiculars had two complete decks plus a quarterdeck and a forecastle and were pierced with 10 or 11 ports on each side on the lower deck for 12pdrs or 8pdrs (although this deck was not usually armed) and with 11 or 12 ports on the upper deck for 6pdrs or 8pdrs. *Flûtes* of 110 to 115ft also had two decks but there was less clearance between decks and they were pierced only on the upper deck with 9 or 10 ports for 4pdr or more commonly 6pdr guns. *Flûtes* of about 100ft in length had only one complete deck plus a quarterdeck and forecastle and carried two or three 4pdrs on each side of the quarterdeck.

A 1773 French list of naval terms referrs to a *flûte d'approvisionnement*, which it defined as a *flûte* loaded with everything necessary to support a squadron or fleet. Usually several *flûtes d'approvisionnement* accompanied squadrons or fleets on extended campaigns at sea. *Flûtes* also carried provisions, rations, munitions, and sometimes troops to an overseas colony or to support a single vessel on a long voyage. British storeships had essentially the same mission. These seaworthy ships had covered gun batteries and orlop decks like frigates but did not have either the strength of armament, size of crew, or speed to serve as warships, except in emergencies.

In 1680 or early 1681 an 'establishment level' of twenty-six *flûtes* was set – with twenty-two *flûtes* on the List in January 1681 there was a shortfall of four vessels. The number of *flûtes* remained at twenty-six or below through 1715 except between 1691 and 1699 when it rose greatly, reaching a wartime peak of sixty in 1696. Following the return of peace, the number of *flûtes* fell from eighteen in 1712 to only two in 1715 and three in 1716.

Navies often commissioned old ships of the line or frigates *en flûte*, landing many of their guns and the crews that served them, to carry out distant supply missions, and the French also built ships especially for this purpose. Note that some of the smaller *flûtes* listed here, particularly before 1715, may actually have been of types like those listed in Chapter 13 because the French used the term *flûte* as a functional designator covering cargo carriers of many configurations besides the big Dutch *fluyt*. The *Barbaut* class hookers of 1669 are among the few *flûtes* for which a specific ship type or rig is recorded.

(A) Vessels in service as at 9 March 1661

CANCRE DORÉ. 400–500 tons. One Dutch 400-ton *flûte* captured in late 1643 or early 1644 was still in French Navy hands in 1661. Her Dutch name may have been *Gulden Kanker*. In May 1661 this *flûte* at Toulon, now of 500 tons, was considered capable of further service.
 Dimensions & tons: dimensions unknown. 400–500 tons. Men: 35/39, +1/5 officers as *flûte*; 25, +1 officer as fireship.
 Guns: 18.
 Accompanied the fleet of Chevalier Paul 3.1663 as a storeship, then converted to a fireship and renamed *Éclat* 3.1663. Struck late 1663 at Toulon, last mentioned 2.1666.

ESPÉRANCE. 200–250 tons. Listed at Toulon on 3 May 1661 with *Licorne*, below, as a 250-ton *flûte* too old to send back to sea without major repairs but suitable for use as a fireship against the port of Algiers. Listed again at Toulon in 1662 as a 200-ton *flûte* with 19 men +1 officer. May have been the *Espérance de Lubeck* listed in 1644 and 1646 as a 400-ton *flûte* with 35 men and 5 officers; this vessel reportedly was acquired in 1642, carried 10 guns and then 4 x 4pdrs in 1665, and was struck 2.1666 at Marseille.

LICORNE. 250 tons. This *flûte*, probably from Hamburg, was purchased 24.4.1655 at Brouage. She may also have been called *Licorne Volante*. Listed at Toulon on 3 May 1661 as a 250-ton vessel too old to send back to sea without major repairs but appropriate for use as a fireship against the port of Algiers. Listed again at Toulon in 1662 as a 250-ton *flûte* with 19 men +1 officer. In port at Toulon in October 1662. 'Very old' and ordered hulked at Toulon 21.8.1663, but in 7–10.1664 participated in the Gigeri expedition. Last mentioned 2.1666.

TÊTE NOIRE. 250 tons. A Dutch vessel built at De Hoorn and named *Neger Hoofd* was purchased in February 1658 at La Rochelle and given the French equivalent of her Dutch name. Listed at Toulon on 3 May 1661 as a 250-ton *flûte* suitable only for sale for commercial use or for use as a fireship agaisst the port of Algiers. 25 men. In port at Toulon in October 1662, unserviceable and sunken at Toulon 8.1663, wreck last mentioned 1666.

FLÛTE ROYALE. 300 tons. A Dutch *flûte* possibly named *Papierenbundel* was purchased in March 1658 at Brouage and named *Balle de Papier*, the equivalent of her Dutch name. She was renamed *Flûte Royale* in 1659 and was also called *La flûte royale de Brouage* and simply *Royale*.
 Dimensions & tons: dimensions unknown. 300 tons. Men: 30 (6/24/) +2 officers.
 Guns: 4 in 1665: 2 x 6pdrs, 2 x 2pdrs. 16 in 1669; 10 from 1671
 L: 1654. Wrecked 12.1665 on the Corsican coast, evidently refloated. Struck in early 1671 at Toulon.

(B) Vessels acquired from 9 March 1661

SEIZED VESSELS (1661). The following *flûtes* ranging from 80 to 400 tons were among the vessels seized from the personal fleet of the Intendant Nicolas Fouquet in late 1661. Fouquet was the *Surintendant général des finances royales* from 1653 to 1661. *Aigle d'Or* was built at Brest in 1658–61 and Fouquet purchased the other four of these *flûtes* in October 1660 at Amsterdam. *Jardin de Hollande* was seized by the King at Morbihan in September 1661 just before leaving for Martinique. *Aigle Noir* was also seized in September 1661. *Aigle d'Or* was seized in November 1661 upon her return from Newfoundland, *Saint Jean Baptiste* (or *Saint Jean*) was seized in December 1661, and *Renommée* was seized in either September 1661 or March 1662 on her return from Martinique.
Jardin de Hollande. Built in Holland.
 Dimensions & tons: dimensions unknown. 400 tons. Men: 40 (8/32/) +2 officers.
 Guns: 24, 16 from 1669, 12 from 1671.
 Built 1657. Renamed *Charente* 24.6.1671. Sold 19.7.1673 at Brest for BU.
Aigle Noir. Built in Holland.
 Dimensions & tons: dimensions unknown. 350 tons. Men: 35
 Guns: 25.
 Built 1660. Renamed *Saint Paul* 1662. Sold 8.1664 at Le Havre to the *Compagnie des Indes Orientales*. Sold by them 3.1672 at Surat.
Aigle d'Or. Built at the Brest Dyd.
 Dimensions & tons: dimensions unknown. 200 tons. Men: 30 (6/24/) +2 officers.

Guns: 26, 16 from 1669, 10 from 1671

K: 1658. L: 1660. C: 1661. Handed over 3.1671 to the *Compagnie des Indies Occidentales*.

Saint Jean Baptiste. Built in Holland.

Dimensions & tons: 60ft 0in x 18ft 6in x 9ft 0in (19.49 x 6.01 x 2.92m). 80 tons (120 in 1672–75). Draught 9ft (2.92m). Men: 30 (6/24/) +2 officers; in 1675, 28 (9/19/), +2 officers.

Guns: 4, 8 from 1672, 6 from 1679, 10 from 1691

Built 1659–1660. Listed in 1671 as *Saint Jean flibot* to distinguish her from *Heux Saint Jean* and was configured as a flyboat or small *flûte*. Renamed *Seine* 24.6.1671. Listed as a 70-ton *caiche* (ketch) at Brest in 1692. Struck 1694, probably at Brest.

Renommée. Built in the Netherlands.

Dimensions & tons: dimensions unknown. 400 tons. Men: 35/40

Guns: 24 (32 ports).

Built 1650. Last mentioned 1667.

PURCHASED VESSELS (1662–1665). Little information is available on these five *flûtes* that were purchased between 1662 and 1665. The first two served in the Mediterranean, the last three were based in the Channel or the Atlantic.

Cheval Marin. Vessel of 300 tons among those remaining in port at Toulon in October 1662. Called very old and heavy under sail in 8.1663. Last mentioned in 1665.

Catherine. Vessel of 150 tons in service at Toulon in March 1663 when she was described as old. 25 men. Last mentioned 2.1666 as unserviceable at Toulon.

Paix. Dutch vessel of 400 tons built in the Netherlands and possibly named *Vrede*, purchased 1663 and put into service at Brouage. Wrecked 9.1665 or 10.1665 at the mouth of the St Lawrence River. Crew returned to France 11.1665 in *Saint Sébastien* (30).

Grand Charles. Vessel of 300 tons purchased 7.1664 at Dunkirk. 14 guns. Handed over in 1666 to the *Compagnie des Indes Orientales*.

Cygne Blanc. Vessel of unknown tonnage, probably Dutch-built, purchased 1665. Wrecked 10.1665 off Zuidcote.

JUSTICE. 300 tons. A Dutch vessel possibly named *Recht* was purchased 1664 soon after completion. She was called a '*magasin*' (storeship) in 1669 in contrast to *Vierge* which was a '*hôpital*' (hospital *flûte*).

Dimensions & tons: dimensions unknown. 300 tons (350 in 1676–79), Draught 14ft. Men: 30 (6/24/) +2 officers; in 1680, 45 (11/34/), +4 officers.

Guns: 8, 10 from 1671, 20 from 1676.

Justice Holland.

Built 1663 to 2.1664. Renamed *Bien Arrivé* 24.6.1671. Unserviceable at Le Havre 8.1681, BU 9.1681.

Ex-BARBARY COAST PRIZES (1664–1666). One 400-ton Barbary Coast vessel was captured from the Algerians by *Saint Louis* under Duquesne in May 1664 and was named *Saint Augustin*, while an 80-ton vessel was captured in 1664 or 1666 and was named *Saint Jean*. These may have been their names prior to capture or acquisition by the North Africans. *Saint Augustin*, a pinnace, was classed in 1663–65 as a combatant warship but was condemned as such on 22 December 1665 and retained as a hospital *flûte*. She was called *Grand Saint Augustin* from 1665 to distinguish her from a fireship of the same name. *Saint Jean* was listed in 1669 and 1671 as *Heux Saint Jean* to distinguish her from another *Saint Jean*; she was also called *Petit Saint Jean*. Her 1669 nomenclature suggests that *Saint Jean* was rigged as a hoy (*heu*).

Saint Augustin Brest Dyd. (possibly).

Dimensions & tons: dimensions unknown. 400 tons. Men: 40 (8/32/) +2 officers.

Guns: 24/38, 16 from 1669, 12 from 1671.

Built 1662–63. Renamed *Large* 24.6.1671. Replaced 2.1672 by *Bretonne* (ex-*Cheval*) as a hospital ship. Sold 19.7.1673 at Brest and BU.

Saint Jean England.

Dimensions & tons: dimensions unknown. 80 tons. Men: 25 (5/20/) +1 officer.

Guns: 6, 4 from 1669.

Built 1661. Renamed *Seine* 24.6.1671, then changed to *Garonne* 7.1671 as the name *Seine* had actually been assigned to another *Saint Jean* on 24.6.1671 and the ship renamed *Garonne* on 24.6.1671 (ex-*Petit Anglais*) had just been lost, making that name available. Service craft at Brest, struck there 1673 or 1674.

Ex-DUTCH PRIZE (1664). One Dutch 200-ton *flûte*, possibly named *Kroon*, was captured in May 1664 and became the French *Couronne*. She was put into service 7.1664 at Dunkirk. In 1666 she was handed over to the *Compagnie des Indes Orientales*. She was sold in 1681 at Port Louis.

CHARIOT D'OR. 300 tons. This vessel was purchased 1665 while under construction in Holland.

Dimensions & tons: dimensions unknown. 300 tons. Men: 30 (6/24/) +2 officers.

Guns: 12, 10 from 1671.

Chariot d'Or Rotterdam (probably).

Built 1665 to 1.1666. Struck 3.1671 at Rochefort.

SAINT HUBERT. 100 tons. Built by Jean-Pierre Brun and Jean Guichard. Not listed before 1671 and may have been purchased in 1670. Called a *flibot*, a flyboat or small *flûte*.

Dimensions & tons: 60ft 0in on keel x 18ft 0in x 9ft 0in (19.49 x 5.85 x 2.92m). 100 tons (80 in 1676–83). Draught 9ft (2.92m). Men: 25 (5/20/) +1 officer; in 1675, 28 (9/19/), +2 officers.

Guns: 6, 4 from 1672.

Saint Hubert. Soubise.

K: 1665. L: 1666. C: 1667. Renamed *Loire* 24.6.1671. Probably captured 6.1684 by the Spanish at Cape Spartel, struck 1684 or 1685.

PURCHASED VESSELS (1666–1667). Little information is available on these two *flûtes* purchased in 1666 and 1667. They were based in the Channel or the Atlantic.

Oranger. Vessel of 200 tons built ?1666 and purchased 1666 or 1667. 25 men (5/20/) +1 officer, 6 guns. Wrecked 1667 off Arcachon but refloated. Struck 3.1671 at Rochefort.

Dauphine. Vessel of 200 tons built 1664 at Amsterdam and purchased 1667. 30 men (6/24/) +2 officers. 6 guns (10 from 1671). Struck 3.1671 at Rochefort.

GRANDE PINASSE. 200 tons. 25 men (5/20/) +1 officer. 6 guns. This vessel was either captured in 1667 or purchased in 1669. She was called *Grande Pinasse* to distinguish her from two smaller (80-ton) unnamed pinnaces captured about the same time. Struck 3.1671 at Rochefort.

FRANÇOIS. 200 tons, 25 men (5/20/) +1 officer, 6 guns. This vessel from Yarmouth was built in 1666, captured from the English in October 1667, and purchased by the Navy. She may previously have been a French merchant vessel taken by the English. Struck 3.1671 at Rochefort.

SOUBISE. 300 tons. Built by Jean-Pierre Brun (?) at Soubise, downriver from Rochefort, and acquired by the Navy in 1668. Considered a good *flûte* but had only one deck.

    Dimensions & tons: dimensions unknown. 300 tons (250 from 1679), Draught 9ft. Men: 30 (6/24/) +2 officers; in 1675, 28 (9/19/), +2 officers.

    Guns: 6, 10 from 1671.

Soubise Soubise.

    Built late 1664 to early 1665 or 1665 to 1667. Renamed *Bien Chargé* 24.6.1671. Hospital ship at the Battle of Solebay 6.1672. Grounded 6.1687 through imprudence and condemned at Toulon.

Ex-ENGLISH NAVAL PRIZE (1668). HMS *Colchester* (72 tons), one of a group of five ketches ordered by the Royal Navy in 1664, participated during 1667 in an attempt to find the North-West Passage. She was captured on 3 April 1668 while bound for the North-West Passage to resupply the English settlements in Hudson's Bay. The French named this small supply vessel *Petit Anglais*.

    Dimensions & tons (English measurements in French feet): 45ft 0in on keel x 15ft 9in x 8ft 5in. 72 tons (60 French tons). Draught 8ft. Men: 25 to 45 in English service

    Guns: 6 x 5pdrs + 2 x 4pdrs in English service, 6 guns in French service.

Petit Anglais John Allin.

    L: 1664. C: 20.5.1665. Renamed *Garonne* 24.6.1671. Hull ripped open accidentally during careening at Brest 7.1671, new name transferred to (*Heux*) *Saint Jean*.

DAUPHIN ROYAL. 300 tons. This Dutch-built *flûte* was purchased in March 1669.

    Dimensions & tons: dimensions unknown. 300 tons. Draught 11½ft. Men: 30 (6/24/) +2 officers.

    Guns: 12.

Dauphin Royal Amsterdam.

    Built 1664–65. Struck 3.1671 at Le Havre and sold to the *Compagnie du Nord* of La Rochelle. Repurchased 1675 and renamed *Éléphant*. Wrecked 2.1678 by a pilot at Sauveterre (Pierres Noires), Sables d'Olonne, while coming from Guadeloupe

ESPÉRANCE. 200 tons. Purchased in May 1669 when new with *Pélican* (below) by Pélicot at Saardam (Zaandam) near Amsterdam.

    Dimensions & tons: 100ft 0in x 23ft 0in (32.48 x 7.47m). 200 tons (250 in 1671). Draught 12½ft (4.06m). Men: 30 (6/24/) +2 officers.

    Guns: 12, 10 from 1671, 8 from 1672, 10 from 1674.

Espérance Saardam.

    Built 1667 to 1669. Completed 6.1669, ready for transit to Brest 31.7.1669. Renamed *Paresseux* 24.6.1671. Wrecked 1674 in the Raz de Sein near Brest.

PÉLICAN. 300 tons. Built at Saardam (Zaandam) near Amsterdam and purchased in May 1669 with *Espérance*, above. Originally called *Sardam*, renamed soon after September 1669.

    Dimensions & tons: dimensions unknown. 300 tons. Draught 12½ft. Men: 30 (6/24/) +2 officers.

    Guns: 12, 10 from 1671.

Pélican Saardam.

    K: 7.1668. L: 15.7.1669. C: 10.1669. To Brest with a French crew 10.1669. Renamed *Bretonne* 24.6.1671 (or *Cheval* 24.6.1671 and *Bretonne* 7.1671). Replaced *Large* as hospital ship at Rochefort 2.1672. Taken by the enemy 1675 with a cargo of timber (reported 18.10.1676).

DON DE DIEU. 200 tons. This *flûte*, originally named *Ostendaise* (*Ostendoise*) and built at Ostend, was purchased or captured during 1669. She was renamed *Don de Dieu* around September 1669; both names appear in a September 1669 list with identical specifications.

    Dimensions & tons: dimensions unknown. 200 tons. Men: 25 (5/20/) +1 officer.

    Guns: 6.

Don de Dieu Ostend.

    Built 1666. Struck 3.1671 at Le Havre, was submerged there 12.1673.

The 5th Rank ship *Vierge* (400 tons), which had been purchased from the *Compagnie des Indes Orientales* in 1666, was re-classed as a hospital *flûte* in 1669, renamed *Profond* on 24.6.1671, and struck in 1678. She is listed in Chapter 5.

PURCHASED VESSELS (1669). Two *flûtes* of between 300 and 500 tons, *Fortune* and *Indienne*, were purchased in 1669 from the *Compagnie des Indes Orientales*, *Indienne* during the summer. Two more *flûtes* were purchased in September 1669 from the company, its *Tersmitte* and *Pagez* becoming the Navy's *Europe* and *Amérique* soon after September 1669.

Fortune Built in the Netherlands.

    Dimensions & tons: dimensions unknown. 300 tons (400 in 1672–75). Draught 14ft. Men: 30 (6/24/) +2 officers.

    Guns: 12, 10 by 1676, 8 in 1677.

    Built 1658. Renamed *Fourgon* 24.6.1671. Was old in 1671 and was used to carry timber. Condemned 11.1676 at Toulon, sold and BU 1677.

Indienne. Built at La Rochelle.

    Dimensions & tons: dimensions unknown. 500 tons (400 in 1671). Men: 30 (6/24/) +2 officers.

    Guns: 12, 16 from 1672.

    Built 1667–68, construction defective. Sailed 3.1670 for the East Indies with the Persia Squadron of Jacob Blanquet de la Haye. Renamed *Portefaix* 24.6.1671 while deployed but never received the order to change her name. Hulked 6.1672 at Trincomalee, captured 19.7.1672 by the Dutch.

Europe. Built at Amsterdam.

Apart from the obvious features of the hull, the Dutch *fluyt* was also characterised by a relatively simple version of the ship rig – since speed under sail was not a prime requirement – and this meant a small crew and another commercial advantage to the owner. The main features persisted into the eighteenth century, as shown by this illustration of the type in Guéroult du Pas's work of 1710.

Dimensions & tons: 106ft 0in on keel x 24ft 4in x 9ft 9in (34.43 x 7.82 x 31.7m). 500 tons. Men: 50 (10/40/) +2 officers.
Guns: 16.
Built 1665 to 9.1666. Sailed 3.1670 for the East Indies with the Persia Squadron of Jacob Blanquet de la Haye. Renamed *Dromadaire* 24.6.1671 while deployed but continued to be called *Europe* until her loss. Captured 2.6.1672 by the Dutch and renamed *De Franse Europa*. Captured 5.1673 by the English and renamed *Europa* (hulk, 406 tons). Burned 19.4.1676 at Malta, apparently by arson.

Amérique. Built at Netherlands.
Dimensions & tons: dimensions unknown. 400 tons. Draught 13ft. Men: 40 (8/32/) +2 officers.
Guns: 16, 12 from 1671, 20 from 1676, 14 from 1677.
Built 1667 to 1668 or 4.1669. Renamed *Coche* 24.6.1671. Wrecked on Îles Aves (in the Caribbean) 11/12.5.1678 with other ships of *Vice-amiral* Jean, Comte d'Estrées's squadron while serving as a hospital ship; she was probably the 'unnamed caïque' of 24 guns and 250 men that was listed as lost on that occasion.

SAINT MARTIN. 200 tons. 25 men (5/20/) +1 officer. 6 guns. This *flûte* was listed at Rochefort in September 1669 and was specified in January 1671 as having been a prize. Her origin and nationality are unknown although she was reportedly built in 1664. Struck 3.1671 at Rochefort.

An English vessel built at Bristol in 1656 or 1660 was captured by *Étoile d'Afrique* in March 1667 and named *Saint Pierre*. She was listed in September 1669 as a 200 ton *flûte* with six guns but by 1671 had become a 60-ton *frégate légère* with six guns that was renamed *Moqueuse* on 24 June 1671. She is listed in Chapter 6.

BARBAUT Class. 160 tons. Ordered on 5 January 1670 by the *Compagnie du Nord* with contract dated 24 January to carry supplies to the Persia Squadron of Jacob Blanquet de la Haye which was to depart for the Indies in February 1670. Purchased by the French Navy in April 1670 and named on 11 April while under construction. Both sailed with supplies for the East Indies on 16 March 1671 (along with the 3rd Rank *Breton*). These two ships were identified in contemporary lists as *oucres*, indicating that they were hookers (French *houcre* or by corruption *hourque*). According to Guillet (1681) and Aubin (1702), hookers were Dutch vessels with flat bottoms and round hulls like *flûtes*, that were rigged like hoys with a single mast and a fore-and-aft sail with in addition bowsprits and spritsails. This rig, traditionally said to have been developed by Erasmus, made it easy to tack and sail close-hauled in the Dutch canals. Hookers then ranged from 50 to 200 tons, even the smaller ones being able to sail to the East Indies with only 5 or 6 men. Typical measurements were (Saverien, 1758) 50ft on the keel, 16ft 6in in breadth, and 8ft depth.
Dimensions & tons: dimensions unknown. 160 tons. Draught 10ft (3.25m). Men: 30 (6/24/), +2 officers.
Guns: 6, 8 from 1672, 12 from 1674 including 6 x 6pdrs.

Barbaut Rochefort Dyd.
K: 2.1670. L: 5.1670. C: 6.1670. Renamed *Dunkerquoise* 24.6.1671 just after sailing for the Indian Ocean, continued to use name *Barbaut* until 2.1673. Wrecked 3.1675 at Fort Dauphin, Madagascar, in a squall. Struck 1676.

Guillot Rochefort Dyd.
K: 2.1670. L: 5.1670. C: 6.1670. Renamed *Dieppoise* 24.6.1671 just after sailing for the Indian Ocean, continued to use the name *Guillot* until the end of 1673. Grounded 11.1673 at São Tomé but refloated. Wrecked 1.1679 off Bénodet in southwestern Brittany.

ROCHELAISE. 300 tons. Named on 24 June 1671. Belatedly described in 1677 as having a large capacity and adequate sailing qualities but by then was badly hogged as she was built of softwood (pine).
Dimensions & tons: dimensions unknown. 300 tons. Men: 30 (6/24/), +2 officers.
Guns: 10, 12 from 1673.

Rochelaise (*Rocheloise*) Rochefort Dyd.
K: 1670. L: 1.1671. C: 2.1671. Ordered hulked at Rochefort 17.1.1673. Condemnation approved 25.8.1673, last mentioned 1674.

SULTANE. 500 tons. This vessel was purchased in January 1670 from the *Compagnie des Indes Orientales*.
Dimensions & tons: Length probably 100ft 0in on keel. 500 tons. Men: 50 (10/40/) +2 officers.
Guns: 16.

Sultane Rochefort Dyd.
K: 3.1668. L: 2.1669. C: 4.1669. Sailed 3.1670 for the East Indies with the Persia Squadron of Jacob Blanquet de la Haye. Renamed *Éléphant* 24.6.1671 but never received news of her new name. Condemned 6.1673 and run ashore at São Tomé.

The hooker rig, as illustrated by Daniel Lescallier in *Traité Pratique du Gréement* (1791 edition). By the end of the eighteenth century these vessels had grown in size – although retaining the main characteristics of the hull – and now carried a form of the square ketch rig. Their smaller seventeenth century ancestors had originally been rigged with a single mast setting a sprit or gaff-headed mainsail, but they soon acquired a small auxiliary mast aft, also setting a fore-and-aft sail, before it grew into a proper mizzen. The development of the hooker into a seagoing cargo-carrier encouraged the adoption of a square rig.

SAINT NICOLAS. 300 tons. Purchased 1670 by Sieur Arnoul at Marseille.
> Dimensions & tons: dimensions unknown. 300 tons. Men: 30 (6/24/) +2 officers.
> Guns: 10.

Saint Nicolas Marseille.
> Built between 1659 and 4.1660. Renamed *Marseilloise* 24.6.1671. Struck 1674 at Rochefort.

BAYONNAISE. 120 tons. Dutch vessel purchased at Brest in April 1671 and called *Galiote Hollandaise* until named *Bayonnaise* on 24 June 1671. *Galiotes* were essentially medium-sized *flûtes* with a two-masted rig (main and small mizzen). Listed as a 70-ton *caiche* (ketch) at Brest in 1692.
> Dimensions & tons: 72ft 0in x 17ft 0in x 8ft 6in (23.29 x 5.52 x 2.76m). 100 tons (130 in 1672–73). Draught 8½ft (2.76m). Men: 30 (6/24/) +2 officers; in 1675, 28 (9/19/), +2 officers
> Guns: 14, 8 from 1672, 4 from 1675, 10 from 1691.

Bayonnaise (*Bayonnoise*) Amsterdam.
> Built 1668. Renamed *Charente* 28.6.1678. Last mentioned 5.1693 at Brest.

Ex-BARBARY COAST PRIZE (1670). A 200-ton Barbary Coast vessel named *Taj Napoli* was captured in November 1670 by the Chevalier de Buons in Vivonne's fleet before Tunis, taken to Toulon 21.11.1670, and renamed *Couronne de Naples*.
> Dimensions & tons: 76ft 0in x 18ft 0in x 11ft 0in (24.69 x 5.85 x 3.57m). 200 tons (300 in 1676–77). Draught 13ft (4.22m). Men: 28 (9/19/) +2 officers.
> Guns: 8, 12 from 1674, 10 from 1675, 16 in 1677.

Couronne de Naples Leghorn.
> Built 1658. Renamed *Normande* 24.6.1671. Condemned 2.1677 at Toulon, struck 1678, BU 1679 and remains sold 2.1681.

BIENVENU. 400 tons. Built by Étienne Salicon, also attributed to Rodolphe Gédéon. Ordered on 10 November 1670, named on 24 June 1671 when nearly complete. In 1677 was considered a very good *flûte* with large capacity and good sailing qualities. The 1680 manning listed below is for long voyages; for ordinary voyages it was reduced to 28 (9/19/), + 2 officers.
> Dimensions & tons: 109ft 0in x 27ft 6in x 13ft 0in (35.40 x 8.93 x 4.22m). 400 tons (350 in 1679–89). Draught 16ft (5.20m). Men: 40 (8/32/), +2 officers; in 1680, 35 (9/26/), +2 officers. From 1696: 150 in war, 55 peace; from 1699: 250 in war, 230 peace (250/50 from 1701)
> Guns: 12, 16 from 1676, 24 from 1690. 10 in war from 1696 (6 peace): 4 x 8pdrs, 6 x 4pdrs. 42 from 1699: LD 18 x 12pdrs, UD 18 x 6pdrs, QD 6 x 4pdrs. 40 from 1704: LD 18 x 12pdrs, UD 16 x 6pdrs, QD 6 x 4pdrs. 14 from 1706: 4 x 8pdrs, 10 x 6pdrs

Bienvenu Toulon Dyd.
> K: 1.1671. L: 30.7.1671. C: 9.1671. Rebuilt 1680–82 at Toulon by Coulomb and 1697–98 at Brest by Hubac. Sometimes called *Royale* between 1685 and 1687. Lent as a privateer in 1689–90 to LG Victor Marie d'Estrées and in 1703 to CFL Duguay-Trouin as part of a squadron of three vessels. Fitted in 1704 as a 400-ton fireship with 8 guns and 60 men. Struck 1706 at Toulon.

AVENANT. 400 tons. Built by Pierre Angallier, also attributed to Rodolphe Gédéon. Named on 24 June 1671 when nearly completed. In

The French purchased a Dutch galiote (*galjoot*) in 1671 and listed her under the name *Galiote Hollandaise* until assigning the name *Bayonnaise* in June. Dutch *galjoots* were two-masted craft with gaff-headed sails and sometimes a topsail on a tall mainmast and with a diminutive pole mast aft on the stern. This rig was also used on the hoy. Lower freeboard variants like those shown in this Van de Velde drawing (possibly by the younger) of about 1665 were common as service craft in Dutch ports and coastal waters. (National Maritime Museum, London PW6833)

1677 was considered a very good *flûte* with large capacity and good sailing qualities.

Dimensions & tons: 109ft 0in x 27ft 6in x 13ft 0in (35.40 x 8.93 x 4.22m). 400 tons (350 in 1679–89). Draught 12/14ft (3.90/4.55m). Men: 40 (8/32/), +2 officers; in 1680, 35 (9/26/), +2 officers.

Guns: 12, 20 from 1676, 16 from 1677, 30 from 1690.

Avenant Toulon Dyd.
K: 1.1671. L: 11.7.1671. C: 9.1671. Unserviceable 1695, but then rebuilt as ship of the 4th Rank at Brest by Blaise Pangalo 1696 (see Chapter 4).

TARDIF. 500 tons. Construction ordered on 7 November 1670, named on 24 June 1671 while on the ways. Built by Laurent Hubac. The 1680 manning listed below is for long voyages; for ordinary voyages it was reduced to 35 (9/26/), + 2 officers.

Dimensions & tons: 112ft 0in x 26ft 0in x 12ft 6in (36.38 x 8.45 x 4.06m). 500 tons (450 from 1680). Draught 12½ft (4.06m). Men: 50 (10/40/), +2 officers; in 1680, 45 (11/34/), +4 officers.

Guns: 16, 20 from 1676, 24 from 1679.

Tardif Brest Dyd.
K: 3.1671. L: 5.9.1671. C: 12.1671. Grounded accidentally 7.1692 at Vannes, sold there 8.1692.

Ex-DUTCH PRIZE (1672). The 300-ton Dutch *flûte Witte Swaan* was captured in late 1672 by the fleet of Châteaurenault in the Straits of Gibraltar and taken into Lisbon. She was put into French service as *Cygne Blanc* (*Cigne Blanc*).

Dimensions & tons: dimensions unknown. 300 tons (400 in 1674–75). Draught 12ft. Men: 28 (9/19/) +2 officers; in 1680, 35 (9/26/), +2 officers.

Guns: 12, 8 from 1679.

Cygne Blanc Holland.
Built 1668. Renamed *Rocheloise* 28.11.1673 and *Françoise* 28.6.1678. Struck 1686 at Toulon.

ÉLÉPHANT. 400 tons. On 12 June 1673 Colbert ordered the purchase of a pinnace to accompany *Dunkerquoise* to replenish the Persia squadron of Jacob Blanquet de la Haye. This vessel was purchased from the *Compagnie du Nord* at Rochefort in June 1673 while fitting out afloat and was named *Éléphant* on 10 July 1673. She was put into service 8.1673 and was to sail with *Rubis* (ex-*Saint Cosme*) but was not ready until January 1674 and was then lost.

Dimensions & tons: 108ft 0in x 24ft 0in x 12ft 0in (35.08 x 7.80 x 3.90m). 400 tons. Men: 80

Guns: 24.

Éléphant Rochefort Dyd.
K: 9.1672. L: 5.1673. C: 8.1673. Wrecked 1.1674 while leaving Rochefort.

GARONNE. 200 tons. Acquired early 1675, ex-*Saint Jean de Rochefort*.
Dimensions & tons: dimensions unknown. 200 or 120 tons. Draught 9ft. Men: 28 (9/19/) +2 officers.

Guns: 10 or 4.

Garonne Rochefort Dyd.
Built 1673. Last mentioned 1675.

CHARIOT. 300 tons. Built by Laurent Hubac.
Dimensions & tons: 90ft 0in x 21ft 0in x 10ft 0in (29.24 x 6.82 x 3.25m). 300 tons (400 in 1674-75). Draught 14ft (4.54m). Men: 28 (9/19/), +2 officers.

Guns: 14, 12 from 1674, 10 from 1676.

Chariot Brest Dyd.
K: 1673. L: 12.1673. C: 1674. Renamed *Large* 28.11.1673. Wrecked 4.1676 (as *Chariot*?) on rocks at Houédic off Brest.

Ex-DUTCH PRIZES (1673–1674). Four Dutch *flûtes* were captured in 1673–74, three probably in Northern Europe and one in the Mediterranean. An 80-ton *caiche hollandaise* (Dutch ketch), described by Brest in March 1674 as a '*cache* or *galiotte*', was captured in December 1673 and called *Caiche Hollandaise* or simply *Hollandaise* until named *Charente* in January 1675. The 300-ton Dutch *Helderberg* was captured in June 1674 and called by the French version of her Dutch name, *Montagne Claire*, until named *Paresseux*, probably also in January 1675. She was assigned to Toulon, and had probably been captured in the Mediterranean. A 400-ton Dutch vessel was captured in 1674 by CV André, Chevalier de Nesmond; she was called *Prise du Chevalier de Nesmond* until named *Dromadaire* later in 1674. Finally, another 400-ton vessel was captured in 1674 by LV or CFL Dantzé, who commanded the *barque longue Hardie* and from 5.1674 the *frégate légère Bouffone* in the Dunkirk area. She was called *Prise de Dantzé* until named *Portefaix* 1.1675.

Hollandaise Holland.
Dimensions & tons: 66ft 0in x 16ft 0in x 8ft 0in (21.44 x 5.20 x 2.60m). 80 tons (60 in 1676–77). Draught 8ft (2.60m). Men: 28 (9/19/) +2 officers.

Guns: 4, 2 from 1677.

Built 1669. Renamed *Charente* 1.1675. Struck 1678 at Brest.

Montagne Claire Saardam, Holland.
Dimensions & tons: dimensions unknown. 300 tons (250 in 1679–86). Draught 12ft (9ft from 1679). Men: 28 (9/19/) +2 officers.

Guns: 10, 12 from 1676, 16 from 1677, 6 from 1679, 5 from 1686.

Built 1664. Renamed *Paresseux* by 1.1675 although old name also used to 4.1675. Assessed in 1677 as having a capacious hull but very poor sailing qualities. Struck 1686 at Toulon.

Dromadaire Holland.
Dimensions & tons: dimensions unknown. 400 tons. Draught 14ft. Men: 28 (9/19/) +2 officers.

Guns: 12.

Built 1670. Named 1674. Struck 1675 at Brest.

Portefaix Holland.
Dimensions & tons: dimensions unknown. 400 tons. Draught 14ft. Men: 28 (9/19/) +2 officers.

Guns: 12.

Built 1670–71. Named 1.1675. Found unsuitable for service 3.1675, sold 11.1675 at Dieppe.

Ex-DUTCH PRIZES (1675). Two more Dutch *flûtes* were captured in 1675. A 400-ton *flûte* possibly named *Paard* had probably been captured in February 1672 and renamed *Cheval* but was recaptured in July 1675 by Dutch or Spanish privateers without appearing on French navy lists. She was retaken or repurchased at the end of 1675 and was listed in the Navy in January 1676 as *Bretonne*, ex-*Cheval*. A small 70-ton *flûte* was captured in 1675 and named *Marseilloise*; her Dutch name is unknown.

Bretonne Holland.
Dimensions & tons: 104ft 0in x 23ft 0in x 11ft 0in (33.78 x 7.47 x 3.57m). 400 tons. Draught 12½ft (4.06m). Men: 28 (9/19/) +2 officers.

Guns: 16, 12 in 1676.

Built 1668. Struck 1676 at Brest.

Marseilloise Holland.
Dimensions & tons: dimensions unknown. 70 tons (80 in 1679). Draught 6ft. Men: 28 (9/19/) +2 officers.

Guns: 4.
Built 1669. Struck 1681, probably at Rochefort.

PORTEFAIX. 500 tons. Construction ordered 8 February 1675, named 3 June 1675. Built by Laurent Hubac. Intended for the transportation of masts from Nantes to Brest. The 1680 manning listed below is for long voyages; for ordinary voyages it was reduced to 40 (10/30/), + 2 officers.
  Dimensions & tons: 121ft 0in x 26ft 0in x 12ft 0in (39.31 x 8.45 x 3.90m). 500 tons. Draught 14ft (4.55m). Men: 28 (9/19/), +2 officers; in 1680, 60 (12/48/), +5 officers. From 1699: 250 in war, 230 peace (250/50 from 1701); from 1706: 60 in war, 60 peace.
  Guns: 20, 12 from 1677, 28 from 1679, 20 from 1681, 24 from 1688. 16 in war from 1696. 42 in war from 1699 (36 peace): LD 18 x 12pdrs, UD 18 x 6pdrs, QD 6 x 4pdrs. 20 from 1704: 20 x 8pdrs. 14 from 1706: 4 x 8pdrs, 10 x 6pdrs
Portefaix Brest Dyd.
  K: 29.3.1675. L: 1.1677. C: 2.1677. Rebuilt at Brest in 1689 and 1699. Lent as a privateer in 1689–90 to Louis Alvarez, Baron de Courçon, to transport supplies for the forces operating in Ireland. May have been submerged at Toulon 7.1707 to avoid mortar fire and refloated 11.1707. Captured 1712 by privateers from Flushing.

GARONNE. 70 tons. 28 men (9/19/) +2 officers. Captured 1676, assigned to Brest after capture. Struck 1678.

SOLEIL. 200 tons. Draught 10ft. 25 men +1 officer. 4 guns. Captured 6.1676, probably with the ex-Tuscan fireship *Saint Rosaire* (*Impudent*). Taken at Palma 3.1678 by privateers from Flushing. May be the same as the fireship *Éclair* of 1676.

The 450-ton 5th Rank ship *Étoile*, captured from the Algerians in 1664, was converted to a *flûte* in 1675, renamed *Bretonne* 12.1675, and struck in 1678. She is listed in Chapter 5.

DROMADAIRE. 550 tons. Built by Jean Guichard.
  Dimensions & tons: dimensions unknown. 550 tons (450 in 1677–79). Draught 14ft. Men: 60 (12/48/), +5 officers.
  Guns: 20, 26 from 1683, 30 from 1688.
Dromadaire Rochefort Dyd.
  K: 9.1676. L: 1677. C: 3.1677. Wrecked on Îles Aves (in the Caribbean) 11/12.5.1678 with other ships of *Vice-amiral* Jean, Comte d'Estrées's squadron but refloated. Capturned 1.1692 by the English at Îles Aves.

Ex-DUTCH PRIZES (1677). The last full year of the 1672–78 Franco-Dutch war saw the capture by the French of five more Dutch *flûtes*. A 250-ton ship whose Dutch name is unknown was captured in January and named *Petit Dauphin*. Three ships were captured in July, the 400-ton *Zoutvat*, the 400-ton *Denneboom*, and the 250-ton *Sint Paulus*. *Zoutvat* was captured by *Moqueuse* 13 July 1677 near Ushant and *Sint Paulus* was captured by Châteaurenault's squadron. All three were initially called by the French equivalents of their Dutch names (*Salière*, *Arbre de Pin*, and *Saint Paul*) until given new French names in 1678. Finally, the Dutch *Konig David* was captured in December. She was a French merchantman from Honfleur named *Roi David* that the Dutch had captured in July 1676.
Petit Dauphin. Holland.
  Dimensions & tons: dimensions unknown. 250 tons. Draught 12ft.
  Guns: 12.
  Struck 10.1678 at Toulon.

Salière Hoorn.
  Dimensions & tons: dimensions unknown. 400 tons. Draught 12ft.
  Men: 45 (11/34/) +4 officers.
  Guns: 6.
  Built *c*.1677. Renamed *Garonne* 1678. Condemned 12.6.1689 and BU at Brest.
Arbre de Pin Hoorn.
  Dimensions & tons: 106ft 0in x 21ft 0in x 11ft 0in (34.43 x 6.82 x 3.57m). 400 tons. Draught 13ft (4.22m). Men: 45 (11/34/) +4 officers. From 1696: 35 in war, 30 peace
  Guns: 6, 8 from 1690. 10 in war (6 peace) from 1691/1696: 4 x 8pdrs, 6 x 4pdrs
  Built 1674. Renamed *Chameau* 1678. In 1683 reportedly carried a mortar with a diameter of 4ft 10in firing a projectile weighing 9,000 *livres*. Unserviceable at Brest 1696 and fitted as accommodation hulk. BU 9.1697.
Saint Paul Rotterdam.
  Dimensions & tons: dimensions unknown. 250 tons (200 in 1680–87). Draught 11ft. Men: 28 (9/19/) +2 officers.
  Guns: 6, 10 from 1688.
  Built 1671–72. Renamed *Mulet* 28.6.1678. Struck 1688 at Rochefort, BU 1689.
Roi David. ?Honfleur
  Dimensions & tons: Unknown. Men: 36
  Guns: 14.
  Wrecked on Îles Aves (in the Caribbean) 11/12.5.1678 with other ships of *Vice-amiral* Jean, Comte d'Estrées's squadron.

FOURGON. 300 tons. Probably designed and built by Laurent Hubac.
  Dimensions & tons: dimensions unknown. 300 tons. Draught 11ft.
  Men: 35 (9/26/), +2 officers.
  Guns: 16, 10 from 1680.
Fourgon Brest Dyd.
  K: 3.1677. L: 1.1678. C: 1678. Captured 6.1684 by the Spanish who reportedly used her until 1703. However, she seems instead to have been bought back at Cadiz in 1685 and then rebuilt at Brest as the 5th Rank ship *Éveillé* (see Chapter 5).

CHARIOT. 350 tons. Designed and built in succession by Benjamin Chaillé, Élie Guichard, and Étienne Salicon, the first two having died while the work was in progress.
  Dimensions & tons: 101ft 6in x 24ft 0in x 12ft 0in (32.97 x 7.80 x 3.90m). 350 tons. Draught 13ft (4.22m). Men: 28 (9/19/), +2 officers; in 1680, 45 (11/34/), +4 officers.
  Guns: 24, 20 from 1681.
Chariot Le Havre.
  K: 5.1677. L: 25.5.1678. C: 8.1678. Loaned 9.1678 to the *Compagnie du Sénégal* for a slaving voyage. Grounded 11.1680 on the isle of São Tomé (Gulf of Guinea). Struck after Seigneley wrote on 23.10.1681 opposing an expedition to recover the *flûtes Baleine* and *Chariot* because of the expense and the poor chance of success.

BALEINE. 450 tons. Designed and built in succession by Benjamin Chaillé, Élie Guichard, and Étienne Salicon.
  Dimensions & tons: 118ft 0in x 27ft 0in x 13ft 6in (38.33 x 8.77 x 4.39m). 450 tons. Draught 15ft (4.87m). Men: 28 (9/19/), +2 officers; in 1680, 60 (12/48/), +5 officers.
  Guns: 30.
Baleine Le Havre.
  K: 5.1677. L: 29.11.1678. C: 2.1679. Loaned 9.1679 to the *Compagnie du Sénégal* for a slaving voyage. Grounded 7.1680 on the

isle of Principe (Gulf of Guinea). Struck after Seigneley wrote on 23.10.1681 opposing an expedition to recover the *flûtes Baleine* and *Chariot* because of the expense and the poor chance of success.

LARGE. 600 tons. Built by Jean Guichard. Named 11 December 1676.
Dimensions & tons: 122ft 6in, 104ft 0in x 27ft 0in x 12ft 6in (39.79 x 8.77 x 4.06m). 600 tons (800 in 1691–92). Draught 13½ft (4.39m). Men: 60 (12/48/), +5 officers.
Guns: 24, 30 from 1688, 10 from 1691.
Large Rochefort Dyd.
K: 10.1677. L: 11.1678. C: 1679 or 8.1680. Sold 12.1693 at Toulon.

Ex-DUTCH PRIZE (1678). The 500-ton Dutch *flûte Sint Jan* was purchased 5.1678 after being captured by Châteaurenault's squadron and was called *Saint Jean* until named *Éléphant* on 28 June 1678.
Dimensions & tons: 107ft 0in x 20ft 0in x 10ft 0in (34.76 x 6.50 x 3.25m). 500 tons. Draught 12ft (3.90m). Men: 60 (12/48/) +5 officers.
Guns: 24.
Éléphant Rotterdam.
Built 1671 of fir wood. Condemned at Brest 31.8.1683 as rotten and sold 9.1683.

COCHE. 500 tons. The mercantile *Saint Jean-Baptiste* was purchased by the King in early 1679 and retained that name until renamed *Coche* in late 1679.
Dimensions & tons: dimensions unknown. 500 tons. Men: 60 (12/48/) +5 officers.
Guns: 20.
Coche Marseille.
Built 1677. Loaned 17.1.1684 to the *Compagnie des Indes Orientales* and sold to them 8.1687. Captured 5.5.1689 by the Dutch at the Cape of Good Hope and became the Dutch *Africa*.

SAINT PAUL. 250 tons. Dutch vessel acquired 1681.
Dimensions & tons: dimensions unknown. 250 tons. Men: 28 (9/19/) +2 officers
Guns: 12.
Saint Paul Holland.
Struck 1682 at Rochefort.

CHARIOT. 750 tons. Built by Laurent Coulomb. Pierced for 36 guns and probably had a round stern.
Dimensions & tons: 115ft 0in, 100ft 0in x 27ft 6in x 14ft 0in (37.36, 32.48 x 8.93 x 4.55m). 750 tons (500 in 1683–90). Draught 17ft (5.52m). Men: 60 (12/48/), +5 officers. In 1696: 150 in war, 50 peace.
Guns: 20, 12 from 1687. 20 in war from 1696 (20 peace): 6 x 12pdrs, 14 x 6pdrs
Chariot Toulon Dyd.
K: 12.1681. L: 18.11.1682. C: 2.1683. Handed over 5.1701 for commercial use at Toulon. Struck 1703.

BALEINE. 800 tons. Built by François Pomet.
Dimensions & tons: 119ft 4in x 28ft 6in x 13ft 0in (38.76 x 9.26 x 4.22m). 800 tons (500 in 1683–86). Draught 17ft (5.52m). Men: 60 (12/48/), +5 officers. In 1696: 60 in war, 60 peace.
Guns: 20, 12 from 1687. 20 in war from 1696 (20 peace): 12 x 14pdrs, 6 x 6pdrs. 20 from 1699: 6 x 12pdrs, 14 x 6pdrs. 20 from 1704: 20 x 6pdrs.
Baleine Toulon Dyd.
K: 12.1681. L: 13.1.1683. C: 3.1683. Intercepted 3.8.1710 while returning to Toulon from Alexandria by Norris's Anglo-Dutch squadron and run ashore and burned at Port Cros to avoid capture.

A contract for the construction at Bordeaux of two *flûtes* measuring 400 tons and 120 x 28 feet was awarded on 20 January 1684 to two Bordeaux shipwrights, Barthélémy and Masson. Upon receipt of a better offer the contract was cancelled in April 1684 and construction was transferred to Rochefort, where they became *Bretonne* and *Profond*.

BRETONNE. 400 tons. Ordered in April 1684 from Honoré and Pierre Malet (father and son). Built by Honoré Malet.
Dimensions & tons: 107ft 0in x 25ft 0in x 12ft 0in (34.76 x 8.12 x 3.90m). 400 tons (300 in 1686–87). Draught 16ft (5.20m). Men: 45 (11/34/), +4 officers.
Guns: 6, 26 from 1688 (20 in the battery and 6 on the *gaillards*).
Bretonne Rochefort Dyd.
K: 6.1684. L: 6.1685. C: 12.1685. Struck 1694 or 1695.

PROFOND. 400 tons. Ordered in April 1684 from Honoré and Pierre Malet (father and son). Built by Honoré Malet, possibly to plans by Jean Guichard.
Dimensions & tons: 120ft 0in x 29ft 0in x 10ft 9in (38.98 x 9.42 x 3.49m). 400 tons (460 in 1699–1701). Draught 14ft (4.55m). Men: 45 (11/34/), +4 officers. In 1696: 200 in war, 60 peace
Guns: 6, 30 from 1688. 40 from 1698: LD 20 x 18pdrs, UD 20 x 8pdrs. 40 from 1699: LD 20 x 12pdrs, UD 20 x 6pdrs. 36 in war from 1700 (24 peace): LD 20 x 12pdrs, UD 16 x 6pdrs. 40 from 1707: LD 20 x 12pdrs, UD 20 x 8pdrs. 32 from 1708: LD 14 x 12pdrs, UD 18 x 6pdrs
Profond Rochefort Dyd.
K: 6.1684. L: 6.1685. C: 1.1686. Lent as a privateer to Louis Alvarez, Baron de Courçon 1692, then lent to René Duguay-Trouin from St Malo in the first *armement mixte* mounted by his family for itself. Operated at Nova Scotia and in Hudson Bay in 1696–97 under CV Le Moyne d'Iberville in a squadron of four vessels. Captured 2.1712 in the Atlantic by the enemy (probably the Dutch) while returning from St Domingue to France.

DIEPPOISE Class. 500 tons. Designed by Laurent Coulomb and built by him and his son François Coulomb. Contract dated 23 May 1685, possibly with Lalemand. Pierced for 28 guns and probably had round sterns.
Dimensions & tons: 105ft 0in, 92ft 0in x 26ft 6in x 13ft 5in (34.11, 29.89 x 8.61 x 4.36m). 500 tons (400 in 1687–89). Draught 15ft (4.87m). Men: 45 (11/34/), +4 officers. In 1696: 140 in war
Guns: 8, 12 from 1687. 26 from 1690: LD 6 x 12pdrs, UD 14 x 6pdrs, QD/Fc 6 x 4pdrs; 24 from 1691: same but 4 x 4pdrs. 20 in war in *Dieppoise* from 1696: same but no 4pdrs.
Dieppoise Toulon Dyd.
K: 5.1685. L: 10.1685. C: 11.1685. Lent as a privateer in 1689–90 to Louis Alvarez, Baron de Courçon, to transport supplies for the forces operating in Ireland. Then lent as a privateer in 1696–97 to CdE Jean Bernard de Saint-Jean, Baron de Pointis, as a hospital ship in a squadron of fourteen vessels, took part in the capture of Cartagena de Indias 5.5.1697. Requisitioned by Jean-Baptiste Ducasse, Governor of St Domingue, who replaced her with *Favori* left there by CV Des Augiers the year before. Struck 10.1697 at Brest.
Marseilloise Toulon Dyd.
K: 5.1685. L: 10.1685. C: 11.1685. Lent as a privateer in 1689 to LV Claude de Forbin-Gardanne. Wrecked 4.1691.

STORESHIPS AND CARGO SHIPS

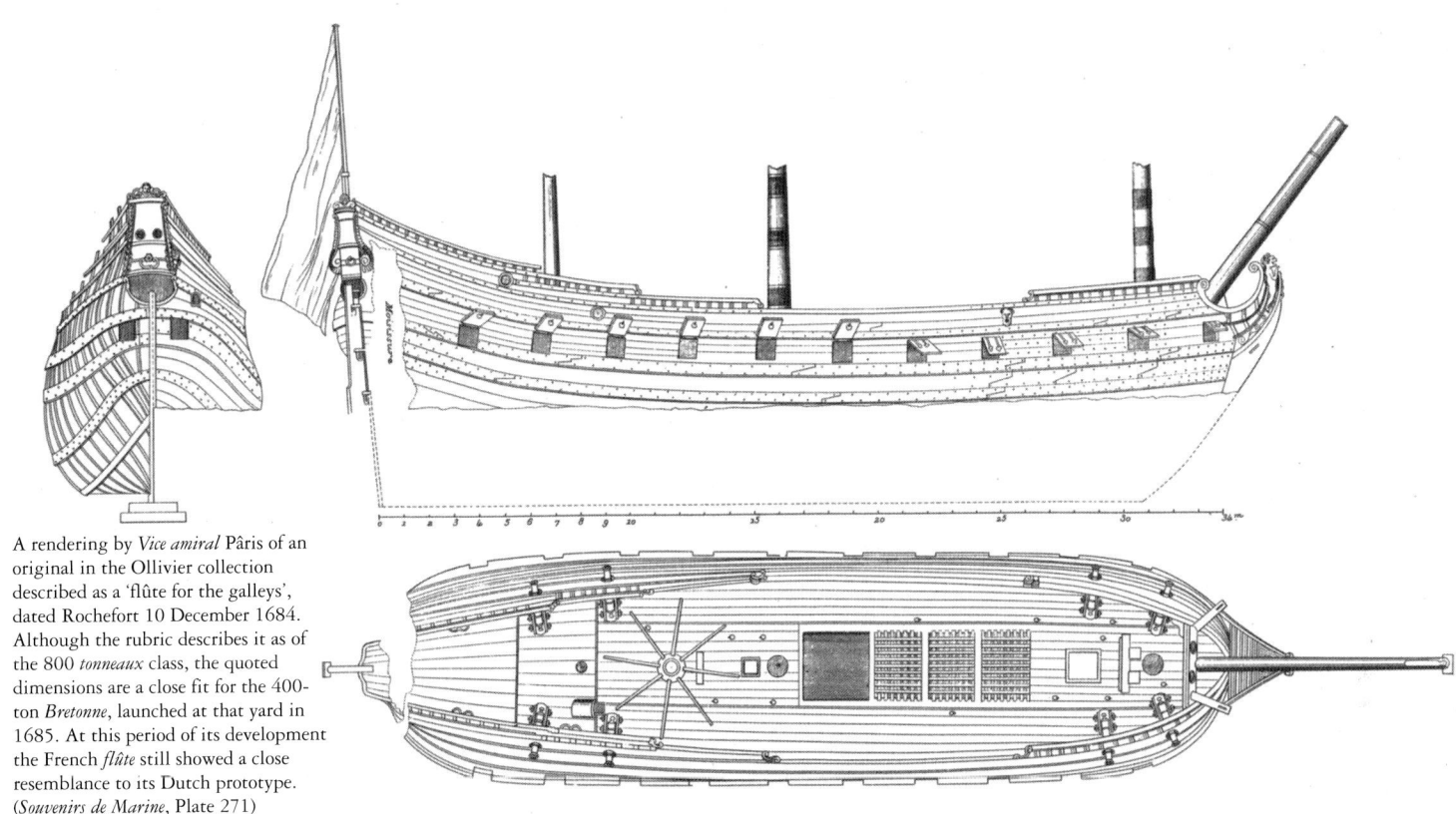

A rendering by *Vice amiral* Pâris of an original in the Ollivier collection described as a 'flûte for the galleys', dated Rochefort 10 December 1684. Although the rubric describes it as of the 800 *tonneaux* class, the quoted dimensions are a close fit for the 400-ton *Bretonne*, launched at that yard in 1685. At this period of its development the French *flûte* still showed a close resemblance to its Dutch prototype. (*Souvenirs de Marine*, Plate 271)

SAINT IGNACE. 500 tons. Put into service 7.1683 at Toulon, may have been a vessel recaptured from the Algerians 2.1683.
>   Dimensions & tons: Dimensions possibly 108ft 0in, 90ft 0in x 22ft 0in x 11ft 0in (35.08, 29.24 x 7.15 x 3.57m). 500 tons. Draught 13ft. Men: 45 (11/34/) +4 officers
>   Guns: 6, 12 from 1687.
> *Saint Ignace* La Rochelle.
>   Built 1667. Renamed *Éléphant* 1.3.1684. Struck 1690 at Toulon.

FOURGON. 400 tons. Dutch vessel acquired 5.1685, possibly captured 6.1684.
>   Dimensions & tons: dimensions unknown. 400 tons (300 in 1687–88). Draught 11ft. Men: 35 (9/26/) +2 officers
>   Guns: 10, 20 from 1688.
> *Fourgon* Amsterdam.
>   Built 1684 to 4.1685. Lent as a privateer in 1688 to Jean-Baptiste Ducasse, Governor of St Domingue, as part of a squadron of four vessels for operations against Surinam. Struck 1691 at Rochefort, after being lost at sea.

NORMANDE. 300 tons. Construction ordered November 1685, named 22 March 1686. Built by Étienne Hubac (Hubac *fils*) or possibly by Blaise Pangalo.
>   Dimensions & tons: dimensions unknown. 300 tons. Draught 12ft. Men: 35 (9/26/), +4 officers.
>   Guns: 30, 20 from 1688.
> *Normande* Brest Dyd.
>   K: 1.1686. L: 4.9.1686. C: 11.1686. Left Pondicherry 2.1689 under charter to the *Compagnie des Indes Orientales*, captured 27.4.1689 by the Dutch at the Cape of Good Hope, the French crew being unaware of the state of war, and renamed *Goede Hoop*.

LOIRE. 500 tons. Construction was ordered November 1685, named 22 March 1686. Built by Étienne Hubac.
>   Dimensions & tons: 110ft 0in x 28ft 8in x 10ft 9in (35.73 x 9.31 x 3.49m). 500 tons. Draught 14ft (4.55m). Men: 60 (12/48/), +5 officers. In 1696: 150 in war, 80 peace
>   Guns: 30. 30 in war from 1696 (16 peace): LD 16 x 12pdrs, UD 14 x 8pdrs. 12 from 1699: 12 x 8pdrs. 24 from 1704: LD 10 x 12pdrs, UD 14 x 8pdrs. 32 from 1706: LD 6 x 12pdrs, 8 x 8pdrs, UD 18 x 6pdrs. 36 from 1707: LD 18 x 8pdrs, UD 18 x 6pdrs. 24 from 1708: LD 8 x 12pdrs, UD 16 x 6pdrs. 32 from 1709: LD 8 x 12pdrs, 6 x 8pdrs, UD 18 x 6pdrs
> *Loire* Brest Dyd.
>   K: 2.1686. L: 18.9.1686. C: 12.1686. Lent as a privateer in 1688 to Jean-Baptiste Ducasse, Governor of St Domingue, as part of a squadron of four vessels for operations against Surinam. Fought off HMS *Chester* (54) 28.1.1694 near Dominica. Sailed in the King's service to the West Indies in 1696 under CV Des Augiers as part of a squadron of nine vessels carrying to the West Indies settlers and young marriageable women. Captured 3.1712 by the British.

ROYALE. 800 tons. Purchased 9.1687 from the *Compagnie des Indes Orientales*, name retained until renamed *Coche* 1688.
>   Dimensions & tons: dimensions unknown. 800 tons. Draught 14ft. Men: 40 (10/30/) +2 officers.
>   Guns: 40.
> *Royale* Le Havre.
>   K: 1671. L: 22.9.1676. C: 7.1677. Renamed *Coche* 1688. Hulked at Brest 1689. Last mentioned 5.1693.

(C) Vessels acquired from 15 April 1689

BIEN ARRIVÉ. The Spanish *San Jose* from Bruges (250 tons) was seized in April 1689 or taken in 1690 by CB Picard and was called *Saint Joseph* until being named *Bien Arrivé* on 3 July 1690. She was also listed as a Dutch prize.

Dimensions & tons: 93ft 0in x 21ft 0in x 8ft 0in (30.21 x 6.82 x 2.60m). 250 tons. Draught 12ft (3.90m). Men: 28 (9/19/) +2 officers. In 1696: 30 in war, 20 peace.

Guns: 4. 6 in war from 1696 (4 peace): 6 x 4pdrs. 4 from 1702: 4 x 4pdrs

Bien Arrivé Holland.

Built 1671. Grounded before Blaye (on the Gironde) 4.1690, refloated. Lent as a privateer in 1694 to Sieur Chaillou, wood merchant at Brest, to carry timber from the Vilaine/Loire area to Brest. Out of service 1702, struck 1702 or 1703.

PURCHASED VESSELS (1690). Two elderly vessels, one of 300 tons and one of 70 tons, were purchased in 1690. *Garonne* was a captured English barque named *Fortune* that may have been taken by a French privateer and then purchased by the King.

Françoise Built at La Rochelle.

Dimensions & tons: dimensions unknown. 300 tons. Draught 14ft. Men: 50 (12/38/) +4 officers.

Guns: 12.

Built 1678. Struck *c.*1693 at Rochefort.

Garonne Built in England.

Dimensions & tons: dimensions unknown. 70 tons. Draught 9ft. Men: 28 (9/19/) +2 officers.

Guns: 4.

Built 1668. Ex *Fortune* 13.12.1690. Struck 7.1692 at Brest, BU there 8–9.1692.

SAINT GUILLAUME. 115 tons. Purchased 12.1690 from the *Compagnie des Indes Orientales*, former name retained. Built by La Villetreux.

Dimensions & tons: 64ft 0in x 19ft 4in x 8ft 0in (20.79 x 6.28 x 2.60m). 115 tons. Draught 9¼ft (3.00m). Men: 40 (10/30/) +2 officers. In 1696: 25 in war

Guns: 10. 8 in war from 1696 (8 peace): 5 x 4pdrs, 3 x 3pdrs

Saint Guillaume Lorient.

K: late 1688. L: 5.1689. C: 1689. Hulked 1700, restored to service 6.1705. Very likely lent as a privateer in 1705 under the name of *Guillaume* to Jacques Cassard from Nantes. Served as a *patache* (*bâtiment interrompu*) at Port Louis from 1707. Last mentioned 6.1713 in very bad condition at Lorient.

Ex-DUTCH PRIZES (1690). Six Dutch *flûtes* ranging from 100 to 360 tons were captured in 1690 and added to the French Navy. Former Dutch names are not recorded except that *Catherine* retained her Dutch name and *Souris* may have been the Dutch *Muis* (both words mean 'mouse').

Bien Chargé Holland.

Dimensions & tons: dimensions unknown. 360 tons. Draught 9ft. Men: 28 (9/19/) +2 officers.

Guns: 4.

Built 1673. In 1677 was assessed as a very good vessel under sail that carried her cargo well. Struck and BU *c.*1694 (possibly wrecked).

Catherine. 200 tons Holland.

Dimensions & tons: dimensions unknown. 200 tons. Draught 10ft. Men: 28 (9/19/) +2 officers.

Guns: 4.

Built 1675. Listed only in 1691, assigned to Brest. May have been captured in 1691 by the English, perhaps becoming the foreign-built merchant ship *Katherine* of 292 tons that the Admiralty purchased for use as a storeship 15.10.1692 from Capt. Nicholas Picket. That ship measured in English feet 97ft 0in x 25ft 1in x 11ft 6in and was sold in 1701. Alternatively, this may have been early and incorrect information on the Dutch *Catherine* that appeared on the list in 1692 as the 3rd Rank ship of the line *Envieux* assigned to Rochefort (see Chapter 3).

Dissimulée Holland.

Dimensions & tons: dimensions unknown. 150 tons. Draught 10ft. Men: 20 (7/13/) +2 officers.

Guns: 4.

Built 1680. Struck 1694.

Éléphant Holland.

Dimensions & tons: dimensions unknown. 300 tons. Draught 9ft. Men: 45 (11/34/) +4 officers.

Guns: 20, 12 from 1691.

Built 1672. Struck 1693–1695 at Toulon.

Paresseux Amsterdam.

Dimensions & tons: 100ft 0in x 23ft 0in x 12ft 6in (32.48 x 7.47 x 4.06m). 350 tons (400 in 1691–92). Draught 15ft (4.87m). Men: 35 (9/26/) +2 officers. In 1696: 40 in war

Guns: 10. 8 from 1696: 8 x 4pdrs

Built 1670. BU 9.1697 at Brest.

Souris Holland.

Dimensions & tons: 89ft 0in x 26ft 6in x 10ft 6in (28.91 x 8.61 x 3.41m). 200 tons (150 in 1691–92). Draught 12ft (3.90m). Men: 28 (9/19/) +2 officers. In 1696: 40 in war, 40 peace.

Guns: 4. 6 in war from 1696: 6 x 6pdrs.

Built 1677. Renamed *Tranquille* 3.1692. Sailed in the King's service to the West Indies in 1696 under CV Des Augiers as part of a squadron of nine vessels carrying to the West Indies settlers and young marriageable women. Grounded and abandoned 1697 at Cap Français in St Domingue. Struck 1697, wreck last mentioned 1701.

Ex-ENGLISH PRIZES (1690–1691). One 200-ton English vessel was captured by the French in 1690 and a 70-ton vessel named *Olive Tree* was captured in July 1691, becoming the French Navy's *Arbre d'Olivier*.

Parti England.

Dimensions & tons: 86ft 0in x 21ft 0in x 11ft 0in (27.94 x 6.82 x 3.57m). 200 tons (300 in 1699–1702). Draught 13½ft (4.39m). Men: 20 (7/13/) +2 officers. In 1699: 40 in war, 26 peace

Guns: 4. 8 in war from 1696 (8 peace): 4 x 6pdrs, 4 x 4pdrs. 8 from 1699: 8 x 4pdrs. 8 from 1700: 8 x 3pdrs

Built 1673. Renamed *Gloutonne* 3.1692. Lent as a privateer in 1695–97 to CV Jean-Baptiste, Comte de Gennes, Seigneur d'Oyac as part of a squadron of six vessels (the others were *Faucon Anglais, Soleil d'Afrique, Séditieux,* the corvette *Félicité,* and the *flûte Fécond*), that destroyed the English Fort James in Gambia, moved to Rio de Janeiro, tried but failed to pass through the Strait of Magellan, and then cruised in the West Indies; she was armed with four or six guns. Captured 25.2.1705 by the English.

Arbre d'Olivier England.

Dimensions & tons: 56ft 0in x 17ft 6in x 8ft 0in (18.19 x 5.68 x 2.60m). 70 tons. Draught 10ft (3.25m). Men: 12 in war, 12 peace. In 1701: 25 in war, 12 peace

Guns: 10. 6 in war from 1696: 6 x 4pdrs

STORESHIPS AND CARGO SHIPS

Once the commercial advantages became evident, the *flûte* hull form was widely adopted by other maritime trading nations. This Jan Peeters painting of 1677 shows an English example in the Levant trade. She is about the size and age of the vessel captured in 1690 that became the *Parti*. (National Maritime Museum, London BHC1930)

Built 1687. Called a corvette in 1701. Struck 1704 or 1705 at Rochefort.

Ex-DUTCH PRIZES (1691). Five Dutch *flûtes* were captured in 1691 and taken into the French service, although two were not added to the Navy until 1692. One of 300 tons, possibly named *Blauw Pot* or *Blauw Kan*, was captured in February and was called *Pot Bleu* until named *Licorne* on 20 April 1691. Another 300-ton *flûte*, possibly named *Hout Handel*, was also captured in February and was called *Marchand de Bois* until named *Mulet* on 20 April 1691. A 350-ton vessel possibly named *San Marco Grande* was captured in April and was called *Grand Saint Marc* until added to the Navy in early 1692 and named *Replète* (*Replette*) on 30 March 1692. A 300-ton *flûte* was captured in May and was called *Saint Jerome* or *Saint Gerosme* (possibly similar to her Dutch name) until added to the Navy and named *Turquoise* in April 1692. Finally, the 350-ton Dutch *Wapen van Polen*, was captured in June and became the Fench *Armes de Pologne*.

Licorne   Holland.
   Dimensions & tons: dimensions unknown. 300 tons. Draught 13ft.
      Men: 30 (8/22/) +1 officer.
   Guns: 8.
   Lost at sea in early 1693, struck 4.1693 at Brest.
Mulet   Holland.
   Dimensions & tons: 100ft 0in x 22ft 0in x 11ft 0in (32.48 x 7.15 x 3.57m). 300 tons (350 in 1698–99). Draught 13ft (4.22m). Men: 30 (8/22/) +1 officer. In 1696: 30 in war, 20 peace
   Guns: 8. 10 in war from 1696 (6 peace): 4 x 8pdrs, 6 x 4pdrs
   Built 1672. Carried, with *Étourdi* and *Providence*, a supply of wheat from Port Louis to Bayonne 1697. Hulked at Brest 1699. Last mentioned 1701 as unserviceable.
Replète   Amsterdam.
   Dimensions & tons: 114ft 0in x 25ft 0in x 11ft 6in (37.03 x 8.12 x 3.74m). 400 tons. Draught 15ft (4.87m). Men: 50 in war, 50 peace
   Guns: 22 to 34. 18 in war from 1696: LD 4 x 12pdrs, UD 14 x 6pdrs
   In January 1693 was classed by Toulon among the 4th Rank ships of the line. Condemned 1697 at Toulon.
Armes de Pologne.   Holland.
   Dimensions & tons: 119ft 0in x 22ft 0in x 10ft 0in (38.66 x 7.15 x 3.25m). 350 tons.
   Guns: unknown.
   Sold 10.1692 at Toulon.
Turquoise   Holland.
   Dimensions & tons: 95ft 0in x 24ft 0in x 11ft 0in (30.86 x 7.80 x 3.57m). 300 tons. Draught 13ft (4.22m). Men: 45 in war, 35 peace; in 1700, 85 in war, 35 peace
   Guns: 14 in war (6 peace): 14 x 4pdrs. 22 from 1698: 14 x 8pdrs, 8 x 4pdrs
   Built 1689. Lent as a privateer in 1696 to LG André, Marquis de Nesmond, as part of a squadron of six to eleven vessels. Armed as a fireship 1704 in the fleet of the Comte de Toulouse with 6 guns, 45 men +1 officer; hulk at Toulon 1705; condemned 15.12.1710, ordered sold 24.12.1710.

VILLE D'EMDEN. 150 tons. The Brandenburgian *Stadt Emden*, which had been captured in 1689 by a French privateer, was purchased by the French Navy in January 1692.
   Dimensions & tons: 77ft 0in x 19ft 0in x 8ft 6in (25.01 x 6.17 x 2.76m). 150 tons (220 in 1698). Draught 10ft (3.25m). Men: 20 in war, 20 peace; in 1699, 30 in war, 20 peace
   Guns: 4 in war (4 peace) from 1696: 4 x 4pdrs; previously 6 x 4pdrs.
Ville d'Emden   Holland.
   Built 1686. Sailed in the King's service to the West Indies in 1696 under CV Des Augiers as part of a squadron of nine vessels carrying to the West Indies settlers and young marriageable women. Struck 1703 at Rochefort.

The *barque longue Inconnue* probably became the *flûte Féconde* 3.1692 but was struck later that year; she is listed in Chapter 10. For a later *Féconde* (1693–97) see the barque *Espérance* in Chapter 11. The 5th Rank ship *Mignon* of 1672 was renamed *Coche* 2.1692 when she was re-classed as an 18-gun *flûte* (with 4 x 8pdrs and 14 x 6pdrs; 45 men); she is listed in Chapter 5.

TONNE DE VICTOIRE. This *flûte* was acquired in August 1692 and handed over in June 1695 at Lorient to the *Compagnie de Guinée*. No other information is available.

Two vessels named *Prodigue* and *Endormie* were carried on a single list dated 1 April 1692 as *flûtes* for use at Brest. They were probably condemned ships of the line or frigates, although one might have been the fireship *Trompeur*. The project was abandoned in June 1692. The fireships *Incommode, Étourdi, Inconnu,* and *Voilé* were re-classed as *flûtes* in March and April 1692 and renamed *Dromadaire, Écrevisse, Paisible,* and *Massue* respectively. They are listed in Chapter 8.

Ex-DUTCH PRIZES (1692). On 31 August 1692 near Mount's Bay, Cornwall, a squadron of three French warships intercepted a homeward-bound Dutch convoy. The Chevalier de Forbin in *Perle* captured three Dutch *flûtes* from the convoy of 80 (*Wijnbergen* belonging to Cornelis van Avenhorn, *Vergulde Melkpot* belonging to Jan Duyf, and *Goude Hoet* belonging to Klaes Bulleper) while *Maure* and *Modéré* engaged and ultimately captured the two escorts (*Castricum* and *Maria-Elizabeth*). By various means the French captured or otherwise acquired eleven Dutch *flûtes* during 1692 that were then taken into the French Navy. *Chagrine* (300 tons), *Cloche Verte* (400 tons, possibly ex-Dutch *Groene Klok*), and *Matrone* (156 tons) were captured in January. The Dutch *Europeaan* (400 tons) was captured in February and became the French *Européen*, although *Européen* may instead have been the English *European* captured in July 1691. A Dutch *flûte* possibly named *Schildpad* (100 tons) was acquired by unknown means in early 1692 and became the French *Tortue*. The Dutch *Juffrouw Maria* (260 tons) was captured in mid-1692 and became the French *Dame Marie*. A 400-ton *flûte* possibly named *Duif* (probably Jan Duyf's *Vergulde Melkpot*) was captured in August 1692 and became the French *Colombe*. Two other Dutch *flûtes* were captured during 1692, a 300-ton vessel (possibly the *Wijnbergen*) named *Ressource* by the French and another *flûte* possibly named *Berg Druif* and called *Montagne au Raisin* by the French until being named *Tardif* late 1692. The Dutch *Pieter Elisabeth* (250 tons) was also captured during 1692; she was called *Pitre-Élisabeth* and possibly *Pierre-Élisabeth* by the French. Finally, a 100-ton Dutch *flûte* was captured around 1692 and was named *Providence*.

Chagrine. Holland.
  Dimensions & tons: dimensions unknown. 300 tons. Draught 12ft. Men: 20, +2 officers
  Guns: 16.
  Built 1673. Struck *c.*1694.

Cloche Verte Holland, probably Rotterdam.
  Dimensions & tons: 100ft 0in x 21ft 0in x 10ft 6in (32.48 x 6.82 x 3.41m). 400 tons. Draught 13ft (4.22m). Men: 70 in war, 30 peace
  Guns: 18 in 1692 (as 1696 less 2 x 8pdrs). 20 in war (10 peace) from 1696: 10 x 8pdrs, 10 x 6pdrs. 12 from 1699: 6 x 8pdrs, 6 x 4pdrs
  Built 1680. Struck 1699 at Brest and sold.

Matrone Holland.
  Dimensions & tons: dimensions unknown. 156 tons. Draught 11ft. Men: 28, +1 officer.
  Guns: 4.
  Struck 6.1692.

Européen Holland, probably Amsterdam.
  Dimensions & tons: 105ft 0in x 24ft 8in x 9ft 0in (34.11 x 8.01 x 2.92m). 400 tons. Draught 13½ft (4.39m). Men: 100 in war; in 1699, 60 in war, 30 peace
  Guns: 24 in war (24 peace): LD 2 x 12pdrs, 10 x 8pdrs, UD 12 x 4pdrs
  Built 1685–86. Lent as a privateer in 1697 to Sieur Beaubriant-L'Évêque, from St Malo to transport supplies to Plaisance in Nova Scotia 1697. Struck 1703 at Port Louis.

Tortue Holland.
  Dimensions & tons: dimensions unknown. 100 tons. Draught 13ft. Men: 19, +3 officers
  Guns: 8.
  Struck 1692 at Rochefort, may have been burned by the enemy at La Hougue.

Dame Marie Holland.
  Dimensions & tons: 96ft 6in x 23ft 8in x 10ft 6in (31.35 x 7.69 x 3.41m). 260 tons. Draught 13ft (4.22m). Men: 30 in war, 28 peace
  Guns: 18. 10 in war (10 peace) by 1696: 6 x 6pdrs, 2 x 4pdrs, 2 x 1pdrs
  Struck 1698 at Toulon.

Colombe Holland.
  Dimensions & tons: 107ft 0in x 25ft 0in x 12ft 0in (34.76 x 8.12 x 3.90m). 400 tons. Draught 13ft (4.22m). Men: 40 in war, 30 peace
  Guns: 6 in war: 6 x 8pdrs. 12 from 1698: 6 x 8pdrs, 6 x 4pdrs. 18 from 1706: 8 x 8pdrs, 10 x 6pdrs. 8 from 1708: 8 x 4pdrs. 12 from 1709: 6 x 8pdrs, 6 x 4pdrs
  Built 1687. Hulked 1.1700 at Brest but restored to service as a *flûte* 8.1701. Sank in the Loire 1.1706 near Paimboeuf, refloated. Handed over 1709 for commercial service, crew mutinied 2.1710 at Cayenne.

Ressource Holland.
  Dimensions & tons: dimensions unknown. 300 tons. Draught 12½ft. Men: 20, +2 officers
  Guns: 16.
  Built 1671. At Dunkirk in 1692. Struck *c.*1694.

Tardif. Holland.
  Lent as a privateer in 1689–90 to Louis Alvarez, Baron de Courçon, to transport supplies for the forces operating in Ireland. Struck 1694, probably at Brest. No other information is available.

Pitre-Élisabeth Holland.
  Dimensions & tons: 76ft 0in x 20ft 0in x 10ft 0in (24.69 x 6.50 x 3.25m). 250 tons. Draught 12ft (3.90m). Men: 45 in peace; in 1698, 25 in peace
  Guns: 10. 4 in war by 1696: 4 x 4pdrs
  Struck 1698 at Toulon.

Providence Holland.
  Dimensions & tons: 64ft 0in x 16ft 0in x 9ft 0in (20.79 x 5.20 x 2.92m). 100 tons. Draught 8ft (2.60m). Men: 15 in war, 10 peace
  Guns: 2 in war: 2 x 4pdrs
  Lent as a privateer in 1694 to Sieur Chaillou, wood merchant at Brest, to carry timber from the Vilaine/Loire area to Brest. Captured 7.1696 near Penmarch by the Flushing privateer *Annie-Jacoba*, recaptured the same month. Lent as a privateer in 1697 to carry, with *Étourdi* and *Mulet*, a supply of wheat from Port Louis to Bayonne. Struck *c.*1703 at Brest, probably after being wrecked at Cap Lévi near Cherbourg.

Ex-ENGLISH PRIZES (1692). Four English vessels were captured in 1692 and added to the French Navy. Three were captured in October: the 100-ton *Elizabeth* and two vessels named *James*, one of 350 tons and one of 300 tons that was described as an East Indiaman. The French named these three ships *Élisabeth de Londres, Jacques I* (or *Premier*), and *Jacques II* (or *Second*). A vessel of 200 tons named *Fleur de Lys* by the French was also captured during the year.

Élisabeth de Londres England, perhaps London.
  Dimensions & tons: 57ft 0in x 15ft 6in x 9ft 0in (18.52 x 5.04 x 2.92m). 100 tons. Draught 10ft (3.25m). Men: 20, +1 officer.
  Guns: 4 in war: 4 x 4pdrs
  Struck 1696 at Toulon and sold.

Jacques I England.
  Dimensions & tons: 101ft 0in x 25ft 0in x 11ft 0in (32.81 x 8.12 x 3.57m). 350 tons. Draught 12ft (3.90m). Men: 45 in war, 45 peace

Guns: 18 in war: 4 x 8pdrs, 14 x 6pdrs
Considered suitable for use as a fireship in 1696. Struck 1698 at Toulon.

Jacques II England.
Dimensions & tons: 92ft 0in x 23ft 0in x 11ft 0in (29.89 x 7.47 x 3.57m). 300 tons. Draught 12ft (3.90m). Men: 45 in war, 45 peace
Guns: 18 in war: 4 x 8pdrs, 14 x 6pdrs
Considered suitable for use as a fireship in 1696. Struck 1696 or 1697 at Toulon.

Fleur de Lys England.
Dimensions & tons: 87ft 0in x 20ft 6in x 9ft 4in (28.26 x 6.66 x 3.03m). 200 tons (250 in 1704). Draught 10½ft (3.41m). Men: 30 in war, 30 peace
Guns: 10 in war: 4 x 8pdrs, 6 x 4pdrs; 10 x 6pdrs from 1702.
Built 1685. Handed over 1697 to the *Compagnie du Sénégal* and struck. Repurchased 1701. Wrecked 8.1702 off Ushant. Struck 1704.

Ex-BARBARY COAST PRIZES (1692). Two Tripolitanian vessels, one of 350 tons and one of 250 tons, were captured in November 1692, becoming the French Navy's *flûtes Postillon de Cadix* and *Armes de Venise*. Their Tripolitanian names may have been *Cadi* and *Tinine Tahior* respectively.

Postillon de Cadix Holland (or Spain?).
Dimensions & tons: dimensions unknown. 350 tons. Men: 45 in war, 45 peace
Guns: 18 in war: 4 x 8pdrs, 14 x 6pdrs
Struck 1698 at Toulon. Given 2.1699 to the *Compagnie Royale de St Domingue*.

Armes de Venise Holland.
Dimensions & tons: 90ft 0in x 23ft 0in x 9ft 10in (29.24 x 7.47 x 3.19m). 250 tons. Draught 12ft (3.90m). Men: 30 in war, 30 peace
Guns: 10 in war: 4 x 8pdrs, 6 x 4pdrs
Struck 1698 at Toulon.

CHARENTE. 600 tons. Built by Pierre Morineau (*père*) and Pierre Masson.
Dimensions & tons: 115ft 0in x 30ft 0in x 13ft 0in (37.36 x 9.75 x 4.22m). 600 tons. Draught 14ft (4.55m). Men: 150 in war, 80 peace; in 1699, 60 in war, 50 peace
Guns: 34 in war (34 peace): LD 2 x 18pdrs, 12 x 12pdrs, UD 20 x 6pdrs. 20 from 1699: LD 6 x 12pdrs, UD 14 x 6pdrs.

Charente Rochefort Dyd.
K: Late 1692. L: 1693. C: 5.1694. Loaned 1699 to carry wheat from Tunisia to Le Havre and wrecked 22.3.1699 near Bizerte (Porto Farina) at night in a storm. Struck 1700, remains sold 1702 to the Bey of Tunis.

Ex-DUTCH PRIZES (1693). Ten Dutch *flûtes* were captured during 1693 and taken into the French Navy. The 400-ton *Sint Jacob* was captured in January and became the French *Saint Jacques* (also called *Saint Jacques de Bayonne*). The 300-ton *Margaretha* was captured on 10 April 1693 and became the French *Marguerite d'Amsterdam*. Five vessels were captured in June: a 100-ton vessel possibly named *Jacobus Benjamin*, a 200-ton vessel possibly named *Agaat*, the 400-ton *Raadhuis van Amsterdam* (taken by Tourville at Lagos), the 300-ton *Prins van Polen*, and a vessel about which little is known that could have been the Dutch *Heiland* or the Spanish *Salvador*. These respectively became the French *Jacques Benjamin, Agathe, Maison de Ville d'Amsterdam, Prince de Pologne*, and *Sauveur*. In October the 300-ton Dutch *Poolster* was taken, becoming the French *Étoile du Nord*. Also captured during 1693 was a 400-ton vessel possibly named *Hollandia* that became the French *Hollande*. Finally, the Dutch *Gouden Berg* of about 200 tons was captured late in 1693 and became the French *Montagne d'Or*.

Saint Jacques Holland.
Dimensions & tons: 98ft 0in x 28ft 0in x 10ft 0in (31.83 x 9.10 x 3.25m). 400 tons. Draught 12ft (3.90m). Men: 40 in war, 40 peace
Guns: 8 in war (8 peace): 8 x 6pdrs
Struck 1698 at Rochefort.

Marguerite d'Amsterdam Holland, probably Amsterdam.
Dimensions & tons: 99ft 0in x 23ft 0in x 9ft 0in (32.16 x 7.47 x 2.92m). 300 tons. Draught 14ft (4.55m). Men: 30.
Guns: 14 in war: 4 x 8pdrs, 10 x 4pdrs
Was old in 1696. Condemned 10.1696 at Toulon, sold 7.1697.

Jacques Benjamin Holland.
Dimensions & tons: 67ft 0in x 19ft 0in x 8ft 8in (21.76 x 6.17 x 2.82m). 100 tons. Draught 9½ft (3.09m). Men: 20, +1 officer.
Guns: 4 in war: 4 x 4pdrs
Struck 1696 or 1697 at Toulon.

Agathe Holland.
Dimensions & tons: 76ft 0in x 20ft 6in x 8ft 6in (24.69 x 6.66 x 2.76m). 200 tons. Draught 11ft (3.57m). Men: 25 in war, 25 peace
Guns: 6 in war: 6 x 4pdrs
Built 1693 (new when taken). Struck 1697 at Toulon.

Maison de Ville d'Amsterdam Amsterdam.
Dimensions & tons: 100ft 0in x 23ft 0in x 12ft 0in (32.48 x 7.47 x 3.90m). 400 tons. Draught 13ft (4.22m). Men: 40 in war
Guns: 10 in 1696: 6 x 8pdrs, 4 x 4pdrs
Built 1689. Lent as a privateer in 1694 to François Saupin, sieur Du Rocher, wood merchant in Brest, to carry timber from the Vilaine/Loire area to Brest. Lent as a privateer in 1696 to LG André, Marquis de Nesmond as part of a squadron of six to eleven vessels. Lent as a privateer in 1696–97 to CdE Jean Bernard de Saint-Jean, Baron de Pointis, as part of a squadron of fourteen vessels; took part in the capture of Cartagena de Indias 5.5.1697. Captured 9.6.1697 by HMS *Warwick* while in use as a hospital ship; the *vomito negro* on board the prize devastated the combined fleet of her captors killing Vice-Adm John Neville, six English captains including George Mees, all but one of the Dutch captains, and 1,300 men.

Prince de Pologne Holland.
Dimensions & tons: 101ft 0in x 22ft 0in x 11ft 0in (32.81 x 7.15 x 3.57m). 300 tons. Draught 10¾ft (3.49m). Men: 45 in war, 45 peace
Guns: 18 in war (18 peace): 4 x 8pdrs, 14 x 6pdrs
Built *c.*1692 (fine new ship when taken). Wrecked 1.1700 at Civita-Vecchia.

Sauveur. Tons unknown, may have been a Spanish vessel. Struck at Toulon 1694 or 1695. No other information is available.

Étoile du Nord Holland.
Dimensions & tons: 90ft 0in x 22ft 0in x 10ft 0in (29.24 x 7.15 x 3.25m). 250 tons (220 in 1706). Draught 10ft (3.25m). Men: 40 in war
Guns: 8 in war (8 peace): 8 x 4pdrs
Built 1681–82. Hulked 1.1701 at Port Louis. Unserviceable 1704, BU 1706.

Hollande Holland.
Dimensions & tons: 96ft 0in x 24ft 0in x 9ft 6in (31.18 x 7.80 x

3.09m). 400 tons. Draught 9½ft (3.09m). Men: 45 in war, 45 peace

Guns: 18 in war: LD 4 x 12pdrs, UD 14 x 6pdrs

Handed over 11.1698 to the *Compagnie Royale de St Domingue*. Returned to the Navy in early 1706, handed over in late 1706 to Canada, wrecked 1710 at Beaumont in Quebec.

Montagne d'Or Holland.

Dimensions & tons: dimensions unknown. *c.*200 tons.

Guns: 10 in war: 10 x 4pdrs

Built *c.*1692 (fine new vessel when taken). Struck 2.1697 and sold at Toulon.

Ex-SPANISH OR DUTCH PRIZES (1693–1694). A vessel about which little is known that probably was Spanish was captured in early 1693, and the Spanish *Fortuna* of 180 tons was captured in May 1693. The first was renamed *Courrier de Cadix* or *Poste de Cadix* by the French Navy while the second was renamed *Fortune de Cadix*. A 250-ton vessel that may have been the Dutch *Regel* or Spanish *Nostra Señora de Regla* was captured in February 1694 and renamed *Règle*.

Courrier de Cadix or *Poste de Cadix*. Tonnage unknown, 45 men, 14 guns. Last mentioned 9.1693.

Fortune de Cadix Holland.

Dimensions & tons: 72ft 0in x 19ft 0in x 7ft 0in (23.39 x 6.17 x 2.27m). 180 tons. Draught 9½ft (3.09m). Men: 20 in war

Guns: 6 in war (6 peace): 2 x 4pdrs, 4 x 3pdrs

Unserviceable 1.1696 and condemned at Port Louis.

Règle Holland.

Dimensions & tons: 92ft 0in x 22ft 6in x 9ft 10in (29.89 x 7.31 x 3.19m). 250 tons. Draught 12ft (3.90m). Men: 30 in war, 30 peace

Guns: 14 in war: 4 x 8pdrs, 10 x 4pdrs

Built *c.*1693 (new when taken). Struck 1696 at Toulon.

GRAND LOUIS. This vessel was acquired *c.*1694 and put into service at Brest. She was wrecked 1695 on the rocks at Minou with heavy loss of life. No other information is available.

Ex-DUTCH PRIZES (1695). Five Dutch *flûtes* were captured during 1695 and added to the French Navy. A 400-ton vessel was named *Ville de Bayonne* by the French. A 150-ton vessel captured by LG André, Marquis de Nesmond was called *Brigantin prise par M. de Nesmond* until named *Providence* in 1696. The 300-ton Dutch *Margaretha* (also called *Marguerite de Staden*) became the French *Marguerite d'Estadem*. A 50-ton ship possibly named *Fortuin* became the French *Fortune de Rotterdam*, and the 260-ton *Kasteel van Breda* became the French Navy's *Château de Breda*.

Ville de Bayonne Holland.

Dimensions & tons: 96ft 0in x 22ft 0in x 10ft 0in (31.18 x 7.15 x 3.25m). 400 tons (250 in 1698). Draught 12ft (3.90m). Men: 60 in war, 40 peace; in 1698, 40 in war, 35 peace

Guns: 24 in war (8 peace): 8 x 8pdrs, 16 x 6pdrs. 10 in war from 1698: 10 x 6pdrs

Renamed *Château de Bayonne* 1696. Wrecked 12.1697 at St Domingue and abandoned. Struck 1698.

Providence Holland.

Dimensions & tons: 65ft 0in x 19ft 0in x 9ft 6in (21.11 x 6.17 x 3.09m). 150 tons (70 in 1696–98). Draught 10ft (3.25m). Men: 20 in war, 15 peace

Guns: 6 in war (4 peace): 6 x 3pdrs. 8 from 1699: 8 x 8pdrs. 6 from 1700: 6 x 4pdrs

Built 1688. Lent as a privateer in 1696–97 to CdE Jean Bernard de Saint-Jean, Baron de Pointis, who called her a *brigantin*, as part of a squadron of fourteen vessels; took part in the capture of Cartagena de Indias 5.5.1697. Abandoned before the return journey, scuttled or more likely sold.

Marguerite d'Estadem Holland.

Dimensions & tons: 95ft 0in x 21ft 9in x 10ft 0in (30.86 x 7.07 x 3.25m). 300 tons. Draught 11ft (3.57m). Men: 30 in war, 30 peace

Guns: 14 in war: 4 x 8pdrs, 10 x 4pdrs

Sold 7.1697 at Toulon.

Fortune de Rotterdam Holland, probably Rotterdam.

Dimensions & tons: 55ft 0in x 15ft 0in x 9ft 0in (17.87 x 4.87 x 2.92m). 50 tons. Draught 8ft (2.60m). Men: 10 in war

Guns: 2 in war: 2 x 3pdrs

Built 1670. BU 9.1697 at Brest.

Château de Breda Holland.

Dimensions & tons: 89ft 0in x 22ft 0in x 9ft 0in (28.91 x 7.15 x 2.92m). 260 tons. Draught 11ft (3.57m). Men: 40 in war, 40 peace.

Guns: 6 in war (6 peace): 6 x 6pdrs

Struck 1696 or 1697 at Rochefort.

Ex-ENGLISH PRIZES (1695). Three small English vessels were captured in 1695 and taken into the French Navy. The 28-ton *Indinio de Bristol* may have been from Bristol, the 180-ton *Aventurier Marin* may have been previously named *Sea Venturer*, and the 120-ton *Sirène de Londres*, captured in August 1695, may have previously been named *Siren* or *Mermaid*.

Indinio de Bristol England, probably Bristol.

Dimensions & tons: dimensions unknown. 44ft 0in x 11ft 6in x 5ft 8in (14.29 x 3.74 x 1.84m). 28 tons. Draught 3½ft (1.14m).

Guns: 3 in war (3 peace): 1 x 3pdr, 2 x 2pdrs

Last mentioned 1696 at Port Louis.

Aventurier Marin England.

Dimensions & tons: 73ft 0in x 20ft 0in x 9ft 0in (23.71 x 6.50 x 2.92m). 180 tons. Draught 9ft 10in (3.19m). Men: 20 in peace

Guns: 6 in war: 6 x 4pdrs

Struck 1698 at Toulon.

Sirène de Londres England, probably London.

Dimensions & tons: 78ft 0in x 23ft 0in x 11ft 0in (25.34 x 7.47 x 3.57m). 120 tons. Draught 12ft (3.90m). Men: 25 in war

Guns: 6 in war (4 peace): 6 x 4pdrs

Struck 6.1697 and sold at Brest.

SAINT MARTIN. This *flûte* was captured *c.*1695. She was an accommodation hulk at Brest by January 1696, being listed as an unserviceable *bâtiment interrompu*, and was BU 9.1697. No other information is available.

GIRONDE. 600 tons. Built by Pierre Masson.

Dimensions & tons: 124ft 0in x 32ft 2in x 12ft 6in (40.28 x 10.45 x 4.06m). 600 tons. Draught 15½ft (5.04m). Men: 150 in war, 100 peace; in 1701, 120 in war, 70 peace

Guns: 42 in war (28 peace): LD 10 x 18pdrs, 12 x 12pdrs, UD 20 x 8pdrs.

Gironde Rochefort Dyd.

K: early 1695. L: 1.1696. C: 4.1696. Scuttled 8.1702 at Léogâne, Haiti, to avoid capture, blew up.

JUSTICE. 120 tons. Dutch vessel purchased 1696, possibly named *Recht* or *Rechtvaardigheid*. She may have been captured on 5 April 1690 by the St Malo privateers *Saint Antoine* and *Comte de Revel*.

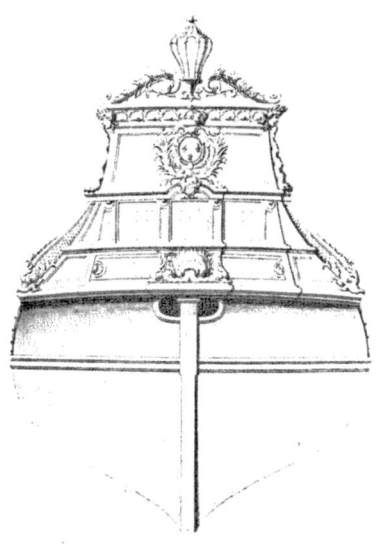

For the French Navy the term *flûte* originally described a vessel similar in appearance to its Dutch model, and was similarly regarded as a load-carrier. However, over time the role remained consistent, but the type of ship underwent a transformation, sometimes being built with a conventional 'square' stern, with a row of lights (windows) under the taffrail. The decorative work of the *Gironde* of 1696 demonstrates the beginning of this process, with the round buttock lines and extreme tumblehome retained but surmounted by a more warship-like taffrail. Although a humble storeship, *Gironde* belonged to the King's Navy and was adorned accordingly. (*Souvenirs de Marine*, Plate 149)

Dimensions & tons: 70ft 0in x 17ft 0in x 9ft 0in (22.74 x 5.52 x 2.92m). 120 tons (130 in 1704–9). Draught 9ft (2.92m). Men: 14 in war, 14 peace

Guns: None until *c*.1703: 4 in war (4 peace): 4 x 4pdrs

Justice Hambourg.
  Built 1688–89. Called a corvette in 1701. Struck 1709 at Brest and handed over for commercial use. Wrecked 1714 in the Bahama Channel.

Ex-DUTCH PRIZES (1696). Two Dutch *flûtes* were captured in July 1696 and added to the French Navy. The 350-ton *Juffrouw Catharina* became the French *Demoiselle Catherine* (also listed as *Demoiselle Catherine d'Amsterdam*) and the 500-ton *Johanna Cornelia* became the French *Jeanne Cornélie* (also listed as *Joanna Cornelia*).

Demoiselle Catherine Amsterdam.
  Dimensions & tons: 93ft 0in x 22ft 6in x 9ft 6in (30.21 x 7.31 x 3.09m). 350 tons (250 in 1699). Draught 10ft (3.25m). Men: 40 in war, 35 peace
  Guns: 8 in war (8 peace) in 1698; 12 in war (6 peace) in 1699: 12 x 4pdrs
  Struck 1699 at Rochefort.

Jeanne Cornélie Holland.
  Dimensions & tons: 110ft 0in x 22ft 6in x 10ft 6in (35.73 x 7.31 x 3.41m). 500 tons (400 in 1701–2). Draught 13½ft (4.39m). Men: 40 in war, 30 peace; in 1701, 80 in war, 50 peace
  Guns: 12 in war (6 peace): 6 x 8pdrs, 6 x 6pdrs, 6 x 4pdrs. 12 from 1699: 6 x 8pdrs, 6 x 4pdrs. 16 from 1702: 8 x 8pdrs, 8 x 4pdrs
  Wrecked 9.1702 or 10.1702 at Bermuda.

Ex-BRANDENBURGIAN PRIZE (1696). The 120-ton Brandenburgian hooker or fireship *Sankt Peter* was captured in 1696 and renamed *Saint Pierre*.
  Dimensions & tons: 70ft 0in x 18ft 0in x 9ft 0in (22.74 x 5.85 x 2.92m). 120 tons. Draught 9½ft (3.09m). Men: 15 in war, 14 peace
  Guns: None (carried 6 or 12 guns prior to capture)

Saint Pierre Hamburg.
  Built 1681 and rebuilt 1685. Struck 1698 and sold at Le Havre.

Aside from one purpose-built ship (*Seine*, below), the French Navy acquired no *flûtes* during the interval between the end of the War of the League of Augsburg in 1697 and the beginning of the War of the Spanish Succession in 1701. Many of the *flûtes* acquired before 1696 were disposed of during this short period of peace, with the result that the Navy's inventory of these ships declined from sixty in January 1696, way above the number of twenty-six authorized by the King in the early 1680s, to fifteen in January 1701, well below that number.

SEINE. 600 tons. Built by Pierre Masson.
  Dimensions & tons: 126ft 0in x 32ft 6in x 13ft 6in (40.93 x 10.56 x 4.39m). 600 tons (640 in 1701–04). Draught 16ft (5.20m). Men: 150 in war, 100 peace; in 1704, 200 in war, 100 peace.
  Guns: 46 in war (30 peace): LD 22 x 12pdrs, UD 24 x 8pdrs. 44 from 1701: LD 10 x 18pdrs, 12 x 12pdrs, UD 11 x 8pdrs, 11 x 6pdrs. 44 from 1702: LD 11 x 18pdrs, 11 x 12pdrs, UD 11 x 8pdrs, 11 x 6pdrs. 44 from 1704: LD 22 x 12pdrs, UD 22 x 6pdrs.

Seine Rochefort Dyd.
  K: 1697. L: 1698. C: 5.1699. While escorting a convoy to Canada with *Loire* on 26.7.1704 engaged and captured by HM Ships *Falkland* (48), *Dreadnought* (66) and *Fowey* (32) off the Azores. Renamed *Falkland Prize* (Fourth Rate, 732 tons, 54 guns). Blown ashore in Sandwich Bay 30.12.1705, wreck sold 22.3.1706.

PURCHASED VESSELS (1701). Three former Dutch *flûtes* were purchased by the Navy in 1701 around the time of the outbreak of the War of the Spanish Succession. *Saint Nicolas* was purchased in June and *Arsenal de Marseille* was bought at Marseille in August. *Dromadaire*, also purchased in 1701, was a prize previously taken by a French privateer. The Dutch names are unknown although *Saint Nicolas* may have been *Sint Nicolaas*.

Saint Nicolas. Purchased 6.1701, ex-Dutch. Built in Holland, was very old in 1702. Renamed *Arche* 9.1701. Captured 6.1702 by the English. No other information is available.

Arsenal de Marseille. Built in Holland.
  Dimensions & tons: 120ft 0in x 24ft 0in x 13ft 0in (38.98 x 7.80 x 4.22m). 550 tons (400 in 1702). Draught 14ft (4.55m). Men: 35 in war, 35 peace; in 1704, 50 in war, 40 peace
  Guns: 18 in war (18 peace): 4 x 8pdrs, 14 x 6pdrs; 12 x 6pdrs from 1704.
  Built 1690–92. Renamed *Chariot* 1701. Struck 8.1704 and resold to her former owner.

Dromadaire Built in Holland.
  Dimensions & tons: 110ft 0in x 21ft 6in x 12ft 0in (35.73 x 6.98 x 3.90m). 400 tons. Draught 13ft (4.22m). Men: 45 in war, 40 peace

Guns: 6 in war (4 peace): 6 x 6pdrs
Struck 1712 at Brest.

ÉLÉPHANT. 300 tons. Built by Antoine Tassy. A 500-ton *flûte* named *Éléphant* was ordered at Brest in January 1699. Construction was adjourned in 1699 or 1700 and the project was transferred to Bayonne in January 1701. Construction of this ship was ordered there on 18 May 1701.
  Dimensions & tons: 98ft 0in x 24ft 0in x 12ft 0in (31.83 x 7.80 x 3.90m). 300 tons. Draught 12½ft (4.06m). Men: 80 in war, 60 peace
  Guns: 12 in war: 6 x 6pdrs, 6 x 4pdrs. 16 from 1704: 16 x 6pdrs
Éléphant Bayonne.
  K: 1701. L: 1702. C: 1702. Captured 25.2.1705 by the English. Purchased 17.8.1705 by the Royal Navy from the Commissioner for Prizes and became the storeship *Elephant*. Hulked 6.1709 at Port Mahon.

CHARENTE. 330 tons. Built by Antoine Tassy.
  Dimensions & tons: 112ft 0in x 26ft 6in x 11ft 2in (36.38 x 8.61 x 3.63m). 430 tons. Draught 15½ft (5.04m). Men: 80 in war, 60 peace; from 1707, 110 in war, 60 peace.
  Guns: 16 in war: 4 x 6pdrs, 12 x 4pdrs. 12 from 1704: 12 x 6pdrs. 24 from 1706: 6 x 8pdrs, 18 x 6pdrs. 28 from 1707: 10 x 8pdrs, 18 x 6pdrs. 24 from 1708: 8 x 8pdrs, 16 x 6pdrs. 32 from 1716: 12 x 8pdrs, 20 x 6pdrs.
Charente Bayonne.
  K: 7.1701. L: 6.2.1703. C: 1703. Struck late 1719 at Rochefort.

Ex-DUTCH PRIZES (1702). Three 350-ton Dutch *flûtes* were captured in 1702–3 and taken into the French Navy. A vessel possibly named *Jacobsput* was taken in April, the *Zuzter Maria* was captured in May, and the *Juffrouw Catharina* was taken in November. The French renamed them *Puits de Jacob*, *Soeur Marie*, and *Demoiselle Catherine* respectively.
Puits de Jacob Amsterdam.
  Dimensions & tons: 113ft 0in x 21ft 0in x 11ft 0in (36.71 x 6.82 x 3.57m). 350 tons. Draught 13ft (4.22m). Men: 45 in war, 40 peace +4 officers.
  Guns: 12 in war (6 peace): 12 x 6pdrs. 4 from 1707: 4 x 6pdrs
  Built 1694–95. Hulk at Brest 1717, condemned 6.1717, BU 1718
Soeur Marie Flushing.
  Dimensions & tons: 105ft 0in x 22ft 0in x 11ft 0in (34.11 x 7.15 x 3.57m). 350 tons. Draught 12½ft (4.06m). Men: 40 in war, 35 peace.
  Guns: 6 in war (4 peace): 6 x 6pdrs
  Was listed as very old in 1709 and was struck in the same year at Brest.
Demoiselle Catherine Amsterdam.
  Dimensions & tons: 93ft 0in x 21ft 0in x 11ft 0in (30.21 x 6.82 x 3.57m). 350 tons (300 in 1709–16). Draught 12½ft (4.06m). Men: 40 in war, 35 peace +2 officers
  Guns: 26 in war: 6 x 8pdrs, 16 x 4pdrs, 4 x 2pdrs. 10 from 1708: 4 x 6pdrs, 6 x 4pdrs
  Built 1696–1697. Also called *Dame Catherine*, name shortened to *Catherine* 1706. Lent as a privateer in 1711–12 to CV Duguay-Trouin, as part of a squadron of thirteen vessels; took part in the Capture of Rio de Janeiro 9.1711. Struck late 1716 at Brest.

Ex-ENGLISH PRIZE (1702). In 1702 the French captured the English *Anne*, a ship that had been purchased by the Royal Navy earlier that year for use as a fireship, and renamed her *Sainte Anne*. The English recaptured her in September 1702. No other information is available.

Ex-DUTCH PRIZES (1703–1704). Three more Dutch *flûtes* were captured and added to the French Navy in 1703 and 1704. Two Dutch whaling ships, the 400-ton *Juffrouw Christina* and the 280-ton *Rusland*, were captured in September 1703 and the 400-ton *Prins Alexander* was taken in 1704. The French rendered their names as *Demoiselle Christine*, *Rusland*, and *Prince Alexandre*.
Demoiselle Christine Amsterdam.
  Dimensions & tons: 98ft 0in x 24ft 0in x 10ft 0in (31.83 x 7.80 x 3.25m). 400 tons. Draught 13ft (4.22m). Men: 45 in war; in 1710, 150 in war, 45 peace
  Guns: 38 in war: 12 x 8pdrs, 20 x 4pdrs, 6 x 2pdrs. 18 from 1706: 8 x 8pdrs, 10 x 6pdrs. 10 from 1709: 10 x 4pdrs
  Built 1696 or 1700. Name shortened to *Christine* 1706. Struck 12.1712 at Port Louis and hulked at Lorient. Sold 1716.
Rusland Holland.
  Dimensions & tons: 88ft 0in x 22ft 0in x 9ft 0in (28.59 x 7.15 x 2.92m). 280 tons. Draught 12ft (3.90m). Men: 45 in war, 45 peace
  Guns: 6 in war: 4 x 4pdrs, 2 x 2pdrs. 6 from 1706: 6 x 4pdrs. 8 from 1708: 8 x 4pdrs
  Built 1692. Service craft at Rochefort 1706, restored to service as a *flûte* 1708, last mentioned 1712 at Rochefort.
Prince Alexandre Holland.
  Dimensions & tons: 109ft 0in x 23ft 0in x 11ft 0in (35.41 x 7.47 x 3.57m). 400 tons. Draught 13ft (4.22m). Men: 50 in war, 40 peace
  Guns: 12 in war (6 peace): 8 x 6pdrs, 4 x 4pdrs
  Listed as very old in 1712 and struck c.1713 at Brest.

SPHÈRE. 500 tons. Construction ordered on 30 July 1704, named on 24 September 1704. Built by Étienne Hubac.
  Dimensions & tons: 116ft 0in x 28ft 0in x 14ft 0in (37.68 x 9.10 x 4.55m). 500 tons. Draught 14ft (4.55m). Men: 220 in war, 60 peace; in 1707: 180 in war, 100 peace
  Guns: 40 in war (16 peace): LD 20 x 12pdrs, UD 20 x 6pdrs. 38 from 1708: LD 18 x 12pdrs, UD 20 x 6pdrs. 36 from 1710: LD 14 x 12pdrs, UD 18 x 6pdrs, QD 4 x 4pdrs
Sphère Brest Dyd.
  K: 8/9.1704. L: 26.1.1705. C: 1705. Lent as a privateer in 1705–6 to CV Henri-Louis, Marquis de Chavagnac, and CV Pierre Le Moyne d'Iberville, as part of a squadron of ten vessels, for operations in the West Indies. Lent as a privateer in 1707–9 to the *Compagnie de l'Asiento* 1707–9. Lent as a privateer in 1711–12 for the transport of alcohols in Brittany. Sold in 1714 to Spain.

Ex-DUTCH PRIZES (1705–1706). The Dutch 300-ton *flûte Hollande* was captured by French privateers and was then purchased by the French Navy in August 1705 and renamed *Cygne Blanc*. The 350-ton *Sommelsdijk* was taken in 1706, being listed by the French as *Sommeldick*, and a 530-ton Dutch ship was captured in 1706 or early 1707 and renamed *Saint Antoine* by the French.
Cygne Blanc Holland.
  Dimensions & tons: 84ft 0in x 23ft 0in x 8ft 6in (27.29 x 7.47 x 2.76m). 300 tons (234 in 1710–12). Draught 12½ft (4.06m). Men: 80 in war, 40 peace
  Guns: 8 in war (4 peace): 8 x 4pdrs. 10 from 1707: 4 x 6pdrs, 6 x 4pdrs. 8 from 1708: 8 x 4pdrs
  Built 1690. Renamed *Cygne* 1706. Struck c.1713 at Rochefort.
Sommeldick Holland.

Dimensions & tons: 92ft 0in x 23ft 0in x 11ft 0in (29.89 x 7.47 x 3.57m). 350 tons. Draught 13½ft (4.39m). Men: 45 in war, 40 peace

Guns: 18 in war (6 peace): 18 x 4pdrs

Struck c.1713 at Brest.

Saint Antoine Holland.

Dimensions & tons: 110ft 0in x 28ft 0in x 11ft 0in (35.73 x 9.10 x 3.57m). 530 tons. Draught 15ft (4.87m). Men: 60 in war, 60 peace

Guns: 20 in war (10 peace): 20 x 6pdrs

Probably submerged at Toulon 7.1707 to avoid mortar fire and refloated 11.1707. Ordered sold 14.8.1709 at Toulon.

Ex-ENGLISH PRIZES (1706). Two English vessels were captured in 1706, the 250-ton *Hampton* late in the year and a similar vessel probably named *Watching Lion* taken in December and called *Lion Veillant* by the French.

Hampton England.

Dimensions & tons: 96ft 0in x 25ft 0in x 11ft 6in (31.18 x 8.12 x 3.74m). 250 tons (350 in 1707). Draught 13½ft (4.39m). Men: 45 in war, 40 peace

Guns: 18 in war (6 peace): 14 x 4pdrs, 4 x 2pdrs. 12 from 1709: 4 x 6pdrs, 8 x 4pdrs

Struck c.1713 at Brest.

Lion Veillant. Probably 250 tons and 10 guns as captured. Repaired 2.1707 at Dunkirk, sold there 9.1707. No other data available.

ATLAS. 650 tons. Built by Pierre Masson. She was named on 24 January 1706.

Dimensions & tons: 125ft 0in x 34ft 0in x 13ft 3in (40.60 x 11.04 x 4.30m). 650 tons. Draught 17½ft (5.68m). Men: 250 in war, 200 peace

Guns: 50 in war (24 peace): LD 22 x 12pdrs, UD 24 x 8pdrs, QD 4 x 4pdrs. 48 from 1709: LD 22 x 12pdrs, UD 22 x 8pdrs, QD 4 x 4pdrs

Atlas Rochefort Dyd.

K: 2.1706. L: Autumn 1707. C: 1.1708. Grounded 7.1708 in the river at Buenos Aires, refloated eight days later. Wrecked 12.1708 in the Rio de la Plata while leaving Buenos Aires. Struck 6.1709 at Rochefort.

Ex-DUTCH PRIZE (1707). The 350-ton Dutch *Ville d'Arkangel* was captured by a French privateer and purchased in February 1707 by the Navy as *Archangel*.

Dimensions & tons: 102ft 0in x 23ft 0in x 11ft 0in (33.13 x 7.47 x 3.57m). 350 tons. Draught 12ft (3.90m). Men: 45 in war, 20 peace

Guns: 14 in war (4 peace): 14 x 4pdrs

Archangel Holland.

Built before 1695. Hulked late 1707 at Dunkirk, struck there 1713.

Ex-ENGLISH PRIZES (1707). A 470-ton English merchant vessel possibly named *Merchant* was captured in early 1707 and the 300-ton English East Indiaman *Elizabeth* was captured in March. The French named them *Marchand* and *Élisabeth*.

Marchand Holland or England.

Dimensions & tons: 105ft 0in x 23ft 6in x 9ft 6in (34.11 x 7.63 x 3.09m). 470 tons. Draught 11ft (3.57m). Men: 20 in war, 20 peace

Guns: 4 in war (4 peace): 4 x 3pdrs

Built in Holland according to lists of 1707–8 and in England according to lists of 1709–10. Considered old in 1708. Struck c.1713 at Rochefort.

Élisabeth England.

Dimensions & tons: 97ft 0in x 25ft 0in x 9ft 0in (31.50 x 8.12 x 2.92m). 300 tons. Draught 13ft (4.22m). Men: 45 in war, 45 peace

Guns: 12 in war (6 peace): 4 x 6pdrs, 8 x 4pdrs. 10 from 1709: 10 x 6pdrs

Built 1691. Struck c.1713 at Rochefort.

(D) Vessels acquired from 1 September 1715

As of 1 June 1716, only three *flûtes* remained on the French fleet list: *Charente*, which 'steered badly', *Puits de Jacob*, in acceptable condition, and *(Demoiselle) Catherine*, called 'very bad'. The last two were off the list by June 1717 and *Charente* was last listed in January 1719. The French support fleet thus had to be rebuilt from scratch in the years following 1715.

PORTEFAIX Class. 650 tons. Designed and built by François Coulomb (who died in 1717). Both ordered on 18 January 1716 to be built from the timbers of the ships of the line *Admirable*, *Magnifique*, and *Orgueilleux* and named 29 June 1716. *Portefaix* was called a 'bâtiment de charge à poupe plate'.

Dimensions & tons: 125ft 0in, 110ft 0in x 29ft 0in x 14ft 0in (40.60, 35.73 x 9.42 x 4.55m). 650/1,000 tons (600 in 1729–41). Draught 15½ft (5.04m). Men: 140 in war, 80 peace +5 officers

Guns: 44 in war (26 peace): LD 22 x 12pdrs, UD 22 x 6pdrs. 42 from 1723: LD 22 x 8pdrs, UD 20 x 6pdrs. 44 in *Portefaix* from 1729: LD 22 x 8pdrs, UD 22 x 6pdrs. 40 in *Dromadaire* from 1729: LD 20 x 12pdrs, UD 20 x 8pdrs. 44 in *Dromadaire* from 1734: LD 22 x 8pdrs, UD 22 x 6pdrs

Portefaix Toulon Dyd.

K: 25.8.1716. L: 18.6.1717. C: 9.1718. Hulk at Rochefort 1736, guard hulk from 1738, struck 1741 as a *flûte*, hulk at Rochefort until BU 1770.

Dromadaire Toulon Dyd.

K: 25.8.1716. L: 28.7.1717. C: 4.1719. Hulk at Rochefort 1736, guard hulk from 1738, struck 1739 or 1740 as a *flûte*, BU 1740 at Rochefort.

CHAMEAU Class. 600 tons. Designed by Étienne Hubac who built *Chameau*, *Éléphant* built by Laurent Hélie to Hubac's plans.

Dimensions & tons: 125ft 0in x 29ft 0in x 14ft 0in (40.60 x 9.42 x 4.55m). 600/1,000 tons (650 in 1723). Draught 15ft (4.87m). Men: 100 in peace +5 officers.

Guns: 48 in war (30 peace): LD 20 x 8pdrs, UD 22 x 6pdrs, QD 6 x 4pdrs. 20 from 1723: LD 20 x 8pdrs, UD 20 x 6pdrs. 46 in *Éléphant* from 1729: LD 20 x 8pdrs, UD 22 x 6pdrs, QD 4 x 4pdrs

Chameau Brest Dyd.

K: 5.1717. L: 1718. C: 1718. Wrecked 27.8.1725 and lost with all hands on Cape Breton near Louisbourg.

Éléphant Brest Dyd.

K: 5.1717. L: 5.1718. C: 8.1718. Wrecked 1.9.1729 at Cape Brulé in the St Lawrence River near Quebec while shifting anchorage, entire crew saved.

SEINE Class. 650 tons. Ordered 4 July 1718, named 6 September 1718. Built by René Levasseur.

Dimensions & tons: 122ft 0in x 32ft 0in x 15ft 6in (39.63 x 10.39 x 5.04m). 650/1,100 tons (700 in 1723–29). Draught 16ft (5.20m). Men: 150 in war, 90 peace; in 1734: 250 in war, 90 peace

Guns: 50 in war (30 peace): LD 22 x 12pdrs; UD 24 x 8pdrs; QD 4 x 4pdrs. 46 guns in 1754.

Seine Toulon Dyd.
K: 10.1718 or 22.5.1719. L: 22.5.1720. C: 8.1720. Under repair in 1754, cut down and hulked 1757–58 at Rochefort. BU 1774.

Loire Toulon Dyd.
K: 10.1718 or 22.5.1719. L: 11.7.1720. C: 1720. In good condition in 1754. Captured 7.1758 by HM Ships *Saint Albans* (60) and *Favourite* (16) in the Mediterranean.

SARCELLE. 300 tons. Designed and built by Laurent Hélie. Described in 1723 as good for transporting masts and in 1739 as being used to transport timbers.

Dimensions & tons: 99ft 6in x 22ft 6in x 11ft 0in (32.32 x 7.31 x 3.57m). 300/420 tons (212 from 1739). Draught 11ft (3.57m). Men: 45 in war, 35 peace +2/4 officers.

Guns: 10 in war (4 peace): 6 x 6pdrs; 4 x 4pdrs

Sarcelle Brest Dyd.
K: 5.1719. L: 6.1720. C: 8.1720. Struck 1752 or 1753 at Brest. BU 1757.

PURCHASED VESSELS (1720–1724). Between 1715 and 1744 all but three of the *flûtes* acquired by the Navy were purpose-built, mostly in Navy dockyards. Few details are available on the three purchased vessels, all of which were acquired in 1720 and 1724.

Demoiselle Suzanne. Purchased 1720, ex-Dutch *Juffrouw Suzanna*. 42 men. Decommissioned 1723 at Dunkirk or at Calais after many voyages to Scandinavia.

Serrurier. Purchased 1720, ex-Dutch *Slotenmaker*. Decommissioned 1723 at Dunkirk or at Calais after many voyages to Scandinavia.

Cygne. Purchased 1.1724 at Le Havre from Sr. Verton, ex-*Schulsembourg* 2.1724. Decommissioned and last mentioned at Brest 8.1724.

PROFOND Class. 600 tons. Designed by Étienne Hubac who built *Profond*, *Baleine* built by Jacques Poirier to Hubac's plans.

Dimensions & tons: 124ft 0in x 32ft 6in x 13ft 6in (40.28 x 10.56 x 4.39m). 600/1,100 tons. Draught 16ft 8in (5.41m). Men: 140 in war, 100 peace.

Guns (*Profond*): 40 in war (30 peace): LD 20 x 12pdrs; UD 20 x 8pdrs. (*Baleine*): 10 in war (4 peace): 6 x 6pdrs, 4 x 4pdrs. 42 from 1734: LD 20 x 12pdrs, UD 22 x 8pdrs. 46 from 1739: LD 20 x 12pdrs, UD 22 x 8pdrs, QD 4 x 4pdrs

Profond Brest Dyd.
K: 5.1724. L: 12.1724. C: 1725 (first commissioned 6.1726). Rebuilt 1738 to 5.1739 at Rochefort. Headquarters hulk at Rochefort 1744, struck from the list of *flûtes* c.1748, replaced 1756 and BU 1757.

Baleine Le Havre.
K: 8.1724. L: 9.11.1725. C: 5.1726. Used in 1729 and 1731 to supply timber to Rochefort. Rebuilt 1735 to 9.1735 at Rochefort. Condemned 1744 at Rochefort and BU.

GIRONDE. 500 tons. Designed and built by Jacques Poirier.

Dimensions & tons: 118ft 0in x 31ft 6in x 11ft 10in (38.33 x 10.23 x 3.84m). 500/1,000 tons. Draught 15½ft (5.04m). Men: 130 in war, 100 peace

Guns: 30: LD 6 x 12pdrs, UD 20 x 8pdrs, 4 x 4pdrs. 28 in war (28 peace) from 1738: LD 4 x 12pdrs, UD 20 x 8pdrs, QD 4 x 4pdrs

Gironde Le Havre.
K: 5.1728. L: 21.8.1728. C: 11.1728. Hauled out 9.1737 for reconstruction at Rochefort (see below).

SOMME. 500 tons. 1729: Designed and built by Jacques Poirier.

Dimensions & tons: 120ft 0in x 32ft 5in x 13ft 3in (38.98 x 10.53 x 4.30m). 500/1,000 tons. Draught 15½ft (5.04m). Men: 130 in war, 100 peace

Guns: 20 in war (2 peace): 20 x 6pdrs. 28 from 1734: LD 6 x 12pdrs, UD 22 x 8pdrs. 30 from 1739: LD 6 x 12pdrs, UD 20 x 8pdrs, QD 4 x 4pdrs

Somme Le Havre.
K: 1729. L: 1729. C: 2.1730. Rebuilt 1736 at Rochefort. Placed in the old dock (*forme*) 1742 for reconstruction by Pierre Morineau but condemned 1745 and BU in the dock.

CHARENTE. 500 tons. Designed and built by Jacques Poirier. Rebuilt at Rochefort in 1738 by Blaise Geslain. Similar to *Somme*.

Dimensions & tons: 119ft 0in x 32ft 3in x 12ft 3in (38.66, 35.73 x 10.48 x 3.98m). 500 tons (530 in 1741–46). Draught 15½ft (5.04m). Men: 130 in war, 100 peace.

Guns: 28 in war (28 peace): LD 6 x 12pdrs, UD 22 x 8pdrs. 28 from 1743: LD 4 x 12pdrs, UD 20 x 8pdrs, QD 4 x 4pdrs. 32 from 1746: LD 4 x 12pdrs; UD 28 x 8pdrs

Charente Le Havre.
K: 4.1731. L: 19.8.1731. C: 1.1732. Hulk at Rochefort 1743, port guardship 1746. Struck 1747 from the list of *flûtes*. Last mentioned 6.1748 as hulk at Rochefort.

OROX. 480 tons. Designed and built by Blaise Geslain.

Dimensions & tons: 124ft 0in, 110ft 0in x 33ft 0in x 13ft 0in (40.28 x 10.72 x 4.22m). 480/1,046 tons (600 in 1741–43). Draught 14¼ft (4.63m). Men: 200 in war, 100 peace; in 1741: 140 in war, 100 peace

Guns: 32 in war (22 peace): LD 8 x 12pdrs, UD 24 x 8pdrs. 28 from 1739: LD 4 x 12pdrs, UD 24 x 8pdrs

Orox Le Havre.
K: 2.1733. L: 28.9.1734. C: 4.1735. In 1743 needed a complete refit, condemned 1745 at Rochefort and BU.

GIRONDE. 560 tons. Poirier's *Gironde* of 1728 rebuilt in 1737–38 by Blaise Geslain.

Dimensions & tons: 120ft 0in x 32ft 0in x 12ft 0in (38.98 x 10.39 x 3.90m). 560/1,000 tons. Draught 15½ft (5.04m). Men: 140 in war, 100 peace; in 1746: 180 in war, 110 peace.

Guns: 28 in war (28 peace): LD 4 x 12pdrs, UD 20 x 8pdrs, QD 4 x 4pdrs. 30 from 1741: LD 4 x 12pdrs, UD 22 x 8pdrs, QD 4 x 4pdrs. 28 from 1743: LD 4 x 12pdrs, UD 20 x 8pdrs, QD 4 x 4pdrs. 32 from 1746: LD 4 x 12pdrs; UD 24 x 8pdrs; QD 4 x 4pdrs

Gironde Le Havre.
K: 9.1737. L: 1.1738. C: 3.1738. Rebuilt 1742–43 at Rochefort. Wrecked 1748 on Le Four off Le Croisic. Her hulk was carried by the currents to Belle-Île where it was BU.

ATLAS. 630 tons. Designed and built by one of both of the Geoffroy brothers (Jean, the elder, and Mathurin-Louis, the younger). She was named 1 December 1737.

Dimensions & tons: 123ft 6in x 32ft 6in x 14ft 6in (40.12 x 10.56 x 4.71m). 630/1,000 tons. Draught 14ft 8in (4.76m). Men: 150 in war, 100 peace

Guns: 50 in war (36 peace): LD 22 x 12pdrs, UD 24 x 8pdrs, QD 4 x 4pdrs

Atlas Brest Dyd.
  K: 8.1736. L: 17.10.1738. C: 2.1739. Wrecked 12.1739 at Ushant, 408 dead.

ÉLÉPHANT. 600 tons. In 1739 Blaise Geslain was sent to Holland under the false name of Dubois ostensibly to build a *flûte* at Saardam but primarily to observe the construction methods used by the Dutch, the procedures they used to conserve timber, and other aspects of their naval architecture. This was one of many foreign trips made by French shipwrights to obtain information on foreign shipbuilding practices, including by Geslain to England in 1729 and by Blaise Ollivier in 1737, though the construction of a ship for the French Navy during such a voyage was exceptional.

  Dimensions & tons: 122ft 0in x 29ft 10in x 11ft 6in (39.63 x 9.69 x 3.74m). 600/950 tons. Draught 14½ft (4.71m). Men: 130 in war, 80 peace

  Guns: 16 in war (16 peace): 16 x 8pdrs

Éléphant Saardam (Holland).
  K: 5.1739. L: 1740. C: 1741. Captured 3.3.1745 by HM Ships *Chester* (50) and *Sunderland* (60) in the Atlantic.

CANADA. 500 tons. Designed and built by René-Nicolas Levasseur.
  Dimensions & tons: 117ft 6in, 106ft 10in x 32ft 0in x 14ft 0in (38.17, 34.70 x 10.39 x 4.55m). 500/950 tons. Draught 14½ft (4.71m). Men: 180 in war, 100 peace.

  Guns: 24 in war (23 peace): LD 4 x 12pdrs; UD 24 x 8pdrs

Canada Quebec.
  K: 9.1739. L: 4.6.1742. C: 6.1742. Needed a considerable refit in 1746, condemned 1.1747 at Rochefort and either BU then or used as a powder hulk to 1786.

CHAMEAU. 560 tons. Ordered in March 1743. Designed and built by Blaise Ollivier with new hull forms based on his study voyage in 1737 to Britain and Holland.
  Dimensions & tons: 141ft 0in, 126ft 0in x 30ft 2in x 12ft 9in (45.80 x 9.80 x 4.14m). 560/1,020 tons. Draught 12½ft (4.06m). Men: 160 in war, 100 peace +7 officers.

Redrawn by László Veres after Plate LIII of Chapman's *Architectura Navalis Mercatoria*, this plan depicts Blaise Ollivier's *Chameau* of 1744. Chapman notes 'The fly-boat Le Chameau is a store-ship belonging to the French crown and sails particularly well.' By this date, the design of the French *flûte* bore little resemblance to its Dutch origins, being far more 'naval' in its appearance. Presumably, in wartime extra gunports were cut to mount the official armament of 24 guns on the lower deck.

Guns: 36 in war (30 peace): LD 24 x 8pdrs; UD 12 x 6pdrs

Chameau Brest Dyd.
  K: 1743. L: 14.8.1744. C: 10.1744. Wrecked 1747 on the Spanish coast while returning from Louisiana.

Ex-BRITISH PRIZES (1744–1745). A British merchant ship named *Ruby* (French *Rubis*) of unknown tonnage but with a large crew was captured on 16 April 1744; she appears to have been in bad condition and was in harbour service by 1746. On 19 July 1745 the frigate *Renommée* captured the British *Prince of Orange* (French *Prince d'Orange*) on the Grand Banks after an action that lasted three hours, she was built in 1744 and was reported as a 495-ton merchant ship with 150 men and pierced for 44 guns, of which 28 were mounted. The French recorded her as a 650-ton ship (900 tons displacement). The 300-ton British merchant ship *Parham* was captured in June 1745, the 250-ton mercantile *Anna Sophia* was captured in July, and the 400-ton privateer frigate *Bristol* was captured on 29 October 1745.

Rubis. Captured 16.4.1744, ex-British merchant ship *Ruby*. 280 men +?8 officers, ?20 guns. Rated *bâtiment interrompu* in 1746, used as stores hulk at Brest 1747, condemned 1748 and BU at Brest.

Prince d'Orange Britain or Boston.
  Dimensions & tons: 110ft 0in x 29ft 0in x 15ft 0in (35.73 x 9.42 x 4.87m), also recorded as 118ft 0in x 30ft 0in x 15ft 0in (38.33 x 9.75 x 4.87m). 650/900 tons. Draught 16ft (5.20m). Men: 80 in war, 40 peace; later 120 men +4 officers.

  Guns: 26 in war (10 peace): 18 x 6pdrs; 8 x 3pdrs. 20 from 1747: 12 x 5pdrs; 8 x 2pdrs. Pierced for 44 guns with only the upper battery armed.

  Used in the 1746 expedition to Nova Scotia under the Duc d'Anville. Repaired 8–9.1747 at Lorient and used for the transport of masts and timbers. Struck 9.1748 at Brest.

Parham Britain.
  Dimensions & tons: 95ft 0in x 23ft 0in x 12ft 0in (30.86 x 7.47 x 3.90m) or 100ft 0in x 25ft 0in x 12ft 0in (32.48 x 8.12 x 3.90m). 300/500 tons (350 in 1766). Draught 11/13ft 6in (3.57/4.39m). Men: 120 +3 officers.

  Guns: 18 x 6pdrs; 20 guns in 1754; 16 x 6pdrs from 1762; 12 x 4pdrs from 1.1771. Pierced for 20 guns.

  Rebuilt 12.1745 to 7.1746 at Lorient, 1761 to 10.1762 at Rochefort, and 1769 to 9.1769 at Rochefort. Chartered commercially 1770 at Rochefort, sold there 1772.

Anna Sophia. Britain.
  Dimensions & tons: 98ft 0in x 25ft 0in x 12ft 0in (31.83 x 8.12 x 3.90m). 250/500 tons (350 in 1749/55). Draught 11/13ft (3.57/4.22m). Men: 50/120, +2/3 officers

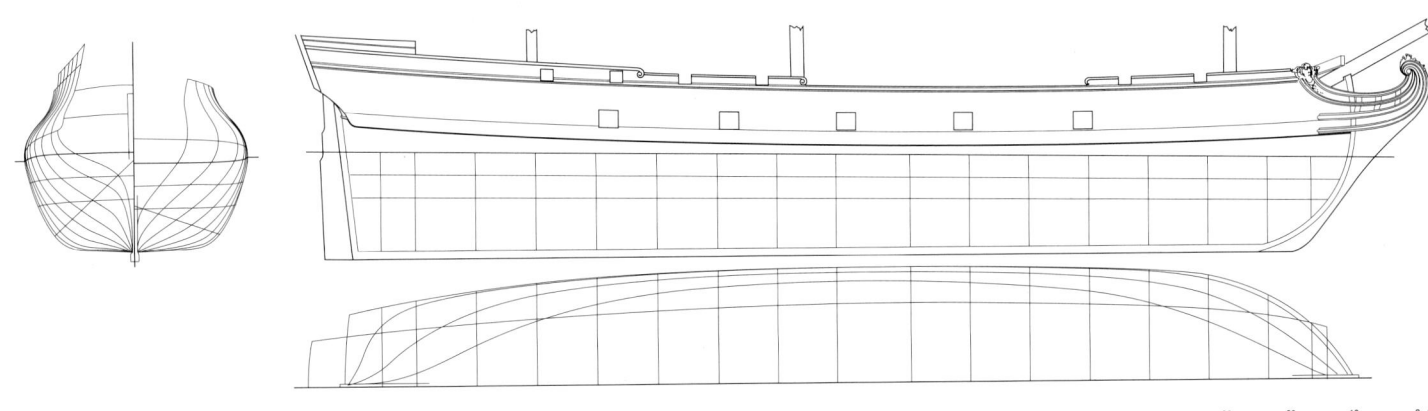

Guns: 18 x 6pdrs; 24 guns including 20 x 6pdrs in 1748, 20 guns in 1754. Pierced for 20 guns

Decomm. 6.1755 at Rochefort, struck 1757.

Bristol Bristol.

Dimensions & tons: 110ft 0in, 100ft 0in x 30ft 0in x 13ft 0in (35.73, 32.48 x 9.75 x 4.22m). 400/750 tons. Draught 16ft (5.20m).

Men: 72/169, +6/10 officers (*Compagnie des Indes* manning).

Guns: 30 (24 in battery, 6 on QD/Fc)

Launched at Bristol *c.*10.1744. Sold 11.1747 at Brest to the *Compagnie des Indes*. Grounded 4.1759 at Pondicherry, captured there 1.1761 by the British.

PIE Class. 320 tons. Designed and built by Pierre Chaillé, Jnr. Classed as *gabarres* from 1746 to 1752, then as *flûtes*.

Dimensions & tons: 104ft 0in x 26ft 4in x 10ft 3in (33.78 x 8.55 x 3.33m). 320/584 tons. Draught 12ft (3.90m). Men: 30/60, +2 officers.

Guns: 16 x 6pdrs, 18 x 6pdrs in 1748 (8 in peace), 20 guns in 1754–58, 10 x 4pdrs from 3.1759.

Pie Le Havre.

K: 4.1746. L: 2.8.1746. C: 8.1748. Rebuilt 1757–58 at Rochefort. Grounded and burned 17.5.1760 at Cap Rouge near Quebec City.

Carpe Le Havre.

K: 4.1746. L: 31.8.1746. C: 11.1746. Wrecked 2.1750.

CHARIOT ROYAL. 650 tons. Built by Pierre Chaillé, Jnr to plans by Jacques-Luc Coulomb.

Dimensions & tons: 140ft 0in x 30ft 0in x 13ft 6in (45.48 x 9.75 x 4.39m). 650/1,000 tons. Draught 14/15½ft (4.55/5.04m). Men: 90/140 men

Guns: 24 x 12pdrs, 6 to 12 x 6pdrs; 24 guns in 1754; 26 guns in 1756.

Chariot Royal Le Havre.

K: 4.1748. L: 19.9.1749. C: 1750. Originally named *Chariot Volant*, renamed *Chariot Royal* 9.1749 to commemorate the presence of Louis XV at her launch. Captured 12.6.1756 with *Arc en Ciel* by HMS *Torbay* (74) near Louisbourg while bringing supplies to Île Royale.

RHINOCEROS. 500 tons. Built by Antoine Groignard. A report to the King, probably in January 1751, noted that there were at Rochefort few ships suitable for supplying the colonies and proposed that a *flûte* of 500 tons be substituted for the *gabarre Abeille* (below) whose construction had been ordered. Four names including *Garonne* were proposed, of which *Rhinoceros* was approved. (The other two were *Magasin volant* and *Messager*.) Rochefort proceeded to build a series of *flûtes* to support the colonies. *Rhinoceros* was pierced for 12 guns on the upper deck.

Dimensions & tons: 125ft 0in x 25ft 0in x 12ft 6in (40.60 x 8.12 x 4.06m). 500 tons. Men: 66/83

Guns: 12 x 6pdrs; 20 guns in 1754; 16 guns in 1756.

Rhinoceros Rochefort Dyd.

K: 1.1751. L: 1751. C: 3.1752. Captured 23.9.1758 by HMS *Isis* (50) in the North Atlantic after dropping out of convoy due to leaks, sank four hours later.

CHÈVRE. 330 tons. Built by Antoine Groignard.

Dimensions & tons: 107ft 0in x 24ft 0in x 12ft 0in (34.76 x 7.80 x 3.90m). 300 tons. Men: 40/70

Guns: 10 to 24, including 10 to 14 x 4pdrs. 22 guns in 1758

Chèvre Rochefort Dyd.

K: 1.1751. L: 6.1751. C: 8.1751. Left Île d'Aix 9.3.1758 in the division of CV Charry des Gouttes to resupply Louisbourg, arrived by 3.5.1758. Scuttled 28 June 1758 to block the channel at Louisbourg

BICHE. A vessel of unknown origin scuttled 28 June 1758 to block the channel at Louisbourg. Upon arrival in Canada in April or May 1758 she was listed with 16 guns and 150 men as was the *flûte Chèvre*, above, although *Chèvre* was listed elsewhere with 22 guns.

CAMÉLÉON Class. 600 to 700 tons. Built by Antoine Groignard.

Dimensions & tons: 130ft 0in, 120ft 8in x 30ft 0in x 15ft 0in (42.23, 39.20 x 9.75 x 4.87m). 600–700/1,260 tons. Draught 14/16ft (4.55/5.20m). Men: 140/160, +5 officers.

Guns: 2 x 12pdrs, 16 x 8pdrs, 4 x 4pdrs; 20 guns in 1754.

Caméléon Rochefort Dyd.

K: 1751. L: 1752. C: 5.1753. Arrived in Louisiana 11.1753. Wrecked 10.9.1754 in the St Lawrence River at Sault de la Chaudière, Quebec.

Outarde Rochefort Dyd.

K: 3.1754. L: 13.3.1755. C: 5.1755. Grounded 12.1758 near Plougastel but refloated. Sold 11.1760 at Pasajes (northern Spain) to the *Compagnie des Indes* and renamed *Beaumont* 17.11.1760. Departed Pasajes 8.6.1761 and captured by the British.

MESSAGER. 400 tons.

Dimensions & tons: 120ft 0in x 25ft 0in x 12ft 6in (38.98 x 8.12 x 4.06m). 500 tons. Draught 13ft 3in/14ft 2in. Men: 70

Guns: 6 x 4pdrs; 20 guns in 1754; also listed with 10 and 12 guns.

Messager Rochefort Dyd.

K: 1752. L: 1753. C: 4.1754. Rammed by *Raisonnable* (64) 13.3.1758, probably causing her loss. The ships had left Rochefort 9.3.1758 in the division of CV Charry des Gouttes to resupply Louisbourg. *Raisonnable* had to put back to Lorient for two months of repairs.

CERF. 300 tons.

Dimensions & tons: dimensions unknown. 300 tons. Men: 90, +4 officers.

Guns: 12 or 14.

Cerf Rochefort Dyd.

K: 1755. L: 6.1756. C: 8.1756. Condemned 1766 and BU at Brest.

FORTUNE. 685 tons. Built by François-Guillaume Clairain-Deslauriers. Listed 1770–71 by Rochefort as snow-rigged. Sometimes confused with *Petite Fortune*, which was the snow-rigged corvette *Fortune* renamed in 1667 and sometimes called a *flûte*.

Dimensions & tons: 140ft 0in x 31ft 0in x 13ft 6in (45.48 x 10.07 x 4.39m). 685/1,050 tons. Draught 13¼/14ft (4.30/4.55m). Men: 145/150, +1/8 officers

Guns: 8 x 12pdrs, 16 x 6pdrs in 1758–59; 24 x 8pdrs, 16 x 4pdrs in 1768–70; 26 x 6pdrs in 1.1771 after refit.

Fortune Rochefort Dyd.

K: 1755. L: 2.2.1757. C: 2.1758. Hauled out 1770 for refitting, relaunched 20.8.1770. Participated 1–9.1772 with the *gabarre Gros Ventre* in an expedition under LV Yves-Joseph de Kerguelen-Trémarec to find a postulated southern continent in the Indian Ocean, resulting in the French discovery of the west coast of Australia. Wrecked 6.1774 at Fort Dauphin, Madagascar.

ADOUR Class. 680 tons. Ordered 7.9.1756 from Mathurin Louis Geoffroy and Ducros; Ducros transferred his contract to the master

STORESHIPS AND CARGO SHIPS

shipwright Étienne Miressou. Both ships were sold to the *Compagnie des Indes* before completion. They were ship-rigged.
  Dimensions & tons: 140ft 0in x 32ft 0in x 10ft 0in (45.48 x 10.39 x 3.25m). 680 tons. Men: 100/150
  Guns: 20 x 8pdrs, 8 x 4pdrs.

Adour (i) Bayonne.
  K: 12.1757. L: 10.4.1759. C: 1759. Sold 1759 to the *Compagnie des Indes*. Repurchased 4.1770 by the Navy while in the Indian Ocean. Condemned 1777 at Île de France and struck.

Utile Bayonne.
  K: 1.1758. L: 24.5.1759. C: 4.1760. Sold 1759 to the *Compagnie des Indes*. Wrecked 31.7.1761 on Île Tromelin in the Indian Ocean with a cargo of 61 slaves, 8 of whom were rescued 29.11.1776 and later freed.

Adour (ii) Bayonne.
  Projected in 1760 to be built to replace the *Adour* sold in 1759 to the *Compagnie des Indes*. Project dropped c. 1763 for lack of funds.

Ex-BRITISH PRIZES (1757–1761). Three prizes captured in 1757 and 1761 were used as *flûtes* by the French Navy. The British *Lady* was captured in 1757 and put into service at Brest in September 1757, while the *Saint Guillaume* of uncertain origin was captured in 1757 and put into service at Brest in February 1758. In March 1761 the British 499-ton Indiaman *Ajax* was captured with a valuable cargo including diamonds while returning from her first voyage to the Indies.

Lady. 29/35 men +4 officers. 10 guns. Recaptured 12.1758 by the British.

Saint Guillaume. 500 tons. 65/75 men +7 officers. 22 guns. Sold 11.1761 at Ferrol to a Bordeaux shipowner and renamed *Guerrier*, captured 3.1762 by the British.

Ajax. Britain.
  Dimensions & tons: 126ft 0in, 112ft 0in x 31ft 6in x 11ft 6in (40.93, 36.38 x 10.23 x 3.74m). 500/1,100 tons. Draught 16ft (5.20m). Men: 130
  Guns: LD 18 x 8pdrs; UD 6 x 8pdrs.
  Built 1757–58. Sold 1762 at Brest to the *Compagnie des Indes*. Repurchased from them 4.1770 at Lorient. Sold 4 or 5.1774 at Lorient for mercantile use.

PURCHASED VESSELS (1758–1761). The French Navy acquired two Bordeaux merchantmen and a privateer frigate for use as *flûtes* between 1758 and 1761. The Bordeaux merchantman *Robuste* was built c.1755 and purchased in May 1758 at Rochefort. The privateer frigate *Cerf* of Sieur Raymond of Bordeaux was purchased by the Navy and renamed *Biche* in February 1759 and entered service at Brest in March. The Bordeaux merchantman *Hardi* was purchased in January 1761.

Robuste. 650–700 tons. May have been built 1755 at Bordeaux. 6 x 8pdrs + 18 x 6pdrs, also listed with 28 guns. 84 men. Captured 7.1758 by the British.

Charles Brooking's oil painting shows an English East Indiaman of the 499-ton class in a gale. The *Ajax* captured in 1761 would have looked very similar. (National Maritime Museum, London BHC1029)

Biche. Built before 1755, possibly at St Malo. 22 guns, 41/45 men +4/6 officers. Converted 8.1760 to floating battery at La Balise, Louisiana. Condemned 8.1761 and fell apart there 7.1762.

Hardi. 400–508 tons. Probably built at Bordeaux between 1758 and 7.1759. 12 guns, 79 men. Captured 3.1761 by the British after three hours of combat.

NORMANDE Class. 710 tons. Designed by Jean-Joseph Ginoux. *Normande* and *Balance* built by Joseph-Louis Ollivier and *Danube* and *Garonne* built by Famin. Called *flûtes sans entrepont* (without 'tween decks). The frames already cut for the cancelled *Ménagère* and *Gourmande* were used to build the *flûtes Bricole* and *Coulisse* of 1764.

    Dimensions & tons: 142ft x 32ft 6in (46.12 x 10.56m). 710/1,350 tons. Draught: 17ft (5.52m). Length of *Danube* and *Garonne* was 145ft (47.10m). Men: 150/184, +7/9 officers

    Guns: LD 14 x 12pdrs; UD 20 x 8pdrs. *Normande*: 18 x 8pdrs in 1774, 20 x 8pdrs from 1780.

Normande Le Havre.
    K: 1.1759. L: 15.5.1759. C: 1760. Grounded 3.1764 at Cayenne, refloated. Loaned 18.4.1774 for a private voyage to Île de France. Struck 1785 or 1786.

Balance Le Havre.
    K: 2.1759. L: 9.1760. C: 11.1761. Foundered 17.1.1768 near the Azores due to multiple leaks in the hull.

Danube Le Havre.
    K: 8.1760. L: 6.1761. C: 10.1761. Condemned 9.1769 at Rochefort, sheer hulk 1771, replaced by *Artésien* 1785 when about to sink.

Garonne Le Havre.
    K: 8.1760. L: 2.7.1761. C: 10.1761. Wrecked 12.1770 in a storm at Île de France, possibly used as hulk until 1783.

Ménagère Le Havre.
    Ordered 1.1759 from Ginoux, cancelled 7.1760.

Gourmande Le Havre.
    Ordered 1.1759 from Ginoux, cancelled 7.1760.

PURCHASED VESSELS (1762). Six merchant vessels that were nearly complete at Nantes were purchased in August 1762 (*Placelière*, later *Étoile*, was purchased on 4 August). All were renamed shortly after completion and *Étoile* took part in a famous voyage of discovery.

Levrette. Built at Nantes.
    Dimensions & tons: dimensions unknown. 250 tons. Men: 41/52, +4 officers
    Guns: 16 in 1762.
    C: 9.1762. Ex-*Volonté* 10.1762. Captured 10.1762 by the British.

Nourrice. Built at Nantes.
    Dimensions & tons: 103ft x 27ft 8in (33.46 x 8.99m). 440 tons. Men: 67/80, +4 officers, later 82/110, +5/6 officers
    Guns: 12 in 1762; 14 in 1766; 20 x 8pdrs in 1768–70; 14 x 4pdrs in 1774.
    C: 9.1762. Ex-*Gaspard* 12.1762. Repaired at Lorient 1774, struck there 1777.

Barbue. Built at Nantes.
    Dimensions & tons: 100ft x 27ft 3in (32.48 x 8.85m). 338 tons (400 in 1766 and 1772). Draught 14ft 8in/16ft 4in (4.77/5.30m). Men: 63/75, +4 officers, later 105/107, +7 officers.
    Guns: 12 in 1762; 12 x 8pdrs in 1767–70; 12 x 6pdrs in 1771.
    K: 1760. L: 1762. Purchased 4.8.1762. C: 9.1762. Decomm. 12.1762 at Brest, ex *Maréchal de Broglie* 3.1763. Grounded 9/10.12.1771 on the rocks at Penmarch, Brittany, struck 1772.

Corisante. Built at Nantes.
    Dimensions & tons: 92ft 9in x 27ft 3in (30.13 x 8.85m). 320 tons (380 in 1766, 350 in 1772). Draught 12ft 10in/13ft 4in (4.17/4.33m). Men: 60/73, +4 officers, later 84/100, +6 officers
    Guns: 12 in 1762; 12 x 6pdrs in 1768–70; 12 x 4pdrs from 1771. Pierced for 14 guns.
    K: 1761. C: 9.1762. Last mentioned 12.1762 out of service at Brest, ex-*Lion* 8.1763. Struck 1772 at Rochefort.

Étoile. Built at Nantes.
    Dimensions & tons: 104ft 0in x 27ft 8in x 13ft 1in (33.80 x 8.99 x 4.25m). 480/794 tons. Draught 13ft 10in/15ft 10in (4.49/5.14m). Men: 70/110, +4 officers (93 +11 officers in 1766–69).
    Guns: 14 in 1762; 20 x 8pdrs from 1766. (May have carried 6pdrs on the Bougainville expedition.)
    K: 1759. C: 9.1762. Ex-*Placelière* 4.1763. Accompanied Bougainville in the frigate *Boudeuse* as storeship for his circumnavigation of the world between 1766 and 1769. Prison ship for prisoners of war at Lorient 5.1779, hulked 1780, last mentioned 1789.

Salomon. Built at Nantes.
    Dimensions & tons: 79ft 0in x 26ft 0in (25.66 x 8.45m). 250 tons. Draught 11ft 2in/13ft 4in (3.63/4.33m). Men: 65/70, +4 officers.
    Guns: 10 in 1762; 12 in 1766; 6 x 4pdrs in 1768–70; 12 x 4pdrs from 1777; 16 x 4pdrs from 1780 (as a hulk)
    K: 1761. L: 1762. C: 9.1762. Gunnery school at Île d'Aix 8.1767. Chartered 7.1768 with the former corvette *Petite Fortune* to the *Compagnie de Cayenne*, headquarters ship at Rochefort 1774, in very bad condition in that port from 1777 until struck in late 1782. These Rochefort records suggest that the *Salomon* that was converted in the Indian Ocean in 9–10.1781 to the fireship *Pulvériseur* for Suffren's squadron was a different ship.

COULISSE Class. 710 tons. Designed in August 1763 and built by Jean-Joseph Ginoux. The frames cut for the cancelled *Ménagère* and *Gourmande* of 1759 were used to build them.

    Dimensions & tons: 144ft 0in, 129ft 0in x 32ft 0in x 14ft 0in (46.78, 41.90 x 10.39 x 4.55m). 700/1,200 tons. Draught 14/15ft (4.55/4.87m). Men: 145/160, +7 officers.
    Guns: LD 14 x 12pdrs; UD 22 x 8pdrs. *Bricole*: 12 x 12pdrs, 20 x 8pdrs in 1771; 20 x 8pdrs from 1773.

Coulisse Le Havre.
    K: 9.1763. L: 18.4.1764. C: 6.1764. Began refit at Rochefort 17.4.1771 but hulked instead, last mentioned 5.1792 as hulk at Rochefort.

Bricole Le Havre.
    K: 9.1763. L: 19.4.1764. C: 6.1764. Rebuilt at Rochefort 1770 to 4.1771. Loaned 31.10.1774 for a private voyage to the Indies. Sold 9.1779 to the South Carolina State Navy which hoped to make her into a 44-gun frigate. Fitted 1.1780 as a floating battery at Charleston. Scuttled there 3.1780 to block the Cooper River.

GAVE Class. 360 tons. Designed, built and purchased in Holland to carry timbers from the Pyrenees, these ships arrived at Brest with Dutch crews in June and August 1765 respectively. The young Jean François de Pérusse, Duc de Cars made several voyages as a junior officer in *Adour* in 1767–68 and wrote in his *Mémoires* that 'This *flûte* and its worthy sister ship *le Gave* were assuredly the two most detestable ships in the royal navy, which they dishonoured. Scurvy Dutch *hourques*, very long and with a flat bottom, an extremely high poop, and a prow absolutely round and very low, they had as their unique quality a capacity for large cargoes; their relatively short masts with few spars required a crew of only 15 or 20 men.'

    Dimensions & tons: 109ft 0in x 20ft 2in x 10ft 8in (35.41 x 6.55 x 3.47m). 360 tons. Draught 10/10ft 4in (3.25/3.56m). Men: 30 +1

officer or 18 +1 master.
Guns: none.
Gave Holland.
K: 1764. L: 3.1765. C: 5.1765. Unserviceable 12.1770 at Brest, hulked there 1771, last mentioned 2.1777.
Adour Holland.
K: 1764. L: 4.1765. C: 6.1765. Condemned 12.1770 at Brest, harbour service. Hulked 7.1771, last mentioned 1772.

Ex-DANISH PRIZE (1765). The Danish privateer *Danoise Église Saint Nicolas* was taken in August 1765 off Larache (Morocco) during the bombardment of that city and was in commission as *Danoise* or *Saint Nicolas* from 6 August to 2 September 1665 when last mentioned.

PURCHASED VESSELS (1766). Two merchant vessels were purchased on 4 February 1766 from the Bordeaux shipowner Abraham Gradis who had offered them to the King on 30 January. *Éléphant* had been built 'in the north'; *David* had just been built at Bordeaux.
Éléphant. 750 tons. Built before 1764. No guns. Condemned 7.1769 at Rochefort, hulked there in 7.1770, last mentioned in 1784.
David. 400 tons. Built 1764. 31 men +2 officers. Wrecked 19.2.1767 at Noirmoutiers while returning from Guadeloupe.

Joseph-Marie-Blaise Coulomb was ordered in 1766 to build a 300-ton 'transport' at Toulon. It was stated in 1767 that she was to serve as a model for merchant ships. She might have been built and handed over in 1767 to a Toulon shipowner.

SEINE. 750 tons. Ordered 1766 at Rochefort, order transferred to Brest in late 1766 and to Le Havre in July 1767 where she was built by Jean-Joseph Ginoux to Blaise Ollivier's plans for the 1744 *Chameau*, which he received from Ollivier's son on 28 July 1767. Named *Seine* on 24 August 1767
Dimensions & tons: 140ft 0in, 126ft 0in x 30ft 0in x 13ft 3in (45.48, 40.93 x 9.75 x 4.30m). 750/1080 tons. Draught 13ft 3in/14ft 5in (4.30/4.71m). Men: 120/160, +6/7 officers.
Guns: 24 x 8pdrs, 12 x 4pdrs; 20 x 6pdrs from 1771 probably with 4 x 4pdrs.
Seine Le Havre.
K: 8.1767. L: 7.1768. C: 8.1768. Struck 1777 at Rochefort and probably sold or loaned to the *Société Roderigue, Hortalez et Cie.* (owned by the writer and polymath Pierre-Augustin Caron de Beaumarchais). Their *Seine* was captured by the British *c.*7.1777 near Martinique or in 1778.

AFRICAIN. 1,000 tons. Built by Louis (or Jacques?) Boux. Named 14 November 1768, designed to transport live cattle.
Dimensions & tons: dimensions unknown. 1,000 tons. Men: 140/180, +6 officers.
Guns: 26 to 40 including 26 x 18pdrs.
Africain Brest Dyd.
K: 7.1768. L: 2.1769. C: 3.1769. Wrecked 4.1772 at Île de France, refloated and repaired 5–7.1772. Hulked 10.1774 at Lorient. BU *c.*1780.

PRUDENT. This vessel was purchased for the *Marine des Colonies* at Île de France in August 1768 from Sieur Nevé. As a colonial vessel she was not carried on naval lists.
Dimensions & tons: dimensions unknown. 460 tons.
Guns: unknown
Prudent Holland.
Built *c.*1760. Destroyed 3.1772 by a cyclone at Île de France.

MARQUIS DE CASTRIES **Class.** 700 tons. The four vessels of this class were built for the *Compagnie des Indes* by François Caro at Lorient and were purchased for the Navy in 1769 and 1770 around the time that the company was dissolved.
Dimensions & tons: 130ft 0in, 112ft 0in x 34ft 0in x 13ft 8in (42.23, 36.38 x 11.04 x 4.44m). 700/1,200 tons. Draught 16½ft (5.36m). Men: 140
Guns: 26 x 12pdrs. *Laverdy*: 20 x 8pdrs in 1774, 26 guns in 1775.
Marquis de Castries Lorient.
K: 4.1765. L: 18.9.1765. C: 1.1766. Purchased 6.1770. Sold 9.1771 for commercial use.
Laverdy Lorient.
K: 2.1766. L: 22.7.1766. C: 10.1766. Purchased 7.1770. Wrecked 10.1777 at Île de France.
Brisson Lorient.
K: 4.1767. L: 27.9.1767. C: 12.1767. Turned over to the King 8.12.1769. Sold 7.1771 to a La Rochelle shipowner for commercial use. Requisitioned 7.1778 by the Navy in the Indian Ocean. Captured 9.1778 by the British at Pondicherry.
Gange Lorient.
K: 2.1768. L: 26.9.1768. C: 3.1769. Purchased 11.1770. Sold 6.1772 for commercial use. Chartered 2.1780 by the Navy. Last mentioned 1782.

PURCHASED VESSELS (1770). Five other vessels of the *Compagnie des Indes* were purchased for the Navy in 1770 around the time that the company was dissolved. Three had been built by the company, while *Outarde* and *Mascarin* were purchased. *Outarde* was named *Duc de Choiseul* until the *Compagnie des Indes* purchased her at Bordeaux in August 1766. *Mascarin* was named *Grand Coureur* until she was bought by the *Compagnie des Indes* in August 1767 and renamed in November 1767.
Outarde. Built at Bordeaux.
Dimensions & tons: dimensions unknown, 500/900 tons. Men: 130
Guns: 24 x 8pdrs (26 in 1775, 24 in 1777)
Built 1755. Purchased by the Navy 4.1770 while at Pondicherry. Assigned to Lorient but kept at Île de France at the disposition of the authorities there. Struck 1777.
Éléphant. Built at Nantes.
Dimensions & tons: dimensions unknown. 650/900 tons. Men: 120/125
Guns: 26 x 12pdrs
K: 1757. L: 1757. C: 3.1758. Purchased by the Navy 4.1770 while in the Indian Ocean. Struck 1777 at Île de France.
Duc de Praslin. Built at Lorient.
Dimensions & tons: 132ft 0in, 112ft 0in x 34ft 0in x 13ft 9in (42.88, 36.38 x 11.04 x 4.47m). 600/1,200 tons. Draught 16ft (5.20m). Men: 140
Guns: 26 x 12pdrs or 8pdrs.
K: 8.1763. L: 21.1.1764. C: 4.1764. Purchased by the Navy 6.1770. Sold 7.1771 for commercial use. Wrecked (as *Breton*) 9.1776 at St Domingue.
Mascarin. Built at Bordeaux.
Dimensions & tons: 120ft 0in x 30ft 0in (38.98 x 9.75m). 350/650 tons. Draught 12ft (3.90m). Men: 126
Guns: 24 x 6pdrs.
Built 1764. Purchased by the Navy 23.8.1770 while in the Indian Ocean. Sailed from Île de France 10.1771 with *Marquis de Castries* (see below) under Marc Joseph Marion Dufresne to find a postulated southern continent in the Indian Ocean, returned to Île de France *c.*5.1773. Last mentioned 1775, reportedly seized by the Spanish at Buenos-Aires for smuggling.

Marquis de Sancé. Built at Lorient by Gilles Chambry *fils*.
  Dimensions & tons: 115ft 0in, 103ft 0in x 31ft 0in x 12ft 4in (37.36, 33.46 x 10.07 x 4.00m). 500/950 tons (700 tons in 1783). Draught 16ft (5.20m). Men: 82/140, +6/8 officers.
  Guns: 24 x 8pdrs; 20 guns in 1785.
  K: 3.1766. L: 3.9.1766. C: 11.1766. Purchased by the Navy 10.1770 at Île de France. Renamed *Île de France* 8.1772, rebuilt 1774 and loaned 31.10.1774 for a private voyage to the Indies. Struck 8.1789 at Lorient, hulk there 6.1790.

PURCHASED VESSELS (1770–1771). Three miscellaneous merchant vessels were purchased or chartered in 1770 and later purchased.

Vaillant. Built at Bordeaux.
  Dimensions & tons: 94ft 0in x 25ft 0in x 11ft 5in (30.53 x 8.12 x 3.71m). 400/550 tons. Draught 11ft 4in/12ft 9in (3.68/4.14m). Men: 47/67, +4/6 officers.
  Guns: none; 16 x 3pdrs in 1779
  Completed 12.1767. Chartered at Bordeaux 10.1770 by the Navy and purchased 1771 or 11.1772. Hulk at Lorient 12.1774–79. Repaired 5.1779 at Lorient and fitted as a *gabarre* (snow-rigged). Left Rochefort 30.9.1779, returned with damage 24.11.1779 and found to be in very bad condition. Off the list at Rochefort by 30.9.1780, there through 3.1783, 'navire' hulked 7.1783 at Lorient, last mentioned 1.1789.

Dragon. Built at Nantes.
  Dimensions & tons: dimensions unknown. 335 tons (440 in 1771). Men: 47/67, + 3/6 officers
  Guns: 12 x 4pdrs.
  Built 1768. Chartered at Nantes 10.1770 and purchased 1.1771. Struck 1774 at Lorient and sold to M. Mauro after refit.

Comte de Menou. Built at Nantes.
  Dimensions & tons: 101ft 6in, 91ft 0in x 28ft 0in x 13ft 6in (32.97, 29.56 x 9.10 x 4.39m). 420/700 tons. Men:56/114, +4/12 officers.
  Guns: 14 x 4pdrs; 16 x 6pdrs in 1777.
  Built 1770. Chartered 10.1770 and purchased 1.1771. Armed as a corvette 1774 for the *Escadre d'Évolutions*. Renamed *Coursier* (*Courtier* in Rochefort lists) 16.12.1775. Struck 1780, headquarters hulk at Rochefort.

MARQUIS DE CASTRIES (ex-*Bruny*). In 1770 Marc Joseph Marion Dufresne proposed to the colonial intendant at Île de France to try to find a postulated southern continent in the Indian Ocean using a ship that he owned and a naval *flûte*. On 6 June 1771 he bought a vessel named *Bruny* and renamed her *Marquis de Castries*. (As a vessel of the *Marine des Colonies* she was not carried on naval lists.) On 12 July 1771 he unloaded from the naval *flûte Mascarin* 109 slaves which he sold to the King; *Mascarin* then became the flagship of his expedition. The expedition sailed on 18 October 1771, found the Crozet islands and then visited Tasmania and New Zealand, where Dufresne and many of his crew were killed and eaten by Maoris. The two ships returned to Île de France via Guam and the Philippines in May 1773.
  Dimensions & tons: 90ft 0in x 25ft 0in (29.24 x 8.12m). 300/400 tons. Draught 10ft (3.25m).
  Guns: 16

Marquis de Castries Unknown.
  Sold 5.1773 at Île de France.

MÉNAGÈRE. 750 tons. Ordered in January 1775. Designed in April 1775 by François-Guillaume Clairin-Deslauriers and built by him. When taken *Ménagère* was carrying 6 x 12pdrs belonging to M. de Beaumarchais, to whom the King had loaned the *flûte*, in addition to her 22 x 8pdrs.

The capture of the French naval *flûte Ménagère* and two mercantile storeships by HMS *Mediator*, 44 guns, on 12 December 1782. Engraving after a painting by Robert Dodd, published 18 September 1783. (Beverley R Robinson Collection, Annapolis 51.7.247)

Dimensions & tons: 144ft 0in, 129ft 0in x 33ft 6in x 14ft 8in (46.78, 41.90 x 10.88 x 4.77m). 750/1,405 tons. Draught 13ft 4in/15ft or 14ft 11in/15ft 8in (4.33/4.87m or 4.85/5.09m). Men: 160.
Guns: 22 x 8pdrs.

Ménagère Rochefort Dyd.
K: 6.1775. L: 27.9.1776. C: 10.1776. Captured 12.12.1782 with the mercantile storeships *Alexandre* and *Eugène* by HMS *Mediator* (44) off Cape Ortegal. The three were carrying naval and ordnance stores to North America. Not struck until 1784.

PINTADE. 300 tons (?). Merchant vessel of unknown origin (possibly from Marseille) purchased and put into service 8.1777 at Pondicherry as *Pintade*. Sold 12.1779 at Île de France for commercial use.

LIVERPOOL. 500 tons. 35 men +5 officers. 16 guns. The British merchant ship *Liverpool* was captured in November 1778 by *Conquérant* (74). She was put into service by the French Navy in June 1779 and sailed from Brest for America 27 June 1779 with *Marie-Thérèse*. She did not appear on lists of ships at Brest until 1781. Struck late 1783 at Brest.

OSTERLEY. 700–800 tons. A ship of the British East India Co captured in the Indian Ocean on 21 February 1779 by the frigate *Pourvoyeuse* while on her third voyage for the Company.
Dimensions & tons: dimensions unknown. 759 tons (British measurement). 90/130 men.
Guns: 24 x 18pdrs (when taken)

Osterley Wells, Deptford
Launched 9.10.1771 for the. Handed over 1.1783 for commercial use at Île de France.

BALEINE Class. 500 tons. A class of four designed by Jean-Joseph Ginoux, 1778–79, all built at Le Havre. They were classed as *gabarres* when built, but re-classed as *flûtes* from 1785. They were pierced for 22 guns. The first two ships were decorated by Jean Baptiste.
Dimensions & tons: 122ft 0in, 112ft 0in x 28ft 8in x 11ft 7in (39.63, 36.38 x 9.31 x 3.76m). 500/920 tons. Draught 12ft 8in/13ft 0in (4.11/4.22m). Men: 93/149, +3/7 officers.
Guns: 20 x 8pdrs.

Baleine Le Havre.
K: 7.1778. L: 3.2.1779. C: 4.1779. Struck 1786 at Rochefort.

Outarde Le Havre.
K: 7.1778. L: 5.3.1779. C: 4.1779. Struck 1788 at Brest, used as a hulk until ordered BU 11.6.1796.

Abondance Le Havre.
K: 1.1780. L: 16.9.1780. C: 11.1780. Captured 12.12.1781 by HMS *Union* (90) of Kempenfelt's squadron in the Bay of Biscay with 15 other ships of her convoy, became HMS *Abondance* (Sixth Rate). Sold 29.4.1784.

Nourrice Le Havre.
K: 1.1780. L: 16.10.1780. C: 12.1780. Struck early 1783, hulk at Brest, sold there 6.1787 for commercial use.

ÉLÉPHANT. 800 tons. The merchant ship *Turgot* was chartered from a Paris shipowner by the Navy in 1778 and named *Bons Amis*, then purchased in January 1779 and renamed *Éléphant*. She was, however, still being called *Les Bons Amis* in Suffren's squadron in India in August 1783.
Dimensions & tons: dimensions unknown. 800 tons. Men: 90/100
Guns: 26 x 8pdrs, 6 x 4pdrs; 20 x 8pdrs from 1781.

Éléphant Lorient.
K: 4.1774. L: 12.1774. C: 3.1775. Left Lorient 16.2.1780 for India with *Protée*, *Ajax*, and *Charmante*. Was probably the transport *Éléphant* that arrived at Lorient in 1785 with timber and masts. Struck 1785.

PURCHASED VESSELS (1779). Four Bordeaux merchantmen were purchased at Bordeaux in May 1779. All four were taken on 24 September 1779 while in a convoy by Hotham's squadron off St Domingue.

Ménagère. Probably built at Bordeaux.
Dimensions & tons: 117ft 0in, 106ft 0in x 29ft 8in x 17ft 0in (38.01, 34.43 x 9.64 x 5.52m). 500/900 tons. Draught 12/14ft (3.90/4.55m).
Guns: ?28 (pierced for 24 guns in the lower battery).

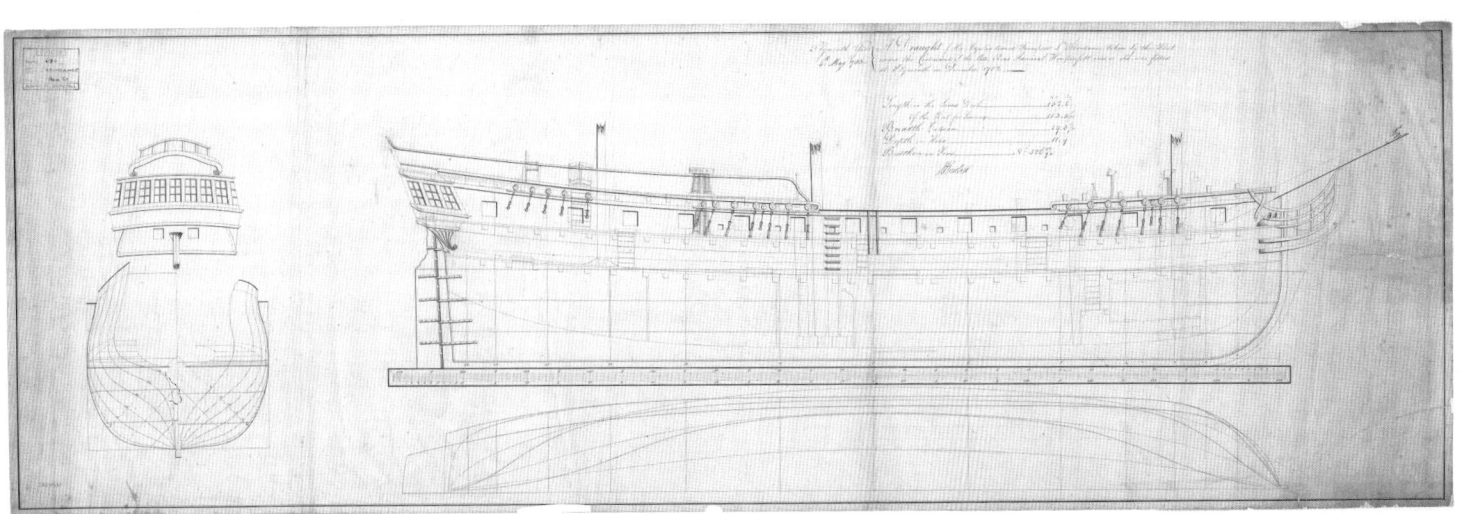

Admiralty draught of 'His Majesty's Armed Transport *L'Abondance*' ... as she was fitted at Plymouth in December 1782', dated 6 May 1783. Above the waterline, this former French *gabarre* is indistinguishable from a small frigate; the only evidence of her original role is the very full underwater shape, which would have made her slower under sail than any purpose-built cruiser. (National Maritime Museum, London J6830)

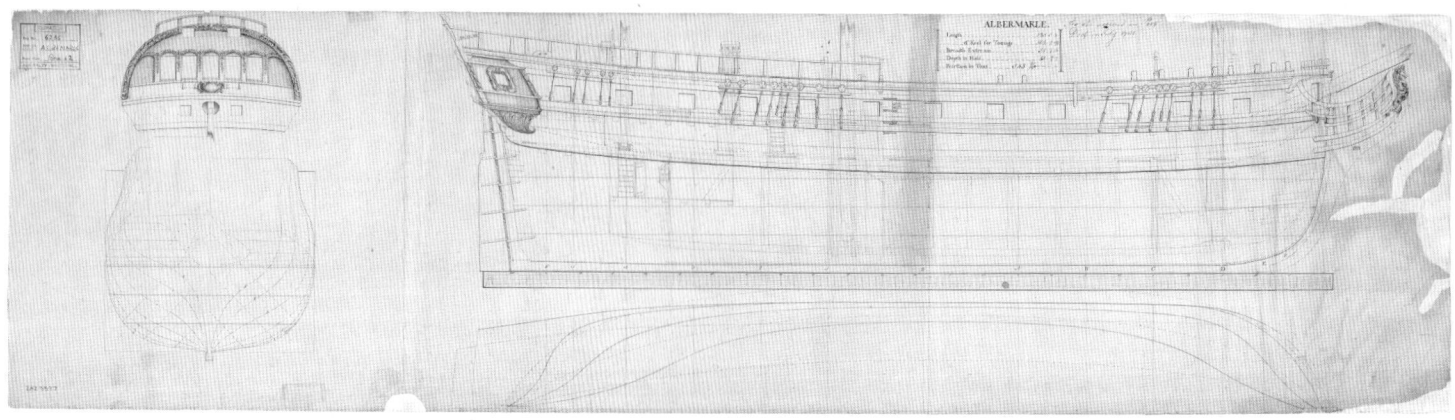

Admiralty draught of the *Albermarle* [*sic*], ex-*Ménagère*. A manuscript note adds: 'As she arrived in Ports. Dock. In July 1781'. This former Bordeaux merchantman had been captured in September 1779 in the West Indies, but despite the passage of time, it is unlikely that there was any opportunity to make substantial alterations before this docking. (National Maritime Museum, London J6407)

Captured 9.1779 by the British upon arrival near St Domingue, became HMS *Albemarle* (Sixth Rate). On 14.8.1782 took the French *flûte Reine de France* along with other prizes. Sold 1.6.1784.

Hercule 600 tons. Captured 9.1779 by the British upon arrival near St Domingue. Later fate unknown.

Président Le Berthon. Captured 9.1779 by the British upon arrival near St Domingue. Later fate unknown.

Maréchal de Mouchy. Captured 9.1779 by the British upon arrival near St Domingue. Repurchased by French merchants, wrecked 5.9.1786 on Mayaguana Island in the Bahamas while engaged in the slave trade between Angola and St Domingue.

Ex-BRITISH PRIZES (1780–1781). The French captured four British merchantmen in 1780 and 1781 that they took into naval service. The first, probably the Indiaman *Gatton*, was taken in September 1780 by the squadron of Chevalier De Monteil and became the French *Gayton*. On 21 March 1781 the 12-gun French brig *Héros* (not on navy lists) commanded by the Chevalier de Coriolis, capitaine de brûlot, captured the British *Union* and took her to St Domingue. She was reported commissioned on 11 April 1781 at Newport, Rhode Island. In April 1781 the corvette *Sylphide* and the *flûte Éléphant* took the Indiaman *Grand Duc de Toscane* (ex-*Britannia*) at the Cape of Good Hope; she was renamed *Toscan*. Finally in August 1781 *Sagittaire* (50) and the frigates *Courageuse* and *Amazone* took the British merchant ship *Briton Lion* which became *Lion Britannique*.

Gayton. 758 tons (British measurement). 18 guns. Built 1771. Last mentioned 1783.

Union. 22 men +2 officers. Sold 12.1781 to Americans at York in Virginia.

Toscan. 500 tons (770 tons British measurement). 80 men. 20 guns. Built 1778 at Bombay. Used as a hospital ship for the French squadron. Recaptured 2.1782 by a British Indiaman at Negapatam with 200 sick on board.

Lion Britannique. 95 men as British ship. 27 guns as captured, including 23 cannons, 4 small carronades and some *pierriers*. Grounded 1.1782 at St Christopher, crew saved but cargo of siege artillery lost.

PURCHASED VESSELS (1781). The mercantile *Philippine* was purchased in March 1781 from Bérard & Cie. at Lorient and put into service there 11.3.1781. On 30 April the merchant vessel *Pérou* was accepted at Lorient from sieur de Monthieu with *Deux Hélènes* and *Malbourough*. *Pérou* may have been purchased in January.

Philippine. 305 tons. 95 men +5 officers. 20 x 6pdrs. Captured 30.9.1781 by a British division in the Antilles.

Pérou. Built at Bordeaux.
  Dimensions & tons: 112ft 0in, 92ft 0in x 28ft 0in x 12ft 6in (36.38, 29.88 x 9.10 x 4.06m). 450/896 tons. Draught 14½/15ft (4.71/4.87m). Men: 74/140
  Guns: 12 x 8pdrs when accepted in 1781, 22 x 8pdrs in 1783
  Built 1774–75. Loaned 6.1786 to the *Compagnie d'Owhère et de Bénin* with a three-year monopoly on trade with Benin, returned 5.1788. Last mentioned 5.1792 at Rochefort.

DROMADAIRE Class. 450 tons. A class of eight designed by Jean-Joseph Ginoux, 1778–79, six built by Ginoux at Le Havre (ordered in pairs) and two built at Bayonne. They were classed as *gabarres* when built, but re-classed as *flûtes* from 1784. They were pierced for 22 guns. *Mulet* and *Portefaix* were listed at 410 tons.

The ships built as *Autruche* and *Portefaix* were renamed *Boussole* and *Astrolabe* in May 1785, and redesignated as frigates, but these two then exchanged names on 28 May; after a refit, each with 112 men and re-armed with 12 x 6pdrs, 3 x 1pdrs and 20 swivels, they sailed from Brest on 1 August 1785 with Comte de Lapérouse's round-the-world scientific expedition, but were both lost with all hands in the Solomon Islands in early 1788 (although not officially declared lost until 14 February 1791); interestingly, a 16-year-old new 2nd Lieut, 'Napolionne' (as then spelt) Buonaparte, was provisionally selected to serve on this voyage, but was finally not appointed.

  Dimensions & tons: 127ft 0in, 112ft 0in x 27ft 3in x 15ft 6in (41.25, 36.38 x 8.85 x 5.04 m). 450/970 tons. Draught 13ft 10in/14ft 7in (4.49/4.74m). Men: 80/210, +4/6 officers.
  Guns: *Lamproie* and *Lourde* in 1783: 24 x 8pdrs. *Mulet* and *Portefaix* in 1783: 20 x 8pdrs. *Dromadaire* and possibly *Mulet* in 1785: 24 x 8pdrs. *Lourde* from 1793: 24 x 8pdrs, 2 x 4pdrs. *Lourde* from 1796: 24 x 6pdrs, 4 x 4pdrs. *Dromadaire* from 1798: 24 x 6pdrs.

Dromadaire Le Havre.
  K: 10.1780. L: 10.5.1781. C: 7.1781. Grounded 11.1798 at Paimboeuf but refloated. Became powder hulk at Brest 1.1800. Condemned 9.1805 and BU.

Chameau Le Havre.
  K: 10.1780. L: 8.6.1781. C: 8.1781. Last mentioned transiting from Toulon to Lorient 2–5.1792, deleted 1793.

Autruche Le Havre.
> K: 6.1781. L: 12.1781. C: 2.1782. Renamed *Boussole* 5.1785 and *Astrolabe* 6.1785. Classed *frégate* in 1786. Wrecked off Vanikoro (Solomon Islands) 26.1.1788.

Lourde Le Havre.
> K: 7.1781. L: 18.12.1781. C: 2.1782. Wrecked 18.5.1797 near Molène Island, Brittany, in fog while returning from St Domingue.

Lamproie Le Havre.
> K: 12.1781. L: 14.5.1782. C: 6.1782. Handed over to Anglo-Spanish forces at the surrender of Toulon 28.8.1793, but turned over to and removed by the Neapolitan Navy in 12.1793; renamed *Lampreda* in their service, burnt 1.1799 at Naples to avoid recovery by the French.

Barbeau Le Havre.
> K: 12.1781. L: 28.5.1782. C: 7.1782. Wrecked during the night of 24/25.2.1792 on the 'Mouchoir Carré' bank at Guadeloupe.

Mulet Bayonne.
> K: 10.1781. L: 5.1782. C: 7.1782. Returned to Lorient 12.6.1784 from a voyage to China armed with 12 x 8pdrs. Handed over to Anglo-Spanish forces at the surrender of Toulon 28.8.1793, decommissioned by the French 14.9.1793, taken by the British as they departed 18.12.1793 and became HMS *Mulette*. For sale 6.1796, apparently sold 1797.

Portefaix Bayonne.
> K: 10.1781. L: 1782. C: 5.1783. Renamed *Astrolabe* 5.1785 and *Boussole* 6.1785. Classed *frégate* in 1786. Wrecked off Vanikoro (Solomon Islands) 26.1.1788.

An otherwise unknown *gabarre* named *Fort* entered Rochefort in September 1781 and departed in October 1781 to become station ship at the bar of the river for the depot of volunteer seamen. Last mentioned in May 1783.

PURCHASED VESSELS (1782–1783). A British merchant vessel was captured in 1779, probably by French privateers, and renamed *Marie-Thérèse*; she was chartered by the Navy from June 1779 to March 1781 and then purchased. The 1,100-ton heavily-armed French merchantman *Apollon* was purchased by the Navy in 1782 at the Cape of Good Hope. A 680-ton vessel built of pine wood in Danzig in 1781 was purchased from Danish owners in November 1782 and named *Nouvelle Entreprise* or *Nouvelle Entreprise de Dantzig*. Finally, the 500-ton merchant ship *Comtesse de Charlus* was purchased by the King in March 1783 for a voyage to China.

Marie-Thérèse. 44 men + 4 officers. Struck late 1783 at Toulon.

Apollon. 1,100 tons. 90 men. ?18 x 18pdrs, 22 x 8pdrs. Her 18pdrs were transferred to the frigate *Cléopâtre* in 5.1783. Listed as a 22-gun frigate in 1785. Decommissioned 5.1785 at Brest, fate unknown.

Nouvelle Entreprise (de Dantzig). 680 tons. Built 1781 in Danzig. Struck 1786, hulk 8.1787 at Lorient, last mentioned 1789.

Sensible. 600 tons. Built at Bordeaux in 1782 as *Comtesse de Charlus*, purchased by the King 3.1783, renamed *Sensible,* and commissioned for a voyage to China on the King's account under the command of M. Bernard de La Gourgue, officer of the *Compagnie des Indes orientales et de la Chine*. Sailed 10.4.1783 with 90 men and armed with 'only' 10 x 6pdrs under the management of the firm Grand Clos Meslé. Returned from China 1.8.1784, decommissioned and struck. Also called *Nouvelle Sensible*, an earlier *Sensible* then being a frigate hulk at Lorient.

Ex-BRITISH PRIZES (1782–1783) The British merchantman *Betzy* was captured in March 1782 by Suffren's squadron in the Indian Ocean. The Indiaman *Fortitude* was taken in June 1782 by the frigate *Fine* off Madras. The 16-gun British armed transport *Resolution* was captured on 10 June 1782 by *Sphinx* (64) and *Annibal* (74) of Suffren's fleet northeast of Negapatam. *Resolution* was previously the exploration ship of Captain James Cook; she had been built as the collier *Marquis of Granby* and became HMS *Drake* in 1770 and *Resolution* in December 1771. Another British armed transport, *Molly* (French *Moolly*), was taken in October 1782 by the frigate *Sémillante* off Madeira, and the Indiaman *Blandford* was captured in January 1783 in the Indian Ocean.

Betzy. 300 tons. Built 1766. Sold at auction 10.1783 at Île de France for commercial service.

Fortitude. 800 tons (758 tons British measurement).
> Guns: 22 x 12pdrs, 6 *pierriers* (pierced for 24 guns in the battery). Built 1780. Sold 6.1783 to Portuguese buyers at Trincomalee.

Résolution Whitby.
> Dimensions & tons: 104ft 0in x 28ft 6in x 12ft 4in (33.78 x 9.26 x 4.01m). 400/700 tons
> Guns: 16
> Sold 1783 for commercial service, probably renamed *Général Conway* in 1789, *Amis Réunis* in 11.1790, and *Liberté* in 1792.

Moolly. 300 tons. 2 x 6pdrs. Ready for sea 12.1782. Sold 12.1783 for commercial use.

Blandford. Sold 5.1783 to Portuguese buyers at Trincomalee.

***SEINE* Class.** 670 tons. A class of four designed by Antoine Groignard in November 1781, two built by Jean-Joseph Ginoux at Le Havre and based at Brest and two built at Bayonne and based at Rochefort. They were pierced for 20 guns in the battery. *Nécessaire* and *Étoile* were listed at 600 tons.
> Dimensions & tons: 132ft 6in, 117ft 6in x 30ft 0in x 14ft 0in (43.04, 38.17 x 9.75 x 4.55 m). 670/1,200 tons. Draught 14½/15¾ft (4.71/5.12m). Men: 48/86, later 135/194.
> Guns: 20 x 6pdrs. The two Brest-based ships may have carried only 4 x 6pdrs while the two Rochefort-based ships carried 16 x 6pdrs at the end of 1783. *Nécessaire* was listed with 10 x 8pdrs by Toulon in late 1783 while *Étoile* was later listed with 20 x 8pdrs and 4 x 4pdrs.

Seine Le Havre.
> K: 5.1782. L: 3.1783. C: 4.1783. Struck in 1788 at Rochefort.

Désirée Le Havre.
> K: 5.1782. L: 23.3.1783. C: 5.1783. Grounded accidentally 6.1784, refloated. Condemned 1788 at Rochefort.

Nécessaire Bayonne.
> K: 1782. L: 5.1783. C: 7.1783. In bad condition and condemned 14.3.1792 at Tenerife after bringing troops there from Lorient. Also reported struck at Martinique in 1792 after bringing troops to St Domingue from Lorient in 11.1791.

Étoile Bayonne.
> K: 1782. L: 6.1783. C: 7.1783. Captured 20.3.1796 by Warren's frigate squadron near the Bec du Raz, Brittany. (Her captor claimed she was armed with 30 x 12pdrs.)

FILLE UNIQUE. 700 tons. Repaired and fitted for sea at Rochefort between February and September 1784, probably after being purchased.
> Dimensions & tons: dimensions unknown. 700 tons. Men: 135–150
> Guns: 24 x 8pdrs; 26 x 12pdrs in 1794–1796.

Fille Unique Bordeaux.
> Built 1782 to 1.1783. Gunnery school at Brest 11.1794 with 26 x 12pdrs. Renamed *Faveur* 1.1795, reverted to *Fille Unique* 1796. Expedition to Ireland 11.1796. Hulk at Brest 3.1797. On sale list 28.5.1797 but not sold, powder hulk 9.1800, BU 4.1804.

CARGO SHIPS (*GABARRES*)

Gabarres (often spelled *gabares*) were originally open (undecked) harbour cargo lighters, which as service craft are not listed here. (Their descendents carry tourists on French rivers today.) Specialized versions of these harbour *gabarres* such as *gabarres portuaires*, *gabarres plates*, and *gabarres à vase* (mud lighters) are also omitted here.

The Navy was dependent on the supply of timber and masts from French forests to its dockyards. Timber was carried by land, then down rivers in rafts, to coastal entrepôts from which coastal shipping delivered it to the dockyards. The main difficulty in freighting timber and masts was that the pieces were large and awkward in shape, and so were not easily accommodated in either the hatches or holds of standard cargo vessels. Small vessels could not carry such timbers at all, and most larger merchant ships could not load them through their hatches. Special vessels had to be built for this purposes. The Dutch built *flûtes* for their trade with Norwegian and Baltic ports that had vertical hatches or ports in the stern through which large timbers and masts could be embarked. The French merchant marine did not participate in this trade and lacked such ships, and until 1715 the Navy relied on suitably fitted ships among its large collection of *flûtes* (see the previous section) for this function.

Soon after 1715 the French Navy began to build *gabarres* with decks (*gabarres pontées*) for the specific purpose of carrying timber along the coast from its timber entrepôts to its dockyards. Ollivier (1735) described these as vessels of about 150 tons capacity and measuring 70ft between perpendiculars. Below the waterline they resembled *flûtes* with square sterns (with lines fuller than in warships) while above the waterline they resembled corvettes. They had one complete deck and a quarterdeck, and some also had a forecastle. Unlike *flûtes* they had no orlop deck. In the deck forward of the mainmast was a hatch 20 to 22ft in length and 6ft wide for loading lumber into the hold. They had carvings on the stern as did corvettes and bomb vessels but they had no quarter galleries. They had standard ship rigs like warships.

The Seven Years' War involved extraordinarily heavy shipping losses for the French and caused a postwar dearth of ships to carry naval timber. To replace wartime losses large shallow-draught flatboats (*bateaux plats*), built during the war to carry troops and munitions for a projected invasion of England, were pressed into the coastal timber traffic as they could also carry large loads of timber. These undecked, flat-bottomed barges and the similar undecked *chattes* at Rochefort are not listed here, although a few decked *chattes* built for the timber trade are listed in Chapter 13. The shortage of shipping in the 1760s which these makeshift craft helped to relieve led to the development by the Navy of a much more numerous auxiliary transport fleet. Financed by the two decades of naval prosperity after the Seven Years' War, this program was designed to obviate reliance on foreign shipping and provide services that French merchant shipowners did not offer. As part of this process the Navy's decked *gabarres* grew in size and came into more general use alongside *flûtes* on both coastal and distant routes. These larger *gabarres* differed from *flûtes* primarily in that they did not have an orlop deck, and some carried their guns in open rather than covered batteries. They were slow but their large cargo capacity, robust hulls, and good seakeeping qualities made them suitable for many purposes, including exploration expeditions.

(A) Vessels acquired from 1714

MARIE-FRANÇOISE Class. 120 tons. Designed and built by Laurent Hélie. These undecked vessels were listed in 1719 with the *Caille* Class, below, as corvettes or *barques longues* destined for the transport of timber. *Grive* and *Bécasse* quickly disappeared from the list but *Marie-Françoise* was re-classed as a *gabarre* between 1719 and 1723, rebuilt in 1724 and listed from 1729 as a decked *gabarre* (*gabarre pontée*) for the same function.

Dimensions & tons: 62ft 0in x 18ft 0in x 9ft 6in (20.14 x 5.85 x 3.09m). 120/200 tons. Draught 9/9½ft (2.92/3.09m). Men: 25, +1 officer.

Guns: none; 2 in *Marie-Françoise* from 1737.

Marie-Françoise Brest Dyd.
K: early 1714. L: 6.1714. C: 7.1714. Rebuilt 1731, hauled out and rebuilt by Hélie 3–5.1737, and rebuilt again 1742. Last mentioned 1758 at Brest.

Grive Brest Dyd.
K: 1714. L: 8.1718. C: 1718. Struck between 1719 and 1723.

Bécasse Brest Dyd.
K: 1714. L: 10.1718. C: 3.1719. Struck between 1719 and 1723.

CAILLE Class. 120 tons. Projected 2 May 1716 to be built on the plan of *Marie-Françoise*. They were probably undecked. Construction ordered 17 June 1716, contract passed with Sieur Garnier 12 August 1716 for the construction of four *gabarres* under the direction of François Coulomb who provided the design. The ships were named 16 October 1716. Listed in 1718 as transport vessels (*bâtiments de transport*) destined for the transport of timber and in 1717 and 1719 as corvettes or *barques longues* destined for the same purpose. In December 1719 they were on loan to a merchant named Chevron for a voyage, probably with timber, from Marseille to Nantes (*Alouette*) or Brest and Le Havre (others). The survivor, *Fauvette*, was re-classed as a *gabarre* between 1719 and 1723.

Dimensions & tons: 62ft 0in x 18ft 0in x 9ft 0in (20.14 x 5.85 x 2.92m). 120/200 tons. Draught 8/9ft (2.60/2.92m). Men: 45, +1 officer.

Guns: 6 x 4pdrs in 1746.

Caille Toulon Dyd.
K: 9.1716. L: 5.2.1717. C: 6.1717. Struck 1721 at Brest.

Perdrix Toulon Dyd.
K: 9.1716. L: 20.2.1717. C: 6.1717. Struck 1721 at Brest.

Alouette Toulon Dyd.
K: 10.1716. L: 23.3.1717. C: 7.1717. Struck 1721 at Brest.

Fauvette Toulon Dyd.
K: 10.1716. L: 13.4.1717. C: 7.1717. Hulked and struck at Brest between 1723 and 1729, BU there in 1746 or 1747.

COLOMBE Class. 150 tons. Designed and built by Laurent Hélie. Initially listed as *gabarres* for transporting timbers, they may initially have been undecked but were specified from 1729 as decked.

Dimensions & tons: 72ft 0in x 19ft 6in x 9ft 10in (23.39 x 6.33 x 3.19m). 150/240 tons. Draught 9ft/9ft 10in (2.92/3.19m). Men: 15/25, +1/2 officers.

Guns: 4 x 4pdrs.

Colombe Brest Dyd.
K: 4.1719. L: 1719. C: 1719. Repaired 3–4.1742 at Le Havre and 1747 at Brest. Removed from service for the last time 7.1748 at Brest.

Tourterelle Brest Dyd.
K: 4.1719. L: 1719. C: 1719. Rebuilt 3–4.1738 at Brest. Removed from service and last mentioned 10.1745.

Pie Brest Dyd.
K: 4.1719. L: 1719. C: 1719. Collided 1724 with the Dutch merchantman *Trouw*, probably in the Loire estuary.

Bécasse Brest Dyd.

K: 1721. L: 1722. C: 1722. Rebuilt at Brest 3–4.1738 and repaired there 1747. Last commissioned at Brest 1748.

ALOUETTE. 200 tons. Designed and built by Jacques Poirier. Listed from 1729 as a decked *gabarre* for transporting timbers and other supplies. Could carry 4,500 square feet of construction timber.
Dimensions & tons: 75ft 0in x 20ft 0in x 10ft 0in (24.36 x 6.50 x 3.25m). 200/280 tons. Draught 9ft 2in (2.98m). Men: 15/25, +1/2 officers.
Guns: 10 x 4pdrs in 1746, 4 x 4pdrs in 1748.
Alouette Le Havre.
K: 6.1723. L: 12.3.1724. C: 5.1724. Rebuilt at Brest 3–4.1738 and repaired there 1747. Last mentioned 1748 at Brest.

CORNEILLE Class. 110 tons. Designed and built by Jacques Poirier, listed from 1729 as decked *gabarres* for transporting timbers.
Dimensions & tons: 64ft 0in x 20ft 6in x 7ft 6in (20.79 x 6.66 x 2.44m). 110/190 tons. Draught 6/7½ft (1.95/2.44m). Men: 10, +1 officer
Guns: none
Corneille Le Havre.
K: 10.1723. L: 5.1724. C: 6.1724. Condemned 2.1732, became headquarters hulk at Le Havre 3.1732 but remained on the list as a *gabarre*, unserviceable 11.1745, sold at Le Havre and BU.
Pintade Le Havre.
K: 4.1725. L: 23.9.1725. C: 1.1726. Wrecked 12.1729 near Cherbourg, wreck sold 1.1730.

CAILLE Class. 150 tons. Designed and built by Blaise Geslain, listed from 1729 as decked *gabarres*.
Dimensions & tons: 70ft 0in x 20ft 8in x 9ft 0in (22.74 x 6.71 x 2.92m). 150/250 tons. Draught 10/11ft (3.25/3.57m). Men: 15/30, +1 officer.
Guns: 6 x 4pdrs in 1746 (*Perdrix*); 12 guns in 1756; 4 guns in 1763
Caille Rochefort Dyd.
K: 1724. L: 1724. C: 1725. Rebuilt 1730 at Rochefort. Rebuilt (*refait à neuf*) in 1739, see below.
Perdrix Rochefort Dyd.
K: 1724, L: 1725. C: 1725. Rebuilt 1734 at Rochefort. Struck 1760 at Rochefort. In 1777–83 Rochefort had a harbour service *gabarre plate* named *Perdrix*, possibly the same vessel cut down.

PALOMBE Class. 130 tons. Designed and built by Jacques Poirier. Listed from 1734 as decked *gabarres* for transporting timbers.
Dimensions & tons: 66ft 0in x 21ft 0in x 8ft 0in (21.44 x 6.82 x 2.60m). 130/200 tons. Draught 7½/9ft (2.44/2.92m). Men: 10/25 +1 officer.
Guns: 4 x 4pdrs
Palombe Le Havre.
K: 3.1730. L: 4.6.1730. C: 7.1730. Repaired 1747 at Brest. Last mentioned 1758.
Pintade Le Havre.
K: 6.1730. L: 29.8.1730. C: 9.1730. Repaired 1747 at Brest. Converted 1756 to headquarters hulk at Le Havre. Unserviceable 2.1761, sold and BU.
Grive Le Havre.
K: 5.1732. L: 5.1733. C: 6.1733. Struck 1746 at Le Havre.

ESPION. A *gabarre* of this name was reportedly built at Toulon between July 1736 and January 1737 by Blaise Coulomb and Louis Boyer. No other information is available.

HEUREUSE MARIE. *Gabarre* built at Brest in 1737 and commissioned there in 1745. Crewed by 8/37 men +2 officers and carried 2 guns. Last mentioned 1758.

CAILLE. 240 tons. The 1724 decked *gabarre Caille* hauled out and enlarged by Pierre Morineau in 1739.
Dimensions & tons: 78ft 0in x 23ft 6in x 10ft 0in (25.34 x 7.63 x 3.25m). 240 tons (200/350 tons in 1746). Draught 11/11½ft (3.57/3.74m). Men: 20/40, +1 officer.
Guns: 8 x 6pdrs
Caille Rochefort Dyd.
K: 1739. L: 6.1740. C: 1740. Repaired 1757 to 11.1757 at Rochefort, struck there 1760. In 1777–83 Rochefort had a harbour service *gabarre plate* named *Caille*, possibly the same vessel cut down.

FAUVETTE. 225 tons. A decked *gabarre* designed and built by Joseph Véronique-Charles Chapelle, notionally replacing the *Fauvette* of 1717 which had been a hulk since before 1729. Rebuilt at Brest by Saucillon in 1757.
Dimensions & tons: 80ft 0in x 20ft 0in x 10ft 2in (25.99 x 6.50 x 3.30m). 225/320 tons. Draught 9ft (2.92m). Men: 25 +1 officer or 15 +1 master.
Guns: 4 x 4pdrs through 1754, 6 guns in 1761; 10 x 4pdrs from 1762.
Fauvette Brest Dyd.
K: 2.1743. L: 9.1743. C: 1.1744. Used as a 10-gun coast guard corvette with 80 men and 4 officers in 1746–47. Rebult 1748 at Brest. To have been loaned to the *Compagnie de Cayenne* in 1768 but was instead hulked at Brest in 1768, struck there 1771, and last mentioned there 11.1775.

DORADE Class. 225 tons. Decked *gabarres* for transporting timbers and other munitions. *Dorade* was built by Venard, who may also have designed the class. *Esturgeon* was built by Geoffroy *aîné* (Jean Geoffroy), *Macreuse* was built by Geoffroy *cadet* (Mathurin-Louis Geoffroy), and *Alose* and *Marne* were built by François-Guillaume Clairain-Deslauriers. In 1767 Geoffroy's original *Esturgeon* was listed, probably in error, with the same dimensions and tonnage as the larger *Gave* class *flûtes* of 1765 (109ft, 360 tons), and she was also reported expanded to these dimensions in 1769–70.
Dimensions & tons: 80ft 0in, ?71ft 0in x 20ft 8in x 10ft 0in (25.99, ?23.06 x 6.71 x 3.25m). 225/330 tons. Draught 9ft 2in/10ft 2in (2.98/3.30m). Men: 15/25, +1 officer.
Guns: 4 x 4pdrs through 1754, 6 guns in *Esturgeon* in 1761; 10 x 4pdrs from 1762.
Dorade Brest Dyd.
K: 1743. L: 11.1743. C: 1.1744. On loan in 1761 as a 12-gun privateer. Grounded 12.1763 on the coast of Morbihan in Brittany, raised 17.1.1764 but unusable and hulk placed on sale. Replaced by *Porteuse*.
Esturgeon Brest Dyd.
K: 1745. L: 10.1746. C: 1.1747. Rebuilt at Brest by Pierre-Augustin Lamothe in 1761 and repaired in 1764. Was to have been loaned to the *Compagnie de Péan de St Gilles* in 1768 but was instead hauled out at Brest 11.1769 and rebuilt, launched 8.1770 and returned to service 10.1770. Wrecked 10.1780 on *Les Morces* at the mouth of the Loire, cargo of timber saved.
Macreuse Brest Dyd.
K: 4.1746, L: 8.1746. C: 9.1746. Taken 9.1755 in the Atlantic in peacetime by the Royal Navy.

Alose Brest Dyd.
   K: 4.1746. L: 8.1746. C: 9.1746. Wrecked 1.1750 on Barfleur Point, near Cherbourg.
Marne Brest Dyd.
   K: 1746. L: 11.1746. C: 1.1747. Wrecked 13.8.1753 near Brest at the Cap de La Chèvre.

ÉCREVISSE. 60 to 80 tons. Designed and built by René-Nicolas Levasseur to support the shipyard at Quebec.
   Dimensions & tons: dimensions unknown. 60–80 tons.
   Guns: none.
Écrevisse Quebec.
   K: 1744. L: 3.1745. C: 4.1745. Fate unknown.

SIRÈNE DU NORD. 160 tons. Credited to Jacques-Luc Coulomb, probably purchased during construction at Stettin and modified by him. Considered well suited to the transportation of timber.
   Dimensions & tons: 89ft 0in x 21ft 0in x 8ft 6in (28.91 x 6.82 x 2.76m). 160/280 tons. Draught 8/9½ft (2.60/3.09m). Men: 40 in war (20 peace), +2/4 officers.
   Guns: 4 x 4pdrs. 8 guns in 1757 as a coast guard vessel.
Sirène du Nord Stettin.
   K: 5.1748. L: early 1749. C: 6.1749. Removed from service 12.1759 at Brest, struck there *c.*1760.

MARIE MAGDELEINE. 180 tons. Credited to Jacques-Luc Coulomb, probably purchased during construction at Stettin and modified by him. Considered unsuited for the transportation of timber because of her 'tween deck.
   Dimensions & tons: 95ft 0in x 22ft 0in x 8ft 6in (30.86 x 7.15 x 2.76m). 180/330 tons. Draught 9½/10ft (3.09/3.25m). Men: 40 in war (20 peace), +4 officers
   Guns: 4 in war: 4 x 4pdrs.
Marie Magdeleine Stettin.
   K: 6.1748. L: 1749. C: 9.1749. Struck *c.*1759 at Brest.

In January 1751 construction of a *gabarre* named *Abeille* at Rochefort was cancelled in order to build the *flûte Rhinoceros* (see above) to resupply the colonies.

MARIE. 200 tons.
   Dimensions & tons: dimensions unknown. 200 tons. Men: 19/33, +1/4 officers
   Guns: Reported with 4 x 4pdrs, 8 x 4pdrs, and 10 guns.
Marie Brest.
   K: 4.1751. L: 10.10.1751. C: 1752. Grounded 5.1760 in the St Lawrence River, refloated. Was at Montreal 9.1760 during the capitulation and was left to the French to repatriate civilians desiring to return to France. Last mentioned in the Vilaine 2.1762, struck before 10.1762.

CIGOGNE Class. 280 tons. Designed by Jacques-Luc Coulomb and built by Pierre-Augustin Lamothe.
   Dimensions & tons: 90ft x 21ft x 11ft (29.24 x 6.82 x 3.57m). 280 tons (200 in 1772). Draught 11ft 4in (3.68m). Men: 20 +1 officer or 12 +1 master.
   Guns: 10 x 4pdrs in *Cigogne*, 4 x 4pdrs in others. 10 guns in *Gelinotte* in 1762.
Cigogne Nantes.
   K: 1.1755. L: 5.1756. C: 7.1756. Sold 3.1761 at Le Havre for commercial use.
Gelinotte Nantes.
   K: 1755. L: 5.1756. C: 1756. On loan in 1761 as an 8-gun privateer. Chartered to M. David 5–7.1768 for a voyage to the Guinea coast. Capsized 4.1769 at Cayenne, refloated. Unserviceable and aground at Brest 6.1772, BU.
Autruche Nantes.
   K: 1755. L: 1756. C: 1756. Struck *c.*1760.
Meuse Nantes.
   K: 1.1755. L: 12.7.1756. C: 1.1757. Last mentioned 25.2.1760 at Paimboeuf.

DOROTHÉE. 200 tons. Probably purchased during construction at Stettin, put into service 4.1757 at Bayonne.
   Dimensions & tons: dimensions unknown. 200 tons. Men: 18/22, +1/2 officers.
   Guns: 4; 6 in 1761; 8 in 1762.
Dorothée Stettin.
   K: 1756. L: 1757. C: 1757. Unserviceable at Brest 4.1764 and struck.

ALOUETTE. 150 tons. Acquired in November 1757 soon after being built at Dunkirk. She was on occasion used as a corvette.
   Dimensions & tons: dimensions unknown. 150 tons. Men: 28, +3 officers (58, +4 officers as corvette)
   Guns: 4
Alouette Dunkirk.
   Built 1756–1757. Last mentioned 3.1760.

PRIZE (1759). A 16-gun *gabarre* named *Thérèse* was captured in around 1759. In 1777–83 Rochefort had a harbour service *gabarre plate* named *Thérèse*, possibly the same vessel cut down.

After 1763 *gabarres* grew in size and took on additional functions. An ordonnance of 1765 distinguished between two types of *gabarres*, the traditional type for coastal navigation and a larger type for long ocean voyages. The coastal type continued to be designed to transport timber and other supplies between French ports while the oceanic type was intended for missions including resupplying the colonies. One physical difference between the two types was that the oceanic *gabarres* tended to lack the big deck hatch used to load timbers into the holds of the coastal vessels. The larger *gabarres* could also be fitted with a temporary orlop deck in the main hold for long voyages, as was evidently done in *Gros Ventre* for her expedition under Yves-Joseph de Kerguelen-Trémarec in 1771–72. Jean-Joseph Ginoux led the way in developing the oceanic *gabarres*, his *Digue*, *Tamponne*, *Officieuse*, *Truite*, and *Adour* classes all being of this type.

DIGUE Class. 450 tons. Designed and built by Jean-Joseph Ginoux to transport timbers from the Pyrenees, pierced for 24 x 6pdrs and 8 x 4pdrs. Both named 26.3.1764. The measurement of *Écluse* was reduced from 450 to 400 tons in 1775 and to 350 tons in 1783.
   Dimensions & tons: 112ft 0in, 100ft 0in x 25ft 0in x 13ft 3in (36.38, 32.48 x 8.12 x 4.30m). 450/700 tons. Draught 12½/13½ft (4.06/4.39m). Men: 50 +1 officer or 30 +1 master.
   Guns: 20 x 6pdrs
Digue Le Havre.
   K: 4.1764. L: 11/16.7.1764. C: 3.1765. In 1768 was operating for the account of and under the command of Sieur Dufresne Marion, *Capitaine de Vaisseau* of the *Compagnie des Indes* (see *Mascarin*, above). At sea in 1770 on a private voyage. Sold 9.1771 at Lorient to Sieur Bourgeois for commercial use.

Écluse Le Havre.
K: 4.1764. L: 8.1764. C: 11.1764. On charter to slave traders in 1770–71. Major repairs in 1773. Burned 5.1779 by the British at Cancale but repaired. Removed from service 5.1788 at Rochefort and condemned.

DORADE Class. 300 tons. Designed and built by Rolland and his son Gaspard-Séraphin Rolland to transport timbers from the Pyrenees. Snow-rigged. Both named 9.7.1764. Tonnages listed for *Dorade* were 300 in 1767, 230 in 1772, 300 in 1776, 200 in 1783–5, 133 in 1786, and 320 in 1787.
Dimensions & tons: 90ft 6in x 22ft 0in x 11ft 0in (29.40 x 7.15 x 3.57m). 300/400 tons. Men: 35 +1 officer or 20 +1 master.
Guns: 12 x 4pdrs.
Dorade Brest Dyd.
K: 5.1764. L: 10.8.1764. C: 8.1764. Left Brest 31.8.1764 to load masts at Bayonne. Hulked at Brest 7.1787, last mentioned 1789.
Dorothée Brest Dyd.
K: 6.1764. L: 29.8.1764. C: 9.1764. Wrecked 16.12.1768 on rocks called *Les Vieux Moines* off the Pointe de Saint Mathieu west of Brest.

FORTE. 400 tons. Ordered 21 May 1764 to replace *Dorothée*, which was in bad condition. Designed and built by Pierre-Auguste Lamothe to transport timbers from the Pyrenees. Named 6 August 1764.
Dimensions & tons: 107ft x 25ft x 12ft (34.76 x 8.12 x 3.90m). 400/550 tons. Draught 13ft (4.22m). Men: 45 +1 officer or 25 +1 master.
Guns: 18 x 6pdrs; 20 x 6pdrs in 1766.
Forte Brest Dyd.
K: 9.1764. L: 5.3.1765. C: 4.1765. Wrecked and lost with all hands 12.1768 on the isle of Quirimba in the Mozambique Channel.

PORTEUSE. 400 tons. Ordered 2 May 1764 to replace *Dorade*, lost on the coast of Morbihan. Named 6.8.1764. Designed and built by C V Segondat or possibly Rolland to transport timbers from the Pyrenees. Snow-rigged. Similar to *Forte*, above.
Dimensions & tons: 104ft 0in x 25ft 0in x 12ft 6in (33.78 x 8.12 x 4.06). 400/550 tons. Draught 13ft (4.22m). Men: 45 +1 officer or 25 +1 master; 70/72 men +5/9 officers as corvette.
Guns: 18 x 6pdrs; 20 x 6pdrs from 1766.
Porteuse Brest Dyd.
K: 9.1764. L: 16.3.1765 C: 4.1765. Struck 1783 and hulked at Lorient. Last mentioned 1789.

TAMPONNE Class. 400 tons. Designed by Jean-Joseph Ginoux and built by Léon Michel Guignace. Both named 31 March 1766. *Gros Ventre* (literally 'big belly') was the first large French *gabarre* to be used in a voyage of exploration; the type was found suitable and others followed.
Dimensions & tons: 112ft 0in, 100ft 0in x 25ft 0in x 13ft 3in (36.40 x 8.13 x 4.31m). 400/600 tons. Draught 11/12ft (3.57/3.90m). Men: 50 +1 officer or 30 +1 master; as corvette 67/69, +7/9 officers.
Guns: 10 x 6pdrs; 16 x 6pdrs by 1771. *Tamponne* listed with 20 x 6pdrs in 1780 as a hulk.
Tamponne Bayonne.
K: 4.1766. L: 18.10.1766. C: 7.1767. Made a scientific cruise in the Baltic in 1777 under Verdun de la Crenne. Hulked 1780 at Brest as guardship, struck 6.1783, sold 1784 for commercial use.
Gros Ventre Bayonne.
K: 4.1766. L: 8.11.1766. C: 8.1767. Participated 1–9.1772 with the *flûte Fortune* in an expedition under LV Yves-Joseph de Kerguelen-Trémarec to find a postulated southern continent in the Indian Ocean, resulting in the French discovery of the west coast of Australia. Condemned and hulked 1777 at Île de France, last mentioned 1779.

PURCHASED VESSELS (1767–1769). The merchant vessel *Heureux* was purchased in September 1767 at Île de France. She was a ship of the Colonial Navy and did not appear on fleet lists. The *gabarre Renée* or *René*, lost in 1770, may not have been a naval vessel although she may have been built at Rochefort.
Heureux. 300/600 tons. Pierced with 30 gunports. Wrecked 2.1769 on a coral reef between the Seychelles and the Comoroes.
Renée or *René*. Possibly built at the Rochefort dockyard. Wrecked in 1770 with a load of construction timbers at Pouliguen in the Loire Estuary.

PURCHASED VESSELS (1770). Six *gabarres* were purchased for the Navy from the *Compagnie des Indes* in April 1770. *Dryade*, *Calypso*, and *Pomone* served only briefly while *Saint Joseph* and the two ships of the *Faune* class lasted until 1777–79.
Dryade. Built for the *Compagnie des Indes* at Lorient.
K: 1747. L: 28.3.1748. C:1748. Condemned 1770 at Lorient and BU.
Calypso. 250 tons. Built for the *Compagnie des Indes* at Nantes. 10 guns.
K: 5.1756. L: 9.1756. C: 11.1756. Designed by Antoine Groignard. Sold 11.1771 at Lorient, BU 1772.

A modern reconstruction of the sheer of the *Gros Ventre* of 1766 by Gérard Delacroix, from his monograph on the ship (see Sources and Bibliography). This drawing shows her as built; later a *faux pont* (orlop deck) was fitted and six more guns were added to the battery. (By courtesy of Gérard Delacroix)

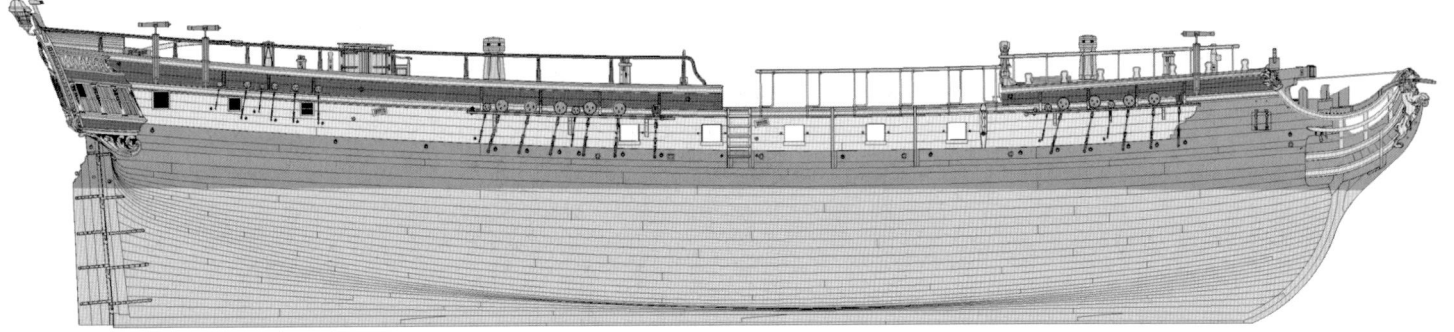

Pomone. 230 tons. Built for the *Compagnie des Indes* at Nantes. 10 guns.
K: 1755. L: 1756. C: 5.1757. Sold 11.1771 at Lorient, BU 1772.

Saint Joseph. 50/150 tons. Tartane built 1755, bought by the *Compagnie des Indes* at Cadiz 1.1756 and modified to a *gabarre*. No guns, 10 men +1 petty officer. Retained 1771 for service in the port and roadstead. Last mentioned 5.1779 at Lorient, BU 1781.

FAUNE Class. 200 tons. Purchased from the *Compagnie des Indes* in April 1770. Both retained 23.9.1771 for transporting munitions from port to port.

Dimensions & tons: dimensions unknown. 200 tons. Men: 20 +1 officer or 12 +1 master.

Guns: none; 8 in *Faune* in 1771, 10 from 1777.

Faune Lorient.
K: 1767. L: 2.1768. C: 4.1768. Struck 1777 at Brest.

Sainte Reine Lorient.
K: 5.1768. L: 8.1768. C: 9.1768. Struck 1777 at Île de France.

COROMANDEL. 50 tons. Origin unknown, was in service in June 1774 at Île de France. 50 tons, possibly 6 guns. Last mentioned 5.1775 at Île de France.

COMPAS Class. 500 tons. Designed and built by Jean-Joseph Ginoux as corvettes for 40 students for the *École de Marine* at Le Havre which was disestablished in March 1775.

Dimensions & tons: 117ft 3in, 106ft 0in x 26ft 0in x 10ft 10in (38.09, 34.43 x 8.45 x 3.52m). 500/740 tons. Draught 11½/13ft (3.74/4.22m). Men: 51/90, +2/10 officers.

Guns: 18 x 6pdrs.

Compas Le Havre.
K: 9.1774. L: 12.9.1775. C: 5.1776. On charter between mid-1779 and early 1780; the report that she was captured 29.8.1779 by HMS *Boreas* (28) at St Domingue appears to be in error. At Rochefort out of service 6.1780, struck there 1781.

Boussole Le Havre.
K: 9.1774. L: 10.11.1775. C: 4.1776. Scientific cruise to the Canary Islands under Jean-Charles de Borda 5.1776 to 2.1777. Loaned 8.1777 to 1784 to the *Compagnie de la Guyane*. Struck 1784 at Brest.

OFFICIEUSE Class. 350 tons. Two-masted vessels sometimes described as snows. Originally to have been a class of ten designed by Jean-Joseph Ginoux, 1776–77, but the design was lengthened for the last seven, which became the *Truite* Class (see below). *Pluvier* and *Saumon* were rearmed in 1779 as bomb vessels with 8 x 8pdrs and 2 x 12-inch mortars. They soon reverted to 6pdr armaments without the mortars and were sometimes listed as brigs.

Dimensions & tons: 113ft 2in, 100ft 0in x 25ft 0in x 12ft 6in (36.76, 32.48 x 8.12 x 4.06 m). 350/700 tons. Draught 12/13ft (3.90/4.22m). Men: 45–182, +1/5 officers; 71 men +6 officers as bomb vessels.

Guns: 20 x 6pdrs. *Pluvier* and *Saumon* as bomb vessels 1779–83: 8 x 8pdrs + 2 x 12in mortars firing to the side, also reported in 1783 as 12 x 4pdrs and 2 x 12-inch mortars in *Saumon* only. *Saumon* arrived at Lorient in late 1782 in need of repair carrying 8 x 6pdrs, 6 x 4pdrs, and 3 x 3½pdr *pierriers*, and by 12.1783 both *Pluvier* and *Saumon* were listed with 16 x 6pdrs. *Pluvier* in 1794–95 had 16 x 6pdrs and 4 *obusiers*.

Officieuse Le Havre.
K: 12.1775. L: 3.8.1776. C: 12.1776. Loaned 12.1776 to the *Compagnie de la Guyane*. Wrecked 11.1781 at Senegal while trying to cross the bar in the Casamance River upon the arrival of a British squadron.

Pluvier Rochefort Dyd.
K: 4.1776. L: 26.9.1776. C: 12.1776. Rebuilt at Rochefort as a bomb vessel 5–7.1779 (fitted with 2 mortars). Repaired 3–4.1780 at Brest. Taken by Allies on occupation of Toulon 8.1793, but restored 9.1793 to evacuate 350 hostile French sailors. Renamed *Commission* 12.1793. Wrecked at Pasages, Spain, 19.6.1795.

Saumon Rochefort Dyd.
K: 4.1776. L: 26.9.1776. C: 12.1776. Rebuilt at Rochefort as a bomb vessel 5–7.1779 (fitted with 2 mortars). Repaired 3–4.1780 at Brest. Struck 1787 at Rochefort.

TRUITE Class. 350 tons. A class of six designed by Jean-Joseph Ginoux, lengthened from the *Officieuse* design. The two Bayonne ships were built as *Paysanne* and *Villageoise*, but renamed *Bayonnaise* and *Pintade* at launch. A possible seventh unit, *Compas*, appeared on the fleet lists of 1780 (with 4 guns) and 1781 (18 guns) at Brest, but she was more likely the *Compas* of 1775. *Barbue* and *Négresse* were listed at 400 and 450 tons respectively.

Dimensions & tons: 116ft 0in, 100ft 0in x 25ft 0in x 12ft 6in (37.68, 32.48 x 8.12 x 4.06 m). 350/700 tons. Draught 12/13¼ft (3.90/4.30m). Men: 46–182, +7 officers.

Guns: 20 x 6pdrs in first three; 16 x 6pdrs in last three and from 1783 in *Barbue*.

Truite Le Havre.
K: 8.1776. L: 9.5.1777. C: 6.1777. Sold to the South Carolina State Navy 9.1779 for use as a 26-gun frigate. Scuttled 3.1780 to block the Cooper River against the advancing British.

Barbue Le Havre.
K: 8.1776. L: 24.5.1777. C: 6.1777. Hulked 1787 at Brest, condemned 20.2.1794, ordered BU 11.6.1796.

Négresse Marion Brillantais, St Malo.
K: 6.1777. L: 4.9.1777. C: 9.1777. Loaned to the *Compagnie de la Guyane* 11.1777 to 1784. Needed repairs 7.1784 at Paimboeuf to prevent sinking, struck in 1785 or 1786.

Guyane Benjamin Dubois, St Malo.
K: 6.1777. L: 8.9.1777. C: 9.1777. Sold 10.1788 at Rochefort for commercial use.

Bayonnaise (Bayonnoise) Bayonne.
K: 1.1779. L: 10.1779. C: 12.1779. Training corvette at Brest from 2.5.1787. Struck 1790.

Pintade Bayonne.
K: 1.1779. L: 10.1779. C: 11.1779. Wrecked 1787 at the entrance to the Loire River.

BOULONNAISE. 100 tons. A small one-off design by Daniel Denys. The artist Pierre Ozanne was embarked in 1783. Brig-rigged from 1788.

Dimensions & tons: 65ft 0in, 56ft 0in x 17ft 0in x 9ft 6in (21.11, 18.19 x 5.52 x 3.09m). 100/180 tons. Draught 7/8ft (2.27/2.60m). Men: 15/20, +1 officer.

Guns: 4 x 4pdrs, later 2 x 6pdrs.

Boulonnaise (Boulonnoise) Nicolas Rivet, Boulogne.
K: 6.1777. L: 3.9.1777. C: 9.1777. Out of service 3.1790, struck 1791 at Brest.

Between 1775 and 1789 many merchant vessels were purchased, requisitioned or captured and inscribed on the fleet list as *gabarres*. They included British merchantmen taken during the War of American Independence and a group of vessels purchased in 1782 at Marseille.

Smaller *gabarres* under about 150 tons could be rigged as snows, brigs, or even cutters. In 1776 naval *gabarres*, which had previously been limited to timber operations on the French coast, ventured for the first time into the Baltic to buy masts at Riga and St Petersburg. The number of naval *gabarres* making these voyages increased in 1783, when they served the additional purpose of providing training for young officers in fleet sailing. Six royal *gabarres* left Riga as a squadron in June 1783 with cargoes of naval stores, and several more such expeditions took place in 1784–86. Thereafter most northen stores again arrived in France in foreign bottoms.

Ex-BRITISH PRIZES (1778–1779). The British merchant schooner *Elisa* and probable privateer *Hunter* or *Hunster* were captured in 1778 and the Liverpool privateer *Rover* was captured by the frigate *Concorde* on 16 February 1779. In addition, the British merchant ships *Dansword* and *London* were captured in 1778 and 1779 respectively and fitted as fireships; they are listed in Chapter 8. They were re-classed as *gabarres* in 1780.

Elisa. 286 tons. 40/50 men +2/4 officers. 8 x 6pdrs, 6 x 4pdrs from 1778; 18 x 4pdrs from 1782. Placed in naval service 11.1778 at St Malo. Removed from service 20.8.1783 at Brest, sold there 1784.

Hunter (Hunster). 31 men +3 officers. 14 x 6pdrs plus 4–6 smaller. Captured 5.1783 by the British after leaving Martinique.

Rover. 240 tons. 14 guns. Sailed for America in 1778, returned to Brest late 1779. Sold 12.1779 at Brest for commercial use.

PAYSANNE Class. These two small *gabarres* are carried on several lists of vessels built, repaired and commissioned at Brest between 1776 and 1782.

Dimensions & tons: dimensions unknown. 200 tons (100 in 1780). Men: 23, +2 petty officers or 16/28, +2 officers.
Guns: unknown.

Paysanne Brest Dyd.
K: 6.1778. L: 3.1779. C: 10.6.1779. Captured 11.9.1781 by the British.

Villageoise Brest Dyd.
K: 6.1778. L: 3.1779. C: 10.6.1779. Captured 27.3.1781 by the British.

PURCHASED VESSELS (1778–1780)
The French purchased three merchant vessels as *gabarres* between 1778 and 1780 including *Ménage*, purchased in 1778, fitted as a fireship, and re-classed as a *gabarre* in 1780; she is listed in Chapter 8.

Terray. Purchased in 1779 from Dessandrais Sébine as a *gabarre* but was hogged and was struck later in 1779 or early in 1780.

Père de Famille. Possibly of 250 tons. Placed in naval service 29.3.1780 at Brest. 29 sailors and 3 officers. Arrived at Puerto Cabello in Central America in 2.1783 and probably sold there that summer.

LOIRE Class. 350 tons. A class of two designed and built by Charles Segondat-Duvernet. Listed with 20 x 4pdrs while building.

Dimensions & tons: 110ft 0in x 25ft 0in x 13ft 6in (35.73 x 8.12 x 4.39m). 350/600 tons. Men: 75–88, +2 officers.
Guns: 20 x 6pdrs.

Loire Lorient Dyd.
K: 2.1780. L: 13.9.1780. C: 10.1780. Struck late 1793 at Brest.

Bretonne Lorient Dyd.
K: 3.1780. L: 25.11.1780. C: 12.1780. Handed over 8.1793 to British Navy at Toulon, retaken by French 12.1793. Became hospital hulk at Toulon 7.1794. Renamed *Basilic* 5.1795 but change not implemented. Struck 1796 at Toulon, still there 8.1802 in sunken condition, sold 1803 for BU.

FORTE. 200 tons. A small one-off design by Charles Segondat-Duvernet.
Dimensions & tons: dimensions unknown. 200 tons. Men: 40/70, +2 officers.
Guns: 12

Forte Lorient Dyd.
K: 12.1780. L: 5.1781. C: 6.1781. Out of service at Brest 11.1786, struck and hulked there 1787, still hulk 1789.

RHÔNE **Class.** 350 tons. A class of two designed by Joseph-Marie-Blaise Coulomb, named on 16 June 1780 and built by Entreprise Aguillon, commercial contractor at Toulon. These were the first *gabarres* or *flûtes* built at Toulon since 1720.

Dimensions & tons: 114ft 0in x 25ft 6in x 14ft 0in (36.98 x 8.28 x 4.55m). 350/750 tons. Draught 12/13ft (3.90/4.22m). Men: 90/100.
Guns: 20 x 6pdrs; 16 x 6pdrs from 1782.

Rhône Aguillon, Toulon.
K: 6.1780. L: 21.7.1781. C: 30.10.1781. Sailed 9.11.1781 with her sister escorted by the frigate *Gracieuse* to replenish the squadron of De Grasse in the Antilles. Wrecked 12.1790 on the Toulinguet Rocks near Brest.

Durance Aguillon, Toulon.
K: 6.1780. L: 14.8.1781. C: 30.10.1781. Renamed *Espérance* 7.1791 for the expedition led by D'Entrecasteaux in *Recherche* (ex-*Truite*, 1787) to find Lapérouse. Seized 10.1793 by the Dutch at Surabaya, Java, recovered by French royalists 2.1794 but handed over to the Dutch 28.10.1794 for unpaid debts and sold at auction 12.1794 at Batavia (Jakarta).

ADOUR **Class.** 350 tons. A class of five *gabarres* designed by Jean-Joseph Ginoux. *Chèvre* was pierced for 24 guns in the battery. Two later ships to the same design (a second *Adour* and *Charente*) were built in 1802–3 – see the 1786–1861 volume.

Dimensions & tons: 112ft 0in, 96ft 6in x 25ft 0in x 14ft 0in (36.38, 31.35 x 8.12 x 4.55m). 350/700 tons. Draught 12/13ft (3.90/4.22m). Men: 75–100, +3 officers.
Guns: 20 x 6pdrs in *Chèvre* in 1780, 16 x 6pdrs in all by 1783.

Adour Bayonne.
K: 2.1781. L: 4.8.1781. C: 1781. Wrecked 13.2.1784 near Île de Ré.

Dordogne Bayonne.
K: 1.1781. L: 1781. C: 1781. Sold 10.1788 at Rochefort.

Chèvre Rochefort Dyd.
K: 1780. L: 1782. C: 12.1782. Struck 1.1788 at Rochefort, BU 2.1788.

Gave Bayonne.
K: 8.1781. L: 12.1781. C: 1.1782. Struck 1792 at Rochefort, sold 8.12.1792.

Cigogne Bayonne.
K: 9.1781. L: 2.1782. C: 4.1782. Struck 1791 at Rochefort.

PURCHASED VESSELS (early 1781). Three merchant ships were purchased for use as *gabarres* in early 1781. *De Grandbourg* or *De Grand-Bourg* was chartered at Brest from March 1779 to February 1781 and then purchased and put into service in March 1781 by the Navy. On 30 April *Deux Hélènes* and *Malbourough* (sic) was accepted at Lorient from sieur de Monthieu with *Pérou*. *Malbourough* may have been taken by French privateers from the British in June 1780 while *Deux Hélènes* may have been purchased in March.

De Grandbourg. 280–327 tons. 35/38 men +2/3 officers. Removed from service 12.1783 at Brest, then struck and sold back to commercial interests at Le Havre. Wrecked 11.1791 off Cherbourg.

Deux Hélènes. 255 tons. 14 men. 8 x 4pdrs when accepted (pierced for 20). Captured 4.1783 by a British squadron off Trincomalee but returned to the French as peace had been signed, struck 1785 or 1786 at Brest.

Malbourough. 287 tons. Had 1 x 9pdr, 11 x 6pdrs, 4 *obusiers* when accepted. Captured 10.1782 by a British frigate while leaving Trincomalee, still listed at Rochefort in 9.1784.

PURCHASED VESSELS (later 1781) Four vessels owned in Le Havre and one of unknown origin were purchased in August and September 1781 for use as *gabarres*. *Deux Soeurs*, *Nouvelle Pauline*, and the former Portuguese *Neptune* or *Neptune Royal* were bought in August. The Havre merchantman *Minerve* and the *Bonne Amitié* of unknown origin followed in September, the latter being put into service at Brest on 5 September 1781 initially as *Amitié No.1*.

Deux Soeurs.
  Dimensions & tons: 85ft 0in, 75ft 0in x 24ft 0in x 9ft 0in. 237–250/430 tons. Draught 10½/12½ft. 29/33 men +4 officers.
  Guns: 1
  Struck 4.1783.

Nouvelle Pauline. 434 tons. Completed 6.1778 at Le Havre. Repaired 9.1781 at Le Havre. Captured 1.1783 by the British.

Neptune or Neptune Royal.
  Dimensions & tons: 73ft 0in keel x 16ft 6in. 228–240/350 tons. 31/44 men +3 officers.
  Guns: unknown
  Was at Île de France in 8.1782. Probably captured 2.1783 by the British.

Minerve or Minerve Royale.
  Dimensions & tons: 300–320 tons. 31/40 men +4 officers.
  Guns: 20.
  Placed out of service 8.1783 at Nantes, struck 1784.

Bonne Amitié. 250 tons. 7 men +4 officers. Wrecked 3.1784 at Île d'Yeu.

PURCHASED VESSELS (early 1782). Four merchant vessels were purchased for use as *gabarres* between January and May 1782. *Sirène* was purchased on 6 January 1782 from Sieur Fournier and sent to Toulon where she completed fitting out for sea in early March 1782. A British merchant sloop possibly named *Friendship* was taken by French privateers, hired by the Navy at St Malo on 12 April 1779, put into service as *Amitié No.2* and then *Amitié,* and then purchased by the King at Granville in April 1782. *Marquis de Castries* was built at Lorient-Bois du Blanc between January and November 1781 for a shipowner in La Rochelle, was requisitioned in September 1781, then purchased in April 1782. Finally, a British merchant ship taken by privateers in December 1779 and purchased in May 1782 at Granville from a Le Havre owner was named *Anonyme*.

Sirène. 473 tons, 6 x 6pdrs. Named *Comte de Stokelberg* between July and October 1785. Grounded 3.1787 at Cherbourg, refloated and loaned 7.1787 for a few months to M. Anthoine at Marseilles to obtain masts at Kherson in the Crimea.

Amitié.
  Dimensions & tons: 52ft 6in x 15ft 10in x 10ft. 85 tons (later 140 tons). 9/18 men +1/2 officers.
  Guns: none.
  Struck at Brest 1791, having been destroyed by the British. A different vessel named *Amitié royale* briefly appeared on lists at Nantes out of service and needing inspection in late 1783.

Marquis de Castries.
  Dimensions & tons: 130ft 0in x 34ft 0in x 16ft 6in (42.23 x 11.04 x 5.36m). 340 tons. Men: 65/74 men +6 officers.
  Guns: 18 x 6pdrs.
  Paquebot 1787. Condemned 3.1789 at Pondicherry, being rotten and sunken, last mentioned 1791.

Anonyme. 402 tons. Removed from service 9.1784 at Cabinda in Angola, struck by Brest 1785 or 1786.

AMPHITRITE. 400 tons. Merchant ship built at Le Havre in 1776–77 and purchased by the Navy 1782. She arrived at Lorient in August 1782.
  Dimensions & tons: dimensions unknown. 400 tons
  Guns: 20 x 8pdrs (pierced for 20 guns). 18 guns in 1785.

Amphitrite Le Havre.
  Conducted a hydrographic mission in 1785 in the Comoro Islands and the Persian Gulf. Struck 1785 or 1786, removed from service 7.1787 at Île de France.

AVENTURE. 200 tons. A British vessel captured *c*.1780 by d'Estaing's squadron and purchased by the King in 1782. 200/350 tons. 6 x 3pdrs (pierced for 20 x 8pdrs). Struck 1786 at Brest.

PURCHASED VESSELS (1782). The following vessels were acquired for use as *gabarres* in 1782 but their purchase dates and their origin are unknown. *Saint Bavo* and *Veuve de Malabar* were very old ships purchased from the Dutch.

Fidèle. 2 guns, snow-rigged. Struck 12.1784 at Brest after returning from a cruise to Newfoundland and Martinique

Petit Cousin. 133 tons. Arrived at Lorient 8.1782. Struck 1785 or 1786 at Lorient and probably sold into merchant service.

Saint Bavo. Purchased 1782.
  Dimensions & tons: 108ft 6in x 20ft 0in x 11ft 0in (35.25 x 6.50 x 3.57m). 240/400 tons.
  Guns: none
  Struck late 1783 or early 1784 and hulked at Cherbourg. Last mentioned 1788.

Veuve de Malabar. 350 tons. Arrived at Lorient 30.8.1783, sold 25.10.1783, last mentioned 1784.

PURCHASED VESSELS (1782, at Marseille). These twelve merchant vessels were purchased by the King at Marseille for use as *gabarres* or *flûtes*, the first nine in August and the last three in September 1782. All were fitted out at Toulon.

Comtesse de la Chaussée d'Eu. Brigantine. 162 tons, 2 x 3pdrs. Ready for sea 8.1782. Repaired 9–10.1783 at Martinique. Entered Rochefort 6.4.1784 under the name *Comtesse d'Eu*, sold 6.1784.

Marie. 187 tons, 6 x 4pdrs + 3 *pierriers*. Ready for sea 8.1782. On sale list 6.1783 at Toulon, sold 9.1783 to Sieur Anthoine.

Jesus-Maria-Joseph. Snow, 2 x 3pdrs, 2 x 1pdrs. Ready for sea 8.1782. On sale list 6.1783, still for sale 11.1683.

Saint Jean Baptiste. Brigantine, 191 tons, 1 x 3pdr + 1 x 1pdr. Ready for sea 8.1782. On sale list 6.1783, sold 9.1783 to Sieur Anthoine.

Gabriel dit le Saint Jean, or *Saint Jean dit le Gabriel*, or *Saint Jean Gabriel*. 270 tons, 8 x 4pdrs + 6 x 1pdr *pierriers*. Ready for sea 8.1782. On sale list 6.1783, sold 9.1783 to Sieur Anthoine.

Modeste Marguerite. 289 tons. 2 x 3pdrs. Ready for sea 8.1782. On sale list 6.1783 at Toulon, sold *c*.10.1783.

Christine-Marguerite. 383 tons, 8 x 6pdrs. Ready for sea 8.1782. Sold 9.1783 to Sieur Anthoine at Toulon.

Bacquencourt. 300 tons, 4 x 4pdrs. Ready for sea 8.1782. Repaired 9–10.1783 at Martinique. Struck in early 1784 at Toulon.

Heureuse Victoire. Brigantine, 4 x 3pdrs. Ready for sea 8.1782. On sale list 6.1783 at Toulon, sold 9.1783 to Sieur Anthoine.

Marius. 225 tons, 2 x 6pdrs. Ready for sea 12.1782. On sale list 11.1783 at Toulon.

Dauphin Royal or *Royal Dauphin*. 325 tons, 2 x 6pdrs. Ready for sea 12.1782. Arrived at Rochefort 15.3.1784, struck there 1787 and sold.

Duc de Crillon. 360 tons, 2 x 6pdrs (2 x 6, 10 x 4 3.1783) . Ready for sea 12.1782. Arrived at Rochefort 4.4.1784, sold 6.1784.

PURCHASED VESSELS (later 1782). These seven miscellaneous merchant vessels were purchased or acquired during 1782 for use as *gabarres*, two in August, two in September, one in October, and two in November.

Holderman or *Holdernetz*. Origin unknown, acquired 8.1782 in North America, was at Boston 1.9.1782. Struck at Brest late 1783 or early 1784.

Dame Victoire. Acquired *c*.8.1782, sailed from Brest 10.9.1782 as a naval vessel. 267 tons. Condemned late 1783 or early 1784 at Brest.

Canada. Dutch-built British merchant vessel captured probably by privateers and purchased 9.1782. 422 tons. She had no forecastle or quarterdeck. Repaired 12.1783 to 1784 at Le Havre as a gunpowder transport, then struck and hulked at Cherbourg. Restored to service at Cherbourg 4.1793 as a bomb vessel with 4 x 24pdrs and 1 mortar and a crew of 20/100 men. Last mentioned 11.1796 out of service at Cherbourg.

Frédéric-Guillaume. Dutch vessel acquired 9.1782 and put into service 12.9.1782 at Brest. 95ft 6in x 26ft 0in x 12ft 3in. 300 tons. 29 men +3 officers. Hulked 1784 at Cherbourg. Last mentioned 1789.

Sally. Acquired 10.1782 in North America. 220 tons, 12 guns. Struck later 1783 or early 1784 at Brest.

Reine de France. American privateer *Queen of France* acquired 11.1782 in North America. 8/12 guns. Captured 1/2.1783 by HMS *Albemarle* in Hood's squadron (ex-French *Ménagère,* above) and taken into Jamaica.

Allegiance. Originally the American merchant vessel *King George*, captured by the Royal Navy in 1779 and renamed *Allegiance*, captured by American privateers 8.1782 and purchased by the French in 11/12.1782 in North America. 14 x 6pdrs. Captured 1/2.1783 by Hood's squadron and taken into Jamaica.

Ex-BRITISH PRIZES (1782). The British merchant vessel *Admiral Keppel* grounded in March 1782 at Waldam near Calais and was taken in May 1782 for the King's service. Another British merchant vessel was captured in September 1782 off the Spanish coast by the frigates *Surveillante* and *Ariel* and became the French Navy's *Grand Duc*.

Amiral Keppel. 96ft 0in x 26ft 6in x 10ft 11in. 300/550 tons. Sold 8.1782 for commercial use, renamed *Comte de Colloredo*. Confiscated 12.1782 by the British during a call at Barbados.

Grand Duc. Removed from service 1783 at Brest, struck and sold there.

***UTILE* Class**. 350 tons. Designed in February 1783 by Jean-Joseph Perrin de Boissieu and built by Raymond-Antoine Haran.
Dimensions & tons: 112ft 0in, 102ft 0in x 27ft 0in x 13ft 6in (36.38, 33.13 x 8.77 x 4.38m). 350/600 tons. Draught 10½/12ft (3.41/3.90m). Men: 73/116, +7 officers.
Guns: 18 x 6pdrs (*Lionne* also had 4 x 4pdrs in 1800–2).

Utile Bayonne.
K: 1783. L: 1.1784. C: 4.1784. Handed over 8.1793 to British Navy at Toulon, retaken by French 12.1793. Renamed *Zibeline* 5.1795 but change not implemented. Captured 9.6.1796 by HMS *Southampton* in the Hyères Islands while escorting a convoy but not added to the RN; sold 6.1798.

Lionne Bayonne.
K: 1783. L: 4.5.1784. C: 16.8.1784. Wrecked 6.1795 at Pasajes, refloated. Removed from service 22.10.1802 and condemned at Rochefort, headquarters hulk. Replaced 7.9.1807 by the corvette *Serpente*, BU 1808.

PORTEUSE. 150 tons. A small brig-rigged *gabarre* or galiote built by Jean-Laurent Beauvoisin at his yard at Le Havre between July and the fall of 1785 for use in the harbour works at Cherbourg. 20 to 45 men, no guns. Primarily a service craft, she also operated along the coast and in April and May 1793 transported artillery and provisions between Brest and Granville. She was struck and placed on sale at Brest in March 1797.

PURCHASED VESSELS (1783). Two more *gabarres* were acquired at the end of the War of American Independence.

Brabant. Vessel of unknown origin that was in service 3.1783 at Brest. 10 guns. Struck 1784 at Brest.

Duc de Lauzun. A British customs vessel acquired by the American Agent of the Marine, Robert Morris, in October 1782 in payment for a debt and outfitted in Nantes as an armed transport of 20 guns for the American Continental Navy. Loaned to the French Navy in April 1783 at Philadelphia to repatriate French troops (Lauzun's Legion and the siege artillery) which she did with the frigates *Astrée, Danaé,* and *Gloire* and the transport *Saint James*. On 21 April 1783 Congress had instructed Morris to sell the ship when she arrived in France, and she was sold at the end of 1783.

10 Corvettes and *Barques Longues*

Barques longues (literally 'long ships') were originally included in a category called *bâtiments interrompus*. These were defined as 'vessels not included among the vessels with official classifications' (Jal, 1848). As of 1675 the Navy officially consisted of four categories: *vaisseaux* (5 ranks), *frégates légères*, *brûlots* (fireships) and *flûtes*. All other craft including smaller combatants, minor cargo vessels, and harbour and dockyard service craft were *bâtiments interrompus* and therefore were not included in official lists or totals. They might be called 'unclassified vessels', the Royal Navy term 'unrated vessels' having a different meaning. The 1674 fleet list mentioned for the first time but without naming them that the Navy had 9 *barques longues de Dunkerque*, these being combatant vessels smaller than *frégates légères*, in addition to the 178 vessels of the four official types. In 1675 it had 13 *barques longues et autres* [and other] *barques*. Beginning in 1676 the *barques longues*, the ancestors of the eighteenth century corvettes, were listed by name and became the fifth category in the officially recorded fleet. (*Galiotes à bombes* or mortar vessels became the sixth category in 1683, producing the fleet structure that lasted to 1719.)

Barques longues had in general developed from the Biscayan double shallops, open or partially-decked craft with lugsails on two masts originally developed for the Basque whaling fleets. (The shallops on the Thames were ancestors of the British sloops but were more heavily built than the Biscay shallops and had square sails.) The category of *barque longue* was first specifically recognised in 1671, and as noted above they were accorded their own class in 1676, when there were nine such vessels in French naval use. By then they were properly decked vessels, able to carry small carriage guns. Unlike the contemporary English sloops, which carried their few guns aft, the French *barque longue* carried its guns in the waist, interspersed with oarports.

The term 'corvette', according to Jal, originated in the Breton *korveten*, but similar words also appeared in other languages. One of the earliest descriptions was that of Guillet in 1678: '*Courvette* is a kind of *Barque-longue* that has only one mast and a small vertical pole forward, and which is propelled by sails and oars. *Courvettes* are common at Calais and at Dunkirk and ordinarily there are some in a naval fleet to scout and to carry news.' The term was introduced into the official nomenclature in 1696 when the category of *barques longues* became *barques longues ou* [or] *corvettes*. The difference between corvettes and *barques longues* was never clearly defined, though illustrations dating from 1710 indicate that the corvettes were essentially large *barques longues*. Between 1743 and 1746 the term *barque longue* was officially dropped and all craft in this category were thereafter labelled as corvettes.

(A) Vessels in service as at 9 March 1661

Small armed vessels prior to 1661 were generally called *frégates* and the one (*Éminante*) that was in service in 1661 is listed in Chapter 6. The first references to *barques longues* in available French naval records date from about 1666.

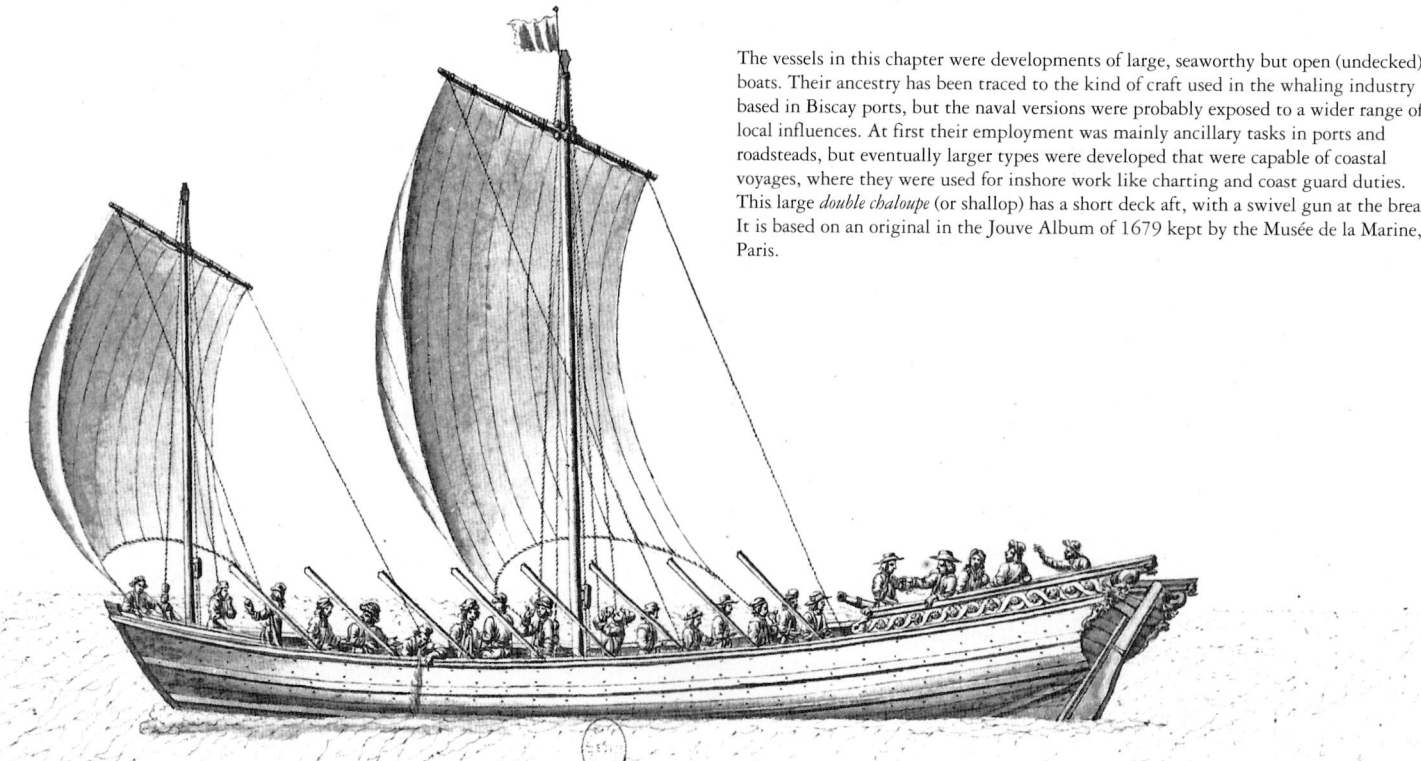

The vessels in this chapter were developments of large, seaworthy but open (undecked) boats. Their ancestry has been traced to the kind of craft used in the whaling industry based in Biscay ports, but the naval versions were probably exposed to a wider range of local influences. At first their employment was mainly ancillary tasks in ports and roadsteads, but eventually larger types were developed that were capable of coastal voyages, where they were used for inshore work like charting and coast guard duties. This large *double chaloupe* (or shallop) has a short deck aft, with a swivel gun at the break. It is based on an original in the Jouve Album of 1679 kept by the Musée de la Marine, Paris.

The imprecision of terminology applied to small craft makes it impossible to tell if there was any objective difference between a *double chaloupe* and the later term *barque longue*. This illustration from du Pas's work of 1710 shows two *barques longues* similar to, if slightly larger than, Jouve's *double chaloupe* above, one being rowed and the other under sail.

(B) Vessels acquired from 9 March 1661

BARQUE LONGUE or BRIGANTIN. This unnamed vessel was described in a compilation of specifications for ships built by Maître François Pomet at Rochefort and Toulon between 1668 and 1675. She was the first French warship to be described as a *barque longue*, and she may have been the vessel called *Barque Longue de Vivonne* in July 1668. (The reference is to Victor de Rochechouart, Comte de Vivonne, then commander of the Mediterranean galleys.) It was originally intended in February 1666 to build six *barques longues* at Toulon, and the remaining five were still planned in 1667, but in the event these were not built.

Dimensions & tons: 48ft 6in x 8ft 0in x 3ft 9in height (15.75 x 2.60 x 1.22m) (with a deck at 2ft 4in/0.76m height). Tons unknown.
Guns: unknown

Barque Longue (Brigantin) Toulon Dyd.
Built 1666. Participated in the expedition to Candia 6.1669. Last mentioned 1.1672 at Toulon.

BARQUE LONGUE. Little is known of this small unarmed vessel with a generic name, which was probably built at Rochefort Dyd between 1669 and February 1672. She accompanied or later joined the Persia Squadron of Jacob Blanquet de La Haye that sailed to the East Indies in March 1670, and was wrecked near Masulipatam in April 1673.

Du Pas also illustrates this 'chaloupe' as used at Toulon. In form it is very similar to his Biscay-rigged example below, but as would be normal in the Mediterranean, it sets a lateen rig, for which a triangular headsail replaces the foremast. In the Mediterranean, as on the Atlantic coast, the *chaloupe* developed into a larger craft termed a *barque longue*, but the lateen-rigged Mediterranean development was more akin to a small galley.

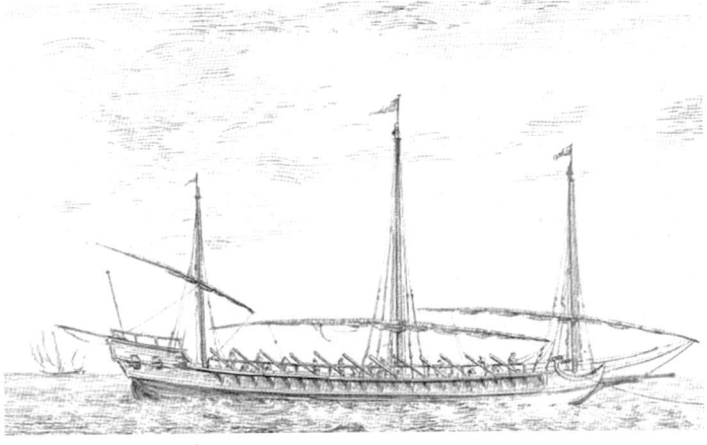

The Mediterranean had an entirely different notion of a *barque longue*, an oared craft similar to galleys shown here by du Pas that was used for privateering along the coasts of the *Levant*. The first ship in this chapter may have been of this type, but otherwise the navy's *barques longues* and corvettes were products of the *Ponant*, with only one unsuccessful one being built in the French *Levant* between the mid-1660s and the late 1760s.

1st DUNKIRK GROUP (1671–1672). The first large-scale production of *barques longues* for the French Navy took place during the Franco-Dutch War of 1672–78, and nearly all of them were designed and built at Dunkirk by the leading shipwright there, Hendryck Houwens. They were mostly armed with 4 guns (4pdrs), and were of 20 to 40 tons. The first group of ten ships reportedly consisted of three classes of three ships (the *Fine*, *Utile*, and *Pouponne* classes) plus one single ship (*Hardi*). The 1674 fleet list showed nine *barques longues de Dunkerque* in service in the northern *Ponant* fleet, each with 30 men: *Hardie*, *Entreprenante*, *Fidèle*, *Assurée*, *Ferme*, *Adroite*, *Pouponne*, *Inconnue*, and *Fine*.

FINE Class. 4 guns. May have been named *Querelleuse*, *Bérénice*, and *Volante* respectively until October 1672.

Dimensions & tons: dimensions unknown. 30 or 20 tons (*Ferme*: 30 tons, 20 from 1679). Draught 5ft (1.62m). Men: 28 (9/19/) +2 officers.

Guns: 4 x 4pdrs except *Ferme*: 2 in 1676, 3 from 1679, and 4 x 4pdrs from 1687.

Fine Dunkirk.
K: 12.1671. L: 22.2.1672. C: 3.1672. Seized 5.1675 by the English at Dover, returned 7.1675. Refitted 1682 at Dunkirk. Struck there 1684.

Ferme Dunkirk.
K: 2.1672. L: 15.3.1672. C: 3.1672. Renamed *Lutine* 28.6.1678. Unserviceable at Rochefort 1695, condemned 1696.

Fidèle Dunkirk.
K: 2.1672. L: 20.4.1672. C: 5.1672. Run ashore 2.1674 on the coast at Boulogne to avoid capture by privateers from Ostend and wrecked.

UTILE Class. 4 guns. *Utile* may have been named *Julie* until October 1672. *Entreprenante* differed from the other two in being frigate-rigged.

Dimensions & tons: dimensions unknown. 40 tons (35 in *Utile*) in 1676, then 30 tons in *Assuré* in 1677 and 20 tons in *Utile* in 1679. Draught 6ft (1.95m). Men: 28 (9/19/) +2 officers.

Guns: 4 x 4pdrs except 3 in *Utile* in 1679 and 6 in *Entreprenante* in 1672–73.

Utile Dunkirk.
K: 3.3.1672. L: 5.1672. C: 6.1672. Captured 18.7.1679 by the Spanish.

Assurée Dunkirk.
K: 7.1672. L: 9.1672. C: 9.1672. With *Vice-amiral* Jean, Comte d'Estrées's squadron in the Antilles. Burned 3.3.1677 in combat with the Dutch at Tobago.

Entreprenante Dunkirk.
K: 7.1672. L: 9.1672. C: 9.1672. Renamed *Bayonnaise* 28.6.1678. Unserviceable 1.1680 and condemned at Dunkirk, BU 3.1680.

POUPONNE Class. 4 guns.

Dimensions & tons: dimensions unknown. 40 tons in 1676 (20 in *Pouponne* and *Inconnue* in 1677, 30 in 1679–82, and 20 from 1683). Draught 5ft (6ft in *Adroite*) (1.62/1.95m). Men: 28 (9/19/) +2 officers.

Guns: 4 x 4pdrs.

Pouponne Dunkirk.
K: 10.1672. L: 12.1672. C: 3.1673. Seized 6.1677 by the English, returned 10.1677 at London. Unserviceable 1.1680 and condemned at Dunkirk, BU 3.1680.

Inconnue Dunkirk.

Du Pas describes this craft as a *double chaloupe*, whose naval roles include advice boat (carrying messages and orders) and 'vedette', or picket boat. The vessel in the background is very similar, although it does not have the decorative weather boards along the gunwales, and is designed to show that such craft could be rowed as well as sailed. Both carry the so-called Biscay rig of single square sails carried on a mainmast and a significantly smaller foremast, common on the Atlantic coast.

K: 10.1672. L: 12.1672. C: 3.1673. Struck 1690 at Dunkirk.
Adroite Dunkirk.
K: 11.1672. L: 12.1672. C: 3.1673. Condemned 1.1677 at Martinique.

HARDIE. 6 guns. This vessel, like *Entreprenante* above, was frigate-rigged.
Hardie Dunkirk.
Dimensions & tons: dimensions unknown. 50 tons. Men: 20/25 +2 officers.
Guns: 6 x 4pdrs.
K: 11.1672. L: 12.1672. C: 3.1673. Wrecked 9.1673 near Dunkirk.

PURCHASED VESSEL (1672). A 50-ton Dunkirk-built *barque longue* was purchased in April 1672 and named *Légère*. She was frigate-rigged and carried 8 x 4pdrs. She was sunk by mistake in March 1673 by an English ship of the line.

LA CORVETTE. 4–6 guns. Designed and built by Benjamin Chaillé, although François Pomet may also have been involved. This vessel first appeared in the 1676 *État abrégé de la Marine* (fleet list) as one of three unnamed Navy-built ships: a *barque longue* called *La Corvette*, a bilander called *La Bellande*, and a gribane called *La Gribane*. The latter two were generic names for types of coastal cargo vessels, and *La Corvette* was probably also a generic name for a large *barque longue*. Recorded in the 1676 list as 'L …' ex-*La Corvette*, she was in service for over a year before getting a 'real' name, *La Folle*, in December 1676; the bilander and the gribane, built around 1670 (see chapter 13), were apparently also called *Madeleine* and *Marie* but these names never appeared in the annual fleet lists. The dimensions below match those of a *courvette* in a compilation of specifications for ships built by Maître François Pomet at Rochefort and Toulon between 1668 and 1675. *Folle* ex-*La Corvette* was increased from a *barque longue* to a *frégate légère* in 1676 (when she was listed as a coast guard vessel with a larger crew) but reverted to a *barque longue* in 1677 or 1678.
Dimensions & tons: 66ft 0in x 14ft 6in x 7ft 0in (21.44 x 4.71 x 2.27m). 50 tons (40 in 1677, 36 from 1679, 25 from 1688). Draught 6ft (1.95m). Men: 28 (9/19/0) +2 officers.
Guns: 6 x 4pdrs. 4 guns from 1677 and 8 from 1688.
La Corvette Rochefort Dyd.
K: 1674. L: 2.1675. C: 3.1675. Renamed *Folle* 11.12.1676. Refitted 1688 at Cayenne. Was immobilized there 3.1691 in need of repairs, struck 1693 at Rochefort.

2ⁿᵈ DUNKIRK GROUP (1674). 4–6 guns. Hendryck Houwens added two more *barques longues* in 1674 to the series that he had begun at Dunkirk in 1671. They replaced two ships that had been lost and took their names.
Hardie Dunkirk.
Dimensions & tons: dimensions unknown. 40 tons (50 from 1677). Draught 6ft (1.95m) (8ft from 1677). Men: 28 (9/19/) +2 officers.
Guns: 4 x 4pdrs. 6 x 4pdrs from 1677.
K: 2.1674. L: 4.1674. C: 5.1674. Renamed *Belle* 28.6.1678. Refitted 1680 at Rochefort. Sunk 9.1680 by a hurricane while at the Petit-Goave anchorage at St Domingue.
Fidèle Dunkirk.
Dimensions & tons: dimensions unknown. 40 tons (30 in 1677, 55 in 1679). Draught 6ft (1.95m). Men: 28 (9/19/) +2 officers.

This is a *barque longue* as illustrated by du Pas. While showing some resemblance to the craft previously described as a *double chaloupe*, this vessel reveals two major developments: firstly, the broadside is now armed (and mounting even small carriage guns requires a deck); and, secondly, the rig is now more elaborate with topsails possible on both masts and a small spritsail carried under a short bowsprit. The caption describes the type as suitable for inshore exploration work, but also the more explicitly naval duty of escorting merchant ships in wartime. These two examples show no evidence of oars.

Guns: 4 x 4pdrs. 6 x 4pdrs or 3pdrs from 1677.
K: 3.1674. L: 4.1674. C: 5.1674. Seized 6.1677 by the English, returned 10.1677 at London. Renamed *Méchante* 28.6.1678. Unserviceable 1.1680 and condemned at Dunkirk, BU 3.1680.

1st **LE HAVRE GROUP (1675).** 4–6 guns. Hendryck Houwens also designed two *barques longues* that were built to the west of Dunkirk at Le Havre. They were built of soft fir (*sapin faible*). They were listed without names in 1676 but were referred to as *Petite Barque Longue* and *Grande Barque Longue* or as *Barque Longue du Sieur Albert* and *Barque Longue du Sieur Moranson* respectively, these gentlemen most likely being their commanders. They received regular names, *Mignonne* and *Subtile*, in June 1676.

Mignonne Le Havre.
  Dimensions & tons: dimensions unknown. 25 tons (40 in 1676). Draught 3½ft (1.14m). Men: 28 (9/19/) +2 officers.
  Guns: 4 x 4pdrs.
  K: 9.1675. L: 8.11.1675. C: 11.1675. Renamed *Rocheloise* 28.6.1678. Condemned 1688 at Le Havre. Sank at her moorings there 1.1689 and BU.

Subtile Le Havre.
  Dimensions & tons: dimensions unknown. 30 tons (40 in 1676). Draught 5½ft (1.79m). Men: 28 (9/19/) +2 officers.
  Guns: 6 x 4pdrs (4 in 1676).
  K: 9.1675. L: 12.11.1675. C: 11.1675. Chartered 1679 for a slaving voyage to Africa. Condemned 1688 at Le Havre, sold there 1.1689.

YACK. 2 guns. Prefabricated at Marseille and assembled at Messina, Sicily, as a yacht for personal use by the Duc de Vivonne, commander of the French fleet there.
  Dimensions & tons: 56ft 0in, 45ft 0in x 14ft 0in x 7ft 0in (18.19, 14.62 x 4.55 x 2.27m). 25 tons. Draught 6ft (1.95m)
  Guns: 2.

Yack (or *Jack*) Marseille/Messina.
  K: 1675. L: 10.1675. C: 11.1675. Returned 5.1679 at Toulon to the Maréchal de Vivonne who had paid for her.

ACQUIRED VESSEL (1675–1676). An 80-ton vessel named *Renommée* of unknown origin was in service at Toulon in March 1676. She carried 6 guns and had a crew of 70 men. She was last mentioned in 1676 at Toulon.

Ex-SPANISH AND DUTCH PRIZES (1675–1677). During this period two Spanish vessels from Ostend and one Dutch vessel were captured in the Channel and one Spanish vessel was probably captured in the Bay of Biscay. The two Ostend vessels, *Surprenante* and *Sibylle*, were listed in January 1677 as a *frégates légères* with larger crews but they were small craft and were re-classed as *barques longues* during 1677 or 1678.

Surprenante Ostend.
  Dimensions & tons: dimensions unknown. 20 tons (25 in 1679). Draught 5½ft (1.79m) (5ft in 1679). Men: 28 (9/19/) +2 officers.
  Guns: 4.
  Built 1672. Captured 7.1675, ex-Spanish *Santa Maria* (probably). Struck 1681, probably at Dunkirk.

Espérance Zeeland.
  Dimensions & tons: dimensions unknown. 25 tons. Draught 4ft (1.30m). Men: 28 (9/19/) +2 officers.
  Guns: 3.
  Built 1666. Captured 1.1675 by French privateers and purchased 5.1676, ex-Dutch *Hoop*. Sold 8.1677 at le Havre to the Duc de Saint-Aignan.

Sibylle Spain.
  Dimensions & tons: dimensions unknown. 30 tons (40 from 1688). Draught 6ft (1.95m). Men: 28 (9/19/) +2 officers.
  Guns: 6, 4 from 1679, and 8 from 1688.
  Built 1673. Captured 1676, ex-Spanish, named 11.12.1676. Struck 1689 at Rochefort.

Rat Ostend.
  Dimensions & tons: unknown.
  Guns: 6.
  Captured 1.1677, ex-Spanish *Rat*. Loaned 4.1678 at Le Havre for commercial use, not further mentioned.

3rd **DUNKIRK GROUP (1677–1678).** 4–6 guns. Hendryck Houwens added three more *barques longues* in 1677–78 to the series that he had begun at Dunkirk in 1671.

Rieuse Dunkirk.
  Dimensions & tons: dimensions unknown. 55 tons. Draught 7ft (2.27m) (8ft from 1687). Men: 28 (9/19/) +2 officers.
  Guns: 6 x 4pdrs. 8 x 4pdrs from 1687.
  K: 1677. L: 1.1678. C: 2.1678. Struck 1694.

Assurée Dunkirk.
  Dimensions & tons: dimensions probably as *Effrontée*. 20 tons (36 in 1687, 40 from 1688, 46 in 1690). Draught 4ft (1.30m) (6½ft in 1687, then 7ft). Men: 28 (9/19/) +2 officers.
  Guns: 4 x 4pdrs. 6 x 4pdrs from 1687.
  K: 3.1678. L: 6.7.1678. C: 10.1678. Named 28.6.1678 while building. Chartered 1681 at Dunkirk to Sieur Omaër for use in Jean Bart's privateering squadron (*Viper*, *Dauphin*, *Assurée*). Struck 1690 at Dunkirk.

Effrontée Dunkirk.
  Dimensions & tons: 54ft 0in x 13ft 6in x 5ft 6in (17.54 x 4.39 x 1.79m). 20 tons (36 from 1687, 40 from 1691, 80 from 1696). Draught 4ft (1.30m) (6½ft from 1687, then 6ft, 7ft from 1696). Men: 28 (9/19/) +2 officers, later 35 in war, 25 peace
  Guns: 4 x 4pdrs. 6 x 4pdrs from 1687. From 1696: 4 in war: 4 x 4pdrs
  K: 3.1678. L: 6.7.1678. C: 10.1678. Named 28.6.1678 while building. Struck 1698 at Toulon.

The *frégates légères Surprenante, Christine,* and *Sans Peur* were listed as *barques longues* near the end of their careers (in 1675, 1677–78, and 1679 respectively).

Ex-SPANISH PRIZES (1682–1684). Two Spanish vessels, one from Catalonia and one from Ostend, were captured and added to the French Navy during this period.

Trône (Trosne) Catalonia.
  Dimensions & tons: dimensions unknown. 80 tons. Draught 7ft (2.27m). Men: 28 (9/19/) +2 officers.
  Guns: 6 guns and 20 *pierriers* in 11.1683, 4 x 4pdrs in 1690–93.
  Built 1672. Captured 1682, ex-Spanish *Trono*. Condemned 1694, probably at Toulon, or possibly burned 5.1695 in combat with Spanish galleys at Ponza.

Ferme Builder unknown.
  Dimensions & tons: dimensions unknown. 30 tons.
  Guns: unknown.
  Captured from Ostend owners 3.1684 and confiscated for the King, probably ex-*Sauveur* (French?). Last mentioned 7.1684 at Brest, probably struck 1685.

BELLE. 6 guns. No *barques longues* were built between the end of the Franco-Dutch War in 1678 and the start of the War of the League of Augsburg in 1688 except for one specialized exploration vessel. The *Belle* was a *barque longue* built at Rochefort in 1684 and entrusted by the King to René-Robert Cavelier, Sieur de La Salle for an ill-fated effort to establish a French colony on the Gulf of Mexico at the mouth of the Mississippi River. She was designed by Pierre Malet under the supervision of Honoré Malet, initially as a kit to be assembled in America although she was ultimately assembled at Rochefort before the voyage. The remains of this *barque longue* were found in 1995 and excavated. They were subsequently fully documented in a monograph by Jean Boudriot. A *Belle* appeared on the French fleet list in January 1687 with a construction date of 1684 and was deleted during 1689, when it was noted that she was on her first cruise. This was probably belated reporting of La Salle's *Belle*.

Dimensions & tons: dimensions unknown. 65 or 50 tons. Draught 7ft (2.27m). Men: 28 (9/19/) +2 officers.
Guns: 6 x 4pdrs. Carried four bronze 4pdrs when lost.
Belle (Rochefort, 1684), Rochefort.
K: 1683. L: early 1684. C: 7.1684. Given by the King 5.1684 to La Salle. Wrecked 1.1686 in Matagorda Bay, Texas.

Ex-ALGERIAN PRIZE (1688). The Algerian *Tinine* was captured in late 1688 and became the French *Dragon Volant*.
Dimensions & tons: dimensions unknown. 60 tons.
Guns: 10.
Dragon Volant Algiers.
Captured 9.6.1689 by HMS *James Galley* (30), became HMS *Dragon Prize*. Her captors reported her as a privateer. Wrecked 22.1.1690 at Kingsgate, Isle of Thanet.

(C) Vessels acquired from 15 April 1689

Construction of *barques longues* resumed shortly after the start of the War of the League of Augsburg in November 1688 and continued in quantity through 1693. At this time vessels with at least 70-foot length and 10 guns were usually *frégates légères* while smaller ships with fewer guns were *barques longues*. In 1689 the 70-foot *Méchante* and *Bayonnaise* were completed as *barque longues*, but *Méchante* became a *frégate légère* by 1696 and *Bayonnaise* would doubtless have followed suit, but for her early loss. The 70-foot *Émeraude* was a *barque longue* in 1692, became a *frégate légère* by 1696, and reverted to a corvette or *barque longue* in 1701 with her sister *Choquante*. The 70-foot *Joyeuse* was designed by Étienne Salicon as a *barque longue* but was re-classed as a *frégate légère* between 1692 and 1695. In contrast the 64-foot *Hautaine*, completed in 1693 as a *frégate légère*, became a *barque longue* during 1696 or 1697. The latter part of the War of the League of Augsburg (1694–97) saw no additional *barques longues* built.

***SURPRENANTE* Class.** 4 guns. *Surprenante* and *Fine* were designed by Étienne Hubac on the lines of the *Ferme* of 1672 and built by Laurent Hélie and Jean-Pierre Brun respectively. They were ordered on 28 February 1689 and named on 21 May.
Dimensions & tons: dimensions unknown. 20 tons (45 in *Fine* from 1691). Draught 7½ft (2.44m). Men: 28 (9/19/) +2 officers.
Guns: 4 x 4pdrs.
Surprenante Brest Dyd.
K: 3.1689. L: 17.5.1689. C: 7.1689. Either destroyed 4.1690 by the English in the Bay of Dublin or wrecked 2.1691 near Barfleur while being pursued by two English vessels, probably in company with the *frégate légère Bayonnaise*.
Fine Brest Dyd.
K: 4.1689. L: 6.1689. C: 7.1689. Struck 7.1692 after being captured by the English, who used her French appearance for inshore ntelligence missions coming regularly to l'Aberwrac'h.

4ᵗʰ DUNKIRK GROUP (1689). 6 guns. This was the last group of *barques longues* built at Dunkirk by Hendryck Houwens before his death later in 1689. One pair of ships from this group is listed separately below as the *Utile* class.
Poupponne Dunkirk.

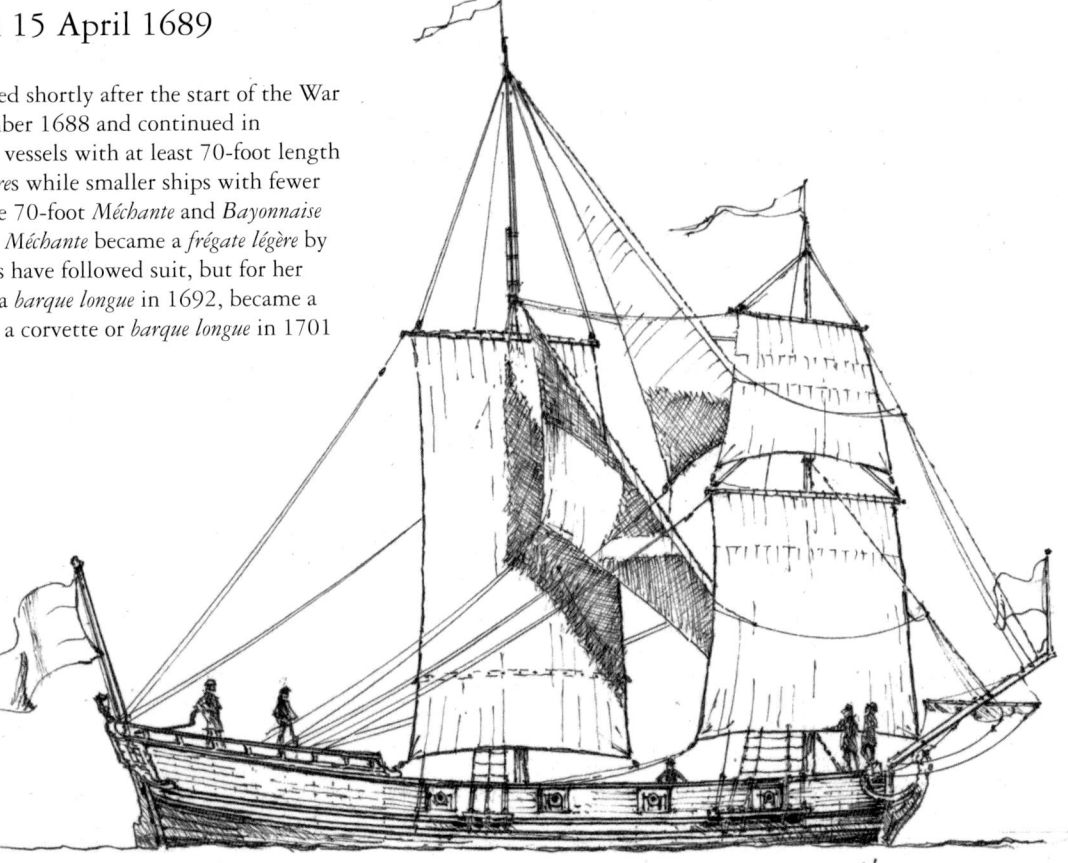

A reconstruction by Ian McLaughlan of the early form of the corvette, a slightly enhanced version of the *barque longue*. Although not obvious in illustrations, by this stage it is likely that in both hull form and structure the corvette has left behind its origins as a boat and become more ship-like, with heavier scantlings and more seaworthy underwater body.

Dimensions & tons: unknown. Men: 30 +2 officers.
Guns: 6.
K: 11.1688. L: 20.2.1689. C: 4.1689. Captured 5.1689 by the Dutch. See the second *Pouponne* below.

Rocheloise Dunkirk.
Dimensions & tons: 62ft 0in x 12ft 0in x 5ft 6in (20.14 x 3.90 x 1.79m). 35 tons (40 from 1691, 60 from 1696). Draught 6¾ft (2.19m). Men: 30 (10/20/) +2 officers, later 50 in war, 45 peace.
Guns: 6 x 4pdrs. From 1696: 8 in war (6 peace): 8 x 4pdrs.
K: 7.1689. L: 10.1689. C: 11.1689. Struck 1697 at Lorient but reconditioned there 11.1698 and given to the *Compagnie Royale de St Domingue*.

Pouponne Dunkirk.
Dimensions & tons: dimensions unknown. 40 tons (50 from 1691). Draught 6ft (1.95m). Men: 30 (10/20/) +2 officers.
Guns: 6 x 4pdrs.
K: 7.1689. L: 1.1690. C: 2.1690. Struck 1694.

Sibylle Dunkirk.
Dimensions & tons: dimensions unknown. 40 tons. Draught 6ft (1.95m). Men: 30 (10/20/) +2 officers.
Guns: 6 x 4pdrs
K: 7.1689. L: 1.1690. C: 2.1690. Struck 1693 or 1694 (possibly wrecked 1694 at La Hougue).

Subtile Dunkirk.
Dimensions & tons: 60ft 6in x 12ft 6in x 5ft 9in (19.65 x 4.06 x 1.87m). 35 tons in 1690, 50 from 1696. Draught 7ft (2.27m). Men: 30 (10/20/) +2 officers; later 35 in war, 25 peace
Guns: 6 x 4pdrs. From 1696: 6 in war (4 peace): 6 x 4pdrs.
K: 7.1689. L: 2.1690. C: 3.1690. Participated in the Lagos campaign of 1693. Lent as a privateer in 1694–96 to *Vice-Amiral* Victor Marie d'Estrées, with *Levrette,* under the command of LFL François-Joseph Marquisan. Unserviceable 1.1702 and condemned at Toulon.

UTILE Class. 8 guns. These apparent sisters were designed by Hendryck Houwens and built at Dunkirk.
Dimensions & tons: 55ft 0in x 15ft 6in x 7ft 0in (17.87 x 5.04 x 2.27m). 30 tons (40 from 1691, 30 from 1696). Draught 7½ft (2.44m). Men: 40 (10/30/) +2 officers, later 30 in war, 25 peace
Guns: 8 x 4pdrs. From 1696: 6 in war (4 peace): 6 x 4pdrs.

Utile Dunkirk.
K: 11.1688. L: 6.2.1689. C: 3.1689. Captured 3.1689 by the Dutch but soon retaken by the French. Sold 10.1691 at St Domingue by the governor there.

Sans Peur Dunkirk.
K: 11.1688. L: 6.2.1689. C: 3.1689. Struck 6/7.1696 at Brest.

2ⁿᵈ LE HAVRE GROUP (1689). 6–8 guns. A few additional *barques longues* were built at Le Havre in 1689, these being designed by Étienne Salicon (who died on 2 December 1691) and/or Pierre Chaillé (who succeeded him). In addition, in 1690 a *barque longue* designed by Salicon in 1670 was captured in 1690 (see *Saint François*, prize).

Entendue Le Havre.
Dimensions & tons: dimensions unknown. 50 tons. Draught 8ft (2.60m). Men: 40 (10/30/) +2 officers.
Guns: 8 x 4pdrs.
K: 12.1689. L: 2/3.1690. C: 3.1690. Designed by Salicon. Struck 1694.

Levrette Le Havre.
Dimensions & tons: dimensions unknown. 40 tons. Draught 7ft (2.27m). Men: 35 (9/26/) +2 officers.
Guns: 6.
L: 2/3.1690. Designed by Chaillé. Lent as a privateer in 1694–95 to *Vice-Amiral* Victor Marie d'Estrées, with *Subtile*, under the command of LFL François-Joseph Marquisan. Struck at Brest 1695.

Blonde Le Havre.
Dimensions & tons: 65ft 0in x 14ft 0in x 5ft 0in (21.11 x 4.55 x 1.62m). 50 tons. Draught 6ft (1.95m). Men: 40 (10/30/) +2 officers, later 35 in war, 25 peace.
Guns: 8 x 4pdrs. From 1696: 6 in war (4 peace): 6 x 4pdrs.
K: 12.1689. L: early 1690. C: 1690. Designed by Chaillé (reported 1691–92) or Salicon (reported 1696–98). Struck 1698 at Toulon, probably BU 1699.

Prompte Le Havre.
Dimensions & tons: dimensions unknown. 40 tons. Draught 7ft (2.27m). Men: 35 (9/26/) +2 officers
Guns: 6 x 4pdrs
K: 12.1689. L: early 1690. C: 1690. Designed by Salicon. Last mentioned 1692, may have been lost at La Hougue.

Ex-SPANISH PRIZES (1689–1691). One Ostend vessel, *Belle*, was captured in November 1689. Three vessels from the Basque region in Spain were also captured, *Inconnue* and the first *Biscayenne* in 1690, and the second *Biscayenne* in June 1691. Their Spanish names are unknown.

Belle Ostend.
Dimensions & tons: dimensions unknown. 80 tons. Draught 9½ft (3.09m). Men: 50 (12/38/) +4 officers.
Guns: 8.
Built 1670–1671. Last mentioned 1694.

Inconnue Vizcaya.
Dimensions & tons: dimensions unknown. 150 tons. Draught 6½ft (2.11m). Men: 28 (9/19/) +2 officers.
Guns: 4.
Built 1672. Struck 3.1692 at Rochefort, probably became the *flûte Féconde* which was struck before the end of 1692 at Rochefort.

Biscayenne San Sebastián.
Dimensions & tons: 41ft 0in x 12ft 0in x 5ft 3in (13.32 x 3.90 x 1.71m). 20 tons (60 from 1696). Draught 6½ft (2.11m). Men: 20 (7/13/) +2 officers, later 45 in war, 30 peace.
Guns: 4. From 1696: 4 in war (4 peace): 4 x 1pdrs.
Built 1671, designed by a shipwright from Vizcaya, Spain. Condemned 1697 at Lorient, sold 1699.

Biscayenne San Sebastián.
Dimensions & tons: 60ft 0in x 15ft 0in x 5ft 6in (19.49 x 4.87 x 1.79m). 20 tons (40 from 1696). Draught 9¼ft (3.00m). Men: 35/40 in war, 30 peace
Guns: 4. From 1696: 8 in war (6 peace): 8 x 4pdrs.
Described by Brest in 11.1692 as new. Unserviceable 6.1697 at Brest, struck 1698.

5ᵗʰ DUNKIRK GROUP (1690–1692). 6–8 guns. Hendryck Houwens died in late 1689 and Toulon was ordered to send a *maître constructeur* (René Levasseur) to replace him. Levasseur concentrated on larger ships while Jean-Nicolas Houwens (1668–1743, probably Hendryck's eldest son), took over the construction of *barques longues*, although Philippe Cochois, who normally built at Le Havre, is also credited with some. Most of these were single ships, but this group also included two pairs of ships with identical specifications that are listed below as the *Flèche* and *Nymphe* classes.

Assurée Dunkirk.
Dimensions & tons: dimensions unknown. 50 tons. Draught 7ft

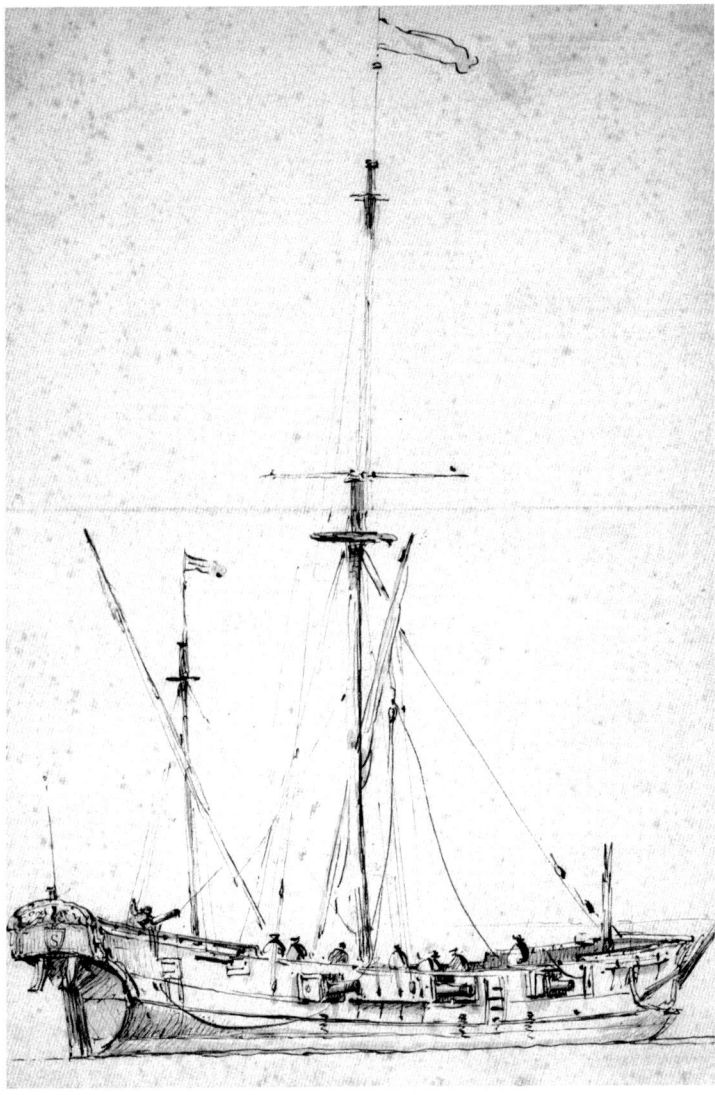

A drawing by Van de Velde the younger of a Dunkirk privateer called *Le Brillant* captured by the English in 1696. Armed with 6 guns, this *barque longue* was ship-rigged (the foremast is missing, presumably lost in action) and probably closely resembled the naval versions built at that port in the 1690s. She was certainly thought to be characteristically French in appearance, because the British government acquired the prize specifically for use in clandestine operations along the Channel coast. (National Maritime Museum, London PW6663)

(2.27m). Men: 40 (10/30/) +2 officers.

Guns: 8 x 4pdrs.

K: 3.1690. L: 6.1690. C: mid-1690. Designed by Jean-Nicolas Houwens. Last mentioned 1692, may have been lost at La Hougue.

Bonne Dunkirk.

Dimensions & tons: dimensions unknown. 50 tons. Draught 6ft (1.94m). Men: 30 (10/20/) +2 officers.

Guns: 6 x 4pdrs.

K: early 1690. L: 10.1690. C: 11.1690. Designed by Jean-Nicolas Houwens. Captured 5.1695 by the English in Acadia, sank the next day.

Brune Dunkirk.

Dimensions & tons: dimensions unknown. 50 tons. Draught 6ft (1.94m). Men: 30 (10/20/) +2 officers.

Guns: 6 x 4pdrs.

K: early 1690. L: 10.1690. C: 11.1690. Designed by Jean-Nicolas Houwens. Captured 11.1695 by a Flemish frigate and sold 12.1695 at Ostend.

Commode Dunkirk.

Dimensions & tons: 60ft 0in x 14ft 0in x 7ft 0in (19.49 x 4.55 x 2.27m). 50 tons. Draught 7ft (2.27m). Men: 36 (10/26/) +2 officers.

Guns: 6 x 4pdrs.

K: 10.1690. L: 1.1691. C: 1691. Designed by 'Houwens' (probably Jean-Nicolas) although also attributed to Philippe Cochois. Cruised under Jean Bart 1692. Lent as a privateer to GM de Belleville L'Étendart, captured 5.1693 by an Ostend privateer.

Rusée Dunkirk.

Dimensions & tons: 60ft 0in x 14ft 0in x 7ft 0in (19.49 x 4.55 x 2.27m). 48 tons. Draught 7ft (2.27m). Men: 36 (10/26/) +2 officers.

Guns: 6 x 4pdrs.

K: 10.1690. L: 1.1691. C: 1691. Designed by Jean-Nicolas Houwens. Last mentioned 1694 at Dunkirk, may have been one of the two corvettes destroyed 5.1694 by the explosion of the fireship *Chasseur* near Conquet.

Biche Dunkirk.

Dimensions & tons: 60ft 0in x 14ft 6in x 7ft 0in (19.49 x 4.71 x 2.27m). 50 tons (60 from 1696). Draught 7½ft (2.44m). Men: 40 (10/30/) +2 officers, later 45/50 in war, 30 peace

Guns: 6 in war: 6 x 4pdrs. From 1699: 8 in war (4 peace): 8 x 4pdrs.

K: early 1691. L: 7.1691. C: 8.1691. Designed by Jean-Nicolas Houwens (credited to Philippe Cochois in 1699). Struck 1699 at Dunkirk. Rearmed at Nantes as a privateer 6.1702 by Jean Saupin.

Boussole Dunkirk.

Dimensions & tons: 60ft 0in x 14ft 0in x 7ft 0in (19.49 x 4.55 x 2.27m). 50 tons. Draught 7ft (2.27m). Men: 40 (10/30/) +2 officers.

Guns: 6 x 4pdrs.

K: early 1691. L: 7.1691. C: 8.1691. Designed by Philippe Cochois. Last mentioned 1692.

Trompette Dunkirk.

Dimensions & tons: 60ft 0in x 14ft 0in x 5ft 0in (19.49 x 4.55 x 1.62m). 50 tons (40 from 1696). Draught 7½ft (2.44m). Men: 40 (10/30/) +2 officers, later 45 in war, 40/20 peace

Guns: 6 x 4pdrs. From 1696: 8 in war (6 peace): 8 x 4pdrs; from 1700: 6 x 4pdrs.

K: early 1691. L: 7.1691. C: 8.1691. Designed by Philippe Cochois. Captured 5.1702 by the English.

Dorade Dunkirk.

Dimensions & tons: 66ft 0in x 14ft 0in x 8ft 0in (21.44 x 4.55 x 2.60m). 50 tons. Draught 9ft (2.92m). Men: 40 (10/30/) +2 officers, later 45 in war, 30 peace

Guns: 8 x 4pdrs. From 1696: 4 in war: 4 x 4pdrs. 8 from 1698: 8 x 4pdrs. 10 from 1700: 10 x 4pdrs. 6 from 1704: 6 x 3pdrs.

K: 1691. L: 12.1691. C: 1.1692. Designed by Jean-Nicolas Houwens. Was in company with *Commode* (below) when she was captured 5.1693 and escaped just in time. Refitted 11.1698 at Brest and handed over there 11.1698 to the *Compagnie Royale de St Domingue*. Returned 1699. Struck 1704 or 1705 at Toulon. Sold 1710 for commercial use.

FLÈCHE Class. 6–8 guns. In 1692 *Vedette* was credited to Jean-Nicolas Houwens while *Flèche* was credited to Philippe Cochois. In 1696 both were credited to Cochois.

An interpretation by László Veres of a French *barque longue* of about 8 guns and 60ft length, based on Guéroult du Pas. In size and characteristics, it is an approximation for a vessel like the *Vedette* of 1691.

Dimensions & tons: 60ft 0in x 14ft 0in x 7ft 0in (19.49 x 4.55 x 2.27m). 50 tons (60 from 1696). Draught 7½ft (2.44m). Men: 40 (10/30/) +2 officers, later 40 in war, 35 peace

Guns: 6 x 4pdrs in *Flèche* and 8 x 4pdrs in *Vedette*. From 1696: 4 in war in *Flèche*: 4 x 4pdrs; and 6 in war in *Vedette*: 6 x 4pdrs.

Flèche Dunkirk.
K: early 1691. L: 7.1691. C: 8.1691. Participated in the Lagos campaign of 1693. Damaged 9.1697 by grounding on the Dogger Bank, took refuge in the Meuse where she was captured by an English frigate.

Vedette Dunkirk.
K: 1691. L: 12.1691. C: 1.1692. Struck 1697. May then have served as a *chaloupe de découverte* (exploration launch) until 1707.

NYMPHE Class. 8 guns. Designed by Guillon.
Dimensions & tons: 60ft 0in x 15ft 4in x 7ft 0in (19.49 x 4.98 x 2.27m). 60 tons. Draught 7ft (2.27m). Men: 60 in war, 40 peace
Guns: 8 in war: 8 x 4pdrs. *Nymphe* from 1699: 10 x 4pdrs. *Prompte* from 1699: 12 x 4pdrs

Nymphe Dunkirk.
K: 7.1692. L: 9.1692. C: 10.1692. Captured 6.1696 by men from Ostend, retaken 8.1696 by the French. Struck 1699 at Dunkirk.

Prompte Dunkirk.
K: 7.1692. L: 9.1692. C: 10.1692. Struck 1699 at Dunkirk.

UTILE. 8 guns. Designed and built by Pierre Masson.
Dimensions & tons: 69ft 4in x 16ft 6in x 6ft 6in (22.52 x 5.36 x 2.11m). 80 tons. Draught 8½ft (2.76m). Men: 35 in war, 25 peace
Guns: 8 in war (6 peace): 8 x 4pdrs.

Utile Bayonne.
K: 1690. L: 1691. C: 10.1691. Unserviceable 1.1702 and hulked at Toulon. Used as gunnery school from 1706, condemned at Toulon 15.12.1710 and ordered sold 24.12.1710.

The barque *Subtile* (1682, 100 tons) was classed as a *barque longue* in 1691 and 1692. She is listed in Chapter 12.

PURCHASED VESSELS (1691). Two merchant vessels or privateers, one built recently at Dieppe and an older one built at Dunkirk, were added to the navy in 1691 as *barques longues*.

Flatteuse. Built 1690 at Dieppe as *Saint Pierre* by Blondel, purchased 9.1691 and renamed *Flatteuse* (*Flateuse*) 10.1691.
Dimensions & tons: 42ft 0in x 12ft 0in x 5ft 0in (13.64 x 3.90 x 1.62m). 20 tons. Draught 5ft (1.62m). Men: 20 in war, 16 peace, +1 officer.
Guns: 2 in war: 2 x 1pdrs.
Loaned as a St Malo privateer 1695–97, struck 1697 at Le Havre.

Agathe. Built 1675–76 at Dunkirk by Hendrick. Purchased 1691, previous names *Chasseur de Grenezé* and *Chasseur de Dunkerque*. Grenezé was the French name for Guernsey.
Dimensions & tons: 54ft 0in x 13ft 6in x 5ft 6in (17.54 x 4.39 x 1.79m). 35 tons. Draught 5ft (1.62m). Men: 19 +1 officer.
Guns: 6 (4 in 9.1692).
Last mentioned 5.1693 at Brest.

Ex-DUTCH PRIZES (1691–1693). *Folâtre* was captured in December 1691, *Flessingoise* was captured in late 1692, and *Dieppoise*, whose origins are unknown but might have been Dutch or Spanish, was captured in March 1693.

Folâtre Flushing.
Dimensions & tons: dimensions unknown. 40 tons. Draught 7½ft (2.44m). Men: 45 +4 officers.
Guns: 8.
Built 1682. Last mentioned 1692, may have been lost at La Hougue.

Flessingoise Flushing or Dunkirk.
Dimensions & tons: 60ft 0in x 15ft 6in x 5ft 6in (19.49 x 5.04 x 1.79m). 40 tons. Draught 9ft (2.92m). Men: 35 in war, 30 peace
Guns: 8 x 4pdrs.
Last mentioned 4.1697 at Port Louis.

Dieppoise Builder unknown.
Specifications unknown.
Placed on sale 5.1693 at Dunkirk, having been found to be very bad under sail.

Ex-ENGLISH MERCANTILE AND PRIVATEER PRIZES (1690–1694). Eight vessels were captured separately and added to the French Navy between 1690 and 1694.

Saint François Le Havre.
Dimensions & tons: dimensions unknown. 20 tons. Draught 5ft (1.62m). Men: 20 (7/13/) +2 officers.
Guns: 4.
Built 1670 (or 1680), designed by Étienne Salicon. Captured 1690. Renamed *Petit Saint François* 1691 and *Lunette* 3.1692. Struck 3.1693. Given to Sieur Sevré Du Tertre, from St Malo, as a replacement for his own vessel, lost in the King's service along the English coast.

Constante. Vessel of unknown origin put into service 10.8.1691 at Dunkirk. Specifications unknown except for crew of 40 men +2 officers. Not mentioned after crew transferred to *Biche* 16.8.1691. May have been the English ketch *Talbot* taken by a French squadron 12.7.1691 while escorting a West Indies-bound convoy and retaken by the English 10.11.1693. The 94-ton *Talbot* was built by Taylor at Cuckolds Point in 1691, measured 62ft (English) x 18ft x 10ft, and carried 10 guns.

Gramon or **Grand Moon** England

Dimensions & tons: 63ft 10in, 56ft 4in x 16ft 11in x 7ft 0in (20.73, 18.30 x 5.50 x 2.27m, English measurements in French feet). 103 tons (bm).
Guns: 6 in RN service.
Captured 1691, possibly ex-English *Great Monck*. Retaken 11.1691 by HMS *Chester* (50) and became HMS *Germoon* [*Prize*], capsized after careening and sank 15.7.1700 in Jamaica.

Volage England.
Dimensions & tons: dimensions unknown. 40 tons. Draught 5ft (1.62m). Men: 45 +4 officers
Guns: 8.
Built 1690 (possibly in Le Havre). Captured late 1691. Retaken 5.1692 by the English in the Channel.

Fleur de la Mer England.
Dimensions & tons: 50ft 0in x 12ft 0in x 6ft 0in (16.24 x 3.90 x 1.95m). 35 tons. Draught 7½ft (2.44m). Men: 30 in war, 25 peace
Guns: 4 in war (4 peace): 4 x 4pdrs. 6 x 4pdrs from 1698
Captured 7.1692, ex-English *Sea Flower*. Captured 7.1702 by Flemish privateers.

Prude England.
Dimensions & tons: 43ft 0in x 13ft 5in x 5ft 0in (13.97 x 4.36 x 1.62m). 30 tons. Draught 6ft (1.95m). Men: 50 in war, 36 peace
Guns: 6 in war: 6 x 4pdrs.
Captured 5.1693 by Sieur Bassanant, ex-English privateer. Named 21.5.1693. Struck 1696 or 1697 at Port Louis (may have been taken by an English privateer).

Hirondelle de Falmouth Falmouth.
Dimensions & tons: 42ft 0in x 22ft 0in x 4ft 9in (13.64 x 7.15 x 1.54m). 23 tons. Draught 5½ft (1.79m).
Guns: unknown.
Captured 10.1693, ex-English *Swallow*. Last mentioned 1696 at Port Louis.

Paquebot England.
Dimensions & tons: 64ft 0in x 18ft 0in x 9ft 0in (20.79 x 5.85 x 2.92m). 90 tons (100 from 1701). Draught 8½ft (2.76m). Men: 50 in war, 28 peace
Guns: 10 in war (2 peace): 10 x 4pdrs. 2 x 4pdrs from 1704.
Built 1687–89. Captured 1694. From 1701 used as service craft at Brest. On escort and patrol duty along the north coast of Brittany in 1702. BU 1705.

6th **DUNKIRK GROUP** (1692–1693). 4–8 guns. The two ships of the *Volage* class, below, were part of this group.

Fine Dunkirk.
Dimensions & tons: 60ft 0in x 15ft 0in x 7ft 0in (19.49 x 4.87 x 2.27m). 60 tons. Draught 7½ft (2.44m). Men: 50 in war, 40 peace
Guns: 8 in war: 8 x 4pdrs. 10 x 4pdrs in 1700.
K: 11.1692. L: 2.1693. C: 3.1693. Designed by Jean-Nicolas Houwens. Rebuilt as new 1698 at Brest by Jean-Pierre Brun, handed over 11.1698 to the *Compagnie Royale de St Domingue*. Seized 7.1699 by the Spanish in the Antilles, returned late 1699 and sold 1700 at Brest.

Farouche ?Dunkirk.
Specifications unknown.
K: 1692. L: 2.1693. C: 3.1693. Lent as a privateer in 1694–95 to LG Victor Marie d'Estrées, under the command of EV Michel de Bellisle. Captured by the English 1695–96.

Fouine Dunkirk.
Dimensions & tons: 62ft 0in x 14ft 6in x 5ft 6in (20.14 x 4.71 x 1.79m). 50 tons. Draught 8ft (2.60m). Men: 50 in war, 40 peace
Guns: 8 in war: 8 x 4pdrs. 12 x 4pdrs in 1699.
K: 2.1693. L: 5.1693. C: 6.1693. Designed by Guillon. Reportedly wrecked 9.1697 off Dunkirk but back in service 1698. Out of service 1.1699, struck 1699 at Dunkirk.

Commode Dunkirk.
Dimensions & tons: 62ft 0in x 16ft 0in x 5ft 3in (20.14 x 5.20 x 1.71m). 45 tons. Draught 7½ft (2.44m). Men: 45 in war, 42 peace
Guns: 8 in war (6 peace): 8 x 4pdrs.
K: 2.1693. L: 5.1693. C: 6.1693. Designed by Guillon. Lent as a privateer to GM de Belleville L'Étendart, captured by the English 9.1696.

Fortune Dunkirk.
Dimensions & tons: 53ft 0in, 42ft 0in x 13ft 0in x 6ft 0in (17.22,

---

One of the earliest known plans of a French corvette-type vessel is preserved in the Danish archives, although without any identification or date. However, it does have a ruler marked in French feet, so despite the topside appearance of a larger ship, it scales out to a length of just under 50ft and a breadth of 13ft. To emphasise its misleading size, Ian McLaughlan redrew this plan with a human figure added to give an empirical measure of proportion. The draught probably dates from the 1690s, and its dimensions would fit the *Discrète* of 1693. The small ports are for oars.

13.64 x 4.22 x 1.95m). 80 tons. Draught 6ft (1.95m). Men: 35 in war, 25 peace

Guns: 6 in war: 6 x 4pdrs.

K: 5.1693. L: 5.8.1693. C: 8.1693. Sold 10.1696 at Toulon, struck 1697.

Discrète Dunkirk.

Dimensions & tons: 48ft 0in x 13ft 0in x 6ft 0in (15.59 x 4.22 x 1.95m). 50 tons. Draught 7ft (2.27m). From 1699: 57ft 0in x 14ft 0in x 5ft 6in (18.52 x 4.55 x 1.79m). 40 tons. Draught 6ft (1.95m). Men: 40 in war, 35 peace

Guns: 4 in war: 4 x 4pdrs. 6 x 4pdrs in 1699, 8 x 3pdrs in 1702.

K: 5.1693. L: 15.8.1693. C: 8.1693. Designed by Guillon. Condemned 1699 and hulked at Dunkirk. Sold 1702, privateer 1702–4.

Allumette Dunkirk.

Dimensions & tons: 47ft 0in x 11ft 6in x 6ft 0in (15.27 x 3.74 x 1.95m). 50 tons. Draught 5½ft (1.79m). From 1699: as *Discrète* in 1699. Men: 40 in war, 35 peace

Guns: 4 in war: 4 x 4pdrs. 6 x 4pdrs in 1699.

K: 6.1693. L: 9.1693. C: 1693. Designed by Jean-Nicolas Houwens. Struck 1699 at Dunkirk.

Galante Dunkirk.

Dimensions & tons: 57ft 0in (keel) x 16ft 6in (18.51 x 5.39m).
Guns: unknown.

K: 1693. L: 10.1693. C: 11.1693. Lost or struck in 1694 or 1695, may have been one of the two corvettes destroyed 5.1694 by the explosion of the fireship *Chasseur* near Conquet.

VOLAGE Class. 8 guns. Designed by René Levasseur. These ships had five gunports per side amidships spaced 5ft apart and measuring 1ft 8in wide and 1ft 4in high, the forward one being 11ft from the bow and the after one 21ft from the stern. They were rigged with two masts and a bowsprit and had a cabin for the captain.

Dimensions & tons: 63ft 6in, 55ft 8in x 16ft x 7ft 6in (20.63, 18.08 x 18.08 x 5.20 x 2.44m). 60 tons. Draught 7ft/8½ft (2.27/2.76m). Men: 40 in war, later 50 in war, 30 peace

Guns: 8 in war: 8 x 4pdrs. From 1699: 12 in war (8 peace): 12 x 4pdrs. 10 x 4pdrs from 1704.

Volage Dunkirk.

K: 11.1692. L: 2.1693. C: 3.1693. Re-classed as a *frégate légère* in 1702–3, refitted at Dunkirk 11–12.1702. Hauled out 7.1706 and rebuilt (see below).

Grenade Dunkirk.

K: 1.1693. L: 3.1693. C: 4.1693. Struck 1694 or 1695, may have been handed over to the navy of James II.

RUSÉE. 4 guns.

Dimensions & tons: 47ft 0in x 12ft 0in x 5ft 0in (15.27 x 3.90 x 1.62m). 35 tons. Draught 7ft (2.27m). Men: 36 in war, 8 peace, +1 officer

Guns: 4 in war (2 peace): 4 x 2pdrs.

Rusée Calais.

Built 1695. Designed by 'Jean' [Jean-Nicolas Houwens?]. Captured 8.1705 by the Dutch, bought back 1706 by the King and returned to service. Struck 1709 at Le Havre.

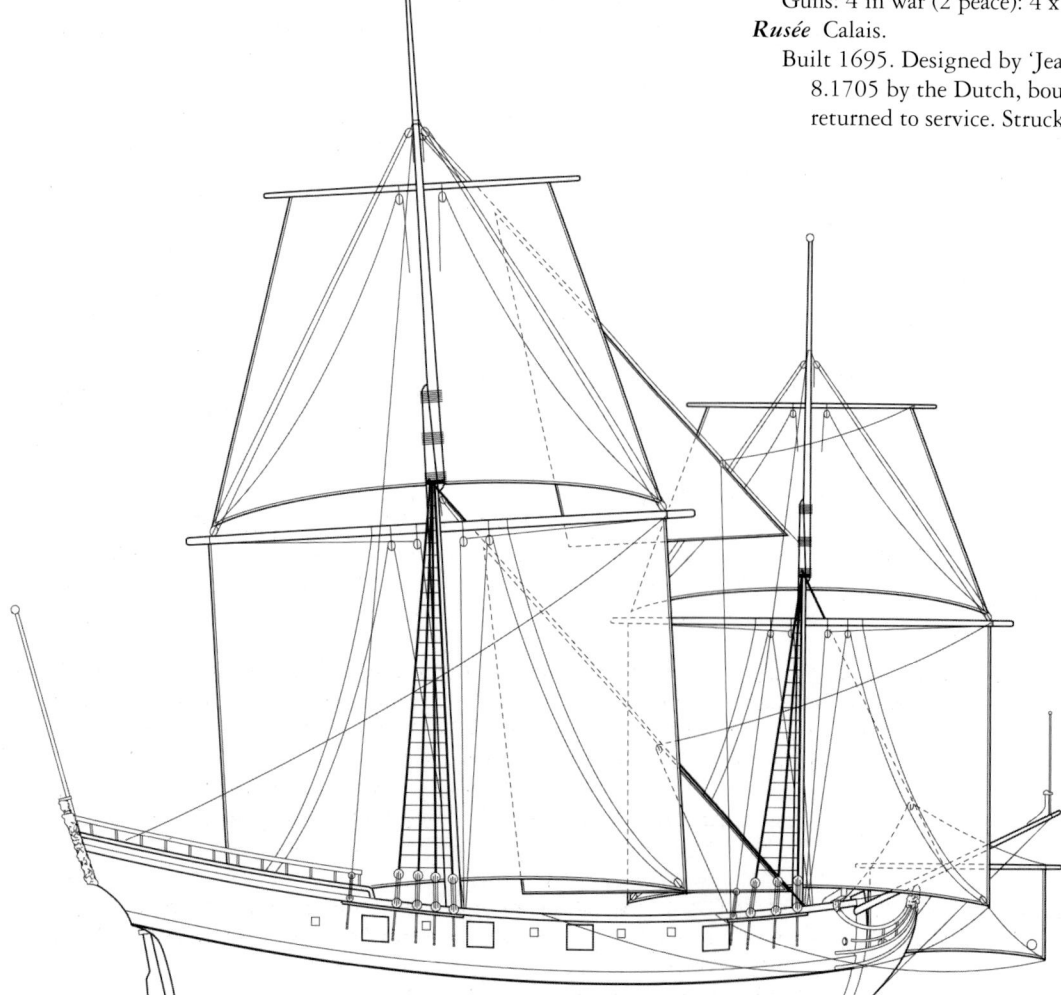

This drawing is an interpretation by László Veres of a French *barque longue* like the *Volage* Class of 1693. The overall appearance is based on an illustration in Guéroult du Pas.

Ex-SPANISH PRIZE (1695). The Ostend (Spanish) privateer *Santa Ana* was captured in 1695 and entered French service as *Sainte Anne*.
  Dimensions & tons: 45ft 6in x 13ft 0in x 5ft 0in (14.78 x 4.22 x 1.62m). 30 tons. Draught 5½ft (1.79m). Men: 30 in war, 26 peace
  Guns: 4 in war (2 peace): 4 x 2pdrs.
Sainte Anne Ostend.
  Built 1690 by Le Fèvre. Struck 10.1696 at Le Havre and sold.

Ex-ENGLISH MERCANTILE OR PRIVATEER PRIZE (1697). The English *Society*, probably from Guernsey (Grenezé in French), was captured on 23 August 1697.
  Dimensions & tons: 50ft 0in x 14ft 4in x 6ft 0in (16.24 x 4.66 x 1.95m). 30 tons. Draught 7½ft (2.44m). Men: 30 in war, 25 peace, +1 officer.
  Guns: 6 x 4pdrs, 4 x 3pdrs. From 1699: 6 in war (4 peace): 6 x 4pdrs.
Societé de Grenezé ?Guernsey.
  Built 1697. Hospital ship, judged 'heavy' at Brest 1699, struck and sold there 1699.

Ex-DUTCH PRIZE (1697). The Dutch *Marie* was captured in around 1697 and may have been new when taken.
  Dimensions & tons: 40ft 0in x 11ft 6in x 6ft 6in (12.99 x 3.74 x 2.11m). 20 tons. Draught 6ft (1.95m). Men: 25 in war, 20 peace, +1 officer.
  Guns: 4 in war (4 peace): 4 x 4pdrs.
Barlonome Maria Flushing.
  Rated as a service craft (a large *bugalet*) until she appeared on the fleet list as a corvette or *barque longue* in 1702 and was renamed *Barlonome* in 1703. She was listed as suitable for escort duty in 1704–6, then became a service craft at Brest in 1706 and was last mentioned in 1707.

The War of the Spanish Succession saw another surge in the construction of *barques longues* or corvettes, although it ended in 1707–8 with the cessation of all new construction for the King's account because of financial distress, well before the war ended in 1713.

CURIEUSE. 6 guns. Designed and built by Philippe Cochois.
  Dimensions & tons: 50ft 0in, 45ft 0in x 11ft 0in x 5ft 6in (16.24, 14.62 x 3.57 x 1.79m). 60 tons. Draught 6ft 4in (2.06m). Men: 30 in war, 15 peace, +1 officer
  Guns: 6 in war (2 peace): 6 x 3pdrs. 6 x 2pdrs in 1704.
Curieuse Le Havre.
  K: 12.1701. L: 2.1702. C: 3.1702. This small vessel was assigned to Toulon by 1706, when it was noted that she could only serve in the summer. In 1707 she was called a *double-chaloupe* and in 1708 her purpose was stated to be carrying orders during the summer. Wrecked 2.1710 at Port Vendres.

Ex-AUSTRIAN PRIZE (1702). A vessel named *Charlotte* was captured in 1702, probably from Imperial Austrian forces, and briefly served the French under the same name. She was removed from service and struck at Toulon later in 1702 and was probably sold around July 1703.

The *flûtes Arbre d'Olivier* and *Justice* were listed as corvettes or *barques longues* for one year only in 1701.

PURCHASED AND ACQUIRED VESSELS (1701–1703). Four privately-owned vessels were added to the French navy as *barques longues* in 1701–3.
Gentille Built 1695 at Dieppe to a design by Vasselin. Abandoned by her mercantile crew at Faro and taken to Algiers where the King sent a *tartane* to bring her to Toulon. Purchased 14.12.1701 by the King from Sieur Chaumel.
  Dimensions & tons: 60ft 0in x 18ft 0in x 6ft 6in (19.49 x 5.85 x 2.11m). 60 tons. Draught 8½ft (2.76m). Men: 40 in war, 25 peace
  Guns: 10 in war: 10 x 4pdrs.
  Sent from Ancona to Toulon 5.1702 in need of major repairs. Sold back to Sieur Chaumel 30.8.1703.
Postillon. Origin unknown. Purchased 7.1701 and fitted out 8.1701 in St Domingue by Joseph de Bouloc, the governor of Grenada.
  Dimensions & tons: 63ft 0in x 18ft 0in x 7ft 4in (20.46 x 5.85 x 2.38m).
  Guns: 10 in English service.
  Captured 10.7.1702 by HMS *Worcester* (50), became HMS *Postillon Prize*. Bilged and sank 18.5.1709 in Ostend harbour.
Diamant. Built at St Martin de Ré, Île de Ré, and acquired in 1702 or 1703.
  Dimensions & tons: 40ft 0in x 14ft 0in x 6ft 0in (12.99 x 4.55 x 1.95m). 25 tons. Draught 7ft (2.27m). Men: 25 in war, 6 peace, +1 officer
  Guns: 4 in war (2 peace): 4 x 4pdrs.
  Struck 1704 at Rochefort.
Victoire. Built at Dunkirk in 1696 and acquired in 1702 or 1703.
  Dimensions & tons: 59ft 6in x 16ft 6in x 7ft 6in (19.33 x 5.36 x 2.44m). 60 tons. Draught 9ft (2.92m). Men: 50 in war, 40 peace, +2 officers
  Guns: 8 in war (6 peace): 8 x 4pdrs.
  Capsized 8.1703 in the bay of Avranches during an English attack, restored to service. Struck 1704 or 1705 at Brest.

Ex-ENGLISH MERCANTILE PRIZES (1703) Two captured English merchantmen were added to the French Navy at Toulon in 1703.
Railleuse England.
  Dimensions & tons: 60ft 0in x 16ft 6in x 7ft 0in (19.49 x 5.36 x 2.27m). 60 tons. Draught 8ft (2.60m). Men: 25 in war, 15 peace
  Guns: 6 in war (4 peace): 6 x 4pdrs.
  Built 1695. Taken by a French privateer and purchased 1703. Struck 8.1704 and placed on sale at Toulon but continued to be used by the Navy until 5.1707.
Abel Isaac England.
  Dimensions & tons: 66ft 0in x 17ft 0in x 6ft 10in (21.44 x 5.52 x 2.22m). 50 tons. Draught 7½ft (2.44m). Men: 50 in war, 25 peace, +1 officer.
  Guns: 8 in war (8 peace): 8 x 4pdrs.
  Built 1703. Captured 1703. Sometimes called *Bel Isaac*. Her function was stated in 1707 to be carrying orders. Struck 1708 at Toulon, captured c.7.1709 in the Mediterranean by the enemy (reported 7.8.1709).

Ex-ENGLISH NAVAL PRIZES (1702–1703). HMS *Prohibition* was captured on 25 August 1702 by an 18-gun French privateer off Land's End and purchased for the French Navy in November 1702. HMS *Shark* was captured on 10 April 1703 by a French 40-gun ship in the Channel off Beachy Head while chasing a French merchantman and renamed *Requin*. Both of these early English sloops were of the *Bonetta* group, lightly armed two- or three-masted sloops with square rigs, fitted to row with 12 oars and intended primarily to enforce the ban on the export of wool. The French generally assessed them as bad under sail and bad ships overall, though they acknowledged that *Prohibition* might be good for commerce raiding or for convoy duty.
Prohibition Sheerness.

Ord: 1.7.1699. L: 5.9.1699. C: 1699.

Dimensions & tons: 56ft 0in, 45ft 4in x 14ft 9in x 5ft 4in (18.19, 14.72 x 4.79 x 1.73m). 50 tons. Draught 7ft (2.27m). Men: 50 in war, 40 peace

Guns: 4 in war: 4 x 2pdrs. From 1707: 10 in war (6 peace): 10 x 3pdrs. Re-classed as a *frégate légère* in 1704–5. Struck 1708 at Brest.

Requin Deptford.

Ord: 1.7.1699. L: 5.9.1699. C: 1699.

Dimensions & tons: 56ft 0in, 45ft 0in x 15ft 0in x 6ft 6in (18.19 x 4.87 x 2.11m). 50 tons. Draught 6ft (1.95m). Men: 50 in war, 10 peace

Guns: 6 in war (4 peace): 6 x 4pdrs. 8 x 4pdrs from 1706, 6 x 3.5pdrs from 1707.

Struck late 1708 at Le Havre.

FINE. 8 guns. Designed and built by Blondel.

Dimensions & tons: 56ft 0in x 15ft 0in x 5ft 4in (18.19 x 4.87 x 1.73m). 50 tons. Draught 7½ft (2.44m). Men: 50 in war, 25 peace.

Guns: 8 in war (6 peace): 8 x 3pdrs. 6 x 3½pdrs in 1707–8.

Fine Dieppe.

K: 9.1702. L: 11.1702. C: 12.1702. Capsized 1703 at Brest, but refloated and returned to service 1704. Was on convoy duty in 1708. Struck 12.1712 at Le Havre and placed on sale there 2.1713.

ACTIVE Class. 2 guns. Designed and built by Blaise Pangalo. Carried 14 pairs of sweeps with probably two men per oar. Described in 1706 as '*chaloupes* with 28 oars built to chase the small privateers of Jersey'. Three similar vessels classified as *bâtiments interrompus* and built at Le Havre and Lorient (see Chapter 12), *Résolu*, *Actif*, and *Félouque*, were described in 1707 as 'good under oars and suitable for use against Jersey privateers'.

Dimensions & tons (all in 1704): 50ft 0in x 10ft 0in x 4ft 6in (16.24 x 3.25 x 1.46m). 15 tons. Draught 4ft (1.30m). Men: 65, +1 officer.

Guns: 2 x 2pdrs, + 6 *pierriers*.

Active Brest Dyd.

K: 1703. L: 1703. C: 1703. Struck 1709 at Brest.

Insensée Brest Dyd.

K: 1703. L: 1703. C: 1703. Struck 1709 at Brest.

Turbulente Brest Dyd.

K: 1703. L: 1703. C: 1703. Struck 1709 at Brest.

GRACIEUSE. 2 guns. Designed by J Drouillart. Both of Drouillart's corvettes were failures, this one being deleted in two years and *Diligente* (below) being almost immediately rebuilt by a different shipwright.

Dimensions & tons: 46ft 0in x 13ft 0in x 5ft 6in (14.94 x 4.22 x 1.79m). 35 tons. Draught 5½ft (1.79m). Men: 30 in war, 20 peace, +1 officer.

Guns: 2 in war (2 peace): 2 x 2pdrs.

Gracieuse Dieppe.

K: 4.1703. L: 6.1703. C: 7.1703. Considered a poor sailer. Struck 1705.

DILIGENTE. 6 guns. Designed by J Drouillart. A *Diligente* belonging to the most Christian (French) King was used at Cadiz in 1705 for the service of the Catholic (Spanish) King at the latter's expense; it is not clear whether this was the same vessel.

Dimensions & tons: 56ft 0in x 16ft 0in x 6ft 0in (18.19 x 5.20 x 1.95m). 50 tons. Draught 6½ft (2.11m). From 1707 after reconstruction: 53ft x 15ft 0in x 6ft 6in (17.22 x 4.87 x 2.11m). 50 tons. Draught 7ft (2.27m). Men: 50 in war, 25 peace

Guns: 6 in war (4 peace): 6 x 4pdrs.

Diligente Dieppe.

K: 4.1703. L: 6.1703. C: 7.1703. Rebuilt 1704 at Le Havre by Philippe Cochois (launched 24.8.1704). Classed as a felucca at Toulon 1713 (see *Sirène* in chapter 12), struck there 1718.

GAILLARDE. This corvette was built at Port Royal (Acadia). Her specifications are unknown except that she was manned by 37 seamen and 1 officer.

K: 1703. L: early 1704. C: June 1704.

Lost on the North American coast, details unknown.

MOUCHE. 8 guns. Designed and built by Laurent Hélie. Ordered on 2 January 1704 with royal authorisation specifically to meet CFL René Duguay-Trouin's requirement for a ship with an English appearance to be used for reconnoitering missions.

Dimensions & tons: (probably) 50ft 0in x 15ft 8in x 6ft 2in (16.24 x 5.09 x 2.00m). Tons unknown. Men: 54 +1 officer.

Guns: 8.

Mouche Brest Dyd.

K: 2.1704. L: 4.1704. C: 5.1704. Lent as a privateer to CFL René Duguay-Trouin who funded the construction. Commissioned 15.7.1704. Departed Brest 25.7.1704 with *Jason* and *Auguste* (both 54), separated from them in bad weather, and captured 12.8.1704 by HM Ships *Revenge* (72) and *Falmouth* (54) at the entrance to the Channel.

MISCELLANEOUS PRIZE (1704). Privateer corvette designed by Philippe Cochois, captured *c*.1703 by an unknown adversary (possibly the English) and recaptured in July 1704 by the French.

Dimensions & tons: 52ft 0in x 16ft 0in x 7ft 0in (16.89 x 5.20 x 2.27m). 60 tons. Draught 8½ft (2.76m). Men: 50 in war, 40 peace, +2 officers

Guns: 8 in war (6 peace): 8 x 2pdrs. 8 x 4pdrs from 1708.

Marie-Françoise Le Havre.

Built 1700. Lent as a privateer in 1704 to CV Marc-Antoine de Saint-Pol Hécourt, as part of a squadron of six vessels, 1704. Wrecked 12.1705 near Lorient, raised and rebuilt 1707 at Brest. On convoy duty in 1708–9. Lent as a privateer in 1711–12 for transporting alcohol in Brittany. Struck 10.1718 at Port Louis and BU. Not to be confused with the 120-ton *gabarre* of the same name built at Brest in 1714.

Ex-ENGLISH MERCANTILE PRIZES (1705–1706). The French naval ports of Toulon, Le Havre, Port Louis (near Lorient) and Brest each acquired one captured English merchantman for naval use during these two years.

Joseph Galle England.

Dimensions & tons: 63ft 0in x 15ft 6in x 8ft 0in (20.46 x 5.04 x 2.60m). 40 tons. Draught 7ft (2.27m). Men: 30 in war, 18 peace

Guns: 10 in war (6 peace): 10 x 3pdrs.

Captured late 1705. Mediocre under sail. Struck 1706 at Toulon.

Cheval Volant Guernsey.

Dimensions & tons: 45ft 0in x 10ft 0in x 5ft 0in (14.62 x 3.25 x 1.62m). 30 tons. Draught 5½ft (1.79m). Men: 30 in war, 8 peace, +1 officer

Guns: 4 in war: 4 x 2pdrs.

Built 1703. Captured 3.1706 (?), probably ex-*Flying Horse*. Struck 1709 at Le Havre.

Jacques Galère. The English *Jacques Galley*, probably from Jersey, was captured 5.1706. 4 x 2pdrs, 40 men +1 officer. Called a brigantine. Struck 1708 at Port Louis.

Marie de Gerzé. A captured vessel named *Marie* probably from Jersey was in service at Brest from 13 September 1706 to 26 October 1706 under the name *Marie de Gerzé*. (Gerzé is a French name for Jersey.) Struck in November or December 1706 at Brest.

Ex-ENGLISH NAVAL PRIZE (1706). HMS *Ferret* was captured on 3 June 1706 by six French galley privateers off Gravelines and became the French Navy's *Furet*. *Ferret* was one of the first English sloops that had enough size and firepower to serve as effective warships. *Ferret* and her sister *Weazle* were designed to 'cruise on the coast of this Kingdom' and to 'row with oars'.

Dimensions & tons: 66ft 0in x 18ft 0in x 6ft 0in (21.44 x 5.85 x 1.95m). 50 tons. Draught 8½ft (2.76m). Men: 70 in war, 30 peace

Guns: 10 in war (6 peace): 10 x 3pdrs.

Furet Edward Dummer, Blackwall.
 Ord: 7.3.1704. L: 9.9.1704. C: 18.12.1704. Captured 7.1707 by Dutch privateers. Reappeared in the January 1708 fleet list (probably recaptured), struck during 1708 at Dunkirk.

TROMPETTE. 6 guns. Designed and built by Blaise Pangalo. Construction proposed by Brest on 22 February 1706, ship named on 31 March 1706. Described in 1707 as good for commerce raiding and in 1712 as good for escort duty.

Dimensions & tons: 56ft 0in x 14ft 6in x 5ft 6in (18.19 x 4.71 x 1.79m). 35 tons. Draught 6½ft (2.11m). Men: 50 in war, 40 peace, +1 officer.

Guns: 6 in war (4 peace): 6 x 3pdrs.

Trompette Brest Dyd.
 K: 3.1706. L: 5.1706. C: 6.1706. Lent as a privateer in 1711–12 for transporting alcohol in Brittany. Unserviceable 6.1716 at Brest, condemned 6.1717, and BU by year end.

VOLAGE. 8 guns. A rebuilding of the *barque longue Volage* of 1693. Designed by René Levasseur.

Dimensions & tons: 63ft 0in x 17ft 6in x 7ft 4in (20.46 x 5.68 x 2.38m). 66 tons. Draught 8ft (2.60m). Men: 60 in war, 20 peace, +1 officer.

Guns: 8 in war (4 peace): 8 x 3.5pdrs (4pdrs from 1709).

Volage Dunkirk.
 K: 7.1706. L: 9.1706. C: 10.1706. Lent as a privateer 3–8.1709 to GM Desgrieux. Struck at Brest late 1709.

HERMINE. 6 guns. Designed and built by Laurent Hélie. Named on 27 October 1706. Listed in 1708 as a *bâtiment interrompu* (unclassified vessel) and as suitable for commerce raiding. Restored to the list of corvettes in January 1709 and listed in 1709 and 1710 as good for convoy duty.

Dimensions & tons: 58ft 0in x 14ft 0in x 7ft 0in (18.84 x 4.55 x 2.27m). 35 tons. Draught 7ft (2.27m). Men: 50 in war, 40 peace.

Guns: 6 in war (4 peace): 6 x 4pdrs.

Hermine Brest Dyd.
 K: 10.1706. L: 1.1707. C: early 1707. Captured by the British 1711.

PURCHASED AND ACQUIRED VESSELS (1706–1707). Two vessels of unknown origin were added to the navy as *barques longues* in 1706–7.

Saint Louis. A vessel possibly of this name was purchased and put into service 10.1706 at Cap Français, St Domingue. The *Saint Louis* was removed from service 2.1713 at Cap Français.

Saint Aubin. Acquired 1707. 30 tons, 50 men, 8 guns +2 *pierriers*. Loaned 8.1707 for commerce raiding at St Malo, then struck from the Navy. Still in use 1709.

LEVRETTE Class. 8 guns. Designed by René Levasseur. *Agile* was listed as *Aigle* in 1707, probably in error. All four were listed in 1708 as *bâtiments interrompus* (unclassified vessels), *Agile* being noted as good for commerce raiding. All but *Agile* (lost) were restored to the list of corvettes in January 1709, the last year in which they were listed.

Dimensions & tons: 64ft 0in x 17ft 6in x 7ft 0in (20.79 x 5.68 x 2.27m). 50 tons. Draught 9ft (2.92m). Men: 70 in war, 30 peace, +2/3 officers.

Guns: 8 in war (6 peace): 8 x 4pdrs.

Levrette Dunkirk.
 K: 12.1706. L: 16.3.1707. C: 5.1707. Lent as a privateer at Dunkerque 1708. Struck 1709 at Dunkirk, either lost or sold.

Agile Dunkirk.
 K: 1.1707. L: 17.3.1707. C: 5.1707. Lent as a privateer at Dunkerque 1708. Grounded 1.1708 on the shore of the dunes near Dunkirk and lost.

Cigale Dunkirk.
 K: 12.1706. L: 19.3.1707. C: 5.1707. Lent as a privateer at Dunkerque 1708. Struck 1709 at Dunkirk, either lost or sold.

Vipère Dunkirk.
 K: 1.1707. L: 24.3.1707. C: 5.1707. Lent as a privateer at Dunkerque 1708. Struck 1709 at Dunkirk, either lost or sold.

Ex-DUTCH PRIZES (1707–1709). Two vessels captured from the Dutch, one ex-French, were briefly used at Brest and in the Channel during 1708–9.

Catherine. Formerly the *Katrijn* from Middelburg, she was captured and taken to Brest by *Gloire* and *Astrée*, two of the King's vessels lent as privateers to CV René Duguay-Trouin. Listed at Brest in 7.1708, she was adjudicated '*de bonne prise*' by the *Amiral de France* on 28.1.1709. She had 8 guns and a crew of 44 men and 3 officers. For reconnoitering missions, Duguay-Trouin was always looking for ships of foreign appearance, and as *Mouche* had been lost, he arranged for this prize to be lent to him as a privateer. Renamed *Catherine*, put under command of Nicolas Daniel de Pradel, Duguay-Trouin's first cousin, she operated within his squadron of nine vessels during two campaigns in 1708. Used as coast guard late 1708 and early 1709. She was wrecked 3.1709 in a storm off the Lizard

Prompte. This vessel, built at Calais in 1706 as the French privateer *Subtile*, was captured in 1708 by Dutch privateers from Flushing. She was recaptured in 1709 by the French and after a brief period of naval service was returned 9.1709 to her former owner at Calais.

AGATHE Class. 8 guns. Designed and built by Pierre Masson. *Étoile* named on 11 August 1708.

Dimensions & tons: 66ft 0in x 16ft 0in x 8ft 0in (21.44 x 5.20 x 2.60m). 75 tons. Draught 7ft (2.27m). Men: 70 in war, 20 peace, +3 officers.

Guns: 8 in war (4 peace): 8 x 4pdrs.

Agathe Rochefort Dyd.
 K: 5.1708. L: 8.1708. C: 1708. Struck 11.1718 at Rochefort.

Étoile Rochefort Dyd.
 K: 5.1708. L: 8.1708. C: 1708. Struck 11.1718 at Rochefort and sold.

BARQUE LONGUE. This 80-ton vessel with a generic name was designed by Le Roux and built slowly at Mobile in the colony of

Louisiana for the governor there, Jean-Baptiste Le Moyne de Bienville.
K: 1702. L: c.1710. C: ?1712.
May have become the traversier *Heureux*, which was in service in Louisiana in 1714–17 (see Chapter 13).

PURCHASED AND ACQUIRED VESSELS (1708–1710). These two newly-built merchant vessels, one from Marseille and one from Majorca, were described as good for coast guard duty in war and for commerce in the Mediterranean. *Saint Jean-Gaëtan* was purchased by the King from the chevalier Marqueze. The only pre-1715 corvettes to remain on the list beyond 1718, they were classed as *barques à voiles latines* in 1718, corvettes or *barques longues* in 1719, and *barques latines* in 1723. *Conception* reverted to a *barque longue* in 1729.

Saint Jean-Gaëtan or *Saint Gaëtan*. Built c.1708 at Marseille and purchased 11.1708.
Dimensions & tons: 65ft 0in x 18ft 6in x 8ft 3in (21.11 x 6.01 x 2.68m). 150 tons. Draught 9ft (2.92m). Men: 80 in war, 30 peace, +2 officers.
Guns: 6 in war (4 peace): 6 x 6pdrs. 8 x 6pdrs from 1723.
Ordered sold 31.1.1724 and sold 2.1724 at Toulon.

Immaculée Conception. Built c.1710 at Majorca as the Spanish *Mayorca* to a design by Blaise Coulomb and purchased 1710.
Dimensions & tons: 68ft 0in x 20ft 0in x 8ft 9in (22.09 x 6.50 x 2.84m). 180 tons. Draught 10ft (3.25m). Men: 110 in war, 30 peace, +2 officers
Guns: 10 in war (4 peace): 10 x 6pdrs.
Name shortened to *Conception* 1722, rebuilt 1727 at Toulon. Ordered sold there 18.2.1732, sold 1733 to Sieur Dominique Carron for commercial use.

(D) Corvettes with 4pdr guns acquired from December 1715

By 1719 only two of the hundreds of corvettes of Louis XIV's navy remained on the fleet list, and they were acquired merchantmen (*Saint Jean-Gaëtan* and *Immaculée Conception*, above). By 1723 the category of corvettes or *barques longues* itself had disappeared from the list, the two ex-merchantmen then being classed as *barques latines*. In 1729 three ships were on the list as *barques longues*, the surviving ex-merchantman (now called *Conception*) and two new vessels, *Sibylle* and *Légère*, that soon became *barques latines* and are listed in Chapter 12. In 1734 the category of corvettes or *barques longues* returned to the fleet list with two ships built that year, *Dryade* and *Naïade*, both armed with 4pdr guns.

The 4pdr had been the standard gun in *barques longues* and corvettes since the 1670s, although the smaller *frégates légères* also carried them as their primary battery but in larger quantities. After 1715 the gap in corvette construction was effectively filled by the construction of a final few 4pdr-armed *frégates légères*. This type effectively merged with subsequent corvette construction and these late 4pdr frigates are listed here instead of in Chapter 6. In addition to the corvettes *Dryade* and *Naïade* mentioned above, the 1734 fleet list included the 4pdr *frégates légères Méduse, Nymphe, Fée, Vipère,* and *Levrette*. Corvettes continued to be built only intermittently and in small quantities, and during wartime the fleet lists tended to be dominated by captured and acquired vessels.

MÉDUSE. A small *frégate légère* of 16 x 4pdr guns, designed by René Levasseur and built by Jacques Poirier alongside the larger *frégate légère Thétis*; however, she was built of deficient material and was taken to pieces in a little more than four years.
Dimensions & tons: 88ft 0in x 20ft 5in x 8ft 9in (28.59 x 6.63 x 2.84m). 150/250 tons. Draught 9½ft (3.09m). Men: 80 in war, 50 peace.
Guns: 16 in war (12 peace): 16 x 4pdrs.
Méduse Le Havre.
K: 3.1722. L: 24.10.1722. C: 1.1723. Condemned at Le Havre 3.1727 and BU there 5–6.1727.

MÉDUSE. A small *frégate légère* of 16 x 4pdr guns, designed and built by Jacques Poirier to replace the previous vessel.
Dimensions & tons: 79ft 6in x 20ft 2in x 10ft 6in (25.82 x 6.55 x 3.41m). 160/250 tons. Draught 11ft (3.57m). Men: 100 in war, 60 peace, +4 officers.
Guns: 16 x 4pdrs.
Méduse Le Havre.
K: 4.1727. L: 16.8.1727. C: 9.1727. Grounded at La Hougue 9.1744 and severely damaged; refloated 10.1744 but sold 1.1745.

NYMPHE. A small *frégate légère* of 14 x 4pdr guns, designed by Jean-Armand Levasseur. She was named on 10 March 1728.
Dimensions & tons: 80ft 0in x 20ft 8in x 9ft 6in (25.99 x 6.71 x 3.09m). 142/250 tons. Draught 9ft 8in/10ft (3.14/3.25m). Men: 110 in war, 60 peace, +6 officers.
Guns: 14 x 4pdrs; also reported with 2 x 6pdrs and 12 x 4pdrs.
Nymphe (*Nimphe*) Toulon Dyd.
K: 3.1728. L: 22.5.1728. C: 6.1728. Participated in the bombardment of Tripoli 7.1728, judged to be badly built and slow under oars, not used again. Condemned at Toulon 24.1.1735, sold 9.6.1735 fully rigged to Sieur Aguillon.

FÉE Class. Small *frégates légères* of 10 x 4pdr guns, designed by Julien Geslain. Pierre Morineau built *Vipère* to Geslain's plans. *Vipère* was re-classed as a corvette or *barque longue* in 1743–45.
Dimensions & tons: 72ft 0in x 21ft 8in x 10ft 0in (23.39 x 7.04 x 3.25m). 140/250 tons. Draught 11ft (3.57m). Men: 90 in war, 40 peace.
Guns: 10 x 4pdrs.
Fée Rochefort Dyd.
K: 1733. L: 1734. C: 1735. Captured by a British ship of the line 10.1740 between Martinique and St Domingue during peacetime, returned to the French 11.1740. Condemned 12.1745 at Martinique and BU.
Vipère Rochefort Dyd.
K: 1733. L: 1734. C: 1735. Condemned 1.1746 at Rochefort, struck and BU.

LEVRETTE. A very small *frégate légère* of 8 x 4pdr guns, designed by Julien Geslain. Two ports were added during repairs in July 1745 increasing the armament to 10 x 4pdrs but the ship was hulked later that year.
Dimensions & tons (in 1734): 66ft 0in x 19ft 6in x 8ft 9in (21.44 x 6.33 x 2.84m). 100/190 tons. Draught 9½/10ft (3.09/3.24m). Men: 80 in war, 30 peace.
Guns: 8 x 4pdrs; 10 x 4pdrs from 7.1745.
Levrette Rochefort Dyd.
K: 1733. L: 1734. C: 1735. Became headquarters hulk at Le Havre 11.1745, last mentioned 1748.

DRYADE. A corvette or *barque longue* of 12 x 4pdr guns, later armed with 3pdrs, designed and built by Blaise Geslain. Re-classed as a *frégate légère* during 1738 but reverted to a corvette or *barque longue* in 1743–45.

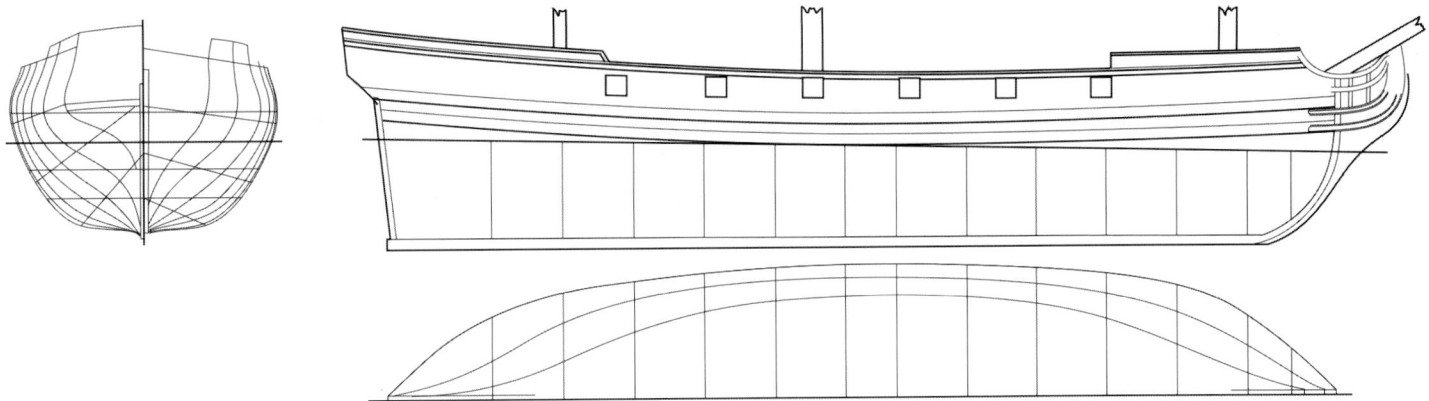

Plan of the 12-gun corvette *Perle* redrawn by László Veres from an original in the Toulon archives. Originally built in 1743, the ship was cut down in 1747 in response to reports of poor sailing qualities. It is difficult to see how this profile could be significantly reduced so the plan may represent the ship after 1747. The details on the plan also list the armament as 4pdrs, which were also changed from 3pdrs in 1747, reinforcing this possibility.

Dimensions & tons: 78ft 0in x 22ft 6in x 8ft 6in (25.34 x 7.31 x 2.76m). 90/200 tons. Draught 7ft 4in/8ft 11in (2.38/2.90m). Men: 90 in war, 50 peace, +2/4 officers.
Guns: 12 in war (8 peace): UD 12 x 4pdrs, QD/Fc nil. (4pdrs replaced in 1738 by 3pdrs)
Dryade Le Havre.
K: 3.1734. L: 7.1734. C: 8.1734. Repaired at Brest 1747, condemned there 1749 and sold.

NAÏADE. A corvette or *barque longue* of 10 x 4pdr guns, later armed with 3pdrs, designed and built by Jacques Poirier. Reconstructed 1741 at Le Havre.
Dimensions & tons: 68ft 0in x 19ft 2in x 7ft 6in (22.09 x 6.23 x 2.44m). 70/150 tons. Draught 8½ft (2.76m). Men: 70 in war, 50 peace.
Guns: 10 in war (6 peace): UD 10 x 4pdrs, QD/Fc nil. (4pdrs replaced around 1738 by 3pdrs)
Naïade (Nayade) Le Havre.
K: 2.1734. L: 9.5.1734. C: 6.1734. Lent as a privateer 2.1745 to Sieur Venard, *sous-constructeur*. Captured by the RN 10.7.1745.

PERLE. 12 guns. Designed by Joseph Véronique-Charles Chapelle and built by Pierre Salinoc. She was cut down (*rasée*) at Brest in 1747 because she did not carry her sails well.
Dimensions & tons: 76ft 0in, 67ft 0in x 20ft 8in x 9ft 0in (24.69, 21.76 x 6.71 x 2.92m). 116/210 tons. Draught 7½ft/9½ft (2.44/3.09m). Men: 90 in war, 50 peace, +4/5 officers.
Guns: 12 x 3pdrs (replaced by 4pdrs in 1747).
Perle Brest Dyd.
K: 12.1743. L: 12.1744. C: 4.1745. Last mentioned 1.1748 at Brest, possibly wrecked at Martinique.

MALIGNE. 6 guns.
Dimensions & tons: unknown. Men: 70, +4 officers
Guns: 6
Maligne Brest Dyd.
K: 1744. L: 1.1745. C: 5.1745. Captured 29.12.1745 by the British, fate unknown.

BADINE. 6 guns. Designed and built by François-Guillaume Clairain-Deslauriers.
Dimensions & tons: 66ft 0in, 60ft 0in x 17ft 6in x 7ft 4in (21.44, 19.49 x 5.68 x 2.38m). 70/124 tons. Draught 5¾ft/6¾ft (1.87/2.19m). Men: 60 in war, 30 peace, +3/4 officers.
Guns: 6 x 3pdrs (later 4pdrs).
Badine Brest Dyd.
K: 11.1744. L: 4.1745. C: 5.1745. Struck 1756 at Brest.

PALME Class. 12 guns. Designed by Joseph-Louis Ollivier, then 15 years old, undoubtedly under the supervision of his father, Blaise Ollivier.

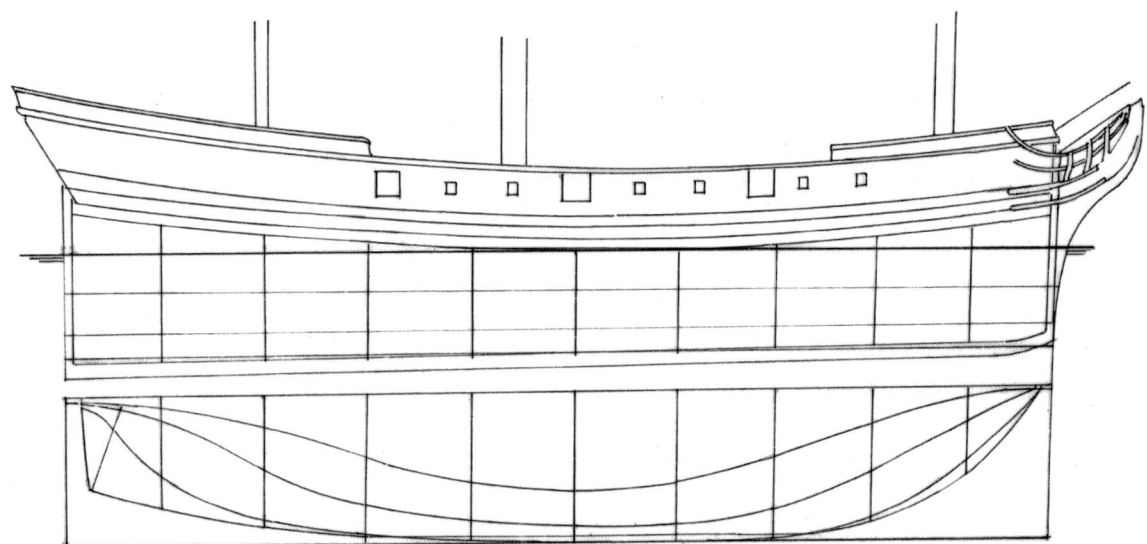

As with the contemporary British sloop of war, the French corvette category contained a wide variety of craft varying in size and firepower, and presumably designed for slightly different functions. This plan of *Badine* (redrawn by Ian McLaughlan from a French original) depicts one of the smaller types, although she carries a three-masted ship rig. The plumb upright stem and sternpost is an unusual feature, but was something of a fashion among some French *constructeurs* of the period – there are a number of such designs in the Danish archives, attributed to Laurent Barbé, an émigré French designer in Danish service.

Dimensions & tons: 84ft 0in, 76ft 0in x 22ft 0in x 9ft 0in (27.29, 24.69 x 7.15 x 2.92 m). 120/232 tons. Draught 9ft/10ft 9in (2.92/3.49m). Men: 90 in war, 50 peace, +4 officers.
Guns: 12 x 4pdrs.

Palme Brest Dyd.
K: 11.1744. L: 4.1745. C: 5.1745. Captured 3.2.1748 by HMS *Surprise* (20) while chartered to the *Compagnie des Indes*.

Amarante Brest Dyd.
K: 3.1747. L: 7.1747. C: 12.1747. Left Dunkirk 15.10.1759 with 5 frigates and 1,200 men under the privateer François Thurot to attempt a landing in Ireland but wrecked 2.1760 near St Malo before reaching Ireland.

Anémone Brest Dyd.
K: 3.1747. L: 7.1747. C: 1.1748. Captured with *Sardoine* (*Sardine*) 13.1.1761 by HM Ships *Mars* (74) and *Orford* (68) in the Bay of Biscay, both being called privateers by their captors.

Ex-BRITISH PRIVATEER PRIZES (1744–1746). Four British privateers were captured and added to the French Navy in 1744–46.

Casimir. Ex-British privateer corvette *Casimir*, built in Britain, completed repairs at Brest 3.1745 after being captured probably in late 1744.
Dimensions & tons: 72ft 0in x 20ft 0in x 10ft 0in (23.38 x 6.50 x 3.25m). 80/150 tons. Draught 7ft 4in/8ft (2.38/2.60m). Men: 80, +3/4 officers.
Guns: 12 x 4pdrs
Last mentioned being removed from service 7.1748 at Brest.

Prince de Galles. Ex-British privateer corvette *Prince of Wales*, captured 2.1745. 8 or 10 guns, 60 men and 3/5 officers, Condemned 1747 at Brest and BU there 1748.

Jeune Cérès. Ex-British privateer corvette, possibly named *Young Ceres*, built in Britain and captured 7.1745. 10 guns, 60/64 men and 3/4 officers. Recaptured 3.1746 by two British privateers off Vannes.

Renard. Ex-British privateer corvette *Fox*, built in Britain and captured 9.1746.
Dimensions & tons: 68ft 8in x 18ft 8in x 8ft 5in (22.31 x 6.06 x 2.74m). 123/200 tons. Draught 11ft (3.57m). Men: 100.
Guns: 14 x 8pdrs, 2 x 3pdrs.
Struck c.1748 at Rochefort.

Ex-BRITISH NAVAL PRIZES (1744–1746). HMS *Falcon*, a *Merlin* class sloop, was captured on 9 October 1745 by the St Malo privateer *Deux Couronnes* and became the French privateer *Falcon* and then the naval *Fortune*. HMS *Mercury*, originally the French merchantman *Mercure*, was purchased by the British in Antigua on 7 October 1744

Plan of the 12-gun corvette *Palme* redrawn by László Veres from an original in the Toulon archives. The 12-gun type was at the upper end of the corvette category in the mid-century French Navy, and resembled light frigates in concentrating the armament amidships, with the fine-lined ends left free of gunports.

and was captured by the French 22-gun *Grand Turc* and a 20-gun brig in the Atlantic on 25 April 1745 while carrying despatches to Plymouth. HMS *Wolf*, a *Wolf* class snow-rigged sloop, was captured on 9 November 1745 by a 32-gun French privateer off the Channel Islands and became the 18-gun French privateer *Loup*. HMS *Albany*, a mercantile brigantine of the same name, was purchased in 1746 by the Royal Navy at Louisbourg and was captured on 30 July 1746 by the French Canadian-built frigate *Castor* (28) in Chedabucto Bay, Nova Scotia.

Fortune John Barnard, Harwich.
Ord: 30.3.1744. K: 15.5.1744. L: 12.11.1744. C: 22.1.1745.
Dimensions & tons: 88ft 0in x 24ft 4in x 11ft 0in (28.59 x 7.90 x 3.57m). 320 tons displacement.
Guns: 14 (10 or 14 x 6pdrs in British service)
Probably purchased by the French Navy from her captor and renamed *Fortune*. Recaptured by the British 17.3.1746, purchased for the RN from her captors 7.4.1746 and renamed HMS *Fortune*. Sold 20.3.1770.

Mercure ?France.
Dimensions & tons: 71ft 0in x 22ft 10in x 10ft 3in (23.06 x 7.42 x 3.33m). 160/300 tons. Draught 10ft 10in (3.52m). Men: 90 in war, 30 peace, +4 officers.
Guns: 14 x 6pdrs
Also listed as *Mercure Anglais* in 1746 and *Petit Mercure* in 1748. Rebuilt by Golain. Struck c.1750 at Brest.

Loup Thomas West, Deptford.
Ord: 21.7.1741. K: 31.7.1741. L: 27.2.1742. C: 15.4.1742.
Dimensions & tons: 85ft 0in x 23ft 6in (27.61 x 7.63m). c.300 tons displacement. Men: 110 (British)
Guns: 14 (14 x 4pdrs in British service)
Probably purchased by the French Navy from her captors. Retaken 12.3.1747 by HM Ships *Amazon* (24) and *Grand Turk* (22) and re-entered RN service as HMS *Wolf*, wrecked 11.1.1749 in Dundrum Bay, Ireland.

Albany Britain or America.
Dimensions & tons: unknown. Men: 90 (British)
Guns: 10 (British)
Probably sent to Quebec, fate unknown. The British sloop HMS *Tavistock* (built 1745, renamed *Albany* 31.8.1747) was a different vessel.

CORVETTES AND *BARQUES LONGUES*

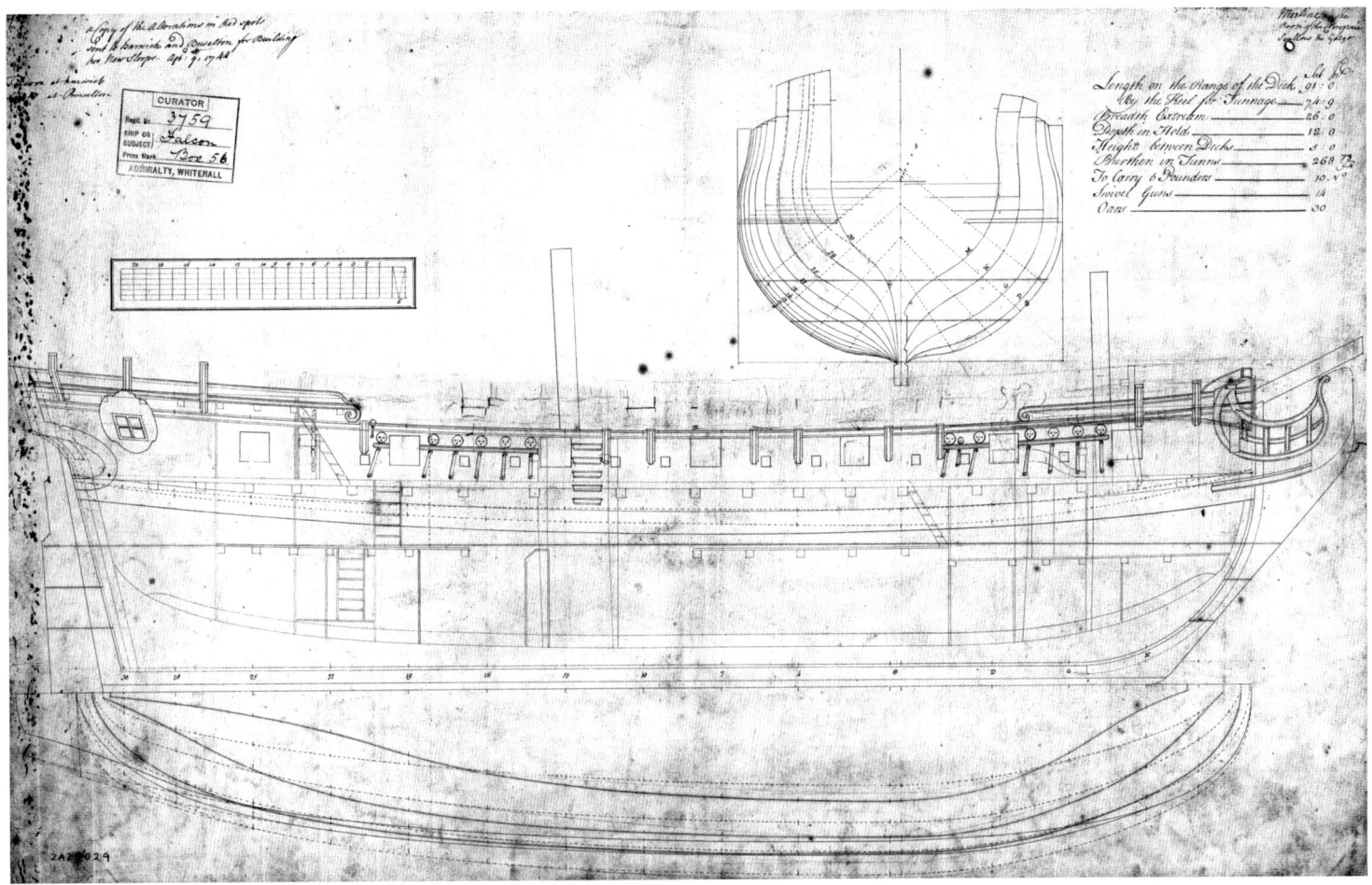

By way of comparison with French corvette design, this is the design draught of the British sloop of war *Falcon*, captured in 1745 and added to the French Navy as *Fortune*. Broader in proportion than her French equivalents, the British ship has less extreme lines – reflected in the gunports being carried nearer to bow and stern – and with the upper deck further from the waterline, there is more freeboard for the gun battery at the expenses of greater topside height and poorer performance to leeward. In general terms, the British sloop is optimised for seakeeping rather than speed. One practical disadvantage of French design philosophy was that the exaggerated tumblehome in the topsides required the channels to be fitted below the line of gunports for a broader supporting spread to the masts; here they were more vulnerable to damage and increased drag in a seaway. (National Maritime Museum, London J4657)

CARCAJOU. Designed and built by René-Nicolas Levasseur in Canada.
  Dimensions & tons: dimensions unknown. 80 tons. Men: 56 +4 officers.
  Guns: 10 or 12 x 4pdrs.
Carcajou Quebec.
  K: 1744. L: 16.6.1745. C: 8.1745. Capsized 10.1745 and lost with all hands near the Île aux Moutons to the north of the Glénans. Hulk later washed ashore at the Pointe de Trevignon.

DILIGENTE. 10 guns. Designed by Jean-Joseph Ginoux. Listed as a snow from 1766.
  Dimensions & tons: unknown. Men: 40
  Guns: 10 x 2pdrs or 3pdrs. Rearmed in 8.1759 as a gunboat with 1 or 2 x 24pdrs. Reduced to 4 x 2pdrs from 1760; later (between 1766 and 1772) 6 x 2pdrs or 6 x 3pdrs.
Diligente Le Havre.
  K: 1755. L: 1.1756. C: 6.1756. In service 10.1756 under a merchant captain to protect coastal traffic. In service 5.1757 as a coast guard vessel with 10 guns patrolling between Cherbourg and Dieppe. Unserviceable 3.1775 at Le Havre and struck, sold 4.1775.

LEVRETTE. 8 guns. Sometimes listed as the first unit of the *Écureuil* class, below, but appears to have been smaller.
  Dimensions & tons: unknown. Men: 66 +5/6 officers (35 as *gabarre*)
  Guns: 8
Levrette ?Nantes.
  K: 1755. L: 7.1756. C: 9.1756. Assigned to Brest and possibly built there. Captured by the British 1758 and became a privateer; retaken 5.1759 and recommissioned as a *gabarre*; lost 1760.

HURAULT. 10 guns. Schooner-rigged corvette on Lake Ontario. Designed and built by Louis-Pierre Poulin de Courval Cressé at Fort Frontenac. Also called *Huron*. Depicted in a contemporary drawing as a two-masted main-topsail schooner
  Dimensions & tons: dimensions unknown. 90 tons. Men: 24 sailors, 40 soldiers, 1 officer
  Guns: 8 x 6pdrs, 4 x 4pdrs, 6 *pierriers*
Hurault Fort Frontenac.
  K: 1755. L: 1755. C: mid-1755. Captured by the British in the fall of Fort Frontenac 28.8.1758 and burned by them 31.8.1758. Her probable forefoot and parts of three other vessels were excavated at Kingston, Ont., on 16.12.1953.

MARQUISE DE VAUDREUIL. 16 guns. Schooner-rigged corvette on

Lake Ontario. Designed and built by the French Canadian Louis-Pierre Poulin de Courval Cressé at Fort Frontenac on the Cataraqui River (now Kingston, Ontario). Depicted as a two-masted main-topsail schooner.
Dimensions & tons: 60ft 0in x 21ft 0in x 7ft 0in (19.49 x 6.82 x 2.27m). 120 tons. Men: 30 sailors, 50 soldiers, 1 officer
Guns: 8 x 8pdrs, 8 x 6pdrs, 8 x 2pdr *pierriers*

Marquise de Vaudreuil Fort Frontenac.
  K: 1755. L: 1756. C: mid-1756. Tried to leave Fort Frontenac early on 27.8.1758 with *Montcalm* and *George* just before it fell but forced ashore by enemy artillery. (British accounts mention only two ships in this action.) The British then loaded captured supplies on two seized vessels (probably *Marquise de Vaudreuil* and *Montcalm* ex-*Halifax*) later that day while razing the fort. The two ships then took the supplies to Oswego and were burned there.

MONTCALM. The former HMS *Halifax*, a snow-rigged corvette, is listed in Chapter 11 with the other ships of the British squadron on Lake Ontario that were captured at Oswego on 14 August 1756.

ÉCUREUIL Class. 12 guns. Designed by Jacques-Luc Coulomb and built by Léon-Michel Guignace (*Écureuil* and *Jacinthe* at Brest) and Pierre-Augustin Lamothe (*Sardoine* and *Renoncule* at Nantes). *Jacinthe* is also listed as built at Nantes, commissioned in February 1757 at Rochefort, and sailing in March 1757 for Martinique with *Hardi* (64). *Sardine* initially operated as a coast guard vessel and convoy escort, departing Rochefort on 27 June 1757 escorting a convoy to Brest with *Friponne, Héroïne, Fidèle, Mutine,* and *Amarante*, and then waiting at Bayonne on 23 August 1757 with *Friponne, Hermine* and *Opale* to escort a convoy to Rochefort and Brest.
Dimensions & tons: 91ft 0in x 23ft 6in x 9ft 6in (29.56 x 7.63 x 3.09 m). 165/300 tons. Draught 9ft/10ft 4in (2.92/3.36m). Men: 100/110.
Guns: 12 x 4pdrs.

Écureuil Brest Dyd.
  K: 5.1756. L: 8.1756. C: 10.1756. Captured 25.2.1762 by HM Ships *Fame* (74) and *Lion* (60).
Jacinthe (*Hyacinthe*) Brest Dyd.
  K: 6.1756. L: 12.1756. C: 3.1757. Captured by the British 1760, details unknown.

Sardoine (*Sardine*) Nantes.
  K: 10.1756. L: 30.3.1757. C: 4.1757. Captured with *Anémone* 13.1.1761 by HM Ships *Mars* (74) and *Orford* (68) in the Bay of Biscay, becoming HMS *Sardoine*; sold 26.4.1768 at Woolwich.
Renoncule Nantes.
  K: 10.1756. L: 4.1757. C: 6.1757. Grounded 5.1759 at Concarneau but refloated. Repaired 8–9.1759 at Lorient. Last mentioned escorting convoys from Île d'Aix to Brest in 1761. Struck before 9.1761, fate unknown.
Arc en Ciel Brest Dyd.
  K: 12.1757. L: 10.4.1758. C: 5.1758. Last mentioned 1759 at Brest, may like *Oracle* below not have been put into service.

CALYPSO Class. 16 guns. Designed by Jacques-Luc Coulomb. The two at Nantes were built by Pierre-Augustin Lamothe to Coulomb's plans.
Dimensions & tons: 100ft 0in x 25ft 0in x 12ft 6in (32.48 x 8.12 x 4.06 m). 200/400 tons. Draught 9ft 8in/10ft 8in (3.14/3.46 m). Men: 90/150 +5 officers.
Guns: 16 x 4pdrs. 18 x 4pdrs in *Calypso* in 1772.

Calypso Brest Dyd.
  K: 6.1756. L: 9.1756. C: 11.1756. Participated in the Battle of Quiberon Bay 20.11.1759, took refuge in the Vilaine and remained there 14 months before returning to Brest 1.1761. Unserviceable at Rochefort 11.1771, struck there 1772.
Escarboucle Brest Dyd.
  K: 7.1756. L: 11.1756. C: 1.1757. Captured 5.9.1757 by HMS *Isis* (50) off Brest.
Mignonne Nantes.
  K: 10.1756. L: 4.1757. C: 5.1757. With *Bizarre* (60) captured HMS *Winchelsea* (24) and 44 merchantmen 10.10.1758 southwest of Ireland. (*Winchelsea* was retaken 27.10.1758 by the Bristol privateer *Duke of Cornwall*.) Captured 19.3.1759 by HM Ships *Aeolus* (32) and *Isis* (50) off the Île d'Yeu.
Éclair Nantes.
  K: 10.1756. L: 4.1757. C: 6.1757. Wrecked 5.1758 on the Houat Rocks.
Oracle Brest Dyd.
  K: end 1757. L: ?1758. Never completed.

LUTINE Class. 16 guns. Designed by Jean-Joseph Ginoux and built by Jouvencourt. French records do not show the dimensions of these ships, those below are British measurements for HMS *Pheasant* converted to French feet. *Pheasant* was ship-rigged. It is possible that *Faisan* and *Tourterelle* were different ships; if so nothing is known of the origins of *Faisan* or of the fate of *Tourterelle* and both were captured at the same

Admiralty draught of the *Sardoine*, dated 29 April 1761. The ship carried only 12 guns in French service, so the two forward pairs of gunports (plus the bridle port) may have been added by the British as the French did not usually fit gunports forward of the foremast. At the time of capture, the three-masted ship rig was still something of a novelty in the British sloop class, so they were unofficially referred to as 'frigates', a designation initially extended to *Sardoine*. (National Maritime Museum, London J4452)

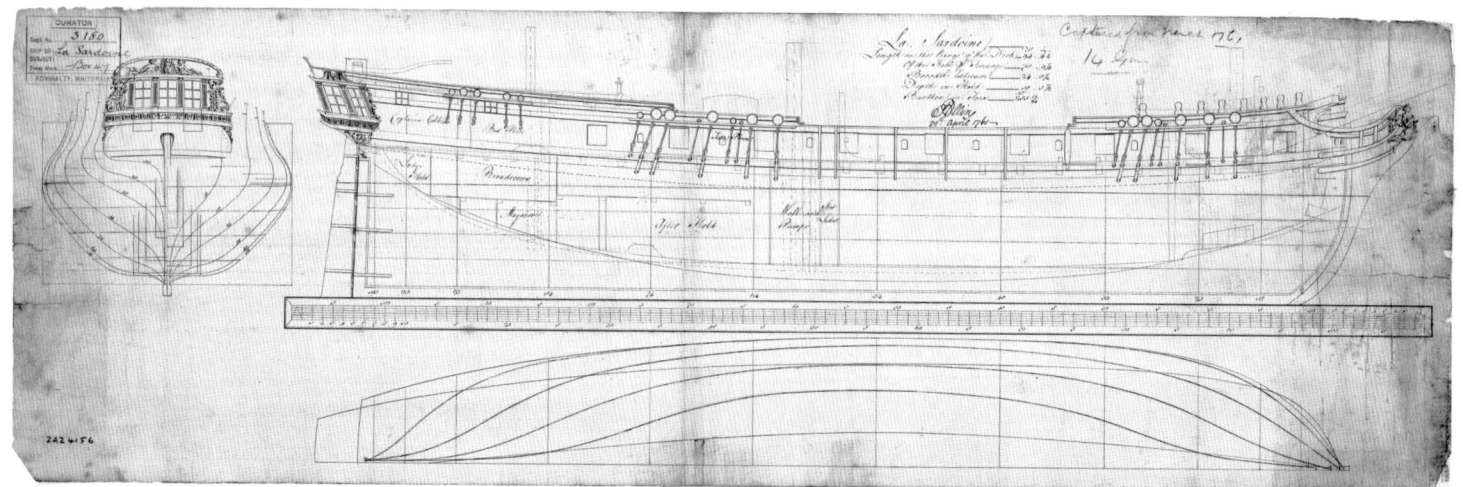

time and place.
- Dimensions & tons: 100ft 1in, 84ft 11in x 23ft 1in x 9ft 11in (32.51, 27.59 x 7.50 x 3.22m). 140/300 tons. Men: 70/100 +4/5 officers.
- Guns: 12 x 4pdrs, 0–4 smaller. As HMS *Pheasant*: 14 x 6pdrs.

Lutine Caen.
- K: 9.1756. L: 10.4.1757. C: 6.1757. Wrecked 10.1757 on the Dogger Bank.

Tourterelle Caen.
- K: 9.1756. L: 10.4.1757. C: 6.1757. Became privateer at Havre 12.1760, possibly under the name *Faisan*. Captured 4.1761 by HMS *Albany* (14) between Jersey and Guernsey, became HMS *Pheasant*. Missing and presumed foundered with all hands in a storm in the Channel 10.10.1761.

Ex-BRITISH MERCANTILE AND PRIVATEER PRIZES (1756–1762). Five British merchant vessels and privateers were captured and used by the French navy during the Seven Years' War.

Hanovre. Ex-British *Duke of Hanover*, probably a packet, captured between 1.1757 and 6.1757. 12 guns, 62/82 men and 4/6 officers. Recaptured 10.1758 by a British frigate off Brest and probably sold.

Hancelot. Ex-British privateer corvette *Hancelot* captured 1757. 10 guns. Last mentioned 1758, fate unknown.

Roi de Prusse. Ex-British merchant or privateer corvette *King of Prussia* captured 6.1758 and put into service at Brest 6.7.1758. 10 guns, 65 men and 4 officers. Recaptured 11.1758 by the British.

Scot. Ex-British *Scot* captured 7.1758. 10 or 12 guns, 80/91 men and 6 officers. Fitted 2.1761 as headquarters hulk at Le Havre, condemned there 10.1761 and sold.

Expédition. Ex-British *Expedition*, captured 6.1762. Built in New England 1750–51 of resinous wood. 165 tons, 4 guns and 1 mortar. Put into service 24.7.1762 in Newfoundland with a crew of 3 petty officers and 24 men. Condemned 5.1765 at Le Havre, the cost of repairs exceeding her value. Sold 1766.

Ex-BRITISH NAVAL PRIZES (1756–1762). HMS *Stork*, an *Alderney* class sloop, was captured on 6 August 1758 by *Palmier* (74) off Cap St Nicolas, St Domingue. The Bayonne privateer *Comtesse de Gramont* was captured by HMS *Tartar* (28) on 29 October 1757, renamed HMS *Gramont* 6 January 1758, and recaptured by the French at the capture of St John's Newfoundland on 27 June 1762. She reverted to her original name in French naval service.

Stork Stow & Bartlett, Shoreham.
- Ord: 14.11.1755. K: early 1756. L: 8.11.1756. C: 26.11.1756.
- Dimensions & tons: 85ft 0in x 23ft 0in x 10ft 2in (27.61 x 7.47 x 3.30m). 250 tons displacement. Draught 10ft 8in/11ft 2in (3.47/3.63m).
- Guns: 14 x 4pdrs, 2 x 3pdrs
- Removed from service 12.1759 at Rochefort, struck c.1760.

Comtesse de Gramont Jean Barrere, Bayonne.
- Dimensions & tons: 95ft 0in x 25ft 10in (30.86 x 8.39m). 500 tons displacement. Men: 120.
- Guns: 18 x 6pdrs.
- K: 7.1756. L: 11.1756. C: 2.1757. Loaned as a privateer 4–6.1763. Condemned 12.1766 at Fort Royal de la Martinique, BU there 1767.

PURCHASED AND ACQUIRED VESSELS (1757–1762). One vessel of unknown origin served briefly at Brest in 1757. Two privateer corvettes were purchased for use by the French Navy in 1759 and four more (including a Bordeaux merchantman acquired in Louisiana) were purchased in 1762.

Princesse de Soubise. Vessel of unknown origin purchased by the Navy 8.1757 and put into service 9.1757 at Brest. 92 men and 4 officers. Captured 10.1757 by the British.

Épreuve. Built at Le Havre as the privateer corvette *Observateur* (20). Purchased by the King 5.1759 and renamed 23.5.1759. Rigged as a snow.
- Dimensions & tons: 89ft 0in x 24ft 0in x 12ft 9in (28.91 x 7.80 x 4.14m). 300 tons displacement.
- Guns: 14 x 6pdrs, 0–6 smaller.
- K: 1757. L: 1758. Loaned 1760 to Sieur Le Vieux of Le Havre for use as a privateer. Captured 25.11.1760 by HMS *Niger* (32) and became HMS *Epreuve*. Sailed for Georgia 24.8.1762, missing and presumed foundered with all hands in the Atlantic returning from Georgia 3.1764.

Turquoise. Built by François Normand at Honfleur as the privateer corvette *Hirondelle* (16) for Sieur Le Griel (probably of Dieppe) under the supervision of Jean-Joseph Ginoux, naval constructor at Le Havre,

Admiralty draught of the *Épreuve*, undated but as captured, with alterations to the below-deck arrangements shown in ticked lines. The extreme hull form and lack of amenities testifies to the vessel's origins as a privateer. The two masts set a snow rig. (National Maritime Museum, London J4614)

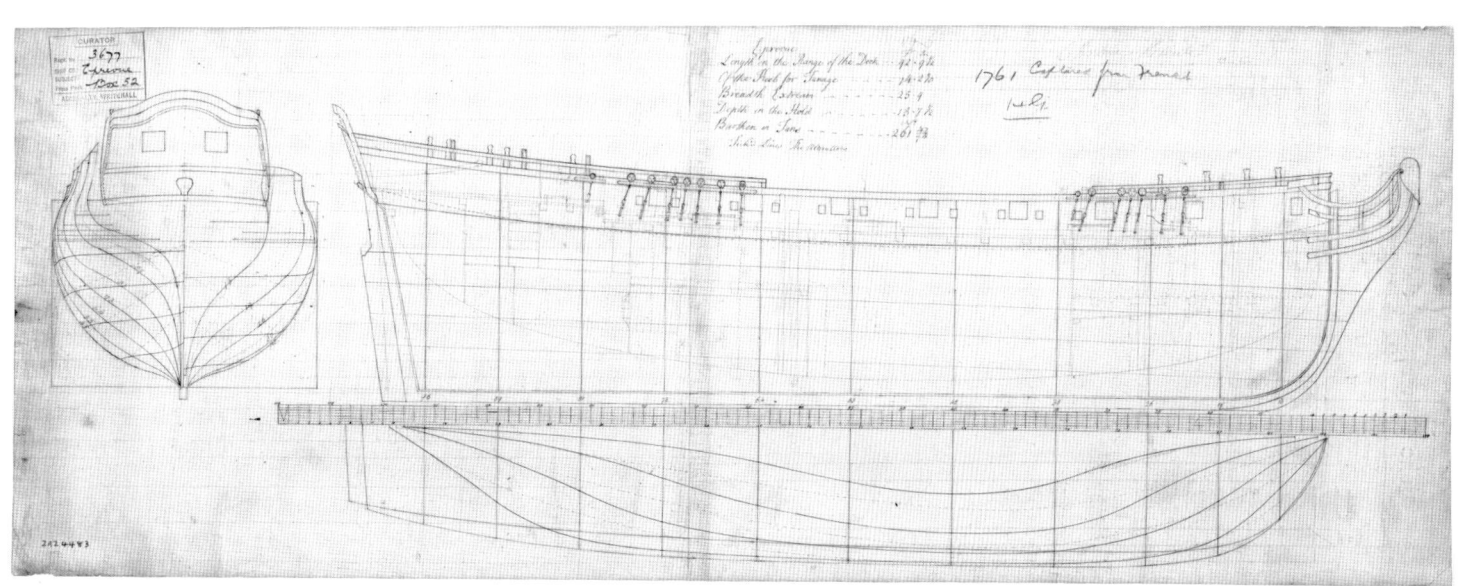

purchased by the King 5.1759 and renamed 23.5.1759. Snow-rigged.
   Dimensions & tons: dimensions unknown. 80 tons. Men: 24/48 +4/6 officers.
   Guns: 4 in 1765, 6 in 1766, 8 x 3pdrs from 1768.
   K: 3.1757. L: 1757. C: 6.1757. Needed major repairs in 1770, struck at Brest 9.1771, BU there 1772.

Fortune. Built at Bordeaux and purchased 7.1762 in Louisiana. Snow-rigged.
   Dimensions & tons: 78ft 0in x 22ft 4in (25.34 x 7.25m). 140 tons. Men: 60 +5 officers.
   Guns: 14 in 1765, 12 x 4pdrs or 3pdrs from 1766 (12 x 4pdrs as *flûte* 1768)
   Renamed *Petite Fortune* 1767. Chartered 7.1768 as a 190-ton *flûte* with the *flûte Salomon* to the *Compagnie de Cayenne*. Was at Rochefort unserviceable with rotten wood 12.1771, struck and sold 1772.

Ambition. Built at Brest as a privateer corvette and purchased there 8.1762 from Sieur Cloinard.
   Dimensions & tons: 88ft 0in x 19ft 7in (28.59 x 6.36m). 150 tons. Men: 70/90 +2/3 officers.
   Guns: 12 to 1766, 20 x 4pdrs from 1768
   K: 1761. L: 7.1762. C: 10.1762. Repaired at Rochefort 1768 and 1771. Condemned and hulked 1.1774 at Île de France, last mentioned 1775.

Bergère. Built at Nantes as a privateer corvette and purchased there 8.1762 (or 22.10.1762 from Sieur André). Originally named *Berger*.
   Dimensions & tons: 81ft x 26ft (26,3 x 8,4m), 190 tons. Men: 60/80 + 4 officers.
   Guns: 12 x 4pdrs.
   L: 1762. C: 9.1762. Assigned 8.1763 to the packet service for the Antilles, carried 6 guns as a packet. Repaired at Rochefort 1.1771. Condemned there late 1773 or early 1774 and struck.

Angélique. Built slowly at Nantes as a privateer corvette and purchased there 4.8.1762.
   Dimensions and tons: dimensions unknown. 180 tons. Men: 45/56 +4 officers
   Guns: 12 in 1762, later 10 x 4pdrs.
   L: 1761. C: 4.1763. Condemned 6.1767 at Rochefort and ordered BU 3.6.1767.

IROQUOISE Class. 10 guns. Schooner-rigged corvettes on Lake Ontario. Ordered after the fall of Fort Frontenac to re-establish French naval power on Lake Ontario. Constructed by Louis-Pierre Poulin de Courval Cressé to a design provided by René-Nicolas Levasseur at Pointe au Baril, located on the St Lawrence River near Maitland, Ontario and across the river and upstream from La Présentation, now Ogdensburg, New York. Rigged as two-masted topsail schooners. On 22 September 1760 Lt. Patrick Sinclair measured the sunken incomplete hull, which appeared identical to *Iroquoise* alongside her, as 84ft x 22ft x 9ft 2in (25.60 x 6.71 x 2.80m), all of these British measurements being for tonnage and producing a tonnage of 160 tons.
   Dimensions & tons: 75ft or 80ft length (24.36/25.99m), 100/250 tons, but see above. Men: 34 + 2 officers + 65 soldiers.
   Guns: 10 x 12pdrs (designed). *Outaouaise* when captured: 1 x 18pdr, 7 x 12pdrs, 2 x 8pdrs.

Iroquoise Pointe au Baril.
   K: 10.1758. L: 9.4.1759. C: 5.1759. Damaged by grounding 1.8.1760, taken to Fort Lévis on Isle Royale (downstream from La Présentation) and scuttled alongside her unfinished sister, her guns being moved to the fort. Captured 25.8.1760 in the fall of Fort Lévis. Raised 28.8.1760 and became HMS *Anson* (schooner-rigged). Ran onto rocks in a gale 23.10.1761 on the Niagara Shoal in the St Lawrence River 20 miles from Lake Ontario while carrying supplies from the former Fort Lévis to Oswego and lost.

Outaouaise Pointe au Baril.
   K: 10.1758. L: 12.4.1759. C: 5.1759. Captured 17.8.1760 while becalmed in the river near Point au Baril by five row-galleys (open boats) with a total of four brass 12pdrs and one howitzer led by Colonel George Williamson, became HMS *Williamson* (brig-rigged). Sunk 20.8.1760 in attack on Fort Lévis, raised. Sprang a leak (partly because of unrepaired battle damage) and run ashore 22.10.1760 near Niagara, could not be salvaged.

(unnamed) Pointe au Baril.
   Incomplete hull taken to Fort Lévis and scuttled at the northern tip of Isle Royale. Captured 25.8.1760 in the fall of the fort. Raised by the British, completed, rigged as snow using material salvaged from HMS *Onondaga* (below), named HMS *Johnson* (snow-rigged), and in service by 22.9.1760. Lost 13.11.1764 in a storm near Oswego en route to Niagara.

Ex-BRITISH NAVAL PRIZE (LAKE ONTARIO, 1760). After taking Fort Niagara from the French, Sir William Johnson on 29 July 1759 ordered the local naval commander, Captain Joshua Loring, to build two snows there. *Mohawk* (16 guns) was launched in October 1759 and *Onondaga* (18 guns, originally called *Apollo* but renamed to please Indian chiefs) was launched on 6 July 1760. *Onondaga* ran aground 23 August 1760 in the British assault on Fort Lévis and was shelled by French artillery and taken by the French, who also rendered her name as *Oneyout*. The ruined *Onondaga* was retaken by the British at the fall of Fort Lévis two days later, and her spars and cordage were used in September to rig HMS *Johnson* (above).

Three ships were ordered on 10 May 1762 from Sieur Le Clerc at Le Havre on plans of Jean-Joseph Ginoux. One was a third frigate of the *Hébé* class (see Chapter 4), one was a corvette with 16 x 6pdrs possibly named *Légère*, and one was a corvette with 12 x 4pdrs named *Bergère*. The contracts were cancelled in June 1762 because the Minister found the prices to be too high. The contracts for the frigate and *Bergère* were reinstated in August 1762 but cancelled around November 1762. The design of *Bergère* was probably modeled on the Lutine of 1757.

SYLPHIDE. 12 guns. Designed and built by Jean-Hyacinthe Raffeau. Named 22 December 1762. Hull pierced with 14 ports.
   Dimensions & tons: 92ft 0in x 24ft 6in x 11ft 6in (29.89 x 7.96 x 3.74m). 190/400 tons. Draught 10ft 4in/11ft 4in (3.36/3.68m). Men: 60/90, +2/8 officers.
   Guns: 12 x 4pdrs.

Sylphide (*Silphide*) Indret (Nantes).
   K: 7.1762. L: 7.1763. C: 10.1763. Rebuilt 1–4.1776 at Rochefort (hauled out, re-launched 5.4.1776). Fitted as a *gabarre* 7.1784, but wrecked 2.9.1784 on the Anse du Toulinguet, near Camaret.

VIGILANT. 12 guns. Designed and built by Arnoux. Purchased on the stocks during summer 1763.
   Dimensions & tons: dimensions unknown. 202 tons. Men: 60/80, +5 officers.
   Guns: 12 x 4pdrs.

Vigilant Indret (Nantes).
   K: 6.1763. L: 9.1763. C: 11.1763. Sold 1777 at Île de France for commercial use. Mentioned 6.1779 at Île de France as a 250-ton merchant snow. Wrecked 27.6.1782 on the Parquette during a transit from Brest to Rochefort.

PURCHASED AND ACQUIRED VESSELS armed with 4pdr guns or smaller (1765–1767). Three probable merchant vessels were acquired for use as smaller corvettes during the years immediately after the Seven Years' War.

Guêpe. Origin unknown, was under repair in 1765 at Lorient for the account of the King. Struck or renamed 1765–1766.

Etoile du Matin. Corvette or brigantine purchased and put into service 2.1767 at Bordeaux, possibly built there. Was part of the *Marine des Colonies* and was not shown on the navy's fleet lists. 27/34 men and 4 officers. Rebuilt 9–12.1769 at Manila. Last mentioned 1773 at Île de France, probably sold for commerce c.1774, mentioned 7.1775 as a merchant brig in the Indian Ocean.

Heure du Berger. Corvette or snow built in Bermuda and purchased 1767 at London. Was part of the *Marine des Colonies* and was not shown on the navy's fleet lists. 47 men and 5 officers. Last mentioned late 1772 in service at Île de France.

AURORE. 6 guns. Designed and built by Nicolas Ozanne for François César le Tellier, marquis de Courtenvaux, at his expense, although her outfitting was partially funded by the Navy. Named *Aurore* 4.1767. Listed as a snow from 1772.

Dimensions & tons: 66ft 6in, 60ft 0in x 18ft 1in x 8ft 2in (21.60, 19.49 x 5.87 x 2.65m). 130 tons displacement. Draught 6½ft/7ft 2in (2.11/2.33m). Men: 30/40

Guns: 6 x 2pdrs; 6 x 3pdrs by 1771.

Aurore Le Havre.
K: 1766. L: 4.1767. C: 5.1767. Renamed *Petite Aurore* 1768. Struck 1775 at Brest.

VERT GALANT. This small vessel was begun in January 1768, probably at Bordeaux, put into service in May 1768 with the *Marine des Colonies*, then repaired in July–October.1768 at Lorient before being sent overseas. 27 men and 3 officers. Last mentioned 1770 out of service at Île de France, destroyed in March 1772 by a typhoon there.

CURIEUX Class. 8 guns. Designed by Nicolas Levesque for the *Compagnie des Indes*, specifically for use by pilots on the Ganges. Snow-rigged. Purchased separately for the French Navy in 1770.

Dimensions & tons: 66ft 0in, 60ft 0in x 20ft 0in x 6ft 7in (21.44, 19.49 x 6.50 x 2.14m). 110/190 tons. Draught 9ft (2.92m). Men: 40/60 +4 officers

Guns: 8 x 4pdrs.

Curieux Lorient.
K: 12.1768. L: 18.4.1769. C: 6.1769. Sent to Cayenne upon completion. Purchased 4.1770. Sold 1775 for commercial use.

Nécessaire Lorient.
K: 12.1768. L: 22.4.1769. C: 6.1769. Purchased 9.1770 while in the Indies. Sold there 11.1778 for commercial use, out of service 18.6.1780 and not further mentioned.

PURCHASED VESSELS armed with 4pdr guns or smaller (1770–1773). Four merchant vessels were acquired for use as smaller corvettes during the period between the Seven Years' War and the War of American Independence during which the construction of new corvettes lapsed.

Sage or *Petit Sage*. Built as as a *gabarre* for Sieur Névé on a new slipway at Bois du Blanc, just above the Lorient dockyard, by the Arnous brothers (René and Nicolas), the first of many ships built there. Purchased 8.1768 by the *Compagnie des Indes*, then purchased from them by the Navy 4.1770 and rebuilt as a corvette by the Lorient dockyard between 1770 and 8.1771.

Dimensions & tons: dimensions unknown, 200 tons. Men: 27 +3/5 officers.

Guns: 10 x 4pdrs

K: 1765. L:2.1766. C:4.1766. Sold 1775 for commercial use, last mentioned 8.1777 at Lorient, later wrecked in the Amazon.

Sirène. Built as the *gabarre Marie* by Nicolas Levesque at Lorient (Caudan) for the *Compagnie des Indes*. Renamed *Sirène* at the end of 1769. Purchased by the Navy 4.1770 and converted into a corvette at Lorient during 1770.

Dimensions & tons: dimensions unknown. 200 or 160 tons. Men: 50/70. (The dimensions sometimes given for this ship, 118ft x 31ft 8in x 16ft 9in, seem much too large for her tonnage and classification.)

Guns: 10 x 4pdrs.

K: 1.1769. L:14.8.1769. C:10.1769.To Île de France 1775. Wrecked 1.1776 near Fort Dauphin in Magagascar.

Postillon. Purchased 2.1773 from Sieur Nicolas Viaud at Nantes and possibly built there. Listed as a brigantine in 1777 and as a schooner in 1778.

Dimensions & tons: dimensions unknown. 90 tons. Men: 42 +2 officers as corvette, 13/18 +3 petty officers as *gabarre*.

Guns: 10 x 3pdrs (4 x 3pdrs in 1776, 2 x 3pdrs from 1780)

Completed 4.1773. Wrecked 8/9.1774 at Ste Marie de Madagascar, refloated 10.1774. Returned to Brest 11.1776. Converted into a *gabarre* in 1780, probably at Brest. Removed from service 5.1781 at Senegal, struck 1784 at Brest.

Dauphine. Purchased 6.1773 while under construction at Île Bourbon or Île de France.

Specifications unknown.

K: 1772, L: 6.1773, C: 8.1773. Rigged as a brig at Île de France 6.1778. Arrived at Lorient c.1779 armed with 8 *pierriers*, recommissioned there early 1780 with 4 x 3pdrs and 12 *pierriers*. Captured 6.1780 by three British privateers.

FAVORITE Class. 10 guns. Designed and built by Jean-Joseph Ginoux. Clinker-built hulls, snow rig. Both cut down (raséed) and re-classed as avisos in July/August 1780 at Brest.

Dimensions & tons: 80ft 0in, 68ft 0in x 20ft 0in x 10ft 6in (25.99, 22.09 x 6.50 x 3.41m). 115/200 tons. Draught 8ft/10ft (2.60/3.25m). Men: 60.

Guns: 10 x 4pdrs; from 8.1780, re-armed with 2 x 3pdrs only.

Favorite Le Havre.
K: 2.1776. L: 27.7.1776. C: 8.1776. Lost 8.1780 at Bertheaume in the approaches to Brest.

Curieuse Le Havre.
K: 2.1776. L: 30.7.1776. C: 8.1776. Struck 1784.

PURCHASED AND ACQUIRED VESSELS armed with 4pdr guns or smaller (1778–1783). Six merchant vessels and privateers were acquired for use as smaller corvettes during the War of American Independence

Les Amis (*Amis*). Built at Lorient by François Caro as *Deux Amis* and purchased 5.1778 upon completion.

Dimensions & tons: dimensions unknown, 100 tons. Men: 30/106 +1/ ? officers.

Guns: 12 x 4pdrs. Listed in 1780–82 (for the *École des Matelots Novices*) variably with 8, 12, and 14 x 4pdrs +6 *pierriers*, and in 7.1782 (no longer on training duty) with 10 x 4pdrs and 4 x 6pdrs.

K: 1.1778. L: 4.1778. C: 5.1778. Used 1780–82 as a training corvette for novices at Lorient (listed by Brest during these years as a cutter at Lorient but may have been brig-rigged). Captured

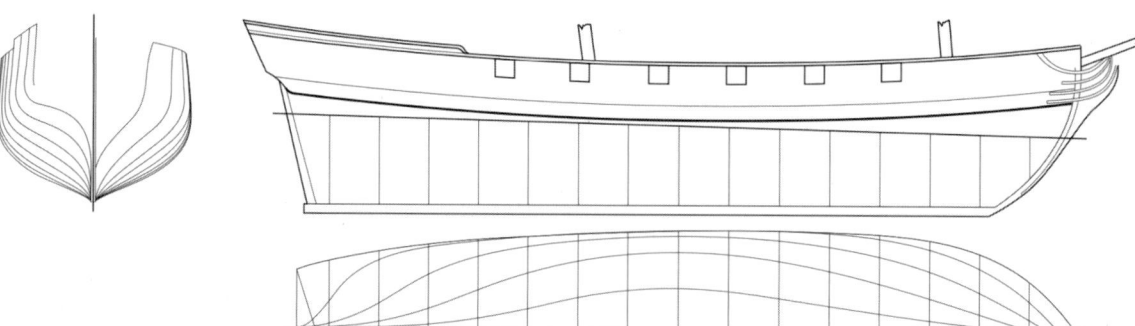

A plan of the *Favorite* Class 10-gun snows of 1776 redrawn by László Veres from an original design draught. Unusually, they are recorded as clinker-built, a technique then in vogue for cutters but rarely tried on larger vessels. It produced a light but relatively fragile hull, so structural weakness may be behind the decision in 1780 to reduce them to 2-gun *avisos* (advice boats).

14.10.1782 by HMS *Eurydice* (24) off Île de Bas.

Arlequin. American merchant vessel, possibly named *Harlequin*, purchased in the Antilles and put into service 22.4.1780.
  Dimensions & tons: 75ft 2in, 66ft 0in x 18ft 10in x 9ft 6in (24.41, 21.44 x 6.12 x 3.09m). 110/205 tons. Draught 8ft 7in/11ft (2.79/3.57m). Men: 25/28 +4 officers.
  Guns: 12 to 16, all of small calibres.
  Captured 6.6.1780 by HMS *Cerberus* (32) off Martinique or 17.6.1780 by HMS *Hind* (24) off Newfoundland and became HMS *Porto*, retaken 11.1780 by the French. Captured 4.1781 off Belle-Isle by a British cutter, renamed HMS *Harlequin* 1782. Sold 19.6.1782.

Duc de Mortemart or ***Mortemart***. Privateer corvette from St Malo chartered there 6–11.1779 and acquired (purchased?) 9.1780 as a training corvette for the Navy. Men: 44 +4 officers and 88 volunteer novice trainees. Wrecked at Granville 10.1780.

Saint Louis. Corvette of unknown origin in service in 1780 at St Domingue. May have been a former patache (tender or advice boat) of the customs service. 14/16 guns, 70 men. With schooner *Petite Minerve* fought off two British privateers 7–8.11.1781 and escorted the leaking French merchantman *Pressigny* into Cap Haïtien. In combat again 7.1782. Last mentioned 1784 as a customs patache in the Antilles.

Duc de Chartres. Privateer 24-gun brig-rigged corvette built between 1779 and 4.1780 at St Malo and purchased by the Navy 9.1782 at Île de France. 80 tons, 14 x 4pdrs. Rebuilt 1785–86, probably at Île de France. Renamed *Coureur* 29.9.1792. Condemned at Île de France 3.1798, last mentioned 1801, wreck still visible there 1808.

Juliette. Nantes merchantman purchased by the Navy at Île de France 4.1783 and put into service as a corvette. 260 tons. Fitted as headquarters hulk at Lorient 3.1787, removed from service 8.1787.

Ex-BRITISH MERCANTILE AND PRIVATEER PRIZES armed with 4pdr guns or smaller (1778–1782).
Seven British merchant vessels and privateers were captured and used by the French navy as small corvettes during the War of American Independence.

Chance (***Chans***). British mercantile or privateer corvette captured 2.9.1778 by *Iphigénie* (32). 12 x 4pdrs, 96 men +4 officers. Listed by Brest from 1778 as a brigantine and by Rochefort after her arrival there 14.3.1780 as a snow, also called a cutter. Used at Rochefort as a school for novices and ratings. Struck early 1783 at Rochefort.

Junon. British mercantile or privateer corvette possibly named *Juno* captured 3.1779 in the Îles de Los off Conakry, Guinea, by the frigate *Nymphe* (32) and the corvette *Épervier*. 14 x 4pdrs. Was in bad condition at Lorient 8.1779 and to be sold.

Finkastle or ***Finkastre***. British privateer corvette *Finkoster* captured 12.1779 by *Précieuse* (32) off Cape St Vincent near the Azores. 14 x 4pdrs, brig-rigged. Captured 7.1781 by a British privateer.

Impératrice de Russie. British privateer from Liverpool (24 guns, 129 men) captured 3.1780 by the frigate *Charmante* (32) and taken into Lorient. 300 tons, 24 guns. Added to the fleet list 1781, then loaned 1781 to Sieur De Launay, sold 1782 and struck.

Diligent. British privateer brigantine *Tanna* or *Danner* from Madras (10 guns, 62 men) captured 1.1781 in the Indian Ocean. Fitted and rearmed with 10 guns as a corvette 11–12.1781 at Île de France. Sank 8.1782 off Gondelour (Cuddalore), India.

Cochrane. British privateer corvette *Cochrane* captured 2.1782 and commissioned 14.3.1782 by the Navy at York (the York River, Virginia?). 150 men +6 officers. Captured 5.2.1783 by the British.

Deux Hélènes or ***Hélène***. Captured 4 or 5.1782 in the Indian Ocean by the frigate *Bellone* (32). 8 guns. Captured 4.1783 by the British off Trincomalee. This may be the same vessel as the *flûte Deux Hélènes* in Chapter 9.

Ex-BRITISH NAVAL AND POST OFFICE PRIZES armed with 4pdr guns or smaller (1778–1782).
Six former merchantmen or privateers that had been commissioned into the Royal Navy and two Post Office packets were captured by the French between 1778 and 1782. HMS *York* was captured on 19 July 1778 off Little Egg Bay, Delaware, by the 90-gun ship *Languedoc*. HMS *Helena* was captured on 16 September 1778 by the frigate *Sensible* (34) in the Channel. HMS *Loyalist* was captured on 30 July 1781 by the frigate *Aigrette* (32) with *Glorieux* (74) off Cape Henry and commissioned on 1 September 1781 by the French. HMS *Sandwich* was captured on 24 August 1781 off Charleston, South Carolina, by *Souverain* (74) of de Grasse's fleet. HMS *Stormont* and HMS *Rodney* were taken by Kersaint's squadron on 3 February 1782 at the surrender of Demerara, *Rodney* being renamed *Jeune Dauphin* in April 1782. Finally the British Post Office packets *Swift* and *Speedy*, which were carrying despatches from Falmouth to the Windward Islands, were captured with four merchantmen and a privateer cutter on 15 July 1782 (report dated 11 August 1782) in sight of Barbados by *Résolue* (40) and *Friponne* (32) and taken into Martinique. Their captor called them advice boats (avisos).

York. Mercantile *Betsy*, possibly sloop rigged and built at Bermuda, purchased by the RN 29.3.1777 in North America and commissioned as HMS *York* 5.1778.
  Dimensions & tons: 61ft 0in x 20ft 8in x 9ft 5in (19.82 x 6.71 x 3.06m). 170 tons displacement.
  Guns: 18 x 4pdrs
  Retaken 23.8.1778 by the British and returned to service. Captured 4.7.1779 by the French at the surrender of Grenada to d'Estaing's squadron and renamed *Duc d'York*. Struck early 1783.

Héléna or ***Hélène***. French schooner *Hélène* purchased by the RN early 1778 and commissioned 5.1778 as HMS *Helena*. Rigged as a schooner when taken, re-rigged as a brigantine by 11.1778 but reverted to a schooner by 1.1779.
  Dimensions & tons: 72ft 0in, 61ft 0in x 25ft 0in x 10ft 0in (23.39, 19.82 x 8.12 x 3.25m). 150/280 tons. Draught 7½ft/13½ft

(2.44/4.39m). Men: 88/89, +3/6 officers.
Guns: 16 x 4pdrs.
Recaptured 22.6.1779 by HMS *Ambuscade* (32) near Ushant and restored to RN service. Wrecked with all hands 3.11.1796 on the Dutch coast in a storm.

Loyaliste. British privateer *Restoration* purchased by the RN 14.11.1779 at New York and commissioned as HMS *Loyalist*.
Dimensions & tons: 93ft 0in x 26ft 0in (3.21 x 8.45m). 400 tons displacement. Men: 87 (including 20 British prisoners), +3 officers.
Guns: Probably 14 guns and 8 *pierriers*.
Given 11.1781 by the French to the Americans.

Sandwich. British mercantile *Marjory* purchased by the RN 10.4.1780 at New York and commissioned as HMS *Sandwich*, a 20-gun unrated 'armed ship'.
Dimensions & tons: dimensions unknown. 150 tons. 30 men +1 officer.
Guns: 24, including some 18pdrs.
Sold 12.1781 in North America.

Stormont. American merchant brig *Pickering* taken by the RN 14.2.1781 at the surrender of St Eustatius and purchased by the RN as HMS *Stormont*.
Dimensions & tons: 75ft 0in x 22ft 1in (24.36 x 7.17m). 126/250 tons.
Guns: 16 x 4pdrs.
Struck 1786, BU at Rochefort.

Jeune Dauphin. Mercantile brig purchased 1781, probably in the Antilles, and commissioned as HMS *Rodney* 29.7.1781.
Dimensions & tons: dimensions unknown. 173 tons.
Guns: 10 x 4pdrs (1783).
Called a *chatte pontée* (decked lighter) when she arrived at Rochefort 17.6.1782. Listed in late 1782 as a brigantine-rigged corvette. Left Rochefort 5.1783 for St Pierre et Miquelon, listed by Rochefort 7-12.1783 both as a corvette and as a *gabarre*. Returned to Rochefort 5.2.1784 in good condition and suitable for use as a packet, sold to a private buyer 6.1784.

Swift. Carried out two round trip voyages between Falmouth and North America as a British Post Office packet between 12.1779 and 6.1781, the first of which took her to the West Indies before calling at New York. Had 16 guns and 80 men when taken. Although reported as sold 11.1782 at Pointe-à-Pitre, *Swift* arrived at Lorient 9.2.1783 and was placed out of service there. The American privateer brig *Middletown* that served as HMS *Swift* between 1779 and 1781 was a different vessel.

Speedy. Carried out two round trip voyages between Falmouth and North America as a British Post Office packet brig 5.1780 to 9.1781. Left Falmouth 18.6.1782 with despatches for Barbados, St Lucia, Antigua, and Jamaica; was then to carry news back to England of the departure of the homeward-bound fleet from Jamaica. Had 16 guns and 80 men when taken. Attached to the French squadron at Martinique, retaken when *Solitaire* (64) was taken 6–7.12.1782 off Martinique by HMS *Ruby* (64) of Hughes's squadron and returned to the British Post Office for further packet service through 1789.

(E) Corvettes with 6pdr (or heavier) guns acquired from 1763

A royal decision in October 1763 stated that in the future there would be two types of corvettes, a 1st Order with 20 x 6pdrs and a 2nd Order with 12 x 4pdrs. This decision officially assigned the 6pdr gun to corvettes for the first time, in effect replacing the category of *frégates légères* which no longer existed, as well as the relatively few 6pdr-armed frigates of the 1740s and 1750s (see Chapter 6). The decision to place 6pdrs in the principal battery of corvettes reflected the fact that these vessels were taking over the role of escort and commerce raiding vessels which the light frigates had held until that time. In 1767 Choiseul went a step further and asked the naval constructors in the ports to develop plans for corvettes carrying 12 x 6pdrs and 18 x 6pdrs, signalling the abandonment of the 4pdr gun for future new construction corvettes.

ISIS. 16 guns. Designed and built by Jean-Hyacinthe Raffeau alongside his 4pdr-armed *Sylphide* (see above); similarly named 22 December 1762. Hull pierced for 18 gunports.
Dimensions & tons: 102ft 0in x 26ft 0in x 13ft 0in (33.13 x 8.45 x 4.22m). 250/500 tons. Draught 10ft 10in/10ft 10in (3.52/3.52m). Men: 90/120.
Guns: 16 x 6pdrs.
Isis Indret (Nantes).
K: 7.1762. L: 10.1763. C: 12.1763. Rebuilt 1767 to 9.1767 at Rochefort. Sold early 1775 at Brest for commercial use.

PURCHASED PRIVATEERS with 6pdr guns or heavier (1762).
Three vessels under construction as privateer corvettes were purchased by the French Navy near the end of the Seven Years' War.

Saint Esprit. Privateer corvette designed and built at Brest by Jean Geoffroy for Sieur Clement & Cie, purchased there 8.1762. Also called *Petit Saint Esprit*.
Dimensions & tons: 90ft 0in x 25ft 6in x 11ft 10in (29.24 x 8.28 x 3.84m), 315/500 tons. Draught 10½ft/11½ft (3.41/3.74m). Men: 56/76 +4 officers.
Guns: 16 x 6pdrs, 6 smaller added later.
K: 1760. L: 1761. C: 9.1762. Captured 1.1763 by the British, returned 2.1763 to the French at Jamaica. Grounded and wrecked 4.1766 near Bayonne, BU 5.1766.

Hirondelle. Privateer corvette *Expédition* built at Nantes, purchased there 8.1762, and renamed *Hirondelle* 10.1762 (or 20.12.1762). Listed as a brigantine in 1778.
Dimensions & tons: 85ft 0in, 70ft 0in x 24ft 0in x 11ft 10in (27.61, 22.74 x 7.80 x 3.84m). 240/458 tons. Draught 9ft 8in/12½ft (3.14/4.06m). Men: 100/141 +4/7 officers.
Guns: 12 to 1765, 16 x 6pdrs from 1766
K: 1761. L: 1762. C: 9.1762. Rebuilt 1770 at Brest. Training ship 1774 for the the École Royale de Marine, part of the *Escadre d'Évolutions* 6–9.1775. Removed from service 18.10.1782 at Brest, struck 1783 at Le Havre.

Petit Mars. Privateer corvette *Mars*, built at St Jean de Luz for Sieur De Lissalde, purchased 8.1762 and put into service 9.1762 at Nantes.
Dimensions & tons: dimensions unknown. 200 tons. Men: 38/52 +4 officers
Guns: 12 x 6pdrs.
K: 1756. L: 1757. C: 1757. Wrecked 7.3.1765 near Gijon on the Spanish coast while returning from Guadeloupe.

LUNETTE. 4 guns. *Corvette-canonnière* of a type proposed by Kerguelen de Trémarec and approved by Choiseul in 1765 with 4 x 24pdr guns on pivoting mounts that could fire to either side. Designed and built by Pierre-Augustin Lamothe. Named 31 March 1766 (contract for workers 12 February). Could make three knots under oars. Listed at Brest in September 1778 as a brigantine with 4 x 24pdrs and from November 1778 to September 1782 as a snow with 10 x 12pdrs; however, lists of 1781 at Brest and 1783 at Rochefort continue to show her with 4 x 24pdrs. Reassigned from Brest to Rochefort 1781.

Dimensions & tons: 90ft 0in x 25ft 0in x 12ft 0in (29.24 x 8.12 x 3.90m). 150/350 tons. Draught 9½ft (3.09m). Men: 70/80, +5 officers.
Guns: 4 x 24pdrs.
Lunette Brest Dyd.
K: 2.1766. L: 19.5.1766. C: 8.1766. Rebuilt at Brest 12.1775–3.1776. Condemned 1784 at Rochefort or possibly in Senegal.

The 6pdr-armed small frigates (ex-privateers) *Étourdie* and *Biche* were re-classed as corvettes in May 1768. They are listed in Chapter 6.

The Navy planned to order the construction of seven new corvettes during 1768, all with 6pdr guns. Brest and Rochefort were each to build one of 16 and two of 12 guns while Toulon was to build one of 12 guns. The few 6pdr corvettes built in 1767–71 were flush-decked vessels, with a continuous orlop deck below, although the constructors at Brest complained that their sizes were too limited for the ordnance and stores which they were expected to stow.

CERF VOLANT. 16 guns. Designed and built by Henri Chevillard.
Dimensions & tons: 100ft 0in x 26ft 0in x 13ft 0in (32.48 x 8.45 x 4.22m). 250/515 tons. Draught 11¾ft/12ft 2in (3.82/3.95m). Men: 100/120.
Guns: 16 x 6pdrs.
Cerf Volant Rochefort Dyd.
K: 2.1768. L: 5.8.1768. C: 4.1769. Sold 1775, probably at Nantes.

ÉCUREUIL. 12 guns. Designed by Jacques-Luc Coulomb and built by C-V Segondat. The vessel, which was ordered in November 1767, was rigged as a snow.
Dimensions & tons: 97ft 0in x 24ft 0in x 12ft 0in (31.51 x 7.80 x 3.90m). 188/400 tons. Draught 10½/12½ft (3.41/4.06m). Men: 70/90, +4 officers (40 as packet).
Guns: 12 x 6pdrs. Later 12 x 6pdrs, 2 to 6 x 4pdrs.
Écureuil Brest Dyd.
K: 2.1768. L: 27.8.1768. C: 1769. Rebuilt at Brest 1776 and as a packet at Rochefort 8–9.1783. Renamed *Courrier de l'Amérique* 10.1783 and used as a translantic packet to New York. Struck 1785 at Lorient.

PERLE. 16 guns. Designed by Pierre-Augustin Lamothe. The vessel was ordered in November 1767.
Dimensions & tons: 100ft 0in, 87ft? x 26ft 0in x 13ft 0in (32.48, 28.26? x 8.45 x 4.22m). 280/480 tons. Draught 10½/11ft (3.41/3.57m). Men: 100/140.
Guns: 16 x 6pdrs. 16 x 6pdrs, 2 x 4pdrs from 1772.
Perle Brest Dyd.
K: 2.1768. L: 30.8.1768. C: 10.1768. Rebuilt at Brest 1779. Captured 6.7.1780 west of Cape Finisterre by HMS *Romney* (50) while escorting a convoy to the Antilles.

EXPÉRIENCE. Experimental corvette or aviso designed and built by Jacques Boux and named in April 1768. In addition to her unusual armament she could carry 18 months of supplies, around three times the usual amount.
Dimensions & tons: dimensions unknown. 250 tons. Men: 59/137 +2/8 officers.
Guns: 4 x 24pdrs (two fore, two aft). Changed 1771 to 16 x 6pdrs and in 1775 to 1 gun + 4 *pierriers*.
Expérience Le Havre.
K: 2.1768. L: 16.7.1768. C: 8.1768. Belonged to the *Marine des Colonies* Hull coppered 6.1772 at Rochefort or Le Havre. Last mentioned 9.1776 after returning from Île de France, probably then sold at Brest for commercial use.

FLÈCHE. 18 guns. Designed by Louis-Hilarion Chapelle and built by Joseph-Marie-Blaise Coulomb. The vessel was ordered on 25 December 1767 and named in February 1768, but on 19 February the Ministry suspended construction (until 18 March) on learning that work had begun without the design being approved. She had pole masts like those in polacres instead of conventional fidded topmasts.
Dimensions & tons: 108ft 0in, 93ft 0in x 27ft 6in x 13ft 8in (35.08, 30.21 x 8.93 x 4.44 m). 326/550 tons. Draught 10¾/11¾ft (3.49/3.82m). Men: 110/130 +6 officers.
Guns: 18 x 6pdrs; by 1794 reduced to 14 x 6pdrs.
Flèche Toulon Dyd.
K: 12.1.1768. L: 19.10.1768. C: 9.1769. Rebuilt 12.1779–1780 at Toulon. Captured 21.5.1794 by the British at the surrender of Bastia and added as HMS *Fleche* (now rigged as a brig); wrecked 12.11.1795 in the bay of San Fiorenzo, Corsica.

ROSSIGNOL. 16 guns. Designed by Joseph-Louis Ollivier. The vessel was ordered in 1769 and named on 25 August 1769 (although work commenced on her earlier). Length also reported as 101ft 6in (32.97m) and draught as 12ft 10in/13ft 8in (4.17/4.44m).
Dimensions & tons: 108ft 0in, 98ft 0in x 28ft 0in x 14ft 0in (35.08, 31.83 x 9.10 x 4.55 m). 350/600 tons. Draught 12ft 1in/13ft 2in (3.93/4.28 m). Men: 100/120.
Guns: 16 x 6pdrs; 18 x 6pdrs by 1772, 20 x 6pdrs by 1775 (the additional guns possibly being 4pdrs).
Rossignol Brest Dyd.
K: 5.6.1769. L: 14.11.1769. C: 11.1770. Rebuilt at Brest 1778. Entered Smyrna 5.1795 incapable of further service, last mentioned there 2.1796.

SÉRIN. 14 guns. Designed by Henri Chevillard. Rigged as a snow. She was set up on the slip in one morning (probably in June 1770) by 200 workers, all the pieces being numbered and arranged in advance.
Dimensions & tons: 96ft 0in, later 99ft 0in x 26ft 0in x 12ft 8in (31.18, 32.16 x 8.45 x 4.11m). 200/400 tons. Draught 10½ft /11ft 2in (3.41/3.63 m). Men: 80/100, +4 officers (43 men as packet).
Guns: 14 x 6pdrs. 18 x 6pdrs by 1783, 16 x 6pdrs from 1784 (the additional guns possibly being 4pdrs instead of 6pdrs).
Sérin Rochefort Dyd.
K: 6.1770. L: 2.3.1771. C: 5.1771. Rebuilt at Brest 1778. Fitted as packet 7–8.1783 at Brest, renamed *Courrier de l'Europe* 9.1783 and employed as transatlantic packet. Transferred 4.1787 to the Régie des Paquebots for service betwee Le Havre and New York or the Antilles. Sold 1.1789 at Le Havre to Sieur Ruellan, resold 1790 and last mentioned 10.1790 at Île de France.

SARDINE. 16 guns (pierced for 18 ports). Designed and built by Broquier (died 26 December 1771) and Joseph-Marie-Blaise Coulomb. This vessel was ordered on 7 February 1770 and named on 25 February 1770.
Dimensions & tons: 106ft 0in x 27ft 0in x 13ft 3in (34.43 x 8.77 x 4.30m). 280/500 tons. Draught 10ft 7in/11ft 4in (3.44/3.68m). Men: 80/100, +6 officers.
Guns: 14 x 6pdrs. 18 guns in 1781: UD 14 x 6pdrs, QD 4 x 4pdrs.
Sardine Toulon Dyd.
K: 6.1770. L: 14.7.1771. C: 1772. Handed over by Royalists to the

British and Spanish at Toulon 29.8.1793, recovered by the French at the surrender of that port in 12.1794, but captured again 9.3.1796 by a British division including HM Ships *Egmont* (74) and *Barfleur* (90) in the neutral port of Tunis and became HMS *Sardine*; sold 1806.

After a barren few years from 1772, construction resumed in 1776 with the last two Navy-built 4pdr corvettes – *Curieuse* and *Favorite*, both built at Le Havre in 1776 and as noted above reduced to lightly-armed avisos in 1780. After a false start in 1776, a larger ship, *Subtile* (immediately below), was built in 1777 to carry 20 x 6pdr guns. Two years later a pair of prototype 8pdr-armed corvettes, *Coquette* and *Naïade*, was built at Toulon (and soon followed by others of the same design). As 8pdr frigate construction had come to an end in the 1770s, the new 6pdr and 8pdr corvettes could be seen to be taking on the role and duties of the smaller frigates.

The construction at Bordeaux of two corvettes with 18 x 6pdr guns, *Philomèle* and *Précieuse*, was planned in 1776 but abandoned in 1777, not having been begun. For another ship with 18 x 6pdrs projected for construction in 1776 at Toulon but not built see the barque *Vigilante* in Chapter 12.

SUBTILE. 18 guns. Designed and built by Raymond-Antoine Haran. Listed with 18 x 6pdrs, pierced for 20 guns.
    Dimensions & tons: 110ft 0in x 28ft 0in x 14ft 6in (35.73 x 9.10 x 4.71m). 320/600 tons. Men: 120/200, +7/8 officers.
    Guns: 18 x 6pdrs. 24 guns by 1786: UD 18 x 6pdrs, QD 6 x 4pdrs.
Subtile Rochefort Dyd.
    K: 4.1777. L: 7.9.1777. C: end 1777. Rebuilt 8.1783–1784 at Lorient. Voyage to China 1786 to 11.1788 with frigate *Résolution* (ex-*Romulus*) under D'Entrecasteaux, renamed *Sainte Catherine* 1.1787 while approaching Macao but original name restored 3.1787. Condemned 12.1788 at Toulon and struck, hulk there 1789, last mentioned 1791.

VALEUR. Although said to have been a sister to *Subtile*, available information suggests that she was a smaller vessel that may have been chartered by the Navy at St Malo in June 1778.
    Dimensions & tons: unknown. Men: 124, +5/8 officers.
    Guns: 6 or 14
Valeur St Malo.
    K: ?1777. L: ?1778. C: 6.1778. Attacked 13.5.1779 at Cancale by a British squadron led by HMS *Experiment* (50) and burned with the *gabarre Écluse* and the cutter *Guêpe*, although the other two ships were later salvaged.

Ex-BRITISH NAVAL PRIZES with 6pdr guns or heavier (1778–1779). HMS *Senegal* was captured on 14 August 1778 by *Hector* (74) of d'Estaing's fleet off Sandy Hook. HMS *Zephyr* was originally HMS *Merlin*, a two-masted sloop that was captured by a French privateer in April 1757 and renamed when recaptured in August 1757. She was captured on 23 August 1778 by *Gracieuse* (28) in the Western Mediterranean. HMS *Ceres* was a one-off British naval ship sloop ordered in 1774 to be copied from the draught of the (ex-French) prize sloop *Chevert* (a Dunkirk privateer taken in 1761 and renamed HMS *Pomona*). She was captured near St Lucia by the frigate *Iphigénie* (32) aided by *Sagittaire* (50) on 17 December 1778. The elderly sloop *Weasel* had originally been purchased by the British Navy in 1745 while building as a two-masted vessel; they completed her as a ship-rigged vessel (the RN's first cruising ship sloop – the earlier *Furnace*, an ex-bomb ketch, was converted to ship rig for a voyage of exploration). After 34 years in RN service, she was captured by the frigate *Boudeuse* (32) off St Eustatius on 13 January 1779 while carrying despatches from Britain. It is unclear whether she was formally added to the French Navy, but she was operated by them in the Antilles for some months under the name *Belette* or *Weasel*. As for other British prizes, all dimensions are as remeasured in French units.

Sénégal. Henry Bird, Rotherhithe.
    Ord:24.4.1760. K: 5.1760. L: 24.12.1760. C: 30.4.1761. Designed by William Bately.
    Dimensions & tons: 91ft 0in, 79ft 3in x 24ft 3in x 12ft 0in (29.56, 25.74 x 7.88 x 3.90m). 350 tons displacement. Draught. 10ft/11ft (3.25/3.57m). Men: 123 +6 officers.
    Guns: 16 x 6pdrs.
    Listed as a brigantine 6.1779. Retaken 2.11.1780 by HMS *Zephyr* (14) and the privateer *Polly* off the Gambia. Recommissioned in the RN but blew up 22.11.1780 while refitting at Gorée. Wreck found 1988.

Zéphyr John Quallett, Rotherhithe.
    Ord: 9.7.1755. K: 18.7.1755. L: 20.3.1756. C: 24.4.1756. Designed by Thomas Slade.
    Dimensions & tons: 81ft 0in x 22ft 10in (26.31 x 7.42m)
    Guns: 4 x 6pdrs, 10 x 4pdrs.
    Removed from service 1.1780 at Toulon and sold 1.4.1780 for privateering. Captured 8.1780 by the British and burned.

Cérès Woolwich Dyd.
    Ord: 16.7.1774. K: 27.5.1776. L: 25.3.1777. C: 1.5.1777.
    Dimensions & tons: 102ft 0in x 25ft 8in (33.13 x 8.34m). 280/450 tons. Men: 140/171, +7/9 officers.
    Guns: 18 x 6pdrs.
    Sometimes called *Petite Cérès*. Retaken in the Mona Passage by HMS *Champion* (24) of Hood's squadron 19.4.1782 and reinstated as HMS *Raven*, but again captured by the French frigates *Nymphe* (36) and *Concorde* (32) off Montserrat 7.1.1783, resuming her name of *Cérès*. Sold at Brest 1791.

Belette or *Weasel* Taylor & Randall, Rotherhithe.
    Purchased 22.4.1745. L: 22.5.1745. C: 24.6.1745.
    Dimensions & tons: 90ft 0in x 25ft 10in (29.24 x 8.39m). 370 tons displacement.
    Guns: 16 x 6pdrs.
    Removed from service 7.1779 in the West Indies (d'Estaing's squadron having commandeered all her guns) and sold 1.1781 at Guadeloupe.

Ex-BRITISH MERCANTILE AND PRIVATEER PRIZES with 6pdr guns or heavier (1778–1779). Eight British merchant vessels and privateers were captured and used by the French navy as larger corvettes during the earlier part of the War of American Independence.

Épervier. British privateer from London probably named *Sparrowhawk* (22 guns, 140 men) captured 7.1778 by the frigate *Oiseau* (34) and put into service 8.1778 at Lorient as *Épervier*. Rigged as a brigantine.
    Dimensions & tons: dimensions unknown. 250/400 tons. Men: 103/135, +4/6 officers.
    Guns: 16 x 9pdrs (British). Listed by Brest 1778–82 with 12 x 4pdrs but probably had the 9pdr armament.
    Placed out of service 12.1782 at Brest, sold early 1783 to Desbordes at Brest for commercial use.

Pilote des Indes. British privateer or merchantman built in Britain or at Lorient captured 10.1778. Rigged as a cutter.
    Dimensions & tons: dimensions unknown. 150 tons. Men: 66/130.
    Guns: in 1779: 1 x 18pdr, 10 x 4pdrs; from 1780: 10 x 6pdrs.

Re-classed from corvette to brig 1787. Wrecked 4.3.1790 on the coast southwest of Finisterre.

Lively. British privateer *Lively* from Bedford captured 10.1778 or 26.7.1779 and purchased by the King from M. de Chaumont at Lorient. Rigged as a snow, originally reported as a cutter.
  Dimensions & tons: dimensions unknown. 100 to 180 tons. Men: 70–130 +5 officers.
  Guns: 16 x 6pdrs.
  Condemned 1.1783 at Fort Royal, Martinique. Struck 1784 by Rochefort.

Jeune Henry. British *Young Henry*, probably a merchantman, captured 11.1778.
  Dimensions & tons: dimensions unknown. 300 tons. Men: 112/154 +5/7 officers
  Guns: (1781): 18 x 6pdrs, 6 x 3pdrs
  Put into service 11.1778. Training corvette at Brest 2.1782 to 3.1783 for 180 boys and novices. Struck 4.1783 at Brest.

Ellis or *Elise*. British privateer *Ellis* captured 1.1779 off Martinique. 20 x 9pdrs, 8 x 4pdrs. Captured 22.12.1779 by a British division in the Antilles.

David. British merchantman or privateer *David* captured 1779. Rigged as a brigantine.
  Dimensions & tons: dimensions unknown. 250 tons. Men: 80/145 +8 officers.
  Guns: 18 x 12pdrs. From 1784: 16 x 6pdrs.
  Removed from service 5.1786 at Brest, then struck.

Argus. British merchantman or privateer *Argus* captured 11.1779. 16 x 6pdrs, 76/86 men +6 officers. Probably rigged as a brigantine.
  Removed from service 6.1782 at Brest, struck 1784.

Tigre. British privateer *Tiger* captured 8.12.1779 by the frigate *Amazone* (32) and purchased 8.2.1780 by the King at Toulon. First appeared on the list at Toulon 6.1781.
  Dimensions & tons: dimensions unknown. 300 tons.
  Guns: from 1779: 2 x 9pdrs, 20 x 6pdrs; from 4.1780: 18 x 6pdrs, 2 x 3pdrs; reduced to 4 x 6pdrs 9.1782.
  Fitted as 300-ton *flûte* 5.1783. Struck 1784 at Toulon.

COQUETTE Class. 18 guns (8pdrs). Designed and built by Joseph-Marie-Blaise Coulomb. The first 8pdr-armed corvettes, following the final building of the last 8pdr frigates a few years earlier. These were equivalent to the contemporary British 9pdr-armed 28-gun Sixth Rates, but these and later large quarterdecked French corvettes were never popular with the British who sometimes reduced their armaments after capture. All eight were built at Toulon. The first two below had names assigned on 23 July 1779; the next four were all ordered on 20 April 1780 and named on 16 June 1780; the final pair were begun in late 1780 as *No.1* and *No.2* respectively and named on 3 March 1781. Most names had previously been carried by frigates, thus emphasizing that they were replacements for the 8pdr-armed frigate type. They had 13 pairs of gunports. During 1781–83 Toulon recorded at least 28 changes in the quarterdeck armaments of these eight ships for totals including the 18 x 8pdrs on the UD ranging from 18 to 24 guns; the reported QD armaments being none, 2 x 6pdrs, 4 x 4pdrs, 2 x 6pdrs + 2 x 4pdrs, 4 x 6pdrs, 6 x 4pdrs, 4 x 6pdrs + 2 x 4pdrs, and 6 x 6pdrs.
  Dimensions & tons: 119ft 0in, 106ft 0in x 30ft 6in x 15ft 6in (38.66, 34.43 x 9.91 x 5.04 m). 400/850 tons. Draught 14ft/15ft (4.55/4.87m). Men: 160, +8 officers (198 men +7/10 officers in *Naïade*, 224 men in *Brune* in 1794).
  Guns: UD 18 x 8pdrs, QD 0 to 6 x 6pdrs and/or 4pdrs (see above). 30 guns in *Badine* 1792: 22 x 8pdrs, 6 x 6pdrs, 2 x 36pdr *obusiers*. *Brune* had 2 (?) mortars added temporarily 9.1792 at Toulon. 26/28 guns in *Brune* 1794: 20/22 x 8pdrs, 6 x 6pdrs. 24 guns in *Badine* 1801: 18/20 x 8pdrs, 6/4 x 6pdrs.

Coquette Toulon Dyd.
  K: 7.1779. L: 11.12.1779. C: 3.1780. Taken 2.3.1783 by HMS *Resistance* (44) off Grand Turk Island in the West Indies, sold by the British for commercial use.

Naïade Toulon Dyd.
  K: 7.1779. L: 21.12.1779. C: 4.1780. Taken 14.4.1783 by HMS *Sceptre* (64) in the East Indies. Commissioned in the RN 4.1783 with UD 22 x 12pdrs, QD 6 x 12pdr carronades, Fc 2 x 18pdr carronades, although never registered on the Navy List. Paid off 6.1784 and sold at Deptford 17.8.1784.

Badine Toulon Dyd.
  K: 5.1780. L: 5.8.1780. C: 12.1780. Decommissioned and condemned at Martinique 18.3.1804 because she could no longer remain afloat. Hulk captured by the British 2.1809.

Sémillante Toulon Dyd.

Admiralty draught of the *Naiade* dated Deptford 14 July 1784. Captured in the East Indies in 1783, the ship served the Royal Navy locally until the end of the war, but was never formally added to the Navy List. This may have been simply the result of the return of peace, but these large quarterdecked corvettes were never popular in the British service: many were captured in later wars and acquired a very poor reputation, in marked contrast to the favourable opinion enjoyed by most French prizes. (National Maritime Museum, London J7149)

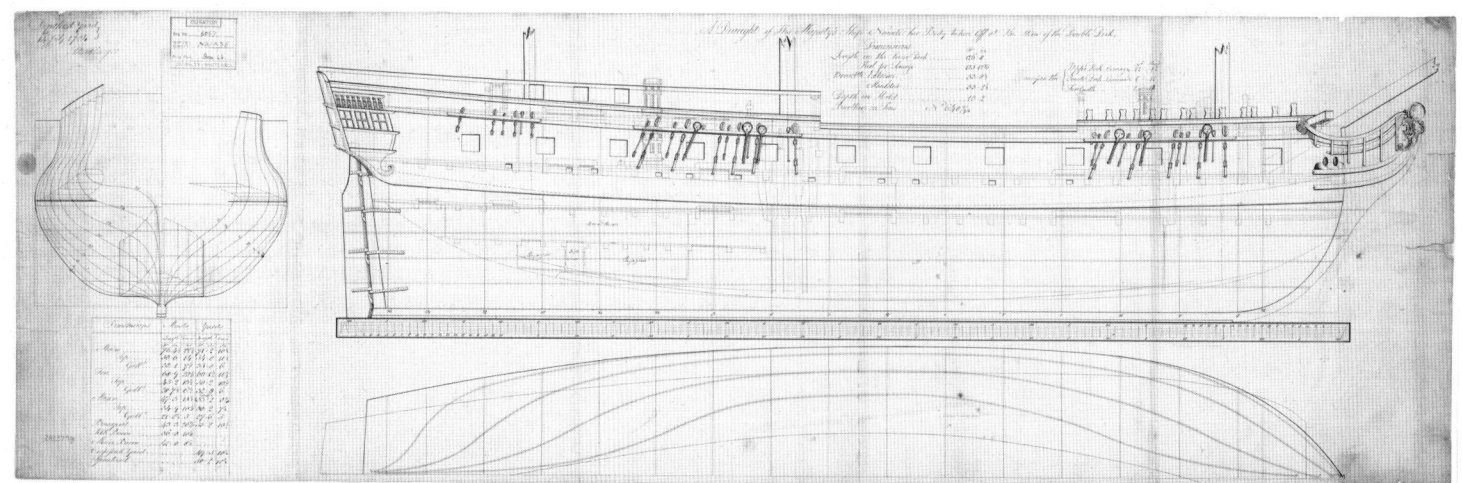

K: 5.1780. L: 11.8.1780. C: 12.1780. Loaned 9.1786 as a storage depot to a Dutch fleet visting Toulon, burnt accidentally 5.1.1787 by a Dutch frigate being careened at Toulon, replaced by *Aigrette* (32) for the summer 1787 cruise of the fleet and struck.

Blonde Toulon Dyd.
K: 8.1780. L: 6.1.1781. C: 2.1781. Taken by HM Ships *Latona* (38) and *Phaeton* (38) off Ushant 27.11.1793. No record of RN service, sold 1794.

Brune Toulon Dyd.
K: 8.1780. L: 20.1.1781. C: 3.1781. Taken with *Leander* (50, ex-British) by the Russians at the fall of Corfu 3.3.1799 and handed over to the Turks. May have been the ex-French Turkish corvette with 10 guns and 18 gunports captured 3.1807 at Tenedos by HMS *Glatton* (50).

Poulette Toulon Dyd.
K: 9.1780. L: 22.3.1781. C: 30.6.1781. Her Royalist crew rallied to the British and Spanish at Toulon 29.8.1793, fled to Porto-Ferrayo 19.9.1793 on the arrival of the Republican army, ship taken away by the RN 18.12.1793 as HMS *Poulette*. Burnt as unserviceable at Ajaccio 20.10.1796.

Belette Toulon Dyd.
K: 10.1780. L: 5.3.1781. C: 17.6.1781. Handed over by Royalists to the British and Spanish at Toulon 29.8.1793, taken away by the RN 18.12.1793 as HMS *Belette*. Burnt as unserviceable at Ajaccio 20.10.1796.

Ex-BRITISH NAVAL PRIZES with 6pdr guns or heavier (1780–1782). During the latter part of the War of American Independence the French captured five units of the *Swan* class, the standard British ship sloop class of the American War, plus four RN vessels that had previously been merchantmen or privateers.

SWAN Class. 25 ships were built for the RN to this 1766 design by John Williams. HMS *Fortune* was captured by frigates *Gentille* (32) and *Iphigénie* (32) of Guichen's squadron off Barbuda 26 April 1780. HMS *Thorn* was captured by the American frigates *Deane* and *Boston* 25 August 1779 and became an American privateer, was then retaken in July 1781 by a British sloop but immediately captured by two French frigates. HMS *Cormorant* was captured 24 August 1781 by *Citoyen* (74) and *Glorieux* (74) of de Grasse's fleet off Charlestown, Maryland, and renamed *Cormoran*. HMS *Bonetta* was surrendered to the Americans at the surrender of Yorktown 19 October 1781 and handed over to the French Navy after carrying letters to New York. Finally, HMS *Alligator* was captured by the frigate *Fée* (32) off the Scilly Isles 26 June 1782. *Fortune* and *Alligator* were converted to transatlantic packets at Lorient in 1783–84 for operation between Lorient and New York, but both were retained on the French Navy list as corvettes; they were transferred in January and May 1787 respectively to the *Régie des Paquebots* for operation from Le Havre until their sale in 1789. The measurements below are in French units.

Dimensions & tons: 94ft 0in, 83ft 0in x 25ft 2in x 12ft 10in (30.53, 26.96 x 8.18 x 4.17m). 300/470 tons. Draught 11ft 4in/12ft (3.68/3.90m). Men: 130/190 +5 officers; as packets 43 men +6 officers.

Guns: 16 x 6pdrs (*Fortune* and *Alligator*), 14 x 6pdrs (others). As packets (1783–84): 16 x 4pdrs in *Courrier de Lorient*, 14 or 18 x 6pdrs in *Courrier de New York*.

Fortune Woolwich Dyd.
Ord: 16.10.1775. K: 19.4.1777. L: 28.7.1778. C: 19.9.1778.
Returned to France 23.8.1783 from the Indian Ocean armed with 16 x 4pdrs under the command of the elder Pierre Bouvet.
Renamed *Courrier de Lorient* 10.1783 and fitted between then and 1.1784 at Lorient as a packet for service between Lorient and New York (between Le Havre and New York or the Antilles after 1.1787); sold at Le Havre 1.1789 to Sieur Ruellan.

Thorn James Betts, Mistleythorn.
Ord: 30.9.1777. K: 12.1777. L: 17.2.1779. C: 15.5.1779 at Sheerness Dyd.
Retaken 20.8.1782 by HMS *Arethusa* (38) and restored to RN service; sold at Deptford 28.8.1816 to BU.

Cormoran John Barnard & Co, Ipswich.
Ord: 30.10.1775. K: 11.1775. L: 21.5.1776. C: 1776.
Last mentioned in the Chesapeake 9.1781, may have been lost.

Bonetta John Perry, Blackwall.
Ord: 16.4.1778. K: 6.1778. L: 29.4.1779. C: 13.7.1779 at Woolwich Dyd.
Retaken 3.1.1782 by HMS *Amphion* (32) in the Chesapeake and restored to RN service; BU at Sheerness 10.1797.

Alligator John Fisher, Liverpool.
Ord: 22.6.1779. K: 10.1779. L: 11.11.1780. C: 5.1781.
Called *Alligator No.1* by Brest 11.1782–1.1783, a cutter named *Alligator* (also designated *Alligator No.2*, see Chapter 11) already being at Brest. Renamed *Courrier de New York* 10.1783 and fitted beween then and 12.1783 at Lorient as a packet for service between Lorient and New York (between Le Havre and New York or the Antilles after 1.1787); sold at Le Havre 1.1789 to Sieur Ruellan.

BARBOUDE. In November 1780 HMS *Boreas* (28) captured and sent into Antigua a Massachusetts vessel named *Charming Sally*. She was commissioned on 11 December 1780 as HMS *Barbuda* and in March 1781, with HMS *Surprize* (ex-American privateer *Bunker Hill*), occupied Demerara and the remainder of Dutch Guiana. She was still at Demerara with HMS *Oronoque, Sylph, Stormont,* and *Rodney* when the colony with the ships surrendered on 3 February 1782 to the squadron of Comte de Kersaint. The five British ships became the French *Vicomte de Damas, Barboude, Sylphe, Stormont,* and *Jeune Dauphin* respectively. The French classed *Barboude* as a 26-gun frigate in 1784–86 but armed and used her as a corvette.

Dimensions & tons: 112ft 0in x 28ft 0in (36.38 x 9.10m). 320/600 tons. Men: 120/200 +8 officers.

Guns: UD 20 x 9pdrs; QD/Fc 6 smaller. From 1793: UD 16 x 6pdrs; QD/Fc 6 x 4pdrs (reported with 22 x 9pdrs when captured 1796)

Barboude ?Massachusetts
Struck at Brest 1786 and sold for commercial use. Became the 22-gun privateer *Inabordable* 1793. Requisitioned by the Navy 5.1793 at Le Havre and renamed *Légère* 6.1793. Grounded in a storm near Cherbourg 12.1793 but refloated. Captured 6.1796 by HM Ships *Apollo* (38) and *Doris* (36) southwest of the Scilly Isles and became HMS *Legere*. Wrecked 2.2.1801 near Cartagena (Colombia).

CHASSEUR. The former French privateer *Chasseur* was purchased by the RN on 1 January 1781 in the East Indies and commissioned in March 1781 as HMS *Chaser*. She was captured on 14 February 1782 by the frigate *Bellone* (32) in the Bay of Bengal and taken into French naval service as *Chasseur*. She was ship-rigged.

Dimensions & tons: 93ft 0in x 26ft 3in (30.21 x 8.53m). Tons unknown.

Guns: 18 (14 x 6pdrs in RN service)

Chasseur ?Bordeaux.
Built 1781. Captured 16.1.1783 by HMS *Medea* (28) in the Indian Ocean and restored to RN service. Sold 28.8.1784 at Deptford.

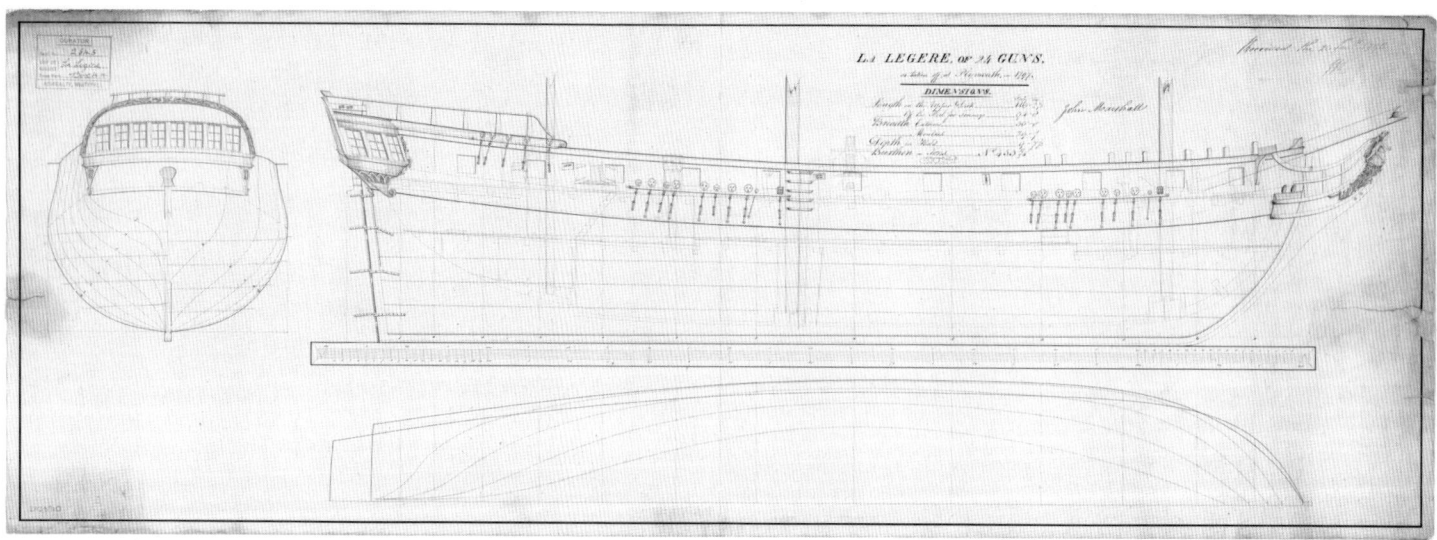

Admiralty draught of the *Legere* (ex-*Barboude*) as taken off at Plymouth in 1797. This American-built vessel had changed hands many times before this plan was made, but at this stage is rated as a 24-gun ship. The ship has a flush open upper deck, with no evidence of a forecastle and only a very short quarterdeck platform. The decorative work looks like it dates from her time in the French Navy. (National Maritime Museum, London J7076)

RAIKES. The troopship HMS *Raikes* was a merchantman of the same name purchased by the RN in September 1780. She was captured 6 June 1782 by *Artésien* (64) and *Sphinx* (64) between Madras and Trincomalee. She was classed as a corvette but was considered a *flûte* in Suffren's Indian Ocean squadron.

　　Dimensions & tons: 94ft 0in, 86ft 0in x 28ft 0in x 12ft 0in (30.53, 27.94 x 9.10 x 3.90m). 240/400 tons.
　　2 x 5pdrs (British 6pdrs added by the French), 10 x 16pdr *obusiers* (her original British 18pdr carronades).

Raikes ?Britain
　　Struck 1784 at Rochefort.

ROVER. The American 20-gun privateer *Cumberland* was captured on 27 January 1779 by HMS *Pomona* and purchased on 2 April 1779 by the Royal Navy. Renamed HMS *Rover*, she was captured on 13 September 1780 by the French frigate *Junon* off Trinidad.

　　Dimensions & tons: 85ft 0in x 21ft 3in (27.61 x 6.90m). 300 tons displacement.
　　Guns: 16 x 6pdrs + 4 *pierriers*.

Rover ?America
　　Retaken 1.1781 by the British privateer *Regulator* and returned to RN service, foundered with all hands *c*.29.10.1781.

Ex-BRITISH MERCANTILE AND PRIVATEER PRIZES with 6pdr guns or heavier (1780–1782). Five British merchant vessels and privateers were captured and used by the French navy as larger corvettes during the later part of the War of American Independence.

Britannia. British *Britannia* captured or purchased at the beginning of 1780. 16 x 6pdrs or 14 x 6pdrs +4 *obusiers*. Sent from Cadiz under orders from Comte d'Estaing and entered Rochefort 6.1.1781 to be careened. Listed by Rochefort as a lugger. Sold 5.1781 at Rochefort, struck 1782. Reappeared on the list late 1783, struck 1784 at Brest.

Hypocrite or *Hipocrite*. British brig captured 10.1781 off the Chesapeake.
　　Dimensions & tons: 66ft 6in, 54ft 8in x 23ft 0in x 10ft 10in (21.60, 17.76 x 7.47 x 3.52m). 97–100/230 tons. Draught 8ft/12ft (2.60/3.90m). men: 70/90.
　　Guns: 10 x 6pdrs in 1783, 16 x 4pdrs from 1785, reduced to 6 x 4pdrs during 1787.
　　Re-classed as a brig from 1785. Struck 1789 at Rochefort.

Martinique. British vessel captured 11.1781.
　　Dimensions & tons: 75ft 6in or 84ft 0in, 63ft 0in x 22ft 6in x 13ft (24.53 or 27.29, 20.46 x 7.31 x 4.22m). 153/300 tons.
　　Guns: 14 x 6pdrs. Listed by Rochefort 12.1783 with 14 x 9pdrs (British) but this appears unlikely.
　　Sailed 20.10.1784 and 20.4.1785 as a packet from Lorient to America. Sold 1785 at Lorient to M. Carosin for commercial use, at Île de France 9.1786.

Vautour. Probably a British privateer named *Vulture*, captured 2.1782.
　　Dimensions & tons: dimensions unknown. 150 tons. Men: 100/150.
　　Guns: 20 x 6pdrs, 6 x 4pdrs, 10 *obusiers*.
　　Arrived at Rochefort from Martinique 15.11.1782. Conducted hydrographic surveys at St Domingue 1784–85. Struck 1786.

Harriot (*Hariot*). Probably the British privateer *Harriot*, captured 30.12.1781 by the French privateer *Robecq* and purchased 3.1782 by the Navy. Listed as a cutter 6.1782.
　　Dimensions & tons: dimensions unknown. 170 tons. Men: 99, +4 officers; as packet 37, +6 officers.
　　Guns: 14 x 6pdrs (7.1782), 12 x 6pdrs (9.1782), 16 guns (early 1783), 18 x 6pdrs (as packet).
　　Arrived at Lorient with *Sérin* 16.8.1783 for conversion to a packet, renamed *Courrier de Port Louis* 10.1783 and fitted as a packet 10–11.1783 at Lorient for a line between Lorient and New York. Wrecked 1.1784 in the ice near Long Island.

TOURTEREAU. 18 guns. Designed by Jean-Denis Chevillard, and named in March 1782.
　　Dimensions & tons: 100ft 0in x 26ft 4in x 13ft 0in (32.48 x 8.55 x 4.22m). 320/550 tons. Draught 12ft/13ft (3.90/4.22m). Men: 120.
　　Guns: 16 x 6pdrs, 2 smaller.

Tourtereau Calais.
　　K: end 1781. L: 27.3.1782. C: 8.1782. Repaired 12.1783–1.1784 at Martinique. Arrived at Rochefort 23.6.1784 for inspection. Struck and BU at Rochefort in 1787.

FAUVETTE Class. 20 guns. Designed by Charles-Étienne Bombelle (Baron de Bombelle) with technical help from Charles Segondat-Duvernet. The design featured a very short forecastle and poop with the upper deck lowered underneath them to accommodate the galley and

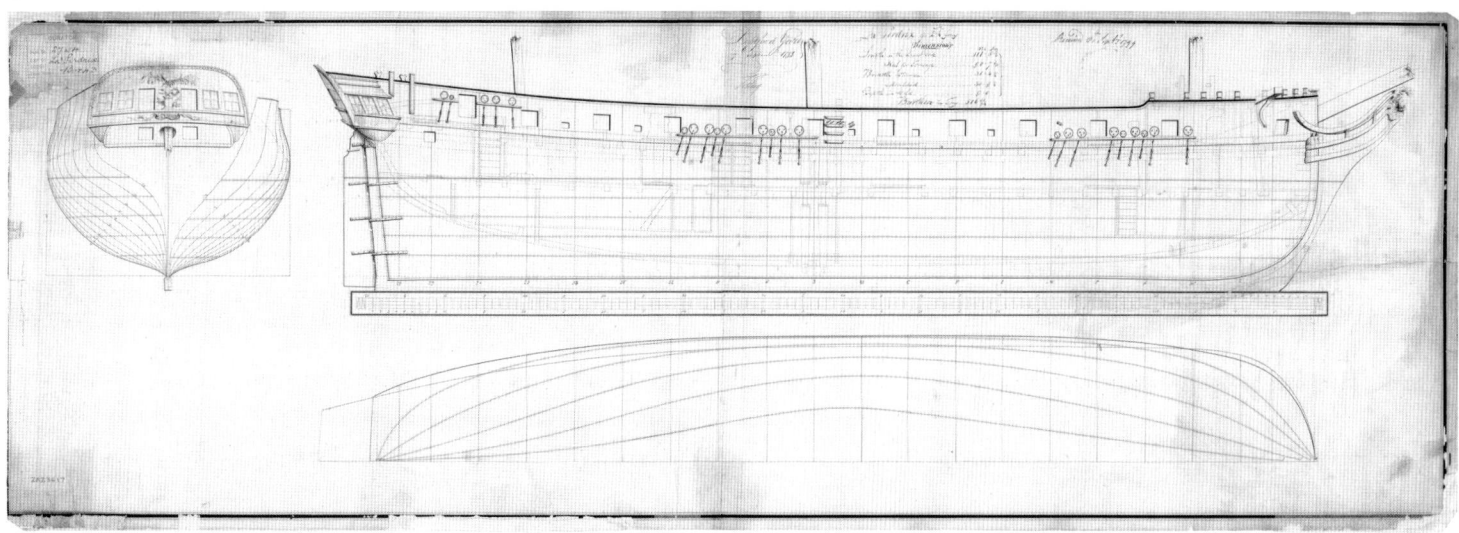

the commander's cabin while making the ships appear flush decked. They had ports for ten pairs of guns and for twelve pairs of oars. The first two were ordered at Rochefort in April 1782 and named on 13 April 1782; they were built by Hubert Pennevert. Two more to the same design were projected at Rochefort – *Enjouée* and *Légère* (and may have been intended to carry 18 x 8pdrs instead of their 20 x 6pdrs), but in the event these were not built. *Favorite* was reportedly built at Bayonne but was probably a Rochefort ship like the others. *Fauvette* was listed in 1793 with 18 x 8pdrs broadside, 2 x 24pdrs chase forward and 2 x 18pdrs aft, but within a year had reverted to 20 x 6pdrs.

Dimensions & tons: 112ft 0in, 101ft 0in x 28ft 0in x 14ft 3in (36.38, 32.81 x 9.10 x 4.63m). 430/752 tons. Draught 12ft/12½ft (3.90/4.06m). Men: 133/150, +8 officers.

Guns: 20 x 6pdrs. *Perdrix* also carried 2 x 36pdr *obusiers* from 1794/95 while *Alouette* added 2 x 6pdrs in 1794/95. *Fauvette* had 20 x 8pdrs from 1798 and 14 x 8pdrs from 1809.

Fauvette Rochefort Dyd.
K: 6.1782. L: 15.6.1783. C: 9.1783. Gunnery school at Toulon 5.1795. Struck 1796 (possibly chartered to Petit & Co. of Toulon for commercial use) but restored to the list in 1798 and rebuilt *c.*1799 at Toulon. Condemned at Toulon and sale approved 16.6.1814, BU 4.1815

Perdrix Rochefort Dyd.
K: early 1783. L: 18.6.1784. C: 2.1785. Taken by HMS *Vanguard* (74) off Antigua 5.6.1795, and added as HMS *Perdrix*. BU at Deptford 10.9.1799.

Favorite Rochefort Dyd.
K: 1784. L: 8.1785. C: 10.1785. Taken by HMS *Alfred* (74) off Cape Finisterre 5.3.1796.

Alouette Rochefort Dyd.
K: early 1785. L: 1.1786. C: 5.1786. Rebuilt at Bayonne 1793 to 9.1793, renamed *Maire Guiton* from 8.1793. Taken by HMS *Hebe* (38) 15.5.1794 but retaken after 4 days. Name restored as *Alouette* 5.1795. Headquarters hulk at Lorient end 1795, last mentioned 1799.

VIGILANTE Class. *Corvette-gabarres* of 16 guns. Designed by Jean-Joseph Perrin de Boissieu, and built by Raymond-Antoine Haran.

Dimensions & tons: 112ft 0in, 102ft 0in x 25ft 0in x 13ft 3in (36.38, 33.13 x 8.12 x 4.30m). 282–350/500 tons. Draught 10ft 4in/10ft 4in (3.36,3.36m). Men: 148/172, +7/8 officers.

Guns: 16 x 6pdrs. 4 x 36pdr *obusiers* added in *Vigilante* 1794/95.

Vigilante Bayonne.

Admiralty draught of the *Perdrix* dated Deptford 7 September 1799. Presumably the survey that accompanied the draught prompted the decision to break up the ship a few days later. At this date the ship has a short forecastle, but no quarterdeck (unless one counts the small step up over the commander's cabin), and the ship was steered with a tiller. There are only five pairs of oarports visible, but there is a pair of large gunports aft for the two 36pdr *obusiers* the ship was recorded as mounting in 1794–95. (National Maritime Museum, London J6197)

K: 4.1783. L: 11.1783. C: 2.1784. Training corvette at Brest from 1788. As a *gabarre* carried guns and timber from Paimboeuf to Brest 5–10.1791. Escorted convoys between Brest and Bordeaux 11.1793, in combat with a British division at La Hougue 3.7.1795. Struck 1796.

Sincère Bayonne.
K: 1783. L: 4.1784. C: 8.1784. Training corvette at Brest from 4.1789. Handed over by Royalists to Anglo-Spanish forces at Toulon 29.8.1793, taken by the RN 18.12.1793 as HMS *Sincere*. Sold 1799.

PURCHASED VESSELS with 6pdr guns or heavier (1783–1785)

Auguste. Bordeaux merchantman of 360/398 tons, purchased 3.1783 in the Indian Ocean by Suffren's squadron. 360 tons, 22 x 6pdrs. Struck 1785 or 1786 at Brest.

Maréchal de Castries. Built in New York by John Peck 1781–83, purchased by the French Navy in February 1785 and named after the current Minister of the Navy.

Dimensions & tons: 107ft 0in (34.76m) length. 250 tons.

Guns: 18 x 6pdrs.

Handed over to the Transatlantic Packet service (*Régie des Paquebots*) 2.1787 for service between Le Havre and New York or the Antilles, returned to the Navy 11.1788. Briefly renamed *Corsaire* 29.9.1792, but name restored to *Maréchal de Castries* in same month. Raised the white (Royalist) flag 10.1792, left Fort Royal, Martinique, 11.1.1793 when the Republicans there revolted and delivered by her officers to the Spanish at Trinidad, unserviceable 2.1793.

A program drafted in 1786 by Jean-Charles de Borda, the Inspector of Naval Shipbuilding, that laid out the types and numbers of ships to be in the new French navy called for 20 corvettes with 24 x 8pdrs and 20 corvettes with 20 x 6pdrs, as well as 20 brigs and other smaller types mounting 12 to 16 x 4pdrs or 6pdrs. However, because of the monarchy's rapidly deteriorating finances no new corvettes were laid down before 1792.

11 Minor Warships – *Ponant* Types
(Barques, Brigantines, Snows, Cutters, Luggers, Schooners, Brigs, etc)

As in other navies, while the principal warship remained the three-masted ship-rigged vessel, there was a constant need for smaller craft for the role of coastal patrol and escort. These types differed in the Atlantic and Channel coasts (referred to by the French as the *Ponant*) and the Mediterranean (called the *Levant*, see Chapter 12), the former tending to have square or fore-and-aft sails and the latter lateen sails, among other differences. Until 1719 all of these small warships along with minor support vessels (see Chapter 13) were shown in fleet lists as *bâtiments interrompus,* or vessels that were not part of the formal structure of the navy. (The Navy structure as approved by the King in the 1680s included only the five ranks of *vaisseaux* plus *frégates légères*, *flûtes*, bomb vessels, fireships, and corvettes or *barques longues*.) After 1719 the smaller warships received full recognition in the lists as members of the fleet, a role they had played in practice since the mid-seventeenth century.

Before 1715 most of the smaller warships were located in the Mediterranean and were of the *Levant* types listed in Chapter 12. Some ships classed as barques and brigantines were also located in ports in the Atlantic region, but these differed somewhat from the similarly classed vessels of the *Levant*. Northern barques tend to be shown in contemporary illustrations with square rather than lateen sails, and northern brigantines were shown as small seaworthy sailing vessels without oars, quite different from the low oar-assisted brigantines of the Mediterranean. By the early eighteenth century the northern brigantine was a two-masted merchant vessel with a mainmast carrying a fore-and-aft mainsail (or brigantine sail) and a square main topsail, a foremast carrying a square foresail and a topsail, and a bowsprit with two or three jibs and sometimes a sprit-topsail. Northern ports also had smaller craft like the *double-chaloupe*, but the name of only one of these (acquired in 1691–92) is known and most were considered harbour service craft. Some *galiotes à rames*, often called *demi-galères* (half-galleys), were used as tugs, for instance to tow decommissioned vessels to and from their wintering location at Landévénec on the river Aulne near Brest.

The number of smaller warships in the *Ponant* increased considerably after 1715 due to the need for such vessels not only on French coasts but in the colonies. From the middle of the century several new specialised types of sailing rigs were developed, of which the principal ones by the 1770s were the schooner, cutter, and lugger. The schooners and luggers tended to be two-or three-masted while the cutters had a single tall mast. A common feature of these otherwise disparate craft was that their hulls were clinker-built. The first armed schooners built by the French Navy (except for a short-lived pair in Canada) were two vessels built at Rochfort by Jean-Denis Chevillard in 1767 (*Afrique* and *Gorée*) and a smaller pair built at Brest by Joseph-Louis Ollivier in 1769 (*Aberwrac'h* and *Nanon*). Three small cutters were built for coast guard service in the late 1750s but it was not until 1770 – much later than the British – that the French Navy decided to emulate their rivals and ordered seven larger cutters for military use at Bordeaux, Dunkirk, St Malo and Lorient. The cutter's rig, coupled with its sharp hull lines, was ideal for speed. These were soon followed by the first French naval lugger, a type also noted for speed. Daniel Denys was the leading French constructor for both French cutters and luggers. (Denys's full name was Étienne Daniel but he signed as Daniel.)

The adoption of cutters and luggers by the French navy quickly led to a major increase in the hull dimensions of these types in an attempt to carry a more powerful armament, reaching lengths of 81 French feet (86 British feet) and armaments of eighteen 6pdrs during the War of the American Revolution. When the rigs of these vessels were scaled up proportionally the single mast and fore-and-aft mainsail of the cutter became too large to handle comfortably and safely, while the labour-intensive lugger rig made the craft very difficult to tack. The solution consisted of applying the two-masted brigantine and later the snow square rig to these hulls, producing the naval brig. In brigs, which unlike brigantines and snows were designed for speed, the rig was further developed by adding topgallant sails, royals, staysails, and more jibs and by expanding the size of most of the sails. Disillusion with the mediocre performance of the oversized cutters built in the late 1770s and problems procuring their single tall masts caused most of them to be completed as, or converted to, brig rig within a few years, and construction of naval luggers ceased at around the same time. By the end of the eighteenth century brigs and schooners were the dominant types of small warships.

(A) Vessels in service as at 9 March 1661

The King's fleet in 1661 consisted of *vaisseaux*, frigates, fireships, *flûtes*, and (in a separate service) galleys. No smaller vessels were listed in 1661, and any that existed were probably considered service craft.

(B) Vessels acquired from 9 March 1661

LÉVRIER. Brigantine, listed as a galiote in May 1669 and also as a *frégate*. Designed by Laurent Hubac.
    Dimensions & tons: dimensions unknown. 30 tons (40 tons in 5.1669). Men: 25 (5/10/10), +1 officer.
    Guns: 2 (4 in 5.1669).
Lévrier Brest
    K: 1.1667. L: 3.1667. C: 4.1667. Sold or BU 1675 at Brest.

LEVRETTE. Brigantine, listed as a galiote in May 1669. Designed by Laurent Hubac.
    Dimensions & tons: dimensions unknown. 30 tons. Men: 25 (5/10/10), +1 officer.
    Guns: 2.
Levrette Brest
    K: 1667. L: 4.1667. C: 4.1667. Struck 9.1676 at Toulon.

SAINT PIERRE. Barque. This may be the vessel listed in May 1669 as the Dutch-built 30-ton *cache* named *Saint Pierre* dating from 1665 with 4 guns and 20 men.
    Dimensions & tons: dimensions unknown. 40/30 tons. Men: 40 + 1 officer
    Guns: 8 small.
Saint Pierre Dieppe
    K: 1666. L: 3.1667. C: 4.1667. Last mentioned 1672 at Le Havre.

MARIE. Barque. This may be the vessel listed in May 1669 as a Dutch-built 40-ton *cache* named *Sainte Anne* dating from 1665 with 4 guns and 40 men.
   Dimensions & tons: dimensions unknown. 40/30 tons. Men: 40 + 1 officer
   Guns: A few small.
Marie Dieppe
   K: early 1667. L: 1667. C: 12.1667. Lost 1675 near Audierne.

FRANÇOISE. This vessel was listed in May 1669 as a Dutch-built 80-ton *caiche* dating from 1665 with 8 guns and 40 men. No other information.

Ex-SPANISH AND DUTCH PRIZES (1674–1676)
Sainte Anne. Barque built at Ostend and captured 9.1674, ex-Spanish *Santa Ana*. 30 tons, 3 x 1pdrs. Sold 10.1675 at Le Havre.
Dieppoise. Old fishing barque possibly built at Dieppe and captured or seized *c*.1675. 10 or 12 tons, no guns. Unserviceable 1.1680 and condemned at Dunkirk, BU 2–3.1680.
Saint Jean. Barque built in Holland 1670 and captured 1676, ex-Dutch *St Jan*. 80 tons, 4 guns. Given by the King 2.1677 to the Duc de Saint Aignan, probably at Le Havre.

BRIGANTIN. Brigantine. Built in Martinique, probably at St Pierre. K: 8.1676. L: 11.1676. C: 1.1677. Last mentioned 1689.

Ex-SPANISH AND DUTCH PRIZES (1677–1689)
Saint Joseph. Barque captured 1677, origin unknown. 10 men. Handed over 1678 to the Spanish by her mutinous French crew. Evidently returned in late 1678, given by the King 7.1679 to the Duc de Noailles.
Saint Pierre. Barque also listed as a *flûte* captured 1672, probably ex-Dutch *St Pieter* built in Holland in 1666.
   Dimensions & tons: dimensions unknown. 60 tons. Draught 6ft (1.94m). Men: 28 (9/19/), +2 officers.
   Guns: None.
   Renamed *Dunkerquoise* 11.12.1676. Sold 6.1677 at Dunkirk.
Roi David. Barque built at Flushing and captured 3.1689, ex-Dutch *capre* (corsair) *Koning David*. 8 guns. Also called *Prise de Mr. de Forbin*. Handed over 9.1691 to the *Compagnie de Guinée*.

PURCHASED VESSEL (1689)
Casque. Fishing barque purchased 1.1689 at Dunkirk to carry out secret missions. No guns. Converted 6.1699 at Dunkirk to a fireship. May have still been in service there in 4.1692.

(C) Vessels acquired from 15 April 1689

VIGILANTE. Brigantine. Designed by Jean-Baptiste Chabert and built at Rochefort. Also called *Brigantin des Galères*.
   K: 3.1690. L: 5.1690. C: 5.1690. Was in service at Le Havre in 5.1692, last mentioned at St Malo in 7.1695.

Ex-ENGLISH MERCANTILE PRIZES (1690–1691).
The English *flibots* or brigantines *White Swan* and *Hope* were captured in 1690 by *Gaillarde* (CB Jean-Baptiste de La Motte Louvard), one of the King's vessels lent for privateering to the Marquis de Seignelay, Secretary of State for the Navy, and were purchased for the French Navy as *Cygne Blanc* and *Espérance*. Another English barque, named *Pearl*, was captured in 1691 and served the French as *Perle de Londres*

The terminology of small craft was always protean, with the precise meaning at any one place and time difficult to pin down. One of the worst examples in northern Europe was 'brigantine', which as an import from the Mediterranean *brigantin* tended to imply a vessel propelled by oars, either as its primary or auxiliary form of propulsion. This illustration from Guéroult du Pas's work of 1710 depicts an English naval brigantine of the kind built in the 1690s (essentially as a fleet tug), but it probably shared its main characteristics with French vessels designated *brigantin*. Of the two similar vessels in the background one is being rowed and the other is under both oars and sails.

Cygne Blanc (Cigne Blanc) England,
   Dimensions & tons: 40ft 0in x 11ft 0in x 7ft 0in (12.99 x 3.57 x 2.27m). 28 tons (15 tons in 9.1692). Draught 5ft (1.62m). Men: 6. In 1696: 8 in war and peace; in 1699; 25 in war, 20 peace, +2 officers.
   Guns: 4 in 1692 and 1696. 7 from 1699: 4 x 4pdrs, 3 x 3pdrs
   Listed in 1696 as a *flûte* with the characteristics shown above and described as quite good under sail. Service craft at Brest 1700, listed 1716 as a 40-ton corvette, last mentioned 1717 as having just been repaired.
Espérance England (possibly London)
   Dimensions & tons: 67ft 0in x 17ft 0in x 8ft 0in (21.76 x 5.52 x 2.60m). 90 tons (40 tons in 9.1692). Draught 9ft (2.92m). Men: 8. In 1696: 15 in war, 15 peace.
   Guns: none in 1692. 4 in 1695: 4 x 4pdrs + 1 mortar; 6 in war in 1696: 6 x 4pdrs
   Built 1687. Also called *Espérance de Londres* and *Petit vaisseau anglais*. Renamed *Féconde* 1.1693 and classed as a *flûte* with the characteristics shown above (she was described in 1696 as miserable under sail). Lent as a privateer in 1695–97 to CV Jean-Baptiste, Comte de Gennes, Seigneur d'Oyac as part of a squadron of six vessels (the others were *Faucon Anglais, Soleil d'Afrique, Séditieux,* the corvette *Félicité,* and the *flûte Gloutonne*), that destroyed the English Fort James in Gambia, moved to Rio de Janeiro, tried but failed to pass through the Strait of Magellan, and then cruised in the West Indies. She was armed with four guns and one mortar. Commanded by Sieur Alain Porée, sieur de La Touche, of St Malo, *Féconde* arrived on her own at Port Louis in April 1696, then went to Rochefort to decommission; the plunder taken from Fort Saint-James was declared at the Amirauté of La Rochelle 26.5.1696. Struck 1696 or 1697 at Rochefort.
Perle de Londres England (possibly London) in 1685 and captured 1691, ex-English *Pearl*.
   Dimensions & tons: 48ft 0in x 14ft 0in x 7ft 0in (15.59 x 4.55 x 2.27m). 80 tons (25 tons in 9.1692). Draught 8½ft (2.76m). Men:

6. In 1696: 10 in war, 10 peace.

Guns: none in 1692. 6 in war in 1696 (6 peace): 4 x 2pdrs, 2 x 1pdrs
Built 1685. Also called *Perle*. Listed in 1696 as a *flûte* with the characteristics shown above and described as bad under sail. Last mentioned 1696 at Port Louis.

PURCHASED AND ACQUIRED VESSELS (1691–1692). Four barques and one '*double-chaloupe* or *barque d'avis*' were added during this period.

Ange Blanc. Barque acquired early 1691 and in service at Brest on 8.4.1691 and 19.9.1692, when described as old. May have been captured or seized in 1688. 55/40 tons, 10 men + 1 master, 2 guns. Last mentioned 1.1694 at Brest.

Oranger. Barque acquired 1691 and in service at Brest on 16.6.1691 and 19.9.1692. May have been captured or seized in 1688. 60/50 tons, 8 men + 1 master, no guns. Struck c.3.1693 at Brest.

Mathieu or *Saint Mathieu*. Barque acquired 1691 and in service at Brest on 3.9.1691. May have been captured or seized in 1688. 50 tons. Struck 1692 at Brest.

Patience. Barque in service at Brest in 1691. May have been captured or seized in 1688. Last mentioned 9.1691 out of service at Brest.

Saint Louis. Double chaloupe or *barque d'avis* built at Dieppe, chartered 7.1691, then purchased early 1692. 30 men, 4 *pierriers*. Struck ca. 1707.

MISCELLANEOUS PRIZES (1692–1693)

Levrette. Brigantine in service at Brest on 19.9.1692; probably the provisions transport *Levrette* that was captured in 7.1691. 20 tons, 10 men, 4 guns. Struck 3.1693 at Brest. May have become the support brigantine *Levrette* for the galley force that was captured 7.1702 by the English.

Saint Joseph. Brigantine captured 1692, ex-Portuguese *São José*. 8 tons. Captured 7.1696 by the English, sold 8.1699 by the English Navy.

Joseph. Brigantine built at Fontarabia and captured c.1693, probably ex-Spanish *Josef*. In service at Port Louis in 1694, last mentioned there 4.1697.

BRIGANTIN. Brigantine. Built in 1692–93 at Port Royal or Port Nascouat in Acadia. Put into service in 1693 by the Sieur de Villebon, governor of Acadia. Probably last mentioned 6.1695. Another craft called *Brigantin*, probably acquired, was put into service at Port Royal c.1708 and sold in Martinique in 3.1710.

CAPTIEUSE Class. Brigantines. Probably designed by Blaise Pangalo.
Dimensions & tons: dimensions unknown. 10 tons.
Guns: 1.

Captieuse Brest
K: 5.1693. L: 7.1693. C: 8.1693. BU 12.1699 at Brest.
Surprenante Brest
K: 5.1693. L: 7.1693. C: 8.1693. BU 12.1699 at Brest.

DEMI-GALÈRE. Brigantine. Built in 1693 at Bayonne. Also called *Galère du Duc de Gramont* and may have had another name. Rebuilt at Bayonne 1700–1, last mentioned 1704 at Bayonne.

PURCHASED AND ACQUIRED VESSELS (1701–1705). Two barques and a brigantine were added during this period.

Revanche. Barque built at Dunkirk 1694–95 and acquired 1701 or 1702. 35/38 tons, 40 men + 1 officer, 4 guns. Last mentioned 9.1705 after being damaged in a storm at Dunkirk.

Gentille. Barque purchased 5.1701 and in service 6.1701 at St Domingue. Repaired there 6–7.1701. Seized 3.1702 by the English at Jamaica.

François. Brigantine acquired 1704/1705 and in service at Rochefort 1705/1706. Struck 1706 at Rochefort.

Between the seventeenth and eighteenth centuries there was a general shift in small-craft description from hull shape or function towards rig. Thus, whereas 'brigantine' had originally implied a vessel with emphasis on oared propulsion, it came to mean a rig – two masts (fore and main), with the main course being a large fore-and-aft sail, often called a 'brigantine sail'; it was set from a tall lower mast, unlike the shorter mainmast of the snow, and later brig. This transference of meaning is an obscure process, but in England it may have resulted from the naval brigantines carrying such a sail. In 1710 Du Pas described the vessel with just such a rig illustrated here as a large English merchant brigantine. She was probably similar to the *Marguerite* captured in 1706.

Ex-ENGLISH PRIZE (1706)

Marguerite. Brigantine captured 4.1706 at Nevis in the Caribbean from the English by the squadron of CV Pierre Le Moyne d'Iberville and put into service 5.1706 at Cap Français. 120 men, 14 guns. Also called by the generic name *Brigantin*. Stuck in the coastal sand in Louisiana 2.1708, restored to service 1709, sold commercially 1710 at La Rochelle, unserviceable at Vera Cruz c1715 and abandoned.

PREMIER (PALME) Class. Brigantines. Designed by René Levasseur. All renamed c.1709 after galleys built at Rochefort in 1690 by the Chevalier de Noailles to support Tourville's fleet.
Dimensions & tons: 43ft 0in x 9ft 9in x 2ft 6in (13.97 x 3.17 x 0.81m). 10/18 tons. Draught 3ft/3ft 6in (0.97/1.14m). Men: 29 + 1 officer.
Guns: 1 x 3pdr + 4 *pierriers*.

Premier, later *Palme* Dunkirk
K: 1.1708. L: 5.1708. C: 6.1708. Last mentioned 1712 at Dunkirk.
Deuxième, later *Triomphante* Dunkirk
K: 1.1708. L: 5.1708. C: 6.1708. Loaned for privateering 1709 at Dunkirk and lost.
Troisième, later *Martiale* Dunkirk
K: 1.1708. L: 5.1708. C: 6.1708. Loaned for privateering 1709 at Dunkirk and lost.
Quatrième, later *Émeraude* Dunkirk
K: 1.1708. L: 5.1708. C: 6.1708. Lost in combat 7.1711.
Cinquième, later *Heureuse* Dunkirk
K: 2.1708. L: 6.1708. C: 8.1708. Last mentioned 1712 at Dunkirk.
Sixième, later *Marquise* Dunkirk
K: 2.1708. L: 6.1708. C: 8.1708. Loaned for privateering 1709 at Dunkirk and lost.

MINOR WARSHIPS – *PONANT* TYPES

The French privateer *barque-canonnière Ruby* commanded by Philippe Plessis (110 men, 6 guns) together with three other French privateers, *Gracieuse* (6 guns, 40 men), *Dragon* (4 guns, 94 men), and *Fortune* (4 guns, 65 men) took and sacked the Dutch island of St Eustache on 11.12.1709. These probably were never naval vessels. *Ruby* was wrecked 2.1713 at Curacao.

(D) Vessels acquired from 1 September 1715

CHASSEUR. Vessel of unknown origin purchased in June 1720 at Martinique and put into service in August. She was also called *Bateau du Roi* or *Patache du Roi*, a *patache* being an advice boat or tender. This 60-ton vessel carried 16 small guns and her hold could carry 150 hogsheads or barrels. She was unserviceable at St Domingue in 1722 despite repairs in 1721 and was placed on sale.

SAINT LOUIS Class. Brigantines. Built at New Orleans, possibly by the master shipwright Adrien Gilbert who was in Louisiana in 1725. The first ship measured 76 tons, other specifications unknown.
Saint Louis New Orleans.
  Built 1731. Wrecked 3.1732 in Bayou Marmotte in Mobile Bay.
Saint Louis New Orleans.
  K: 1731. L: 26.3.1732. C: 1732. Repaired at New Orleans 6.1733. Wrecked 9.1733 in Louisiana.
Saint Louis New Orleans.
  K: 1732. L: 6.1733. C: 1733. Probably had a different name until the second *Saint Louis* was lost. Sold 3.1741 in Louisiana, probably being unserviceable.

SAINT ANNE. Barque. Built at Rochefort or La Rochelle in 1732–33 and sent to Louisiana. Last mentioned in that colony 9.1735.

VAUTOUR. Brigantine (brig) designed and built by Gilles Cambry for the Governor of St Domingue. She was probably a colonial vessel as she does not appear in any navy fleet lists.
  Dimensions & tons: dimensions unknown. 130 tons
  Guns: 12 (probably)
Vautour Lorient
  K: 10.1734. L: 7.4.1735. C: 5.1735. May have lasted until 1754.

PURCHASED AND ACQUIRED VESSELS (1739–1745). Two brigantines were added to the navy during this period.
Brigantin du Roi. Brigantine acquired in St Domingue and sent to Louisiana in 5.1739 to serve there. Wrecked 9.1740 at La Balise during a hurricane.
Bien Trouvé. Brigantine in service 12.1745 at Dunkirk. Captured 6.1746 by the British off the Scottish coast.

Ex-BRITISH NAVAL PRIZE (1745). HMS *Hazard*, a snow, was captured by Jacobite rebels in Montrose harbour on 5 December 1745 and handed over to the French in the same month.
  Dimensions & tons: 90ft 0in x 24ft 4in (29.24 x 7.90m). 350 tons.
  Men: 57 + 4 officers.
  Guns: 14.
Hasard Buxton at Rotherhithe
  K: 4.1744. L: 11.12.1744. C: 1745. Commissioned 6.3.1746 as *Prince Charles* by the 'Young Pretender' at Dunkirk. Retaken by the British 5.4.1746 off Buchan Ness while running supplies to the Jacobites and reverted to HMS *Hazard*. Sold 18.9.1749.

A drawing by Ian McLaughlan of the British snow-rigged sloop of war *Hazard* captured in 1745. Related to both the earlier brigantine and the later brig, the snow carried a smaller fore-and-aft sail on the mainmast; it was often set in lieu of the square main, so might be regarded as secondary, unlike the equivalent of a brigantine or brig, where the fore-and-aft sail was primary. One feature that later became a defining characteristic of the snow was employment of a separate trysail mast or stout hawser to which the luff of the gaff main sail was laced or hooped.

Ex-BRITISH MERCANTILE PRIZE (1745). A French mercantile schooner of 55 tons built at Quebec in 1741 by Duperé was captured by the British in 1744 and retaken by the French in early 1745.
  Dimensions & tons: 51ft 0in x 16ft 0in x 6ft 1in (16.57 x 5.20 x 1.98m). 50/80 tons. Draught 8ft 6in (2.76m). Men: 40 + 4 officers
  Guns: 10 x 4pdrs + 4 *pierriers*.
Marianne or Marie-Anne Quebec
  Built 1741. Rebuilt at Quebec in early 1745, then sent to Le Havre and repaired there 12.1745–1.1746. Loaned 6.1747 for commercial use, then struck.

The Canadian Great Lakes were large enough to encourage the deployment of significant naval squadrons during the Seven Years' War. This contemporary French map of Lake Ontario shows the main sites of the actions in 1756–57, but also included vignettes of the opposing flotillas. At bottom, the French vessels (left to right) are: *Marquise de Vaudreuil*, a main-topsail schooner, *Victor* a sloop, *Hurault*, a main-topsail schooner and *Louise*, a schooner. Details of *Marquise de Vaudreuil* and *Hurault*, rated as corvettes, can be found in Chapter 10. (The British Library)

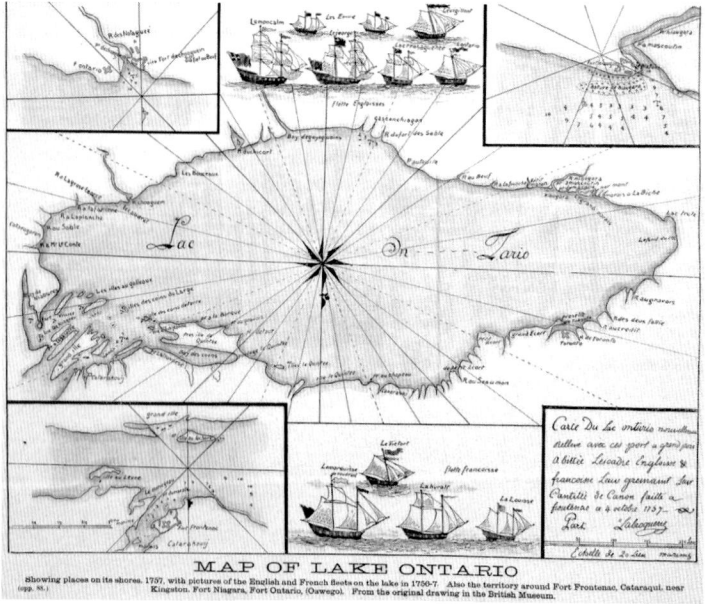

ROCHEFORT. Brigantine designed by François-Guillaume Clairain-Deslauriers. This may be the same as the yacht *Rochefort* of 1750 (see Chapter 13) which, however, was built to a design by Blaise Geslain.
  Dimensions & tons: dimensions unknown. 45 tons. Men: 46 + 4 officers
  Guns: 2 or 4.
Rochefort Rochefort
  K: 1751. L: 1751. C: 10.1751. Last mentioned 12.1771 at Rochefort.

LOUISE. Schooner on Lake Ontario. Depicted as a two masted schooner.
  Dimensions & tons: dimensions unknown. 50 tons. Men: 16 crew, 25 soldiers, 2 sergeants
  Guns: 6 x 4pdrs and 3pdrs, 4 *pierriers*.
Louise Fort Frontenac
  Built in 1750. Captured by the British at the capitulation of Fort Frontenac 28.8.1758 and burned by them 31.8.1758.

VICTOR. Sloop or *bateau* on Lake Ontario. Depicted as a single-masted gaff-rigged fore-and-aft sloop.
  Dimensions & tons: dimensions unknown. 40 tons. Men: 12 crew, 20 soldiers, 2 sergeants
  Guns: 2 x 6pdrs, 4 x 2pdrs, 4 *pierriers*.
Victor Fort Frontenac
  Built 1749. Captured by the British at the capitulation of Fort Frontenac 28.8.1758 and burned by them 31.8.1758. A second sloop was also reportedly captured and burned at the same time, she has not been identified.

PURCHASED VESSEL (*c.*1755)
Heureuse. Schooner wrecked 6.1755 in Louisiana, no other information.

Ex-BRITISH NAVAL PRIZES (LAKE ONTARIO, 1756). In 1754 Governor William Shirley of Massachusetts ordered the construction of several warships at Oswego on Lake Ontario to compete with the French fur trade and protect British settlements from the French and their Indian allies. Workers and supplies were brought from New York and Boston. The ships were reportedly built to designs by Sir Jacob Acworth, Surveyor of the Navy until his death in 1749. The first ships built were the snow-rigged

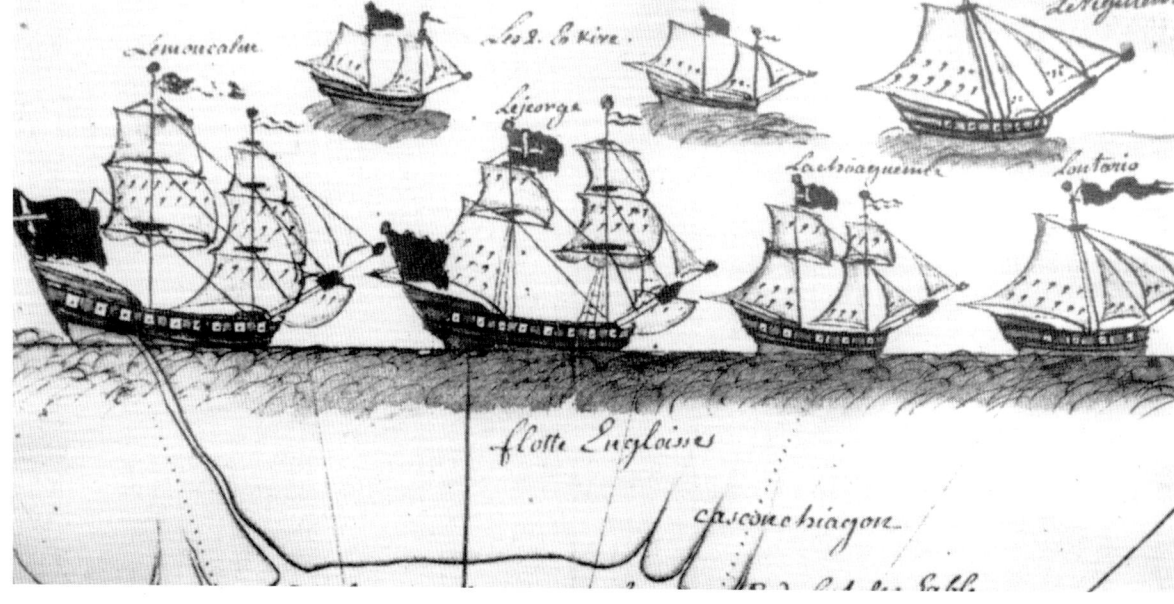

An enlargement from the map of Lake Ontario shown previously, depicting the British flotilla as renamed after capture by the French. In the bottom row are: the snow *Montcalm*, brigantine *George*, two-topsail schooner *Choueguen*, and sloop *Ontario*; those above are identified simply as '2 skiffs', with the sloop *Vigilant* to the right.

sloops *Oswego* and *Ontario*. They may have been originally been sisters rigged as brigs or two-masted schooners, although *Oswego* was later depicted as a two-masted topsail schooner and *Ontario* as a single-masted gaff-rigged fore-and-aft sloop. *Mohawk* was also depicted as a single-masted gaff-rigged fore-and-aft sloop. *George* was named for Fort George, one of the three forts at Oswego along with Fort Ontario and Fort Oswego. She and *Vigilant* were fitted with oars and depicted as small two-masted schooners; *George* was undecked. *Lively* was a schooner 'not bigger than a four-cord boat'.

Oswego, *Ontario*, and *Lively* encountered four French vessels on 27/28 June 1756 and avoided combat as *Oswego* and *Ontario* each had only 5 guns and 45 men. *Lively* fell behind and was captured by *Louise* and *Victor* (above) and renamed *Farquer* (*Farquhar*?). The other seven ships of the British squadron on Lake Ontario were captured on 14.8.1756 by a French expedition against Oswego (known by the French as Chouegen) led by Montcalm. Because the French did not have enough seamen to man the captured British vessels they decided to burn all but two of them (probably HM Ships *London* and *Halifax*) which they kept for transport purposes. The dimensions are of British origin.

Montcalm. Snow. Ex-HMS *Halifax*. Oswego
K: 1756. L: 7.1756. Probably complete but not outfitted when Oswego fell.
Dimensions & tons: 80ft 0in on deck, 66ft 0in keel x 22ft 0in x 8ft 7in (24.54, 20.12 x 6.71 x 2.62m). 172 tons.
Guns: 18 (designed, probably 9pdrs)
Renamed *Montcalm* and taken to Fort Frontenac. Tried to leave Fort Frontenac with *Marquise de Vaudreuil* and *George* early on 27.8.1758 just before it fell but forced ashore by enemy artillery. The British then loaded captured supplies on two seized vessels (probably *Montcalm* and *Marquise de Vaudreuil*) later that day while razing the fort. The two ships then took the supplies to Oswego and were burned there.

George. Brigantine (brig). Ex-HMS *London*. Oswego
K: 1756. L: 3.7.1756. C: 29.7.1756.
Dimensions & tons: 60ft 0in keel x 21ft 0in x 7ft (18.29 x 6.40 x 2.13m). 160 tons.
Guns: 6 x 6pdrs, 8 x 4pdrs + 8 swivels in 7.1756. (Designed for 16 guns)
Renamed *George* and taken to Fort Frontenac. Tried to leave Fort Frontenac early on 27.8.1758 with *Marquise de Vaudreuil* and *Montcalm* just before it fell but forced ashore by enemy artillery. Burned by the British 31.8.1758.

Choueguen. Schooner. Ex-HMS *Oswego*. Oswego
K: 1755. L: 10.7.1755. C: late 1755.
Dimensions & tons: 43ft 0in (or 55ft?) x 15ft 0in x 7ft 0in (13.11 or 16.76 x 4.57 x 2.13m). 60 tons. Men: 45.
Guns: 10 (9pdrs and 12pdrs) + swivels as designed. Had only 4 x 4pdrs, 1 x 3pdr in action on 28.6.1756.
Renamed *Choueguen* but burned by the French at Oswego.

Ontario. Sloop or *bateau*. Ex-HMS *Ontario*. Oswego
K: 1755. L: 28.6.1755. C: late 1755.
Dimensions & tons: 43ft 0in (or 55ft?) x 15ft 0in x 7ft 0in (13.11 or 16.76 x 4.57 x 2.13m). 60 tons. Men: 45.
Guns: 10 (9pdrs and 12pdrs) + swivels as designed. Had only 4 x 4pdrs, 1 x 3pdr in action on 28.6.1756, 6 x 4pdrs in 7.1756.
Retained name *Ontario* but burned by the French at Oswego.

Vigilant. Sloop or *bateau*. Ex-HMS *Mohawk*. Oswego
K: 1756. L: 3.7.1756. C: 29.7.1756.
Dimensions & tons: 45ft 0in x 18ft 0in x 7ft 0in (13.71 x 5.49 x 2.13m). 80 tons
Guns: 4 x 4pdrs, 2 x 3pdrs + 4 swivels in 7.1756. Designed for 8 guns and 2 swivels.
Renamed *Vigilant* but burned by the French at Oswego.

Ex-George. Schooner or skiff. Ex-HMS *George* Oswego
Built 6.1755–late 1755.
Dimensions & tons: 38ft 0in (11.58m). 40 tons.
Guns: 8 swivels (designed), also listed with 4 swivels.
The French reassigned the names of *George* and *Vigilant* to larger vessels and did not give these two *esquifs* new names. Burned by the French at Oswego.

Ex-Vigilant. Schooner or skiff. Ex-HMS *Vigilant*. Oswego
Built 1755.
Dimensions & tons: 38ft 0in (11.58m). 40 tons
Guns: 8 swivels (designed), also listed with 4 swivels.
Received no French name. Burned by the French at Oswego.

Lively. Schooner. Ex-HMS *Lively*. Oswego
Built 1755–56.
Dimensions & tons: unknown. Men: 6 sailors and 8 soldiers when captured
Guns: 6 swivels when captured.
Retaken by the British at Fort Niagara 1759.

In addition, the French found one dispatch vessel or schooner, not launched, burned by the British on the building ways.

VIGILANTE. Schooner. Designed and built by Pierre Levasseur in Quebec on a river that flows into Lake Champlain, where she became part of the French flotilla.
Dimensions & tons: dimensions unknown. 60 to 80 tons.
Guns: 10 x 4pdrs
Vigilante Fort St Jean, Quebec
K: 1756. L: 1757. C: 1757. Rebuilt at Fort St Jean 1758–59. Captured 1760 by the British on Lake Champlain and became HMS *Vigilant* (8 guns). Last mentioned 1778 beached in Lake Champlain.

MOUCHE. Snow, also listed as a sloop or cutter and sometimes as a corvette or schooner.
Dimensions & tons: dimensions unknown. 50 tons. Men: 30/55 men + 3/4 officers.
Guns: 2 or 4
Mouche Brest
K: early 1756. L: 5.1756. C: 6.1756. Struck 12.1763 at Brest. May have been converted to a *chatte* at Rochefort that served until 1767.

AGATHE. Cutter. Pierced for 12 guns and 12 *pierriers*.
Dimensions & tons: unknown. Men: 51/63
Guns: 6 x 4pdrs + 8 *pierriers*.
Agathe Brest
K: 1756. L: 1.8.1756. C: 10.1756. Last mentioned 1759 as a coast guard vessel at Rochefort.

TIERCELET Class. Cutters. During 1756 one or more cutters were ordered built at Dunkirk for coast guard duty, probably by the *commissaire-ordonnateur* at Dunkirk. *Tiercelet* was designed and built by Daniel Denys. She was named on 27.11.1756 and was stated by Denys to have been the first clinker-built cutter built in France. She was designed for 6 x 4pdrs but because of the chronic shortage of guns in Dunkirk the purchase of some 3pdrs and 2pdrs was authorized. *Épervier* is usually listed as a sister but, as Denys did not claim to have built her, her origins and specifications are not entirely clear.
Dimensions & tons: dimensions unknown. 48 tons.
Guns: 4 or 6 x 4pdrs
Tiercelet Daniel Denys, Dunkirk

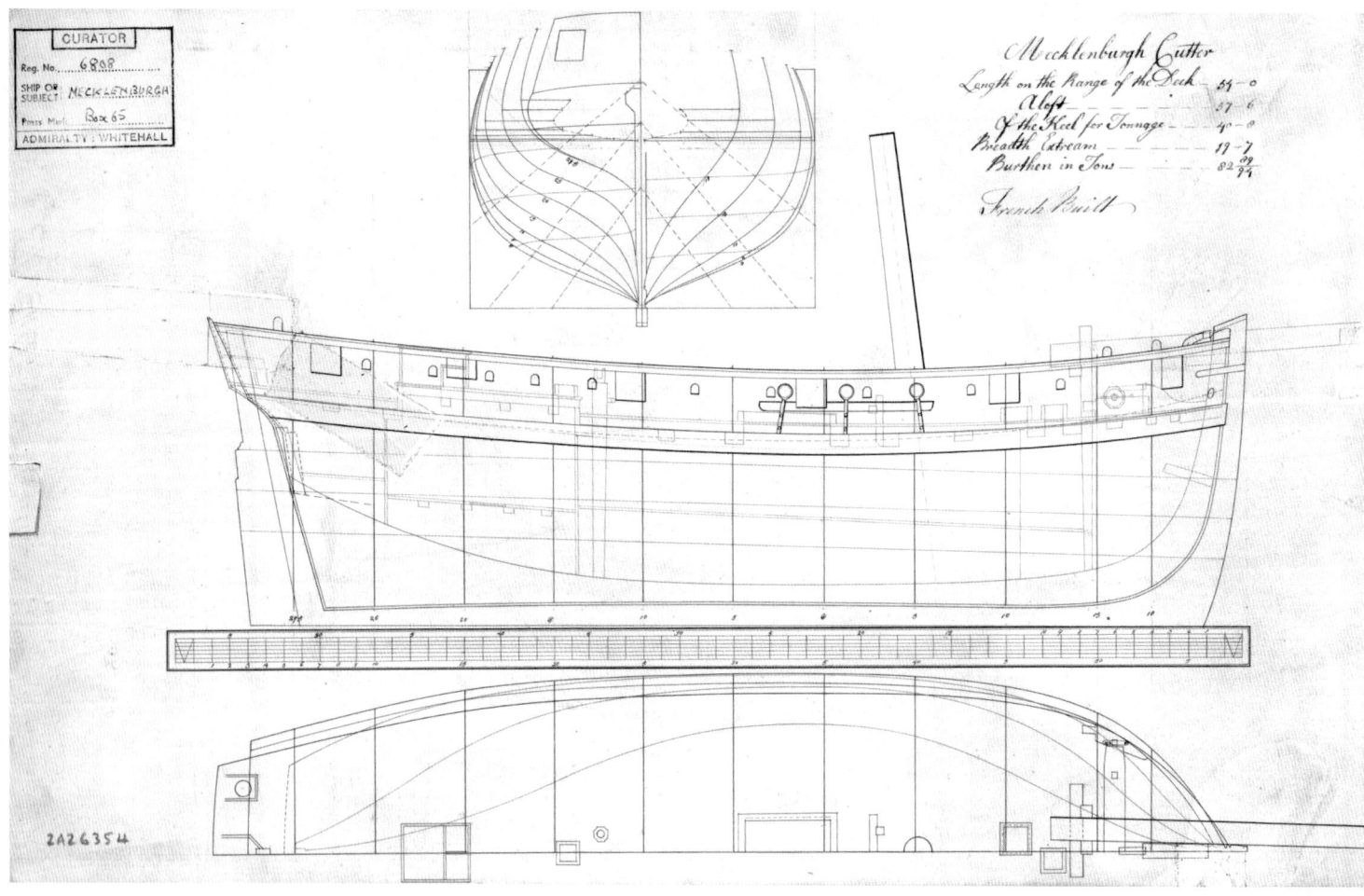

Admiralty draught of the privateer cutter *Mecklenburg* purchased in 1763. This French-built vessel was reckoned to be about five years old, so a contemporary of the *Tiercelet* Class, the first clinker-built cutters in the French Navy, which she probably closely resembled. (National Maritime Museum, London J0568)

K: 9.1756. L: 12.1756. C: 1757. Last mentioned when removed from service 1.1760 at Dunkirk.

Épervier Dunkirk
K: 9.1756. L: 12.1756. C: 1757. Captured 7.1759 by the British in the North Sea.

Ex-BRITISH MERCANTILE AND PRIVATEER PRIZES (1756–1757)

Dauphin. Ex-Guernsey privateer cutter captured 9.1756. 2 guns. Last mentioned 1758 at Brest.

Pucelle. Ex-British cutter *Virgin* captured 1757 and put into service at Brest 4.9.1757. 25 tons, 17/20 men + 2 officers, 4 guns. Was the only cutter at Brest in 1761 and was assigned to the invasion force of the Duc d'Aiguillon. Struck 12.1763 at Brest.

PURCHASED AND ACQUIRED VESSELS (1757–1759).

Three brigantines were added during this period, one in the colonies.

Origni. Brigantine. Put into service in 1757 at Rochefort. Later fate unknown.

Cabriolet. Brigantine put into service in 1757 at Brest. 14 men + 2 officers. Last mentioned 1758.

Janny or *Jouanis*. Brigantine purchased 1.1759 and put into service in French Guiana. Last mentioned 2.1759 when sent to St Christopher.

Ex-BRITISH NAVAL PRIZE (1759).

The cutter HMS *Hawk* was captured on 9 December 1759 by the French privateer *Duc de Choiseul* by musket fire in a storm that prevented the use of either ship's guns and was taken into the French Navy as *Faucon*.

Dimensions & tons (British): 89ft 0in x 24ft 10in x 10ft 7.5in (28.91 x 8.07 x 3.45m). 225 tons. Men (French) 36:
Guns (French): 8 or 10 x 4pdrs

Faucon. Batson, Limehouse.
K: 7.1755. L: 1.4.1756. C: 5.1756. Captured 2.1761 by the British and reverted to HMS *Hawk*. Sold 8.1781 by the Royal Navy.

Two unnamed French schooners, one large and one small, were built at Niagara but were not launched before Niagara was captured by the British in 7.1759. The British completed them as *Mississaga* and *Farquhar* but they were lost in December 1759.

Ex-BRITISH MERCANTILE PRIZES (1760–1762)

Goélette de Leroy (*Goélette du Roy?*). Ex-British schooner captured 5.1760 on the Canadian coast. Recaptured 6.1760 by the British.

Marie. Ex-British schooner *Mary* captured 6.1762 and put into service 11.7.1762 at Newfoundland. 90 tons, 23 men + 2 officers, 4 guns. Struck at Brest 10.1764. Also called a snow.

Crozon. Ex-British schooner captured 6.1762 and put into service 22.6.1762 at Newfoundland. 16/31 men + 3/4 officers, 6 guns.

Captured 10.1762 by HMS *Venus*.

Neptune. Brigantine captured 6.1762, ex-British *Neptune*. Put into service 17.7.1762 at Newfoundland. 90 tons, 22 men + 2 officers, 4 guns. Struck at Brest 10.1764. Also called a corvette and a snow.

PURCHASED AND ACQUIRED VESSELS (1761–1765). Two snows, a schooner, and two brigantines were added during this period. In addition four snows were acquired in 1762 at Rochefort for use as fireships and then re-classed as snows in 1762 or 1763. These (*Grand Saint Louis*, *Saint Jean Baptiste*, *Sainte Élisabeth*, and *Ville de Bilbao*) are listed in Chapter 8.

Aimable. Snow acquired 1761 and put into service at Lorient or Port Louis. Last mentioned 10.1762 out of service at Port Louis.

Désir. Snow captured 1.1762 by the *Compagnie des Indes* and ceded 9.1767 by them to the *Marine des Colonies* at Île de France. Last mentioned there 9.1769.

Denise. Schooner in service 11.1763 at Guyane and wrecked there in the Kourou River c.12.1763.

Anna. Brigantine purchased 8.1764 at Cayenne. Last mentioned at Philadelphia 6.1765.

Manon. Brigantine of merchant construction launched 8.1765 at Nantes, purchased 8.1765 and in service 9.1765. 60 tons, 20 men with an officer or 12 men with a master, 0 to 4 guns. Called a snow in 1765 at Brest though also listed as a brigantine, often used as a *gabarre*. Wrecked near Brest 1.1779. Not to be confused with the schooner *Nanon*.

GUYANE. Schooner. Designed by Augustin Pic. Specifications probably similar to *Afrique*, below.

Guyane Rochefort.
K: 3.1764. L: 8.1764. C: 10.1764. Last mentioned 12.1766 after having been found unsuited for service in Guyane and ordered back to Rochefort via Martinique.

AFRIQUE Class. Schooners. Designed by Jean-Denis Chevillard (cadet). Originally called *caiches* (ketches) or *bateaux*. They were designed with a Bermuda rig but were completed with a schooner rig that based on reports of their commanders were not successful (the maximum speed was 5 knots close-hauled).
Dimensions & tons: 55ft 0in x 16ft 0in x 8ft 6in (17.87 x 5.20 x 2.76m). 45/80 tons. Draught 6ft/7ft 2in (1.95/2.33m).
Guns: 8 x 4pdrs; 4 x 3pdrs (*Afrique*, 1774); 4 x 4pdrs (*Afrique*, 1780)

Afrique Rochefort
K: 1766. L: 1767. C: 1767. Listed in Rochefort inventories as a snow or schooner with 4 x 3pdrs from 1774 to 1778. This or a new *Afrique* built in 1780 was listed by Rochefort from 1780 to 1784 as a schooner for harbour service with 4 x 4pdrs. She was also called a 60-ton *gabarre* or *bateau*. Ceded 6.1786 to the *Compagnie d'Owhère et de Bénin* with the *flûte Pérou* and an otherwise unknown *Petite Charlotte* (40 tons, 12 pierriers) for an expedition to Benin.

Gorée Rochefort.
K: 1766. L: 4.1767. C: 6.1767. Probably replaced by a 60-ton *bateau* of the same name with a snow rig designed by François-Guillaume Clairain-Deslauriers and built at Rochefort in 1773. Captured 5.1779 by the British.

SAINT NICOLAS. Snow. Designed and built by Antonio Attuna at Bordeaux and purchased on the building ways 9.1767, being renamed from *Vermudien* or *Bermudien*. She belonged to the *Marine des Colonies* and not the regular navy.
Dimensions & tons: 82ft 1in, 70ft 3in x 23ft 4in x 10ft (26.66, 22.82 x 7.58 x 3.25m). 180/300 tons.
Guns: Unknown.

Saint Nicolas Bordeaux.
K: 1767. L: 12.1767. C: 2.1768. Was in service 9.1768 at Port au Prince, St Domingue, later fate unknown.

ACQUIRED VESSELS (1767–1768). These six ships (four schooners, a barque, and an Indian Ocean *palle*) were transferred from the *Compagnie des Indes* during these years. They probably all became part of the colonial navy, which did not appear on regular navy fleet lists.

Danaé. Schooner ceded 9.1767 at Île de France to the *Marine des Colonies* by the *Compagnie des Indes*. 30 tons. Wrecked 4.1768 on a reef in the Indian Ocean.

Pouponne. Schooner identical to *Danaé* above ceded 9.1767 at Île de France to the *Marine des Colonies* by the *Compagnie des Indes*. Wrecked 3.1772 in a storm at Île de France.

Comtesse de Mark. Schooner ceded 9.1767 at Île de France to the *Marine des Colonies* by the *Compagnie des Indes*. 26 tons. Wrecked 3.1772 in a storm at Île de France.

Créole. Barque of the *Compagnie des Indes* ceded to the King in 9.1767 or 4.1770 at Île de France. Last mentioned there 10.1773.

Iphigénie. Palle, ex-*Sainte Iphigénie*, of the *Compagnie des Indes*, ceded to the King in 9.1767 or 4.1770. Last mentioned at Île de France 11.1776 in bad condition.

Curieuse. Schooner that was in service 9.1768 at Île de France with the *Marine des Colonies*. Last mentioned there 1772.

ABERWRAC'H Class. Schooners or brigantines. Designed by Joseph-Louis Ollivier. *Aberwrac'h* was used as a school ship for pilots and as a hydrographic ship, her light draught being only 1ft 10in/2ft 8in (0.60/0.87m).
Dimensions & tons: 48ft 5in, 43ft 6in x 10ft 3in x 5ft 8in (15.73, 14.13 x 3.33 x 1.84m). 20/35 tons. Men: 11/12 + 3 officers
Guns: 6 x 4pdrs in *Aberwrac'h*, 4 x 3pdrs in *Nanon*.

Aberwrac'h Brest
K: 2.1769. L: 11.8.1769. C: 11.1769. Called a brigantine with *Manon* (acquired) in 1772. Last mentioned 1774, probably struck 4.1775 at Brest. Name spelled many ways including *Abbrewrack* and *Aberrack*.

Nanon Brest
K: 2.1769. L: 11.8.1769. C: 1769. Called a schooner in 1772. Listed as a schooner at Brest 11.1775 at the end of the *gabarre* section of the list and just ahead of the acquired brigantine *Manon*, last mentioned 6.1778, still in the *gabarre* section and in need of a refit.

LÉVRIER Class. Cutters. On 14 October 1770 the Minister of Marine, having been impressed by a model of a British cutter provided by CV de Kearney, decided to build eight cutters including four at Bordeaux. These were to be built at the Chantiers du Roi (the royal slipways within the city) under the direction of *ingénieur-constructeur* Leon Michel-Guignace. The minister supplied a model and plans, which Guignace was to use to design a clinker-built cutter of 40–45ft. *Lévrier* was completed with 6 x 4pdrs but by 1772 had exchanged them for 3pdrs. She and *Moucheron* (below) were called sloops (*seloups*) when first listed at Brest in 1771. *Furet* and *Milan* were stationed at Brest where cutters (including *Moucheron* and *Puce*, below) were called *caiches* (ketches) between 1775 and 1778.
Dimensions & tons: 45ft 6in x 19ft 4in x 7ft 3in (14.78 x 6.28 x 2.36m). 40/70 tons. Men: 17/28 + 2 officers.
Guns: 6 x 3pdrs; 4 x 3pdrs from 1776.

Lévrier Bordeaux.
K: 12.1770. L: 5.1771. C: 7.1771. Was serviceable at Rochefort

12.1774, Last mentioned when removed from service at Morlaix 9.1775, unsuccessful sale attempt there 8.12.1775.
Furet Bordeaux.
   K: 12.1770. L: 6.1771. C: 8.1771. Out of service mid-1778 at Brest, struck there late 1782.
Lézard Bordeaux.
   K: 12.1770. L: 6.1771. C: 8.1771. Struck 1777 at Île de France.
Milan Bordeaux.
   K: 12.1770. L: 6.1771. C: 8.1771. Out of service mid-1778 at Brest, struck there late 1782.

SAUTERELLE Class. Cutters. The Minister of Marine decided on 14 October 1770 to build eight cutters of 40–45ft length including four at Boulogne-sur-mer. These were reassigned on 28 October to St Malo and Lorient. When Daniel Denys proposed to build one cutter to the minister's specifications at Dunkirk the Minister reduced the orders at St Malo and Lorient to one ship each. The vessels were designed by *ingénieur-constructeur* Antoine Groignard, then residing at Lorient.
   Dimensions & tons: 45ft 0in, 40ft 0in x 21ft 0in x 9ft 0in (14.62, 12.99 x 6.82 x 2.92m). 40 tons. Draught 5ft 6in/9ft 6in (1.79/3.09m). Men: 18/24 + 3 officers.
   Guns: 6 x 4pdrs (*Moucheron*, 1771–81), both also listed from 1772 with 6 x 3pdrs or from 1776 with 4 x 3pdrs.
Sauterelle Lorient
   K: 12.1770. L: 4.1771. C: 6.1771. Struck 1777 at Île de France.
Moucheron St Malo
   K: 12.1770. L: 6.1771. C: 7.1771. Out of service mid-1778 at Brest, struck there late 1782.

PUCE. Cutter. On 14 October 1770 the Minister of Marine decided to build four cutters at Boulogne (soon moved to St Malo and Lorient) and four at Bordeaux. Étienne Daniel Denys responded by proposing to build a 40–45ft cutter to the minister's specifications at Dunkirk. (Note that Daniel's first cousin, Jacques François, with whom Daniel built some larger ships, did not participate in Daniel's work on cutters and luggers.) The Minister accepted this proposal on 1 November and reduced the orders at St Malo and Lorient to one ship each. By 14 November the Minister had approved Denys' design and approved its construction. Considerable money was saved by building her in the Navy's *parc de la Marine* within the city and not in Denys's shipyard. She was clinker-built to make her as light as possible and was regarded as highly successful. This success caused the Navy to make Denys a *sous-ingénieur-constructeur sans appointements* in the *Génie maritime*, the Navy's professional constructor's corps, on 24 December 1771.
   Dimensions & tons: 45ft 2in, 38ft 2in x 16ft 1in x 8ft 0in (14.67, 12.40 x 5.22 x 2.60m). 37/67 tons. Draught 6ft 8in/8ft 4in (2.17/2.71m). Could mount 7 pairs of oars. Men: 22 + 1 officer
   Guns: 6 x 3pdrs; 4 x 3pdrs from 1776.
Puce Dunkirk
   K: 12.1770. L: 30.4.1771. C: 9.1771. Sold *c.*10.1779 at Brest.

SYLPHIDE. Schooner. Designed by Henri Chevillard (the elder) and built at Rochefort in 1771. Wrecked in the harbour at Cayenne 1.1774.

ESPIÈGLE. Lugger. In 1772 CV de Kearney recommended building luggers, a type of which the British thought highly. In June 1772 a British lugger fortuitously arrived in Dunkirk in need of repairs, and while she was hauled out the *commissaire-ordonnateur* at Dunkirk had Denys take off her lines. The Navy authorities at Brest approved the construction of luggers based in part on plans received from Denys but asked that the designers take into account the plans of another British lugger obtained by the Comte d'Estaing and the experience gained by LV Claude-Antoine-François-Marie de Bavre who had travelled to Britain to study British cutters and luggers. The minister received the contract from Denys on 26 December 1772 and responded on 23 January 1773 by sending the final plans for the ship to Dunkirk. The ship was named on 16 April. De Bavre oversaw the construction of the ship and took command of her on 21 June 1773.
   Dimensions & tons: 45ft 2in x 16ft 0in x 8ft 0in (14.67 x 5.20 x 2.60m). 112 tons displacement. Men: 33 + 2 officers
   Guns: 6 x 3pdrs; 4 x 3pdrs from 1778. Also reported with 6 x 4pdrs in 1776 and 4 x 4pdrs in 1781.
Espiègle Dunkirk.
   K: 12.1772. L: 4.6.1773. C: 7.1773. Repaired 8.1780. Struck at Brest in early 1783.

PURCHASED AND ACQUIRED VESSELS (1772–1775). These miscellaneous additions included a brigantine or snow, another snow, and two schooners. At least two served in the colonies.
Africain. Brigantine acquired *c.*1772. In service 1,1774 at Rochefort as a snow or brigantine requiring inspection, last mentioned 12.1774 as requiring a major refit.
Lazare. Schooner that was in service 12.1773 at Gorée. Last mentioned 3.1774.
Coureur. Snow purchased 9.1774 at Madagascar. Last mentioned there 3.1775.
Badine. Schooner that was in service 5.1775, no other information.

CHASSEUR. Lugger. In December 1773 the Minister of Marine was considering building a lugger somewhat larger than *Espiègle*, but the proposed lugger remained unfunded in 1775 until the advent of Sartine as Minister. He wrote to Dunkirk on 13 October 1775 that the King had decided to build two luggers similar to *Espiègle* and wanted them to be commissioned during the next summer. In submitting his plans on 3

The dimensions accompanying this plan by *Vice amiral* Pâris exactly match the cutter *Puce* built, as Pâris correctly states, at Dunkirk in 1771. The lines do not make it clear that the cutter was clinker-built. (*Souvenirs de Marine*, Plate 250)

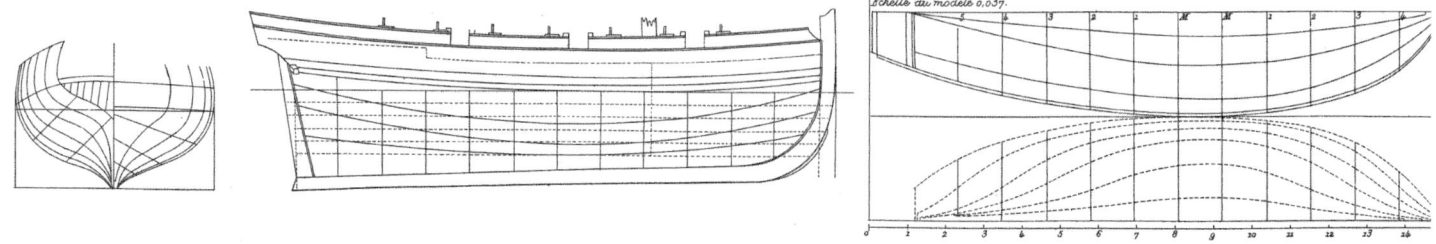

MINOR WARSHIPS – *PONANT* TYPES

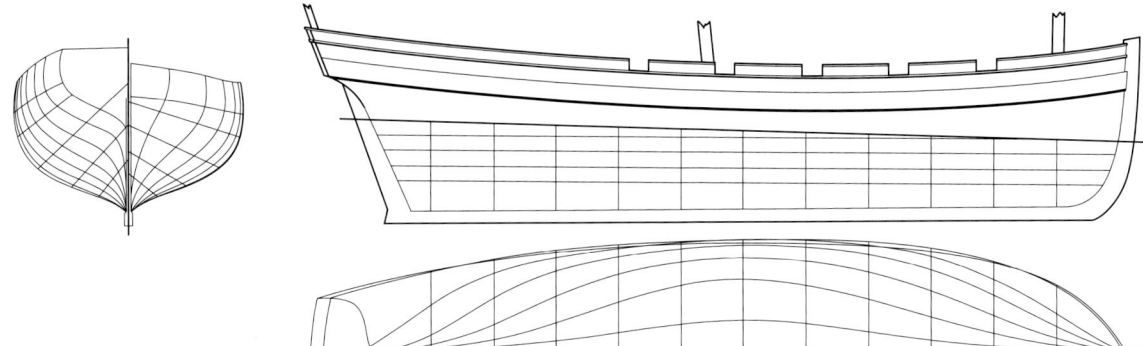

Lines plan of the 10-gun lugger *Chasseur*, of 1776, drawn by László Veres after an original in the Dunkirk archives.

November 1775 Daniel Denys pointed out the advantages of the additional 4 feet of length of the new ship compared to *Espiègle*. The contract was signed on 6 December and plans were approved on 22 December for a 72-foot lugger (*Chasseur*) to be completed in early May and for a 66-foot lugger (*Coureur*).

Dimensions & tons: 72ft 0in, 63ft 0in x 20ft 6in x 10ft 6in (23.39, 20.46 x 6.66 x 3.41m). 72/130 tons. Draught 7ft 2in/9ft 4in (2.33/3.03m). Men: 53/80 + 3 or 4 officers.

Guns: 8 x 4pdrs + 6 *pierriers*. Also reported with 8 x 3pdrs in 1778.

Chasseur Dunkirk.
K: 12.1775. L: 8.5.1776. C: 8.1776. Condemned 7.1784 at Fort Royal, Martinique, and made into a supply hulk.

COUREUR. Lugger. This ship was part of a program for the construction by Daniel Denys of two luggers to follow *Espiègle* that is described in the entry for *Chasseur*, above. They were both designed for 10 x 4pdrs which Dunkirk planned to get from England; the minister proposed 3pdrs, but neither calibre was available at Brest and Britain had embargoed exports of guns in May 1776 as war approached. *Coureur* actually carried the lighter armament shown below according to Jean Boudriot's monograph on the ship.

Dimensions & tons: 66ft 0in, 56ft 6in x 20ft 4in x 11ft 0in (21.44, 18.35 x 6.61 x 3.57m). 65/120 tons. Draught 6ft 10in/9ft 3in (2.22/3.00m). Men: 47 + 3 officers; 60 + 3 officers when taken.

Guns: 2 x 3pdrs and 6 x 2pdrs + 6 *pierriers*; had two more 2pdrs when taken.

Coureur Dunkirk.
K: 12.1775. L: 8.5.1776. C: 8.1776. While supporting frigate *Belle Poule* was captured 18.6.1778 by the British cutter *Alert* (12 x 6pdrs) in the Channel. Rerigged as a schooner, she became HMS *Coureur*. Taken 21.6.1780 by the American privateer brigs *Fortune* (16) and *Griffin* (14) off Newfoundland. Reportedly retaken 25.2.1782, and an aviso or 10-gun lugger named *Coureur* was briefly listed along with the new *Courrier* in the port at Brest between 9.1782 and 1.1783.

SERVICE SCHOONERS AT ROCHEFORT (1777). Inventories of vessels at Rochefort between March 1777 and November 1784 include a

Admiralty draught of the lugger *Coureur* dated 18 September 1778, as captured but with some proposed alterations outlined. Unusually, below the body plan is a structural section showing the clinker planking of the hull. (National Maritime Museum, London J0873)

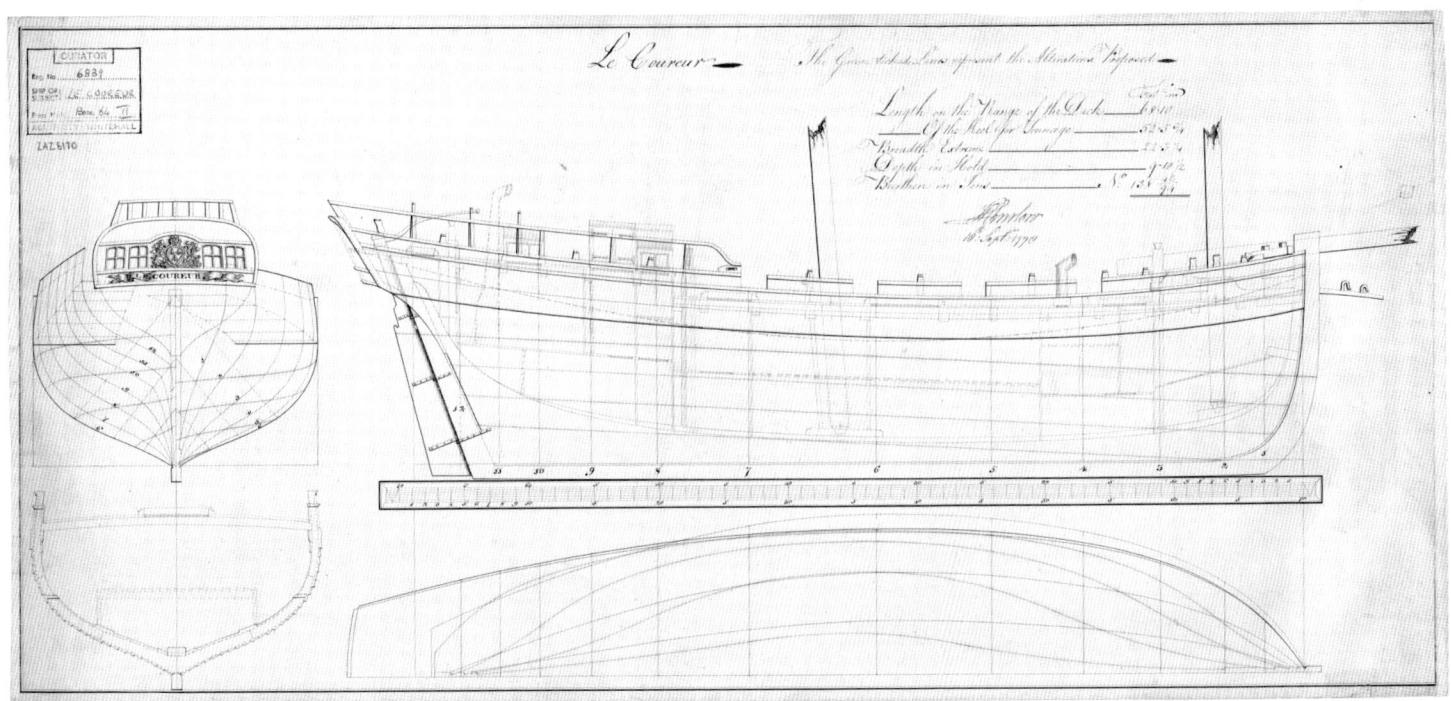

group of harbour service schooners (*goélettes de servitude*) whose function was to make daily deliveries of provisions from Rochefort to the ships in the roadstead at Île d'Aix. The four on the list in 1777 were *Ambulante*, *Artésienne*, *Avant-garde*, and *Va et Vient*. *Ambulante* was launched on 28 February 1777 and *Artésienne* (ex-*Céleste*) in May 1777, the others were probably older. A new *Céleste* was launched in July 1780, and *Va et Vient* was re-launched on 5.7.1781 after lengthy repairs. *Afrique* and the prize *Vanneau* (see below), previously in regular service, joined this group of service craft in late 1782 but the deteriorated *Vanneau* was struck in 1783. A *Caprice* that entered Rochefort on 29.11.1783 was briefly listed with this group, then deleted. The remaining six harbour service schooners were all in good condition when these inventories ended in November 1784. One more schooner was listed as under construction in July 1783; she was probably the *Légère* that was begun at Rochefort in June 1783, in service in 1784, and last mentioned in 1786. *Va et Vient* was removed from service at Brest in 1787 and *Céleste* was last mentioned at Rochefort in 1792. Other service craft also supported the ships in the roadstead, notably the yachts listed in Chapter 13 which acted as personnel ferries.

    Dimensions & tons (*Ambulante*): 49ft 6in, 45ft 0in x 14ft 0in x 6ft 0in (16.08, 14.62 x 4.55 x 1.95m). 42/70 tons. Draught 5ft/6ft (1.62/1.95m).
    Guns: None, and no gunports.

PURCHASED AND ACQUIRED VESSELS (1777–1778). Two schooners were added during this period, both in the colonies.
Goélette des Colonies. Schooner that was in service 8.1777 in French Guiana. Also called *Goélette du Roi* or possibly *Mutine*. No other information.
Fourmi. Schooner that was in service in the Indian Ocean 7.1778. 16 men + 1 officer, no guns. Decomm. 9.1778 at Île de France and then condemned because of age.

Ex-BRITISH NAVAL PRIZES (1778). Three Royal Navy cutters were taken by the French in 1778. HMS *Folkestone* was captured on 24 June 1778 by the frigate *Surveillante* off Ushant before the declaration of war, the French initially believing that she was a privateer. HMS *Alert* was captured 17.7.1778 by the frigate *Junon* in the Channel and became the French *Alerte* while HMS *Jackall* was delivered at Calais 11.1779 by her mutinous Irish crew.
Folkestone Hall, Folkestone.
    Ord: 30.4.1763. K: 8.1763. L: 13.10.1764. C: 31.1.1765.
    Dimensions & tons: 45ft 0in x 20ft 1in (14.62 x 6.52m). 60/100 tons. Men: 37/94 + 2/4 officers.
    Guns: 8 x 3pdrs
    Struck 1782 or early 1783.

Alerte Ladd, Dover
    Ord: 14.12.1776. K: 1.1777. L: 24.6.1777. C: 25.8.1777.
    Dimensions & tons: 65ft 0in x 24ft 0in (21.11 x 7.80m). 200 tons displacement. Men: 102 + 5 officers
    Guns: 14 x 4pdrs
    Designated *Alerte No.1* after a second HMS *Alert* was captured in 1780 (below). Lost with all hands 15.12.1779 off the American coast, struck from the list at Brest *c*.10.1780.
Jackall. Purchased by the Royal Navy 4.1778
    Dimensions & tons: 69ft 0in x 23ft 9in x 9ft 8in (22.41 x 7.71 x 3.14m). 180 tons displacement.
    Guns: 14 x 4pdrs; 10 x 4pdrs as French privateer.
    Turned over to French privateers, retaken 5.1780 by the British, and either captured by the American frigate *Deane* in 4.1782 or sold by the RN in 6.1785.

Ex-BRITISH MERCANTILE AND PRIVATEER PRIZES (1778)
Guêpe. Ex-British merchant cutter *Wasp* seized 2.1778 before war began. 14 x 6pdrs in 1779; 10 x 6pdrs in 1781. In late 1778 it was proposed to use her as a model for three cutters to be built at St Malo but the plans of Daniel Denys for *Serpent* were used instead. Burned by the British at Cancale 5.1779 but repaired, to Brest from St Malo *c*.1.1780 and to sea 2.5.1780, wrecked 2.1781 at Cape Charles in Chesapeake Bay.
Shallow. Ex-British merchant or privateer cutter *Shallow* captured 6.1778 and put into service 7.1778 at Granville. 8 x 3pdrs. Struck 1781 at Brest. Name also spelled *Slhawo*, *Sibawo*, *Shalouw*, and *Shalow*.
Trial. Ex-British privateer cutter *Tryal* from Plymouth (6 x 6pdrs) captured 6.1778 and put into service 12.1778 by the Navy at Le Havre. 25 tons, 20/39 men + 1/3 officers, 8 x 4pdrs. Struck in early 1783 at Brest.
Vanneau. Ex-British privateer schooner captured 10.6.1778 by the corvette *Rossignol* and taken to La Rochelle. 8 x 3pdrs, 8 x 6pdrs by 1.1780. Fast under sail and reserved for the King's service. Ordered sold at Rochefort 24.4.1781 but instead became a harbour service schooner there in 1782 (see above), struck 1783.
Expédition. Ex-British merchant or privateer cutter *Expedition* captured 7.1778. 77/90 men + 4/5 officers, 14 x 4pdrs. Towed the frigate *Surveillante* to Brest after the frigate's epic battle with HMS *Quebec* on 7.10.1779. Run ashore at Tranquebar 4.1782 to avoid capture by a British squadron.
Stanley. Ex-British brig *Stanley*, probably mercantile, captured 8.1778 by the ship of the line *César* on the North American coast. 10–16 guns. Recaptured 11.1778 by the British.

CERF Class. Cutters. On 15 May 1778 the Minister of Marine, Sartine, proposed that Daniel Denys built two cutters. On 26 May he

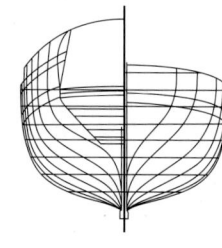
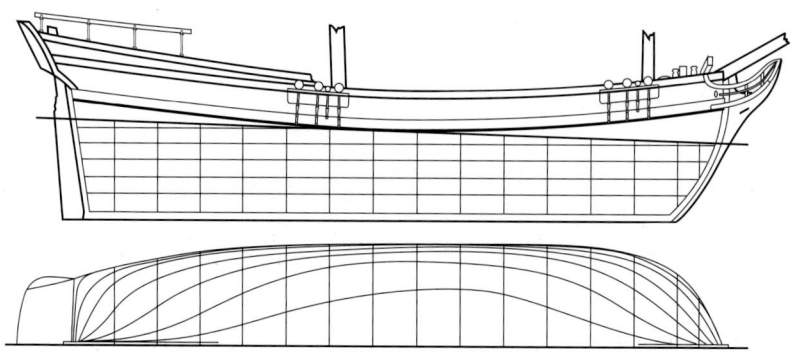

A lines plan of a service schooner built at Rochefort in 1777, redrawn by László Veres after a reconstruction by Jean Boudriot based an original in the Rochefort archives – in design, a merchant schooner but in naval service. The dimensions in French feet are 57ft 5in x 17ft 4in x 8ft 4in.

Admiralty design draught for the *Alert* Class cutters of 1777. The armament is listed as 'ten carriage guns' and some carried more 12pdr carronades later, but if *Alert* ever carried the fourteen guns attributed to her after capture by the French, it would have been necessary to permanently arm the bow-chase ports. This was an extreme design with almost nothing by way of rails or weather protection above deck level, in contrast with the substantial bulwarks carried by their French equivalents; it would have made them fast and weatherly, but wet and uncomfortable for the crew, who would have been very exposed in action. Although nominally Navy-designed by this date, they were still constructed by specialist South Coast shipyards and adopted many of their practices – note, for example the rockered keel, with its slight upward curve at bow and stern. (National Maritime Museum, London J7946)

wrote that in addition to these he needed two luggers like *Chasseur*, although if Denys thought he could augment the qualities of cutters and make them faster he should send plans. The initial plans were dated 28 May 1778. Sartine changed his mind on 31 May stating that he wanted only the luggers (although he wrote on 2 June that he liked Denys's plans for the cutters). On 12 June Sartine wrote that he had not approved the plan of the two luggers of 10 x 4pdrs each because he was interested in increasing these to 16 or 18 x 6pdrs. He thought no such vessels had been yet built but trusted the talents of Denys

to produce a design. If this proved impossible Denys was to draw plans for two cutters to carry the same 16 to 18 x 6pdrs. The ships were to be clinker-built. Fifteen days later Sartine accepted the plans of two smaller cutters and two larger cutters and stated that they must be built quickly. The four units were named on 13 September 1778, *Pilote* and *Mutin* having 14 x 6pdrs and *Serpent* and *Levrette* having 18 x 6pdrs.

In October 1778 the construction of cutters with 16 to 18 x 6pdrs was envisaged at St Malo. During that year the British cutter *Wasp* was captured and became *Guêpe* and the *commissaire-ordonnateur* there, prompted by LV de Bavre, proposed to build the new cutters on the model of the *Guêpe*. However, Denys's plans for *Serpent* arrived at St Malo at the end of October and were ultimately used to build all three of the St Malo cutters.

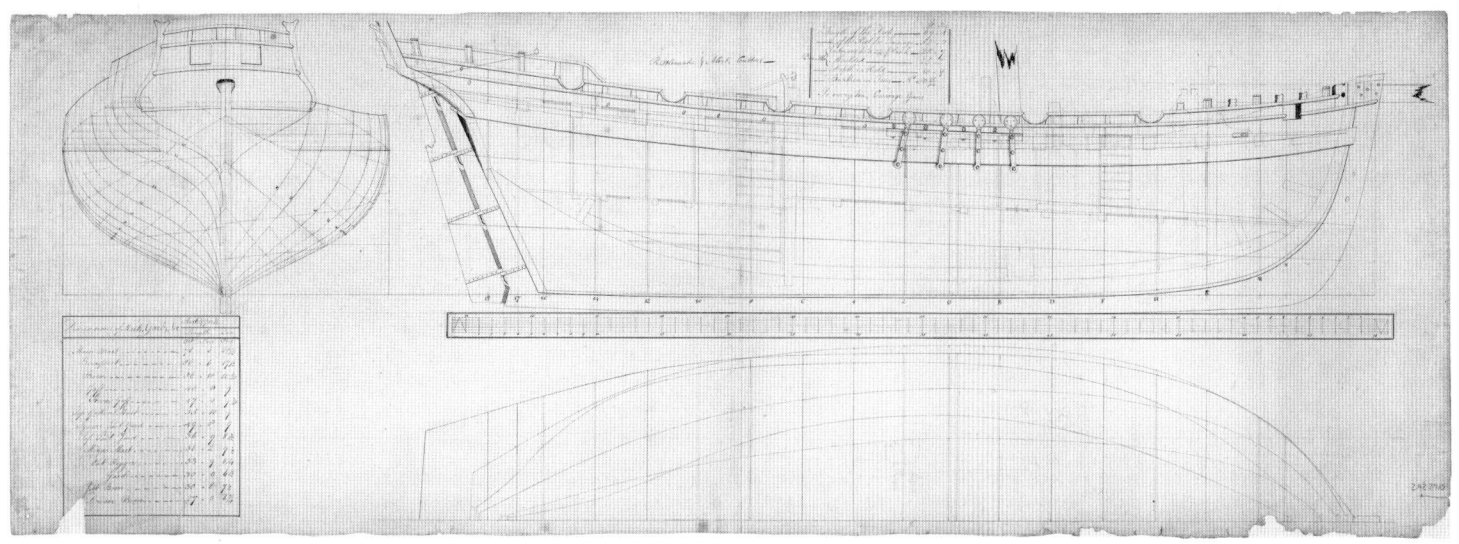

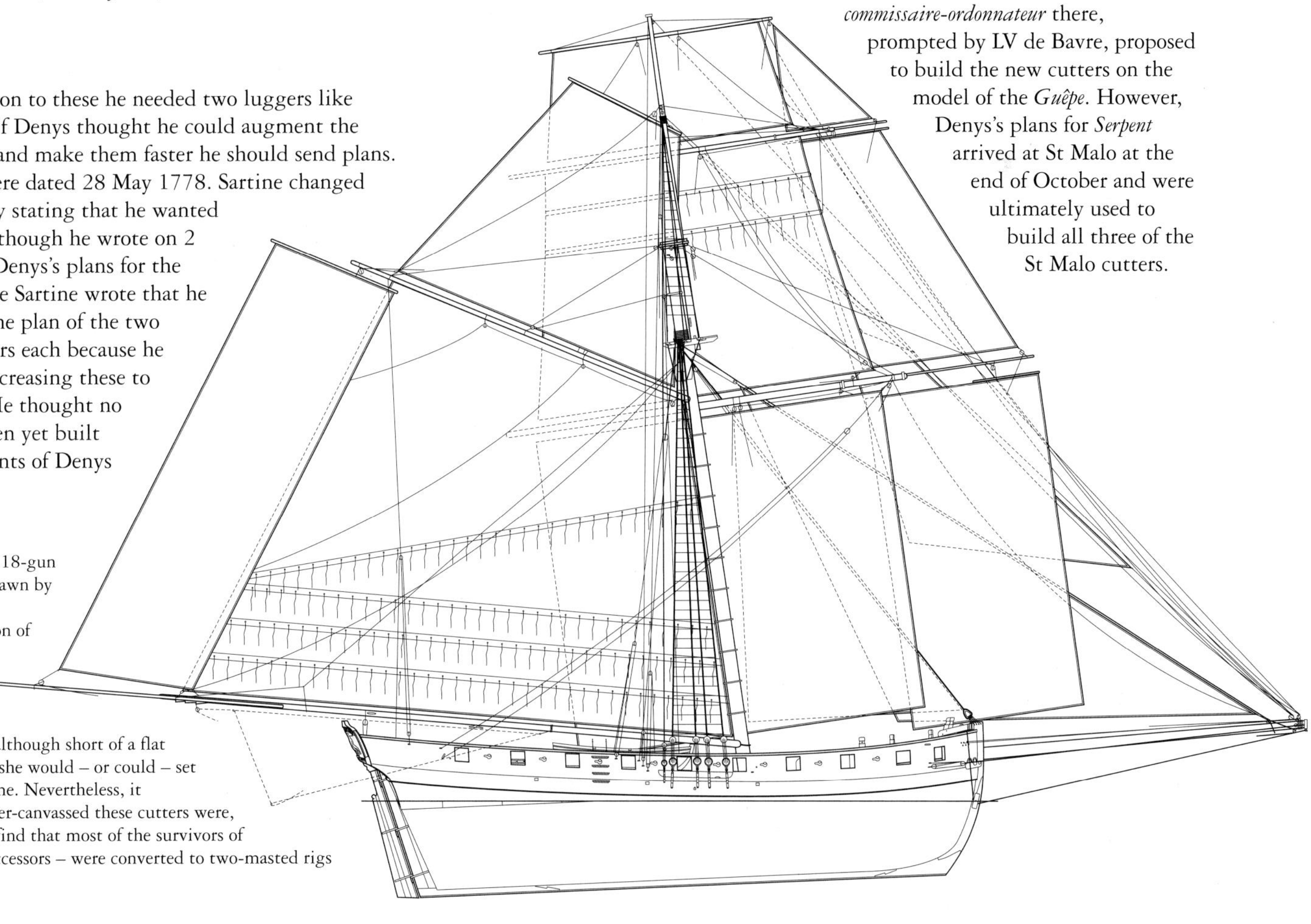

The sail plan of the big 18-gun cutter *Cerf* of 1779 redrawn by László Veres after Jean Boudriot's reconstruction of the rig. It shows every stunsail and 'flying kite' theoretically available to the vessel, although short of a flat calm it is unlikely that she would – or could – set them all at the same time. Nevertheless, it emphasizes just how over-canvassed these cutters were, and it is no surprise to find that most of the survivors of the class – and their successors – were converted to two-masted rigs (brigs or luggers).

The lack of small warships remained critical at the end of 1779. On 15 September Sartine announced his intention to build at Dunkirk in the following year two cutters of 18 x 6pdrs on the plans of *Serpent* and *Levrette*, and despite growing controversy over the poor sailing performance of the large cutters Versailles wrote on 23 May 1780 that the King's intention was to build four, which were to be carvel- rather than clinker-built to permit coppering. On 4 August the Minister approved the *devis* (specifications) for the new ships which he named *Espion*, *Fanfaron*, *Malin* and *Lézard*. The copper sheathing was not included in Denys's contract but at least *Malin* and *Lézard* were reportedly coppered. The gun foundry at Indret furnished 28 x 6pdrs for the four new ships.

Dimensions & tons: 81ft 0in, 68ft 6in x 25ft 10in x 11ft 6in (26.31, 22.25 x 8.38 x 3.73 m.). 130/256 tons. Draught 8ft 6in/12ft (2.76/3.90m). Men: 104–135 + 4/5 officers.

Guns: 18 x 6pdrs. *Fanfaron* in 1783: 16 x 6pdrs; in 1796: 6 x 3pdrs. *Levrette* in 1795: 18 x 6pdrs, 2 *obusiers*; in 1800: 20 x 6pdrs;

Serpent Daniel Denys, Dunkirk.
K: 11.1778. L: 3.4.1779. C: 5.1779. Condemned 4.1783 at Fayal, struck 1783 at Brest, BU 1798.

Levrette Daniel Denys, Dunkirk.
K: 11.1778. L: 16.4.1779. C: 7.1779. Re-rigged as brig (brigantine) 1783 at Brest. Hired out as a privateer 4.1793 and renamed *Patriote de Brest* but returned to the Navy 5.1793. Condemned 6.1793 at Brest, then hauled out 6.1793 at St Malo, re-launched 9.1793 as a corvette, renamed *Levrette* 9.1793, and completed 3.1794. Training corvette 1799. Replaced by the corvette *Festin* and in 7.1806 became target ship for the gunnery school at Brest.

Cerf St Malo.
K: 10.1778. L: 1.3.1779. C: 4.1779. Named 4.12.1778. Placed under the orders of the American John Paul Jones at Lorient 6.1779 and sometimes called *Stag*, returned 9.1779. Damaged 8.2.1780 in combat with a 24-gun British privateer which she drove off, decomm at Martinique 7.1780 and left in the care of the colony, later fate unknown.

Chevreuil St Malo.
K: 10.1778. L: 1.3.1779. C: 4.1779. Named 4.12.1778. Re-rigged as a brig 7.1779 (see notes for *Mutin* class below). Attacked 17.12.1780 in the Atlantic by HM Ships *Foudroyant*, *Courageous*, and *Monsieur* and taken by *Monsieur*, not added to the Royal Navy.

Hussard St Malo.
K: 12.1778. L: 1.4.1779. C: 5.1779. Named 4.12.1778. Re-rigged as a brig 7.1779. Captured 5.7.1780 by HMS *Nonsuch* off Ushant and became HMS *Echo*. Foundered 13.12.1781 in Plymouth Sound after colliding with a privateer in a gust of wind and then striking a rock.

Lézard Daniel Denys, Dunkirk.
K: 10.1780. L: 10.3.1781. C: 6.1781. Captured 10.1782 by HMS *Sultan* in the neutral Danish port of Tranquebar, taken to Bombay, and became HMS *Lizard*. Restored to the French at the end of the war in 1783 but struck by them in 1784 and back in British service the same year. Sold by the British in the East Indies in 1785.

Malin Daniel Denys, Dunkirk.
K: 10.1780. L: 12.3.1781. C: 6.1781. Was part of the Squadron of Evolutions reviewed by Louis XVI at Cherbourg on 24.6.1786 and was visited by the King the following day. Disappeared 11.1786 during a storm in the Gulf of Gascony.

Espion Daniel Denys, Dunkirk.
K: 12.1780. L: 22.6.1781. C: 10.1781. Captured 24.1.1782 by HMS *Lizard* (28) off St Kitts and became HMS *Espion*. Sold 25.3.1784 at Deptford.

Fanfaron Daniel Denys, Dunkirk.
K: 12.1780. L: 23.6.1781. C: 9.1781. Re-rigged as brig at Lorient 1783. Scuttled in the Scheldt 21.3.1793 but salved and repaired at Antwerp. Re-rigged as lugger at Le Havre 5.1797. For sale at Dunkirk 1.1802.

MUTIN Class. Cutters. These four ships were smaller 14-gun versions of the large 18-gun cutters desired by Sartine that became the *Cerf* class above. At the end of June 1778 Sartine accepted plans of Daniel Denys dated 28.5.1778 for two smaller cutters along with two larger cutters and stated that they must be built quickly. The four units were named on 13 September 1778, the two smaller cutters becoming *Pilote* and *Mutin*. France continued to have an urgent need for small warships, and on 3 December 1779 Sartine added to a new program for 18-gun cutters two of 14 x 6pdrs on the plans of *Pilote* and *Mutin*. On 9 June 1780 the Minister named the two new cutters *Pandour* and *Clairvoyant*; they were launched on 15 and 18 June 1780 and were copper sheathed. The masts of both failed during their delivery voyage from Dunkirk to Le Havre in September 1780.

Dimensions & tons: 75ft, 65ft x 24ft x 11ft (24.36, 21.11 x 7.80 x 3.57m). 115/212 tons. Draught 8ft/11ft 9in (2.60/3.82m). Men: 85–115.

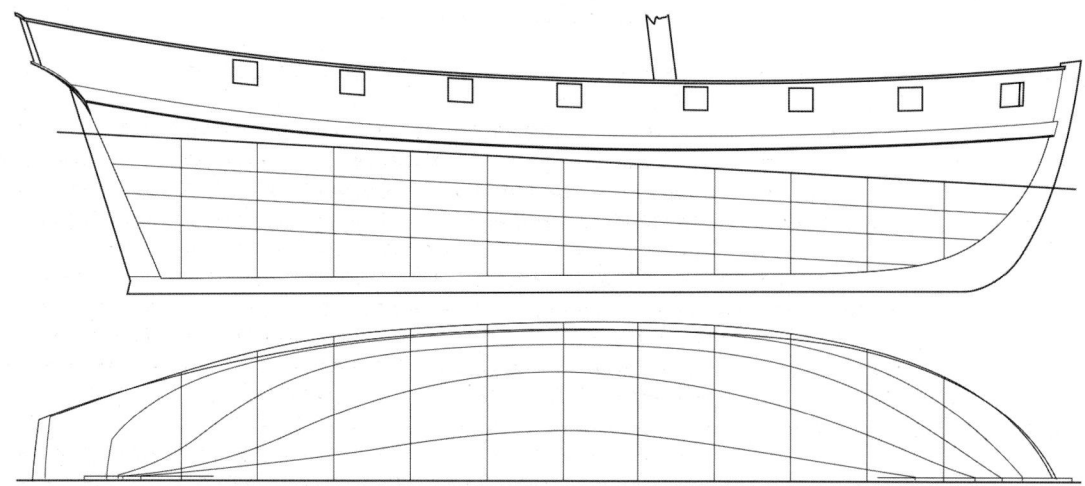

Lines plan for the 14-gun cutters of the *Mutin* Class, redrawn by László Veres after an original in the Service Historique de la Défense, Vincennes. Although smaller than the 18-gun type, it is significant that three of the four cutters of this class were converted to brigs, including one after capture by the British.

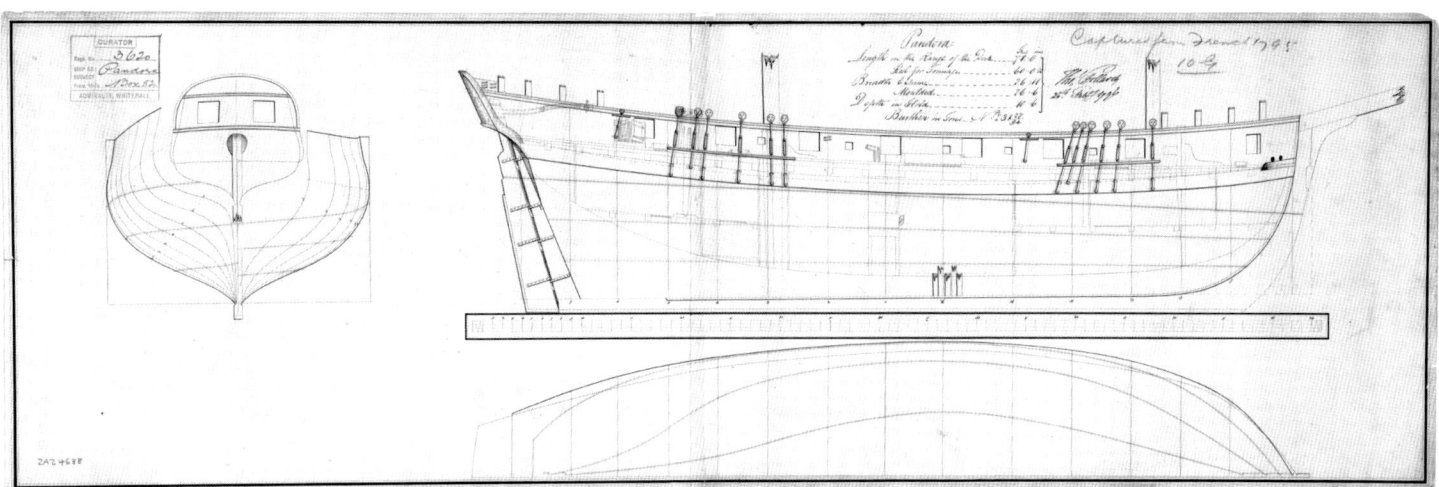

Admiralty draught of the *Pandora* [actually *Pandour*] as captured, dated 24 February 1796. By 1782 the French Navy had converted its two remaining cutters of this class, *Pandour* and *Clairvoyant*, to a brig rig, as shown here. (National Maritime Museum, London J4829)

Guns: 14 x 6pdrs.

Mutin Daniel Denys, Dunkirk.
K: 6.1778. L:11.1778. C: 3.1779. Dismasted and captured with *Pilote* 2.10.1779 by HMS *Jupiter* (50) in the Channel, became HMS *Mutine*. Retaken by the French 1781 and by the British 1782. Renamed HMS *Pigmy* 20.1.1798. Wrecked 9.8.1805 in St Aubin's Bay, Jersey.

Pilote Daniel Denys, Dunkirk.
K: 7.1778. L: 11.1778. C: 5.1779. Captured 2.10.1779 with *Mutin* by HMS *Jupiter* (50) in the Channel, became HMS *Pilote*. Re-rigged as a brig 1794. Sold 5.1799 at Sheerness.

Pandour Daniel Denys, Dunkirk.
K: 4.1780. L: 16.6.1780. C: 9.1780. Re-rigged and re-classed as a brig (brigantine) in 1782. Captured 31.8.1795 by HMS *Caroline* off Dunkirk and became HMS *Pandour* (also recorded as *Pandora*). Foundered with all hands 6.1797 in the North Sea.

Clairvoyant Daniel Denys, Dunkirk.
K: 4.1780. L: 18.6.1780. C: 9.1780. Re-rigged and re-classed as a brig (brigantine) in 1782. Wrecked 10.1784 on the rocks at Audierne, Brittany, hulk sold 28.9.1785.

In early 1779 the large cutters were proving to be problematic. *Chevreuil* and *Hussard* transited from St Malo to Lorient in June 1779 and their commanders complained of their slow speed and their inability to catch the small privateers they they had encountered off Ouessant. The *ingénieur-constructeur* at Lorient, Segondat-Duvernet, and the commander of that port asked Sartine for permission to re-rig them as brigs, and the conversion was completed in late July 1779 with favourable results. At Dunkirk, however, the cutter rig was retained for a time. On 14 April 1780 Sartine replied to a memoir in which Denys stated that the luggers and cutters that he had been charged to build could be faster if crew size was reduced, less equipment was embarked, and hammock netting was substituted for the heavy bulwarks along the deck edges. He in effect regarded reduction of weight and hull height, not a change of rig, as the answer to the speed problems of the cutters. However, the rig of cutters also produced resupply problems, as the masts had to be cut from scarce high-quality trees normally used for the topmasts of ships of 74 or 80 guns. The big cutters proved to be highly vulnerable to dismasting, further increasing the demand they placed on scarce timber supplies. Competition with 74s for timber, more than the supposed speed problems, probably led to the abandonment of the large cutters in favour of brigs. In the early 1780s the Dunkirk-built *Levrette*, *Malin*, *Pandour*, *Clairvoyant*, and *Fanfaron* were re-rigged as brigs. Of these *Levrette* was re-rated as a corvette in 1794 and *Fanfaron* was re-rated as a lugger in 1797.

TAPAGEUR. The origins of this cutter are unknown, she may have been a privateer launched at Dunkirk in December 1778 that resembled the Navy's *Mutin* class. The dimensions below are those measured by the British after her capture converted to French feet.

Dimensions & tons: 69ft 0in, 51ft 5in x 26ft 0in x 10ft 2in (22.41, 16.70 x 8.45 x 3.30m). 224 tons. Men: 70
Guns: 14 x 4pdrs + 10 *pierriers*.

Tapageur Unknown.
Captured 4.1779 by HMS *Milford* off Plymouth and became the cutter HMS *Tapageur*. Wrecked while trying to warp into Careenage Bay, St Lucia, 3.1780, though there is a later reference to her at Porto Praya 16.4.1781.

ÉTOILE. Lugger.

Dimensions & tons: dimensions unknown. Men: 25/32 + 3/4 officers
Guns: 8 x 3pdrs

Étoile Nantes.
K: 1779. L: 2.1780. C: 3.1780. Struck 1784 at Brest, may have later been used as a *gabarre* hulk at Rochefort.

PURCHASED AND ACQUIRED VESSELS (1779). These miscellaneous wartime additions included two brigs or brigantines, a lugger, and six schooners. The brig *Vengeance* was purchased by the French to serve in a squadron under the American John Paul Jones that also included the former Indiaman *Duc de Duras* (renamed *Bonhomme Richard*) and the privateer frigate *Pallas*, chartered by the French in May 1779. *Vengeance* and *Pallas* reverted to French control (along with the captured *Serapis*) in October 1779 in order to leave the neutral Dutch port in which the squadron had taken refuge after the Battle of Flamborough Head and return to France. The six schooners all served in the Antilles.

Vengeance. Brig or brigantine purchased 1.1779 by the French Navy at Bordeaux. 80 tons, 12 x 4pdrs or 3pdrs. Arrived at Dunkirk 1.1780 and sold.

Joyeuse. Schooner that was in service in the Antilles 3.1779. No other information.

Marie-Christine. Schooner that was in service in the Antilles 3.1779. No other information.

Actif. Schooner that was in service in the Antilles 3.1779. Last mentioned 7.1792 while in service at Martinique.

Éclair. Schooner that was in service in the Antilles 3.1779. No other information.

Guêpe or *Petite Guêpe*. Lugger of unknown origin put into service on 3.5.1779 at St Malo. 7–15 men + 1 officer. Was at Granville when last mentioned in 1781.

Saint Jean. Brigantine of unknown origin put into service 8.1779 at Rochefort. 105 tons, 4 *pierriers*. Last mentioned 6.1780 at Cayenne.

Éther. Schooner of unknown origin put into service 9.1779. Lost with all hands 10.1779 in the Antilles.

Combel. Schooner of unknown origin put into service *c*.1779. Disappeared at sea 1780 in the Antilles.

Ex-BRITISH MERCANTILE AND PRIVATEER PRIZES (1779)

Barrington. Ex-British mercantile or privateer schooner *Barrington* captured 1.1779. 50 tons, 18 guns. Participated in the recapture of Grenada 7.1779. Overwhelmed by a squall 10.1779 off Savannah where she had come from Martinique.

Alerte No.2. Ex-British privateer schooner *Alert* with 44 men and 8 guns captured 2.1779 by the ships of the line *Bien Aimé* and *Palmier* and put into service in the same month. 70 tons, 33/37 men + 1/4 officers, 4 x 4pdrs in 1779 and 8 x 4pdrs in 1780. Designated *Alerte No.2* to distinguish her from the cutters *Alerte* and *Alerte No.1*, both also assigned to Brest, and changed to *Alerte No.1* after that cutter was struck in 11.1780. Captured 29.11.1780 by the British west of Ushant, though not struck at Brest until mid-1782.

Charmante Betzy. Probably a captured British schooner that was in service in the Antilles 3.1779. No other information.

Reprisal. Ex-British privateer brig *Reprisal* captured 4.1779 by the frigate *Cérès* off Barbados. 14 guns, may have been a cutter. Used by d'Estaing's squadron 6.1779 in the Antilles. Struck 1780.

Lively. Ex-British privateer cutter *Lively* taken 26.7.1779 by a French privateer and purchased by the French Navy from M. de Chaumont in 1779 at Lorient. 40 tons, 14 x 4pdrs (or 6 guns). Last listed 6.1782 at Brest out of service and in bad condition.

Sprightly. Ex-Jersey privateer lugger *Sprightly* boarded and captured 15.8.1779 west of Ushant by boats from the French frigate *Atalante* and the Spanish frigate *Santa Catarina*. 33/44 men + 4/5 officers; 8 x 3pdrs, then 4 x 3pdrs from 1780. Struck at Brest in early 1783.

Actif. Ex-British privateer cutter *Active* (12 guns) boarded and captured on 18.8.1779 by the French cutter *Mutine* which had just left Brest with orders for the combined French-Spanish fleet. 30/38 men + 2 officers, 8 x 4pdrs. Sometimes called *Actif No.1* in 1782 to distinguish her from another cutter named *Actif* at Brest taken in 1780 (below) and *Actif No.2*, a merchantman chartered at Brest in 7.1782. Off the list at Brest between 3.1782 and 6.1782.

Sans Pareil. Ex-British privateer cutter *Non Such* (18 guns) captured 11.1779 by the frigate *Concorde*. 77 men, 14 x 4pdrs. Captured 26.6.1780 by *Phoenix* (44) and two frigates in the Antilles.

Repulse. A British merchant vessel taken in 1779 and included in the 1779 fleet list as a cutter. No further information; she was probably not naval.

Fame. Ex-British brig or brigantine *Fame* captured 1779 and in service 1780 at Martinique. Wrecked 10.1780 at St Vincent in a hurricane with the frigate *Junon*.

Comète. Ex-British schooner captured 1779 by the squadron of d'Estaing in America. No other information.

Dauphin. Ex-British schooner captured 1779 by the squadron of d'Estaing in America. No other information.

FACTEUR Class. Cutters. In 1779 six cutters with 18 x 6pdr guns were ordered on plans of Charles Segondat-Duvernet. Carried on fleet lists as avisos with much reduced armaments, these were called *côtre-avisos* but were suitable equally for conversion as schooners or *goélette-avisos*. Their breadth was substantially less than that of the cutters of the *Serpent/Cerf* class while the lengths of the two types were about the same. All were built at a yard founded by the Arnous family in 1757 in a cove of the Scorff River at Lorient, upstream from the naval dockyard. On 5 August 1785 its owner, Nicolas Arnoux Dessaulsays, signed an agreement with the new *Compagnie des Indes Orientales et de la Chine* that made his 'chantier naval du Blanc' the chief shipbuilding facility for the company.

Of this class only one, *Facteur*, was ultimately rigged as a cutter. Based on the experience with *Chevreuil* and *Hussard* (above), the second of the new *Facteur* class cutters building at Lorient, *Lévrier*, was re-rigged as a schooner. In comparative trials at Lorient of the cutter, schooner, and brig rigs the brig was found to be the most successful, and Sartine authorized the brig rig for the remaining *Facteur* class cutters under construction or located at Lorient.

Dimensions & tons: 80ft 0in, 65ft 0in x 20ft 0in x 8ft 4in (25.99, 21.11 x 6.50 x 2.71m). 150/220 tons. Men: 50/51 + 3 officers
Guns: 2 x 4pdrs; 4 x 3pdrs from 1783/84.

Facteur Lorient Dyd.
K: 3.1780. L: 19.6.1780. C: 8.1780. Listed as a brig with 8 x 4pdrs in 4.1783. Sold 6.1783 at Lorient and became mercantile *Madagascar*, 150 tons. Was at Île de France 9.1785.

Lévrier Lorient Dyd.
K: 3.1780. L: 3.7.1780. C: 8.1780. Schooner-rigged. Struck 1784 at Brest.

Bienvenu Lorient Dyd.
K: 7.1780. L: 28.10.1780. C: 12.1780. Brig-rigged. Captured 5.1.1781 by the British privateer *Thamer* (20) while departing Lorient for Brest.

Téméraire Lorient Dyd.
K: 7.1780. L: 13.11.1780. C: 12.1780. Brig-rigged. Taken 7.1782 by HMS *Cormorant* off Brest but retaken in 1783. Struck 1784 at Brest or at Toulon.

Papillon Lorient Dyd.
K: 2.1781. L: 27.4.1781. C: 8.1781. Brig-rigged. Disappeared at sea after departing Lorient 7.2.1782, struck 1783 at Lorient.

Espérance Lorient Dyd.
K: 3.1781. L: 19.6.1781. C: 7.1781. Brig-rigged. At Lorient awaiting coppering 1.1782. Captured 7.1782 by the British, later fate unknown.

PURCHASED AND ACQUIRED VESSELS (1780–1781).

Miscellaneous additions during these two years included four brigs or brigantines, a snow, a lugger, and four schooners. Five of these vessels were acquired overseas.

Lièvre. Brigantine of unknown origin put into service 1780 at St Domingue. Participated in the Franco-Spanish landings at Pensacola on 21.4.1781 under the Baron de Monteil, then repaired 5–6.1781 at Havana. Last mentioned returning to Cap Français 7.1781.

Prudence. Schooner of unknown origin put into service 11.4.1780 at Brest. 26 men + 2 officers, 8 guns. Decommissioned 12.1782 or early 1783, struck at Brest.

Émeraude. Snow of unknown origin captured and put into service

8.8.1780 at Brest. 160 tons, 13/19 men + 1 officer, probably no guns. Described as old at Brest 9.1781, sent to Toulon, condemned there 11.1783 and struck.

Duchesse de Chartres. St Malo privateer brig chartered from 6.1779 to 11.1779, then purchased 8.1780 and put into service 1.9.1780. 250 tons, 26/93 men + 3/7 officers, 12 guns. Captured by the British privateer *Seacome*, plundered, and returned to her crew 2.1781, captured again 3.1781 and taken to Ireland.

Breteuse (*Bretteuse*). Schooner of unknown origin put into service 9.1780 at St Pierre de la Martinique. May have been lost 10.1780 in a hurricane at St Vincent.

Souris. Schooner that served as a *mouche* (scout or aviso) for the fleet in the Antilles 12.1780. Last mentioned 5.1781 in the fleet departing Havana to attack Pensacola.

Petite Minerve. Schooner of unknown origin put into service 1780 and was at St Domingue 2.1781. With the small corvette *Saint Louis* fought off two British privateers 7–8.11.1781 and escorted the leaking French merchantman *Pressigny* into Cap Haïtien. 8 guns. Last mentioned 1.1782.

Huron. Brig of unknown origin that was operating as a 'Brick du Roi' in 3.1781 between Île de France and Île Bourbon. Fate unknown.

Tartare. Lugger purchased at Granville and put into service 13.8.1781. 78 men + 3 officers, 4 x 3pdrs. Stationed at Brest. May have been the 4-gun British lugger taken 6.1781 by the *chaloupes-canonnières Martinique* and *Sainte Lucie*. Wrecked 1784 and struck at Brest.

Royale. Brigantine or brig of 85 tons built in 1781 by Daniel Denys at Dunkirk as a small privateer with 4 ports for 12pdr guns and evidently purchased by the Navy. A *Royale* of 60 tons, 56 men and 5 guns was recorded in 1781–82 as a Dunkirk privateer under the command of Jacques Perret; she may have been the same vessel.

Ex-BRITISH NAVAL PRIZES (1780–1781). The cutter HMS *Alert* was captured on 25 September 1780 by the frigate *Diligente* off the Gironde while the cutter HMS *Pigmy* went ashore at Dunkirk on 27 December 1781 and was captured.

Alerte. King, Dover
K: 10.1778. L: 1.10.1779. C: end 1779.
Dimensions & tons: 74ft 0in, 63ft 0in x 23ft 6in x 10ft 4in. 220 tons displacement. Draught 9ft 0in/10ft 6in (2.92/3.41m). Men: 80.
Guns: 6 x 18pdrs + 12 x 18pdr *obusiers*, probably sailed for America 3.1781 with 14 x 4pdrs.
Repaired 12.1780 at Brest. Captured 11.1781 in northern American waters by the British frigate *Perseverance* after a long resistance, struck from the list at Brest *c*. 2.1783. HMS *Alert* sold 10.1792 at Deptford.

Pigmy. King, Dover.
K: 5.1780. L: 2.1781. C: 5.1781.
Dimensions & tons: 65ft 0in x 24ft 0in x 10ft 1in (21.11 x 7.80 x 3.27m). 200 tons displacement.
Guns: 10 (10 x 4pdrs in British service)
Retaken 22.7.1782 by HM Ships *Crown* (64) and *Panther* (60), renamed *Lurcher* 31.5.1783 but reverted to *Pigmy* 7.1783. Wrecked 16.12.1793.

Ex-BRITISH MERCANTILE AND PRIVATEER PRIZES (1780)

Succès. Ex-British privateer schooner-rigged felucca from Minorca captured 1.1780 and put into service 2.1781 at Toulon. 1 x 3pdr, 4 x 1pdrs. Out of service in good condition 21.8.1782, ordered sold at Toulon 23.3.1783.

Aigle. Ex-British privateer brig *Eagle* captured 3.1780 at St Eustache in the Antilles. May have been a 220-ton vessel built in Bombay in 1776. 16 guns + 6 *pierriers*. Arrived at Lorient 1.1782 and listed as a corvette with 20 x 6pdrs. Captured 9.8.1782 by HMS *Duc de Chartres* off the American coast.

Victor. Ex-British brig *Victor*, possibly a privateer, captured 3.1780. 80/100 men. Left Cap Français for France 3.1780. Reportedly rebuilt 1.1782 as a 310-ton *gabarre* with 37 men + 3 officers but listed by Toulon 4.1782 as a brig with 10 x 4pdrs + 16 x ½pdrs, changed 1.1783 to 2 x 6pdrs + 6 x 12pdr *obusiers* + 7 x ½pdrs. Listed at Brest from 6.1783 as a *gabarre*, out of service by 10.1783, sold 9.1784 at Brest.

Actif. Ex-British cutter taken in 1780 and on the list at Brest between 3.1780 and 6.1780. 4 x 3pdrs or 12 x 3pdrs. Commanded by a pilot and probably small. Last mentioned 3.1783 out of service at Brest.

Neptune. Ex-British privateer schooner *Neptune* captured 4.1780 by the frigate *Aurore*. 42 men, 6 guns + 12 *pierriers* as privateer. In service at Toulon between 8.1780 and 4.1781 but never on the fleet list there. Last mentioned 8.1782.

Alerte No.3. British privateer schooner *Alert* captured in 1780. 28 tons, 10 x 3pdrs in 1780, 8 x 4pdrs in 1781, and 10 x 4pdrs in 1783. With three other ships named *Alerte* already on the list at Brest she was designated *Alerte No.3*, becoming *Alerte No.2* after the cutter *Alerte No.1* was struck in 11.1780. Off the list at Brest mid-1782, struck in late 1783.

Swallow. Ex-British cutter *Swallow*, possibly a privateer, captured 6.1780. 16 men and 3 petty officers. Removed from service 6.1780, either sold or retaken later by the British.

Renard. Ex-British privateer lugger *Fox* captured 7.1780 in the Channel by the corvette *Pilote des Indes*.
Dimensions & tons: 47ft 0in x 8ft 0in x 3ft 0in (15.27 x 2.60 x 0.97m). 20/40 tons.
Guns: 8 *pierriers*.
Wrecked and recaptured by the British during the landing on Jersey on 6.1.1781 by the Baron de Rullecourt.

Rodney (?). Ex-British schooner captured by the French privateer *Moustic* and purchased 8.1780 at Cherbourg for use as a discovery vessel. Fate unknown.

Chien de Chasse. Ex-British privateer cutter *Lurcher* captured *c*.8.1780. Listed by Rochefort from 1781 to 1783 as *Chien de Chasse*, then as *Lurchers*, followed by the discovery after she returned to Rochefort from the colonies on 16.6.1784 that *Chien de Chasse* was her real name. Remained *Lurchers* on other lists through 1786.
Dimensions & tons: 86ft 0in, 74ft 0in x 27ft 0in x 12ft 6in (27.94, 24.04 x 8.77 x 4.06m). 200/350 tons. Draught 7ft/14ft (2.27/4.55m).
Guns: 22 x 9pdrs + 8 x 6pdr *obusiers*.
Condemned 6.1787 at Tobago as worn out.

Levrette. Ex-British privateer brig *Leveret* captured 18.9.1780 off St Domingue by the cutter *Serpent*. ?10/14 guns. Wrecked early 1781 in the Azores.

Tartare. Ex-British privateer cutter *Tartar* captured 9.1780 by the frigates *Aimable* and *Diligente* off the Gironde.
Dimensions & tons: 70ft 0in x 23ft 11in x 8ft 5in (22.74 x 7.77 x 2.74m). 200 tons displacement.
Guns: 14 x 6pdrs or 10 x 6pdrs + 4 *obusiers*.
Re-rigged as a brig (brigantine). Recaptured 2.1782 by the British frigate *Arethusa* and became HMS *True Briton*.

TRIOMPHE. Ex-British privateer lugger *Triumph* captured October 1780. 36 tons, 4 x 3pdrs. This obscure vessel, which was to have its moment in history, was first listed in French records in January 1781 as out of commission at Brest in need of repair. Her name was initially recorded as *Triomphant* and *Triomph* but was soon corrected to *Triomphe*.

She was put into service in June 1781 and conducted local operations from Brest through December 1781. Ready for sea after repairs in April 1782, she departed Brest on 8 July for the Île d'Aix to join the convoy forces there. Still at Île d'Aix on 8 August, probably without a commanding officer, she was apparently sent to Martinique and then escorted a convoy from there to Cadiz, joining the squadron of Comte d'Estaing upon arrival. LV Pierre Claude, Chevalier Duquesne reported on board as commanding officer in late 1782. After the signature of the preliminaries of peace between Britain and America on 20 January 1783 d'Estaing on 10 February ordered Duquesne to carry the news from Cadiz to America, correctly believing that *Triomphe* might arrive sooner than any packet from Brest or Lorient. The lugger delivered her news at Philadelphia on 16 March 1783 and remained there at the disposal of the minister of France until 17 June 1783. Reportedly she was then sent to Martinique and was wrecked at Bermuda on 3 July 1783, but a *Triomphe* reappeared at Brest out of commission in June 1783 and was so listed through the end of 1783, while Rochefort listed a *Triomphe* as in America from March 1783 through February 1784.

Ex-BRITISH MERCANTILE AND PRIVATEER PRIZES (1781)

Alligator. Ex-British privateer cutter *Alligator* captured in late 1780 and put into service 29.5.1781 at Lorient. 46 men + 3/4 officers. Listed in 1781 as an aviso with 2 x 4pdrs, at Lorient as a snow with 6 x 4pdrs, and at Brest as a cutter, later corvette. Called *Alligator No.2* at Brest after the corvette *Alligator* was captured in 1782. Sold before 7.1783 at Lorient to Sieur Collier.

Levrette. British cutter captured in America in 1781 and struck there near the end of that year. Mentioned in only one source.

Aigle. Ex-British privateer lugger *Eagle* captured at St Eustache and put into service 12.7.1781 at Rochefort. 6 x 3pdrs. Converted to *gabarre* 1783, hulked at Cherbourg and struck 7.1784. Last mentioned 1788 or 1793.

Suzanne. Ex-British brig captured 9.1781 off Yorktown, possibly a privateer and possibly named *Susan* or *Susanna*. 80 tons, 120 men, 16 x 4pdrs + 10 x ¼ pdrs. Was at Pointe-à-Pitre, Guadeloupe, in 11.1785, struck 3.1786 at Martinique and crew returned to Toulon in *Iris* and *Flèche*.

Défiance or *Défiante*. Ex-British privateer brig *Defiance* captured by a French privateer 1779, then purchased and put into service 13.11.1781 by the French Navy in North America. 70 men + 3 officers, from 1782 had 42 men + 1 officer. Removed from service 11.1782 in the colonies and struck early 1783.

Dragon. Ex-British brig or brigantine built at Boston, taken 11.1781 and put into service 10.12.1781 at Croisic. 96 men + 5 officers, 16 x 4pdrs + 4 *obusiers*. Listed from 1782 as a corvette. Attacked 22.1.1783 by a British divison and run ashore on the coast of Montechristo, St Domingue. Burned there by her crew to avoid capture and blew up.

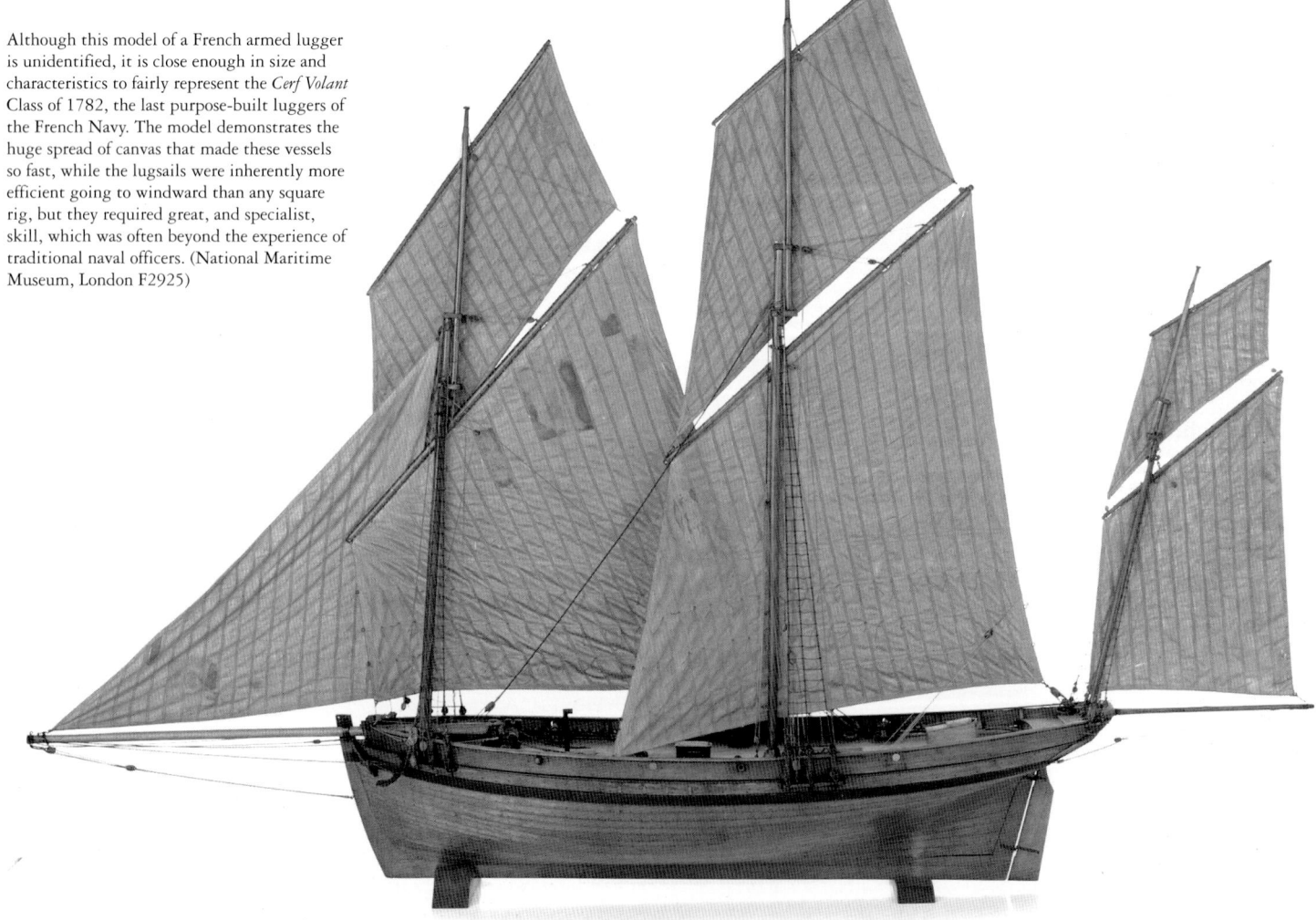

Although this model of a French armed lugger is unidentified, it is close enough in size and characteristics to fairly represent the *Cerf Volant* Class of 1782, the last purpose-built luggers of the French Navy. The model demonstrates the huge spread of canvas that made these vessels so fast, while the lugsails were inherently more efficient going to windward than any square rig, but they required great, and specialist, skill, which was often beyond the experience of traditional naval officers. (National Maritime Museum, London F2925)

***CERF VOLANT* Class**. Luggers. On 10 December 1781 Daniel Denys and LV de Bavre sent to the Minister of Marine a plan bearing the same date for a lugger of 4 x 3pdrs and a proposal to build four of these vessels. Castries approved the project on 19 December 1781. In addition, contracts were agreed with Nicolas Rivet and Pierre Sauvage at Boulogne and Jacques Rivet at Calais for the construction of four more luggers on the plans of those ordered from Denys at Dunkirk. The ships were named on 23 February 1782, the guns were ready on 24 April, and the commanders chosen on 8 June. *Pivert* and *Vanneau* and probably the others were coppered. On 26 September the acceptance documents were prepared for *Cerf Volant* at Calais and the three built at Boulogne, *Courrier*, *Silphe* (*Sylphe*), and *Ballon*. The ships of this class were carried on fleet lists as avisos in 1783 and as cutters from 1784 but all eight were actually rigged as luggers and their armament was much reduced compared to previous classes. Some were later re-rigged as brigs and no more luggers were ordered.

    Dimensions & tons: 67ft 0in, 59ft 0in x 17ft 8in x 8ft 8in (21.76, 19.17 x 5.74 x 2.82m). 50/113 tons. Draught 6ft 9in / 9ft 7in (2.19/3.11m). Men: 52/70.

    Guns: 4 x 3pdrs, 10 x 3pdrs from 1784 except 8 x 4pdrs in *Vanneau* from 1784 and 6 x 3pdrs in *Courrier* from 1786 as a packet, then 4 x 3pdrs in 1789 and 10 guns in 1793.

Cerf Volant Jacques Rivet, Calais.
    K: 2.1782. L: 9.7.1782. C: 9.1782. Decommissioned at Brest 6.1786 and struck at the end of 1786.

Pivert Daniel Denys, Dunkirk.
    K: 1.1782. L: 24.7.1782. C: 9.1782. Struck at Brest 1787 after returning from St Domingue.

Vanneau Daniel Denys, Dunkirk.
    K: 1.1782. L: 25.7.1782. C: 9.1782. Captured 6.6.1793 by HMS *Colossus* in the Bay of Biscay and became HMS *Vanneau*, possibly later re-rated as a gunbrig. Wrecked 21.10.1796 at Porto-Ferrajo, Elba. Not to be confused with the schooner of the same name (1778–81).

Tiercelet Daniel Denys, Dunkirk.
    K: 2.1782. L: 22.8.1782. C: 9.1782. Sold at Rochefort 4.1797, became privateer, captured 8.1797 by the British.

Gerfaut Daniel Denys, Dunkirk.
    K: 2.1782. L: 24.8.1782. C: 9.1782. Run ashore in the roadstead at Tunis 9.3.1796 to avoid capture by a British division including HMS *Egmont*; the French frigate *Nemesis* and corvettes *Postillon* and *Sardine* were taken.

Sylphe Pierre Sauvage, Boulogne.
    K: 3.1782. L: 7.9.1782. C: 9.1782. Captured 18.10.1782 by HMS *Jackall* (14), not taken into the RN.

Courrier Sauvage or Rivet, Boulogne.
    K: 3.1782. L: 7.9.1782. C: 9.1782. Renamed *Courrier des Indes* 1786 for service as a packet, soon reverted. Taken 23.5.1794 by the British in the Channel, then scuttled.

Ballon Nicolas Rivet, Boulogne.
    K: 3.1782. L: 21.9.1782. C: 10.1782. Named to recognize the success of the balloonist Pilâtre de Rozier. Lost 11.1795 at Maingueneau in the Vendée.

Ex-BRITISH NAVAL PRIZES (1782). The brigs HMS *Sylph* and HMS *Oronoque* were captured on 3 February 1782 by Kersaint's squadron at the surrender of Demerara in Dutch Guiana. *Oronoque* was renamed *Vicomte de Damas*. The brig HMS *Racoon* was captured 12.9.1782 by the frigates *Aigle* and *Gloire* off the Delaware River. The French *Poisson Volant* was probably HMS *Flying Fish*, a purchased merchant cutter that grounded near Dunkirk 31.12.1782 and was taken by French troops.

Sylphe. Formerly the British mercantile cutter *Active* purchased by the British Navy 5.1780, renamed and re-rigged as a brig.
    Dimensions & tons: 74ft 0in, 63ft 0in x 24ft 9in x 9ft 10in (24.04, 20.46 x 8.04 x 3.19m). 173/300 tons. Draught 8ft 2in/12ft (2.65/3.90m).
    Guns: 18 x 4pdrs.
    Returned to Lorient 6.1784 after one voyage as a packet. Repaired at Rochefort 9–10.1785, struck there 1788.

Vicomte de Damas. Previously the French privateer *Orénoque* commissioned at French Guiana in 1781 and taken by the British 1.1782.
    Guns: 18 x 9pdrs + 4 *pierriers* (10 x 9pdrs + 10 x 3pdrs in British service).
    Placed on sale 9.1784 at Honfleur, then at Le Havre.

Racoon. Previously the mercantile brig *Lovely Sally* purchased at Boston 27.4.1782 and commissioned by the British 8.1782.
    Guns: 18 x 6pdrs
    Also listed as a cutter. Struck late 1783 at Rochefort, last mentioned there 1785.

Poisson Volant. A British mercantile cutter purchased by the Royal Navy 4.1778.
    Dimensions & tons: 70ft 0in x 24ft 0in x 10ft 0in. (22.74 x 7.80 x 3.25m). 100/200 tons. Men: 50–70.
    Guns: 18 x 6pdrs.
    Put into service 12.6.1783 at Dunkirk. Was out of commission at St Domingue 7.1785, struck 1785 or 1786.

SURPRISE. Cutter of uncertain origin, *c*.1782. She is said to have been the former HMS *Surprize* (the American privateer *Bunker Hill* taken by the British in December 1778) that was sold by the Royal Navy in 1783 at Sheerness, but the French *Surprise* was already under repair at Rochefort in November 1782 and left on a cruise in December 1782 before the British ship was sold.
    Dimensions & tons: dimensions unknown. 106 tons, 50/70 men.
    Guns: 14 x 4pdrs or 8 x 4pdrs + 6 x 3pdrs.
    Struck 1789 at Rochefort.

Ex-BRITISH MERCANTILE AND PRIVATEER PRIZES (1782–1783)

Tartare. Ex-British privateer brig *Tartar* captured, then put into service 17.1.1782 at Brest. 150 tons, 70/130 men, 10 x 8pdrs + 10 x 12pdr *obusiers*, from 1783 14 x 6pdrs. Entered Rochefort 19.8.1782, sailed from there 9.11.1782, wrecked by an 'ignorant' pilot 4.1783 on the northern coast of St Domingue. Struck by Rochefort *c*.3.1784. Another cutter named *Tartare* with 4 x 3pdrs appeared on Rochefort lists in 3.1783 as 'on the coasts' and then 'at sea'. The 9.1784 list stated that her location was unknown, and the 11.1784 list stated that no further mention of her would be made.

Lord Cornwallis. British cutter (perhaps a privateer) *Lord Cornwallis* captured 1.1782 and put into service 17.2.1782 in the colonies. 65 men + 4 officers, 2 x 6pdrs or 6 x 6pdrs. Often called an aviso. Out of service 14.11.1782 in the colonies. Listed by Rochefort late 1783 as an aviso with 2 x 4pdrs, struck from the list at Rochefort 1784.

Railleur. Ex-British brig, captured 6.1782. 14 guns. Recaptured 11.1.1783 by HMS *Cyclops* (28) in the Atlantic.

Tarleton. Ex-British brig *Tarleton*, probably a privateer built at Bristol in 1780, captured by the French *Aigrette* 19.10.1782 and taken into Cap François. 50 men, 14 x 6pdrs, by 7.1783 had 14 x 4pdrs. Conducted surveys of the Ottoman coast 1784–88 under CF Comte Laurent-Jean-François Truguet. Rallied to the Anglo-Spanish forces 8.1793 during the occupation of Toulon, fled to Portoferraio 19.9.1793 on the approach of the Republicans, taken by the British 18.12.1793 on the evacuation of Toulon and added to the Royal Navy as a fireship. Sold 12.1796.

Petit Argus. Ex-British privateer lugger from Jersey *Argus* captured in 1782 by the frigate *Fée* and put into service as an aviso 6.9.1782 at Brest.

Dimensions & tons: 58ft 0in, 52ft 0in x 17ft 8in x 8ft 0in (18.84 x 5.74 x 2.60m). 86/150 tons. Draught 7ft 5in/10ft 8in (2.41/3.46m). Men: 41 + 3 officers.

Guns: Pierced for 10 x 3pdrs + 14 small *pierriers*, carried 2 x 4pdrs as an aviso in 1783.

Out of service 7.1783 at Rochefort, struck there 1784.

Alexander. Ex-British privateer brig *Alexander* captured, then put into service 17.9.1782 at Cap Françoise and assigned to Brest. 150 tons, 100/130 men + 3 officers, 18 x 6pdrs or 4pdrs. Also called *Alexandre No.2* in 1782–83, *Alexandre No.1* being a merchant ship chartered at Brest between 7.1782 and 5.1783. Struck 1785 or 1786 at Brest.

Warwick. Ex-British privateer brig *Warwick* captured, then put into service 16.11.1782 at Boston. 87 men + 4 officers, 16 x 6pdrs, by 8.1783 had 18 x 4pdrs. Sailed from Lorient as a packet in 1784 and 1785, struck there late 1785 or 1786.

Lise. Ex-British schooner captured in 1782 or 1783 and in service at Demerara in 1783. Last mentioned 1784 when out of service at Le Havre.

PURCHASED AND ACQUIRED VESSELS (1782–1786). These vessels included two brigantines, three cutters, a lugger, and five schooners. Four of the schooners were acquired at Martinique.

Fouine. Brigantine of unknown origin acquired 7.1782 and put into service 1.8.1782 at Brest. 65 men + 5 officers. Decommissioned 24.6.1783 at Brest and struck.

Passe Partout. Lugger of unknown origin acquired 1782. 100 tons displacement, 50/70 men, 8 x 4pdrs (these specifications uncertain). Listed at Brest in 1783 as an aviso with 2 x 4pdrs, listed at Lorient at the same time as a lugger with 4 x 3pdrs. Struck 1785 or 1786.

Hasard. Cutter of unknown origin unknown put into service in 1782 at Lorient. Captured 9.1782 by a British privateer.

Guerrier. Cutter of unknown origin acquired 1782 or 1783. 100 tons, 50/70 men, 16 or 18 x 6pdrs. Struck 1784 at Brest.

Mouche. Cutter inscribed on the list at Brest 2.1783. 35/100 tons, 70/90 men, 10 to 14 x 4pdrs, then 4 x 3pdrs. Condemned at Brest 1784.

Utile. Schooner that was in service 10.1783 at Martinique as coast guard vessel. Last mentioned in service there 9.1785.

Levrette. Schooner acquired 1784, ex-*Levrette de Saint Malo*, possibly purchased at St Malo.

Dimensions & tons: 66ft 4in x 18ft 5in x 7ft 10in (21.55 x 5.99 x 2.54m). 170 tons disp. Draught 8ft 4in/10ft 8in (2.71/3.47m)

Guns: 16 x 4pdrs; 14 x 4pdrs from 1786.

Repaired at Brest 1790. For sale 5.1792 at Rochefort.

Louise. Schooner probably purchased in Martinique 10–11.1784. Sent to France via Cayenne to serve as a model, last mentioned 1.1786.

Témérité. Brigantine of unknown origin put into service in 1785 at Brest. Fate unknown.

Légère. Schooner built in North America 1784–85 and purchased 7.1785 from an American at Fort Royal de la Martinique. 62 men, 4 x 6pdrs in 1785 and 14 x 6pdrs in 1786. Wrecked 3.1786 at Pointe-à-Pitre, Guadeloupe.

Nymphe. Schooner possibly purchased 10.1785, in service at Martinique 11.1786. 9–11 men. Last mentioned 1788 in the Antilles.

12 Minor Warships – *Levant* types

(Barques, Brigantines, Tartanes, Feluccas, Xebecs, etc)

While the minor warships on the Atlantic and Channel coasts (referred to by the French as the *Ponant*, see Chapter 11) tended to have square or fore-and-aft sails, those on the Mediterranean coast (called the *Levant*) tended to have lateen sails and in many cases oars. Vessels carrying lateen sails (triangular sails, attached to a long yard or boom set diagonally fore-and-aft) had been prominent in the Mediterranean for centuries. Many such vessels were built for or taken into service with the French naval forces in the Mediterranean, and a smaller number were also used in Atlantic ports.

Early *Levant* types used as minor warships included the *barque à voiles latines*, the *brigantin* (brigantine), and the *galiote à rames*, the latter being a miniature galley, as was the *demi-galère* (half-galley). The *Levant* types most commonly used by France (and also by the Spanish and Italian navies) however, were the tartane and the felucca. The former was a small (the name literally means 'small ship') two-masted vessel which typically had a prominent forward-projecting bluff bow, and was lateen-rigged on both pole masts, with the foremast raked sharply forward. The felucca was similar but was also fitted with oars as an alternative to sail. Up to 1719 all of these small warships along with minor support vessels (Chapter 13) were shown in fleet lists as *bâtiments interrompus,* or vessels that were not part of the formal structure of the navy.

Before 1715 most of the French Navy's minor warships were in the Mediterranean and were of the types listed in this chapter. After 1715 this situation reversed, and northern types like the cutter, schooner and, from the 1780s, the brig not only proliferated in Atlantic ports but came to dominate the small warship forces in the Mediterranean as well. The main exception was the xebec or zebec (*chébec*), a relatively large, fast, and heavily armed vessel with three lateen-rigged masts that appeared in the French navy in 1750 and that militarily was as powerful as some of the 8pdr- and 6pdr-armed frigates in northern waters. The xebecs took over patrol duties from the last of the galleys. The large xebec was in favour for only a short time, however, as Toulon built the last of its eight big xebecs in 1762, only twelve years after its first one.

(A) Vessel in service as at 9 March 1661

LÉGÈRE. Felucca built at Toulon. She had a crew of 216 men in 1669, presumably including many rowers.
    K: 4.1660. L: 1660. C: end 1660. Repaired 5–6.1663 at Toulon. Renamed *Volante* in early 1669. Struck *c.*1670.

The elusive nature of terminology for northern small-craft was equally applicable in the Mediterranean. This engraving by Claude Randon is one of a series done to illustrate *Plan de Plusieurs Batiments de Mer avec leurs Proportions* by Henri Sbonski de Passebon, published in Marseille in 1700. It is described as a *brigantin* giving chase to a felucca, both types being essentially oared craft that also carried a sailing rig – in the case of this mercantile felucca, just a short mast with a spritsail and jib, whereas the *brigantin* has the lateen sails so common in the Mediterranean. *Brigantin* was a term applied to a wide variety of small galley-like vessels, but unlike in northern waters, it never suggested a rig; *felucca* was often stretched even further, sometimes up to half-galley type vessels. In this example, the felucca, with only three pairs of oars, is noticeably smaller than the chasing *brigantin*, with nine – although the rowers in the first three banks have abandoned their oars to take up their small-arms and prepare for boarding. (National Maritime Museum, London PZ4898)

(B) Vessels acquired from 9 March 1661

SUBTILE Class. Galiotes (*galiotes à rames*) built at Toulon to support the galley fleet. These may be the two 'very successful' feluccas built at Toulon in early 1664 from the timbers of the *Saint Jean* and the old *Régine* (both galleys), one of which might have been named *Africaine*. Had 20 banks of oars.

Dimensions & tons: 108ft 0in x 14ft 5in x 5ft 3in (35.08 x 4.68 x 1.71m). 80 tons. Men: 212 in *Subtile*, 204 in *Vigilante*.

Subtile Toulon.
K: 11.1663. L: 4.1664. C: 5.1664. Her captain in 1672 was the Chevalier de la Vidalle. On fleet lists in 1672 and 1673. Struck c.1676 and replaced by a new *Subtile* (below) at Marseille (possibly struck in 1674 and another *Subtile* used in 1675–76)

Vigilante Toulon.
K: 11.1663. L: 4.1664. C: 5.1664. Served in the siege of Candia 1669. Her captain in 1672–73 was the Chevalier de Valbelle. On fleet lists in 1672 and 1673. Struck c.1675 and replaced by a new *Vigilante* at Marseille (possibly struck in late 1671 and another *Vigilante* used in 1672–75)

AVENTURE (name uncertain). Felucca built at Rochefort. One of two *galiotes à rames* listed in 5.1669 as *L'une* and *L'autre*, this one being *L'une*. Had 14 banks of oars.

Dimensions & tons: 48ft 6in x 8ft 0in x 3ft 9in (15.75 x 2.60 x 1.22m). 30 tons. Men: 30.
Guns: 3.

Aventure Rochefort.
K: 5.1666. L: 1666. C: end 1666. Last mentioned 1672 at Rochefort. May have been the *Aventure* BU at Rochefort in 1688.

ESPÉRANCE. Felucca built at Rochefort. One of two *galiotes à rames* listed in 5.1669 as *L'une* and *L'autre*, this one being *L'autre*. Had 16 banks of oars.

Dimensions & tons: 50ft 0in x 10ft 0in (16.24 x 3.25m). 30 tons. Men: 40
Guns: 3.

Espérance Rochefort.
K: 6.1666. L: 1667. C: 1667. *Barque de servitude* at Rochefort 1672. Reconditioned 1684 at Rochefort and sold for commercial use.

SAINT JEAN (?). Tartane built at Martigues in 1666 or 1667. 30 tons, 12 men, no armament (except 2 guns in 5.1669). Listed in 5.1669 as *La Petite Tartane*. Last mentioned 1677 at Toulon and may have been wrecked in Corsica in 11.1676.

SAINT JOSEPH. Tartane built at Brest. Listed in 5.1669 as *La Grande Tartane*.

Dimensions & tons: 45ft 0in on keel x 15ft 0in x 7ft 6in (14.62 x 4.87 x 2.44m). 30 tons. Men: 12
Guns: None (2 small in 5.1669).

Saint Joseph Brest.
Built 1667–68. Last mentioned 4.1676 at Brest.

LÉGÈRE. Galiote (*galiote à rames*) built at Marseille in 1670–71 to support the galley fleet. She was probably similar to the *Subtile* class above. Her captain in 1672 was the Chevalier de Rancé. On fleet lists in 1672 and 1673. Replaced by a new *Légère* in 1677.

PURCHASED VESSELS (1671–1675)

Brigantin. Brigantine possibly built at Marseille. Was in the service of the Comte de Vivonne, General of the Galleys, in July 1671.

Félouque. Brigantine possibly built at Marseille. Was in the service of the Comte de Vivonne, General of the Galleys, in July 1671.

Félouque du Marquis de Centurion. Felucca possibly built at Genoa. Arrived at Toulon 2.5.1672. The King terminated his contract with the Marquis de Centurion to operate galleys in 8.1672.

Sainte Anne. Tartane built at Martigues and purchased 10.1675. 7 men, no guns. Wrecked 12.1675 near the Strait of Bonifacio.

Saint Roche. Tartane built at Martigues and purchased 10.1675. Wrecked 1.1676 on the coast of Languedoc.

Ex-SPANISH PRIZES (1673–1675)

Notre Dame. Barque captured 11.1673, ex-Spanish. 80 tons, 70 men, 4 guns. Last mentioned 1676 at Toulon. Probably became in 12.1675 the fireship *Notre Dame de Bon Voyage* (see Chapter 8).

Notre Dame du Mont Carmel. Barque captured 11.1673 or early 1674, ex-Spanish. 80 tons, 30/70 men, 4 guns. Last mentioned 2.1676 at Messina.

Marie or *Sainte Marie*. Brigantine captured 9.1675 or 4.1676, ex-Spanish *Santa Maria*. 20 soldiers and 30 rowers, possibly 10 *pierriers*. Sold 4.1677 at Toulon.

VIGILANTE Class. Feluccas built at Marseille. Had 14 banks of oars.
Dimensions & tons: unknown. Men: 17, + 1 officer, + 56 rowers.
Guns: unknown.

Vigilante Marseille.
Built in 1675. Rebuilt at Toulon 1677–78. Condemned 1683 at Marseille.

Subtile Marseille.
Built in 1676. Rebuilt at Toulon 1677–78. Condemned 1683 or 1686 at Marseille.

Ex-SPANISH PRIZE (1676)

Sainte Anne. Tartane captured 5.1676, probably ex-Spanish. 14 men. Last mentioned 1688 at Toulon.

LÉGÈRE. Felucca designed by Laurent Coulomb. Had 15 pairs of oars, 2 rowers each.
Dimensions & tons: 60ft 0in, 51ft 3in x 9ft 11in x 3ft 3in (19.49, 16.65 x 3.22 x 1.06m). 25 tons.
Guns: 1 x 8pdrs, with 4 or 5 *pierriers*.

Légère Toulon.
K: 2.1677. L: 5.4.1677. C: 4.1677. Rebuilt 3–4.1684 at Toulon. Struck c.1690.

FIDÈLE. Felucca (also called a *galiote à rames* or brigantine) designed by Laurent Coulomb. Had 15 pairs of oars, 2 rowers each.
Dimensions & tons: 60ft 0in, 40ft 0in x 10ft 6in x 4ft (19.49, 12.99 x 3.41 x 1.30m). 30 tons. Men: 73, + 2 officers
Guns: 1 x 8pdrs, with 5 *pierriers*.

Fidèle Toulon.
K: 2.1677. L: 13.4.1677. C: 4.1677. Rebuilt 3–4.1684 at Toulon. Condemned 1693 or 1694 and BU at Toulon.

SAINT JEAN. Tartane built at Martigues in 1677. 14 men. Mentioned for the last time in 1690 in the *Ponant*.

GALANTE Class. Feluccas designed by Jean-Baptiste Chabert. They were laid down in early 12.1677 at Marseille but on orders of the Minister were taken up and laid down again at Toulon in 12.1677.

Dimensions & tons: Probably 57ft 0in, 46ft 8in x c.10ft x 4ft 6in (4ft

8in in *Galante*) (18.52, 15.16 x 3.25 x 1.46/1.52m). Men: 73, + 2 officers (83, + 5 officers in *Galante*)
Guns: 1 x 8pdrs, with 4 or 5 *pierriers*.
Galante Toulon.
K: 12.1677. L: 26.2.1678. C: 3.1678. Rebuilt 3–4.1684 at Toulon. Struck 1690 at Toulon
Brillante Toulon.
K: 12.1677. L: 26.2.1678. C: 3.1678. Rebuilt 3–4. 1684 at Toulon. Struck 1690 at Toulon

FERME. Felucca (also called a *galiote à rames* or brigantine) designed by Laurent Coulomb.
Dimensions & tons: 60ft 0in, 51ft 3in x 9ft 11in x 3ft 3in (19.49, 16.65 x 3.22 x 1.06m)
Guns: probably 1 x 8pdrs, with 4 or 5 *pierriers*.
Ferme Toulon.
K: 12.1677. L: early 3.1678. C: 3.1678. Rebuilt 3–4.1684 at Toulon. Condemned 1693 or 1694 and BU at Toulon.

PURCHASED VESSELS (1677–1682)

Thérèse. Brigantine from Cannes purchased 4.1677. 1 gun and several *pierriers*. Last mentioned 4.1684 at Toulon.
Saint Pierre. Barque acquired *c*.1678. 20 tons. Was in service at Toulon in 6.1681, last mentioned there 12.1681.
Saint Jacques. Barque acquired 1680 and put into service 12.1680 at Toulon. Repaired there 3.1681 and last mentioned there 12.1681.
Saint Cyprien. Tartane put into service 1680 at Toulon. Last mentioned there 1680.
Saint Esprit. Tartane put into service 10.1680 at Toulon. Repaired there 9–10.1681, sold there 11.1682 for merchant service.
Saint Sébastien. Tartane put into service 1681 at Toulon. 60 tons, 12/15 men + 1 officer, 4 guns. In service at Brest 9.1692. Struck *c*.3.1693 at Brest.
Saint Antoine. Tartane built at Martigues and in commission at Toulon in 1682–83. 70 tons, 9 men, 1 x 3pdr + 10 *pierriers*. Last mentioned late 1683 at Toulon, may have been wrecked in 1689 at the Îles d'Hyères.
Notre Dame de Bon Voyage or *Bon Voyage*. Tartane put into service 1682 at Toulon. Last mentioned there 1685.

Ex-BARBARY COAST PRIZES (1680–1682)

Saint Joseph. Tartane built at La Ciotat, captured 9.1680 from the Tripolitanians, and put into service 12.1680 at Toulon. 15 men + 1 officer. Last mentioned 1686.
Sainte Anne. Merchant tartane built at Martigues 1680, taken by the Algerians 1682, and recaptured and taken into the Navy 7.1683. 40 tons, 6 men, no guns.
Saint Jean. Merchant tartane built at Martigues 1679, taken by the Algerians 1682, and recaptured and taken into the Navy 7.1683. 35 tons, 8 men, no guns. Returned in early 1684 to her former owner, Claude Audibert.
Saint Pierre. Merchant tartane built at Martigues 1679, taken by the Algerians 1682, and recaptured and taken into the Navy 7.1683. 40 tons, 8 men, no guns.

SUBTILE. Barque designed by Jean Martinenc and built at Toulon. 100 tons, 30/60 men + 2 officers, and 6 guns.
K: 1682. L: 6.1682. C: 7.1682. Classed as a *barque longue* in 1691 and 1692. Condemned 1701 at Toulon.

SAINTES RÉLIQUES, or *Notre Dame des Saintes Réliques*. Tartane built at Toulon.
K: 11.1682. L: early 1683. C: 1683. Last mentioned 1686 at Toulon.
SAINTE BARBE. Tartane built at Toulon. 15/17 men.
K: 11.1682. L: early 1683. C: 5.1683. Last mentioned 1693 at Marseille where she was serving with the galleys.

PURCHASED VESSEL (1683)

Jesus-Maria-Joseph. Tartane put into service 9.1683 at Toulon. 11 men + 1 officer. Last mentioned when she returned to Toulon 11.1683.

SUBTILE. Felucca or *galiote à rames* built at Marseille in 1684. 1 gun. Struck 1690 at Marseille.

PURCHASED VESSELS (1684–1687)

Tartane. Tartane put into service 1684 at Toulon. Last mentioned 1684, may have been renamed.
Pêcheur. Tartane put into service 1685 at Toulon. Last mentioned 1693 at Toulon.
Providence. Barque acquired and equipped for the King's service 7.1685 at Marseille. Last mentioned 1688.
Saint Barthelemy. Tartane put into service in 1687 (probably 4.1687) at Toulon. Last mentioned 1687.

VIGILANTE. Felucca built at Marseille in 1687. 1 gun. Struck 1690 at Marseille.

DEMI-GALÈRE DORÉE or *Petite Galère*. Felucca built at Brest in 1687. Struck 1698 at Brest and BU there 11.1699.

SAINT FRANÇOIS. Tartane designed by Laurent or François Coulomb.
Dimensions & tons: 59ft 0in x 16ft 0in x 9ft 0in (19.17 x 5.20 x 2.92m). 70 tons. Draught 7ft (2.27m). Men: 20 in war, 15 peace, + 1 officer
Guns: 4 in war (2 peace): 4 x 4pdrs. 6 from 1699: 6 x 4pdrs
Saint François Toulon.
K: early 1687. L: 4.1687. C: 4.1687. Renamed *Saint François l'Ardent* 1692. Listed at Brest in 9.1692 as a *tartane* (60 tons, 15 men, 4 guns). Classed as a *flûte* 1695, on fleet list 1696, became service craft at Brest 1699, last mentioned 1704.

POSTILLON Class. Tartanes designed by Pierre Rousquet.
Postillon Toulon.
Ord: 5.7.1687. K: 7.1687. L: 9.1687. C: 9.1687. Last mentioned 1688 at Toulon.
Saint Joseph Toulon.
Ord: 8.9.1687. K: 9.1687. L: 11.1687. C: 12.1687. Last mentioned 9.1691 at Brest.
Gracieuse Toulon.
Ord: 3.10.1687. K: 10.1687. L: 11.1687. C: 11.1687. Last mentioned 1688.
Gentille Toulon.
Ord: 15.11.1687. K: 11.1687. L: 1.1688. C: 2.1688. Last mentioned 1688.

(C) Vessels acquired from 15 April 1689

PURCHASED VESSELS (1689)

Dorade. Tartane put into service in 1689 at Toulon. Last mentioned 11.1695 at Toulon.

This small galley with twelve banks of oars is described as a felucca in Daniel Lescallier's late eighteenth century treatise on rigging. As with so many technical works of this era, much of the information is backward-looking, so this might well represent what was understood by the term much earlier in the century.

Folle. Tartane put into service 12.1689 at Toulon. Last mentioned 1.1693 at Toulon.

FÉLOUQUE. Felucca designed by Laurent Coulomb. Described in 1707 with *Résolu* and *Actif* (below) as good under oars and suitable for use against Jersey privateers. Had 11 banks of oars. The three similar vessels of the *Active* class (see Chapter 10) were described in 1707 as as 'double chaloupes with 28 oars suitable for chasing the small privateers of Jersey'.

Dimensions & tons: 50ft 0in, 40ft 0in x 9ft 6in x 3ft 9in (16.24 x 3.09 x 1.22m). 18 tons. Draught 4ft (1.30m). Men: 40
Guns: 1 x 2pdr.

Félouque Lorient.
K: 7.1691. L: 9.9.1691. C: 9.1691. Built 1693. Appeared on fleet lists 1704 as unserviceable, rebuilt 1705. Listed from 1709 as a corvette or *barque longue*. Unserviceable 1.1712 at Port Louis.

ENTREPRENANTE. Tartane designed by Pierre Rousquet.
Dimensions & tons: dimensions unknown. 80 tons (60 tons in 9.1692). Men: 20 in war, 15 peace + 1 officer
Guns: 4 x 4pdrs.

Entreprenante Toulon.
K: 1692. L: 3.1692. C: 4.1692. Listed at Brest 9.1692. Appeared on fleet lists 1704. Struck 1705 at Toulon and became service craft. Handed over for privateering 1709.

Ex-SPANISH PRIZE (1692). The Spanish tartane *San Lorenzo* was captured in late 1692 and first named *Saint Laurent* or *Petit Saint Laurent* and then *Bécasse* or *Bégasse*. She was shown in 1704, probably in error, as a new ship designed by François Coulomb (he may have rebuilt her) but this was changed back in 1706, probably correctly, to a Spanish prize. The similarity in the 1696 and 1704 dimensions (both shown above) suggests these are all the same vessel.

Dimensions & tons (1696): 51ft 0in x 16ft 0in x 9ft 0in (16.57 x 5.20 x 2.92m), 45 tons, Draught 8ft (2.60m); (1704): 55ft 0in x 16ft 0in x 9ft 6in (17.87 x 5.20 x 3.09m). 70 tons. Draught 7½ft (2.44m); (1706) same but 50 tons. Men: 8; 20/15 in 1704, 15/7 in 1706.
Guns: none, 4 x 4pdrs in 1704, 2 x 4pdrs in 1706.

Bécasse Spain
Listed as *flûte* in 1696–98, as a *bâtiment interrompu* (*tartane*) in 1704–6, and as a hulk in 1710. Struck and hulked 1706, BU 1710–11. A *bécasse* was a small undecked Spanish craft with one mast and oars, it was also the name of a bird.

SAINTE ANNE. Tartane built 1692–93 at Toulon. Last mentioned 1706, may have been wrecked at Agde 1704.

A two-masted tartane as illustrated by Guéroult du Pas in 1710. These were originally coastal trading craft (often with only a single mast) later adapted for minor naval roles by the addition of a few guns. Like so many lateen-rigged types, they featured a long protruding beak – known in French as an *éperon* – which served in lieu of a bowsprit to secure the lower end of the fore lateen yard.

ACTIF **Class.** Brigantines or half-galleys designed by Jean-Baptiste Chabert. See note on *Félouque*, above.
>Dimensions & tons: 63ft 0in x 10ft 0in x 3ft 6in (20.46 x 3.25 x 1.14m). 25 tons. Draught 4½ft (1.46m). Men: 60
>Guns: 1 x 2pdr.

Actif Le Havre.
>K: 1.1693. L: 3.1693. C: 4.1693. Appeared on fleet lists 1704 as unserviceable, rebuilt 1705 at Lorient. Listed from 1709 as a corvette or *barque longue*. Unserviceable 1.1712 at Port Louis.

Résolu Le Havre.
>K: 1.1693. L: 3.1693. C: 4.1693. Appeared on fleet lists 1704 as unserviceable, rebult 1705 at Lorient. Listed from 1709 as a corvette or *barque longue*. Unserviceable 1.1712 at Port Louis.

LÉGÈRE **Class.** Feluccas or half-galleys (also called *galiotes à rames* and *brigantins*), the first two designed by François Coulomb.
>Dimensions & tons: 60ft 0in, 40ft 0in x 10ft 0in x 4ft 0in (19.49, 12.99 x 3.25 x 1.30m). 25/30 tons. Men: 70 (except *Légère*, unknown)

Légère Marseille or Toulon.
>K: 1694. L: 1694. C: 1694. Condemned 1702 at Toulon.

Ferme Toulon.
>K: 4.1695. L: 5.5.1695. C: 5.1695. Condemned c.1703 at Toulon

Fidèle Toulon.
>K: 4.1695. L: 5.5.1695. C: 5.1695. Condemned c.1703 at Toulon

PURCHASED VESSELS (1693–1695)

Sainte Marie. Brigantine put into service 1693 at Toulon. Handed over for privateering 6.1695.

Pêcheuse. Tartane, 12 men, put into service 1693 at Toulon. Last mentioned 1701 at Toulon.

Françoise. Tartane put into service 1693 at Toulon. Last mentioned 1694 at Toulon.

Sainte Thérèse. Tartane put into service 1693 at Toulon. Last mentioned 1693 at Toulon.

Saint Pierre. Tartane put into service 1693 at Toulon. Last mentioned 1693 at Toulon.

Sainte Élisabeth. Tartane put into service 1693 at Toulon. Last mentioned 1693 at Toulon.

Saint Jean. Tartane put into service 1693 at Toulon. May have been the tartane *Saint Jean et Saint Thomas* captured 9.1692. Sunk 1694 at Martigues or at the Îles d'Hyeres.

Saint Jacques. Tartane put into service 1694 at Toulon. Last mentioned 1694 at Toulon.

Saint Antoine. Barque in service at Toulon on 21.6.1695. Last mentioned 1697.

Paresseuse. Tartane put into service 1695 at Toulon. Last mentioned 1695 at Toulon.

MISCELLANEOUS PRIZE (1695)

Jean et Richard. Captured tartane of unknown origin in service 6.1695 at Le Havre. Handed over 8.1695 to a private shipowner.

PURCHASED VESSELS (1700–1702)

Saint Jean. Tartane in service at Toulon in 6.1700. Last mentioned 1702 at Toulon.

Saint Joseph. Tartane put into service 1702 at Toulon. Wrecked 12.1705 at Cassis.

Saint Michel. Tartane put into service 1702 at Toulon. Last mentioned 1702 at Toulon.

Saint Antoine or *Saint Antoine de Padoue*. Tartane put into service 1702

A single-masted tartane as illustrated by Guéroult du Pas in 1710. The large jib secured spread between the mast and the extended *éperon* on the bow takes the place of the foremast and its lateen sail on the two-masted type. Tartanes were normally small coasters that were sailed rather than rowed, although du Pas shows a few crewmen struggling to row one here.

at Toulon. Probably captured by Tunisians 7.1704 and returned to the French 10.1704. Last mentioned 1706 at Toulon.

NOTRE DAME DES SAINTES RÉLIQUES. Tartane built at Toulon (?) in 1702. Last mentioned 1706 at Toulon.

NOTRE DAME DE GRÂCE. Tartane built at Toulon (?) in 1702. Last mentioned 1707 (?) at Toulon.

CHASSEUR **Class.** Feluccas or half-galleys, probably designed by Jean-Baptiste Chabert). Had 25-foot oars, 3 rowers per oar. Half-galleys were small galleys with 20 or fewer banks of oars and only two masts.
>Dimensions & tons: dimensions unknown. 40/50 tons. Men: 130.
>Guns: 1 x 18pdr forward, flanked by 2 x 4pdrs; also 6 *pierriers*.

Chasseur Dunkirk.
>K: 5.1702. L: 15.7.1702. C: 11.1702. Struck 1706, probably lost 7.1706 on the Scheldt or at Ostend.

Effronté Dunkirk.
>K: 5.1702. L: 15.7.1702. C: 11.1702. Struck 1706, probably lost 7.1706 on the Scheldt or at Ostend.

Farouche Dunkirk.
>K: 5.1702. L: 15.7.1702. C: 11.1702. Struck 1706, probably lost 7.1706 on the Scheldt or at Ostend.

Furet Dunkirk.
>K: 5.1702. L: 15.7.1702. C: 11.1702. Struck 1706, probably lost 7.1706 on the Scheldt or at Ostend.

Ex-ENGLISH MERCANTILE PRIZE (1702). Her name indicates that this former English vessel was a half-galley.
>Dimensions & tons: 64ft 0in x 16ft 0in x 5ft 0in (20.79 x 5.20 x 1.62m). 36 tons. Draught 7ft (2.27m). Men: 50 in war, 20 peace
>Guns: 4 in war (4 peace): 4 x 3pdrs. 6 x 3pdrs from 1706.

Demy Galère England.
>Built 1701. Captured 6.1702. Struck 2.1706 at Le Havre.

NOTRE DAME DE BON VOYAGE **Class.** Barques built at Toulon. Had square sterns and quarterdecks extending forward to the mainmast.
>Dimensions & tons: dimensions unknown. 70 tons. Men: 35 + 1 officer.

The Mediterranean barque illustrated by Guéroult du Pas in 1710. It closely resembles the known details of the three barques of the *Notre Dame de Bon Voyage* Class built in 1703, with a square stern and long quarterdeck to the mainmast. The background views, in the usual convention of ship portraiture, show the same vessel on different points of sailing, but the one to the left shows the ship setting a square main (*voile de fortune carré*) instead of the lateen, often done in vessels with fore-and-aft or lateen rigs when the wind was from astern or in foul weather.

Guns: 4 guns or 2 small mortars.
Notre Dame de Bon Voyage Toulon.
  K: 1702. L: 1.1703. C: 1.1703. Wrecked 1.1708 near Cape Roux.
Notre Dame du Mont Carmel Toulon.
  K: 1702. L: 1.1703. C: 1.1703. Last mentioned 1703 at Toulon.
Saint Jean Toulon.
  K: 1702. L: 1.1703. C: 1.1703. Probably handed over for privateering 1709.

SIRÈNE. Brigantine or felucca designed by Jean-Baptiste Chabert. Also referred to as *La Félouque*. Had 16 banks of oars, 2 rowers per oar.
  Dimensions & tons: 64ft 0in x 9ft 6in x 3ft 0in (20.79 x 3.09 x 0.97m). 25 tons. Draught 4ft (1.30m). Men: 75 in war, 75 peace, + 1 officer.
  Guns: 1.
Sirène Marseille.
  K: 7.1703. L: 1.1704. C: 2.1704. Off the list *c.*1711, probably service craft at Toulon. On the list in 1717 with 35 men in war, 30 peace, and as unable to serve except in summer, then off the list again. Struck *c.*1720 at Toulon. The 1717 list also contained a *Diligente* with identical information except she had the original 75/75 men and was in need of a refit.

BRIGANTIN DES GALÈRES. Felucca built at Dunkirk.
  Dimensions & tons: 64ft 0in x 9ft 0in x 4ft 0in (20.79 x 2.92 x 1.30m). 25 tons. Draught 3ft (0.97m). Men: 50
  Guns: 1 x 4pdr.
Brigantin des Galères Dunkirk.
  Built in 1703 or 1706. Wrecked 2.1707 on the Banc des Dunes, probably near Dunkirk, while in combat with a Dutch frigate.

LÉGÈRE. One barque and one brigantine designed by François Coulomb. The dimensions and designer listed for these two vessels were identical and they were probably sisters.
  Dimensions & tons: 40ft 0in x 11ft 6in x 3ft 6in (12.99 x 3.74 x 1.14m). 20 tons. Men: 52 (53 in *Fidèle*)
  Guns: probably 1.
Légère Toulon.
  K: 6.1703. L: 7.1703. C: 7.1703. Barque. Used as service craft at Toulon in 1713, last mentioned 1717.
Fidèle Toulon.
  Built 1705. Brigantine. Hulked at Toulon 1709, condemned *c.*1713, still listed as hulk 1719.

PROMPTE Class. Four barques (one also called a *chaloupe garde-côtes*) and one brigantine designed by François Coulomb. All were listed with the same dimensions and designer and were probably sisters.
  Dimensions & tons: 34ft 0in x 10ft 0in x 3ft 4in (11.04 x 3.25 x 1.08m). 14 tons. Men: 37; *Sainte Claire* 35; *Vigilante* 42 (33 from 1709); *Ferme* 33, *Prompte* 32
  Guns: probably 1.
Prompte Toulon.
  Built 6–7.1703. *Chaloupe garde-côtes* or barque. Became service craft at Toulon in 1713, last mentioned 1717.
Sainte Claire Toulon.
  Built 1705. Barque. Used as service craft at Toulon from 1713, struck *c.*1717.
Subtile Toulon.
  Built 1705. Barque. Used as service craft at Toulon from 1713, struck *c.*1717.
Vigilante Toulon.
  Built 1705. Barque. Used as service craft at Toulon from 1713, last mentioned 1721.
Ferme Toulon.
  Built 1705. Brigantine. Used as service craft at Toulon from 1713, struck *c.*1717.

PURCHASED VESSELS (1706–1708)
Saint Pierre or *Pinque Saint Pierre*. Barque or pink built in Catalonia and acquired in 1706.
  Dimensions & tons: 59ft 0in x 18ft 0in x 7ft 4in (19.17 x 5.85 x 2.38m). 86 tons. Draught 8ft (2.60m). Men: 70 in war, 30 peace + 1 officer

Lescallier's illustration of a large pink (*pinque*), a vessel generally resembling the barque. Traditionally, the distinguishing mark of the *pinque* was a high narrow stern, as in this example, but it was a custom more honoured in the breach than the observance. These vessels, like other fore-and-aft rigged ships, often carried alternative rigs: short square yards for running before the wind, and lateens for working to windward.

Guns: (6 in war, 2 peace) 6 x 4pdrs.

Also referred to as *Pink Saint Pierret* and *Le pinck S. Pierre*. Built in Catalonia and may have been called *Catalan*. Burned 6.1708 by the British near Marseille.

Sainte Croix. Tartane put into service 1706 at Toulon. Last mentioned 1706.

Jesus-Maria-Sainte Anne. Barque put into service 1706 at Toulon. Wrecked 1.1708 at La Ciotat.

Saint Alexis. Barque put into service *c*.1707 at Toulon. Handed over for privateering 1709.

Saint Hyacinthe. Barque put into service *c*.1707 at Toulon. Handed over for privateering 1709.

Sainte Anne. Barque put into service *c*.1707 at Toulon. Last mentioned 1710 at Toulon.

Notre Dame Des Anges. Brigantine put into service *c*.1707 at Toulon. Built at Oneille, 21 men. Struck 1710 at Toulon.

Sainte Marie. Barque put into service *c*.1708 at Toulon. Last mentioned 1709 in service as a privateer at Toulon.

(D) Vessels acquired from 1 September 1715

PURCHASED VESSELS (1719–1720)

Saint Joseph. Tartane from Marseille put into service 10.1719 at Toulon. 12/44 men + 1 officer. Out of service and last mentioned 5.1721 at Toulon. Called a 'chaloupe' in 1721.

Sainte Croix. Tartane put into service 16.12.1719 at Toulon. 25 men + 1 officer. Out of service 1.1720, probably at Toulon.

Saint Paul. Barque put into service 27.9.1720 at Toulon. 11/12 men + 1 officer. Last mentioned 11.1722 out of service at Toulon.

Saint Pierre. Barque put into service 27.9.1720 at Toulon. 11/12 men + 1 officer. Last mentioned 5.1721 out of service at Toulon.

Crucifix. Tartane put into service 10.12.1720 at Toulon. 19 men + 2 officers. Out of service 29.12.1720.

Saint Joseph Bonaventure. Tartane put into service 10.12.1720 at Toulon. 50 men + 3 officers. Out of service 29.12.1720.

St Joseph et St Clement. Tartane put into service 10.12.1720 at Toulon. 36 men + 2 officers. Out of service 29.12.1720.

Saint Ginier. Tartane put into service 10.12.1720 at Toulon. 19 men + 2 officers. Out of service 25.12.1720.

Ex-SPANISH PRIZE (1719)

Saint Jacques de Galice. Tartane, ex-Spanish *San Yago a Horcajadas*, captured in 1719 and put into service 10.12.1720 at Toulon. Out of service 29.12.1720.

Brigantines or half-galleys shown by Guéroult du Pas under sail and being rowed. The functions of these smaller oared craft and the similar *galiotes à rames* in both the *Levant* and *Ponant* varied from coastal warfare to supporting the galley fleets and towing sailing warships out of port against contrary winds. They were part of the regular Navy, not the Galley Corps.

The later version of the Mediterranean barque as illustrated by Lescallier, which retained the traditional bow shape and fore lateen, but adopted conventional square main and mizzen masts. These may have been traditional fidded masts with separate topmasts, but barques also employed the single-piece pole masts that were even more commonly used in polacres. The polacre illustrated in Chapter 13 is in fact very similar to this barque. Presumably, the term *barque latine*, as for the *Sibylle* Class of 1728, was used deliberately to denote barques with at least a partial lateen rig and the associated hull form.

ÉPERVIER Class. Brigantines, some also called half-galleys (*demi-galères*). Designed by Pierre Chabert. Had 13 banks of oars with 52 rowers. The first four were all in service in 1739 with the summer galleys of the Château d'If, a fortification in the Bay of Marseille.

Dimensions & tons: 63ft 6in x 11ft 5in x 4ft 3in (20.63 x 3.71 x 1.38m). 30/50 tons (7 tons in 1746). Men: 75–110 + 2–4 officers.
Guns: 1 x 6pdr forward.

Épervier Marseille.
K: 1727. L: 1727. C: 1728. Also called a *demi-galère*. Last mentioned 1740.

Vautour Marseille.
K: 1727. L: 1727. C: 1728. Last mentioned 1740.

Faucon Marseille.
K: 1727. L: 1727. C: 1728. Last mentioned 1739 at Marseille.

Effronté Marseille.
K: 1727. L: 1727. C: 1728. Last mentioned 1739 at Marseille.

Inconnu Marseille.
K: 1728. L: 1728. C: 6.1729. Reported struck 1746 at Toulon but listed in 1759 as in good condition.

Assuré Marseille.
K: 1728. L: 1728. C: 7.1729. Reported struck 1746 at Toulon but listed in 1759 as in good condition.

SIBYLLE Class. *Barques latines* (classed as *barques longues* between 1723 and 1729, reverted to *barques latines* by 1734). Designed by Blaise Coulomb, built to chase Algerian privateers. Both named 14.2.1729.

Dimensions & tons: 76ft 0in x 23ft 3in x 8ft 1in (24.69 x 7.55 x 2.63m). 156/300 tons. Draught 10ft (3.25m). Men: 120 in war, 40 peace + 4 officers
Guns: 14 in war (6 peace) 14 x 4pdrs. *Légère*: 16 guns in 1754, 24 in 1757, 12 from 1759, 14 in 1768.

Sibylle Toulon.
Ord: 3.11.1728. K: 16.11.1728. L: 27.3.1729. C: 4.1729. Wrecked 8.1742 on the Barbary Coast near La Galite.

Légère Toulon.
Ord: 15.11.1728. K: 22.11.1728. L: 4.1729. C: 1729. Listed as a barque from 1752. Struck and hulked at Toulon in 1759, listed as a *corps de garde* (harbour guard station) at Toulon 1766–70.

Ex-BARBARY COAST PRIZE (1728)
Thérèse. Barque put into service 18.8.1728 in the harbour of Tunis, probably after being taken as a prize. 69 men + 2 officers. Last mentioned 11.1728 out of service at Malta.

PURCHASED VESSELS (1728–1735)
Notre Dame de Porto-Salvo or *Notre Dame de Port-Salut*. Barque (probably purchased) put into service 11.1728 at Malta. Last mentioned 6.1729 departing Toulon for Île Royale in Canada.

Saint Antoine. Tartane put into service 1735 at Toulon. Fate unknown.

DILIGENTE Class. *Tartanes pontées*. Designed by Laurent Marchand and ordered 1.1.1738. Ex-*Tartane No.1* and *No.2* 6.1738 and 7.1738 respectively

Dimensions & tons: 66ft 0in, 50ft 0in x 19ft 6in x 7ft 6in (21.44, 16.24 x 6.33 x 2.44m). 70–100/160 tons. Men: 100 in war + 2 officers.
Guns: 4 x 4pdrs.

Diligente Toulon.
Ord: 1.1.1738. K: 2.1738. L: 9.6.1738. C: 29.6.1738. Condemned 7.11.1761 at Toulon to be sold or BU.

Gaillarde Toulon.
K: 23.6.1738. L: 25.10.1738. C: 7.1740. Wrecked 12.2.1741 on San Salvador Island near Cuba.

CHASSE Class. Half-galleys or *galiotes à rames*. Designed by Augustin Scolaro de Malte (Augustin Nicolas de Malte) with the same dimensions as the vessels of this type that Scolaro had built at Malta in the previous year. Ex-*Demi-galère No.1* and *No.2* respectively 11.1742.

Dimensions & tons: 98ft 0in x 13ft 2in x 4ft 4in (31.83 x 4.28 x 1.41m). 75/100 tons. Draught 4ft (1.30m). Men: 200 in war, 150 peace
Guns: 3 in war (2 peace) 3 x 4pdrs. 1 gun in 1759 and 1761. 3 guns in 1767: 1 x 6pdr; 2 x 2pdrs. 1 gun in 1768.

Chasse Toulon.
K: 5.1742. L: 13.8.1742. C: 1742. First commissioned 4.1747, then used as harbour tug. Repaired early 1755. Listed as *Embuscade c.* 1757 and as *Chasse* 1761. In need of major repairs 1768, struck 1770 at Toulon.

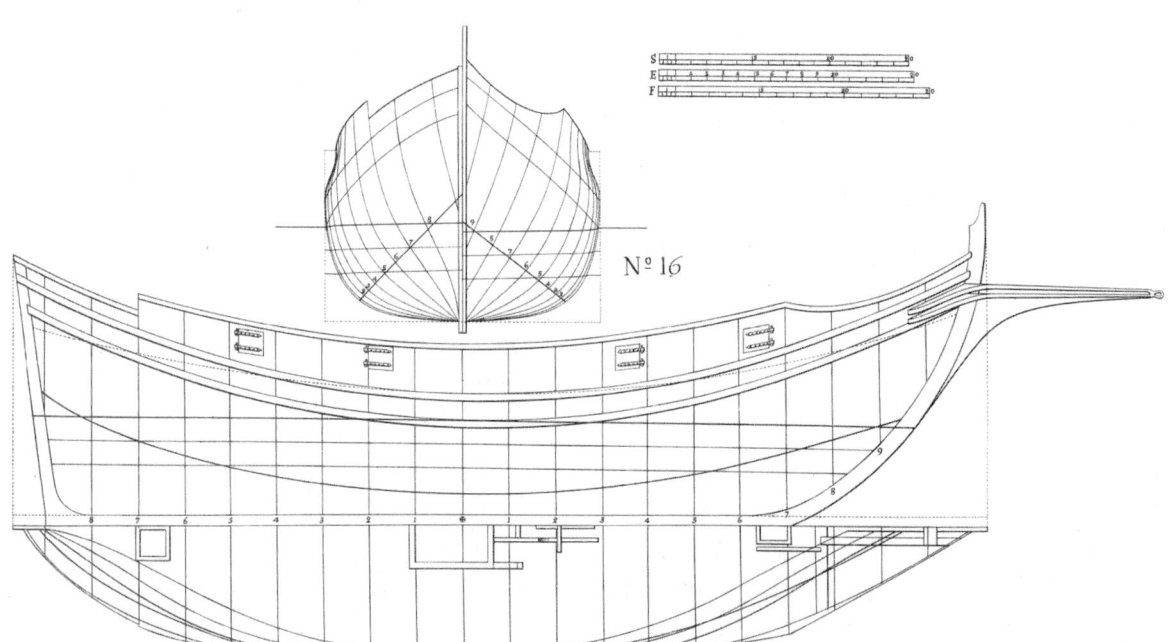

Lines plan of a mid-century tartane from F H Chapman's *Architectura Navalis Mercatoria*, published in 1768. This example is described as a French warship armed with eight 4pdrs and four swivels. It may be a privateer as no known French naval tartane fits this description, although several carried four 4pdrs. The development of the type for naval purposes can be inferred by comparison with the du Pas drawing on page 355.

Découverte Toulon.
  K: 5.1742. L: 2.10.1742. C: 1742. First commissioned 4.1747, then used as harbour tug. Repaired early 1755. In need of major repairs 1768, struck 1770 at Toulon.

HIRONDELLE. *Barque latine*. Designed by Augustin Scolaro de Malte (Augustin Nicolas de Malte). Ordered 4.7.1742 and named 23.10.1742. A report of November 1754 stated that 'the two barques at Toulon [*Hirondelle* and *Légère*, above] were little suited for war, however they could be used as escorts on the coast.'
  Dimensions & tons: 92ft 0in x 26ft 7in x 11ft 6in (29.89 x 8.64 x 3.74m). 160/370 tons. Draught 12ft (3.90m). Men: 130 in war, 80 peace + 4 officers.
  Guns: 24 in war (16 peace): 18 x 8pdrs, 6 x 4pdrs. 18 x 6pdrs from 1766 and probably from 1759, 16 x 6pdrs from 1768, 18 x 6pdrs from 1772.
Hirondelle Toulon.
  K: 4.10.1742. L: 8.6.1743. C: 3.1744. Rebuilt by Landré 1752 (hauled out 8.1752 and re-launched 20.10.1752). Rated as a barque from 1752. Was on commercial loan at Vigo in 1761. Was serving as a *patache* in 1767. Listed as a *barque de guerre* in 1768 with a second to be built on the same lines (see *Éclair* below). Returned from sea in good condition 1770. Condemned 1775 and used as a *patache* at Toulon. Sank at Toulon 5.1786 from neglect, raised and BU.

PURCHASED VESSEL (1747)
Victoire. Felucca put into service 17.4.1747 at Toulon. 18 men + 1 officer. Last mentioned 6.1747 arriving at Toulon after having participated in the recapture of the Île Sainte Marguerite off Cannes.

Ex-BRITISH MERCANTILE OR PRIVATEER PRIZE (1748)
Savoyarde. British tartane captured 1748. Lost 6.1748 with all hands between Civita-Vecchia and Toulon.

REQUIN Class. Xebecs. Designed by Joseph Coubet de Majorque. Ordered 13.2.1750, built to defend against the Barbary raids on the Mediterranean coast. Named 11.6.1750. A report of November 1754 states that 'the four *chébecks* that a constructor from Minorca has come to build at Toulon were tried last year with success and they can serve usefully against the Barbary corsairs, some more will be built following them.'
  Dimensions & tons: 115ft 0in, 95ft 0in x 26ft 0in x 8ft 0in (37.36, 30.86 x 8.44 x 2.60m), 260/350 tons. Draught 9ft (2.92m). Men: 170 in war, 115 peace + 5 officers
  Guns: 24 x 8pdrs.
Requin Toulon.
  K: 13.7.1750. L: 13.3.1751. C: 10.1752. Condemned 30.9.1770 at Toulon, ordered sold 25.10.1770, sold 15.12.1770 and BU.
Indiscret Toulon.
  K: 21.6.1750. L: 26.3.1751. C: 8.1753. Sold 1759 or 1761 at Cartagena to the Spanish Navy and renamed *Caballo Blanco*. Still in service as such 1770.

RUSÉ Class. Xebecs. *Rusé* designed by Joseph Coubet de Majorque and *Serpent* by Roux de Majorque. Ordered 13.2.1750, built to defend against the Barbary raids on the Mediterranean coast. Named 11.6.1750.
  Dimensions & tons: 103ft x 22ft 6in x 7ft 6in (33.46 x 7.31 x 2.44m), 150/240 tons. Men: 120 in war, 85 peace + 5 officers
  Guns: 18 x 6pdrs.
Rusé Toulon.
  K: 3.1751. L: 9.6.1751. C: 6.1753. Unserviceable 9.1774 at Toulon, condemned 1775.
Serpent Toulon.
  K: 3.1751. L: 23.6.1751. C: 9.1753. Condemned 1775 and used as an artillery polygon at Toulon. Last mentioned 1779.

Ex-BRITISH PRIVATEER PRIZE (1752)
Revanche. Xebec. Ex-British privateer xebec *Revenge*, built in Spain in 1752, commissioned in Spain, and captured 7.1757 by the galleys *Brave* and *Duchesse*.
  Dimensions & tons: 76ft x 16ft 6in (24.69 x 5.36m). 70/150 tons. Men: 70 in war, 50 peace
  Guns: 2 x 6pdrs, 10 x 4pdrs. 14 x 3pdrs from 1768.
  Used in 1764 to train seamen gunners at Toulon, participated in operations in Corsica 10.1768. Listed in 1770 as 'in condition but bad ship'. Struck 1772 at Toulon.

Lines plan of the *Requin* Class xebecs of 1751 redrawn by László Veres from an original in the Danish archives. Built to fight fire with fire, this class was a direct counter to similar vessels that had been used almost with impunity by the so-called Barbary corsairs. They sailed far better than galleys, but could be rowed when circumstances dictated, while their broadside armament put them on a par with corvettes.

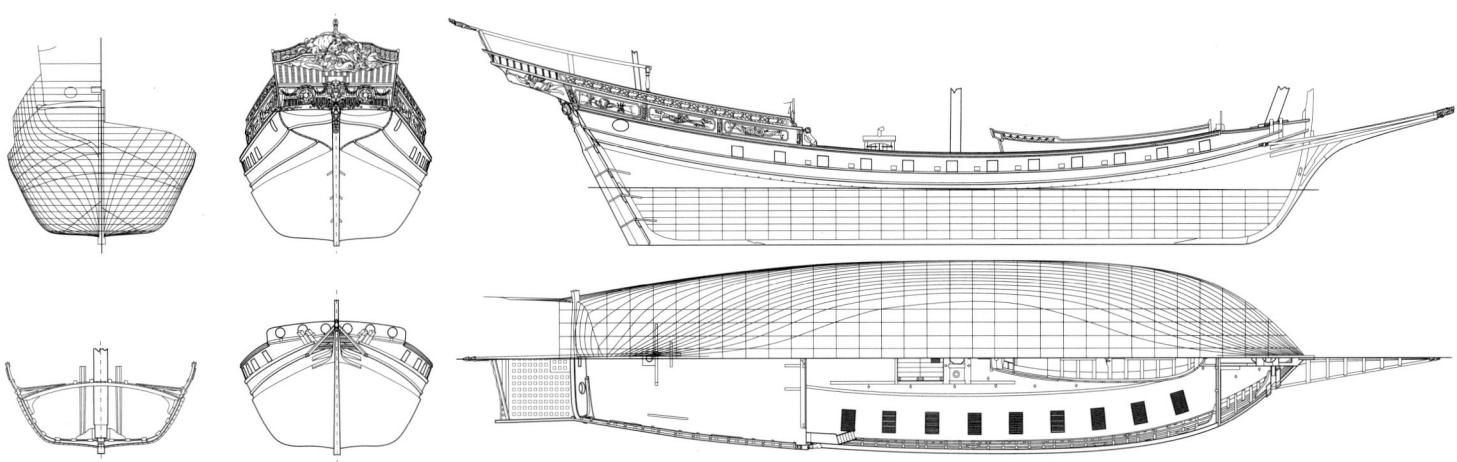

Xebecs were also built in Spain and proved popular with Mediterranean privateers, some even operating under British letters of marque in wars against France, like the *Revenge* captured in 1757. This is Lescallier's illustration of a Spanish xebec.

PURCHASED VESSELS (1753–1754)
Sainte Barbe. Tartane put into service 1753 at Toulon. Fate unknown.
Sainte Marguerite. Tartane put into service 1753 at Toulon. Fate unknown.
Belle Maguelonne. Tartane put into service 1754 at Toulon. Fate unknown.
Tamise. Tartane in service at Toulon in 1754, sometimes called a pink. Last mentioned 1758 at Toulon.

ESPION. Felucca, also called a *trincadour*. Designed by S Journe (or Journa). Ordered 8.7.1758. Was one of three feluccas at Marseille in 1768, the other two being unnamed. Had 7 banks of oars.
   Dimensions & tons: 58ft 0in, 44ft 0in x 10ft 7in x 3ft 2in (18.84, 14.29 x 3.44 x 1.03m). 20/35 tons.
   Guns: 2 x 2pdrs.
Espion Toulon.
   K: 1757. C: 1758. C: 5.6.1761. Wrecked 6.1769 at Portiglio in Corsica.

BROCHET Class. Xebecs. Designed by Pierre Levasseur and built on Lake Champlain. Like other colonial craft, not carried in regular French fleet lists. One of the three scuttled xebecs was initially named *Amherst* by the British.
   Dimensions & tons: unknown. Men: 50
   Guns: 2 x 6pdrs (forward), 6 x 4pdrs.
Brochet Fort St Jean (Lake Champlain).
   K: 10.1758. L: 6.1759. C: 7.1759. Scuttled 10.1759 in Missisquoi Bay in Lake Champlain to avoid capture. Raised by the British 10–11.1759 and became sloop HMS *Brochette* (6 guns). Last mentioned 1778.
Esturgeon Fort St Jean (Lake Champlain).
   K: 10.1758. L: 1.9.1759. C: 9.1759. Scuttled 10.1759 in Missisquoi Bay in Lake Champlain to avoid capture. Raised by the British 10–11.1759 and became sloop HMS *Lochegeon* (6 guns). Last mentioned 1778.
Maskalonge Fort St Jean (Lake Champlain).
   K: 10.1758. L: 6.1759. C: 7.1759. Scuttled 10.1759 in Missisquoi Bay in Lake Champlain to avoid capture. Raised by the British 10–11.1759 and became sloop HMS *Musquenonge* (6 guns). Last mentioned 1778.
Gardon (or *Goujon*?) Fort St Jean (Lake Champlain).
   K: 10.1758. L: 12.1759. C: 1760. Captured 1760 by the British on Lake Champlain and renamed HMS *Waggon*. Last mentioned beached on Lake Champlain.

PURCHASED VESSEL (1759)
Génoise. Felucca (also called a *trincadour*) built in Genoa in 1759 and purchased 7.1768 at Toulon.
   Dimensions & tons: 51ft 0in x 11ft 0in (16.57 x 3.57m)
   Guns: Unknown.
   Renamed *Corse* 1769. Wrecked 6.1769 at Portiglio in Corsica, refloated and removed from service at Calvi. Still out of service in Corsica in 1772, wrecked at Calvi 1773.

RENARD. Xebec. Designed by Louis-Hilarion Chapelle (*fils*). Ordered 9.12.1761, named 5.6.1762.
   Dimensions & tons: 115ft 0in x 26ft 0in x 7ft 6in (37.36 x 8.45 x 2.44m), 260/350 tons (145 tons in 1773). Draught 10ft 6in/10ft 10in (3.41/3.52m). Men: 140 in war, 95 peace + 5 officers
   Guns: 20 x 8pdrs.
Renard Toulon.
   K: 3.1762. L: 23.6.1762. C: 8.1762. Sale approved 27.12.1779, sold 3.1780 to Sieur Blaise Piguier for commercial use. Possibly captured 1780 by HMS *Brune*.

SINGE. Xebec. Designed by Jean-Baptiste Doumet-Revest. Ordered 9.12.1761, named 5.6.1762. Pole-masted.
   Dimensions & tons: 115ft 0in x 28ft 0in x 10ft 0in (37.36 x 9.10 x 3.25m). 260/350 tons (126 tons in 1773). Draught 10ft 6in/10ft 10in (3.41/3.52m). Men: 140 in war, 95 peace + 5 officers
   Guns: 20 x 8pdrs.
Singe Toulon.
   K: 3.1762. L: 3.7.1762. C: 8.1762. Sale approved 27.12.1779, sold 1780 at Toulon.

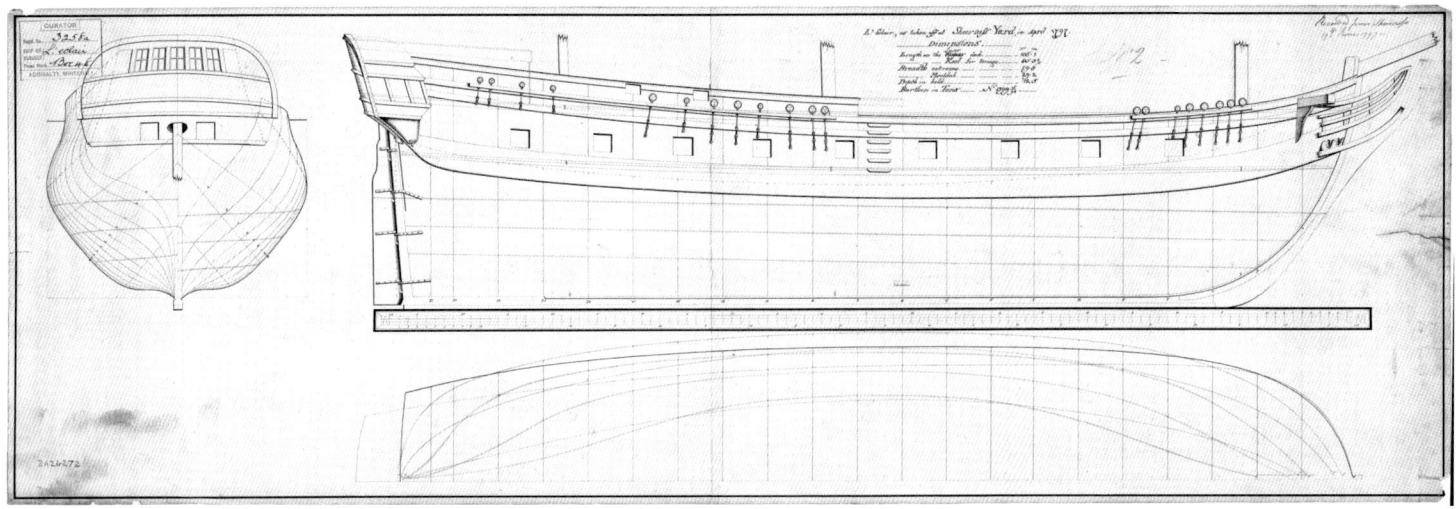

SÉDUISANT. Xebec. Designed by Jean-François Étienne. Ordered 9.12.1761, named 5.6.1762.
  Dimensions & tons: 115ft 0in x 28ft 2in x 10ft 0in (37.36 x 9.15 x 3.25m), 260/350 tons (127 tons in 1773). Draught 10ft 6in (3.41m). Men: 140 in war, 95 peace + 5 officers
  Guns: 20 x 8pdrs.
Séduisant Toulon.
  K: 3.1762. L: 14.7.1762. C: 9.1762. Struck 1780 at Toulon, sold 1781.

CAMÉLÉON. Xebec. Designed by Claude Saucillon. Ordered 9.12.1761, named 5.6.1762.
  Dimensions & tons: 115ft 0in x 27ft 0in x 10ft 0in (37.36 x 8.77 x 3.25m), 260/350 tons (144 tons in 1773). Draught 8ft 8in/9ft 6in (2.82/3.09m). Men: 140 in war, 95 peace + 5 officers
  Guns: 20 x 8pdrs.
Caméléon Toulon.
  K: 3.1762. L: 27.7.1762. C: 9.1762. Condemned 1780 at Toulon and struck.

PURCHASED VESSEL (1763)
Louvine. Tartane purchased c.6.1763 at Toulon. 22 men + 2 officers. Listed in 12.1766 as at sea. Struck c.10.1769.

ÉCLAIR Class. Barques (*barques latines*, *barques de guerre*), *Éclair* rated as a corvette from 1783. Designed by Jean-Baptiste Doumet-Revest to the same proportions as *Hirondelle*, above. Ordered 7.2.1770, named 25.2.1770. Had eight pairs of small ports for oars.
  Dimensions & tons: 98ft 0in, 80ft 0in x 27ft 0in x 12ft 0in (31.83, 25.99 x 8.77 x 3.90m). 230/395 tons. Draught 11ft 6in / 11ft 10in (3.74/3.84m). Men: 5/6 officers, 160 ratings.
  Guns: 18 x 6pdrs. 20 x 6pdrs from 1780.
Éclair Toulon Dyd.
  K: 4.1770. L: 5.7.1771. C: 1772. Rebuilt at Toulon 1781, listed as corvette from 1783. Captured by HM Ships *Illustrious* and *Leda* south of Marseille 9.6.1793, and added as HMS *Éclair*; powder hulk at Sheerness 4.1797, sold 27.8.1806.
Vigilante Toulon Dyd.
  This probable sister to *Éclair* with 18 x 6pdrs was to have been laid down at Toulon in 1776 but was abandoned not having been begun. Listed in 1776 and 1777.

Admiralty draught of *Éclair* as taken off at Sheerness in April 1797. Although captured in 1793, the vessel had probably not been in British dockyard hands before this period at Sheerness, so is essentially as captured. *Éclair* had been re-rated as a corvette in 1783, which presumably involved conversion to the conventional ship rig seen here, but her origins as a Mediterranean barque are evident in the hull shape with its swept-up bow; the stern is also rather awkward with the row of stern lights at a higher level than the obviously false quarter galleries, perhaps the result of grafting on a conventional warship stern to the original barque shape when the vessel was converted to a corvette. The underwater lines, however, are fine and resemble the body of a small French frigate. (National Maritime Museum, London J4582)

PURCHASED VESSELS (1774–1780)
Légère. Felucca in service at Corsica in 1774. Fate unknown.
Notre Dame or *Notre Dame de Miséricorde*. Tartane purchased 5.1780 and put into service at Toulon. Carried 6 x 6pdrs in 1781–82. Struck 12.1783 at Toulon.

Ex-BRITISH PRIVATEER AND MERCANTILE PRIZES (1779–1781)
Tartare. Felucca, ex-British privateer *Tartar* from Minorca, captured 2.1779 by the French. 4 x 1pdrs. In service at Toulon from 8.1780 to 8.1782, ordered sold there 23.3.1783.
Mahounoise (*Mahonnaise*) or *Port de Citadella*. Felucca, ex-British privateer *Port de Citadella* or *Porto de Cuidadella* from Minorca, captured 4.1780 by the French. 4 x 1pdrs. In service at Toulon from 7.1780 to 10.1781, ordered sold there 23.3.1783. The ports of Mahon and Ciutadella are at opposite ends of the island of Minorca.
Légère. Felucca, ex-British privateer from Minorca, captured 5.1780 by the French. 2 x 3pdrs + 2 x 1pdrs, later 4 x 1pdrs. In service at Toulon from 9.1780 to 10.1781, ordered sold there 23.3.1783.
Sainte Barbe. Felucca, ex-British privateer from Minorca, captured 5.1780 by the French. 2 x 4pdrs, 2 x 3pdrs, 2 x 1pdrs; later 4 x 1pdrs. In service at Toulon from 9.1780 to 9.1782, ordered sold there 23.3.1783.
Succès. Felucca, ex-British privateer *Success* from Minorca, captured 1.1781 by the French. 1 x 3pdr, 4 x 1pdrs. In service at Toulon from 2.1781 to 8.1782, ordered sold there 23.3.1783.
Pêcheur. British *bateau* or felucca captured 1781 by the French. 1 x 6pdr, 2 x 3pdr, 4 x 1pdr. In service at Toulon from 8.1781 to 8.1782, struck there 3.1783.

13 Minor Support Vessels

This chapter contains a variety of smaller naval craft used for many subsidiary purposes, particularly cargo carrying. Until 1719 they were listed in the fleet lists with the smaller combatant ships in Chapters 11 and 12 as *bâtiments interrompus,* or vessels that were not part of the formal structure of the navy. (The Navy structure as approved by the King in the 1680s included only the five ranks of *vaisseaux* plus *frégates légères, flûtes,* bomb vessels, fireships, and corvettes or *barques longues.*) In general, these minor support vessels were vessels of below 200 tons with a wide variety of rigs and designations. Some of the smaller *flûtes* in Chapter 9, particularly before 1715, may actually have been of types like those in this chapter because the French used the term *flûte* as a functional designator covering cargo carriers of many configurations besides the big Dutch *fluyt*. This chapter includes only ships with known names; there were undoubtedly many other vessels of these miscellaneous types that lacked names or that escaped the historical record altogether.

CARGO VESSELS

The portion of this section up to 1715 contains *bélandres* or *bellandres* (bilanders), *caiches* or *quaiches* (ketches), *dogres* or *dogrebots* (doggers), *flibots* (flyboats), *galiotes* (galiotes), *gribanes* or *gribannes* (gribanes), *heux* (hoys), *pinasses* or *pinnaces* (pinnaces), *pinques* or *pingues* (pinks), *polacres* (polacres), *smacks, semales* or *semaques* (smacks), *transports* (transports), and *chaloupes, seloups* or *saloupes* (launches or barges). The portion of this section after 1715 adds *chattes pontées* (decked or covered lighters), while many of the earlier types disappear. *Chattes* were cargo craft that were round at the stern as well as at the bow, their rudders could be fitted at either end. The *chattes pontées* at Rochefort were used as *gabarres* to carry timber, in contrast with the *chattes non-pontées* (undecked or open lighters, service craft not listed here) which carried barrels of water to the large warships in the Île d'Aix roadstead and brought their guns to them when they were being commissioned.

(A) Vessels in service as at 9 March 1661

FORTUNE. This 60-ton *flibot* was built at Brest in 1658. She was sold at Brest 1669 as old and worn out. The existence of this vessel is unconfirmed.

SEIZED VESSEL (1661). *Petit Chalain*, possibly a galiote and probably built at Concarneau in 1658–60, was confiscated 9.1661 from Nicolas Fouquet. She was last mentioned in March 1669 at Toulon.

(B) Vessels acquired from 9 March 1661

PURCHASED VESSELS (1668–1669)
Prophète Daniel or *La Bellandre*. Bilander built at Le Havre and acquired 1668. 90 tons, no guns. Renamed *La Vieille Bellandre* 1669. Struck 1672, in sunken condition at Le Havre 12.1673.
La Gribane. Gribane built at Le Havre probably by Jean Esnault and completed 1.1669. Acquired 1668 while under construction. 50 tons, no guns. Renamed *La Vieille Gribane* 6.1670. Unserviceable 5.1680 at Le Havre.

LA BELLANDE. Bilander. Probably designed and built by Jean Esnault.
  Dimensions & tons: dimensions unknown. 80 tons. Draught 7ft (2.27m). Men: 28 (9/19/) +2 officers.
  Guns: 4 or none.
La Bellande Le Havre
  K: 1668. L: 3.1669. C: 5.1670. Appeared in fleet lists only in 1676 where she was shown as 'La ...' ex-*La Bellande*, built in 1665 and assigned to Le Havre. Listed elsewhere as *Madeleine*, 90 tons and without armament. Wrecked 10.1678 in the harbour of Le Havre, evidently raised, struck after 7.1679.

LA GRIBANE. Gribane. Probably designed and built by Jean Tortel. *Gribane*s were flat-bottomed vessels without keels that were used mainly in Picardy and on the Somme River.
  Dimensions & tons: 60ft 0in x 17ft 0in x 7ft 6in (19.49 x 5.52 x 2.44m). 60 tons. Draught 7ft (2.27m). Men: 28 (9/19/) +2 officers.
  Guns: 4 or none.
La Gribane Le Havre
  K: 1670. L: 3.7.1670. C: 7.1670. Appeared in fleet lists only in 1676 where she was shown as 'La ...' ex-*La Gribane*, built in 1666 and assigned to Le Havre. Listed elsewhere as *Marie* or *La Grande Gribane*, 50 tons with the dimensions shown above and without armament. Captured 1.1678 by the enemy.

Modern maritime historians owe a great debt to Guéroult du Pas. His 1710 publication *Recüeil des veiies de tous les differens Bastimens de la mer Mediterrannée et de l'Ocean avec leurs noms et usages* is almost the only source of reliable illustrations from a period that is a 'dark ages' for the visual representation of ships. It is particularly valuable for small craft and although the engraving is relatively crude, his understanding of ships is rather more profound. This is his rendering of a *flibot*, understood in France to be a smaller version of a *flûte*.

MINOR SUPPORT VESSELS

Lescallier's illustration of a bilander, a small cargo-carrier originating in the Baltic. Its characteristic feature was the main course, a sail like the old ship-rig's lateen mizzen, but with the luff cut off vertically. This endowed the sail with some of the advantages of both fore-and-aft and square canvas, depending on the point of sailing.

CACHE DE L'ADMIRAL (?). *Cache* (*caiche*). Built at Brest in 1666, 30/40 tons. Last mentioned 1671 at Brest.

GALIOTE. Galiote. Built at Quebec. 120 tons. Renamed *Suisse* in 1669.
K: 11.1666. L: 1667. C: 1668. Believed to have been lost at sea *c.*1672.

DUNKERQUOISE Class. Heux (hoys). Probably designed and built by Hendryck Houwens along with two unnamed *chaloupes-canonnières-galiotes* that were built for the defence of the *fosse* (an offshore channel) at Mardick.
Dimensions & tons: Unknown
Guns: 4 x 3pdrs.
Sainte Anne Dunkirk
K: 3.1678. L: 15.5.1678. C: 5.1678. Condemned 10.1680 and put on sale at Le Havre, still on sale 12.1680.
Dunkerquoise Dunkirk
K: 3.1678. L: 15.5.1678. C: 5.1678. Rebuilt 3–5.1680 at Dunkirk, then reinforced 11–12.1681 and fitted with a 12-inch mortar to conduct trials with this weapon before placing it on the new *galiotes à mortiers* (bomb vessels) of the *Foudroyante* class. Last mentioned 1692.

MARIE. Gribane. Built at Le Havre, probably designed by Étienne Salicon. Carried no guns.
K: 4.1678. L: 6.1678. C: 7.1678. Abandoned by her crew in a storm in the Channel 10.1678 and captured by the Dutch, bought back by the King 12.1678 at Flushing and returned to service at Le Havre. Last mentioned there 1692.

PURCHASED VESSELS (1679)
Saint Jean. Smack built in Flanders in 1679, repaired 1.1682 at Dunkirk, last mentioned there 1682.
Diligent. Smack built in Flanders in 1679 and completed before 2.1680, last mentioned 1682 at Dunkirk.

GALIOTE ROYALE or *Galiote du Roy*. Galiote built at Dunkirk, decorated by Pierre Dirubi.
K: 3.1680. L: 6.1680. C: 7.1680. Last mentioned 1692.

SAINT LOUIS Class. Gribanes, apparently with keels. Designed and built by Étienne Salicon.

Hoys (*Heux*) as drawn by Guéroult du Pas. The leeboards mark these as the original Dutch hoys, which were fishing boats and coastal traders. They were essentially single-masted with a sprit mainsail but they began to add a small mast aft (like the example on the left), which probably helped to balance the rig as hoys grew larger. The sprit sail was later replaced by a gaff-headed sail as shown here.

Like so many small-craft types, the *gribane* was originally a local design (in this case hailing from Picardy and the Somme river), whose success in its specific environment led to wider employment. These small coasters were square-rigged with two masts, originally without a fore topsail, but as shown here by Guéroult du Pas they later acquired one.

The polacre carried a hybrid rig that combined lateen and square sails, but not always in the combination shown here by Guéroult du Pas. In this example, the square-rigged masts have separate topmasts, but polacres later became characterised by one-piece pole masts. By the end of the eighteenth century many polacres had three square-rigged masts of which the fore and main were poles.

Dimensions & tons: 69ft 6in, 60ft 0in x 16ft 0in x 8ft 6in (22.58, 19.49 x 5.20 x 2.76m). 70 or 80 tons. Draught 7ft (2.27m).
Guns: Unknown.

Saint Louis Le Havre
  K: 2.1680. L: 6.5.1680. C: 5.1680. Wrecked 1689 or 1690 at Plougonvelin.
Madeleine Le Havre
  K: 4.1682. L: 20.6.1682. C: 7.1682. In sunken condition at the entrance to Le Havre 9.1694, BU 11.1694.
Sans Peur Le Havre
  K: 2.1683. L: 5.1683. C: 6.1683. Captured 6.1692 by the English and Dutch at La Hougue.

PURCHASED VESSEL (1682)

Marie. Polacre put into service at Toulon in 1682. Carried 2 guns and some *pierriers*. Wrecked 2.1687 in the vicinity of Barcelona.

Ex-SPANISH AND DUTCH PRIZES (1684–1689)

Prophète Daniel. Bilander captured 2.1684, ex-Spanish *Profeet Daniel* from Nieuport. 40 tons, 3 men + 1 master. Sold 4.1685 at Le Havre.
Bourg Couronné. Flibot, probably ex-Dutch, captured 11.1688 and put into service at Dunkirk 12.1688. 100 tons. Sold 4.1689 at Boulogne.
Saint François d'Ostende. Galiote or *caiche* built at Ostend and captured 4.1689, ex-Spanish *San Francisco*.
  Dimensions & tons: 55ft 0in x 16ft 0in x 7ft 0in (17.87 x 5.20 x 2.27m). 80 tons. Draught 8ft (2.60m). Men: 8 in 1692, 25 in 1696
  Guns: none in 1692, 4 x 4pdrs in 1696
  Described as old when listed at Brest in 9.1692. Last mentioned 12.1699 at Brest.

(C) Vessels acquired from 15 April 1689

Ex-SPANISH AND DUTCH PRIZES (1689–1694)

Espérance. Dogger seized 4.1689, probably ex-Spanish *Esperanza* from Nieuport and built at Ostend. 60 or 70 tons, 10 men, no guns. In Tourville's fleet 6–8.1691, in service at Brest 9.1692. Last mentioned 5.1693 at Brest.
San Yago. Flibot built at Ostend and captured 1691, ex-Spanish *San Yago*. 50 or 70 tons, 10 men, 4 guns. In service at Brest 9.1692. Unserviceable 3.1693 at Brest and struck.
Unité. Flibot built in Holland and captured in early 1691, probably ex-Dutch *Eenheid*.
  Dimensions & tons: 60ft 0in x 16ft 0in x 8ft 0in (19.49 x 5.20 x 2.60m). 80 tons. Draught 8ft (2.60m). Men: 10
  Guns: 4.
  Described as old when listed at Brest in 9.1692 and as an 'old mediocre sailer' in 1696. Struck 10.1696 and sold at Brest.
Marie de Redo. Pinasse probably built in northern Spain (Redo being a village in Cantabria), captured from the Spanish, and in service at Port Louis in 1694. Last mentioned there 4.1697.

Ex-ENGLISH NAVAL PRIZE (1690)

The ketch (*caiche*) HMS *Kingfisher* was captured on 2 April 1690 in the Channel and renamed *Pêcheur du Roi*.
  Dimensions & tons: 53ft 6in, 44ft 10in x 14ft 6in x 7ft 11in (17.38, 14.56 x 4.71 x 2.57m). 40 tons. Draught 7ft/8ft (2.27/2.60m). Men: 10
  Guns: 4.
Pêcheur du Roi. Purchased by the Royal Navy in 1684. In service at Brest 9.1692. Commissioned 7.1694 at Brest as a privateer *caiche* of 50 tons with 56 men + 4 officers and 6 guns + 6 *pierriers*. Subsequent fate unknown.

PURCHASED VESSELS (1691–1692)

Sainte Croix. Flibot in service at Brest in 12.1691. 70 tons. Struck 1692, probably lost.
Catherine. Dogger in service at Brest in 12.1691 and 9.1692. 60 or 70 tons, 10 men, no guns. Last mentioned 5.1693 at Brest.
Isabelle. Ketch (*caiche*) in service at Brest in 1.1692 and 9.1692 when described as old. 30 or 80 tons, 8 men, no guns. Struck 3.1693 at Brest.

Ex-ENGLISH MERCANTILE PRIZE (1696)

Bety. *Caiche* (ketch) captured 1696, ex-English *Bety* (probably *Betty*). Condemned 9.1697 at Brest, BU there 11.1699.

Doggers were the archetypal Dutch fishing craft (the large area of shallows in their North Sea fishing grounds is called the Dogger Bank). They had a single principal mast but also set a small auxiliary sail aft, which was useful in keeping the vessel's head to wind when fishing. Illustration by Guéroult du Pas.

This small Mediterranean pink (*pinque*) bears a family resemblance to many of the lateen-rigged types of the area. Pinks were usually differentiated from craft like *barques à voiles latines* by the narrow stern. They were normally used as commercial craft and were not designed to be rowed. Illustration by Guéroult du Pas.

Ex- DUTCH PRIZE (1702)

Dogre de Flessingue. Dogger built at Flushing captured 6–7.1702, ex-Dutch. Repaired at Le Havre 8–9.1702. 6 guns in 1702, 4 guns in 1703. Probably renamed *Subtile* in early 1703. Struck 11 or 12.1703 at Le Havre.

Ex-ENGLISH MERCANTILE PRIZE (1702).

The English *flibot* (flyboat) *Orange Tree* was captured in August 1702 by a French privateer and confiscated for the Navy in September 1702.

Dimensions & tons: 56ft 0in x 18ft 0in x 8ft 0in (18.19 x 5.85 x 2.60m). 50 tons. Draught 8ft (2.60m). Men: 12 in war, 8 peace
Guns: none.

Oranger England
Built 1688. Based at Le Havre. Struck 1706.

PURCHASED VESSELS (1707–1708)

Saint Jean. Pinque put into service at Toulon c.1707. Also called *Pinck Saint Jean*, simply called *La Pinck* in 1712. Last mentioned 1717 at Toulon.

Sainte Anne. Pinque in service at Toulon in 1708. Also called *Pinck Sainte Anne*. Last mentioned when loaned 1708 at Toulon for use as a privateer.

Saint François Xavier. Vessel of unknown type in service at Toulon in 1708. Last mentioned when loaned 1708 at Toulon for use as a privateer.

Espérance. One of three privateers that participated with four French warships in the capture of HMS *Salisbury* on 21 April 1703. 150 tons, 130 men, 12 to 20 guns. Commissioned 1708 as a *flûte* for Forbin's expedition to land James III Stuart ('the Old Pretender') in Scotland, returned to owner 4.1708. Captured 26.11.1710 by the British in the Antilles en route to Mississippi after a 7-hour fight.

MISCELLANEOUS PRIZES (1707–1710)

Comtesse de Forbin. Dogger or *quèche* captured 7.1707, ex-*Constance Galley* from Hamburg. 70 tons, 20/75 men + 1 officer, 8 to 10 guns + 4 *pierriers*. Turned over 12.1707 to CdE Claude, Comte de Forbin shortly after he returned to Brest with a captured British convoy. Chartered 3.1708 by the King as an exploration ship but the charter was cancelled 5.1708 and the ship was sold 7.1708 at Dunkirk.

Marianne. Caiche captured 5.1710, ex-Tunisian *Marianna*. Departed the Îles d'Hyères 29.3.1712 with the ships of the line *Neptune*, *Téméraire*, and *Rubis* and three frigates to raid British, Dutch, and Portuguese colonies in the Antilles. Returned to Toulon and on 11.3.1713 judged worth retaining there.

(D) Vessels acquired from 1 September 1715

Ex-RUSSIAN PRIZE (1734)

Moscovite. Ex-Russian galiote *Kars-Maker*, built 1723 at St Petersburg as the private galiote of Peter the Great and captured 5.1734 off Danzig. 9 men + 1 officer. Retaken 18.6.1734 by the Russians off Danzig, wrecked 12.9.1734 off Revel.

PURCHASED VESSELS (1744–1749)

Vierge. Caïque or quèche put into service at Toulon in 3.1744 and on 12.9.1744. 2 tons. Initially called *Caiche du Roi*, named *Vierge* 11.12.1744. Last mentioned 1.1745 as out of service at Brest.

Sibylle. Pinque put into service 7.1748 at Toulon. 5 tons. Last mentioned 8.1748 as out of service at Toulon.

Conception. Pinque put into service 10.1749 at Toulon. 3 tons. Fate unknown.

CÉSAR. Chatte pontée. Built in 1756–57 at Port d'Envaux by Augustin Pic and used at Rochefort.

Dimensions & tons: 75ft 0in x 20ft 0in x 10ft 0in (24.36 x 6.50 x 3.25m). 130/220 tons. Men: 12 +3 petty officers.
Guns: none.

César Port d'Envaux
K: 1756. L: 1756. C: 1757. Commissioning for use as a *patache de santé* (quarantine ship) 12.1770, located in the Île d'Aix roadstead 1.1771. Left Rochefort for sea 14.11.1781, last mentioned in 1784 as BU.

GRUË. Chatte, probably pontée (decked). Built at Rochefort in 1756 and last listed there 5.1768 with *César*, *Mouche*, and *Ours*, all of which were pontées.

Ex-BRITISH MERCANTILE PRIZE

Belette. Caiche built in Britain and captured 7.1758, ex-British *Weasel* (?). Last mentioned 2.1760 at Le Havre.

OURS. Chatte pontée. Launched 4.1768 at Rochefort and completed 5.1768. 180 or 230 tons burthen. In commercial use by Sr Raymon (?) 12.1770. In 1.1771 was considered better for coastal voyages than for port service. Sold 1784 at Bayonne and BU.

PURCHASED VESSELS (1758–1765)

Superbe. Polacre in service at Toulon in 1758. Fate unknown.
Saint Jacques. Polacre in service at Toulon in 1759. Fate unknown.
Saint Philippe. Polacre in service at Toulon in 1759. Fate unknown.
Languedocienne. Polacre chartered 1765, perhaps to carry troops to Corsica. Fate unknown.

MOUCHE. Chatte pontée. Launched at Rochefort 4.1768 and completed 5.1768. 120 tons burthen. Repaired 1771 at Rochefort and 1776 at Cayenne. Left Rochefort for sea 6.9.1781, last mentioned 2.1782.

PÉRINE. Chatte pontée. Under construction 9.1778 and in service by 1.1780. 100/200 tons (may have been the first of the *Paix* group, below). In good condition when last listed 11.1784.

Ex-BRITISH MERCANTILE PRIZES (1778–1779)

Intéressant. British cutter captured 24.10.1778 by *Neptune* (74) and *Glorieux* (74) and put into service 2.4.1779 at Brest as a transport. 41 men + 5 officers. Condemned 1.1781 at Grenada because of her bad condition.

Rosalie. Captured British *flûte* put into service 12.6.1779 at St Malo as a transport. 41/56 men + 1 to 5 officers. Recommissioned 7.1781 at Lorient, last mentioned 9.1783 at Pondicherry.

MICHELLE. Chatte pontée. Replaced an old 70-ton non-decked *Michel* in mid-1780. Originally not decked but after being re-launched 24.10.1781 after repairs and completion of work on her *plats bords* and *gaillards* she was listed with the *chattes pontées*.
  Dimensions & tons: 61ft 2in x 17ft x 9ft 3in (19.87 x 5.52 x 3.00m). 80/160 tons. Draught 4ft 11in/5ft 4in (1.60/1.73m).
  Guns: Probably none.
Michelle Rochefort
  In good condition when last listed 11.1784.

PURCHASED VESSELS (1780–1783)

Aimable Marie. Transport of unknown origin put into service 4.1.1780 at Brest. 10/14 men + 1 officer. Wrecked 2.1782 on the 'Île des Saints', either the Île de Sein off Brittany or the Saintes in the Antilles.

Septentrion. Transport of unknown origin put into service 11.8.1780 at Brest. 130 tons, 10/15 men + 1 officer. Removed from service at Brest in 1783 or 1784.

Guillaume Tell. Transport of unknown origin put into service 12.1781 at Brest. Captured 12.1781 or 1.1782 by the British off Brest.

Drack. Transport of unknown origin in service in 7.1783 in the Indian Ocean as a *Flûte du Roi*. Fate unknown.

Ex-BRITISH MERCANTILE PRIZE (1782)

Rose. British merchant vessel captured 6.1782 by the frigate *Surveillante* and put into service as a transport. 14 men + 1 officer. Removed from service 11.1784 at Morlaix and stricken after having served as a cartel ship.

ESPÉRANCE. Chatte pontée. Launched 17.1.1783 at Rochefort. Left Rochefort for St Pierre et Miquelon 5.1783, last mentioned 1787.

PAIX Class. Chattes pontées.
  Dimensions & tons: 62ft 0in x 19ft 6in x 9ft 9in (20.14 x 6.33 x 3.17m). 100/200 tons. Draught 8ft/8ft 3in (2.60/2.68m).
  Guns: probably none.
Paix Rochefort
  Built 1783. In good condition when last listed 11.1784.
Élisabeth Rochefort
  Launched 6.7.1784. In good condition when last listed 11.1784.
Sorcière (?)Rochefort
  First listed in 2.1784 as *No.1* in the early stages of construction at Rochefort, probably completed in 1785. Her name is not certain and her fate is unknown.

SUPPLY AND PATROL VESSELS.

This section contains two types that were sometimes used for coastal patrol and escort duties as well as carrying supplies. *Chasse-marées* (fishing or coasting luggers) were originally sturdy and fast vessels that brought freshly-caught fish to shore from the fishing grounds; their ample cargo holds also made them suitable for use as harbour service craft and many were so used. (Until 1990 the official plural form of *chasse-marée* was *chasse-marée*, we use the more recent *chasse-marées* which is also customary in English.) Sloops (*sloups*, *sloops* or *cheloupes*) were single-masted vessels used mostly as harbour service craft. Military *lougres* (luggers) and *côtres* (cutters) inherited some features from the humble *chasse-marées* and *sloops* respectively. Both the *chasse-marées* and *sloops* probably inherited their coastal resupply function from smaller harbour service craft like *bugalets*, vessels with two masts that transported passengers, powder, merchandise and provisions within naval harbours and along the coasts. One unusually large *bugalet* that was also used as a gunboat is included here.

Listed at the end of this section are *garde-côtes* (literally coast guard vessels), whose nominal function was coastal escort but whose configuration was not recorded. These were all purchased or captured, though some naval craft (listed in their original categories) were also assigned to coast guard duty. The list here is probably only a sampling of the local defence craft in use during the period of this book. Some local defence craft, possibly including some shown here, were probably not naval, being instead operated by local authorities.

(C) Vessels acquired from 15 April 1689

GAILLARDE Class. Chaloupes garde-côtes. These two vessels may not be sisters; alternatively they might both be sisters to *Prompte*, below.
  Dimensions & tons: dimensions unknown. 10 tons. Men: 32
  Guns: probably 1 small.
Gaillarde Toulon
  K: 6.1703. L: 7.1703. C: 7.1703. Last mentioned 1704 on the coast of Languedoc.
Jolie Toulon
  K: 1703. L: 12.1703. C: 12.1703. Last mentioned 1704 on the coast of Languedoc.

PROMPTE. Chaloupe garde-côtes or barque. Designed by François Coulomb.
  Dimensions & tons: 34ft 0in x 10ft 0in x 3ft 4in (11.04 x 3.25 x 1.08m). 10 tons. Men: 32
  Guns: probably 1 small.
Prompte Toulon
  K: 6.1703. L: 7.1703. C: 7.1703. Also called a *tartane*. Reduced to service craft at Toulon 1713. Last mentioned 1717.

Ex-ENGLISH MERCANTILE PRIZE (1703). An English vessel possibly named *Montserrat* was captured by the French in 1703 and used as a coast guard vessel. Her name was variously rendered by the French as *Montsarat*, *Montsara*, *Monsarrat*, and *Monserra*
  Dimensions & tons: 46ft 0in, 40ft 0in x 13ft 6in x 7ft 0in (14.94, 12.99 x 4.39 x 2.27m). 45 tons. Draught 8ft (2.60m). Men: 20 in war, 10 peace
  Guns: 4 in war (2 peace) 4 x 2pdrs.
Montsarat Britain
  Struck early 1707 at Brest.

(D) Vessels acquired from 1 September 1715

POSTILLON. Bugalet. Designed by Chapelle *fils* (probably Joseph-Véronique-Charles) and built in 1744 with the specifications shown below. In 1746 she was described as steering well and behaving well at sea. Reconfigured in 1748 at Toulon as a *chaloupe-canonnière* and still

The *bugalet* was another local type pressed into naval service, this one coming from Brittany and in particular the area round Brest. As Brest was the main base of the French *Ponant* fleet, it is not surprising that the local coaster was adopted for supply duties, carrying stores, water and victuals to warships lying in the roadstead. As depicted by Guéroult du Pas, they were substantial decked vessels, with two square-rigged masts and a topsail on the main.

listed as such in a register maintained at Toulon in the late 1750s and early 1760s, although no details of this configuration are available.
  Dimensions & tons: 48ft 0in x 14ft 0in x 6ft 6in (15.59 x 4.55 x 2.11m). 70 tons.
  Men: 20 in war, 6 peace
  Guns: (4 in war) 4 x 4pdrs.
Postillon Toulon
  K: 1.1744. L: 3.1744. C: 1744. Used as a *chaloupe-canonnière* (gunboat) from 1748 to the late 1750s, had reverted to a *bugalet* by 1761. Hulked 10.1762 at Toulon as a *corps de garde* (harbour guard station), condemned between 1766 and 1768 although remained in use as a *corps de garde*. Last mentioned 1778.

PURCHASED VESSELS (1744–1756)
Cerf Volant Chasse-marée launched 10.1747 at Lorient for the *Compagnie des Indes* and purchased from them 4.1770. 18 tons. Sold 9.1770 for commercial use.
Chargeur. Chasse-marée ponté launched 8.1756 at Lorient, for the *Compagnie des Indes* and purchased from them 4.1770. 28 or 40 tons, 8 men. Last mentioned 12.1770 at Lorient.

Ex-BRITISH MERCANTILE PRIZES (1757)
Anne. Sloop captured from the British and put into service 9.1757 at Brest. 9 men + 2 petty officers. Re-captured 10.1757 by the British. May have been called *Arme* or *Anne-Marie*.
Gloucester. Sloop captured 8.1757 from the British and put into service 9.1757 at Brest. 3 men. Out of service at Brest 11.1758, last mentioned 1759.

MARINGOUIN. Chasse-marée. Completed 11.1767, probably built at Rochefort. 20/25 tons. Re-rigged as a schooner 2.1768, was in Cayenne by mid-1769. Last mentioned 1770.

MARMOUTH. Bugalet built at Brest by Ollivier cadet and in service there 5.1768. According to Blaise Ollivier the *bugalet*s at Brest in 1736 measured 36ft x 10ft x 5ft or 5ft 6in (11.70 x 3.25 x 1.62/1.79m). Last mentioned 1771.

HERVÉ. Bugalet in service at Brest 5.1768. Last mentioned 1773.

PURCHASED VESSELS (1768–1771)
Oiseau. Chasse-marée ponté launched in early 7.1768 at Lorient for the *Compagnie des Indes* and purchased from them 4.1770. 46 tons, 8 men, 10 gunports. Listed from 7.1779 as a *chasse-marée [armé] en guerre* (fitted for combat) stationed at Belle-Île with *Belleislois* (below) as a coast guard vessel and armed with 2 x 12pdrs, 2 x 4pdrs, and 4 *pierriers*. From January 1783 also listed by Brest as one of its coastal supply ships. Last mentioned 4.1783 at Rochefort and 11.1783 at Brest.
Faucon. Chasse-marée ponté launched 7.1768 at Lorient for the *Compagnie des Indes* and purchased from them 4.1770. 40 tons, 8 men. Last mentioned 1770.
Épervier. Chasse-marée ponté launched in late 1769 at Lorient for the *Compagnie des Indes* and purchased from them 4.1770. 40 tons, 8 men. LP1770. Sister to *Oiseau* and *Faucon*. Last mentioned 1770.
Sainte Anne. Chasse-marée put into service 1.1771 at Brest. Last mentioned 2.1771, out of service.

CHASSE-MARÉES AT BREST. Between March 1777 and November 1778 a group of 30-ton *chasse-marées* appeared on the inventories of ships at Brest. These were used for coastal navigation in the vicinity of Brest and as far as Lorient or Nantes to bring supplies to Brest, and they also provided support within the port. The first four of these were built at Brest in two groups (the second pair repeating the names of two *chasse-marées* acquired from the *Compagnie des Indes* in 1770), one of the others was acquired and the origin of the other two is unclear. These were joined in mid-1783 by two *chasse-marées* from Lorient, *Oiseau* and *Belleislois*, that had been performing coast guard duty at Belle-Île until the end of the American war.
  Dimensions & tons: dimensions unknown. 30 tons. Men: 7/9, +1 petty officer.
  Guns: None.
Turbot Brest
  Built 11.1776, initially listed as *Chasse-marée No.1* and named 11.4.1777. Last mentioned 1789.
Cormoran Brest
  Built 11.1776, initially listed as *Chasse-marée No.2* and named 11.4.1777. Last mentioned 1789.
Faucon Brest
  K: 1778. L: 7.4.1778. C: 4.1778. Last mentioned 2.1783.
Épervier Brest
  K: 1.1778. L: 8.4.1778. C: 4.1778. Also called *Épervier No.2* in 1782, *Épervier No.1* being a corvette that was also at Brest. Captured 2.1783 by the British.
Marie-Françoise Rhuis (a town on the Oise River in northern France)
  Built in 1776, purchased 31.5.1778 at Brest. Last mentioned at Brest 1789.
Grondin Unknown
  Formerly named *Saint Esprit*, probably acquired, put into service 5.1778 at Brest. Last mentioned at Brest 1789.
Félicité Unknown
  In service as of 11.1778. Renamed *Fabuleux* in May 1795, last mentioned 9.1796 at Lorient.

SAINT FRANÇOIS. Chasse-marée. Launched 11.1778 at the Chantier du Blanc at Lorient just upriver from the naval dockyard and completed in 11.1778. 75 tons. Last mentioned 1789 in service at Brest.

BELLEISLOIS. Chasse-marée. Launched 4.1779 at Lorient and completed in 5.1779. 30 tons. Joined the acquired *Oiseau* (above) at the

The *chasse-marée* was rigged like a lugger but with smaller masts and sails in relation to hull size. Originating as coastal fishing craft and local traders in south Brittany, they also had a less refined and more capacious hull form than the luggers favoured as privateers and minor warships. Nevertheless, they showed some variety in size, with the smaller versions having only two masts and the larger ones capable of carrying a few guns. This is a large, and late, example from Baugean's *Receuil de Petites Marines*, published in 1819 (although many of his illustrations reflect earlier practice).

beginning of 1780 as a *chasse-marée [armé] en guerre* stationed at Belle-Île as a coast guard vessel and armed with 2 x 12pdrs, 2 x 4pdrs, and 4 *pierriers*. From January 1783 she was also listed by Brest as one of its coastal supply ships. Last mentioned 4.1783 at Rochefort, struck there 1784.

PURCHASED VESSEL (1779)
Sainte Anne. Chasse-marée of unknown origin put into service at Brest 7.1779. Used as a service craft and struck before 1783.

SAINT GUILLAUME or *Guillaume*. Chasse-marée. Built at Brest in 1784, last mentioned there 1789.

CHASSE-MARÉES AT CHERBOURG.
Twenty or more numbered *chasse-marées* of 90/150 tons were built in 1785 for use in the construction works at Cherbourg. These were initially service craft but some were armed during the 1790s. They are described in the 1786–1861 volume.

PURCHASED COAST GUARD VESSELS (1715–1783)
Marie-Anne. In use in 11–12.1715 at St Domingue. Seized 6.1716 by the British at Jamaica.
Princesse du Ciel. In use in 1716 at St Domingue. Seized 6.1716 by the British at Jamaica.
Sainte Marie. In use in 1716 at St Domingue. Seized 6.1716 by the British at Jamaica.
Surprenant. Put into service 11.1717 at St Domingue for service at Grenada. Last mentioned 12.1721 in the Antilles.
Saint Jacques. Pinque put into service 3.1719 at Toulon for coastal defence. 50 men + 3 officers. Probably removed from service 2.1720.
Saint Michel. Pinque put into service 3.1719 at Toulon for coastal defence. 50 men + 3 officers. Probably removed from service 2.1720.
Notre Dame du Paradis. Chaloupe chartered at Hennebont 11.1719 for coastal surveillance. Returned to her owner 3.1720.
États du Languedoc. Merchant vessel from Cette (Sète) put into service 10.1720 at Martinique. Returned to her owner 12.1720 or in 1721.
Triomphant. Purchased in Martinique 4.1722. Condemned there 11.1724 and last mentioned 1.1725. Also referred to under the generic name of *Bateau du Roi*.
Saint Esprit. Put into service in 1728 by the Chamber of Commerce of Marseille. Crew included 25 men and 1 officer from the King's navy. Last mentioned 6.1729 out of service.
Saint Michel. Purchased in Martinique 6.1735. Wrecked 2.1737 off Saint Lucia. Also called *Bateau du Roi*.
Soleil de Nantes. Put into service 6.1744 at Paimbeuf. 190/200 tons, possibly 20 guns + 10 *pierriers*. Last mentioned 8.1744.
Royal. Was in service at St Domingue in 1747. Last mentioned there 1748.
Entreprenant. Bateau probably put into service at Le Havre *c.*1749 for escort duty. Wrecked 4.1750 at La Hougue.
Province de Guyane. Purchased at Martinique, then put into service in French Guiana 11.1753. Returned to Martinique 9.1756, wrecked in a hurricane 10.1756.
Maréchal de Thomond. Frigate purchased and put into service by the Chamber of Commerce of Bordeaux. 250 tons, 87 men, 24 x 8pdrs + 12 *pierriers*. Fate unknown.
Notre Dame de Boulogne. Put into service at Dunkirk in 1757. Fate unknown.
Mélampe. Privateer frigate built at Bayonne and requisitioned in 1757. 500 tons, 320/400 men, 26 x 12pdrs + 10 x 6pdrs. Captured 2.11.1757 by HMS *Tartar* after a stiff fight and served as HMS *Melampe* until 1764.
Rostan. Privateer frigate built at Bordeaux and requisitioned in 10.1757. 460 tons, 320 men, 26 guns. Captured 3.2.1758 by HM Ships *Torbay* and *Chichester* and served as HMS *Crescent* until 1774.
Comte de Saint Florentin. 60-gun ship put into service 4.1758 by the Chamber of Commerce of Bordeaux. 800 tons, 463 men, LD 24 x 24pdrs, UD 26 x 12pdrs, QD/Fc 10 x 5pdrs. Captured 4.4.1759 by HMS *Achilles* off Cape Finisterre and served as HMS *Saint Florentine* until 1771.
Marquis de Marigny. Privateer frigate from Bordeaux chartered 4.1758. 350 tons, 130 men, 24 guns. Returned to her owners at Bordeaux 3.1759.

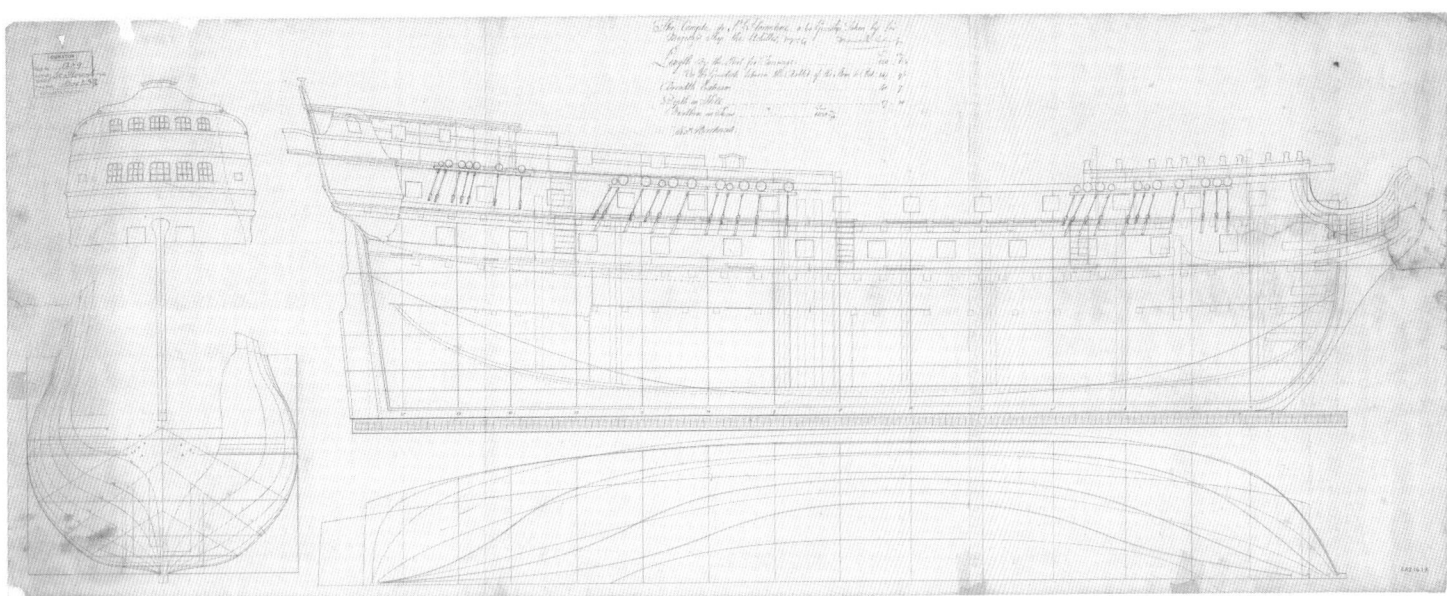

Admiralty draught of the *Comte de Saint Florentine*, undated but probably as captured. The origins of this small two-decker are obscure, as she was put into service by the Bordeaux Chamber of Commerce for local protection duties. (National Maritime Museum, London J3468)

Conquérant. Small privateer requisitioned 1758. 2 guns + 6 *pierriers*. Captured 8.1758 at Cherbourg by the British and burned.

Duc de Penthièvre. Privateer used in 1758 as a coast guard vessel at Cherbourg. Last mentioned 8.1758.

Duc de Choiseul. Frigate put into service at St Malo 5.1759. 32 guns. Returned to her owners 1761 after being in combat with the British in 10.1760.

Quatre Frères. Bordeaux merchant ship requisitioned at Quebec 5.1759. 500 tons, 10 guns (20 ports). Used as a stationary gun battery resting on the bottom for the defence of Quebec, lost there 9.1759.

Angélique. Bordeaux merchant ship requisitioned at Quebec 5.1759. 450 tons, 10 guns (18 ports). Used as a stationary gun battery resting on the bottom for the defence of Quebec, lost there 9.1759.

Trois Amis. Chasse-marée requisitioned 3.1760 at Vieille-Roche in the Vilaine. 43 men + 2 officers. Fitted as a bomb vessel with 1 x 8in mortar. Removed from service 4.1760 and probably returned to her owner.

Malice. Privateer corvette used in 5.1762 as a coast guard vessel at Le Havre. 60 tons, 60 men, 8 guns. Returned to her owner 8.1762.

Saint Louis. In service at Martinique in 1.1765. 42 men + 2 officers. Last mentioned in early 1773 at Martinique.

Gédéon. Put into service at Martinique in 5.1766. 25 men + 2 officers. Last mentioned in early 1773 at Martinique.

Surveillant. Acquired 11.1769, probably a Bordeaux merchant vessel. 23 men + 1 officer. Last mentioned in early 1773 at Martinique.

Grand Bourbon. The ship of the Governor of Île de France in 8.1773. Last mentioned 1774.

Bateau du Roi de la Colonie. In service 4.1774 at Guadeloupe and made two voyages from Guadeloupe to French Guiana in that year. Last mentioned 1774.

Superbe. Put into service 12.1778 at Cayenne, possibly requisitioned. Last mentioned 1779.

Judith. A small vessel chartered 4.1779 at Bordeaux and sent to French Guiana. In service at Cayenne in 7.1779 and at Martinique in 10.1783. Fate unknown.

Tourlourou. Boarding cutter in service in 1779 at Cherbourg. Lost 2.1781 when crushed against a naval *gabarre* in a squall in the Cherbourg roadstead.

Terrible. In service 10.1783 at Martinique. Fate unknown.

Saint Christophe. In service 10.1783 at Martinique. Fate unknown.

Aigle Royal. In service 10.1783 at Martinique. Fate unknown.

Ex-BRITISH MERCANTILE PRIZES (COAST GUARD, 1756–1783)

Trial. Captured from the British 8.1756 and placed in coast guard service at St Pierre de Martinique. Wrecked 10.1756 in a hurricane in the Antilles.

Entreprenant. Sloop captured in 1757 and placed in coast guard service 1757 at Le Havre. Fate unknown.

Henry. Ex-British *Henry* captured 1 or 2.1782 at Demerary. 8 x 4pdrs. Was in coast guard service 10.1783 at Martinique, fate unknown.

William. Ex-British *William*, in coast guard service 10.1783 at Martinique. Fate unknown.

YACHTS, *TRAVERSIERS*, AND *PAQUEBOTS*

Yacs, *iacs* or *yacks* (yachts), *traversiers* (ferries) and *paquebots* (packets) carried specialized cargo and personnel and generally operated in sheltered waters. The *yachts de port* at Rochefort were working, not luxury, craft that carried delicate cargoes, mainly gunpowder, munitions, and biscuits (hardtack) to the ships anchored out in the Île d'Aix roadstead. *Traversiers* typically crossed back and forth between two points on the shore while *paquebots* made somewhat longer voyages. Two of these obscure types are documented in monographs, a Rochefort yacht in *Le Rochefort* (1787) by Gérard Delacroix, and a *traversier* at Brest in *Le bateau de Lanvéoc* by Jean Boudriot and Hubert Berti.

(B) Vessels acquired from 9 March 1661

PURCHASED VESSEL
Illustre. Traversier. A letter of 15.8.1672 from the Intendant at Dunkirk indicated that the King's *traversier Illustre* had occasioned some expenses in England when accompanying the French fleet. No further information.

A '*jaq*' measuring 56ft x 14ft x 7ft built at Rochefort was in service there in 1674. These dimensions were very similar to those in use a century later.

Two *yacks* (yachts) were ordered 31.7.1680 to be built at Dunkirk but were probably cancelled *c*.9.1680.

MATROU and *SOUBISE*. 25 tons. Built at Rochefort and in service from 1687 to 1713 (*Matrou*) and 1692 (*Soubise*).

ROCHEFORT and *VERGEROUX*. 20 tons. Built at Rochefort and in service from 1687 to 1692.

(C) Vessels acquired from 15 April 1689

PURCHASED VESSELS (1690–1698)
Saint Hubert. Traversier acquired 1690 and in service at Brest on 16.6.1691 and 19.9.1692. 20 tons, 7 men, no guns. Last mentioned 5.1693 at Brest.

Biscayenne. Traversier purchased mid-1698, ex-Spanish. Built at Vizcaya. Last mentioned 9.1698.

Précieux. Traversier purchased mid-1698, probably built at La Rochelle. Renamed *Précieuse* 1699. Wrecked 1705 on Massacre Island, Louisiana (now Dauphin Island, Alabama).

Ten yachts, names unknown, were built at Rochefort between 1690 and 1704 and served until between 1700 and 1713.

Possibly the most appropriate modern translation of *traversier* would be 'ferry' since the usual definition suggests a craft sailing back and forth between fixed points, but judging by their employment in the French Navy, they were also used as tenders to large ships – one accompanied the French fleet to England in 1672, for example, while one Rochefort-built example crossed the Atlantic (surely accompanied by a larger vessel) to be wrecked in Louisiana in 1707. In this illustration by Guéroult du Pas the *traversier* is shown with a single square sail (one example also has a topsail) plus jibs; this is not a rig ideally suited for making long open-water crossings unescorted.

ESPÉRANCE. Traversier. Put into service 1701 at Rochefort and possibly built there 1700–1. Wrecked 8.1707 in a hurricane in Louisiana.

PAGE. Traversier.
  Dimensions & tons: 47ft 0in x 14ft 0in x 6ft 0in (15.27 x 4.55 x 1.95m). 40 tons. Men: 15
  Guns: none.
Page Rochefort
  Built in 1706. Described as 'good for nothing'. Struck 1707 at Toulon.

SUZANNE. *Paquebot* designed by Desjumeaux and built at Bayonne 1707–8. 70 tons, 14 men, 2 guns. Had the dimensions of a corvette. Ceded 1708 to Sr Forsant, wrecked 9.1713 at the entrance to the Loire River.

HEUREUX. *Traversier*. Was in service in Louisiana in 1714, may have been the *Barque Longue* built in 1702/1712 at Mobile by Le Roux (see Chapter 10). Crew reduced to 10 men in 1716, last mentioned 1717

Traversiers were also purchased for use as landing craft and bomb vessels during the raids against Cartagena de Indias in 1696–97 and Rio de Janeiro in 1711–12. These are listed with the bomb vessels in Chapter 7.

(D) Vessels acquired from 1 September 1715

ESPION. Yacht built at Rochefort in 1749. Struck 12.1770 at Rochefort. She is also reported as a British prize taken in 1756.

ROCHEFORT. Yacht built to a design by Blaise Geslain, who died in 1748. The dimensions below were taken from the draught of this ship preserved in the port archives at Rochefort.

In English usage 'packet' denoted a fast-sailing vessel, of no specific form or rig, that carried the mails and a few passengers between specific ports, often across oceans. The French *paquebot* (at least those in the service of the French Navy) seems to have been more restricted in its range. This illustration by Guéroult du Pas labelled a *paquebot* shows a vessel carrying the seventeenth century square ketch rig.

Dimensions & tons: 54ft 0in x 14ft 8in x 7ft 6in (17.54 x 4.76 x 2.44m). 60 tons.
Guns: none.
Rochefort Rochefort
   Built in 1750. In port service at Rochefort 12.1770 and 1.1771 with *Saint Louis* and *Saint Jean*. Rebuilt in 1775, see *Rochefort* class below.

PURCHASED VESSEL (1757)
Corbeau. Traversier put into service 1757 at Rochefort. Last mentioned 1757.

SAINT LOUIS. Yacht in service at Rochefort 1757 and probably built there 1756. 100 tons. In port service at Rochefort 12.1770 and 1.1771. A new *Saint Louis* reported laid down *c.*1769 at Rochefort and launched 1.1771 was probably this vessel rebuilt. Condemned by 1777, BU 1779–80.

SAINT JEAN. Yacht built at Rochefort 1755–56 by Augustin Pic and in service 8.1756. 60 tons. In commercial use by Sr Raymon (?) at Lorient 12.1770, back at Rochefort 1.1771 and last mentioned there 2.1771.

CORMORAN. Traversier built at Rochefort 1756–57 by Augustin Pic. Carried 4 x 4pdrs, two firing forward and two firing aft. Last mentioned 5.1759 in service at Rochefort.

ROCHEFORT Class. Yachts. This class consists of the *Rochefort* of 1750 rebuilt, a new vessel, and a replacement for the condemned *Saint Louis*. Specifications probably similar to the *Rochefort* of 1750.
Rochefort Rochefort.
   Rebuilt 1775. In good condition 3.1777 and when last listed 11.1784. BU 1786 and replaced 1787 by a similar *Rochefort* designed by Hubert Pennevert.
Camille Rochefort.
   K: 3.1777. L: 12.1777. C: early 1778. Needed routine repairs when last listed 11.1784.
Saint Louis Rochefort.
   K: 1779. L: 23.12.1779. C: 1780. In good condition when last listed 11.1784.

YACHT DE LA REINE. Luxury yacht built 1785 at Paris or St Cloud. Sold at Paris 2.1793.

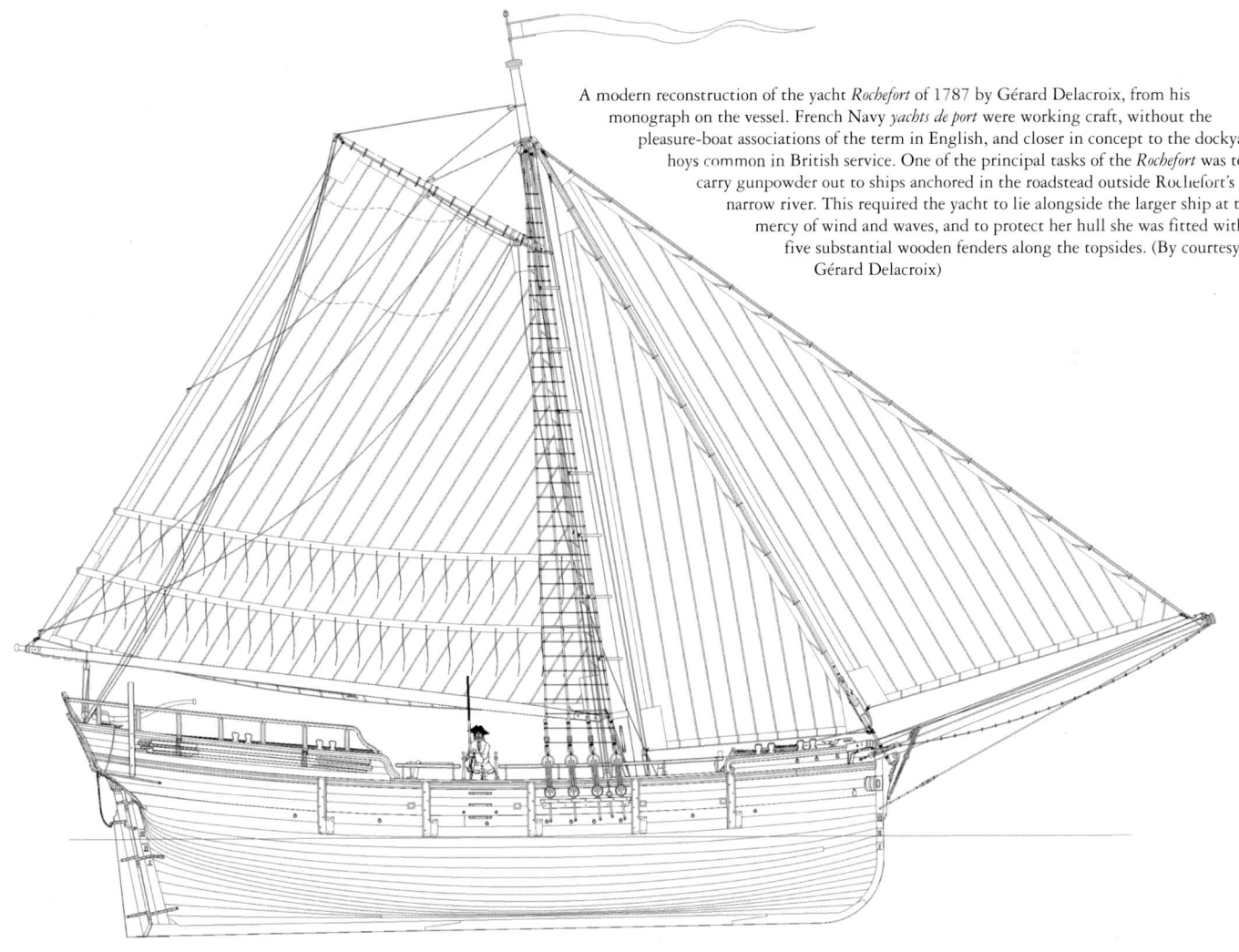

A modern reconstruction of the yacht *Rochefort* of 1787 by Gérard Delacroix, from his monograph on the vessel. French Navy *yachts de port* were working craft, without the pleasure-boat associations of the term in English, and closer in concept to the dockyard hoys common in British service. One of the principal tasks of the *Rochefort* was to carry gunpowder out to ships anchored in the roadstead outside Rochefort's narrow river. This required the yacht to lie alongside the larger ship at the mercy of wind and waves, and to protect her hull she was fitted with five substantial wooden fenders along the topsides. (By courtesy of Gérard Delacroix)

Addendum: The Galley Corps

(Corps des galères)

The French galley fleet has to be considered separately from the French maritime defence establishment because, until 30 September 1748 (when an *ordonnance* to merge the separate service with the *Levant* Fleet was issued), the galley fleet did not form part of the French Navy *per se*, but formed an independent body – the Galley Corps – under its own command structure. Consequently, this summary of the galleys' construction and organisation is provided as an Addendum rather than as a Chapter of this volume. Note that, in French, the expression '*les galères de la Religion*' referred not to French galleys but to the galleys of the sovereign Order of St John (the Knights of Malta).

The office of *Général des galères* (General of the Galleys), was held consecutively from 1572 by five members of the *Maison de Gondi* – Albert, Charles, Charles II, Philippe-Emmanuel and Pierre II – until March 1635, when Armand du Plessis, Cardinal and Duc de Richelieu, the King's *Principal Ministre*, compelled Pierre Gondi to sell (for 560,000 *livres*) the office of the *Généralat* to his nephew Francois de Vignerod, Marquis de Pont de Courlay.

That was the second step of Richelieu's long-term plan which aimed to give the Crown full authority over all the means of maritime defence. This followed his own appointment, ten years earlier in 1626, to the post specially created for him of *Grand-Maître, Chef et Surintendant de la Navigation et Commerce de France*. At the same time, to extend his authority over all of the regional admiralties, notably the one of Brittany, the King appointed him as Governor of that province.

The third step occurred on 17 February 1636 when, again with Louis XIII's approval, Richelieu merged the offices of *Général des galères* and *Grand-Maître* in his own hands. Discontented with that solution, in 1639 he split them again, retaining the *Grande-Maîtrise* when giving the *Généralat* and the '*survivance*' (right to inherit) of the *Grande-Maîtrise* to another nephew, Jean-Armand Maillé, Marquis de Brézé who, sadly, died in action at Orbitello in 1646.

The *Généralat* passed then to Pont de Courlay's son, Armand Jean de Vignerod du Plessis, who held it until July 1661, when it was purchased (for 200,000 *livres*) by Nicolas Fouquet who conferred it on François de Blanchefort, Marquis de Créqui. Following Fouquet's arrest on 5 September 1661 and his subsequent downfall, Créqui was rapidly deprived of his office and banished; on 3 March 1669, he finally resigned and sold the *Généralat* for 700,000 *livres* (note the variations in the value of this office!) to Louis-Victor de Rochechouart, Duc de Mortemart et de Vivonne, brother of Françoise Athénaïs de Rochechouart de Mortemart, Marquise de Montespan. In 1688, Vivonne conferred the *Généralat* on his own nephew, Louis-Auguste de Bourbon, Duc du Maine, a legitimised son of Louis XIV and his favourite. The subsequent holders were: in 1694, Louis-Joseph de Bourbon, Duc de Vendôme; in 1712, René-Mans de Froulay, Maréchal de Tessé, who resigned in 1716; and then Jean-Philippe, Grand Prieur d'Orléans (the legitimised son of the Regent), who died in office on 16 June 1748. Three months after Orleans' death (during which the post was left vacant), the Galley Corps was merged into the French Navy and the office superseded.

The Royal Standard for the Galley Corps was red, adorned with fleurs-de-lys with the coat of arms of France surrounded by the necklaces of the King's two honorific orders, the one of the Holy Spirit (*Ordre du Saint Esprit*) and the other of Saint Michel. The ranks of the officers of the Galley Corps (and their equivalent to ranks in the Navy) were as follows: *Lieutenant général des galères* (LGGal / LG), *Chef d'escadre des galères* (CdEGal / CdE), *capitaine de galère* (CGal / CV), *lieutenant de galère* (LGal / LV) and *enseigne de galère* (EGal / EV). In the early 1690s, the budget of the Galley Corps was about a tenth of that of the Navy. In 1692, two offices of *trésorier général des galères* were established, at 353,000 *livres* each.

Essentially there were two categories of galley: the **galères ordinaires**, which comprised the bulk of the force, and the **galères extraordinaires**, which served as flagships for the galley squadrons. The latter came in two varieties – the 'Réale', which was the flagship of the *Général des galères*, and the 'Patronne', which served the same function for the *Lieutenant-Général des galères*; these words were usually used as the vessels' names. Throughout this Addendum, a vessel is a *galère ordinaire* except where expressly described as a *galère extraordinaire*. Unlike classical times, all these galleys were monoremes, with a single level of benches, each bench responsible for one oar per side.

Unlike sailing warships, for which the designs tended to grow over the years, the dimensions of the ordinary galley remained very constant over the period covered by this book. As the design had been established in past centuries, the standard galley in French service comprised 26 benches per side, each of five oarsmen pulling on a single oar or sweep. Each bench, carved from a solid length of pine, measured 7ft in length by 6in in width and was 5in thick (2.28m x 16cm x 14cm). It was covered in old material tied up to form a cushion. One of the benches – the ninth row from the bow on the port side – was replaced by the galley's stove (*fougon*) – so that the galley had 51 oars in use rather than 52 (although enough oarsmen were aboard to man 52 oars – or 260 in all); thus in the entries throughout this Addendum the number of rows is generally described as 25/26. Given the length of two benches abreast of each other, there was room for only a narrow centerline gangway (the *coursier*) between them, and each oarsman had a space of about 16½ inches in width in which to sit.

The oarsmen came from three sources: volunteers (*bonevoglies*); prisoners of the 'Barbary' coast – depending on the treaties signed with the Dey of Algiers, the Bey of Tunis or the king of Morocco; and the various categories of convicts. According to criminal law, the '*peine des galères*', sometimes for life, was indeed a corporal and defamatory punishment covering a wide range of crimes, including some under civil law (salt smuggling, begging, etc), some under military law (desertion, service for another country, etc) and some under religious law (profaning the consecrated Host or, after 1685, being an adherent of the *Religion Prétendue Réformée* or RPR). After the return of the squadron that raided Cartagena de Indias, the *intendant* at Brest, Hubert de Champy, Seigneur Desclouzeaux, wrote to Louis de Pontchartrain, the Secretary of State for the Navy, to report that he was amazed that CdE Jean-Bernard de Saint-Jean, Baron de Pointis, had not experienced more disciplinary problems with his men and added '*aucun n'a été condamné aux galères*'.

As the number of volunteers declined over the years (the volunteers were shackled in the same manner as the other categories), the preponderance increasingly came from the latter two categories. Of the five oarsmen on a bench, the physically strongest was seated nearest to the centerline and was the leader (*vogue-avant*) of the five – the whole group chained together being labelled a *brancade* (the name also of the many-

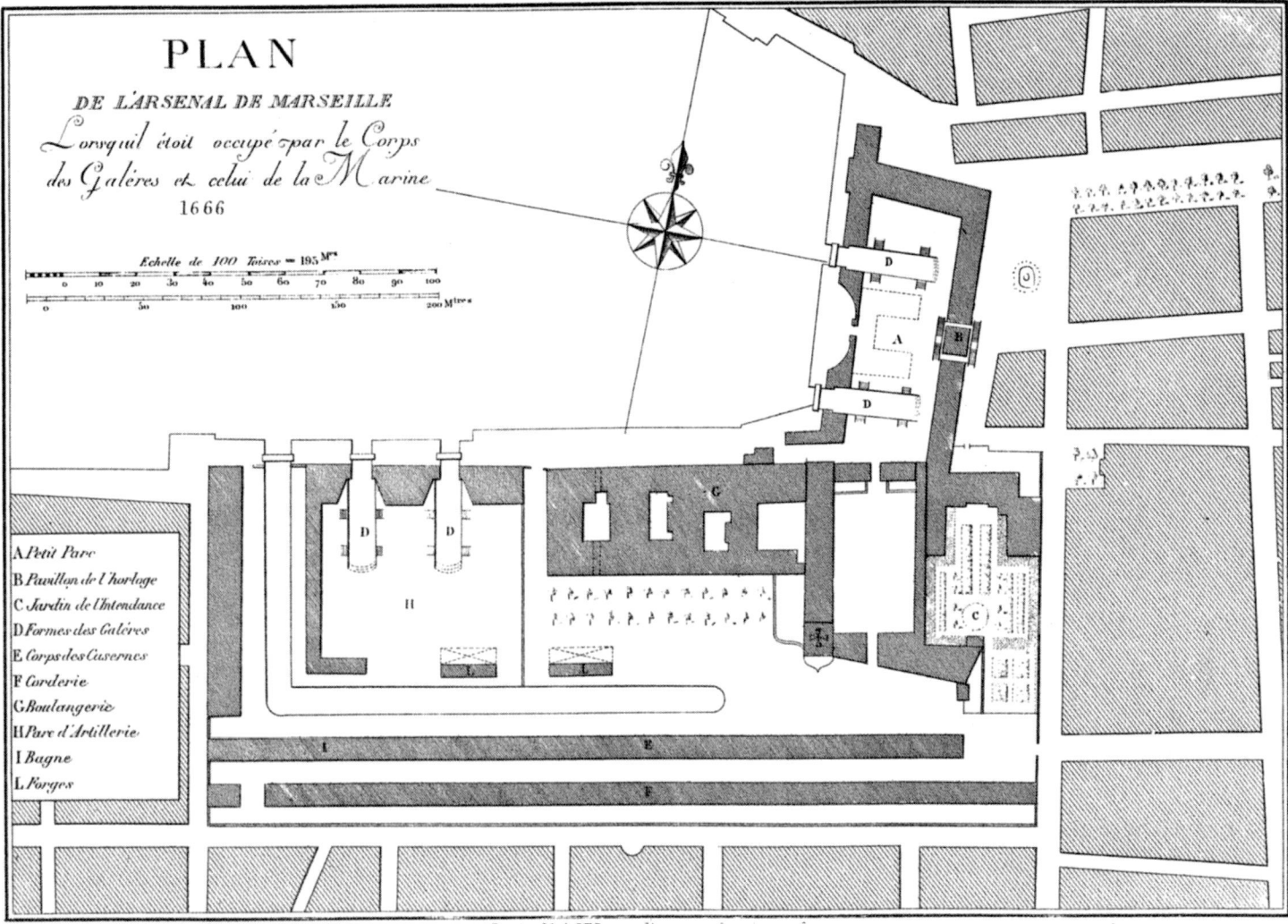

Plan of the Arsenal at Marseille, purpose-built as the headquarters of the Galley Corps after it was transferred from Toulon to Marseille in 1665. The galleys moored in a row abreast with their sterns to the quay wall above the top of the image. The harbour office of the Arsenal – the *Capitainerie des galères* – survives to this day; it is now an Etap hotel. (*Souvenirs de Marine*, Plate 310)

branched chain to which oarsmen's shackles were secured); the other four, who had to follow the *vogue-avant*'s stroke, were chosen so that the most powerful were towards the centreline, with diminishing strength required from the others; their positions were consecutively labelled the *apostis*, *tiercerol*, *quarterol* and *quinterol* (the latter closest to the galley's side). The pair of *vogue-avants* closest to the prow (the *conillers*) and the pair closest to the poop (the *espaliers*) had special responsibilities – the latter setting the pace or stroke for the whole vessel.

The *galères extraordinaires* were necessarily larger and longer; the *réale* had seven men on each bench forming a *brancade*, and the *patronne* had six men, and they usually had 30 rows of oars (again, one fewer on the side where the stove was placed). Their oars were similarly longer – typically 44ft (14.3m) compared with the 37ft 8.5in (12.25m) of a *galère ordinaire*. The cutting of oars, from beech, was a specialized trade; as with timber for ship construction, the oar-maker (*rémolat*) left the 'blank' cut wood, taken from the thickest part of the tree trunk, to dry out before working on it; it had to be shaped so that the thickest part of the oar was inboard, in order that the weight was balanced at the fulcrum or thole.

All galleys carried a similar armament of heavy guns, all carried on the foredeck and firing forward. The heaviest, traditionally a 36pdr (called the *coursier*, thus bearing the same name as the vessel's central gangway), was mounted on the centreline, and was flanked by on each side by an 8pdr (known as the *moyenne*) and usually also by a 6pdr or 4pdr (the *batarde*); a number of light guns (*pierriers*) – usually about a dozen – could be mounted on stocks along the sides. In October 1695, LG Sébastien Le Prestre, Marquis de Vauban, suggested replacing the main guns by one 36pdr *coursier* of 10 to 12 feet in length and two 18pdr *moyennes* of 8 feet in length.

(A) Vessels acquired before 9 March 1661

The precise details of galleys built prior to 1661 are somewhat uncertain, as ordinary galleys were not usually given a name of their own, but generally were known by the name of their appointed commander. As a result, the same galley may appear under a number of names, while conversely one name may cover a number of different galleys. Thus, as Jan Glete has emphasised (see Bibliography), contemporary French archives give contradictory details as to whether a galley is new, reconstructed, or renamed, and any calculation of numbers (both as regards constructions and strengths in service) is highly uncertain. The following section is believed to provide a record of known galleys built for France (all at Marseille unless otherwise indicated below) or acquired by her, but the precise details must remain problematic.

During the early part of the sixteenth century, France maintained a sizeable galley fleet in the Mediterranean, comparable with that of Hapsburg Spain. However, the Italian wars, and the Wars of Religion during the latter decades of the century, resulted in the destruction of French naval strength, and in particular the total disappearance of the royal galley fleet by the time that Henri IV established the Bourbon Dynasty in 1589.

A modest revival began around 1600, and by 1610 a dozen new vessels had been acquired – the *galères extraordinaires* listed as *Réale* and *Régine* (both launched in 1608, the latter probably being the 'Patronne' of its day) and ten *galères ordinaires*. However, a further decline then set in, and over the next few decades Marseille and other Mediterranean ports sought the protection of galley squadrons provided by local entrepreneurs. It is easier to treat the two categories separately during the next 50 years.

A new *Réale* was built at Marseille from 1618 to July 1620, when it replaced the 1610 vessel of that name. Both in turn were commanded by Philippe-Emmanuel de Gondi, Comte de Joigny. The 1620 *Réale* in turn was replaced by a new vessel of that name in 1628, which lasted until a further *Réale* was built in 1650.

In 1626 Richelieu proposed the creation of a fleet of forty galleys. When the naval threat from Spain to the coasts of Provence and Languedoc grew in the mid-1630s, he came up with a practical scheme to raise the number from the existing level of less than a dozen to twenty, with fresh orders placed in November 1634. By 1635 seven new galleys were brought into service. Gondi's three galleys came under Richelieu's control with the change in *Général des galères* – the *Réale*, *Patronne* and *Contine*. The new galleys built were the *Cardinalle* and *Richelieu* (both begun in March 1635 as the personal property of Richelieu), *Séguirane*, *Forbine*, *Servianne*, *Mazergue* and *Cabries*. Two more were built in 1636 – the *Valbelle* and *Montréale* – to reach the target of twenty. This total was approximately maintained, chiefly by rebuilding, over the next quarter-century.

In February 1660 Louis XIV inspected the galleys at Toulon with the Duc de Richelieu, saw that some of them were 'entirely ruined', and struck eleven of them, keeping only nine. The construction of eight replacements was ordered and the *maître constructeur* Chabert *père* was recalled from Malta for this purpose by a letter dated 16 February 1660. The eleven galleys struck (*cassées*) in February 1660 were *Réale, Patronne, Cardinale, Pillière, Ducale, Allemagne, Manse, Bailliebauilt, Sainte Marie, Bois d'Arnas*, and *Villeneuve*. The ones retained were *Régine, Mazarine, Marquise, Fiesque, Princesse, Grimaldi, Collongue, Vendôme*, and *Montoliéu*.

(B) Vessels acquired from 9 March 1661

As part of Colbert's drive to improve France's maritime security, dependence on entrepreneurs was terminated, and the galleys brought under state control. Numbers had declined since the *Fronde* period, and by 1660 there were only some fifteen galleys in existence. By March 1661 only ten remained, of which six were in service. A period of rebuilding began which saw a doubling of the overall strength in the Mediterranean, so that by 1689 there were some three dozen in use. Although galley-building was undertaken by a few specialist constructors, notable the Chabert family at Toulon and subsequently at Marseille, details of the changes in design are unknown and the early vessels below are grouped according to known dimensions as well as by builders. The numbers of oars quoted below reflects the difference between the port and starboard banks, so that there was always an odd number of oars.

SAINT LOUIS Group. Designed and built at Toulon by Chabert *père* (except *Victoire* and *Fortune* by Simon Chabert and *Saint Dominique* by Pierre Hubac). 25/26 rows of oars.

Dimensions & tons: 141ft 0in, 115ft 6in x 17ft 6in x 6ft 11in (45.80, 37.52 x 5.68 x 2.25m). 200 tons. Draught 5½ft/6ft (1.79/1.95m). Men: 130, +4 officers and 260 oarsmen.

Guns: 1 x 36pdr forward, flanked by 2 x 8pdrs and 2 x 6pdrs; also 12 *pierriers*.

Saint Louis Toulon.
K: early 1661. L: 1661 or 1662. C: 4.1662. Struck 1674.
France Toulon.
K: 8.1662. L: 12.1662. C: 1663. Condemned and hulked 1675 at Marseille, renamed *Vieille France* 1675.
Vendôme Toulon.
K: 10.1662. L: 11.5.1663. C: 5.1663. Renamed *Couronne* 1665. Struck 1675 and BU.
Victoire Toulon.
K: 5.1663. L: 19.1.1664. C: 3.1664. Condemned 1673.
Saint Dominique Toulon.
K: 6.1663. L: 2.3.1665. C: 4.1666. Renamed *Ferme* 8.1671. Condemned 1675 at Marseille and BU 1676.
Renommée Toulon.
K: 7.1664. L: 15.3.1665. C: 6.1665. Condemned 1676 at Marseille.
Fortune Toulon.
K: 7.1664. L: 3.1665. C: 4.1666. Renamed *Heureuse* 8.1671. Condemned 1676 at Messina.

DAUPHINE Group. Somewhat smaller galleys built at Toulon by Chabert *père*, with one fewer oar on each side. The *Fleur de Lys* was ordered and named on 17 October 1662.

Dimensions & tons: 135ft 0in, 110ft 0in x 17ft 6in x 6ft 0in (43.85, 35.73 x 5.68 x 1.95m). 180 tons. Men: 130, +4 officers and 250 oarsmen.

Guns: 1 x 36pdr forward, flanked by 2 x 8pdrs and 2 x 6pdrs; also 10 or 12 *pierriers*.

Dauphine Toulon.
K: late 1661. L: 8.1662. C: 10.1662. Condemned and hulked 9.1671 at Marseille. Renamed *Fidèle* 1672.
Fleur de Lys Toulon.
K: 1.1663. L: 17.5.1663. C: 5.1663. Condemned and struck 1674 at Marseille.

RÉALE DE FRANCE. Galère extraordinaire, designed and built by Chabert *père*. Ordered in 1661 and originally named *Capitaine* as the flagship of the *Capitaine général des galères de France*, but renamed *Réale de France* or *Réale* in 1662 as flagship of the *Général des galères*. Luxuriously appointed, with marquetry flooring and gold-covered sculptures, this served as the flagship of LG Jean Despincha, Marquis de Ternes, for the 1663 operation against North African corsair ports. 28/29 rows of oars.

Dimensions & tons: 157ft 0in, 130ft 0in x 19ft 0in x 6ft 5in (51.00, 42.23 x 6.17 x 2.08m). 250 tons. Draught 7ft (2.27m).

Guns: 1 x 36pdr forward, flanked by 2 x 8pdrs and 2 x 6pdrs; also 14 *pierriers*.

Réale de France Toulon.
K: end 1661. L: 6.1662. C: 4.1663. Condemned 1667, but possibly became the *Sovereign*.

In addition to the foregoing, two galleys were purchased on the stocks at Genoa in early 1663, both having been begun in September 1662. The *Croix de Malte* of 200 tons (with 25/26 rows of oars) was purchased in January 1663 and launched in the same month, while the *Saint Jean*

Baptiste (or *Saint Jean*) of 180 tons (with 24/25 rows of oars) was purchased on 27 March and launched on 25 April 1663. They were renamed *Souveraine* and *Thérèse* respectively in August 1671. In January 1673 the *Thérèse* became a hospital vessel at Marseille; she was struck and BU during 1676. The *Souveraine* was condemned and BU in 1674. Alternatively an otherwise unrecorded galley named *Saint Jean* that was hulked around 1673 at Marseille and struck and BU there in 1691 may have been the 1663 *Saint Jean Baptiste*.

RÉGINE. Galère extraordinaire, designed and built by Chabert *père* and/or Pierre Hubac. The *Régine* was probably equivalent to the later *Patronne* as the flagship of the *Lieutenant général des galères*.

Dimensions & tons: dimensions unknown. 230 tons. Men: 105, +4 officers and 392 oarsmen (in 1669).

Guns: 1 x 36pdr forward, flanked by 2 x 8pdrs and 2 x 6pdrs; also 14 *pierriers*.

Régine Toulon.
K: 28.5.1663. L: 13.12.1663. C: 12.1663. Renamed *Patronne* or *Patronne de France* 4.1666. Condemned 9.1671 at Marseille and struck 1680.

In August 1663 a squadron of galleys under LG Jean Despincha, Marquis de Ternes, was deployed against corsair bases on the North African ('Barbary') coast, returning to Toulon on 10 October. The squadron comprised the galleys *Réale*, *Vendôme*, *Saint Dominique*, *Dauphine* and *Fleur de Lis*, plus the older *Saint Jean* (built 1655–56 as the *Collongue* and renamed 1660).

FORCE Group. Designed and built by Simon Chabert (*Force*, *Brave* and *Grande*), Pierre Hubac (*Valeur* and *Thérèse*) and Chabert *père* (*Duchesse Royale*). 25/26 rows of oars. The first three were all begun in April 1666, but their construction was then suspended from November 1666 until July 1667. The first five were all given names on 10 September 1668. The *Valeur*, *Brave* and *Grande* all wintered at Messina 1677–78.

Dimensions & tons: 141ft 0in, 115ft 6in x 17ft 6in x 6ft 11in (45.80, 37.52 x 5.68 x 2.25m). 200 tons. Draught 5½ft/6ft (1.79/1.95m). Men: 130, +4 officers and 260 oarsmen.

Guns: 1 x 36pdr forward, flanked by 2 x 8pdrs and 2 x 6pdrs; also 10 or 12 *pierriers*.

Force Marseille.
K: 4.1666. L: 1.1668. C: 4.1668. Renamed *Forte* 1673. Hulked 1677 at Marseille, and BU *c*.1679.

Valeur Marseille.
K: 4.1666. L: 1.1668. C: 4.1668. Condemned 1679 at Marseille and replaced.

Thérèse Marseille.
K: 4.1666. L: 1.1668. C: 4.1668. Condemned 1677 at Marseille and BU

Galante Marseille.
K: 1668. L: 1669. C: 1669. Condemned 1675 at Marseille and BU.

Duchesse Royale Marseille.
K: 1668. L: 5.1669. C: 1669 or 1670. Renamed *Hardie* 8.1671. Condemned 1678.

Brave Marseille.
K: 1669. L: 12.1670. C: 3.1671. Condemned 1679 at Marseille and replaced.

Although galleys lost their position as the ultimate arbiters of sea power to the ship of the line during the seventeenth century, in one particular area of operations they retained a tactical advantage – coastal land attacks. Galleys were of very shallow draught, highly manoeuvrable and carried powerful forward-firing guns that could give close support to amphibious landings. However, they could only operate safely where they were free from possible intervention by the greater firepower of a sailing battlefleet. This was why, for example, the French used galleys to raid Teignmouth in August 1690 after the Battle of Beachy Head: it had no tactical significance but was a humiliating demonstration of the strategic reality that the Anglo-Dutch allies had lost control of the Channel. This French engraving illustrates the use of galleys in one such 'littoral warfare' scenario – in support of the Duc de Vivonne's siege of Scaletta Zanclea (which surrendered in November 1676) during the French intervention in Sicily. (Beverley R Robinson Collection, Annapolis 51.7.66)

Grande Marseille.
>K: 1669. L: 12.1670. C: 3.1671. Condemned 1679 at Marseille and replaced.

CAPITANE. Galère extraordinaire, designed and built by Jean-Baptiste Chabert.
>Dimensions & tons: 154ft 0in, 131ft 0in x 20ft 0in x 7ft 6in (50.03, 42.55 x 6.50 x 2.44m). 230 tons. Draught 6ft/6½ft (1.95/2.11m). Men: 130, +7 officers and 280 (later 305) oarsmen.
>Guns: 1 x 36pdr forward, flanked by 2 x 8pdrs and 2 x 6pdrs; also 14 *pierriers*.

Capitane Marseille.
>K: 1667. L: 29.5.1668. C: 7.1668. Renamed *Capitane du Marquis de Centurion* 7.1670, then *Dauphine* 12.1671. Struck 1680 at Marseille.

RÉALE. Galère extraordinaire, designed and built by Chabert *père*.
>Dimensions & tons: 170ft 0in, 135ft 0in x 21ft 0in x 8ft 0in (55.22, 43.85 x 6.82 x 2.60m). 270 tons. Draught 7ft 10in (2.55m). Men: 160, +7 officers and 410 oarsmen.
>Guns: 1 x 36pdr forward, flanked by 2 x 8pdrs and 2 x 6pdrs; also 16 *pierriers*.

Réale Marseille.
>K: 3.1668. L: 12.1668. C: 6.1669. Renamed *Grande Réale* 1678, and hulked at Marseille. Replaced by new *Réale* 1691 at Marseille.

CAPITANE DU MARQUIS DE CENTURION. Galère extraordinaire, designed and built by Pierre Hubac. 25/26 rows of oars.
>Dimensions & tons: 170ft 0in, 135ft 0in x 21ft 0in x 8ft 0in (55.22, 43.85 x 6.82 x 2.60m). 270 tons. Men: 145, +8 officers and 360 oarsmen.
>Guns: 1 x 36pdr forward, flanked by 2 x 8pdrs and 2 x 6pdrs; also 16 *pierriers*.

Capitane Toulon.
>K: 6.1670. L: 4.1671. C: 5.1671. Renamed *Réale Neuve* 1673. Rebuilt as *Réale* 1678–79 at Marseille.

PATRONNE DU MARQUIS DE CENTURION. Galère extraordinaire, designed and built by Pierre Hubac.
>Dimensions & tons: 170ft 0in, 135ft 0in x 21ft 0in x 8ft 0in (55.22, 43.85 x 6.82 x 2.60m). 270 tons. Men: 130, +7 officers and 290 (later 360) oarsmen.
>Guns: 1 x 36pdr forward, flanked by 2 x 8pdrs and 2 x 6pdrs; also 14 *pierriers*.

Patronne Toulon.
>K: 7.1670. L: 6.1671. C: 9.1671. Named shortened to *Patronne* 8.1672 when the King terminated his contract with the Marquis de Centurion to operate galleys. Struck 1680 at Marseille.

BELLE Group. Designed and built by Pierre Hubac and Chabert *père* respectively. 25/26 rows of oars. Precursors of the numerous galleys built from late 1671 until 1676, which all appear to have been built to the same design (with the sole exception of the slightly smaller *Madame* below).
>Dimensions & tons: 141ft 9in, 118ft 6in x 16ft 6in x 7ft 1in (46.55, 38.49 x 5.36 x 2.30m). 200 tons. Men: 175, +3 officers and 260 oarsmen.
>Guns: 1 x 36pdr forward, flanked by 2 x 8pdrs and 2 x 6pdrs; also 10 or 12 *pierriers*.

Belle Marseille.
>K: 12.1670. L: 4.1671. C: 5.1671. Condemned 1679 at Marseille and replaced.

Favorite Marseille.
>K: 12.1670. L: 1671. C: 1672. Condemned 1679 at Marseille and replaced.

MADAME. Designed and built by Jean-Bapiste Chabert, slightly shorter and broader than the 'standard' design of the 1670s and with one fewer pair of oars.
>Dimensions & tons: 139ft 0in, 118ft 6in x 17ft 6in x 6ft 6in (45.15, 38.49 x 5.68 x 2.11m). 190 tons. Men: 130, +4 officers and 250 oarsmen.
>Guns: 1 x 36pdr forward, flanked by 2 x 8pdrs and 2 x 6pdrs; also 10 or 12 *pierriers*.

Madame Marseille.
>K: 10.1671. L: 3.1672. C: 4.1672. Out of service 12.1679 at Marseille.

PRINCESSE Group (1671–1676 orders). Designed and built by Jean-Baptiste Chabert ('Chabert jeune'), Simon Chabert and Pierre Hubac (as indicated below), these all appear to have been built to the same design. 25/26 oars.
>Dimensions & tons: 141ft 9in, 118ft 6in x 16ft 6in x 7ft 1in (46.55, 38.49 x 5.36 x 2.30m). 200 tons. Men: 175, +3 officers and 260 oarsmen.
>Guns: 1 x 36pdr forward, flanked by 2 x 8pdrs and 2 x 6pdrs; also 10 or 12 *pierriers*.

Princesse Marseille (J-B Chabert).
>K: 10.1671. L: 3.1672. C: 4.1672. Condemned 1679 at Marseille and replaced.

Invincible Marseille (J-B Chabert).
>K: early 1673. L: 9.1673. C: 3.1674. Struck 1679 at Marseille and replaced.

Perle Marseille (Pierre Hubac).
>K: early 1673. L: 9.1673. C: 1674. Condemned 1682 at Marseille and replaced.

Reine Marseille (J-B Chabert).
>K: 9.1673. L: 11.1674. C: 1674. Struck early 1679 at Marseille and replaced.

Sirène Marseille (Simon Chabert).
>K: 9.1673. L: 11,1674. C: 1674. Struck late 1681 at Marseille and replaced.

Superbe Marseille (J-B Chabert).
>K: 1673. L: 12.1674. C: 4.1675. Struck 1679 at Marseille and replaced.

Fleur de Lys Marseille (Pierre Hubac).
>K: 9.1674. L: 12.1674. C: 4.1675. Struck early 1682 at Marseille and replaced.

Victoire Marseille (Simon Chabert).
>K: 9.1674. L: 12.1674. C: 4.1675. Struck 1681 at Marseille and replaced.

Fidèle Marseille (Pierre Hubac).
>K: 12.1674. L: 1675. C: 3.1676. Struck 1687 at Marseille and replaced.

Fortune Marseille (Simon Chabert).
>K: 12.1674. L: 1675. C: 3.1676. Struck 1681 at Marseille and replaced.

Amazone Marseille (J-B Chabert).
>K: 12.1674. L: 2.1676. C: 4.1676. Struck 1687 at Marseille and replaced.

France Marseille (Simon Chabert).
>K: 1675. L: 1675. C: 3.1676. Struck 1684 at Marseille and replaced.

Galante Marseille (Pierre Hubac).

K: 10.1675. L: 2.1676. C: 4.1676. Struck early 1687 at Marseille and replaced.

Heureuse Marseille (?).
K: 1675. L: 7.1676. C: 4.1677. Blew up by accident off Civitavecchia 7.1677, with all crew killed.

Souveraine Marseille (Simon Chabert).
K: 9.1676. L: 12.1676. C: 2.1677. Condemned 1687 at Marseille and replaced.

Couronne Marseille (Pierre Hubac).
K: 1676. L: 8.1677. C: 11.1677. Condemned 1687 at Marseille and replaced.

Hardie Marseille (Simon Chabert).
K: 1676. L: 1677. C: 1677. Condemned 1687 at Marseille and replaced.

Forte Marseille (J-B Chabert).
K: 1676. L: 1677. C: 3.1678. Condemned early 1687 at Marseille and replaced.

CAPITANE. Galère extraordinaire. Designed and built by Jean-Baptiste Chabert.
Dimensions & tons: 154ft 6in, 128ft 6in x 19ft 9in x 7ft 6in (50.19, 41.74 x 6.42 x 2.44m). 240 tons. Draught 8ft (2.60m). Men: 130, +7 officers and 360 oarsmen.
Guns: 1 x 36pdr forward, flanked by 2 x 8pdrs and 2 x 6pdrs; also 14 *pierriers*.

Capitane Marseille.
K: 9.1676. L: 3.1677. C: 7.1677. Renamed *Patronne* early 1680. Struck 1683 at Marseille and replaced.

GALÉASSE DE VIVONNE. Built at Messina to the order of the Duc de Vivonne, this vessel's details appear to coincide with the standard dimensions of other *galères ordinaires*. A similar *Ferme* may also have been built at Messina in 1677–78 but her existence is unconfirmed.

Galéasse de Vivonne Messina.
K: 1677. L: 8.1677. C: 2.1678. Renamed *Saint Louis* 1678. Struck 1680 at Marseille and replaced.

REINE Class (1677 orders). Designed and built by Jean-Baptiste Chabert. 25/26 rows of oars. Both vessels took part in the Bombardment of Genoa 18–28 May 1684.
Dimensions & tons: dimensions unknown. 200 tons. Men: 130, +4 officers and 260 oarsmen.
Guns: 1 x 36pdr forward, flanked by 2 x 8pdrs and 2 x 6pdrs; also 12 *pierriers*.

Reine Marseille.
K: 1677. L: 1678. C: early 1679. Condemned 1687 at Marseille.

Invincible Marseille.
K: 1677. L: 1678. C: early 1679. Condemned 1687 at Marseille.

FAVORITE Class (1678 orders). Galleys of reduced length. The first two were built by Simon Chabert, the next two by Jean-Baptiste Chabert, the following three by Pierre Hubac, and the eighth – which was ordered on 26 August 1678 and prefabricated in six months – by Simon and Jean-Baptiste Chabert together. 25/26 rows of oars (of 36ft length). Most took part in the Bombardment of Genoa 18–28.5.1684.
Dimensions & tons: 139ft 6in, 114ft 0in x 17ft 6in x 6ft 10in (45.315, 37.03 x 5.68 x 2.22m). 200 tons. Men: 130, +4 officers and 260 oarsmen.
Guns: 1 x 36pdr forward, flanked by 2 x 8pdrs and 2 x 6pdrs; also 12 *pierriers*.

Favorite Marseille.
K: 1678. L: 1679. C: 1679. Condemned 1687 at Marseille and replaced.

Heureuse Marseille.
K: 1678. L: 1679. C: 1679. Grounded and lost 3.1680.

Brave Marseille.
K: 1678. L: 1679. C: 1679. Condemned early 1687 at Marseille and replaced.

Sirène Marseille.
K: 1678. L: 1679. C: 1679. Condemned 1687 at Marseille and replaced.

Belle Marseille.
K: 1678. L: 1679. C: 1679. Condemned 1688 at Marseille and replaced.

Princesse Marseille.
K: 1678. L: 1679. C: 1679. Condemned early 1687 at Marseille and replaced.

Valeur Marseille.
K: 1678. L: 1679. C: 1679. Condemned early 1687 at Marseille and replaced.

Grande Marseille.
K: 25.10.1678. L: 1679. C: 10.1679. Condemned 11.1689 at Marseille.

RÉALE. Galère extraordinaire, designed and built by Jean-Baptiste Chabert.
Dimensions & tons: 173ft 3in, 143ft 0in x 22ft 6in x 7ft 8in (56.28, 46.45 x 7.31 x 2.49m). 260 tons. Men: 145, +7 officers and 360 oarsmen.
Guns: 1 x 36pdr forward, flanked by 2 x 8pdrs and 2 x 6pdrs; also 14 *pierriers*.

Réale Marseille.
K: 10.1681. L: 1683. C: 1683. Renamed *Invincible* 1.1688. Condemned 4.1690 at Marseille; hulked 1691 and variously called *Grande Réale* and *Vieille Invincible*; not mentioned after 1715.

PATRONNE. Galère extraordinaire, designed and built by Jean-Baptiste Chabert.
Dimensions & tons: 154ft 6in, 127ft 9in x 19ft 9in x 7ft 6in (50.19, 41.50 x 6.42 x 2.44m). 240 tons. Draught 8ft/9ft (2.60/2.92m). Men: 130, +7 officers and 360 oarsmen.
Guns: 1 x 36pdr forward, flanked by 2 x 8pdrs and 2 x 6pdrs; also 14 *pierriers*.

Patronne Marseille.
K: 1682. L: 1682. C: 4.1683. Condemned 1693 at Marseille and replaced.

DAUPHINE Class. Twelve galleys, probably all to similar design, built Simon Chabert, Pierre Hubac and Jean-Baptiste Chabert.
Dimensions & tons: 143ft 0in, 117ft 0in x 18ft 0in x 6ft 11in (46.45, 38.01 x 5.85 x 2.25m). 200/300 tons. Men: 130, +4 officers and 260 oarsmen.
Guns: 1 x 36pdr forward, flanked by 2 x 8pdrs and 2 x 6pdrs; also 12 *pierriers*.

Dauphine Marseille (Simon Chabert).
K: 11.1679. L: 2.1680. C: 5.1680. Condemned early 1692 at Marseille.

Saint Louis Marseille (Simon Chabert)
K: 1679. L: 1680. C: 5.1680. Hulked at Marseille 4.1690 (renamed *Vieille Saint Louis* 1691). Not mentioned after 2.1692.

Madame Marseille (Pierre Hubac).
K: 11.1679. L: 1680. C: 1680. Condemned 3.1692 at Marseille.

Ferme Marseille (J-B Chabert).
  K: 11.1679. L: 1680. C: 9.1680. Condemned 4.1690 at Marseille, then RB 1690-91.
Renommée Marseille (J-B Chabert).
  K: 12.1679. L: 4.1680. C: 5.1680. Condemned 4.1690 at Marseille and BU 1691.
Victoire Marseille (Pierre Hubac).
  K: 12.1679. L: 1680. C: 1680. Probably ex-*Fière* 1682. Condemned 4.1690 at Marseille and BU 1691.
Fortune Marseille (Simon Chabert).
  K: 1679. L: 1681. C: 9.1681. Condemned 1688 at Marseille and replaced.
Fière Marseille (Simon Chabert).
  K: 1680. L: 1681. C: 6.1681. Probably ex-*Victoire* 1682. Condemned 4.1690 at Marseille, then RB 1690-91.
Fleur de Lys Marseille (J-B Chabert).
  K: 1680. L: 1681. C: 5.1680. Condemned 2.1692 at Marseille.
Superbe Marseille (J-B Chabert).
  K: 9.1681. L: 1682. C: 9.1682. Condemned 1693 at Marseille and replaced.
Perle Marseille (Simon Chabert).
  K: 9.1681. L: 1682. C: 1682. Condemned late 1693 at Marseille.
France Marseille (Simon Chabert).
  K: 1683. L: 1684. C: 1685. Condemned 1694 at Marseille and rebuilt by Simon Chabert. Condemned 1723 at Marseille.
Magnifique Marseille (Simon Chabert).
  K: 1684. L: 1.1685. C: 2.1685. Condemned 1.1698 at Marseille and hulked, last mentioned 1701.
Galante Marseille (Simon Chabert).
  K: 1684. L: 3.1685. C: 4.1685. Condemned in the fall of 1693 at Marseille and rebuilt 1693–94 by Jean Reynoir. Condemned 6.1701 at Marseille.

ILLUSTRE Class. Designed and built by Pierre Hubac. 25/26 rows of oars (of 36ft 5in length – 11.83m)
  Dimensions & tons: 144ft 0in, 121ft 1in x 18ft 0in x 6ft 10in (46.78, 39.33 x 5.85 x 2.22m). 200/300 tons. Men: 130, +4 officers and 260 oarsmen.
  Guns: 1 x 36pdr forward, flanked by 2 x 8pdrs and 2 x 6pdrs; also 12 *pierriers*.
Illustre Marseille.
  K: 1684. L: 1.1685. C: 2.1685. Condemned 8.1695 and rebuilt by Jean Reynoir at Marseille 1695–96. Struck and hulked at Marseille 1700, BU 1701.
Fidèle Marseille.
  K: 1684. L: 1686. C: 1687. Condemned 1691 at Marseille, then rebuilt 1691–92.
Éclatante Marseille.
  K: 5.1685. L: 2.1686. C: 8.1686. Condemned early 1695 at Marseille.
Couronne Marseille.
  K: 6.1686. L: 1686. C: 5.1687. Condemned late 1695 at Marseille and rebuilt there by Jean-Baptiste Chabert 1695–97. Condemned 2.1716 at Marseille and sold or BU.
Brave Marseille.
  K: 11.1686. L: 1687. C: 1687. Condemned and hulked 1699 at Marseille. Ceded to Genoa 1702. Chartered by the French 3.7.1715, purchased 3.1716, and restored to service as *Brave*. Condemned 1726 at Marseille.
Forte Marseille.
  K: 11.1686. L: 1687. C: 1687. Condemned 5.1701 at Marseille and BU.
Sirène Marseille.
  K: 11.1686. L: 1687. C: 1687. Condemned 5.1701 at Marseille and BU.

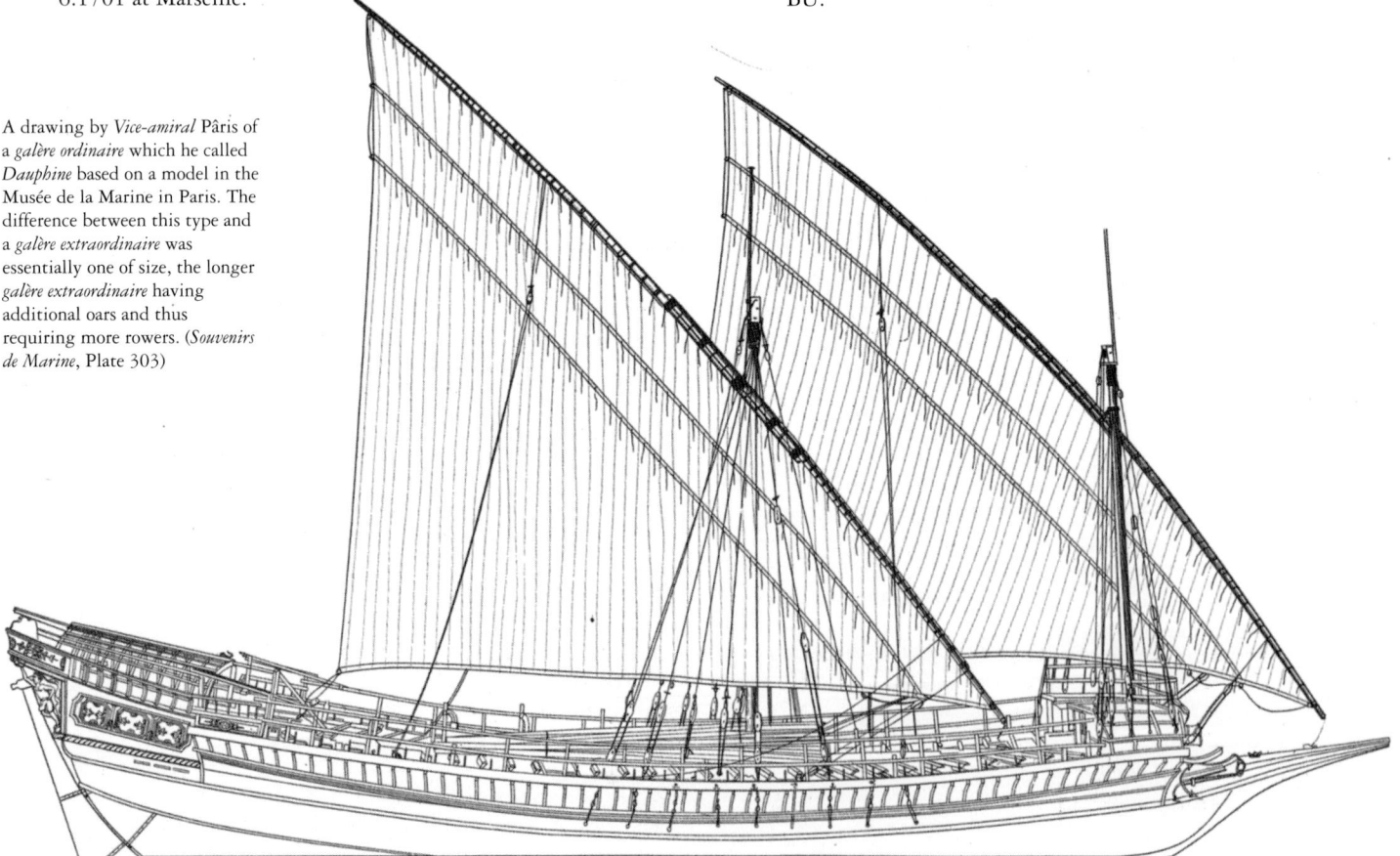

A drawing by *Vice-amiral* Pâris of a *galère ordinaire* which he called *Dauphine* based on a model in the Musée de la Marine in Paris. The difference between this type and a *galère extraordinaire* was essentially one of size, the longer *galère extraordinaire* having additional oars and thus requiring more rowers. (*Souvenirs de Marine*, Plate 303)

Valeur Marseille.
- K: 1687. L: 1687. C: 1.1688. Rebuilt by Jean-Baptiste Chabert at Marseille 1694–95 and condemned there 1713. The original *Valeur* was condemned and BU at Marseille in 1696.

Reine Marseille.
- K: 1687. L: 4.1688. C: 5.1688. Condemned 6.1701 at Marseille.

Belle Marseille.
- K: 1688. L: 4.1688. C: 5.1688. Condemned 6.1701 at Marseille.

Favorite Marseille.
- K: 1688. L: 1688. C: 1688. Condemned 5.1704 at Marseille, but rebuilt 1704–5 and in service until 1719. Replaced 1724.

Héroïne Marseille.
- K: 1688. L: 7.1688. C: 8.1688. Condemned 1720 at Marseille and rebuilt 1722.

Dauphine Marseille.
- K: 3.1689. L: 10.1689. C: 2.1692. Renamed *Madame* 1693. Condemned 7.1718 at Marseille and sold or BU.

DUCHESSE Class. Built by Simon Chabert, although the design was probably identical to Hubac's contemporary *Illustre* Class (see above). The *Amazone* was built by Jean-Baptiste Chabert and the *Grande* was begun by him but was completed by Simon Chabert after the former moved to Rochefort in June 1689 to organise the construction of galleys at that dockyard. 25/26 rows of oars (of 36ft 5in length – 11.83m)
- Dimensions & tons: 144ft 0in, 121ft 0in x 18ft 0in x 7ft 0in (46.78, 39.31 x 5.85 x 2.27m). 200/300 tons. Men: 130, +4 officers and 260 oarsmen. Draught 8ft/9ft (2.60/2.92m).
- Guns: 1 x 36pdr forward, flanked by 2 x 8pdrs and 2 x 6pdrs; also 12 *pierriers*.

Duchesse Marseille.
- K: 5.1685. L: 2.1686. C: 5.1686. Condemned 5.1704 and reconstructed 1704–5. Condemned 1723.

Amazone Marseille.
- K: 1685. L: 6.1686. C: 5.1687. Struck 1694 at Marseille, BU 1695.

Princesse Marseille.
- K: 6.1686. L: 1686. C: 5.1687. Condemned early 1695 at Marseille and BU in 1696.

Souveraine Marseille.
- K: 6.1686. L: 1686. C: 5.1687. Condemned 6.1704 and reconstructed 1704–5. Condemned 7.1718.

Hardie Marseille.
- K: 11.1686. L: 1687. C: 1687. Struck at Marseille 1700. Ceded to Genoa 1702. Chartered by the French 3.7.1715, purchased 3.1716, and restored to service as *Hardie*. Condemned 1723 at Marseille.

Fortune Marseille.
- K: 9.1688. L: 12.1688. C: 7.1689. Struck at Marseille 1700.

Magnanime Marseille.
- K: 9.1688. L: 12.1688. C: 7.1689. Condemned 5.1704 and reconstructed 1704–5. Condemned 2.1716 and BU.

Grande Marseille.
- K: 1689. L: 29.10.1689. C: 11.1689. Condemned at Marseille 5.1701.

RÉALE. Galère extraordinaire, designed and built by Jean-Baptiste Chabert. 30/31 rows of oars (of 42ft 7in length – 13.83m).
- Dimensions & tons: 175ft 0in, 147ft 0in x 24ft 0in x 8ft 0in (57.47, 47.75 x 7.88 x 2.63m). 280 tons. Draught 9ft (2.92m). Men: 145, +8 officers and 432 oarsmen.
- Guns: 1 x 36pdr forward, flanked by 2 x 8pdrs and 2 x 6pdrs; also 16 *pierriers*.

Réale Marseille.
- K: 1687. L: 11.1688. C: 8.1689. Condemned 1693. Hulked at Marseille and renamed *Vielle Réale* 5.1694. Not mentioned after 1715.

(C) Vessels acquired from 15 April 1689

Until the outbreak of the war against England and the Netherlands in 1689, French galleys had almost always been confined to the smoother waters of the Mediterranean. However, in 1689 it was decided to create a northern galley fleet to support Tourville in his campaign against the English Navy.

The *galères de l'Atlantique* (the 'patronne' *Glorieuse* and 14 *Bellone* class ordinary galleys) were all built at Rochefort in 1689–90, and left there as a squadron under the command of LGGal Jacques de Noailles, called the *Bailli de Noailles*, on 14 June 1690, but were too late to take part in the Battle of Beachy Head. On 5 August the squadron raided Teignmouth in Devon, where they landed 1,570 soldiers (the last successful occupation of England by hostile troops). On 18 August they returned to Le Havre, before moving up the Seine as far as Rouen on 4 September, where they remained to winter. They were not commissioned for the *Campagne du large* in 1691, but they were used later for the defence of the approaches to Brest against Anglo-Dutch threats such as those from Berkeley's fleet in 1694 and Rooke's fleet in 1696.

HALF-GALLEYS. Half-galleys (*demi-galères*) were typically small galleys with 20 or fewer banks of oars (with three oarsmen per oar), each oar being 25ft in length, and with only two masts. They tended to be part of the regular Navy rather than of the Galley Corps and are listed in Chapter 12. In addition to supporting the regular galleys, the half-galleys and other small oared craft at Brest were used as tugs to tow inactive ships to or from their wintering stations at Landévenec or operational vessel in or out the Brest Narrows when the wind was blowing from the wrong direction. The regular galleys were sometimes used for the same duties. When the departure of CV Des Augiers' squadron for the second campaign in 1696 was delayed by strong westerly winds, Louis de Pontchartrain, Secretary of State for the Navy, ordered Hubert de Champy, Seigneur Desclouzeaux, the *intendant* at Brest, to use the galleys of the Chevalier de Rochechouart to tow the vessels out of the port of Brest into the bay of Bertheaume from where they could get to sea.

ILLUSTRE/DUCHESSE Class (1689 and later orders). The following fifteen galleys were a continuation of the vessels built in the period to 1688, with the same characteristics and seemingly the same design. Seven were built by Simon Chabert, five by Jean-Baptiste Chabert and three by Pierre Hubac. *Perle* was rebuilt at Marseille in 1703.

Conquérante Marseille (Simon Chabert).
- K: 5.1689. L: 12.1689. C: 3.1690. Condemned 7.1718 at Marseille, and sold or BU.

Guerrière Marseille (Simon Chabert).
- K: 9.1689. L: 11.1689. C: 12.1689. Condemned and hulked 7.1718 at Marseille. No mention after 1720.

Gloire Marseille (Simon Chabert).
- K: 1690. L: 1691. C: 5.1691. Condemned 1726 at Marseille and replaced.

Fidèle Marseille (Simon Chabert).
- K: 1690. L: 1691. C: 3.1692. Condemned 7.1718 at Marseille, and sold or BU.

Saint Louis Marseille (Pierre Hubac).
- K: 1690. L: 1691. C: 3.1692. Condemned 6.1701 at Marseille.

Renommée Marseille (Pierre Hubac).
  K: 1690. L: 5.1691. C: 6.1691. Condemned 6.1701 at Marseille.
Ferme Marseille (J-B Chabert).
  K: 1690. L: 5.1691. C: 6.1691. Struck 1694 at Marseille, either lost or sold to the Order of Malta.
Ambitieuse Marseille (J-B Chabert).
  K: late 1690. L: early 1692. C: 4.1693. Struck 1694 at Marseille, either lost or sold to the Order of Malta.
Fière Marseille (Simon Chabert).
  K: 1.1691. L: 1691. C: 12.1691. Condemned and hulked 7.1718 at Marseille. No mention after 1720.
Invincible Marseille (J-B Chabert).
  K: early 1691. L: 5.1691. C: 6.1691. Condemned and hulked 7.1718 at Marseille. No mention after 1720.
Superbe Marseille (J-B Chabert).
  K: late 1691. L: 1692. C: 4.1693. Rebuilt 1695–96 at Marseille by Jean-Baptiste Chabert. Condemned 7.1718 at Marseille and sold or BU.
Victoire Marseille (Pierre Hubac).
  K: early 1691. L: 10.1691. C: 12.1691. Struck 1694 at Marseille, either lost or sold to the Order of Malta.
Madame Marseille (Simon Chabert).
  K: 9.1691. L: 3.1692. C: 4.1692. Renamed *Dauphine* 1693. Condemned 6.1701 at Marseille.
Fleur de Lys Marseille (J-B Chabert).
  K: 9.1691. L: 3.1692. C: 5.1692. Condemned 7.1718 at Marseille, and sold or BU.
Perle Marseille (Simon Chabert).
  K: 1692. L: 1694. C: 1694. Condemned 1724 at Marseille, and replaced.

GLORIEUSE. Galère extraordinaire ('Patronne' role). Designed and built by Jean-Baptiste Chabert, and built at Rochefort as 'command ship' for LGGal Jacques de Noailles. 29/30 banks of oars.
  Dimensions & tons: 170ft 0in, 144ft 4in x 21ft 6in x 7ft 4in (55.22, 46.89 x 6.98 x 2.41m). 250/ tons. Men: 131, +4/8 officers and 360 oarsmen.
  Guns: 1 x 36pdr forward, flanked by 2 x 8pdrs and 2 x 6pdrs; also 14 *pierriers*.
Glorieuse Rochefort.
  K: 10.1689. L: 3.1690. C: 5.1690. Condemned 1.1696 at Rouen, and BU 1–4.1696.

BELLONE Class. Designed and built by Jean-Baptiste Chabert. 25/26 rows of oars (of 37ft length)
  Dimensions & tons: 142ft 0in x 18ft 0in x 7ft 0in (46.13 x 5.85 x 2.27m). 200/300 tons. Men: 131, +4 officers and 260 oarsmen.
  Guns: 1 x 36pdr forward, flanked by 2 x 8pdrs and 2 x 6pdrs; also 12 *pierriers*.
Bellone Rochefort.
  K: 10.1689. L: 18.3.1690. C: 5.1690. Condemned 1.1696 at Rouen, and BU 1–4.1696.
Combattante Rochefort.
  K: 12.1689. L: 28.3.1690. C: 5.1690. Condemned 1.1696 at Rouen, and BU 1–4.1696.
Constante Rochefort.
  K: 10.1689. L: 10.3.1690. C: 5.1690. Name sometimes rendered as *Constance*. Condemned 5.1696 at Le Havre, and BU there 6.1696.
Émeraude Rochefort.
  K: 1.1690. L: 20.4.1690. C: 5.1690. Condemned 5.1696 at Bordeaux, and BU there in same year.
Heureuse Rochefort.
  K: 12.1689. L: 10.4.1690. C: 5.1690. Condemned 1.1696 at Rouen, and BU 1–4.1696.
Marquise Rochefort.
  K: 2.1690. L: 20.3.1690. C: 5.1690. Condemned 10.1696 at Brest, and BU there in same year.
Martiale Rochefort.
  K: 11.1689. L: 20.4.1690. C: 5.1690. Condemned 5.1696 at Bordeaux, and BU there in same year.
Néréide Rochefort.
  K: 1.1690. L: 15.4.1690. C: 5.1690. Condemned 1.1696 at Rouen, and BU 1–4.1696.
Palme Rochefort.
  K: 10.1689. L: 13.3.1690. C: 5.1690. Condemned 1.1696 at Rouen, and BU 1–4.1696.
Précieuse Rochefort.
  K: 12.1689. L: 4.1690. C: 5.1690. Condemned 1.1696 at Rouen, and BU 1–4.1696.
Prudente Rochefort.
  K: 11.1689. L: 25.3.1690. C: 5.1690. Condemned 1.1696 at Rouen, and BU 1–4.1696.
Sensible Rochefort.
  K: 2.1690. L: 30.4.1690. C: 5.1690. Condemned 1.1696 at Rouen, and BU 1–4.1696.
Sublime Rochefort.
  K: 10.1689. L: 3.1690. C: 5.1690. Condemned 5.1696 at Le Havre, and BU there 6.1696.
Triomphante Rochefort.
  K: 10.1689. L: 3.1690. C: 5.1690. Condemned 10.1696 at Brest, and BU there in same year.

In September 1691, the Marseille (galley) Construction Council met to consider fixing the standard dimensions for all future building of *galères ordinaires*. They decided that all future building should be: 144ft 0in, 121ft 3in x 18ft 0in x 7ft 2in (46.78, 39.39 x 5.85 x 2.33m). The displacement was fixed at 316 tons.

PATRONNE. Galère extraordinaire, designed and built by François Cadière and Jean-Baptiste Chabert. 29/30 rows of oars. When first ordered in March 1691, this was originally intended to have 28/29 rows of oars (*i.e.* one pair fewer) and to measure 160ft x 20ft x 7ft 10in. Rebuilt in 1706 (completed in November)
  Dimensions & tons: 170ft 0in, 144ft 4in x 21ft 6in x 7ft 4in (55.22, 46.89 x 6.98 x 2.38m). 250 tons. Draught 7ft 4in (2.38m). Men: 130, +8 officers and 360 oarsmen (6 per oar).
  Guns: 1 x 36pdr forward, flanked by 2 x 8pdrs and 2 x 6pdrs; also 14 *pierriers*.
Patronne Marseille.
  K: 4.1691. L: 4.1694. C: 5.1694. Renamed *Valeur* 1713. Struck 1733 at Marseille and replaced.

RÉALE. Galère extraordinaire, designed and built by Jean-Baptiste Chabert, and known as *Réale Neuve* until launched. 30/31 rows of oars.
  Dimensions & tons: 175ft 7in, 148ft 0in x 23ft 10in x 7ft 2in (57.04, 48.08 x 7.74 x 2.33m). 280 tons. Draught 7ft 10in (2.54m). Men: 145, +7 officers and 432 oarsmen (7 per oar).
  Guns: 1 x 36pdr forward, flanked by 2 x 8pdrs and 2 x 6pdrs; also 16 *pierriers*.
Réale Marseille.
  K: 12.1692. L: 4.1694. C: 5.1694. Condemned 1720 at Marseille and replaced 1722.

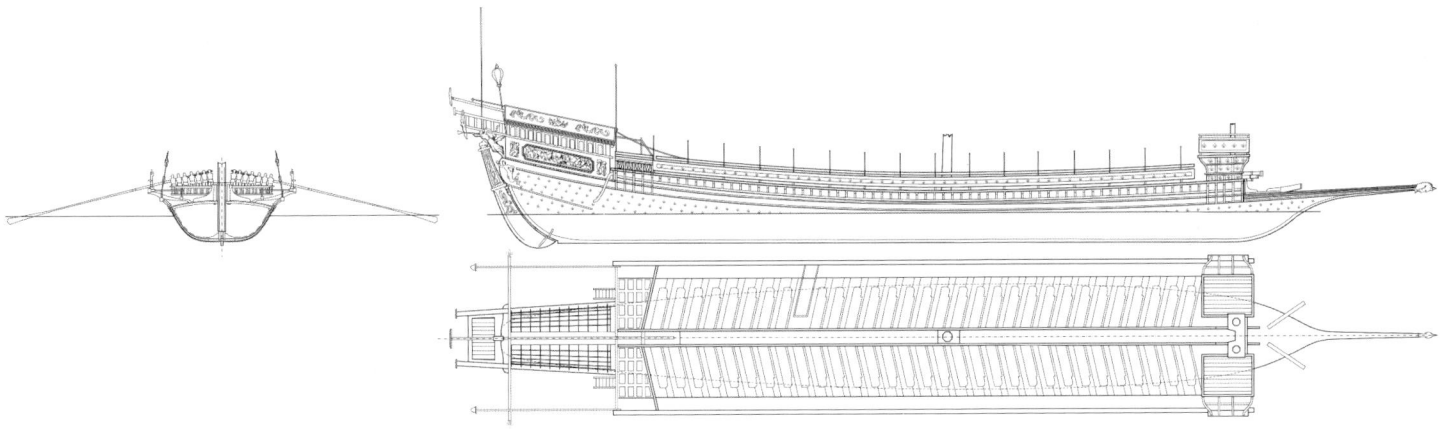

A drawing by László Veres after Björn Landström's reconstruction from various sources of a *Réale* of the late seventeenth century. The stern decoration is based on the surviving sculpture conceived by Pierre Puget and executed by the court artist Jean Bérain, now preserved in the Musée de la Marine in Paris. The sculptural ensemble is representative of the ornate decoration of the period, designed to 'shine forth at sea the magnificence of His Majesty' – hence the exaggerated lines and the excessive use of gilt and paint over the carved walnut, lime and poplar bas-reliefs. With 61 banks of oars (note the galley on the port side), this *galère extraordinaire* was one of the largest examples.

HEUREUSE Class. Designed and built by Jean-Baptiste Chabert in pairs at various ports, as replacements for those galleys of the same names built in 1690. 25/26 rows of oars (of 37ft length). On completion, the *Heureuse* and *Palme* were first moved to St Malo, the *Émeraude* and *Martiale* to Bordeaux. When the Peace of Ryswick was concluded, all six were stored at Rochefort. All six were renamed in June 1699 (as shown below), but their original names were restored in November (last four) and December (first two) 1700.

In June 1701 they were recommissioned and moved to Dunkirk, where they were reconstructed from October until early 1702, then placed under the overall command of CGal Charles-Martial Davy, Bailli de La Pailléterie. On 4 July 1702 the squadron – *Heureuse* (Maulévrier-Langeron), *Triomphante* (Valence), *Émeraude* (Fontette), *Palme* (La Pailleterie), *Martiale* (Lévy) and *Marquise* (Montuillies) – captured the Dutch 46-gun *Wapen van Hoorn* (or *Eenhorn*) of the Noorderkwartier Admiralty off the Flanders coast, which was added to the French Navy and renamed *Licorne* (see Chapter 3); following this feat of arms, La Pailléterie was promoted to CdEGal. All six were again rebuilt at Dunkirk, the *Triomphante* and *Martiale* from May 1704 until January 1705, and the other four from July 1705 to May 1706.

Dimensions & tons: 144ft 0in, 121ft 6in x 19ft 0in x 5ft 0in (46.78, 39.47 x 6.17 x 1.62m). 200/300 tons. Men: 130, +4 officers and 260 oarsmen.

Guns: 1 x 36pdr forward, flanked by 2 x 8pdrs and 2 x 6pdrs; also 12 *pierriers*.

Heureuse Le Havre
  K: 2.1696. L: 19.5.1696. C: 6.1696. Renamed *Victoire* 6.1699 until 12.1700. Sold 6.1713 at Dunkirk, and BU there 5.1714.

Palme Le Havre
  K: 2.1696. L: 19.5.1696. C: 6.1696. Renamed *Ferme* 6.1699 until 12.1700. Sold 6.1713 at Dunkirk, and BU there 5.1714.

Émeraude Rochefort
  K: 6.1696. L: 10.1696. C: 4.1697. Renamed *Ambitieuse* 6.1699 until 11.1700. Sold 6.1713 at Dunkirk, and BU there 5.1714.

Martiale Rochefort
  K: 6.1696. L: 10.1696. C: 4.1697. Renamed *Princesse* 6.1699 until 11.1700. Sold 6.1713 at Dunkirk, and BU there 5.1714.

Marquise Brest Dyd
  K: 10.1696. L: 20.4.1697. C: 17.5.1697. Renamed *Brave* 6.1699 until 11.1700. Sold 6.1713 at Dunkirk, and BU there 5.1714.

Triomphante Brest Dyd
  K: 10.1696. L: 22.4.1697. C: 17.5.1697. Renamed *Éclatante* 6.1699 until 11.1700. Sold 6.1713 at Dunkirk, and BU there 5.1714.

AMBITIEUSE Class. Designed by Jean Reynoir, who built the first two; the other pair were built by Jean-Baptiste Chabert and Simon Chabert respectively. *Éclatante* was reconstructed in 1713 at Marseille.

Dimensions & tons: 144ft 0in, 121ft 6in x 18ft 6in x 7ft 4in (46.78, 39.47 x 6.01 x 2.38m). 200/300 tons. Draught 6ft 4in/8ft 4in (2.06/2.71m). Men: 130, +4 officers and 260 oarsmen.

Guns: 1 x 36pdr forward, flanked by 2 x 8pdrs and 2 x 6pdrs; also 12 *pierriers*.

Ambitieuse Marseille.
  K: 1696. L: 1699. C: 1700. Condemned 1720 at Marseille, and replacement built 1724–25 (see below).

Éclatante Marseille.
  K: 1696. L: 1699. C: 1700. Condemned 1725 at Marseille, but reconstructed 1727 and put back into service until struck in 1734.

Amazone Marseille.
  K: 1698. L: 1699. C: 4.1702. Condemned 2.1716 at Marseille and BU.

Princesse Marseille.
  K: 1698. L: 1699. C: 1700. Condemned 7.1718 at Marseille and BU.

ÉCLATANTE. Designed by Jean Reynoir. 26 rows of oars. One large and two ordinary galleys were ordered at Marseille on 8 October 1706, possibly to be named *Patronne*, *Éclatante* and *Fortune*. All three were laid down. The large galley may have been the rebuilt *Patronne* of 1694 while one of the ordinary galleys, probably *Éclatante*, seems to have lasted at Marseille until 1734. There is no evidence that the third was completed.

Dimensions: 144ft 0in, 121ft 6in x 18ft 6in x 7ft 4in (46.78, 39.47 x 6.01 x 2.38m). 200 tons. Men: 130, +4 officers and 260 oarsmen.

Guns: 1 x 36pdr forward, flanked by 2 x 8pdrs and 2 x 4pdrs; also 12 *pierriers*.

Éclatante (?) Marseille.
  K: 11.1706. L: 1713. C: 1713 or 1714. Name not confirmed. Condemned 1724 at Marseille but returned to service 1727. Struck 1734 at Marseille and replaced.

(D) Vessels acquired from 1 September 1715

In March 1716, four *galères ordinaires* were purchased from Genoa – and were named *Victoire*, *Ferme*, *Hardie* and *Brave*. The *Hardie* and *Brave* were former French galleys of 1687, listed above, while *Victoire* and *Ferme* were former Genoese galleys chartered from the Duc de Tursi on 3 July 1715 and purchased in March 1716. *Victoire* was condemned in July 1718 while *Ferme* was condemned in 1723.

In 1718 the established strength of the galley corps was fixed at fifteen vessels, and this level was nominally maintained until 1748; in practice the number of serviceable galleys was generally below this established strength.

HÉROÏNE. Designed and built by Jean-Baptiste Chabert. 25/26 banks of oars.

Dimensions & tons: 145ft 0in, 121ft 0in x 18ft 0in x 6ft 5in (47.10, 39.31 x 5.85 x 2.09m). 200/300 tons. Men: 152, +4 officers and 260 oarsmen.

Guns: 1 x 36pdr forward, flanked by 2 x 18pdrs.

Héroïne Marseille.
K: 1719. L: 1722. C: 1723. Hulked 1753 at Toulon, and sold (with *Fortune*) 29.10.1758.

RÉALE. Galère extraordinaire, designed and built by Jean-Baptiste Chabert. 28/29 rows of oars.

Dimensions & tons: dimensions unknown. 280/450 tons. Men: 210, +10 officers and 402 oarsmen.

Guns: 1 x 36pdr forward, flanked by 2 x 18pdrs and 2 x 4pdrs.

Réale Marseille.
K: 1719. L: 1722. C: 1723. May have been renamed *Valeur* 8.1733 (not confirmed). Struck 1743.

FERME Class. Designed and built by Pierre Chabert. 25/26 banks of oars.

Dimensions & tons: 145ft 0in, 121ft 0in x 18ft 8in x 7ft 8in (47.10, 39.31 x 6.06 x 2.49m). 185/300 tons. Men: 156, +4/7 officers and 260 oarsmen.

Guns: 1 x 36pdr forward, flanked by 2 x 18pdrs.

Ferme Marseille.
K: early 1723. L: 1723. C: 4.1724. Struck 1738.

Hardie Marseille.
K: early 1723. L: 1723. C: 1724. Struck 1739 at Marseille.

Favorite Marseille.
K: early 1724. L: 1724. C: 1725. Struck 1751.

Perle Marseille.
K: early 1724. L: 1724. C: 1725. Struck 1743 and BU 1749.

FRANCE Class. Designed and built by Jean Reynoir. 25/26 banks of oars.

Dimensions & tons: 145ft 0in, 121ft 0in x 18ft 11in x 6ft 3in (47.10, 39.31 x 6.15 x 2.03m). 185/300 tons. Men: 156, +4/7 officers and 260 oarsmen.

Guns: 1 x 36pdr forward, flanked by 2 x 18pdrs.

France Marseille.
K: early 1723. L: 1723. C: 1724. Probably BU 1749 at Marseille.

Duchesse Marseille.
K: early 1723. L: 1723. C: 1724. Struck 1742 at Marseille.

Ambitieuse Marseille.
K: early 1724. L: 1724. C: 1725. Struck 1744 at Marseille.

Brave Marseille.
K: 1725. L: 1726. C: 1726. Struck 1746 at Marseille.

Gloire Marseille.
K: 1725. L: 1726. C: 1726. Out of service 11.1747 at Marseille, probably BU there 1749.

Fortune Marseille.
K: 1729. L: 1730. C: 1731. Hulked 1753 at Toulon. Sold 10.1758 for BU, BU 1759

RÉALE. Galère extraordinaire, designed and built by Pierre Chabert. 28/29 rows of oars.

Dimensions & tons: 164ft 0in, 136ft 10in x 21ft 0in x 8ft 7.5in (53.27, 44.45 x 6.82 x 2.80m). 280/450 tons. Men: +8 officers.

Guns: 1 x 36pdr forward, flanked by 2 x 18pdrs and 2 x 4pdrs.

Réale Marseille.
K: 1.1733. L: 8.1733. C: 4.1734. Employed as a tug at Toulon 9.1749. Condemned and hulked there 4.1755; not mentioned after 1773.

ÉCLATANTE. Designed and built by Germain Baudillon. 25/26 rows of oars.

Dimensions & tons: 145ft 0in, 120ft 6in x 18ft 11in x 6ft 3in (47.10, 39.14 x 6.15 x 2.03m). 185–200/300 tons. Men: 156, +4 officers and 260 oarsmen.

Guns: 1 x 36pdr forward, flanked by 2 x 18pdrs

Éclatante Marseille
K: 11.1732. L: 1734. C: 5.1734. Tug at Toulon 1749. Refitted 1754 at Toulon (prison hulk 1761). Hulk at Toulon 1758. Last mentioned 1775.

PATRONNE. Galère extraordinaire, designed and built by Jean Reynoir. 28/29 rows of oars.

Dimensions & tons: 163ft 0in, 136ft 0in x 21ft 0in x 8ft 7.5in (52.95, 44.18 x 6.82 x 2.80m). 277/450 tons. Men: 165, +8 officers and 402 convicts.

Guns: 1 x 36pdr forward, flanked by 2 x 18pdrs and 2 x 4pdrs; unarmed from 1767.

Patronne Marseille.
K: 6.1735. L: 15.9.1736. C: early 1737. Renamed *Dauphine* 1.1749. Employed as a tug at Toulon 10.1749. Condemned and hulked at Toulon 1767. Sale ordered 11.1783, but she was not sold, and was employed as a hospital hulk at Toulon until at least 1793 (renamed *Espérance* 10.1792).

HARDIE Class. Designed and built by Pierre Chabert. 25/26 rows of oars. The *Patience* (originally *Duchesse*) was in summer 1799 the last galley to put to sea militarily.

Dimensions & tons: 145ft 0in, 121ft 0in x 18ft 8in x 7ft 8in (47.10, 39.31 x 6.06 x 2.49m). 185/300 tons. Men: 156, +4/7 officers and 260 oarsmen.

Guns: 1 x 36pdr forward, flanked by 2 x 18pdrs (*Patience* 1 x 24pdr only in 1799).

Hardie Marseille.
K: 4.1737. L: 1739. C: 1739. Disarmed 1767, and became convict hulk at Marseille. To Toulon in 1778, where employed until at least 1795.

Duchesse Marseille.
K: 4.1740. L: 1742. C: 1742, Renamed *Patience* 10.1792, Refitted at Toulon in summer 1798 and 5.1799. Disarmed (again) 10.1799 at Toulon, where remained until broken up in 1814.

Brave Marseille.
K: 1744. L: 1746. C: 1746. Refitted at Toulon 1757. Disarmed 1776, and became convict hulk at Toulon, where remained until at least 10.1802.

FERME Class. Designed and built by the Reynoir Brothers. 25/26 rows of oars. *Valeur* was initially to have been named *Héroïne*.

Dimensions & tons: 145ft 0in, 121ft 0in x 18ft 11in x 6ft 3in (47.10, 39.31 x 6.14 x 2.03m). 185/300 tons. Men: 156, +4/7 officers and 260 oarsmen.
Guns: 1 x 36pdr forward, flanked by 2 x 18pdrs.

Ferme Marseille.
K: 1739. L: 1740. C: 1740. Disarmed 1768, and became convict hulk at Marseille. To Toulon 1781, where remained until broken up in 1814.

Valeur Marseille.
K: 8.1740. L: 1742. C: 1743. Used as tug at Toulon 5.1749. To Marseille 10.1762, and hulked there 5.1768. Renamed *Écarlate* 1779, then sold to BU 9.1781.

Ambitieuse Marseille.
K: 10.1742. L: 1744. C: 1745. Used as tug at Toulon 5.1749. To Marseille 10.1762, and hulked there 5.1768. Returned 9.1781 to Toulon, where sold 1786.

As mentioned above, the Galley Corps was suppressed in 1748, and the surviving vessels and personnel were absorbed into the French Navy. In practice, no further vessels were obtained for the *Levant* Fleet (although one *galère extraordinaire* was projected but not built in 1755), while on the Atlantic coast only two new galleys were built (both at Brest).

AMAZONE. Designed and built by Reynoir (Jnr). 25/26 rows of oars.
Dimensions & tons: 146ft 0in x 19ft 0in x 6ft 6in (47.43 x 6.17 x 2.11m). 200/300 tons. Draught 4ft/5½ft (1.30/1.79m). Men: 156, +4 officers and 255 oarsmen.
Guns: 1 x 36pdr forward, flanked by 2 x 18pdrs.

Amazone Brest Dyd.
K: 12.1750. L: 10.2.1751. C: 8.1751. Converted to transport in 1762, and condemned 1763 at Brest.

BRETONNE. Designed and built by Claude Saucillon. 25/26 rows of oars.
Dimensions & tons: 149ft 0in x 21ft 0in (48.40 x 6.82m). 280/ tons. Men: 156, +4 officers and 255 oarsmen.
Guns: 1 x 36pdr forward, flanked by 2 x 18pdrs.

Bretonne Brest Dyd.
K: 1754. L: 20.10.1755. C: 12.1755. Converted to transport in 1762, and condemned 29.8.1765 at Brest.

RÉALE. Galère extraordinaire, ordered in April 1755 to be built by Jouve at Toulon, to have been identical to the previous *Réale* of 1733 (see above). 28/29 rows of oars.
Dimensions & tons: 164ft 0in, 136ft 10in x 21ft 0in x 8ft 7.5in (53.27, 44.45 x 6.82 x 2.80m). 280/450 tons. Men: ? +8 officers.
Guns: 1 x 36pdr forward, flanked by 2 x 18pdrs and 2 x 4pdrs.

Réale Toulon Dyd.
Not built. Order cancelled later in 1755.

The remaining Mediterranean galleys were phased out over the following years (replaced as patrol vessels by xebecs – see Chapter 12), and continued as harbour hulks for the *galériens* (the term continued to be used colloquially for the convicts) at Toulon and Marseille until they were replaced by shore-based facilities. By 1768 all of the remaining galleys had become prison hulks at Toulon or Marseilles except for the *Brave* and *Duchesse*, which followed in 1776 and 1778 respectively. A few of the last galleys continued in harbour service into the nineteenth century, the last (*Patience* and *Ferme*) being broken up in 1814. With no naval function after 1748, they were mentioned only briefly in our 1786–1861 volume.

Appendix A Strength of the French Navy, 1660–1786

Reign of Louis XIV

Year	1st	2nd	3rd	4th	5th	Total Rated	Frigates	Fireships	Corvettes	Bomb Vessels	Storeships	Small
1660	–	–	5	3	1	9	–	–	–	–	3	–
1661	–	–	7	4	4	15	1	–	–	–	3	–
1662	–	–	7	6	4	17	1	–	–	–	3	–
1663	1	–	8	7	4	20	2	–	–	–	3	–
1664	1	–	9	7	8	25	4	1	–	–	6	–
1665	2	1	9	8	12	32	7	13	–	–	7	–
1666	2	2	9	9	13	35	11	17	–	–	9	–
1667	2	6	10	10	16	44	14	18	–	–	25	–
1668	2	12	12	13	19	58	15	18	–	–	27	–
1669	8	13	20	16	21	78	14	21	–	–	33	–
1670	–	–	–	–	–	–	–	–	–	–	–	–
1671	16	16	33	25	29	119	22	16	–	–	37	–
1672	11	22	35	23	29	120	30	20	–	–	24	–
1673	11	22	37	21	29	120	30	20	–	–	24	–
1674	11	24	35	18	28	116	23	17	9	–	22	–
1675	11	23	37	18	29	118	26	19	13	–	23	–
1676	12	27	33	22	23	117	17	16	19	–	24	–
1677	12	26	30	22	26	116	28	17	14	–	24	–
1678	13	21	32	27	20	113	29	17	21	–	31	–
1679	12	20	33	25	19	109	24	14	16	–	21	–
1680	12	19	35	26	21	113	24	14	13	–	23	–
1681	12	21	36	26	20	115	24	8	10	–	22	–
1682	12	20	36	26	21	115	24	7	10	–	20	–
1683	12	20	39	25	21	117	25	7	17	–	20	–
1684	12	21	39	27	22	121	25	7	10	10	19	–
1685	12	22	41	26	20	121	23	9	10	10	21	–
1686	10	21	39	26	19	115	21	9	9	10	23	–
1687	10	21	43	22	16	112	19	11	10	10	23	–
1688	10	23	36	30	19	118	19	11	10	10	21	–
1689	9	21	35	28	22	115	26	10	10	10	21	–
1690	9	24	38	26	23	120	26	30	16	10	18	–
1691	17	26	42	20	22	127	27	36	24	10	30	–
1692	22	27	46	16	21	132	32	31	32	10	28	–
1693	–	–	–	–	–	–	–	–	–	–	–	–
1694	26	30	50	13	9	128	34	47	56	10	50	–
1695	26	29	50	11	21	137	26	26	42	10	55	–
1696	26	30	46	13	20	135	27	22	29	8	60	–
1697	26	27	49	19	16	137	33	22	26	11	57	–
1698	26	27	47	18	17	135	23	15	20	9	40	–
1699	26	20	51	19	16	132	20	12	13	5	30	–
1700	26	20	47	18	18	129	20	11	9	6	21	–
1701	25	18	50	18	19	130	19	9	12	7	15	–
1702	25	18	54	17	21	135	21	8	11	7	26	–
1703	25	10	46	18	18	117	19	6	9	8	22	–
1704	24	30	34	18	22	128	25	8	13	5	22	–
1705	24	17	42	22	24	129	33	10	12	6	25	–
1706	23	29	39	17	12	120	24	9	13	7	19	–
1707	22	20	48	22	10	122	26	10	18	7	20	–
1708	22	21	47	21	10	121	26	10	16	8	22	–
1709	22	19	43	24	12	120	20	10	21	8	23	–
1710	21	18	36	21	9	105	17	7	12	6	17	–

APPENDIX A

Year	1st	2nd	3rd	4th	5th	Total Rated	Frigates	Fireships	Corvettes	Bomb Vessels	Storeships	Small
1711	21	18	33	16	10	98	18	6	11	6	18	–
1712	21	18	32	15	10	96	18	5	11	6	18	–
1713	–	–	–	–	–	–	–	–	–	–	–	–
1714	–	–	–	–	–	–	–	–	–	–	–	–
1715	16	16	27	14	7	80	14	7	7	3	2	–

Reign of Louis XV

Year	1st	2nd	3rd	4th	5th	Total Rated	Frigates	Fireships	Corvettes	Bomb Vessels	Storeships	Small
1716	11	11	24	15	5	66	13	3	7	2	3	–
1717	5	8	19	13	4	49	11	1	3	1	8	–
1718	4	7	22	13	3	49	11	1	5	1	9	–
1719	5	7	21	13	3	49	10	1	2	1	14	–
1723	2	13	14	14	1	44	9	–	2	1	12	–
1727	1	14	12	11	3	41	7	–	0	2	19	–
1729	1	15	15	14	–	45	10	–	3	3	19	–
1734	1	14	18	13	–	46	13	–	2	5	22	4
1735	1	14	19	13	–	47	13	–	2	5	22	4
1736	1	12	19	12	–	44	12	–	2	5	22	4
1738	1	14	19	12	–	46	12	–	2	5	24	4
1739	1	14	20	12	–	47	13	–	1	5	23	6
1740	1	14	22	13	–	50	13	–	1	5	22	6
1741	2	14	23	12	–	51	15	–	1	5	21	6
1742	2	14	21	11	–	48	15	–	1	5	21	5
1743	0	16	22	11	–	49	15	–	1	5	22	6
1746	1	15	20	12	–	48	18	–	6	5	21	6
1751	5	20	19	8	–	52	24	–	–	–	–	–
1752	5	21	28	10	–	64	24	–	3	1	2	8
1753	6	23	24	8	–	61	24	–	–	–	–	–
1754	5	22	23	9	–	59	22	–	2	3	19	8
1755	6	24	31	12	–	73	31	–	5	–	19	4
1757	7	27	28	7	–	69	48	–	18	6	30	4
1758	11	32	30	9	–	82	43	–	15	6	27	4
1759	10	30	24	5	–	69	38	–	10	6	8	10
1761	5	20	20	4	–	49	20	–	6	5	11	7
1762	7	22	19	8	–	56	22	–	7	3	11	11
1763	7	23	21	9	–	60	20	-	6	3	12	9
1764	7	23	22	9	–	61	18	-	12	3	14	9
1765	8	24	26	4	–	62	21	–	15	3	24	21
1766	8	24	27	4	–	63	25	–	19	3	24	19
1767	8	24	23	8	–	63	29	–	9	3	26	29
1768	8	28	26	4	–	66	41	–	14	3	29	9
1769	8	28	21	8	–	65	34	–	16	3	28	11
1770	8	28	24	4	–	64	36	–	14	3	25	9
1771	8	29	31	4	–	72	37	–	21	3	23	9
1772	8	29	25	4	–	66	35	–	21	3	23	9
1773	8	26	28	4	–	66	36	–	18	3	11	16
1774	8	29	26	4	–	67	37	–	17	3	12	15

Reign of Louis XVI

Year	1st	2nd	3rd	4th	5th	Total Rated	Frigates	Fireships	Corvettes	Bomb Vessels	Storeships	Small
1775	8	30	22	6	–	66	34	–	12	3	25	16
1776	8	30	22	6	–	66	41	–	18	3	25	15
1777	8	32	22	4	–	66	41	–	18	3	31	14
1778	7	32	22	3	–	64	48	–	15	3	21	12
1779	12	41	23	3	–	79	67	–	21	5	23	37
1780	13	37	24	5	–	79	67	–	26	5	27	41
1781	12	38	24	6	–	80	62	–	33	5	36	52
1782	12	42	23	6	–	80	56	–	33	5	48	66
1783	14	45	18	6	–	83	66	–	39	5	60	83
1784	12	35	10	6	–	63	55	–	37	5	56	65
1785	13	38	10	6	–	67	57	–	19	3	48	36
1786	12	38	7	3	–	60	67	–	17	3	45	28

Notes: The above dates up to 1743 refer to the situation pertaining on 1 January of the year stated, except for 1669 (when it was in September), 1716–17 (1 June), and 1718 (1 September). The dates for later États are generally not specified except for the year, but they were probably also as at 1 January (although the 1753 one was as at April). Most of the États after 1746 do not give the ranks of ships of the line; they have been distributed here according to other sources that do. The column for 1st Rank ships includes 80-gun two-deckers from 1746 (one is in the 2nd Rank in 1743). The frigate column includes all frigates with single gun decks, both the *frégate légères* and the larger 'true' (single-decked) frigates that were introduced in 1740. The storeship column includes both *flûtes* and *gabarres*. The expansion of the 'small' column beginning in the later 1770s reflects the advent of cutters and other new small combatant types. Named ships under construction were generally included from the 1740s and a few were included previously; we have generally excluded unnamed ships under construction from this tabulation. Note that the system of five ranks was introduced only in 1670 and first appeared in the 1671 État, so we have distributed the data for ranked vessels before 1671 among the ranks using the same parameters that were used in the 1671 État. Also, note that these figures are taken from contemporary sources and may not match comparable figures compiled from modern works including this book.

Sources: Data for 1660–1743 are taken from the *État général des Vaisseaux, Frégates, Brûlots, Galiotes à Bombes, Flûtes, Corvettes, Barques Longues, & autres Bâtiments interrompus du Roi* (in Archives Nationales file B5-2), a chart compiled on 30 September 1745 from the *États abrégés* ('petits Agenda de la Marine') then in the *Dépôt de la Marine*. (An earlier version of this document is in AN B5-3.) Nineteen of these annual volumes were then missing (1670, 1681, 1693, 1699, 1713, 1714, 1720, 1721, 1722, 1723, 1724, 1725, 1726, 1728, 1730, 1731, 1732, 1733 and 1737); since then fifteen more (1674, 1678, 1680, 1684–85, 1694–95, 1697, 1703, 1705, 1711, 1715, 1727, 1735 and 1740) have disappeared and three (1681, 1699, and 1723) have been found. A 1 January 1693 edition was noted in private collections in 1819 and at Dunkirk in 1861, but its location today is unknown. Data to 1717 are exactly as given in the source; data for 1718–43 were modified to add the *gabarres* to the storeship column to match subsequent years and the corvette listings in 1718–19 were also adjusted. Data for 1746 and later are from *États abrégés* at the Archives Nationales, the Service Historique de la Défense, the Bibliothèque Nationale, the Bibliothèque Municipale de Versailles, the Bibliothèque Mazarine, and the Bibliothèque Municipale du Havre, plus for years with no surviving *États* (1746, 1752, 1754-5, 1758, 1761-2, 1764, 1767-71, and 1774-6) lists in files B5-2 through B5-10 and G34 at the Archives Nationales. The 1764 figures are interpolated from the 1763 and 1765 *États*.

Appendix B Financial Expenditures on the French Navy, 1662–1789

The following list sets out the expenditures for the Navy (in *livres tournois*) for each year. Also shown are the figures for the Galley Corps until its abolition in 1748, for the colonies after they first appeared as a separate budget item in 1691, and the totals for the three maritime accounts.

Year	Expenditures, Navy	Expenditures, Galleys	Expenditures, Colonies	Total Expenditures
1662	2,285,403	552,917	–	2,838,320
1663	2,006,148	682,230	–	2,688,378
1664	3,651,637	664,657	–	4,316,294
1665	5,529,068	919,377	–	6,448,445
1666	10,556,748	1,126,763	–	11,683,511
1667	10,225,361	1,084,817	–	11,310,178
1668	8,081,629	1,255,175	–	9,336,804
1669	11,272,761	1,623,718	–	12,896,479
1670	11,703,425	1,693,449	–	13,396,874
1671	10,556,154	1,875,155	–	12,431,309
1672	8,787,770	1,856,473	–	10,644,243
1673	9,799,864	1,761,326	–	11,561,190
1674	9,308,717	2,208,675	–	11,517,392
1675	7,934,318	2,226,428	–	10,160,746
1676	–	–	–	7,990,000
1677	–	–	–	12,000,000
1678	–	–	–	10,659,260
1679	6,753,195	2,735,431	–	9,488,626
1680	7,818,693	3,304,694	–	11,123,387
1681	5,764,816	2,794,530	–	8,559,346
1682	8,069,738	2,858,821	–	10,928,559
1683	9,335,377	3,230,390	–	12,565,767
1684	9,942,037	3,091,134	–	13,033,171
1685	8,494,337	3,348,056	–	11,842,393
1686	8,832,029	2,889,818	–	11,721,847
1687	8,885,435	3,145,891	–	12,031,326
1688	10,542,979	3,233,377	–	13,776,356
1689	20,669,950	3,487,983	–	24,157,933
1690	23,732,650	4,741,288	–	28,473,938
1691	28,525,992	4,378,119	802,744	33,706,855
1692	28,401,411	3,881,682	834,182	33,117,275
1693	28,163,020	3,650,031	997,494	32,810,545
1694	18,719,510	4,203,669	896,270	23,819,449
1695	14,293,488	4,174,446	888,401	19,356,335
1696	18,287,070	4,021,875	937,842	23,246,787
1697	17,645,053	4,062,465	978,941	22,686,459
1698	10,293,734	3,662,927	858,405	14,815,066
1699	10,448,648	3,662,259	800,693	14,911,600
1700	9,118,696	3,031,615	868,455	13,018,766
1701	17,463,771	3,503,667	1,006,686	21,974,124
1702	24,735,850	3,786,976	791,330	29,314,156
1703	19,822,353	3,778,897	1,125,092	24,726,342
1704	20,967,587	3,455,042	927,214	25,349,843
1705	21,575,242	3,204,762	894,270	25,674,274
1706	19,768,199	2,996,640	808,485	23,573,324
1707	14,225,016	2,855,258	860,616	17,940,890
1708	*15,727,793	2,680,118	816,647	*19,224,558
1709	10,251,070	2,290,090	814,841	13,356,001
1710	9,110,831	2,500,909	844,910	12,456,650
1711	6,685,192	1,873,048	652,504	9,210,744
1712	7,986,041	1,911,978	859,080	10,757,099
1713	7,213,116	2,191,755	708,592	10,113,463
1714	5,842,403	2,003,260	886,361	8,732,024
1715	6,016,108	2,095,625	943,035	9,054,768
1716	6,172,465	1,917,874	1,198,540	9,288,879
1717	5,570,778	1,464,922	896,588	7,932,288
1718	5,281,652	1,618,381	759,313	7,659,346
1719	6,017,997	1,427,250	983,197	8,428,444
1720	8,209,968	2,494,850	972,752	11,677,570
1721	7,087,416	1,576,082	1,119,142	9,782,640
1722	7,978,518	1,718,039	907,351	10,603,908
1723	9,869,660	2,550,508	1,255,662	13,675,830
1724	9,856,440	1,926,139	1,238,281	13,020,860
1725	8,458,159	1,772,429	1,085,279	11,315,867
1726	6,774,998	1,562,960	995,210	9,333,168
1727	8,809,323	1,683,004	1,055,363	11,547,690
1728	8,006,178	1,746,130	1,369,868	11,122,176
1729	7,759,741	2,032,829	1,073,534	10,866,104
1730	7,964,565	1,697,832	1,267,057	10,929,454
1731	8,309,478	1,805,686	1,343,398	11,458,562
1732	8,495,597	1,717,441	1,734,871	11,947,909
1733	10,339,621	1,605,974	1,924,896	13,870,491
1734	14,499,808	2,058,844	2,033,784	18,592,436
1735	12,026,612	1,630,842	2,053,819	15,711,273
1736	6,664,219	1,460,418	2,207,287	10,331,924
1737	8,543,158	1,621,770	2,373,965	12,538,893
1738	9,415,194	1,714,202	2,716,700	13,846,096
1739	9,406,653	1,707,069	3,342,923	14,456,645
1740	15,440,452	1,632,931	2,753,932	19,827,315
1741	19,366,171	1,684,020	3,113,500	24,163,691
1742	12,490,413	1,765,843	3,102,345	17,358,601
1743	14,132,954	1,544,127	3,314,940	18,992,021
1744	27,486,558	1,700,354	3,726,061	32,912,973
1745	21,658,500	1,642,463	3,860,202	27,161,165
1746	25,821,586	1,528,936	5,418,648	32,769,170
1747	23,244,603	1,851,224	5,208,377	30,304,204
1748	18,414,669	1,496,305	4,898,188	24,809,162
1749	15,562,555	–	7,591,832	23,154,387
1750	18,217,772	–	12,063,992	30,281,764
1751	16,510,653	–	11,673,378	28,184,031
1752	16,278,498	–	13,138,447	29,416,945
1753	14,603,542	–	14,499,550	29,103,092

Year	Expenditures, Navy	Expenditures, Galleys	Expenditures, Colonies	Total Expenditures	Year	Expenditures, Navy	Expenditures, Galleys	Expenditures, Colonies	Total Expenditures
1754	15,424,262	–	12,819,564	28,243,826	1772	18,578,380	–	27,019,382	45,597,762
1755	24,897,472	–	16,748,723	41,646,195	1773	19,500,000	–	25,914,391	45,414,391
1756	42,949,888	–	27,144,334	70,094,222	1774	17,680,831	–	24,937,894	42,618,725
1757	49,712,985	–	35,347,554	85,060,539	1775	20,522,129	–	25,816,555	46,338,684
1758	40,949,164	–	40,309,944	81,259,108	1776	27,179,944	–	34,720,904	61,900,848
1759	51,800,243	–	40,567,519	92,367,762	1777	41,130,401	–	43,847,746	84,978,147
1760	17,289,289	–	20,204,243	37,493,532	1778	74,086,949	–	61,434,261	135,521,210
1761	16,722,415	–	–	–	1779	105,355,790	–	65,889,469	171,245,259
1762	30,529,650	–	19,682,961	50,212,611	1780	123,288,832	–	64,804,352	188,093,184
1763	21,631,914	–	26,263,221	47,895,135	1781	113,566,736	–	70,621,137	184,187,873
1764	16,199,414	–	29,307,582	45,506,996	1782	184,474,500	–	91,183,149	275,657,649
1765	17,360,458	–	26,115,794	43,476,252	1783	–	–	–	147,588,938
1766	21,400,684	–	24,588,828	45,989,512	1784	–	–	–	63,724,996
1767	19,877,456	–	23,223,586	43,101,042	1785	–	–	–	62,911,620
1768	21,607,207	–	25,058,177	46,665,384	1786	–	–	–	52,726,829
1769	19,033,510	–	31,436,767	50,470,277	1787	–	–	–	69,272,986
1770	20,114,537	–	31,796,562	51,911,099	1788	–	–	–	82,525,475
1771	21,504,303	–	–	–	1789	–	–	–	49,287,186

*The 1708 figure in the original source ('727,793') appears to be missing the first two digits; we have estimated them from other figures for 1707–1709.

Sources:
1662–1675: BN, n.a.f. 4223 to 4226, 'États de Finances, Années 1662–1675'.
1676–1678: Martine Acerra, *Rochefort et la construction navale française, 1661–1815* (Paris, 1993), pp623–29, 791–92, 906–8; taken from AN, K 1360, 'Mémoires de Usson de Baurepas. Dépenses de 1672 à 1709'.
1679–1782: BN, n.a.f. 5399, 'Matériaux pour servir à l'histoire des finances de la marine, 1678–1811'.
1783: Alain Demerliac, *Nomenclature des navires français de 1774 à 1792* (Nice, 1996), p5.
1784–1789: Pierre Victor, baron Malouet, *Collection des opinions de M. Malouet, député à l'Assemblée Nationale*, t. 1, Paris, 1791, p224.

Appendix C French Warship Ranks and Changes in Ranks, 1669–1786

One feature of the French Navy in the late 1600s and early 1700s was the frequent reassignment of its ships among the five ranks of vaisseaux. A *règlement* of 1670 attempted to define the parameters of the five ranks, but it was soon departed from although it and a later ordinance of 1689 continued to be cited as guidance until the mid-1700s.

Part 1: Ranking by tonnage, 1669–1690

Tonnage was the organizing factor in the 1669 to 1675 annual *États abrégés* (herafter simply called États). The ships were listed in these États in descending order of tonnage, with the next rank taking over where the previous left off without any overlap in tonnages between ranks. Although the ships were not listed in order of number of guns, in this early period the number of guns (see Table III) behaved almost as well as an indicator of rank as did tonnage, with the main overlap being a small one between the 1st and 2nd Ranks. As new ships were added to the list this orderly structure began to fray at the edges, first with more overlaps in the number of guns beginning in 1675 and then with overlaps in tonnages beginning in 1676. Tonnage probably continued to be the primary determinant of a ship's rank up to 1690, but after 1675 tonnages and ranks were modified for reasons that to a large extent remain unexplained.

The 1688 État cleaned up the overlaps in tonnages that had accrued since 1675. Once again the ships are listed in descending order of tonnage, with the next rank taking over where the previous left off without any overlap in tonnages. This pattern is largely repeated in 1689 and 1690. Note that there are significant overlaps in the number of guns (in Table III), as the close correlation between the number of guns and hull size apparent in the early 1670s had largely disappeared by 1690. Table I shows the tonnages of each rank in all existing États between 1669 and 1716 while Table II shows the individual re-rankings that took place between 1671 and 1690.

Note that the year in the left column in these tables is that of the État in which the re-ranking was first recorded (usually on 1 January of that year). The next column in Tables II and IV shows the year(s) in which the actual action is estimated to have taken place. In the chapters in this book we cite the estimated years of the actual re-rankings rather than the État years, although it should be noted that we cite the État years for armament changes.

Table I: Rankings by tons

État	1st Rank	2nd Rank	3rd Rank	4th Rank	5th Rank	Fre. Lég.
1669	2000–1200	1100–1000	900–600	550–350	–	200–30
1671	2400–1400	1300–1100	1050–800	800–600	550–300	200–30
1672	2400–1500	1500–1050	1050–800	750–550	550–300	300–30
1673	2400–1500	1500–1050	1050–800	750–550	550–300	300–30
1674	2400–1500	1500–1050	1050–800	750–550	550–300	300–30
1675	2400–1500	1500–1050	1050–800	750–600	550–300	500–50
1676	2400–1400	1500–1050	1000–800	750–450	550–250	500–60
1677	2400–1400	1500–1000	1000–700	750–350	600–250	350–30
1679	2500–1400	1500–1000	1100–600	750–350	500–250	300–70
1680	2500–1400	1500–1000	1100–600	750–350	500–250	300–70
1681	2500–1400	1500–1000	1100–600	750–350	500–250	300–70
1682	2500–1400	1500–1000	1100–600	750–350	500–250	300–70
1683	2500–1400	1500–1000	1100–600	750–350	500–250	300–70
1686	2500–1400	1500–900	1100–600	750–350	500–250	300–70
1687	2500–1400	1500–900	1100–600	750–350	600–250	300–70
1688	2500–1500	1400–1100	1050–800	750–410	400–200	300–70
1689	2500–1500	1400–1100	1050–800	750–410	400–200	380–70
1690	2500–1500	1400–1100	1050–800	750–400	400–200	380–70
1691	2500–1300	1500–1000	1100–700	800–250	500–180	280–70
1692	2500–1400	1500–1000	1100–600	600–250	400–180	250–40
1696	2600–1400	1400–800	1000–400	800–330	400–200	300–40
1698	2600–1400	1400–800	1000–400	800–300	400–200	380–50
1699	2600–1400	1400–950	1050–480	800–280	420–150	250–60
1700	2600–1400	1400–950	1050–390	800–280	360–150	250–60
1701	2600–1400	1400–950	1100–480	800–290	600–245	250–60
1702	Unknown	Unknown	Unknown	Unknown	Unknown	Unknown
1704	2600–?	?–600	1050–330	600–330	450–230	220–80 (50)
1706	Unknown	Unknown	Unknown	Unknown	400–240	Unknown
1707	2600–1400	1500–700	1100–390	600–350	350–180	500–90
1708	Unknown	Unknown	Unknown	Unknown	Unknown	Unknown
1709	2600–1300	1550–800	1200–460	700–350	400–200	250–90
1710	2200–1300	1550–800	1100–460	700–350	300–177	300–90
1712	2600–1300	1550–800	1100–420	700–236	300–177	420–90
1716	2600–1350	1550–880	1100–600	700–263	300–200	470–90

The 1670 *Règlement* increased the number of ranks from four to five by inserting a new 3rd Rank. As a result, in 1671 47 ships were re-ranked, with some smaller 2nd Rank ships moving to the new 3rd Rank, many of the former 3rd Rank ships moving to the 4th Rank, and nearly all of the former 4th Rank ship moving to the 5th Rank. The next largest re-ranking before 1691 was in 1688, when 21 ships were re-ranked to clean up the rank structure. Many of these re-rankings were accompanied by tonnage changes; the tonnages accompanying the re-rankings are indicated below. Tonnage changes are generally not shown in the main body of this work; consequently, some of the tonnages shown below may not appear in the text.

Table II: Ships Re-ranked, 1671–1690

État	Est. Year	Re-ranking	Ships re-ranked (tons)
1671	1670	From 2nd to 1st Rank	*Paris* (1500), *Île de France* (1500)
1671	1670	From 2nd to 3rd Rank	*Bourbon* (1050), *Princesse* (1050), *Sophie* (1000), *Diamant* (1000), *Reine* (1000), *Lys* (950), *Navarre* (950), *Royale* (950), *Rochefort* (950), *Saint Louis* (950), *Breton* (800)
1671	1670	From 3rd to 4th Rank	*Triomphe* (800), *Mazarin* (750), *Toulon* (750), *Cheval Marin* (750), *Sirène* (750), *Provençal* (750), *Dunkerquois* (750), *Duc* (700), *Galant* (700), *Hercule* (700), *Jules* (700), *Flamand* (650), *Soleil* (650), *Beaufort* (600), *Mercœur* (600), *Le Havre* (600), *Tigre* (550)
1671	1670	From 4th to 5th Rank	*Sauveur* (550), *Ville de Rouen* (550), *Bayonnais* (500), *Dragon* (500), *Écureuil* (500), *Hermine* (500), *Étoile* (450), *Perle* (450), *Soleil d'Afrique* (450), *Croissant d'Afrique* (450), *Hirondelle* (450), *Lion Rouge* (450), *Saint Joseph* (400), *Ligournois* (400), *Palmier* (400), *Lion d'Or* (350), *Saint Sébastien* (350)
1672	1671	From 1st to 2nd Rank	*Saint Philippe* (1500), *Pompeux* ex-*Madame* (1400), *Henry* ex-*Joli* (1400), *Florissant* ex-*Rubis* (1400)
1672	1671	From 3rd to 2nd Rank	*Éclatant* ex-*Bourbon* (1050), *Triomphant* ex-*Princesse* (1050)
1672	1671	From 4th to 3rd Rank	*Courageux* ex-*Triomphe* (800)
1672	1671	From 4th to 5th Rank	*Léger* ex-*Saint Antoine de Gênes* (550)
1673	1672	From 4th to 3rd Rank	*Maure* ex-*Artois* (800), *Fendant* ex-*Grâces* (800)
1673	1673	From fireship to 5th Rank	*Émerillon* ex-*Actif* (350), *Vigilant* ex-*Entreprenant* (350)
1674	1673	From 3rd to 2nd Rank	*Saint Michel* ex-*Fier* (1050), *Furieux* (1050)
1674	1673	From 4th to 3rd Rank	*Apollon* ex-*Saint Michel* (850)
1674	1673	From fireships to 5th Rank	*Arrogant* ex *Caché* (450), *Dragon* ex *Entreprenant* (450)
1675	1674	From 2nd to 3rd Rank	*Furieux* (1050)
1675	1674	From fireships to 5th Rank	*Croissant* ex *Brutal* (500) and probably *Entendu* ex *Fâcheux* (500)
1676	1675	From 3rd to 2nd Rank	*Fier* ex-*Alsace* (1050), *Parfait* ex-*Indien* (1050)
1676	1675	From 5th to 4th Rank	*Entendu* ex-*Dauphin* (600), *Croissant* ex-*Brutal* (500), *Hasardeux* (450), *Faucon* (450)
1676	1675	From fireship to 4th Rank	*Étoile* ex-*Actif* (450)
1676	1675	From fireship to 5th Rank	*Soleil d'Afrique* ex-*Éclair* (350)
1677	1676	From 4th to 5th Ranks	*Neptune* ex-*Beaufort* (600), *Trident* ex-*Mercœur* (600)
1677	1676	From *frégates légères* to 4th Rank	*Arc en Ciel* ex-*Rieuse* (500), *Ferme* ex-*Serpente* (500)
1679	1678	From 1st to 2nd Rank	*Admirable* ex-*Souverain* (1500)
1679	1677–78	From 2nd to 3rd Rank	*Constant* ex-*Triomphant* (1100), *Ferme* ex-*Fier* (1050), *Parfait* ex-*Indien* (1050)
1679	1677–78	From 4th to 3rd Rank	*Capable* ex-*Mignon* (750), *Fidèle* ex-*Joli* (750), *Opiniâtre* ex-*Galant* (600)
1679	1677–78	From 5th to 4th Rank	*Maure* ex-*Neptune* (600), *Trident* ex-*Mercœur* (600), *Aventurier* ex-*Galante* (400), *Bizarre* ex-*Mignonne* (400), *Capricieux* ex-*Hermine* (400)
1681	1680	From 5th to 4th Rank	*Sérieux* (350)
1683	1682	From 4th to 5th Rank	*Sérieux* (350)
1686	1685	From 5th Rank to *frégate légère*	*Bien Aimée* (250)
1688	1687	From 2nd to 1st Rank	*Grand* (1600)
1688	1687	From 1st to 2nd Rank	*Couronne* (1400)
1688	1687	From 3rd to 2nd Rank	*Courtisan* (1150), *Bourbon* (1150), *Constant* (1100), *Sérieux* (1100)
1688	1687	From 2nd to 3rd Rank	*Sans Pareil* (1000), *Furieux* (1000), *Vermandois* (1000), *Saint Louis* (1000)
1688	1687	From 3rd to 4th Rank	*Hardi* (750), *Fidèle* (750), *Capable* (750), *Duc* (700), *Oriflamme* (700), *Opiniâtre* (600)
1688	1687	From 5th to 4th Rank	*Gaillard* (600), *Prompt* (500)
1688	1687	From 4th to 5th Rank	*Triton* (400), *Tigre* (400), *Croissant* (300)
1689	1688	From 4th to 3rd Rank	*Hardi* (900)

Part II: Ranking by number of guns, 1691–1716

The 1691 État shows a sudden shift from tonnage to the number of guns as the organizing factor. In this État the ships were listed in descending order of number of guns, with the next rank taking over where the previous left off. Now there is no overlap in the gun ranges while the tonnages, probably unavoidably, have significant overlaps. Note that the relevant number of guns was that for wartime, not peacetime. In 1699 overlaps begin to creep back in, and they were quite sizeable between 1704 and 1712. In 1716, excluding two prizes, all of the overlaps were eliminated. Table III shows the figures for number of guns for all existing États between 1669 and 1716 plus the *Règlement* of 1670 while Table IV shows the re-rankings that took place between 1691 and 1716, including the estimated years in which they occurred.

Table III: Rankings by guns

État	1st Rank	2nd Rank	3rd Rank	4th Rank	5th Rank	Fre. Lég.
1669	120–64	66–50	50–36	36–24	—	16–02
1670 Reg.	120–70	70–56	50–40	40–30	28–18	16–08
1671	120–66	68–62	60–48	44–36	34–24	18–04
1672	120–70	70–64	56–48	44–36	34–28	18–02
1673	120–70	76–60	56–48	44–36	34–28	18–04
1674	120–70	78–60	60–50	46–36	34–28	24–06
1675	120–70	78–60	60–50	46–36	40–28	30–06
1676	120–74	78–60	56–50	46–38	36–22	38–08
1677	120–74	78–60	60–48	48–40	42–20	28–06
1679	120–76	80–60	64–46	48–36	36–20	28–06
1680	120–76	80–60	64–46	48–36	40–20	28–06
1681	120–76	80–60	64–46	48–36	40–20	28–06
1682	120–76	80–60	64–46	48–36	36–20	28–06
1683	120–76	80–60	64–46	48–36	36–20	28–06
1686	120–76	78–60	64–46	48–36	40–20	28–10
1687	120–76	80–54	64–46	48–38	44–28	28–10
1688	108–76	78–62	60–50	50–34	40–20	28–10
1689	108–76	78–62	60–48	50–34	40–28	34–10
1690	110–80	86–62	68–54	58–36	40–28	34–10
1691	110–76	76–64	60–50	50–40	36–24	34–10
1692	110–80	76–64	60–50	46–40	36–24	34–10
1696	110–80	76–64	62–50	48–40	36–30	28–08
1698	110–80	76–64	62–50	48–40	38–30	28–10
1699	110–80	76–62	62–46	46–34	38–28	36–10
1700	110–80	76–64	64–46	50–38	40–28	34–10
1701	110–80	76–64	68–46	50–36	38–30	32–06
1702	110–80	76–64	64–46	46–36	40–28	24–06
1704	110–80	76–50	60–46	48–36	46–28	30–10
1706	112–80	76–52	68–44	50–30	40–24	30–10
1707	110–76	74–60	68–38	50–30	40–20	40–6
1708	110–76	84–60	68–38	50–30	36–18	40–6
1709	110–76	84–64	72–38	56–34	36–18	34–10
1710	110–76	84–64	72–48	56–34	44–18	34–10
1712	110–76	84–64	72–48	48–36	44–18	40–10
1716	110–84	74–64	66–50	52–38	38–16	42–10

The shift in 1691 to number of guns as the organizing factor caused the ranks of 21 ships of the line to be changed. It is worth noting that all of these ships were promoted in rank except for one 4th Rank ship which was demoted. Another major re-ranking took place in 1704 when 18 ships were re-ranked, of which 15 went from the 3rd to 2nd Rank. This change was essentially reversed in 1707 when 14 ships moved from the 2nd to the 3rd Rank. Changes in the number of guns sometimes accompanied re-rankings; the gun counts accompanying the re-rankings are indicated below. Most armament changes including most of those shown here are described in the main body of this work.

Table IV: Ships Re-ranked, 1691–1716

État	Est. Year	Re-ranking	Ships re-ranked (guns)
1691	1690	From 2nd to 1st Rank	*Monarque ex-Saint Esprit* (94), *Conquérant* (84), *Magnifique* (84), *Intrépide* (84), *Saint Philippe* (84), *Couronne* (76), *Tonnant* (76), *Fier* (76), *Triomphant* (76)
1691	1690	From 3rd to 2nd Rank	*Aimable* (70), *Content* (66), *Ardent* (66), *Brillant* (64)
1691	1690	From 4th to 3rd Rank	*Maure* (54), *Trident* (50), *Brusque* (50), *Duc* (50)
1691	1690	From 5th to 4th Rank	*Alcyon* (40), *Mignon* (40), *Triton* (40)
1691	1690	From 4th to 5th Rank	*Prompt* (36)
1692	1691	From 1st to 2nd Rank	*Couronne* (76), *Tonnant* (76), *Fier* (76), *Triomphant* (76)
1692	1691	From 4th to 3rd Rank	*Fidèle* (50), *François* (50), *Neptune* (50), *Arc en Ciel* (50)
1696	1692–95	From 3rd to 2nd Rank	*Écueil* (66), *Parfait* (64)
1696	1692–95	From 3rd to 4th Rank	*Heureux Retour* (46), *Arc en Ciel* (46)
1696	1692–95	From 5th to 4th Rank	*Adroit* (44), *Poli* (40), *Opiniâtre* (40)
1696	1692–95	From 4th to 5th Rank	*Aventurier* (36), *Étoile* (36)
1696	1692–95	From *frégates légères* to 5th Rank	*Gaillarde* (32), *Badine* (32), *Jalouse* (30)
1696	1694	From fireship to 5th Rank	*Lutin* (32)
1696	1694	From 5th Rank to fireship	*Éveillé* (6)
1698	1696–97	From 2nd to 3rd Rank	*Laurier* (60), *Sirène* (60)
1699	1698	From 2nd to 3rd Rank	*Juste* (62), *Sérieux* (62), *Parfait* (62), *Éole* (62), *Saint Louis* (60), *Content* (60)
1699	1699	From 4th to 3rd Rank	*Faucon Anglais* (50)
1699	1698	From 3rd to 4th Rank	*Sainte Croix Galion* (40)
1699	1698	From 5th to 4th Rank	*Palmier* (40)
1699	1698	From *galiote à mortier* to 5th Rank	*Bellone* (30), *Martiale* (28)
1701	1700	From 3rd to 2nd Rank	*Ferme* (66)
1701	1700	From 2nd to 3rd Rank	*Bizarre* (68), *Écueil* (66), *Ardent* (64), *Glorieux* (64)
1701	1700	From 3rd to 4th Rank	*Mignon* (48), *Jerzé* (46)
1701	1700	From 4th to 5th Rank	*Héroïne* (38), *Alcyon* (36)
1701	1700	From 5th Rank to *galiote à mortier*	*Martiale* (28)
1702	1701	From 3rd to 2nd Rank	*Bizarre* (68)
1702	1701	From 2nd to 3rd Rank	*Henry* (64)
1702	1701	From 4th to 3rd Rank	*Hasardeux* (50), *Mignon* (48), *Heureux Retour* (46)
1702	1701	From *frégate légère* to 5th Rank	*Milfort* (32)
1702	1701	From fireship to 5th Rank	*Éveillé* (32)
1704	1703	From 1st to 2nd Rank	*Magnanime* (70)
1704	1702–03	From 3rd to 2nd Rank	*Écueil* (66), *Ardent* (64), *Glorieux* (64), *Henri* (64), *Content* (62), *Furieux* (62), *Vermandois* (62), *Ville de Médemblick* (62), *Juste* (60), *Zélande* (60), *Éole* (58), *Sérieux* (58), *Saint Louis* (58), *Saint Michel* (58), *Fendant* (56)
1704	1702–03	From 3rd to 4th Rank	*Mignon* (48)
1704	1702–03	From 5th to 4th Rank	*Alcyon* (38)
1706	1704–05	From 4th to 3rd Rank	*Mignon* (48), *Héros* (46)
1706	1704–05	From 5th to 3rd Rank	*Dryade* (44)
1706	1704–05	From 5th Rank to *frégate légère*	*Méduse* (28)
1707	1706	From 2nd to 1st Rank	*Couronne* (76)
1707	1706	From 1st to 2nd Rank	*Grand* (72)
1707	1706	From 2nd to 3rd Rank	*Glorieux* (66), *Écueil* (66), *Brillant* (66), *Achille* (64), *Toulouse* (62), *Vermandois* (60), *Zélande* (60), *Ville de Médemblick* (60), *Sérieux* (58), *Saint Louis* (58), *Éole* (58), *Furieux* (58), *Fendant* (56), *Content* (54)
1707	1706	From 4th to 3rd Rank	*Jerzé* (46)
1707	1706	From 3rd to 4th Rank	*Mignon* (48), *Dryade* (44)
1707	1706	From 5th to 4th Rank	*Rozendal* (34)
1709	1708	From 2nd to 3rd Rank	*Élisabeth* (72), *Oriflamme* (60)
1709	1708	From 3rd to 4th Rank	*Licorne* (56), *Héros* (42), *Jerzé* (40)
1709	1708	*Frégate légère* to 4th Rank	*Amazone* (40)
1709	1708	From 4th to 5th Rank	*Palmier* (30)
1709	1708	*Frégate légère* to 5th Rank	*Méduse* (28)
1712	1710–11	From 4th to 5th Rank	*Rozendal* (34)
1715	1712	From 1st to 2nd Rank	*Conquérant* (70)
1715	1712–14	From 2nd to 3rd Rank	*Grafton* (66)
1715	1712–14	From 3rd to 4th Rank	*Blakoual* (52), *Protée* (46), *François* (46)
1715	1712–14	From 4th to 3rd Rank	*Licorne* (56/hulk)

Part III: Rank changes, 1717–1786

The changes in 1716 and some adjustments to the armaments recorded for some other ships essentially resulted in the elimination of the overlaps between ranks in numbers of guns. Two overlaps remained, each of 2 guns, because the captured *Grafton* (66 guns) and *Blackwall* (52 guns) did not quite fit in the 3rd and 4th Ranks to which they were respectively assigned. Without them the resulting rank structure looked as follows.

1st Rank: 110 to 84 guns
2nd Rank: 74 to 68 guns (and two old 64s)
3rd Rank: 64 to 50 guns.
4th Rank: 50 to 38 guns.
5th Rank: 38 to 16 guns.

With the main parameters of the rank structure in place there were relatively few re-rankings after 1716. Most of these involved the smallest two-deckers (those with fewer than 60 guns) as the Navy struggled to figure out where they fitted in a fleet increasingly dominated by 64- and 74-gun ships. These later re-rankings were generally not accompanied by a change in the number of guns on the ships.

Table V: Ships Re-ranked, 1717–1786

Est. Year	Re-ranking	Ships re-ranked (guns)
1723–28	From 5th to 4th Rank	*Ludlow* (32)
1743–46	From 3rd to 4th Rank	*Diamant* (50)
1746–48	From 4th Rank to frigate	*Aquilon* (42), *Anglesea* (42), *Junon* (40)
1748–52	From 3rd to 4th Rank	*Arc en Ciel* (56), *Oriflamme* (54) *Hippopotame* (50), *Apollon* (50), *Aigle* (50)
1748–52	From frigate to 4th Rank	*Anglesea* (50), *Junon* (46), *Aquilon* (46)
1753	From 3rd to 2nd Rank	*Northumberland* (70)
1753	From 3rd to 4th Rank	*Amphion* (50)
1756	From 3rd to 4th Rank	*Fier* (50)
1764	From 4th to 3rd Rank	*Bordelais* class (56)
1766	From 1st to 2nd Rank	*Orient* (74, rebuilt from 80)
1766	From 4th to 3rd Rank	*Amphion* (50), *Sagittaire* (50)
1767	From 3rd to 2nd Rank	*Actif* (74, rebuilt from 64)
1768	From 3rd to 2nd Rank	*Bordelais* class (56)
1771	From 2nd to 3rd Rank	*Bordelais* class (56)
1771	From 4th to 3rd Rank	*Hippopotame* (50), *Fier* (50)
1772	From 3rd to 4th Rank	*Hippopotame* (50), *Fier* (50), *Amphion* (50), *Sagittaire* (50)
1776	From 3rd to 4th Rank	*Bordelais* (56), *Flamand* (56)

Appendix D Standard Armaments of French Ships, 1674 and 1689

Regulation of 10 February 1674.

First Rank: 80 guns.
LD: 12 x 24pdrs bronze, 14 x 18pdrs bronze.
MD: 14 x 18pdrs iron, 12 x 12pdrs iron.
UD: 22 x 8pdrs bronze.
QD: 6 x 4pdrs bronze.

Second Rank: 64 guns.
LD: 10 x 24pdrs bronze, 12 x 18pdrs iron.
MD: 8 x 12pdrs bronze, 20 x 12pdrs iron.
UD: 6 x 6pdrs bronze, 8 x 6pdrs iron.

Third Rank: 50 guns.
LD: 12 x 18pdrs bronze, 10 x 12pdrs iron.
UD: 6 x 12pdrs bronze, 6 x 12pdrs iron, 10 x 8pdrs iron.
QD: 6 x 6pdrs iron.

Fourth Rank: 40 guns.
LD: 4 x 12pdrs bronze, 6 x 12pdrs iron, 10 x 8pdrs iron.
UD: 6 x 6pdrs bronze (see note), 12 x 6pdrs iron.
QD: 2 x 4pdrs iron.
Note that the AN manuscript has 6 x 8pdrs bronze vice 6 x 6pdrs bronze (a copyist's error?).

Fifth Rank: 30 guns.
LD: 4 x 12pdrs bronze, 12 x 8pdrs iron.
UD: 4 x 6pdrs bronze, 10 x 6pdrs iron.

Ordinance of 15 April 1689.

First Rank: 100 guns. Note that all guns are bronze.
LD: 28 x 36pdrs bronze.
MD: 26 x 18pdrs bronze.
UD: 24 x 12pdrs bronze.
QD/Fc: 22 x 6pdrs bronze.

Second Rank: 80 guns.
LD: 12 x 24pdrs bronze, 14 x 18pdrs iron.
MD: 14 x 12pdrs bronze, 12 x 12pdrs iron.
UD: 22 x 6pdrs bronze.
QD: 6 x 4pdrs bronze.

Third Rank: 60 guns.
LD: 6 x 24pdrs bronze, 16 x 18pdrs iron.
UD: 14 x 12pdrs bronze, 10 x 12pdrs iron.
QD: 10 x 6pdrs bronze.
Fc: 4 x 4pdrs iron.

Fourth Rank: 44 guns.
LD: 4 x 18pdrs bronze, 16 x 12pdrs iron.
UD: 8 x 8pdrs bronze, 12 x 8pdrs iron.
QD: 4 x 4pdrs bronze.

Fifth Rank: 36 guns.
LD: 6 x 8pdrs bronze, 12 x 8pdrs iron.
UD: 6 x 6pdrs bronze, 12 x 4pdrs iron.

Sources:
1674: BNF: FR. 25,377 and AN: MAR/A/1/14 (n°9).
1689: AN: AD/VII/11 (printed edition page 272).
Note that these documents specified only the number and types of guns to be carried; we have distributed them on decks based on the work of J C Lemineur on the first three ranks and on the distribution of actual armaments in the 1696 *État abrégé* for all five ranks.

Appendix E French Monarchs, Political and Naval Leaders, 1626–1786

FRENCH MONARCHS – THE BOURBON DYNASTY

King	Born	Acceded	Died	
Henri IV	13.12.1553	2.8.1589	14.5.1610	(assassinated)
Louis XIII	27.9.1601	14.5.1610	14.5.1643	
Louis XIV	5.9.1638	14.5.1643	1.9.1715	
Louis XV	15.2.1710	1.9.1715	10.5.1774	
Louis XVI	23.8.1754	10.5.1774	21.1.1793	(executed)
Louis XVII	27.3.1785	28.1.1793	8.6.1795	(in captivity)
Louis XVIII	17.11.1755	8.6.1795	16.9.1824	

Notes: Louis XIII was King under the Regency of his mother, Marie de Médicis, until 1617. Louis XIV was similarly King under the Regency of his mother, Anne of Austria, until 1651. Louis XVI was deposed and a republic proclaimed on 21 September 1792. His son, Louis XVII, was proclaimed King by exiled monarchists a week after his father's execution, but never reigned. Louis XVIII (the younger brother of Louis XVI) did not reign until 1814, when he recovered the throne – only to lose it again briefly in 1815 during Napoleon's 'Hundred Days'.

CHIEF MINISTER OF FRANCE

1624	(12 Aug)	[Cardinal] Armand-Jean du Plessis, Duc de Richelieu et de Fronsac (died in office)
1642	(4 Dec)	[Cardinal] Jules Raymond Mazarin (died in office)
1661	(9 Mar)	Louis XIV became absolute ruler, announcing that he would be his own First Minister
1715	(1 Sept)	[the Regent] Philippe II, Duke of Orléans
1722	(23 Aug)	[Cardinal] Guillaume Dubois (died in office)
1723	(10 Aug)	Philippe II, Duke of Orléans (died in office)
	(2 Dec)	Louis Henri, Duke of Bourbon
1726	(11 June)	[Cardinal] André-Hercule de Fleury
1743	(29 Jan)	Louis XV became absolute ruler, announcing that he would be his own First Minister
1758	(3 Dec)	Étienne François de Choiseul, Duke of Choiseul
1770	(24 Dec)	René Nicolas Charles Augustin de Maupeou
1774	(14 May)	Jean-Frédéric Phélypeaux, Comte de Maurepas (died in office)
1781	(21 Nov)	Charles Gravier, Comte de Vergennes (died in office 13 Feb 1787)

GRAND-MAÎTRE, CHEF ET SURINTENDANT GÉNÉRAL DE LA NAVIGATION ET COMMERCE DE FRANCE

The post was created by Richelieu for himself in 1626 to consolidate the former positions of Admiral of France (held by Henri, Duc de Montmorency from 2 July 1612 to 20 Oct 1626) and the other Admiralties – of the Levant (the Mediterranean coastline), of Brittany, and of Guyenne (covering the Atlantic coastline south of Brittany), all of which were abolished (*i.e.* bought out). Only the role of General of the Galleys (which were based in Marseille) was retained, as this service was not added to the Navy until 1748.

1626	(20 Oct)	Armand-Jean du Plessis, Cardinal de Richelieu
1642	(5 Dec)	Jean Armand de Maillé-Brézé, Duc de Fronsac (killed in action 14 June 1646)
1646	(4 July)	Anne d'Autriche (widow of Louis XIII and Queen Regent of France)
1650	(12 May)	César de Bourbon-Vendôme, Duc de Vendôme, Duc d'Étampes.
1665	(22 Oct)	François de Bourbon-Vendôme, Duc de Beaufort (killed in action 25 June 1669).

AMIRAL DE FRANCE

The post, nominally the supreme post within the Navy, was revived by Colbert on taking its political powers into his own hands as Secretary of State for the Navy, and used as a sinecure to be given to and held in succession by infants of royal blood, to prevent any genuine naval officer aspiring to it – note the holders' ages on taking office. Even mere aristocrats were excluded. The short-lived Comte de Vermandois was an illegitimate son of Louis XIV and Louise de la Vallière; the Comte de Toulouse was an illegitimate son of Louis XIV and Françoise-Athénaïs, Marquise de Montespan; the Duc de Penthièvre was the son of the Comte de Toulouse, and was dismissed from office only during the Revolution, father and son between them having held the post continuously for well over a century. The Comte de Toulouse was the only one to have seen seagoing service, and was in command of the French fleet at the Battle of Vélez-Málaga in 1704.

Holder	Born	Appointed	Died
Louis de Bourbon, Comte de Vermandois	2.10.1667	25. 6.1669	18.11.1683
Louis Alexandre de Bourbon, Comte de Toulouse	6. 6.1678	18.11.1683	1.12.1737
Louis Jean Marie de Bourbon, Duc de Penthièvre	16.11.1725	1.12.1737	4. 3.1793

As the office of Admiral (*Amiral de France*) was effectively a lucrative honour, and – the Comte de Toulouse, briefly, apart – was not an actual naval post, in practice most senior naval posts were those of the Vice-Admirals. The two posts, which had been in abeyance since the 1620s, were re-established on 12 November 1669.

Vice-Amiral des Mers du Levant (responsible for the Mediterranean coast):

1669	Anne Hilarion de Costentin, Comte de Tourville (shared until 1689 with Duquesne, who died in 1688).
1701	François-Louis Rousselet, Marquis de Châteaurenault.
1716	Alain-Emmanuel, Marquis de Coëtlogon.
1730	Charles, Marquis de Sainte-Maure.
1745	Gaspard de Goussé de La Roche-Allard (who died after one week in post).
1750	Vincent de Salaberry de Benneville.
1751	Pierre de Blouet de Camilly.
1753	Jean-André Barrailh.
1762	Emmanuel-Auguste de Cahideux, Comte Dubois de La Motte.
1764	Claude-Louis, Marquis de Massiac.
1770	Ann-Antoine, Comte d'Aché de Marbeuf.
1780	Charles-Alexandre Morel, Comte d'Aubigny.
1781	Aymar-Joseph, Comte de Roquefeuil.
1782	Henri-François de La Rochefoucauld, Comte de Cousages.
1784	Louis-Armand-Constantin de Rohan, Prince de Montbazon (to 1792).

Vice-Amiral des Mers du Ponant (responsible for the Atlantic and Channel coasts):

1669		Jean, Comte d'Estrées.
1707		Victor Marie, Duc d'Estrées (son of the foregoing).
1737		Antoine François de Pardaillan de Gondrin, Marquis d'Antin.
1741		François de Bricqueville, Comte de La Luzerne (to 1746).
1746		Claude-Élisée de Court de La Bruyère.
1752		François-Cornil Bart (the son of Jean Bart).
1755		Charles-Félix de Poilvilain, Comte de Cresnay.
1756		Jean-Baptiste Mac Nemara (who died the day following his nomination).
1756		Hubert de Brienne, Comte de Conflans.
1777		Joseph de Bauffremont, Prince de Listenois.
1781		Paul-Hippolyte de Beauvilliers, Marquis de La Ferté-Saint-Aignan.
1788		Pierre-Antoine de Raymond, Bailli d'Éoux (to 1792).

In 1778 a third Vice-Admiral's post (*Vice-Amiral des Mers d'Asie et d'Amérique*) was created specifically for Charles Henry d'Estaing, and in 1784 another post (*Vice-Amiral des Mers d'Inde*) was created for Pierre-André de Suffren. Until 1791 these four appointments were honorific and rarely sea-going, most of the holders being in their 70s or even 80s at the time of appointment. The existing posts were abolished in 1792, after the existing rank of *lieutenant general* was renamed *Vice-Amiral*.

Below the level of Vice-Admiral were two further ranks of flag officers (*officiers généreux*), the higher being that of *lieutenant général* (which in 1791 was renamed *vice-amiral*) – in practice the usual commander of a battlefleet – and the lower being *chef d'escadre* (which in 1791 was renamed *contre-amiral*). In general, these were the effective sea-going flag officers. These ranks are abbreviated in this volume to LG and CdE respectively where they precede an officer's name.

Richelieu created the post of *chef d'escadre* in 1627, to remove responsibility for defence of the French coasts – traditionally left to its feudal overlords in the semi-independent provinces of Brittany, Guyenne and Normandy – into the hands of competent military leaders (*officiers d'épée*). The first new *chefs d'escadres* were created for Brittany, for Guyenne and for Normandy. They took over control of the ports of Brest, Brouage and Le Havre respectively, as well as the King's ships based on those ports. Each was aided by an administrative officer (*officier de plume*) with the title of *commissaire général*.

Further *chefs d'escadres* were created in 1635 for Provence (with responsibility for the port of Toulon and its fleet), in 1647 for Flanders (Dunkirk) and for Catalonia, in 1663 for Poitou-Saintonge, in 1673 for Picardy and for Languedoc, in 1689 for Aunis, in 1701 for 'America' (for the Caribbean and Arcadian territories) and in 1707 for Roussillon. After 1715, having run out of littoral provinces, the title was altered to *chef d'escadre des armées navales*, and there were no longer references to geographical territories.

For ranks below that of *chef d'escadre*, see Introduction.

CONTROLEUR-GÉNÉRAL DES FINANCES

The post, while of long standing, was augmented in 1661 to replace the former position of *Surintendant-général des finances royales*, whose last holder, Nicolas Fouquet, was disgraced, dismissed from office on 5 September 1661 (and imprisoned) by Louis XIV after the King became his own Chief Minister; subsequent holders of the new post were as follows:

1657	(20 Oct)	Louis Le Tonnelier de Breteuil.
1665	(12 Dec)	Jean-Baptiste Colbert.
1687	(6 Sept)	Claude Le Pelletier de Morfontaine.
1689	(20 Sept)	Louis Phélypeaux, Comte de Pontchartrain.
1699	(5 Sept)	Michel Chamillart.
1708	(1 Oct)	Nicolas Desmarets
1715	(15 Sept)	Adrien Maurice, Duc de Noailles, *Président du Conseil des Finances*.
1718	(28 July)	Marc-René de Voyer de Paulmy, Marquis d'Argenson, *Directeur de l'administration principale des finances*.
1720	(12 Dec)	Félix Le Peletier de la Houssays.
1722	(21 Apr)	Charles Gaspard Dodun.
1756	(24 Apr)	François Marie Peyrenc de Moras.
1757	(25 Aug)	Jean de Boullongne.
1759	(4 Mar)	Étienne de Silhouette.
	(23 Nov)	Henri Léonard Jean Baptiste Bertin.
1763	(13 Dec)	Clément Charles François de L'Averdy.
1768	(22 Sept)	Étienne Maynon d'Invault.
1769	(22 Dec)	Abbé Joseph Marie Terray.
1774	(20 July)	Anne Robert Jacques Turgot, Baron de l'Aulne.
1776	(21 May)	Jean Étienne Bernard Clugny de Nuits.
	(21 Oct)	Louis Gabriel Taboureau des Réaux (nominally, Jacques Necker, *Directeur-général du Trésor*, actually held control).
1777	(29 June)	Jacques Necker, *Directeur-général des Finances*.
1781	(21 May)	Jean-François Joly de Fleury, *Administrateur-général des Finances*.
1783	(29 Mar)	Henri Lefèvre d'Ormesson.
	(3 Nov)	Charles Alexandre de Calonne (to 8 Apr 1787).

SECRETARIES OF STATE (FOR FOREIGN AFFAIRS):

(The office of Secretary of State, dating back several centuries, including responsibility for naval matters until 7 March 1669, when the separate office of Secretary of State for the Navy was created for Colbert. The office of Secretary of State continued thereafter, but was retitled Secretary of State for Foreign Affairs in September 1718.)

1616	(30 Nov)	Armand-Jean du Plessis, Bishop of Luçon – later Duc (and Cardinal) de Richelieu.
1617	(24 Apr)	Pierre Brûlart, Vicomte de Puisieux.
1626	(11 Mar)	Raymond Phélypeaux, Seigneur d'Herbault et La Vrillière.
1629	(2 May)	Claude Bouthillier, Seigneur du Pont et de Fossigny.
1632	(18 Mar)	Léon Bouthillier, Comte de Chavigny et de Buzançais.
1643	(23 June)	Henri Auguste de Loménie, Seigneur de la Ville aux Clercs.
1663	(3 Apr)	Hugues de Lionne, Marquis de Fresnes.
1671	(1 Sept)	Simon Arnauld, Marquis de Pomponne (to 18 November 1679).
1680	(12 Feb)	Charles Colbert, Marquis de Croissy.
1696	(28 July)	Jean-Baptiste Colbert, Marquis de Torcy.
1715	(23 Sept)	Nicolas du Blé, Marquis d'Huxelles.
1718	(24 Sept)	Guillaume Dubois.
1723	(16 Aug)	Charles Jean-Baptiste Fleuriau, Comte de Morville.
1727	(23 Aug)	Germain Louis Chauvelin.
1737	(22 Feb)	Jean-Jacques Amelot de Chaillou.
1744	(26 Apr)	Adrien Maurice, Duc de Noailles.
1744	(19 Nov)	René de Voyer de Paulmy, Marquis d'Argenson.
1747	(27 Jan)	Louis Philogène Brûlart, Vicomte de Puisieulx.
1751	(11 Sept)	François Dominique de Barberie de Saint-Contest.
1754	(24 July)	Antoine Louis Rouillé.
1757	(28 June)	François Joachim de Pierre de Bernis.

1758	(3 Dec)	Étienne François, Duc de Choiseul.
1761	(13 Oct)	César Gabriel de Choiseul-Chevigny, Duc de Praslin.
1766	(10 Apr)	Étienne François, Duc de Choiseul.
1770	(24 Dec)	Louis Phélypeaux, Duc de La Vrillère.
1771	(6 June)	Emmanuel Armand de Vignerot du Plessis de Richelieu, Duc d'Aiguillon.
1774	(2 June)	Henri Léonard Jean Baptiste Bertin.
1774	(21 July)	Charles Gravier, Comte de Vergennes (to February 1787).

(Note that Charles Colbert was the younger brother of Le Grand Colbert. He was followed by his son, named after his uncle, who was granted the survivence or right of inheritance of his father in 1689.)

SECRETARIES OF STATE FOR THE NAVY

The post of *Sécretaire d'État à la Marine* was created by Louis XIV on 7 March 1669, at the instigation of Colbert, in order to allow the development of a Navy 'worthy of the King'. Prior to that date, the responsibility for the Navy had nominally been under the Secretary of State for Foreign Affairs but was effectively under the First Minister.

1669	(7 Mar)	Jean-Baptiste Colbert (I).
1683	(4 Dec)	Jean-Baptiste Antoine Colbert (II), Marquis de Seignelay.
1690	(7 Nov)	Louis Phélypeaux, Comte de Pontchartrain.
1699	(6 Sept)	Jérôme Phélypeaux, Comte de Pontchartrain.
1715	(1 Oct)	Louis-Alexandre de Bourbon, Comte de Toulouse (was Admiral of France, and thereby Head of the Navy Council, not Secretary of the Navy; the President of the Navy Council during this period was Victor, Comte d'Estrées.)
1718	(24 Sept)	Joseph Fleuriau d'Armenonville.
1722	(28 Feb)	Charles Fleuriau d'Armenonville, Comte de Morville.
1723	(16 Aug)	Jean-Frédéric de Phélypeaux, Comte de Maurepas.
1749	(30 Apr)	Antoine-Louis Rouillé, Comte de Jouy.
1754	(24 July)	Jean-Baptiste de Machault, Seigneur d'Arnouville.
1757	(1 Feb)	François Marie Peyrenc de Moras.
1758	(31 May)	Claude Louis d'Espinchal, Marquis de Massiac.
1758	(31 Oct)	Nicolas-René Berryer, Comte de la Ferrière.
1761	(15 Oct)	Étienne-François, Duc de Choiseul-Stainville.
1766	(10 Apr)	César Gabriel de Choiseul-Chevigny, Duc de Praslin (cousin of Choiseul).
1770	(24 Dec)	Joseph-Marie Terray, Abbé Terray
1771	(9 Apr)	Pierre-Étienne Bourgeois, Marquis de Boynes
1774	(20 July)	Anne-Robert-Jacques Turgot, Baron de Laune
1774	(24 Aug)	Antoine Raymond Jean Gualbert Gabriel de Sartine, Comte d'Alby
1780	(13 Oct)	Charles Eugène de La Croix, Marquis de Castries

Note that Colbert, on his death in 1683, was succeeded by his son, who bore the same given first name (Colbert believed in continuity!); the latter is thus referred to under his title of Marquis de Seignelay and so appears throughout this volume. The other notable recurrence is the family of Phélypeaux, whose descendents held various posts of Ministers of State throughout much of the *Ancien Régime*; Louis Phélypeaux (1643–1727) was the grandson of Raymond Phélypeaux's brother; Louis's son Jérôme (1674–1747) succeeded his father in office (like Seignelay did *his* father); Jérôme's own son Jean-Frédéric (1701–1781), better known as Comte de Maurepas, was Secretary of State for the Navy for a quarter-century from 1723, including the Wars of the Polish and Austrian Successions.

Appendix F Selected French Master Shipwrights and Master Sculptors, 1661–1786

1. MASTER SHIPWRIGHTS

This table shows the shipwrights named in this book as designers or chief constructors of ships. Most worked for the King in his naval dockyards although a few were commercial shipbuilders. The dates shown in the 'active' column are not the dates of their careers but are instead the dates during which the ships listed in this book that they designed or built were under construction. These were the years during which the shipwrights had enough seniority and experience to be assigned such responsibilities; other shipwrights in the dockyards who never reached this level are not listed. The chapters in which the shipwrights are mentioned are also shown, giving an indication of the types of ships that they built. Shipbuilding at this time was a family trade, handed down from one generation to the next, and some of the relationships between the succeeding generations are shown here.

The original title of the senior shipbuilder in each dockyard was *maître-charpentier* (master carpenter). During the late 1670s grades of master carpenters appeared with one *premier maître-charpentier* at each of the three major dockyards assisted by *second maître charpentiers* and *sous-maître charpentiers*. The designation *constructeur* began to appear in the late 1690s in the titles *maître-charpentier constructeur*, *constructeur*, and *sous-constructeur*. In 1740 the leading constructor in each port became the *premier constructeur*, assisted by *constructeurs ordinaires* and *sous-constructeurs* (sub-constructors). By an Ordinance of 25 March 1765 the designation *ingénieur-constructeur* (engineer-constructor) replaced that of *constructeur* while the *premier constructeur* became the *ingénieur-constructeur en chef*.

Family Name	Given name(s)	Active	Port(s)	Chapters	Relationships
Angallier	Pierre	1671–1671	Toulon	9	
Arnaud	Félix	1691–1694	Bayonne	2, 3, 4, 5, 6	
Arnoux		1763–1763	Indret	10	
Attuna	Antonio	1767–1768	Bordeaux	11	
Aubier (Aubin?)	Abraham	1672–1673	Rochefort	5, 8	
Audibert	Charles	1665–1678	Toulon, Marseille	1, 4	
Audibert	Louis	1667–1674	Toulon, Marseille	1, 3, 5	
Barthe		1691–1692	Bayonne	6	
Beaugeard de Segrey		1777–1778	St Malo	4	
Beauvoisin	Jean-Laurent	1785–1785	Le Havre	9	
Blondel		1690–1702	Dieppe	10	
Bombelle	Charles-Étienne	1778–1787	Rochefort	4, 10	
Bonvoisin	Jean-Philippe	1756–1759	Le Havre	5	
Boux	Louis (or Jacques?)	1768–1769	Brest	9	
Boux	Jacques	1768–1776	Le Havre, Lorient	4, 10	
Boyer	René	1738–1740	Toulon	3	
Brillantais	Marion	1777–1778	St Malo		
Broquier		1770–1771	Toulon	10	
Brouillan	Jacques	1704–1707	Port Royal, Acadia	6	
Brun	François	1691–1699	Brest, Port Louis	4, 6, 7	Son of Jean-Pierre. Last name usually rendered as Lebrun or Le Brun
Brun	Jean-Pierre	1656–1670	Tonnay-Charente, Soubise	1, 2, 3, 4, 5, 6, 9, 10	Nephew of Laurent Hubac and son of François
Cambry	Gilles	1734–1778	Lorient	3, 4, 7, 11	
Cardinaal	Hendrik	1666–1699	A'dam Admy.	3	
Caro	François	1762–1778	Lorient	3, 4	
Carteret	Georges	1655–1660	Brest	4, 5	
Chabert	Jean-Baptiste	1667–1723	Rochefort, Toulon, Le Havre, Dunkirk, Marseille	11, 12, 14	
Chabert	Pierre	1723–1746	Marseille	12, 14	Oldest son of Simon
Chabert	Simon	1663–1700	Marseille	14	
Chabert		1661–1672	Toulon, Marseille	14	
Chaillé	Benjamin	1667–1679	Rochefort, Le Havre	4, 5, 6, 9, 10	
Chaillé	Pierre	1744–1748	Le Havre	4, 5, 9	Jnr (grandson of Pierre, his father was also named Pierre)
Chaillé	Pierre	1688–1704	Le Havre	2, 4, 5, 6, 10	Younger brother of Benjamin
Chapelle	François	1670–1728	Toulon	2, 3, 4, 6, 8	

Family Name	Given name(s)	Active	Port(s)	Chapters	Relationships
Chapelle	François	1747–1754	Toulon	2, 3, 4, 5, 7	Son of Nicolas.
Chapelle	Joseph Véronique-Charles.	1740–1769	Toulon, Brest	2, 3, 4, 9, 10, (13	Son of the younger François
Chapelle	Louis-Hilarion	1762–1769	Toulon	10, 12	Son of the younger François.
Chapelle	Nicolas	1690–1692	Toulon	8	Son of the elder François
Chevillard	Jean-Denis	1759–1782	Rochefort (Bordeaux, Calais)	1, 2, 4, 7, 10, 11	Cadet (the second oldest brother)
Chevillard	Henri	1768–1787	Rochefort	2, 4, 7, 10, 11	The elder
Clairain-Deslauriers	François-Guillaume	1744–1780	Rochefort	1, 2, 3, 5, 7, 9, 10, 11	Nephew of Pierre Morineau Jnr
Cochois	Philippe	1690–1715	Le Havre	2, 3, 4, 5, 6, 7, 10	
Coubet de Majorque	Joseph	1750–1753	Toulon	12	
Coulomb	Blaise	1723–1734	Toulon	2, 3, 4, 9, 10, 12	Son of Laurent
Coulomb	François	1689–1716	Toulon	1, 2, 3, 4, 6, 7, 8, 9, 12, 13	Son of Laurent
Coulomb	François	1725–1751	Toulon	1, 2, 3, 4, 6, 7	Jnr, son of François Snr.
Coulomb	Jacques-Luc	1743–1769	Brest, Toulon, etc	1, 2, 3, 4, 5, 6, 7, 9, 10	Son of Blaise
Coulomb	Joseph-Marie-Blaise	1752–1783	Toulon	1, 2, 3, 4, 5, 7, 9, 10	Son of Joseph
Coulomb	Laurent	1661–1692	Toulon	1, 2, 3, 4, 5, 6, 7, 8, 9, 12	
Coulomb	Pierre	1691–1717	Port Louis/Lorient	1, 3, 4, 5, 6, 8	
Coulomb	Pierre-Blaise	1727–1753	Toulon	2, 3, 6	Son of Blaise
Couturier	Jean-André	1756–1763	Marseille	4	
d'Estival	Henri	1664–1664	Brouage	6	
Daviaud		1662–1671	Libourne	8	
de Langeron	Joseph Andrault	1682–1692	n/a	2, 3	
de Werth	Jean	1640–1644	Indret	4, 5	
Debast		1665–1667	Dunkirk	4	
Denys (Denÿs)	Daniel	1756–1782	Dunkirk	6, 9, 11	
Denys (Denÿs)	Jacques	1757–1758	Dunkirk	6	Cousin of Daniel
Depeches	Guillemant	1777–1778	St Malo		
Desjumeaux		1702–1709	Bayonne	3, 4, 6, 13	
Deslandes		1782–1782	Granville	4	
Deviot		1640–1643	Indret	4	
Doley	Jacques	1681–1686	Le Havre	3	
Donard/Donnard	Alain	1706–1706	Lorient	3, 4	
Doumet-Revest	Jean-Baptiste	1762–1774	Toulon	4, 5, 12	
Drouillart	J	1703–1703	Dieppe	10	
Dubois	Geoffroy and Benjamin	1777–1781	St Malo	4, 9	
Duclos-Guyot	Nicolas-Pierre	1759–1759	Quebec	7	
Dupuy	Fromy	1777–1778	St Malo	4	
Esnault	Jean	1665–1670	Le Havre	3, 4, 13	
Étienne	Jean	1660–1661	Marseille	5	
Étienne	Jean-François	1762–1774	Toulon	3, 4, 12	
Eustache	(sieurs)	1760–1760	Rouen	7	
Famin		1760–1761	Le Havre	9	
Forfait	Pierre-Alexandre-Laurent	1777–1778	Brest	4	
Gassies	Pierre & Dominique	1762–1764	Bayonne	6	
Gauthier (Gautier)	Jean-François	1763–1763	Toulon	3	
Gédéon	Rodolphe	1646–1673	Toulon	1, 3, 4, 5, 8, 9	
Geoffre		1683–1683	Trever (Holland)	8	
Geoffroy	Antoine	1778–1778	Brest	7	
Geoffroy	Jean	1739–1766	Brest	1, 2, 3, 4, 5, 6, 9, 10	Aîné (the oldest brother)
Geoffroy	Mathurin-Louis	1744–1756	Brest	3, 5, 6	Cadet
Geslain	Blaise	1734–1748	Rochefort	2, 6, 7, 9, 10, 11, 13	Son of Julien, cadet
Geslain	Julien	1711–1735	Rochefort	2, 3, 5, 10	
Ginoux	Jean-Joseph	1749–1783	Le Havre	4, 5, 7, 9, 10	
Gobert	Louis	1702–1706	Brest, Port Louis	2	

Family Name	Given name(s)	Active	Port(s)	Chapters	Relationships
Golain		1746–1746		10	
Groignard	Antoine	1751–1785	Brest, Lorient, Rochefort, etc	1, 2, 3, 4, 5, 7, 9	
Guérouard	Jean	1668–1672	Toulon	2, 3	
Guéroult	Jean	1701–1702	Dieppe	6	
Guichard	Elie	1677–1678	Le Havre	5	Brother of Jean
Guichard	Jean	1665–1693	Rochefort	1, 2, 3, 4, 5, 6, 8, 9	
Guignace	Léon-Michel	1757–1780	Brest (Bordeaux, Bayonne)	1, 2, 3, 4, 5, 9, 10, 11	
Guillon		1692–1693	Dunkirk	10	
Haran	Raymond-Antoine	1777–1785	Rochefort (Bayonne, Bordeaux)	4, 7, 9, 10	
Hélie	Jean-Marie	1735–1744	Brest	2, 3	Son of Laurent
Hélie	Laurent	1689–1730	Brest	1, 2, 3, 4, 6, 7, 9, 10	
Hontabat	Jean	1666–1673	Bayonne, Brest	3, 5	
Houwens	Hendryck	1663–1689	Dunkirk	2, 3, 4, 5, 6, 7, 10, 13	
Houwens	Jean-Nicolas	1690–1693	Dunkirk	6, 10	
Hubac	Étienne	1676–1726	Brest	1, 2, 3, 5, 6, 8, 9, 10	Son of Laurent (called Hubac le jeune)
Hubac	Laurent	1646–1682	Brest	1, 2, 3, 4, 5, 6, 8, 9, 11	
Hubac	Pierre	1661–1692	Toulon, Marseille	14	
Imbert		1665–1665	Marseille	6	
Journe (or Journa)	S	1757–1761	Toulon	12	
Jouve		1755–1755	Toulon	14	
Jouvencourt		1756–1759	Caen	10	
La Villetreux		1688–1689	Lorient	9	
Lamothe	Pierre-Augustin	1755–1788	Brest	4, 5, 9, 10	Snr.
Lamothe	Pierre-Augustin	–	Toulon		Jnr, son of Pierre-Augustin Snr.
Landré		1752–1752	Toulon	12	
Laure	Jean	1656–1671	Soubise, Brouage, Rochefort	2, 3	
Le Brun (Lebrun)		1691–1699			See Brun
Le Roux		1702–1712	Mobile	10	
Lemarchand		1777–1778	St Malo	4	
Levasseur	Jean-Armand	1728–1734	Toulon	4, 10	
Levasseur	Pierre	1756–1760	Lake Champlain, Quebec	11, 12	
Levasseur	René	1690–1727	Dunkirk (Toulon, Le Havre)	2, 3, 4, 6, 9, 10	
Levasseur	René-Nicolas	1739–1759	Quebec, Pointe-au-Baril	2, 3, 4, 5, 7, 9, 10	
Levesque	Nicolas	1752–1770	Lorient	4, 10	
Malet	Honoré	1670–1700	Rochefort	1, 2, 3, 4, 5, 6, 8, 9, 10	
Malet	Pierre	1673–1694	Rochefort	4, 5, 10	Son of Honoré
Marchand	Laurent	1738–1740	Toulon	12	
Martinenc	Jean	1682–1682	Toulon	12	
Masson	Pierre	1687–1720	Rochefort	1, 2, 3, 4, 5, 6, 9, 10	Cousin of Pierre Malet/son-in-law of Honoré Malet
Morineau	Pierre	1692–1694	Rochefort	9	Snr.
Morineau	Pierre	1729–1757	Rochefort	2, 3, 4, 5, 9, 10	Related to Pierre Masson
Niou	Joseph	1784–1788	Rochefort	2	
Nissard	Jean	1665–1667	Toulon	3	
Normand	François	1757–1757	Honfleur	10	
Ollivier	Joseph	1720–1732	Brest (initially Rochefort)	3, 6	Father of Blaise
Ollivier	Blaise	1720–1746	Brest (initially Rochefort)	1, 2, 3, 4, 5, 6, 7, 9	Full name was Blaise-Joseph
Ollivier	Joseph-Louis	1744–1777	Brest	1, 2, 3, 5, 7, 9, 10, 11	Son of Blaise
Ozanne	Nicolas	1766–1769	(Le Havre) Brest	5, 10	
Pangalo	Joseph	1705–1705	Brest	4	Son of Blaise
Pangalo	Blaise	1682–1706	Toulon, Brest	1, 2, 3, 4, 5, 6, 7, 8, 9, 10, 11	
Pennevert	Hubert	1782–1787	Rochefort	4, 10, 13	
Perrin de Boissieu	Jean-Joseph	1783–1784	Rochefort (Bayonne)	9, 10	
Pic	Augustin	1756–1764	Rochefort	7, 11, 13	

Family Name	Given name(s)	Active	Port(s)	Chapters	Relationships
Poirier	Jacques	1722–1740	Le Havre	4, 6, 9, 10	
Pomet	François	1662–1683	Toulon, Rochefort	1, 2, 3, 4, 6, 9, 10	
Pomet	Joseph	1690–1692	Toulon	8	
Pomet	Noël	1749–1767	Toulon	2, 3	
Poulin de Courval Cressé	Louis-Pierre	1755–1759	Fort Frontenac	10	
Raffeau	Jean-Hyacinthe	1762–1767	Indret	4, 5, 10	
Rati	Ange-Marie	1754–1761	Genoa	3	
Renau d'Eliçagaray	Bernard	1689–1696	Brest	2, 3, 6	
Reynoir	(brothers)	1739–1745	Marseille	14	
Reynoir	Jean	1696–1751	Marseille	14	
Richot	Michel	1646–1646	Elbeuf	5	
Rolland	Gaspard-Séraphin	1764–1765	Brest	9	
Rolland	Pierre-Élisabeth	1785–1787	Brest	4	Possibly son of Gaspard-Séraphin
Rolland		1764–1765	Brest	9	Father of Gaspard-Séraphin
Rollin		1637–1638	Le Havre	5	
Rousquet	Pierre	1687–1692	Toulon	12	
Roux de Majorque		1751–1753	Toulon	12	
Saboulin	Joseph	1666–1676	Bayonne, Brest, Rochefort	3, 4, 5, 6	
Salicon	Étienne	1678–1691	Le Havre	2, 3, 4, 6, 7, 8, 9, 10, 13	
Salinoc	Pierre	1743–1759	Brest	2, 3, 6, 10	
Sané	Jacques-Noël	1775–1786	Brest	2, 4	
Saucillon (Saussillon)	Claude	1754–1768	(Brest) Toulon	5, 12, 14	
Scolaro	Augustin	1742–1744	Toulon	12	
Segondat	C V or C-V	1764–1769	Brest	9, 10	
Segondat-Duvernet	Charles	1778–1787	Lorient	2, 4, 9, 10,11	Brother of M. Segondat, commissaire de la marine
Serrin	Jean	1667–1670	Toulon	1	
Sterein	Pierre	1726–1731	Toulon	3	
Tanguy		1655–1657	St Malo	4	
Tassy	Antoine	1697–1705	Bayonne	3, 4, 5, 9	
Tortel	Barthélémy	1665–1673	Toulon, Le Havre	3, 4	Father of Jean
Tortel	Jean	1670–1671	Le Havre	6, 13	
Train	Pierre	1772–1788	(Lorient) Rochefort	4	
Venard		1740–1745	Le Havre, Brest, Bayonne	5, 6, 7, 9, 10	

2. MASTER SCULPTORS

Master Sculptors (*maître-sculpteurs*) were responsible for the decoration, specifically the carved work, which adorned sailing warships. Charles Le Brun was made responsible for overseeing all of the decorative work on Louis XIV's ships; upon his death in 1690, he was succeeded in this role by Jean Bérain. A master sculptor was appointed from 1674 at each of the dockyards, who took responsibility for the design and completion of all the work on new or repaired ships at that port.

This list contains the Master Sculptors in the French dockyards from 1669 to 1786. It also contains the three Master Overseers, a post discontinued in 1736, and several Sculptors who were the senior artists in their dockyards for extended periods (more sculptors are listed in the note following the table). The position of Master Sculptor was vacant at Toulon from 1679 to 1711 and Rochefort had no regularly assigned Master Sculptor or Sculptor between 1694 and 1712, although the Master Sculptor at Port Louis near Lorient (who moved to Rochefort in 1712) may have filled this gap. More information on French naval sculptors and their work is available in Andrew Peters, *Ship Decoration, 1630–1780* (Barnsley, 2013), pages 38–64.

Family name	Given name(s)	Lifespan	Position(s)
Bérain	Jean	1639–1711	Overseer 1690–1711
Bourguignon	Victor	1719–?	Master sculptor at Rochefort in the 1750s.
Buirette	Claude	1639–1694	Sculptor at Rochefort 1669–1694
Buirette	Claude-Ambroise	1663–1743	Master sculptor at Port Louis 1698–1712 and at Rochefort 1712–1743
Caffieri	Charles-Philippe	1695–1766	Master sculptor at Dunkirk 1717–1729 and at Brest 1729–1766
Caffieri	François	1667–1729	Master sculptor at Dunkirk 1714–1717 and at Brest 1717–1729 (also stood in at Rochefort 1720–1724 and at Le Havre 1726)
Caffieri	Philippe	1634–1714	Master sculptor at Dunkirk 1687–1716
Caravaque	Jean	1673–1754	Master sculptor at Marseille 1706–1748
D'Augère	René	1643–1703	Master sculptor at Brest 1674–1683
Gibert	Antoine	1716–1789	Master sculptor at Toulon 1760–1789
Lange	Jean	1671–1761	Master sculptor at Toulon 1736–1760
Le Brun	Charles	1619–1690	Overseer 1669–1690
Legeret	Jean	1628–1688	Master sculptor at Brest 1683–1688
Levasseur	Pierre-Noël	1719–1770	Sculptor at Rochefort 1746–1763
Lubet	Pierre Philippe	1721–1797	Sculptor at Bordeaux 1744–1766, master sculptor at Brest 1766–1797
Mathias	Jean	16??–1706	Master sculptor at Marseille 1676–1706
Puget	Pierre	1620–1694	Master sculptor at Toulon 1670–1679
Renard	Nicolas	1654–1720	Master sculptor at Brest 1688–1717
Vassé	Antoine-François	1681–1736	Overseer and master sculptor at Toulon 1711–1736

Note: Other known sculptors during this period include:

At Brest: Jacques-Étienne Collet (1721–1808, active 1752–1800), Yves-Étienne Collet (1761–1843, master sculptor 1797–1840 and the navy's last master sculptor)

At Le Havre: Philippe Caffieri, jnr (1671–1734, active 1690)

At Rochefort: Pierre Turreau (1638–1676)

At Marseille: Jean-Baptiste Olérys (active 1688), François Caravaque (active/died 1698), and Antoine Gibert (1716–1789, active 1743–1750)

At Toulon: Christopher Veyrier (1637–1689), François Girardon (1628–1715), Romaut Longueneux (1638–1718), Bernard Toro (1661–1731, active 1718–1731), Jean-Ange Maucard (active 1731–1760), and Nicolas Delizy (1758–1814, to Rochefort as master sculptor 1789)

Appendix G Action stations of the 80-gun ship of the line *Foudroyant* of 1750

The following table set out the combat posts for the 805 men aboard this typical 80-gun ship

Lower deck (*Premier batterie*) – 243
    Signalsmen (*gardes du pavillon*) — 3
    Master gunner (*maître canonnier*) — 1
    2nd Master gunners (*seconds maîtres canonniers*) — 2
    15 pair of 36pdrs (@ 15 men per pair) — 225
    Sentries at hatchways (*sentinelles aux écoutilles*) — 6
    Entries to powder supply (*passage des poudres*) — 6
Upper deck (*Second batterie*) – 184
    Signalsmen (*gardes du pavillon*) — 3
    Master gunner (*maître canonnier*) — 1
    2nd Master gunners (*seconds maîtres canonniers*) — 2
    16 pair of 18pdrs (@ 11 men per pair) — 176
    Entries to powder supply (*passage des poudres*) — 2
Forecastle (*Gaillard d'avant*) – 32
    Signalsman (*garde du pavillon*) — 1
    Gunner's mate (*aide canonnier*) — 1
    5 pair of 8pdrs (@ 6 men per pair) — 30
Quarterdeck (*Gaillard d'arrière*) – 26
    Signalsman (*garde du pavillon*) — 1
    Gunner's mate (*aide canonnier*) — 1
    4 pair of 8pdrs (@ 6 men per pair) — 24
Marines and Snipers (*mousqueterie*) – 135
    Poop deck (2 signalsmen, 30 marines) — 32
    Quarterdeck (2 signalsmen, 22 marines, 1 armourer) — 25
    Waist (30 marines) — 30
    Forecastle (3 signalsmen, 24 marines, 1 armourer) — 28
    In the tops (8 main top, 8 fore top, 4 mizzen top) — 20

Ship handling (*manoeuvre*) – 107
    Main top (*grand hune*) — 4
    Fore top (*hune de misaine*) — 4
    Mizzen top (*hune d'artimon*) — 2
    Poop deck (*dunette*) — 10
    Quarterdeck (*gaillard d'arrière*) — 35
    Helmsmen (*à la barre*) — 2
    Waist (*coursive*) — 20
    Forecastle (*gaillard d'avant*) — 30
Powder distribution – 38
    Forward magazine (2 gunners' mates, 4 crew) — 6
    Bosun's stores (1 guard, 4 crew) — 5
    Aft magazine (2 gunner's mates, 6 crew) — 9
    Lantern-room — 1
    [?translation] *Couloir de valets* — 8
    Bread room (8 victuallers, 2 crew) — 10
Orlop deck and below – 22
    Carpenters (*charpentiers*) — 2
    Caulkers (*calfats*) — 3
    Surgeons (*chirurgiens*) — 6
    Surgeons' crew (*valets*) — 8
    Stowage trimmer (*égalier*) — 1
    Guard in cable tier (*gardien*) — 1
    Seaman in cable tier — 1
Others (*canot armé*) – 18

Note the disposition of the *gaillards* ordnance is at odds with the known gunports arrangement; in fact, the *Gaillard d'avant* had 3 pairs of gunports and the *Gaillard d'arrière* had 6 pairs of gunports.

Appendix H Colbert's mass ship renamings of 24 June 1671

As an integral part of his comprehensive re-organisation of the French Navy, Colbert instigated a pattern of changes in ships' names which all took effect on 24 June 1671. This affected most of the vessels in the Navy; in many cases, new names were chosen, while in other cases names were moved from one vessel to another. Following on the re-classifications of Ranks which took place at the start of the year, this produced confusion in the French archives. The following list, which groups vessels according to the Rank under which they were now classed, shows for each ship what name they held before 24 June and the name they were assigned thereafter.

Guns	Former name	New name
1st Rank		
120	Soleil Royal	unchanged
120	Royal Louis	unchanged
104	Royal Duc	Reine
100	Dauphin Royal	Royal Dauphin
84	Monarque	unchanged
82	Couronne	unchanged
80	Sceptre	unchanged
74	Henri	Souverain
70	Île de France	Lys
70	Paris	Royale Thérèse
70	Courageux	Magnanime
70	Saint Philippe	unchanged
70	Madame	Pompeux
70	Rubis	Florissant
70	Joli	Henri
66	Vendôme	Victorieux
2nd Rank		
68	Vermandois	Superbe
68	Faucon	Orgueilleux
68	Terrible	unchanged
68	Royale Thérèse	Saint Esprit
68	Fort	Foudroyant
68	Tonnant	unchanged
64	Charente	Belliqueux
64	Frédéric	Admirable
64	Invincible	unchanged
64	Conquérant	unchanged
64	Intrépide	Grand
64	Normand	Saint Louis
64	Neptune	Illustre
64	Courtisan	Magnifique
62	Prince	Sans Pareil
62	Français	Glorieux
3rd Rank		
60	Bourbon	Éclatant
60	Princesse	Triomphant
56	Furieux	unchanged
56	Fier	Saint Michel
56	Fidèle	unchanged
56	Glorieux	Agréable
56	Navarrais	Excellent
56	Alsace	Fier
54	Sophie	Fort
54	Diamant	unchanged
54	Maure	Fougueux
54	Indien	Parfait
54	Ardent	Temeraire
54	Émerillon	Fortuné
54	Lys	Assuré
54	Navarre	Constant
52	Royale	Ferme
50	Comte	Prudent
50	Rochefort	Sage
50	Anjou	Vaillant
48	Reine	Brave
48	Saint Louis	Aimable
48	Dauphin	Vermandois
48	Brave	Prince
48	Fleuron	unchanged
48	Oriflamme	unchanged
48	Trident	Aquilon
48	Louvre	Bourbon
48	Breton	Courtisan
48	César	Rubis
48	Wallon	Duc
48	Brillant	Précieux
48	Heureux	unchanged
48	Saint Esprit	Intrépide
4th Rank		
44	Saint Michel	Apollon
44	Toulon	Joli
44	Cheval Marin	unchanged
44	Sirène	unchanged
44	Provençal	Mignon
44	Dunkerquois	Brusque
44	Assuré	Français
44	Constant	Oiseau
42	Mazarin	Bon
42	Duc	Comte
42	Grâces	Fendant
42	Artois	Maure
40	Galant	unchanged
40	Saint Antoine de Genes	Léger
40	Flamand	Arc en Ciel
40	Basque	Brillant
38	Triomphe	Courageux
38	Hercule	Marquis
36	Jules	Indien
36	Soleil	Hercule
36	Françoise	Éole
36	Beaufort	Neptune
36	Mercœur	Trident

Guns	Former name	New name
36	Havre	Alcyon
36	Infante	Écueil
36	Tigre	unchanged

5th Rank

Guns	Former name	New name
34	Sauveur	Lion
34	Ville de Rouen	Hasardeux
34	Princesse de Gênes	Prompt
34	Bayonnais	Adroit
34	Dragon	unchanged
34	Écureuil	Orage
34	Hermine	Capricieux
34	Galante	Aventurier
34	Mignonne	Bizarre
34	Saint Augustin de Genes	Palmier
32	Étoile	unchanged
32	Perle	unchanged
32	Soleil d'Afrique	unchanged
32	Croissant d'Afrique	unchanged
28	Hirondelle	unchanged
28	Lion Rouge	Entendu
28	Saint Joseph	Dur
28	Bouffonne	Drôle
28	Trompeuse	Triton
28	Victoire	Arrogant
28	Périlleux	Hardi
28	(Les) Jeux	unchanged
28	Lion d'Or	Vigilant
28	Saint Sébastien	Faucon
28	Laurier	unchanged
28	Tourbillon	unchanged
24	Ligournois	Émerillon
24	Palmier	Actif
24	Dur	Éveillé

Light frigates

Guns	Former name	New name
18	Dangereux	Bouffonne
18	Embuscade	Dangereux
18	Hameçon	Trompeuse
14	Friponne	unchanged
14	Maligne	unchanged
14	Mutine	unchanged
14	Notre Dame des Anges	Subtile
12	Dieppoise	Lutine
12	Gaillarde	unchanged
12	Diligente	unchanged
12	Bretonne	Tempête
10	Normande	Aurore
10	Petite Infante	Légère
10	Belle-Île	Fée
10	Fontarabie	Folle
6	Madeleine	Belle
6	Aurore	Sibylle
6	Marguerite	Jolie
6	Saint Pierre	Moqueuse
6	Christine	Sans Peur
6	Saint Jean	Gentille
4	Morine	Surprenante

Guns	Former name	New name
(new, at Rochefort)		Favorite
(new)		Railleuse
(new)		Rieuse
(new)		Bien Aimée
(new)		Gracieuse
(new)		Sorcière
(new)		Serpente
(new)		Mignonne

Flûtes (tons)

Guns	Former name	New name
500	Sultane	Éléphant
500	Europe	Dromadaire
400	Indienne	Portefaix
400	Amérique	Coche
400	Saint Augustin	Large
400	Vierge	Profond
400	(new, at Toulon)	Avenant
400	(new, at Toulon)	Bienvenu
400	(new, at Brest)	Tardif
400	Jardin de Hollande	Charente
400	Fortune	Fourgon
300	Rochelaise	unchanged
300	Soubise	Bien Chargé
300	Justice	Bien Arrivé
300	Saint Nicolas	Marseilloise
300	Pélican	Bretonne
250	Espérance	Paresseux
200	Couronne de Naples	Normande
160	Guillot	Dieppoise
160	Barbaut	Dunkerquoise
	Galiote Hollandaise	Bayonnaise
	Saint Jean flibot	Seine
	Saint Hubert	Loire
	Heux Saint Jean	Garonne

Fireships

Guns	Former name	New name
10	Justice	Hameçon
6	Bilbaut	Inquiet
6	Saint Antoine [de Padoue]	Ardent
6	Flambeau	Entreprenant
6	Symbole	Impudent
6	Petit Saint Augustin	Éclair
6	Concorde	Fin
6	Auguste	Fanfaron
6	Tigre	Inconnu
6	Sauvage	Voilé
6	(new, by Daniau)	Trompeur
	(new, by Daniau)	Serpent
	(new, by Daniau)	Déguisé
	(new, at Toulon)	Périlleux
	(new, at Toulon)	Dangereux
	(new)	Incommode
	(new)	Fâcheux
	(new)	Brutal
	(new)	Caché

Appendix J Lists of the French Fleet

The following lists set out the composition as detailed in the annual Fleet Lists (*États abrégés*), and do not take account of corrections included in the main chapters of this book. The twelve lists we have selected are at roughly ten-year intervals (dependent upon availability – *États abrégés* are not available for some years.

1. List of the French Fleet as at 1 January 1672

1st Rank (11 vessels)
(a) Levant Fleet
- 120 *Royal Louis* (1668)
- 100 *Royal Dauphin* (1668)
- 84 *Monarque* (1668)
- 80 *Sceptre* (1670)
- 70 *Royale Thérèse* (1670)
- 70 *Lys* (1669)
- 70 *Magnanime* (building at Marseille)

(b) Ponant Fleet – Brest Dept
- 120 *Soleil Royal* (1668)
- 104 *Reine* (1668)
- 82 *Couronne* (1668)

(c) Ponant Fleet – Rochefort Dept
- 76 *Souverain* (1668)

2nd Rank (20 vessels)
(a) Levant Fleet
- 70 *Florissant* (1670)
- 70 *Henry* (1670)
- 70 *Pompeux* (1670)
- 68 *Saint Esprit* (1670)
- 64 *Éclatant* (1665)
- 64 *Magnifique* (1666)
- 64 *Triomphant* (1667)

(b) Ponant Fleet – Brest Dept
- 70 *Saint Philippe* (1663)
- 68 *Terrible* (1670)
- 64 *Glorieux* (1669)
- 64 *Tonnant* (1670)

(c) Ponant Fleet – Rochefort Dept
- 68 *Foudroyant* (1670)
- 68 *Orgueilleux* (1671)
- 68 *Superbe* (1671)
- 64 *Admirable* (1666)
- 64 *Belliqueux* (1667)
- 64 *Conquérant* (1666)
- 64 *Grand* (1666)
- 64 *Illustre* (1666)
- 64 *Invincible* (1666)
- 64 *Saint Louis* (1666)
- 64 *Sans Pareil* (1667)

3rd Rank
(a) Levant Fleet
- 56 *Agréable* (1671)
- 56 *Fidèle* (1670)
- 56 *Furieux* (1671)
- 56 *Saint Michel* (1671)
- 54 *Assuré* (1666)
- 54 *Diamant* (1663)
- 54 *Fortuné* (1671)
- 54 *Fougueux* (1671)
- 54 *Parfait* (1671)
- 50 *Ferme* (1661)
- 50 *Prudent* (1666)
- 48 *Fleuron* (1667)
- 48 *Vermandois* (1664)

(b) Ponant Fleet – Brest Dept
- 54 *Téméraire* (1670)
- 52 *Vaillant* (1670)
- 50 *Courtisan* (1666)
- 48 *Bon* (1671)
- 48 *Bourbon* (1669)
- 48 *Brave* (1647)
- 48 *Duc* (1669)
- 48 *Oriflamme* (1670)
- 48 *Rubis* (1648)

(c) Ponant Fleet – Rochefort Dept
- 56 *Excellent* (1670)
- 56 *Fier* (1670)
- 54 *Constant* (1666)
- 54 *Fort* (1666)
- 48 *Aimable* (1659)
- 48 *Aquilon* (1666)
- 48 *Courageux* (1671)
- 48 *Intrépide* (1671)
- 48 *Prince* (1668)
- 48 *Sage* (1669)

(d) Ponant Fleet – Le Havre Dept
- 48 *Heureux* (1671)
- 48 *Précieux* (1671)

(e) Ponant Fleet – Dunkirk Dept
- 48 Unnamed (*Incertain*) (1672)

4th Rank
(a) Levant Fleet
- 44 *Brusque* (1665)
- 44 *Cheval Marin* (1667)
- 44 *Joli* (1666)
- 44 *Mignon* (1667)
- 44 *Sirène* (1667)
- 42 *Comte* (1664)
- 36 *Neptune* (1662)
- 36 *Trident* (1662)

(b) Ponant Fleet – Brest Dept
- 38 *Hercule* (1657)
- 36 *Éole* (1656)
- 36 *Indien* (1661)
- 36 *Marquis* (1642)

(c) Ponant Fleet – Rochefort Dept
- 46 *Arc-en-Ciel* (1664)
- 44 *Apollon* (1671)
- 42 *Fendant* (1671)
- 42 *Galant* (1667)
- 42 *Maure* (1671)
- 40 *Brillant* (1670)
- 36 *Écueil* (1665)
- 36 *Tigre* (1666)

(d) Ponant Fleet – Le Havre Dept
- 36 *Alcyon* (1668)

(e) Ponant Fleet – Dunkirk Dept
- 44 *François* (1670)
- 44 *Oiseau* (1670)

5th Rank
(a) Levant Fleet
- 34 *Aventurier* (1671)
- 34 *Bizarre* (1671)
- 34 *Léger* (1662)
- 34 *Orage* (1658)
- 34 *Palmier* (1658)
- 34 *Prompt* (1663)
- 32 *Croissant (d'Afrique)* (1654)
- 32 *Étoile* (1657)
- 32 *Perle* (1658)
- 32 *Soleil d'Afrique* (1656)
- 28 *Drôle* (1670)
- 28 *Dur* (1661)
- 28 *Triton* (1670)

(b) Ponant Fleet – Brest Dept
- 32 *Arrogant* (1670)
- 32 *Dragon* (1646)
- 32 *Hardi* (1670)
- 28 *Laurier* (1669)
- 28 *Tourbillon* (1669)

(c) Ponant Fleet – Rochefort Dept
- 34 *Adroit* (1666)
- 34 *Capricieux* (1664)
- 34 *Hasardeux* (1659)
- 28 *Émerillon* (1658)
- 28 *Faucon* (1658)
- 28 *Hirondelle* (1664)
- 28 *Les Jeux* (1670)
- 28 *Vigilant* (1661)

(d) Ponant Fleet – Le Havre Dept
- 34 *Lion* (1660)
- 30 *Entendu* (1656)

(e) Ponant Fleet – Dunkirk Dept
- 28 *Éveillé* (1670)

Light Frigates
(a) Levant Fleet
- 11 *Gentille* (1666)
- 8 *Bien Aimée* (1671)
- 8 *Gracieuse* (1671)

(b) Ponant Fleet – Brest Dept
- 14 *Tempête* (1670)
- 12 *Aurore* (1670)
- 10 *Railleuse* (1671)
- 6 *Moqueuse* (1660)
- 6 *Surprenante* (1656)

(c) Ponant Fleet – Rochefort Dept
- 14 *Friponne* (1670)
- 14 *Maligne* (1670)
- 14 *Mutine* (1670)
- 12 *Légère* (1659)
- 10 *Favorite* (1671)
- 10 *Fée* (1655)
- 10 *Folle* (1662)
- 6 *Belle* (1667)
- 6 *Sibylle* (1665)

(d) Ponant Fleet – Le Havre Dept
- 18 *Bouffonne* (1670)
- 18 *Embuscade* (1670)
- 14 *Subtile* (1659)
- 12 *Diligente* (1666)
- 12 *Gaillarde* (1666)
- 12 *Lutine* (1666)
- 10 *Jolie* (1658)
- 10 *Sans Peur* (1666)

(e) Ponant Fleet – Dunkirk Dept
- 18 *Trompeuse* (1670)

Fireships
(a) Levant Fleet
- 12 *Dangereux* (1671)
- 12 *Incommode* (1671)
- 10 *Hameçon* (1658)
- 10 *Inquiet* (1662)
- 6 *Ardent* (1662)

(b) Ponant Fleet – Brest Dept
- 12 *Actif* (1654)
- 12 *Déguisé* (1671)
- 12 *Périlleux* (1671)

(c) Ponant Fleet – Rochefort Dept
- 12 *Entreprenant* (1671)
- 12 *Fin* (1671)
- 10 *Serpent* (1671)
- 10 *Trompeur* (1671)
- 6 *Fanfaron* (1670)
- 6 *Inconnu* (1662)
- 6 *Voilé* (1659)

(e) Ponant Fleet – Dunkirk Dept
- 12 *Brutal* (1672)
- 12 *Fâcheux* (1672)
- 6 *Impudent* (1662)

Flûtes

(a) Levant Fleet
- 12 *Avenant* (1671)
- 12 *Bienvenu* (1671)
- 12 *Profond* (1660)
- 8 *Normande* (1658)

(b) Ponant Fleet – Brest Dept
- 16 *Tardif* (1671)
- 12 *Fourgon* (1658)
- 12 *Large* (1654)
- 10 *Bretonne* (1668)
- 8 *Bayonnoise* (1668)
- 8 *Paresseux* (1668)
- 4 *Garonne* (1661)
- 4 *Loire* (1665)

(c) Ponant Fleet – Rochefort Dept
- 16 *Dromadaire* (1669)
- 16 *Éléphant* (1669)
- 16 *Portefaix* (1668)
- 12 *Charente* (1657)
- 12 *Coche* (1668)
- 10 *Bien Arrivé* (1664)
- 10 *Bien Chargé* (1665)
- 10 *Marseilloise* (1662)
- 10 *Rocheloise* (1670)
- 8 *Dieppoise* (1669)
- 8 *Dunkerquoise* (1669)
- 8 *Seine* (1661)

2. List of the French Fleet as at 1 January 1682

1st Rank (12 vessels)
(a) Levant Fleet
- 104 *Royal Dauphin* (1668)
- 104 *Royal Louis* (1668)
- 80 *Monarque* (1668)
- 80 *Royale Thérèse* (1669)
- 76 *Lys* (1669)
- 76 *Magnanime* (1671)
- 76 *Sceptre* (1670)

(b) Ponant Fleet – Brest Dept
- 120 *Soleil Royal* (1669)
- 104 *Reine* (1668)
- 80 *Couronne* (1668)
- 80 *Souverain* (1677)

(c) Ponant Fleet – Rochefort Dept
- 100 *Victorieux* (1673)

2nd Rank (20 vessels)
(a) Levant Fleet
- 80 *Henri* (1671)
- 76 *Saint Esprit* (1676)
- 72 *Magnifique* (1666)
- 70 *Florissant* (1671)
- 70 *Pompeux* (1670)
- 64 *Éclatant* (1667)
- 64 *Saint Michel* (1671)

(b) Ponant Fleet – Brest Dept
- 78 *Saint Philippe* (1665)
- 76 *Belliqueux* (1677)
- 76 *Foudroyant* (1670)
- 76 *Triomphant* (1677)
- 72 *Terrible* (1680)
- 70 *Fier* (1680)
- 70 *Tonnant* (1680)
- 60 *Glorieux* (1678)

(c) Ponant Fleet – Rochefort Dept
- 76 *Admirable* (1667)
- 76 *Orgueilleux* (1670)
- 76 *Superbe* (1670)
- 70 *Grand* (1680)
- 70 *Illustre* (1664)

3rd Rank (36 vessels)
(a) Levant Fleet
- 64 *Constant* (1667)
- 60 *Agréable* (1671)
- 60 *Assuré* (1667)
- 60 *Ferme* (1670)
- 60 *Fougueux* (1672)
- 60 *Parfait* (1672)
- 58 *Brillant* (1672)
- 58 *Prudent* (1666)
- 56 *Aimable* (1660)
- 56 *Fort* (1676)
- 54 *Vaillant* (1669)
- 54 *Vigilant* (1664)
- 52 *Aquilon* (1666)
- 52 *Content* (1671)
- 52 *Fortuné* (1671)
- 52 *Sage* (1669)
- 50 *Hardi* (1672)
- 48 *Capable* (1665)
- 48 *Fidèle* (1672)
- 48 *Fleuron* (1669)

(b) Ponant Fleet – Brest Dept
- 56 *Diamant* (1664)
- 56 *Intrépide* (1675)
- 54 *Bon* (1671)
- 54 *Prince* (1680)
- 52 *Heureux* (1671)
- 50 *Duc* (1669)
- 50 *Entreprenant* (1678)
- 50 *Oriflamme* (1670)
- 48 *Téméraire* (1669)
- 46 *Opiniâtre* (1668)

(c) Ponant Fleet – Rochefort Dept
- 54 *Fendant* (1676)
- 50 *Courageux* (1679)
- 50 *Excellent* (1679)

(d) Ponant Fleet – Le Havre Dept
- 50 *Ardent* (1680)
- 50 *Arrogant* (1681)
- 50 *Précieux* (1679)

4th Rank (26 vessels)
(a) Levant Fleet
- 46 *Cheval Marin* (1664)
- 46 *Sirène* (1664)
- 44 *Brusque* (1668)
- 44 *Éole* (1673)
- 44 *Indien* (1678)
- 42 *Bizarre* (42)
- 40 *Aventurier* (1671)
- 40 *Entendu* (1664)
- 40 *Laurier* (1676)
- 40 *Sérieux* (1679)
- 36 *Maure* (1662)
- 36 *Trident* (1662)

(b) Ponant Fleet – Brest Dept
- 48 *François* (1670)
- 48 *Oiseau* (1670)
- 44 *Alcion* (1669)
- 44 *Neptune* (1678)
- 40 *Comte* (1677)
- 40 *Tigre* (1664)
- 40 *Triton* (1670)
- 38 *Étoile* (1673)

(c) Ponant Fleet – Rochefort Dept
- 44 *Faucon* (1673)
- 44 *Hasardeux* (1674)
- 40 *Arc en Ciel* (1676)

(d) Ponant Fleet – Le Havre Dept
- 40 *Croissant* (1673)
- 40 *Écueil* (1678)
- 40 *Léger* (1679)

5th Rank (21 vessels)
(a) Levant Fleet
- 34 *Prompt* (1667)
- 32 *Poli* (1664)
- 20 *Gaillard* (1670)
- 20 *Mercure* (1669)

(b) Ponant Fleet – Brest Dept
- 36 *Dragon* (1673)
- 32 *Lion* (1679)
- 30 *Galant* (1673)
- 30 *Mignon* (1674)
- 28 *Hirondelle* (1679)
- 28 *Marquis* (1678)
- 28 *Pétillant* (1670)
- 24 *Éveillé* (1679)
- 20 *Hercule* (1676)

(c) Ponant Fleet – Rochefort Dept
- 40 *(Les) Jeux* (1670)
- 36 *Émerillon* (1671)
- 34 *Joli* (1671)
- 32 *Perle* (1670)
- 28 *Marin* (1679)
- 28 *Soleil d'Afrique* (1681)

(d) Ponant Fleet – Le Havre Dept
- 36 *Palmier* (1676)

(e) Ponant Fleet – Dunkirk Dept
- 36 *Adroit* (1676)

Light Frigates (24 vessels)
(a) Levant Fleet
- 20 *Bien Aimé* (1672)
- 6 *Gentille* (1666)
- 6 *Gracieuse* (?)

(b) Ponant Fleet – Brest Dept
- 28 *Fée* (1676)
- 28 *Mutine* (1676)
- 18 *Bouffonne* (1678)
- 14 *Aurore* (1670)
- 10 *Moqueuse* (1676)
- 10 *Pressante* (1676)

(c) Ponant Fleet – Rochefort Dept
- 28 *Tempête* (1676)
- 26 *Diligente* (1676)
- 16 *Friponne* (1670)
- 12 *Favorite* (1678)
- 12 *Gaillarde* (1678)

(d) Ponant Fleet – Le Havre Dept
- 24 *Jolie* (1675)
- 24 *Trompeuse* (1675)
- 24 *Maligne* (1670)
- ? *Embuscade*

(e) Ponant Fleet – Dunkirk Dept
- 26 *Sorcière* (1678)
- 16 *Sorcière* (1676)
- 14 *Vipère* (1676)
- 10 *Badine* (1678)
- 10 *Charmante* (1678)
- 10 *Mignonne* (1673)

Fireships (7 vessels)
(a) Levant Fleet
- 10 *Fin*
- 8 *Espion*
- 6 *Voilé*

(b) Ponant Fleet – Brest Dept
- 10 *Déguisé* (1672)
- 10 *Fanfaron* (1672)
- 10 *Périlleux* (1671)

(c) Ponant Fleet – Rochefort Dept
- 6 *Brutal* (1670)

Flûtes (20 vessels)
(a) Levant Fleet
- 16 *Bienvenu* (1670)
- 8 *Françoise* (1668)
- 6 *Bien Chargé* (1665)
- 6 *Paresseux*

(b) Ponant Fleet – Brest Dept
- 24 *Éléphant*
- 24 *Tardif* (1671)
- 20 *Coche*
- 20 *Portefaix* (1677)
- 10 *Fourgon*
- 6 *Chameau*
- 6 *Garonne*
- 6 *Seine* (1661)
- 4 *Charente* (1669)

(c) Ponant Fleet – Rochefort Dept
- 24 *Large* (1679)
- 20 *Dromadaire* (1676)
- 12 *Saint Paul*
- 6 *Mulet*
- 4 *Loire* (1668)

(d) Ponant Fleet – Le Havre Dept
- 20 *Bien Arrivé* (1664)
- 16 *Avenant* (1670)

Barques Longues (10 vessels)
(b) Ponant Fleet – Brest Dept
  3   *Lutine*
(c) Ponant Fleet – Rochefort Dept
  4   *Folle*
  4   *Sibylle*
(d) Ponant Fleet – Le Havre Dept
  4   *Rocheloise*
  6   *Subtile*
(e) Ponant Fleet – Dunkirk Dept
  4   *Assuré*
  4   *Effrontée*
  4   *Fine*
  4   *Inconnue*
  6   *Rieuse*

3. List of the French Fleet as at 1 January 1692

1st Rank (22 vessels)
(a) Levant Fleet
 104 *Royal Louis* (1668)
  84 *Magnanime* (1672)
  80 *Lys* (1691)
  80 *Sceptre* (1691)
(b) Ponant Fleet – Brest Dept
 110 *Soleil Royal* (1669)
 104 *Royal Dauphin* (1669)
  94 *Monarque* (1690)
  88 *Orgueilleux* (1690)
  86 *Grand* (1680)
  84 *Conquérant* (1688)
  84 *Foudroyant* (1691)
  84 *Magnifique* (1680)
  84 *Saint Philippe* (1665)
  84 *Souverain* (1677)
  80 *Formidable* (1691)
  80 *Merveilleux* (1691)
(c) Ponant Fleet – Rochefort Dept
  88 *Victorieux* (1691)
  84 *Intrépide* (1690)
  80 *Ambitieux* (1691)
  80 *Fulminant* (1691)
(d) Ponant Fleet – Port Louis (Lorient) Dept
  84 *Admirable* (1690)
  80 *Vainqueur* (1691)

2nd Rank (27 vessels)
(a) Levant Fleet
  70 *Constant* (1690)
  70 *Éclatant* (1687)
  70 *Heureux* (1690)
  70 *Invincible* (1690)
  70 *Superbe* (1690)
  66 *Ardent* (1682)
(b) Ponant Fleet – Brest Dept
  76 *Belliqueux* (1677)
  76 *Couronne* (1668)
  76 *Fier* (1680)
  76 *Florissant* (1666)
  76 *Terrible* (1686)
  76 *Tonnant* (1680)
  76 *Triomphant* (1676)
  74 *Pompeux* (1666)
  66 *Content* (1687)
  64 *Brillant* (1690)
  64 *Glorieux* (1672)
  64 *Sérieux* (1686)
(c) Ponant Fleet – Rochefort Dept
  74 *Illustre* (1665)
  70 *Aimable* (1690)
  70 *Henri* (1688)
  70 *Saint Esprit* (1691)
  64 *Bourbon* (1684)
  64 *Courtisan* (1687)
  64 *Laurier* (1691)
  64 *Sirène* (1691)
(d) Ponant Fleet – Le Havre (completing)
  64 *Juste* (1691)

3rd Rank (46 vessels)
(a) Levant Fleet
  60 *Fortuné* (1688)
  60 *Marquis* (1684)
  60 *Prudent* (1667)
  58 *Précieux* (1672)
  56 *Bon* (1671)
  56 *Sage* (1669)
  54 *Aquilon* (1668)
  54 *Hardi* (1673)
  50 *Arc en Ciel* (1678)
(b) Ponant Fleet – Brest Dept
  60 *Arrogant* (1681)
  60 *Diamant* (1687)
  60 *Écueil* (1690)
  60 *Entendu* (1690)
  60 *Ferme* (1671)
  60 *Fort* (1676)
  60 *Furieux* (1688)
  60 *Parfait* (1666)
  60 *Sans Pareil* (1685)
  54 *Heureux Retour* (1691)
  54 *Maure* (1688)
  50 *Brusque* (1674)
  50 *Fidèle* (1665)
  50 *Modéré* (1684)
  50 *Perle* (1690)
(c) Ponant Fleet – Rochefort Dept
  60 *Agréable* (1670)
  60 *Apollon* (1672)
  60 *Assuré* (1690)
  60 *Courageux* (1680)
  60 *Excellent* (1679)
  60 *Fougueux* (1672)
  60 *Saint Louis* (1681)
  58 *Fleuron* (1688)
  56 *Téméraire* (1678)
  54 *Fendant* (1672)
  54 *Vaillant* (1689)
  54 *Vigilant* (1668)
  50 *Envieux* (1691)
  50 *François* (1686)
  50 *Neptune* (1680)
  50 *Trident* (1686)
(d) Ponant Fleet – Port Louis (Lorient) Dept
  60 *Brave* (1685)
  60 *Entreprenant* (1678)
  60 *Prince* (1680)
  60 *Saint Michel* (1687)
  60 *Vermandois* (1684)
(e) Ponant Fleet – Le Havre Dept
  60 *Gaillard* (1690)

4th Rank (16 vessels)
(a) Levant Fleet
  40 *Aventurier* (1671)
  40 *Étoile* (1678)
(b) Ponant Fleet – Brest Dept
  44 *Emporté* (1683)
  40 *Triton* (1670)
(c) Ponant Fleet – Rochefort Dept
  46 *Cheval Marin* (1666)
  46 *Éole* (1673)
  44 *Bizarre* (1671)
  44 *Solide* (1684)
  40 *Faucon* (1672)
  40 *Hasardeux* (1684)
  40 *Léger* (1680)
  40 *Mignon* (1673)
(d) Ponant Fleet – Port Louis (Lorient) Dept
  46 *Oiseau* (1670)
(e) Ponant Fleet – Le Havre Dept
  40 *Charles II* (1682)
(f) Ponant Fleet – Dunkirk Dept
  40 *Alcion* (1689)
  40 *Comte* (1677)

5th Rank (21 vessels)
(a) Levant Fleet
  32 *Hirondelle* (1680)
  30 *Croissant* (1679)
  24 *Curieux* (1688)
(b) Ponant Fleet – Brest Dept
  36 *Palmier* (1676)
  30 *Éveillé* (1670)
  30 *Mercure* (1670)
(c) Ponant Fleet – Rochefort Dept
  36 *Adroit* (1691)
  36 *Émerillon* (1683)
  34 *Opiniâtre* (1691)
  34 *Poli* (1691)
  30 *Marin* (1680)
  30 *Pétillant* (1670)
  30 *Soleil d'Afrique* (1691)
(d) Ponant Fleet – Port Louis (Lorient) Dept
  36 *Joli* (1671)
  32 *Lion* (1673)
  30 *Dragon* (1673)
(f) Ponant Fleet – Dunkirk Dept
  36 *(Les) Jeux* (1689)
  36 *Tigre* (1689)
  30 *Hercule* (1678)
(g) Ponant Fleet – Bayonne (bldg)
  36 *Aigle* (1691)
  36 *Favori* (1691)

Light Frigates (32 vessels)
(a) Levant Fleet
  28 *Jalouse* (1678)
(b) Ponant Fleet – Brest Dept
  34 *Badine* (1688)
  34 *Gaillarde* (1688)
  28 *Favorite* (1678)
  28 *Mutine* (1676)
  28 *Tempête* (1671)
  20 *Vipère* (1675)
  16 *Friponne* (1691)
  12 *Bonne* (1691)
  12 *Choquante* (1691)
  12 *Fée* (1690)
  12 *Trompeuse* (1690)
  10 *Bouffonne* (1678)
  10 *Jolie* (1675)
  10 *Mignonne* (1673)
(c) Ponant Fleet – Rochefort Dept
  26 *Légère* (1682)
  10 *Embuscade* (1682)
  10 *Pressante* (1676)
(d) Ponant Fleet – Port Louis (Lorient) Dept
  12 *Charmante* (1688)
  10 *Maligne* (1673)
(e) Ponant Fleet – Le Havre Dept
  34 *Diligente* (1691)
  14 *Gentille* (1688)
  14 *Gracieuse* (1688)
  14 *Serpente* (1691)
  10 *Chasse* (1691)
(f) Ponant Fleet – Dunkirk Dept
  24 *Sorcière* (1676)
  20 *Aurore* (1690)
  20 *Bien Aimée* (1672)
  18 *Railleuse* (1690)
  12 *Audacieuse* (1691)
  12 *Naïade* (1691)
  12 *Suffisante* (1691)

Mortar Vessels (10 vessels)
(a) Levant Fleet
  8 *Belliqueuse* (1684)
  8 *Éclatante* (1684)
  8 *Terrible* (1684)
  6 *Ardente* (1683)
  6 *Fulminante* (1683)
  4 *Bombarde* (1682)
  4 *Brûlante* (1682)
  4 *Cruelle* (1682)
  4 *Foudroyante* (1682)

4   *Menaçante* (1682)

Fireships (31 vessels)
(a) Levant Fleet
  10   *Caché* (1660)
  10   *Éclair* (1686)
  10   *Fourbe* (1691)
  10   *Lutin* (1691)
   6   *Dangereux* (1684)
   6   *Espion* (1674)
   6   *Indiscret* (1690)
   6   *Violent* (1690)
(b) Ponant Fleet – Brest Dept
   8   *Incommode* (1670)
   6   *Boutefeu* (1677)
   6   *Déguisé* (1670)
   6   *Dévorant* (1674)
   6   *Drôle* (1668)
   6   *Dur* (1675)
   6   *Fâcheux* (1684)
   6   *Fin* (1670)
   6   *Inconnu* (1675)
   6   *Insensé* (1678)
   6   *Orage* (1682)
   6   *Rusé* (1675)
   6   *Voilé* (1674)
(c) Ponant Fleet – Rochefort Dept
  10   *Impertinent* (1672)
  10   *Séditieux* (1682)
   8   *Inquiet* (1684)
   6   *Brutal* (1670)
   6   *Enflammé* (1687)
   6   *Étourdi* (1683)
   6   *Fanfaron* (1673)
(d) Ponant Fleet – Port Louis (Lorient) Dept
  10   *Périlleux* (1671)
   8   *Serpent* (1672)
   6   *Hameçon* (1675)

Flûtes (28 vessels)
(a) Levant Fleet
  12   *Baleine* (1682)
  12   *Chariot* (1682)
  12   *Éléphant* (1672)
  10   *Large* (1676)
(b) Ponant Fleet – Brest Dept
  30   *Avenant* (1670)
  26   *Bretonne* (1685)
  24   *Bienvenu* (1680)
  24   *Dieppoise* (1685)
  24   *Portefaix* (1677)
  24   *Tardif* (1671)
  10   *Chameau* (1674)
  10   *Paresseux* (1670)
  10   *Seine* (1672)
   8   *Licorne* (1691)
   8   *Mulet* (1691)
   4   *Bien Arrivé* (1671)
   4   *Garonne* (1668)
   4   *Parti* (1673)
(c) Ponant Fleet – Rochefort Dept
  30   *Dromadaire* (1676)
  30   *Loire* (1686)
  12   *Françoise* (12)
  10   *Normande* (1670)
   4   *Dissimulée* (1680)
   4   *Souris* (1677)
   4   *Volante* (1670)
(d) Ponant Fleet – Port Louis (Lorient) Dept
  10   *Saint Guillaume* (1688)
(f) Ponant Fleet – Dunkirk Dept
  30   *Profond* (1684)
   4   *Bien Chargé* (1673)

Barques Longues (32 vessels)
(a) Levant Fleet
   6   *Subtile* (1682)
   4   *Trône* (1672)
(b) Ponant Fleet – Brest Dept
  10   *Méchante* (1689)
   6   *Effrontée* (1682)
   4   *Fine* (1689)
   4   *Petit Saint François* (1670)
(c) Ponant Fleet – Rochefort Dept
   8   *Belle* (1670)
   8   *Folle* (1674)
   4   *Biscayenne* (1671)
   4   *Inconnue* (1672)
(d) Ponant Fleet – Port Louis (Lorient) Dept
   4   *Lutine* (1679)
(e) Ponant Fleet – Le Havre Dept
  10   *Joyeuse* (1691)
   8   *Blonde* (1689)
   8   *Entendue* (1689)
   6   *Levrette* (1689)
   6   *Prompte* (1689)
   6   *Rocheloise* (1689)
(f) Ponant Fleet – Dunkirk Dept
   8   *Assurée* (1690)
   8   *Dorade* (1691)
   8   *Émeraude* (1691)
   8   *Rieuse* (1678)
   8   *Vedette* (1691)
   6   *Biche* (1691)
   6   *Bonne* (1690)
   6   *Boussole* (1691)
   6   *Brune* (1690)
   6   *Commode* (1691)
   6   *Fleche* (1691)
   6   *Pouponne* (1690)
   6   *Rusée* (1691)
   6   *Sibylle* (1689)
   6   *Trompette* (1691)

4. List of the French Fleet as at 1 January 1702

1st Rank (25 vessels)
(a) Levant Fleet
  90   *Saint Philippe* (1693)
  90   *Tonnant* (1693)
  84   *Lys* (1690)
  84   *Sceptre* (1690)
  82   *Admirable* (1692)
  80   *Conquérant* (1687)
(b) Ponant Fleet – Brest Dept
 110   *Royal Louis* (1692)
 104   *Soleil Royal* (1692)
 104   *Foudroyant* (1694)
 100   *Terrible* (1692)
  98   *Fulminant* (1691)
  98   *Merveilleux* (1692)
  98   *Triomphant* (1694)
  90   *Formidable* (1691)
  88   *Monarque* (1689)
  88   *Orgueilleux* (1690)
  84   *Grand* (1680)
  84   *Vainqueur* (1691)
  80   *Magnanime* (1668)
  80   *Souverain* (1677)
(c) Ponant Fleet – Rochefort Dept
  94   *Victorieux* (1691)
  92   *Ambitieux* (1693)
  90   *Fier* (1694)
  86   *Magnifique* (1693)
  82   *Intrépide* (1690)

2nd Rank (18 vessels)
(a) Levant Fleet
  76   *Parfait* (1700)
  68   *Bizarre* (1692)
  68   *Constant* (1689)
  68   *Invincible* (1689)
(b) Ponant Fleet – Brest Dept
  76   *Belliqueux* (1677)
  76   *Couronne* (1669)
  76   *Prompt* (1691)
  70   *Fort* (1693)
  68   *Éclatant* (1686)
  68   *Heureux* (1691)
  68   *Superbe* (1691)
(c) Ponant Fleet – Rochefort Dept
  76   *Saint Esprit* (1691)
  70   *Aimable* (1690)
  68   *Bourbon* (1693)
  68   *Ferme* (1700)
  64   *Brillant* (1689)
  64   *Courtisan* (1687)
  63   *Espérance d'Angleterre* (-)

3rd Rank (54 vessels)
(a) Levant Fleet
  64   *Henry* (1687)
  64   *Oriflamme* (1699)
  62   *Écueil* (1691)
  60   *Sérieux* (1686)
  60   *Saint Louis* (1693)
  60   *Éole* (1690)
  60   *Content* (1695)
  60   *Prudent* (1697)
  60   *Assuré* (1697)
  60   *Trident* (1695)
  60   *Marquis* (1684)
  60   *Entreprenant* (1680)
  56   *Fleuron* (1688)
  56   *Fortuné* (1688)
  56   *Laurier* (1691)
  54   *Téméraire* (1695)
  52   *Perle* (1691)
  50   *Neptune* (1678)
  46   *Heureux Retour* (-)
(b) Ponant Fleet – Brest Dept
  64   *Ardent* (1692)
  64   *Glorieux* (1678)
  62   *Juste* (1690)
  62   *Furieux* (1684)
  62   *Vermandois* (1684)
  60   *Saint Michel* (1687)
  58   *Courageux* (1684)
  58   *Hardi* (1680)
  56   *Diamant* (1687)
  50   *Solide* (1695)
  50   *Mercure* (1697)
(c) Ponant Fleet – Rochefort Dept
  60   *Phénix* (1693)
  60   *Excellent* (1679)
  56   *Sirène* (1691)
  58   *Capable* (1691)
  58   *Arrogant* (-)
  56   *Apollon* (1683)
  58   *Prince de Frise* (-)
  58   *Pelican* (-)
  56   *Prince* (1682)
  52   *Gaillard* (1693)
  52   *Modéré* (1687)
  50   *François* (1688)
  54   *Faucon Anglais* (-)
(d) Ponant Fleet – Port Louis (Lorient) Dept
  50   *Ville de Médemblick* (1689)
  60   *Zélande* (1688)
  50   *Agréable* (1661)
  52   *Bon* (1694)
  54   *Sage* (1700)
  50   *Hasardeux* (1698)
(f) Ponant Fleet – Dunkirk Dept
  58   *Fendant* (1701)
  54   *Maure* (1687)
  48   *Mignon* (1691)
  52   *Stadenland* (1686)
  50   *Amphitrite* (1699)

4th Rank (17 vessels)
(a) Levant Fleet
  44   *Adélaïde* (1698)
(b) Ponant Fleet – Brest Dept
  36   *Volontaire* (1695)
  40   *Dauphine* (1697)
(c) Ponant Fleet – Rochefort Dept
  44   *Thetis* (1697)
  42   *Avenant* (1696)
  44   *Renommée* (1698)
  36   *Poli* (1691)
  42   *Emporté* (1680)

40   *Cheval Marin* (1668)
40   *Palmier* (1676)
40   *Indien* (-)
42   *Africain* (-)
(d) Ponant Fleet – Port Louis (Lorient) Dept
40   *Mutine* (1695)
44   *Triton* (1696)
42   *Faucon Français* (1674)
(f) Ponant Fleet – Dunkirk Dept
42   *Adroit* (1692)
46   *Jersey* (1688)

5th Rank (21 vessels)
(a) Levant Fleet
36   *Hirondelle* (-)
(b) Ponant Fleet – Brest Dept
32   *Favori* (1689)
32   *Bellone* (1695)
32   *Oiseau* (1695)
30   *Méduse* (1699)
(c) Ponant Fleet – Rochefort Dept
34   *Aigle* (1692)
32   *Badine* (1689)
30   *Zeripsée* (-)
32   *Weeps* (-)
32   *Dragon* (1673)
38   *Sérieux* (1679)
34   *Marin* (1678)
32   *Éveillé* (-)
(d) Ponant Fleet – Port Louis (Lorient) Dept
32   *Gaillarde* (1687)
30   *Hercule* (1678)
28   *Hermione* (1698)
(f) Ponant Fleet – Dunkirk Dept
36   *Tigre* (1689)
36   *Les Jeux* (1689)
32   *Milford* (-)
40   *Alcyon* (1688)
(g) Ponant Fleet – Bayonne
38   *Héroïne* (1699)

Light Frigates (21 vessels)
(a) Levant Fleet
20   *Galatée* (1695)
20   *Salamandre* (1696)
(b) Ponant Fleet – Brest Dept
14   *Fée* (1690)
(c) Ponant Fleet – Rochefort Dept
24   *Nieuport* (-)
22   *Atalante* (1693)
20   *Néréide* (1696)
16   *Fourbe* (1693)
6   *Enflammé* (1668)
(d) Ponant Fleet – Port Louis (Lorient) Dept
20   *Naïade* (1697)
18   *Tempête* (1692)
18   *Vipère* (1678)
16   *Bonne* (1692)

14   *Saint Paul d'Ostende* (1691)
(e) Ponant Fleet – Le Havre Dept
22   *Aurore* (1697)
16   *Gracieuse* (1701)
12   *Gentille* (1701)
12   *Joyeuse* (1692)
(f) Ponant Fleet – Dunkirk Dept
18   *Railleuse* (1689)
14   *Audacieuse* (1690)
(g) Ponant Fleet – Bayonne
22   *Entreprenante* (1691)
16   *Jolie* (1693)

Mortar Vessels (7 vessels)
(a) Levant Fleet
6   *Proserpine* (1696)
6   *Vulcain* (1696)
4   *Ardente* (1682)
4   *Fulminante* (1682)
(b) Ponant Fleet – Brest Dept
8   *Belliqueuse* (1686)
(e) Ponant Fleet – Le Havre Dept
28   *Martiale* (1696)
(f) Ponant Fleet – Dunkirk Dept
-    *Tonnerre* (1694)

Fireships (8 vessels)
(a) Levant Fleet
8   *Éclair* (1686)
6   *Espion* (1689)
6   *Fâcheux* (1684)
6   *Lion* (1684)
(b) Ponant Fleet – Brest Dept
6   *Dangereux* (1690)
6   *Indiscret* (1690)
6   *Violent* (1690)
(d) Ponant Fleet – Port Louis (Lorient) Dept
6   *Périlleux* (1678)

Flûtes (26 vessels)
(a) Levant Fleet
20   *Baleine* (1682)
18   *Chariot* (1696)
18   *Coche* (-)
10   *Fleur de Lys* (1692)
(b) Ponant Fleet – Brest Dept
42   *Bienvenu* (1682)
42   *Portefaix* (1675)
22   *Turquoise* (1691)
12   *Colombe* (-)
6   *Providence* (1688)
4   *Ville d'Emden* (1689)
4   *Bien Arrivé* (1689)
-    *Arche* (-)
-    *Dromadaire* (-)
(c) Ponant Fleet – Rochefort Dept
44   *Seine* (1698)
42   *Gironde* (1695)
36   *Profond* (1685)
16   *Jeanne Cornélie* (-)
12   *Loire* (1685)

8   *Gloutonne* (-)
6   *Arbre d'Olivier* (-)
4   *Ville d'Emden* (1689)
(d) Ponant Fleet – Port Louis (Lorient) Dept
24   *Européen* (1686)
8   *Étoile du Nord* (1682)
8   *Saint Guillaume* (1690)
(g) Ponant Fleet – Bayonne
12   *Éléphant* (1701)
16   *Charente* (1701)

Corvettes or Barques Longues (11 vessels)
(a) Levant Fleet
10   *Gentille* (1695)
8   *Utile* (-)
6   *Subtile* (-)
(b) Ponant Fleet – Brest Dept
10   *Choquante* (1690)
10   *Dorade* (1692)
10   *Émeraude* (1692)
6   *Fleur de la Mer* (1693)
(e) Ponant Fleet – Le Havre Dept
6   *Trompette* (1691)
(f) Ponant Fleet – Dunkirk Dept
12   *Hautaine* (1693)
12   *Volage* (1693)
8   *Discrète* (1693)

5. List of the French Fleet as at 1 January 1712

1st Rank (21 vessels)
(a) Levant Fleet
104 *Foudroyant* (1693)
104 *Soleil Royal* (1693)
104 *Terrible* (1693)
94   *Fier* (1694)
94   *Triomphant* (1693)
92   *Saint Philippe* (1693)
90   *Orgueilleux* (1690)
88   *Admirable* (1692)
88   *Magnifique* (1693)
88   *Sceptre* (1690)
86   *Vainqueur* (1691)
84   *Intrépide* (1691)
84   *Monarque* (1690)
80   *Conquérant* 1687)
76   *Couronne* (1661)
(b) Ponant Fleet – Brest Dept
110 *Royal Louis* (1692)
98   *Merveilleux* (1692)
96   *Ambitieux* (1692)
90   *Formidable* (1694)
(c) Ponant Fleet – Rochefort Dept
96   *Fulminant* (1691)
92   *Victorieux* (1691)

2nd Rank (18 vessels)

(a) Levant Fleet
74   *Saint Esprit* (1691)
72   *Parfait* (1700)
72   *Neptune* (1703)
68   *Invincible* (1689)
68   *Bizarre* (1704)
66   *Éclatant* (1687)
64   *Henry* (1687)
(b) Ponant Fleet – Brest Dept
84   *Cumberland* (1707)
72   *Grand* (1680)
72   *Magnanime* (1706)
72   *Lys* (1706)
70   *Saint Michel* (1706)
(c) Ponant Fleet – Rochefort Dept
72   *Pompeux* (1707)
70   *Constant* (1691)
64   *Juste* (1691)
(d) Ponant Fleet – Port Louis (Lorient) Dept
68   *Aimable* (-)
(f) Ponant Fleet – Dunkirk Dept
68   *Grafton* (-)
64   *Hampton Court* (-)

3rd Rank (32 vessels)
(a) Levant Fleet
60   *Vermandois* (1685)
58   *Sérieux* (1688)
58   *Saint Louis* (1693)
58   *Entreprenant* (1702)
58   *Diamant* (1687)
58   *Furieux* (1684)
56   *Trident* (1695)
56   *Fendant* (1700)
56   *Rubis* (-)
54   *Content* (1695)
52   *Fleuron* (1688)
50   *Téméraire* (1706)
(b) Ponant Fleet – Brest Dept
72   *Elizabeth* (1704)
66   *Glorieux* (1678)
66   *Brillant* (1689)
64   *Achille* (1705)
60   *Dauphine* (1706)
60   *Hercule* (1705)
54   *Jason* (1704)
50   *Mercure* (1697)
(c) Ponant Fleet – Rochefort Dept
62   *Phénix* (1693)
60   *Oriflamme* (1703)
58   *Fidèle* (1703)
58   *Prince* (1682)
52   *Ville de Médemblick* (-)
50   *François* (1688)
(d) Ponant Fleet – Port Louis (Lorient) Dept
56   *Apollon* (1686)
50   *Triton* (1708)
(f) Ponant Fleet – Dunkirk Dept
54   *Mars* (1705)

54 *Auguste* (1707)
54 *Blackwall* (1697)
48 *Amphitrite* (1700)

4th Rank (15 vessels)
(a) Levant Fleet
42 *Cheval Marin* (1668)
40 *Vestale* (1705)
40 *Parfaite* (1704)
36 *Adélaïde* (1698)
(b) Ponant Fleet – Brest Dept
44 *Argonaute* (1709)
40 *Amazone* (1707)
40 *Jersey* (-)
(c) Ponant Fleet – Rochefort Dept
48 *Renommée* (1699)
44 *Africain* (1692)
44 *Indien* (-)
44 *Atalante* (1707)
42 *Amphitrite* (1697)
42 *Héros* (1701)
38 *Alcyon* (-)
36 *Poli* (1691)

5th Rank (10 vessels)
(a) Levant Fleet
31 *Rozendal* (1698)
28 *Méduse* (1700)
(b) Ponant Fleet – Brest Dept
36 *Bellone* (1695)
32 *Milford* (-)
30 *Fowey* (1704)
(c) Ponant Fleet – Rochefort Dept
38 *Aigle* (1692)
30 *Ludlow* (-)
18 *Venus* (1705)
(e) Ponant Fleet – Le Havre Dept
44 *Gaillarde* (1688)
(f) Ponant Fleet – Dunkirk Dept
30 *Tigre* (1689)

Light Frigates (18 vessels)
(b) Ponant Fleet – Brest Dept
24 *Victoire* (-)
24 *Astrée* (1707)
24 *Paon* (1705)
18 *Nieuport* (-)
14 *Concorde* (1711)
10 *René* (1709)
(c) Ponant Fleet – Rochefort Dept
40 *Valeur* (1707)
-   *Nymphe* (-)
22 *Sirène* (1691)
22 *Néréide* (-)
18 *Aurore* (-)
(d) Ponant Fleet – Port Louis (Lorient) Dept
34 *Galatée* (1710)
18 *Cavalier de Flessingue* (1699)
16 *Sphère d'Angleterre* (-)
(e) Ponant Fleet – Le Havre Dept

12 *Amarante* (1709)
10 *Flore* (1708)
(f) Ponant Fleet – Dunkirk Dept
24 *Zéphyr* (1706)
20 *Fortune* (1704)

Mortar Vessels (6 vessels)
(a) Levant Fleet
6   *Proserpine* (1696)
6   *Vulcain* (1696)
4   *Ardente* (1682)
4   *Fulminante* (1684)
(b) Ponant Fleet – Brest Dept
-   *Belliqueuse* (1686)
(f) Ponant Fleet – Dunkirk Dept
-   *Tonnerre* (1694)

Fireships (5 vessels)
(a) Levant Fleet
8   *Éclair* (1686)
8   *Violent* (1691)
6   *Aigle Volant* (-)
(c) Ponant Fleet – Rochefort Dept
34 *Samslaack* (-)
(d) Ponant Fleet – Port Louis (Lorient) Dept
6   *Impudent* (1702)

Flûtes (18 vessels)
(a) Levant Fleet
14 *Portefaix* (-)
(b) Ponant Fleet – Brest Dept
18 *Sommeldick* (1706)
12 *Prince Alexandre* (1704)
12 *Hampton* (1707)
10 *Catherine* (1696)
6   *Dromadaire* (1701)
4   *Puits de Jacob* (-)
(c) Ponant Fleet – Rochefort Dept
32 *Profond* (1685)
32 *Loire* (1685)
32 *Dragon* (1673)
24 *Charente* (1700)
10 *Elizabeth* (-)
8   *Cigne* (-)
8   *Rusland* (-)
4   *Marchand* (-)
(d) Ponant Fleet – Port Louis (Lorient) Dept
36 *Sphère* (1708)
10 *Christine* (1700)
(f) Ponant Fleet – Dunkirk Dept
14 *Archangel* (-)

Corvettes or Barques Longues (11 vessels)
(a) Levant Fleet
-   *Immaculée Conception* (-)
6   *Saint Jean-Gaëtan* (-)
-   *Diligente* (-)
(b) Ponant Fleet – Brest Dept

6   *Trompette* (1706)
(c) Ponant Fleet – Rochefort Dept
8   *Étoile* (1708)
8   *Agathe* (1708)
(d) Ponant Fleet – Port Louis (Lorient) Dept
8   *Marie-Françoise* (-)
-   *Actif* (-)
-   *Résolu* (-)
-   *Félouque* (-)
(e) Ponant Fleet – Le Havre Dept
8   *Fine* (1702)

Bâtiments interrompus (15 vessels)
(a) Levant Fleet
-   *Subtile* (-)
-   *Sainte Claire* (-)
-   *Légère* (-)
-   *Prompte* (-)
-   *Vigilante* (-)
-   *Ferme* (-)
(b) Ponant Fleet – Brest Dept
-   *Agréable* (-)
-   *Licorne* (-)
-   *Étourdi* (-)
-   *Orage* (-)
-   *Dévorant* (-)
-   *Saint Jean de Plymouth* (-)
-   *Cigne Blanc* (-)
(d) Ponant Fleet – Port Louis (Lorient) Dept
-   *Tempête* (-)
-   *Saint Guillaume* (-)

6. List of the French Fleet as at 1 January 1723

1st Rank (2 vessels)
(a) Levant Fleet – nil
(b) Ponant Fleet – Brest Dept
110 *Royal Louis* (1692)
100 *Foudroyant* (building)

2nd Rank (13 vessels)
(a) Levant Fleet
74 *Duc d'Orléans* (1722)
74 *Espérance* (1722)
74 *Ferme* (1722)
74 *Phénix* (1722)
72 *Parfait* (1700)
70 *Conquérant* (1687)
68 *Invincible* (1684)
64 *Henri* (1687)
(b) Ponant Fleet – Brest Dept
74 *Bourbon* (1719)
74 *Neptune* (bldg)
74 *Sceptre* (1719)
72 *Lys* (1706)
(c) Ponant Fleet – Rochefort Dept

74 *Saint Philippe* (1720)

3rd Rank (14 vessels)
(a) Levant Fleet
64 *Solide* (1722)
62 *Toulouse* (1714)
58 *Entreprenant* (1702)
56 *Rubis* (1704)
(b) Ponant Fleet – Brest Dept
66 *Élisabeth* (1722)
66 *Grafton* (1707)
62 *Achille* (1705)
62 *Éclatant* (1721)
60 *Hercule* (1705)
60 *Mercure* (1697)
56 *Content* (1717)
(c) Ponant Fleet – Rochefort Dept
62 *Ardent* (1720)
62 *Saint Louis* (1720)
60 *Oriflamme* (1703)

4th Rank (14 vessels)
(a) Levant Fleet
42 *Cheval Marin* (1688)
40 *Vestale* (1705)
(b) Ponant Fleet – Brest Dept
48 *Griffon* (1705)
46 *Amphitrite* (1699)
46 *Argonaute* (1722)
46 *Parfaite* (1722)
42 *Amazone* (1707)
(c) Ponant Fleet – Rochefort Dept
50 *François* (1688)
46 *Héros* (1701)
46 *Renommée* (1699)
42 *Africain* (1692)
40 *Atalante* (1707)
40 *Néréide* (1722)
(e) Ponant Fleet – Le Havre Dept
50 *Jason* (bldg)

5th Rank (1 vessel)
(c) Ponant Fleet – Rochefort Dept
30 *Ludlow* (1703)

Light Frigates (9 vessels)
(b) Ponant Fleet – Brest Dept
26 *Victoire* (1704)
22 *Fortune* (1704)
12 *Amarante* (1707)
10 *Flore* (1706)
(c) Ponant Fleet – Rochefort Dept
18 *Paon* (1705)
14 *Sphère* (1707)
(e) Ponant Fleet – Le Havre Dept
26 *Thetis* (1722)
26 *Vénus* (bldg)
16 *Méduse* (1722)

Mortar Vessels (1 vessel)
(a) Levant Fleet

4   *Ardente* (1682)

Flûtes (7 vessels)
(a) Levant Fleet
50   *Loire* (1719)
50   *Seine* (1719)
(b) Ponant Fleet – Brest Dept
10   *Sarcelle* (1720)
(c) Ponant Fleet – Rochefort Dept
42   *Dromadaire* (1717)
42   *Portefaix* (1717)
40   *Chameau* (1718)
40   *Éléphant* (1718)

Barques latines (2 vessels)
(a) Levant Fleet
10   *Immaculée Conception* (1710)
8   *Saint Jean-Gaëtan* (-)

Gabarres (5 vessels)
(b) Ponant Fleet – Brest Dept
-    *Colombe* (1719)
-    *Fauvette* (1717)
-    *Marie-Françoise* (1714)
-    *Pie* (1719)
-    *Tourterelle* (1719)

7. List of the French Fleet as at 1st January 1734

First Rank (1 vessel)
(a) Levant Fleet – nil
(b) Ponant Fleet – Brest Dept
110   *Foudroyant* (1724)

Second Rank (14 vessels)
(a) Levant Fleet
74   *Duc d'Orléans* (1720)
74   *Phénix* (1720)
74   *Ferme* (1722)
74   *Espérance* (1722)
74   *Saint Esprit* (1724)
68   *Conquérant* (1687)
-    *Henri* (1687)
(b) Ponant Fleet – Brest Dept
74   *Neptune* (1723)
74   *Sceptre* (1719)
74   *Bourbon* (1719)
72   *Lys* (1706)
70   *Aimable* (1725)
(c) Ponant Fleet – Rochefort Dept
74   *Saint Philippe* (1721)
74   *Juste* (1724)

Third Rank (18 vessels)
(a) Levant Fleet
64   *Solide* (1722)
64   *Éole* (1722)
62   *Leopard* (1726)
62   *Toulouse* (1714)
60   *Heureux* (1727)
50   *Diamant* (1733)
(b) Ponant Fleet – Brest Dept
64   *Ardent* (1723)
64   *Éclatant* (1721)
64   *Achille* (1705)
64   *Elizabeth* (1722)
64   *Fleuron* (1730)
62   *Grafton* (1707)
60   *Mercure* (1697)
60   *Hercule* (1705)
60   *Content* (1717)
60   *Triton* (1727)
56   *Brillant* (1724)
(c) Ponant Fleet – Rochefort Dept
62   *Saint Louis* (1720)

Fourth Rank (13 vessels)
(a) Levant Fleet
50   *Alcyon* (1724)
50   *Tigre* (1724)
42   *Aquilon* (1733)
(b) Ponant Fleet – Brest Dept
50   *Jason* (1724)
50   *Griffon* (1705)
46   *Argonaute* (1722)
46   *Parfaite* (1722)
46   *Gloire* (1726)
42   *Amazone* (1707)
(c) Ponant Fleet – Rochefort Dept
50   *Héros* (1701)
50   *François* (1688)
50   *Rubis* (1728)
42   *Néréide* (1722)

Light Frigates (12 vessels)
(a) Levant Fleet
26   *Flore* (1728)
26   *Zéphyr* (1728)
14   *Nymphe* (1728)
(b) Ponant Fleet – Brest Dept
30   *Astrée* (1727)
26   *Vénus* (1723)
16   *Méduse* (1727)
(c) Ponant Fleet – Rochefort Dept
34   *Victoire* (1704)
16   *Paon* (-)
14   *Sphère* (-)
10   *Fée* (1734)
10   *Vipère* (1734)
8   *Levrette* (1734)
(e) Ponant Fleet – Le Havre Dept
18   *Gazelle* (1732)

Mortar Vessels (5 vessels)
(a) Levant Fleet
8   *Ardente* (1725)
8   *Foudroyante* (1727)
8   *Tempête* (1725)
(b) Ponant Fleet – Brest Dept
-    *Salamandre* (-)
-    *Tonnante* (-)

Flûtes (11 vessels)
(a) Levant Fleet
50   *Loire* (1719)
50   *Seine* (1719)
(b) Ponant Fleet – Brest Dept
10   *Sarcelle* (1720)
(c) Ponant Fleet – Rochefort Dept
44   *Dromadaire* (1717)
44   *Portefaix* (1717)
42   *Baleine* (1724)
40   *Profond* (1724)
28   *Charente* (1731)
28   *Gironde* (1728)
20   *Somme* (1729)
(e) Ponant Fleet – Le Havre Dept
32   *Orox* (1733)

Corvettes or Barques Longues (2 vessels)
(e) Ponant Fleet – Le Havre Dept
12   *Dryade* (1734)
10   *Naïade* (1734)

Barques latines (2 vessels)
(a) Levant Fleet
14   *Sibylle* (1728)
14   *Légère* (1728)

Brigantines (2 vessels)
(a) Levant Fleet
-    *Inconnu* (1729)
-    *Assuré* (1729)

Gabarres (11 vessels)
(b) Ponant Fleet – Brest Dept
-    *Colombe* (1719)
-    *Tourterelle* (1719)
-    *Bécasse* (1722)
-    *Alouette* (1724)
-    *Marie-Françoise* (1714)
(c) Ponant Fleet – Rochefort Dept
-    *Caille* (1724)
-    *Perdrix* (1724)
(e) Ponant Fleet – Le Havre Dept
-    *Corneille* (1723)
-    *Palombe* (1730)
-    *Pintade* (1730)
-    *Grive* (1732)

Careening Hulks (2 vessels)
(e) Ponant Fleet – Le Havre Dept
-    *Grand Ponton* (1722)
-    *Petit Ponton* (1722)

8. List of the French Fleet as at 1st January 1743

First Rank
(none)

Second Rank (17 vessels)
(a) Levant Fleet
78   *Terrible* (1739)
74   *Duc d'Orléans* (1720)
74   *Espérance* (1722)
74   *Ferme* (1722)
74   *Phoenix* (1720)
74   *Saint Esprit* (1724)
(b) Ponant Fleet – Brest Dept
74   *Dauphin Royal* (1735)
74   *Juste* (1724)
74   *Neptune* (1723)
74   *Saint Philippe* (1721)
74   *Sceptre* (1719)
74   *Superbe* (1735)
72   *Lys* (1706)
(c) Ponant Fleet – Rochefort Dept
74   *Invincible* (1741)
74   *Magnanime* (1741)
68   *Conquérant* (1687)

Third Rank (22 vessels)
(a) Levant Fleet
64   *Éole* (1733)
64   *Sérieux* (1741)
64   *Solide* (1722)
64   *Trident* (1742)
62   *Borée* (1735)
62   *Leopard* (1726)
62   *Toulouse* (1714)
60   *Heureux* (1727)
50   *Diamant* (1733)
(b) Ponant Fleet – Brest Dept
64   *Éclatant* (1720)
64   *Elizabeth* (1722)
64   *Fleuron* (1729)
64   *Grafton* (1707)
64   *Mars* (1739)
64   *Saint Louis* (1723)
64   *Saint Michel* (1738)
60   *Content* (1717)
60   *Mercure* (1697)
60   *Triton* (1727)
58   *Brillant* (1724)
(c) Ponant Fleet – Rochefort Dept
64   *Ardent* (1720)
56   *Apollon* (1738)

Fourth Rank (11 vessels)
(a) Levant Fleet
50   *Alcyon* (1724)
50   *Tigre* (1724)
48   *Aquilon* (1733)
(b) Ponant Fleet – Brest Dept
52   *Auguste* (1739)
50   *Griffon* (1705)
46   *Argonaute* (1722)
46   *Parfaite* (1722)

(c) Ponant Fleet – Rochefort Dept
   54   *Rubis* (1737)
   52   *Jason* (1724)
   44   *Gloire* (1742)
   44   *Néréide* (1733)

Light Frigates (15 vessels)
(a) Levant Fleet
   32   *Atalante* (1741)
   28   *Zéphyr* (1728)
   26   *Flore* (1728)
   24   *Volage* (1741)
(b) Ponant Fleet – Brest Dept
   26   *Medee* (1740)
   26   *Venus* (1727)
   18   *Gazelle* (1729)
   16   *Méduse* (1727)
   12   *Dryade* (1739)
(c) Ponant Fleet – Rochefort Dept
   22   *Victoire* (1736)
   16   *Paon* (--)
   10   *Fée* (1734)
   10   *Vipère* (1734)
   8   *Levrette* (1734)
(d) Ponant Fleet – Le Havre Dept
   20   *Subtile* (1741)

Mortar Vessels (5 vessels)
(a) Levant Fleet
   8   *Ardente* (1725)
   8   *Foudroyante* (1727)
   8   *Tempête* (1725)
(b) Ponant Fleet – Brest Dept
   8   *Salamandre* (1734)
   8   *Tonnante* (1734)

Flûtes (11 vessels)
(a) Levant Fleet
   50   *Loire* (1719)
   50   *Seine* (1719)
(b) Ponant Fleet – Brest Dept
   10   *Sarcelle* (1720)
(c) Ponant Fleet – Rochefort Dept
   46   *Baleine* (1726)
   40   *Profond* (1724)
   28   *Canada* (1740)
   28   *Charente* (1738)
   28   *Gironde* (1737)
   28   *Orox* (1734)
   28   *Somme* (1736)
   16   *Éléphant* (1740)

Barque latine (1 vessel)
(a) Levant Fleet
   14   *Légère* (1728)

Corvette (1 vessel)
(d) Ponant Fleet – Le Havre Dept
   10   *Naïade* (1734)

Brigantines (2 vessels)

(a) Levant Fleet
   1   *Assuré* (1729)
   1   *Inconnu* (1729)

Half Galleys (2 vessels)
(a) Levant Fleet
   3   *Chasse* (1742)
   3   *Découverte* (1742)

Tartane (1 vessel)
(a) Levant Fleet
   4   *Diligente* (1738)

Decked Gabarres (11 vessels)
(b) Ponant Fleet – Brest Dept
   --   *Alouette* (1724)
   --   *Bécasse* (1722)
   --   *Colombe* (1719)
   --   *Marie-Françoise* (1714)
   --   *Tourterelle* (1719)
(c) Ponant Fleet – Rochefort Dept
   --   *Caille* (1730)
   --   *Perdrix* (1725)
(d) Ponant Fleet – Le Havre Dept
   --   *Corneille* (1723)
   --   *Grive* (1732)
   --   *Palombe* (1730)
   --   *Pintade* (1730)

Careening Hulks (2 vessels)
(d) Ponant Fleet – Le Havre Dept
   --   *Grand Ponton* (1722)
   --   *Petit Ponton* (1722)

9. List of the French Fleet as at 1752

Second Rank, First Order (5 vessels)
(a) Levant Fleet
   80   *Foudroyant* (1750)
(b) Ponant Fleet – Brest Dept
   80   *Soleil Royal* (1749)
   80   *Formidable* (1751)
   80   *Tonnant* (1744)
(c) Ponant Fleet – Rochefort Dept
   80   *Duc de Bourgogne* (1751)

Second Rank, Second Order (21 vessels)
(a) Levant Fleet
   74   *Sceptre* (1747)
   74   *Couronne* (1749)
   74   *Téméraire* (1749)
   74   *Redoutable* (1752)
   74   *Guerrier* (bldg – 1753)
   74   *Hector* (bldg – 1753)
   74   *Ferme* (1722)
(b) Ponant Fleet – Brest Dept
   74   *Magnifique* (1749)

   74   *Intrépide* (1746)
   74   *Conquérant* (1746)
   74   *Entreprenant* (1751)
   74   *Courageux* (bldg – 1753)
   74   *Défenseur* (bldg – 1753)
   74   *Palmier* (bldg – 1752)
   74   *Héros* (bldg – 1752)
   74   *Superbe* (1736)
   74   *Espérance* (1722)
   70   *Dauphin Royal* (1736)
(c) Ponant Fleet – Rochefort Dept
   74   *Florissant* (1750)
   74   *Prudent* (bldg – 1753)
   74   *Juste* (1724)

Third Rank (28 vessels)
(a) Levant Fleet
   64   *Hercule* (1748)
   64   *Orphée* (1749)
   64   *Achille* (1747)
   64   *Triton* (1747)
   64   *Content* (1746)
   64   *Sage* (1752)
   64   *Lion* (1751)
   60   *Saint Laurent* (1748)
   60   *Fier* (1746)
(b) Ponant Fleet – Brest Dept
   66   *Northumberland* (1743)
   64   *Protée* (1748)
   64   *Lys* (1746)
   64   *Dragon* (1747)
   64   *Illustre* (1750)
   64   *Bizarre* (1751)
   64   *Opiniâtre* (1750)
   64   *Alcide* (1744)
   64   *Actif* (bldg – 1752)
   64   *Bienfaisant* (bldg – 1753)
   64   *Sphinx* (bldg – 1754)
   60   *Saint Michel* (1740)
   60   *Leopard* (1726)
   50   *Amphion* (1749)
(c) Ponant Fleet – Rochefort Dept
   66   *Hardi* (1750)
   64   *Inflexible* (bldg – 1752)
   64   *Éveillé* (bldg – 1752)
   64   *Capricieux* (bldg – 1753)
   60   *Heureux* (bldg – 1727)

Fourth Rank (10 vessels)
(a) Levant Fleet
   54   *Oriflamme* (1745)
   50   *Hippopotame* (1749)
   46   *Junon* (1747)
(b) Ponant Fleet – Brest Dept
   56   *Arc en Ciel* (1745)
   54   *Alcion* (1724)
   50   *Tigre* (1724)
   50   *Apollon* (1740)
   50   *Anglesea* (1745)
   46   *Aquilon* (1730)
(c) Ponant Fleet – Rochefort Dept

   50   *Aigle* (1750)

Frigates (24 vessels)
(a) Levant Fleet
   30   *Pomone* (1749)
   30   *Rose* (1752)
   26   *Flore* (1728)
   24   *Gracieuse* (1750)
   22   *Maréchal de Saxe* (1748)
(b) Ponant Fleet – Brest Dept
   36   *Favorite* (1747)
   30   *Émeraude* (1744)
   30   *Comète* (1752)
   30   *Sirène* (1744)
   24   *Topaze* (1750)
   24   *Cumberland* (1747)
   24   *Galathée* (1744)
   24   *Mutine* (1744)
   24   *Thétis* (1751)
   24   *Héroïne* (bldg – 1752)
(c) Ponant Fleet – Rochefort Dept
   34   *Atalante* (1741)
   30   *Diane* (1744)
   30   *Mégère* (1744)
   30   *Zéphyr* (1728)
   26   *Fidèle* (1747)
   26   *Hermione* (1749)
   24   *Friponne* (1747)
   22   *Martre* (1746)
   20   *Nymphe* (1751)

Corvettes (3 vessels)
(a) Ponant Fleet – Brest Dept
   12   *Anémone* (1734)
   12   *Amarante* (1734)
   6   *Badine* (1734)

Flûtes (2 vessels)
(a) Levant Fleet
   50   *Loire* (1719)
(b) Ponant Fleet – Brest Dept
   50   *Seine* (1719)

Barques (2 vessels)
(a) Levant Fleet
   24   *Hirondelle* (1743)
   14   *Légère* (1728)

Xebecs (4 vessels)
(a) Levant Fleet
   24   *Requin* (1751)
   24   *Indiscret* (1751)
   18   *Rusé* (1751)
   18   *Serpent* (1751)

Half Galleys (2 vessels)
(a) Levant Fleet (Marseille)
   3   *Chasse* (1742)
   3   *Découverte* (1742)

Mortar Vessel (1 vessel)

(a) Levant Fleet
  6   *Foudroyante* (1727)

10. List of the French Fleet as at 1765

First Rank (8 vessels)
(a) Levant Fleet
  80 *Languedoc* (bldg)
  80 *Tonnant* (1744)
(b) Ponant Fleet – Brest Dept
 116 *Royal Louis* (1759)
 100 *Bretagne* (bldg)
  92 *Ville de Paris* (1764)
  80 *Duc de Bourgogne* (1751)
  80 *Orient* (1756)
  80 *Saint Esprit* (bldg)

Second Rank (24 vessels)
(a) Levant Fleet
  74 *Bourgogne* (bldg)
  74 *Guerrier* (1753)
  74 *Hector* (1755)
  74 *Marseillais* (bldg)
  74 *Protecteur* (1760)
  74 *Souverain* (1757)
  74 *Zélé* (1763)
(b) Ponant Fleet – Brest Dept
  74 *Citoyen* (1764)
  74 *Conquérant* (1746)
  74 *Couronne* (1749)
  74 *Défenseur* (1754)
  74 *Diadème* (1756)
  74 *Diligent* (1763)
  74 *Glorieux* (1756)
  74 *Intrépide* (1747)
  74 *Magnifique* (1749)
  74 *Minotaure* (1757)
  74 *Palmier* (1752)
  74 *Robuste* (1758)
  74 *Sceptre* (1747)
  74 *Six Corps* (1762)
  74 *Zodiaque* (1756)
  70 *Northumberland* (1744)
(c) Ponant Fleet – Rochefort Dept
  70 *Dauphin Royal* (1736)

Third Rank (26 vessels)
(a) Levant Fleet
  64 *Altier* (1761)
  64 *Aventurier* (purchased 1760)
  64 *Content* (1746)
  64 *Fantasque* (1758)
  64 *Hasard* (purchased 1760)
  64 *Lion* (1751)
  64 *Provence* (1763)
  64 *Rencontre* (purchased 1760)
  64 *Sage* (1752)
  64 *Triton* (1747)
  64 *Vaillant* (1755)
(b) Ponant Fleet – Brest Dept
  64 *Actif* (1752)
  64 *Brillant* (1757)
  64 *Éveillé* (1752)
  64 *Protée* (1748)
  64 *Solitaire* (1758)
  64 *Sphinx* (1755)
  64 *Union* (1763)
  60 *Artésien* (bldg)
  60 *Saint Michel* (1741)
(c) Ponant Fleet – Rochefort Dept
  64 *Bizarre* (1751)
  64 *Hardi* (1750)
  56 *Bordelais* (1763)
  56 *Ferme* (1763)
  56 *Flamand* (bldg)
  56 *Utile* (1764)

Fourth Rank (4 vessels)
(a) Levant Fleet
  50 *Sagittaire* (1751)
(c) Ponant Fleet – Rochefort Dept
  50 *Amphion* (1749)
  50 *Fier* (1746)
  50 *Hippopotame* (1749)

Frigates (23 vessels)
(a) Levant Fleet
  30 *Sultane* (bldg)
  26 *Chimère* (1758)
  26 *Fortune* (purchased 1761)
  26 *Pléiade* (1756)
  24 *Gracieuse* (1750)
  24 *Topaze* (1750)
(b) Ponant Fleet – Brest Dept
  30 *Héroïne* (1752)
  30 *Licorne* (1755)
  30 *Malicieuse* (1758)
  30 *Terpsichore* (1763)
  30 *Thétis* (1751)
  26 *Biche* (1752 prize)
  26 *Danaé* (1763)
  24 *Folle* (1763)
  20 *Étourdie* (purchased 1761)
(c) Ponant Fleet – Rochefort Dept
  30 *Aigrette* (1756)
  30 *Comète* (1752)
  30 *Diligente* (purchased 1760)
  24 *Bayonnaise* (1764)
(d) Under construction
  30 *Belle Poule* (Bordeaux)
  30 *Dédaigneuse* (Bordeaux)
  30 *Infidèle* (Le Havre)
  30 *Légère* (Le Havre)

Corvettes (15 vessels)
(b) Ponant Fleet – Brest Dept
  18 *Comtesse de Gramont*
      (prize 1762)
  12 *Hirondelle* (1762)
(c) Ponant Fleet – Rochefort Dept
  16 *Calypso* (1756)
  16 *Isis* (1756)
  16 *Saint Esprit* (1756)
  14 *Fortune* (1764)
  12 *Ambition* (1762)
  12 *Bergère* (1762)
  12 *Petit Mars* (1762)
  12 *Sylphide* (1763)
  10 *Angélique* (1762)
(d) Ponant Fleet – Le Havre Dept
   4 *Diligente* (1755)
   4 *Expedition* (1762)
   4 *Turquoise* (1757)
(e) Ponant Fleet – Nantes
  12 *Vigilant* (1763)

11. List of the French Fleet as at 1772

First Rank (8 vessels)
(a) Levant Fleet
  80 *Languedoc* (1766)
  80 *Tonnant* (1744)
(b) Ponant Fleet – Brest Dept
 116 *Royal Louis* (1759)
 100 *Bretagne* (1766)
  90 *Ville de Paris* (1764)
  80 *Couronne* (1766)
  80 *Duc de Bourgogne* (1762)
  80 *Saint Esprit* (1765)

Second Rank (29 vessels)
(a) Levant Fleet
  74 *Bertin* (?)
  74 *Bourgogne* (1764)
  74 *César* (1768)
  74 *Guerrier* (1751)
  74 *Hector* (1752)
  74 *Marseillais* (1764)
  74 *Protecteur* (1757)
  74 *Souverain* (1755)
  74 *Zélé* (1763)
(b) Ponant Fleet – Brest Dept
  74 *Actif* (1767)
  74 *Bien Aimé* (1769)
  74 *Citoyen* (1764)
  74 *Conquérant* (1765)
  74 *Défenseur* (1754)
  74 *Diadème* (1766)
  74 *Diligent* (1763)
  74 *Glorieux* (1756)
  74 *Intrépide* (1747)
  74 *Magnifique* (1749)
  74 *Minotaure* (1766)
  74 *Orient* (1765)
  74 *Palmier* (1766)
  74 *Robuste* (1758)
  74 *Sceptre* (1762)
  74 *Six Corps* (1763)
  74 *Victoire* (1770)
  74 *Zodiaque* (1767)
  70 *Dauphin Royal* (1750)
  68 *Northumberland* (1744)

Third Rank (21 vessels)
(a) Levant Fleet
  64 *Aventurier* (1760)
  64 *Caton* (1771)
  64 *Fantasque*
  64 *Hardi* (1764)
  64 *Lion* (1769)
  64 *Provence* (1763)
  64 *Triton* (1746)
  64 *Vaillant* (1752)
(b) Ponant Fleet – Brest Dept
  64 *Alexandre* (1771)
  64 *Artésien* (1765)
  64 *Bizarre* (1751)
  64 *Éveillé* (1752)
  64 *Protée* (1747)
  64 *Roland* (1771)
  64 *Sphinx* (1755)
  64 *Union* (1763)
  64 *Vengeur* (1765)
  60 *Saint Michel* (1751)
(d) Ponant Fleet – Lorient Dept
  64 *Actionnaire* (1767)
  64 *Indien* (1768)
  64 *Mars* (1769)

Fourth Rank (8 vessels)
(a) Levant Fleet
  50 *Sagittaire* (1761)
(c) Ponant Fleet – Rochefort Dept
  56 *Bordelais* (1763)
  56 *Ferme* (1763)
  56 *Flamand* (1763)
  56 *Utile* (1763)
  50 *Amphion* (1763)
  50 *Fier* (1746)
  50 *Hippopotame* (1749)

Frigates (35 vessels)
(a) Levant Fleet
  26 *Atalante* (1768)
  26 *Aurore* (1768)
  26 *Chimère* (1757)
  26 *Engageante* (1766)
  26 *Gracieuse* (1750)
  26 *Pléiade* (1756)
  26 *Sultane* (1765)
  24 *Topaze* (1750)
(b) Ponant Fleet – Brest Dept
  32 *Flore* (1768)
  32 *Folle* (1761)
  32 *Licorne* (1753)
  32 *Malicieuse* (1758)
  32 *Zéphyr* (1768)
  30 *Amphitrite* (1768)
  30 *Renommée* (1767)
  30 *Terpsichore* (1763)

30	*Tourterelle* (1770)
28	*Indiscrète* (1767)
28	*Sensible* (1767)
26	*Blanche* (1766)
26	*Boudeuse* (1765)
26	*Danae* (1763)
26	*Diligente* (1761)
26	*Enjouée* (1766)
26	*Inconstante* (1766)
26	*Infidèle* (1765)
26	*Légère* (1765)
26	*Mignonne* (1767)
26	*Sincere* (1766)
26	*Sultane* (1765)
24	*Thetis* (1750)

(c) Ponant Fleet – Rochefort Dept
30	*Dédaigneuse* (1766)
26	*Aigrette* (1756)
26	*Oiseau* (1769)

(d) Ponant Fleet – Lorient Dept
| 26 | *Triton* (1770) |

Hydrography service in the Indian Ocean
| 30 | *Belle Poule* (1766) |

Corvettes (21 vessels)
(a) Levant Fleet
18	*Fleche* (1768)
16	*Perle* (1768)
14	*Sardine* (1771)

(b) Ponant Fleet – Brest Dept
22	*Biche* (1762)
20	*Étourdie* (1762)
16	*Cerf Volant* (1768)
16	*Hirondelle* (1762)
16	*Rossignol* (1768)
12	*Écureuil* (1768)
4	*Lunette* (1765)

(c) Ponant Fleet – Rochefort Dept
20	*Ambition* (1762)
18	*Calypso* (1756)
16	*Isis* (1763)
14	*Sérin* (1771)
12	*Bergère* (1762)
12	*Fortune* (1762)
12	*Sylphide* (1763)

(d) Ponant Fleet – Lorient Dept
10	*Sirène* (1769)
5	*Nécessaire* (1769)
3	*Curieux* (1769)

Service in the Indian Ocean
| 12 | *Vigilant* (1763) |

Xebecs – 7 vessels (all with Levant Fleet)
20	*Caméléon* (1762)
20	*Renard* (1762)
20	*Séduisant* (1762)
20	*Singe* (1762)
18	*Rusé* (1752)
18	*Serpent* (1752)

| 12 | *Revanche* (1757) |

Barques – 2 vessels (both with Levant Fleet)
| 18 | *Éclair* (1770) |
| 16 | *Hirondelle* (1742) |

Bomb vessels – 3 vessels (all with Levant Fleet)
6	*Etna* (1754)
6	*Salamandre* (1754)
6	*Tempête* (1727)

Flûtes – 11 vessels
(b) Ponant Fleet – Brest Dept
  Seine (1768)
(c) Ponant Fleet – Rochefort Dept
  Ambulante (1762)
  Barbue (1760)
  Bricole (1759)
  Corisante (1762)
  Étoile (1762)
  Fortune (1757)
  Normande (1759)
  Nourrice (1762)
  Parham (1762)
  Salomon (1762)

Gabarres – 12 vessels
(a) Levant Fleet
  Tamponne (1766)
(b) Ponant Fleet – Brest Dept
  Dorade (1765)
  Écluse (1764)
  Esturgeon (1746)
  Gelinotte (1756)
  Gros Ventre (1766)
  Porteuse (1764)
Also (unassigned):
  Calypso
  Faune
  Pomone
  Saint Joseph
  Sainte Reine

Galleys – 9 vessels (all with Levant Fleet)
5	*Dauphine* (1734)
5	*Reine* (1732)
3	*Ambitieuse* (1744)
3	*Brave* (1746)
3	*Duchesse* (1742)
3	*Éclatante* (1767)
3	*Ferme* (1767)
3	*Hardie* (1739)
3	*Valeur* (1767)

12. List of the French Fleet as at 1786

The reform which took effect from 1 January 1786, put into effect by the Navy Minister (*Secrétaire d'Etat de la Marine*), the Marquis de Castries, divided the ships of the Brest Department into 5 squadrons, the ships of the Toulon Department into another 2 squadrons, and the ships of the Rochefort Department into a further 2 squadrons; see our 1786-1861 volume for more details.

First Rank (12 vessels)
(a) Levant Fleet
| 80 | *Couronne* (1781) |
| 80 | *Triomphant* (1779) |

(b) Ponant Fleet – Brest Dept
110	*Bretagne* (1766)
110	*Invincible* (1780)
110	*Majesteux* (1780)
110	*Royal Louis* (1780)
110	*Terrible* (1780)
80	*Auguste* (1778)
80	*Deux Frères* (1784)
80	*Duc de Bourgogne* (1751)
80	*Languedoc* (1766)
80	*Saint Esprit* (1765)

(c) Ponant Fleet – Rochefort Dept
There were no 1st Rank ships based on Rochefort

Second Rank (44 vessels)
(a) Levant Fleet
74	*Alcide* (1782)
74	*Centaure* (1782)
74	*Conquérant* (1765)
74	*Destin* (1778)
74	*Dictateur* (1782)
74	*Guerrier* (1753)
74	*Héros* (1778)
74	*Heureux* (1782)
74	*Mercure* (1783)
74	*Puissant* (1782)
74	*Séduisant* (1783)
74	*Souverain* (1757)
74	*Suffisant* (1782)
74	(unnamed, became *Commerce de Bordeaux*)
74	(unnamed, became *Commerce de Marseille*, then *Lys*)

(b) Ponant Fleet – Brest Dept
74	*Achille* (1778) – named *Annibal* until 21.1.1786
74	*America* (1782)
74	*Argonaute* (1781)
74	*Audacieux* (1784)
74	*Borée* (1785)
74	*Brave* (1781)
74	*Citoyen* (1764)
74	*Diadème* (1756)
74	*Fougueux* (1785)

74	*Hercule* (1778)
74	*Illustre* (1781)
74	*Léopard* (bldg – 1787)
74	*Magnanime* (1779)
74	*Neptune* (1778)
74	*Northumberland* (1780)
74	*Pluton* (1778)
74	*Sceptre* (1780)
74	*Superbe* (1784)
74	*Téméraire* (1782)
74	*Victoire* (1770)
74	*Zélé* (1762)
74	(unnamed, became *Ferme*)
74	(unnamed, became *Patriote*)

(c) Ponant Fleet – Rochefort Dept
74	*Censeur* (1782)
74	*Généreux* (1785)
74	*Impétueux* (projected – 1787)
74	*Marseillais* (1766)
74	*Orion* (bldg – 1787)
74	*Protecteur* (1760)

Third Rank (7 vessels)
(a) Levant Fleet
| 64 | *Réfléchi* (1776) |

(c) Ponant Fleet – Rochefort Dept
64	*Brillant* (1774)
64	*Éveillé* (1772)
64	*Provence* (1763)
64	*Sphinx* (1776)
64	*Triton* (1747)
60	*Saint Michel* (1741)

Fourth Rank (3 vessels)
(b) Ponant Fleet – Brest Dept
| 50 | *Amphion* (1749) |
| 50 | *Sagittaire* (1761) |

(c) Ponant Fleet – Rochefort Dept
| 50 | *Annibal* (1782) |

Frigates (66 vessels)
(a) Levant Fleet
26	*Alceste*
26	*Aurore*
26	*Boudeuse*
26	*Flore*
26	*Flore Américaine*
26	*Friponne*
26	*Iris*
26	*Junon*
26	*Lutine*
26	*Mignonne*
26	*Minerve*
26	*Modeste*
26	*Montréal*
26	*Pléiade*
26	*Précieuse*
26	*Reunion*
26	*Sérieuse*
26	*Sultane*
26	*Vestale*

(b) Ponant Fleet – Brest Dept
44 *Résolution* (2 batteries)
40 *Expériment* (2 batteries)
26 *Aigrette*
26 *Amazone*
26 *Amphitrite*
26 *Astrée*
26 *Atalante*
26 *Barboude*
26 *Bellone*
26 *Calypso*
26 *Cléopâtre*
26 *Consolante*
26 *Danaé*
26 *Didon*
26 *Dryade*
26 *Émeraude*
26 *Engageante*
26 *Fine*
26 *Galatée*
26 *Gentille*
26 *Gloire*
26 *Iphigénie*
26 *Méduse*
26 *Nimphe*
26 *Proselyte*
26 *Proserpine*
26 *Résolue*
26 *Richemont*
26 *Surveillante*
26 *Venus*
24 *Active*
24 *Crescent*
20 *Ariel*
12 *Astrolabe*
12 *Boussole*
(c) Ponant Fleet – Rochefort Dept
26 *Andromaque*
26 *Cérès*
26 *Fée*
26 *Félicité*
26 *Fleur de Lys*
26 *Gracieuse*
26 *Guadeloupe*
26 *Hermione*
26 *Medée*
26 *Néréide*
26 *Pomone*
26 *Railleuse*

Corvettes (17 vessels)
(a) Levant Fleet
20 *Éclair*
18 *Badine*
18 *Belette*
18 *Blonde*
18 *Brune*
18 *Flèche*
18 *Poulette*
18 *Sémillante*
14 *Sardine*
(b) Ponant Fleet – Brest Dept
22 *Auguste*
20 *Rossignol*
16 *David*
(c) Ponant Fleet – Rochefort Dept
24 *Subtile*
20 *Cérès*
20 *Fauvette*
20 *Perdrix*
16 *Tourtereau*

Brigs, Cutters, and Luggers (21 vessels)
(a) Levant Fleet
16 *Suzanne*
(b) Ponant Fleet – Brest Dept
18 *Levrette*
18 *Poisson Volant*
16 *Hypocrite*
14 *Pandour*
14 *Sylphe*
14 *Tarleton*
10 *Ballon*
10 *Cerf Volant*
10 *Gerfaut*
10 *Pilote des Indes*
10 *Pivert*
10 *Tiercelet*
(c) Ponant Fleet – Rochefort Dept
22 *Lurchers*
16 *Stormont*
14 *Levrette de Saint Malo*
8 *Surprise*
(d) Ponant Fleet – Lorient Dept
16 *Courrier de l'Europe*
16 *Courrier de Lorient*
14 *Courrier de New York*
(f) Ponant Fleet – Dunkirk
18 *Fanfaron*

Bomb vessels (3 vessels)
(a) Levant Fleet
8 *Etna*
8 *Salamandre*
8 *Tempête*

Chaloupes-canonnières (6 vessels)
(b) Ponant Fleet – Brest Dept
3 *Arrogante*
1 *Rusée*
(c) Ponant Fleet – Rochefort Dept
3 *Mégère*
(e) Ponant Fleet – Le Havre
3 *Martinique*
3 *Sainte Lucie*
(g) Ponant Fleet – Cherbourg
1 *Violente*

Flûtes and Gabarres (45 vessels)
(Note that fleets and ports were not assigned; the numbers below are tonnages and do not refer to number of guns)
800 *Éléphant*
700 *Fille Unique*
700 *Île de France*
680 *Nouvelle Entreprise de Dantzig*
670 *Désirée*
670 *Seine*
600 *Étoile*
600 *Nécessaire*
500 *Dromadaire*
473 *Sirène*
450 *Barbeau*
450 *Barbue*
450 *Lamproie*
450 *Lourde*
450 *Mulet*
402 *Anonyme*
400 *Loire*
400 *Pérou*
350 *Bayonnaise*
350 *Bretonne*
350 *Chèvre*
350 *Cigogne*
350 *Dordogne*
350 *Durance*
350 *Écluse*
350 *Gave*
350 *Guyane*
350 *Pintade*
350 *Pluvier*
350 *Rhône*
350 *Saumon*
345 *Lionne*
345 *Utile*
325 *Dauphin Royal*
287 *Malbourough*
286 *Amphitrite*
282 *Sincère*
282 *Vigilante*
255 *Deux Hélènes*
200 *Aventure*
200 *Forte*
133 *Dorade*
133 *Petit Cousin*
100 *Boulonnaise*
85 *Amitié*

Sources: AN Marine G-2 (1672), G-6-ter (1682), G-10-bis (1692), G-13 (1702), G-19 (1712), G-24 (1723), G-26 (1734), G-32 (1743), B5-3 (1752), Bibliothèque Municipale du Havre Ms 275 (1765), AN Marine G-37 (1772), Service historique de la défense SH-30 (1786).

Index to Named Vessels

This index lists alphabetically all named vessels referenced in this book, but only for their primary entry (mention elsewhere in the book is not noted). Each is noted along with its year of launch (or of acquisition for ships not ordered for the French Navy) and the year in which it ceased to be known under that name, its original type, and the appropriate page number. Vessels which were renamed while remaining in French naval service (even if hulked) also appear under that name. Vessels which were numbered only are not included.

Abeille, 1751 (canc), Gabarre, 296
Abel Isaac, 1703–1709, Barque longue, 313
Abénakise, 1756–1757, 4th Rank, 174
Aberwrac'h, 1769–1775, Schooner, 339
Abondance, 1780–1781, Flûte, 291
Abondante, 1692–1692, Light frigate, see *Normande* 1670–1671, 218
Achille, 1705–1743, 2nd Rank, 94
Achille, 1747–1761, 3rd Rank, 142
Achille, 1786–1794, 2nd Rank, see *Annibal* 1778–1786, 108
Acis, 1711–1711, Light frigate, 233
Actif, 1671–1672, 5th Rank, see *Palmier* 1665–1671, 192
Actif, 1672–1673, 5th Rank, see *Émerillon* 1673–1694, 195
Actif, 1673–1673, Fireship, see *Fanfaron* 1673–1685, 256
Actif, 1675–1676, Fireship, 256
Actif, 1676–1678, Fireship, 256
Actif, 1690–1691, Fireship, 259
Actif, 1692 (canc), Fireship, 262
Actif, 1693–1712, Brigantine, 355
Actif, 1752–1767, 3rd Rank, 143
Actif, 1767–1784, 2nd Rank, 106
Actif, 1779–1782, Cutter, 346
Actif, 1779–1782, Schooner, 346
Actif, 1780–1783, Cutter, 347
Actionnaire, 1770–1782, 3rd Rank, 150
Active, 1703–1709, Barque longue, 314
Active, 1778–1794, 8pdr frigate, 214
Adélaïde, 1699–1714, 4th Rank, 166
Adélaïde, 1761–1763, Gunboat, 250
Admirable, 1671–1677, 2nd Rank, see *Frédéric* 1666–1671, 80
Admirable, 1678–1689, 1st Rank, see *Henri* 1669–1671, 57
Admirable, 1691–1692, 1st Rank, 65
Admirable, 1692–1716, 1st Rank, 67
Adour, 1759–1777, Flûte, 287
Adour, 1763 (canc), Flûte, 287
Adour, 1765–1772, Flûte, 289

Adour, 1781–1784, Gabarre, 299
Adriatique, 1665–1665, Light frigate, 217
Adroit, 1671–1673, 5th Rank, see *Bayonnais* 1667–1671, 193
Adroit, 1677–1689, 5th Rank, 197
Adroit, 1691–1704, 4th Rank, 163
Adroite, 1672–1677, Barque longue, 305
Africain, 1701–1723, 4th Rank, 167
Africain, 1769–1780, Flûte, 289
Africain, 1772–1774, Brigantine, 340
Afrique, 1767–1786, Schooner, 339
Agaçante, 1762–1762, Gunboat, 250
Agathe, 1691–1693, Barque longue, 310
Agathe, 1693–1697, Flûte, 279
Agathe, 1708–1718, Barque longue, 315
Agathe, 1756–1759, Cutter, 337
Agile, 1707–1708, Barque longue, 315
Aglaé, 1760–1767, Prame, 247
Agréable, 1671–1717, 3rd Rank, 120
Agricola, 1794–1803, 2nd Rank, see *Borée* 1785–1794, 111
Aigle d'Or, 1661–1671, Flûte, 267
Aigle Noir, 1661–1662, Flûte, 267
Aigle Royal, 1783–?, Coast guard vessel, 369
Aigle Volant, 1704–1712, Fireship, 263
Aigle, 1628–1644, Dragon, 51
Aigle, 1692–1712, 5th Rank, 201
Aigle, 1750–1765, 3rd Rank, 153
Aigle, 1780–1782, 18pdr frigate, 187
Aigle, 1780–1782, Brig, 347
Aigle, 1781–1788, Cutter, 348
Aigrette, 1756–1789, 8pdr frigate, 208
Aimable Marie, 1780–1782, Transport, 366
Aimable Mélanie, 1759–1766, Bomb vessel, 246
Aimable, 1671–1690, 3rd Rank, see *Saint Louis* 1658–1671, 115
Aimable, 1690–1714, 2nd Rank, 89
Aimable, 1695–1697, Gunboat, 248
Aimable, 1725–1736, 2nd Rank, 99
Aimable, 1761–1762, Snow, 339
Aimable, 1776–1782, 8pdr frigate, 213
Ajax, 1761–1774, Flûte, 287
Ajax, 1779–1801, 3rd Rank, see *Maréchal de Broglie* 1778–1779, 150
Albany, 1746–?, Corvette, 318
Alceste, 1780–1799, 12pdr frigate, 181
Alcide, 1743–1755, 3rd Rank, 141
Alcide, 1782–1795, 2nd Rank, 111
Alcmène, 1774–1779, 8pdr frigate, 213
Alcyon, 1671–1696, 4th Rank, see *Le Havre* 1669–1671, 159
Alcyon, 1689–1718, 4th Rank, 163
Alcyon, 1726–1759, 4th Rank, 171
Alcyon, 1760 (canc), 3rd Rank, 146
Alerte No 2, 1779–1782, Schooner, 346

Alerte No 3, 1780–1782, Schooner, 347
Alerte, 1778–1780, Cutter, 342
Alerte, 1780–1781, Cutter, 347
Alexander, 1782–1786, Brig, 350
Alexandre, 1771–1782, 3rd Rank, 148
Algonkin, 1753–1784, 2nd Rank, 104
Allegiance, 1782–1783, Gabarre, 301
Alligator No 2, 1782–1783, Cutter, see *Alligator* 1781–1782, 348
Alligator, 1781–1782, Cutter, 348
Alligator, 1782–1783, Corvette, 329
Allumette, 1693–1699, Barque longue, 312
Almirante, 1638–1650, Vaisseau, 51
Alose, 1746–1750, Gabarre, 296
Alouette, 1717–1721, Gabarre, 294
Alouette, 1724–1748, Gabarre, 295
Alouette, 1757–1760, Gabarre, 296
Alouette, 1786–1799, Corvette, 331
Alsace, 1670–1671, 3rd Rank, see *Fier* 1671–1678, 118
Altier, 1760–1772, 3rd Rank, 146
Amarante, 1708–1724, Light frigate, 233
Amarante, 1747–1760, Corvette, 318
Amazone, 1676–1687, Galley, 376
Amazone, 1686–1695, Galley, 379
Amazone, 1699–1716, Galley, 391
Amazone, 1707–1748, 4th Rank, 169
Amazone, 1751–1763, Galley, 393
Amazone, 1778–1797, 12pdr frigate, 179
Ambassadeur, 1759–1759, Fireship, 264
Ambitieuse, 1692–1694, Galley, 380
Ambitieuse, 1699–1700, Galley, see *Émeraude* 1696–1714, 391
Ambitieuse, 1699–1724, Galley, 391
Ambitieuse, 1724–1744, Galley, 392
Ambitieuse, 1744–1786, Galley, 393
Ambitieux, 1691–1692, 1st Rank, 65
Ambitieux, 1692–1713, 1st Rank, 67
Ambition, 1762–1775, Corvette, 322
Amélie, 1759–1759, Fireship, 264
America, 1782–1786, 2nd Rank, 112
Américain, 1759–1759, Fireship, 264
Amérique, 1669–1671, Flûte, 270
Améthyste, 1754–1771, 8pdr frigate, 207
Amiral Keppel, 1782–1782, Gabarre, 301
Amitié, 1710–1711, Light frigate, 234
Amitié, 1782–1791, Gabarre, 300
Amour, 1769 (canc), 8pdr frigate, 213
Amphion, 1749–1787, 3rd Rank, 143
Amphitrite, 1696–1713, 4th Rank, 164
Amphitrite, 1700–1705, 3rd Rank, 134
Amphitrite, 1741–1742, Mortar boat, 248
Amphitrite, 1744–1745, 8pdr frigate, 204
Amphitrite, 1768–1791, 12pdr frigate, 178
Amphitrite, 1782–1787, Gabarre, 300

Amsterdam, 1689–1690, 3rd Rank, see *Vaillant* 1690–1692, 128
Andromaque, 1777–1796, 12pdr frigate, 180
Andromède, 1704–1709, Light frigate, 230
Anémone, 1747–1761, Corvette, 318
Ange Blanc, 1691–1694, Barque, 334
Ange, 1691–1699, Fireship, 260
Angélique, 1718–1718, Light frigate, see *Cosse d'Angélique* 1715–1718, 234
Angélique, 1759–1759, Coast guard vessel, 369
Angélique, 1762–1767, Corvette, 322
Anglesea, 1745–1771, 4th Rank, 173
Anglois, 1673–1673, Fireship, see *Caché* 1673–1676, 256
Anglois, 1673–1673, Fireship, see *Voilé* 1673–1676, 256
Anguille, 1756–1769, Gunboat, 249
Anjou, 1671–1671, 3rd Rank, see *Vaillant* 1671–1691, 122
Anna Sophia, 1745–1757, Flûte, 285
Anna, 1650–1678, 4th Rank, 156
Anna, 1763–1763, Brigantine, 339
Anne, 1757–1757, Sloop, 367
Annibal, 1778–1786, 2nd Rank, 108
Annibal, 1782–1792, 3rd Rank, 151
Anonyme, 1673–1673, 4th Rank, see *Indien* 1673–1692, 160
Anonyme, 1782–1786, Gabarre, 300
Anti-Fédéraliste, 1794–1795, 1st Rank, see *Languedoc* 1766–1794, 77
Apollon, 1671–1678, 3rd Rank, 121
Apollon, 1683–1719, 3rd Rank, 125
Apollon, 1740–1758, 3rd Rank, 152
Apollon, 1782–1785, Flûte, 293
Aquilon, 1670 (canc), 3rd Rank, 120
Aquilon, 1671–1697, 3rd Rank, see *Trident* 1666–1671, 117
Aquilon, 1702–1707, 3rd Rank, 134
Aquilon, 1733–1757, 4th Rank, 171
Arbre de Pin, 1677–1678, Flûte, 273
Arbre d'Olivier, 1691–1705, Flûte, 276
Arc en Ciel, 1671–1673, 4th Rank, see *Flamand* 1667–1671, 158
Arc en Ciel, 1675–1676, 3rd Rank, see *Constant* 1674–1675, 123
Arc en Ciel, 1678–1699, 4th Rank, 161
Arc en Ciel, 1745–1756, 3rd Rank, 152
Arc en Ciel, 1758–1759, Corvette, 320
Archangel, 1707–1715, Flûte, 283
Arche de Noé, 1692–1693, 4th Rank, see *Éole* 1673–1692, 160
Arche, 1701–1702, Flûte, see *Saint Nicolas* 1701–1701, 281
Ardent, 1671–1671, 3rd Rank, see *Téméraire* 1671–1694, 122
Ardent, 1671–1676, Fireship, see *Saint Antoine de Padoue* 1661–1671, 252
Ardent, 1676–1678, Fireship, 256
Ardent, 1680–1705, 2nd Rank, 85
Ardent, 1723–1746, 3rd Rank, 139
Ardent, 1779–1782, 3rd Rank, 150

Ardente, 1683–1714, Bomb vessel, 241
Ardente, 1726–1757, Bomb vessel, 245
Aréthuse, 1757–1758, 8pdr frigate, 210
Argo, 1783–1783, 3rd Rank, 154
Argonaute, 1708–1746, 4th Rank, 169
Argonaute, 1722–1762, 4th Rank, 170
Argonaute, 1781–1794, 2nd Rank, 110
Argus, 1779–1784, Corvette, 328
Ariel, 1779–1793, 8pdr frigate, 214
Arlequin, 1780–1781, Corvette, 324
Armes de France, 1677–1678, Light frigate, 221
Armes de Pologne, 1691–1692, Flûte, 277
Armes de Velasque, 1696–1697, Light frigate, 228
Armes de Venise, 1692–1698, Flûte, 279
Arrogant, 1671–1673, 5th Rank, 195
Arrogant, 1673–1678, 5th Rank, 195
Arrogant, 1682–1705, 3rd Rank, 125
Arrogante, 1781–1792, Gunboat, see *Nantaise* 1779–1792, 251
Arsenal de Marseille, 1701–1701, Flûte, 281
Artésien, 1765–1785, 3rd Rank, 148
Artésienne, 1762 (canc), 3rd Rank, 153
Artois, 1670–1671, 4th Rank, see *Maure* 1672–1678, 121
Artois, 1780–1780, 18pdr frigate, 187
Aspic, 1759–1766, Gunboat, 249
Assuré, 1670–1671, 4th Rank, see *François* 1671–1686, 159
Assuré, 1671–1689, 3rd Rank, see *Lys* 1667–1671, 118
Assuré, 1689–1692, 3rd Rank, 128
Assuré, 1697–1702, 3rd Rank, 130
Assuré, 1728–1758, Brigantine, 358
Assurée, 1672–1677, Barque longue, 304
Assurée, 1678–1690, Barque longue, 306
Assurée, 1690–1692, Barque longue, 308
Astrée, 1707–1719, Light frigate, 232
Astrée, 1728–1743, Light frigate, 237
Astrée, 1780–1795, 12pdr frigate, 180
Astrolabe, 1785–1785, Flûte, see *Portefaix* 1782–1785, 293
Astrolabe, 1785–1788, Flûte, see *Autruche* 1781–1785, 293
Astronome, 1760 (canc), 2nd Rank, 106
Atalante, 1696–1705, Light frigate, see *Salamandre* 1693–1696, 226
Atalante, 1707–1733, 4th Rank, 169
Atalante, 1741–1760, 4th Rank, 173
Atalante, 1768–1794, 12pdr frigate, 178
Atlas, 1707–1709, Flûte, 283
Atlas, 1738–1739, Flûte, 284
Atlas, 1776–1781, 2nd Rank, see *Northumberland* 1744–1776, 101
Attendant, 1672–1672, 4th Rank, see *Marquis* 1673–1677, 160
Audacieuse, 1692–1706, Light frigate, 225
Audacieux, 1784–1803, 2nd Rank, 111
Auguste, 1670–1671, Fireship, 254
Auguste, 1704–1705, 3rd Rank, 137
Auguste, 1707–1720, 3rd Rank, 138

Auguste, 1741–1746, 4th Rank, 172
Auguste, 1778–1793, 1st Rank, 77
Auguste, 1783–1786, Corvette, 331
Aurore, 1665–1671, Light frigate, 217
Aurore, 1671–1688, Light frigate, see *Normande* 1670–1671, 218
Aurore, 1690–1697, Light frigate, 224
Aurore, 1693–1694, Light frigate, 226
Aurore, 1695–1697, Gunboat, 248
Aurore, 1697–1697, Light frigate, 228
Aurore, 1697–1720, Light frigate, 228
Aurore, 1745–1753, 4th Rank, 173
Aurore, 1767–1768, Corvette, 323
Aurore, 1768–1793, 12pdr frigate, 178
Autruche, 1692 (canc), Light frigate, 225
Autruche, 1756–1760, Gabarre, 296
Autruche, 1781–1785, Flûte, 293
Avenant, 1671–1695, Flûte, 271
Avenant, 1696–1704, 4th Rank, 164
Aventure, 1665–1666, Light frigate, 217
Aventure, 1666–1672, Felucca, 352
Aventure, 1756–1763, Gunboat, 249
Aventure, 1782–1786, Gabarre, 300
Aventurier Marin, 1695–1698, Flûte, 280
Aventurier, 1671–1697, 5th Rank, 195
Aventurier, 1764–1772, 3rd Rank, see *Saint François de Paule* 1760–1764, 147
Bacquencourt, 1782–1784, Gabarre, 300
Badine, 1678–1684, Light frigate, 221
Badine, 1689–1705, 5th Rank, 199
Badine, 1745–1756, Corvette, 317
Badine, 1761–1766, Gunboat, 250
Badine, 1775–1775, Schooner, 340
Badine, 1780–1809, 8pdr corvette, 328
Balance, 1760–1768, Flûte, 288
Baleine, 1678–1681, Flûte, 273
Baleine, 1683–1710, Flûte, 274
Baleine, 1725–1744, Flûte, 284
Baleine, 1779–1786, Flûte, 291
Balle de Papier, 1658–1659, Flûte, see *Flûte Royale* 1659–1671, 267
Ballon, 1786–1795, Lugger, 349
Barbaut, 1670–1671, Flûte, 270
Barbeau, 1782–1792, Flûte, 293
Barbude, 1782–1786, 8pdr corvette, 329
Barbue, 1762–1772, Flûte, 288
Barbue, 1777–1796, Gabarre, 298
Barlonome Maria, 1697–1707, Barque longue, 313
Baronne, 1640–1652, Frigate, 51
Barque Longue, 1666–1672, Barque longue, 303
Barque Longue, 1669–1673, Barque longue, 303
Barque Longue, 1710–1714, Barque longue, 315
Barrington, 1779–1779, Schooner, 346
Basilic, 1795–1795, Gabarre, see *Bretonne* 1780–1803, 299
Basque, 1671–1671, 4th Rank, 159
Bateau du Roi de la Colonie, 1774–1774, Coast guard vessel, 369
Batilde, 1760–1781, Prame, 247
Bayonnais, 1667–1671, 5th Rank, 193

Bayonnaise, 1671–1678, Flûte, 271
Bayonnaise, 1689–1691, Light frigate, 223
Bayonnaise, 1764–1765, 6pdr frigate, 236
Bayonnaise, 1779–1790, Gabarre, 298
Bayonne, 1692–1692, Light frigate, see *Jolie* 1692–1693, 226
Beaufort, 1662–1671, 4th Rank, 157
Beaumont, 1770–1772, 4th Rank, 185
Bécasse, 1692–1711, Tartane, 354
Bécasse, 1718–1723, Gabarre, 294
Bécasse, 1722–1748, Gabarre, 294
Bel Isaac, 1703–1709, Barque longue, see *Abel Isaac* 1703–1709, 313
Belette, 1758–1760, Caiche, 365
Belette, 1779–1779, Corvette, 327
Belette, 1781–1793, 8pdr corvette, 329
Bélier, 1770 (canc), 3rd Rank, see *Jason* 1779–1782, 149
Bellande, 1669–1679, Bilander, 362
Belle Île, 1663–1671, Light frigate, 216
Belle Maguelonne, 1754–?, Tartane, 360
Belle Poule, 1766–1780, 12pdr frigate, 177
Belle, 1671–1674, Light frigate, see *Madeleine* 1668–1671, 218
Belle, 1671–1679, Galley, 376
Belle, 1676 (canc), Light frigate, 221
Belle, 1676–1678, Light frigate, 221
Belle, 1678–1680, Barque longue, see *Hardie* 1674–1678, 305
Belle, 1679–1688, Galley, 377
Belle, 1684–1684, Barque longue, 307
Belle, 1688–1701, Galley, 379
Belle, 1689–1694, Barque longue, 308
Belleislois, 1779–1784, Chasse-marée, 367
Belliqueuse, 1684–1712, Bomb vessel, 241
Belliqueux, 1671–1678, 2nd Rank, see *Charente* 1669–1671, 82
Belliqueux, 1678–1708, 2nd Rank, see *Courtisan* 1676–1678, 85
Belliqueux, 1756–1758, 3rd Rank, 144
Bellone, 1690–1696, Galley, 380
Bellone, 1696–1741, Bomb frigate, 242
Bellone, 1742–1744, Fireship, 263
Bellone, 1757–1759, 8pdr frigate, 209
Bellone, 1778–1798, 12pdr frigate, 179
Bergère, 1762 (canc), Corvette, 322
Bergère, 1762–1774, Corvette, 322
Berryer, 1770–1773, 4th Rank, 184
Bertin, 1770–1773, 4th Rank, 185
Beschermer, 1703–1704, 3rd Rank, 135
Bety, 1686–1699, Caiche, 364
Betzy, 1782–1783, Flûte, 293
Biche, 1691–1702, Barque longue, 309
Biche, 1706–1709, Light frigate, 231
Biche, 1758–1758, Flûte, 286
Biche, 1759–1762, Flûte, 288
Biche, 1762–1774, 6pdr frigate, 236
Bien Aimé, 1769–1783, 2nd Rank, 108
Bien Aimée, 1672–1688, Light frigate, 219
Bien Aimée, 1685–1693, 5th Rank, see *Éveillé* 1671–1685, 194

Bien Aimée, 1685–1693, Light frigate, 222
Bien Arrivé, 1671–1681, Flûte, see *Justice* 1664–1671, 268
Bien Arrivé, 1690–1703, Flûte, 276
Bien Chargé, 1671–1687, Flûte, see *Soubise* 1668–1671, 269
Bien Chargé, 1690–1694, Flûte, 276
Bien Trouvé, 1745–1746, Brigantine, 335
Bienfaisant, 1754–1758, 3rd Rank, 144
Bienvenu, 1671–1706, Flûte, 271
Bienvenu, 1780–1781, Cutter, 346
Bilbaut, 1666–1671, Fireship, 253
Biscayenne, 1667–1671, Light frigate, see *Fontarabie* 1667–1671, 217
Biscayenne, 1690–1699, Barque longue, 308
Biscayenne, 1691–1698, Barque longue, 308
Biscayenne, 1698–1698, Traversier, 370
Bizarre, 1671–1692, 5th Rank, 195
Bizarre, 1692–1727, 2nd Rank, 91
Bizarre, 1751–1782, 3rd Rank, 144
Blakoual, 1709–1720, 3rd Rank, 136
Blanche, 1766–1779, 12pdr frigate, 177
Blandford, 1755–1755, 8pdr frigate, 209
Blandford, 1783–1783, Flûte, 293
Blekoualle, 1705–1709, 3rd Rank, see *Blakoual* 1709–1720, 136
Blonde, 1690–1699, Barque longue, 308
Blonde, 1755–1760, 8pdr frigate, 208
Blonde, 1781–1793, 8pdr corvette, 329
Bombarde, 1682–1710, Bomb vessel, 240
Bon Succès (de Londres), 1692–1697, Fireship, 261
Bon, 1671–1671, 4th Rank, see *Mazarin* 1647–1671, 156
Bon, 1672–1692, 3rd Rank, 122
Bon, 1693–1703, 3rd Rank, 128
Bonetta, 1781–1782, Corvette, 329
Bonhomme Richard, 1779–1779, 3rd Rank, see *Duc de Duras* 1769–1771, 154
Bonne Amie, 1759–1759, Fireship, 264
Bonne Amitié, 1781–1784, Gabarre, 300
Bonne, 1690–1695, Barque longue, 309
Bonne, 1692–1707, Light frigate, 225
Bonnet Rouge, 1793–1794, 2nd Rank, see *Commerce de Bordeaux* 1785–1793, 112
Bordelais, 1763–1779, 3rd Rank, 148
Borée, 1734–1746, 3rd Rank, 140
Borée, 1785–1794, 2nd Rank, 111
Boudeuse, 1766–1800, 12pdr frigate, 178
Bouffonne, 1670–1671, 5th Rank, 194
Bouffonne, 1671–1678, Light frigate, see *Dangereux* 1671–1681, 218
Bouffonne, 1678–1696, Light frigate, 221
Bouffonne, 1758–1761, 8pdr frigate, 210
Boulonnaise, 1777–1791, Gabarre, 298
Bourbon, 1665–1671, 2nd Rank, 79
Bourbon, 1671–1678, 3rd Rank, 120
Bourbon, 1683–1692, 2nd Rank, 86
Bourbon, 1692–1702, 2nd Rank, 91
Bourbon, 1703–1705, Fireship, 262
Bourbon, 1706–1707, 3rd Rank, 137

Bourbon, 1720–1741, 2nd Rank, 98
Bourg Couronné, 1688–1689, Flibot, 364
Bourg, 1688–1689, Fireship, see *Incommode* 1689–1692, 258
Bourgogne, 1766–1783, 2nd Rank, 107
Boussole, 1691–1692, Barque longue, 309
Boussole, 1775–1784, Gabarre, 298
Boussole, 1785–1785, Flûte, see *Autruche* 1781–1785, 293
Boussole, 1785–1788, Flûte, see *Portefaix* 1782–1785, 293
Boutefeu, 1689–1697, Fireship, 259
Boutique de Loux, 1703–1705, Light frigate, 230
Brabant, 1783–1784, Gabarre, 301
Branche d'Olivier, 1690–1690, Fireship, see *Fin* 1690–1693, 261
Brave, 1670–1671, 3rd Rank, 118
Brave, 1670–1679, Galley, 375
Brave, 1671–1674, 3rd Rank, see *Reine* 1647–1671, 113
Brave, 1672–1681, 3rd Rank, 122
Brave, 1674–1675, 2nd Rank, see *Constant* 1675–1678, 85
Brave, 1679–1687, Galley, 377
Brave, 1683–1697, 3rd Rank, 125
Brave, 1687–1726, Galley, 378
Brave, 1699–1700, Galley, see *Marquise* 1697–1714, 391
Brave, 1726–1746, Galley, 392
Brave, 1746–1802, Galley, 392
Brave, 1749–1751, 1st Rank, see *Duc de Bourgogne* 1751–1792, 76
Brave, 1762–1766, Gunboat, 250
Brave, 1781–1798, 2nd Rank, 110
Bretagne, 1766–1793, 1st Rank, 72
Breteuse, 1780–1780, Schooner, 347
Breton, 1666–1674, 3rd Rank, 117
Breton, 1783 (canc), 3rd Rank, 150
Bretonne, 1665–1678, 5th Rank, see *Étoile* 1664–1675, 192
Bretonne, 1670–1671, Light frigate, 218
Bretonne, 1671–1675, Flûte, see *Pélican* 1669–1671, 269
Bretonne, 1675–1676, Flûte, 272
Bretonne, 1685–1695, Flûte, 274
Bretonne, 1755–1765, Galley, 393
Bretonne, 1780–1803, Gabarre, 299
Brézé, 1647–1665, 3rd Rank, 114
Bricole, 1764–1780, Flûte, 288
Brigantin des Galères, 1703–1707, Felucca, 356
Brigantin du Roi, 1739–1740, Brigantine, 335
Brigantin, 1671–?, Brigantine, 352
Brigantin, 1676–1689, Brigantine, 333
Brigantin, 1693–1695, Brigantine, 334
Brillant, 1671–1678, 4th Rank, see *Basque* 1671–1671, 159
Brillant, 1690–1719, 2nd Rank, 89
Brillant, 1724–1748, 3rd Rank, 151
Brillant, 1757–1771, 3rd Rank, 146
Brillant, 1774–1797, 3rd Rank, 149

Brillante, 1678–1690, Felucca, 353
Brisson, 1769–1778, Flûte, 289
Bristol, 1745–1761, Flûte, 286
Britannia, 1780–1784, Corvette, 330
Brochet, 1759–1759, Xebec, 360
Brûlante, 1682–1712, Bomb vessel, 240
Brûlot du Capitaine d'Auberville, 1690–1690, Fireship, 260
Brune, 1690–1695, Barque longue, 309
Brune, 1755–1761, 8pdr frigate, 208
Brune, 1781–1799, 8pdr corvette, 329
Brusque, 1671–1693, 4th Rank, see *Dunkerquois* 1667–1671, 158
Brusque, 1689–1697, 3rd Rank, 128
Brusque, 1695–1697, Gunboat, 248
Brutal, 1671–1674, Fireship, see *Croissant* 1675–1693, 160
Brutal, 1675–1693, Fireship, see *Ruben* 1672–1675, 257
Brutus, 1782–1797, 2nd Rank, see *Diadème* 1756–1792, 105
Bruyante, 1778–1784, Gunboat, 250
Ça Ira, 1792–1796, 1st Rank, see *Couronne* 1781–1792, 78
Ça Ira, 1794–1794, 2nd Rank, see *Borée* 1785–1794, 111
Cabriolet, 1757–1758, Brigantine, 338
Cache de l'Amiral, 1666–1671, Cache, 363
Caché, 1673–1673, Fireship, 255
Caché, 1673–1676, Fireship, 256
Caché, 1684–1692, Fireship, 257
Caille, 1717–1721, Gabarre, 294
Caille, 1724–1739, Gabarre, 295
Caille, 1740–1760, Gabarre, 295
Calypso, 1756–1772, Corvette, 320
Calypso, 1770–1772, Gabarre, 297
Calypso, 1785–1793, 12pdr frigate, 184
Caméléon, 1752–1754, Flûte, 286
Caméléon, 1762–1780, Xebec, 361
Camille, 1777–1784, Yacht, 371
Canada, 1742–1786, Flûte, 285
Canada, 1782–1796, Gabarre, 301
Canadien, 1673–1676, 5th Rank, 194
Canard de Feu, 1689–1690, Light frigate, see *Tempête* 1690–1726, 223
Cancre Doré, 1643–1663, Flûte, 267
Capable, 1678–1691, 4th Rank, see *Provençal* 1667–1671, 158
Capable, 1692–1706, 3rd Rank, 128
Capitane du Marquis de Centurion, 1670–1671, Galley, see *Capitane* 1668–1670, 376
Capitane, 1668–1670, Galley, 376
Capitane, 1671–1673, Galley, 376
Capitane, 1677–1680, Galley, 377
Capricieuse, 1761–1766, Gunboat, 250
Capricieuse, 1779–1780, 12pdr frigate, 182
Capricieuse, 1786–1800, 12pdr frigate, 182
Capricieux, 1671–1686, 5th Rank, see *Hermine* 1664–1671, 193
Capricieux, 1682 (canc), 4th Rank, 162
Capricieux, 1689–1690, 5th Rank, 199

Capricieux, 1691 (canc), 5th Rank, 200
Capricieux, 1753–1758, 3rd Rank, 144
Captieuse, 1693–1699, Brigantine, 334
Caravelle, 1683–1684, Light frigate, 222
Carcajou, 1745–1745, Corvette, 319
Cardinal, 1638–1662, 4th Rank, 155
Caribou, 1744–1757, 3rd Rank, 152
Carpe, 1746–1750, Flûte, 286
Casimir, 1744–1748, Corvette, 318
Casque, 1689–1699, Barque, 333
Castor, 1745–1747, 8pdr frigate, 206
Castricum, 1692–1701, 3rd Rank, 132
Caterlan, 1703–1704, 3rd Rank, 135
Catherine, 1663–1666, Flûte, 268
Catherine, 1690–1691, 3rd Rank, see *Envieux* 1691–1699, 128
Catherine, 1690–1692, Flûte, 276
Catherine, 1691–1693, Dogger, 364
Catherine, 1706–1716, Flûte, see *Demoiselle Catherine* 1702–1706, 282
Catherine, 1707–1709, Barque longue, 315
Catholique, 1628–1632, Vaisseau, 51
Caton, 1777–1782, 3rd Rank, 149
Caton, 1794–1801, 1st Rank, see *Duc de Bourgogne* 1751–1792, 76
Cavalier de Flessingue, 1703–1713, Light frigate, 230
Cavalier, 1713–1717, Light frigate, see *Cavalier de Flessingue* 1703–1713, 230
Célèbre, 1757–1758, 3rd Rank, 146
Censeur, 1782–1799, 2nd Rank, 111
Centaure, 1757–1759, 2nd Rank, 105
Centaure, 1782–1793, 2nd Rank, 111
Cerbère, 1779–1784, Gunboat, 250
Cérès, 1778–1791, Corvette, 327
Cérès, 1779–1787, 12pdr frigate, 182
Cerf Volant, 1628–1635, Dragon, 51
Cerf Volant, 1747–1770, Chasse-marée, 367
Cerf Volant, 1768–1775, Corvette, 326
Cerf Volant, 1782–1786, Lugger, 349
Cerf, 1756–1766, Flûte, 286
Cerf, 1779–1780, Cutter, 344
César, 1648–1671, 3rd Rank, 114
César, 1756–1784, Chatte pontée, 365
César, 1765–1765, Gunboat, 250
César, 1768–1782, 2nd Rank, 107
César-Auguste, 1744–1748, Light frigate, 238
Chagrine, 1692–1694, Flûte, 278
Chameau, 1678–1697, Flûte, see *Arbre de Pin* 1677–1678, 273
Chameau, 1718–1725, Flûte, 283
Chameau, 1744–1747, Flûte, 285
Chameau, 1781–1793, Flûte, 292
Chance, 1778–1783, Corvette, 324
Changeant, 1673–1673, 4th Rank, see *Éole* 1673–1692, 160
Charente, 1669–1671, 2nd Rank, 82
Charente, 1671–1673, Flûte, see *Jardin de Hollande* 1661–1671, 267
Charente, 1675–1678, Flûte, see *Hollandaise* 1673–1675, 272

Charente, 1678–1693, Flûte, see *Bayonnaise* 1671–1678, 271
Charente, 1693–1700, Flûte, 279
Charente, 1703–1719, Flûte, 282
Charente, 1731–1748, Flûte, 284
Chargeur, 1756–1770, Chasse-marée, 367
Chariot d'Or, 1665–1671, Flûte, 268
Chariot Royale, 1749–1756, Flûte, 286
Chariot Volant, 1748–1749, Flûte, see *Chariot Royale* 1749–1756, 286
Chariot, 1673–1673, Flûte, 272
Chariot, 1678–1681, Flûte, 273
Chariot, 1682–1703, Flûte, 274
Chariot, 1701–1704, Flûte, see *Arsenal de Marseille* 1701–1701, 281
Charles II, 1691–1694, 4th Rank, 163
Charlotte, 1702–1703, Barque longue, 313
Charlotte, 1760–1766, Prame, 247
Charmante Betzy, 1779–?, Schooner, 346
Charmante Rachel, 1759–1759, Fireship, 264
Charmante, 1678–1684, Light frigate, 221
Charmante, 1689–1692, Light frigate, 223
Charmante, 1762–1764, Gunboat, 250
Charmante, 1777–1780, 12pdr frigate, 180
Chasse, 1691–1702, Light frigate, 224
Chasse, 1702–1709, Light frigate, 230
Chasse, 1742–1770, Half-galley, 358
Chasseur, 1647–1660, Vaisseau, 53
Chasseur, 1691–1694, Fireship, 261
Chasseur, 1702–1706, Felucca, 355
Chasseur, 1720–1722, Patache, 335
Chasseur, 1776–1784, Lugger, 340
Chasseur, 1782–1783, Corvette, 329
Chat, 1673–1674, Light frigate, see *Trompeuse* 1674–1675, 219
Château de Bayonne, 1696–1698, Flûte, see *Ville de Bayonne* 1695–1696, 280
Château de Breda, 1695–1697, Flûte, 280
Cher Ami, 1666–1667, Fireship, 254
Cheval Marin, 1662–1665, Flûte, 268
Cheval Marin, 1666–1729, 4th Rank, 157
Cheval Volant, 1706–1709, Barque longue, 314
Cheval, 1671–1671, Flûte, see *Pélican* 1669–1671, 269
Chèvre, 1751–1758, Flûte, 286
Chèvre, 1782–1788, Gabarre, 299
Chevreuil, 1779–1780, Cutter, 344
Chien de Chasse, 1780–1786, Cutter, 347
Chimère, 1758–1783, 12pdr frigate, 176
Choquante, 1692–1702, Light frigate, 225
Choueguen, 1756–1756, Schooner, 337
Christ (Chrisot), 1697–1697, 4th Rank, 166
Christine, 1666–1671, Light frigate, 217
Christine, 1689–1690, Fireship, 260
Christine, 1706–1716, Flûte, see *Demoiselle Christine* 1703–1706, 282
Christine, 1760–1783, Prame, 247
Christine-Marguerite, 1782–1783, Gabarre, 300
Cigale, 1707–1709, Barque longue, 315
Cigogne, 1756–1761, Gabarre, 296
Cigogne, 1782–1791, Gabarre, 299

Citoyen, 1764–1790, 2nd Rank, 106
Citoyenne Française, 1793–1795, 12pdr frigate, see *Flore Américaine* 1784–1787, 183
Clairvoyant, 1780–1784, Cutter, 345
Clément, 1683–1684, Fireship, see *Hameçon* 1684–1694, 257
Cléopâtre, 1781–1793, 12pdr frigate, 183
Cloche Verte, 1692–1699, Flûte, 278
Coche, 1671–1678, Flûte, see *Amérique* 1669–1671, 270
Coche, 1679–1687, Flûte, 274
Coche, 1688–1693, Flûte, see *Royale* 1687–1688, 275
Coche, 1692–1704, 5th Rank, see *Vigilant* 1673–1678, 195
Cochrane, 1782–1783, Corvette, 324
Coeur Doré, 1664–1666, Fireship, 253
Colibri, 1759–1759, Fireship, 264
Colombe, 1692–1709, Flûte, 278
Colombe, 1719–1748, Gabarre, 294
Colosse, 1692–1694, 5th Rank, see *Bizarre* 1671–1692, 195
Combattante, 1690–1696, Galley, 380
Combel, 1779–1780, Schooner, 346
Comète, 1706–1709, Bomb vessel, 243
Comète, 1752–1767, 8pdr frigate, 207
Comète, 1762–1763, 8pdr frigate, see *Danaé* 1763–1779, 211
Comète, 1779–?, Schooner, 346
Commerce de Bordeaux, 1785–1793, 2nd Rank, 112
Commerce de Marseille, 1783 (canc), 1st Rank, 74
Commission, 1793–1795, Gabarre, see *Pluvier* 1776–1793, 298
Commode, 1691–1693, Barque longue, 309
Commode, 1693–1696, Barque longue, 311
Compas, 1775–1781, Gabarre, 298
Comte d'Argenson, 1770–1771, 4th Rank, 184
Comte de Menou, 1771–1775, Flûte, 290
Comte de Saint Florentin, 1758–1759, Coast guard vessel, 368
Comte de Stokelberg, 1785–1785, Gabarre, see *Sirène* 1782–1787, 300
Comte, 1667–1671, 3rd Rank, 117
Comte, 1671–1677, 4th Rank, see *Duc* 1666–1671, 157
Comte, 1677–1698, 4th Rank, 161
Comtesse de Forbin, 1707–1708, Dogger, 365
Comtesse de Gramont, 1762–1766, Corvette, 321
Comtesse de la Chaussée d'Eu, 1782–1784, Gabarre, 300
Comtesse de Mark, 1767–1772, Schooner, 339
Comtesse, 1695–1697, Gunboat, 248
Conception, 1722–1733, Barque longue, see *Immaculée Conception* 1710–1722, 316
Conception, 1749–?, Pink, 365
Concorde, 1631–1633, Vaisseau, 51
Concorde, 1666–1671, Fireship, 254
Concorde, 1692–1693, 4th Rank, see *Indien* 1673–1692, 160
Concorde, 1711–1717, Light frigate, 234

Concorde, 1755–1756, 8pdr frigate, 207
Concorde, 1777–1783, 12pdr frigate, 181
Condé, 1770–1773, 4th Rank, 184
Conquérant, 1666–1679, 2nd Rank, 81
Conquérant, 1688–1712, 2nd Rank, 89
Conquérant, 1712–1743, 2nd Rank, 95
Conquérant, 1744–1764, 2nd Rank, 101
Conquérant, 1758–1758, Coast guard vessel, 369
Conquérant, 1765–1798, 2nd Rank, 106
Conquérante, 1689–1718, Galley, 379
Consolante, 1775–1804, 18pdr frigate, 185
Constant, 1670–1671, 4th Rank, see *Oiseau* 1671–1693, 159
Constant, 1671–1673, 3rd Rank, see *Navarre* 1666–1673, 117
Constant, 1674–1675, 3rd Rank, 123
Constant, 1675–1678, 2nd Rank, 85
Constant, 1678–1690, 2nd Rank, see *Princesse* 1667–1671, 80
Constant, 1690–1714, 2nd Rank, 90
Constante, 1690–1696, Galley, 380
Constante, 1691–1693, Barque longue, 310
Constante, 1762–1764, Gunboat, 250
Content, 1678–1685, 3rd Rank, see *Maure* 1672–1678, 121
Content, 1686–1695, 2nd Rank, 88
Content, 1695–1712, 2nd Rank, 93
Content, 1717–1747, 3rd Rank, 151
Content, 1747–1793, 3rd Rank, 142
Convention, 1792–1800, 2nd Rank, see *Sceptre* 1780–1792, 110
Coq, 1628–1643, Vaisseau, 51
Coquette, 1695–1697, Gunboat, 248
Coquette, 1761–1764, Gunboat, 250
Coquette, 1769 (canc), 12pdr frigate, 178
Coquette, 1769 (canc), 8pdr frigate, 212
Coquette, 1779–1783, 8pdr corvette, 328
Corail, 1626–1641, Vaisseau, 49
Corbeau, 1757–1757, Traversier, 371
Corisante, 1762–1772, Flûte, 288
Cormoran, 1756–1759, Traversier, 371
Cormoran, 1777–1789, Chasse-marée, 367
Cormoran, 1781–1781, Corvette, 329
Corneille, 1724–1745, Gabarre, 295
Coromandel, 1774–1775, Gabarre, 298
Corossol, 1692–1693, Fireship, 260
Corsaire, 1792–1792, Corvette, see *Maréchal de Castries* 1785–1793, 331
Corse, 1769–1773, Felucca, see *Génoise* 1768–1769, 360
Corvette, 1675–1676, Barque longue, 305
Cosse d'Angélique, 1715–1718, Light frigate, 234
Couleuvre, 1759–1763, Gunboat, 249
Couleuvre, 1778–1784, Gunboat, 250
Coulisse, 1764–1792, Flûte, 288
Courageuse, 1778–1799, 12pdr frigate, 181
Courageux, 1670–1671, 1st Rank, see *Magnanime* 1673–1705, 60
Courageux, 1671–1674, 3rd Rank, see *Triomphe* 1661–1671, 115

Courageux, 1679–1705, 3rd Rank, 124
Courageux, 1753–1761, 2nd Rank, 104
Coureur, 1774–1775, Snow, 340
Coureur, 1776–1778, Lugger, 341
Coureur, 1792–1801, Corvette, see *Duc de Chartres* 1782–1792, 324
Couronne de Naples, 1670–1671, Flûte, 271
Couronne Ottomane, 1761–1762, 2nd Rank, 106
Couronne, 1632–1643, Vaisseau, 51
Couronne, 1664–1666, Flûte, 268
Couronne, 1665–1675, Galley, see *Vendôme* 1663–1665, 374
Couronne, 1669–1712, 1st Rank, 60
Couronne, 1677–1687, Galley, 377
Couronne, 1686–1716, Galley, 378
Couronne, 1749–1766, 2nd Rank, 102
Couronne, 1768–1781, 1st Rank, 77
Couronne, 1781–1792, 1st Rank, 78
Courrier de Cadix, 1693–1693, Flûte, 280
Courrier de l'Amérique, 1783–1785, Corvette, see *Écureuil* 1768–1783, 326
Courrier de l'Europe, 1783–1789, Corvette, see *Sérin* 1771–1783, 326
Courrier de Levant, 1783–1789, Corvette, see *Fortune* 1780–1783, 329
Courrier de New York, 1783–1789, Corvette, see *Alligator* 1782–1783, 329
Courrier de Port Louis, 1783–1784, Corvette, see *Harriot* 1782–1783, 330
Courrier des Indes, 1786–1794, Lugger, see *Courrier* 1782–1786, 349
Courrier, 1782–1786, Lugger, 349
Coursier, 1775–1780, Flûte, see *Comte de Menou*, 290
Courtisan, 1666–1671, 2nd Rank, 81
Courtisan, 1671–1674, 3rd Rank, see *Breton* 1666–1674, 117
Courtisan, 1676–1678, 2nd Rank, 85
Courtisan, 1686–1702, 2nd Rank, 88
Coventry, 1704–1709, 4th Rank, 168
Coventry, 1783–1785, 8pdr frigate, 214
Créole, 1767–1773, Barque, 339
Crescent, 1781–1786, 8pdr frigate, 214
Croissant d'Afrique, 1665–1675, 5th Rank, 192
Croissant d'Espagne, 1694–1697, Light frigate, 227
Croissant, 1652–1652, Vaisseau, 53
Croissant, 1675–1693, 4th Rank, 160
Croissant, 1688–1689, 2nd Rank, see *Sérieux* 1687–1718, 88
Croissant, 1690–1704, 5th Rank, see *Sérieux* 1679–1690, 197
Croix de Malte, 1663–1671, Galley, 374
Crozon, 1762–1762, Schooner, 338
Crucifix, 1720–1720, Tartane, 357
Cruelle, 1682–1712, Bomb vessel, 240
Cumberland, 1707–1715, 2nd Rank, 97
Cumberland, 1747–1758, Light frigate, 238
Cunéginde, 1760–1774, Prame, 247
Curieuse, 1702–1710, Barque longue, 313

Curieuse, 1768–1772, Schooner, 339
Curieuse, 1776–1784, Corvette, 323
Curieux, 1690–1692, 5th Rank, 200
Curieux, 1770–1775, Corvette, 323
Cybèle, 1783 (canc), 12pdr frigate, 183
Cyclope, 1779–1784, Gunboat, 251
Cygne Blanc, 1665–1665, Flûte, 268
Cygne Blanc, 1672–1673, Flûte, 272
Cygne Blanc, 1690–1717, Brigantine, 333
Cygne Blanc, 1705–1706, Flûte, 282
Cygne, 1706–1713, Flûte, see *Cygne Blanc* 1705–1706, 282
Cygne, 1724–1724, Flûte, 284
d'Oquendo, 1638–1650, Vaisseau, 51
Dame Marie, 1692–1698, Flûte, 278
Dame Victoire, 1782–1796, Gabarre, 301
Danaé, 1756–1759, 12pdr frigate, 176
Danaé, 1760–1768, Gunboat, 249
Danaé, 1763–1779, 8pdr frigate, 211
Danaé, 1767–1768, Schooner, 339
Danaé, 1782–1795, 18pdr frigate, 187
Dangereux, 1671–1681, Light frigate, 218
Dangereux, 1672–1676, Fireship, 256
Dangereux, 1685–1709, Fireship, 258
Danoise, 1765–1765, Flûte, 289
Danube, 1761–1785, Flûte, 288
Daphné, 1760 (canc), 8pdr frigate, 210
Dashwood, 1779–1783, Fireship, 265
Dauphin Royal, 1668–1671, 1st Rank, 57
Dauphin Royal, 1669–1671, Flûte, 269
Dauphin Royal, 1691–1700, 1st Rank, see *Dauphin Royal* 1668–1671, 57
Dauphin Royal, 1738–1787, 2nd Rank, 99
Dauphin Royal, 1782–1787, Gabarre, 301
Dauphin, 1628–16230, Dragon, 51
Dauphin, 1638–1661, 5th Rank, 190
Dauphin, 1664–1671, 3rd Rank, 116
Dauphin, 1674–1675, 5th Rank, 196
Dauphin, 1675–1675, 4th Rank, see *Entendu* 1675–1692, 161
Dauphin, 1756–1758, Cutter, 338
Dauphin, 1770–1771, 4th Rank, 185
Dauphin, 1779–?, Schooner, 346
Dauphine, 1662–1672, Galley, 374
Dauphine, 1667–1671, Flûte, 268
Dauphine, 1671–1680, Galley, see *Capitane* 1668–1670, 376
Dauphine, 1680–1692, Galley, 377
Dauphine, 1689–1693, Galley, 379
Dauphine, 1693–1701, Galley, see *Madame* 1692–1693, 380
Dauphine, 1697–1702, 4th Rank, 166
Dauphine, 1703–1705, Light frigate, 230
Dauphine, 1706–1721, 3rd Rank, 137
Dauphine, 1749–1792, Galley, see *Patronne* 1736–1749, 392
Dauphine, 1773–1780, Corvette, 323
David, 1766–1767, Flûte, 289
David, 1779–1786, Corvette, 328
De Grandbourg, 1781–1791, Gabarre, 299
Découverte, 1742–1770, Half-galley, 359

Dédaigneuse, 1766–1784, 12pdr frigate, 177
Défenseur, 1677–1678, 3rd Rank, 124
Défenseur, 1754–1778, 2nd Rank, 104
Défenseur, 1775 (canc), 2nd Rank, 108
Défiance, 1781–1783, Brig, 348
Déguisé, 1671–1673, Fireship, 255
Déguisé, 1674–1677, Fireship, 257
Déguisé, 1676–1678, Fireship, 256
Déguisé, 1678–1693, Fireship, 257
Demi-Galère Dorée, 1687–1699, Felucca, 353
Demi-Galère, 1693–1704, Brigantine, 334
Demoiselle Catherine, 1696–1699, Flûte, 281
Demoiselle Catherine, 1702–1706, Flûte, 282
Demoiselle Christine, 1703–1706, Flûte, 282
Demoiselle Suzanne, 1720–1723, Flûte, 284
Demy Galère, 1702–1706, Half-galley, 355
Denise, 1763–1763, Schooner, 339
Désir, 1762–1769, Snow, 339
Désirée, 1783–1788, Flûte, 293
Destin, 1777–1793, 2nd Rank, 107
Deux Frères, 1784–1792, 1st Rank, 78
Deux Hélènes, 1781–1786, Gabarre, 300
Deux Hélènes, 1782–1783, Corvette, 324
Deux Soeurs, 1781–1783, Gabarre, 300
Dévorant, 1690–1716, Fireship, 260
Diable, 1759–1759, Floating battery, 247
Diadème, 1756–1792, 2nd Rank, 105
Diamant, 1664–1685, 3rd Rank, 116
Diamant, 1687–1724, 3rd Rank, 127
Diamant, 1733–1747, 3rd Rank, 152
Diamont, 1702–1704, Barque longue, 313
Diane, 1704–1705, Light frigate, 231
Diane, 1707–1711, 4th Rank, 169
Diane, 1744–1758, 4th Rank, 173
Diane, 1779–1780, 12pdr frigate, 180
Dictateur, 1782–1792, 2nd Rank, 111
Didon, 1785–1792, 18pdr frigate, 189
Dieppoise, 1668–1671, Light frigate, 218
Dieppoise, 1671–1679, Flûte, see *Guillot* 1670–1671, 270
Dieppoise, 1675–1680, Barque, 333
Dieppoise, 1685–1697, Flûte, 274
Dieppoise, 1693–1693, Barque longue, 310
Digue, 1764–1771, Gabarre, 296
Diligent, 1679–1682, Smack, 363
Diligent, 1762–1779, 2nd Rank, 106
Diligent, 1781–1782, Corvette, 324
Diligente, 1666–1674, Light frigate, 217
Diligente, 1676–1691, Light frigate, 221
Diligente, 1692–1694, Light frigate, 226
Diligente, 1703–1718, Barque longue, 314
Diligente, 1717–?, Brigantine, see *Sirène* 1704–1717, 356
Diligente, 1738–1761, Tartane, 358
Diligente, 1746–1763, Mortar boat, 248
Diligente, 1756–1775, Corvette, 319
Diligente, 1761–1782, 8pdr frigate, 211
Discrète, 1693–1702, Barque longue, 312
Dissimulée, 1690–1694, Flûte, 276
Dogre de Flessingue, 1702–1703, Dogger, 365
Don de Dieu, 1648–1652, Vaisseau, 53

Don de Dieu, 1669–1671, Flûte, 269
Dorade, 1689–1695, Tartane, 353
Dorade, 1691–1710, Barque longue, 309
Dorade, 1743–1764, Gabarre, 295
Dorade, 1764–1789, Gabarre, 297
Dordogne, 1781–1788, Gabarre, 299
Dorothée, 1757–1764, Gabarre, 296
Dorothée, 1764–1768, Gabarre, 297
Drack, 1783–?, Transport, 366
Dragon No 5, 1628–?, Dragon, 51
Dragon No 6, 1628–?, Dragon, 51
Dragon No 7, 1628–1629, Dragon, 51
Dragon No 8, 1628–?, Dragon, 51
Dragon No. 1 (Dragon de Rumare), 1627–1628, Dragon, 50
Dragon No. 2 (Dragon de La Rochelle), 1627–?, Dragon, 50
Dragon No. 3 (Dragon de Puygareau), 1627–1628, Dragon, 50
Dragon No. 4 (Dragon de Letier), 1627–1630, Dragon, 50
Dragon Volant, 1688–1689, Barque longue, 307
Dragon, 1646–1684, 5th Rank, 190
Dragon, 1673–1712, 5th Rank, 195
Dragon, 1747–1762, 3rd Rank, 142
Dragon, 1771–1774, Flûte, 290
Dragon, 1781–1783, Brig, 348
Droite, 1695–1708, Gunboat, 248
Drôle, 1671–1678, 5th Rank, see *Bouffonne* 1670–1671, 194
Drôle, 1690–1695, Fireship, 260
Dromadaire, 1671–1672, Flûte, see *Europe* 1669–1671, 269
Dromadaire, 1674–1675, Flûte, 272
Dromadaire, 1677–1678, Flûte, 273
Dromadaire, 1692–1693, Fireship, see *Incommode* 1689–1692, 258
Dromadaire, 1701–1712, Flûte, 281
Dromadaire, 1717–1740, Flûte, 283
Dromadaire, 1781–1805, Flûte, 292
Dryade, 1702–1709, 4th Rank, 167
Dryade, 1734–1749, Corvette, 317
Dryade, 1770–1770, Gabarre, 297
Dryade, 1783–1801, 18pdr frigate, 187
Duc de Bourgogne, 1751–1792, 1st Rank, 76
Duc de Chartres, 1782–1792, Corvette, 324
Duc de Choiseul, 1759–1761, Coast guard vessel, 369
Duc de Choiseul, 1770–1772, 4th Rank, 185
Duc de Crillon, 1782–1784, Gabarre, 301
Duc de Duras, 1769–1771, 3rd Rank, 154
Duc de Lauzun, 1783–1783, Gabarre, 301
Duc de Mortemart, 1780–1780, Corvette, 324
Duc de Penthièvre, 1758–1758, Coast guard vessel, 369
Duc de Penthièvre, 1769–1771, 3rd Rank, 154
Duc de Praslin, 1770–1771, Flûte, 289
Duc d'Harcourt, 1760–1760, Gunboat, see *Victoire* 1760–1762, 249
Duc d'Orléans, 1671–1691, 3rd Rank, see *Wallon* 1669–1671, 118

Duc d'Orléans, 1722–1766, 2nd Rank, 98
Duc d'York, 1779–1783, Corvette, see *York* 1778–1778, 324
Duc, 1666–1671, 4th Rank, 157
Duc, 1692 (canc), 3rd Rank, see *Téméraire* 1695–1722, 133
Duchesse de Chartres, 1780–1781, Brig, 347
Duchesse Royale, 1669–1671, Galley, 375
Duchesse, 1686–1723, Galley, 379
Duchesse, 1723–1742, Galley, 392
Duchesse, 1742–1792, Galley, 392
Dugommier, 1797–1805, 2nd Rank, see *Pluton* 1778–1797, 109
Dunkerquois, 1667–1671, 4th Rank, 158
Dunkerquoise, 1665–1665, Light frigate, see *Adriatique* 1665–1665, 217
Dunkerquoise, 1671–1676, Flûte, see *Barbaut* 1670–1671, 270
Dunkerquoise, 1676–1677, Barque, see *Saint Pierre* 1672–1676, 333
Dunkerquoise, 1678–1692, Hoy, 363
Dur, 1671–1678, 5th Rank, see *Saint Joseph* 1666–1671, 193
Dur, 1689–1690, Fireship, 259
Dur, 1690–1699, Fireship, 259
Durance, 1781–1791, Gabarre, 299
Dursley Galley, 1746–1748, 8pdr frigate, 206
Dutchesse Thérèse, 1745–1747, Light frigate, 238
Écarlate, 1779–1781, Galley, see *Valeur* 1742–1779, 393
Echo, 1758–1758, 8pdr frigate, 210
Éclair, 1671–1671, Fireship, see *Saint Augustin* 1664–1671, 252
Éclair, 1673–1675, 5th Rank, see *Soleil d'Afrique* 1675–1678, 195
Éclair, 1675–1676, 5th Rank, see *Écureuil* 1661–1671, 191
Éclair, 1686–1721, Fireship, 258
Éclair, 1757–1758, Corvette, 320
Éclair, 1771–1793, Barque, 361
Éclair, 1779–?, Schooner, 346
Éclat, 1663–1666, Fireship, see *Cancre Doré* 1643–1663, 267
Éclatant, 1671–1684, 2nd Rank, see *Bourbon* 1665–1671, 79
Éclatant, 1688–1713, 2nd Rank, 88
Éclatant, 1721–1764, 3rd Rank, 139
Éclatante, 1684–1697, Bomb vessel, 241
Éclatante, 1686–1695, Galley, 378
Éclatante, 1699–1700, Galley, see *Triomphante* 1697–1714, 391
Éclatante, 1699–1734, Galley, 391
Éclatante, 1713–1734, Galley, 391
Éclatante, 1734–1775, Galley, 392
Écluse, 1764–1788, Gabarre, 297
Économe, 1692–1692, 5th Rank, see *Mercure* 1690–1692, 200
Écrevisse, 1692–1692, Fireship, see *Étourdi* 1688–1712, 258
Écrevisse, 1745–?, Gabarre, 296

Écueil, 1671–1673, 4th Rank, see *Infante* 1661–1671, 157
Écueil, 1678–1678, 3rd Rank, 123
Écueil, 1678–1699, 4th Rank, 162
Écueil, 1691–1710, 2nd Rank, 91
Écureuil, 1661–1671, 5th Rank, 191
Écureuil, 1694–1695, Light frigate, 227
Écureuil, 1706–1708, Light frigate, 232
Écureuil, 1756–1762, Corvette, 320
Écureuil, 1768–1783, Corvette, 326
Effronté, 1702–1706, Felucca, 355
Effronté, 1727–1739, Brigantine, 358
Effrontée, 1678–1698, Barque longue, 306
Église, 1636–1636, Vaisseau, see *Trois Rois* 1626–1641, 50
Élair, 1676–1678, Fireship, 257
Élair, 1759–1768, Gunboat, 249
Elbeuf, 1646–1688, 5th Rank, 190
Éléphant, 1671–1673, Flûte, see *Sultane* 1670–1671, 270
Éléphant, 1673–1674, Flûte, 272
Éléphant, 1675–1678, Flûte, see *Dauphin Royal* 1669–1671, 269
Éléphant, 1678–1683, Flûte, 274
Éléphant, 1684–1690, Flûte, see *Saint Ignace* 1683–1684, 275
Éléphant, 1690–1695, Flûte, 276
Éléphant, 1702–1705, Flûte, 282
Éléphant, 1718–1729, Flûte, 283
Éléphant, 1740–1745, Flûte, 285
Éléphant, 1766–1784, Flûte, 289
Éléphant, 1770–1777, Flûte, 289
Éléphant, 1774–1785, Flûte, 291
Elisa, 1778–1784, Gabarre, 299
Élisabeth de Londres, 1692–1696, Flûte, 278
Élisabeth, 1704–1720, 2nd Rank, 96
Élisabeth, 1707–1713, Flûte, 283
Élisabeth, 1722–1756, 3rd Rank, 139
Élisabeth, 1760–1783, Prame, 247
Élisabeth, 1784–1784, Chatte pontée, 366
Ellis, 1779–1779, Corvette, 328
Embuscade, 1670–1678, Light frigate, 218
Embuscade, 1680 (canc), Light frigate, 222
Embuscade, 1681–1698, Light frigate, 222
Embuscade, 1704–1707, Light frigate, 230
Embuscade, 1745–1746, 8pdr frigate, 205
Embuscade, 1757–1761, Half-galley, see *Chasse* 1742–1770, 358
Embuscade, 1779–1784, Gunboat, 251
Émeraude, 1690–1696, Galley, 380
Émeraude, 1692–1702, Light frigate, 225
Émeraude, 1696–1714, Galley, 391
Émeraude, 1708–1711, Brigantine, 334
Émeraude, 1744–1757, 8pdr frigate, 204
Émeraude, 1779–1797, 12pdr frigate, 180
Émeraude, 1780–1783, Snow, 346
Émerillon, 1671–1671, 3rd Rank, see *Fortuné* 1671–1688, 118
Émerillon, 1671–1672, 5th Rank, see *Ligournois* 1666–1671, 193
Émerillon, 1673–1694, 5th Rank, 195

Éminent, 1647–1661, 4th Rank, 156
Éminente, 1658–1666, Light frigate, 216
Emporté, 1683–1704, 4th Rank, 162
Endormie, 1692–1692, Flûte, 277
Enflammé, 1690–1692, Fireship, 259
Enflammé, 1694–1710, Light frigate, see *Jeanette* 1689–1694, 223
Enflammé, 1747–1747, Fireship, 264
Engageante, 1766–1794, 12pdr frigate, 178
Enjouée, 1695–1697, Gunboat, 248
Enjouée, 1766–1783, 12pdr frigate, 177
Entendu, 1671–1675, 5th Rank, see *Lion Rouge* 1666–1671, 193
Entendu, 1675 (canc), 4th Rank, 160
Entendu, 1675–1675, 4th Rank, 160
Entendu, 1675–1692, 4th Rank, 161
Entendu, 1691–1701, 3rd Rank, 128
Entendue, 1690–1694, Barque longue, 308
Entreprenant, 1671–1671, Fireship, see *Flambeau* 1666–1671, 254
Entreprenant, 1671–1673, Fireship, see *Vigilant* 1673–1678, 195
Entreprenant, 1672–1673, 5th Rank, see *Vigilant* 1673–1678, 195
Entreprenant, 1674–1678, Fireship, 256
Entreprenant, 1680–1738, 3rd Rank, 124
Entreprenant, 1749–1750, Coast guard vessel, 368
Entreprenant, 1751–1758, 2nd Rank, 102
Entreprenant, 1757–?, Coast guard vessel, 369
Entreprenante, 1672–1680, Barque longue, 304
Entreprenante, 1692–1709, Tartane, 354
Entreprenante, 1693–1702, Light frigate, 227
Entreprise, 1759–1759, 8pdr frigate, 211
Envieux, 1691–1699, 3rd Rank, 128
Éole, 1671–1674, 4th Rank, see *Françoise* 1656–1671, 156
Éole, 1673–1692, 4th Rank, 160
Éole, 1693–1710, 2nd Rank, 92
Éole, 1733–1745, 3rd Rank, 140
Épervier, 1727–1740, Brigantine, 358
Épervier, 1756–1759, Cutter, 338
Épervier, 1770–1770, Chasse-marée, 367
Épervier, 1778–1783, Chasse-marée, 367
Épervier, 1778–1783, Corvette, 327
Épreuve, 1759–1760, Corvette, 321
Érasme, 1778–1778, Fireship, 265
Escarboucle, 1756–1757, Corvette, 320
Espérance d'Angleterre, 1695–1702, 2nd Rank, 93
Espérance en Dieu, 1627–1640, Vaisseau, 49
Espérance, 1644–1666, Flûte, 267
Espérance, 1667–1684, Felucca, 352
Espérance, 1669–1671, Flûte, 269
Espérance, 1676–1677, Barque longue, 306
Espérance, 1690–1697, Brigantine, 333
Espérance, 1691–1693, Dogger, 364
Espérance, 1701–1707, Traversier, 370
Espérance, 1708–1710, Flûte, 365
Espérance, 1724–1755, 2nd Rank, 98
Espérance, 1756–1757, Gunboat, see *Aventure* 1756–1763, 249

Espérance, 1779–1780, 12pdr frigate, 183
Espérance, 1781–1782, Cutter, 346
Espérance, 1783–1787, Chatte pontée, 366
Espérance, 1791–1794, Gabarre, see *Durance* 1781–1791, 299
Espérance, 1792–1793, Galley, see *Patronne* 1736–1749, 392
Espiègle, 1773–1783, Lugger, 340
Espion, 1678–1683, Fireship, see *Ardent* 1676–1678, 256
Espion, 1687–1688, Fireship, 258
Espion, 1690–1702, Fireship, 259
Espion, 1702–1711, Fireship, 262
Espion, 1736–1737, Gabarre, 295
Espion, 1749–1770, Yacht, 370
Espion, 1758–1769, Felucca, 360
Espion, 1781–1782, Cutter, 344
Ester, 1697–1697, Bomb vessel, 243
Esther-Marie, 1693–1694, Fireship, see *Sainte Marie* 1693–1694, 262
Esturgeon, 1746–1780, Gabarre, 295
Esturgeon, 1759–1759, Xebec, 360
États du Languedoc, 1720–1721, Coast guard vessel, 368
Éther, 1779–1779, Schooner, 346
Etna, 1703–1710, Fireship, 263
Etna, 1754–1786, Bomb vessel, 245
Étoile de Matin, 1767–1774, Corvette, 323
Étoile du Nord, 1693–1706, Flûte, 279
Étoile, 1664–1675, 5th Rank, 192
Étoile, 1673–1697, 4th Rank, 160
Étoile, 1695–1697, Gunboat, 248
Étoile, 1703–1704, Light frigate, 230
Étoile, 1708–1718, Barque longue, 315
Étoile, 1745–1747, 4th Rank, 173
Étoile, 1762–1789, Flûte, 288
Étoile, 1767 (canc), 8pdr frigate, 212
Étoile, 1780–1784, Lugger, 345
Étoile, 1783–1796, Flûte, 293
Étourdi, 1678–1681, Fireship, see *Entreprenant* 1674–1678, 256
Étourdi, 1688–1712, Fireship, 258
Étourdi, 1692 (canc), Fireship, 262
Étourdie, 1762–1783, 6pdr frigate, 236
Europa, 1681–1683, Fireship, see *Inquiet* 1683–1684, 257
Europe, 1626–1629, Vaisseau, 49
Europe, 1669–1671, Flûte, 269
Européen, 1692–1703, Flûte, 278
Éveillé, 1671–1685, 5th Rank, 194
Éveillé, 1685–1702, 5th Rank, 198
Éveillé, 1752–1770, 3rd Rank, 144
Éveillé, 1772–1787, 3rd Rank, 148
Excellent, 1671–1675, 3rd Rank, 120
Excellent, 1679–1710, 3rd Rank, 124
Expédition, 1762–1766, Corvette, 321
Expédition, 1778–1782, Cutter, 342
Expérience, 1768–1776, Corvette, 326
Expériment, 1779–1802, 3rd Rank, 154
Extravagant, 1689–1691, Fireship, 259
Fabuleux, 1795–1796, Chasse-marée, see *Félicité* 1778–1795, 367
Fâcheux, 1671–1674, Fireship, see *Entendu* 1675–1675, 160
Fâcheux, 1675–1675, 5th Rank, see *Croissant d'Afrique* 1665–1675, 192
Fâcheux, 1685–1705, Fireship, 258
Facteur de Bristol, 1695–1698, Fireship, 262
Facteur de Bristol, 1696–1698, Fireship, 262
Facteur, 1780–1783, Cutter, 346
Falmouth, 1704–1706, 4th Rank, 168
Fame, 1779–1780, Brig, 346
Fanfaron, 1671–1673, Fireship, see *Auguste* 1670–1671, 254
Fanfaron, 1673–1685, Fireship, 256
Fanfaron, 1686–1697, Fireship, 258
Fanfaron, 1781–1802, Cutter, 344
Fantasque, 1692 (canc), Fireship, 262
Fantasque, 1695–1697, Gunboat, 248
Fantasque, 1758–1784, 3rd Rank, 146
Fantasque, 1761–1766, Gunboat, 250
Farouche, 1690–1690, Fireship, 259
Farouche, 1693–1696, Barque longue, 311
Farouche, 1702–1706, Felucca, 355
Faucon Anglais, 1694–1708, 4th Rank, 164
Faucon, 1638–1661, 5th Rank, 190
Faucon, 1669–1671, 2nd Rank, see *Superbe* 1671–1687, 83
Faucon, 1671–1673, 5th Rank, see *Saint Sébastien* 1661–1671, 191
Faucon, 1674–1708, 4th Rank, 160
Faucon, 1727–1739, Brigantine, 358
Faucon, 1759–1761, Cutter, 338
Faucon, 1770–1770, Chasse-marée, 367
Faucon, 1778–1783, Chasse-marée, 367
Faune, 1768–1777, Gabarre, 298
Fauvette, 1717–1747, Gabarre, 294
Fauvette, 1743–1775, Gabarre, 295
Fauvette, 1783–1815, Corvette, 331
Favorite, 1671–1674, Light frigate, 219
Favorite, 1671–1679, Galley, 376
Favorite, 1674–1676, Light frigate, 219
Favorite, 1676–1676, 5th Rank, see *Palmier* 1676–1709, 196
Favorite, 1676–1678, Light frigate, 220
Favorite, 1678–1694, Light frigate, 222
Favorite, 1679–1687, Galley, 377
Favorite, 1688–1724, Galley, 379
Favorite, 1692–1702, 5th Rank, 201
Favorite, 1724–1751, Galley, 392
Favorite, 1747–1771, 12pdr frigate, 175
Favorite, 1776–1780, Corvette, 323
Favorite, 1783 (canc), 12pdr frigate, 182
Favorite, 1785–1796, Corvette, 331
Favour, 1795–1796, Flûte, see *Fille Unique* 1784–1804, 293
Fée, 1671–1674, Light frigate, see *Belle Île* 1663–1671, 216
Fée, 1676–1685, Light frigate, 221
Fée, 1689–1703, Light frigate, 223
Fée, 1734–1745, Corvette, 316
Fée, 1780–1789, 12pdr frigate, 182
Félicité, 1756–1761, 8pdr frigate, 208
Félicité, 1778–1795, Chasse-marée, 367
Félicité, 1785–1809, 12pdr frigate, 184
Félouque du Marquis de Centurion, 1672–1672, Felucca, 352
Félouque, 1671–?, Brigantine, 352
Félouque, 1691–1712, Felucca, 354
Fendant, 1672–1702, 3rd Rank, 121
Fendant, 1701–1713, 3rd Rank, 134
Fendant, 1776–1784, 2nd Rank, 108
Ferme, 1671–1676, 3rd Rank, see *Royale* 1661–1671, 115
Ferme, 1671–1676, Galley, see *Saint Dominique* 1665–1671, 374
Ferme, 1672–1696, Barque longue, 304
Ferme, 1678–1678, 4th Rank, see *Laurier* 1678–1692, 161
Ferme, 1678–1694, Felucca, 353
Ferme, 1678–1700, 3rd Rank, see *Fier* 1671–1678, 118
Ferme, 1680–1690, Galley, 378
Ferme, 1684–1685, Barque longue, 306
Ferme, 1691–1694, Galley, 380
Ferme, 1695–1703, Felucca, 355
Ferme, 1699–1700, Galley, see *Palme* 1696–1714, 391
Ferme, 1700–1702, 2nd Rank, 93
Ferme, 1705–1717, Barque, 356
Ferme, 1716–1723, Galley, 391
Ferme, 1723–1738, Galley, 392
Ferme, 1723–1774, 2nd Rank, 98
Ferme, 1740–1814, Galley, 393
Ferme, 1762 (canc), 3rd Rank, 153
Ferme, 1763–1774, 3rd Rank, 148
Ferme, 1785–1792, 2nd Rank, 112
Fidèle, 1671–1676, 3rd Rank, 120
Fidèle, 1672–1672, Galley, see *Dauphine* 1662–1672, 374
Fidèle, 1672–1674, Barque longue, 304
Fidèle, 1674–1678, Barque longue, 305
Fidèle, 1675–1687, Galley, 376
Fidèle, 1677–1677, 4th Rank, see *Comte* 1677–1698, 161
Fidèle, 1677–1694, Felucca, 352
Fidèle, 1678–1696, 4th Rank, see *Toulon* 1667–1671, 158
Fidèle, 1686–1691, Galley, 378
Fidèle, 1691–1718, Galley, 379
Fidèle, 1695–1697, Gunboat, 248
Fidèle, 1695–1703, Felucca, 355
Fidèle, 1704–1712, 3rd Rank, 130
Fidèle, 1705–1719, Brigantine, 356
Fidèle, 1748–1758, 8pdr frigate, 206
Fidèle, 1761–1766, Gunboat, see *Reine du Maroc* 1761–1766, 250
Fidèle, 1782–1784, Gabarre, 300
Fier Rodrigue, 1779–1784, 3rd Rank, see *Hippopotame* 1749–1777, 153
Fier, 1671–1678, 3rd Rank, 118
Fier, 1682–1692, 2nd Rank, 86
Fier, 1694–1713, 1st Rank, 69

Fier, 1745–1782, 3rd Rank, 153
Fière, 1681–1690, Galley, 378
Fière, 1691–1720, Galley, 380
Fille Unique, 1784–1804, Flûte, 293
Fin, 1671–1671, Fireship, see *Concorde* 1666–1671, 254
Fin, 1671–1673, Fireship, 255
Fin, 1674–1676, Fireship, 257
Fin, 1676–1686, Fireship, 257
Fin, 1690–1691, Fireship, 260
Fin, 1690–1693, Fireship, 261
Fine, 1672–1684, Barque longue, 304
Fine, 1689–1692, Barque longue, 307
Fine, 1693–1700, Barque longue, 311
Fine, 1702–1713, Barque longue, 314
Fine, 1744–1745, 8pdr frigate, 204
Fine, 1769 (canc), 8pdr frigate, 212
Fine, 1779–1794, 12pdr frigate, 180
Finkastle, 1779–1781, Corvette, 324
Flamand, 1667–1671, 4th Rank, 158
Flamand, 1765–1786, 3rd Rank, 148
Flamande, 1761–1768, Gunboat, 249
Flambeau, 1666–1671, Fireship, 254
Flatteuse, 1691–1697, Barque longue, 310
Flèche, 1691–1697, Barque longue, 310
Flèche, 1759–1763, Gunboat, 249
Flèche, 1768–1794, Corvette, 326
Flessingoise, 1692–1697, Barque longue, 310
Flessingoise, 1703–1706, Light frigate, 230
Fleur de Blé, 1689–1689, Fireship, 259
Fleur de la Mer, 1692–1702, Barque longue, 311
Fleur de Lys, 1628–1636, Vaisseau, 51
Fleur de Lys, 1659–1662, 5th Rank, 191
Fleur de Lys, 1663–1674, Galley, 374
Fleur de Lys, 1674–1682, Galley, 376
Fleur de Lys, 1681–1692, Galley, 378
Fleur de Lys, 1692–1702, Flûte, 279
Fleur de Lys, 1692–1718, Galley, 380
Fleur de Lys, 1754–1760, 8pdr frigate, 207
Fleur de Lys, 1785–1792, 12pdr frigate, 182
Fleuron, 1668–1688, 3rd Rank, 117
Fleuron, 1689–1722, 3rd Rank, 127
Fleuron, 1730–1745, 3rd Rank, 140
Flibustier, 1794–1795, 2nd Rank, see *Argonaute* 1781–1794, 110
Flore Américaine, 1784–1787, 12pdr frigate, 183
Flore, 1708–1724, Light frigate, 233
Flore, 1728–1761, Light frigate, 237
Flore, 1766 (canc), 12pdr frigate, 177
Flore, 1768–1787, 8pdr frigate, 212
Flore, 1787–1793, 12pdr frigate, see *Flore Américaine* 1784–1787, 183
Florissant, 1671–1696, 2nd Rank, 82
Florissant, 1750–1762, 2nd Rank, 103
Flûte Royale, 1659–1671, Flûte, 267
Folâtre, 1691–1692, Barque longue, 310
Folkestone, 1778–1783, Cutter, 342
Folle, 1671–1673, Light frigate, see *Fontarabie* 1667–1671, 217

Folle, 1674–1676, Light frigate, 220
Folle, 1676–1691, Barque longue, see *Corvette* 1675–1676, 305
Folle, 1689–1693, Tartane, 354
Folle, 1761–1780, 8pdr frigate, 211
Fontarabie, 1667–1671, Light frigate, 217
Force, 1668–1673, Galley, 375
Formidable, 1691–1714, 1st Rank, 65
Formidable, 1751–1759, 1st Rank, 76
Fort, 1645–1652, Vaisseau, 53
Fort, 1669–1671, 2nd Rank, 82
Fort, 1671–1677, 3rd Rank, see *Sophie* 1666–1671, 117
Fort, 1678–1692, 3rd Rank, see *Écueil* 1678–1678, 123
Fort, 1693–1702, 2nd Rank, 93
Fort, 1781–1783, Gabarre, 293
Forte, 1673–1679, Galley, see *Force* 1668–1673, 375
Forte, 1677–1687, Galley, 377
Forte, 1687–1701, Galley, 378
Forte, 1765–1768, Gabarre, 297
Forte, 1781–1789, Gabarre, 299
Fortitude, 1782–1783, Flûte, 293
Fortune de Cadix, 1693–1696, Flûte, 280
Fortune de Rotterdam, 1695–1697, Flûte, 280
Fortune, 1626–1629, Vaisseau, 49
Fortune, 1658–1669, Flibot, 362
Fortune, 1665–1671, Galley, 374
Fortune, 1669–1671, Flûte, 269
Fortune, 1675–1681, Galley, 376
Fortune, 1681–1688, Galley, 378
Fortune, 1688–1700, Galley, 379
Fortune, 1693–1697, Barque longue, 311
Fortune, 1704–1728, Light frigate, 231
Fortune, 1706 (canc), Galley, 391
Fortune, 1730–1759, Galley, 392
Fortune, 1745–1746, Corvette, 318
Fortune, 1757–1772, 4th Rank, 174
Fortune, 1757–1774, Flûte, 286
Fortune, 1762–1767, Corvette, 322
Fortune, 1780–1783, Corvette, 329
Fortuné, 1671–1688, 3rd Rank, 118
Fortuné, 1689–1707, 3rd Rank, 127
Fortunée, 1695–1697, Gunboat, 248
Fortunée, 1759–1769, Prame, 247
Fortunée, 1777–1779, 12pdr frigate, 181
Fouay, 1704–1720, 5th Rank, 203
Foudre, 1759–1768, Gunboat, 249
Foudroyant, 1671–1690, 2nd Rank, see *Fort* 1669–1671, 82
Foudroyant, 1691–1692, 1st Rank, 64
Foudroyant, 1693–1714, 1st Rank, 68
Foudroyant, 1724–1742, 1st Rank, 70
Foudroyant, 1750–1758, 1st Rank, 75
Foudroyante, 1682–1695, Bomb vessel, 240
Foudroyante, 1696–1696, Bomb frigate, 242
Foudroyante, 1728–1746, Bomb vessel, 245
Fougueux, 1671–1691, 3rd Rank, 122
Fougueux, 1692 (canc), 3rd Rank, see *Fougueux* 1695–1696, 133

Fougueux, 1695–1696, 3rd Rank, 133
Fougueux, 1747–1747, 3rd Rank, 142
Fougueux, 1785–1805, 2nd Rank, 111
Fouine, 1693–1699, Barque longue, 311
Fouine, 1782–1783, Brigantine, 350
Fourbe, 1691–1691, Fireship, 261
Fourbe, 1691–1703, Fireship, 261
Fourgon, 1671–1677, Flûte, see *Fortune* 1669–1671, 269
Fourgon, 1678–1684, Flûte, 273
Fourgon, 1685–1691, Flûte, 275
Fourmi, 1778–1778, Schooner, 342
Fournaise, 1756 (canc), Bomb vessel, 245
Fox, 1778–1779, 8pdr frigate, 214
France, 1662–1675, Galley, 374
France, 1676–1684, Galley, 376
France, 1684–1723, Galley, 378
France, 1723–1749, Galley, 392
François, 1667–1671, Flûte, 268
François, 1669–1671, 2nd Rank, 82
François, 1671–1686, 4th Rank, 159
François, 1687–1736, 4th Rank, 162
François, 1704–1706, Brigantine, 334
Françoise, 1656–1671, 4th Rank, 156
Françoise, 1669–?, Caiche, 333
Françoise, 1678–1686, Flûte, see *Cygne Blanc* 1672–1673, 272
Françoise, 1690–1693, Flûte, 276
Françoise, 1693–1694, Tartane, 355
Françoise, 1711–1711, Bomb vessel, 243
Françoise, 1760–1783, Prame, 247
Frédéric, 1666–1671, 2nd Rank, 80
Frédéric-Guillaume, 1782–1789, Gabarre, 301
Frégate Royale, 1661–1671, 3rd Rank, see *Royale* 1661–1671, 115
Fringante, 1761–1766, Gunboat, 250
Friponne, 1670–1690, Light frigate, 218
Friponne, 1691–1697, Light frigate, 224
Friponne, 1747–1762, 8pdr frigate, 206
Friponne, 1780–1796, 12pdr frigate, 182
Fulminant, 1691–1719, 1st Rank, 65
Fulminante, 1683–1713, Bomb vessel, 241
Furet, 1702–1706, Felucca, 355
Furet, 1706–1708, Barque longue, 315
Furet, 1771–1782, Cutter, 340
Furieuse, 1779–1784, Gunboat, 250
Furieux, 1671–1688, 3rd Rank, 120
Furieux, 1680 (canc), 2nd Rank, 85
Furieux, 1684–1727, 2nd Rank, 88
Gaillard, 1678–1682, 5th Rank, see *Bouffonne* 1670–1671, 194
Gaillard, 1684–1699, 4th Rank, 162
Gaillard, 1690–1691, Light frigate, see *Gaillarde* 1678–1690, 222
Gaillard, 1690–1692, 2nd Rank, 90
Gaillard, 1693–1710, 3rd Rank, 133
Gaillarde, 1668–1678, Light frigate, 218
Gaillarde, 1676–1676, Light frigate, 220
Gaillarde, 1678–1690, Light frigate, 222
Gaillarde, 1689–1712, 5th Rank, 199
Gaillarde, 1703–1704, Coast guard sloop, 366

Gaillarde, 1704–?, Barque longue, 314
Gaillarde, 1738–1741, Tartane, 358
Galant, 1668–1678, 4th Rank, 159
Galant, 1678–1684, 5th Rank, see *Arrogant* 1673–1678, 195
Galant, 1688–1689, 5th Rank, see *Soleil d'Alger* 1687–1688, 198
Galant, 1691 (canc), 5th Rank, 200
Galante, 1669–1675, Galley, 375
Galante, 1670–1671, 5th Rank, see *Aventurier* 1671–1697, 195
Galante, 1675–1684, Galley, 376
Galante, 1678–1690, Felucca, 353
Galante, 1685–1701, Galley, 378
Galante, 1693–1694, Barque longue, 312
Galatée, 1696–1708, Light frigate, 228
Galatée, 1708–1712, Light frigate, 233
Galatée, 1741–1742, Mortar boat, 248
Galatée, 1744–1758, 6pdr frigate, 235
Galatée, 1779–1795, 12pdr frigate, 182
Galéasse de Vivonne, 1677–1678, Galley, 377
Galiote Hollandaise, 1671–1671, Flûte, see *Bayonnaise* 1671–1678, 271
Galiote Royale, 1680–1692, Galiote, 363
Galiote, 1667–1669, Galiote, 363
Gange, 1770–1782, Flûte, 289
Gardon, 1759–1760, Xebec, 360
Garonne, 1671–1671, Flûte, see *Petit Anglais* 1668–1671, 269
Garonne, 1671–1674, Flûte, see *Saint Jean* 1664–1671, 268
Garonne, 1675–1675, Flûte, 272
Garonne, 1676–1678, Flûte, 273
Garonne, 1678–1689, Flûte, see *Salière* 1677–1678, 273
Garonne, 1690–1692, Flûte, 276
Garonne, 1761–1783, Flûte, 288
Gave, 1765–1777, Flûte, 289
Gave, 1781–1792, Gabarre, 299
Gayton, 1780–1783, Flûte, 292
Gazelle, 1733–1748, Light frigate, 235
Gédéon, 1766–1773, Coast guard vessel, 369
Gelinotte, 1756–1772, Gabarre, 296
Généreux, 1785–1800, 2nd Rank, 111
Génoise, 1768–1769, Felucca, 360
Gentille, 1671–1684, Light frigate, see *Saint Jean* 1666–1671, 217
Gentille, 1687–1688, Tartane, 353
Gentille, 1689–1698, Light frigate, 222
Gentille, 1701–1702, Barque, 334
Gentille, 1701–1703, Barque longue, 313
Gentille, 1702–1702, Light frigate, 229
Gentille, 1702–1708, Light frigate, 230
Gentille, 1778–1795, 12pdr frigate, 179
George, 1756–1758, Brigantine, 337
Gerfaut, 1782–1796, Lugger, 349
Gift of God, 1625–1626, Vaisseau, 49
Gironde, 1696–1702, Flûte, 280
Gironde, 1728–1737, Flûte, 284
Gironde, 1738–1748, Flûte, 284
Gloire, 1691–1718, Galley, 379

Gloire, 1707–1709, 4th Rank, 169
Gloire, 1725–1736, 4th Rank, 171
Gloire, 1727–1749, Galley, 392
Gloire, 1742–1747, 4th Rank, 172
Gloire, 1778–1795, 12pdr frigate, 179
Glorieuse, 1690–1696, Galley, 380
Glorieux, 1671–1671, 3rd Rank, see *Agréable* 1671–1717, 120
Glorieux, 1671–1677, 2nd Rank, see *François* 1669–1671, 82
Glorieux, 1679–1719, 2nd Rank, 85
Glorieux, 1756–1782, 2nd Rank, 105
Gloucester, 1709–1711, 3rd Rank, 138
Gloucester, 1757–1758, Sloop, 367
Gloutonne, 1692–1705, Flûte, see *Parti* 1690–1692, 276
Goélette de LeRoy, 1760–1760, Schooner, 338
Goélette des Colonies, 1777–?, Schooner, 342
Gorée, 1767–1779, Schooner, 339
Gosse, 1662–1666, Fireship, see *Petit Hercule* 1662–1666, 252
Gourmande, 1760 (canc), Flûte, 288
Grâces, 1670–1671, 4th Rank, see *Fendant* 1672–1702, 121
Gracieuse, 1672–1675, Light frigate, 219
Gracieuse, 1676–1676, 5th Rank, see *Adroit* 1676–1689, 197
Gracieuse, 1676–1687, Light frigate, 220
Gracieuse, 1679 (canc), Light frigate, 222
Gracieuse, 1687–1688, Tartane, 353
Gracieuse, 1689–1697, Light frigate, 223
Gracieuse, 1702–1702, Light frigate, 229
Gracieuse, 1703–1705, Barque longue, 314
Gracieuse, 1750–1781, 12pdr frigate, 175
Gracieuse, 1762–1764, Gunboat, 250
Grafton, 1707–1744, 2nd Rank, 96
Gramon, 1691–1691, Barque longue, 310
Grand Adrien, 1756–1756, Fireship, 264
Grand Anglais, 1643–1649, Vaisseau, 52
Grand Anglais, 1665–1666, 5th Rank, see *Lion Rouge* 1666–1671, 193
Grand Anglais, 1666–1667, Fireship, see *Justice* 1667–1671, 253
Grand Bourbon, 1773–1774, Coast guard vessel, 369
Grand Charles, 1664–1666, Flûte, 268
Grand Duc, 1782–1783, Gabarre, 301
Grand Louis, 1694–1695, Flûte, 280
Grand Maltais, 1645–1657, Vaisseau, 53
Grand Ponton, 1676–1686, 5th Rank, see *Sauveur* 1666–1671, 193
Grand Saint Augustin, 1665–1671, Flûte, see *Saint Augustin* 1663–1665, 268
Grand Saint Jean, 1626–1638, Vaisseau, see *Saint Jean de Hollande* 1626–1638, 50
Grand Saint Louis, 1646–1649, Vaisseau, see *Navire du Roi* 1627–1646, 49
Grand Saint Louis, 1762–1770, Fireship, 264
Grand, 1671–1678, 2nd Rank, see *Intrépide* 1666–1671, 82
Grand, 1680–1717, 2nd Rank, 85

Grande Gribane, 1670–1678, Gribane, see *Gribane* 1670–1678, 362
Grande Pinasse, 1667–1671, Flûte, 268
Grande Réale, 1678–1691, Galley, see *Réale* 1668–1678, 376
Grande, 1670–1679, Galley, 376
Grande, 1679–1689, Galley, 377
Grande, 1689–1701, Galley, 379
Greenwich, 1757–1758, 3rd Rank, 146
Grenade, 1693–1695, Barque longue, 312
Gribane, 1669–1670, Gribane, 362
Gribane, 1670–1678, Gribane, 362
Griffon, 1628–1641, Dragon, 51
Griffon, 1705–1748, 4th Rank, 167
Grive, 1718–1723, Gabarre, 294
Grive, 1733–1746, Gabarre, 295
Grondeuse, 1695–1708, Gunboat, 248
Grondin, 1778–1789, Chasse-marée, 367
Gros Ventre, 1766–1779, Gabarre, 297
Gruë, 1756–1768, Chatte pontée, 365
Guadeloupe, 1781–1794, 8pdr frigate, 214
Gualbert, 1778–1791, 3rd Rank, see *Pondichéry* 1769–1771, 154
Guêpe, 1765–1766, Corvette, 323
Guêpe, 1778–1781, Cutter, 342
Guêpe, 1779–1781, Lugger, 346
Guerrier, 1753–1798, 2nd Rank, 102
Guerrier, 1782–1784, Cutter, 350
Guerrière, 1689–1720, Galley, 379
Guerrière, 1693–1693, Light frigate, 226
Guillaume de Londres, 1693–1694, Fireship, 260
Guillaume Tell, 1781–1782, Transport, 366
Guillaume, 1666–1671, Fireship, 253
Guillot, 1670–1671, Flûte, 270
Guirlande, 1757–1758, 6pdr frigate, 236
Guirlande, 1760–1762, 6pdr frigate, 236
Guyane, 1764–1766, Schooner, 339
Guyane, 1777–1788, Gabarre, 298
Haarlem, 1625–1625, Vaisseau, 49
Hameçon, 1670–1671, Light frigate, 218
Hameçon, 1671–1676, Fireship, see *Justice* 1667–1671, 253
Hameçon, 1676–1681, Fireship, 256
Hameçon, 1684–1694, Fireship, 257
Hampton Court, 1707–1712, 2nd Rank, 96
Hampton, 1706–1713, Flûte, 283
Hancelot, 1757–1758, Corvette, 321
Hanovre, 1757–1758, Corvette, 321
Hardenbroek, 1706–1706, 3rd Rank, 137
Hardi, 1671–1678, 5th Rank, 195
Hardi, 1678–1709, 3rd Rank, see *Apollon* 1671–1678, 121
Hardi, 1750–1798, 3rd Rank, 143
Hardi, 1761–1761, Flûte, 288
Hardie, 1671–1678, Galley, see *Duchesse Royale* 1669–1671, 375
Hardie, 1672–1673, Barque longue, 305
Hardie, 1674–1678, Barque longue, 305
Hardie, 1677–1687, Galley, 377
Hardie, 1687–1723, Galley, 379
Hardie, 1723–1739, Galley, 392

Hardie, 1739–1795, Galley, 392
Harmonie, 1757–1760, 12pdr frigate, 176
Harpe, 1693–1695, Light frigate, 226
Harriot, 1782–1783, Corvette, 330
Hasard, 1744–1749, Snow, 335
Hasard, 1762–1771, 3rd Rank, see *Notre Dame du Rosaire* 1760–1762, 147
Hasard, 1782–1782, Cutter, 350
Hasardeux, 1671–1673, 5th Rank, see *Ville de Rouen* 1666–1671, 193
Hasardeux, 1674–1695, 4th Rank, 160
Hasardeux, 1698–1698, 4th Rank, see *Maurepas* 1698–1705, 166
Hasardeux, 1699–1703, 3rd Rank, 133
Haston, 1707–1708, Light frigate, 232
Hautaine, 1693–1702, Light frigate, 226
Hébé, 1757–1763, 12pdr frigate, 176
Hébé, 1782–1782, 18pdr frigate, 187
Hector, 1755–1782, 2nd Rank, 104
Hélène, 1778–1779, Corvette, 324
Henri, 1630–1637, Vaisseau, 51
Henri, 1669–1671, 1st Rank, 57
Henri, 1671–1687, 2nd Rank, 82
Henri, 1688–1726, 2nd Rank, 88
Henry, 1782–1783, Coast guard vessel, 369
Hercule, 1626–1627, Vaisseau, 50
Hercule, 1655–1673, 4th Rank, 156
Hercule, 1671–1671, 4th Rank, see *Soleil* 1642–1671, 155
Hercule, 1673–1678, 3rd Rank, 123
Hercule, 1679–1704, 5th Rank, 197
Hercule, 1705–1746, 3rd Rank, 137
Hercule, 1749–1761, 3rd Rank, 143
Hercule, 1778–1795, 2nd Rank, 109
Hercule, 1779–1779, Flûte, 292
Hermine, 1664–1671, 5th Rank, 193
Hermine, 1707–1711, Barque longue, 315
Hermine, 1757–1761, 8pdr frigate, 209
Hermione, 1699–1705, 5th Rank, 201
Hermione, 1706–1707, Light frigate, 232
Hermione, 1708–1714, Light frigate, 233
Hermione, 1749–1759, 12pdr frigate, 175
Hermione, 1779–1793, 12pdr frigate, 181
Héroïne, 1688–1722, Galley, 379
Héroïne, 1692–1694, Light frigate, 226
Héroïne, 1696–1697, Light frigate, 227
Héroïne, 1699–1702, 5th Rank, 201
Héroïne, 1704–1708, Light frigate, 231
Héroïne, 1722–1758, Galley, 392
Héroïne, 1752–1766, 8pdr frigate, 206
Héros, 1702–1740, 4th Rank, 167
Héros, 1752–1759, 2nd Rank, 104
Héros, 1778–1794, 2nd Rank, 109
Hervé, 1768–1773, Bugalet, 367
Heure du Berger, 1767–1772, Corvette, 323
Heureuse Marie, 1737–1758, Gabarre, 295
Heureuse Marthe, 1779–1780, Bomb vessel, 246
Heureuse Victoire, 1782–1783, Gabarre, 300
Heureuse, 1676–1677, Galley, 377
Heureuse, 1679–1680, Galley, 377
Heureuse, 1690–1696, Galley, 380

Heureuse, 1692–1693, Light frigate, 226
Heureuse, 1696–1714, Galley, 391
Heureuse, 1708–1712, Brigantine, 334
Heureuse, 1755–1755, Schooner, 336
Heureux Retour, 1691–1708, 3rd Rank, 131
Heureux Succès, 1692–1697, Fireship, see *Bon Succès* 1692–1697, 261
Heureux, 1671–1676, Galley, see *Fortune* 1665–1671, 374
Heureux, 1671–1693, 3rd Rank, 121
Heureux, 1690–1710, 2nd Rank, 90
Heureux, 1714–1716, Traversier, 370
Heureux, 1730–1768, 3rd Rank, 152
Heureux, 1767–1769, Gabarre, 297
Heureux, 1782–1798, 2nd Rank, 111
Hippopotame, 1749–1777, 3rd Rank, 153
Hirondelle de Falmouth, 1693–1696, Barque longue, 311
Hirondelle, 1664–1679, 5th Rank, 193
Hirondelle, 1679–1687, 5th Rank, 197
Hirondelle, 1688–1699, 5th Rank, see *Trois Roses* 1687–1688, 198
Hirondelle, 1699–1704, 5th Rank, 201
Hirondelle, 1743–1786, Barque latine, 359
Hirondelle, 1762–1783, Corvette, 325
Holderman, 1782–1784, Gabarre, 301
Holdernetz, 1782–1784, Gabarre, see *Holderman* 1782–1784, 301
Hollandaise, 1673–1675, Flûte, 272
Hollande, 1693–1710, Flûte, 279
Hunter, 1778–1783, Gabarre, 299
Hurault, 1755–1758, Corvette, 319
Huron, 1781–?, Brig, 347
Hussard, 1762–1762, 8pdr frigate, 212
Hussard, 1779–1780, Cutter, 344
Hydre, 1795–1799, 2nd Rank, see *Hercule* 1778–1795, 109
Hypocrite, 1781–1789, Corvette, 330
Île de France, 1669–1671, 1st Rank, 59
Île de France, 1772–1790, Flûte, see *Marquis de Sancé* 1770–1772, 290
Illustre, 1671–1698, 2nd Rank, see *Neptune* 1666–1671, 82
Illustre, 1672–?, Traversier, 369
Illustre, 1685–1701, Galley, 378
Illustre, 1750–1761, 3rd Rank, 143
Illustre, 1781–1791, 2nd Rank, 110
Immaculée Conception, 1710–1722, Barque longue, 316
Impératrice de Russie, 1780–1782, Corvette, 324
Impérieuse, 1695–1708, Gunboat, 248
Impérieuse, 1787–1793, 18pdr frigate, 188
Impertinent, 1690–1699, Fireship, 260
Impétueux, 1755–1762, 1st Rank, see *Ville de Paris* 1764–1782, 70
Impudent, 1671–1676, Fireship, see *Symbole* 1668–1671, 254
Impudent, 1676–1678, Fireship, 257
Impudent, 1686–1690, Fireship, 258
Impudent, 1690–1691, Fireship, 259
Impudent, 1693–1698, Fireship, 262

Impudent, 1705–1715, Fireship, see *Bourbon* 1703–1705, 262
Impudente, 1778–1784, Gunboat, 251
Incendiaire, 1747–1747, Fireship, 263
Incommode, 1672–1675, Fireship, 256
Incommode, 1678–1681, Light frigate, see *Gaillarde* 1668–1678, 218
Incommode, 1689–1692, Fireship, 258
Inconnu, 1671–1673, Fireship, see *Tigre* 1667–1671, 254
Inconnu, 1673–1673, 4th Rank, see *Faucon* 1674–1708, 160
Inconnu, 1674–1676, Fireship, 256
Inconnu, 1678–1678, Light frigate, see *Gaillarde* 1668–1678, 218
Inconnu, 1689–1692, Fireship, 260
Inconnu, 1692 (canc), Fireship, 262
Inconnu, 1728–1759, Brigantine, 358
Inconnue, 1672–1690, Barque longue, 304
Inconnue, 1690–1692, Barque longue, 308
Inconstante, 1766–1781, 12pdr frigate, 177
Indien, 1671–1673, 4th Rank, see *Jules* 1661–1671, 157
Indien, 1673–1692, 4th Rank, 160
Indien, 1692–1698, 3rd Rank, 128
Indien, 1701–1719, 4th Rank, 167
Indien, 1770–1784, 3rd Rank, 150
Indien, 1777–1779, 18pdr frigate, 186
Indienne, 1669–1671, Flûte, 269
Indinio de Bristol, 1695–1696, Flûte, 280
Indiscret, 1690–1702, Fireship, 261
Indiscret, 1751–1761, Xebec, 359
Indiscrète, 1767–1784, 12pdr frigate, 178
Indomptable, 1760 (canc), 1st Rank, 72
Industry, 1625–1626, Vaisseau, 49
Infante, 1661–1671, 4th Rank, 157
Infidèle, 1765–1783, 12pdr frigate, 177
Inflexible, 1752–1763, 3rd Rank, 143
Inquiet, 1671–1676, Fireship, see *Bilbaut* 1666–1671, 253
Inquiet, 1674–1676, Fireship, 256
Inquiet, 1676–1681, Fireship, 256
Inquiet, 1683–1684, Fireship, 257
Inquiet, 1690–1691, Fireship, 259
Inquiet, 1691–1692, Fireship, 259
Insensé, 1689–1692, Fireship, 259
Insensée, 1703–1709, Barque longue, 314
Intéressant, 1779–1781, Transport, 366
Intrépide, 1666–1671, 2nd Rank, 82
Intrépide, 1671–1686, 3rd Rank, 121
Intrépide, 1690–1717, 1st Rank, 63
Intrépide, 1747–1781, 2nd Rank, 102
Invincible, 1666–1681, 2nd Rank, 82
Invincible, 1673–1679, Galley, 376
Invincible, 1678–1687, Galley, 377
Invincible, 1688–1715, Galley, see *Réale* 1683–1688, 377
Invincible, 1690–1727, 2nd Rank, 89
Invincible, 1691–1720, Galley, 380
Invincible, 1744–1747, 2nd Rank, 101
Invincible, 1780–1808, 1st Rank, 73

Iphigénie, 1767–1776, Palle, 339
Iphigénie, 1777–1795, 12pdr frigate, 179
Iris, 1781–1784, 12pdr frigate, 183
Iris, 1781–1793, 12pdr frigate, 181
Iroquoise, 1759–1760, Corvette, 322
Isabelle, 1692–1693, Caiche, 364
Isis, 1763–1775, Corvette, 325
Jacinthe, 1756–1760, Corvette, 320
Jackall, 1778–1780, Cutter, 342
Jacobin, 1793–1794, 1st Rank, see *Auguste* 1778–1793, 77
Jacques Benjamin, 1693–1697, Flûte, 279
Jacques Galère, 1706–1708, Barque longue, 315
Jacques I, 1692–1698, Flûte, 278
Jacques II, 1692–1697, Flûte, 279
Jalouse, 1690–1698, Light frigate, see *Fée* 1676–1685, 221
Jalouse, 1692–1698, 5th Rank, 201
Janny, 1759–1759, Brigantine, 338
Jardin de Hollande, 1661–1671, Flûte, 267
Jason, 1704–1720, 3rd Rank, 136
Jason, 1724–1747, 4th Rank, 170
Jason, 1779–1782, 3rd Rank, 150
Jean et Richard, 1695–1695, Tartane, 355
Jeanne Cornélie, 1696–1702, Flûte, 281
Jeannette, 1689–1694, Light frigate, 223
Jerzé, 1691–1717, 3rd Rank, 131
Jesus-Maria-Joseph, 1683–1683, Tartane, 353
Jesus-Maria-Joseph, 1782–1783, Gabarre, 300
Jesus-Maria-Sainte Anne, 1706–1708, Barque, 357
Jeune Cérès, 1745–1746, Corvette, 318
Jeune Dauphin, 1782–1784, Corvette, 325
Jeune Henry, 1778–1783, Corvette, 328
Jeux, see Les Jeux, 194
Joli, 1669–1671, 2nd Rank, see *Henri* 1671–1687, 82
Joli, 1671–1678, 4th Rank, see *Toulon* 1667–1671, 158
Joli, 1678–1692, 5th Rank, see *Hardi* 1671–1678, 195
Jolie, 1671–1671, Light frigate, see *Favorite* 1671–1674, 219
Jolie, 1671–1674, Light frigate, 219
Jolie, 1675–1692, Light frigate, 220
Jolie, 1692–1693, Light frigate, 226
Jolie, 1693–1702, Light frigate, 226
Jolie, 1703–1704, Coast guard sloop, 366
Jolie, 1762–1763, Gunboat, 250
Joseph Galle, 1705–1706, Barque longue, 314
Joseph, 1693–1697, Brigantine, 334
Joyeuse, 1691–1709, Light frigate, 225
Joyeuse, 1702–1703, Light frigate, 230
Joyeuse, 1779–?, Schooner, 346
Judith, 1779–1783, Coast guard vessel, 369
Jules, 1648–1650, Vaisseau, 53
Jules, 1661–1671, 4th Rank, 157
Juliette, 1783–1787, Corvette, 324
Junon, 1709–1709, 5th Rank, 203
Junon, 1747–1757, 4th Rank, 173
Junon, 1778–1780, 12pdr frigate, 180

Junon, 1779–1779, Corvette, 324
Junon, 1782–1799, 18pdr frigate, 188
Jupiter, 1647–1658, Vaisseau, 53
Juste, 1691–1719, 2nd Rank, 91
Juste, 1725–1759, 2nd Rank, 99
Juste, 1792–1794, 1st Rank, see *Deux Frères* 1784–1792, 78
Justice, 1664–1671, Flûte, 268
Justice, 1667–1671, Fireship, 253
Justice, 1696–1714, Flûte, 280
La Galéasse, 1651–1664, 5th Rank, see *Sainte Anne* 1651–1664, 191
Lady, 1757–1758, Flûte, 287
Lamproie, 1782–1793, Flûte, 293
Languedoc, 1766–1794, 1st Rank, 77
Languedocienne, 1765–?, Polacre, 365
Large, 1671–1673, Flûte, see *Saint Augustin* 1663–1665, 268
Large, 1673–1676, Flûte, see *Chariot* 1673–1673, 272
Large, 1678–1693, Flûte, 274
Laurier, 1670–1677, 5th Rank, 194
Laurier, 1678–1692, 4th Rank, 161
Laurier, 1690–1707, 2nd Rank, 90
Laverdy, 1770–1777, Flûte, 289
Lazare, 1773–1774, Schooner, 340
Le Havre, 1669–1671, 4th Rank, 159
Léger, 1671–1679, 4th Rank, see *Saint Antoine de Gênes*, 1669–1671, 159
Léger, 1679–1696, 4th Rank, 162
Légère, 1660–1669, Felucca, 351
Légère, 1670–1677, Galoite à rames, 352
Légère, 1671–1678, Light frigate, see *Petite Infante* 1666–1671, 217
Légère, 1672–1673, Barque longue, 305
Légère, 1677–1690, Felucca, 352
Légère, 1680 (canc), Light frigate, 222
Légère, 1682–1693, Light frigate, 222
Légère, 1703–1717, Barque, 356
Légère, 1729–1770, Barque latine, 358
Légère, 1746–1763, Mortar boat, 248
Légère, 1760–1763, Gunboat, 249
Légère, 1762 (canc), Corvette, 322
Légère, 1762–1764, Gunboat, 250
Légère, 1765–1780, 12pdr frigate, 177
Légère, 1774–?, Felucca, 361
Légère, 1780–1783, Felucca, 361
Légère, 1785–1786, Schooner, 350
Légère, 1793–1796, Corvette, see *Barbude* 1782–1786, 329
Légère. 1694–1702, Felucca, 355
Léopard, 1642–1651, Vaisseau, 51
Léopard, 1667–1668, Fireship, 254
Léopard, 1693–1695, Fireship, 262
Léopard, 1727–1757, 3rd Rank, 139
Léopard, 1787–1793, 2nd Rank, 112
Léopold, 1702–1703, Light frigate, 230
Les Amis, 1778–1782, Corvette, 323
Les Jeux, 1670–1687, 5th Rank, 194
Les Jeux, 1689–1689, 5th Rank, 199
Les Jeux, 1689–1706, 5th Rank, 200

Levrette, 1628–1649, Dragon, see *Dragon No. 1*, 50
Levrette, 1667–1676, Brigantine, 332
Levrette, 1690–1695, Barque longue, 308
Levrette, 1692–1693, Brigantine, 334
Levrette, 1707–1709, Barque longue, 315
Levrette, 1734–1748, Corvette, 316
Levrette, 1756–1760, Corvette, 319
Levrette, 1762–1762, Flûte, 288
Levrette, 1778–1786, Gunboat, 250
Levrette, 1779–1806, Cutter, 344
Levrette, 1780–1781, Brig, 347
Levrette, 1781–1781, Cutter, 348
Levrette, 1784–1792, Schooner, 350
Lévrier, 1667–1675, Brigantine, 332
Lévrier, 1771–1775, Cutter, 339
Lévrier, 1780–1784, Cutter, 346
Lezard, 1771–1777, Cutter, 340
Lézard, 1780–1784, Cutter, 344
Liberté, 1792–1793, 2nd Rank, see *Dictateur* 1782–1792, 111
Licorne, 1626–1643, Vaisseau, 50
Licorne, 1638–1638, Vaisseau, 51
Licorne, 1655–1666, Flûte, 267
Licorne, 1691–1693, Flûte, 277
Licorne, 1702–1720, 3rd Rank, 135
Licorne, 1755–1778, 8pdr frigate, 209
Licorne, 1780–1781, 8pdr frigate, 215
Lièvre, 1780–1781, Brigantine, 346
Ligournois, 1666–1671, 5th Rank, 193
Ligournois, 1676–1676, Fireship, 257
Lion Britannique, 1781–1782, Flûte, 292
Lion d'Or, 1623–1624, Vaisseau, 49
Lion d'Or, 1625–1641, Vaisseau, 49
Lion de Smaaland, 1647–1647, 4th Rank, see *Éminent* 1647–1661, 156
Lion d'Or, 1666–1671, 5th Rank, 193
Lion Rouge, 1666–1671, 5th Rank, 193
Lion Veillant, 1706–1707, Flûte, 283
Lion, 1638–1638, Vaisseau, 51
Lion, 1671–1676, 5th Rank, see *Sauveur* 1666–1671, 193
Lion, 1676–1677, 5th Rank, see *Canadien* 1673–1676, 194
Lion, 1678–1678, 4th Rank, see *Écueil* 1678–1699, 162
Lion, 1678–1678, 5th Rank, see *Orage* 1675–1680, 196
Lion, 1678–1710, 5th Rank, see *Soleil d'Afrique* 1675–1678, 195
Lion, 1751–1785, 3rd Rank, 144
Lionne de Honfleur, 1628–1646, Dragon, see *Dragon No. 3*, 50
Lionne, 1780–1784, Gunboat, 251
Lionne, 1784–1808, Gabarre, 301
Lise, 1782–1784, Schooner, 350
Lively, 1778–1781, 8pdr frigate, 214
Lively, 1778–1784, Corvette, 328
Lively, 1779–1782, Cutter, 346
Liverpool, 1779–1783, Flûte, 291
Loire, 1671–1684, Flûte, see *Saint Hubert*

1670–1671, 268
Loire, 1686–1712, Flûte, 275
Loire, 1720–1758, Flûte, 284
Loire, 1780–1793, Gabarre, 299
London, 1779–1783, Fireship, 265
Lord Cornwallis, 1782–1784, Cutter, 349
Louise, 1623–1625, Vaisseau, 49
Louise, 1750–1758, Schooner, 336
Louise, 1760–1783, Prame, 247
Louise, 1784–1786, Schooner, 350
Loup, 1745–1747, Corvette, 318
Lourde, 1781–1797, Flûte, 293
Louvine, 1763–1769, Tartane, 361
Louvre, 1670–1671, 3rd Rank, see *Bourbon* 1671–1678, 120
Loyaliste, 1781–1781, Corvette, 325
Loyalty, 1625–1626, Vaisseau, 49
Ludlow, 1703–1729, 5th Rank, 203
Lune, 1641–1664, 4th Rank, 155
Lunette, 1692–1693, Barque longue, see *Saint François* 1690–1691, 310
Lunette, 1766–1784, Corvette, 325
Lurchers, 1780–1786, Cutter, see *Chien de Chasse*, 347
Lutin, 1692–1697, Fireship, 262
Lutine, 1671–1675, Light frigate, see *Dieppoise* 1668–1671, 218
Lutine, 1676–1678, Light frigate, 220
Lutine, 1757–1757, Corvette, 321
Lutine, 1779–1793, 12pdr frigate, 181
Lynx, 1779–1797, Gunboat, 251
Lys, 1667–1671, 3rd Rank, 118
Lys, 1671–1691, 1st Rank, see *Île de France* 1669–1671, 59
Lys, 1691–1705, 1st Rank, 65
Lys, 1706–1747, 2nd Rank, 95
Lys, 1746–1755, 3rd Rank, 141
Lys, 1785–1792, 2nd Rank, 112
Macreuse, 1746–1755, Gabarre, 295
Madame, 1670–1671, 2nd Rank, 82
Madame, 1672–1679, Galley, 376
Madame, 1680–1692, Galley, 377
Madame, 1692–1693, Galley, 380
Madame, 1693–1718, Galley, see *Dauphine* 1689–1693, 379
Madeleine, 1629–1634, Dragon, 51
Madeleine, 1629–1634, Vaisseau, 51
Madeleine, 1668–1671, Light frigate, 218
Madeleine, 1669–1679, Bilander, see *Bellande* 1669–1679, 362
Madeleine, 1682–1694, Gribane, 364
Madona del Popolo, 1675–1676, 4th Rank, 161
Magicienne, 1778–1781, 12pdr frigate, 181
Magnanime, 1673–1705, 1st Rank, 60
Magnanime, 1688–1716, Galley, 379
Magnanime, 1706–1712, 2nd Rank, 95
Magnanime, 1744–1748, 2nd Rank, 101
Magnanime, 1779–1793, 2nd Rank, 110
Magnifique, 1671–1680, 2nd Rank, see *Courtisan* 1666–1671, 81
Magnifique, 1685–1692, 2nd Rank, 87

Magnifique, 1685–1701, Galley, 378
Magnifique, 1692–1716, 1st Rank, 67
Magnifique, 1749–1782, 2nd Rank, 102
Mahonnaise, 1780–1783, Felucca, 361
Maire Guiton, 1793–1795, Corvette, see *Alouette* 1786–1799, 331
Maison de Ville d'Amsterdam, 1693–1697, Flûte, 279
Majestueux, 1760 (canc), 1st Rank, 72
Majestueux, 1780–1797, 1st Rank, 74
Malbourough, 1781–1784, Gabarre, 300
Malgue, 1665–1671, Fireship, 253
Malice, 1762–1762, Coast guard vessel, 369
Malicieuse, 1758–1777, 8pdr frigate, 210
Maligne, 1670–1693, Light frigate, 218
Maligne, 1745–1745, Corvette, 317
Malin, 1781–1786, Cutter, 344
Manon, 1765–1779, Brigantine, 339
Maquaido, 1638–1644, Vaisseau, 51
Marabout, 1651–1654, Vaisseau, 53
Marchand de Bois, 1691–1691, Flûte, see *Mulet* 1691–1701, 277
Marchand, 1707–1713, Flûte, 283
Maréchal de Broglie, 1778–1779, 3rd Rank, 150
Maréchal de Castries, 1785–1793, Corvette, 331
Maréchal de Mouchy, 1779–1779, Flûte, 292
Maréchal de Saxe, 1748–1755, 8pdr frigate, 206
Maréchal de Thomond, 1756–?, Coast guard vessel, 368
Maréchal Phébus, 1666–1676, Fireship, 254
Marengo, 1800–1811, 2nd Rank, see *Sceptre* 1780–1792, 110
Marguerite d'Amsterdam, 1693–1697, Flûte, 279
Marguerite d'Estadem, 1695–1697, Flûte, 280
Marguerite, 1627–1645, Dragon, 51
Marguerite, 1629–1633, Vaisseau, 51
Marguerite, 1706–1715, Brigantine, 334
Marianne, 1689–1691, Fireship, 259
Marianne, 1710–1713, Caiche, 365
Marianne, 1745–1747, Schooner, 336
Marie de Gerzé, 1706–1706, Barque longue, 315
Marie de Redo, 1694–1697, Pinnace, 364
Marie Magdeleine, 1749–1759, Gabarre, 296
Marie Rose, 1691–1692, 3rd Rank, see *Vaillant* 1692–1698, 131
Marie, 1667–1675, Barque, 333
Marie, 1675–1677, Brigantine, 352
Marie, 1678–1692, Gribane, 363
Marie, 1682–1687, Polacre, 364
Marie, 1751–1762, Gabarre, 296
Marie, 1762–1764, Schooner, 338
Marie, 1782–1783, Gabarre, 300
Marie-Anne, 1697–1697, Bomb vessel, 243
Marie-Anne, 1715–1716, Coast guard vessel, 368
Marie-Christine, 1779–?, Schooner, 346
Marie-Élisabeth, 1692–1697, 4th Rank, 164
Marie-Françoise, 1704–1718, Barque longue, 314
Marie-Françoise, 1714–1758, Gabarre, 294

Marie-Françoise, 1778–1789, Chasse-marée, 367
Marie-Thérèse, 1781–1783, Flûte, 293
Marin, 1678–1678, 4th Rank, see *Écueil* 1678–1699, 162
Marin, 1679–1705, 5th Rank, 197
Maringouin, 1767–1770, Chasse-marée, 367
Marius, 1782–1783, Gabarre, 301
Marmouth, 1768–1771, Bugalet, 367
Marne, 1746–1753, Gabarre, 296
Marquis de Castries, 1770–1771, Flûte, 289
Marquis de Castries, 1770–1773, Flûte, 290
Marquis de Castries, 1782–1791, Gabarre, 300
Marquis de Marigny, 1758–1759, Coast guard vessel, 368
Marquis de Sancé, 1770–1772, Flûte, 290
Marquis, 1671–1671, 4th Rank, see *Hercule* 1655–1673, 156
Marquis, 1671–1672, 4th Rank, see *Soleil* 1642–1671, 155
Marquis, 1673–1677, 4th Rank, 160
Marquis, 1679–1684, 5th Rank, 197
Marquis, 1685–1705, 3rd Rank, 125
Marquise de La Fayette, 1780–1783, 8pdr frigate, 215
Marquise de Vaudreuil, 1756–1758, Corvette, 319
Marquise, 1640–1648, Frigate, 51
Marquise, 1690–1696, Galley, 380
Marquise, 1697–1714, Galley, 391
Marquise, 1708–1709, Brigantine, 334
Mars, 1705–1721, 3rd Rank, 137
Mars, 1740–1746, 3rd Rank, 141
Mars, 1770–1773, 3rd Rank, 150
Marseillais, 1766–1794, 2nd Rank, 107
Marseilloise, 1671–1674, Flûte, see *Saint Nicolas* 1670–1671, 271
Marseilloise, 1675–1681, Flûte, 272
Marseilloise, 1685–1691, Flûte, 274
Martiale, 1690–1696, Galley, 380
Martiale, 1696–1703, Bomb frigate, 242
Martiale, 1696–1714, Galley, 391
Martiale, 1708–1709, Brigantine, 334
Martinique, 1779–1792, Gunboat, 251
Martinique, 1781–1785, Corvette, 330
Martre, 1746–1757, 8pdr frigate, 206
Marygold, 1625–1626, Vaisseau, 49
Mascarin, 1770–1775, Flûte, 289
Maskalonge, 1759–1759, Xebec, 360
Massiac, 1770–1771, 4th Rank, 184
Massue, 1692–1693, Fireship, see *Voilé* 1690–1692, 260
Mathieu, 1691–1692, Barque, 334
Matrone, 1692–1692, Flûte, 278
Matrou, 1687–1713, unknown type, 370
Maure, 1672–1678, 3rd Rank, 121
Maure, 1678–1678, 4th Rank, see *Neptune* 1678–1702, 161
Maure, 1679–1686, 4th Rank, see *Beaufort* 1662–1671, 157
Maure, 1688–1710, 4th Rank, 162

Maurepas, 1698–1705, 4th Rank, 166
Mauresque, 1695–1697, Gunboat, 248
Mazarin, 1647–1671, 4th Rank, 156
Méchante, 1678–1680, Barque longue, see
  Fidèle 1674–1678, 305
Méchante, 1689–1699, Light frigate, 223
Médée, 1704–1708, Light frigate, 231
Médée, 1741–1744, 8pdr frigate, 204
Médée, 1778–1800, 12pdr frigate, 179
Médiateur, 1760 (canc), 1st Rank, 72
Méduse, 1699–1713, 5th Rank, 202
Méduse, 1722–1727, Corvette, 316
Méduse, 1727–1745, Corvette, 316
Méduse, 1782–1796, 18pdr frigate, 188
Méfiance, 1760 (canc), 8pdr frigate, 210
Méfiante, 1778–1786, Gunboat, 250
Mégère, 1744–1753, 8pdr frigate, 204
Mégère, 1779–1795, Gunboat, 251
Mélampe, 1757–1757, Coast guard vessel, 368
Melanide, 1761–1769, Gunboat, 250
Menaçante, 1682–1711, Bomb vessel, 240
Ménage, 1778–1783, Fireship, 264
Ménagère, 1760 (canc), Flûte, 288
Ménagère, 1776–1782, Flûte, 290
Ménagère, 1779–1779, Flûte, 291
Mercoeur, 1661–1671, 4th Rank, 157
Mercure Volante, 1711–1711, Light frigate, 234
Mercure, 1678–1690, 5th Rank, see *Trompeuse*
  1670–1671, 194
Mercure, 1690–1692, 5th Rank, 200
Mercure, 1696–1746, 3rd Rank, 133
Mercure, 1705–1707, 4th Rank, 169
Mercure, 1745–1750, Corvette, 318
Mercure, 1783–1798, 2nd Rank, 111
Méridienne, 1795–1797, Gunboat, see *Mégère*
  1779–1795, 251
Merveilleux, 1691–1692, 1st Rank, 64
Merveilleux, 1692–1713, 1st Rank, 67
Mesny, 1780–1781, 8pdr frigate, 215
Messager, 1753–1758, Flûte, 286
Meuse, 1756–1760, Gabarre, 296
Michelle, 1780–1784, Chatte pontée, 366
Mignon, 1671–1678, 4th Rank, see *Provençal*
  1667–1671, 158
Mignon, 1678–1692, 5th Rank, see *Vigilant*
  1673–1678, 195
Mignon, 1693–1709, 3rd Rank, 132
Mignonne, 1670–1671, 5th Rank, see *Bizarre*
  1671–1692, 195
Mignonne, 1673–1694, Light frigate, 219
Mignonne, 1676–1678, Barque longue, 306
Mignonne, 1695–1711, Gunboat, 248
Mignonne, 1757–1759, Corvette, 320
Mignonne, 1767–1794, 8pdr frigate, 212
Milan, 1771–1782, Cutter, 340
Milfort, 1693–1709, Light frigate, 226
Milfort, 1703–1720, 5th Rank, 203
Minerve (Royale), 1781–1784, Gabarre, 300
Minerve, 1756–1762, 8pdr frigate, 208
Minerve, 1778–1781, 12pdr frigate, 183
Minerve, 1782–1794, 18pdr frigate, 188

Minotaure, 1757–1787, 2nd Rank, 105
Mittau, 1734–1734, 4th Rank, 171
Modéré, 1685–1702, 3rd Rank, 126
Modeste Marguerite, 1782–1783, Gabarre, 300
Modeste, 1759–1759, 3rd Rank, 145
Modeste, 1786–1793, 12pdr frigate, 181
Monarque, 1664–1665, 4th Rank, see *Sirène*
  1666–1684, 157
Monarque, 1668–1685, 1st Rank, 58
Monarque, 1689–1717, 1st Rank, 63
Monarque, 1747–1747, 2nd Rank, 102
Monarque, 1783 (canc), 1st Rank, 78
Monique, 1760–1769, Prame, 247
Monsieur de Beauvoir, 1760–1760, Gunboat, see
  Pallas 1760–1768, 249
Monsieur de Berville, 1760–1760, Gunboat, see
  Légère 1760–1763, 249
Montagne Claire, 1674–1675, Flûte, 272
Montagne d'Or, 1693–1697, Flûte, 280
Montcalm, 1756–1758, Snow, 337
Montréal, 1779–1793, 12pdr frigate, 183
Montsarat, 1703–1707, Coast guard sloop, 366
Moolly, 1782–1783, Flûte, 293
Moqueuse, 1671–1673, Light frigate, see *Saint
  Pierre* 1667–1671, 217
Moqueuse, 1674–1676, Light frigate, 219
Moqueuse, 1676–1685, Light frigate, 221
Moqueuse, 1688–1691, Light frigate, 222
Moqueuse, 1692 (canc), Light frigate, 225
Morian, 1685–1687, Light frigate, 222
Morine, 1665–1671, Light frigate, 217
Moscovite, 1734–1734, Galiote, 365
Mouche, 1704–1704, Barque longue, 314
Mouche, 1756–1763, Snow, 337
Mouche, 1768–1782, Chatte pontée, 365
Mouche, 1783–1784, Cutter, 350
Moucheron, 1771–1782, Cutter, 340
Mucius Scévola, 1791–1794, 2nd Rank, see
  Illustre 1781–1791, 110
Mucius Scévola, 1793–1793, 2nd Rank, see *Orion*
  1787–1793, 111
Mucius Scévola, 1793–1804, 2nd Rank, see *Orion*
  1787–1793, 111
Mulet, 1678–1689, Flûte, see *Saint Paul* 1677–
  1678, 273
Mulet, 1691–1701, Flûte, 277
Mulet, 1782–1793, Flûte, 293
Mutin, 1778–1782, Cutter, 345
Mutine, 1670–1675, Light frigate, 218
Mutine, 1675–1675, Light frigate, 220
Mutine, 1676–1694, Light frigate, 221
Mutine, 1692 (canc), Fireship, 262
Mutine, 1693–1693, 5th Rank, 201
Mutine, 1695–1707, 4th Rank, 164
Mutine, 1744–1758, 6pdr frigate, 235
Naïade, 1692–1695, Light frigate, 225
Naïade, 1696–1705, Light frigate, 228
Naïade, 1706–1710, Light frigate, 232
Naïade, 1734–1745, Corvette, 317
Naïade, 1760 (canc), 8pdr frigate, 210
Naïade, 1779–1783, 8pdr corvette, 328

Nanon, 1769–1778, Schooner, 339
Nantaise, 1779–1792, Gunboat, 251
Nassau, 1638–1638, Vaisseau, 51
Navarre, 1666–1673, 3rd Rank, 117
Navarrois, 1670–1671, 3rd Rank, see *Excellent*
  1671–1675, 120
Navire de la Reine, 1627–1639, Vaisseau, 49
Navire du Roi, 1627–1646, Vaisseau, 49
Nécéssaire, 1770–1778, Corvette, 323
Nécéssaire, 1783–1792, Flûte, 293
Négresse, 1777–1786, Gabarre, 298
Neptune (Royal), 1781–1783, Gabarre, 300
Neptune, 1628–1641, Dragon, 51
Neptune, 1650–1652, Vaisseau, 53
Neptune, 1666–1671, 2nd Rank, 82
Neptune, 1671–1679, 4th Rank, see *Beaufort*
  1662–1671, 157
Neptune, 1678–1702, 4th Rank, 161
Neptune, 1697–1699, Light frigate, 228
Neptune, 1704–1713, 2nd Rank, 95
Neptune, 1723–1747, 2nd Rank, 99
Neptune, 1762–1764, Brigantine, 339
Neptune, 1778–1795, 2nd Rank, 108
Neptune, 1780–1782, Schooner, 347
Néréide, 1690–1696, Galley, 380
Néréide, 1696–1713, Light frigate, 228
Néréide, 1724–1743, 4th Rank, 170
Néréide, 1779–1810, 12pdr frigate, 180
Neuf Thermidor, 1794–1795, 1st Rank, see
  Auguste 1778–1793, 77
Nieuport, 1696–1697, Light frigate, 227
Noix, 1689–1691, Light frigate, see *Bayonnaise*
  1689–1691, 223
Nonsuch, 1695–1696, 4th Rank, 164
Normand, 1666–1671, 2nd Rank, 82
Normande, 1670–1671, Light frigate, 218
Normande, 1671–1679, Flûte, see *Couronne de
  Naples* 1670–1671, 271
Normande, 1686–1689, Flûte, 275
Normande, 1759–1786, Flûte, 288
Northumberland, 1744–1776, 2nd Rank, 101
Northumberland, 1780–1794, 2nd Rank, 109
Notre Dame (de Miséricorde), 1780–1783,
  Tartane, 361
Notre Dame de Bon Voyage, 1675–1676,
  Fireship, 257
Notre Dame de Bon Voyage, 1682–1685, Tartane,
  353
Notre Dame de Bon Voyage, 1703–1708, Barque,
  356
Notre Dame de Boulogne, 1757–?, Coast guard
  vessel, 368
Notre Dame de Grâce, 1702–1707, Tartane, 355
Notre Dame de Grâce, 1759–1764, Bomb vessel,
  246
Notre Dame de Lumière, 1675–1676, Fireship,
  256
Notre Dame de Miséricorde, 1675–1676, Fireship,
  see *Fin* 1676–1686, 257
Notre Dame de Port-Salut, 1728–1729, Barque,
  358

Notre Dame des Anges, 1665–1671, Light frigate, 217
Notre Dame des Anges, 1674–1676, Light frigate, see *Favorite* 1676–1678, 220
Notre Dame des Anges, 1707–1710, Brigantine, 357
Notre Dame des Carmes, 1675–1676, Fireship, 257
Notre Dame des Saintes Réliques, 1702–1706, Tartane, 355
Notre Dame du Mont Carmel, 1673–1676, Barque, 352
Notre Dame du Mont Carmel, 1703–1703, Barque, 356
Notre Dame du Paradis, 1719–1720, Coast guard vessel, 368
Notre Dame du Rosaire, 1760–1762, 3rd Rank, 147
Notre Dame, 1661–1675, 5th Rank, 191
Notre Dame, 1673–1676, Barque, 352
Nourrice, 1762–1777, Flûte, 288
Nourrice, 1780–1787, Flûte, 291
Nouvelle Entreprise (de Dantzig), 1782–1789, Flûte, 293
Nouvelle Pauline, 1781–1783, Gabarre, 300
Nymphe, 1692–1699, Barque longue, 310
Nymphe, 1702–1719, Light frigate, 229
Nymphe, 1728–1735, Corvette, 316
Nymphe, 1752–1757, 8pdr frigare, 206
Nymphe, 1769 (canc), 8pdr frigate, 213
Nymphe, 1777–1780, 12pdr frigate, 180
Nymphe, 1782–1793, 18pdr frigate, 188
Nymphe, 1785–1788, Schooner, 350
Océan, 1756–1759, 1st Rank, 76
Officieuse, 1776–1781, Gabarre, 298
Oiseau, 1671–1693, 4th Rank, 159
Oiseau, 1695–1704, 5th Rank, 201
Oiseau, 1757–1762, 8pdr frigate, 208
Oiseau, 1769–1779, 8pdr frigate, 213
Oiseau, 1770–1783, Chasse-marée, 367
Olivarez, 1638–1648, Vaisseau, 51
Ontario, 1756–1756, Sloop, 337
Opale, 1757–1762, 8pdr frigate, 209
Opiniâtre, 1678–1689, 4th Rank, see *Galant* 1668–1678, 159
Opiniâtre, 1689–1690, 5th Rank, 199
Opiniâtre, 1691–1699, 4th Rank, 163
Opiniâtre, 1750–1758, 3rd Rank, 143
Oracle, 1758 (canc), Corvette, 320
Orage, 1671–1675, 5th Rank, see *Écureuil* 1661–1671, 191
Orage, 1675–1680, 5th Rank, 196
Orage, 1690–1712, Fireship, 260
Oranger, 1666–1671, Flûte, 268
Oranger, 1691–1693, Barque, 334
Oranger, 1702–1706, Flibot, 365
Orgueilleux, 1671–1688, 2nd Rank, 83
Orgueilleux, 1691–1715, 1st Rank, 64
Orient, 1756–1782, 1st Rank, 76
Oriflamme, 1670–1691, 3rd Rank, 120
Oriflamme, 1692 (canc), 3rd Rank, see *Gaillard* 1693–1710, 133
Oriflamme, 1699–1702, 3rd Rank, 133
Oriflamme, 1704–1727, 2nd Rank, 94
Oriflamme, 1744–1761, 3rd Rank, 152
Oriflamme, 1783 (canc), 3rd Rank, 150
Orignal, 1750–1750, 3rd Rank, 142
Origni, 1757–?, Brigantine, 338
Orion, 1760 (canc), 2nd Rank, 106
Orion, 1787–1793, 2nd Rank, 111
Orox, 1734–1745, Flûte, 284
Orphée, 1749–1758, 3rd Rank, 142
Ostendoise, 1669–1669, Flûte, see *Don de Dieu* 1669–1671, 269
Osterley, 1779–1783, Flûte, 291
Ours, 1768–1784, Chatte pontée, 365
Outaouaise, 1759–1760, Corvette, 322
Outarde, 1755–1760, Flûte, 286
Outarde, 1770–1777, Flûte, 289
Outarde, 1779–1796, Flûte, 291
Page, 1706–1707, Traversier, 370
Paisible, 1692–1699, Fireship, see *Inconnu*, 260
Paix, 1663–1665, Flûte, 268
Paix, 1770–1780, 4th Rank, 184
Paix, 1783–1784, Chatte pontée, 366
Pallas, 1760–1768, Gunboat, 249
Pallas, 1778–1778, 8pdr frigate, 213
Palme, 1690–1696, Galley, 380
Palme, 1696–1714, Galley, 391
Palme, 1708–1712, Brigantine, 334
Palme, 1745–1748, Corvette, 318
Palmier, 1665–1671, 5th Rank, 192
Palmier, 1671–1678, 5th Rank, see *Saint Augustin de Gênes* 1669–1671, 194
Palmier, 1676–1709, 5th Rank, 196
Palmier, 1752–1766, 2nd Rank, 104
Palmier, 1766–1782, 2nd Rank, 106
Palombe, 1730–1758, Gabarre, 295
Pandour, 1780–1795, Cutter, 345
Panthère, 1744–1745, 6pdr frigate, 235
Panthère, 1779–1784, Gunboat, 251
Paon, 1692–1694, Light frigate, 224
Paon, 1705–1711, Light frigate, 231
Paon, 1712–1744, Light frigate, 234
Papillon, 1781–1783, Cutter, 346
Paquebot, 1694–1705, Barque longue, 311
Paresseuse, 1695–1695, Tartane, 355
Paresseux, 1671–1674, Flûte, see *Espérance* 1669–1671, 269
Paresseux, 1675–1686, Flûte, see *Montagne Claire* 1674–1675, 272
Paresseux, 1690–1697, Flûte, 276
Parfait, 1671–1699, 3rd Rank, 122
Parfait, 1701–1726, 2nd Rank, 94
Parfaite, 1704–1718, 4th Rank, 167
Parfaite, 1723–1746, 4th Rank, 170
Parfaite, 1761–1766, Gunboat, 250
Parham, 1745–1772, Flûte, 285
Paris, 1669–1671, 1st Rank, 59
Parti, 1690–1692, Flûte, 276
Passe Partout, 1782–1786, Lugger, 350
Patience, 1691–1691, Barque, 334
Patience, 1792–1814, Galley, see *Duchesse* 1742–1792, 392
Patient, 1711–1711, Bomb vessel, 243
Patriote de Brest, 1793–1793, Cutter, see *Levrette* 1779–1806, 344
Patriote, 1785–1821, 2nd Rank, 112
Patronne (de France), 1666–1680, Galley, see *Régine* 1663–1666, 375
Patronne, 1671–1680, Galley, 376
Patronne, 1680–1683, Galley, see *Capitane* 1667–1680, 377
Patronne, 1682–1693, Galley, 377
Patronne, 1694–1713, Galley, 390
Patronne, 1736–1749, Galley, 392
Paysanne, 1779–1781, Gabarre, 299
Pearl, 1625–1626, Vaisseau, 49
Pêcheur du Roi, 1692–?, Caiche, 364
Pêcheur, 1685–1693, Tartane, 353
Pêcheur, 1781–1783, Felucca, 361
Pêcheuse, 1693–1701, Tartane, 355
Pégase, 1781–1782, 2nd Rank, 110
Pèlerin, 1666–1671, Fireship, 254
Pélican, 1669–1671, Flûte, 269
Pélican, 1689–1690, Light frigate, 223
Pélican, 1693–1697, 3rd Rank, 132
Pélican, 1701–1706, 3rd Rank, 134
Pelletier, 1793–1795, 2nd Rank, see *Séduisant* 1783–1796, 111
Pembroke, 1710–1711, 3rd Rank, 138
Pénélope, 1787–1788, 18pdr frigate, 189
Perdrix, 1717–1721, Gabarre, 294
Perdrix, 1725–1760, Gabarre, 295
Perdrix, 1784–1795, Corvette, 331
Père de Famille, 1780–1783, Gabarre, 299
Périlleux, 1670–1671, 5th Rank, see *Hardi* 1671–1678, 195
Périlleux, 1672–1702, Fireship, 255
Périne, 1778–1784, Chatte pontée, 365
Perle (de Londres), 1691–1696, Barque, 333
Perle, 1629–1645, Vaisseau, 51
Perle, 1663–1676, 5th Rank, 191
Perle, 1673–1682, Galley, 376
Perle, 1675–1690, 5th Rank, see *Dauphin* 1674–1675, 196
Perle, 1682–1693, Galley, 378
Perle, 1690–1710, 3rd Rank, 131
Perle, 1694–1724, Galley, 380
Perle, 1695–1708, Gunboat, 248
Perle, 1724–1749, Galley, 392
Perle, 1744–1748, Corvette, 317
Perle, 1746–1748, 4th Rank, 173
Perle, 1768–1780, Corvette, 326
Péron, 1781–1792, Flûte, 292
Persée, 1654–1654, Vaisseau, 53
Peter–and–John, 1625–1626, Vaisseau, 49
Pétillant, 1678–1694, 5th Rank, see *Tourbillon* 1670–1678, 194
Petit Anglais, 1666–1666, Fireship, see *Guillaume* 1666–1671, 253
Petit Anglais, 1668–1671, Flûte, 269
Petit Annibal, 1782–1792, 3rd Rank, see

Annibal 1782–1792, 151
Petit Argus, 1782–1784, Lugger, 350
Petit Chalain, 1661–1669, Galiote, 362
Petit Cousin, 1782–1786, Gabarre, 300
Petit Dauphin, 1677–1678, Flûte, 273
Petit Hercule, 1662–1666, Fireship, 252
Petit Mars, 1762–1765, Corvette, 325
Petit Sage, 1770–1775, Corvette, see *Sage* 1770–1775, 323
Petit Saint Augustin, 1664–1671, Fireship, see *Saint Augustin* 1664–1671, 252
Petit Saint Esprit, 1762–1766, Corvette, see *Saint Esprit* 1762–1766, 325
Petit Saint François, 1691–1692, Barque longue, see *Saint François* 1690–1691, 310
Petit Saint Louis, 1626–1640, Vaisseau, see *Saint Louis de Hollande* 1626–1640, 50
Petite Aurore, 1768–1775, Corvette, see *Aurore* 1767–1768, 323
Petite Fortune, 1767–1772, Corvette, see *Fortune* 1762–1767, 322
Petite Frégate de Brest, 1664–1668, Light frigate, 216
Petite Infante, 1666–1671, Light frigate, 217
Petite Minerve, 1780–1782, Schooner, 347
Petite Royale, 1670–1671, Light frigate, see *Favorite* 1671–1674, 219
Peuple Souverain, 1792–1798, 2nd Rank, see *Souverain* 1757–1792, 105
Peuple, 1792–1794, 1st Rank, see *Duc de Bourgogne* 1751–1792, 76
Phébus, 1666–1676, Fireship, see *Maréchal Phébus* 1666–1676, 254
Phénix, 1667–1670, Fireship, 254
Phénix, 1692–1714, 3rd Rank, 129
Phénix, 1723–1751, 2nd Rank, 98
Philippine, 1781–1781, Flûte, 292
Philomèle, 1777 (canc), Corvette, 327
Phocion, 1792–1794, 2nd Rank, see *Ferme* 1785–1792, 112
Picarde, 1761–1762, Gunboat, 249
Pie, 1719–1724, Gabarre, 294
Pie, 1746–1760, Flûte, 286
Pigmy, 1781–1782, Cutter, 347
Pilote des Indes, 1778–1790, Corvette, 327
Pilote, 1778–1779, Cutter, 345
Pimpante, 1761–1766, Gunboat, 250
Pindenize, 1705–1706, 3rd Rank, 136
Pintade, 1725–1729, Gabarre, 295
Pintade, 1730–1761, Gabarre, 295
Pintade, 1777–1779, Flûte, 291
Pintade, 1779–1787, Gabarre, 298
Pique, 1792–1795, 12pdr frigate, see *Fleur de Lys* 1785–1792, 182
Pitre-Élisabeth, 1692–1698, Flûte, 278
Pivert, 1782–1787, Lugger, 349
Planète, 1760 (canc), 8pdr frigate, 210
Pléiade, 1755–1787, 8pdr frigate, 208
Pluton, 1778–1797, 2nd Rank, 109
Pluvier, 1776–1793, Gabarre, 298
Poder, 1744–1744, 3rd Rank, 141

Poisson Volant, 1782–1786, Cutter, 349
Poli, 1678–1692, 5th Rank, see *Saint Joseph* 1666–1671, 193
Poli, 1691–1717, 4th Rank, 163
Pomone, 1749–1760, Light frigate, 238
Pomone, 1770–1772, Gabarre, 298
Pomone, 1785–1794, 18pdr frigate, 189
Pompeux, 1671–1696, 2nd Rank, see *Madame* 1670–1671, 82
Pompeux, 1707–1719, 2nd Rank, 95
Pondichéry, 1769–1771, 3rd Rank, 154
Portefaix, 1671–1672, Flûte, see *Indienne* 1669–1672, 269
Portefaix, 1675–1675, Flûte, 272
Portefaix, 1677–1712, Flûte, 273
Portefaix, 1717–1770, Flûte, 283
Portefaix, 1782–1785, Flûte, 293
Porteuse, 1765–1789, Gabarre, 297
Porteuse, 1785–1797, Gabarre, 301
Poste de Cadix, 1693–1693, Flûte, see *Courrier de Cadix* 1693–1693, 280
Postillon de Cadix, 1692–1699, Flûte, 279
Postillon, 1665–1669, Light frigate, 216
Postillon, 1687–1688, Tartane, 353
Postillon, 1701–1702, Barque longue, 313
Postillon, 1734–1778, Bugalet, 366
Postillon, 1773–1784, Corvette, 323
Pot Bleu, 1691–1691, Flûte, see *Licorne* 1691–1693, 277
Poulette, 1781–1793, 8pdr corvette, 329
Pouponne, 1672–1680, Barque longue, 304
Pouponne, 1689–1689, Barque longue, 307
Pouponne, 1690–1694, Barque longue, 308
Pouponne, 1767–1772, Schooner, 339
Pourvoyeuse, 1772–1794, 18pdr frigate, 185
Précieuse, 1690–1696, Galley, 380
Précieuse, 1766–1767, 8pdr frigate, see *Mignonne* 1767–1794, 212
Précieuse, 1777 (canc), Corvette, 327
Précieuse, 1778–1814, 12pdr frigate, 181
Précieux, 1671–1678, 3rd Rank, 121
Précieux, 1679–1694, 3rd Rank, 124
Précieux, 1698–1705, Traversier, 370
Premier Bâtiment, 1780–1785, Gunboat, 251
Président Le Berthon, 1779–1779, Flûte, 292
Pressante, 1678–1696, Light frigate, see *Subtile* 1676–1678, 221
Prince Alexandre, 1704–1713, Flûte, 282
Prince de Conti, 1777–1778, 8pdr frigate, see *Pallas* 1778–1778, 213
Prince de Frise, 1694–1703, 3rd Rank, 132
Prince de Galles, 1745–1748, Corvette, 318
Prince de Pologne, 1693–1700, Flûte, 279
Prince d'Orange, 1745–1748, Flûte, 285
Prince, 1664–1665, 4th Rank, see *Cheval Marin* 1666–1729, 157
Prince, 1666–1671, 2nd Rank, 79
Prince, 1671–1678, 3rd Rank, see *Brave* 1670–1671, 118
Prince, 1680–1717, 3rd Rank, 124
Prince, 1706–1706, Fireship, 263

Princesse Anne de Danemark, 1695–1697, Fireship, 262
Princesse d'Angole, 1758–1758, Fireship, 264
Princesse de Gênes, 1669–1671, 5th Rank, 194
Princesse de Soubise, 1757–1757, Corvette, 321
Princesse du Ciel, 1716–1716, Coast guard vessel, 368
Princesse, 1667–1671, 2nd Rank, 80
Princesse, 1672–1679, Galley, 376
Princesse, 1679–1687, Galley, 377
Princesse, 1686–1696, Galley, 379
Princesse, 1699–1700, Galley, see *Martiale* 1696–1714, 391
Princesse, 1699–1718, Galley, 391
Princesse, 1704–1706, 4th Rank, see *Sylvie* 1703–1704, 167
Prise de Dantzé, 1674–1675, Flûte, see *Portefaix* 1675–1675, 272
Prise de la Preille, 1673–1674, Light frigate, see *Surprenante* 1674–1676, 219
Prise de M de Forbin, 1689–1691, Barque, see *Roi David* 1689–1691, 333
Prise de Messine, 1675–1676, Fireship, see *Fin* 1676–1686, 257
Prise de Montortié, 1674–1674, Light frigate, see *Favorite* 1674–1674, 219
Prise du Chevalier de Nesmond, 1674–1674, Flûte, see *Dromadaire* 1674–1675, 272
Prodige, 1692–1692, Flûte, 277
Profond, 1671–1678, 5th Rank, see *Vierge* 1666–1671, 193
Profond, 1685–1712, Flûte, 274
Profond, 1724–1757, Flûte, 284
Prohibition, 1702–1708, Barque longue, 313
Prompt, 1671–1691, 5th Rank, see *Princesse de Gênes* 1669–1671, 194
Prompt, 1692–1702, 2nd Rank, 93
Prompte, 1690–1692, Barque longue, 308
Prompte, 1692–1699, Barque longue, 310
Prompte, 1703–1717, Barque, 356
Prompte, 1703–1717, Coast guard sloop, 366
Prompte, 1709–1709, Barque longue, 315
Prophète Daniel, 1668–1669, Bilander, 362
Prophète Daniel, 1684–1685, Bilander, 364
Proserpine, 1696–1720, Bomb vessel, 243
Proserpine, 1785–1796, 18pdr frigate, 188
Protée, 1705–1722, 3rd Rank, see *Amphitrite*, 134
Protée, 1748–1770, 3rd Rank, 143
Protée, 1772–1780, 3rd Rank, 148
Provençal, 1667–1671, 4th Rank, 158
Provence, 1763–1786, 3rd Rank, 148
Providence, 1685–1688, Barque, 353
Providence, 1692–1703, Flûte, 278
Providence, 1695–1697, Flûte, 280
Province de Guyane, 1753–1756, Coast guard vessel, 368
Prude, 1693–1697, Barque longue, 311
Prudence, 1780–1783, Schooner, 346
Prudent, 1671–1696, 3rd Rank, see *Comte* 1667–1671, 117

Prudent, 1697–1702, 3rd Rank, 130
Prudent, 1753–1758, 2nd Rank, 103
Prudent, 1768–1772, Flûte, 289
Prudente, 1690–1696, Galley, 380
Prudente, 1778–1779, 12pdr frigate, 179
Psyché, 1762–1764, Gunboat, 250
Psyché, 1769 (canc), 8pdr frigate, 213
Puce, 1771–1779, Cutter, 340
Pucelle, 1645–1654, Vaisseau, 53
Pucelle, 1695–1687, Gunboat, 248
Pucelle, 1757–1763, Cutter, 338
Puissant, 1782–1793, 2nd Rank, 111
Puits de Jacob, 1702–1718, Flûte, 282
Pulvériseur, 1781–1784, Fireship, 265
Quatre Frères, 1702–1709, Light frigate, 230
Quatre Frères, 1759–1759, Coast guard vessel, 369
Québec, 1758–1759, 4th Rank, 174
Querelleuse, 1780–1784, Gunboat, 251
Racoon, 1782–1785, Brig, 349
Raikes, 1782–1784, Corvette, 330
Railleuse, 1671–1681, Light frigate, 219
Railleuse, 1677–1689, Light frigate, 222
Railleuse, 1683 (canc), Light frigate, 222
Railleuse, 1683–1683, 4th Rank, see *Solide* 1683–1694, 162
Railleuse, 1690–1703, Light frigate, 224
Railleuse, 1703–1707, Barque longue, 313
Railleuse, 1779–1798, 12pdr frigate, 182
Raisonnable, 1756–1758, 3rd Rank, 145
Rameau, 1759–1759, Fireship, 264
Rat, 1677–1678, Barque longue, 306
Réale de France, 1662–1667, Galley, 374
Réale Neuve, 1673–1678, Galley, see *Capitane* 1671–1673, 376
Réale, 1668–1678, Galley, 376
Réale, 1683–1688, Galley, 377
Réale, 1688–1694, Galley, 379
Réale, 1694–1722, Galley, 390
Réale, 1722–1743, Galley, 392
Réale, 1733–1773, Galley, 392
Réale, 1755 (canc), Galley, 393
Redoutable, 1706 (canc), 2nd Rank, 97
Redoutable, 1752–1759, 2nd Rank, 104
Réfléchi, 1776–1793, 3rd Rank, 149
Régine, 1647–1667, 4th Rank, 156
Régine, 1663–1666, Galley, 375
Règle de l'Espérance, 1682–1684, Fireship, see *Caché* 1684–1692, 257
Règle, 1694–1696, Flûte, 280
Reine de France, 1782–1783, Gabarre, 301
Reine du Maroc, 1761–1766, Gunboat, 250
Reine, 1647–1671, 3rd Rank, 113
Reine, 1671–1688, 1st Rank, see *Royal Duc* 1668–1671, 59
Reine, 1674–1679, Galley, 376
Reine, 1678–1687, Galley, 377
Reine, 1688–1701, Galley, 379
Reine, 1787–1787, 3rd Rank, see *Romulus* 1781–1784, 154
Renard, 1690–1691, Fireship, see *Christine* 1689–1690, 260
Renard, 1692 (canc), Fireship, 262
Renard, 1746–1748, Corvette, 318
Renard, 1762–1780, Xebec, 360
Renard, 1780–1781, Lugger, 347
Rencontre, 1762–1769, 3rd Rank, see *Vierge de Santé* 1760–1762, 147
René, 1709–1713, Light frigate, 233
Renée, 1769–1770, Gabarre, 297
Renommée, 1661–1667, Flûte, 268
Renommée, 1665–1676, Galley, 374
Renommée, 1676–1676, Barque longue, 306
Renommée, 1680–1691, Galley, 378
Renommée, 1691–1701, Galley, 380
Renommée, 1698–1712, 4th Rank, 166
Renommée, 1744–1747, 8pdr frigate, 205
Renommée, 1767–1783, 12pdr frigate, 178
Renoncule, 1757–1761, Corvette, 320
Replète, 1692–1697, Flûte, 277
Reprisal, 1779–1780, Brig, 346
Républicain, 1792–1794, 1st Rank, see *Royal Louis* 1780–1792, 73
Républicain, 1797–1803, 1st Rank, see *Majestueux* 1780–1797, 74
Repulse, 1779–?, Cutter, 346
Requin, 1703–1708, Barque longue, 314
Requin, 1751–1770, Xebec, 359
Réserve, 1805–1806, 2nd Rank, see *Zélé* 1763–1805, 106
Résolu, 1693–1712, Brigantine, 355
Résolu, 1760 (canc), 3rd Rank, 146
Résolue, 1778–1798, 12pdr frigate, 179
Résolution, 1782–1783, Flûte, 293
Résolution, 1784–1789, 3rd Rank, see *Romulus* 1781–1784, 154
Ressource, 1692–1694, Flûte, 278
Réunion, 1786–1793, 12pdr frigate, 181
Réussite, 1760 (canc), 8pdr frigate, 210
Revanche, 1701–1705, Barque, 334
Revanche, 1757–1772, Xebec, 359
Revêche, 1760 (canc), 8pdr frigate, 210
Révolutionnaire, 1793–1796, 1st Rank, see *Bretagne* 1766–1793, 72
Reyne des Anges, 1665–1671, Light frigate, see *Notre Dame des Anges* 1665–1671, 217
Rhinoceros, 1751–1758, Flûte, 286
Rhône, 1781–1790, Gabarre, 299
Richemont, 1781–1793, 12pdr frigate, 183
Rieuse, 1674–1676, 4th Rank, see *Arc en Ciel* 1678–1699, 161
Rieuse, 1678–1694, Barque longue, 306
Robecq, 1780–1782, 8pdr frigate, 215
Robuste, 1756 (canc), 3rd Rank, 145
Robuste, 1758–1758, Flûte, 287
Robuste, 1758–1784, 2nd Rank, 106
Rochefort, 1669–1671, 3rd Rank, 118
Rochefort, 1687–1692, unknown type, 370
Rochefort, 1750–1775, Yacht, 370
Rochefort, 1751–1771, Brigantine, 336
Rochefort, 1775–1786, Yacht, 371
Rochefort, 1787–?, Yacht, 371
Rochelaise, 1671–1674, Flûte, 270
Rocheloise, 1673–1678, Flûte, see *Cygne Blanc* 1672–1673, 272
Rocheloise, 1678–1689, Barque longue, see *Mignonne* 1676–1678, 306
Rocheloise, 1689–1698, Barque longue, 308
Rodney, 1780–?, Schooner, 347
Rohan Soubise, 1780–1781, 8pdr frigate, 215
Roi David, 1666–1671, Fireship, 254
Roi David, 1677–1678, Flûte, 273
Roi David, 1689–1691, Barque, 333
Roi de Pruse, 1758–1758, Corvette, 321
Roland, 1771–1779, 3rd Rank, 148
Romulus, 1781–1784, 3rd Rank, 154
Rosalie, 1779–1783, Transport, 366
Rose, 1750 (canc), 8pdr frigate, 207
Rose, 1752–1758, 4th Rank, 174
Rose, 1782–1784, Transport, 366
Rossignol, 1707–1708, Light frigate, 232
Rossignol, 1769–1796, Corvette, 326
Rostan, 1757–1758, Coast guard vessel, 368
Rotterdam, 1703–1706, 4th Rank, 168
Rouen, 1668–1670, 3rd Rank, 117
Rover, 1746–1749, 8pdr frigate, 206
Rover, 1779–1779, Gabarre, 299
Rover, 1780–1781, Corvette, 330
Royal Dauphin, 1671–1691, 1st Rank, see *Dauphin Royal* 1668–1671, 57
Royal Dauphin, 1782–1787, Gabarre, see *Dauphin Royal* 1782–1787, 301
Royal Duc, 1668–1671, 1st Rank, 59
Royal Louis Vieux, 1692–1697, 1st Rank, see *Royal Louis* 1668–1692, 56
Royal Louis, 1668–1692, 1st Rank, 56
Royal Louis, 1692–1727, 1st Rank, 65
Royal Louis, 1740–1742, 1st Rank, 70
Royal Louis, 1759–1773, 1st Rank, 70
Royal Louis, 1779 (canc), 1st Rank, 73
Royal Louis, 1780–1792, 1st Rank, 73
Royal Thérèse, 1671–1690, 1st Rank, see *Paris* 1669–1671, 59
Royal, 1747–1748, Coast guard vessel, 368
Royale Thérèse, 1670–1671, 2nd Rank, 82
Royale, 1661–1671, 3rd Rank, 115
Royale, 1685–1687, Flûte, see *Bienvenu* 1671–1706, 271
Royale, 1687–1688, Flûte, 275
Royale, 1781–1782, Brigantine, 347
Rozendal, 1703–1709, 5th Rank, 202
Ruben, 1672–1675, Fireship, 257
Rubis, 1664–1666, 3rd Rank, 115
Rubis, 1669–1671, 2nd Rank, see *Florissant* 1671–1696, 82
Rubis, 1671–1673, 3rd Rank, see *César* 1648–1671, 114
Rubis, 1672–1677, 3rd Rank, 123
Rubis, 1704–1729, 3rd Rank, 136
Rubis, 1728–1747, 4th Rank, 171
Rubis, 1744–1748, Flûte, 285
Rusé, 1690–1692, Fireship, 260
Rusé, 1751–1774, Xebec, 359

Rusée, 1691–1694, Barque longue, 309
Rusée, 1695–1709, Barque longue, 312
Rusée, 1778–1793, Gunboat, 250
Rusland, 1703–1712, Flûte, 282
Sage, 1671–1692, 3rd Rank, see *Rochefort* 1669–1671, 118
Sage, 1701–1707, 3rd Rank, 134
Sage, 1751–1768, 3rd Rank, 144
Sage, 1770–1775, Corvette, 323
Sage, 1783–1783, Gunboat, 251
Sagittaire, 1761–1790, 3rd Rank, 146
Saint Alexis, 1707–1709, Barque, 357
Saint André, 1630–1640, Vaisseau, 51
Saint Antoine de Gênes, 1669–1671, 4th Rank, 159
Saint Antoine de Padoue, 1661–1671, Fireship, 252
Saint Antoine, 1654–1670, 5th Rank, 191
Saint Antoine, 1675–1675, 5th Rank, see *Orage* 1675–1680, 196
Saint Antoine, 1682–1683, Tartane, 353
Saint Antoine, 1695–1697, Barque, 355
Saint Antoine, 1702–1706, Tartane, 355
Saint Antoine, 1706–1709, Flûte, 283
Saint Antoine, 1735–?, Tartane, 358
Saint Aubin, 1707–1709, Barque longue, 315
Saint Augustin de Gênes, 1669–1671, 5th Rank, 194
Saint Augustin, 1650–1650, Vaisseau, 53
Saint Augustin, 1663–1665, Flûte, 268
Saint Augustin, 1664–1671, Fireship, 252
Saint Barthelemy, 1687–1687, Tartane, 353
Saint Basile, 1624–1625, Vaisseau, see *Lion d'Or* 1624–1625, 49
Saint Bavo, 1782–1788, Gabarre, 300
Saint Benoît, 1677–1678, Fireship, see *Déguisé* 1678–1693, 257
Saint Charles, 1620–1625, Vaisseau, 49
Saint Charles, 1666–1670, 5th Rank, 193
Saint Christophe, 1783–?, Coast guard vessel, 369
Saint Cyprien, 1665–1668, Fireship, 253
Saint Cyprien, 1680–1680, Tartane, 353
Saint Dominique, 1665–1671, Galley, 374
Saint Edme, 1629–1633, Vaisseau, 51
Saint Esprit, 1627–1627, Vaisseau, 49
Saint Esprit, 1671–1691, 2nd Rank, see *Royale Thérèse* 1670–1671, 82
Saint Esprit, 1680–1682, Tartane, 353
Saint Esprit, 1691–1718, 2nd Rank, 91
Saint Esprit, 1726–1761, 2nd Rank, 99
Saint Esprit, 1728–1729, Coast guard vessel, 368
Saint Esprit, 1762–1766, Corvette, 325
Saint Esprit, 1765–1795, 1st Rank, 77
Saint François d'Ostende, 1689–1699, Galiote, 364
Saint François de Paule, 1760–1764, 3rd Rank, 147
Saint François l'Ardent, 1692–1704, Tartane, see *Saint François* 1687–1692, 353

Saint François Xavier, 1708–1708, type unknown, 365
Saint François, 1620–1625, Vaisseau, 49
Saint François, 1687–1692, Tartane, 353
Saint François, 1690–1691, Barque longue, 310
Saint François, 1778–1789, Chasse-marée, 367
Saint Gaëtan, 1708–1724, Barque longue, see *Saint Jean–Gaëtan* 1708–1724, 316
Saint Ginier, 1720–1720, Tartane, 357
Saint Guillaume, 1690–1713, Flûte, 276
Saint Guillaume, 1758–1762, Flûte, 287
Saint Guillaume, 1784–1789, Chasse-marée, 368
Saint Hubert, 1670–1671, Flûte, 268
Saint Hubert, 1690–1693, Traversier, 370
Saint Hyacinthe, 1707–1709, Barque, 357
Saint Ignace, 1683–1684, Flûte, 275
Saint Jacques de Dunkerque, 1646–1649, Vaisseau, see *Saint Jacques* 1643–1646, 52
Saint Jacques de Galice, 1720–1720, Tartane, 357
Saint Jacques du Portugal, 1643–1648, Vaisseau, 52
Saint Jacques, 1643–1646, Vaisseau, 52
Saint Jacques, 1680–1681, Barque, 353
Saint Jacques, 1693–1698, Flûte, 279
Saint Jacques, 1694–1694, Tartane, 355
Saint Jacques, 1719–1720, Coast guard pink, 368
Saint Jacques, 1759–?, Polacre, 365
Saint Jean (Baptiste), 1663–1671, Galley, 374
Saint Jean Baptiste, 1661–1671, Flûte, 268
Saint Jean Baptiste, 1674–1674, Fireship, see *Fin* 1674–1676, 257
Saint Jean Baptiste, 1679–1679, Flûte, see *Coche* 1679–1687, 274
Saint Jean Baptiste, 1762–1767, Fireship, 264
Saint Jean Baptiste, 1782–1783, Gabarre, 300
Saint Jean de Bayonne, 1667–1671, 5th Rank, see *Bayonnais* 1667–1671, 193
Saint Jean de Bordeaux, 1638–1641, Vaisseau, see *Saint Jean de Hollande* 1626–1638, 50
Saint Jean de Hollande, 1626–1638, Vaisseau, 50
Saint Jean de Plymouth, 1696–1712, Fireship, 262
Saint Jean d'Espagne, 1692–1697, 3rd Rank, 132
Saint Jean Gabriel, 1782–1783, Gabarre, 300
Saint Jean, 1620–1625, Vaisseau, 49
Saint Jean, 1664–1671, Flûte, 268
Saint Jean, 1666–1671, Light frigate, 217
Saint Jean, 1666–1676, Tartane, 352
Saint Jean, 1676–1677, Barque, 333
Saint Jean, 1677–1690, Tartane, 352
Saint Jean, 1678–1678, Flûte, see *Éléphant* 1678–1683, 274
Saint Jean, 1679–1682, Smack, 363
Saint Jean, 1683–1684, Tartane, 353
Saint Jean, 1693–1694, Tartane, 355
Saint Jean, 1700–1702, Tartane, 355
Saint Jean, 1703–1709, Barque, 356

Saint Jean, 1707–1717, Pink, 365
Saint Jean, 1756–1771, Yacht, 371
Saint Jean, 1779–1780, Brigantine, 346
Saint Jean-Gaëtan, 1708–1724, Barque longue, 316
Saint Joseph Bonaventure, 1720–1720, Tartane, 357
Saint Joseph et Saint Clement, 1720–1720, Tartane, 357
Saint Joseph, 1666–1671, 5th Rank, 193
Saint Joseph, 1667–1676, Tartane, 352
Saint Joseph, 1677–1679, Barque, 333
Saint Joseph, 1680–1686, Tartane, 353
Saint Joseph, 1687–1691, Tartane, 353
Saint Joseph, 1689–1690, Flûte, see *Bien Arrivé* 1690–1703, 276
Saint Joseph, 1692–1696, Brigantine, 334
Saint Joseph, 1702–1705, Tartane, 355
Saint Joseph, 1719–1721, Tartane, 357
Saint Joseph, 1770–1781, Gabarre, 298
Saint Laurent, 1748–1753, 3rd Rank, 142
Saint Louis, 1626–1640, Vaisseau, 49
Saint Louis, 1652–1652, Vaisseau, 53
Saint Louis, 1658–1671, 3rd Rank, 115
Saint Louis, 1661–1674, Galley, 374
Saint Louis, 1671–1680, 2nd Rank, see *Normand* 1666–1671, 82
Saint Louis, 1678–1680, Galley, see *Galéasse de Vivonne* 1677–1678, 377
Saint Louis, 1680–1690, Gribane, 364
Saint Louis, 1680–1691, Galley, 377
Saint Louis, 1681–1692, 3rd Rank, 125
Saint Louis, 1691–1701, Galley, 379
Saint Louis, 1692–1707, Barque, 334
Saint Louis, 1692–1712, 2nd Rank, 92
Saint Louis, 1697–1697, Bomb vessel, 243
Saint Louis, 1706–1713, Barque longue, 315
Saint Louis, 1723–1748, 3rd Rank, 139
Saint Louis, 1731–1732, Brigantine, 335
Saint Louis, 1732–1733, Brigantine, 335
Saint Louis, 1733–1741, Brigantine, 335
Saint Louis, 1757–1780, Yacht, 371
Saint Louis, 1765–1773, Coast Guard vessel, 369
Saint Louis, 1779–1784, Yacht, 371
Saint Louis, 1780–1784, Corvette, 324
Saint Martin, 1669–1671, Flûte, 270
Saint Martin, 1695–1697, Flûte, 280
Saint Michel, 1620–1625, Vaisseau, 49
Saint Michel, 1673–1687, 3rd Rank, 121
Saint Michel, 1686–1704, 3rd Rank, 127
Saint Michel, 1702–1702, Tartane, 355
Saint Michel, 1706–1719, 2nd Rank, 95
Saint Michel, 1719–1720, Coast guard pink, 368
Saint Michel, 1735–1737, Coast guard vessel, 368
Saint Michel, 1741–1787, 3rd Rank, 141
Saint Nazaire, 1676–1683, Fireship, 257
Saint Nicolas, 1670–1671, Flûte, 271
Saint Nicolas, 1701–1701, Flûte, 281

Saint Nicolas, 1765–1765, Flûte, see *Danoise*, 289
Saint Nicolas, 1767–1768, Snow, 339
Saint Paul d'Ostende, 1696–1704, Light frigate, 228
Saint Paul, 1662–1664, Flûte, see *Aigle Noir* 1661–1662, 267
Saint Paul, 1677–1678, Flûte, 273
Saint Paul, 1681–1682, Flûte, 274
Saint Paul, 1720–1722, Barque, 357
Saint Philippe, 1663–1692, 1st Rank, 56
Saint Philippe, 1693–1714, 1st Rank, 68
Saint Philippe, 1722–1746, 2nd Rank, 98
Saint Philippe, 1759–?, Polacre, 365
Saint Pierre, 1667–1671, Light frigate, 217
Saint Pierre, 1667–1672, Barque, 332
Saint Pierre, 1672–1676, Barque, 333
Saint Pierre, 1678–1681, Barque, 353
Saint Pierre, 1683–?, Tartane, 353
Saint Pierre, 1693–1693, Tartane, 355
Saint Pierre, 1696–1698, Flûte, 281
Saint Pierre, 1697–1697, Bomb vessel, 243
Saint Pierre, 1706–1708, Barque, 356
Saint Pierre, 1720–1721, Barque, 357
Saint Pierre, 1742–1744, Fireship, 263
Saint Roche, 1675–1676, Tartane, 352
Saint Rosaire, 1676–1676, Fireship, see *Impudent* 1676–1678, 257
Saint Sébastien, 1661–1671, 5th Rank, 191
Saint Sébastien, 1681–1693, Tartane, 353
Saint Vincent, 1632–1633, Vaisseau, 51
Sainte Anne, 1651–1664, 5th Rank, 191
Sainte Anne, 1661–1670, Light frigate, 216
Sainte Anne, 1674–1675, Barque, 333
Sainte Anne, 1675–1675, Tartane, 352
Sainte Anne, 1676–1688, Tartane, 352
Sainte Anne, 1678–1680, Hoy, 363
Sainte Anne, 1683–?, Tartane, 353
Sainte Anne, 1692–1706, Tartane, 354
Sainte Anne, 1695–1696, Barque longue, 313
Sainte Anne, 1702–1702, Flûte, 282
Sainte Anne, 1707–1710, Barque, 357
Sainte Anne, 1708–1708, Pink, 365
Sainte Anne, 1733–1735, Barque, 335
Sainte Anne, 1760–1761, 3rd Rank, 147
Sainte Anne, 1771–1771, Chasse-marée, 367
Sainte Anne, 1779–1783, Chasse-marée, 368
Sainte Barbe, 1683–1693, Tartane, 353
Sainte Barbe, 1753–?, Tartane, 360
Sainte Barbe, 1780–1783, Felucca, 361
Sainte Catherine, 1666–1669, Light frigate, 217
Sainte Claire, 1705–1717, Barque, 356
Sainte Croix, 1691–1692, Flibot, 364
Sainte Croix, 1696–1699, 4th Rank, 165
Sainte Croix, 1706–1706, Tartane, 357
Sainte Croix, 1719–1720, Tartane, 357
Sainte Élisabeth, 1693–1693, Tartane, 355
Sainte Élisabeth, 1762–1763, Fireship, 264
Sainte Geneviève, 1629–1645, Vaisseau, 51
Sainte Lucie, 1779–1801, Gunboat, 251
Sainte Marguerite, 1753–?, Tartane, 360

Sainte Marie, 1693–1694, Fireship, 262
Sainte Marie, 1693–1695, Brigantine, 355
Sainte Marie, 1708–1709, Barque, 357
Sainte Marie, 1716–1716, Coast guard vessel, 368
Sainte Reine, 1768–1777, Gabarre, 298
Sainte Thérèse, 1674–1676, Light frigate, see *Gracieuse* 1676–1687, 220
Sainte Thérèse, 1693–1693, Tartane, 355
Saintes Réliques, 1683–1686, Tartane, 353
Salamandre, 1629–1644, Dragon, see *Dragon No. 7*, 51
Salamandre, 1693–1696, Light frigate, 226
Salamandre, 1696–1709, Bomb vessel, 243
Salamandre, 1734–1750, Bomb vessel, 245
Salamandre, 1754–1785, Bomb vessel, 245
Salière, 1677–1678, Flûte, 273
Salisbury, 1703–1708, 3rd Rank, 136
Sally, 1782–1784, Gabarre, 301
Saloman, 1762–1782, Flûte, 288
Salvador, 1675–1676, Fireship, see *Ligournois* 1676–1676, 257
Samslaack, 1703–1720, 5th Rank, 202
Samson, 1651–1652, Vaisseau, 53
San Giovanni Battista (Maltese), 1718–1765, 3rd Rank, 139
San Yago, 1692–1693, Flibot, 364
Sandwich, 1781–1781, Corvette, 325
Sans Pareil, 1671–1679, 2nd Rank, see *Prince* 1666–1671, 79
Sans Pareil, 1685–1698, 3rd Rank, 125
Sans Pareil, 1696–1697, 4th Rank, see *Nonsuch* 1695–1697, 164
Sans Pareil, 1760 (canc), 1st Rank, 72
Sans Pareil, 1779–1780, Cutter, 346
Sans Peur, 1671–1681, Light frigate, see *Christine* 1666–1671, 217
Sans Peur, 1683–1692, Gribane, 364
Sans Peur, 1689–1696, Barque longue, 308
Sarah-Elisabeth, 1689–1690, Fireship, see *Drôle* 1690–1695, 260
Sarcelle, 1720–1757, Flûte, 284
Sardine, 1771–1796, Corvette, 326
Sardoine, 1757–1761, Corvette, 320
Saumon, 1776–1787, Gabarre, 298
Sauterelle, 1759–1763, Gunboat, 249
Sauterelle, 1771–1777, Cutter, 340
Sauvage, 1670–1671, Fireship, 254
Sauvage, 1673–1673, Fireship, 256
Sauvage, 1756–1759, 8pdr frigate, 209
Sauveur, 1666–1671, 5th Rank, 193
Sauveur, 1693–1695, Flûte, 279
Savoyarde, 1748–1748, Tartane, 359
Sceptre Vieux, 1691–1692, 1st Rank, see *Sceptre* 1670–1691, 60
Sceptre, 1670–1691, 1st Rank, 60
Sceptre, 1691–1718, 1st Rank, 65
Sceptre, 1720–1745, 2nd Rank, 97
Sceptre, 1747–1779, 2nd Rank, 102
Sceptre, 1780–1792, 2nd Rank, 110
Scévola, 1794–1796, 2nd Rank, see *Illustre*

1781–1791, 110
Scipion, 1778–1782, 2nd Rank, 109
Scot, 1758–1761, Corvette, 321
Seaford, 1744–1744, Light frigate, 238
Second Bâtiment, 1781–1781, Gunboat, 251
Séditieux, 1691–1698, Light frigate, see *Gaillarde* 1678–1690, 222
Séduisant, 1762–1780, Xebec, 361
Séduisant, 1783–1796, 2nd Rank, 111
Seine, 1671–1694, Flûte, see *Saint Jean Baptiste* 1661–1671, 268
Seine, 1698–1706, Flûte, 281
Seine, 1720–1774, Flûte, 284
Seine, 1768–1778, Flûte, 289
Seine, 1783–1788, Flûte, 293
Sémillante, 1780–1787, 8pdr corvette, 328
Sénégal, 1778–1780, Corvette, 327
Sensible, 1690–1696, Galley, 380
Sensible, 1767–1789, 12pdr frigate, 178
Sensible, 1783–1784, Flûte, 293
Sept Provinces, 1708–1708, Fireship, 263
Septentrion, 1780–1784, Transport, 366
Serapis, 1779–1781, 3rd Rank, 154
Sérieuse, 1695–1702, Gunboat, 248
Sérieuse, 1779–1798, 12pdr frigate, 181
Sérieux, 1679–1690, 5th Rank, 197
Sérieux, 1687–1718, 2nd Rank, 88
Sérieux, 1740–1747, 3rd Rank, 140
Sérin, 1771–1783, Corvette, 326
Serpent, 1671–1673, Fireship, 254
Serpent, 1674–1676, Fireship, 256
Serpent, 1676–1678, Fireship, 256
Serpent, 1690–1696, Fireship, 260
Serpent, 1751–1779, Xebec, 359
Serpent, 1779–1798, Cutter, 344
Serpente, 1674–1678, 4th Rank, see *Laurier* 1678–1692, 161
Serpente, 1678–1691, Light frigate, 221
Serpente, 1692–1692, Light frigate, 225
Serpente, 1693–1697, Light frigate, 226
Serrurier, 1720–1723, Flûte, 284
Sévère, 1779–1784, 3rd Rank, 150
Severn, 1746–1747, 4th Rank, 173
Shallow, 1778–1781, Cutter, 342
Sibylle, 1671–1675, Light frigate, see *Aurore* 1665–1671, 217
Sibylle, 1676–1689, Barque longue, 306
Sibylle, 1690–1694, Barque longue, 308
Sibylle, 1704–1704, Light frigate, 231
Sibylle, 1729–1742, Barque latine, 358
Sibylle, 1748–1748, Pink, 365
Sibylle, 1777–1783, 12pdr frigate, 180
Sincère, 1766–1777, 12pdr frigate, 177
Sincère, 1784–1793, Corvette, 331
Singe, 1762–1780, Xebec, 360
Sirène de Londres, 1695–1697, Flûte, 280
Sirène du Nord, 1749–1760, Gabarre, 296
Sirène, 1666–1684, 4th Rank, 157
Sirène, 1674–1681, Galley, 376
Sirène, 1679–1687, Galley, 377
Sirène, 1687–1701, Galley, 378

Sirène, 1691–1702, 2nd Rank, 90
Sirène, 1703–1712, Light frigate, 230
Sirène, 1704–1717, Brigantine, 356
Sirène, 1744–1760, 8pdr frigate, 205
Sirène, 1770–1776, Corvette, 323
Sirène, 1782–1787, Gabarre, 300
Six Corps, 1762–1779, 2nd Rank, 106
Societé de Grenezé, 1697–1699, Barque longue, 313
Soeur Marie, 1702–1709, Flûte, 282
Solebay, 1744–1746, Light frigate, 238
Soleil d'Afrique, 1665–1676, 5th Rank, 192
Soleil d'Afrique, 1675–1678, 5th Rank, 195
Soleil d'Afrique, 1676–1676, 5th Rank, see *Palmier* 1676–1709, 196
Soleil d'Afrique, 1681–1698, 5th Rank, 197
Soleil d'Alger, 1687–1688, 5th Rank, 198
Soleil de Nantes, 1744–1744, Coast guard vessel, 368
Soleil Royal, 1669–1692, 1st Rank, 60
Soleil Royal, 1692–1714, 1st Rank, 67
Soleil Royal, 1749–1759, 1st Rank, 75
Soleil, 1642–1671, 4th Rank, 155
Soleil, 1676–1678, Flûte, 273
Solide, 1683–1694, 4th Rank, 162
Solide, 1695–1702, 3rd Rank, 133
Solide, 1722–1771, 3rd Rank, 139
Solitaire, 1756 (canc), 3rd Rank, 145
Solitaire, 1758–1771, 3rd Rank, 146
Solitaire, 1774–1782, 3rd Rank, 149
Somme, 1729–1742, Flûte, 284
Sommeldick, 1706–1713, Flûte, 282
Sophie, 1666–1671, 3rd Rank, 117
Sophie, 1760–1767, Prame, 247
Sorcière (?), 1784–?, Chatte pontée, 366
Sorcière, 1673 (canc), Light frigate, 219
Sorcière, 1676–1695, Light frigate, see *Gaillarde* 1676–1676, 220
Sorlingue, 1705–1711, 5th Rank, 203
Soubise, 1668–1671, Flûte, 269
Soubise, 1687–1692, unknown type, 370
Sourdis, 1641–1661, 5th Rank, 190
Souris, 1690–1692, Flûte, 276
Souris, 1780–1781, Schooner, 347
Souverain, 1671–1678, 1st Rank, see *Henri* 1669–1671, 57
Souverain, 1678–1706, 1st Rank, 62
Souverain, 1757–1792, 2nd Rank, 105
Souveraine, 1671–1674, Galley, see *Croix de Malte* 1663–1671, 374
Souveraine, 1676–1687, Galley, 377
Souveraine, 1686–1718, Galley, 379
Speedy, 1782–1782, Corvette, 325
Sphère d'Angleterre, 1707–1717, Light frigate, 232
Sphère, 1693–1695, 5th Rank, see *Mutine* 1693–1693, 201
Sphère, 1705–1714, Flûte, 282
Sphère, 1717–1741, Light frigate, 232
Sphinx, 1755–1755, 3rd Rank, 144
Sphinx, 1776–1802, 3rd Rank, 149

Sphinx, 1779–1779, 8pdr frigate, 215
Sprightly, 1779–1783, Lugger, 346
Stadenland, 1694–1702, 3rd Rank, 132
Stanley, 1778–1778, Brig, 342
Stork, 1758–1760, Corvette, 321
Stormont, 1782–1786, Corvette, 325
Sublime, 1690–1696, Galley, 380
Subtile, 1664–1676, Galiote à rames, 352
Subtile, 1671–1674, Light frigate, see *Notre Dame des Anges* 1665–1671, 217
Subtile, 1674–1675, Light frigate, 219
Subtile, 1676–1678, Light frigate, 221
Subtile, 1676–1689, Barque longue, 306
Subtile, 1677–1686, Felucca, 352
Subtile, 1682–1701, Barque, 353
Subtile, 1684–1690, Felucca, 353
Subtile, 1690–1702, Barque longue, 308
Subtile, 1705–1717, Barque, 356
Subtile, 1741–1746, Light frigate, 235
Subtile, 1777–1791, Corvette, 327
Succès, 1780–1783, Schooner, 347
Succès, 1781–1783, Felucca, 361
Suffisant, 1782–1793, 2nd Rank, 111
Suffisante, 1692–1695, Light frigate, 225
Suisse, 1669–1672, Galiote, see *Galiote* 1667–1669, 363
Sultane, 1670–1671, Flûte, 270
Sultane, 1765–1793, 12pdr frigate, 177
Superbe, 1671–1687, 2nd Rank, 83
Superbe, 1674–1679, Galley, 376
Superbe, 1682–1693, Galley, 378
Superbe, 1690–1702, 2nd Rank, 89
Superbe, 1692–1718, Galley, 380
Superbe, 1708–1710, 3rd Rank, 138
Superbe, 1738–1759, 2nd Rank, 99
Superbe, 1758–?, Polacre, 365
Superbe, 1778–1779, Coast guard vessel, 369
Superbe, 1779–1779, 3rd Rank, 150
Superbe, 1784–1795, 2nd Rank, 111
Surprenant, 1717–1721, Coast guard vessel, 368
Surprenante, 1671–1673, Light frigate, see *Morine* 1665–1671, 217
Surprenante, 1674–1676, Light frigate, 219
Surprenante, 1675–1681, Barque longue, 306
Surprenante, 1689–1689, Barque longue, 307
Surprenante, 1693–1699, Brigantine, 334
Surprise, 1760 (canc), 8pdr frigate, 210
Surprise, 1782–1789, Cutter, 349
Surveillant, 1769–1773, Coast guard vessel, 369
Surveillante, 1778–1797, 12pdr frigate, 179
Suzanne, 1708–1713, Paquebot, 370
Suzanne, 1781–1786, Brig, 348
Swallow, 1780–1780, Cutter, 347
Swift, 1782–1783, Corvette, 325
Sylphe, 1782–1782, Lugger, 349
Sylphe, 1782–1788, Brig, 349
Sylphide, 1763–1784, Corvette, 322
Sylphide, 1771–1774, Schooner, 340
Sylvie, 1703–1704, 4th Rank, 167

Symbole, 1668–1671, Fireship, 254
Syrène, 1741–1742, Mortar boat, 248
Tamise, 1754–1758, Tartane, 360
Tamponne, 1766–1784, Gabarre, 297
Tapageur, 1778–1779, Cutter, 345
Tardif, 1671–1692, Flûte, 272
Tardif, 1692–1694, Flûte, 278
Tarleton, 1782–1793, Brig, 349
Tartane, 1684–1684, Tartane, 353
Tartare, 1780–1782, Cutter, 347
Tartare, 1780–1783, Felucca, 361
Tartare, 1781–?, Lugger, 347
Tartare, 1782–1784, Brig, 349
Téméraire, 1671–1694, 3rd Rank, 122
Téméraire, 1695–1722, 3rd Rank, 133
Téméraire, 1749–1759, 2nd Rank, 102
Téméraire, 1780–1784, Cutter, 346
Téméraire, 1782–1803, 2nd Rank, 111
Témérité, 1785–?, Brigantine, 350
Tempête, 1671–1675, Light frigate, see *Bretonne* 1670–1671, 218
Tempête, 1676–1690, Light frigate, 221
Tempête, 1690–1726, Light frigate, 223
Tempête, 1726–1786, Bomb vessel, 245
Tempête, 1759–1768, Gunboat, 249
Tenare, 1784 (canc), Bomb vessel, 246
Terpichore, 1763–1787, 12pdr frigate, 176
Terpsichore, 1758–1760, 6pdr frigate, 236
Terray, 1779–1780, Gabarre, 299
Terre-Neuvier, 1689–1689, Fireship, 259
Terreur, 1755–1762, Bomb vessel, 245
Terrible, 1670–1678, 2nd Rank, 84
Terrible, 1680–1692, 2nd Rank, 85
Terrible, 1684–1697, Bomb vessel, 241
Terrible, 1693–1714, 1st Rank, 67
Terrible, 1739–1747, 2nd Rank, 100
Terrible, 1780–1804, 1st Rank, 74
Terrible, 1783–?, Coast guard vessel, 369
Terron, 1662–1665, 5th Rank, 191
Teste de More, 1688–1689, 3rd Rank, see *Brusque* 1689–1697, 128
Tête Noire, 1658–1663, Flûte, 267
Thérèse, 1665–1669, 3rd Rank, 116
Thérèse, 1668–1677, Galley, 375
Thérèse, 1671–1676, Galley, see *Saint Jean (Baptiste)* 1663–1671, 374
Thérèse, 1677–1684, Brigantine, 353
Thérèse, 1728–1728, Barque, 358
Thérèse, 1759–1783, Gabarre, 296
Thérèse, 1760–1783, Prame, 247
Thérèse, 1762–1766, Gunboat, 250
Thésée, 1759–1759, 2nd Rank, 106
Thétis, 1697–1705, 4th Rank, 166
Thétis, 1705–1711, 4th Rank, 167
Thétis, 1722–1730, Light frigate, 234
Thétis, 1741–1742, Mortar boat, 248
Thétis, 1751–1777, 8pdr frigate, 206
Thétis, 1788–1808, 18pdr frigate, 188
Thorn, 1781–1782, Corvette, 329
Tiercelet, 1756–1760, Cutter, 337
Tiercelet, 1782–1797, Lugger, 349

Tigre, 1642–1664, 5th Rank, 190
Tigre, 1666–1697, 4th Rank, 157
Tigre, 1667–1671, Fireship, 254
Tigre, 1689–1713, 5th Rank, 200
Tigre, 1724–1754, 4th Rank, 171
Tigre, 1758–1762, 8pdr frigate, 211
Tigre, 1779–1781, 18pdr frigate, 187
Tigre, 1780–1784, Corvette, 328
Timoléon, 1794–1798, 2nd Rank, see *Commerce de Bordeaux* 1785–1793, 112
Toison d'Or, 1673–1674, Light frigate, see *Subtile* 1674–1675, 219
Toison d'Or, 1759–1759, Fireship, 264
Tonnant, 1670–1678, 2nd Rank, 84
Tonnant, 1681–1692, 2nd Rank, 86
Tonnant, 1693–1714, 1st Rank, 68
Tonnant, 1743–1780, 1st Rank, 74
Tonnante, 1735–1750, Bomb vessel, 245
Tonne de Victoire, 1692–1695, Flûte, 277
Tonnerre, 1696–1713, Bomb vessel, 243
Tonnerre, 1759–1768, Gunboat, 249
Topaze, 1750–1775, 8pdr frigate, 206
Tortue, 1692–1692, Flûte, 278
Toscan, 1781–1782, Flûte, 292
Toulon, 1667–1671, 4th Rank, 158
Toulouse, 1703–1711, 2nd Rank, 94
Toulouse, 1714–1755, 3rd Rank, 130
Tourbillon, 1670–1678, 5th Rank, 194
Tourlourou, 1779–1781, Coast guard vessel, 369
Tourtereau, 1782–1787, Corvette, 330
Tourterelle, 1719–1745, Gabarre, 294
Tourterelle, 1757–1761, Corvette, 321
Tourterelle, 1770–1783, 12pdr frigate, 178
Tranquille, 1692–1697, Flûte, see *Souris* 1690–1692, 276
Trial, 1756–1756, Coast guard vessel, 369
Trial, 1778–1783, Cutter, 342
Tricolore, 1792–1793, 2nd Rank, see *Lys* 1785–1792, 112
Trident, 1666–1671, 3rd Rank, 117
Trident, 1671–1686, 4th Rank, see *Mercoeur* 1661–1671, 157
Trident, 1685–1720, 3rd Rank, 129
Trident, 1688–1695, 4th Rank, 162
Trident, 1742–1747, 3rd Rank, 141
Trinité, 1666–1671, Fireship, 254
Triomphant, 1671–1678, 2nd Rank, see *Princesse* 1667–1671, 80
Triomphant, 1678–1692, 2nd Rank, see *Constant* 1675–1678, 85
Triomphant, 1688–1689, 4th Rank, 163
Triomphant, 1693–1726, 1st Rank, 68
Triomphant, 1722–1725, Coast guard vessel, 368
Triomphant, 1779–1805, 1st Rank, 78
Triomphante, 1690–1696, Galley, 380
Triomphante, 1697–1714, Galley, 391
Triomphante, 1708–1709, Brigantine, 334
Triomphe, 1638–1661, 5th Rank, 190
Triomphe, 1661–1671, 3rd Rank, 115
Triomphe, 1780–1784, Cutter, 347

Triton, 1628–1632, Vaisseau, 51
Triton, 1637–1652, Vaisseau, 51
Triton, 1663–1667, Fireship, 252
Triton, 1671–1678, 5th Rank, see *Trompeuse* 1670–1671, 194
Triton, 1678–1694, 4th Rank, see *Basque* 1671–1671, 159
Triton, 1697–1702, 4th Rank, 166
Triton, 1703–1720, 3rd Rank, 135
Triton, 1728–1745, 3rd Rank, 139
Triton, 1747–1791, 3rd Rank, 142
Triton, 1769–1782, 12pdr frigate, 178
Trois Amis, 1760–1760, Coast guard vessel, 369
Trois Poignards, 1694–1697, Light frigate, 227
Trois Rois, 1626–1641, Vaisseau, 50
Trois Rois, 1666–1669, Fireship, 254
Trois Roses, 1687–1688, 5th Rank, 198
Trompette, 1691–1702, Barque longue, 309
Trompette, 1706–1717, Barque longue, 315
Trompeur, 1671–1673, Fireship, 254
Trompeur, 1676–1678, Fireship, 257
Trompeur, 1690–1691, Fireship, 259
Trompeur, 1692 (canc), Fireship, 262
Trompeuse, 1670–1671, 5th Rank, 194
Trompeuse, 1671–1674, Light frigate, see *Hameçon* 1670–1671, 218
Trompeuse, 1674–1675, Light frigate, 219
Trompeuse, 1675–1683, Light frigate, 220
Trompeuse, 1683–1683, 4th Rank, see *Emporté* 1683–1704, 162
Trompeuse, 1684–1685, Light frigate, 222
Trompeuse, 1689–1696, Light frigate, 223
Trône, 1682–1695, Barque longue, 306
Truite, 1777–1780, Gabarre, 298
Turbot, 1777–1789, Chasse-marée, 367
Turbulente, 1703–1709, Barque longue, 314
Turquoise, 1692–1710, Flûte, 277
Turquoise, 1762–1772, Corvette, 321
Union, 1756–1756, Fireship, 264
Union, 1763–1782, 3rd Rank, 147
Union, 1781–1781, Flûte, 292
Unité, 1692–1696, Flibot, 364
Upton, 1705–1706, Light frigate, 232
Utile, 1672–1679, Barque longue, 304
Utile, 1689–1691, Barque longue, 308
Utile, 1691–1710, Barque longue, 310
Utile, 1759–1761, Flûte, 287
Utile, 1764–1792, 3rd Rank, 148
Utile, 1783–1785, Schooner, 350
Utile, 1784–1796, Gabarre, 301
Vaillant, 1671–1691, 3rd Rank, 122
Vaillant, 1690–1692, 3rd Rank, 128
Vaillant, 1692–1698, 3rd Rank, 131
Vaillant, 1755–1792, 3rd Rank, 145
Vaillant, 1771–1789, Flûte, 290
Vaillante, 1666–1666, Fireship, 254
Vaillante, 1780–1783, Gunboat, 251
Vainqueur, 1692–1722, 1st Rank, 65
Vainqueur, 1743–1744, Fireship, 263
Vaisseau de la Reine, 1627–1639, Vaisseau, see *Navire de la Reine* 1627–1639, 49

Vaisseau du Roi, 1627–1646, Vaisseau, see *Navire du Roi* 1627–1646, 49
Valeur, 1668–1679, Galley, 375
Valeur, 1679–1687, Galley, 377
Valeur, 1687–1713, Galley, 379
Valeur, 1704–1710, Light frigate, 231
Valeur, 1707–1720, Light frigate, 232
Valeur, 1713–1733, Galley, see *Patronne* 1694–1713, 390
Valeur, 1742–1779, Galley, 393
Valeur, 1754–1759, 8pdr frigate, 208
Valeur, 1778–1779, Corvette, 327
Vanguard, 1625–1626, Vaisseau, 49
Vanneau, 1778–1783, Schooner, 342
Vanneau, 1782–1793, Lugger, 349
Vautour, 1727–1740, Brigantine, 358
Vautour, 1735–1754, Brigantine, 335
Vautour, 1779–1783, Gunboat, 251
Vautour, 1782–1786, Corvette, 330
Vedette, 1691–1707, Barque longue, 310
Vendôme, 1651–1671, 1st Rank, 56
Vendôme, 1663–1665, Galley, 374
Vengeance, 1779–1780, Brigantine, 345
Vengeur du Peuple, 1794–1794, 2nd Rank, see *Marseillais* 1766–1794, 107
Vengeur, 1765–1785, 3rd Rank, 148
Vénus, 1704–1722, 5th Rank, 202
Vénus, 1723–1745, Light frigate, 234
Vénus, 1780–1781, 12pdr frigate, 183
Vénus, 1782–1788, 18pdr frigate, 187
Vergeroux, 1687–1692, unknown type, 370
Vermandois, 1669–1671, 2nd Rank, see *Orgueilleux* 1671–1688, 83
Vermandois, 1671–1678, 3rd Rank, see *Dauphin* 1664–1671, 116
Vermandois, 1684–1727, 3rd Rank, 125
Vert Galant, 1768–1772, Corvette, 323
Vestale, 1705–1739, 4th Rank, 167
Vestale, 1756–1761, 8pdr frigate, 208
Vestale, 1780–1799, 12pdr frigate, 181
Vésuve, 1755–1762, Bomb vessel, 245
Vésuve, 1784 (canc), Bomb vessel, 246
Veuve de Malabar, 1782–1784, Gabarre, 300
Vicomte de Damas, 1782–1784, Brig, 349
Victoire, 1637–1652, Vaisseau, 51
Victoire, 1658–1666, 5th Rank, 191
Victoire, 1664–1673, Galley, 374
Victoire, 1670–1671, 5th Rank, see *Arrogant* 1671–1673, 195
Victoire, 1674–1681, Galley, 376
Victoire, 1680–1691, Galley, 378
Victoire, 1691–1694, Galley, 380
Victoire, 1699–1700, Galley, see *Heureuse* 1696–1714, 391
Victoire, 1702–1705, Barque longue, 313
Victoire, 1704–1743, Light frigate, 231
Victoire, 1716–1718, Galley, 391
Victoire, 1737–1743, Light frigate, 235
Victoire, 1747–1747, Felucca, 359
Victoire, 1757–1758, 8pdr frigate, 210
Victoire, 1760–1762, Gunboat, 249

Victoire, 1770–1793, 2nd Rank, 108
Victoire, 1795–1799, 1st Rank, see *Languedoc* 1766–1794, 77
Victor, 1749–1758, Sloop, 336
Victor, 1780–1784, Brig, 347
Victorieuse, 1762–1766, Gunboat, 250
Victorieux, 1673–1685, 1st Rank, 61
Victorieux, 1691–1717, 1st Rank, 63
Vielle Bellandre, 1669–1673, Bilander, see *Prophète Daniel* 1668–1669, 362
Vielle France, 1675–1675, Galley, see *France* 1662–1675, 374
Vielle Gribane 1670–1680, Gribane, see *Gribane* 1669–1670, 362
Vielle Réale, 1694–1715, Galley, see *Réale* 1688–1694, 379
Vielle Saint Louis, 1691–1692, Galley, see *Saint Louis* 1680–1691, 377
Vierge de Santé, 1760–1762, 3rd Rank, 147
Vierge, 1620–1625, Vaisseau, 49
Vierge, 1637–1660, Vaisseau, 51
Vierge, 1646–1657, Vaisseau, 53
Vierge, 1666–1671, 5th Rank, 193
Vierge, 1744–1745, Caiche, 365
Vieux Constant, 1690–1704, 2nd Rank, see *Princesse* 1667–1671, 80
Vigilance, 1703–1712, 5th Rank, 202
Vigilant, 1671–1673, 5th Rank, see *Lion d'Or* 1666–1671, 193
Vigilant, 1673–1678, 5th Rank, 195
Vigilant, 1678–1700, 3rd Rank, see *Dauphin* 1664–1671, 116
Vigilant, 1744–1745, 3rd Rank, 141
Vigilant, 1756–1756, Sloop, 337
Vigilant, 1763–1782, Corvette, 322
Vigilante, 1664–1675, Galiote à rames, 352
Vigilante, 1677–1683, Felucca, 352
Vigilante, 1687–1690, Felucca, 353
Vigilante, 1690–1695, Brigantine, 333
Vigilante, 1705–1721, Barque, 356
Vigilante, 1757–1778, Schooner, 337
Vigilante, 1777 (canc), Barque, 362
Vigilante, 1783–1796, Corvette, 331
Villageoise, 1779–1781, Gabarre, 299
Ville de Bayonne, 1695–1696, Flûte, 280
Ville de Bilbao, 1762–1767, Fireship, 264
Ville de Cadiz, 1693–1693, Fireship, 262
Ville de Hambourg, 1706–1709, 3rd Rank, 137
Ville de Médemblick, 1693–1712, 3rd Rank, 129
Ville de Paris, 1764–1782, 1st Rank, 70
Ville de Paris, 1783 (canc), 1st Rank, 74
Ville de Rouen, 1666–1671, 5th Rank, 193
Ville d'Emden, 1692–1703, Flûte, 277
Ville du Havre, 1760–1760, Gunboat, see *Danaé* 1760–1768, 249
Villevault, 1770–1771, 4th Rank, 185
Violent, 1690–1712, Fireship, 261
Violente, 1778–1793, Gunboat, 250
Vipère, 1678–1703, Light frigate, see *Lutine* 1676–1678, 220
Vipère, 1707–1709, Barque longue, 315
Vipère, 1734–1746, Corvette, 316
Vipère, 1759–1766, Gunboat, 249
Vive, 1759–1763, Gunboat, 249
Vivonne, 1665–1665, 3rd Rank, see *Comte* 1667–1671, 117
Voilé, 1671–1673, Fireship, see *Sauvage* 1670–1671, 254
Voilé, 1673–1676, Fireship, 256
Voilé, 1676–1685, Fireship, 257
Voilé, 1690–1692, Fireship, 260
Volage, 1691–1692, Barque longue, 311
Volage, 1693–1706, Barque longue, 312
Volage, 1706–1709, Barque longue, 315
Volage, 1741–1753, 8pdr frigate, 204
Volage, 1762–1763, Gunboat, 250
Volante, 1669–1670, Felucca, see *Légère*, 351
Volante, 1688–1692, Light frigate, see *Normande* 1670–1671, 218
Volante, 1708–1708, Light frigate, 233
Volontaire, 1693–1695, 4th Rank, 164
Volontaire, 1695–1702, 4th Rank, 164
Vulcain, 1696–1715, Bomb vessel, 243
Wallon, 1669–1671, 3rd Rank, 118
Warwick, 1756–1761, 3rd Rank, 146
Warwick, 1782–1786, Brig, 350
Weasel, 1778–1779, Corvette, see *Belette* 1779–1779, 327
Weps, 1694–1705, 5th Rank, 201
William, 1783–?, Coast guard vessel, 369
Winchelsea, 1758–1758, 8pdr frigate, 211
Yacht de la Reine, 1785–1793, Yacht, 371
Yack, 1675–1679, Barque longue, 306
Yack, 1690–1697, Light frigate, 223
Yack, 1691–1692, Light frigate, see *Serpente* 1692–1692, 225
York, 1778–1778, Corvette, 324
Zélande, 1693–1708, 3rd Rank, 129
Zélé, 1763–1805, 2nd Rank, 106
Zénobie, 1759–1762, 8pdr frigate, 211
Zéphyr, 1706–1713, Light frigate, 232
Zéphyr, 1728–1762, Light frigate, 237
Zéphyr, 1766 (canc), 12pdr frigate, 177
Zéphyr, 1768–1779, 8pdr frigate, 212
Zéphyr, 1778–1780, Corvette, 327
Zeripsée, 1694–1705, 5th Rank, 201
Zodiaque, 1756–1784, 2nd Rank, 105